P9-CJX-028

Fodor's
ESSENTIAL
GREECE

Portions of this book appear in *Fodor's Greek Islands*.

4/24

WELCOME TO GREECE

A visit to the land of Homer, Aristotle, and Sophocles is a journey to the dawn of classical civilization, with archaeological splendors from Athens to Crete. The towering monasteries of Meteora and soaring Mt. Olympus inspire awe, while relaxing islands like Corfu and Santorini invite simple pleasures and a taste of the good life on the Aegean Sea. The Greek countryside presents the perfect coda with idyllic landscapes of cypress groves, vineyards, and olive trees, as well as dramatic coves with sparkling white sand and rugged mountains that plunge into the sea.

TOP REASONS TO GO

★ **Athens.** Spread out below the towering Acropolis, Greece's capital pulses with excitement.

★ **Islands.** Spiritual Patmos, peaceful Naxos, medieval Rhodes, sylvan Skopelos, and more.

★ **Stunning Beaches.** Some 9,000 miles of shoreline means a beach for every interest.

★ **Ancient Splendors.** Sacred Delphi, ancient Olympia, and the Minoan palaces of Crete.

★ **Food and Drink.** Succulent lamb, freshly grilled fish, fiery ouzo, and flavorful wines.

★ **Nightlife.** The world parties at the beaches of Mykonos and seaside clubs of Glyfada.

22 ULTIMATE EXPERIENCES

Greece offers terrific experiences that should be on every traveler's list. Here are Fodor's top picks for a memorable trip.

1 Sunset in Santorini

The crescent-shaped Cycladic island offers dramatic views over the Aegean Sea. The town of Ia, perched on an 1,100-foot cliff, provides some spectacular—and wildly popular—sunset-watching opportunities across the bay. *(Ch. 6)*

2 The Acropolis of Athens

Every city-state in ancient Greece had a fortress on a hill. But there is only one Acropolis, built in 5 BC and rightly considered the jewel of Athenian civilization. *(Ch. 2)*

3 The Palace of Knossos, Crete

The palace of the wise King Minos reveals a gentrified people some 5,000 years ago in possession of advanced technology, a written language, and intellectual prowess. *(Ch. 7)*

4 Pine-Covered Skopelos

One of the greenest Greek islands, which also offers aquamarine waters and a picturesque church perched high on a rock, was the setting for the film *Mamma Mia!* (Ch. 4)

5 Greece's First Capital

Nafplion, the first capital of Greece in 1821, retains its picturesque, Venetian-era historic center. It's ideal for exploring the Peloponnese. *(Ch. 13)*

6 Greece's Second City

Historic sites such as the Medieval White Tower have made Thessaloniki a UNESCO World Heritage Site, while vibrant nightlife draws partiers. *(Ch. 12)*

7 Low-Key Folegandros

With one of the prettiest towns in the Cyclades perched upon a windswept cliff, the archetypal island is rocky and tiny and still largely untouched by mass tourism. *(Ch. 6)*

8 A Treasure Trove

The National Archaeological Museum in Athens holds the most important findings from excavations around Greece. It's a must-see for first-time visitors. *(Ch. 2)*

9 Mountain of the Gods

The tallest mountain in Greece is the mythical sanctuary of the Olympian Gods. These days it's an impressive national park with numerous hiking trails. *(Ch. 12)*

10 Keep the Flame Alive

Olympia is a must-do day trip when touring the Peloponnese. The sanctuary dedicated to Zeus will forever be associated with the Olympic Games, which began here. *(Ch. 13)*

11 Partying in Mykonos

Greece's most famous island is the quintessential party paradise, attracting an impressive roster of jet-setters and A-listers, but it also has a quieter side. *(Ch. 6)*

12 Delos, the Sacred Island

A short boat trip from Mykonos lies the abandoned birthplace of Apollo, once a religious capital and a safe port for incoming vessels, now an archaeological site. *(Ch. 6)*

13 Live the Middle Ages

The narrow alleyways of Monemvasia transport you five centuries back in time to the clashes between the Byzantine empire and the Franks. *(Ch. 13.)*

14 Rhodes Town

The oldest populated medieval town in the world draws you into its mazelike, traffic-free streets with beautiful restored buildings and cobbled lanes. *(Ch. 8)*

15 Beaches Everywhere

With 8,498 miles of coastline, you are never too far away from a beach in Greece. Several of the most beautiful white-sand beaches, including Elafonissi, are in Crete. *(Ch. 7)*

16 Get Closer to Heaven

There is something out-of-this-world about Meteora and the determination of the human spirit, which willed that there would be monasteries nestled atop of these impressive rocks. *(Ch. 10)*

17 Places of Worship

Thousands of churches are scattered around Greece, ranging in style from the Cycladic (with blue and white domes) to the Venetian style of Panayia Evangelistria on Tinos. *(Ch. 6)*

18 Italianate Style in Corfu

The lush green slopes, protected coves, and mild climate lured Ulysses, but also a string of Byzantine, Venetian, and British settlers (including the literary Durrells). *(Ch. 5)*

19 Island of the Apoclypse

It is not easy to get to Patmos, so the atmosphere remains serene, sophisticated, and relaxed, just as when St. John wrote the Revelation here in AD 95. *(Ch. 8)*

20 Enter Warrior Country

The Mani is the land of warriors, from where many Greek heroes hail, an isolated, barren land dotted with stone towers and fortresses that is still strangely beautiful. *(Ch. 13)*

21 Car-Free Hydra

The approach to the harbor is spectacular as the crescent-shaped, hilly settlement is slowly revealed. Life on this simply beautiful island follows a relaxed, slow pace. *(Ch. 3)*

22 Respect the Oracle

For ancient Greeks, Delphi, with its oracles, was the center of the world. Today, the sanctuary has one of the highest concentrations of ancient ruins and a wonderful museum. *(Ch. 9)*

Fodor's ESSENTIAL GREECE

Editorial: Douglas Stallings, *Editorial Director*; Margaret Kelly, Jacinta O'Halloran, *Senior Editors*; Kayla Becker, Alexis Kelly, Amanda Sadlowski, *Editors*; Teddy Minford, *Content Editor*; Rachael Roth, *Content Manager*

Design: Tina Malaney, *Design and Production Director*; Jessica Gonzalez, *Production Designer*

Photography: Jennifer Arnow, *Senior Photo Editor*

Maps: Rebecca Baer, *Senior Map Editor*; Mark Stroud and Henry Colomb (Moon Street Cartography), David Lindroth, *Cartographers*

Production: Jennifer DePrima, *Editorial Production Manager*; Carrie Parker, *Senior Production Editor*; Elyse Rozelle, *Production Editor*

Business & Operations: Chuck Hoover, *Chief Marketing Officer*; Joy Lai, *Vice President and General Manager*; Stephen Horowitz, *Director of Business Development and Revenue Operations*; Tara McCrillis, *Director of Publishing Operations*; Eliza D. Aceves, *Content Operations Manager and Strategist*

Public Relations and Marketing: Joe Ewaskiw, *Manager*; Esther Su, *Marketing Manager*

Writers: Alexia Amvrazi, Stephen Brewer, Natasha Giannousi-Varney, Liam McCaffrey, Hillary Whitton Paipeti, Marissa Tejada, Adrian Vrettos

Editor: Douglas Stallings

Production Editor: Carrie Parker

1st Edition

ISBN 978-1-64097-020-5

ISSN 2574–349X

All details in this book are based on information supplied to us at press time. Always confirm information when it matters, especially if you're making a detour to visit a specific place. Fodor's expressly disclaims any liability, loss, or risk, personal or otherwise, that is incurred as a consequence of the use of any of the contents of this book.

SPECIAL SALES

This book is available at special discounts for bulk purchases for sales promotions or premiums. For more information, e-mail SpecialMarkets@fodors.com.

PRINTED IN THE UNITED STATES OF AMERICA

10 9 8 7 6 5 4 3 2 1

CONTENTS

Fodor's Features

ABOUT THIS GUIDE

Fodor's Recommendations
Everything in this guide is worth doing—we don't cover what isn't—but exceptional sights, hotels, and restaurants are recognized with additional accolades. **Fodor's Choice★** indicates our top recommendations. Care to nominate a new place? Visit Fodors.com/contact-us.

Trip Costs
We list prices wherever possible to help you budget well. Hotel and restaurant price categories from **$** to **$$$$** are noted alongside each recommendation. For hotels, we include the lowest cost of a standard double room in high season. For restaurants, we cite the average price of a main course at dinner or, if dinner isn't served, at lunch. For attractions, we always list adult admission fees; discounts are usually available for children, students, and senior citizens.

Hotels
Our local writers vet every hotel to recommend the best overnights in each price category, from budget to expensive. Unless otherwise specified, you can expect private bath, phone, and TV in your room. For expanded hotel reviews visit Fodors.com.

Top Picks
★ Fodor's Choice

Listings
⊠ Address
⊠ Branch address
☎ Telephone
🖷 Fax
⊕ Website
✎ E-mail
🎫 Admission fee
⊙ Open/closed times
Ⓜ Subway
✛ Directions or Map coordinates

Hotels & Restaurants
🏨 Hotel
🛏 Number of rooms
⊠⊙⊠ Meal plans
✕ Restaurant
⊜ Reservations
🏛 Dress code
⊟ No credit cards
Ⓢ Price

Other
⇨ See also
☞ Take note
⅄ Golf facilities

Restaurants
Unless we state otherwise, restaurants are open for lunch and dinner daily. We mention dress code only when there's a specific requirement and reservations only when they're essential or not accepted.

Credit Cards
The hotels and restaurants in this guide typically accept credit cards. If not, we'll say so.

EUGENE FODOR

Hungarian-born Eugene Fodor (1905–91) began his travel career as an interpreter on a French cruise ship. The experience inspired him to write *On the Continent* (1936), the first guidebook to receive annual updates and discuss a country's way of life as well as its sights. Fodor later joined the U.S. Army and worked for the OSS in World War II. After the war, he kept up his intelligence work while expanding his guidebook series. During the Cold War, many guides were written by fellow agents who understood the value of insider information. Today's guides continue Fodor's legacy by providing travelers with timely coverage, insider tips, and cultural context.

EXPERIENCE GREECE

WHAT'S NEW

Responding to Crisis

It doesn't take someone with a job on the Athens Stock Exchange to tell you that times are tough in the cradle of democracy—but don't be spooked by the headlines. The Acropolis isn't for sale, and all the natural beauty and updated tourism and cultural sites are still open. Life goes on—in colorful Greek style—but the country's changing finances have brought other changes to Greek society.

Greece became synonymous with the words "economic crisis" when its public debt topped €350 billion. The dire situation caused by overspending on infrastructure, services, and public-sector wages worsened further thanks to rampant tax dodging. Although the roots of the country's financial crisis were decades in the making, the response by the financial markets was not. Large financial institutions were suddenly reluctant to invest further in Greece until the country got its financial house in better order. As a result, the country's borrowing costs skyrocketed, and by 2010, Greece found itself in need of a bailout.

The European Union, International Monetary Fund, and European Central Bank—collectively known as "the troika"—agreed to help Greece in its hour of need, but this financial rescue came with significant strings attached. While Greece was offered huge loans to bridge its budgetary chasm, EU authorities required the country to implement stringent austerity measures to cut down on government spending. The Greeks did not like these measures at all and showed their frustration. Protests, strikes, and even some violent riots, hit the capital as the government slashed pay and benefits for state employees, reduced incomes, and

raised taxes. Unemployment soared, and hundreds of thousands working in the private sector didn't see paychecks for months at a time.

In response to the uncertain economic and social climate, Greek leadership changed hands. In 2012, Andreas Papandreou's Panhellenic Socialist Movement (PASOK) collapsed. Antonis Samaras, the president of New Democracy, became the new prime minister. Unexpectedly, a new, controversial far-right political party, Golden Dawn, gained seats in parliament. Golden Dawn's members had been accused of violent attacks against immigrants and are said to follow neo-Nazi philosophies. But the situation is not entirely grim.

Family and Forward Thinking

While the bleak economy and high unemployment have meant that some Greeks have left their homeland for better opportunities abroad, a strong sense of family has allowed others to weather this storm. Families worked together to provide child care and help to their elders. With less income, trips abroad became a dream. Nevertheless, for Greeks, summer vacations are considered a birthright so in tough times many tap their family networks to head out to a cousin's cottage by the sea. Greeks are strongly connected to their roots and enjoy spending holidays at traditional village homes, away from the city.

In fact, many Greeks began to look at their villages in a new way. They have learned that local agricultural products, which provide cheap, healthy, and delicious sustenance for Greeks at home, can also be marketed with success abroad. While Greece remains the world's top olive oil consumer, they have fallen behind competing producers, Spain and Italy. Instead of packaging their oil in bulk, producers have begun to bottle and market their quality extra virgin olive oil abroad for the first time. This move has spurred new entrepreneurship in one of the oldest and largest agriculture markets of the country.

Starting Up

Greece has always shown strong entrepreneurship, but the country has remained mostly unproductive and associated with corruption. Although most ventures still follow the failed principles of the past, there are a few high-impact start-ups that have succeeded, and these have had an impact on tourism.

Mobile apps like TaxiBeat, Bug Sense, and Pinnatta and high-tech companies like Workable are setting a high bar. Meanwhile, the eco-minded furniture company Coco-Mat and successful cosmetics companies like Apivita and Korres continue to establish their worldwide presence, setting the bar for success. Agribusiness and tourism, Greece's most promising sectors, continue to move forward with companies like Fage, Mastiha Shop, and Hotelbrain.

A Bright Light for Tourism?

Despite the vast political, social, and economic upheaval, Greeks remain optimistic by nature and remain hospitable hosts. No matter what challenges they face as a country, they're a proud, warm-hearted, and outgoing people that continue to be as welcoming as ever. One-fifth of the population of Greece works in tourism, and more than 18 million tourists visit Greece annually. Greeks are moving forward with innovative ideas to showcase the country's beautiful landscape and islands.

The Annual Spetses Mini-Marathon has gathered a considerable following since it started in 2010, and other islands have begun to offer sporting events, spurring new waves of island sport tourism.

Back in the capital, Greeks are going back to their roots to survive the downturn. In the center of Athens, restaurant, bar, and café owners are bringing new life to once-abandoned squares and streets in the commercial center, including Ayias Irinis Square. Steady as ever above the modern city built around it, the Acropolis continues to welcome tourists daily as it undergoes a seemingly endless renovation plan. Nearby, the Acropolis Museum elegantly showcases its ancient wares.

By night, there is no sign of crisis, as the country's nightlife remains as vibrant as ever. Traditional and often pricey Greek music clubs called *bouzoukia* pump with live music that inspires flower throwing and tabletop dancing into the early morning hours. For the first time, Greek pop music bands are headlining on its raised stages to attract a wider audience. In the summer, outdoor clubs that hug the coastline of the Athens Riviera open up for the season with refurbished, glamorous seaside balconies welcoming posh Greek clubbers who still prefer to smoke and stare, rather than dance.

And while some businesses struggle, new hotels and business open all over Greece, including on the islands.

WHAT'S WHERE

1 Athens. Contemporary Athens has a sleek subway, a brand new culture center (financed by the Stavros Niarchos Foundation), that comes complete with much needed outdoor green space, a thriving art scene and a happening nightlife. But for 5 million Athenians, it's still the tried-and-true pleasures that put the spin on urban life here: the endless parade of cafés, the charming Plaka district, and, most of all, the glorious remnants of one of the greatest civilizations the West ever produced, such as the Acropolis.

2 The Saronic Gulf Islands. When Athenians want a break, they often make a quick crossing to the idyllic islands of the Saronic Gulf. You're well advised to follow suit. The most popular of these destinations are Aegina, Hydra, and Spetses.

3 The Sporades. The northern Sporades deliver quintessential Greek-island pleasures: villages spilling down hillsides like giant sugar cubes, Byzantine monasteries, and ageless paths, where the tinkle of goat bells may be the only sound for miles. Weekenders savor Skiathos, but Skopelos has great beaches, and Skyros is washed by some of the clearest waters in Greece.

BULGARIA

erresO

Kavala

Amphipolis

Alexandroupolis

THASSOS

Thracian Sea

Kamariotissa

11

Ouranoupolis

SAMOTHRAKI

Mt. Athos

SITHONIA

Mirina

TURKEY

KASSANDRA Paliouri

LIMNOS

THE

S P O R A D E S

A e g e a n   S e a

SKIATHOS

Elios O

3

SKOPELOS

SKYROS

LESVOS

Skyros Town

Khalkis

EVIA

Chios

Marathon

CHIOS

Megara

ATHENS

Karystos

THE

AEGINA

Gavrio O O Andros

C Y C L A D E S

Saronic

Temple of

Poseidon

KEA

ANDROS

TINOS

IKARIA

Gulf

Portochelion

KYTHNOS

SYROS

Mykonos

DELOS MYKONOS

TSES HYDRA

2

SERIFOS

PAROS

5

NAXOS

SIFNOS ANTIPAROS

IOS

MILOS

FOLEGANDROS

ANAFI

SANTORINI

4 Corfu. Temperate, multi-hued Corfu—of turquoise waters lapping rocky coves, and jacaranda spread over cottages—could have inspired impressionism. The island has a history equally as colorful, reflecting the commingling of Venetians, French, and British. First stop, of course, is Corfu town—a stage set for a Verdi opera.

5 The Cyclades. The ultimate Mediterranean archipelago, the Cyclades easily conjure up the magical words "Greek islands." Santorini, with its ravishing caldera, is the most picturesque; Mykonos, with its sexy jet-set lifestyle, takes the prize for hedonism. Mountainous Folegandros, verdant Naxos, idyllic Sifnos, church-studded Tinos, and Brad Pitt–discovered Antiparos have their own distinct charms, and all center on ancient Delos, birthplace of Apollo.

6 Crete. Crete is Greece's southernmost and largest island, and the claims to superlatives don't stop there. Here, too, are some of Greece's tallest mountains, its deepest gorge, many of its best beaches, and a wealth of Venetian and Byzantine wonders. Treasure of treasures is the Palace of Knossos—the high point of Minoan civilization.

WHAT'S WHERE

7 Rhodes and the Dodeca-nese. Wrapped enticingly around the shores of Turkey, the Dodecanese ("Twelve Islands") have attracted some notable visitors. St. John the Divine received his *Revelation* on Patmos, Hippocrates estab-lished a healing center on Kos, and the Crusader Knights of St. John lavished their wealth on palaces in Rhodes, still famed for its glitzy resorts.

8 Northern Aegean Islands. Flung like puzzle pieces into the Aegean, each of these green and gold islands is distinct: Chios retains an eerie beauty amid its fortified villages and Byzantine monasteries; Lesvos is a getaway favored by artists and writers, and has happily lent a helping hand to high numbers of war-torn Middle East refugees; and lush, mountainous Samos whispers of the classical wonders of antiquity.

9 Attica. Some of the most important remains of ancient Greece are only an hour away from Athens. Delphi was center of the universe for the ancients; at Marathon, the Athenians defeated the Persians; and the Temple of Poseidon hovers between sea and sky at Sounion.

10 Epirus and Thessaly.
Epirus is a land of stark mountains and swift rivers, where Ali Pasha ruled an 18th-century kingdom from the handsome lakeside city of Ioannina. The route east to Thessaly leads into the Meteora—the name derives from "to hang in midair," which is what the region's mountaintop Byzantine monasteries spectacularly do.

11 Thessaloniki and Central Macedonia. This northern region includes two sacred places, Mount Olympus, the stormy heights where Zeus reigned, and Mount Athos, a male-only sanctuary dedicated, ironically, to the Virgin Mary. The hub of the region is Thessaloniki, Greece's second-largest city—a cosmopolitan crossroads leading to remnants of Alexander the Great's Macedonian empire.

12 The Peloponnese. The rugged mountains that loom here cradle some of Greece's most important ancient sites—Olympia, Corinth, Mycenae, and Ancient Messene. Gorgeous Nafplion is the work of later empire builders—Byzantines, Venetians, and Turks—and is as mellow as wines from the region's vineyards. Southward lies rugged Sparta and the often inhospitable but hauntingly beautiful Mani Peninsula.

NEED TO KNOW

AT A GLANCE

Capital: Athens

Population: 10,815,197

Currency: Euro

Money: ATMs are common, but some smaller places don't take credit cards

Language: Greek

Country Code: 30

Emergencies: 166

Driving: On the right

Electricity: 200v/50 cycles; electrical plugs have two round prongs

Time: Six hours ahead of New York

Documents: Up to 90 days with valid passport; Schengen rules apply

Mobile Phones: GSM (900 and 1800 bands)

Major Mobile Companies: Cosmote, Vodafone, Wind

WEBSITES

Greece: ⊕ www.visitgreece.gr

Greek Ministry of Culture: ⊕ www.culture.gr

GETTING AROUND

✈ **Air Travel:** Most flights are to Athens (or Thessaloniki). Crete, Mykonos, Corfu, Zante, Cephallonia, Paros, Naxos, and Santorini also have international airports.

🚌 **Bus Travel:** There is an extensive network of inexpensive, KTEL buses that are fairly modern and depart from Athens for major sites such as Sounion, Delphi, and Olympia.

🚗 **Car Travel:** If you want to explore at your own pace on the mainland or islands, a car is a good idea.

🚆 **Train Travel:** Except for the Athens metro, trains in Greece are limited and dated.

PLAN YOUR BUDGET

	HOTEL ROOM	MEAL	ATTRACTIONS
Low Budget	€80	€10	90-minute Athens metro ticket, €1.40
Mid Budget	€120	€25	Ticket for the Athens Concert Hall (Megaron Mousikis), €25
High Budget	€400	€120	Night out at a Greek music club (*bouzoukia*), €100

WAYS TO SAVE

Share a platter of *mezedes*. Typical small plates with a bit of wine make a great meal.

Visit the local farmers' market. Weekly farmers' markets sell fresh ingredients for a home-cooked Greek meal.

Take advantage of air ticket offers. Even with the merger of Aegean and Olympic Air, there are still frequent sales on domestic flights.

Unification of Archaeological Sites ticket. The combined ticket (€30) includes five days of access to major sights in Athens.

PLAN YOUR TIME	
Hassle Factor	Medium. Flights to Athens are frequent, but most require a change in Europe; in the summer, cheaper charter flights go directly to the islands.
3 days	Visit Athens and venture out to watch the sun set over the Temple of Poseidon at Sounion, or you can do a short island escape.
1 week	Combine a short trip to Athens with an island stay and perhaps an overnight stay at Delphi.
2 weeks	You can visit two or three islands of your choice before heading back to Athens to visit the Acropolis and its museum.

WHEN TO GO

High Season: June through August is the most expensive and popular time to visit Greece. Athens is fairly empty in August, except for the mobs of tourists.

Low Season: Most island hotels are closed in the low season, from mid-October to the middle of April, although this is the perfect time to discover the mountainous regions of the mainland, including the ski resorts not too far from Delphi. Athens is cold and humid.

Value Season: May, September, and October offer the best combination of mild Mediterranean weather and value. The Aegean may still be too cold for swimming in May, but things get better in early June, when you are still beating the crowds. Some island hotels are open until the start of November; others close in early October. An Athenian city break is a good, affordable option all year round.

BIG EVENTS

April/May: Greek Easter is a movable feast: a traditional highlight is lamb roasting on the spit.

May to October: The Athens and Epidavros Festival invites global artists to perform in magnificent surroundings ⊕ www.greekfestival.gr.

August: The Assumption of Mary on August 15 marks the height of the summer vacation for Greeks.

November: Run in what the Greek's call the "authentic" Athens Marathon ⊕ www.athensauthenticmarathon.gr.

READ THIS

■ *Eurydice Street: A Place in Athens,* Sofka Zinovieff. The author adapts to life in Athens.

■ *Sunlight in the Wine,* Robert Leigh. An Englishman moves to the island of Andros for a simpler life.

■ *The Island,* Victoria Hislop. Cretan family saga set on the leprosy colony of Spinalonga.

WATCH THIS

■ *Mamma Mia!* A feel-good Abba musical.

■ *Captain Corelli's Mandolin.* A WWII Italian officer falls in love on Cephallonia.

■ *Zorba the Greek.* Anthony Quinn brings the Greek spirit to life.

EAT THIS

■ *Feta cheese*: crumbly aged sheep or goat cheese

■ *Greek salad*: country salad with feta

■ *Moussaka*: layered eggplant, potato, ground meat, and béchamel

■ *Fava*: a traditional dip made of pureed yellow split peas

■ *Pita me gyro*: spit-roasted meat, in pita with tomatoes, onions, and tzatziki

■ *Lamb kleftiko*: slow-roasted leg of lamb

GREECE'S BEST BEACHES

With some 9,000 miles of exposed shoreline, Greece's beaches are to Europeans what Florida's are to Americans. But choosing Greece's best is a task of almost Herculean proportions. For us *xènos* (foreigners), Greek beaches may be simply sandy playgrounds that live up to their promise of sun, sand, and azure seas. But for the Greeks, the beach becomes the center of Greek social life from May through October, when seas are warm and sunshine can be taken for granted.

Best for Families

Ayia Marina, Aegina, Saronic Gulf Islands. Shallow waters, paddleboat rentals, and other amenities make this beach outside Aegina Town especially popular with Athenian families.

Elafonisi, Crete. Turquoise waters, pure-white sandbars, with a sea shallow enough to create a beautiful wading pool for youngsters. Young explorers love to wade across the "bathtub" to Elafonisi islet.

Santa Maria, Paros, Cyclades. Windsurfers love the winds here, and parents will welcome the warm, shallow waters and those beautiful dunes that are irresistible to the sandbox set.

Best for Partiers

Aegina Town, Saronic Gulf Islands. A party scene prevails at a parade of bars on the coast just outside town, where a spectacular sunset kicks off a night of cocktails and notched-up music.

Pounta Beach, Paros, Cyclades. Dancing on the sand and tabletops is just part of the scene at this beach, which is also a major windsurfing destination.

Skiathos Town, Skiathos, Sporades. For those who prefer drinking and dancing next to the sea, come evening the lively harbor front becomes a big party, one long row of hopping clubs and bars.

Super Paradise Beach and Paradise Beach, Mykonos, Cyclades. Greece's celebrated party island lives up to its reputation at a string of bars that line these soft sands, where an international crowd lingers until dawn.

Best Off the Beaten Path

Ayios Georgios, Rhodes, Dodecanese. Shaded with heavenly scented cedars, this pristine strand is the loveliest beach on Rhodes and well worth the harrowing, four-wheel drive down a cypress-lined track.

Moni Beach, Moni, Saronic Gulf Islands. Five km (3 miles) off the coast of Aegina, this little island is now a nature preserve, where you can swim off a little sandy beach in the marvelously green waters while you wait for your boatman to return.

Psili Amos, Patmos, Dodecanese. A caïque ride or half-hour hike are the ways to reach the island's most beautiful stretch of sand.

Red Beach, Matala, Crete. A beautiful hike from Matala allows you to plunge into the surf at this delightfully isolated strand. Nearby caves have sheltered everyone from prehistoric nomads to hippies.

Best for History Buffs

Kommos Beach, Matala, Crete. This mile-plus-long strand of golden sand is justifiably popular with sunbathers, who would be humbled to know ancient Minoans once inhabited this now-being-excavated spot.

Olous, Elounda Peninsula, Crete. Strap on a snorkel mask, dive into the crystal-clear waters, and regard the Roman settlement on the sandy seafloor—finds from this seafloor are on view at the nearby archaeological museum in Ayios Nikolaos.

Best for Water Sports

Chrissi Akti (Golden Beach), Paros, Cyclades. The long stretch of golden sand is Greece's windsurfing capital, hosting the International Windsurfing World Cup every August.

Paleokastritsa, Corfu. This stretch of sand-rimmed coves and seaside grottoes rewards divers and snorkelers with crystal-clear waters. Korfu Diving and other outfitters provide all the necessary equipment for underwater fun.

Paradise Beach, Mykonos, Cyclades. Mykonos is considered to be the diving center of the Aegean, and Mykonos Diving Center is the place for serious instruction and rewarding dives.

Best for Natural Beauty

Kolimbithres, Paros, Cyclades. Smooth boulders whimsically shaped by the wind create a string of coves backed by golden sands. The calm, warm waters are ideal for swimming.

Lemonakia, Kokkari, Samos. Beauty and the Beach describes this winner, with its perfect half-moon crescent magnificently framed by rocky promontories green with pine trees.

Mavra Volia, Chios, Northern Aegean Islands. A "wine-dark sea" washes the black volcanic shores of a cove nestled between sheltering cliffs—little wonder the hauntingly appealing place is aptly called "Black Pebbles."

Milia Beach, Skopelos, Sporades. With brilliant white sands and clear turquoise waters, this gorgeous beach is ensconced by vibrant green pine trees, making for a breathtaking sight.

Myrtidiotissa, Corfu. Sheer cliffs shelter soft sands backed by olive groves; Lawrence Durrell was not exaggerating when, in Prospero's Cell, he described this spot as "perhaps the loveliest beach in the world."

Plaka, Naxos, Cyclades. The most beautiful beach of all on an island of beautiful beaches is backed by sand dunes and bamboo groves, an exotic setting enhanced by a predictably spectacular sunset almost every evening.

Vai, Crete. A grove of palm trees provides an MGM-worthy backdrop to a beach that even the ancients raved about.

CRUISING IN GREECE

Travelers have been sailing Greek waters ever since 3500 BC. The good news is that today's visitor will have a much, much easier time of it than Odysseus, the world's first tourist and hero of Homer's Odyssey. Back in his day, exploring the Greek islands—1,425 geological jewels thickly scattered over the Aegean Sea like stepping-stones between East and West—was a fairly daunting assignment. Zeus would often set the schedule (during the idyllic days in midwinter the master of Mt. Olympus forbade the winds to blow during the mating season of the halcyon or kingfisher); waterlogged wooden craft could be tossed about in summer, when the meltemi, the north wind, would be a regular visitor to these waters; and pine-prow triremes often embarked with a scramble of 170 oarsmen, not all of them pulling in the right direction.

Itineraries

Most itineraries that focus on Greece last 7 to 10 days. They may be round-trip cruises that begin and end in Piraeus, or they may begin in Venice (usually ending in Piraeus) or Piraeus (usually ending in Istanbul). Some cruises concentrate on covering an area that includes the Greek islands, Turkish coast, Cyprus, Israel, and Egypt, while others reach from Gibraltar to the Ionian isles, the western Peloponnese, and Athens.

For an overview of Greece's top sights, choose an itinerary that includes port calls in Piraeus for a shore excursion to the Acropolis and other sights in Athens; Mykonos, a sparkling Cycladic isle with a warren of whitewashed passages, followed by neighboring Delos, with its Pompeii-like ruins; Santorini, a stunning harbor that's actually a partially submerged volcano; Rhodes, where the Knights of St. John built their first walled city before being forced to retreat to Malta; and Heraklion, Crete, where you'll be whisked through a medieval harbor to the reconstructed Bronze Age palace at Knossos. Port calls at Katakolon and Itea mean excursions to Olympia and the Temple of Apollo at Delphi. Some cruises call at Epidavros and Nafplion, offering an opportunity for visits to the ancient theater and the citadel of Mycenae, or at Monemvasia or Patmos, the island where St. John wrote the *Book of Revelation.*

Some lines allow you to spend extra time (even stay overnight) in Mykonos to experience the party scene, or Santorini, so that you can see the island after the crush of cruise-ship tourists leaves for the day.

When to Go

When to go is as important as where to go. The Greek cruising season is lengthy, starting in March and ending in November. In July or August, the islands are crowded with Greek and foreign vacationers, so expect sights, beaches, and shops to be crowded. High temperatures could also limit time spent on deck. May, June, September, and October are the best months—warm enough for sunbathing and swimming, yet not so uncomfortably hot as to make you regret the trek up Lindos. Cruising in the low seasons provides plenty of advantages besides discounted fares. Availability of ships and particular cabins is greater in the low and shoulder seasons, and the ports are almost completely free of tourists.

Major Ports

The cruise ports of Greece vary in size and popularity, and some require passengers on larger ships to take a smaller tender to go ashore. In some ports, the main sights may be an hour or more away by car or bus, so plan your day appropriately. At virtually every port listed, a beach stop can be found nearby if you prefer to relax by the sea instead of exploring a village or archaeological site.

Ayios Nikolaos, Crete. A charming and animated port town, Ayios Nikolaos is a dramatic composition of bare mountains, islets, and deep blue sea. Its hilly streets offer fantastic views over Mirabello Bay, and the "bottomless" Lake Voulismeni remains its core. There aren't any significant beaches in the town but a few nice bays. Its streets are lined with simple tavernas, and its architecture reflects Venetian and Byzantine influences.

Chania, Crete. This elegant city of eucalyptus-lined avenues features miles of waterfront promenades and shady, cobbled alleyways lined with Venetian and Ottoman homes. There's a lighthouse; the waterfront Firka Fortress, once a Turkish prison, is now a maritime museum. A converted Turkish mosque now hosts art exhibitions. You can tour several monasteries on Agia Triada, an area that extends into the sea from the east side of Chania. A short walk west of the harbor takes you to Chania's main beach. Buses and tours depart for Samaria, known for its deep, breathtaking gorge that cuts through Crete's mountains.

Corfu. Stroll through the narrow, winding streets and steep stairways that make up the Campiello, the traffic-free medieval area. Head to the center of town, known as the Spianada, where seven- and eight-story Venetian and English Georgian houses line the way. Wander through the maze inside the New Fort, which was built by the Venetians. There's also the 15th-century Old Fort. Other highlights include the Church of St. George, St. Spyridon Cathedral, and Antivouniotissa church, which dates back to the 15th century. The archaeological museum houses collections from Kanoni, the site of Corfu's ancient capital.

Delos. During a stop in Mykonos, a short boat ride takes you to the tiny uninhabited island of Delos, a well-preserved archaeological site that was once a holy sanctuary for a thousand years, the fabled birthplace of Apollo and Artemis. Walk through formerly luxurious villas including the House of Cleopatra and the House of Dionysus to see 2,500-year-old mosaic floors and remnants of magnificent marble sculptures. Other highlights include the Sacred Way, the Temple of Apollo, and the marbled and imposing Avenue of Lions. Smaller cruise ships can anchor nearby and tender their passengers ashore.

Gythion. This small port located right on the southernmost peninsula in the Peloponnese is in a unique geographical and cultural area called the Mani. Gythion is known for its seaside cafés, restaurants, and beaches. The Diros caves, accessible by underground boat tours, are located 37 km (22 miles) southwest. Tours also head out to other Peloponnese towns popular for their beauty and history including Mystras, Sparta, and Monemvasia.

Heraklion, Crete. This port gives you access to visit the nearby Palace of Knossos, the Minoan king's residence as well as the religious center for the whole region. Right in the center of the Heraklion, near the main Platia Eleftherias, you can find the Archaeological Museum of Heraklion, which displays artifacts from Minoan culture discovered during the excavations of Knossos. The streets of the capital are lined with Venetian buildings, promenades, and outdoor cafés. In the port's inner harbor you'll find Koules, the massive fortress.

Katakolon. This small port is known as "the door to Olympia" since it is the closest port to the Greek city known for the most important sanctuaries of ancient Greece, the birthplace of the ancient Olympic Games. The ancient site includes the remains of the original 20,000-spectator stadium, and its archaeological museum houses prehistoric, archaic, and classical statues from ancient times. If you don't want to make the trip to Olympia, then Katakolon is an ideal place for a leisurely Greek lunch.

Kos. Ships dock in Kos Town, putting you within walking distance to the main sights of the birthplace of Hippocrates, father of modern medicine. You can stop by the archaeological museum located in the central Eleftherias Square and explore the impressive 15th-century Castle of Neratzia (Knight's castle). You may also want to see Hippocrates's Tree, where the ancient Greek physician lectured his students in its shade. In wooded foothills 3½ km (2 miles) west of Kos Town you can discover the ruins of the ancient Greek hospital of Asklepieion.

Monemvasia. Cruise ships tender you close to this unique medieval island town, which is actually a natural rock fortress that has been inhabited since AD 583. A narrow road connects you to the town, and from that point on you must travel by foot or donkey. Once inside, explore the nooks, grottoes, tiny alleys, and homes carved into the rock. In Lower Town you'll find Elkomenos Square, where the medieval Elkomenos Christos church and a small museum stand. Follow the remains of the medieval fortress to Upper Town to stand at the top of the rock. There you'll bask in memorable sea views right where Agia Sophia church is located.

Mykonos. Cruise ships drop anchor at Tourlos, where a small boat shuttles you to the island's main town called Mykonos Town, a well-preserved whitewashed Cycladic village comprised of a maze of narrow, small, and winding streets lined with shops, restaurants, bars, and cafés. Other ships dock in the modern cruise port and shuttle passengers into Mykonos Town by bus. Once in town, you'll be within walking distance of several highlights, including one of the most photographed churches in the world, Panagia Paraportiani, as well as the town's picturesque waterfront district called Little Venice. At night, Mykonos Town comes alive as a cosmopolitan nightlife and dining destination.

Mytilini, Lesvos. Mytilini, or Lesvos, is Greece's third-largest island known as the birthplace of ancient Greek poet Sappho. It's also known for its landscapes that produce fine olive oil and ouzo. Once your ship docks in harbor you'll be right near the waterfront mansions and bustling streets of Mytilini, which are lined with shops, taverns, and good ouzeries serving up local ouzo. A 15-minute walk up a pine-clad hill stands one of the largest castles in the Mediterranean, the Fortress of Mytilini. The Archaeological Museum of Mytilene, housed in a 1912 neoclassical mansion, is located behind the ferry dock.

Nafplion. Ships anchor off the coast of Nafplion and shuttle you to the main village, where you'll pass the picturesque Bourtzi islet, where a tower fortress seems to stand in the center of the sea. The top attraction of Nafplion is the Palamidi Fortress built by the Venetians in 1711. Getting to it requires a climb up 899 stairs to the entrance, where you'll have fantastic views of the region. The village itself is a picturesque maze of Venetian and Byzantine architecture lined with colorful bougainvillea, sidewalk cafés, tavernas, and shops. In the center of it all is Syntagma Square where you'll find a beautiful 18th-century Venetian arsenal and the archaeological museum.

Patmos. Smaller ships can dock in pretty, mountainous Patmos. At the port of Skala you can venture on a scenic 20-minute hike up to Kastelli hill to the town's 6th- to 4th-century BC stone remains. A quick taxi or bus ride 4 km (2½ miles) away takes you to neighboring Patmos Town, where you'll discover the religious significance of the island; it was where St. John the Divine was once exiled and where he wrote the *Book of Revelation*. Traditional whitewashed homes surround the bottom of the exterior walls of the Monastery of St. John the Divine, dating back to 1088. It's also where the Sacred Grotto is found, the sacred place where St. John received his visions that he recorded in the *Book of Revelation*.

Piraeus. The port of Piraeus is located 11 km (7 miles) southwest of Central Athens. You can easily catch the metro or a taxi to reach the worthy sites of the city, including the Acropolis, the ancient core of the modern capital. On its southwest slope you'll see the Odeon of Herodes Atticus, an ancient and impressive stone theater. Within the perimeter you'll find yourself in the heart of Old Athens and can easily stroll through Plaka and visit the bazaars of Monastiraki. The birthplace of democracy called the ancient Agora is at the northern edge of the Plaka. In the city, you can browse the impressive collections at the Acropolis Museum, the Benaki Museum, and the National Archaeological Museum. In central Syntagma Square you'll find parliament, formerly King Otto's royal palace, and have the opportunity to watch the Changing of the Evzone Guards at the Tomb of the Unknown Soldier.

Rhodes. Ships dock at the cruise port east of St. Catherine's Gate, bringing you close to the island's historical center. For two centuries Rhodes Town was ruled by the Knights of St. John. The monuments of that era are the island's highlights, including its 4-km (2½-mile) fortress walls; Palace of the Grand Master of the Knights of Rhodes; and the Mosque of Süleyman, dedicated to a Turkish sultan, that dates back to the 1522. You'll also discover where the ancient wonder called the Colossus once towered above the harbor in 280 BC. A 48-km (30-mile) trip away from Rhodes Town leads to the whitewashed medieval village of Lindos known for its grand hilltop acropolis.

Santorini. Cruise ships anchor near the cliffs of Fira, offering memorable views of the whitewashed mountaintop villages of Santorini. Once a tender shuttles you to the Old Port, you'll find a picturesque, romantic village with whitewashed homes and churches topped with bright blue roofs. The Museum of Prehistoric Fira gives insight into the island's prehistoric and archaeological history. If you want to venture 11 km (7 miles) farther into the island you'll find yourself taking in the view in Ia, another beautiful village that's built on a steep slope of the island's impressive cliffs. The remains of Akrotiri, destroyed millennia ago by a massive volcanic eruption, are on the island's southeastern tip.

GREAT ITINERARIES

CLASSICAL SITES

Lovers of art, antiquity, and mythology journey to Greece to make a pilgrimage to its great archaeological sites. Here, at Delphi, Olympia, and Epidauros, the gods of Olympus were revered, Euripides's plays were first presented, and some of the greatest temples ever built still evoke the genial atmosphere of Greece's golden age (in spite of 2,500 years of wear and tear). Take this tour and you'll learn that it's not necessary to be a scholar of history to feel the proximity of ancient Greece.

2 Days: Athens

Begin at the beginning—the Acropolis plateau—where you can explore the greatest temple of Periclean Greece, the Parthenon, while drinking in heart-stopping views over the modern metropolis. After touring the ancient Agora, the Monument of Lysikrates, and the Odeon of Herod Atticus, finish up at the National Archaeological Museum (check opening hours). *Chapter 3.*

Logistics: *Your Acropolis ticket also gets you into the other archaeological sites in Athens. Use the efficient Metro to avoid constant traffic slowdowns.*

1 Day: Sounion

Sun, sand, art, and antiquity all lie southeast of Athens in Sounion. Here, the spectacular Temple of Poseidon sits atop a cliff 195 feet over the Saronic Gulf. Pay your own respects to the god of the sea at the beach directly below or enjoy the coves of the Apollo coast as you head back west to the seaside resort of Vouliagmeni for an overnight. *Attica in Chapter 4.*

Logistics: *If you don't want to go on your own, most travel agencies offer tours to Sounion, and then you can spend another night in Athens.*

1 Day: Eleusis and Corinth

Heading west of Athens, make a stop at Eleusis (*Elefsina* in modern Greek), home of the Sanctuary of Demeter and the haunted grotto of Hades, god of the Underworld. Past the isthmus of Corinth—gateway to the Peloponnese—Ancient Corinth and its sublime Temple of Apollo beckon. Head south to the coast and Nafplion; en route, stop at a roadside stand for some tasty Nemean wine. *Attica in Chapter 4 and Argolid and Corinthiad in Chapter 10.*

Logistics: *Stopping briefly at Eleusis is easier if you have a car. Otherwise, you are at the mercy of bus schedules.*

2 Days: Nafplion, Tiryns, Mycenae, Epidauros

Nafplion is a stage set of spectacular Venetian fortresses, Greek churches, and neoclassical mansions, and you can explore the mysteries of forgotten civilizations in nearby Tiryns (*Tiryntha* in modern Greek), Mycenae, and Epidauros. North is Tiryns, where Bronze Age ramparts bear witness to Homer's "well-girt city." Farther north is Agamemnon's blood-soaked realm, the royal citadel of Mycenae, destroyed in 468 BC. Then take a day trip east to the famous ancient Theater at Epidauros, where a summer drama festival still presents the great tragedies of Euripides. *Argolid and Corinthiad in Chapter 11.*

Logistics: *Set up base in Nafplion and visit the nearby sights at your leisure. It's obviously easier to do this if you have a car.*

2 Days: Olympia and Bassae

After your third overnight in Nafplion, head west to Olympia—holiest site of the ancient Greek religion, home to the Sanctuary of Zeus, and birthplace of the Olympics. Walk through the olive groves

of the sacred precinct; then get acquainted with Praxiteles' *Hermes* in the museum. Overnight here and then make a trip south to the remote Temple of Apollo at Bassae (if traveling by car, look for road signs to *Vasses*). *Argolid/Corinthiad and Arcadia in Chapter 11.*

Logistics: *From Nafplion, you can get to Olympia via Argos by train or Tripoli by car (on the E65).*

1 Day: Delphi

Set aside a day to discover Delphi, whose noble dust and ancient ruins are theatrically set amid cliffs. Despite the tour buses, it is still possible to imagine the power of the most famous oracle of antiquity. From here, head back to Athens. *In Delphi and Environs in Chapter 4.*

Logistics: *From Olympia, head north through verdant forests of the Elis (Ilieia) region to Patras or nearby Rion for the ferry or bridge across the Corinthian gulf; travel east along the coast and overnight in chic Galaxidi, with its elegant stone seafarers' mansions.*

GREAT ITINERARIES

MARVELS OF CENTRAL GREECE

With a rich wilderness of mountains, rocky gorges, and white-water rivers crossed by stone-arch bridges, Epirus is the antithesis of what most people think about Greece. Take a tour of the region that sweeps down from the borders of Albania, and drive south into Central Greece almost to the Gulf of Corinth to discover a stunning landscape that shows off Greece's mountainous character at its best.

1 Day: Ioannina

Ioannina, which was a crossroads of trading, is the handsome capital of Epirus and reflects its Balkan, Ottoman, and Byzantine roots that are preserved in its Old Town. You can soak in the panoramic view of the city from its castle walls that date back to AD 528 and visit the city's Byzantine Museum within the city's citadel. Take a boat ride and glide to the city's landmark, Lake Pamvotis, for a stop at Nissi Island. Visit the little village on Nissi, which is free of most vehicular traffic, then head to the museum that unveils the historical details of enigmatic Ottoman ruler Ali Pasha during his dramatic reign of the region from 1788 until he was deposed by the Turks in 1821. It's housed in the 16th-century era Pandelimonos Monastery, where Ali Pasha lived until he was killed. *Chapter 8.*

Logistics: *A bus from Athens to Ioannina can take 7 hours; it's much easier to fly.*

1 Day: Zagorohoria

In the Zagorohoria region north of Ioannina, numerous traditional villages defined by stone, wood, and slate rock hug the mountain slopes. Admire the handicrafts in Monodendri village, at

altitude 3,400 feet, where you can also enter the depths of the Vikos Gorge, the deepest in the world, and walk the cobblestone trail to the 15th-century Aghia Paraskevi Monastery. *Chapter 8.*

Logistics: *Drive from Ioannina to Zagorohoria (1 hour), or take a bus. There are just a few places to stay in Zagorohoria, so you may want to remain for a second night in Ioannina and visit on a day-trip, especially if you have a car. The area can be especially busy during summer weekends in July and August, so plan ahead if visiting during that time.*

1 Day: Metsovo

Metsovo is a traditional village cascading down a mountainside in the heart of the Pindos mountain range (below the Katara pass marking the highest point in Greece and the border between Epirus and Thessaly), where outdoor aficionados can hike and raft. Even during the summer, the temperatures at this altitude will be considerably cooler than in other parts of Greece, with highs in the 70s F. Wind down in the village and walk through its stone-paved streets. Be sure to see the Tositsa Museum, the home of one of the village's most prominent families. Stop to sample local wines and cheeses; the Katogi-Averoff Winery is an important regional winery and produces fine red wines. *Chapter 8.*

Logistics: *Metsovo is another 1½ hours from Zagorohoria; drive to Kalambaka (1 hour farther), just outside Meteora, for an overnight stay.*

1 Day: Meteora

Wake up ready to spend the day exploring Meteora's sky-high monasteries built on seemingly inaccessible sandstone peaks. In an awe-inspiring effort, Byzantine emperors funded the construction of these

aeries, and monks settled on these rock towers from the 11th century onwards. At one point there were 16 monasteries. Today only six remain, and they are on the UNESCO World Heritage list. *Chapter 8.*

Logistics: *Two or three monasteries are usually enough for anyone. After your visit, drive to the next stop, Delphi (3½ hours), in the early afternoon.*

2 Days: Delphi and Environs

Wake up in the land that was once regarded as the center of the world by Ancient Greeks. Spend the day touring the archaeological site of Delphi. Positioned on the slopes of Mt. Parnassos the site housed the ancients' most famous oracle. Next, visit Arachova, also perched on the slopes of Mt. Parnassos, and stop at the monastic complex of Osios Loukas before returning to either Delphi or Arachova for the night. *Chapter 6.*

Logistics: *It's 3 to 4 hours back to Athens by car, longer if you are going by bus.*

TIPS

■ Points in Epirus may be quite high in altitude, and those who are sensitive to heights may be affected. Mountain roads may have numerous blind curves and they can be steep. Drive with caution.

■ The preferred route back to Athens takes you back through Levadia; if you want a short detour, follow the signs for the ancient springs of Lethe and Mnemosyne.

■ Guided tours can get you to Delphi and back, but to do this full itinerary, you will need to rent a car or take multiple buses.

GREAT ITINERARIES

GREECE'S GREAT NORTH

Northern Greece sparkles with the sights, sounds, and aromas of a melting-pot history and crossroads geography. The region's seaside capital, Thessaloniki, impresses with its stylish young, hip nightlife, diverse culture, and easy-going nature. Just east of the metropolis is the trident-shaped arch of Halkidiki, the summer playground for northern Greeks and southeastern Europeans. The landmass juts out into the Aegean, offering spectacular beaches lined with aquamarine waters and green rolling hills and mountains. The Sporadic island chain including its southernmost island, Skyros, matches that nature with the same loveliness with the charm only a Greek island can offer. To get the most out of your trip around northern Greece's coast and on Skyros island, plan your flights in advance and consider the drive times between each destination.

3 Days: Skyros

Fly from Athens directly to Skyros. Once your flight gets in, rent a car and get settled in. Time your next few days to explore the sights of this island of the Sporades chain that resembles a Cycladic island due to its whitewashed architecture, and a Dodecanese island due to its rugged landscape. Its main town was built like an amphitheater around the Byzantine-era Monastery of St. George, where an ancient acropolis remains on the highest point of the Old Town. Weave in through its alleyways, where much of the island's population lives, and be sure to visit the outstanding Faltaits Historical and Folklore Museum. Choose one of the golden sandy beaches, typically surrounded by the green hills covered with lush pine trees. Take a day-trip to the tiny Sarakino island and feel calmly isolated on its white-sand beach, Glyfada. *Chapter 6.*

Logistics: *If you don't want to fly, you can get a ferry to Skyros from Evia, but that requires a bus ride from Athens.*

2 Days: Thessaloniki

Wake up early and take a flight to Greece's second-largest city, Thessaloniki. Walk around the port where the icon of the city, a 15th-century White Tower stands by the sea. Stop at the city's grand monuments including the 5th-century Church of Agios Dimitrios, the impressive Roman Rotunda, and the 3rd-century palace ruins of Roman emperor Galerius. Much of the city's charm lies in its ever-changing character, since it's been conquered and rebuilt so many times of the year; its modern appeal lies in part in its warmth, accessibility, and languid pace; an opportunity to slow down and relax for a couple of days. By night, enjoy the city's vibrant nightlife and great restaurants. *Chapter 8.*

Logistics: *You'll need to fly from Skyros to Thessaloniki; there's just no other way to do the trip in a reasonable amount of time.*

1 Day: Alexander the Great Country

After enjoying Greece's second city, rent a car and explore some of the fascinating sights in Central Macedonia. These include Pella, Alexander the Great's birthplace; the royal tombs of Vergina, where his father was buried after his assassination; and Dion at the base of Mount Olympus, an underrated temple city named after Zeus that is not widely visited. *Chapter 8.*

Logistics: *If you want to see everything here, you must have a car. If you want to rely on buses, choose either Vergina or Dion, not both, but keep your hotel base in Thessaloniki; there are not very many places to stay in this area.*

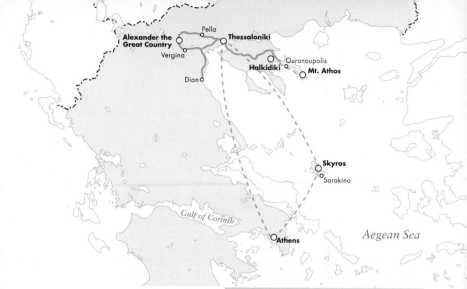

2 Days: Halkidiki and Mt. Athos

Reserve some time to explore Halkidiki's third leg, Mt. Athos. Drive from Thessaloniki to Ouranoupolis, which will be your base, and give yourself some time to simply wind down. That's why the Greeks come here. The village, which is on the final point of land that separates the secular world from the sacred sanctuaries of Mt. Athos, is noted for its tapestry and rug weaving. On the second day, the men in your group can make a pilgrimage to the monastery of Mt. Athos, which is open only to men who seek advance permission to enter. But anyone can enjoy a scenic boat ride around the peninsula, which is like no other in the world. All boats depart from the docks in Ouranoupolis. *Chapter 8.*

Logistics: *Drive back to Thessaloniki (2 hours) in the afternoon, and take a 1-hour flight back to Athens.*

TIPS

Athens to Skyros flights leave at least three times per week and more frequently (currently six times daily) during peak season on Olympic Air. Skyros to Thessaloniki flights depart two times per week on Sky Express.

There is an abundance of flights leaving daily between Athens and Thessaloniki on Olympic Air, Ellinair, and Ryanair.

Also note that the Thessaloniki Airport is not within Thessaloniki city center limits. Schedule 30-minute drive time from the airport to and from the Thessaloniki city center.

GREAT ITINERARIES

WONDERS OF THE PELOPONNESE COAST

The Peloponnese remains generally unknown to most Americans, but for those who take the leap to explore it the rewards are great. The coastline is divine, showcasing the natural and rural beauty of Greece from rugged cliffs that meet the sparkling seas swirling in bright shades of turquoise. Peloponnese port cities also give off a special Greek island–like charm with their small village atmosphere, beautiful architecture, and expansive views of the sea. If you have time, an excursion here will be well rewarded.

1 Day: Epidavros

Epidavros has Greece's best-preserved ancient theater, which still amazes audiences with its perfect acoustics. You can literally hear a pin drop on the stage from 55 rows up. Seating 14,000 people, with a breathtaking view of the mountains and valleys directly behind its stage, the venue gets packed each summer (June through August) for the Athens Epidauros Festival, which features notable actors from all over the world. Also visit the Sanctuary of Asklepios, the supposed birthplace of Apollo's son, the world's greatest healer, which has been a major place of healing since the 4th century. Take a break by the port with an orange juice, freshly squeezed from oranges grown in the area's famous orange groves. *Chapter 10.*

Logistics: *This itinerary really needs to be done by car; it's 1 ½ hours from Athens to Epidauros. During the festival, however, buses run to and from Nafplion especially for the performances, and that's where you should base yourself for the night.*

1 Day: Nafplion

The first capital of Greece is often described as the most cultural, historic, and romantic port city in the country. Discover its Old Town, a peninsula that juts out into the Gulf of Argos and where Greek, Venetian, and Turkish architecture melds in harmony in its little streets and tree-shaded plazas. It deserves at least a day of your undivided attention, but you could certainly spend more time if you have it. *Chapter 10.*

Logistics: *The drive from Epidauros to Nafplion is just 40 minutes, but if you are staying the night, you'll likely want to start this itinerary in Nafplion, which is 2 hours from Athens by toll road.*

1 Day: Monemvasia

From afar it's incredible to think people live in the massive rock, towering at 1,148 feet, just ahead of you. One narrow bridge connects the Peloponnese landmass to Monemvasia, where a little walled community has thrived since AD 600. Its name translates as *one entrance*, and it's a perfectly preserved medieval town filled with shops, small hotels, and restaurants. Its alleyways lined with traditional homes are a delight to explore with viewing spots, including at Agia Sofia Church, that offer sweeping views of both the town and sea. *Chapter 10.*

Logistics: *An overnight here allows you to enjoy this strange place when the tour groups have departed. Just be aware that cars are not allowed, so you will have to carry your luggage in (have your hotel's staff meet you to help).*

1 Day: Mystras and Sparta

Although not on the coast, Mystras is not to be missed. While modern Sparta may be disappointing to many because of its paucity of ruins, not so for Mystras, which has the most impressive ruins in the Peloponnese, albeit from the 14th century rather than from ancient times. The abandoned palaces, churches, and monasteries are well worth the detour. *Chapter 10.*

Logistics: *The Kinsterna Hotel & Spa in Agios Stefanos is one of the most distinctive hotels in Greece, but there are less expensive options near Mystras.*

2 Days: Mani

Mani is one of the most unique areas of Greece. Byzantine chapels, towered houses, and stories of lawless locals are connected with a rocky, wild, dry yet strikingly handsome landscape. Walk to the mythical gate to the end of the world and the southernmost point of mainland Greece, Cape Tenaro. Then, explore seaside villages of Gerolimenas and Areopolis, trying Mani's famous local olive oils and honey along the way. *Chapter 10.*

Logistics: *You can stay in a distinctive property in either Areopolis or Gerolimenas. It's a 3-hour drive back to Athens from here.*

TIPS

Driving through the Peloponnese is pleasant, scenic, and easy. Roads are typically traffic-free and safe, and exits are marked with the Latin alphabet.

An overnight stay at one of the small hotels situated within "the rock" of Monemvasia is a unique experience, but you have to carry your luggage into town, which is not accessible to cars.

If you are up for a scenic, rocky but easy-to-follow hike, head toward the lighthouse at the tip of Cape Tenaro. The amazing views from the very tip of mainland Greece will be your reward.

ISLAND-HOPPING: CYCLADES TO CRETE

There is no bad itinerary for the Greek islands. Whether you choose the Sporades, the Dodecanese, or any of those other getaways floating in the Aegean, the leading isles in Greece differ remarkably, and they are all beautiful. But the needle flies off the beauty-measuring gauge when it comes to the Cyclades. It might be possible to "see" any of these famous islands in a day: the "must-see" sights—monasteries or ancient temples—are often few. Still, it is best to take a slower pace and enjoy a sumptuous, idyllic 14-day tour. Planning the details of this trip depends on your sense of inclusiveness, your restlessness, your energy, *and* your ability to accommodate changing boat schedules. Just be warned: the danger of sailing through the Cyclades is that you will never want to leave them. From these suggested landfalls, some of the most justly famous, you can set off to find other idyllic retreats on your own.

2 Days: Mykonos

Jewel of the Cyclades, this island manages to retain its seductive charm. Spend the first day and evening enjoying appealing Mykonos Town, where a maze of beautiful streets is lined with shops, bars, restaurants, and clubs; spend time on one of the splendid beaches; and, if you want to indulge in some hedonism, partake of the wild nightlife. The next morning take the local boat to nearby Delos for one of the great classical sites in the Aegean. *Mykonos in Chapter 11.*

Logistics: *Mykonos is one of the main transport hubs of the Greek islands, with many ferries, boats, and planes connecting to Athens and its port of Piraeus. For a short stay like this, it's best to be in or near Mykonos Town.*

2 Days: Naxos

Sail south to Naxos, arriving from Mykonos in the late afternoon or evening, and begin with a pre-dinner stroll around Naxos town, visiting the Portara (an ancient landmark), the castle, and other sights in the old quarter. The next morning, visit the Archaeological Museum; then drive through the island's mountainous center for spectacular views. Along the way, visit such sights as the Panayia Drosiani, a church near Moni noted for 7th-century frescoes; the marble-paved village of Apeiranthos; and the Temple of Demeter. If you have time, stop for a swim at one of the beaches facing Paros, say Mikri Vigla. *Naxos in Chapter 11.*

Logistics: *During high season in summer, there are many ferries to Naxos from Mykonos, but there are many fewer in the off-season. The fast-ferry trip (by Seajet) takes less than an hour.*

3 Days: Paros

Go west, young man, to Paros, where the large spaces provide peace and quiet. Paros town has delights profane—buzzing bars—and sacred, such as the legendary Hundred Doors Church. But the highlight will be a meal in the impossibly pretty little fishing harbor of Naousa or, on a morning drive around the island, a visit to the lovely mountain village of Lefkes. Then spend an extra night of magic on the neighboring isle of Antiparos, where off-duty Hollywood celebs bliss out with all the white sands, pink bougainvillea, and blue seas. *Paros in Chapter 11.*

Logistics: *It's a very short hop from Naxos to Paros.*

2 Days: Folegandros

This smaller isle is not only beautiful but, rarer in these parts, authentic. It boasts one of the most stunning Chora towns, deliberately downplayed touristic development, several good beaches, quiet evenings, traditional local food, and respectful visitors. The high point, literally and figuratively, is the location of the main town—on a towering cliff over the sea, its perch almost rivals that of Santorini. *Folegandros in Chapter 11.*

3 Days: Santorini

Take a ferry from Folegandros south to the spectacle of all spectacles. Yes, in summer the crowds will remind you of the running of the bulls in Pamplona, but even they won't stop you from gasping at the vistas, the seaside cliffs, and stunning Cycladic cubist architecture. Once you've settled in, have a sunset drink on a terrace overlooking the volcanic caldera. You can also find many view-providing watering holes in Fira, the capital, or Ia, Greece's most photographed village. The next day, visit the Museum of Prehistoric Thera; the Akrotiri excavation; then enjoy a third day just swimming one of the black-sand beaches at Kamari or Perissa. *Santorini in Chapter 11.*

2 Days: Crete

Despite the attractions of sea and mountains, it is still the mystery surrounding Europe's first civilization and empire that draws many travelers to Crete. Like them,

you can discover stunning testimony to the island's mysterious Minoan civilization, particularly at the legendary Palace of Knossos. Along these shores are blissful beaches as well as the enchanting Venetian-Turkish city of Hania. Spinalonga, the last leper island colony of Greece, lies peacefully opposite the sleepy fishing village of Plaka. From Heraklion, Crete's main port, there are frequent flights and ferries back to Piraeus, Athens, and reality. *Crete in Chapter 12.*

ON THE CALENDAR

	Many celebrations throughout the year revolve around Greek Orthodox holidays and saint days. But Greeks also love any good excuse to dance and feast, and they love to celebrate the arts, including film, dance, and drama.
JANUARY	**Epiphany, January 6.** To commemorate the day of Christ's baptism, a sizable gathering in Athens takes place at the port of Piraeus (and every other port nearby). A priest throws a large crucifix into the water, and young men brave the cold to recover it. The finder is rewarded with a blessing.
FEBRUARY	**Apokries.** Thousands take to the streets of Greece, prancing and dancing in costume, drinking, and just being merry during the country's three-week pre-Lenten Carnival season. The islands of Skyros and Crete attract some of the largest crowds, but the Greek Carnival capital is Patras in the northern Peloponnese. ⊕ *carnival-in-rethymnon-crete-greece.com* or ⊕ *carnivalpatras.gr.*
MARCH	**Thessaloniki International Documentary Festival.** Documentary filmmakers from all over the world screen their work at this March festival that's gaining a name for itself in the industry. ⊕ *tdf.filmfestival.gr.* **Greek Independence Day, March 25.** A military parade that commemorates the start of the War of Greek Independence of 1821 is held with pomp and circumstance. It marches straight through the heart of Athens in Syntagma Square. **Feast of the Annunciation, March 25.** While Greece celebrates its independence, the islands of Tinos and Hydra hold special religious festivities to honor the news that Mary would be the mother of Christ.
APRIL–MAY	**Holy Easter Week Celebrations, April or May.** Throughout the country, church services and processions are scheduled during the most important holiday in Greece. On Easter midnight, families gather at local churches, candles in hand. The rest of the day is dedicated to feasting on roasted lamb and other traditional food. On Holy Thursday, "The Last Supper" is reenacted at the Monastery of St. John the Divine on the island of Patmos.
MAY	**Dora Stratou Dance Troupe in Athens.** The 75-member dance troupe performs a full repertoire of Greek folk dances wearing traditional costumes and jewelry beginning

in May. Frequent performances light the stage at the group's open-air theater near the Acropolis. The season continues through September. ⊕ *www.grdance.org*.

International Museums Day, May 18. A day established by the International Council of Museums encourages public awareness of the importance of museums in today's society. Some of the best museums in Greece including the Acropolis Museum, the Benaki Museum, and the National Archeological Museum offer free admission. ⊕ *network. icom.museum/international-museum-day*.

Art Athina Festival. One of the longest-lasting contemporary art fairs in Europe takes place in Athens each May. International artists gather to collaborate and present their work to more than 30,000 visitors over a four-day period. ⊕ *www.art-athina.gr*.

Anastenaria Fire Walking Festival, May 21–23. Outside of Thessaloniki, in the northern Greek villages of Agia Eleni and Langadas, the pagan ritual of walking over fire still goes on. Today, however, it is dedicated and attached to the Christian faith and always begins on St. Constantine Day, lasting for three days.

JUNE

Athens and Epidavros Festival, June to October. A full schedule of classical Greek dramas, opera, orchestra, and dance performances fills venues across Athens, including the ancient Odeon of Herodes Atticus next to the Acropolis. Over the years a roster of famous actors including Helen Mirren, Ethan Hawke, and Kevin Spacey have graced the stage at the magnificent ancient Theatre of Epidauros in the Peloponnese. ⊕ *www.greekfestival.gr*.

Nafplion Festival. Established as one of the most successful classical music events in Greece, the festival is set in various venues in the beautiful seaside Peloponnese city and attracts the brightest ensembles and artists from around the world. ⊕ *www.nafplionfestival.gr*.

Rockwave Festival. The Black Eyed Peas, Megadeth, Oasis, and Guns N' Roses are just a few headliners that have taken the stage at Terravibe Park, north of Athens, since this festival began in 1995. Crowds pack the outdoor venues for four days of performances, rocking on to established and upandcoming bands. ⊕ *www.rockwavefestival.gr*.

JULY	**Medieval Rose Festival.** The gorgeous medieval town of Rhodes is the perfect backdrop for well-rehearsed reenactments from Byzantine and medieval times. Musical and art events add to the program with the aim to educate and entertain. ⊕ *www.medievalfestival.gr.*
	Festival of the Aegean. Hundreds of singers and dancers from all over the world, including more than a dozen choirs, gather in Syros, the capital of the Cyclades, each summer. Their inspiring performances pack audiences at beautiful venues including the elegant Apollo Theatre and St. Nicholas Church. ⊕ *www.festivaloftheaegean.com.*
AUGUST	**Feast of the Assumption of the Virgin, August 15.** On this national holiday, thousands of pilgrims crowd Tinos to ask for a special blessing or a miracle. In crowds, they crawl on their hands and knees to the cathedral of Panagia Evangelistria.
	Sani Festival. With sections like "Jazz on the Hill" and "Greek Variations," the fun music fest gathers significant artists from around the world for a jam-packed program of concerts in the Halkidiki Peninsula of northern Greece. Performances take place at various venues, including Sani Hill, a small islet surrounded by the lapping waves of the Aegean. ⊕ *sanifestival.gr.*
	Renaissance Festival at Rethymnon. In a celebration of art, theater, and music, hundreds of artists from around the globe act, sing, and dance in venues throughout the most picturesque Cretan town in performances that begin in August and continue through September. Each performance aims to honor of the spirit of the Renaissance era. ⊕ *www.rfr.gr.*
	Megaro Gyzi Festival. A combination of classical music, traditional Greek performances, and art exhibitions add to the already beautiful atmosphere on Santorini. A 17th-century mansion called Megaro Gyzi, located in the cliff-hugging village of Fira, houses each event. ⊕ *www.megarogyzi.gr.*
SEPTEMBER	**Aegina Pistachio Festival.** Go dance, sing, and enjoy your share of delicious pistachio products as you learn about the Aegina's appreciation for the nut that has helped their island thrive. ⊕ *www.aeginafistikifest.gr.*
	Dionysia Wine Festival. One of Naxos island's key events, with music, theater, and art exhibitions, celebrates the

	island's ties to the Ancient Greek God of Wine, Dionysus, during the first week of September.
OCTOBER	**Spetses Mini Marathon.** The biggest island sporting event in Greece features running and swimming races and a children's run. Social events are also open for those who want to feel the energetic vibe of the island during the action-packed weekend. Get a welcoming taste of the savory homemade pies baked and handed out by local women. ⊕ *spetsesmarathon.com.*
	Ochi Day, October 28. *Ochi* means *no* in Greek, a word that sums up Greece's defiance to the Italian invasion of 1940. The day is a national holiday that's widely celebrated and honored. Major cities like Athens and Thessaloniki hold military parades, and coastal villages schedule naval parades.
NOVEMBER	**Thessaloniki International Film Festival.** For more than 50 years, the sophisticated city has hosted independent filmmakers from all over the world, who compete for the event's highest award, the Golden Alexander. ⊕ *www.filmfestival.gr.*
	Athens Marathon. Tens of thousands of runners head to Greece in early November to run the course based on the original marathon from Ancient Greek times. The 26.2-mile course begins in Marathon and finishes at the grand marble Panathenaic Stadium in Athens. ⊕ *www.athensauthenticmarathon.gr.*
	November 17th. The widely observed anniversary commemorates the 1973 uprising by Athens Polytechnic University students, who were killed for protesting the Greek military junta. Metro stations close down, and protests typically take to the streets, making it a difficult day for travel and sightseeing.
DECEMBER	**Christmas.** Athens gets festive, especially for kids. The National Gardens and Syntagma Square are transformed into a Christmas village, where activities are scheduled during school vacation. Additional city venues and public spaces hold events as well. ⊕ *www.cityofathens.gr.*

ATHENS

WELCOME TO ATHENS

TOP REASONS TO GO

★ **The Acropolis:** A beacon of classical glory rising above Athens's architectural mishmash, this iconic citadel represents everything the Athenians were and still aspire to be.

★ **Evzones on Syntagma Square:** Unmistakable in tasseled hats and pom-pom shoes, elite Evzones guards act out a traditional changing of the guard that falls somewhere between discipline and performance art.

★ **The Ancient Agora and Monastiraki:** Socrates and Plato once philosophized at the Agora, and today you can do the same perambulating around the nearby Monastiraki marketplace.

★ **Opa!:** Whether jamming to post-Grunge in Gazi-Kerameikos, drinking cocktails til dawn around Syntagma, or dirty dancing on the tables at live-bouzoukia clubs, the Athenians party like no one else.

★ **Thriving Culture:** Galleries, cooperatives, artistic events, performances, museums and the new Stavros Niarchos Cultural Center have put Athens on the road to being the new Berlin.

Athens's main grid consists of three parallel streets—Stadiou, Eleftheriou Venizelou (known as Panepistimiou by locals), and Akadimias—that link two main squares, Syntagma and Omonia.

1 **Acropolis, Makriyianni, and Koukaki.** The massive citadel and its architecturally sophisticated structures rise majestically above the city. Just below is Makriyianni, an increasingly trendy neighborhood with the Acropolis Museum. Koukaki is one of the city's hippest districts.

2 **Plaka and Anafiotika.** Touristy and tranquil at once, old-fashioned Plaka is dotted by Byzantine churches, ancient Greek monuments, and souvenir shops. Above it is the whitewashed minivillage of Anafiotika, with Cycladic-inspired architecture and splendid city views.

3 **Monastiraki and Psirri.** Adjacent to the ancient Agora is where you'll find Athens's Central Market, not to mention flea markets, shops, and a chaotic buzz. To the south, Psirri is a diverse area of low-key eateries, traditional grocery shops, and artisanal workshops.

4 **Thissio.** Graced by classical ruins, Thissio is lined with pretty cafés, restaurants, and galleries.

5 **Syntagma.** The heart of modern Athens, surrounded by the Parliament House, the city's top restaurants and bars, and Ermou shopping boulevard.

2

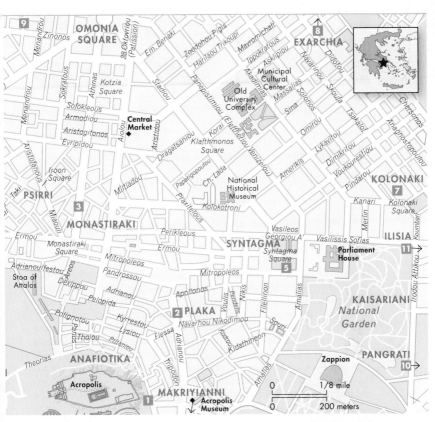

6 Gazi-Kerameikos.
Home to the city's Technopolis gasworks and a popular arts and nightlife hub.

7 Kolonaki. East of Syntagma Square lies this fashionable residential area loaded with see-and-be-seen cafés, glossy boutiques, and top museums.

8 Exarchia. In the northern reaches of the city, the offbeat area is home to the famed National Archaeological Museum.

9 Omonia and Metaxourgeio. Omonia is an important transport hub with good hotels but can be sketchy at night; Metaxourgeio is popular for its arts scene and nightlife.

10 Pangrati. The mostly residential neighborhood of Pangrati has a blossoming nightlife scene.

11 Ilisia. Home to the Athens Concert Hall, the U.S. Embassy, and nearby nightlife spot Mavili Square.

12 Piraeus. Athens's busy port also has some recommendable restaurants.

Updated by Alexia Amvrazi

It's no wonder that all roads lead to the fascinating and maddening metropolis of Athens. Lift your eyes 200 feet above the city to the Parthenon, its honey-colored marble columns rising from a massive limestone base, and you'll behold architectural perfection that has not been surpassed in 2,500 years. Today, this shrine of classical form dominates a 21st-century boomtown.

One of the world's oldest cities, Athens is home to 4.5 million souls, many of whom spend the day discussing the city's faults, including budget woes, red tape, overcrowding, transport strikes, immigration problems, and unemployment. These complaint sessions are usually accompanied by good coffee, food, or cocktails since Athenians refuse to stay indoors in any weather or mood. But while Athens is a difficult city to love, it's also a difficult city to leave, and many temporary visitors end up settling there for years without ever having expected to. As damaging as it has been to the Greek psyche and businesses alike, the financial crisis has also served to inspire Greeks to try out new jobs and start innovative and sophisticated entrepreneurial pursuits, while the blossoming urban arts scene has earned the Greek capital the title of being "the new Berlin." Over the last five years it has undergone a huge transformation, and almost every day an innovative new shop, gallery, or eatery pops up.

To experience Athens—Athìna in Greek—fully is to understand the essence of Greece: ancient monuments surviving in a sea of cement, startling beauty amid the squalor, folkish tradition juxtaposed with ultramodern concepts. A priest in flowing robes looks entranced as he studies his iPhone while waiting on the platform of the sleek, space-age metro. To appreciate Athens is to appreciate life with all its surprises and complexities.

THE NEW ATHENS

Many splendid features were created for the city's 2004 Olympics. In 2000, Athens opened its still-expanding metro, many of whose gleaming stations display ancient artifacts and modern artworks and installations by famous artists. High-tech Eleftherios Venizelos International Airport serves as the country's efficient entry point. New infrastructure blessings also include a (somewhat slow) tram line running from the city center to the south-coast beaches; an express train running to the airport and far-flung suburbs; and a ring-road beltway and the repaving and expansion of most of the city's potholed highways.

Within the city, beautification projects took priority. The most successful has been the completion of Athens's Archaeological Park, which links the capital's ancient sites in a pedestrian network that includes the Panathenaic stadium, the Temple of Olympian Zeus, the Acropolis, Filopappou hill, the ancient Greek and Roman agoras, Hadrian's Library, and Kerameikos.

Two major new projects include the long-awaited National Museum of Contemporary Art (EMST) on Syngrou Avenue, housed in a massive, 19th-century beer factory, and the Stavros Niarchos Foundation Cultural Center (SNFCC) in the southern suburbs, housing the National Opera House of Greece and the National Library.

While various museums have received renovations, such as the National Archaeological Museum and the Benaki Museum, one museum garnered headlines around the world when it finally opened in June 2009: the spectacularly modern Acropolis Museum, which showcases some of the most venerated ancient statues in the world. And the invigorating buzz that seized Athens pre-2004 has also helped transform entire neighborhoods like Gazi-Kerameikos, Thissio, Metaxourgeio, Kerameikos, and Psirri from industrial warehouse districts to hot spots of hip restaurants and happening nightclubs.

THE AGELESS CITY

Happily, you can still wander into less-touristy areas to discover pockets of timeless charm. Here, in the lovelier Athenian neighborhoods, you can delight in the pleasures of strolling—*Peripatos,* the Athenians call it, and it's as old as Aristotle, whose students learned as they roamed about in his Peripatetic school. This ancient practice survives in the modern custom of the evening *volta,* or stroll, taken along the pedestrianized Dionyssiou Areopagitou Street skirting the base of the Acropolis.

Along your way, be sure to stop in a taverna to observe Athenians in their element. They are lively and expressive, their hands fiddling with worry beads (a trend recently reborn among youths) or gesturing excitedly. Although often expansively friendly, they can be combative when they feel threatened, but they're also insatiably curious.

Amid the ancient treasures and the 19th-century delights of neighborhoods such as Anafiotika and Plaka, the pickax, pneumatic drill, and cement mixer have given birth to countless office buildings and modern apartments. Hardly a monument of importance attests to the city's history between the completion of the Temple of Olympian Zeus 19 centuries ago and the present day. That is the tragedy of Athens: the long vacuum in its history, the centuries of decay, neglect, and even oblivion. But within the last 150 years the Greeks have created a modern capital out of a village centered on a group of ruined marble columns and have gone far in transforming Athens into a sparkling modern metropolis that the ancients would strain to recognize but would heartily endorse. Its joyous spirit remains unscathed even in the face of financial adversity and shrinking public coffers.

PLANNING

WHEN TO GO

Athens often feels like a furnace in summer, due to the capital's shortage of parks and millions of circulating cars. Mornings between 7 am and 9 am or evenings after 5 pm are often pleasant, but temperatures can still hover in the 90s during heat waves. The capital is far more pleasant in spring and fall, when the air is crisp and the sunlight bearable. Winters are mild here, just as they are in all of Greece: it rains but rarely snows, but in deep winter the cold can cut to the bone.

GETTING HERE AND AROUND

Many major sights, as well as hotels, cafés, and restaurants, are within a fairly small central area of Athens. It's easy to walk everywhere, though sometimes cars and bikes obstruct sidewalks. Most far-flung sights, such as beaches, are reachable by metro, bus, and tram.

AIR TRAVEL

Athens's sleek Eleftherios Venizelos International Airport has made air travel around the country much easier. Greece is so small that few in-country flights take longer than an hour or cost more than €200 round-trip. Aegean Airlines and Olympic Airways have regular flights between Athens, Thessaloniki, and most major cities and islands in Greece. *For further information, see Air Travel in Travel Smart.*

AIRPORT TRANSFERS

The best way to get to or from the airport and Athens is by metro or light-rail. Single tickets cost €10 and include transfers within 90 minutes of the ticket's initial validation to bus, trolley, or tram. Multi-passenger tickets for groups of two (€18) or three (€24) passengers are also available; if you're just making a stopover in Athens, opt for a round-trip ticket (€18), valid for trips to and from the airport made within a week.

In Athens four reliable express buses connect the airport with the metro (Nomismatokopeio, Ethniki Amyna, and Dafni stations), Syntagma Square, Kifissos Bus Station, and Piraeus. Express buses leave the arrivals level of the airport every 15 minutes and operate 24 hours a day. Bus X95 will take you to Syntagma Square (Amalias Avenue); Bus X96 takes the Vari–Koropi road inland and links with the coastal road, passing through Voula, Glyfada, and Alimos; it then goes on to Piraeus (opposite Karaiskaki Square), and this is the best option if you are getting directly on a cruise ship. Bus X97 goes to the Dafni metro stop, while X93 brings voyagers to the dusty Kifissos intercity bus station. The Attiki Odos ring road and the expansion of the city's network of bus lanes have made travel times more predictable.

Bus tickets to and from the airport cost €5 and are valid on all forms of transportation in Athens for 24 hours from the time of validation. Purchase tickets (and get bus schedules) from the airport terminal, kiosks, metro stations, or even on the express buses.

Taxis are readily available at the arrivals level of the Athens airport; it costs an average of €35 to get into downtown Athens. (If you fear you have been overcharged, insist on a receipt with the driver's details and contact the tourist police.) Prestige Limousine Service and Central VIP Services provide service; an evening surcharge of up to 50% often applies, and you should call in advance. Prices range between €60 and €90 one-way from the airport to a central hotel for four people.

Contacts Central VIP Services. ☎ *210/924–9500* ⊕ *www.centralvip.gr.*
Prestige Limousine Service. ☎ *210/323–4151* ⊕ *www.prestigegreece.com.*

BOAT AND FERRY TRAVEL

Boat travel in Greece is common and reasonably priced. Every weekend thousands of Athenians set off on one- and two-hour trips to islands like Aegina, Hydra, and Andros, while in summer ferries are weighed down with merrymakers on their way to Mykonos, Rhodes, and Crete. Cruise ships, ferries, and hydrofoils from the Aegean and most other Greek islands dock and depart every day from Athens's main port, Piraeus, 10 km (6 miles) southwest of Central Athens. Ships for Corfu sail from ports nearer to it, such as Patras and Igoumenitsa. Connections from Piraeus to the main island groups are good, while connections from main islands to smaller ones within a group are less so.

Boat schedules are published in *Kathimerini,* an insert in *The New York Times International Edition,* but it's often more convenient to book tickets through a travel agent; it's what Greeks do as well. Schedules can be found online or by calling the Piraeus Port Authority. Just realize that timetables change according to seasonal demand, and boats may be delayed by weather conditions, so your plans should be flexible. Ideally, buy your tickets at least two or three days in advance, especially if you are traveling in summer or taking a car. Reserve your return journey or continuation soon after you arrive. *For further information, see Boat Travel in Travel Smart.*

GETTING TO AND FROM PIRAEUS AND RAFINA

To get to and from Piraeus, you can take the Green Line metro (Line 1) from Central Athens directly to the station at the main port. The trip takes 25 to 30 minutes, but there may be a rather long walk to your dock from there. A taxi can take longer because of traffic and costs around €15–€18. Express bus line X80 links the OLP cruise terminal to the Acropolis and Syntagma Square in the center of Athens and runs daily every 30 minutes from 7 am until 9:30 pm.

Athens's other main port is Rafina, which serves some of the closer Cyclades and Evia. KTEL buses run every 45 minutes between the Mavromateon bus terminal in Central Athens and the port, from 5:40 am until 10:30 pm, and cost €2.40 At Rafina, the buses arrive and depart from an area slightly uphill from the port. The trip takes about one hour depending on traffic. *(See Bus and Tram Travel).*

Contacts Rafina KTEL Buses. ☎ *22940/23440 bus terminal* ⊕ *www.ktelattikis.gr.*

BUS AND TRAM TRAVEL WITHIN ATHENS

Athens and its suburbs are covered by a good network of buses, with express buses running between Central Athens and major neighborhoods, including nearby beaches. During the day, buses tend to run every 15 to 30 minutes, with reduced service at night and on weekends. Buses run daily from about 5 am to midnight.

A tram link between downtown Athens and the coastal southern suburbs features two main lines. Line A runs from Syntagma to Glyfada; Line B traces the shoreline from Glyfada to the Peace & Friendship Stadium on the outskirts of Piraeus. Single tickets cost €1.40 and are sold at machines on the tram platforms.

Main bus stations are at Akadimias and Sina and at Kaningos Square. Bus and trolley tickets cost €1.20 for one ride. A more expensive €1.40 ticket is valid for 90 minutes of travel on all modes of public transport (bus, trolley, tram, and metro). Remember to validate the ticket (insert it in the ticket machine in the ticket area of the metro or aboard the train or bus) when you begin your journey and keep it until you've exited the bus or tram station. Day passes for €4.50, and five-day tickets for €9 are also popular with tourists, but they don't include airport transport; a three-day tourist ticket costs €22 and does include one round-trip for the airport train. Monthly passes are also sold at special booths at the main terminals on the first and last week of each month.

Maps of bus routes are available at terminal booths or from EOT. The website of the Organization for Urban Public Transportation (OASA) has a helpful English-language section.

Contacts City tram. ⊕ www.stasy.gr. **Organization for Urban Public Transportation (OASA).** ☎ 11185 Call center ⊕ www.oasa.gr.

BUS TRAVEL BEYOND ATHENS

Travel around Greece by bus is inexpensive and usually comfortable; most buses are now air-conditioned. Make reservations at least one day before your planned trip, earlier for holiday weekends.

Most buses to the east Attica coast, including those for Sounion €6.20 for inland route, €6.90 on coastal road) and Marathon €4.10), leave from the KTEL terminal in Pedion Areos.

The journey from Athens to Thessaloniki takes roughly the same time as the regular train (around 6 hours), though the InterCity Express train covers the distance 1¼ hours faster. Make reservations at least one day before your planned trip, earlier for holiday weekends. To reach the Peloponnese, buses are as fast as trains thanks to Proastiakos, the high-speed suburban rail to Corinth and beyond. Information and timetables are available at tourist information offices and metro stations.

Terminal A—aka Kifissos Station—is the arrival and departure point for bus lines that serve parts of northern Greece, including Thessaloniki, and the Peloponnese destinations of Epidauros, Mycenae, Nafplion, Olympia, and Corinth. Terminal B serves Evia, most of Thrace, and central Greece, including Delphi. Tickets for these buses are sold only at this terminal, so you should call to book seats well in advance in high season or holidays. *For more detailed bus information, see Bus Travel in Travel Smart.*

Contacts KTEL Attica. ✉ *Patission 68 and Kotsika 2, Aigyptou Sq., at corner of Mavromateon and Leoforos Alexandras near Pedion Areos Park, Pedion Areos* ☎ *210/880–8000 all information* ⊕ *ktelattikis.gr.*

CAR TRAVEL IN ATHENS

Greek drivers can be feisty, but standards today are the closest they've ever been to standard European style—except on the coastal roads late at night. Locals have welcomed the accessible and generally reliable public transport, while taxi fares remain affordable, and cycling is in fashion, so driving (especially with gasoline at high prices) is less popular. Driving is on the right, and although the vehicle on the right has the right-of-way, don't always expect this to be obeyed; in fact, be prepared to discover how creatively the rules can be bent.

The speed limit is 50 kph (31 mph) in town. Seat belts are compulsory, as are helmets for motorcyclists, though many flagrantly ignore the laws. In the downtown sectors of the city do not drive in the bus lanes marked by a yellow divider; if caught, you may be fined. You're better off leaving your car in the hotel garage and walking or taking a cab. Gas pumps and service stations are everywhere, but be aware that all-night stations are few and far between.

CAR TRAVEL BEYOND ATHENS

Greece's main highways to the north and the south link up in Athens; both are called Ethniki Odos (National Road). Take the Attiki Odos, a beltway around Athens that also accesses Eleftherios Venizelos International Airport, to speed your travel time entering and exiting the city. The toll is €2.80 for cars, payable upon entering this privately owned highway. At the city limits, signs in English clearly mark the way to both Syntagma Square and Omonia Square in the city center. Leaving Athens, routes to the highways and Attiki Odos are well marked; green signs usually name Lamia for points north, and Corinth or Patras for points southwest. From Athens to Thessaloniki, the distance is 515 km (319 miles); to Kalamata, 257 km (159 miles); to Corinth, 84 km (52 miles); to Patras, 218 km (135 miles); to Igoumenitsa, 472 km (293 miles).

Most car rental offices are around Syngrou and Syntagma Square in Central Athens, but it can be cheaper to book from your home country; small-car rentals start at around €20/day. *For more information, see Car Rental in the Travel Smart chapter.*

CRUISE TRAVEL

Chinese-owned Piraeus is the port of Athens, 11 km (7 miles) southwest of the city center, and is itself the third-largest city in Greece, with a population of about 500,000. In anticipation of a flood of visitors during the 2004 Olympics, the harbor district was given a general sprucing up. The cruise port has 12 berths, and the cruise terminal has duty-free shops, information, and refreshments.

The cheapest (and often fastest) way to get to Athens from Piraeus is to take the metro. Line 1 (Green Line) reaches the downtown Athens stops most useful to tourists, including Platia Victorias, near the National Archaeological Museum; Omonia Square; Monastiraki, in the old Turkish bazaar; and Thission, near the ancient Agora. The trip takes 25 to 30 minutes. The Piraeus metro station for Line 1 (Piraeus-Kifissia) is off Akti Kallimasioti on the main harbor, a 20-minute walk from the cruise port, and you must walk all the way around the harbor to reach these piers.

You can also take the express X80 bus line, leaving the OLP cruise terminal for Acropolis and Syntagma Square (for info, visit ⊕ *www.oasa.gr*).

Taxis wait outside the terminal entrance. Taxis into the city are not necessarily quicker than public transport because of traffic, and cost around €15 to €18. Make sure the meter is running from the moment you start your ride. If a driver wishes to pick up other passengers if there is room in the cab, you have the right to refuse having others cramp your style. Taxis are also readily available at the port to get you to the airport for around €45.

METRO (SUBWAY) TRAVEL

The best magic carpet ride in town is the polished metro, which is fast, cheap, and convenient; its three lines go to all the major spots in Athens. Line 1, or the Green Line, of the city's metro system is often called the *elektrikos* (or the electrical train) and runs from Piraeus to the northern suburb of Kifissia, with several downtown stops (including Victoria Square, near the National Archaeological Museum; Omonia Square; Monastiraki, in the old Turkish bazaar; Thissio, near Kerameikos; the ancient Agora; and the nightlife districts of Psirri, Gazi-Kerameikos, and Thissio).

The other two lines are newer and more modern but cover limited territory. Line 2, or the Red Line, cuts northwest across the city, starting from suburban Anthoupoli and passing through such useful stops as Syntagma Square, opposite the Greek Parliament; Panepistimiou (near the Old University complex and the Numismatic Museum); Omonia Square; Metaxourgeio; the Stathmos Larissis stop next to Athens's central train station; Acropolis, at the foot of the famous site; and finishing off at the south suburb of Elliniko.

Line 3, or the Blue Line, runs from the suburb of Ayia Varvara (the Ayia Marina terminal station) through Kerameikos (the stop for bustling Gazi-Kerameikos) and Monastiraki; some trains on this line go all the way to the airport, but they only pass about every half hour and require a special ticket. The stops of most interest for visitors are Evangelismos, near the Byzantine and Christian Museum, Hilton Hotel, National Gallery of Art, and Megaron Mousikis, next to the U.S. Embassy and the concert hall.

The fare is €1.40, except for tickets to the airport, which are €10. A 24-hour travel pass, valid for use on all forms of public transportation, is €4.50. You must validate all tickets at the machines in metro stations before you board (if you're caught without a valid ticket you will be fined, so retain your ticket until you reach your final destination); however, the system is transitioning to paper and plastic smartcards similar to the London Oyster cards or those used on the Washington, DC Metro. Until the transition is complete, paper tickets will still be available (and will still need to be validated) Trains run between 5:30 am and 1 am. Maps of the metro are available in stations.

Contacts Athens Transport. ⊕ *www.athenstransport.com.*

2

TAXI TRAVEL

Most drivers in Athens speak basic English. Although you can find an empty taxi on the street, it's often faster to call out your destination to one carrying passengers; if the taxi is going in that direction, the driver will pick you up. Likewise, don't be alarmed if your driver picks up other passengers (although he should ask your permission first). Each passenger pays full fare for the distance he or she has traveled. Make sure the driver turns on the meter and that the rate listed in the lower corner is 1, the normal rate before midnight; after midnight, the rate listed is 2.

Taxi drivers know the major central hotels, but if your hotel is less well known, show the driver the address written in Greek and make note of the hotel's phone number and, if possible, a nearby landmark. If all else fails, the driver can call the hotel from his mobile phone or a kiosk. Athens has thousands of short side streets, and few taxi drivers have maps, although newer taxis have GPS installed. Neither tipping nor bargaining is generally practiced; if your driver has gone out of the way for you, a small gratuity (10% or less) is appreciated.

The local ride-hailing app is Taxibeat, allowing you to choose your driver and follow your ride on your phone. Uber has reached Athens, too. Booking and payment can be done via the Uber Android or IOS app, with choices for Economy, Premium, Accessibility (for wheelchair users), and Pool rides.

The Athens taximeter starts at €1.19 and, even if you join other passengers, you must add this amount to your final charge. The minimum fare is €3.16. The basic charge is €0.68 per kilometer (½ mile); this increases to €1.19 between midnight and 5 am or if you go outside city limits. There are surcharges for holidays (€1), trips to and from the airport (€3.84), and rides to (but not from) the port, train stations, and bus terminals (€1.07). There is also a €0.40 charge for each suitcase over 10 kilos (22 pounds), but drivers expect €0.40 for each bag anyway. Waiting time is €10.85 per hour. Radio taxis charge an additional €2 to €5.65 for the pickup, depending on time of day requested.

Contacts Athens 1 Intertaxi. ☎ *210/921–2800* ⊕ *www.athens1.gr.* **Ermis Taxi Service.** ☎ *210/411–5200* ⊕ *www.radiotaxiermis.gr.* **Radio Taxi Hellas.** ☎ *210/645–7000* ⊕ *www.radiotaxihellas.gr.* **Taxibeat.** ⊕ *taxibeat.gr.*

TRAIN TRAVEL

The *Proastiakos* ("suburban"), a light-rail network offering travelers a direct link from Athens Eleftherios Venizelos Airport to Kiato (en route to Patras for €12), has introduced Athenians to the concept of commuting. The trains now serve the city's northern and eastern suburbs as well as western Attica. The Athens-to-Corinth fare is €9; lower fares apply for points in between. If you plan on taking the train while in Athens, call the Greek Railway Organization (OSE) to find out which station your train leaves from, and how to get there. Trains from the north and international trains arrive at, and depart from, Stathmos Larissis, which is connected to the metro. If you want to buy tickets ahead of time, it's easier to visit a downtown railway office. *For further information, see Train Travel in the Travel Smart chapter.*

Contacts Stathmos Larissis Train Station. ☎ *14511 customer service (daily 6 am–11 pm).*

VISITOR INFORMATION

Greek National Tourism Organization has a new information center in Central Athens near the Acropolis Museum. The website of the city of Athens has a growing section in English. The English-speaking tourist police can handle complaints, steer you to an open pharmacy or doctor, and locate phone numbers of hotels and restaurants.

Contacts City of Athens. ⊕ *www.cityofathens.gr.* **Greek National Tourism Organisation.** ✉ *18-20 Dionyssiou Aeropagitou Street, Plaka* ☎ *210/331–0529* ⊕ *http://www.visitgreece.gr.*

TOURS

Most travel agencies offer excursions at about the same prices, but CHAT is reputed to have the best service and guides. You can take traditional day or night tours of Athens by bus and be picked up at your hotel. Full- and half-day tours go to many destinations in Attica, including Sounion, Corinth, Delphi; longer tours go to Meteora, Naf-plion, and the Peloponnese. It's best to reserve a few days in advance. *For a full list of agencies that offer tours—including CHAT—see Travel Agents in Travel Smart.*

BICYCLE TOURS

FAMILY **Athens City Electric Bike Tours.** Let the eco-friendly bike do all the work
Fodor'sChoice and enjoy the breeze, choosing between the Athens Grand City Tour,
★ Old City Tour, and City to Coast Tour. ✉ *11 Lempessi* ☎ *210/921–5620* ⊕ *www.solebike.eu.*

BUS TOURS

City Sightseeing. The easiest way to get quickly acquainted with Athens is to opt for a ride on the Athens City Sightseeing Bus, a typical tour-ist double-decker with open top floors that stops at all the city's main sights. Those buses run by City Sightseeing run every 15 minutes and tickets cost €20. The full tour takes 90 minutes, but you can hop on and off as you please at any of the 18 stops (including Syntagma Square) throughout the day. There is also a new combined tour of Piraeus and Athens, lasting 70 minutes, departing from the harbor terminal in Akti Miaouli. ✉ *Athens* ☎ *210/922–0604* ⊕ *www.citysightseeing.gr.*

GUIDED TOURS

FAMILY **Alternative Athens.** Tours are centered on food, nightlife, local experi-ences, and kid-friendy locations, presented in a fresh, colorful way. ✉ *28 Karaiskaki* ☎ *6951–518589* ⊕ *www.alternativeathens.com.*

Union of Certified Guides. The Union of Official Guides provides licensed guides for individual or group tours, for a four-hour tour of the Acropolis and its museum. Prices start at around €200 for this tour. ☎ *210/322–9705, 210/322–0090* ⊕ *www.tourist-guides.gr.*

WALKING TOURS

It's easy to arrange for a private or small-group tour in Athens.

Athens Walking Tours. The 19 certified guides of the Athens Walking Tours company offer walking tours of the Acropolis, as well as a culinary Food Tour around the city's central food market. ✉ *Athens* ☎ *210/884–7269, 69458/59662* ⊕ *www.athenswalkingtours.gr.*

Personality Journeys. The company offeres walking tours in the historical center, Anafiotika, and the Athenian Riviera as well as food tours. ✉ *1 Orfeos* ☎ *215/215–1629* ⊕ *www.personalityjourneys.com.*

EXPLORING

Although Athens covers a huge area, the major landmarks of the ancient Greek, Roman, and Byzantine periods are close to the modern city center. You can easily walk from the Acropolis to many other key sites, taking time to browse in shops and relax in cafés and tavernas along the way. From many quarters of the city you can glimpse the Acropolis looming above the horizon, but only by actually climbing that rocky precipice can you feel its power. The Acropolis and Filopappou, two verdant hills sitting side by side; the ancient Agora (marketplace); and Kerameikos, the first cemetery, form the core of ancient and Roman Athens. Along the Unification of Archaeological Sites promenade, you can follow stone-paved, tree-lined walkways from site to site, undisturbed by traffic. Cars have also been banned or reduced in other streets in the historical center. In the National Archaeological Museum, vast numbers of artifacts illustrate the many millennia of Greek civilization; smaller museums such as the Museum of Cycladic Art and the Byzantine and Christian Museum beautifully and elaborately illuminate the history of particular regions or periods.

Athens may seem like one huge city, but it is really a conglomeration of neighborhoods with distinctive characters. The Eastern influences that prevailed during the 400-year rule of the Ottoman Empire are still evident in Monastiraki. On the northern slope of the Acropolis, stroll through Plaka to get the flavor of the 19th century's gracious lifestyle. The narrow lanes of Anafiotika thread past tiny churches and small color-washed houses recalling a Cycladic island village. Vestiges of the older city are everywhere: crumbling stairways lined with festive tavernas, occasionally a court garden enclosed within high walls and filled with magnolia trees, ancient ruins scattered in sun-blasted corners.

Makriyianni and Koukaki are prime real estate, the latter recently voted sixth-best neighborhood in the world by Airbnb. Formerly run-down old quarters, such as Kerameikos, Gazi-Kerameikos, and Psirri, popular nightlife areas filled with bars and *mezedopoleio,* have undergone some gentrification, although they retain much of their post-industrial edge. The newly trendy area around Syntagma Square, including the buzzing, gay-friendly café scene at Monastiraki's Ayias Irinis Square, and bleak, noisy Omonia Square, form the commercial heart of the city. Athens is distinctly European, having been designed by the court architects of King Otto, a Bavarian, in the 19th century. The chic shops and bistros of ritzy Kolonaki nestle at the foot of Mt. Lycabettus, Athens's highest hill (909 feet), with a man-made forest. Each of the city's outlying suburbs has a distinctive character: Pangrati, Ambelokipi, and Ilisia are more residential in nature, densely populated, with some lively night-life hotspots and star attractions like the Panathenaic Stadium and the Athens Concert Hall (Megaron Mousikis).

Just beyond the southern edge of the city is Piraeus, a bustling port city of waterside fish tavernas and Saronic Gulf views that is still connected to Central Athens by metro. And beyond Athens proper, in Attica to the south and southeast, lie Glyfada, Voula, and Vouliagmeni, with their sandy beaches, seaside bars, and lively summer nightlife.

THE ACROPOLIS, MAKRIYIANNI, AND KOUKAKI
ΑΚΡΟΠΟΛΗ, ΜΑΚΡΥΓΙΑΝΝΗ, ΚΟΥΚΑΚΙ

Although Athens, together with its suburbs and port, sprawls across the plain for more than 240 square km (150 square miles), most of its ancient monuments cluster around the Acropolis, which rises like a massive sentinel, white and beautiful, out of the center of the city. In mountainous Greece, most ancient towns were backed up by an acropolis, an easily defensible upper town (which is what the word means), but when spelled with a capital *A* it can only refer to antiquity's most splendid group of buildings.

Towering over the modern metropolis of 4.5 million as it once stood over the ancient capital of 50,000, it has remained Athens's most spectacular attraction ever since its first settlement around 5000 BC. It had been a religious center long before Athens became a major city-state in the 6th century BC. It has been associated with Athena ever since the city's mythical founding, but virtually all of the city's other religious cults had temples or shrines here as well. As Athens became the dominant city-state in the 5th century BC, Pericles led the city in making the Acropolis the crowning symbol of Athenian power and successful democracy.

An elegant and tranquil neighborhood on the foothills of the Acropolis, Makriyianni was really put on the map by the opening of the nearby Acropolis Museum and is one of the most coveted residential areas of the city, both for its exclusive ambience and beautiful examples of neoclassical architecture; indeed, it is now considered one of the most up-and-coming districts of the capital. Explore the streets south of the museum to discover artsy new shops like Athena Design Workshop, Greek delis like Ellinika Kaoudia and Pelasgea, galleries (the Eleni Marnieri Galerie is a treasure trove of modern jewelry designs to ogle at or buy), the classic Ilias Lalaounis Jewelry Museum, and hip "third-wave" coffee shops like Coffee Dive. Stop for lunch at Strofi, Peloponnesian cuisine–centered Mani Mani or Attalos Greek House Restaurant.

Adjacent, and serviced by Fix and Acropolis metro stations, Koukaki is one of the most sought-after residential areas of Athens. In recent years it has become one of the most fashionable places for seeing and being seen (also recently eulogized by Vogue), at bars like Bobo Winebar and Bel Ray Cafe in popular Faliron Square. A resurgence of the area, also inspired by the spanking-new Museum of Contemporary Art (EMST), a massive structure that was once a beer factory, has followed the pedestrianization of G. Olympiou Street on Koukaki Square.

THE ACROPOLIS ΑΚΡΟΠΟΛΗ
TOP ATTRACTIONS

Fodor's Choice
★

Acropolis. Towering above all—both physically and spiritually—is the Acropolis, the ancient city of upper Athens and the prime source of Western civilization. The Greek term *Akropolis* means "High City," and most of the notable structures on this flat-top limestone outcrop, 512 feet high, were built from 461 to 429 BC, when Athens's intellectual and artistic life flowered under the statesman Pericles. With most of the major restoration work now completed, a visit evokes the spirit of the ancient heroes and gods who were once worshipped here. Highlights include the **Parthenon**, dedicated to the goddess Athena; the **Temple of Athena Nike**; the imposing **Propylaea**, showing the first use of the Attic style; and the **Erechtheion**, the prime exemplar of the graceful Ionic order. Walking through the Acropolis takes about four hours, depending on the crowds, including an hour spent in the Acropolis Museum at the base of the hill. The earlier you start out the better, or visit after 5 pm in summer. ⊠ *Dionyssiou Areopagitou, Acropolis* ☎ *210/321–4172 ticket information* ⊕ *www.culture. gr* ⊠ *€20 Acropolis and Theater of Dionysus; €30 joint ticket for all Unification of Archaeological Sites* Ⓜ *Acropolis.*

Fodor's Choice
★

Acropolis Museum. Making world headlines when it opened in June 2009, the museum nods to the fabled ancient hill above it but speaks—thanks to a spectacular building—in a contemporary architectural language. The ground-floor exhibit features objects from the sanctuaries and settlements around the Acropolis, including theatrical masks and vases from the sanctuary of the matrimonial deity Nymphe. The first floor is devoted to the Archaic period (650 BC–480 BC), with rows of precious statues mounted for 360-degree viewing, including stone lions gorging a bull from 570 BC and the legendary five Caryatids (or Korai). The second floor is devoted to the terrace and restaurant/coffee shop, with an eagle eye's view of the Acropolis. In the top-floor atrium, don't miss the star gallery devoted to the temple's Pentelic marble decorations, consisting of a suitably magnificent, rectangle-shaped room tilted to align with the Parthenon itself and empty spaces that can hold the pieces Lord Elgin whisked off to the British Museum in London. Floor-to-ceiling windows provide magnificent vistas of the temple just a few hundred feet away. ⊠ *Dionyssiou Areopagitou 15, Acropolis* ☎ *210/900–0900* ⊕ *www.theacropolismuseum.gr* ⊠ *€5* Ⓜ *Acropolis.*

Odeon of Herodes Atticus. Hauntingly beautiful, this ancient theater was built in AD 160 by the affluent Herodes Atticus in memory of his wife, Regilla. Known as the Irodion and visited throughout the summer by culture vultures, it is nestled Greek-style into the hillside, but with typically Roman arches in its three-story stage building and barrel-vaulted entrances. The circular orchestra has now become a semicircle, and the long-vanished cedar roof probably covered only the stage and dressing rooms, not the 34 rows of seats. The theater, which holds 5,000, was restored and reopened in 1955 for the Athens and Epidaurus Festival. To enter you must hold a ticket to one of the summer performances, which range from the Royal Ballet to ancient tragedies usually performed in Modern Greek. Contact the festival's box office for

Continued on page 70

THE ACROPOLIS
ASCENT TO GLORY

One of the wonders of the world, the Acropolis symbolizes Greece's
Golden Age. Its stunning centerpiece, the Parthenon, was commissioned in the 5th century BC by the great Athenian leader Pericles as
part of an elaborate building program designed to epitomize the apex
of an iconic culture. Thousands of years later, the Acropolis pulls the
patriotic heartstrings of modern Greeks and lulls millions of annual visitors back to an ancient time.

You don't have to look far in Athens to encounter perfection. Towering above all—both physically and spiritually—is the Acropolis, the ancient city of upper Athens and womb of Western civilization. Raising your eyes to the crest of this *ieros vrachos* (sacred rock), the sight of the Parthenon will stop you in your tracks. The term Akropolis (to use the Greek spelling) means "High City," and today's traveler who climbs this table-like hill is paying tribute to the prime source of civilization as we know it.

A TITANIC TEMPLE
Described by the 19th-century French poet Alphonse de Lamartine as "the most perfect poem in stone," the Acropolis is a true testament to the Golden Age of Greece. While archaeological evidence has shown that the flat-top limestone outcrop, 512 feet high, attracted settlers as early as Neolithic times, most of its most imposing structures were built from 461 to 429 BC, when the intellectual and artistic life of Athens flowered under the influence of the Athenian statesman, Pericles. Even in its bleached and silent state, the Parthenon—the Panathenaic temple that crowns the rise—has the power to stir the heart as few other ancient relics do.

PERICLES TO POLLUTION
Since the Periclean Age, the buildings of the Acropolis have been inflicted with the damages of war, as well as unscrupulous transformations into, at various times, a Florentine palace, an Islamic mosque, a Turkish harem, and a World War II sentry. Since then, a more insidious enemy—pollution—has emerged. The site is presently undergoing conservation measures as part of an ambitious rescue plan. Today, the Erechtheion temple and Temple of Athena Nike have been completely restored, and work on the Parthenon and the Propylaea is due for completion by the end of 2014. A final phase, involving massive landscaping works, will last through 2020. Despite the ongoing restoration work, a visit to the Acropolis today can evoke the spirit of the ancient heroes and gods who were once worshiped here.

THE PARTHENON

PINNACLE OF THE PERICLEAN AGE

DEDICATED TO ATHENA

At the loftiest point of the Acropolis stands the Parthenon, the architectural masterpiece conceived by Pericles and executed between 447 and 438 BC by the brilliant sculptor Pheidias, who supervised the architects Iktinos and Kallikrates in its construction. It not only raised the bar in terms of sheer size, but also in the perfection of its proportions.

Dedicated to the goddess Athena (the name Parthenon comes from the Athena Parthenos, or the virgin Athena) and inaugurated at the Panathenaic Festival of 438 BC, the Parthenon served primarily as the treasury of the Delian League, an ancient alliance of cities formed to defeat the Persian incursion. In fact, the Parthenon was built as much to honor the city's power as to venerate Athena. Its foundations, laid after the victory at Marathon in 490 BC, were destroyed by the Persian army in 480–479 BC. In turn, the city-state of Athens banded together with Sparta to rout the Persians by 449 BC.

To proclaim its hegemony over all Greece, Athens envisioned a grand new Acropolis. After a 30-year building moratorium, the titanic-scale project of reconstructing the temple was initiated by Pericles around 448 BC.

490 BC
/ Foundation for Acropolis laid

447–438 BC
/ The Parthenon is constructed

420 BC
/ Temple of Athena Nike is completed

TIMELINE

EDIFICE REX: PERICLES

His name means "surrounded by glory." Some scholars consider this extraordinary, enigmatic Athenian general to be the architect of the destiny of Greece at its height, while others consider him a megalomaniac who bankrupted the coffers of an empire and an elitist who catered to the privileged few at the expense of the masses.

Indeed, Pericles (460–429 BC) plundered the treasury of the Athenian alliance for the Acropolis building program. One academic has even called the Periclean building program the largest embezzlement in human history.

MYTH IN MARBLE

But Pericles's masterstroke becomes more comprehensible when studied against the conundrum that was Athenian democracy.

In truth an aristocracy that was the watchdog of private property and public order, this political system financed athletic games and drama festivals; it constructed exquisite buildings. Its motto was not only to live, but to live well. Surrounded by barbarians, the Age of Pericles was the more striking for its high level of civilization, its qualities of proportion, reason, clarity, and harmony, all of which are epitomized nowhere else as beautifully as in the Parthenon.

To their credit, the Athenians rallied around Pericles' vision: the respect for the individualistic character of men and women could be revealed through art and architecture.

Even jaded Athenians, when overwhelmed by the city, feel renewed when they lift their eyes to this great monument.

TRICK OF THE TRADE

One of the Parthenon's features, or "refinements," is the way it uses meiosis (tapering of columns) and entasis (a slight swelling so that the column can hold the weight of the entablature), deviations from strict mathematics that breathed movement into the rigid marble. Architects knew that a straight line looks curved, and vice versa, so they cleverly built the temple with all the horizontal lines somewhat curved. The columns, it has been calculated, lean toward the center of the temple; if they were to continue into space, they would eventually converge to create a huge pyramid.

1456
Converted to mosque by occupying Turks

September 26, 1687
The Parthenon, used for gunpowder storage, explodes after being hit by a mortar shell

The Acropolis in Pericles's Time

RAISING A HUE
"Just my color—beige!" So proclaimed Elsie de Wolfe, celebrated decorator to J. Pierpont Morgan, when she first saw the Parthenon. As it turns out, the original Parthenon was anything but beige. Especially ornate, it had been covered with a tile roof, decorated with statuary and marble friezes, adorned with gilded wooden doors and ceilings, and walls and columns so brightly hued that the people protested, "We are adorning our city like a wanton woman" (Plutarch). The finishing touch was provided by the legendary sculptor Pheidias, who created some of the sculpted friezes—these were also brightly colored.

THE ERECHTHEION

PARTHENON

ATHENA PROMACHOS
Pheidias's colossal bronze statue of Athena Promachos, one of the largest of antiquity at 30' (9 m) high, could be seen from the sea. It was destroyed after being moved to Constantinople in 1203.

THE PROPYLAEA

TOURING THE ACROPOLIS

Most people take the metro to the Acropolis station, where the New Acropolis Museum opened in 2009. They then follow the pedestrianized street Dionyssiou Areopagitou, which traces the foothill of the Acropolis to its entrance at the Beulé Gate. Another entrance is along the rock's northern face via the Peripatos, a paved path from the Plaka district.

THE BEULÉ GATE

You enter the Acropolis complex through this late-Roman structure named for the French archaeologist Ernest Beulé, who discovered the gate in 1852. Made of marble fragments from the destroyed monument of Nikias on the south slope of the Acropolis, it has an inscription above the lintel dated 320 BC, dedicated by "Nikias son of Nikodemos of Xypete." Before Roman times, the entrance to the Acropolis was a steep processional ramp below the Temple of Athena Nike. This Sacred Way was used every fourth year for the Panathenaic procession, a spectacle that honored Athena's remarkable birth (she sprang from the head of her father, Zeus).

THE PROPYLAEA

This imposing structure was designed to instill the proper reverence in worshipers as they crossed from the temporal world into the spiritual world of the sanctuary, for this was the main function of the Acropolis. Conceived by Pericles, the Propylaea was the masterwork of the architect Mnesicles. Conceived to be the same size as the Parthenon, it was to have been the grandest secular building in Greece. Construction was suspended

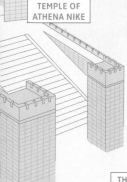

TEMPLE OF
ATHENA NIKE

THE BEULÉ GATE

during the Peloponnesian War, and it was never finished. The structure shows the first use of both Doric and Ionic columns together, a style that can be called Attic. Six of the sturdier fluted Doric columns, made from Pendelic marble, correspond with the gateways of the portal. Processions with priests, chariots, and sacrificial animals entered via a marble ramp in the center (now protected by a wooden stairway), while ordinary visitors on foot entered via the side doors. The slender Ionic columns had elegant capitals, some of which have been restored along with a section of the famed paneled ceiling, originally decorated with gold eight-pointed stars on a blue background. Adjacent to the Pinakotheke, or art gallery (with paintings of scenes from Homer's epics and mythological tableaux), the south wing is a decorative portico. The view from the inner porch of the Propylaea is stunning: the Parthenon is suddenly revealed in its full glory, framed by the columns.

THE TEMPLE OF ATHENA NIKE

The 2nd-century traveler Pausanias referred to this fabled temple as the Temple of Nike Apteros, or Wingless Victory, for "in Athens they believe Victory will stay forever because she has no wings." Designed by Kallikrates, the mini-temple was built in 427–424 BC to celebrate peace with Persia. The bas-reliefs on the surrounding parapet depicting the Victories leading heifers to be sacrificed must have been of exceptional quality, judging from the section called "Nike Unfastening Her Sandal" in the New Acropolis Museum. In 1998, Greek archaeologists began dismantling the entire temple for conservation. After laser-cleaning the marble to remove generations of soot, the team reconstructed the temple on its original site.

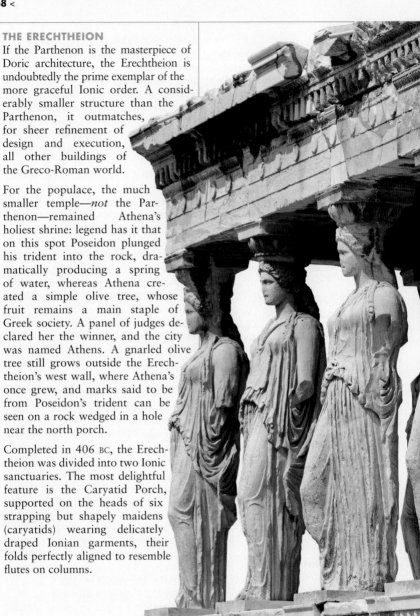

THE ERECHTHEION

If the Parthenon is the masterpiece of Doric architecture, the Erechtheion is undoubtedly the prime exemplar of the more graceful Ionic order. A considerably smaller structure than the Parthenon, it outmatches, for sheer refinement of design and execution, all other buildings of the Greco-Roman world.

For the populace, the much smaller temple—*not* the Parthenon—remained Athena's holiest shrine: legend has it that on this spot Poseidon plunged his trident into the rock, dramatically producing a spring of water, whereas Athena created a simple olive tree, whose fruit remains a main staple of Greek society. A panel of judges declared her the winner, and the city was named Athens. A gnarled olive tree still grows outside the Erechtheion's west wall, where Athena's once grew, and marks said to be from Poseidon's trident can be seen on a rock wedged in a hole near the north porch.

Completed in 406 BC, the Erechtheion was divided into two Ionic sanctuaries. The most delightful feature is the Caryatid Porch, supported on the heads of six strapping but shapely maidens (caryatids) wearing delicately draped Ionian garments, their folds perfectly aligned to resemble flutes on columns.

Now replaced by casts, the originals of the Erechtheion's famous Caryatid maidens are in the New Acropolis Museum.

PLANNING YOUR VISIT

Dionysiou Areopagitou, Acropolis

☎ 210/321–4172 or 210/321–0219

🌐 www.culture.gr

🎫 Joint ticket for all Unification of Archaeological Sites €12. Good for five days—and for free admission—to the Ancient Agora, Theatre of Dionysus, Kerameikos cemetery, Temple of Olympian Zeus, and the Roman Forum.

🕙 Apr.–Oct., daily 8–6:30; Nov.–Mar., daily 8–3

Ⓜ Acropolis

When exploring the Acropolis, keep the below pointers in mind. As the hill's stones are slippery and steep, it is best to wear rubber-soled shoes.

What Are the Best Times to Go? Such is the beauty of the Acropolis and the grandeur of the setting that a visit in all seasons and at all hours is rewarding. In general, the earlier you start out the better. In summer, by noon the heat is blistering and the reflection of the light thrown back by the rock and the marble ruins is almost blinding. An alternative, in summer, is to visit after 5 PM, when the light is best for taking photographs. In any season the ideal time might be the two hours before sunset, when occasionally the fabled violet light spreads from the crest of Mt. Hymettus (which the ancients called "violet-crowned") and gradually embraces the Acropolis. After dark the hill is spectacularly floodlighted, creating a scene visible from many parts of the capital. A moonlight visit—sometimes scheduled by the authorities during full moons in summer—is highly evocative. In winter, if there are clouds trailing across the mountains, and shafts of sun lighting up the marble columns, the setting takes on an even more dramatic quality.

How Long Does a Visit Usually Run? Depending on the crowds, the walk takes about three hours, plus several more spent in the nearby Acropolis Museum.

Are Tour Guides Available? The Union of Official Guides (Apollonos 9A, Syntagma, 210/322-9705, 210/322-0090) offers licensed guides for tours of archaeological sites within Athens. However, most tour companies and travel agents can set up group or private tours. Guides will also help kids understand the site better.

What's the Handiest Place to Refuel? The Tourist Pavilion (Filoppapou Hill), a landscaped, tree-shaded spot soundtracked by chirping birds is just outside the Beulé Gate. It serves drinks, snacks, and a few hot dishes.

DON'T FORGET:

■ If it's hot, remember to bring water, sunscreen, and a hat to protect yourself from the sun.

■ Get a free bilingual pamphlet guide (in English and Greek) at the entrance gate. It is packed with information, but staffers usually don't bother to give it out unless asked.

■ An elevator now ascends to the summit of the Acropolis, once inaccessible to people with disabilities.

■ All large bags, backpacks, and shopping bags will have to be checked in the site cloakroom.

Temple of Olympian Zeus

Grand Promenade

One of the most popular features created in Athens for the 2004 Olympics was the Grand Promenade, a pedestrian walkway meant to beautify some of the traffic-choked streets much favored by tourists. Part of the city's Archaeological Unification Project, the promenade connects fabled ancient sites along a landscaped walkway paved with gneiss cobblestones from Naxos and marble slabs from Tinos. It stretches through several neighborhoods but is often accessed near the Acropolis since its pedestrian ribbon includes the roads around its southern end.

Start out at the Acropolis metro stop, surface and walk north, and then left to find Dionyssiou Areopagitou, the famed road running below the hill. You'll first pass the Acropolis Museum on your left and the Theater of Diony- sus and Odeon of Herodes Atticus on your right. You can begin your climb here up to the Beulé Gate entrance to the Acropolis but, instead, take the marble walkway up Filopappou Hill— its summit flaunts Cinerama views of the Acropolis and Lycabettus hill side by side. Head back down to Apostolou Pavlou to find some of the best café real estate in the world.

Farther down the road is the Thissio metro station, Ayion Asomaton Square, and Ermou Street, which heads down to the great ancient cemetery of Kerameikos, and ends on Pireus Street and the Technopolis and the Gazi- Kerameikos district across the road.

Keep the following restaurants and cafés in mind if you want to enjoy food-with-a-view, and not just any old view, but the Acropolis itself: Dionysos Zonars; Filistron mezedopoleio- restaurant (especially the rooftop on summer nights); Strofi restaurant (perfect for a summer post-perfor- mance dinner at the ancient Odeon of Herodes Atticus); Kuzina (for a wonderful view from its rooftop); and Orizontes (seen from another angle, this one from Lycabettus hill). Last but not least, the café and restaurant of the Acropolis Museum, which can be visited without a museum entry ticket, with its huge glass windows and extensive verandas, is a definite must for spectacular photo ops of the ancient landmark. Some hotels in the area, for example Herodion, Athens Was, and the Grande Bretagne in Syntagma, also have rooftop restau- rants with mouthwatering views.

ticket information. Children under six are not allowed except at some special performances. ⊠ *Dionyssiou Areopagitou, Acropolis* ✧ *Near Propylaion* ☎ *210/324–1807* ⊕ *www.greekfestival.gr* Ⓜ *Acropolis.*

WORTH NOTING

Filopappou. This summit includes **Lofos Mousson** (Hill of the Muses), whose peak offers the city's best view of the Parthenon. Also there is the **Monument of Filopappus,** depicting a Syrian prince who was such a generous benefactor that the people accepted him as a distinguished Athenian. The marble monument is a tomb decorated by a frieze show- ing Filopappus driving his chariot. In 294 BC a fort strategic to Athens's defense was built here, overlooking the road to the sea. On the hill of the **Pnyx** (meaning "crowded"), the all-male general assembly (Ecclesia) met during the time of Pericles. Originally, citizens of the Ecclesia faced the Acropolis while listening to speeches, but they tended to lose their concentration as they gazed upon the monuments, so the positions of the speaker and the audience were reversed. The speaker's platform is still visible on the semicircular terrace. Farther north is the **Hill of the Nymphs**, with a 19th-century observatory designed by Theophilos Hansen. He was so satisfied with his work, he had *servare intaminatum* ("to remain intact") inscribed over the entrance. ⊠ *Acropolis* ✢ *Enter from Dionyssiou Areopagitou or Apostolou Pavlou* Ⓜ *Acropolis*.

Theater of Dionysus. It was on this spot in the 6th century BC that the Dionysia festivals took place; a century later, dramas such as Sophocles's *Oedipus Rex* and Euripides's *Medea* were performed for the entire population of the city. Visible are foundations of a stage dating from about 330 BC, when it was built for 15,000 spectators as well as the assemblies formerly held on Pnyx. In the middle of the orchestra stood the altar to Dionysus; a fantastic throne in the center was reserved for the priest of Dionysus. On the hillside above the theater stand two columns, vestiges of the little temple erected in the 4th century BC by Thrasyllus the Choragus. ⊠ *Dionyssiou Areopagitou, Acropolis* ✢ *Across from Mitsaion St.* ☎ *210/322–4625* 🎫 *€20 Acropolis and Theater of Dionysus; €30 joint ticket for all Unification of Archaeological Sites* Ⓜ *Acropolis*.

MAKRIYIANNI ΜΑΚΡΥΓΙΑΝΝΗ

TOP ATTRACTIONS

Hadrian's Arch. One of the most important Roman monuments surviving in Athens, Hadrian's Arch has become, for many, one of the city's most iconic landmarks. This marble gateway, built in AD 131 with Corinthian details, was intended both to honor the Hellenophile emperor Hadrian and to separate the ancient and imperial sections of Athens. ⊠ *Vasilissis Amalias at Dionyssiou Areopagitou, Makriyianni* 🎫 *Free* Ⓜ *Acropolis*.

Fodor'sChoice
★ **Ilias Lalaounis Jewelry Museum.** Housing the creations of internationally renowned artist-jeweler Ilias Lalaounis, this private foundation also operates as an international center for the study of decorative arts. The collection includes 4,000 pieces inspired by subjects as diverse as the Treasure of Priam of Troy to the wildflowers of Greece. Many of the works are eye-catching, especially the massive necklaces evoking the Minoan and Byzantine periods. Besides the well-made videos that explain jewelry making, craftspeople in the workshop demonstrate ancient and modern techniques, such as chain weaving and hammering. The company also operates several jewelry stores in Athens. ⊠ *Kallisperi 12, at Karyatidon, Makriyianni* ☎ *210/922–1044* ⊕ *www.lalaounis-jewelrymuseum.gr* 🎫 *€5* ☉ *Closed Mon.* Ⓜ *Acropolis*.

Temple of Olympian Zeus. Begun in the 6th century BC, this gigantic temple was completed in AD 132 by Hadrian, who also commissioned a huge gold-and-ivory statue of Zeus for the inner chamber and another, only slightly smaller, of himself. Only 15 of the original Corinthian columns remain, but standing next to them may inspire a sense of awe at their bulk, which is softened by the graceful carving on the acanthus-leaf capitals. The site is floodlighted on summer evenings, creating a majestic scene when you turn round the bend from Syngrou Avenue. On the outskirts of the site to the north are remains of Roman houses, the city walls, and a Roman bath. Hadrian's Arch lies just outside the enclosed archaeological site. ✉ *Vasilissis Olgas 1, Makriyianni* ☎ *210/922–6330* ⊕ *www.culture.gr* ✉ *€6; €30 joint ticket for all Unification of Archaeological Sites* Ⓜ *Acropolis.*

PLAKA AND ANAFIOTIKA ΠΛΑΚΑ ΑΝΑΦΙΩΤΙΚΑ

Fanning north from the slopes of the Acropolis, picturesque Plaka is the last corner of 19th-century Athens. Set with Byzantine accents provided by churches, the Old Town district extends north to Ermou Street and eastward to the Leofóros Amalias. During the 1950s and '60s, the area became garish with neon as nightclubs moved in and residents moved out, but locals, architects, and academicians joined forces in the early 1980s to transform a decaying neighborhood. Noisy discos and tacky pensions were closed, streets were changed into pedestrian zones, and old buildings were restored. At night merrymakers crowd the old tavernas, which feature traditional music and dancing; many have rooftops facing the Acropolis.

Set in the shadow of the Acropolis and often compared to the whitewashed villages of the rural Greek islands, the Anafiotika section of the Plaka is populated by many descendants of the Anafi stonemasons who arrived from that small Cycladic island in the 19th century to work in the expanding capital. It remains an enchanting area of simple stone houses, many nestled right into the bedrock, most little changed over the years, others stunningly restored. Cascades of bougainvillea and pots of geraniums and marigolds enliven the balconies and rooftops, and the prevailing serenity is in blissful contrast to the cacophony of modern Athens. In classical times, this district was abandoned because the Delphic Oracle claimed it as sacred ground. The original residents erected their homes overnight, as they took advantage of an Ottoman law decreeing that if you could put up a structure between sunset and sunrise, the property was yours.

Today, the residents are seldom seen—only a line of wash hung out to dry, the lace curtains on the tiny houses, or the curl of smoke from a wood-burning fireplace indicates human presence. Perched on the bedrock of the Acropolis is **Ayios Georgios tou Vrachou** (St. George of the Rock), which marks the southeast edge of the district. One of the most beautiful churches of Athens, it is still in use today. **Ayios Simeon,** a neoclassical church built in 1847 by the settlers, marks the western boundary and contains a copy of a famous miracle-working icon from Anafi, Our Lady of the Reeds. The **Church of the Metamorphosis Sotiros** (Transfiguration), a high-dome 14th-century stone chapel, has a rear grotto carved right into the Acropolis.

PLAKA ΠΛΑΚΑ

TOP ATTRACTIONS

Kanellopoulos Museum. The stately Michaleas Mansion, built in 1884, now showcases the Kanellopoulos family collection. It spans Athens's history from the 3rd century BC to the 19th century, with an emphasis on Byzantine icons, jewelry, and Mycenaean and Geometric vases and bronzes. Note the painted ceiling gracing the first floor. ✉ *Theorias 12* *and Panos, Plaka* ☎ *210/321–8873, 210/321–2313* ⊕ *www.pakanel-lopoulosfoundation.org* ✉ *Free* ⊙ *Closed Mon.* Ⓜ *Monastiraki.*

NEED A BREAK ✕ **Cafe Oionos.** Stop for an ice-cold frappé (Nescafé instant coffee frothed with sugar and condensed milk) and a game of backgammon at Cafe Oionos. **Known for:** freshly made salads; pastas and sandwiches; relaxing atmosphere. ✉ *Kydathinaion and Geronta 7, Plaka* ☎ *210/322-3139* ⊕ *www.oionos-cafe.gr.*

Little Mitropolis. This church snuggles up to the pompous Mitropolis (on the northern edge of Plaka), the ornate Cathedral of Athens. Also called Panayia Gorgoepikoos ("the virgin who answers prayers quickly"), the chapel dates to the 12th century; its most interesting features are its outer walls, covered with reliefs of animals and allegorical figures dating from the classical to the Byzantine period. Light a candle for a loved one and then look for the ancient frieze with zodiac signs and a calendar of festivals in Attica. Most of the paintings inside were destroyed, but the famous 13th- to 14th-century Virgin, said to perform miracles, remains. ✉ *Mitropolis Sq., Plaka* Ⓜ *Syntagma.*

NEED A BREAK ✕ **Melina Cafe.** Melina is dedicated to its namesake, the dynamic *Never on Sunday* actress turned Minister of Culture, Melina Mercouri. Set on a scenic, village-style Plaka street framed by pink bougainvillea, the tables are always packed. **Known for:** buzzy atmosphere; good food you can linger over; traditional desserts. ✉ *Lysiou 22, Plaka* ☎ *210/324-6501.*

Roman Agora. The city's commercial center from the 1st century BC to the 4th century AD, the Roman Market was a large rectangular courtyard with a peristyle that provided shade for the arcades of shops. Its most notable feature is the west entrance's Bazaar Gate, or Gate of Athena Archegetis, completed around AD 2. On the north side stands one of the few remains of the Turkish occupation, the **Fethiye** (Victory) **Mosque;** eerily beautiful, it dates from the late 15th century. Now used as a storehouse, it is closed to the public. Surrounded by a cluster of old houses on the western slope of the Acropolis, the world-famous **Tower of the Winds** (Aerides), now open to the public for visits, is the most appealing and well preserved of the Roman monuments of Athens, keeping time since the 1st century BC. Its eight sides face the direction of the eight winds into which the compass was divided. ✉ *Pelopidas and Aiolou, Plaka* ☎ *210/321-6690* ⊕ *www.culture.gr* ✉ *€6; €30 joint ticket for all Unification of Archaeological Sites* Ⓜ *Monastiraki.*

WORTH NOTING

NEED A BREAK ✕ **Kapnikarea.** A perfect stop while exploring Ermou Street's shops and the Monastiraki area, Kapnikarea serves up tasty meze with a live sound track of the Greek blues (*rembetika*), especially between 6 and 11 pm, in a relaxed, authentic setup reflective of the owner's heritage from "longevity island," Ikaria. **Known for:** rembetika music played by skilled musicians; great location. ✉ *Hristopoulou 2, at Ermou 57, Monastiraki* ✛ *Behind Kapnikarea church* ☎ *210/322-7394.*

STEP-BY-STEP: A WALK THROUGH PLAKA

Begin your stroll at the ancient, jewel-like **Monument of Lysikrates,** one of the few remaining supports (334 BC) for tripods (vessels that served as prizes) awarded to the producer of the best play in the ancient Dionyssia festival. Take Herefondos to Plaka's central square, Filomoussou Eterias (or Kidathineon Square), a great place to people-watch.

The **Greek Folk Art Museum,** one of Athens's most rewarding cultural stops, is currently closed to the public, with plans for an ultramodern new museum that will hold its collection and more exhibits to open around 2019. Across from the former museum on Kidathineos Street is the 11th- to 12th-century church of Metamorfosi Sotira Tou Kottaki, in a tidy garden with a fountain that was the main source of water for the neighborhood until sometime after Turkish rule. Down the block and around the corner on Angelikis Hatzimichali is the **Center of Folk Art and Tradition.** Continue west to the end of that street, crossing Adrianou to Hill, then right on Epimarchou to the striking Church House (on the corner of Scholeiou), once a Turkish police post and home to Richard Church, who led Greek forces in the War of Independence.

At the top of Epimarchou is Ayios Nikolaos Rangavas, an 11th-century church built with fragments of ancient columns. The church marks the edge of the **Anafiotika** quarter, a village smack-dab in the middle of the metropolis. Wind your way through the narrow lanes off Stratonos, visiting the churches Ayios Georgios tou Vrachou, Ayios Simeon, and Metamorphosis Sotiros.

Another interesting church is 8th-century Ayioi Anargyroi, at the top of Erechtheos. From the church, make your way to Theorias, which parallels the ancient *peripatos* (public roadway) that ran around the Acropolis. The collection at the **Kanellopoulos Museum** spans Athens's history; nearby on Panos you'll pass the Athens University Museum (Old University, otherwise known as the Kleanthis Residence), the city's first higher-learning institution. Walk down Panos to the **Roman Agora,** which includes the Tower of the Winds and the Fethiye Mosque. Nearby visit the engaging **Museum of Greek Popular Musical Instruments,** where recordings will take you back to the age of *rembetika* (Greek blues). Also next to the Agora is Athens's only remaining Turkish bathhouse, providing a glimpse into a daily social ritual of Ottoman times. On your way back to Syntagma Square, cut across to Mitropoleos Square to see the newly renovated cathedral and the beautiful 12th-century church of **Little Mitropolis.** From there, walk the tiny Benizelou Paleologou Street (recently opened to the public) to admire the **Benizelou Mansion,** among the city's oldest abodes and once the home of the city's patron saint, Aghia Filothei on Adrianou Street.

FAMILY **Museum of Greek Popular Musical Instruments.** An entertaining crash course in the development of Greek music, from regional *dimotika* (folk) to rembetika (blues), this museum has three floors of instruments. Headphones are available so you can appreciate the sounds made by such unusual delights as goatskin bagpipes and discern the differences in tone between the Pontian lyra and Cretan lyra, string instruments often featured on world-music compilations. ⊠ *Diogenous 1–3, Plaka* ☎ *210/325–0198* ⊕ *www.instruments-museum.gr* ☞ *Free* ☉ *Closed Mon.* Ⓜ *Monastiraki.*

NEED A BREAK

✕ **Vyzantino.** Vyzantino is directly on Plaka's main square—good for a reasonably priced, flavorsome, and traditional bite to eat with a front seat to all the action. **Known for:** creamy pastitsio; friendly service; central location. ⊠ *Kidathineon 18, Plaka* ☎ *210/322–7368* ⊕ *www.vyzantinorestaurant.gr* Ⓜ *Acropolis.*

MONASTIRAKI AND PSIRRI ΜΟΝΑΣΤΗΡΑΚΙ ΨΥΡΗ

The Agora was once the focal point of urban life. All the principal urban roads and country highways traversed it; the procession of the great Panathenaea Festival, composed of chariots, magistrates, virgins, priests, and sacrificial animals, crossed it on the way to the Acropolis; the Assembly met here first, before moving to the Pnyx; it was where merchants squabbled over the price of olive oil; the forum where Socrates met with his students; and centuries later, where St. Paul went about his missionary task. Lying just under the citadel of the Acropolis, it was indeed the heart of the ancient city and a general meeting place, where news was exchanged and bargains transacted, alive with all the rumors and gossip of the marketplace. The Agora became important under Solon (6th century BC), founder of Athenian democracy; construction continued for almost a millennium. Today, the site's sprawling confusion of stones, slabs, and foundations is dominated by the best-preserved Doric temple in Greece, the Hephaistion, built during the 5th century BC, and the impressive reconstructed Stoa of Attalos II, which houses the Museum of the Agora Excavations.

You can still experience the sights and sounds of the marketplace in Monastiraki, which retains vestiges of the 400-year period when Greece was subject to the Ottoman Empire. The Varvakeios Agora (Central Market) in the heart of Athinas Street sells fish, meat, and produce from all over Greece and is the major supplier for the city. Not for the squeamish, the bustling market is where you'll see every variety of fish, skinned goats, and cow's tongues. It is a bustling and colorful complex of both indoor and outdoor stalls and shops scattered around the back streets.

For anyone who may have explored the city even only a few years ago, Monastiraki today is unrecognizable, especially at night. Cool, artsy bars, some managed by savvy mixologists, tiny street food eateries, dessert places, third-generation cafés making designer coffee, restaurants, yoga schools, and vintage or design stores have mushroomed across the area in the true style of a European capital. It's a great idea to head down Ermou and cross into the heart of Monastiraki's mazelike streets without any map or any plan, just a thirst for adventure and to gain a new understanding of what Athens's real center is all about.

During his stint in Athens, Lord Byron stayed in Psirri, adjacent to Monastiraki, and this is where he supposedly met Thiresia-Tereza Makri, who inspired him to write "The Maid of Athens." Over the last 20 years an influx of artists, designers, bakers, and organic grocers took advantage of the available rental opportunities, changing the area's profile and bringing the rents up considerably.

Defined by Ermou, Kerameikou, Athinas, Evripidou, Epikourou, and Pireos streets, Psirri has many buildings older than those in picturesque Plaka. Although nowhere near as fashionable as it was in the late 1990s–early 2000s, it still draws the crowds for its plethora of tavernas, *mezedopoleio* (Greek tapas bars), nightspots, and cafés, while a small number of artsy shops and modern hotels, including the O&B Hotel, can be found in the area. Peek over the wrought-iron gates of the old houses on the narrow side streets between Ermou and Kerameikou to see the pretty courtyards bordered by long, low buildings, whose many small rooms were rented out to different families. Linger on into the evening if you want to dance on tabletops to live Greek music or sing along with a soulful accordion player. The classic old Athens eatery Diporto is well hidden in the corner basement of an olive shop (with no sign) on Platia Theatrou. The regulars know where it is, and that's good enough (you can ask). Just follow your nose to Evripidou Street, where the city's best spice and herb shops are. If you're feeling adventurous (during the day only) get lost in the border between Psirri and Omonia to discover the immigrant zone brimming with Indian and Pakistani restaurants and grocers, Chinese clothes shops, and Middle Eastern barbers.

MONASTIRAKI ΜΟΝΑΣΤΗΡΑΚΙ

TOP ATTRACTIONS

Fodor's Choice ★ **Ancient Agora.** Ancient Athens's commercial hub, the Agora was once lined with statues and expensive shops, the favorite strolling ground of fashionable Athenians as well as a mecca for merchants and students. Under the arches of the long colonnades, Socrates discussed matters with Plato, and Zeno expounded the philosophy of the Stoics (whose name comes from the six stoa, or colonnades of the Agora). The Agora's showpiece was the **Stoa of Attalos II,** where Socrates once lectured and incited the youth of Athens to adopt his progressive ideas on mortality and morality. Some of the most easily distinguished buildings include the circular **Tholos,** the principal seat of executive power in the city; the **Mitroon,** shrine to Rhea, the mother of gods, which included the vast state archives and registry office; the **Bouleterion,** where the council met; the **Monument of Eponymous Heroes,** the information center; and the Sanctuary of the Twelve Gods, a shelter for refugees and the point from which all distances were measured. In the Agora's northwest corner stands the best-preserved Doric temple in all Greece, the **Hephaistion,** which is slightly older than the Parthenon. ✉ *3 entrances: from Monastiraki on Adrianou;*

from Thission on Apostolou Pavlou; and descending from Acropolis on Polygnotou St. (near the church of Ayion Apostolon), Monastiraki ☎ *210/321–0185* ⊕ *www.culture.gr* 🎫 *€8; €30 joint ticket for all Unification of Archaeological Sites* Ⓜ *Thissio.*

Fodor'sChoice **Varvakeios Agora** (*Central Market*). Athens's cacophonous Central
★ Market runs along Athinas Street: on one side are open-air stalls selling fruit and vegetables, with a few stores selling mainly eastern European foods tucked at the back. Across the street, in the huge neoclassical covered market, built between 1870 and 1884 (and renovated in 1996), are the meat market next to the fish market, juxtaposing the surrealistic composition of suspended carcasses and shimmering fish on marble counters. The shops at the north end of the market, to the right on Sofokleous, sell the best cheese, olives, halvah, bread, spices, and cold cuts—including *pastourma* (spicy cured beef)—available in Athens. Nearby is Evripidou Street, lined with herb and spice shops all the way down. Small restaurants serving traditional fare and *patsa* (tripe soup), dot the market; these stay open until almost dawn and are popular stops with weary clubbers trying to ease their hangovers. ✉ *Athinas Street, Monastiraki* ⊗ *Closed Sun.* Ⓜ *Monastiraki.*

WORTH NOTING

Flea Market. Here is where the chaos, spirit, and charm of Athens turn into a feast for the senses. The Sunday-morning market has combined sight, sound, and scent into a strangely alluring little world where everything is for sale: 1950s-era scuba masks, old tea sets, antique sewing machines, old tobacco tins, gramophone needles, old matchboxes, army uniforms, and lacquered eggs. Get there before the crowd becomes a throng at 11 am, and practice your haggling skills. ✉ *Along Ifestou, Kynetou, and Adrianou Sts., Monastiraki* Ⓜ *Monastiraki.*

Monastiraki Square. One of Athens's most popular meeting places, the square is always alive with fruit sellers, bunches of youths hanging out, and street dance performances. If you are coming by metro, look for the special glassed-in view revealing the ancient Iridanos riverbed, where the water still flows. The square takes its name from the small Panayia Pantanassa Church, commonly called Monastiraki ("Little Monastery"). It once flourished as an extensive convent, perhaps dating to the 10th century, and once stretched from Athinas to Aiolou. The nuns took in poor people, who earned their keep weaving the thick textiles known as *abas*. The buildings were destroyed during excavations, and the train (and later metro) line construction that started in 1896. The convent's basic basilica form, now recessed a few steps below street level, was altered through a poor restoration in 1911, when the bell tower was added. ✉ *Monastiraki* ✛ *South of Ermou and Athinas junction* Ⓜ *Monastiraki.*

NEED A BREAK

✕ **Thanasis.** With the hands-down best kebab (especially the traditional *yiaourtlou*, i.e., with yogurt sauce) in town, and open since 1950, Thanasis is always crowded with hungry Greeks who crave the specially spiced ground meat, along with a nicely oiled pita bread, yogurt, onions, and tomatoes. **Known for:** kebabs with all the trimmings; popular with both locals and visitors; reasonable prices. ✉ *Mitropoleos 82, Monastiraki* ☎ *210/325–3845* ⊕ *www.othanasis.gr.*

THISSIO ΘΗΣΕΙΟ

On the opposite side of the Agora is another meeting place of sorts: Thissio, a former red-light district that has been one of the most sought-after residential neighborhoods since the early 1990s. Easily accessible by metro and offering a lovely view of the Acropolis, it has become one of the liveliest café and restaurant districts in Athens. Mainly on Adrianou Street along the rail track, you'll find excellent *rakadika* and *ouzeri*—publike eateries that offer plates of appetizers to go with *raki,* a fiery spirit made from grape must; *rakomelo,* a mix of raki and honey heated to boiling; the ever-appealing ouzo; as well as barrels of home-made wine. On a summer evening, walk to the main strip on the Nileos pedestrian zone to sit at an outdoor table in summer in local style, or perch yourself under the Acropolis on Apostolou Pavlou Street. The rest of the neighborhood is quiet, an odd mix of mom-and-pop stores and dilapidated houses that are slowly being renovated.

SYNTAGMA ΣΥΝΤΑΓΜΑΤΟΣ

From the Tomb of the Unknown Soldier to Queen Amalia's National Garden, to the top of Mt. Lycabettus, to a cluster of top museums, this center-city sector is packed with cultural marvels and wonders of old. Paradoxically, in crisis-hit Athens it has also blossomed into a newly stylish and popular hangout for coffee, dinner, and drinks. Sooner or later, everyone passes through the capital's heart, the spacious Syntagma (Constitution) Square, which is surrounded by remnants of Athens's history from the days of the Roman emperors to King Otto's reign after the 1821 War of Independence. Some may have likened his palace (now the Parliament) to a barracks, but things could have been much worse: Otto's father, King Ludwig I of Bavaria, vetoed plans for a royal residence atop the Acropolis itself, a plan that would have used one end of the Parthenon as the entrance and blown up the rest. The palace was finished just in time for Otto to grant the constitution of 1843, which gave the square its name. Besides culture-hopping, you can spend time window-shopping and people-watching; nursing a single coffee for hours remains not only socially acceptable but a vital survival tactic in frequently stressful modern Greek life.

TOP ATTRACTIONS

FAMILY **National Garden.** When you can't take the city noise anymore, step into this oasis completed in 1860 as part of King Otto and Queen Amalia's royal holdings. Here old men on the benches argue politics, children

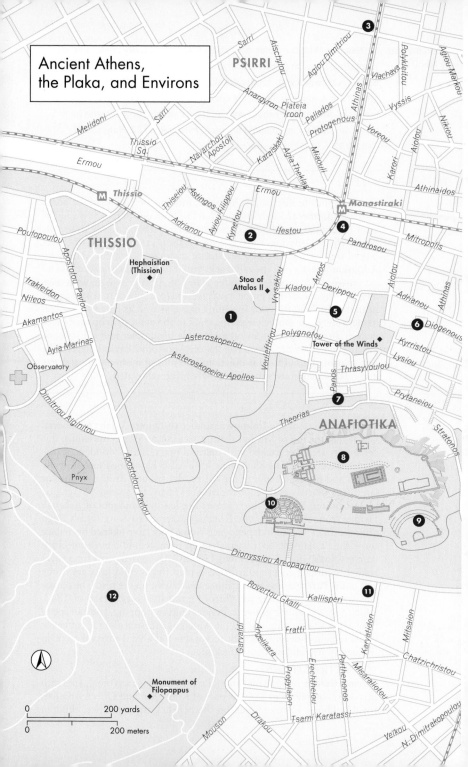

Ancient Athens, the Plaka, and Environs

PSIRRI

Sarri
Aischylou
Agiou Dimitriou
Vlachava
Polykleitou
Agiou Markou

Anargyron Plateia
Iroon
Pallados
Athinas
Vyssis
Nikiou

Melidoni
Sarri
Navarchou Apostoli
Karaiskaki
Agia Theklas
Miaouli
Protogenous
Voreou
Karori
Aiolou

Thissio Sq.
Ermou

Ermou
Thiseiou
Astingos
Ayiou Filippou
Kynetou
Ermou
Athinaidos

Ⓜ Thissio
Adrianou
❷
Ifestou
Ⓜ Monastiraki
Mitropolis

THISSIO
❹
Pandrosou

Poutopoulou
Apostolou Pavlou
Hephaistion (Thission)
Stoa of Attalos II
Vrysakiou
Kladou
Areos
Dexippou
❺
❻ Diogenous
Adrianou
Athinas

Irakleidon
Nileos
Akamantos
Asteroskopeiou
Polygnotou
Tower of the Winds
Kyrristou
Lysiou

Ayia Marinas
Asteroskopeiou Apollos
Vouleftiron
Panos
Thrasyvoulou
Prytaneiou

Observatory
❼
Theorias
ANAFIOTIKA
Stratonos

Dimitriou Aiginitou
Apostolou Pavlou
❽

Pnyx
❿
❾

Dionyssiou Areopagitou

⓬
Rovertou Gkalli
Kallisperi
⓫

Garvaldi
Angelikara
Fratti
Karyatidon
Mitsaion
Chatzichristou

◈
Propylaion
Erechtheiou
Parthenonos
Misaraliotou

Monument of Filopappus
Mouson
Drakou
Tsami Karatassi
Veikou
N. Dimitrakopoulou

0   200 yards
0   200 meters

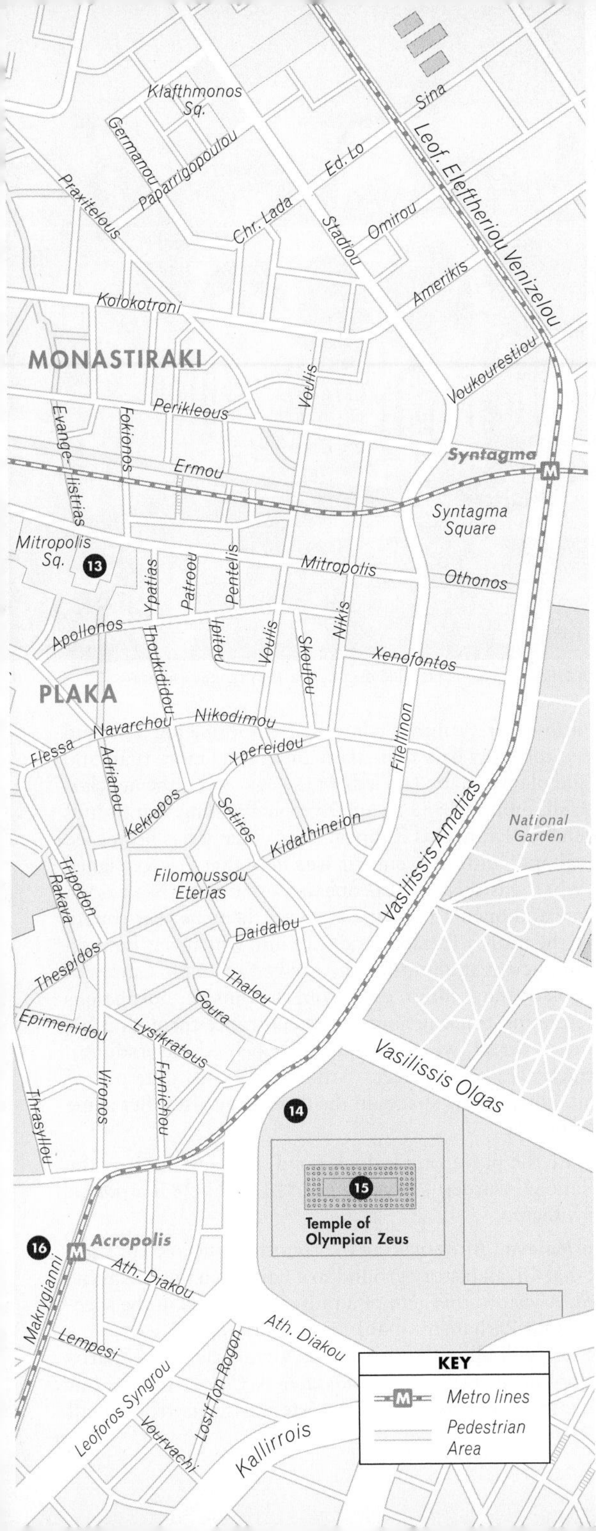

Klafthmonos Sq.
Germanou
Paparrigopoulou
Praxitelous
Sina
Leof. Eleftheriou Venizelou
Ed. Lo
Chr. Lada
Stadiou
Omirou
Amerikis
Kolokotroni
MONASTIRAKI
Voukourestiou
Voulis
Perikleous
Evange-listrias
Fokionos
Ermou
Syntagma
Syntagma Square
Mitropolis Sq.
13
Ypatias
Patroou
Pentelis
Mitropolis
Othonos
Apollonos
Thoukididou
Ipitou
Voulis
Skoufou
Nikis
Xenofontos
PLAKA
Nikodimou
Navarchou
Flessa
Adrianou
Ypereidou
Filellinon
Kekropos
Sotiros
Kidathineion
Vasilissis Amalias
National Garden
Tripodon
Rakava
Filomoussou Eterias
Daidalou
Thespidos
Thalou
Goura
Epimenidou
Lysikratous
Vasilissis Olgas
Vironos
Frynichou
Thrasyllou
14
15
Temple of Olympian Zeus
16
Acropolis
Ath. Diakou
Makrygianni
Lempesi
Ath. Diakou
Leoforos Syngrou
Iosif Ton Rogon
Vourvachi
Kallirrois
KEY
Metro lines
Pedestrian Area

Acropolis 8
Acropolis Museum 16
Ancient Agora 1
Filopappou 12
Flea Market 2
Hadrian's Arch 14
Ilias Lalaounis Jewelry Museum 11
Kanellopoulos Museum 7
Little Mitropolis 13
Monastiraki Square 4
Museum of Greek Popular Musical Instruments 6
Odeon of Herodes Atticus 10
Roman Agora 5
Temple of Olympian Zeus 15
Theater of Dionysus 9
Varvakeios Agora 3

One of the hearts of the center city, Monastiraki Square is presided over by the 18th-century Tzistarakis Mosque.

run free among lush nature, runners count early-morning jog laps, and animal lovers feed the stray cats that roam among the more than 500 species of trees and plants, many labeled. At the east end is the neoclassical **Zappeion Hall,** built in 1888 as an Olympic building (with funds from Greek benefactor Evangelos Zappas). Since then it has been used for major political and cultural events: it was here that Greece signed its accession to what was then the European Community. Next door, the leafy Aegli café and open-air cinema attract Athenians year-round. Cross the road to the nearby Panathenaic Stadium, which was built on the very site of an ancient stadium for the revived Olympic Games in 1896. You can look at the stadium only from the outside, but there is an elevated dirt running track behind it (free entrance through a big gate on Archimidous Street, which runs directly behind the stadium). The tree-lined track area and adjacent Ardittos hill constitute one of the most pleasant, quiet public spaces in the city—they also offer some stunning vantage points.

Children appreciate the playground, duck pond, and small zoo at the east end of the National Garden. ⊠ *Syntagma* ☎ *210/323–7830* ⊕ *www. zappeion.gr* Ⓜ *Syntagma.*

National Historical Museum. After making the rounds of the ancient sites, you might think that Greek history ground to a halt when the Byzantine Empire collapsed. A visit to this gem of a museum, housed in the spectacularly majestic Old Parliament mansion (used by parliamentarians from 1875 to 1932), will fill in the gaps, often vividly, as with Lazaros Koyevina's copy of Eugene Delacroix's *Massacre of Chios,* to name but one example. Paintings, costumes, and assorted artifacts from small arms to flags and ships' figureheads are arranged in a chronological display tracing Greek history from the mid-16th century and the Battle of Lepanto through World War II and the Battle of Crete. A small gift shop near the main entrance—framed by a very grand neoclassical portico of columns—has unusual souvenirs, like a deck of cards featuring Greece's revolutionary heroes. ✉ *Stadiou 13, Syntagma* ☎ *210/323–7617* ⊕ *www.nhmuseum.gr* 💶 *€3* ⊘ *Closed Mon.* Ⓜ *Syntagma.*

NEED A BREAK

✕ **Aeglí Zappiou.** Visit the elegant Aeglí Zappiou, an excellent spot for a classic Greek coffee experience. Nestled among fountains and flowering trees next to the Zappio Exhibition Hall in the National Garden, it's an ideal spot to sample a fresh dessert or some haute cuisine, or watch a movie at the open-air Cine Aegli next door. **Known for:** good desserts; great coffee; views of open-air Cine Aegli next door. ✉ *Zappio Megaro, Syntagma* ☎ *210/336–9300* ⊕ *www.aeglizappiou.gr.*

Fodor's Choice
★

Numismatic Museum Iliou Melathron. Even those uninterested in coins might want to visit this museum to see the former home of Heinrich Schliemann, who famously excavated Troy and Mycenae in the 19th century. Built by the Bavarian architect Ernst Ziller for the archaeologist's family and baptized the "Iliou Melanthron" (or Palace of Troy), it flaunts an imposing neo-Venetian facade. Inside are some spectacular rooms. Today, you can see more than 600,000 coins; displays range from the archaeologist's own coin collection to 4th-century BC measures employed against forgers to coins grouped by what they depict—animals, plants, myths, and famous buildings. ✉ *Panepistimiou 12, Syntagma* ☎ *210/363–2057, 210/361–2834* ⊕ *www.nma.gr* 💶 *€6; €15 for unified museum ticket (includes National Archaeological Museum, Epigraphical Museu, Byzantine and Christian Museum)* Ⓜ *Syntagma or Panepistimiou.*

NEED A BREAK

✕ **Le Greche.** There's nothing like an ice cream to revive flailing, sweaty spirits on a hot day of touring the city. Le Greche serves fresh, handmade ice cream made with pure ingredients and inspired from Italian gelato, as well as cakes and sorbets. **Known for:** high-quality ice cream and sorbet; central location; good coffee. ✉ *16 Mitropoleos, Syntagma* ☎ *216/700–6458.*

Syntagma Square (*Constitution Square*). At the top of the city's main square stands the Greek Parliament, formerly King Otto's royal palace, completed in 1838 for the new monarchy. It seems a bit austere and heavy for a southern landscape, but it was proof of progress, the symbol of the new ruling power. The building's saving grace is the stone's magical change of color from off-white to gold to rosy-mauve as the day progresses. Here you can watch the **Changing of the Evzones Guards at the Tomb of the Unknown Soldier**—in front of Parliament on a lower level—which takes place at intervals throughout the day. On a wall behind the Tomb of the Unknown Soldier, the bas-relief of a dying soldier is modeled after a sculpture on the Temple of Aphaia in Aegina. In recent years the square has become the new frontline of

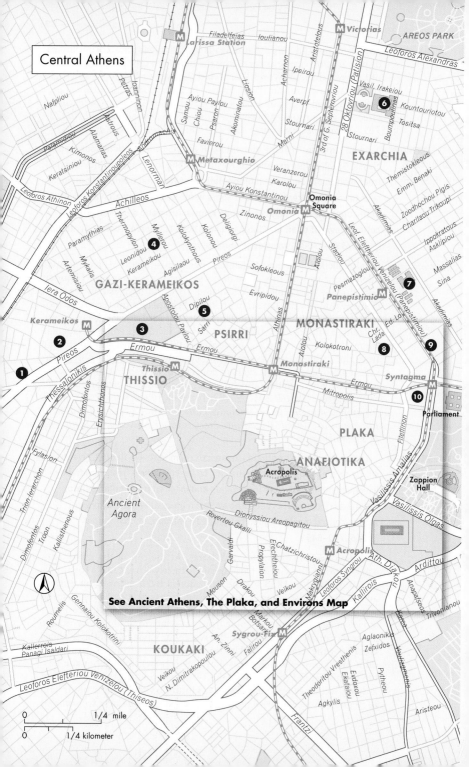

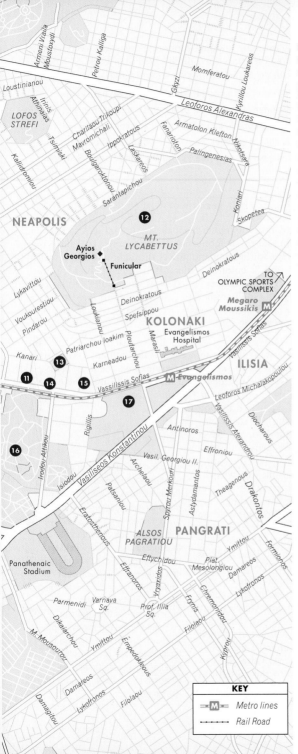

mass protests against the ongoing economic crisis in Greece. It also hosts Europe's longest-established public Wi-Fi network. ⊠ *Vasilissis Amalias and Vasilissis Sofias, Syntagma* Ⓜ *Syntagma.*

NEED A BREAK

✗ **Café Voulis.** Café Voulis is among the top-10 espresso bars in the country, but its aficionados also swear by the fresh sandwiches and salads for an easy lunch break, and a live DJ set and cocktails at night. It is also remarkably cool in summer. **Known for:** youthful, fun atmosphere; well-mixed cocktails; excellent coffee. ⊠ *Voulis 17 and Ermou, Syntagma* ☎ *210/323–4333.*

GAZI-KERAMEIKOS ΓΚΑΖΙ-ΚΕΡΑΜΕΙΚΟΣ

Gazi-Kerameikos takes its name from the industrial gas works that even today dominate the neighborhood's landscape. The plant that used to provide gas for lighting and power throughout the city (called Technopolis) is now a cultural center offering festivals, temporary exhibitions, and open-air concerts. A slew of bars, clubs (with a zone popular among the LGBT community), and restaurants have made the neighborhood a lively nightlife area conveniently served by the sleek Kerameikos metro station.

TOP ATTRACTIONS

Kerameikos Cemetery. At the western edge of the modern Gazi district lies the wide, ancient green expanse of Kerameikos, the main cemetery in ancient Athens until Sulla destroyed the city in 86 BC. The name is associated with the modern word "ceramic": in the 12th century BC the district was populated by potters who used the abundant clay from the languid Iridanos River to make funerary urns and grave decorations. From the 7th century BC onward, Kerameikos was the fashionable cemetery of ancient Athens. During succeeding ages cemeteries were superimposed on the ancient one until the latter was discovered in 1861. From the main entrance, you can still see remains of the **Makra Teixi** (Long Walls) of Themistocles, which ran to Piraeus, and the largest gate in the ancient world, the **Dipylon Gate,** where visitors entered Athens. The walls rise to 10 feet, a fraction of their original height (up to 45 feet). Here was also the **Sacred Gate,** used by pilgrims headed to the mysterious rites in Eleusis and by those who participated in the Panathenaic

> **CHANGING OF THE GUARDS**
>
> Near the Parliament, you can watch the **Changing of the Evzones Guards** at the Tomb of the Unknown Soldier—in front of Parliament on a lower level—which takes place at intervals throughout the day. On Sunday the honor guard of tall young men don a dress costume—a short white and very heavy *foustanella* (kilt) with 400 neat pleats, one for each year of the Ottoman occupation, and red shoes with pom-poms—and still manage to look brawny rather than silly. A band accompanies them: they all arrive by 11:15 am in front of Parliament.

For patriotic Greeks, the Changing of the Guard in front of the Tomb of the Unknown Soldier is always a heart-stirring ceremony.

procession, which followed the Sacred Way. Between the two gates are the foundations of the **Pompeion,** the starting point of the Panathenaic procession. It is said the courtyard was large enough to fit the ship used in the procession. On the **Street of Tombs,** which branches off the Sacred Way, plots were reserved for affluent Athenians. A number of the distinctive *stelae* (funerary monuments) remain, including a replica of the marble relief of Dexilios, a knight who died in the war against Corinth (394 BC); he is shown on horseback preparing to spear a fallen foe. To the left of the site's entrance is the **Oberlaender Museum,** also known as the Kerameikos Museum, whose displays include sculpture, terra-cotta figures, and some striking red-and-black-figured pottery. The extensive grounds of Kerameikos are marshy in some spots; in spring, frogs exuberantly croak their mating songs near magnificent stands of lilies. ⊠ *Ermou 148, Gazi-Kerameikos* ☎ *210/346–3552* 🖥 *Full: €8 site and museum; €30 joint ticket for all Unification of Archaeological Sites* Ⓜ *Kerameikos.*

WORTH NOTING

Benaki Museum of Islamic Art. Housed in a gleaming white neoclassical mansion with a sweeping view of the Kerameikos cemetery (that can be relished over coffee at the rooftop café), this annex of the Benaki Museum provides a welcoming home to its extensive Islamic art collection (which is considered among the most important in the world). More than 8,000 pieces of art hail from regions as widely spread geographically as North Africa, India, Persia, Asia Minor, Arabia, Mesopotamia, and even Sicily and Spain. ⊠ *Dipilou 12, at Ag. Asomaton*

22, Gazi-Kerameikos ☎ *210/325–1311* ⊕ *www.benaki.gr* ✉ *Permanent collection €9; temporary exhibitions €7* ⊘ *Closed Mon.–Wed.*

Benaki Museum Pireos Street Annexe. The eye-knocking Benaki Museum Annexe is located at one of the busiest and most industrially developed points in the city. The minimalist exterior is covered in smooth pink stone—a kind of beacon of modernity—with creatively designed clean lines on the dusty, loud avenue. Inside, all is high-ceilinged atriums, transparent walkway ascents, and multiple levels, a dramatic setting for the museum's temporary exhibitions (many of which are far more avant-garde in character than those housed in the main building). ✉ *Pireos 138, Gazi-Kerameikos* ✢ *At Andronikou St.* ☎ *210/345–3111* ⊕ *www.benaki.gr* ✉ *€6–€8 (varies by special exhibit)* ⊘ *Closed Mon.– Wed. and Aug.* Ⓜ *Kerameikos.*

Technopolis. Gazi, the neighborhood surrounding this former 19th-century-gasworks–turned–arts complex, takes its name from the toxic gas fumes that used to spew from the factory's smokestacks. Today Gazi district is synonymous with an intellectual gallery scene and buzzy nightlife, with a special LGBT-friendly zone to boot. The smokestacks are now glowing crimson referential landmarks anchoring a burgeoning stretch that runs from the central neighborhood of Kerameikos to the once-decrepit neighborhood of Rouf. Since the city of Athens bought the disused gasworks in the late 1990s, it was converted, retaining the original brick architecture, into Technopolis, where large art exhibitions and events centered on gastronomy, social history, lifestyle, and culture (like the annual European Jazz Festival) regularly take place, and where the Industrial Gas Museum is housed. ✉ *Pireos 100, Gazi-Kerameikos* ☎ *210/347–5518* ⊕ *www. technopolis-athens.com* ✉ *Technopolis free, Gas Museum €1* ⊘ *Closed Mon.* Ⓜ *Kerameikos.*

KOLONAKI ΚΟΛΩΝΑΚΙ

Kolonaki was named after a marble column dating from the Middle Ages, probably a memento of a religious procession, that was discovered in Dexameni Square, on the foot of Mt. Lycabettus. On its southwestern edge is Syntagma Square and the Parliament building; the neighborhood extends all the way to Lycabettus and beyond. It is a posh neighborhood with lots of upmarket boutiques, glossy cafés, and upscale restaurants, galleries, and museums. At the bottom edge of Kolonaki on Vas. Sophias Avenue, you can pay homage to the power of movement and clean lines of the impressive *Runner,* a glass sculpture of impressive proportions by local artist Kostas Varotsos across from the Hilton Hotel.

TOP ATTRACTIONS

Fodor'sChoice ★

Benaki Museum. Greece's oldest private museum, which emphasizes the country's later heritage, received a spectacular face-lift in the year of the Athens Olympics with the addition of a hypermodern wing. Established in 1926, it is in an imposing neoclassical mansion in the posh Kolonaki neighborhood. The permanent collection (more than 20,000 items are on display in 36 rooms) moves chronologically from the ground floor upward, from prehistory to the formation of the modern Greek state. You might see anything from a 5,000-year-old hammered-gold bowl to an austere Byzantine icon of the Virgin Mary to Lord Byron's pistols. Topping the complex off is a state-of-the-art amphitheater. ☒ *Koumbari 1, Kolonaki* ☏ *210/367–1000* ⊕ *www.benaki.gr* 🎫 *€7 (free Thurs.)* ☾ *Closed Mon. and Tues.* Ⓜ *Syntagma or Evangelismos, Kerameikos for the New Wing on Pireos.*

NEED A BREAK

✕ **Clemente VIII.** Located on pedestrian Voukourestiou Street, where all the most luxurious fashion boutiques are, the Italian-style café serves freshly ground, high-quality espresso and cappuccino and a fresh daily platter of sandwiches and sweets. It is named after the 16th-century pope who gave his blessing to the then-exotic coffee bean. **Known for:** chichi coffee drinking; elegant location; good, albeit expensive, sandwiches and desserts. ☒ *City Link Mall, Voukourestiou 3, Kolonaki* ☏ *210/321–9340.*

FAMILY
Fodor'sChoice
★

Mt. Lycabettus. Myth claims that Athens's highest hill came into existence when Athena removed a piece of Mt. Pendeli, intending to boost the height of her temple on the Acropolis. While she was en route, a crone brought her bad tidings, and the flustered goddess dropped the rock in the middle of the city. Dog-walkers and joggers have made it their daily stomping grounds, and kids love the ride up the steeply inclined *teleferique* (funicular) to the summit, crowned by whitewashed Ayios Georgios chapel with a bell tower donated by Queen Olga. Lovers head to the top to watch the sunset and then turn to watch the moon rise over "violet-crowned" Mt. Hymettus as the lights of Athens blink on all over the city. Events are held at the hill's open-air theater during summer months. ☒ *Kolonaki* ✛ *The base is a 15-min walk northeast of Syntagma Sq.; funicular runs every 30 mins (10 mins during rush hour) from corner of Ploutarchou and Aristippou (take Minibus 060 from Kanari or Kolonaki Sq.); then the terminal is at the end of Aristippou St.* ☏ *210/721–0701 Funicular information* ⊕ *www.lycabettushill.com* 🎫 *Funicular €7 (round-trip).*

FAMILY
Fodor'sChoice
★

Museum of Cycladic Art. Also known as the Nicholas P. and Dolly Goulandris Foundation, and funded by one of Greece's richest families, this museum has an outstanding collection of 350 Cycladic artifacts dating from the Bronze Age, including many of the enigmatic marble figurines whose slender shapes fascinated such artists as Picasso, Modigliani, and Brancusi. Along with Cycladic masterpieces, a wide array from other eras is also on view, ranging from the Bronze Age through the 6th century AD. The third floor is devoted to Cypriot art, while the fourth floor showcases a fascinating exhibition on "scenes from daily life in antiquity." A glass corridor connects the main building to the gorgeous 19th-century neoclassical Stathatos Mansion, where temporary exhibits are mounted. ☒ *Neofitou Douka 4, Kolonaki* ☏ *210/722–8321* ⊕ *www. cycladic.gr* 🎫 *€7; €10 (including temporary exhibitions)* ☾ *Closed Tues.* Ⓜ *Evangelismos.*

Try to catch the purple glow of sundown from atop Mt. Lycabettus, Athens's highest hill.

✕ **Zonar's Café d'Athenes.** One of Athens's most established and elegant cafés, where a multitude of film stars and politicians have sipped their coffee since 1939, grandiosely renovated Zonar's serves plush brunches, mouthwatering pastries, and chic snacks. Get there before 11 am to have your eggs Benedict in virtual solitude. **Known for:** brunch in classy-café environs; wonderful cakes; elegant service. ✉ *Attica Department Store, Panepistimiou and Voukourestiou, Kolonaki* ☎ *210/325–1430* ⊕ *www.zonarsathens.gr* ☉ *No dinner.*

WORTH NOTING

B&M Theocharakis Foundation. A key reference point for Athens's culture vultures, this private nonprofit foundation focuses on the visual arts and music, with a special interest in modernism. The driving force behind the imposing cultural center, housed in a neoclassical building beside the Greek Parliament, is Basil Theocharakis, a prominent businessman who is also an avid and talented painter, and his wife, Marina. Temporary exhibitions, classical concerts, and educational workshops are held here on a regular basis, while Cafe Merlin, the elegant first-floor café, offers a welcome respite from the city's hustle and bustle. ✉ *Vassilissis Sofias 9, at Merlin 1, Kolonaki* ☎ *210/361–1206* ⊕ *www.thf.gr* ☎ *Free* ☉ *Closed Aug.*

Byzantine and Christian Museum. One of the few museums in Europe focusing exclusively on Byzantine art displays an outstanding collection of icons, mosaics, tapestries, and sculptural fragments (the latter provides an excellent introduction to the architecture of the period).

The permanent collection is divided into two main parts: the first is devoted to Byzantium (4th through 15th century AD) and contains 1,200 artifacts, while the second is entitled "From Byzantium to the Modern Era" and presents 1,500 artworks dating from the 15th to the 21st century. ⊠ *Vasilissis Sofias 22, Kolonaki* ☎ *213/213–9572* ⊕ *www. byzantinemuseum.gr* 🎟€8; €30 for unified museum ticket (includes National Archaeological Museum, Epigraphical Museu, Numismatic Museum)* ⊗ *Closed Mon.* Ⓜ *Evangelismos.*

Kolonaki Square. To see and be seen, Athenians gather not on Kolonaki Square—hub of the chic Kolonaki district—but at the cafés on its periphery and along the Tsakalof and Milioni pedestrian zones. Clothespin-thin models, slick talk-show hosts, middle-aged executives, elegant pensioners, university students, and expatriate teen queens can be spotted lounging at the square (officially known as Filikis Eterias). ⊠ *Intersection of Patriarchou Ioakeim and Kanari, Kolonaki* Ⓜ *Syntagma or Evangelismos, then 10- to 15-min walk.*

NEED A BREAK

✕ **Caffe Da Capo.** Enjoy a cappuccino and an Italian panini standing inside Caffe Da Capo, or if you have more time, watch the world go by at an outside table. This place is usually packed with trendsetters and stern policy makers. **Known for: people-watching; hangout for Greek movers and shakers; excellent cappuccino.** ⊠ *Tsakalof 1, Kolonaki* ☎ *210/360–2497.*

Old University Complex. In the sea of concrete that is Central Athens, this imposing group of white marble buildings, known as the Athenian Trilogy, gleams majestically under perfect azure skies like an illusion of classical antiquity. The three dramatic buildings belonging to the University of Athens were designed by the Hansen brothers in the period after independence in the 19th century and are built of Pendelic marble, with tall columns and decorative friezes. In the center is the **University,** after which Panepistimiou (*panepistimio* means university) Street is named, with its huge colorful mural. To the right is the **Academy,** flanked by two slim columns topped by statues of Athena and Apollo; paid for by the Austro-Greek Baron Sina, it is a copy of the Parliament in Vienna. Frescoes in the reception hall depict the myth of Prometheus. At the left end of the complex is a griffin-flanked staircase leading to the **National Library,** which has been housed in the building since 1903 and contains more than 2 million Greek and foreign-language volumes; the books are now being transferred to their new home, the Stavros Niarchos Foundation Cultural Center. ⊠ *Panepistimiou, between Ippokratous and Sina, Kolonaki* ☎ *210/368–9765 Senate, 210/366–4700 Academy, 210/360–8185 Library* ⊕ *www.nlg.gr* ⊗ *Closed Sun. and Aug.* Ⓜ *Panepistimiou.*

EXARCHIA ΕΞΑΡΧΕΙΑ

The neighborhood of Exarchia is full of life and largely student-central, as the National Technical University of Athens (Polytechneio) is located just a few hundred yards away from Exarchia Square down tech-friendly Stournari Street. The area is also infamous for the anarchist groups that use it as a base for their demonstrations, although in recent years peace and quiet have largely prevailed. The National Archaeological Museum (the neighborhood's biggest draw) is next to the Polytechnic, where the historic student uprising of 1973, which led to the ousting of the junta, took place. Look for the "Blue" building in Exarchia Square, which is a prime example of the modernist movement in Greek architecture. Rembetika music clubs, vintage record shops, comic-book shops, musical instrument stores, quaint little bars, traditional tavernas, and cheap souvlaki corners all coexist in the area, which is always buzzing with creative—one might dare say revolutionary—energy.

TOP ATTRACTIONS

Fodor'sChoice ★ **National Archaeological Museum.** Many of the greatest achievements in ancient Greek sculpture and painting are housed here in the most important museum in Greece. Artistic highlights from every period of its ancient civilization, from Neolithic to Roman times, make this a treasure trove beyond compare. The most celebrated display is the Mycenaean Antiquities, stunning gold treasures from Heinrich Schliemann's 1876 excavations of Mycenae's royal tombs. Also not to be missed are the beautifully restored frescoes from Santorini, delightful murals depicting daily life in Minoan Santorini, and the works of Geometric and Archaic art (10th to 6th century BC) and kouroi and funerary stelae (8th to 5th century BC). The collection of classical art (5th to 3rd century BC) contains some of the most renowned surviving ancient statues: the bareback *Jockey of Artemision*; from the same excavation, the bronze *Artemision Poseidon* (some say Zeus); and the *Varvakios Athena*, a half-size version of the gigantic gold-and-ivory cult statue in the Parthenon. ⊠ *28 Oktovriou (Patission) 44, Exarcheia* ☎ *213/214–4800, 213/214–4891* ⊕ *www.namuseum.gr* ✉ *€10; €15 for unified museum ticket (includes Byzantine and Christian Museum, Epigraphical Museum, Numismatic Museum)* Ⓜ *Victoria, then 10-min walk.*

OMONIA AND METAXOURGEIO ΟΜΟΝΟΙΑΣ ΜΕΤΑΞΟΥΡΓΕΙΟ

Omonia is the meeting point of several vital avenues: Stadiou, Panepistimiou, Ayiou Konstantinou, 3rd September, Pireos, and Athinas. The commercial hot spots of the pedestrianized Aiolou Street and Patission Avenue are also within walking distance. It's a major transport hub, the meeting place of lines 1 (from Kifissia to Piraeus) and 2 (the red metro line). Omonia Square was built at the request of King Otto in 1846, and it quickly became one of the busiest meeting points in the young capital. Soon, however, the low and elegant neoclassical buildings gave way to the gray concrete blocks that dominate the urban horizon today. In recent years, the economic crisis has meant that the once-lively commercial square (a symbol of the economic development of the 1960s) is struggling to find its character after the dramatic influx of illegal immigrants and rise in drug addiction and petty crime.

In Kotzia Square, one can admire the imposing Old Town Hall (now the city's registry office), an ongoing archaeological excavation in the middle of the square, and some lovely neoclassical buildings scattered around (one of them is the National Bank of Greece's Cultural Centre). The Gregotel Pallas Athena hotel is right here, and Omonia Square is just a couple of hundred yards away.

Once ignored as simply a transient neighborhood, Metaxourgeio has acquired its own character as an emerging artist hub. The Municipal Gallery of Athens set up shop here. The surrounding urban grid is an assorted collection of crumbling buildings and renovated houses that pays equal tribute to the glorious past and the hopeful future. But this is definitely a transitional neighborhood filled with recent immigrants (a small Chinatown of grocery and clothing shops is located between Kolonou and Kolokynthous streets), so always be mindful of your surroundings. You may wish to admire the Metaxourgeio metro station even if you don't have to go anywhere in particular, if only to admire the wall mural "The myth of my neighborhood" by renowned Greek painter Yiannis Moralis. Just up the road from traffic-ladden Metaxourgeio Square, on Ayiou Konstantinou Street, is the headquarters of the Greek National Theatre.

METAXOURGEIO ΜΕΤΑΞΟΥΡΓΕΙΟ

TOP ATTRACTIONS

New Municipal Gallery of Athens. One of Athens's oldest neoclassical buildings became the new home of the city's Municipal Art Collection in 2010. The former silk factory, designed in 1833 by Danish architect Hans Christian Hansen, now houses almost 3,000 important art works from leading 19th- and 20th-century mainly Greek artists (most of the works were acquired during the 1930s and '40s). The museum also hosts archaeological and cultural tours. ⊠ *Leonidou and Myllerou, Metaxourgeio* ☎ *210/323–1841* ✉ *Free* ☼ *Closed Mon.*

PANGRATI ΠΑΓΚΡΑΤΙ

Just behind the marble Panathenaic Stadium, which hosted the first Olympic Games of modern times in 1896, Pangrati is filled with concrete apartment blocks as well as such leafy squares as Platia Proskopon and Platia Varnava. Unfortunately, only a few neoclassical buildings from the turn of the 20th century survived the building boom of the 1960s. This is a safe and quiet neighborhood, with Central Athens a comfortable half-hour walk (there is also good bus service). The First Cemetery of Athens is located in Mets, which borders Pangrati, and notable politicians and personalities in recent Greek history are buried here; the artful marble statues and tombs made in their memory are worth a visit. The neighborhood also has a few noteworthy tavernas and restaurants. In recent years its nightlife scene has sprung up, too.

ILISIA ΙΛΙΣΙΑ

On the outskirts of Central Athens, this densely populated neighborhood takes its name from the river Ilisos, which once flowed here (between the streets Michalakopoulou and Kalirrois) before it was drained in the 1960s to create space for the construction of apartment blocks and the expansion of the city's road network. It is also known for its many hospitals built early in the 20th century. It is still within easy reach of the main sights (via Megaron Mousikis metro station) and a bit closer to the Eleftherios Venizelos Airport than more central neighborhoods like Monastiraki and Plaka, and offers some excellent accommodation and dining options. The most important museum in the area is the National Gallery of Art, which is closed for renovation until at least 2019. The area also encompasses the mostly residential neighborhood of Ambelokipi, which is bounded by Kifissias, Vassilissis Sofias, and Alexandras avenues, and has the dubious honor of being the second most densely populated district (after Kypseli) in Athens. The United States Embassy is here, while lively Mavili Square is a popular nightlife haunt.

PIRAEUS ΠΕΙΡΑΙΑΣ

When you think of Piraeus, you'll most likely visualize a massive (Europe's largest) passenger port with every kind of ship and thousands of bag-pulling travelers scurrying about. It's Greece's main gateway to its many islands. More than that, it is also a city within a city (locals don't consider themselves Athenians) that has charming pockets with traditional eateries and attractive architecture.

WHERE TO EAT

Doesn't anybody eat at home anymore? When you're on vacation, travelers don't have much choice in the matter, but these days—even in the throes of the current economic crisis—Athenians are going out to restaurants (many of which have lowered their prices accordingly) in record numbers. And it's easy for visitors to the capital to become a part of the clatter, chatter, and song, especially at the city's neighborhood tavernas.

These Athenian landmarks were famous for their wicker chairs that inevitably pinched your bottom, wobbly tables that needed coins under one leg, and *hima* wine drawn from the barrel. There are still plenty of them around, but today some of their clientele has moved up to a popular new restaurant hybrid: the "gastro-taverna," which serves traditional fare in surroundings that are more modern and creative. Most are located in the up-and-coming industrial-cum-arty districts of Central Athens, such as Gazi-Kerameikos and Metaxourgeio and attract youths who stay nibbling, sipping *tsipouro* (a distilled grape spirit), and laughing for hours. At the same time, enduring in popularity are the traditional *magereia* ("cookeries"): humble, no-frills eateries where the food, usually displayed behind glass windows, is cooked in grandma's style—it's simple, honest, time-tested, filling comfort food. Some noteworthy magereia are located around the bustling Ayias Irinis Square in the heart of Monastiraki. Of course cheap, filling, and delicious souvlaki is more popular than ever, and local favorites still have queues. Meanwhile, Athenians' evolving taste for exotic foods, combined with a tighter budget, has led to the opening of numerous ethnic street food restaurants—some just holes in the wall—serving expertly made, authentic options.

Trends? Athens has them. Health-centric restaurants specializing in vegan, vegetarian, and raw food seem to be blossoming more, as well as sophisticated juice bars. These would have stood out just a few years

The Greek Fish Taverna

Enjoying the bounty of the seas that wash against Greek shores can be a fishy business. The waters have been overfished for decades and much "Greek" fish served today is often frozen from other waters. Take heart, though. You can still feast on delicious fish in Greece—it's just a question of what you order, and where.

Patrons of fish restaurants are usually greeted with iced displays of the catch of the day. Proprietors will often spout some mumbo-jumbo about the fish being caught only an hour earlier—allow the shills some poetic license and go for the operative word here: *fresco*, fresh, as opposed to *katepsigmeno*, frozen.

The fish you choose will be sold by the portion, *merida*, and priced by the kilo. Expect to pay at least €55 a kilo for such popular fish as *xifia*, swordfish; *lavraki*, sea bass; *tsipoura*, sea bream; and *barbounia*, red mullet.

Yes, fish is expensive in Greece, but remember: that price is per kilo, and the portion you order may well weigh, and cost, less.

WHAT TO ORDER

Garides, shrimp, are often served deliciously as *saganaki*, baked with fresh tomatoes and feta cheese and brought to the table sizzling.

Sardelles, sardines, are grilled, fried, or eaten salt-baked and marinated. *Papalina* are small sardines, and

atherina are very small sardines usually fried crisp.

Gavros, anchovies, are almost always marinated in lemon and vinegar or deep-fried.

Kalamari, squid, are often fried, but they are sometimes grilled on the fire. A tasty relative is the *soupia*, cuttlefish, usually cooked in its own ink and wine.

Htapodi, octopus, is grilled, marinated in vinegar and oil, or stewed with tomatoes and onions.

Mydia, mussels, are usually steamed, and are often taken out of their shells and served in risotto, seafood pasta, or salads.

OLD-TIME FAVORITES

In addition to fresh fish, keep an eye out for these old standards. *Taramosalata*, fish roe salad, is a tasty spread, a poor man's caviar made from carp eggs, blended with olive oil, lemon juice, and garlic.

Kakavia and *psarosoupa* are velvety variations of fish soup, usually made from pieces of whatever fish is available, simmered in broth with vegetables, and always embellished with the special flourishes of the individual cook.

Bakaliaros, cod, is often served as *bakaliaros skordalia*, dipped in batter, deep-fried, and drizzled with garlic sauce.

ago; now they have competitors. Organic food stores can be found in every neighborhood, many selling Greek-grown concoctions made in the traditional style by small producers, many of whom returned to the rural homeland after facing unemployment; look for local truffle oils, unpasteurized craft beer, and gold leaf honey. Most Greeks value pure, high-quality, and easily accessible staples like the seasonal vegetables and fruit, medicinal handpicked herb teas, and nuts that they hunt for at the weekly neighborhood *laiki* market, as well as the multitude of Greek product stores. With less money to spend, Athenians now order more discerningly and in smaller quantities, but they resolutely linger outside, which never seems to be a problem for restaurant owners.

But some things remain eternal. Athenian dining is seasonal. In August, when residents scatter to the hills and seaside, many restaurants and tavernas close, with the hippest bar-restaurants reopening at choice seaside positions. And visitors remain shocked by how late Greeks dine. It's normal (even on a weekday) to show up for a meal at 9 or 10 and to leave long after midnight, only to head off for drinks. Hotel restaurants, seafood places, and Plaka tavernas keep very late hours. Most places serve lunch from about noon to 4 (and sometimes as late as 6) and dinner from about 8 or 9 until at least midnight. When in Athens, don't hesitate to adopt this Zorbaesque lifestyle. Eat, drink, party, and enjoy life—knowing full well that, as a traveler, there can always be a siesta the next day.

DINING, ATHENS STYLE

Taverna culture is all about sharing. People often order their own main meat, fish, or vegetable courses, but often share a plethora of salads, and appetizers, which may be placed in the middle of the table for easy access by the entire dinner party. It's a nice alternative to being stuck with just one choice. Vegetarians will find plenty of options, including rice-stuffed dolmades or tomatoes, tomato and garlic-baked aubergines, fried zucchini, and tomato-stewed okra, as well as several bean dishes—and of course the classic Greek salad. Tipping is less strict than in many countries. There is a service charge on the bill, but it doesn't necessarily go to the staff, so Athenians usually leave a tip of 10%. Feel free to request tap water in a pitcher (it's good in Athens) as opposed to bottled water, which may be brought automatically to your table without your request. Although Athens is informal (and none of the restaurants listed here requires a jacket or tie), locals usually dress up when out on the town, so you may feel more comfortable following suit, especially at more expensive places. One of the tragedies of eating out in Athens is that, although smoking is no longer legally permitted inside bars and restaurants, owners and staff turn a blind eye to it in order to keep clientele, and outdoors it's fair play for all—and Greeks smoke a lot! It's best to check a restaurant's smoking policy by phone first. Children are welcome in most places, but it's best to check in advance for upscale establishments.

Restaurant reviews have been shortened. For full information, visit Fodors.com. Use the coordinate (✣ B2) at the end of each listing to locate a site on the corresponding map.

DINING PRICES IN EUROS			
	$	$$	$$$	$$$$
Restaurants	under €15	€15–€25	€26–€40	over €40

Restaurant prices are the average cost of a main course at dinner or, if dinner is not served, at lunch.

THE ACROPOLIS, MAKRIYIANNI, AND KOUKAKI
ΑΚΡΟΠΟΛΗ, ΜΑΚΡΥΓΙΑΝΝΗ, ΚΟΥΚΑΚΙ

MAKRIYIANNI ΜΑΚΡΥΓΙΑΝΝΗ

Makriyianni eateries have the distinct advantage of a prestigious location with an exclusive vibe and unbeatable views of the Acropolis; the food is also highly recommended by the locals.

$$$
MEDITERRANEAN
Fodor's Choice
★

✕ **Dionysos Zonars.** This famous, historic restaurant just happens to be the spot where movies are often filmed because of its astounding location, looking out to exquisite views of the Acropolis, and it has been an idyllic dining spot for the world's glitterati for decades. Today's plush, renovated establishment serves high-quality, traditional Greek and international dishes with a creative twist. **Known for:** exclusive ambience; magnificent Acropolis views; a mix of Greek and international food. $ *Average main: €30* ⊠ *Rovertou Galli 43, Makriyianni* ☎ *210/923–3182* ⊕ *www.dionysoszonars.gr* ⊹ *C5.*

$$
GREEK
Fodor's Choice
★

✕ **Manhmanh.** Featuring inspired recipes—and many ingredients—from the southern Peloponnese's Mani region, Manhmanh strikes the perfect balance between sophistication and heartiness. The food and extensive regional wine list take center stage, and its comforting food sweetly screams "village." The chef adds delicate new fruity or spicy touches to dishes and embraces organic products. **Known for:** authentic Peloponnesian cuisine; farm-to-table ingredients; good wine list. $ *Average main: €18* ⊠ *Falirou 10, Makriyianni* ☎ *210/921–8180* ⊕ *www. manimani.com.gr* ⊹ *D5.*

$$
GREEK
Fodor's Choice
★

✕ **Strofi.** It's the place where the likes of Rudolph Nureyev, Maria Callas, and Elizabeth Taylor dined after performances at the Odeon of Herodes Atticus nearby, and its walls are lined with images attesting to its glamorous past. Once a humble taverna with a fantastic Acropolis view, its current modernist renovated version and simple traditional Greek menu are still pleasing to tourists and politicians alike. **Known for:** a magnificent view of the Parthenon; a reliable Greek menu; grilled meats. $ *Average main: €25* ⊠ *Rovertou Galli 25, Makriyianni* ☎ *210/921–4130* ⊕ *www.strofi.gr* ☽ *Closed Mon.* ⊹ *C5.*

PLAKA AND ANAFIOTIKA ΠΛΑΚΑ ΑΝΑΦΙΩΤΙΚΑ

PLAKA ΠΛΑΚΑ

Popular Plaka delights in its traditional homes, winding alleys, and bustling cafés and gift shops.

$$$
GREEK

✕ **Daphne's.** Daphne's is one of the most exclusive (and at times priciest) destinations in Plaka. The Pompeian frescoes on the walls, the fragments of an ancient Greek building in the garden, and the tasteful restoration of the neoclassical building in terra-cotta and ocher hues also contribute to a pleasant and romantic evening. **Known for:** refined cuisine based on quality produce; exclusive surroundings; rabbit in Mavrodaphne wine sauce. $ *Average main: €35* ⊠ *Lysikratous 4, Plaka* ☎ *210/322–7991* ⊕ *www.daphnesrestaurant.gr* ⊹ *D5.*

$$
GREEK

✕ **O Platanos.** On a picturesque pedestrianized square, this is one of the oldest tavernas in Plaka (established 1932). Although not as good as it

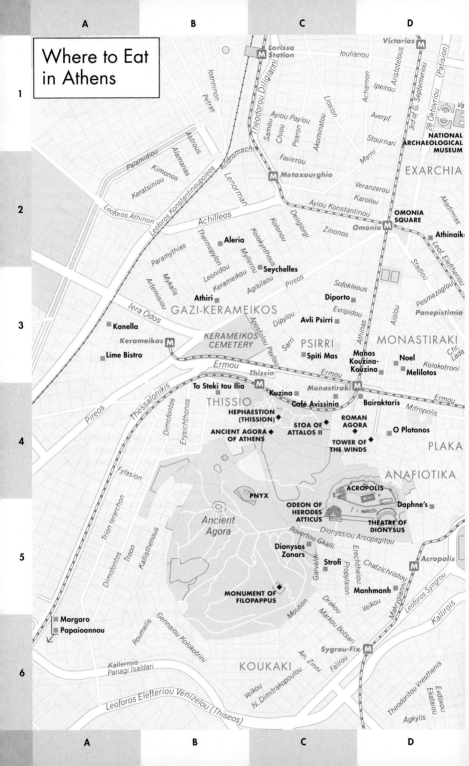

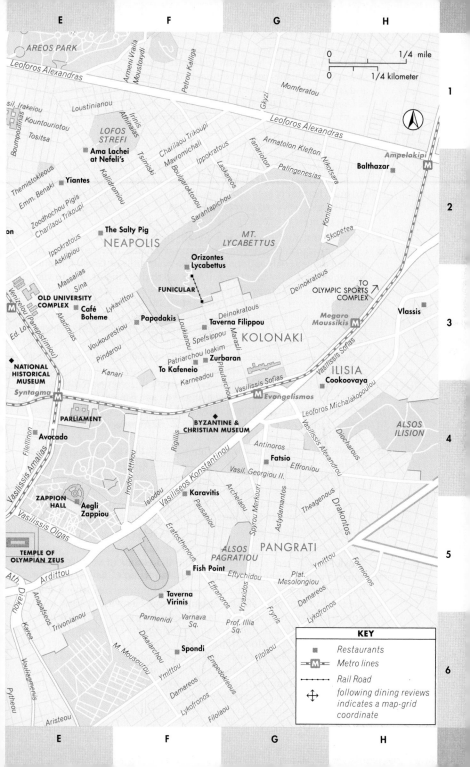

was during its glory years when intellectuals and artists sat here sipping retsina until the early hours, it's still worth a stop. **Known for:** beautiful setting under plane trees; traditional Greek cooking like stuffed squid and lamb casserole; pitchers of the house retsina. [$] *Average main: €17* ✉ *Diogenous 4, Plaka* ☎ *210/322–0666* 🌐 *eleinitsa.wixsite.com/platanos* 💳 *No credit cards* ⏲ *Closed Sun. June–Aug. No dinner Sun.* ✣ *D4.*

MONASTIRAKI AND PSIRRI ΜΟΝΑΣΤΗΡΑΚΙ ΨΥΡΡΗ

Although constantly transforming, Monastiraki retains the gritty charm of an Anatolian bazaar to magnetize the city's hard-core café and bar crowd. The former warehouse district of Psirri, between Omonia and Monastiraki, has lively tavernas and bars.

MONASTIRAKI ΜΟΝΑΣΤΗΡΑΚΙ

$ GREEK 🍴 **Bairaktaris.** Run by the same family since 1879, this is an almost legendary souvlaki eatery in Monastiraki Square. After admiring the painted wine barrels and the black-and-white stills of Greek film stars and politicians who have lunched here, go to the window case to view the day's *magirefta* (stove-top-cooked dish, usually made earlier)—possibly a delicious *pastitsio*. **Known for:** traditional kebabs and gyros; historic setting; simple food for reasonable prices. [$] *Average main: €10* ✉ *Monastiraki Sq. 2, Monastiraki* ☎ *210/321–3036* 🌐 *www.bairaktaris.gr* ✣ *D4.*

$ GREEK FAMILY 🍴 **Manas Kouzina-Kouzina.** Homey cuisine, served at a counter (there's no table service), with prices lower than a fast-food meal are the secrets that keep Mother's Kitchens successful. Every dish comes in three sizes, so you can choose based on how hungry you are. **Known for:** traditional oven-baked dishes; easy, with a central location; low prices for great tastes. [$] *Average main: €10* ✉ *Aiolou 27A, Monastiraki* ☎ *210/325–2335* ✣ *D3.*

$$ GREEK 🍴 **Melilotos.** In the city's main shopping district, the compact but modern Melilotos offers a large variety of refreshing, quick-bite options based on traditional Greek dishes with influences from other cuisines. The menu offers a large array of dishes at reasonable prices. **Known for:** a modern take on traditional Greek; healthy options; reasonable prices. [$] *Average main: €20* ✉ *Kalamiotou 19, Monastiraki* ☎ *210/322–2458* 🌐 *www.melilotos.gr* ✣ *D3.*

PSIRRI ΨΥΡΡΗ

$ GREEK 🍴 **Avli Psirri.** A very well-kept secret until a couple of years ago, Avli remains well under the radar even today. But if you walk past its inconspicuous entrance, you'd be missing out on uniquely satisfying small plates and bottomless carafes of barrel wine. **Known for:** basic grills, from fried liver to meatballs; simple authenticity; completely original village atmosphere. [$] *Average main: €5* ✉ *Aghiou Dimitriou 12, Psirri* ☎ *210/324–4117* [M] *Monastiraki* ✣ *C3.*

$$ GREEK Fodor's Choice ★ 🍴 **Café Avissinia.** Facing hoary and merchant-packed Abyssinia Square, this timeworn but exceptional eatery is popular with locals who want home-cooked traditional food with heavy Asia Minor influences and endless servings of the excellent barrel wine and ouzo. Diners love to settle within the elegant glass-and-wood interior to sample mussels and

rice pilaf, wine-marinated octopus with pasta, fresh garden salad, or any of the dips. **Known for:** delicious moussaka and grilled sardines; an air of nostalgia but with style; live music on weekend afternoons. $ *Average main: €18* ⊠ *Abyssinia Sq., Kinetou 7, Psirri* ☎ *210/321–7047* ⊕ *www.avissinia.gr* ⊗ *Closed Mon.* ✛ *C4.*

$ ✕ **Spiti Mas.** With a name that means "our house" in Greek, Spiti Mas
MEDITERRANEAN   is designed like the interior of a home, with a bed, a dining area, a "balcony" out on the street, a nice homey bathroom, and a living room. The menu changes by the day, as it would at home, and light meals (omelets, sandwiches, etc.) are prepared according to the day's fresh groceries. **Known for:** breakfast and brunch; spinach pie; friendly, homelike setting. $ *Average main: €12* ⊠ *Navarchou Apostoli 10, Psirri* ☎ *210/331–4751* ⊕ *spitimas.net* ✛ *C3.*

THISSIO ΘΗΣΕΙΟ

Thissio's pedestrianized streets are perfect meeting points for coffee lovers, but the mezedopoleia there are also of a high caliber and offer beautiful Acropolis views.

$$$ ✕ **Kuzina.** Kuzina may be sleek, dazzlingly decorated, and moodily
GREEK FUSION   lighted, but is not just a pretty face. The food—especially the inven-
Fodor'sChoice   tive seafood and pasta dishes—is among the best in Athens, standing
★   out on touristy Adrianou. **Known for:** 12-hour pork with pineapple salad; value-priced prix-fixe menu; scenic rooftop for delicious drinks. $ *Average main: €30* ⊠ *Adrianou 9, Thissio* ☎ *210/324–0133* ⊕ *www. kuzina.gr* ✛ *C4.*

$$ ✕ **To Steki tou Ilia.** Unpretentious and overall unremarkable, this restau-
STEAKHOUSE   rant is justifiably famous for its freshly grilled *paidakia* (lamb chops),
FAMILY   to be eaten with unabashed gusto by hand. It's always busy and always a great escape from an increasingly modernized city, but avoid the *hima* wine, which almost certainly leads to a headache. **Known for:** lamb chops with thick fries and tzatziki; a relaxed village vibe in the heart of the city; cash only. $ *Average main: €17* ⊠ *Eptachalkou 5, Thissio* ☎ *210/345–8052* ▭ *No credit cards* ⊗ *No lunch Tues.–Fri.; no dinner Sun.* ✛ *B4.*

SYNTAGMA SQUARE ΠΛΑΤΕΙΑ ΣΥΝΤΑΓΜΑΤΟΣ

Syntagma, a bustling central square between Parliament and Ermou Street, is also popular with tourists.

$$$ ✕ **Aegli Zappiou.** The lush Zappeion Gardens have always been a tran-
MODERN GREEK   quil green oasis for stressed-out Athenians, who head here to gaze at the
Fodor'sChoice   distant views of the Parthenon and Temple of Olympian Zeus or chill
★   out at this landmark café. Sharing the same premises, a chic, full-service restaurant is a must during summer with its beautiful garden—shady in daytime, beautifully lighted at night. **Known for:** a refreshing and historic location; elegant atmosphere; reasonable prices for upscale cuisine. $ *Average main: €30* ⊠ *Zappio Megaro, Syntagma* ☎ *210/336–9364* ⊕ *www.aeglizappiou.gr* ✛ *F5.*

$$ ✕**Avocado.** For such a tiny spot in a narrow street just off Syntagma
VEGETARIAN Square, this small but stylish vegetarian favorite has many devoted fans.
FAMILY The veg and vegan comfort food appeals to health-conscious diners
who appreciate the friendly atmosphere and internationally focused
menu. **Known for:** vegan and vegetarian cuisine; delicious smoothies
and juices; macrobiotic and gluten-free options. $ *Average main: €17*
✉ *Nikis 30, Syntagma* ☎ *210/323–7878* ⊕ *www.avocadoathens.com*
⊙ *No dinner Sun.* ✛ *E4.*

$$ ✕**Noel.** A recent addition to the trendy Syntagma nightlife scene, Noel
MEDITERRANEAN is the kind of bar-restaurant that people talk about with a smile on
their face. The casual and modern Mediterranean menu is wide ranging and internationally oriented, including everything from pizzas to
pastas to chicken curry. **Known for:** cheerful holiday theme; excellent
and innovative cocktails; brunch. $ *Average main: €20* ✉ *Kolokotroni
59B, Syntagma* ☎ *211/215–9534* ⊕ *noelbar.gr* Ⓜ *Syntagma* ✛ *D3.*

GAZI-KERAMEIKOS ΓΚΑΖΙ-ΚΕΡΑΜΕΙΚΟΣ

West of Psirri, Gazi-Kerameikos has turned into the city's hottest art,
culture, and nightlife zone. The new Kerameikos metro station has also
made it ultraconvenient.

$$ ✕**Athiri.** Once you step into the lush and peaceful urban garden of this
MODERN GREEK popular restaurant (with a Michelin star), you'll relax immediately.
FAMILY The casual elegance of the setting is perfectly matched by the creative
Fodor'sChoice Greek cuisine on the menu, which changes by the season and is very
★ reasonably priced. **Known for:** innovative preparations of Greek clas-
sics; fresh, locally sourced, seasonal ingredients; all-Greek wine list.
$ *Average main: €18* ✉ *Plateon 15, Gazi-Kerameikos* ☎ *210/346–2983*
⊕ *www.athirirestaurant.gr* ⊙ *Closed Mon. No lunch Tues.–Sat. No din-
ner Sun.* ✛ *B3.*

$$ ✕**Kanella.** Housed in a cool, airy building with modern and traditional
MODERN GREEK touches, this lively example of a neo-taverna serving mama's cook-
FAMILY ing but infused with Gazi's creative energy. Regional specialties, great
barrel wine served in lovely carafes, and a familial atmosphere make
dining here a pleasure. **Known for:** traditional home-style favorites like
slow-cooked lamb and stuffed grape leaves; lively atmosphere great for
groups of friends; excellent house wine. $ *Average main: €25* ✉ *Kon-
stantinoupoleos 70, at Evmolpidon, Gazi-Kerameikos* ☎ *210/347–6320*
⊕ *www.kanellagazi.gr* ✛ *A3.*

$ ✕**Lime Bistro.** Athenians have been known historically as meat lovers,
VEGETARIAN but they are beginning to discover the merits of creative, sophisticated,
FAMILY and delicious vegetarian cuisine. The popularity of this bistro attests to
the fact with a modern and playful layout that includes a charming back
garden and a seasonal menu packed with guilt-free, nutritious vegan and
vegetarian choices. **Known for:** raw vegan homemade cheeses; fresh,
crispy salads and vegan burgers; gluten-free and raw options. $ *Average
main: €10* ✉ *Dekeleon 23, Gazi-Kerameikos* ☎ *210/347–4423* ✛ *A3.*

KOLONAKI ΚΟΛΩΝΑΚΙ

Located east of Plaka, Kolonaki is an old-money neighborhood that's a haunt for politicians, expats, and high-maintenance ladies who lunch (and shop).

$$ MEDITERRANEAN 🍴 **Café Boheme.** This popular restaurant offers everything from a homey breakfast to a business lunch, from a sneaky late-afternoon expensive whisky to a long dinner accompanied by plenty of wine and creative cocktails. The Mediterranean bistro-inspired menu changes by the season but always features excellent quality (and properly cooked) seafood, mouthwatering risottos, organic salads, and rich desserts with imaginative touches. **Known for:** seafood and risotto; all-day menu; popular bar that goes late into the night. [$] *Average main: €15* ✉ *Omirou 36, Kolonaki* ☎ *210/360–8018* 🌐 *www.cafeboheme.gr* ✣ *E3.*

$$$ MEDITERRANEAN 🍴 **Orizontes Lycabettus.** As you are handed the menu, you'll find it nearly impossible to avert your eyes from the stunning view from the very top of verdant Lycabettus Hill, the highest point in Athens; the Acropolis glitters below, and beyond it, the metropolis unfolds like a map out to the Saronic Gulf. The restaurant centers on gourmet Mediterranean cuisine with bold French elements and is beautiful to look at, but the chef also cooks up playful renditions of classic Greek dishes. **Known for:** sea bream; high-quality service; some of the most romantic views in Athens. [$] *Average main: €35* ✉ *Lycabettus Hill, Kolonaki* ☎ *210/721–0701* 🌐 *www.orizonteslycabettus.gr* ✣ *F3.*

$$$$ SEAFOOD Fodor's Choice ★ 🍴 **Papadakis.** Picture this: it's twilight and you're sitting under bitter-orange trees at one of Athens's best fish restaurants, in the heart of Kolonaki, overlooking the Parthenon as you sip a perfectly chilled glass of wine and wait for your order of succulent seafood to arrive. There's muted conversation at the gleaming white-tableclothed tables around you, where opinion makers, theater directors, and loyal customers relax. **Known for:** high-profile dining at high quality; fresh, artfully prepared seafood. [$] *Average main: €50* ✉ *Voukourestiou 47, at Fokylidou 15, Kolonaki* ☎ *210/360–8621* 🌐 *www.papadakisrestaurant.com* ✣ *F3.*

$$ GREEK FAMILY 🍴 **Taverna Filippou.** This unassuming urban taverna is hardly the sort of place you'd expect to find in chic Kolonaki, yet its devotees (since 1923) have included cabinet ministers, diplomats, actresses, and film directors. The appeal is simple: well-prepared Greek classics, mostly *ladera* (casseroles cooked in an olive oil and tomato sauce), *moussaka* (layered eggplant and ground beef in béchamel sauce), and delicious side dishes like shrimps in a mayonnaise sauce. **Known for:** moussaka; familial atmosphere; sophisticated clientele. [$] *Average main: €20* ✉ *Xenokratous 19, Kolonaki* ☎ *210/721–6390* ⏲ *Closed Sun. and mid-Aug. No dinner Sat.* ✣ *F3.*

$$ GREEK 🍴 **To Kafeneio.** A Kolonaki institution, this bistro-style traditional restaurant is slightly fancier and more costly than the normal mezedopoleio, with cloth napkins, candles on the tables, and walls decorated with writings by its famous patrons. The menu centers on delicate Greek classics (such as lamb with lemon or roast suckling pig) but also some international fare. **Known for:** reliably good Greek classics; an excellent location in the heart of Kolonaki; sophisticated setting. [$] *Average main: €25* ✉ *Loukianou 26, Kolonaki* ☎ *210/723–9600* ⏲ *Closed Sun. and 3 wks in Aug.* ✣ *F3.*

$$$ ✕ **Zurbaran.** This new, ultramodern spot just minutes from Kolonaki
MEDITERRANEAN Square draws the city's fashionistas and moneyed good-timers like
bees to honey. A solid, modern Greek and Mediterranean menu, funky
decor, and high-resonance sound track set the right mood. **Known for:**
trendy, modern setting; innovative cuisine and good cocktails; uneven
service. Ⓢ *Average main: €30* ⊠ *Patriarchou Ioakeim 38, Kolonaki*
☎ *210/723–8334* ⊕ *zurbaranathens.gr* ✢ *F3.*

EXARCHIA ΕΞΑΡΧΕΙΑ

The student district of Exarchia offers some casual and more adventurous dining options.

$ ✕ **Ama Lachei at Nefeli's.** Step out of Kallidromiou Street in edgy Exar-
MODERN GREEK cheia and find yourself in a large, lovely courtyard full of little tables
FAMILY and abundant greenery. Ama Lachei has gained a loyal following for
its decently priced, delectable Greek dishes always made with a fanci-
ful flourish and with bona fide ingredients. **Known for:** large selection
of fish, meat, and vegetable *mezedes* (small plates); a good choice of
regional wines; verdant courtyard setting. Ⓢ *Average main: €13* ⊠ *Kal-
lidromiou 69, Exarcheia* ☎ *210/384–5978* Ⓜ *Omonia* ✢ *E2.*

$ ✕ **The Salty Pig.** If you're looking for meat and don't mind the street-
BARBECUE side setting, this self-service restaurant offers chef-driven food in a very
FAMILY casual setting. Using high-quality local ingredients, the abundant menu
Fodor'sChoice celebrates New World cuisine, offering everything from ribs prepared
★ in a custom-built smoker to robust, saucy sandwiches, and homemade
pies baked in a wood-fired oven. **Known for:** barbecue and smoked
meats; excellent quality at low prices; tantalizing street food. Ⓢ *Aver-
age main: €8* ⊠ *Ippokratous 36, Exarcheia* ☎ *210/364–7445* ⊕ *www.
thesaltypig.gr* ✢ *E2.*

$$ ✕ **Yiantes.** In a flower-filled courtyard—fashionably green and framed
GREEK by wisteria and jasmine—you peruse a menu that, despite some modern
FAMILY influences, reads like an honest culinary journey through the far reaches
of Greece. Almost everything is fresh and delicious, as the chef estimates
that about 90% of the ingredients he uses are organic (the owners are
organic farmers), including the house wine. **Known for:** mainly organic
ingredients; beautiful garden setting; bargain prix-fixe menu. Ⓢ *Average
main: €20* ⊠ *Valtetsiou 44, Exarcheia* ☎ *210/330–1369* ⊗ *Closed Mon.
and 1st 2 wks in Aug.* ✢ *E2.*

OMONIA AND METAXOURGEIO ΟΜΟΝΟΙΑΣ ΜΕΤΑΞΟΥΡΓΕΙΟ

North of Monastiraki, Omonia, the city's main square, is busy by day
and seedy by night, but its side streets burst with cultural diversity
from the huge influx of immigrants, and trendy art spaces and galleries are scattered around. To the west, the former red-light district of
Metaxourgeio gets the green light when it comes to award-winning and
avant-garde dining.

2

OMONIA ΟΜΟΝΟΙΑΣ

$$ GREEK 🍴 **Athinaikon.** Choose among classic specialties at this old-fashioned mezedopoleio founded in 1932: grilled octopus, shrimp croquettes with white sauce, broad beans simmered in thick tomato sauce, fresh grilled calamari, and *ameletita* (sautéed lamb testicles). All goes well with the light barrel red or ouzo. **Known for:** small-plates menu; old-fashioned charm and decor; good house-made wine. [$] *Average main: €20* ✉ *Themistokleous 2, Omonia Sq.* ☎ *210/383–8485, 210/383–5905* 🌐 *www.athinaikon.gr* 🕒 *Closed Sun. and Aug.* ✥ *D2.*

$ GREEK 🍴 **Diporto.** It's the savvy locals' treasured secret—and one of Athens's oldest tavernas—where everyone wandering around Omonia Square has been welcomed through the years. Owner-chef Barba Mitsos keeps everyone happy with his handful of simple, delicious, and dirt-cheap homemade dishes, from the always exceptional *horiatiki* (Greek salad) and buttery *gigantes* (giant beans in tomato sauce) to saucy boiled meats with vegetables and tiny fried fish. **Known for:** an authentic, legendary old-school taverna; wine barrels and the wine in them; dirt-cheap prices (and cash only) for excellent food. [$] *Average main: €10* ✉ *Platia Theatrou, Socratous 9, Omonia Sq.* ☎ *210/321–1463* 💳 *No credit cards* 🕒 *Closed Sun. No dinner* ✥ *C3.*

METAXOURGEIO ΜΕΤΑΞΟΥΡΓΕΙΟ

$$$ MEDITERRANEAN 🍴 **Aleria.** Restaurants, including this award-winning gem of neoclassical design and inventive Mediterranean cuisine, are one reason Metaxourgeio's star is rising. Chef Gikas Xenakis's cooking is a serious candidate for notoriety. **Known for:** elaborate tasting menus; elegant setting but reasonable prices; Wine Wednesdays featuring small Greek producers. [$] *Average main: €38* ✉ *Meg. Alexandrou 57, Metaxourgeio* ☎ *210/522–2633* 🌐 *www.aleria.gr* 🕒 *Closed Sun. No lunch* ✥ *B2.*

$$ GREEK 🍴 **Seychelles.** Although it's named after one of the world's most exotic destinations, this restaurant is almost provincially Greek in its ingredients and culinary attitude. You may experience some exciting moments of surprise, however, when scanning the menu and spotting old favorites like smoked swordfish, hot and sweet little steaks, baked beetroot stuffed with garliky *skordalia* sauce, and pappardelle with *kavourmas* (terrine). **Known for:** home-style cooking with contemporary flair; an excellent assortment of regional cheeses; artistic following. [$] *Average main: €15* ✉ *Kerameikou 49, Metaxourgeio* ☎ *211/183–4789* 🌐 *www.seycheles.gr* ✥ *C3.*

PANGRATI ΠΑΓΚΡΑΤΙ

Urbane without being snobby or expensive, mostly residential Pangrati is a haven for academics, artists, and expats who bask in the homey if somewhat shabby warmth of this neighborhood in the southeastern quarter of the city.

$ GREEK FAMILY 🍴 **Fatsio.** Don't be fooled by the Italian name: the food at this old-fashioned (practically unchanged since 1949), family-owned restaurant is all home-style Greek, albeit with an influence from Constantinople. Walk past the kitchen and look through the window at the *ladera* (casserole) dishes of the day to point at what you like, or select a fresh fish, stewed

CLOSE UP

Greek Fast Food

Souvlaki is the original Greek fast food: spit-roasted or grilled meat on a *kalamaki* stick (mainly pork or chicken), tomatoes, onions, and garlicky tzatziki wrapped in a pita. The financial crisis made this cheap, filling, and not terribly unhealthy food even more accessible with souvlaki restaurants popping up almost around every corner. Greeks on the go have always eaten street food, such as the endless variations of *tiropita* cheese pie, *koulouri* (sesame-covered bread rings), roasted chestnuts or ears of grilled corn, and palm-size paper bags of nuts. But modern lifestyles and the arrival of foreign pizza, sandwich, and burger chains, and in more recent years ethnic street food from Asia and South America (mainly located around Syntagma, with falafel shops being the latest rage), have made busy

Athenians particularly reliant on fast food. In almost every neighborhood you'll come across a handful of Greek fast-food chains. **Goody's** serves burgers and spaghetti as well as some salads and sandwiches. **Everest** is tops when it comes to *tost*—oval-shaped toasted sandwich buns with any combination of fillings, from omelets to smoked turkey breast, and various spreads (it also sells sweet and savory pies, coffee, and desserts). **Grigoris**, the main rival to Everest, is a chain of sandwich and pie shops that also serves freshly squeezed orange juice and *cappuccino freddo*, which is so beloved to Greeks. If you want to sit down while you eat your fast food, look for a **Flocafe**, where you can find a great choice of coffees as well as a selection of pastries, cookies, and sandwiches.

meat, or pasta dish from the menu. **Known for:** homemade traditional casseroles and stews; strictly nonsmoking space; quick service. $ *Average main: €9* ⊠ *Effroniou 5–7, Pangrati* ⊹ *Off Rizari* ☎ *210/725–0028* ⊕ *www.fatsio.gr* ⊗ *Closed 1 wk in mid-Aug.* ⊹ *G4.*

$$
SEAFOOD
✕**Fish Point.** At first glance you may think this is just an ordinary fishmonger, with all its glistening goods laid out in ice boxes like jewels, unless you look to the right and see that next to the display of the day's catch is a modern, polished restaurant. You'll find wonderful seafood at very reasonable prices in an increasingly exciting neighborhood spot just off Plastira Square. **Known for:** superfresh fish and many raw fish choices (ceviche, sushi, etc.); attached fish market and seafood deli; seafood pastas. $ *Average main: €20* ⊠ *Archimidous 8, Pangrati* ☎ *210/756–5321* ⊕ *www.fishpoint.gr* ⊹ *F5.*

$$
GREEK
✕**Karavitis.** This very traditional taverna has been around since 1926 and doesn't seem to have changed a bit in that span, serving classic, well-prepared Greek cuisine. Pungent *tirokafteri* (a peppery cheese dip), *stamnaki* (beef baked in a clay pot), and *bekri mezes* (lamb in a zesty tomato sauce) are among the taverna's specialty. **Known for:** plenty of prewar charm; beef baked in a clay pot and lamb cooked in zesty tomato sauce; cash only. $ *Average main:* ⊠ *Arktinou 35, at Pausaniou, Pangrati* ☎ *210/721–5155* ⊕ *www.karavitistavern.gr* ▭ *No credit cards* ⊗ *Closed 1 wk mid-Aug. No lunch Mon.–Sat.* ⊹ *F4.*

$$$$ MODERN FRENCH Fodor's Choice ★ 🍴 **Spondi.** What is perhaps the capital's top restaurant is justly celebrated as a feast for both the eyes and the taste buds, and eating here is a serious affair. Chef Anghelos Lantos uses French techniques to create his inspired culinary art. **Known for:** langoustines served with caviar and citrus sauce; lamb with eggplant; elaborate prix-fixe menus with wine pairings. [$] *Average main: €50* ✉ *Pirronos 5, at Varnava Sq., Pangrati* ☎ *210/756–4021* 🌐 *www.spondi.gr* ⏲ *No lunch* ✥ *F6.*

$$ GREEK FAMILY 🍴 **Taverna Virinis.** In summer, Athenian couples, families, and groups of all ages find refuge in the pleasant, open-air garden of this taverna, as they chomp on grilled meats, tasty homemade ladera, salads, and dips. Run by the third generation of the same family, who provide you with very friendly service, the taverna has an effervescent atmosphere and sees a lot of excellent house wine flowing with every meal. **Known for:** good lamb; friendly service and laid-back atmosphere; excellent housemade wine. [$] *Average main: €20* ✉ *Archimidou 11, Pangrati* ☎ *210/701–2153* ⏲ *No dinner Sun.* ✥ *F5.*

ILISIA ΙΛΙΣΙΑ

Ilisia is close to the center, and its open spaces are an excellent base for some easily accessible restaurants offering tastes of Greek regional cuisine.

$$ CONTEMPORARY 🍴 **Balthazar.** In an airy neoclassical mansion with a leafy, minimalist courtyard—paved with original painted tiles, canopied by huge date palms, and illuminated by colored lanterns—Balthazar truly feels like a summer oasis in the middle of Athens. Acclaimed chef Christophoros Peskias keeps the quality and flavor high on the up-to-the-minute Mediterranean menu, adding exotic touches from Asia in menus of finger food, summer dishes, and sushi—all of which go brilliantly with a few well-mixed cocktails. **Known for:** glamorous garden setting; sophisticated, Asian-influenced dishes; fashionable clientele. [$] *Average main: €24* ✉ *Tsoha 27, Ilisia* ✥ *At Vournazou* ☎ *210/644–1215* 🌐 *www.balthazar.gr* ⏲ *Closed Sun. No lunch* ✥ *H2.*

$$$ MODERN GREEK 🍴 **Cookoovaya.** This buzz-worthy restaurant has become known for its delicate, eclectic, and creative cuisine and expertly cooked food. A brainchild of five chefs, they have divided the menu into four different styles of preparation: wood oven–baked, charcoal-grilled, fried, and stewed. **Known for:** bougatsa (vanilla cream and cinnamon ice cream–filled phyllo); large portions; creative Greek cuisine. [$] *Average main: €30* ✉ *Chatzigianni Mexi 2, Ilisia* ☎ *210/723–5005* 🌐 *cookoovaya.gr* ✥ *G4.*

$$ GREEK FAMILY 🍴 **Vlassis.** Relying on traditional recipes from northern Greece and the islands, as well as gourmet Mediterranean creations, the chefs here whip up some noteworthy home-style cooking in the heart of the city. With a menu that changes every winter and summer, this family-run restaurant, which opened in 1983, always centers on fresh regional ingredients such as fish, seafood, vegetables, cheeses, and meats. **Known for:** well-prepared fresh fish; garbanzo bean soup starter; seasonally changing menu. [$] *Average main: €25* ✉ *Maiandrou 15, Ilisia* ☎ *210/646–3060* 🌐 *www.vlassisrestaurant.gr* ⏲ *Closed Aug.–mid-Sept. No dinner Sun.* ✥ *H3.*

PIRAEUS ΠΕΙΡΑΙΑΣ

Athenians enjoy going to Piraeus for a change of scene and fresh fish, usually to be enjoyed at tavernas by the sea. Urban explorers can also discover small, rustic tavernas reminiscent of the one created for the hit film *Never on Sunday,* in which Melina Mercouri sang "Ta Paidia Tou Peirea" (to the boys of Piraeus) in one of the town's little pockets.

$ SEAFOOD Fodor's Choice ★ 🍴 **Margaro.** With one of the most refreshingly simple menus in Athens (which is limited to fresh, fried sea bream, red mullet, and shrimps with a side of Greek salad and house wine), this taverna is always busy. On weekends lines form, as there is a no-reservation policy. **Known for:** basic yet rewarding menu; very fresh fish, fried to a perfect crisp; delicious Greek salad. [$] *Average main: €10* ✉ *Marias Chatzikiriakou 126* ☎ *210/451–4226* 🕓 *No dinner Sun.* ✥ *A6.*

$$ SEAFOOD FAMILY 🍴 **Papaioannou.** Elegant but unpretentious and located in Piraeus's prettiest spot—the Mikrolimano (little port) marina where sailboats, fishing boats, and yachts bob up and down in the sea—Papaioannou is a classic fish restaurant for those craving every kind of seafood (from mouthwatering razor clams, crawfish with spinach, and sea urchin to marinated, grilled calamari and fried giant shrimp). For romantics, the ideal time to visit is sunset, although this is a great place to take your family for a fish feast or even have a stylish and tasty business lunch. **Known for:** daily-changing menu according to what's available and fresh; beautiful seafront setting. [$] *Average main: €20* ✉ *Akti Koumoundourou 42* ☎ *210/422–5059* 🕓 *No dinner Sun.* ✥ *A6.*

WHERE TO STAY

Greeks pride themselves for their *philoxenia,* or hospitality. Even in antiquity, many of them referred to Zeus as Xenios Zeus—the God in charge of protecting travelers. Today, Greek philoxenia is alive and well in the capital city, whether displayed in the kindness of strangers you ask for directions or in the thoroughness of your hotel receptionist's care. With 18.5% of the small country's GDP derived from tourism, philoxenia is vital, and since the advent of the financial crisis almost a decade ago, Greeks have woken up to a whole new level of awareness when it comes to quality service and customer satisfaction.

The city is full of hotels, many of which were built in Greek tourism's heyday in the 1960s and '70s. In the years prior to the 2004 Athens Olympic Games, financial incentives were provided to hoteliers to upgrade and renovate their facilities, to the effect that many hotels—such as the Athens Hilton—completely renovated themselves inside and out as they increased their range of services.

But while prices have increased since the Olympics, accommodations are still available at all price levels. In Athens you can find everything from boutique hotels dreamed up by prestigious designers and decorated by well-known artists to no-fuss youth hostels that for decades have served the backpacking crowds on their way to their island adventures. Airbnb has shaken the waters for the hotel industry, with many visitors now preferring apartment and studio rentals over hotels, and

2

this has also catalyzed the hotel industry to raise its standards. Athens's budget hotels—once little better than dorms—now almost always have air-conditioning and a TV in all rooms, along with prettier public spaces and Wi-Fi. In the post-Olympics years, there was a notable increase in the number of good-quality, middle-rank family hotels, and over a decade later the newest trend is the so-called "micro hotel," a style of accommodation that throws standard hotel features like an entrance lobby, set breakfast hours, and standard hotel layouts to the wind, offering guests the feeling of staying in a beautiful, homelike space (often a restored mansion or building) with exquisite furnishings and modern facilities. At the same time, the city's classic luxury hotels, such as the Grande Bretagne and the King George, continue to be considered the cream of the crop for anyone seeking the full package in hotel pampering, and not least because of their impressive spas, restaurants, and bars.

The most convenient hotels for travelers are in the heart of the city center. Some of the older hotels in charming Plaka and near gritty Omonia Square are comfortable and clean, their appeal inherent in their age, while there's also an enticing range of choices in Syntagma, an ideally central location for exploring the city. Makriyianni, the area that includes the Acropolis, makes for an idyllic location for those seeking elegant tranquility away from the hubbub of the city and morning jogs. Beware that as charming as some of the smaller, cheaper hotels may have become, you're bound to come across some lapses in the details—take a good look at the room before you register. The thick stone walls of neoclassical buildings keep them cool in summer, but few of the budget hotels have reliable central heating, and Athens can be devilishly cold in winter.

PRICES

Along with higher quality have come higher hotel prices: room rates in Athens are not much less than in many European cities. Still, there are bargains to be had. It's also a good idea to bargain in person at smaller hotels, especially off-season. When negotiating a rate, note that the longer the stay, the lower the nightly rate, so it may be less expensive to spend six consecutive nights in Athens than to stay two or three nights at either end of your trip through Greece.

Bear in mind that usually hotels will charge extra for a view of the Acropolis, and that breakfast is not always included. It is sometimes best to book through an agent for better bulk rates (this can lead to cost savings of up to 20%). Often it is also well worth checking the websites of hotels for special seasonal offers or bargain packages. In the off-season months (October to April) it is possible to negotiate for, and achieve, better rates.

Hotel reviews have been shortened. For full information, visit Fodors. com. Use the coordinate (✛ B2) at the end of each listing to locate a site on the corresponding map.

	PRICES IN EUROS			
	$	$$	$$$	$$$$
Hotels	under €125	€125–€225	€226–€275	over €275

Hotel prices are the lowest cost of a standard double room in high season.

THE ACROPOLIS, MAKRIYIANNI, AND KOUKAKI
ΑΚΡΟΠΟΛΗ, ΜΑΚΡΥΓΙΑΝΝΗ, ΚΟΥΚΑΚΙ

MAKRIYIANNI ΜΑΚΡΥΓΙΑΝΝΗ

$$$ **Athens Was.** Athens's first lustrous and refreshingly modern design
HOTEL hotel is only minutes from the Acropolis and its museum, and since the
hotel opened in 2015 its rooftop café-restaurant has been a hot spot
for locals and others looking for a drink or meal with a view. **Pros:**
excellent location near the Acropolis; modern bathrooms with a lot of
perks; fantastic views from rooftop café-restaurant. **Cons:** passersby on
the pedestrian street below can be noisy; arranging things via email can
be tricky; reception staff a little flat. $ *Rooms from: €250* ⊠ *Dionissiou Aeropagitou 5, Makriyianni* ☎ *210/924–9954* ⊕ *www.athenswas.
gr* ⤴ *21 rooms* ⦿| *No meals* Ⓜ *Acropolis* ✛ *D5.*

$$ **Hera Hotel.** Attention to elegant detail—the lobby's marble floors,
HOTEL dark wood paneling, and leather sofas—reigns at this small and elegant
hotel, a good value that is perfectly located just down the street from
the Acropolis Museum. **Pros:** unbeatable location; the Acropolis view
from the dreamy roof garden; cleanliness and service. **Cons:** breakfast
not automatically included (depends on booking); rooms at the back
have no views; lofty restaurant prices. $ *Rooms from: €130* ⊠ *Falirou
9, Makriyianni* ☎ *210/923–6682* ⊕ *www.herahotel.gr* ⤴ *38 rooms*
⦿| *No meals* ✛ *D5.*

KOUKAKI ΚΟΥΚΑΚΙ

$ **Acropolis Select.** For not significantly more per night than many basic
HOTEL budget options, you get to stay in a slick-looking hotel with an artfully
modernized lobby full of designer furniture in the residential and newly
fashionable neighborhood of Koukaki, a 10-minute walk from the
Acropolis (and literally around the corner from the Acropolis Museum).
Pros: comfortable rooms; friendly staff; good value for money. **Cons:**
no Acropolis views; small elevator; some noise from the street at night.
$ *Rooms from: €95* ⊠ *Falirou 37–39, Koukaki* ☎ *210/921–1610*
⊕ *www.acropoliselect.gr* ⤴ *72 rooms* ⦿| *No meals* ✛ *D5.*

$$ **Herodion Hotel.** A good compromise between the area's budget venues and deluxe digs, this hospitable hotel is down the street from the
HOTEL Odeon of Herodes Atticus, where Athens Festival performances are
held in summer, and a few minutes from the Acropolis. **Pros:** tastefully
designed rooms; wide choice at buffet breakfast; great Acropolis views
from some rooms. **Cons:** rooms a bit small; no free in-room Wi-Fi; a
little pricey if you're on a budget. $ *Rooms from: €150* ⊠ *Rovertou
Galli 4, Makriyianni* ☎ *210/923–6832 through 210/923–6836* ⊕ *www.
herodion.gr* ⤴ *90 rooms* ⦿| *Breakfast* ✛ *D5.*

2

$ **Marble House.** This welcoming guesthouse has a steady clientele who
B&B/INN don't mind the basic accommodations and facilities in return for gracious, welcoming service, a convenient location, and unbeatable prices.
Pros: unbeatable price for the budget traveler; quiet neighborhood ideally located for sightseeing; friendly staff. **Cons:** a bit outdated, no-frills interiors; breakfast costs extra; cramped bathrooms (not en suite).
$ *Rooms from: €45* ✉ *Anastassiou Zinni 35, Koukaki* ☎ *210/923–4058, 210/922–8294* ⊕ *www.marblehouse.gr* ⟳ *16 rooms, 11 with bath* ⟨⊙⟩ *No meals* ✛ *C6.*

$$ NLH Fix - **Neighborhood Lifestyle Hotels.** Right behind the brand-new
HOTEL National Museum of Contemporary Art (EMST), this new seven-
FAMILY story hotel opened in 2017 and has already received rave reviews for
Fodor's Choice its large, light-filled, and modern rooms that are ideal for families
★ or small groups of friends (up to four). **Pros:** wonderfully spacious,
airy, and light-filled rooms; staff offer exceptional insider tips; excellent value for families. **Cons:** breakfast not included in price (and
only in-room); on Syngrou Avenue so a little noisy; rooms don't have
Acropolis views. $ *Rooms from: €150* ✉ *Syggrou 64, Koukaki* ✛ *At
Stratigou Kontouli* ☎ *210/920–0170* ⊕ *nlh.gr* ⟳ *13 rooms* ⟨⊙⟩ *No
meals* Ⓜ *Syngrou Fix* ✛ *D6.*

PLAKA AND ANAFIOTIKA ΠΛΑΚΑ ΑΝΑΦΙΩΤΙΚΑ

PLAKA ΠΛΑΚΑ

$ **Adrian Hotel.** This comfortable pension offers friendly service and an
HOTEL excellent location in the heart of Plaka—incurable romantics should
ask for one of just three rooms looking toward the Acropolis. **Pros:**
great central location; friendly staff; excellent value for the money.
Cons: Adrianou Street can be noisy during the summer months; smallish
rooms; bathroom and some interior details (i.e., carpets) need updating.
$ *Rooms from: €98* ✉ *Adrianou 74, Plaka* ☎ *210/322–1553* ⊕ *www.
douros-hotels.com* ⟳ *22 rooms* ⟨⊙⟩ *Breakfast* ✛ *D4.*

$ **Alice Inn.** One of a new breed of micro-hotels (and not quite a
RENTAL hotel at that but more like a comfortable restored neoclassical
home) offers four suites, each with its own advantage, including a
kitchenette. **Pros:** stylish, unconventional home away from home;
central location; scenic rooftop and pretty courtyard. **Cons:** no services except tea and coffee; unsuitable for families; not ideal for
elderly guests (lots of stairs). $ *Rooms from: €120* ✉ *9 Tsatsou,
Plaka* ☎ *210/323–7139* ⊕ *www.aliceinnathens.com* ⟳ *4 suites* ⟨⊙⟩ *No
meals* Ⓜ *Acropolis* ✛ *D4.*

$$$ **AVA Hotel & Suites.** On a quiet side street in the Plaka, this lovely small
HOTEL hotel (fully renovated in 2016) is ideally located for all the major Athens
attractions and has become a firm favorite among leisure and business
travelers alike. **Pros:** spacious rooms; elegant furnishings; impeccable
service. **Cons:** lacks big-hotel amenities and a restaurant; small elevator; the breakfast could be richer. $ *Rooms from: €250* ✉ *Lyssicratous 9–11, Plaka* ☎ *210/325–9000* ⊕ *www.avahotel.gr* ⟳ *16 rooms*
⟨⊙⟩ *Breakfast* ✛ *D5.*

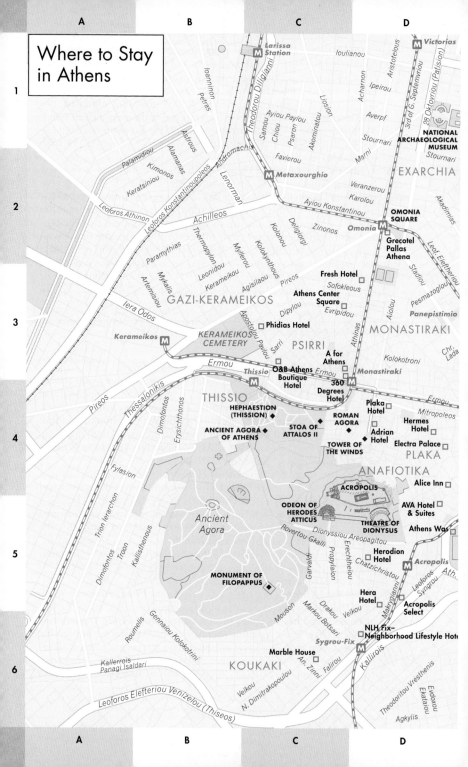

Where to Stay in Athens

A **B** **C** **D**

1

Larissa Station Ⓜ

Ⓜ Victorias

Ioulianou

Ioanninon

Petras

Astrous

Palamidiou

Kimonos

Keratsiniou

Alamanas

Leoforos Konstantinoupoleos

Leoforos Athinon

Andromachis

Lenorman

Theodorou Diligianni

Samou

Chiou

Psaron

Ayiou Paylou

Favierou

Ⓜ Metaxourghio

Liosion

Akominatou

Acharnon

Ipeirou

Ioulianou

Averpf

Stournari

Marni

NATIONAL
ARCHAEOLOGICAL
MUSEUM

Stournari

EXARCHIA

3rd of G. Septemvriou

28 Oktovriou (Patision)

Aristotelous

2

Achilleos

Paramythias

Thermopylon

Mylerou

Leonidou

Artemisiou

Mykalis

Kerameikou

Agisilaou

Kolonou

Kolokynthous

Deligiorgi

Zinonos

Pireos

Dipylou

Evripidou

Ayiou Konstantinou

Veranzerou

Karolou

OMONIA
SQUARE

Ⓜ Omonia

Grecotel
Pallas
Athena

Akadimias

Leof. Eleftheriou

Stadiou

Pesmazoglou

Aiolou

Athinas

Panepistimio

MONASTIRAKI

Chr. Lada

GAZI-KERAMEIKOS

Iera Odos

3

Kerameikos Ⓜ

KERAMEIKOS
CEMETERY

Apostolou Paylou

Sarri

PSIRRI

Fresh Hotel ▫

Sofokleous

Athens Center
Square ▫

▫ **Phidias Hotel**

A for
Athens ▫

Kolokotroni

4

Pireos

Thessalonikis

Dimofontos

Erysichthonos

Ⓜ Thissio

Ermou

O&B Athens ▫
Boutique
Hotel

Ermou

360
Degrees
Hotel ▫

Ⓜ Monastiraki

Ermou

Mitropoleos

THISSIO

HEPHAESTION
(THISSION) ◆

ANCIENT AGORA ◆
OF ATHENS

STOA OF ◆
ATTALOS II

◆ **ROMAN**
AGORA ▪

Plaka
Hotel ▫

Hermes
Hotel ▫

Adrian
Hotel ▫

Electra Palace ▫

TOWER OF
THE WINDS ▪

PLAKA

ANAFIOTIKA

5

Trion Ierarchon

Fylasion

Dimofontos

Troon

Kallisthenous

Ancient
Agora

ACROPOLIS

ODEON OF
HERODES
ATTICUS

Rovertou Gkalli

THEATRE OF
DIONYSUS

Dionyssiou Areopagitou

Erechtheiou

Garivaldi

Propylaion

Herodion
Hotel ▫

Chatzichristou

▫ **Alice Inn**

AVA Hotel ▫
& Suites

Athens Was ▫

Ⓜ Acropolis

Ath

Leoforos Syngrou

MONUMENT OF
FILOPAPPUS ◆

Mouson

Markou Botsari

Drakou

Veikou

Hera
Hotel ▫

Acropolis
Select ▫

Makrogianni

NLH Fix–
Neighborhood Lifestyle Hote

6

Roumelis

Gennaiou Kolokotrini

Kallerrois
Panagi Isaldari

Marble House ▫

KOUKAKI

An. Zinni

Falirou

Ⓜ Sygrou-Fix

Kallirois

Veikou

N. Dimitrakopoulou

Leoforos Elefteriou Venizelou (Thiseos)

Theodoritou Vresthenis

Evdoxou
Ekatalou

Agkylis

A **B** **C** **D**

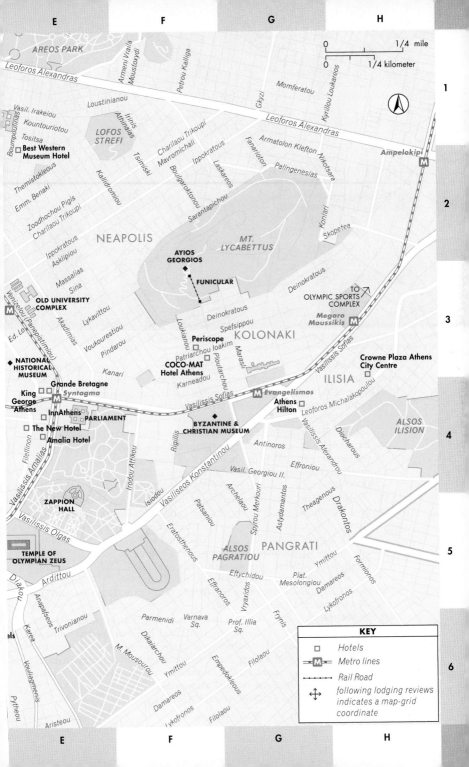

Most restaurants in the heart of Athens offer tables out on the street, where you can dine under an umbrella or a spreading plane tree. Few sections of the city are as picturesque as the Plaka district.

$$ 🏨 Electra Palace. If you want luxurious elegance, good service, and a great

HOTEL location, this is the hotel for you—rooms from the fifth floor up have a

Fodor'sChoice view of the Acropolis—and in summer you can bask in the sunshine at the

★ outdoor swimming pool as you take in the view of Athens's greatest monument or catch the sunset from the rooftop garden, if you're not enjoying some serious pampering in the excellent spa. **Pros:** gorgeous rooms; great location; shady garden and rooftop pool. **Cons:** air-conditioning can be problematic; free Wi-Fi for only first half hour; breakfast buffet is unimpressive. $ *Rooms from: €200* ⊠ *Nikodimou 18–20, Plaka* ☎ *210/337–0000* ⊕ *www.electrahotels.gr* ➷ *175 rooms* ᠬᠥᠯ *Breakfast* ✛ *D4.*

$$ 🏨 Hermes Hotel. Athens's small, modestly priced establishments have

HOTEL generally relied on little more than convenient central locations to

FAMILY draw visitors, but the Hermes goes further, with sunny guest rooms

Fodor'sChoice with brightly colored decorative details that feel warm and welcoming

★ and marble bathrooms. **Pros:** great staff; sleek, clean decor; free Wi-Fi. **Cons:** some smallish rooms, some without a balcony (check availability); on a sometimes noisy street; room walls are thin. $ *Rooms from: €135* ⊠ *Apollonos 19, Plaka* ☎ *210/323–5514* ⊕ *www.hermeshotel.gr* ➷ *45 rooms* ᠬᠥᠯ *Breakfast* ✛ *D4.*

$$ 🏨 Plaka Hotel. The guest rooms in this charming, centrally located hotel

HOTEL offer a comfortable place to rest your head while in the heart of old Athens. **Pros:** view of the Acropolis from the roof garden; diligent staff; good breakfast and lounge areas. **Cons:** small and sometimes stuffy rooms; no pets allowed; cleanliness standards could be higher. $ *Rooms from: €130* ⊠ *Kapnikareas 7 and Mitropoleos, Plaka* ☎ *210/322–2706* ⊕ *www.plakahotel.gr* ➷ *67 rooms* ᠬᠥᠯ *Breakfast* ✛ *D4.*

MONASTIRAKI AND PSIRRI ΜΟΝΑΣΤΗΡΑΚΙ ΨΥΡΡΗ

MONASTIRAKI ΜΟΝΑΣΤΗΡΑΚΙ

$
HOTEL
Fodor'sChoice
★
A for Athens. One of Athens's hippest hotels is as fresh a concept as its name, a restored 1960s building with minimalist rooms with wood floors and all the modern amenities (including both air-conditioning and free Wi-Fi). **Pros:** central location next to a metro stop; comfortable rooms with a contemporary design; breathtaking views. **Cons:** some noise from the street and the bar; no gym or pool; half the rooms have shared baths. $ *Rooms from: €90* ⊠ *Miaouli 2–4, Monastiraki* ☎ *210/324–4244* ⊕ *www.aforathens.com* 🗭 *35 rooms* ❑ *Breakfast* ✛ *C3.*

$$
HOTEL
360 Degrees Hotel. You can't get more central than this, nor can you get better views than those from the rooftop café-restaurant, which is so popular among Athenian youth. **Pros:** in the heart of the city; friendly, helpful staff; cool design and style. **Cons:** noise from the square; noise from rooftop bar if you're right below it; some beds not large enough. $ *Rooms from: €200* ⊠ *Monastiraki Sq., Monastiraki* ☎ *210/324–0034* ⊕ *www.360hotelathens.com* 🗭 *20 rooms* ❑ *Breakfast* Ⓜ *Monastiraki* ✛ *C3.*

PSIRRI ΨΥΡΡΗ

$$
HOTEL
Athens Center Square. This surprisingly peaceful, modern hotel nevertheless blends nicely into the iconic, bustling landscape of the Athens Central Market. **Pros:** knowledgeable, friendly staff; rooftop with Acropolis views; excellent price-to-quality ratio. **Cons:** a safe, albeit inner-city, location that may not be to everyone's taste; free Wi-Fi can be slow in rooms; cheapest rooms have shower only. $ *Rooms from: €130* ⊠ *Aristogeitonos 15, Psirri* ✛ *At Athinas* ☎ *210/321–1770* ⊕ *www.athenscentersquarehotel.gr* 🗭 *54 rooms* ❑ *Breakfast* ✛ *C3.*

$$$
HOTEL
Fodor'sChoice
★
O&B Athens Boutique Hotel. Each room in this boutique hotel with a sleek design and an outstanding restaurant-bar is a little haven of urban cool, thanks to flat-screen TVs, personal stereo/DVD systems, Molton Brown bath products, high-drama high-design color schemes, black minimalistic headboards, and soft white Egyptian cotton sheets. **Pros:** beautiful rooms; excellent food; personalized service. **Cons:** all rooms but the penthouse have limited views; street not very attractive; pricey. $ *Rooms from: €260* ⊠ *Leokoriou 7, Psirri* ☎ *210/331–2940* ⊕ *www.oandbhotel.com* 🗭 *27 rooms* ❑ *Breakfast* ✛ *C3.*

THISSIO ΘΗΣΕΙΟ

$
HOTEL
Phidias Hotel. Stay here, and you may develop the impression that Athens is all fun and not a car-packed, frantic metropolis—simply put, there's no better spot to stay, location-wise, on Athens's most beautiful pedestrian walkway. **Pros:** top location with proximity to metro and shopping; a particularly good value; pets OK. **Cons:** public and private spaces could use a makeover; old elevator; sometimes the nearby Thissio partying is loud. $ *Rooms from: €85* ⊠ *Apostolou Pavlou 39, Thissio* ☎ *210/345–9511* ⊕ *www.phidias.gr* 🗭 *15 rooms* ❑ *Breakfast* ✛ *C3.*

For food-with-a-view, the Plaka district is famed for its lovely garden restaurants with front-row seats to the Acropolis Hill.

SYNTAGMA ΣΥΝΤΑΓΜΑΤΟΣ

$$ HOTEL FAMILY

Amalia Hotel. The central location and competitive prices are the main attractions here for most visitors, with a location right on one of Athens's biggest, busiest streets, directly across from Parliament, but double-glazed windows (fortunately) and a view to the pretty National Garden keep things peaceful inside. **Pros:** perfect central location; easy access to transport, to Plaka, and to the pretty National Garden; free Wi-Fi. **Cons:** on a busy thoroughfare; no restaurant at the hotel, just a snack bar; front rooms can be a bit noisy. [$] *Rooms from: €160* ✉ *Amalias 10, Syntagma* ☎ *210/323-7300* 🌐 *www.amalia.gr* 🛏 *99 rooms* 🍴 *Breakfast* ✥ *E4.*

$$$$ HOTEL FAMILY Fodor's Choice ★

Grande Bretagne. With a guest list that includes more than a century's worth of royals, rock stars, and heads of state, the landmark Grande Bretagne remains the most exclusive hotel in Athens. **Pros:** all-out luxury; exquisite rooms; excellent café, spa, and pool lounge. **Cons:** expensive; no free Wi-Fi; demonstrations sometimes take place right in front of the hotel. [$] *Rooms from: €320* ✉ *Vasileos Georgiou A'1 at Syntagma Sq., Syntagma* ☎ *210/333-0000, 210/331-5555 through 210/331-5559 reservations* 🌐 *www.grandebretagne.gr* 🛏 *377 rooms* 🍴 *Breakfast* ✥ *E4.*

$$ HOTEL FAMILY Fodor's Choice ★

InnAthens. Five minutes' walk from Syntagma Square is a homey 20-room boutique hotel built from a renovated neoclassical building with minimalist decor that draws travelers with its helpful, friendly service and great, included breakfast. **Pros:** excellent service; great location; delicious breakfast made with fresh, seasonal ingredients. **Cons:** some rooms a bit boxy; not ideal for wheelchair users; water pressure is low. $ *Rooms from: €165* ✉ *Georgiou Sourri 3, Syntagma* ✛ *At Filellinon* ☎ *210/325–8555* ⊕ *www.innathens.com* ⤴ *22 rooms* ⦿ *Breakfast* ✛ *E4*.

$$$$ ▦ **King George Athens.** One of the most historic and luxurious hotels in
HOTEL Athens, the King George is where Madonna and Woody Allen stayed
Fodor's Choice while visiting Athens (in the same Royal Penthouse suite, but not at the
★ same time!), and first impressions tell you why: a spacious lobby done
in marble, mahogany, velvet, leather, and gold trim lures you into a
world where antique crystal lamps and frosted glass shower stalls with
mother-of-pearl tiles raise standards of luxury to dizzying heights. **Pros:**
outstanding food; luxurious rooms; attentive service. **Cons:** slow elevators; thin walls in rooms; in-room Wi-Fi at a charge. $ *Rooms from:*
€350 ✉ *Vasileos Georgiou A' 2, Syntagma* ☎ *210/322–2210* ⊕ *www.*
kinggeorgeathens.com ⤴ *102 rooms* ⦿ *No meals* ✛ *E4*.

$$ ▦ **The New Hotel.** This cutting-edge New Hotel was heralded as an
HOTEL aesthetic triumph in the inner city's ever-changing landscape when
Fodor's Choice it opened in 2011, and it has maintained its edge, attracting guests
★ who still prefer something avant-garde. **Pros:** helpful staff; sumptuous
breakfast; great spa. **Cons:** pricey pay-per-view TV; front-facing rooms
can be noisy; may be a bit too avant-garde for some. $ *Rooms from:*
✉ *Filellinon 16, Syntagma* ☎ *210/327–3000* ⊕ *www.newhotel.gr* ⤴ *79*
rooms ⦿ *Breakfast* ✛ *E4*.

KOLONAKI ΚΟΛΩΝΑΚΙ

$$ ▦ **COCO-MAT Hotel Athens.** In a first, a manufacturer of luxury mat-
HOTEL tresses has opened up its own boutique hotel right above the com-
pany's mattress showroom, offering chic, minimalist rooms centered
on the bed. **Pros:** blissfully comfortable beds; just off Kolonaki Square;
friendly, helpful service. **Cons:** breakfast could be better; some rooms
have little natural light; bathroom lighting can be low. $ *Rooms from:*
€180 ✉ *Patriarchou Ioakeim 36, Kolonaki* ☎ *210/723–0000* ⊕ *www.*
cocomatathens.com ⤴ *39 rooms* ⦿ *Breakfast* Ⓜ *Syntagma* ✛ *F3*.

$$ ▦ **Periscope.** This sleek concept hotel combines minimalist urban-chic
HOTEL design, amenity-filled rooms, and exceptional service for a truly relaxing
experience. **Pros:** outstanding service; eatery (PBox) created by award-
winning chef; great breakfast. **Cons:** rooms are a bit on small side and
have limited views; only suites have balconies; no parking. $ *Rooms*
from: €180 ✉ *Haritos 22, Kolonaki* ☎ *210/729–7200* ⊕ *periscope.gr*
⤴ *21 rooms* ⦿ *Breakfast* ✛ *F3*.

OMONIA ΟΜΟΝΟΙΑΣ

$$ ▦ **Fresh Hotel.** Reveling in minimalist glam, this attractive and uncon-
HOTEL ventional boutique hotel has relaxing and expertly decorated rooms, a
plugged-in staff, and two restaurants that feature nouvelle-Mediterra-
nean cuisine—in a centrally located, albeit somewhat dodgy neighborhood (by night, at least). **Pros:** Air Lounge Bar restaurant has great
food and views; central location; plugged-in staff. **Cons:** surrounding
neighborhood is a bit dodgy at night; only a few rooms have great
views; noisy if you keep your window open. $ *Rooms from: €150*

✉ *Sofokleous 26, Omonia Sq.* ☎ *210/524–8511* ⊕ *www.freshhotel.gr* ⇌ *133 rooms* ⦿ *Breakfast* ✣ *D3.*

$$ ⬚ **Grecotel Pallas Athena.** Fun yet posh, this is a crazy/cool boutique
HOTEL   art hotel in a slightly sketchy but strategic location near City Hall,
FAMILY   Omonia, and the Central Market. **Pros:** reliable Wi-Fi; attentive staff;
excellent in-house food. **Cons:** many rooms have poor views; run-down
neighborhood that is especially unpleasant at night; some rooms are
poorly decorated. Ⓢ *Rooms from: €140* ✉ *Athinas 65, at Lykourgou,*
Omonia Sq. ☎ *210/325–0900* ⊕ *www.grecotelpallasathena.com* ⇌ *63*
rooms ⦿ *Breakfast* ✣ *D2.*

EXARCHIA ΕΞΑΡΧΕΙΑ

$ ⬚ **Best Western Museum Hotel.** If you'd like to stay just a few blocks from
HOTEL   the National Archaeological Museum, this reliable hotel offers elegant
FAMILY   rooms in good, clean condition, as well as friendly, helpful service, free
Wi-Fi, and a satisfying breakfast. **Pros:** clean, well-maintained rooms;
pleasant, central location; a good breakfast included. **Cons:** unexciting
in terms of ambience and decor; a little dated; not near the ancient sites.
Ⓢ *Rooms from: €70* ✉ *Bouboulinas 16, Exarcheia* ☎ *210/380–5611*
⊕ *www.museum-hotel.gr* ⇌ *93 rooms* ⦿ *Breakfast* ✣ *E1.*

ILISIA ΙΛΙΣΙΑ

$$ ⬚ **Athens Hilton.** Although the impressive Hilton is one of the city's ven-
HOTEL   erable architectural landmarks, characteristically covered in Egyptian
FAMILY   hieroglyphics, it's also been kept up to date with modern, glossy, and
Fodor's Choice minimalist design. **Pros:** outstanding service; huge pool surrounded by
★   palm trees; excellent buffet breakfast. **Cons:** very expensive restaurants;
extra fee to use the pool, spa, and gym, unless you are staying in one of
the suites; high extra charge for Internet access. Ⓢ *Rooms from: €170*
✉ *Vasilissis Sofias 46, Ilisia* ☎ *210/728–1000* ⊕ *www.athens.hilton.com*
⇌ *517 rooms* ⦿ *No meals* ✣ *G4.*

$$ ⬚ **Crowne Plaza Athens City Centre.** On the site of the city's former Hol-
HOTEL   iday Inn (it opened its doors in mid-2008), this is among the most
FAMILY   technology-friendly Athens hotels. **Pros:** high-tech infrastructure; out-
door swimming pool (closes at 7 pm); spacious rooms and bathrooms.
Cons: costly breakfast; not central, so you'll need to take taxis; the
pool is on the small side. Ⓢ *Rooms from: €130* ✉ *Michalakopoulou*
50, Ilisia ☎ *210/727–8000* ⊕ *www.cpathens.com* ⇌ *193 rooms* ⦿ *No*
meals ✣ *H3.*

NIGHTLIFE AND PERFORMING ARTS

From ancient Greek tragedies in quarried amphitheaters under the stars
to progressive DJ sets at the coolest dance clubs or themed street par-
ties to performances around the town, Athens rocks at night, and like
New York, it could be described as a city that never sleeps. Several of
the former industrial districts are enjoying a renaissance, and large
spaces have filled up with galleries, restaurants, and theaters—providing
one-stop shopping for an evening's entertainment. The Greek weekly

Athinorama (also online) covers current performances, gallery openings, and films, as does English-language *Kathimerini,* inserted in the *International New York Times* (available Monday through Saturday).

You can also find out everything that's going on in the city by visiting English-language websites like ⊕ *www.ThisIsAthens.org,* ⊕ *www.Elculture.gr,* and ⊕ *www.DeBop.com,* while websites like ⊕ *www.lifo.gr,* ⊕ *www.athensvoice.gr,* and ⊕ *www.Popaganda.gr* (all translatable via Google) offer an in-depth look at events, places, and people.

NIGHTLIFE

Despite demanding working hours, significantly tighter budgets, and family obligations, Athenians simply refuse to stay home, and will always find good reasons to sit out with friends at a bar until the middle of the night. Athens's heady nightlife starts late. Most bars and clubs don't get hopping until midnight and they stay open at the very least until 3 am. Drink prices can be rather steep (about €9–€13), but the pours are generous, and in recent years the cocktails have become exciting and sophisticated. Often there is a cover charge on weekends at the most popular clubs, which also have bouncers (aptly called "face-control" by Greeks because they tend to let only the "lookers" in). For a uniquely Greek evening, visit a club featuring rembetika music, a type of blues, or the popular *bouzoukia* (clubs with live bouzouki, a stringed instrument, music). Few clubs take credit cards for drinks.

Nightclubs in Greece migrate with the seasons. From October through May, they're in vast, throbbing venues in Central Athens and the northern suburbs; from June through September, many relocate to luxurious digs on the south coast for moonlit beach views. The same spaces are used from year to year, but owners and names tend to bounce around. Before heading out, check local listings or talk to your hotel concierge, especially during the summer. One way to avoid both lines and cover charges—since partying doesn't get going until after 1 am—is to make an earlier dinner reservation at one of the many clubs that have restaurants as well.

BOUZOUKIA

Many tourists think Greek social life centers on large clubs where live bouzouki music plays while patrons smash up the plates. Plate-smashing has been prohibited since 1976, but plates of flowers (at high prices) are sold for scattering over the performer or your companions when they take to the dance floor. Upscale bouzoukia clubs line the middle section of Pireos Avenue and stretch out to the south coast, where top entertainers command top prices. Be aware that bouzoukia food is overpriced and often second-rate. There is a per-person minimum (around €25) or a prix-fixe menu; a bottle of whiskey may cost around €100. For those who choose to stand at the bar, a drink runs about €15 to €20 at a good bouzoukia place.

REMBETIKA

The Greek equivalent of the urban blues, rembetika music is rooted in the traditions of Asia Minor and was brought to Greece by refugees from Smyrna in the 1920s. It filtered up from the lowest economic levels to become one of the most enduring genres of Greek popular music, still enthralling clubgoers today. At these thriving clubs, you can catch a glimpse of Greek social life and even join the dances (but remember, it's considered extremely rude to interrupt a solo dance). The two most common dances are the *zeimbekiko*, in which the man improvises in circular movements that become ever more complicated, and the belly dance–like *tsifteteli*. Most of the clubs are closed in summer; call in advance. Drink prices range from €10 to €15, a bottle of whiskey from €70 to €90, and the food is often expensive and unexceptional; it's wisest to order a fruit platter or a bottle of wine.

PLAKA AND ANAFIOTIKA ΠΛΑΚΑ ΑΝΑΦΙΩΤΙΚΑ

BARS

Brettos. With walls adorned with brightly lighted bottles in all colors of the spectrum, Brettos is a dated choice for most locals and is mainly popular among tourists who have seen photos of it over the years. Locals who still choose to come here do so to relish the memories of the oldest distillery in town (going strong since 1909) and the second-oldest bar in the whole of Europe. The huge barrels store head-spinning spirits produced on the premises even today—ouzo, cognac, liqueurs (like top picks cinnamon or mango), tsipouro, and more. Order a *mezedes* platter to accompany your beverage of choice. ⊠ *Kydathinaion 41, Plaka* ☎ *210/323–2110* ⊕ *www.brettosplaka.com.*

TAVERNAS WITH MUSIC

FAMILY **Neos Rigas.** At this traditional music taverna you can get a taste of folk dances and costumes from throughout Greece. At the end of the night the music turns more "Eastern," and everybody is invited to show off their own dance moves (if you don't want to dance, pick your seat accordingly). The price of this slice of old-style Greek entertainment is fair; there's a reasonably priced prix-fixe menu and wine by the bottle. ⊠ *Agg. Hatzimihali 13, at Adrianou, Plaka* ☎ *210/324–0830* ⊕ *www.newrigas.gr.*

FAMILY **Palia Taverna** (*Old Tavern of Stamatopoulos*). This taverna has everything: good food, barrel wine, an acoustic duo with guitar and bouzouki playing old Athenian songs in an 1882 house. In summer the show moves to the garden. Whatever the season, Greeks will often get up and dance, beckoning you to join them (don't be shy). Live music starts at about 8:30 and goes on until 1 am. ⊠ *Lysiou 26, Plaka* ☎ *210/321–8734* ⊕ *www.stamatopoulostavern.gr.*

KOLONAKI ΚΟΛΩΝΑΚΙ

CLUBS

Minnie the Moocher. Just two minutes walk from Kolonaki Square, this sleek, Prohibition-era-themed bar is always kicking with a mixed crowd sipping excellently mixed cocktails. Chesterfield-style sofas, high padded stools, and elaborately tiled floors as well as a vibrant sound track keep customers there until the late hours. ⊠ *Tsakalof 6, Kolonaki* ☎ *210/364–1686* Ⓜ *Syntagma.*

MONASTIRAKI AND PSIRRI ΜΟΝΑΣΤΗΡΑΚΙ ΨΥΡΡΗ

BARS

Baba Au Rum. Rum is the star at this trendy, popular bar in the heart of Monastiraki. All the liqueurs, syrups, and essences to flavor highly original and delicious cocktails are made in-house. The vibe is buzzy both indoors—where the decor has stylish yet quirky vintage touches like stained-glass lamps and antique drinking glasses—and out, where crowds gather especially on weekends. From tiki-inspired beverages to dark rum, chocolate, and lemon creations, you can spend hours experimenting here. ⊠ *Klitiou 6, Monastiraki* ☎ *211/710–9140* ⊕ *babaaurum.com.*

Couleir Locale. This youthful, scenic, and modish bar offers a different kind of local color than the usual walk-in or street-level place, as you'll have to walk into an arcade selling antiques and take the elevator to the top floor of an old building to reach it. As you step out onto the roof, you'll come face to face with a stunning view of the Acropolis, the National Observatory, and the Anafiotika area—and after sunset all of them beautifully lighted up. The cocktails are creative, the finger foods tasty, the music loud (there are regular DJ sets hosted), and the service friendly. ⊠ *Normanou 3, Monastiraki* ☎ *216/700–4917* ⊕ *www.couleurlocaleathens.com* Ⓜ *Monastiraki.*

Six d.o.g.s. You can choose to lounge at the bar or squeeze yourself into a bopping crowd to watch a top DJ or alternative electronica band do their thing. Or if you're the quiet-loving type, simply walk down the stairs to find yourself in a huge urban garden, where you can sip a cold beer and chat until late into the night. Since it opened in the early 2000s, this bar/club has never for a moment lost its edge, or popularity. ⊠ *Avramiotou 6–8, Monastiraki* ☎ *210/321–0510* ⊕ *sixdogs.gr* Ⓜ *Monastiraki.*

360 Cocktail Bar. With a menu of more than 70 cocktails and an extensive wine list, there is something for everyone at this rooftop bar in the heart of lively Monastiraki Square. An unexpected bonus is the magical view of the Acropolis. ⊠ *Ifaistou 2, Monastiraki Sq., Monastiraki* ☎ *210/321–0006* ⊕ *www.three-sixty.gr.*

BREWERIES

Beertime. Over the last few years Greece has exploded with microbreweries, with even ordinary supermarkets now selling at least a handful of exceptionally fresh, sometimes unpasteurized and always interestingly flavored beers. The ideal place for choosing among hundreds of labels of Greek craft beers is this pub in Psirri, where you can relax for hours watching the world go by. ⊠ *Iroon Sq. 1, Psirri* ☎ *210/322–8443* ⊕ *www.beertime.gr* Ⓜ *Thisseio.*

TAVERNAS WITH MUSIC

The Clumsies. Located between Syntagma and Psirri, this innovative bar-restaurant is among the best and most popular in Athens. The impressively decorated, multilevel venue even has a private room (for 10, which must be prebooked), where clients can order bespoke drinks. Despite its popularity among people of all ages and styles, The Clumsies is unpretentious, and the unique cocktails (there's a degustation menu that offers the chance of tasting four to five smaller versions) are top quality. ⊠ *Praxitelous 30, Psirri* ☎ *210/323–2682* ⊕ *www.theclumsies. gr* Ⓜ *Monastiraki, Syntagma.*

FAMILY **Klimataria.** On Wednesdays, Fridays, and Saturday evenings, a rembetika or traditional *laiko* band plays sing-along favorites much appreciated by the largely Greek crowd. The price of the old-style Greek entertainment at this century-old taverna is surprisingly reasonable. Meanwhile, the food at this all-day taverna is displayed on big trays, which allows you to choose the dish of your choice with help from owners Mario and Pericles (who is also a noted rembetika singer). ⊠ *Platia Theatrou 2, Psirri* ☎ *210/321–6629* ⊕ *www.klimataria.gr.*

SYNTAGMA ΣΥΝΤΑΓΜΑΤΟΣ

BARS

Heteroclito. This small and elegant wine bar focuses exclusively on Greek wines, and has knowledgeable owners who will help you navigate their extensive wine list. The vibe is breezy and relaxed, somewhat reminiscent of a Parisian street café, where you can dawdle for hours sipping a perfect glass of wine. ⊠ *Fokionos 2, at Petraki 30, Syntagma* ☎ *210/323–9406* ⊕ *www.heteroclito.gr.*

Fodor'sChoice **Oinoscent.** If you'd like to learn about Greek wine both using your mind
★ and your taste buds, this modern bar with bold-yellow walls and high stools is the place for you. Serving some 50 Greek labels by the glass among a selection of 500, this wine cellar–turned–wine bar/restaurant is popular for its high-quality wines, educationally minded staff (it is run by a team of wine experts), and foods that pair well with what you choose to drink. ⊠ *Voulis 45–47, Syntagma* ☎ *210/322–9374* ⊕ *oinoscent.com* Ⓜ *Syntagma.*

GAZI-KERAMEIKOS ΓΚΑΖΙ-ΚΕΡΑΜΕΙΚΟΣ

BARS

Sodade2. This gay-friendly bar-club-lounge attracts a standing-room-only crowd every weekend. The draw is the great music, the joyous vibe, and the very fact that it's in Gazi, where a number of LGBT-friendly spots are located. ⊠ *Triptolemou 10, Gazi-Kerameikos* ☎ *210/346–8657.*

CLUBS

Bios. Cool architects and graphic designers, arty students and hipster DJs, revolutionaries and experimental philosophers: they all hang out in the cavernous basement of this Bauhaus building in the Kerameikos neighborhood, part of the greater Gazi district. Expect to hear the best electronica music in town. In summer, relish the view of the Acropolis from the postmodern, neon-lighted roof terrace. A handful of "multispace" imitators have emerged, offering offbeat film/video and music events in painfully hip industrial spaces—but Bios remains the standard. ⊠ *Pireos 84, Gazi-Kerameikos* ☎ *210/342–5335* ⊕ *www.bios.gr.*

OMONIA ΟΜΟΝΟΙΑΣ

SHOWS

Rex Music Theatre. Over-the-top is the way to describe a performance at Rex Music Theatre—it's a laser-light show, multi-costume-change extravaganza, with headlining pop and bouzouki stars. Programs and performances change every season, so do check out the local press for the most current listings. ✉ *Panepistimiou 48, Omonia Sq.* ☎ *210/330–5074.*

EXARCHIA ΕΞΑΡΧΕΙΑ

BARS

Alexandrino. This elegant Parisian-style bar and café is frequented by fashion personalities, academics, and thespians alike, who come to unwind over a few cocktails. During the day you'll find a great range of teas and coffees served in porcelain cups. Bistro-style food is also served. ✉ *Benaki 69A, Exarcheia* ☎ *210/382–7780.*

ILISIA ΙΛΙΣΙΑ

BARS

Balthazar. Athenians of all ages come to escape the summer heat at this stylish, upscale bar-restaurant in a neoclassical house with a lush garden courtyard and subdued music. Reservations are essential for the popular restaurant. ✉ *Tsoha 27, at Vournazou, Ilisia* ☎ *210/644–1215* ⊕ *www.balthazar.gr.*

Baraonda. Beautiful people, breakneck music, and a slightly gaudy VIP vibe have made this club-restaurant a perennial city favorite all year-round. The food here is also top-line and there's a beautiful garden when you need a breather. Reservations are highly recommended for both the club and the restaurant. ✉ *Tsoha 43, Ilisia* ☎ *210/644–4308* ⊕ *www.baraonda.gr.*

Fodor's Choice
★

O Kyrios. Unlike Briki next door, where the younger generations go to flirt and down shots, O Kyrios caters to an older, more deeply glamorous crowd seeking sophisticated cocktails and finger foods to match. Dress up, perch yourself on a gold stool, and order a bottle of Prosecco or a potent martini in a tiny glass. ✉ *Dorileou 4, Ilisia* ☎ *210/640–0615* ⊕ *kyriosathens.com.*

FAMILY
Fodor's Choice
★

To Parko Eleftherias. With low-key music and a romantic setting, Parko is located in the hilly park above the Megaron Mousikis (Athens Concert Hall) and the U.S. Embassy. It's a summer favorite for snacks, food, and drink by day and night. ✉ *Eleftherias Park, Ilisia* ☎ *210/722–3784* ⊕ *www.toparko.gr.*

LEAVE THE DRIVING TO THEM

Looking for some summer nightlife? Most of the popular clubs (and even some restaurants) relocate to the beach for the long, hot days and nights of Greek summer. The best way to get to Athens's seaside nightclubs is by taxi—driving on the coastal road can be a nightmare. Just tell the taxi the name of the club; drivers quickly learn the location of the major spots once they open each year.

PERFORMING ARTS

Athens's energetic year-round performing arts scene kicks into a higher gear from June through September, when numerous stunning outdoor theaters host everything from classical Greek drama (in both Greek and English), opera, symphony, and ballet, to rock, pop, and hip-hop concerts. In general, dress for summer performances is fairly casual, though the city's glitterati get decked out for events such as a world premiere opera at the Odeon of Herodes Atticus. From October through May, when the arts move indoors, the Megaron Mousikis/ Athens Concert Hall is the biggest venue, but there are literally hundreds of theaters and performance venues around the city. Performances at outdoor summer venues, stadiums, and the Megaron tend to be priced between €15 to €120 for tickets, depending on the location of seats and popularity of performers.

FESTIVALS

Every summer, the city center is covered with posters for a host of big-name music festivals.

FAMILY

Fodor's Choice

★

Athens and Epidaurus Festival. The city's primary artistic event (formerly known as the Hellenic Festival) runs from June through August at over 50 venues, from ancient sites and museums to gritty factories and public spaces. The most widely beloved venue is the ancient Odeon of Herodes Atticus at the foot of the Acropolis. The festival has showcased performers such as Norah Jones, Dame Kiri Te Kanawa, Luciano Pavarotti, and Diana Ross; such dance troupes as the Royal London Ballet, the Joaquin Cortes Ballet, and Maurice Béjart; symphony orchestras; and local groups performing ancient Greek drama. Usually a major world premiere is staged during the festival. Starting in 2006, the then creative director Yiorgos Loukos rejuvenated the festival, adding more youthful venues and bringing a wider gamut of performances, including world musicians, modern dance, and multimedia artists. The Odeon makes a delightful backdrop, with the floodlighted Acropolis looming behind the audience and the Roman arches behind the performers. The upper-level seats have no cushions, so bring something to sit on, and wear low shoes, since the marble steps are steep. For viewing most performances, the *Gamma* zone is the best seat choice. Tickets go on sale three weeks before performances but sell out quickly for popular shows; they are available from the festival box office in Syntagma Square, at the box office outside the Odeon theater, and at major bookshops in Athens (for a full list, check the website). Prices range from €15 to as high as €120 for the big names; student and youth discounts are available. ✉ *Athens* 🕾 *210/928–2900 general information* ⊕ *www.greekfestival.gr.*

Ejekt Festival. The Ejekt Festival, which brings together pop, rock, and electronica bands, usually takes place every June in one of the Olympic venues in the southern suburb of Faliro. ⊕ *www.ejekt.gr.*

Festival Vrahon "In the Shadow of the Rocks". Performances by well-known Greek performers and ancient Greek theater classics are staged in an attractively remodeled old quarry, now known as the Theatro Vrahon *Melina Merkouri* (and its sister stage nearby, the *Anna Synodinou*). The festival begins in early June and lasts until the end of September every year; most performances start at 9 pm. Buy tickets (€20–€100) at the theater before the show. 🕾 *210/762–6438, 210/760–9340* ⊕ *www. festivalvraxon.gr.*

ARTS PERFORMANCES

Two Athens 2004 Olympic venues located about 20 to 30 minutes from the city center by taxi or public transportation host the biggest concerts. Madonna, Jennifer Lopez, and U2 have performed at the open-air Athens Olympic Sports Complex (OAKA), while Brazilian star Caetano Veloso and an international company presenting *West Side Story* are among the many troupes that have appeared inside the Badminton Theater. There are other important performing arts venues around town.

TICKETS

It's easiest to buy tickets through ticket vendors like Ticket House or at Public (an electronics store that sells music CDs).

Public. You can buy tickets for popular concerts and performing arts events at this electronics store chain with convenient locations in Central Athens. ⊠ *Karageorgi Servias 1, Syntagma* ☎ *80111/40000* ⊕ *www.public.gr.*

Ticket House. Like Ticketmaster in the United States, Ticket House sells all sorts of performing arts and popular music concert tickets. ⊠ *Panepistimiou 42, Kolonaki* ☎ *210/360–8366* ⊕ *www.tickethouse.gr.*

DANCE

Fodor's Choice
★

Dora Stratou Dance Theater. The country's leading folk dance company performs exhilarating and sublime Greek folk dances (from all regions) in eye-catching, authentic costumes in programs that change every two weeks. Performances are held Wednesday through Sunday from the end of May through September. ⊠ *Arakinthou and Voutie, Filopappou* ☎ *210/324–4395* ⊕ *www.grdance.org.*

PERFORMANCE VENUES

Onassis Cultural Centre. The Onassis Cultural Centre hosts events from across the whole spectrum of the arts, mainly in their highly contemporary version, from theater, dance, and music to performances of the written word. Inside the airy rectangular shell are two amphitheaters, a Greek bistro (Hytra Apla), an award-winning restaurant, a rooftop bar (in summer), and exhibition spaces that occupy more than 18,000 square meters and can be seen bustling with activity from October to June. ⊠ *Syngrou 107–109, Neos Kosmos* ☎ *213/017–8000* ⊕ *www.sgt.gr.*

FULL-MOON FESTIVAL IN ATHENS

On the night of August's full moon (believed to be the brightest moon of the year), the Ministry of Culture celebrates by offering free, nighttime access to various museums and ancient sites in and around the city. In the past, venues including the Acropolis, Roman Agora, and the Odeon of Herodes Atticus have been open for free, with music and dance performances held amid the ancient columns by moonlight. Check the ministry's site (⊕ *www.culture.gr*) and local English-language publications to see if you're lucky enough to be there in a year when this must-see is happening.

FILM

One of the most delightful aspects of summer in Athens is sitting al fresco to watch a film on the silver screen at an old outdoor cinema. Sipping a homemade *vyssinada* (sour cherry drink) or an icy beer, munching on popcorn, and occasionally diverting your eyes off-screen only to see the gold-lighted Acropolis in the distance is a precious experience. Films are shown in original-language versions with Greek subtitles (except for major animated films), a definite boon for foreigners. Tickets run about €9. To see what's playing, walk past the cinema during the day or check their websites.

Fodor'sChoice
★
Cine Paris. This rooftop-garden movie theater, which offers Dolby Digital sound, is the oldest (dating from 1920) and most romantic in Athens. It's located on pedestrianized Kydathinaion Street, which also means it's close to many hotels and tavernas. In the lobby there's a store selling vintage film posters. It is open from May to October. ⊠ *Kidathineon 22, Plaka* ☎ *210/322–2071* ⊕ *www.cineparis.gr.*

Fodor'sChoice
★
Cine Thisio. Films at this open-air theater, among the oldest in Athens (dating from 1935), comes complete with a view of the Acropolis. It's on the Unification of Archaeological Sites walkway and conveniently offers tables among the seating, for your film-munchies spread. In fact, the bar sells homemade cheese pie, sour cherry juice, and tsipouro accompanied with bottarga fish roe from Messolonghi. ⊠ *Apostolou Pavlou 7, Thissio* ☎ *210/342–0864, 210/347–0980* ⊕ *www.cine-thisio.gr.*

SHOPPING

For serious retail therapy, most Athenians head to the shopping streets that branch off central Syntagma and Kolonaki Squares. Syntagma is the starting point for popular Ermou, a pedestrian zone where large, international chains like Zara, Sephora, H&M, Massimo Dutti, Mothercare, Replay, Nike, Accessorize, and Marks & Spencer have edged out small, independent retailers. You'll find local shops on streets parallel and perpendicular to Ermou: Mitropoleos, Voulis, Nikis, Perikleous, and Praxitelous among them. Poke around here for real bargains, like strings of freshwater pearls, loose semiprecious stones, or made-to-fit hats. Much ritzier is the Kolonaki quarter, with boutiques and designer shops on fashionable streets like Anagnostopoulou, Tsakalof, Skoufa, Solonos, and Kanari. Voukourestiou, the pedestrianized link between Kolonaki and Syntagma, is where you'll find luxury boutiques: Louis Vuitton, Hermes, Polo Ralph Lauren, and similar brands. In Monastiraki Flea Market on Pandrossou (which also operates on Sundays) there's a mishmash of tourist trinkets, clothing, footwear, jewelry, and rugs; in Psirri you'll find coppersmiths selling wine jugs, candlesticks, cookware, and more for next to nothing. Athinas Street is loaded with stores selling everything from homewear to DIY tools, leather goods, plastic flowers, incense, and foods, and if you walk down "the spice street" of Evripidou and turn into Menandrou, you'll discover an area where migrants mainly from India and Pakistan have set up a whole different style of stores, barbershops, and restaurants (only venture there by day). Meanwhile, to get a feel of the local shopping lifestyle of Athens it's well worth getting lost in the mazelike backstreets of Monastiraki (start from Aiolou and turn anywhere). This area has flourished over recent years and is packed with quirky stores, eateries, bars, and yoga studios.

Many stores in Athens are open from 9 am to 3 pm on Monday, Wednesday, and Saturday, while on Tuesday shops on Ermou Street remain open until 5 pm. On Thursday and Friday, shops operate from 9 to 2 and then again from 5:30 to 9.

WHAT TO BUY

Antiques are always in vogue, so the prices of these items can be high. On Sunday mornings, antique hunters gather at Avyssinias Square from the crack of dawn to grab the best offers. Shops on Pandrossou sell small antiques and icons, but always check for authenticity. You must have government permission to export genuine objects from the ancient Greek, Roman, or Byzantine periods.

Greece is known for its well-made shoes (most shops are clustered around the Ermou pedestrian zone and in Kolonaki), its furs (Mitropoleos near Syntagma), its jewelry (Voukourestiou and Panepistimiou), and its durable leather items (Pandrossou in Monastiraki). In Plaka shops you can find sandals (currently making a fashionable comeback), fishermen's caps, and the wool, hand-knit sweaters worn by Greek fishermen; across the United States these can sell at triple the Athens prices. Mainly organic and almost completely chemical-free Greek skin-care lines, which include Korres and Apivita, are also much more affordable in Athens than abroad, and most pharmacies sell Korres products at excellent prices.

Discover touristy treasures in the numerous souvenir shops along the streets of Plaka and Monastiraki—in particular, look for them in the Monastiraki flea market and the shops along Adrianou Street, behind the Monastiraki train station.

Prices are much lower for gold and silver in Greece than in many Western countries, and the jewelry is of high quality. Many shops in Plaka carry original pieces available at a good price. For those with more expensive tastes, the Voukourestiou pedestrian mall off Syntagma Square has a number of the city's leading jewelry shops.

If you're looking for a cheap and iconic gift to take back home, pick up a string of *komboloi* (worry beads)—made of wood, semiprecious gems, or stone—which have had a comeback, especially among stressed-out youths and ex-smokers, who wish to keep their hands busy and their nerves in check. You can pick them up very cheaply in Monastiraki, or look in antiques shops for more-expensive versions, with amber, silver, or black onyx beads (each stone is said to have its own healing properties). Another popular gift option is the *mati,* the good-luck charm (usually turquoise or cobalt blue) depicting a symbol that wards off the evil eye.

THE ACROPOLIS, MAKRIYIANNI, AND KOUKAKI
ΑΚΡΟΠΟΛΗ, ΜΑΚΡΥΓΙΑΝΝΗ, ΚΟΥΚΑΚΙ

GIFTS

FAMILY **Athena Design Workshop.** One of the neighborhood's most original stores is a design shop run by artist Krina Vronti, from whom you can buy original printed T-shirts, home decor items, and cloth bags—all handmade, original prints with traditional Greek themes, sometimes made with a quirkily droll take on the area's classic, kitschy tourist shops. ⊠ *Parthenonos 30, Makriyianni* ☎ *210/924–5713.*

JEWELRY

Eleni Marnieri Galleie. Greece's only contemporary jewelry museum and shop features creations by over 40 Greek and foreign designers. Original jewelry and home decor designs can be admired at a distance or bought. The gallery also presents themed exhibitions and video installations. ⊠ *Lebessi 5–7* ✛ *At Porniou 16* ☎ *210/861–9488* ⊕ *www.elenimarneri. com* ☾ *Closed Mon* Ⓜ *Acropolis.*

PLAKA AND ANAFIOTIKA ΠΛΑΚΑ ΑΝΑΦΙΩΤΙΚΑ

ANTIQUES AND ICONS

Elliniko Spiti. For over 40 years, art restorer Dimitris Koutelieris has been inspired by his home island of Naxos. He salvages most of his materials from houses under restoration, then fashions them into picture frames, little wooden boats, small chairs, and other decorative objects. In his hands objects like cabin doors or window shutters gain a magical second life. ⊠ *Kekropos 14, Plaka* ☎ *210/323–5924.*

FOOD

Malotira. Named after an herb that grows in the higher reaches of Crete, this deli has expanded to include authentic, pure products of the traditional as well as modern variety. The friendly staff will be happy to offer you various foods to taste as you explore the shelves. ⊠ *Apollonos 30, Plaka* ☎ *210/324–6008* ⊕ *www.malotira.gr.*

Taste of Greece. This ethnic grocery store is a treasure trove of traditional delicacies from all over Greece—from the unique-tasting *mastiha* liqueur from the island of Chios to truffle-flavored extra virgin olive oil from Kalamata. The friendly owner is eager to offer little tastes of everything and chat about the provenance of all the products he has painstakingly picked for his quaint little shop. ⊠ *Adrianou 67, Plaka* ☎ *210/321–0550.*

GIFTS

Fine Wine. Elegant wine gift packs are available at this old-fashioned wineshop, where you can browse a broad selection of Greek wines and liqueurs. The couple who own this place are veritable wine lovers themselves and will be eager to offer any advice you need. ⊠ *Lysikratous 3, Plaka* ☎ *210/323–0350* ⊕ *www.finewine.gr.*

Fodor's Choice ★ **Forget Me Not.** This inspirational "cultural goods" shop has gained a loyal following for its unique souvenirs and gifts. Here, you can buy gifts with a contemporary Greek design twist and a sense of humor, created by local designers Greece is for lovers, Beetroot, Yiorgos Drakos, Studiolav, AC Design, and more. From a leather skateboard made in sandal style to unique bags that look like they're made from fishmonger's paper and Plexiglass evil-eye charms, this is contemporary Greek design at its best. ⊠ *Adrianou 100, Plaka* ☎ *210/325–3740* ⊕ *www.forgetmenotathens.gr.*

HANDICRAFTS

Amorgos. Wood furniture and ceramics, all hand-carved and hand-painted by the shop's owners—a creative couple specializing in antique furniture restoration and interior design—beautifully feature motifs from regional Greek designs. Needlework, hanging ceiling lamps, shadow puppets, and other decorative accessories like cushions, fabrics, wooden carved chests, and traditional low tables called *sofras,* are also for sale. ⊠ *Kodrou 3, Plaka* ☎ *210/324–3836* ⊕ *www.amorgosart.gr.*

The Loom. A cornucopia of fantastically embroidered cushion covers, blankets, and tapestries as well as beautiful carpets (including vintage, stone-washed rugs). This is the kind of shop where you can browse at your leisure. The store can ship your merchandise home to you as well. ⊠ *Adrianou 94, Plaka* ☎ *210/323–8540* Ⓜ *Monastiraki.*

The Olive Tree Store. This unique shop sells items made exclusively of olive wood, such as salad bowls and tongs, wall clocks, jewelry, and even backgammon sets. Alas, the beautiful specially made olive wood Gibson-style guitar is not for sale. ⊠ *Adrianou 67, Plaka* ☎ *210/322–2922.*

SPAS

Al Hammam. Sumptuous massages are offered here with Greek olive oil and raki or with Eastern ingredients. And the option of overlooking the Acropolis during your treatment, which can be carried out by two skilled therapists, is all part of the Al Hammam experience. And that's after relaxing in an Ottoman-style, circular marble steam room. It's a relaxing ritual that's ideal after a day of shopping and sightseeing. The Hammam also offers mani-pedis and beauty treatments. ⊠ *Tripodon 10, at Ragava, Plaka* ☎ *211/012–9099* ⊕ *alhammam.gr.*

MONASTIRAKI AND PSIRRI ΜΟΝΑΣΤΗΡΑΚΙ ΨΥΡΗ

ANTIQUES AND ICONS

Old Market. Old coins, from Greece and around the world, are for sale at this antiques shop, along with stamps, engravings, antique toys and radios, musical instruments, and medals. ⊠ *Normanou 7, Monastiraki* ☎ *210/331–1638* ⊕ *www.oldmarket.gr.*

CLOTHING

Pantelis Melissinos. Pantelis follows in the steps of his father, Stavros, aka "the poet sandalmaker," a legendary cultural figure in his own right, gentle soul, and longtime fixture of the Monastiraki scene, as well as artist shoemaker, whose shop was once visited by the Beatles, Elizabeth Taylor, Maria Callas, and Jackie O. Pantelis also writes poetry, but his main claim to fame remains the handmade sandals that continue to delight countless tourists and celebrities. ⊠ *Ayias Theklas 2, Monastiraki* ☎ *210/321–9247* ⊕ *www.melissinos-art.com.*

HANDICRAFTS

Center of Hellenic Tradition. The center is an outlet for quality handicrafts—ceramics, weavings, sheep bells, wood carvings, prints, and old paintings. Take a break from shopping in the center's quiet and quaint I Oraia Ellas café to enjoy a salad or mezedes in clear view of the Parthenon. Upstairs is an art gallery hosting temporary exhibitions of Greek art. ⊠ *Mitropoleos 59, at Pandrossou 36, Monastiraki* ☎ *210/321–3023* ⊕ *www.kelp.gr.*

THISSIO ΘΗΣΕΙΟ

SPAS

Fodor'sChoice ★ **Hammam Baths.** For an ancient-modern steam bath experience head to Hammam Baths, a gorgeous neoclassical house that has been converted into a full-amenities day spa with Eastern decorative undertones and excellent service. ⊠ *Ayion Asomaton 17, Thissio* ☎ *210/322–3073* ⊕ *www.hammam.gr.*

SYNTAGMA ΣΥΝΤΑΓΜΑΤΟΣ

ACCESSORIES

Ippolito. Luxurious bags, handcrafted in Athens using Italian leather, are sold here in addition to elegant straw and linen backpacks (with men's designs thrown into the mix) and even a back-friendly maternity range. Prices are as high as the quality. ⊠ *Voulis 38, Syntagma* ☎ *210/331–5051* ⊕ *www.ippolito.gr.*

FOOD

Fodor'sChoice ★ **Aristokratikon.** Athens's oldest and finest chocolatier (since 1928) has catered to the most high-profile and demanding chocolate lovers since it opened, and its luxuriant quality remains high. Greek ingredients (pistachios from Aegina, prunes from Skopelos, chestnuts from Pelion, and more) are produced by hand. Try the dark chocolate fondant covered in white chocolate, the sour cherry and brandy chocolates, and the milk chocolates with croquant centers. ⊠ *Voulis 7, Syntagma* ☎ *210/322–0546* ⊕ *www.aristokratikon.com* Ⓜ *Syntagma.*

GIFTS

Fodor'sChoice ★ **Diplous Pelekys.** A large variety of handwoven articles, genuine folk art, ceramics from all over Greece, and traditional and modern jewelry all on show here make excellent, and affordable, gifts. The cozy and tasteful shop is run by third-generation weavers and is the oldest folk art shop in Athens (established 1925). ⊠ *Bolani Arcade, Voulis 7 and Kolokotroni 3, Syntagma* ☎ *210/322–3783* ⊕ *diplouspelekis.gr.*

Fresh Line. Among the solid shampoo cakes, body oils, lotions, and face packs sold here are a tremendous number of organic Greek-made soaps, most sliced from big blocks or wheels, which you pay for by weight. Try the watermelon soap, shimmering fizzing ball, and the soothing body souffle. ⊠ *Ermou 30, Syntagma* ☎ *210/324–6500* ⊕ *www.freshline.gr.*

Korres. The flagship store of this cosmetics line sells a broad variety of the company's popular namesake cosmetics, from body lotions and soaps to shower gels and makeup. ⊠ *Ermou 4, Syntagma* ☎ *210/321–0054.*

2

Mastiha Shop. Medical research lauding the healing properties of gum mastic, a resin from trees found only on the Greek island of Chios, has spawned a range of exciting wellness products, from chewing gum and cookies to liqueurs and cosmetics. ⊠ *Panepistimiou 6, at Kriezotou, Syntagma* ☎ *210/363–2750.*

Tanagrea. Hand-painted ceramic pomegranates—a symbol of fertility and good fortune—are one of the most popular of the multitude of Greek decor items in one of the city's oldest gift shops. ⊠ *Petraki 3, Syntagma* ⚓ *Enter from Ermou 11* ☎ *210/321–6783* ⊕ *tanagrea.gr.*

JEWELRY

Fodor's Choice ★ **Lalaounis.** This world-famous Greek jewelry house experiments with its designs, taking ideas from nature, biology, African art, and ancient Greek pieces—the last are sometimes so close to the original that they're mistaken for museum artifacts. The pieces are mainly in gold, some in silver—look out for the decorative objects inspired by ancient Greek housewares. ⊠ *Panepistimiou 6, at Voukourestiou, Syntagma* ☎ *210/361–1371* ⊕ *www.lalaounis.gr.*

Zolotas. Since it opened in 1895, this jewelry boutique has been favored by Athens's crème de la crème, visiting dignitaries, and grateful receivers of magnificent gold gifts. Designs inspired by ancient Greece and Byzantium are as stunning as the modern ones. ⊠ *Panepistimiou 10, Kolonaki* ☎ *210/360–1272* ⊕ *www.zolotas.gr.*

KOLONAKI ΚΟΛΩΝΑΚΙ

ANTIQUES AND ICONS

Fodor's Choice ★ **Martinos.** Antiques collectors should head here to look for items such as exquisite dowry chests, old swords, precious fabrics, and Venetian glass. You will certainly discover something you like in the four floors of this renovated antiques shop that has been an Athens landmark for the past 100 years. There's another branch in Monastiraki, at Pandrossou 50. ⊠ *Pindarou 24, Kolonaki* ☎ *210/360–9449* ⊕ *www.martinosart.gr.*

ART GALLERIES

Zoumboulakis Art-Design-Antiques. The art shop of this respected private art gallery stocks some beautiful objets d'art, including candlesticks and other decor, in addition to gifts like limited-edition silkscreens by famous Greek painters Yiannis Moralis, Nikos Xatzikyriakos-Gikas, Yiannis Tsarouchis, and many more. ⊠ *Kriezotou 6, Kolonaki* ☎ *210/363–4454* ⊕ *www.zoumboulakis.gr.*

CLOTHING

Parthenis. Fashion designer Dimitris Parthenis opened his first boutique in 1970. Today his daughter Orsalia continues the family tradition of creating urban chic fashion with a Bohemian hint. Natural fibers, such as wool, silk, and cotton are used to create relaxed, body-hugging silhouettes. There is an eyewear line and a wedding collection, too. ⊠ *Dimokritou 20, at Tsakalof, Kolonaki* ☎ *210/363–3158* ⊕ *www. orsalia-parthenis.gr.*

GIFTS

Fodor's Choice ★ **Benaki Museum Gift Shop.** The airy museum shop has excellent copies of Greek icons, jewelry, and folk art—at fair prices. You will also find embroideries, ceramics, stationery, art books, small reliefs, and sculpture pieces. The new Benaki Museum Annex on Pireos Street has its own shop with an interesting collection of modern Greek jewelry. The gift shop is also open on Monday (even though the museum is closed). ✉ *Benaki Museum, Koumbari 1, at Vasilissis Sofias, Kolonaki* ☎ *210/367–1045* ⊕ *www.benaki.gr.*

Fodor's Choice ★ **Kombologadiko.** From real amber, or pinhead-size "evil eyes," to 2-inch-diameter wood, sugarcane, or shell beads, you'll find a dizzying selection of beads and styles here to string your own *komboloi* (worry beads). You'll admire the variety of this unique Greek version of a rosary, which can be made from traditional amber, but also from coral root, camel bone, semiprecious stones, and many more materials. ✉ *Amerikis 9, Kolonaki* ☎ *212/700–0500* ⊕ *www.kombologadiko.gr.*

JEWELRY

Elena Votsi. Elena Votsi designed jewelry for Gucci and Ralph Lauren before opening her own boutiques, where she sells exquisite, larger-than-life creations in coral, amethyst, aquamarine, and turquoise. In 2003 she designed the Athens 2004 Olympic Games gold medal; in 2009 her handmade 18-karat gold ring with diamonds won a Couture Design Award in the Best in Haute Couture category in Las Vegas. Brava! ✉ *Xanthou 7, Kolonaki* ☎ *210/360–0936* ⊕ *www.elenavotsi. com.*

Fanourakis. Original gold masterpieces can be had at these shops, where Athenian masters, prompted by jewelry designer Lina Fanouraki, use gold almost like a fabric—creasing, scoring, and fluting it. There's another branch at Panagitsas 6 (*210/623–2334*) in the Kifissia neighborhood. ✉ *Patriarchou Ioakeim 23, Kolonaki* ☎ *210/721–1762* ⊕ *www. fanourakis.gr.*

Museum of Cycladic Art Shop. Exceptional modern versions of ancient jewelry designs are available in the gift shop of this museum, where you can also find museum replicas and inspired ceramics. ✉ *Museum of Cycladic Art, Neofitou Douka 4, Kolonaki* ☎ *210/722–8321* ⊕ *www.cycladic.gr.*

Pentheroudakis. Browse among the classic designs in gold, diamond, and gemstones but, happily, there are less expensive trinkets, like silver worry beads that can be personalized with cubed letters in Greek or Latin and with the stone of your choice. ✉ *Voukourestiou 19, Kolonaki* ☎ *210/361–3187* ⊕ *www.pentheroudakis.com.*

EXARCHIA ΕΞΑΡΧΕΙΑ

GIFTS

Eftychia. Mainly nature-inspired ceramics (representing birds, flowers, trees, and the sea) are created and sold by artist Eftychia Barzou in her pretty shop. The top seller is a pomegranate, considered a good luck charm for abundance and fertility in Greece. ✉ *Ippokratous 32, Exarcheia* ☎ *210/363–9110.*

Continued on page 136

GREEK BY DESIGN

Shopping is now considered an Olympic sport in Greece. Many get the urge to splurge in the chic shops of Mykonos, Rhodes, and Crete, the islands that launched a thousand gifts. But if you really want to bag the best in Greek style, Athens is where to get the goods.

The Greeks had a word for it: *tropos*. Style. You would expect nothing less from the folks who gave us the Venus de Milo, the Doric column, and the lyre-back chair. To say that they have had a long tradition as artisans and craftsmen is, of course, an understatement. Even back in ancient Rome, Greece was the word. The Romans may have engineered the stone vault and perfected the toilet, but when it came to style and culture, they were perfectly content to knock off Grecian dress, sculpture, décor, and architecture, then considered the height of fashion. Fast-forward 2,500 years and little has changed. Many works of modern art were conceived as an Aegean paean, including the statues of Brancusi and Le Corbusier's minimalistic skyscrapers—both art-

ists were deeply influenced by ancient Cycladic art. Today, the goddess dress struts the runways of Michael Kors and Valentino while Homer has made the leap to Hollywood in such box-office blockbusters as *300* and *Troy*.

Speaking of which, those ancient Trojans may have once tut-tutted about Greeks bearing gifts but would have second thoughts these days. Aunt Ethel has now traded in those plastic souvenir models of the Parthenon for a new Athenian bounty: pieces of Byzantine-style gold jewelry; hand-woven bedspreads from Hydra; strands of amber *komboloi* worry beads; and reproductions of red-figure ceramic vases. These are gifts you cannot resist and will be forever be glad you didn't.

(above) Byzantine design jewelry

BEARING GIFTS?

Seeing some of the glories of Aegean craftsmanship is probably one of the reasons you've come to Greece. The eggshell-thin pottery Minoans were fashioning more than 3,500 years ago, Byzantine jewelry and icons, colorful rugs that were woven in front of the fire as part of a dowry, not to mention all those bits of ancient masonry—these comprise a magnificent legacy of arts and crafts.

LEATHER SANDALS

Ancient Greek women with means and a sense of style wore sandals with straps that wrapped around the ankles—what today's fashion mags call "strappy sandals," proof that some classics are always in vogue. The most legendary maker is Athens's very own Stavros Melissinos, whose creations were once sported by the Beatles and Sophia Loren. He has been crafting sandals for more than 50 years.

TAVLÍ BOARDS

No matter where you are in Greece, follow the sound of clicking dice and you'll probably find yourself in a kafenion. There, enthusiasts will be huddled over Greece's favorite game, a close cousin to backgammon. Tavlí boards are sold everywhere in Greece, but the most magnificent board you'll ever see is not for sale—a marble square inlaid with gold and ivory, crafted sometime before 1500 BC for the amusement of Minoan kings and now on display at the archaeological museum in Heraklion, Crete.

WORRY BEADS

Feeling fidgety? Partake of a Greek custom and fiddle with your worry beads, or komboloi. The amber or coral beads are loosely strung on a long strand and look like prayer beads, yet they have no religious significance. Even so, on a stressful day the relaxing effect can seem like divine intervention. Particularly potent are beads painted with the "evil eye."

ICONS

Icon painting flourished in Greece as the Renaissance took hold of Western Europe, and panels of saints and other heavenly creatures are among the country's greatest artistic treasures. Some, like many of those in the 799 churches on the island of Tinos, are said to possess miraculous healing powers, attracting thousands of cure-seeking believers each year. Icons attract art buyers too, but if you can easily afford one, it's almost certainly a modern reproduction.

WEAVING

Even goddesses spent their idle hours weaving (remember Arachne, so proud of her skills at the loom that Athena turned her into a spider?). From the mountains of Arcadia to such worldly enclaves as Mykonos, mortals sit behind handlooms to clack out folkloric rugs, bedspreads, and tablecloths.

BARGAINING FOR BEGINNERS

In Greece there is often the "first price" and the "last price." Bargaining is still par for the course (except in the fanciest stores). And if you're planning a shopping day, leave those Versace shoes at home—shopkeepers often decide on a price after sizing up the prospective buyer's income bracket.

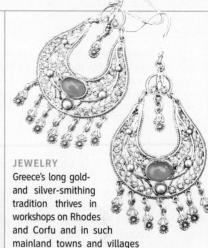

JEWELRY

Greece's long gold- and silver-smithing tradition thrives in workshops on Rhodes and Corfu and in such mainland towns and villages as Ioannina and Stemnitsa. Many artisans turn to the past for inspiration—Bronze Age cruciform figures, gold necklaces from the Hellenistic period dangling with pomegranates, Byzantine-style pendants—while others tap out distinctly modern creations using age-old techniques.

CERAMICS

Ancient Greek pottery was a black-and-red medium: the Spartans and Corinthians painted glossy black figures on a reddish-orange background; later ceramists switched the effect with stunning results, reddish-hued figures on a black background. Artisans still create both, and potters on Crete and elsewhere in Greece throw huge terracotta storage jars, pithoi, that are appealing, if no longer practical, additions to any household.

PANGRATI ΠΑΓΚΡΑΤΙ ·

CLOTHING

Jujudekokimo. Billowy silks, soft cotton, and fluffy wool are the raw materials for the designer's luxuriantly abstract, handmade creations. Kimono-style tops and asymmetrical dresses, coats inspired by 1920s-era Japan, leather bags, and jewelry made from a variety of materials. All pieces are limited editions and unique. ✉ *Archelaou 20, Exarcheia* ☎ *210/722–0021* ⊕ *www.jujudekokimo.gr.*

GIFTS

Boxes N Foxes. A clean, colorful, and minimalist space offers illuminated shelves full of handmade Greek crafts, boxes, and other decorative and utilitarian objects, from tablewear to accessories. ✉ *Archelaou 23, Exarcheia* ☎ *210/724–1223* ⊕ *www.boxesnfoxes.gr.*

Fodor's Choice ★ **Korres Pharmacy.** Natural beauty products blended in traditional recipes using Greek herbs and flowers have graced the bathroom shelves of celebrities like Rihanna and Angelina Jolie, but in Athens they are available at most pharmacies for regular-folk prices. Korres also maintains a traditional laboratory for herbal preparations such as tinctures, oils, capsules, and teas. ✉ *Eratosthenous 8, at Ivikou, Pangrati* ☎ *210/756–0600* ⊕ *www.korres.com.*

THE SARONIC
GULF ISLANDS

WELCOME TO THE SARONIC GULF ISLANDS

TOP REASONS TO GO

★ **Handsome Hydra:** The place for the jet-setter who appreciates walking more than showing off new wheels, Hydra offers both tranquility and sociability—a bustling main town and abundant walking trails. What's here (stone houses set above a welcoming harbor) and what's not (cars) provide a relaxing retreat.

★ **Ship-Shape Spetses:** A fine jumping-off point for the Peloponnesian shore, cosmopolitan Spetses is famed for its Spetsiot seafaring tradition—not surprisingly, the Old Town harbor is car-free and picture-perfect.

★ **Ancient Aegina:** Not far from this vast island's medieval Paliachora—with nearly 20 churches—is the Temple of Aphaia, one of Greece's best-preserved Archaic sites. Aegina's isle is the closest Saronic island to Athens's port of Piraeus.

★ **Pistachio Perfection:** You can already taste them—salty, sweet, mellow—and the best pistachio nuts anywhere may come from Aegina.

Bounded on three sides by sea, Attik (Attica) has an indented, sun-gilded coastline fringed with innumerable sandy beaches and rocky inlets. Just to the south of Athens, straddling the gulf between its bustling port of Piraeus and the Peloponnese, are the Saronic Gulf islands, the aristocracy of the Greek isles. Riddled with coves and natural harbors ideal for seafaring, the islands of Aegina, Hydra, and Spetses are enveloped in a patrician aura that is the combined result of history and their more recent cachet as the playgrounds of wealthy Athenians. Owing to their proximity and beauty, they can get swamped with vacationers during the summer, yet they retain their distinct cultural traditions, perhaps best appreciated out of season.

1 Aegina. The largest of the Saronic islands, Aegina is a land of contrasts—from its crowded beach towns to its isolated, rugged mountain peaks, scattered ruins, and forgotten monasteries. Take in the main town's famous fish market, visit the pre-Hellenic Temple of Aphaia, and then explore the ghost town of Palia-chora, still spirit-warm thanks to its 20 chapels.

2 Hydra. Noted for its 19th-century *archontika* (mansions), its crescent-shaped waterfront, and fashionable boutiques, Hydra has been catnip to writers and artists for decades—visit the isle's galleries or bring along your easel and let your own creative juices flow. For Hydriot splendor in excelsis, visit the 1780 Lazaros Koundouriotis Mansion or buy a glittering jewel or two at Elena Votsi's harbor-front jewelry shop.

3 Spetses. The island, with regular boat service to pine-lined beaches, is perfect for beach-hopping. It's also top contender for the most dining and night-life offerings of the Saronic isles. As for sights, Bouboulina's museum in the main town offers fascinating details about the island's storied history.

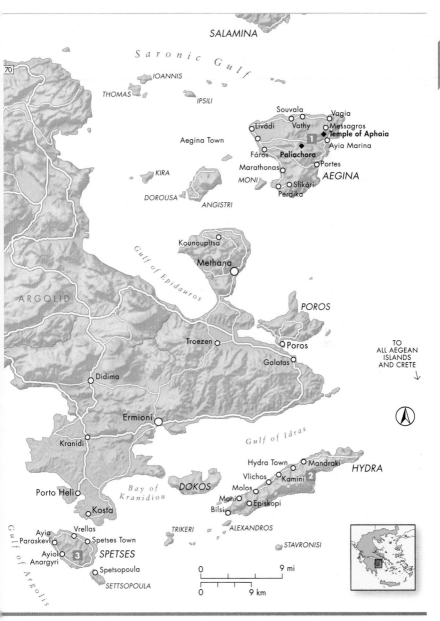

3

SALAMINA

Saronic Gulf

IOANNIS

THOMAS

IPSILI

Souvala

Vagia

Livádi   Vathy   Messagros

Aegina Town   ◆ Temple of Aphaia

1

◆ Paliachora

Fáros   **Paliachora**   Ayia Marina

KIRA   Portes

Marathonas   **AEGINA**

MONI

DOROUSA   Sfikári

ANGISTRI   Perdika

Kounoupitsa

Methana

POROS

ARGOLID

Gulf of Epidauros

Troezen   Poros

Galatas

TO
ALL AEGEAN
ISLANDS
AND CRETE
↓

Didima

Ermioni

Gulf of Idras

Kranidi

Hydra Town   Mandraki

Vlichos   **HYDRA**

DOKOS   Molos   Kamini   2

Porto Heli   Moni

Bay of Kranidiou   Bilsi   Episkopi

Kosta

TRIKERI   ALEXANDROS

Ayia   STAVRONISI
Paraskevi   Vrellas
Ayioi   3   Spetses Town
Anargyri   **SPETSES**

Spetsopoula

SETTSOPOULA

0   9 mi

0   9 km

Updated by
Natasha
Giannousi-
Varney

Only have a few days in Greece but need a taste of island life? Hopping over to one of the Saronic isles is the perfect solution. Called the "offshore islands" by day-tripping Athenians, they are treasured for their proximity to the burly city. Just south of hectic Piraeus, Aegina still feels like another world. Heading southward you'll find chic and cosmopolitan Hydra, a fitting stage for one of Sophia Loren's first forays into Hollywood. Finally, there is splendid Spetses, anchored off mainland Kosta—a playground prized by carefree vacationing Greeks.

The Saronic Gulf islands, whose ancient city-states rivaled Athens, are now virtually a part of the capital. Aegina, one of the most-visited islands in Greece because of its proximity to the capital, is 30 minutes from Piraeus by hydrofoil, while Spetses, the most "remote" and the greenest of the Saronic islands, is 120 minutes away. South of the Argolid, the peninsula that divides the Saronic Gulf from the Gulf of Argolis, rests Hydra, poor in beaches but rich in charm.

Aegina's pretty country villas have drawn shipping executives, who often commute daily from the island to their offices in Piraeus. Here pine forests mix with groves of pistachio trees, a product for which Aegina is justly famous. Hydra and Spetses are farther south and both ban automobiles. Hydra's stately mansions, restaurants, and boutiques cater to the sophisticated traveler and art lover. Spetses has both broad forests and regal, neoclassical buildings. Rather than being spoiled by tourism, all four islands have managed to preserve their laid-back attitude, well suited to the hedonistic lifestyle of weekend pleasure-seekers arriving by yacht and hydrofoil.

PLANNING

WHEN TO GO

The weather on the islands tends to be the same as in Athens, though the heat can feel more intense on the arid peaks of Aegina and Hydra. The island breeze—felt on all the Saronic isles, particularly later in the day—makes these vacation destinations more refreshing than the mainland on summer evenings (and in winter, more bitter, due to the lower humidity). There is a risk of summer fires, so do not wander into forested areas in the hot-weather months. Check the forecast before heading to Aegina, Hydra, or Spetses at any time of year—bad weather in the off-season or strong August winds (*meltemia*) may strand you on the island you only intended to visit briefly.

PLANNING YOUR TIME

The Saronic isles make fabulous day trips, though an overnight stay—or hop to a second isle—is recommended if you have the time. To ease into the pace of island life probably requires at least two days per island; however, you can visit all the islands in as few as four days. Aegina—the closest to Piraeus—is the easiest to do in a day since it has the most regular traffic to and fro, especially if your time is very limited. Although all the Saronic islands have swimming beaches, those on Spetses are the best, so you may want to linger. In three days you can explore most of Hydra or Spetses, or really get to know Aegina. Is island-hopping on your agenda? Devote the first two days to the small main town and beautiful beaches of Spetses. In the next two, wander Hydra's port town, and if you're ambitious (and in shape), hike to a monastery. Then give Aegina its day's due. One no-sweat tip to keep in mind: In July and August visit Saronic island archaeological sites like the Temple of Aphaia as early in the day as possible. There is little shade at such sites, and the midday heat can be withering. And, of course, an early start may help you avoid crowds.

GETTING HERE AND AROUND

A car is only truly useful on Aegina, as cars are prohibited on the islands of Hydra and (except by special permit) Spetses. Renting scooters, mopeds, and bicycles is popular with tourists on Aegina and Spetses. But extreme caution is advised: roads can be narrow, winding and treacherous, and some drivers are scornful of your safety. Always wear a helmet! If braving the road isn't part of your plan, never fear: on Aegina, there is regular bus service between towns and beaches. But on Hydra, you can famously travel only by water taxi, mule, bike, horse, or donkey—no cars or buses allowed. On Spetses, get around by buggy, bike, scooter, boat, and two buses. But, as with any personal transportation in Greece, it's best to confirm prices first, so you don't get taken for a different kind of ride.

BOAT AND FERRY TRAVEL

Spetses is so close to the Peloponnese mainland that you can drive there from Athens, park, and cross the channel in any of a number of caïques (price negotiable) at the ports, but to get to any of the other Saronic Gulf islands, you must take to the sea in a ferry. You can get a weekly boat schedule from the Greek National Tourism Organization

(⊕ *www.visitgreece.gr*). You can get detailed info about ferry schedules at ⊕ *www.ferries.gr* or ⊕ *ferriesingreece.com*, and you can also reserve through a travel agent. Large ferries are the leisurely and least expensive way to travel; however, most people prefer the speedier passenger-only and "flying dolphins" (and be aware that there's also a ferry company called "Aegean Flying Dolphins") and hydrofoils.

Hellenic Seaways, ANES Ferries, and Nova Ferries will carry you and your car from the main port in Piraeus (Gate E8), about a thousand feet from the metro, to Aegina (1 hour). There are approximately a half dozen daily departures, and boat fares begin at about €8 per person for Aegina, from €20 for cars (there are no slow ferries to Hydra or Spetses). Speedier Hellenic Seaways and Aegean Flying Dolphins ferries and hydrofoils also depart from Piraeus (Gate E8 or E9). These faster ferries can get you to Aegina in 40 minutes (€13), to Hydra in 90 minutes (€28), and to Spetses in just under two hours (€38.50). There are about a half dozen departures daily to each island, but make reservations ahead of time—boats fill quickly.

What about boats and ferries between the various Saronic Gulf islands? Hellenic Seaways fast-ferry routes connect Piraeus to Hydra and Spetses year-round. There are about five daily round-trips from October to April, more the rest of the year. In summer, Saronic Ferries offers daily service that connects Aegina with the tiny islands of Angistri, Poros, and Methana. But plan your Argo-Saronic island-hopping carefully in the off-season. During that time, boats between the islands are much less frequent, and you may have to combine several ferries to reach your destination, some fast and some slow. And connecting service is not available every day; on some days (and in some seasons), you will have to backtrack to the main port at Piraeus to catch another boat. *For information regarding specific ferry companies, see Boat and Ferry Travel in Travel Smart.*

CAR TRAVEL

On Aegina, there is a good network of mostly narrow rural roads (two lanes at best). Drivers should be prepared for occasional abrupt turns; major towns and sites are well marked. Cars are not allowed on Hydra. Unlike on Hydra, cars are not banned outright on Spetses: residents are permitted to ferry their autos to the island. Sadly, the presence of cars seems to be getting more pronounced every year, despite the wishes of many inhabitants. Karagiannis Klimi Travel, on Aegina, rents both cars and motorcycles. *(See Tour Options, below.)*

HOTELS

Accommodations on the Saronic Gulf islands range from elegant 19th-century mansions—usually labeled as "traditional settlements"—to boutique-style hotels to spare rental rooms overlooking a noisy waterfront. Rented rooms can be less expensive than hotels and offer an easy option for fly-by-the-seaters: just follow signs, or solicitors who show up when boats come in. (And note that it's okay to check out the room before committing.) From June to September, book far in advance. Off-season (October–April), you'll have fewer hotels to choose from, as many close during the colder months. Souvala and

Ayia Marina are suitable lodging alternatives to Aegina's main town, but on the other islands it's best to stay in or around the main ports, the hubs of these islands. If you want to plan a great off-season trip with minimum hassle, putting your itinerary in the hands of a professional is your best bet. On Aegina we recommend Karagiannis Klimi Travel *(see Tour Options, below)*. Also note that during certain times of the year (most notably summer), you may get better deals on weekdays than on Athenian-heavy weekends.

RESTAURANTS

The cuisine of the Saronic islands resembles that of Athens, Attica, and the Peloponnese. Local ingredients predominate, with fresh fish perhaps the greatest (and most expensive) delicacy. Because much of Attica's vegetation is used to support herds of grazing sheep and the omnivorous goat, the meat of both animals is also a staple in many country tavernas. Although it is becoming increasingly difficult to find the traditional Greek taverna with large stew pots full of the day's hot meal, or big *tapsi* (pans) of *pastitsio* (layers of pasta, meat, and cheese laced with cinnamon) or *papoutsakia* (eggplant slices filled with minced meat), market towns still harbor the occasional rustic haunt, offering tasty, inexpensive meals. Always ask to see the *kouzina* (kitchen) to look at the day's offerings, or to even peer inside the pots. Informal dress is appropriate at all but the very fanciest restaurants and, unless noted, reservations are not necessary.

Restaurant and hotel reviews have been shortened. For full information, visit Fodors.com.

WHAT IT COSTS IN EUROS			
$	**$$**	**$$$**	**$$$$**
Restaurants	under €15	€15–€25	€26–€40	over €40
Hotels	under €125	€125–€225	€226–€275	over €275

Restaurant prices are the average cost of a main course at dinner or, if dinner is not served, at lunch. Hotel prices are the lowest cost of a standard double room in high season.

VISITOR INFORMATION

There are few main official tourist offices for the Saronic Gulf islands, though you'll find an information center on Aegina that is operated by the Aegina Municipality. Keep in mind that in lieu of official agencies, there is an array of private travel agencies (usually based in offices near each island's harbor port), and these offer myriad services, tickets, car rentals, and guided tours. Top agencies include Key Tours based in Athens, Karagiannis Klimi Travel on Aegina, and Hydreoniki Travel on Hydra *(see Tour Options, below, for contact information)*.

TOUR OPTIONS

Most agencies run tour excursions at about the same prices, but CHAT and Key Tours have the best service and guides. A full-day cruise from Piraeus, with either CHAT or Key Tours, visits Aegina, Poros, and

Hydra, and costs around €98 (including buffet lunch on the ship). Karagiannis Klimi Travel on Aegina and Hydreoniki Travel on Hydra also offer local tours.

Contacts Hydreoniki Travel. ✉ *Hydra Port, Hydra Town* ☎ *22980/54007, 22980/53812* ⊕ *www.hydreoniki.gr.* **Karagiannis Klimi Travel.** ✉ *Panayi Irioti 44, Aegina Town* ☎ *22970/25664, 22970/28780* ⊕ *aeginatravel.gr.* **Key Tours.** ✉ *Athanasiou Diakou 26, Athens* ☎ *210/923–3166* ⊕ *www.keytours.gr.*

AEGINA ΑΙΓΙΝΑ

30 km (19 miles) south of Piraeus by ferry.

The eastern side of Aegina is rugged and sparsely inhabited today, except for Ayia Marina, a former fishing hamlet now studded with hotels. The western side of the island, where Aegina Town lies, is more fertile and less mountainous than the east; fields are blessed with grapes, olives, figs, almonds, and, above all, the treasured pistachio trees. Idyllic seascapes, quaint backstreets, and a number of beautiful courtyard gardens make Aegina Town attractive.

Although it may seem hard to imagine, by the Archaic period (7th to 6th centuries BC), Aegina was a mighty maritime power. At that time it introduced the first silver coinage (marked with a tortoise), the first proper coins of the "western world'." By the 6th century BC, Egina—to use its alternative spelling—had become a major art center, known in particular for its bronze foundries (worked by such sculptors as Kallon, Onatas, and Anaxagoras) and its ceramics, which were exported throughout the Mediterranean. Testimony to its great glory is the Temple of Aphaia, one of the most extant of the great Greek temples and famed for its spectacular Doric columns.

As it turns out, this powerful island, lying so close to the Attica coast, could not fail to come into conflict with Athens. As Athens's imperial ambitions grew, Aegina became a thorn in its side. In 458 BC Athens laid siege to the city, eventually conquering the island. In 455 BC the islanders were forced to migrate, and Aegina never again regained its former power.

From the 13th to the 19th century, Aegina ping-ponged between nations. A personal fiefdom of Venice and Spain after 1204, it was fully claimed by Venice in 1451. Less than a century later, in 1537, it was devastated and captured by the pirate Barbarossa and repopulated with Albanians. Morosini recaptured Aegina for Venice in 1654, but Italian dominance was short-lived: the island was ceded to Turkey in 1718. Its Greek roots flourished again in the early 19th century, when it experienced a rebirth as an important base in the 1821 War of Independence, briefly holding the fledgling Greek nation's government (1826–28). By happenstance the first modern Greek coins were minted here. At this time many people from the Peloponnese, plus refugees from Chios and Psara, immigrated to Aegina, and many of the present-day inhabitants are descended from them.

GETTING HERE AND AROUND

Aegina is so close to the port of Piraeus (less than an hour) that some Athenians live on the island and commute. Two well-known companies that offer boat service to Aegina are Hellenic Seaways and Aegean Flying Dolphins.

To get around while in Aegina, use the KTEL buses that leave from the main bus station on Ethneyersias Square (✉ *Platia Ethneyersias* ☎ *22970/22787*), just left of the main port; purchase tickets here, not on the bus. Routes stop at many spots, including Ayia Marina and Perdika; a popular destination is the Temple of Aphaia, with nearly hourly departures in summer (€2.50). Service on the island becomes infrequent from late October to early May.

VISITOR INFORMATION

Contacts Aegina Municipality. ✉ *Town hall, Xristou Lada 1, Aegina Town* ☎ *22973/20026* ⊕ *www.discoveraegina.gr.*

AEGINA TOWN ΑΙΓΙΝΑ ΠΟΛΗ

84 km (52 miles) southwest of Piraeus by ferry.

As you approach from the sea, your first view of Aegina Town takes in the sweep of the harbor, punctuated by the tiny white chapel of Ayios Nikolaos. A large population of fishermen adds character to the many waterfront café-taverna hybrids serving ouzo and beer with pieces of grilled octopus, home-cured olives, and other *mezedes* (appetizers).

Much of the ancient city lies under the modern, although the world-famous ancient Temple of Aphaia looms over the entire island from its hilltop perch. Although some unattractive contemporary buildings (and some less well-preserved older ones) mar the harborscape, a number of well-preserved neoclassical buildings and village houses are found on the backstreets.

EXPLORING

Aegina Archaeological Museum. This small but choice collection of archaeological artifacts was the first ever to be established in Greece (1829). Finds from the famed Temple of Aphaia and excavations throughout the island, including early and middle Bronze Age pottery, are on display. Among the Archaic and classical works of art is the distinctive Ram Jug, which depicts Odysseus and his crew fleeing the Cyclops, and a 5th-century BC sphinx, a votive monument with the head of a woman and a body that is half-eagle, half-lion.

Aegina was one of the best schools of pottery and sculpture in antiquity and the exhibits here prove it. Just above the Archaeological Museum is the ancient site of the **Acropolis of Aegina,** the island's religious and political center. The settlement was first established in the Copper Age, and was renamed Kolona, or "column," in the Venetian era, after the only remaining pillar of the Temple of Apollo that once stood there. While in great disarray—11 successive cities once stood here—it remains a true treat for those into archaeology. Examine ruins and walls dating back to 1600–1300 BC, as well as Byzantine-era buildings. ✉ *Harbor front, 350 feet from ferry dock* ☎ *22970/22248* 🎫 *€4* ⊘ *Closed Mon.*

FAMILY **Aegina Museum of History and Folklore.** Within a 1828 neoclassical house endowed to the municipality of Aegina, this museum colorfully allows you to experience home and working life in a traditional Aegina house. On the second floor discover exhibits of authentic old furniture, paintings, costumes, and lace in a typical island setting. On the first floor, the Fisherman's house features fishery and sponge-fishing equipment, while the Cottage house displays farm tools of the old days. The first-floor hall regularly hosts temporary exhibitions. ✉ *Spyrou Rodi 16* ✢ *Behind the harbor road* ☎ *22970/26401* 🌐 *laografiko.gr* 🕘 *Closed Mon. and Tues.*

Ayios Nikolaos. As you approach from the sea, your first view of Aegina Town takes in the sweep of the harbor, with quaint neoclassical buildings in the background, the lovely vista punctuated by the gleaming white chapel of Ayios Nikolaos Thalassinos (St. Nicholas the Seafarer). ✉ *Harbor front.*

Markelon Tower. During the negotiations for Greece during the War of Independence, Ioannis Kapodistrias, the first president of the country, conducted meetings in the Markelon Tower, which dates back to the late 17th century. Today, the pink- and ocher-hued tower is being looked after by the municipality and occasionally houses cultural events and exhibitions. ✉ *Corner of Thomaidou and Pileos.*

Psaragora. A trip to (not to mention a bite to eat at) the covered fish market is a must in Aegina Town. A small dish of grilled octopus or sea urchin salad at the World War II–era Tavernas Agora or To Steki is perfect with an ouzo—if you aren't averse to the smell of raw fish wafting over. Fishermen gather mid-afternoon and early evening on the pedestrian-only street, worrying their beads while seated beside glistening octopus hung up to dry—as close to a scene from the movie *Zorba the Greek* as you are likely to see in modern Greece. ✉ *Panayi Irioti* ☎ *22970/27308.*

BEACHES

Kolona Beach. Aegina Town's beaches, notably the pine-surrounded Kolona, are pleasant enough with their shallow waters—and crowds—for a refreshing dip after a hot day. This largely undeveloped beach is within easy walking distance to a few tavernas and the archaeological site of Kolona (hotel Rastoni is also not too far away); you can find some precious shade in the adjacent pine forest. **Amenities:** none. **Best for:** swimming. ✉ *Aegina Town* ✢ *Near Kolona site.*

WHERE TO EAT

$$ SEAFOOD 🍴 **O Skotadis.** Since 1945 O Skotadis has been serving a large selection of *mezedes* for starters and mostly fresh fish dishes, usually to be accompanied by ouzo, the classic Greek anise drink. Try to snag a table (reservation is best) on the second-floor terrace with its panoramic view of Aegina's harbor. **Known for:** local fresh fish that is grilled, baked, or steamed; prime harbor-front location. [$] *Average main: €20* ✉ *Dimokratias Ave.* ✢ *Across from the floating grocers at the harbor* ☎ *22970/24014.*

$ SEAFOOD 🍴 **Pelaisos.** One of the oldest tavernas on the busy harbor strip of Aegina Town, Pelaisos is now in the capable hands of Vagelis, the third generation. His father still cooks in the morning, preparing such homey dishes of the day as stuffed zucchini, usually locally sourced, but fresh fish is the mainstay of this old-school establishment, from affordable grilled sardines to the more expensive sea bass or mullet priced by the kilo. **Known for:** great fish and seafood; popular with locals and Athenians alike; homegrown vegetables. $ *Average main: €13* ✉ *Dimokratias 41* ✛ *Opposite the 2 landmark floating grocers* ☎ *22970/23897* ⊕ *pelaisos.gr.*

$$
SEAFOOD

✕ **Tsias.** For a light bite, try this harborside *ouzeri* restaurant, a hangout for locals as well as tourists, where warm yellow walls are decorated with stencils. Except for the 30 varieties of ouzo, everything is homemade, including palate-pleasing Vouta Vouta (Dip Dip), a shrimp-and-pink-spicy-sauce concoction, and the real don't-miss dishes: baked apple in cognac and custom omelets for breakfast. **Known for:** good friendly service; tasty and inventive Greek fare. $ *Average main: €15* ✉ *Dimokratias 47* ☎ *22970/23529.*

$$
GREEK
Fodor's Choice
★

✕ **Vatzoulias.** Ask a local to name the best restaurant in Aegina, and the response is invariably Vatzoulias. In summer the garden is a pleasant oasis, scented with jasmine and honeysuckle; in winter, nestle inside the cozy dining room to dine on expertly prepared taverna classics. **Known for:** local rustic dishes; a favorite with locals. $ *Average main: €20* ✉ *Aphaias 75, Ayioi Asomatoi* ☎ *22970/22711* ▭ *No credit cards* ⊗ *Closed Mon., Tues., Thurs., and Fri.*

WHERE TO STAY

$
B&B/INN

⌂ **Aeginitiko Archontiko.** Staying at this small bed-and-breakfast, within a neoclassical house from the 1700s that has historical connections, feels like a crash course in Greek history, and its owner, Kyria Rena, is bubbly, sociable, and adored by all guests. **Pros:** homey feeling, with bright, feel-good colors; historic mansion; central location in town. **Cons:** book early or risk not finding a room; small basic rooms; some rooms still need a makeover. $ *Rooms from: €65* ✉ *Ayiou Nikolaou, Thomaidou and Liakou 1* ✛ *Behind Markelon Tower* ☎ *22970/24968* ⊕ *www.aeginitikoarchontiko.gr* ⊲ *12 rooms* ⊚ *Breakfast.*

$$
B&B/INN
Fodor's Choice
★

⌂ **Rastoni.** Quiet and secluded, this boutique hotel's peaceful quality is heightened by the landscaped mature Mediterranean garden filled with aromatic herbs, wild flowers, and pistachio trees. **Pros:** views of the garden, the pistachio groves and beyond; beautiful four-poster beds; excellent and restrained service. **Cons:** few hotel amenities; best hotel on the island fills in summer, so book early; 10-minute walk to the beach. $ *Rooms from: €150* ✉ *Dimitriou Petriti 31* ☎ *22970/27039* ⊕ *www. rastoni.gr* ⊲ *12 rooms* ⊚ *Breakfast.*

NIGHTLIFE

Greek bars and clubs frequently change names, so it's sometimes hard to keep up with the trends.

Avli. The ever-popular Avli, which goes from café-bistro by day to bar (playing Latin rhythms) by night, serves delicious appetizers in a small courtyard, crowned by an impressively tall palm tree. Free Wi-Fi is available. ✉ *Panayi Irioti 17* ☎ *22970/26438.*

Caps Love. Probably the coolest bar on Aegina, on the southern edge of the main town. Enjoy the lounge vibe with a gourmet pizza or burger

An often overlooked wonder of ancient Greece, Aegina's Temple of Aphaia boasts more than 25 of its original 32 columns and spectacularly perches atop a promontory.

downstairs in this creatively restored old town house with exposed stonework, and then head upstairs where most of the action is after dark. ⊠ *Achilleas 4* ✚ *Past Panagitsa church* ☎ *22970/29418.*

Inn on the Beach. On the outskirts of Aegina Town, this multilevel venue draws an early crowd with its sunset seafront cocktails and chill-out music, before notching up the music to a beach-party tempo. ⊠ *Akti Toti Hatzi* ☎ *6947/205283.*

SHOPPING

Aegina's famous pistachios, much coveted by Greeks, can be bought from stands along the town harbor. At Fistikato, one of the better vendors you can get these Moorish nuts, along with a whole host of other pistachio products like pesto, honey nut balls, and pistachio butter; gifts your loved ones will be eternally grateful for, if indeed these hellishly addictive snacks make it all the way home (best buy a couple of pistachio shower gels, just in case). Another treat found at some of the Aegean Town bakeries behind the harbor is *amygdalota*, rich almond macaroons sprinkled with orange flower water and powdered sugar. If you want to have a picnic lunch on the island or on the ferryboat while en route to another Saronic island, check out the luscious fruit displayed on several boats that double as picturesque floating groceries, in the center of the harbor.

Animal Respect. Cheap secondhand items, from lamps to undergarments, can be found at the Animal Respect charity store and information center. Run by the nonprofit organization *Animal Protection Aegina-Angistri* (FAZA), which cares for stray animals on the islands, the store also sells fashionable pet accessories. ✉ *Panayi Irioti 67* ⊹ *Behind the town hall* ☎ *22970/27049* 🕙 *Closed Sun.*

Ceramics Art Workshop. Sisters Martha and Maria Kottaki are talented examples of the new generation of Aegina potters (following on the footsteps of their equally talented mother, Triantafyllia). They create utilitarian yet elegant household items such as colorful salad bowls and country-chic fruit platters. ✉ *Spyrou Rodi 33* ☎ *22970/26484 shop, 22970/25152 workshop.*

Cool Soap. The locally created handmade natural soaps here are all made from the finest extra virgin olive oil and scented with expertly blended Mediterranean essential oils. The workshop also doubles as a selling point. Check out the fun and colorful mood-of-the-day boxes. ✉ *Agiou Nektariou 5* ☎ *22970/29359* ⊕ *www.coolgreeksoap.com.*

Egina Aigina. Naïf paintings by local artists, monochromatic ceramics, and minimalist sculptures can be found in this petite yet refined art gallery. ✉ *Thermopilon 12* ☎ *22970/23967.*

Fistiki. Flip-flops, shoes, bikinis, jewelry, papier-mâché figures, dangling Turkish charms, and kitchenware form the rainbow of items available at Fistiki. The shop's small entrance opens into a maze of boxy rooms filled with everything you could possibly need to stay stylish on your trip. ✉ *Panayi Irioti 15* ☎ *22970/28327.*

SPORTS AND THE OUTDOORS

BOATING AND SAILING

Aegean Sailing School. Learn to sail a yacht, try power boating, or join this lively international group of sailors on one of their day trips to nearby islands of Moni and Angistri. ✉ *Martyros Leontiou 8* ☎ *22970/25852* ⊕ *www.aegeansailingschool.com.*

> **BEACH BUMMED?**
>
> If Aegina's beaches don't wow you, climb aboard one of the many daily boats from Aegina's harbor to the smaller nearby isle of **Angistri**. Without cars, but with food, drink, and small coves to swim in, Angistri has a relaxed, out-of-the-way feel, and more than its share of lovely beaches. A closer alternative is the tiny **Moni island**, which can be reached in less than 10 minutes from the fishing village of Perdika.

SOUVALA ΣΟΥΒΑΛΑ

10 km (6 miles) northeast of Aegina Town.

Souvala is a sleepy fishing village that comes to life in summer, as it is a favorite resort of many Athenians. The tamarisks and pine trees offer natural shade on the beach, or you can head to Vagia Beach, 3 km (2 miles) farther down the seaside road.

BEACHES

FAMILY **Souvala.** The sandy and pebbled beach of Souvala is one the nicest on the island and used to be famous for its therapeutic hot and cold springs (which dried up a while back). Close to the Souvala village, it offers umbrellas, sun beds, and the Banio Banio beach bar. Elsewhere along the coastline here are many other spots where you can sunbathe and swim off the rocks. Windsurfing is available near the hotel Irides. **Amenities:** food and drink; lifeguards; showers; water sports. **Best for:** swimming; windsurfing. ✉ *Souvala* ☎ *22970/54140.*

Vagia Beach. This is a sandy beach next to a picturesque little harbor. The quaint beachfront taverna O Thisavros tis Vagias looks after the beach, renting sun beds and umbrellas, and serves coffee, drinks, and food all day long. A few pine trees provide much-needed shade, and there's easy parking nearby. The taverna is also open during winter weekends, with lunch and dinner served by a fireplace. Look for an even quieter stretch of beach at the right side of the little harbor. **Amenities:** food and drink. **Best for:** solitude; swimming; walking. ✉ *Vagia* ✥ *13 km (8 miles) northeast of Aegina Town* ☎ *22970/71191 O Thisavros tis Vagias.*

WHERE TO STAY

$ B&B/INN 🏨 **Aethrio Guesthouse.** About 9 km (5½ miles) from Aegina Town, at the small port of Souvala, this modern bed-and-breakfast is popular with Athenians seeking relaxing weekends away from the city and its studios (including one larger suite) can accommodate two to five people each. **Pros:** homey; clean and modern; decent breakfast. **Cons:** few hotel-type facilities; no in-room Wi-Fi; small rooms. [$] *Rooms from: €60* ✉ *Souvala Beach, Alipranti 154* ☎ *22970/52030* 🌐 *www.aethrioguesthouse.gr/en* 💳 *No credit cards* 🛏 *12 rooms* 🍴 *Breakfast.*

$ B&B/INN FAMILY Fodor's Choice ★ 🏨 **Irides Luxury Apartments Hotel.** It all started a few years ago, when a derelict house around 3 km (2 miles) to the east of the port of Souvala was rebuilt into a friendly little hotel by the same family that operates the Rastoni hotel in Aegina Town; then, in 2009, Irides Luxury Studios expanded into a slightly quirky brand new building, just 100 feet from the seafront, so all guest rooms and studios here enjoy a sea view. **Pros:** great for families; excellent breakfast; friendly owners. **Cons:** rocky beach; somewhat isolated; patchy Wi-Fi in some of the rooms. [$] *Rooms from: €110* ✉ *Agii, Odos Thermopilon* ☎ *22970/52215, 22970/52183* 🌐 *www.irides.gr* ⏲ *Closed Dec.–Feb.* 🛏 *25 rooms.*

$ B&B/INN 🏨 **Vagia Hotel.** The well-sized and simply decorated white rooms of this quaint little hotel have cool stone floors and king-size beds, and the balconies have either sea views or views of the forested mountain, home to the temple of Afaia, rising behind the building. **Pros:** only five-minute walk from the beach; quiet and laid-back; excellent breakfast. **Cons:** Vagia is a little off the beaten track; bathrooms are a little dated; difficult to find a room in high season. [$] *Rooms from: €55* ✉ *Vagia* ✥ *On main village road leading to the beach* ☎ *22970 /71179* 🌐 *www.vagiahotel.gr* 🛏 *21 rooms* 🍴 *Breakfast.*

FESTIVALS

Ayios Nektarios Monastery. Two of the most important festivals held at Ayios Nektarios Monastery are Whit Monday, or the day after Pentecost (the seventh Sunday after Easter), and the November 9th Saint's nameday, when the remains of Ayios Nektarios are brought down from the monastery and carried in a procession through the streets of town, which are covered in carpets and strewn with flowers. ✥ *7 km (4½ miles) southeast of Aegina Town* ☎ *22970/53806 monastery.*

Panayia Chrysoleontissa. On the Assumption of the Virgin Mary, August 15th—the biggest holiday of the Christian summer throughout Europe—a celebration is held at Panayia Chrysoleontissa, a mountain monastery built between 1403 and 1614. ✠ *6 km (4 miles) east of Aegina Town.*

AYIA MARINA ΑΓΙΑ ΜΑΡΙΝΑ

13 km (8 miles) east of Aegina Town, via small paved road below Temple of Aphaia.

The small, somewhat-overrun port of Ayia Marina has many hotels, cafés, restaurants, and a family-friendly beach with shallow waters. On the opposite side of the Ayia Marina harbor, you'll find small bays with deeper waters, ideal for diving. Ayia Marina is easily accessible by regular KTEL bus service from Aegina Town (about a 25-minute trip).

EXPLORING

Fodor'sChoice ★ **Temple of Aphaia.** One of the great glories of ancient Greek art, the Temple of Aphaia is among the most extant examples of classical Doric architecture. Once adorned with an exquisite group of pedimental sculptures (now in the Munich Glyptothek) it still proudly bears 25 of its original 32 columns, which were either left standing or have been reconstructed. The structure is perched on a pine-clad promontory, offering superb views of Athens and Piraeus across the water—with binoculars you can see both the Parthenon and the Temple of Poseidon at Sounion. The saying goes that the Ancient Greeks built the Temple of Aphaia in Aegina, the Parthenon in Athens, and the Temple of Poseidon at Sounion as the tips of a perfect equidistant triangle (called Antiquity's Perfect Triangle). This site has been occupied by many sanctuaries to Aphaia; the ruins visible today are those of the temple built in the early 5th century BC. Aphaia was apparently a pre-Hellenic deity, whose worship eventually converged with that of Athena.

You can visit the museum for no extra fee. The exhibit has a reconstructed section of the pediment of the temple, many fragments from the once brilliantly colored temple interior, and the votive tablet (560 BC) on which is written that the temple is dedicated to the goddess Aphaia. From Aegina Town, catch the KTEL bus for Ayia Marina on Ethneyersias Square, the main Aegina Town bus station; ask the driver to let you off at the temple. A gift and snack bar across the road is a comfortable place to have a drink and wait for the return bus to Aegina Town or for the bus bound for Ayia Marina and its pebbled beach. ⊠ *Ayia Marina* ✠ *15 km (9 miles) east of Aegina Town* ☎ *22970/32398* ⊕ *www.culture.gr* ☟ *€6* ☾ *Museum closed Mon.*

BEACHES

FAMILY **Ayia Marina Beach.** The best sandy beach on the island, Ayia Marina is popular with the parenting set, as the shallow water is ideal for playing children. A more rocky beach lies to the north of the marina that is good for diving and snorkeling. There are plenty of tavernas and cafés along the bay, while Hotel Apollo is not too far away. **Amenities:**

food and drink; lifeguards; toilets; water sports. **Best for:** snorkeling; swimming; walking. ⊠ *Ayia Marina.*

WHERE TO EAT

$$ ✕ **Kiriakakis.** This seafront taverna, the oldest and most established one
GREEK in Ayia Marina, has been here since 1950, when Kyriakos Haldaios brought out a gas stove and started frying fish and fries under the pine trees for local sunbathers. Today, it is owned by his grandson, also named Kyriakos, and offers traditional Greek specialties like *moussaka,* the famous dish of layered eggplant and ground meat, and plenty of fresh fish, especially gilthead and sea bass. **Known for:** fresh fish; dinner overlooking the sea. $ *Average main: €18* ⊠ *Ayia Marina* ☎ *22970/32165* ⊕ *kiriakakis-aegina.gr.*

$$ ✕ **O Kostas.** Hollowed-out wine barrels used for decorative purposes are
GREEK more kitsch than antique, but they match the lightheartedness of this country tavern. Cooks showily prepare *saganaki* over live flames by the table as waiters pull wine (red and retsina) from the barrels lining the walls. **Known for:** table-side saganaki presentation; decent house wines; good spot for outdoor dining in good weather. $ *Average main: €18* ⊠ *Aegina–Alones road* ☎ *22970/32424.*

$ ✕ **Tholos.** The go-to Taverna for the islanders, Tholos is nestled in the
GREEK pine forest spilling down from the temple of Afaia on the road down to Ayia Marina. The wonderful views through the trees down to the sea are complemented by the flavorsome rustic dishes served at this establishment. **Known for:** authentic Greek village fare; warm friendly service. $ *Average main: €11* ⊠ *Ayia Marina* ✛ *On the road from Afaia to Ayia Marina* ☎ *22970/32129.*

WHERE TO STAY

$ ⛉ **Hotel Apollo.** Take advantage of this hotel's beautiful hillside location
HOTEL over a beach by relaxing on the restaurant terrace or renting a boat to
Fodor's Choice water-ski in the clear blue waters; not surprisingly, guest rooms at this
★ gracefully aging hotel, built in a typical 1970s style, have balconies and most of them sea views. **Pros:** panoramic views of the Saronic Gulf; pool with saltwater; crystal sea waters set against a dramatic volcanic backdrop. **Cons:** room decor a bit on the spartan side; rocky beach; Wi-Fi doesn't cover all the hotel. $ *Rooms from: €80* ⊠ *Ayia Marina Beach* ☎ *22970/32271, 210/323–4292 Nov.–Mar.* ⊕ *www.apollohotel. gr* ☉ *Closed Nov.–Mar.* ⇝ *107 rooms* ⦿ *Breakfast.*

MARATHONAS ΜΑΡΑΘΩΝΑΣ

6 km (4 miles) south of Aegina Town.

This small village a few miles south of Aegina Town is reachable by bicycle or bus. The beach is just beyond.

BEACHES

Aeginitissa Beach. After Marathonas, Aeginitissa is a small, sandy bay with crystalline green waters surrounded by huge eucalyptus trees. The shallow water makes it accessible to novice swimmers. There's a bar, a beach volleyball court, and umbrellas and lounge chairs are available for

Be at the regal Ayios Nektarios Monastery on November 9 to see the saint's day celebration, when the streets are covered with carpets and strewn with flowers.

rent. **Amenities:** food and drink; showers; water sports. **Best for:** sunset; swimming. ✉ *Paliachora ✢ 7 km (4½ miles) south of Aegina Town.*

FAMILY **Marathonas Beach.** There's a good swimming spot at the sandy Marathonas A beach on the west side of the island. Beyond the village lies another nice beach, Marathonas B; both beaches get very busy during the summer months, and both have sun beds and umbrellas for rent, so be sure to arrive early if you want to beat the crowds (and pick the perfect spot!). **Amenities:** food and drink; lifeguards. **Best for:** sunset; swimming. ✉ *Marathon ☎ 22970/28160 Ammos Taverna, 22970/27677 Ostria Taverna.*

PERDIKA ΠΕΡΔΙΚΑ

9 km (5½ miles) south of Aegina Town.

Follow the lead of the locals and visiting Athenians and, for an excursion, take a bus (a 25-minute ride from Ethneyersias Square) to the pretty port village of Perdika to unwind and eat lunch at a seaside taverna. Places to eat in Perdika have multiplied over the years but are still low-key and have a strong island flavor, transporting you light-years away from the bustle of much of modern Greece. Try O Nontas, the first fish taverna after the bus station, for a meal on the canopied terrace overlooking the little bay, the sailing boats, and the islet of Moni. Antonis, the famous fish tavern, draws big-name Athenians year-round. Across the bay, and only a short walk away, stands the sole modern building of a camera obscura. Inside, the cylindrical chamber allows the light to enter and projects an inverted image of the landscape outside—a technique that is now thought to have been used by many celebrated artists, including Leonardo and Vermeer. It is definitely worth a visit.

EXPLORING

FAMILY Fodor's Choice ★ **Hellenic Wildlife Hospital** (*EKPAZ*). At the foot of Mt. Oros, half a mile southeast of the village of Pachia Rachi, the Hellenic Wildlife Hospital (EKPAZ) is a nonprofit institution, the oldest and largest wildlife rehabilitation center in Greece and southern Europe. It treats 2,000 wild animals from all over Greece every year, many of which are released back into the wild. You can visit the sanctuary and adopt a wild animal, such as Obelix, the wild boar, and a black vulture, the third-largest bird of prey in the world, for €50 per year. This wildlife hospital is one of the few that doesn't euthanize animals that are handicapped, caring for them into their old age. ✉ *Mt. Oros, Pachia Rachi* ☎ *22970/31338, 6979/914851* 🌐 *www.ekpaz.gr.*

BEACHES

Klima. A semisecluded sandy beach, Klima, which is just south of Perdika, has a finely pebbled bay of crystal-clear waters. To reach it, turn left at the intersection toward Sfentouri before entering Perdika, and then go right at the crossroads and continue until you reach Klima. It is also a popular destination for yachts. There's a beach bar that rents sun beds and umbrellas during the summer months. **Amenities:** food and drink. **Best for:** snorkeling; swimming. ✉ *Perdika* ✣ *10 km (6 miles) south of Aegina Town.*

Fodor's Choice ★ **Moni Beach.** In summer, caïques make frequent 10-minute trips from the fishing port of Perdika to the little island of Moni, a real heaven-on-earth inhabited only by peacocks, wild deer, relocated *kri-kri* (Cretan goats), and some remains of a 1960s campground. Shadowed by pine trees, hiking trails wind their way through the island's pristine landscape. Once the property of the Monastery of Chrysoleontissa, it is now a nature preserve. After your hike, take a most refreshing swim off the little sandy beach in the marvelously clear green waters by the quay. Note that the boatmen come back every hour, allowing you to leave whenever you wish (the round-trip ticket costs €5). A small beach bar operates in summer, offering cool drinks and toasted sandwiches, but if you plan to spend the day here, you would be better off bringing a full picnic lunch. In crowded peak season, Moni is a lovely way to escape the madding crowds. **Amenities:** food and drink. **Best for:** swimming; walking. ✉ *Moni.*

WHERE TO EAT

$$ SEAFOOD 🍴 **Antonis.** Seafood is the word at this famed taverna run by Antonis and his sons, and the octopus grilled in front of the establishment lures bathers and other visitors who tuck into options ranging from teeny fried smelt to enormous lobsters. People-watching is as much of a draw as the food, since the tables afford a view of all the comings and goings of the harbor's small boats as well as some sleek yachts. **Known for:** catch of the day from local fishermen; great harbor-front location. [$] *Average main: €15* ✉ *Perdika* ✣ *Waterfront* ☎ *22970/61443* 🌐 *www.antonisperdika.gr.*

FESTIVALS

Ayios Sostis. On September 6 and 7, the feast of the martyr Sozon is observed with a two-day *paniyiri* (saint's day festival), celebrated at the church of Ayios Sostis in Perdika. ✉ *Perdika ✚ 9 km (5½ miles) south of Aegina Town.*

HYDRA ΥΔΡΑ

139 km (86 miles) south of Aegina by ferry.

As the full length of Hydra stretches before you when you round the easternmost finger of the northern Peloponnese, your first reaction might not, in fact, be a joyful one. Gray, mountainous, and barren, Idra (to use its alternative spelling) has the gaunt look of a saintly figure in a Byzantine icon. But as the island's curved harbor—one of the most picturesque in all of Greece—comes into view, delight will no doubt take over. Because of the nearly round harbor, the town is only visible from a perpendicular angle, a quirk in the island's geography that often saved the island from attack, since passing ships completely missed the port. Although there are traces of an ancient settlement, the island was sparsely inhabited until the Ottoman period. Hydra took part in the Greek War of Independence, begun in 1821, by which time the island had developed an impressive merchant fleet, creating a surge in wealth and exposing traders to foreign cultures. Their trade routes stretched from the mainland to Asia Minor and even America.

In the middle of the 20th century the island became a haven for artists and writers like Arthur Miller, Canadian singer-songwriter Leonard Cohen, and the Norwegian novelist Axel Jensen. In the early 1960s, an Italian starlet named Sophia Loren emerged from Hydra's harbor waters in the Hollywood flick *Boy on a Dolphin*. The site of an annex of Athens's Fine Arts School, today Hydra remains a favorite haunt of new and established artists.

The arrival of world-famous contemporary art collector Dakis Joannou (who set up an exhibition space at the island's former slaughterhouse in 2009 for his DESTE Foundation) means that Hydra is now a magnet for today's chic art crowd. Every summer, the opening night of the Slaughterhouse is one of the art world's most coveted invitations; modern art lovers flock here to catch a glimpse of the most avant-garde artworks, refreshed by the Hydriot breeze. In summer there are ongoing art exhibitions in many venues around the island, from the town's schools (where curator Dimitrios Antonitsis organizes his annual collaborative Hydra School Projects) to the Melina Mercouri exhibition space right by the Hydra harbor, opposite the hydrofoil dock. The Hydra Workshop is a waterfront art space that puts together an annual exhibition inspired by the collection of London-based art patron Pauline Karpidas.

There are many reasons to love Hydra, not the least of which is the fact that all motor traffic is banned from the island (except for several rather noisy garbage trucks). After the racket of inner Athens and ear-splitting assaults on the eardrums by motorbikes in Aegina and Spetses, Hydra's blissful tranquility, especially off-season, is a cause for rejoicing.

GETTING HERE AND AROUND

At this writing the only ferry company that travels to Hydra is Hellenic Seaways. Due to high-season demand, it is essential to make reservations for boat tickets on weekends. It takes about 90 minutes to get to Hydra. These depart from Gate E8 or E9 in the port of Piraeus. There are eight departures per day during high season. Scheduled itineraries become scarcer during the winter months. The price of the ticket starts at €25.50 for economy class. You can get detailed information about departures on the websites ⊕ *www.hellenicseaways.gr* or ⊕ *www.ferries.gr.*

Famously, cars are not allowed on Hydra—and that means there are no public buses either! Mules are the time-honored and most practical mode of transportation up to the crest; you may see mules patiently hauling anything from armchairs and building materials to cases of beer. When you arrive, mule tenders in the port will rent you one of their fleet to carry your baggage—or better yet, you—to your hotel, for around €10 (be sure to agree on a price before you leave).

Other modes of transportation include water taxis and bicycles for rent—hotel concierges can give you information.

VISITOR INFORMATION

Contacts Hydra Tourist Information. ⊠ *Town Hall, Hydra Harbor, Hydra Town* ☎ *22980/53003, 22980/52184* ⊕ *www.hydra.gr.*

HYDRA TOWN ΥΔΡΑ ΠΟΛΗ

Even though Hydra's beautiful harbor is flush with bars and boutiques, Hydra Town seems as fresh and innocent as when it was "discovered." The two- and three-story gray-and-white houses with red tile roofs, many built from 1770 to 1821, climb the steep slopes around Hydra Town harbor. The noble port and houses have been rescued and placed on the Council of Europe's list of protected monuments, with strict ordinances regulating construction and renovation. Although Hydra has a landmass twice the size of Spetses, only a fraction is habitable, and after a day or so on the island, faces begin to look familiar—and not just because you saw them in last month's *Vanity Fair.*

EXPLORING

Church of the Dormition. Founded in 1643 as a monastery, the Church of the Dormition has since been dissolved and the monks' cells are now used to house municipal offices and the small ecclesiastical museum "Ayios Makarios Notaras." The church's most noticeable feature is an ornate, triple-tier bell tower made of Tinos marble, likely carved in the early 19th century by traveling artisans. There's also an exquisite marble iconostasis. ⊠ *Hydra Town ✛ Along central section of harbor front* ☎ *22980/54071 museum* ⊕ *www.imhydra.gr* ✍ *Church free (donations accepted), museum €2* ☉ *Museum closed Nov. 16–Mar. 31 and Mon. Apr.–Nov.*

Fodor's Choice ★   **Hydra Historical Archives and Museum.** Housed in an impressive mansion, this collection of historical artifacts and paintings has exhibits that date back to the 18th century. Heirlooms from the Balkan wars as well as from World War I and II are exhibited in the lobby. A small upstairs room contains figureheads from ships that fought in the 1821 War of Independence. There are old pistols and navigation aids, as well as portraits of the island's heroes and a section devoted to traditional local costume, including the dark *karamani* pantaloons worn by Hydriot men. Temporary art exhibits are also showcased from time to time. ⊠ *Hydra Town* ⊹ *On east end of harbor* ☏ *22980/52355* ⊕ *www.iamy.gr* ✉ *€5*.

Lazaros Koundouriotis Mansion. Impressed by the architecture they saw abroad, shipowners incorporated many of the foreign influences into their *archontika*, old, gray-stone mansions facing the harbor. The forbidding, fortresslike exteriors are deliberately austere, the combined result of the steeply angled terrain and the need for buildings to blend into the gray landscape. One of the finest examples of this Hydriot architecture is the Lazaros Koundouriotis Mansion, built in 1780 and beautifully restored in the 1990s as a branch of Greece's National Historical Museum. The interior is lavish, with hand-painted ceiling borders, gilt moldings, marquetry, and floors of black-and-white marble tiles. Some rooms have pieces that belonged to the Koundouriotis family, who played an important role in the War of Independence; other rooms have exhibits of costumes, jewelry, wood carvings, and pottery from the National Museum of Folk History. The basement level has three rooms full of paintings by Periklis Vyzantinos and his son, friends of the Koundouriotis family ⊠ *Hydra Town* ⊹ *On a graded slope above the port, on west headland* ☏ *22980/52421* ⊕ *www.nhmuseum.gr* ✉ *€4* ⊘ *Closed Nov.–Feb. and Mon. Mar.–Oct.*

Slaughterhouse/DESTE Foundation Project Space. Internationally renowned modern art collector Dakis Joannou acquired this former Hydra slaughterhouse, a leisurely 10-minute walk from the town (toward Mandraki), in 2009 to host artistic events and projects organized by his budding DESTE Foundation. Surprisingly, this is not what one might expect a chic and modern art gallery to look like: housed in an unassuming small building on a cliff by the sea, it can be missed if you don't actively look for it. But perhaps that is exactly the point that Joannou wanted to make with the Slaughterhouse, which has already acquired a leading role in Hydra's cultural life. Starting with the 2009 multimedia project "Blood of Two" by Matthew Barney and Elizabeth Peyton (which paid homage to the space's morbid past), every summer the space is now assigned to a different artist who is invited to stage a site-specific exhibition. Since then Doug Aitken, Urs Fischer, Paul Chan, Pawel Althamer, and Kara Walker, among others, have had works and installations exhibited there. ⊠ *Hydra Town* ⊹ *10-min walk east of the port, toward Mandraki* ☏ *210/275–8490* ⊕ *www.deste.gr*.

SEEING HYDRA'S MONASTERIES

If you're staying for more than a day, you have time to explore Hydra's monasteries. Hire a mule (the donkey rank is located just outside the Alpha Bank in the western corner of Hydra's harbor; be sure to check prices with the muleteers first, as these can soar to more than €70 for some routes) for the ascent up Mt. Klimaki, where you can visit the **Profitis Ilias Monastery** (about two hours by mule from Hydra Town) and view the embroidery work of an inhabitant of the nearby nunnery of **Ayia Efpraxia**. Experienced hikers might be tempted to set off for the **Zourvas Monastery** at Hydra's tip. It's a long and difficult hike, but compensation comes in the form of spectacular views and a secluded cove for a refreshing dip.

An alternative: hire a water taxi to Zourvas.

The convent of **Ayios Nikolaos Monastery** is to the southeast of Hydra Town, after you pass between the monasteries of Ayios Triadas and Ayias Matronis (the latter can be visited). Stop here for a drink and a sweet (a donation is appropriate), and to see the beautiful 16th-century icons and frescoes in the sanctuary. When hiking, wear sturdy walking shoes, and in summer start out early in the morning—even when traveling by mule—to minimize exposure to the midday sun. Your reward: stunning vistas over the island (resplendent with wildflowers and herbs in spring), the western and eastern coasts, and nearby islets on the way to area monasteries.

BEACHES

Beaches are not the island's main attraction; the only sandy beach on Hydra is at Mandraki, east of Hydra Town. There are small, shallow coves at Kamini and Vlichos, both west of the harbor. And a few mostly pebble beaches are found on the southern coast, also reachable by water taxi.

At Hydroneta beach bar and café, just underneath the Hydriot cannons, the gray crags have been blasted and laid with cement to form sundecks. Sunbathing, socializing at the cocktail bar, and the views of the harbor may take priority over swimming, but old-timers can attest to the fact that diving off the rocks into the deep water is truly exhilarating, and it's the closest spot to Hydra Town where you can take a refreshing dip.

Ayios Nikolaos. Boats ferry bathers from Hydra Town harbor near the Mitropolis church to pebble beaches on the island's southern coast, the best of which is Ayios Nikolaos, where there are sun beds and umbrellas for a charge (starting at €3) and you can also rent canoes. Ayios Nikolaos is located on the south side of the island, facing the Aegean Sea, and it is the largest organized beach on the island. It is mostly pebbled with some small sandy stretches that are ideal for children's play. The large boats heading to and from here have set fees (to Ayios Nikolaos from Hydra Town is €8); water taxis, whose rates you should negotiate in advance, start at €12. **Amenities:** food and drink; water sports. **Best for:** snorkeling; swimming.

Hydra is a shore thing—who needs a beach when you have waters as electric-blue as this?

WHERE TO EAT

$$$
MEDITERRANEAN
Fodor's Choice
★

×**Omilos.** The spot where Aristotle Onassis and Maria Callas once danced is now a vision in minimalist island white, now run by one of Enalion's owners. Tables nestle in the small, high-ceilinged Hydra Nautical Club and wind around the deck outside, which affords an exquisite sea view. **Known for:** excellent service; popular with visiting high society. $ *Average main: €35* ✉ *Hydra port* ✛ *On the way to Hydronetta* ☎ *22980/53800* ⊕ *www.omilos-hydra.com* ☉ *Closed Mon.–Thurs. Oct.–Apr.*

$$
GREEK

×**To Geitoniko.** Christina and Manolis, the former owners, have now passed the baton to their son Constantinos, who has elevated the home-style Greek dishes served here, in a typical old Hydriot house with stone floors and wooden ceilings, where time seems to have been standing still since the 1950s. If it's available, try the fresh fish that is prepared to perfection, but check the prices so you don't have any surprises. **Known for:** popular with the discerning locals; cool roof terrace dining; tasty Greek food. $ *Average main: €15* ✉ *Spiliou Harami* ✛ *Opposite Pension Antonis* ☎ *22980/53615* ▭ *No credit cards* ☉ *No lunch Sept.–June; no dinner Dec.–mid-Apr.*

WHERE TO STAY

$$
HOTEL

🛏 **Angelica Hotel.** A three-minute walk from Hydra's bustling port, this alluring place is composed of two villas in Hydra stone, with red barrel-tile roofs and garden areas; both have been restored and renovated to a high standard. **Pros:** the Jacuzzi on the veranda (free use for VIP Villa rooms); generously sized rooms; friendly owners. **Cons:** no elevator; limited variety of breakfast options; slow Wi-Fi.

Continued on page 164

EAT LIKE A GREEK

Hailed for its healthfulness, heartiness, and eclectic spicing, Greek cuisine remains one of the country's greatest gifts to visitors. From gyros to galaktoboureko, moussaka to myzthira, and soutzoukakia to snails, food in Greece is rich, exotic, and revelatory.

To really enjoy communal meals of fresh fish, mama's casseroles, flavorful salads, house wine, and great conversation, keep two ground rules in mind.

what the day's catch is (you can often inspect it in the kitchen). Note that waiters in Greece tend to be impatient—so don't waffle while you're ordering.

ORDER LIKE A NATIVE
Go for *tis oras* (grilled fish and meat "of the hour") or *piato tis imeras* (or "plate of the day," often stews, casseroles, and pastas). Remember that fish is always expensive, but avoid frozen selections and go for the freshest variety by asking the waitstaff

DINE LIKE A FAMILY
Greeks share big plates of food, often piling bites of *mezedes*, salads, and main dishes on small dishes. It's okay to stick your fork into communal platters but not in each other's personal dishes (unless you're family or dear friends).

(top) lunching alfresco; (bottom) Kadalee with cinnamon

GRECIAN BOUNTY

Can't understand the menu? Just point!

Greece is a country of serious eaters, which is why there are so many different kinds of eateries here. Here is a list of types to seek out.

Estiatorio: You'll often find fine tablecloths, carefully placed silverware, candles, and multipage menus at an *estiatorio*, or restaurant; menus range from traditional to nouvelle.

Oinomageirio: Now enjoying a retro resurgence, these simple eateries were often packed with blue-collar workers filling up on casseroles and listening to *rembetika*, Greece's version of the blues.

Taverna: This is vintage Greece—family-style eateries noted for great spreads of grilled meat *tis oras* (of the hour), thick-cut fried potatoes, dips, salads, and wine—all shared around a big table and with a soundtrack of *bouzouki* music.

Psarotaverna: Every bit like a regular taverna, except the star of the menu is fresh fish. Remember that fish usually comes whole; if you want it filleted, ask "*Mporo na exo fileto?*" Typical fish varieties include *barbounia* (red mullet), *perka* (perch), *sardella* (sardine), *bakaliaros* (cod), *lavraki* (sea bass), and *tsipoura* (sea bream).

Mezedopoleia: In this Greek version of tapas bars, you can graze on a limited menu of dips, salads, and hot and cold mezedes. Wildly popular with the pre-nightclub crowd.

Ouzeri and Rakadiko: *Ouzo* and the Cretan firewater *raki* (also known as *tsikoudia*) are the main attractions here, but there's always a generous plate of hot or cold mezedes to go with the spirits. A mix of old-timers and young scenesters make for great people-watching.

Kafeneio (café): Coffee rules here—but the food menu is usually limited to sandwiches, crepes, *tiropites* (cheese pies), and *spanakopites* (spinach pies).

Zacharoplasteio (patisserie): Most dessert shops are "to go," but some old-style spots have a small klatch of tables to enjoy coffee and that fresh slice of *galaktoboureko* (custard in phyllo dough).

FOR THOSE ON THE GO

Greeks are increasingly eating on the run, since they're working longer (right through the afternoon siesta that used to be a mainstay) and happy that eateries have adapted to this lifestyle change. *Psitopoleia* (grill shops) have the most popular takeaway food: the wrapped-in-pita *souvlaki* (pork, lamb, or chicken chunks), *gyros* (slow-roasted slabs of pork and lamb, or chicken), or *kebabs* (spiced, grilled ground meat). Tzatziki, onions, tomatoes, and fried potatoes are also tucked into the pita. Toasted sandwiches and tasty hot dogs are other satisfying options.

Gyros: a take-away treat

ON THE GREEK TABLE

Mezedes Μεζέδες (appetizers): Eaten either as a first course or as full meals, they can be hot (pickled octopus, chickpea fritters, dolmades, fried squid) or cold (dips like *tzatziki; taramosalata*, puree of salted mullet roe and potato; or the spicy whipped feta called *htipiti*). Start with two or three, then keep ordering to your heart's content.

Tzatziki (cucumber in yogurt)

Salata Σαλάτα (salad): No one skips salads here since the vegetables burst with flavor, texture, and aroma. The most popular is the *horiatiki*, or what the rest of the world calls a "Greek salad"—this country-style salad has tomato, onion, cucumber, feta, and Kalamata olives. Other popular combos include *maroulosalata* (lettuce tossed with fresh dill and fennel) and the Cretan *dakos* (bread rusks topped with minced tomato, feta, and onion).

Horiatiki (Greek salad)

Kyrios Piato Κύριο Πιάτο (main course): Main dishes were once served family-style, like mezedes, but the plates are now offered as single servings at many restaurants. Some places serve the dishes as they are ready while more Westernized eateries bring all the plates out together. Order all your food at the same time, but be sure to tell the waiter if you want your main dishes to come after the salads and mezedes. Most grilled meat dishes come with a side of thick-cut fried potatoes, while seafood and casseroles such as *moussaka* are served alone. *Horta*, or boiled greens, drenched in lemon, are the ideal side for grilled or fried fish.

Sardines with rice, potatoes, and salad

Epidorpio Επιδόρπιο (dessert): Most restaurants give diners who have finished their meals a free plate of fresh seasonal fruit or some homemade *halva* (a cinnamony semolina pudding-cake with raisins).

Krassi Κρασί (wine): Greeks almost always have wine with a meal, usually sharing a carafe or two of *hima* (barrel or house wine) with friends. Bitter resinated wine, or *retsina*, has become less common in restaurants. Instead, the choice is often a dry Greek white wine that goes well with seafood or poultry.

Moussaka

Psomi Ψωμί (bread): Bread, often pita-fashion, always comes with a meal and usually costs 1 to 2 euros—a *kouver* (cover) charge—regardless of whether you eat it.

Nero Νερό (water): If you ask for water, waitstaff will usually bring you a big bottle of it—and charge you, of course. If you simply want tap water (free and safe to drink) ask for a *kanata*—or a pitcher.

Galaktoboureko (custard-filled phyllo pastry)

LIKE MAMA USED TO MAKE

Nearly all Greek restaurants have the same homey dishes that have graced family dinner tables here for years. However, some of these dishes are hardly ever ordered by locals, who prefer to eat them at home—most Greeks just avoid moussaka and pastitsio unless they're made fresh that day. So if you order the following foods at restaurants, make sure to ask if they're fresh ("*tis imeras*").

■ **DOLMADES**—grape leaves stuffed with rice and herbs

■ **KOTOPOULO LEMONATO** —whole chicken roasted with thickly sliced potatoes, lemon, and oregano

■ **MOUSSAKA**—a casserole of eggplant and spiced beef topped with béchamel

■ **PASTITSIO**—tube-shaped pasta baked with spiced beef, béchamel, and cheese

Best bet: Grape leaves

■ **PSARI PLAKI**—whole fish baked with tomato, onions, garlic, and olive oil

■ **SOUPA AVGOLEMONO**— an egg-lemon soup with a chicken stock base

COFFEE CULTURE

Greek coffee: tiny but strong

A *kafeneio* coffeehouse

Greeks go out for coffee not because of caffeine addiction but because they like to spend at least two hours mulling the world with their friends. *Kafeneia*, or old-style coffeehouses, are usually full of courtly old men playing backgammon and sipping tiny but strong cups of *elliniko* (Greek coffee). Modern cafés (*kafeterias*) are more chic, packed with frappé-loving office workers, freddo-swilling college

students, and arty hipsters nursing espressos. Order your coffee *sketos* (without sugar), *metrios* (medium sweet), or *glykos* (sweet).

■ **Frappé**—a frothy blend of instant coffee (always Nescafé), cold water, sugar, and evaporated milk

■ **Elliniko**—the strong traditional coffee made from Brazilian beans ground into a fine powder

Frappé

■ **Freddo**—an iced cappuccino or espresso

■ **Nes**—instant coffee, often served with froth

Ⓢ *Rooms from: €130* ✉ *Andrea Miaouli 43* ☎ *22980/53202* ⊕ *www. angelica.gr* ↻ *21 rooms* ⓘⓞ *Breakfast.*

$$$$
HOTEL

▦ **Bratsera Hotel.** An 1860 sponge factory was transformed into this charming character hotel (doors made out of old packing crates still bearing the "Piraeus sponge" stamp, etc.), which has a bevy of alluring delights, including guest-room decor accented with framed portraits, old engravings, four-poster ironwork beds, and cozy natural wood lofts, and the hotel restaurant—considered one of the island's best—which is set in the oleander-and-bougainvillea-graced courtyard. **Pros:** helpful staff; the relaxing-by-the-pool experience; free Wi-Fi. **Cons:** some basic, tired rooms; some small dark bathrooms; patchy Wi-Fi in some of the rooms. Ⓢ *Rooms from: €290* ✉ *Hydra Town* ✛ *On left of port up Tompazi, then follow the alley straight ahead as Tompazi veers to the right* ☎ *22980/53971, 22980/52794 restaurant* ⊕ *www.bratserahotel. com* ☺ *Closed mid-Oct.–Mar.* ↻ *25 rooms* ⓘⓞ *Breakfast.*

$$
B&B/INN
Fodor'sChoice
★

▦ **Cotommatae 1810 Guesthouse.** This old mansion has been refurbished into a lovely boutique hotel by a descendant of the original owners, a wealthy and well-known Hydriot shipping family, without losing its original charm. **Pros:** relaxing, elegant atmosphere; easy walking distance from the port; welcoming staff. **Cons:** no swimming pool, just a small plunge pool in the garden; no sea views; slow Internet at times. Ⓢ *Rooms from: €200* ✉ *Votsi* ☎ *22980/53873* ⊕ *www.cotommatae.gr* ↻ *7 rooms* ⓘⓞ *Breakfast.*

$$$
HOTEL

▦ **Hotel Hydra.** In an idyllic setting, this boutique hotel with eight relaxing, modern, and beautifully decorated guest suites offers panoramic views of the port and separate living and bedroom areas (as well as a small kitchenette). **Pros:** suites feel more like small apartments rather than rooms; friendly host; fast Wi-Fi. **Cons:** about 150 steps to get to the hotel from the port; not all rooms have great panoramic views of the harbor; need to book far in advance to get a room with the best view. Ⓢ *Rooms from: €250* ✉ *Petrou Voulgari 8* ✛ *Close to the Lazaros Koundouriotis mansion* ☎ *22980/53420* ⊕ *www.hydra-hotel.gr* ☺ *Closed Nov.–late Mar.* ↻ *8 rooms* ⓘⓞ *Breakfast.*

$$
HOTEL

▦ **Hotel Leto Hydra.** Right in the middle of Hydra Town, this small upscale hotel has sparkling interiors with an elegant "old Greece" touch provided by an array of antique Hydriot rugs, mirrors, and lanterns—and some modern artworks by well-known Greek painters (Papanikolaou and Akrithakis to name two) thrown in to liven things up. **Pros:** the distinguished feel of an old mansion; spacious, shady rooms; marble bathrooms. **Cons:** a bit pricey; no views and no significant outside spaces; can be difficult to find on your own (ask for directions at the port). Ⓢ *Rooms from: €150* ✉ *Corner of Miaouli and Mandrakiou-Molou* ☎ *22980/53385* ⊕ *www.letohydra.gr* ☺ *Closed Nov.–mid-Mar.* ↻ *30 rooms* ⓘⓞ *Breakfast.*

$$
B&B/INN

▦ **Miranda Hotel.** Antiques lovers might feel right at home among the 18th- and 19th-century furniture and decor (Oriental rugs, wooden chests, nautical engravings, ceilings painted in detailed Venetian motifs) decorating this traditional Hydriot home, now a gracious small hotel. **Pros:** peaceful garden; precious artworks on display; lovely breakfast with homemade elements. **Cons:** somewhat dated and smallish rooms;

thin doors do not provide enough sound insulation; the cramped bathrooms could do with a makeover. [$] *Rooms from: €140* ⊠ *Miaouli* ✛ *2 blocks inland from port center* ☎ *22980/52230* ⊕ *www.mirandahotel. gr* ⊗ *Closed Nov.–Feb.* ⤴ *14 rooms* ⟮◎⟯ *Breakfast.*

$$
B&B/INN
Fodor's Choice
★

⊡ **Orloff Boutique Hotel.** Commissioned in 1796 by Catherine the Great for her lover Count Orloff—who came to Greece with a Russian fleet to try to dislodge the Turks—this *archontiko* mansion retains its splendor now that it has been turned into a small boutique hotel. **Pros:** homey feeling with lovely decor; friendly owners; excellent breakfast. **Cons:** slightly noisy air-conditioning; no balconies; minimum two-night stay. [$] *Rooms from: €165* ⊠ *Rafalia 9 and Votsi* ✛ *350 feet from the port* ☎ *22980/52564* ⊕ *www.orloff.gr* ⊗ *Closed Nov.–Mar.* ⤴ *9 rooms* ⟮◎⟯ *Breakfast.*

FESTIVALS

Its image as a weekend destination has made Hydra a popular venue for all sorts of events, from trail races and art exhibitions to sailing events and regattas. Exhibitions, concerts, and performances are usually held from June through August to coincide with the busy summer season. The international *rembetika* (Greek blues) music festival takes place here in October. Plus the new and ever-growing contemporary art scene here is sure to be highlighted with happenings that will draw an international art crowd.

FAMILY
Fodor's Choice
★

Hydra's Trail Event. During one long weekend in April the whole of Hydra lives and breathes trail running. The locals have embraced the vertical trail race that sees runners starting at the top of the mountain by the monastery of Profitis Hlias (individual starts every minute ensure their safety) and finishing after a steep downhill 3.2 km (2 miles) later, in the heart of the harbor. Other trail races and plenty of side activities take place, too, most of them good for kids. ⊠ *Hydra Town* ☎ *6932/271106* ⊕ *www.hydrastrail.gr.*

Fodor's Choice
★

Miaoulia. The island celebrates its crucial role in the War of Independence with the Miaoulia, which takes place the last weekend of June. At around 10 o'clock on Saturday night, Hydra's small port goes dark, and a journey into history commences as the day's festivities culminate in a reenactment of the night Admiral Miaoulis loaded a vessel with explosives and sent it upwind to the Turkish fleet back in 1821. Naturally, the model enemy's ship goes down in flames. Fireworks, music, traditional dancing, treasure hunts, and sports competitions all accompany the burning of the fleet, a glorious part of Hydra's Naval Week. ⊠ *Hydra Town.*

NIGHTLIFE

Bars often change names, ownership, and music—if not location—so check with your hotel for what's in vogue.

Amalour. On the first floor of an early 19th-century mansion, Amalour attracts millennials who sip expertly made and reasonably priced cocktails (especially the exquisite daiquiris) and listen to ethnic, jazz, soul, and funk music. ⊠ *Tombazi* ✛ *Behind the port* ☎ *22980/53775.*

Andy's Bar. Greek music jam sessions are hosted here. ⊠ *Hydra Town* ✛ *West of harbor* ☎ *6944/541374.*

Beach Club Spilia. Tucked into the seaside rocks just below the Hydroneta bar, Spilia provides a nice escape from the midday sun and is a popular nocturnal haunt, too. The view toward the port is impressive and the deck chairs are comfortable. The steps down to the refreshing sea are especially inviting on hot summer days, which means you can end up spending a whole day here without realizing it, enjoying coffee, nibbles, and then drinks. ⊠ *Hydra Town* ⊹ *After Omilos, on the way to the Cannons* ☎ *22980/54166.*

Hydroneta. The minuscule Hydroneta bar-restaurant has an enchanting view from its perch above the harbor. Embraced by rocks and surrounded by water, it is jam-packed during the day, and it is *the* place to enjoy a glass of chilled beer or fruity long drink at sunset. Hydroneta's trademark events are its "Full Moon" parties, fun-filled events under Hydra's starlit skies. ⊠ *Hydroneta Beach* ⊹ *West of Hydra Town, on the way to Kamini, past the Canons* ☎ *22980/54160* ⊕ *www.hydronetta.gr.*

Papagalos. On the western tip of the harbor toward Mandraki, where the first disco club of the island used to be, Papagalos is a cocktail and tapas bar (created by the owners of locally renowned Amalour) with a panoramic view of the harbor action. Rock and ethnic music are the staples on the decks, while live events are held here on a regular basis. Free Wi-Fi is available. ⊠ *Harbor front* ☎ *22980/52626.*

Fodor'sChoice **The Pirate Bar.** Café-bar Pirate has been a fixture of the island's nightlife
★ since the mid-1970s. Over the years, it's gotten face-lifts, added some mainstream dance hits to its onetime rock music–only playlist, and remains popular and raucous. The spot is actually open all day with delicious home-cooked dishes (burgers, salads, and lemon pies) but it is at night that the fun really takes off, often with the help of one of the popular house drinks, such as the fruity Tropical Sun. ⊠ *Hydra Town* ⊹ *South end of harbor* ☎ *22980/52711.*

SHOPPING

A number of elegant shops (some of them offshoots of Athens stores) sell fashionable and amusing clothing and jewelry, though you won't save much by shopping here.

Elena Votsi. Worth a visit, the stylish store of local jewelry designer Elena Votsi showcases her exquisite handmade pieces—more works of art than accessories—which sell well in Europe and New York. She was the creator of the 2004 Athens Olympic medals and the design has been used in all subsequent games. ⊠ *Ikonomou 3* ☎ *22980/52637* ⊕ *www.elenavotsi.com.*

Fodor'sChoice **The Hydra Trading Company and the Hydra Gallery.** French mother-and-
★ son team Veronique and Tom Powell (himself a talented painter) have created an eclectic boutique/gallery offering a wide selection of pure white linen, ceramics in all shades of Aegean blue, lucky charms, and household items exuding island chic and a bit of country flair. Painting exhibitions are also organized regularly in this charming third-floor shop. ⊠ *Old police station* ☎ *22980/29700.*

Speak Out Hydra. This boutique is so hip the owners run an art and fashion blog (speakouthydra.blogspot.com). Most of the stock is by up-and-coming Greek designers. ⌧ *Harbor front* ☏ *22980/52099* ⊕ *www.speakout-hydra.com.*

Spoiled! Hydra's trendoisie head to Spoiled! for a top selection of glamorous evening togs in the latest fashion. ⌧ *Tombazi* ☏ *22980/52363* ⊕ *www.spoiled.gr.*

Studio Hydra. Not simply your typical tourist gift shop, this is a treasure trove of stylish fashion finds, chic mementos, and even dreamy Hydra watercolors. ⌧ *Harbor front* ☏ *22980/52132.*

Fodor'sChoice ★ **Tsagkaris Hydriot Macaroons.** Don't leave Hydra without some traditional almond macaroons in your suitcase. The Tsagkaris family, led by octogenarian matriarch Anna Tsagkari, have been lovingly making them in their workshop for more than 70 years. ⌧ *Miaouli ⊕ 100 feet from the harbor front* ☏ *22980/52314.*

SPORTS AND THE OUTDOORS
HORSEBACK RIDING

Fodor'sChoice ★ **Harriet's Hydra Horses.** Discover Hydra by riding one of Harriet's goodnatured horses; the friendly Hydra native leads rides over the island's brown/gray arid mountains to mysterious monasteries and gorgeous beaches. Prices start at €25 (plus tax) for a 60-minute clip to Kaminia village, suitable for all levels. ⌧ *Hydra Town ⊕ 300 feet from harbor, past Phaedra Hotel* ☏ *6980/323347.*

SCUBA DIVING

Hydra Diving Center. For those who love the great outdoors, snorkeling and scuba diving in the rocky seabeds of Hydra, especially around the Bay of Bisti, could be a highlight of a Greek vacation. Diving tuition is available, too. The center is located at the back of taverna Enalion, in Vlichos, whose owner, Yiannis Kitsos, also passionately runs the dive school. His boat can also pick up divers from Hydra's port. ⌧ *Taverna Enalion* ☏ *6977/792493* ⊕ *www.hydra.com.gr/diving-center.*

KAMINI KAMINI

1 km (mile) west of Hydra Town.

A small fishing hamlet built around a shallow inlet, Kamini has much of Hydra Town's charm but none of its bustle—except on Orthodox Good Friday, when the entire island gathers here to follow the funerary procession of Christ. On a clear day, the Peloponnese coast is plainly visible across the water, and spectacular at sunset. Take the 20-minute stroll from Hydra Town west; a paved coastal track gives way to a staggered, white path lined with fish tavernas; Kamini's small beach also has restaurants nearby, which you can spot arriving by boat or sea taxi.

BEACHES

FAMILY **Mikro Kamini.** Kamini's small gray-pebbled beach, known as Mikro Kamini, is about 1,000 feet beyond the sleepy fishing port, just in front of the Castello Bar & Restaurant, where you can rent sun beds and umbrellas. There are more tavernas nearby, from where you can spot arriving boats and water taxis. The water here is calm and shallow, so the beach is good for families with small children. **Amenities:** food and drink. **Best for:** swimming; walking.

WHERE TO EAT

$$$

MEDITERRANEAN

Fodor's Choice

★

✕ **Castello Bar and Restaurant.** Set right on Mikro Kamini, a leisurely 15-minute walk from the port (or 5 minutes by mule or 1 minute by water taxi), this fully renovated 18th-century fortress is a popular bar-restaurant offering some of the most fortifying dining on the island. Castello is the only place where you can find sushi, or if you are craving a snack, try the whole-wheat pizza with pesto sauce. **Known for:** gourmet Mediterranean food; stunning views from the old fortress; sophisticated yet laid-back atmosphere. $ *Average main: €27* ☎ *22980/54101* ⊕ *www.castellohydra.gr* ⊗ *Closed Dec.–Feb.*

$$$

SEAFOOD

✕ **Kodylenia's Taverna.** Kodylenia's Taverna looks like a whitewashed fisherman's cottage on a promontory overlooking the little harbor of Kamini, with a veranda terrace charmingly set with folkloric pennants and communal tables—it's the perfect perch to catch some sublime sunsets. It is also an irresistibly alluring (if a little pricey) place that has enraptured town folk and off-duty billionaires alike. **Known for:** whole grilled fish; kirtamos (rock samphire); squid in tomato sauce. $ *Average main: €26* ✛ *On the headland above Kamini harbor* ☎ *22980/53520* ⊕ *www.hydra-kodylenia.gr* ⊗ *Closed Nov.–Feb.*

$$

MEDITERRANEAN

✕ **Pirofani.** The half-Greek, half-Danish host of this taverna in Kamini, the second-largest village in Hydra, likes to cook for and entertain all his visitors himself. Being the life of the party that he is, by the time you leave after a heartening dinner, you will feel as if you've made a new friend. **Known for:** hangout for island's artists; good-humored eccentricities of the owner; spontaneous outbreaks of live music and dance. $ *Average main: €25* ☎ *22980/53175* ⊕ *www.pirofani.com* ⊗ *Closed Mon. and Tues. and Oct.–Apr.*

VLICHOS ΒΛΥΧΟΣ

6 km (4 miles) west of Hydra Town.

From Kamini, the coastal track continues to Vlichos, another pretty village with tavernas, a historic bridge, and a gray-pebbled beach on a bay. It's a 5-minute water-taxi ride from the Hydra Town port or a 40-minute walk (25 minutes past Kamini).

BEACHES

FAMILY

Vlichos Beach. This scenic little gray-pebble beach west of Kamini is a good dive destination (ask at Enalion taverna) as well as a nice swimming spot for families due to its shallow waters. Sun beds and umbrellas can be rented from the beachfront tavernas. **Amenities:** food and drink. **Best for:** swimming; walking. ✉ *Vlichos.*

WHERE TO EAT

$$

MEDITERRANEAN

Fodor's Choice

★

✕ **Enalion.** The charming young trio of owners—Yiannis, Kostas, and Alexandros—have imbued this beach taverna just 100 feet from Vlichos Beach with energy and attentive service. The traditional taverna fare includes favorite Greek dishes like fried tomato balls, beet salad, fried calamari, and stuffed tomatoes and peppers, which all go perfectly with a glass of house wine or a cold beer. **Known for:** tasty Greek fare; large portions; friendly service. $ *Average main: €18* ✉ *Vlichos* ☎ *22980/53455* ⊕ *www.enalion-hydra.gr* ⊗ *Closed Dec.–Mar.*

WHERE TO STAY

$$$$ 🏨 **Four Seasons Luxury Suites.** No, this is not one of the famous chain's
HOTEL hotels but rather a tiny hotel inspired by the magical colors of the four
seasons (the Sun Suite is the cream of the crop) sweetly set in an atmospheric, fully renovated 150-year-old stone mansion. **Pros:** alluring interiors; next to the beach; excellent à la carte breakfast. **Cons:** challenging
distance from town; slightly expensive for Hydra; limited number of
suites. $ *Rooms from: €380* ✉ *Vlichos Beach* ☎ *22980/53698* ⊕ *www.
fourseasonshydra.gr* ⊗ *Closed Nov.–late Mar.* ↵ *6 rooms* ⊙ *Breakfast.*

MANDRAKI ΜΑΝΔΡΑΚΙ

4 km (1 miles) east of Hydra Town.

The only sandy beach on Hydra is an activity-centered beach by the
Miramare Hotel, near Mandraki, which is currently closed (but you can
still visit the beach with one of the boats or water taxis that regularly
depart from Hydra Town; the nearby taverna is also open).

BEACHES

Mandraki Beach. One of the few sandy beaches of Hydra, Mandraki is a
leisurely 2-km (1-mile) walk west of the town, but you can also come
here by small boat or water taxi from the main port. The hotel right on
the beach (Miramare Hotel) is closed, but you can still enjoy the fine
sand and the sun beds. More amenities (such as water sports) should
be available once the hotel reopens. **Amenities:** food and drink. **Best
for:** swimming; walking. ✉ *Mandraki, Hydra Town.*

SPETSES ΣΠΕΤΣΕΣ

24 km (15 miles) southwest of Hydra.

Spetses shows evidence of continuous habitation through all of antiquity. From the 16th century BC, settlers came over from the mainland
and, as on Hydra, they soon began to look to the sea, building their
own boats. They became master sailors, successful merchants, and fear-
some pirates, and later, during the Napoleonic Wars, they were skilled
blockade runners, earning fortunes that they poured into building larger
boats and grander houses. With the outbreak of the War of Independence in 1821, the Spetsiots dedicated their best ships and brave men
(and women) to the cause.

In the years leading up to the revolution, Hydra's great rival and ally
was the island of Spetses. Lying at the entrance to the Argolic gulf, off
the mainland, Spetses was known even in antiquity for its hospitable
soil and verdant pine tree–covered slopes. The pines on the island today,
however, were planted by a Spetsiot philanthropist dedicated to restor-
ing the beauty stripped by the shipbuilding industry in the 18th and
19th centuries. There are far fewer trees than there were in antiquity,
but the island is still well watered, and prosperous Athenians who have
made Spetses their second home compete to have the prettiest gardens
and terraces. Today's visitor can enjoy spotting this verdant beauty all
over the island.

GETTING HERE AND AROUND

Hellenic Seaways' Flying Dolphins hydrofoils and catamarans travel regularly, year-round, from Piraeus (Gate E8 or E9) to Spetses (usually stopping at Poros and Hydra as well). There are half a dozen such daily rounds from April to October, and fewer the rest of the year. You can get to Spetses (€38.50 economy) in just under two hours. Make reservations ahead of time—boats fill quickly. You can get detailed info about departure times on ⊕ *www.hellenicseaways.gr.*

The island of Spetses is so close to the Peloponnese mainland that you also can drive to the small port of Kosta (200 km [124 miles] from Athens), park your car, and ferry across the channel in any of a number of caïques (price at around €5 per person, but you have to wait for the boat to fill up before it leaves for the 20-minute crossing). You can also take a water taxi on demand 24 hours a day (€23 for the five-minute crossing). For water taxi information, call ☎ 22980/72072.

Only homeowners are usually allowed to bring cars onto the island. Visitors must rent bikes, scooters, or mopeds, hire water taxis or carriages, or use one of the two high-season-only (June 15–September) municipal buses: one bus line goes from Ayios Mamas Beach to Ayioi Anargyroi and Ayia Paraskevi; the other, with regular departures during the day, from Poseidonion Grand Hotel to Ligoneri and Vrellos beach. Tickets range from €1 to €3. For bus schedule information you can contact the two bus drivers directly on their cell phones (for Ayios Mamas and Ayioi Anargyroi, call Anargyros Kotzias at ☎ 69/4480–2536; for Ligoneri and Vrellos, call Konstantinos Mouratis at ☎ 69/7894–9722). It is worth going on one of the buses if only for the scenic route.

VISITOR INFORMATION

Contacts Spetses Tourist Information. ✉ *Town hall, Spetses Town* ☎ *22980/72255, 22983/20010 info line (daily 8–3)* ⊕ *www.spetses.gr.*

SPETSES TOWN ΣΠΕΤΣΕΣ ΠΟΛΗ

91 km (56 miles) southwest of Hydra.

By most visitors' standards, Spetses Town is small—no larger than most city neighborhoods—yet it's nevertheless divided into districts populated with many well-to-do neoclassical mansions and 19th-century villas. You will arrive in Dapia, the modern harbor. Kastelli, the oldest quarter, extends toward Profitis Ilias and is marked by the 18th-century Ayia Triada Church, the town's highest point. The area along the coast to the north is known as Kounoupitsa, a residential district of pretty cottages and gardens with pebble mosaics in mostly nautical motifs.

EXPLORING

Anargyrios and Korgialenios School. Known as the inspiration for the school in John Fowles's *The Magus*, this institution was established in 1927 as an English-style boarding school for the children of Greece's Anglophile wealthy elite. Until 2010, tourism management students studied amid the elegant amphitheaters, black-and-white-tile floors, and huge windows. Today, the buildings are used for conferences, private seminars, and summer schools. Nevertheless, visitors can still take a peek (free) inside the school and stroll around the fabulous gardens throughout the year. ⊠ *Spetses Town* ✛ *½ km (¼ mile) west of Dapia* ☎ *22980/74306* ⊕ *www.akss.gr.*

Ayios Mamas. The town's stone promontory is the site of the little 19th-century church, Ayios Mamas—take your photos from a distance as the church is privately owned and often locked. Bring a swimsuit, as the beach here is great for a dip. ⊠ *Spetses Town* ✛ *Above the harbor.*

Fodor'sChoice
★
Bouboulina's Museum. In front of a small park is Bouboulina's House, now a museum, where you can take a 45-minute guided tour (available in English) and learn about this interesting heroine's life. Laskarina Bouboulina was the bravest of all Spetsiot revolutionaries, the daughter of a Hydriot sea captain, and the wife—then widow—of two more sea captains. Left with a considerable inheritance and nine children, she dedicated herself to increasing her already substantial fleet and fortune. On her flagship, the *Agamemnon,* the largest in the Greek fleet at the time, she sailed into war against the Ottomans at the head of the Spetsiot ships. Her fiery temper led to her death in a family feud many years later. It's worth visiting the mansion, which is run by her fourth-generation grandson, just for the architectural details, like the carved-wood Florentine ceiling in the main salon. Tour times (in groups of up of 35 visitors) are posted on the museum website, in front of the museum, and in announcement boards at the port of Dapia. The museum closes for maintenance during winter. ⊠ *Spetses Town* ✛ *Behind Dapia* ☎ *22980/72416* ⊕ *www.bouboulinamuseum-spetses. gr* ⊠ *€6* ⊗ *Closed Nov.–late Mar.*

Dapia. Ships dock at the modern harbor, Dapia, in Spetses Town. This is where the island's seafaring chieftains met in the 1820s to plot their revolt against the Ottoman Turks. A protective jetty is still fortified with cannons dating from the War of Independence. Today, the town's waterfront strip is packed with cafés, and the navy-blue-and-white color scheme adopted by Dapia's merchants hints of former maritime glory. The harbormaster's offices, to the right as you face the sea, occupy a building designed in the simple two-story, center-hall architecture typical of the period and this place. ⊠ *Dapia.*

Ekklisia Ayios Nikolaos. On the headland sits Ayios Nikolaos, the current cathedral of Spetses, and a former fortified abbey. Its lacy white-marble bell tower recalls that of Hydra's port monastery. It was here that the islanders first raised their flag of independence. ⊠ *Spetses Town* ✛ *On road southeast on waterfront* ☎ *22980/72423.*

Palio Limani (*Balitiza*). Take a horse and carriage or stroll the seafront promenade to the old harbor, Palio Limani, from the bustling new harbor, Dapia. As you wander by the waterfront, you might imagine it as it was in its 18th- and 19th-century heyday: the walls of the mansions resounding with the noise of shipbuilding and the streets humming with discreet whisperings of revolution and piracy. Today, the wood keels in the few remaining boatyards are the backdrop for cosmopolitan bars, cafés, and restaurants; the sailing boats linger lazily in the bay. Walk up the hill to the ocher-hued chapel of Panayia

Armata for unforgettable sunset views. ⊠ *Spetses Town* ✛ *Waterfront, 1½ km (1 mile) southeast of Dapia.*

Poseidonion Grand Hotel. This 1914 waterfront landmark, a fitting backdrop to the defiant bronze statue of Bouboulina, was the scene of glamorous Athenian society parties and balls in the era between the two world wars. It was once the largest resort in the Balkans and southeastern Europe. The hotel was the brainchild of Sotirios Anargyros, a visionary benefactor who was responsible for much of the development of Spetses. After extensive renovations were completed in 2009, it recaptured its former glory and is once again the focal point of most Spetsiot cultural and social events. ⊠ *Spetses Town* ✛ *West side of Dapia* ☎ 22980/74553 ⊕ *www.poseidonion.com.*

Fodor's Choice ★ **Spetses Museum.** A fine and impressive late 18th-century *archontiko*, owned by the locally renowned Hatziyianni-Mexi family and built in a style that might be termed Turko-Venetian, contains the town's municipal museum. It holds articles from the period of Spetses's greatness during the War of Independence, including the bones of the town's heroine, Bouboulina, and a revolutionary flag. A small collection of ancient artifacts consists mostly of ceramics and coins. Also on display are representative pieces of furniture and household items from the period of the Greek revolution. ⊠ *Archontiko Hatziyianni-Mexi* ✛ *600 feet south of harbor* ☎ 22980/72994 ⊠ €3 ⊘ *Closed Mon.*

BEACHES

Spetses's best beaches are on the west side of the island, and most easily reached by water taxi or the daily boats from Spetses Town. You can ask for caïques information directly at the port. Water taxis at Dapia (the New Port) make scheduled runs to the most popular outlying beaches but can also be hired for trips to more remote coves. The rides can be pricey, ranging from €7 to go from Dapia to the Old Port, up to €30 to the Ayia Paraskevi Beach, and €60 for a tour of the island—but the experience is unique. There are currently seven water taxis serving Spetses.

Kaiki. Trendy Kaiki Beach (otherwise known as Scholes or College beach due to its proximity to the Anargyros School) is a triangular patch of sandy beach that draws a young crowd with its beach volleyball court, water-sports activities (about €40 for 20 minutes of Jet Skiing), and the Kaiki Beach bars (yes, there are two of them!) and restaurant, the hippest one on the beach in Spetses. It will cost you about €10 for a huge umbrella, two bamboo sun beds, two beach towels, and a bottle of water for a relaxing day on the beach. You can even rent an iPad (€5 per 20 minutes) or get a beach massage. **Amenities:** food and drink; lifeguards; toilets; water sports. **Best for:** swimming; walking. ⊠ *Spetses Town* ✛ *Opposite Anargyrios and Korgialenios School* ☎ 22980/74507 *Kaiki Beach Bar Restaurant.*

WHERE TO EAT

$$ SEAFOOD ✕ **Akrogialia.** Enjoy a meal at this down-to-earth—well, almost in the sea—Greek taverna. As the beach location would suggest, seafood dominates the simple menu, and it is prepared to perfection by the chef. **Known for:** fresh fish; superb location. $ *Average main: €16*

✉ *Anargirou, Kounoupitsa* ✣ *10-min walk from the new harbor* ☎ *22980/74749* 🌐 *www.akrogialia-restaurant.gr.*

$$$ MEDITERRANEAN Fodor's Choice ★ 🍴 **Liotrivi Restaurant.** Spetses's best restaurant has been morphing and evolving since it first opened 25 years ago, and the owner, Giorgos—a local who grew up on the island working in his father's taverna—still loves what he does and it shows! Everyone from fishermen to Hollywood headliners know him by his first name, and a meal here is not to be missed, not only for the innovative upscale Mediterranean dishes and thoughtful wine list, but also for the dreamy seafront setting and candlelit tables on a little pier jutting into the bay. **Known for:** mayiatiko à la spetsiota, a variation of the local fish specialty made with yellowtail tuna; live Latin music; excellent service. [$] *Average main: €26* ✉ *Palio Limani* ☎ *22980/72269* 🌐 *www.liotrivi-restaurant.gr* ⏲ *Closed Nov.–Mar.*

$$ MEDITERRANEAN 🍴 **Mourayo.** This highly regarded restaurant and music "boit" is right on the water in Dapia and is *the* all-time classic bar and nightclub of Spetses (running since 1975). The food in the restaurant is pretty decent, too, and it's probably one of the better choices on the island. **Known for:** live music (piano) every night; very good service; dining alfresco on a seafront terrace. [$] *Average main: €22* ✉ *Palio Limani* ☎ *22980/73700.*

$$$ GREEK FUSION 🍴 **On the Veranda.** Dine in style at the iconic Poseidonion Grand Hotel, where the restaurant serves local island dishes that have been inventively redefined. Many ingredients come straight from the hotel's own organic farm, harmoniously complementing the headlining fresh seafood. **Known for:** silver service; organic produce and fresh seafood. [$] *Average main: €35* ✉ *Poseidonion Grand Hotel, Dapia* ☎ *6957/507267, 22980 /74553.*

$$ SEAFOOD Fodor's Choice ★ 🍴 **Patralis.** Sit on the seaside veranda and savor seafood mezedes and fresh fish right from the sea in one of the more affordable restaurants on this sometimes overpriced (for Greece) island. As the very friendly waiters will tell you, the house specialties are the fish soup, *astakomakaronada* (lobster with spaghetti), and a kind of paella with mussels, shrimp, and crayfish. *Magirefta* (oven-baked dishes) include stuffed aubergines; oven-baked lamb; and roast scarpine fish with tomato and garlic. **Known for:** superbly prepared fresh fish; great service; sea view. [$] *Average main: €25* ✉ *Kounoupitsa* ✣ *Near Spetses Hotel* ☎ *22980/72134* 🌐 *www.patralis.gr* ⏲ *Closed Nov. and Dec.*

$ GREEK 🍴 **Stelios Restaurant.** Swift service and good value for your money more than make up for a lack of atmosphere at this little restaurant. Pass up the grilled dishes for the magirefta, like goat slowly cooked in a clay pot and oven-roasted potatoes lightly flavored with lemon and oregano. **Known for:** inexpensive and decent food; great location, in the heart of Spetses's buzzy waterfront strip. [$] *Average main: €10* ✉ *Dapia* ☎ *22980/73748* ⏲ *Closed mid-Nov.–mid-Mar.*

WHERE TO STAY

$ B&B/INN 🏨 **Niriides Guesthouse.** With cheerful, renovated exteriors surrounded by myriad flowers, this charming boutique-style B&B is only a few minutes' walk from the main harbor and offers decent value, especially in the off-season. **Pros:** on a central, quiet side street; hospitable owners; nice breakfast served in pretty, cool courtyard. **Cons:** bathrooms a bit on the small side; aside from breakfast, offers few hotel-style amenities; no 24-hour reception. $ *Rooms from: €100* ✉ *Dapia* ✛ *Near the clock tower square* ☎ *22980/73392* ⊕ *www.niriides-spetses.gr* ↘ *7 rooms* �’⊚’ *Breakfast.*

$$$ ⚏ **Orloff Resort.** A complex of renovated early-20th-century-listed build-
RESORT ings, set around a garden courtyard with a 72-foot swimming pool, comprise these lodgings. **Pros:** friendly down-to-earth staff; architectural splendor of aristocratic Spetses; pickup from the harbor on arrival. **Cons:** the double rooms are on the small side; Wi-Fi doesn't reach all spaces; a 20-minute trek to Dapia, the main part of town. $ *Rooms from: €230* ✉ *Spetses Old Town* ☎ *22980/75444* ⊕ *www.orloffresort. com* ↘ *31 rooms* ❙⊚❙ *Breakfast.*

$$$ ⚏ **Poseidonion Grand Hotel.** Set with fin-de-siècle cupolas, imposing man-
HOTEL sard roof, and elegant neoclassical facade, this landmark mansion was
Fodor'sChoice acclaimed as the Saronic gulf's own Hotel Negrescu in 1914—like that
★ Nice landmark, this hotel was built to attract the cosmopolitan ocean-liner set and, today, the Poseidonion has been hailed as the most elegant hotel in all the Greek islands. **Pros:** the beautiful landmark building is "the place to stay"; impeccable service; simple but elegant guest rooms with high ceilings. **Cons:** not all rooms have a sea view; occasional hot-water issues in the grand old building; fills quickly in high season, so book early. $ *Rooms from: €240* ✉ *Dapia* ☎ *22980/74553* ⊕ *www. poseidonion.com* ↘ *52 rooms* ❙⊚❙ *Breakfast.*

$$ ⚏ **Spetses Hotel.** Enjoy both privacy—surrounded by greenery, beach, and
HOTEL water—and proximity (about a 20-minute walk) to town at this spot, which dates back to the 1970s. **Pros:** free Wi-Fi in common areas; nice café on the beach; view of the harbor and Spetses Town. **Cons:** rooms quite basic; not the most charming building; a little bit of a hike to and from town. $ *Rooms from: €130* ✉ *Kounoupitsa beachfront* ✛ *1 km (½ mile) west of Dapia* ☎ *22980/72602, 22980/72603, 22980/72604* ⊕ *www.spetses-hotel.gr* ⊘ *Closed Nov.–Mar.* ↘ *77 rooms* ❙⊚❙ *Breakfast.*

FESTIVALS

Fodor'sChoice **Armata Festival.** Thousands flock in from all over Greece to attend the
★ Armata Festival celebrations on Spetses, held in honor of Panayia Armata (Virgin Mary "of the Army"), in what is probably the most glorious weekend on the island's calendar. During the second week of September Spetses mounts an enormous harbor-front reenactment of a War of Independence naval battle (the epic battle took place on September 8, 1822), complete with costumed fighters and burning ships. Book your hotel well in advance if you wish to see this popular event. There are also concerts and exhibitions during the week leading up to it. ✉ *Spetses Town.*

Saronic Chamber Festival. The Saronic Chamber Music Festival features the excellent Leondari ensemble, an international group of world-class musicians who perform on the island of Spetses in August. There are also concerts in Galatas, Hydra, Poros, and Kythera. All performances start at 9 pm. ✉ *Kapodistrian Cultural Hall* ✛ *Near Ag. Mamas* ⊕ *www. saronicfestival.com.*

Spetses is studded with extravagant mansions, such as this one, built for Sotirios Anargyros, owner of the famed Poseidonion Grand Hotel.

NIGHTLIFE

For the newest "in" bars, ask at your hotel or, even better, take a stroll on the seafront promenade to the old harbor or Kounoupitsa; you'll be sure to find the spot with the right vibes for you.

Bikini Cocktails & Snacks. This bar in a redesigned neoclassical building stands out for its romantic surroundings. Sip one of the imaginative cocktails, with names like Oki Monkey and Inferno, while sitting at a candlelit table right by the water. Things get more lively later in the evening, as this is one of *the* happening places on the island. ⊠ *Palio Limani* ☎ *22980/74888.*

Marine Club. Enjoy your drink on a veranda while taking in a picturesque view of the Palio Limani (old harbor) before going back inside to resume a night of dancing to popular Greek and international hits. ⊠ *Palio Limani waterfront* ☎ *22980/75245.*

Mosquito Bar. Spetses's take on the gastro pub serves tasty grub that can be washed down by one (or more) of the many cool craft beers sourced from microbreweries throughout Greece. The sunset views from the roof garden, overlooking the sea, are magical. ⊠ *Kounoupitsa, Anargirou* ☎ *22980/29572.*

Spetsa Bar. The island's all-time-classic hangout, where Kostas likes to play music from the 1960s and '70s. It's a perfect choice for a pre-dinner drink (bar opens at 8 pm). ⊠ *Platia Ag. Mamas* ☎ *22980/74131* ⊕ *www.barspetsa.org* ⊘ *Closed Nov.–Mar.*

Throubi. DJ sets from little-known, creative young Athenian talent set this little bar on the seafront promenade abuzz. The down-to-earth prices attract a less flashy crowd of nighttime fun seekers. ⊠ *Spetses Town* ⚓ *At the entrance of the old harbor* 🕿 *69/4895 7398.*

Votsalo. Tiny, cozy, and cute, Votsalo is a great meeting point for breakfast (it serves excellent espresso), but is equally popular after sunset, when you can order dreamy cocktails and listen to cool acid jazz tunes. ⊠ *Stavrou Niarchou 79, Dapia* 🕿 *22980/073031.*

SHOPPING

Isola di Spezzie. At this traditional Greek grocery on the Clock Square, you can find aromatic herbs and spices, homemade jams, dried pasta, sumptuous olives, and other local delicacies that you can taste on the spot before taking them home with you. ⊠ *Platia Roloi, Dapia* 🕿 *22980/73982.*

Rota. Locally sourced objects, from silver jewelry and kitchen bowls to souvenirs and decorative gifts, some of them handmade by the owner himself, are showcased here. ⊠ *High At., Dapia* 🕿 *22980/74013.*

Spetza. A classic boutique, stocking stylish clothes and accessories by top Greek designers, this is a great place to top up your chic island look. ⊠ *Dapia* 🕿 *22980/73353* ⊕ *www.spetza-spetses.gr.*

White Spetses. For a healthy dose of retail therapy, head to this clothing boutique, which offers a wide selection of caftans, bikinis, sandals, and other casual chic clothing. ⊠ *Dapia* 🕿 *22980/73308.*

SPORTS AND THE OUTDOORS

BIKING

The lack of cars and the predominantly level roads make Spetses ideal for cycling. One good trip is along the coastal road that circles the island, going from the main town to Ayia Paraskevi Beach.

Nikitas Rent-A-Bike. Head here to rent well-maintained mountain bikes (about €7 per day), motorbikes, and other equipment. A handy drop-off and pickup service is available. ⊠ *Spetses Town* ⚓ *Above the new port, 150 feet from Clock Sq.* 🕿 *22980/75305.*

BOATING

Fodor's Choice
★

Spetses Classic Yacht Race. For a long weekend in late June, Spetses fills with skippers and sailors who participate in this popular regatta celebrating the island's seafaring tradition. ⊠ *Spetses Town* 🕿 *210/422–0506 race organizers, in Piraeus* ⊕ *spetsesclassicregatta.com.*

RUNNING

Spetses Mini Marathon. At this mid-October running event, you can choose between a 5K (3.1-mile) fun run or a more demanding 25K (15½ miles), though the latter is also more scenic, taking in a whole lap around the island. You can also take part in the endurance swimming competitions taking place over the same weekend: a 3-km (1.8-mile) race from Kosta to Spetses and a 5-km (3.1-mile) round-trip to Kosta and back. ⊠ *Spetses Town* ⊕ *www.spetsesmarathon.com.*

Ayia Marina Beach is one of the sizzling reasons why people love Spetses.

AYIA MARINA ΑΓΙΑ ΜΑΡΙΝΑ

2 km (1 mile) southeast of Spetses Town.

Ayia Marina is the most cosmopolitan beach on the island, so head here if you want to see and be seen.

BEACHES

Ayia Marina. Favored by fashionable Greek socialites, the mostly sandy beach at Ayia Marina is the home of the elegant Paradise Beach Bar, tavernas, and many water-sports activities. Sun beds and umbrellas are available for a fee. You can hire a horse-drawn buggy from town to arrive in style, or you can come by caïque. Warning: this beach can get pretty busy during the summer months with a younger, party-loving crowd. **Amenities:** food and drink; showers; toilets; water sports. **Best for:** partiers; swimming; walking. ⊠ *Ayia Marina* ☎ *22980/72195 Paradise Beach Bar.*

AYIOI ANARGYROI ΑΓΙΟΙ ΑΝΑΡΓΥΡΟΙ

6 km (4 miles) west of Spetses Town.

With plenty of water-sports options, this popular beach is set against a luscious green backdrop, offering the added prospect of exploring the nearby Bekiris cave at your own pace.

BEACHES

Ayioi Anargyroi. A clean and cosmopolitan beach, Ayioi Anargyroi has a gently sloped seabed with deep waters suitable for snorkeling, water-skiing, and other water sports (rentals are available on-site). It is the island's best-known beach, 6 km (4 miles) away from town. You can also swim (or take a path) to beautiful Bekiris cave, a famous historical spot as Greek revolutionaries used it as a hiding place during the 1821 revolution. Look for the taverna Manolis by the beach; nearby you can rent two sun beds and an umbrella for about €8 a day. There is also a pretty hotel (Acrogiali) right on the beach. **Amenities:** lifeguards; showers; water sports. **Best for:** snorkeling; swimming; walking; windsurfing.

ZOGERIA ΖΩΓΕΡΙΑ

7 km (4½ miles) west of Spetses Town.

A pine-edged cove with deep sapphire waters, Zogeria has a gorgeous natural setting that more than makes up for the lack of amenities—there's just a tiny church and the modest Loula taverna, where you can taste an incredible chicken stew in tomato sauce.

BEACHES

Zogeria. This is, in fact, two beaches split by a verdurous little peninsula. On the right, the larger beach offers a day of relaxation away from the cosmopolitan crowds, with few amenities other than the beautiful water. You can rent sun beds and umbrellas from Taverna Loula (June–September). On a clear day you can see all the way to Nafplion. **Amenities:** food and drink. **Best for:** solitude; swimming. ☎ *69446/27851 Taverna Loula.*

AYIA PARASKEVI ΑΓΙΑ ΠΑΡΑΣΚΕΥΗ

10 km (6 miles) west of Spetses Town.

In a sheltered cove and easily accessible by bus or water taxi, this is a favorite with locals and visitors alike. In the height of summer the pine trees offer some much needed natural shade.

BEACHES

Ayia Paraskevi. Pine trees, a canteen, sun beds, and umbrellas line Ayia Paraskevi, a sheltered and popular beach with a mostly sandy shore (and coarse pebbles in other parts). Look for the cubic Ayia Paraskevi chapel at the back—it has given its name to the bay. Many locals consider this beach the most beautiful on the island; it can be reached either via road or with a caïque. The beach gets fairly busy during the summer months, and if you don't manage to snag a sun bed, you can sun yourself on the red rocks bordering the sandy beach. **Amenities:** food and drink. **Best for:** snorkeling; swimming; walking. ✉ *Ayia Paraskevi.*

4

THE SPORADES

Skiathos, Skopelos, and Skyros

Visit Fodors.com for advice, updates, and bookings

WELCOME TO THE SPORADES

TOP REASONS TO GO

★ **Sun-and-Fun Skiathos:** Thousands of international sunseekers head here to enjoy famous beaches and show off their tans in the buzzing nightclubs.

★ **Skyros's Style:** Set against a dramatic rock, the main town of Skyros is a showstopper of Cycladic houses colorfully set with folk wood carvings and embroideries.

★ **Sylvan Skopelos:** Tucked into verdant forests are 40 picturesque monasteries, while Skopelos Town is almost sinfully picturesque.

★ **Golden Sands:** The beaches are best on Skiathos, the star location being Koukounaries, whose luscious sands are famous throughout Greece.

★ **"Forever England":** The grave of Edwardian poet Rupert Brooke draws pilgrims to Vouno on Skyros.

This small cluster of islands off the coast of central Greece is just a short hop from the mainland and, consequently, often overrun in high season. Obviously, the Cyclades aren't the only Greek islands that serve up a cup of culture and a gallon of hedonism to travelers looking for that perfect tan. Each of the Sporades is very individual in character. Due east of tourism-oriented Skiathos are lesser-visited eco-blessed Skopelos and folk-craft-famous Skyros.

1 Skiathos. The 3,900 residents are eclipsed by the 50,000 visitors who come here each year for clear blue waters and scores of beaches, including the world-famous Koukounaries. Close to the mainland, this island has some of the aura of the Pelion Peninsula, with red-roof villages and picturesque hills. Beauty spots include the Monastery of Evangelistria and Lalaria Beach.

2 Skopelos. Second largest of the Sporades, this island is lushly forested and more prized by ecologists than fun seekers. The steep streets of Skopelos Town need mountain-goat negotiating skills, but the charming alleys are irresistible, as are the island's monasteries, the famous cheese pies, and

4

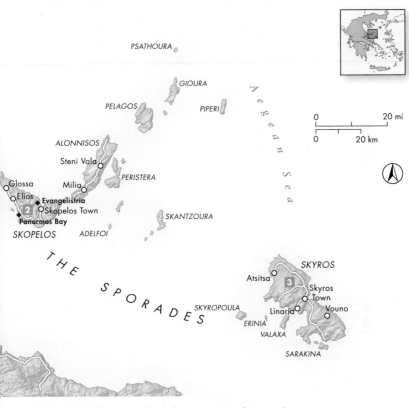

PSATHOURA

GIOURA

PELAGOS

PIPERI

Aegean Sea

ALONNISOS

Steni Vala

Milia

PERISTERA

Glossa

Elios

Evangelistria

Skopelos Town

Panormos Bay

SKOPELOS

ADELFOI

SKANTZOURA

2

0   20 mi

0   20 km

THE SPORADES

SKYROS

Atsitsa

Skyros Town

SKYROPOULA

Linaria

Vouno

ERINIA

VALAXA

SARAKINA

3

the traditional *kalivia* farmhouses around Panormos Bay.

3 Skyros. Located at the virtual center of the Aegean Sea, this Sporades Shangri-la is the southernmost of the island group. The top half is covered with pine forests and is home to Skyros Town,

a cubic masterpiece that climbs a spectacular rock peak and is a tangle of lanes, whitewashed houses, and Byzantine churches. The arid southern half is the site of noted Edwardian poet Rupert Brooke's grave, at Vouno.

Updated
by Stephen
Brewer

Little mentioned in mythology or history, the Sporades confidently rely on their great natural beauty and cultural history to attract visitors. Some locals poetically claim them to be the handful of colored pebbles the gods were left with after creating the world, and as an afterthought, they flung them over the northwestern Aegean.

Bustling with visitors, Skiathos sits closest to the mainland; it has a pretty harbor area and the noisiest nightlife, international restaurants and pubs, and resort hotels. Due east is Skopelos, covered with dense, fragrant pines, where you can visit scenic villages, hundreds of churches, and lush beaches. Much less contemporary than Skiathos, it is the most naturally beautiful of the Sporades and has a fascinating old hill town.

Then there is traditional Skyros. Some visitors return year after year to this mythical isle, southeast of the other islands, for its quiet fishing villages, expansive beaches, and stunning cubist eagle's nest of a town that seems to spill down a hill. This remote island is a little hard to reach, so a visit is all the more rewarding for those who make the effort.

Like emerald beads scattered on sapphire satin, the aptly named Sporades ("scattered ones") are resplendent with pines, ripe fruit, and olive trees. The lush countryside, marked with sloping slate roofs and wooden balconies, reflects the aura of the neighboring, hauntingly beautiful Pelion Peninsula, to which the islands were once attached. Only on Skyros, farther out in the Aegean, will you see windswept, treeless landscapes.

The Sporades have changed hands constantly throughout history, and wars, plunder, and earthquakes have eliminated all but the strongest ancient walls. A few castles and monasteries remain, but Skiathos and Skopelos are better suited for relaxing and having fun than for sightseeing. Skiathos is the most touristy, in some cases to the point of overkill, while less-developed Skopelos has fewer (but purer) beaches, a far less contrived nightlife, and a main town that is said to be the most beautiful in the Sporades, if not in all of Greece. Late to attract tourists, Skyros is the least traveled of the Sporades (probably because it is hardest to reach). It's also the quirkiest, and the most traditional, with its distinct ways and customs.

Quintessential Greek-island delights beckon on all three islands: sun, sand, and surf, along with starlit dinners. Almost all restaurants have outside seating, often under cooling trees, where you can watch the passing classically Greek, ubiquitous dramas of daily life.

PLANNING

WHEN TO GO

Winter is least desirable, as the weather turns cold and rainy; most hotels, rooms, and restaurants are closed, and ferry service is minimal. If you do go from November through April, book in advance and leave nothing to chance. The same advice applies to July and August peak season, when everything is open but overcrowded, except on Skyros. The *meltemi*, the brisk northeasterly summer wind of the Aegean, keeps things cooler than on the mainland even on the hottest days. Late spring and early summer are ideal, as most hotels are open, crowds have not arrived, the air is warm, and the roadsides and fields of flowers are incredible; September is also mild.

If you want to catch one of the famous religious and cultural festivals on your visit, keep the following dates in mind. The lively Carnival (February) traditions of Skopelos, although not as exotic as those of Skyros, parody the expulsion of the once-terrifying Barbary pirates. August 15 is the day of the *Panayia* (Festival of the Virgin), celebrated on Skyros at Magazia Beach and on Skopelos in the main town; cultural events there continue to late August. Skiathos hosts several cultural events in summer, including a dance festival in July. Feast days? Skiathos: July 26, for St. Paraskevi; Skopelos: February 25, for St. Riginosi.

PLANNING YOUR TIME

You can hop between Skiathos and Skopelos easily, since there are several-times-a-day ferry connections between them, and they are relatively near each other. Traveling between these islands and Skyros, however, requires advance planning, since there are no direct ferries to Skyros but instead boats leave from Kimi, on the island of Evia. Four days can be just enough for touching down on Skiathos and Skopelos, but you need more days if you want to include Skyros, since reaching it means a flight through Athens or a drive or bus trip to the port of Kimi.

How to choose if you're only visiting one of the Sporades? If you're the can't-sit-still type and think crowds add to the fun, Skiathos is your island. By day you can take in the beautiful, thronged beaches and Evangelistria Monastery or the fortress-turned-cultural-center, and at night stroll the port to find the most hopping nightclub. Day people with a historical bent should explore Skopelos's many monasteries and churches and its 18th-century Folk Art Museum. Skyros should be at the top of your list if you're a handicraft collector, as the island's furniture, embroidery, and pottery are admired throughout the country and can be bought and sent abroad from several shops.

GETTING HERE AND AROUND

AIR TRAVEL

During the summer Aegean and Olympic fly daily—or even twice a day, depending on the period—to Skiathos from Athens International Airport. The trip takes 45 minutes. In summer there are also weekly flights from Athens and Thessaloniki to Skyros Airport; the flights take 40 minutes. Fares vary dramatically depending on how far in advance you book.

Skiathos Airport also has direct charter flights from many European cities.

BOAT AND FERRY TRAVEL

Ferry travel to Skiathos and Skopelos requires that you drive or take a bus to Agios Konstantinos, about two hours north of Athens; if arriving from central or northern Greece, however, it's easiest to board a ferry at Volos or Thessaloniki. For all ferries, it's best to call a travel agency ahead of time to check schedules and prices and to book your ferry in advance—especially if you are bringing a car—as boat times change seasonally; to check schedules, go to the Greek Travel Pages (⊕ *www.gtp.gr*). Tickets are also available from several travel agents on the dock.

There are at least three to four ferries per day in the summer from Agios Konstantinos to Skiathos, often continuing on to Skopelos (these may be regular ferries or the so-called Flying Dolphin and Flyingcat ferries, which are smaller, faster, and more expensive but do not take cars). There are significantly fewer departures in winter.

Fast ferries from Agios Konstantinos to Skiathos take approximately 90 minutes and cost €32–€37; many continue to Skopelos in another 60 minutes and cost €40–€49.50. Regular ferries from Agios Konstantinos to Skiathos take about three hours and cost €30.50; they continue to Skopelos in another hour and 45 minutes and cost €38. From Volos, the travel time is slightly less and has similar pricing. On Skopelos, ferries usually make two stops, at Loutraki (port for the town of Glossa) and in Skopelos Town.

Getting to Skyros from Athens or elsewhere on the mainland requires driving or taking a bus to Kimi—on the giant island of Evia, connected by bridges to the mainland—and then catching one of the two daily ferries (or less-frequent hydrofoils) to Skyros. You can buy ferry tickets at the Kimi dock when you get off the bus; the trip to Skyros takes two hours and costs €9.

In summer only, there are three ferries weekly ferries between Skopelos and Skyros; the trip takes about five hours and the ticket price is €22. *For information on ferry companies, see Boat and Ferry Travel in Travel Smart.*

Contacts Port Authority. ☎ *22350/31759 in Agios Konstantinos, 22220/22606 in Kimi, 24270/22017 in Skiathos Town, 24240/22180 in Skopelos Town, 22220/91475 in Skyros Town.*

BUS TRAVEL

From Central Athens, buses leave every hour to Agios Konstantinos, the main port for the Sporades (except Skyros, for which ferries leave from Kimi on the island of Evia). Fares are about €15.70, and travel time is about 2½ hours. Buses from Athens to Kimi, on Evia island (the only port from which boats depart for Skyros) cost €15.30 and take 2½ hours. Schedules and fares change, so be sure to verify them with KTEL or a travel agent.

Bus service is available throughout the Sporades, although on some islands buses run more frequently than on others.

CAR TRAVEL

To get to Skiathos and Skopelos by car, you must drive to the port of Agios Konstantinos (Agios), and from there, take the ferry. The drive to Agios from Athens takes about two hours. For high-season travel you should reserve a place on the car ferry well in advance. Boats for Skyros leave from the port of Kimi on the big island of Evia. From Athens, take Athens–Lamia National Road to Skala Oropou, and make the 30-minute ferry crossing to Eretria on Evia (every half hour in the daytime). No reservations are needed. You can drive directly to Evia over a short land bridge connecting Agios Minas on the mainland with Halkidha, about 80 km (50 miles) from Athens (take National Road 1 to the Schimatari exit, and then follow the signs to Halkidha). From Halkidha it's another 80 km (50 miles) to Kimi; total driving time from Athens is about 2½ hours, but on weekend crowds can slow traffic across the bridge.

The best way to get around the islands is by renting a car, but in the busy summer months, parking can be hard to come by in the main towns and villages. Car rentals cost €30–€70 per day, while scooters cost €14–€30 (with insurance). Scooters are ubiquitous, but if you rent a scooter, be extra cautious: scooter accidents provide the island clinics with 80% of their summer business.

See the individual island sections for detailed contact information.

TAXI TRAVEL

Taxis throughout the Sporades are unmetered, so be sure to negotiate your fare in advance or (better) check with your hotel for correct fares. You will find "Piatsa" taxi ranks next to all the harbor ports and airports, and taxis will be lined up even late at night if there is a boat or flight coming in. On the other hand, your hotel can usually arrange a taxi for you, but if you need one in the wee hours of the morning make sure you book it in advance. The prices on the islands are not cheap (compared to Athens or Thessaloniki), and can be as much as €10 to €20 for a 10-minute drive.

HOTELS

Skopelos has a fair number of hotels, Skiathos a huge number, and Skyros has relatively few. Most hotels close from October or November to April or May. Reservations are a good idea, though you may learn about rooms in pensions and private homes when you arrive at the airport or ferry landing. The best bet, especially for those on a budget, is to rent a room in a private house—look for the Greek National Tourism Organization (EOT or GNTO) license displayed in windows. Owners meet incoming ferries to tout their location, offer rooms, and negotiate the price. In Skyros most people take lodgings in town or along the beach at Magazia and Molos; accommodations are basic, and not generally equipped with TVs. Always negotiate rates off-season.

RESTAURANTS

Most tavernas are opened from midday until just past midnight, and welcome guests to stay as long as they like. Traditional recipes such as *mageirefta* (home-cooked) dishes based on local meat and vegetables, and a variety of fresh fish, reign supreme. Look for local specialties such as the *Skopelitiki tiropita,* or cheese pie (a spiral of tubed phyllo pastry filled with creamy white feta and fried to a crispy texture), or the fluffy *avgato* yellow plums in light syrup that can be savored as a dressing for fresh yogurt or on a small plate as *glyko koutaliou* (spoon sweet). Be sure to ask the waiter what fresh fish they serve and what the dishes of the day are, and don't hesitate to go inside and see the food for yourself before ordering. As with everywhere in Greece, the *hima* (homemade) house wine is usually good enough, sometimes excellent; the waiter will not mind if you order a taste before deciding.

Restaurant and hotel reviews have been shortened. For full information, visit Fodors.com.

DINING AND LODGING PRICES IN EUROS			
	$	$$	$$$	$$$$
Restaurants	under €15	€15–€25	€26–€40	over €40
Hotels	under €125	€125–€225	€226–€275	over €275

Restaurant prices are the average cost of a main course at dinner, or if dinner is not served at lunch. Hotel prices are the lowest price for a standard double room in high season.

VISITOR INFORMATION

There are few official tourist offices for the Sporades. The closest you'll come is the Skiathos Municipality agency. In lieu of official agencies, however, there is an array of private travel agencies, and these offer myriad services, tickets, car rentals, and guided tours. *See the individual islands sections for specific recommendations.*

SKIATHOS ΣΚΙΑΘΟΣ

Part sacred (scores of churches), part profane (lots of nightlife), the hilly, wooded island of Skiathos is the closest of the Sporades to the Pelion Peninsula. The island covers an area of only 42 square km (16 square miles) but has some 70 beaches and sandy coves. A jet-set island 25 years ago, today Skiathos teems with European—mostly British—tourists on package deals promising sun, sea, and late-night revelry. Higher prices and a bit of Mykonos's attitude are part of the deal, too.

In winter most of the island's 5,000 or so inhabitants live in its main city, Skiathos Town, built after the War of Independence on the site of the colony founded in the 8th century BC by the Euboean city-state of Chalkis. Skiathos was on good terms with the Athenians, prized by the Macedonians, and treated gently by the Romans. Saracen and Slav raids left the island virtually deserted during the early Middle Ages, but it started to prosper during the later Byzantine years.

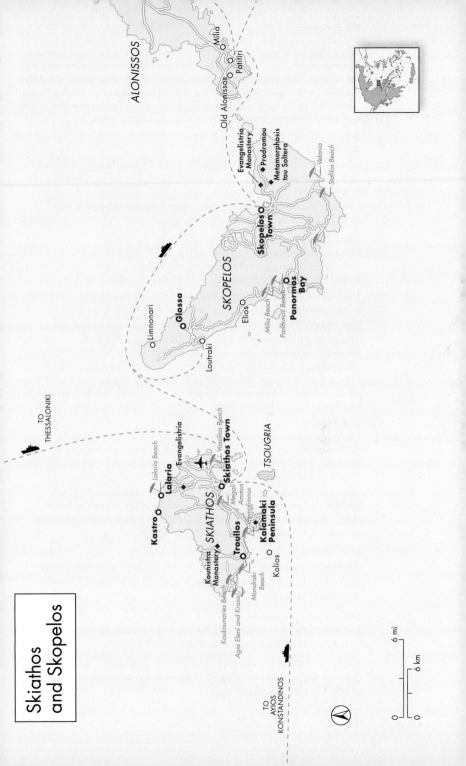

Skiathos and Skopelos

TO THESSALONIKI

ALONISSOS

Milia
Patitiri
Old Alonissos

Evangelistria Monastery
Prodromou
Metamorphosis tou Soltera
Velania
Staflios Beach

Skopelos Town

SKOPELOS

Limonari
Glossa
Loutraki
Elios
Milia Beach
Panormos Beach
Panormos Bay

Lalaria Beach
Lalaria
Kastro
Evangelistria
SKIATHOS
Skiathos Town
Vassilias Beach
Megali
Ammos
Troullos
Kounistra Monastery
Kalamaki Peninsula
TSOUGRIA
Kolios
Mandraki Beach
Kanapitsa
Koukounaries Beach
Agia Eleni and Krassa

TO AXIOS KONSTANDINOS

6 mi
6 km

When the Crusaders deposed their fellow Christians from the throne of Constantinople in 1204, Skiathos and the other Sporades became the fief of the Ghisi, knights of Venice. One of their first acts was to fortify the hills on the islet separating the two bays of Skiathos harbor. Now connected to the shore, the Bourtzi castle-fortress still has a few stout walls and buttresses shaded by some graceful pine trees.

GETTING HERE AND AROUND

AIR TRAVEL

The island airport is located 1 km (½ mile) northeast of Skiathos Town; buses to town are very infrequent so plan on jumping in a taxi to get to your hotel.

Contacts Skiathos Airport. ✛ *1 km (½ mile) northeast of Skiathos Town* ☎ *24270/29100, 24270/29101.*

BOAT TRAVEL

Ferries run regularly to Skiathos from both Agios Konstantinos and Volos, and these generally continue to Skopelos. There is also a daily hydrofoil to Thessaloniki.

Caïques leave from the main port for the most popular beaches; captains have signs of their destinations and departure times posted.

BUS TRAVEL

The main bus route follows the southern coast and makes 25 stops between Skiathos Town and the famed beach at Koukounaries (Maratha), a 30-minute ride. Fares are €1.50 to €3, with service from 7:30 am to 1 am in high season. This widely used service provides an easy and hassle-free way to get to towns and beaches along the southern side of the island.

CAR TRAVEL

Many companies, most of them local businesses, operate on Skiathos. To ensure a car is available in July and August, it's best to book in advance. *For information on international car-rental firms, see Car Travel in Travel Smart.*

Contacts The First. ✉ *Papadiamantis St., Skiathos Town* ☎ *24270/22810, 69424/43165 mobile* ⊕ *www.skiathoshire.com.* **Skiathos Cheap Car Rental.** ✉ *Port of Skiathos, Skiathos Town* ☎ *24270/21246* ⊕ *www.skiathoscheapcar-rental.gr.*

TAXI TRAVEL

Arrange taxis through your hotel, or you can call operators directly.

Contacts Skiathos Taxi Rank (*Skiathos Piasta*). ✉ *Port of Skiathos, Skiathos Town* ☎ *24270/24461.*

TRAVEL AGENCIES

Contacts Dolphin of Skiathos. ✉ *Parodos Evaggelistrias, Skiathos Town* ☎ *24270/21910* ⊕ *www.dolphin-skiathos.gr.*

VISITOR INFORMATION

Contacts Municipality of Skiathos. ✉ *Nikotsara 12, Skiathos Town* ☎ *24273/50100* ⊕ *www.skiathos.gr.*

On Skiathos, the coast is always clear.

SKIATHOS TOWN ΣΚΙΑΘΟΣ (ΠΟΛΗ)

2½ hours by ferry from Agios Konstantinos.

The harbor is especially picturesque from a ferry docking at sunset, when a violet-orange light casts a soft glow and the lights on the hills behind the quay start twinkling like faint stars. Onshore, magenta bougainvillea, sweet jasmine, and the casual charm of brightly painted balconies and shutters add to the experience of wandering through narrow lanes and up steep steps that serve as streets. Activity centers on the waterfront or on Papadiamantis, the main drag, while shops, bars, and restaurants line the cobbled side streets. Watching over the east side of the port (known as the New Port) is the little church and clock tower of Ayios Nikolaos, reached by steps so steep they're almost perpendicular to the earth.

EXPLORING

Bourtzi. This lovely presence on Skiathos harbor stands on a small, pine-covered peninsula that divides the main port and was built in 1207 by the Venetian Gyzi brothers to protect Skiathos from pirate attacks. Not much remains of the original fortress (also called the castle of St. George), but a cultural center at the site hosts concerts in the summer, as well as art and antiquities exhibitions. Many tranquil, refreshing spots provide views over the busy waterfront. ⊠ *Skiathos Town ⊹ End of causeway extending from port.*

Papadiamantis Museum. The modest home of one of Greece's finest writers, Alexandros Papadiamantis (1851–1911), lauded by some as "the Greek Dostoyevsky," is filled with his modest furniture, personal belongings, and vintage photographs. The author's native Skiathos played a prominent role in his essays, short stories, and novels, as did his Greek Orthodox faith and simple rural life. Several of his novels have been translated into English, including the internationally acclaimed *The Murderess.* ✉ *Skiathos Town* ✥ *Right off Papadiamantis St. at the fork* ☎ *24270/23843* 🎟 *€1.50.*

BEACHES

Skiathos is known for its beaches, and on the beautiful, pine-covered 14-km (9-mile) stretch of coast running south of the town to famed, gold-sand Koukounaries, one beach succeeds another. Along this coast, the beaches—**Megali Ammos, Vassilias, Achladia, Tzaneria, Vromolimnos,** and **Platania**—all offer water sports, umbrellas, lounge chairs, and plenty of company. Most are on popular bus routes so a car or scooter rental is unnecessary if you are just looking for a day at the beach.

Megali Ammos. Within walking distance of Skiathos Town, the sandy stretch of Megali Ammos is an easy option. The bars and eating options lining the back of the beach have sun lounges reaching down to the water's edge, and many of the bars offer a free drink when you rent one for the day. There is a water-sports school on the busier right side of the beach where you can enjoy white-knuckle rides on giant inflatable bananas and doughnuts pulled at high speeds by little motorboats. **Amenities:** food and drink; lifeguard; showers; toilets; water sports. **Best for:** swimming. ✉ *Skiathos Town* ✥ *Walk west over the hill then on the coastal road* [M] *Bus Stop 5.*

Vassilias Beach. On one of the better beaches close to Skiathos Town, Vassilias is lined by pine trees that lean thirstily toward the shallow seashore, providing shade under their aromatic branches. A rustic canteen and some beachside restaurants serve refreshments, outfitters offer all sorts of sea-based adventures, and rows of shaded sun lounges are lined up for rent. **Amenities:** food and drink; parking (no fee); showers; toilets; water sports. **Best for:** snorkeling; swimming; walking. ✉ *Skiathos Town* ✥ *2 km (1 mile) from Skiathos Town* [M] *Bus Stop 8.*

Vromolimnos. One of the most popular and busiest beaches on Skiathos has a party vibe, along with waterskiing, which is especially good in the afternoon when the sea usually calms to a lakelike smoothness. On the far end of the beach, away from the pulsating tunes and rumbling boat engines, there's space to lay out a towel and soak up the sun. There's also a decent little taverna. **Amenities:** food and drink; lifeguard; parking (no fee); showers; toilets; water sports. **Best for:** partiers; sunset; swimming. ✥ *Kolios, 8 km (5 miles) southwest of Skiathos Town* [M] *Bus Stop 13.*

WHERE TO EAT

$ SEAFOOD 🍴 **Amfiliki.** The balcony pairs inviting breezes and sprawling views, a perfect setting in which to enjoy fresh local fish. Owner Christos also takes pride in the organic vegetables he serves, all from his own garden. **Known for:** views; fresh fish; ekmek (custard cake) with mastic ice cream. [$] *Average main: €12* ✉ *Agia Triada* ✥ *Opposite the health center* ☎ *24270/22839* 🌐 *www.amfiliki.gr* ⏲ *Closed Oct.–May.*

$$ ✕ **The Final Step.** At this aerie atop Skiathos Town, enjoy spectacular
CONTEMPORARY views of the harbor while enjoying some of the best food on the island,
Fodor'sChoice if not the Aegean. The menu offers an artful blend of Mediterranean
★ flavors with a slight hint of Asian influence. **Known for:** spectacular
views; the spot to be at sunset; accomplished cuisine. $ *Average main:*
€18 ⊠ *St. Nikolas Sq.* ☎ *24270/21877, 69718/84249* ⊕ *www.final-*
steprestaurant.com.

$$ ✕ **The Windmill.** A beautifully restored 1880s mill offers awesome views
INTERNATIONAL of the moonlit harbor along with a gourmet rendition of British pub
dishes. Breezy Mediterranean and Asian twists make themselves known
in dishes like calamari with Parmesan crumb and ginger dip, and salmon
with a lemon-lime sauce that alone will have you coming back. **Known
for:** views; best cooking on the island; delightful setting. $ *Average
main: €20* ⊠ *Skiathos Town* ✛ *Above the clock tower* ☎ *24270/24550*
⊕ *www.skiathoswindmill.gr.*

WHERE TO STAY

$$$$ 🛏 **Aegean Suites.** Romantically inclined twosomes who settle into this
RESORT couples-only hideaway on a hillside outside town will be excused for
thinking they've landed in their own grand Mediterranean villa, since
that's what the large, comfortable suites, lovely gardens, and pampering all are meant to do. **Pros:** outstanding service; luxurious amenities;
very attractive surroundings. **Cons:** no elevator and lots of stairs; walk
into town is along busy road; not on the beach. $ *Rooms from: €450*
⊠ *Megali Ammos Beach* ☎ *24270/24066* ⊕ *www.aegeansuites.com*
☉ *Closed Nov.–Apr.* 🛏 *20 suites* ⦿| *Breakfast* Ⓜ *Bus Stop 5.*

$$ 🛏 **Bourtzi Boutique Hotel.** Contemporary style and relaxing, luxurious
HOTEL ambience comes to the fore in the island's bastion of chic, with a snazzy
cocktail lounge and public rooms, crisp, cool, spotless accommoda-
tions, and a laid-back courtyard pool that could hold its own in South
Beach. **Pros:** stylish sophistication; restful and quiet accommodations;
convenient town center location. **Cons:** not on the beach; pool area
is often in shade; minimum-stay requirement some periods. $ *Rooms
from: €175* ⊠ *Moraitou 8* ☎ *24270/21304* ⊕ *www.hotelbourtzi.gr*
🛏 *38 rooms* ⦿| *Breakfast.*

$ 🛏 **Mouria Hotel and Taverna.** A big dose of Greek hospitality comes with
HOTEL a provenance in these simple but cheerful rooms surrounding a bou-
gainvillea-scented courtyard and downstairs taverna in premises that
have been a bastion of Skiathos hospitality since 1830. **Pros:** delightful
atmosphere; immaculate surroundings; extremely hospitable owners
and staff. **Cons:** rooms overlooking Papadiamantis Street can be noisy;
more charm than luxury; no sea views. $ *Rooms from: €80* ⊠ *Papa-
diamantis St.* ✛ *Behind the National Bank* ☎ *24270/23069* ⊕ *www.
mouriahotel.com* ☉ *Closed Oct.–May* 🛏 *12 rooms* ⦿| *Breakfast.*

NIGHTLIFE

Skiathos is filled with night owls, and bars for all tastes line main and
side streets, from pubs run by Brits to quintessential Greek bouzouki
joints in beach tavernas. Most of the nightlife in Skiathos Town is
centered along the waterfront and on Papadiamanti, Politechniou, and
Evangelistrias streets.

4

FILM

Cinema Attikon. Enjoy three different films per week under the summer stars; two English-language films are screened some nights, with a regular tribute to *Mamma Mia.* ✉ *Papadiamantis St.* ☎ *24270/22352.*

MUSIC AND NIGHTCLUBS

The Borzoi. If you were one of the jet-setters who touched down on Skiathos in the 1970s, you'll be delighted to find this reincarnation of an old-time, legendary favorite going strong, serving sophisticated cocktails as well as excellent meals in a beautiful white-walled courtyard and an atmospheric club room. Those who are in the mood to linger can come for dinner and stay until the break of dawn. ✉ *Papadiamantis St.* ☎ *69442/47349.*

Bourtzi Café. The tip of the promontory beneath the fortress (Bourtzi) is a quiet spot for a coffee or sunset cocktail and can come with a swim off the rocks below the bar terrace. ✉ *Bourtzi.*

Kahlua. Sooner or later clubbers head to this island mainstay for indoor and outdoor dancing. Doors open at 10:30 pm—the action doesn't usually get going till after midnight—and it goes until at least 3 am. ✉ *Tasos Antonaros (New Port)* ☎ *69780/11870* ⊕ *www.kahluaclub. com* ⊗ *Closed Sept.–June.*

Kentavros Bar. A young professional crowd gathers for rhythm and blues, funk, soul, and classic rock starting at 9:30 pm. ✉ *Papadiamantis Sq.* ☎ *24270/22980* ⊗ *Closed Oct.–Apr.*

SPORTS AND THE OUTDOORS

SAILING

Active Yachts. The way to explore the Sporades in style is aboard these weekly sailboat charters. ✉ *Skiathos Town* ⊹ *Portside* ☎ *69722/45391* ⊕ *activeyachts.gr* ⊠ *From €2,700 per wk* ⊗ *Closed Oct.–Apr.*

SCUBA DIVING

Dolphin Diving Center. Several popular beaches have diving-equipment rentals and instructors on hand. Dolphin offers single or multiple dives, as well as full-certification programs. ✉ *Hotel Nostos, Tzaneria Beach* ☎ *69449/99181* ⊕ *www.ddiving.gr* ⊠ *Diving courses from €60* ⊗ *Closed Nov.–Apr.*

SHOPPING

ANTIQUES AND CRAFTS

Galerie Varsakis. Kilims, embroideries, jewelry, icons, and hundreds of antiques from around the world are available here, all set off by proprietor Charalambos Varsaki's impressive surrealistic paintings and prints. Also noteworthy is his collection of guns and swords dating to 1780–1820 and used in the Greek War of Independence. ✉ *Trion Hierarchon Sq.* ☎ *24270/22255* ⊕ *www.varsakis.com.*

JEWELRY

Phaedra. Silver and gold pieces that are part of collections by noteworthy Greek designers celebrate jewelry making with an artsy twist. ✉ *Papadiamantis 23* ☎ *24270/21233.*

Simos. Jewelry in 14-karat and 18-karat yellow and white gold, and more recently in silver, are specialties, from simple designs to classical Greece-inspired baubles encrusted with precious stones. ✉ *Papadiamantis 29* ☎ *24270/23232.*

KALAMAKI PENINSULA ΚΑΛΑΜΑΚΙ (ΧΕΡΣΟΝΗΣΟΣ)

6 km (4 miles) south of Skiathos Town.

On the least-developed part of the south coast, villas are tucked above tiny, isolated coves. Access to most of the shoreline is by boat only. Motor launches run at regular intervals to the most popular beaches from Skiathos Town, and you can also hire a boat and find your own private beach.

WHERE TO STAY

$$$ HOTEL Fodor's Choice ★

🏨 **Atrium Hotel.** This stunning hillside retreat tucked away in gardens and pine groves above the south coast seems like a private villa, with lots of wood and stone enhancing the airy public spaces, a beautiful pool terrace, and sharply decorated rooms and suites—all with balconies and patios, some with private pools, and most with extensive sea views. **Pros:** beautiful design by architect-owners; very attractive and comfortable guest rooms; extremely pleasant lounges and pool area. **Cons:** beach is nearby but across the busy road; stairs on property may be difficult for some guests; not all rooms have sea views. [$] *Rooms from: €250* ✉ *Ayia Paraskevi Platanias* ✣ *On the coastal road 8 km (5 miles) from Skiathos Town* ☎ *24270/49345* 🌐 *atriumhotel.gr* 🕓 *Closed Nov.–Apr.* 🛏 *75 rooms* 🍴 *Breakfast* [M] *Bus Stop 16.*

$$$$ RESORT FAMILY

🏨 **Skiathos Princess.** Understated glamour and polished island chic rule at this luxurious getaway spreading above Ayia Paraskevi Beach—from guest rooms that are fit for the pages of design magazines to an absolute "wow" of a pool area to three polished restaurants. **Pros:** beautiful grounds and facilities; wonderful views; five-star treatment from most staff. **Cons:** some rooms are in need of renovation .; bathrooms tend to be small; not all rooms have sea views. [$] *Rooms from: €325* ✉ *Ayia Paraskevi Platanias* ✣ *On the coastal road 8 km (5 miles) from Skiathos Town* ☎ *24270/49731* 🌐 *www.skiathosprincess.com* 🕓 *Closed Nov.–Apr.* 🛏 *158 rooms* 🍴 *Breakfast* [M] *Bus Stop 16.*

TROULLOS ΤΡΟΥΛΛΟΣ

4 km (2½ miles) west of Kalamaki Peninsula, 8 km (5 miles) west of Skiathos Town.

West of the Kalamaki Peninsula the coast road rounds Troullos Bay and comes to Koukounaries Beach—famous and beautiful but not a remote hideaway.

EXPLORING

Kounistra Monastery. The dirt road north of Troullos leads to beaches and to the small, now deserted, Kounistra Monastery. It was built in 1655 on the spot where a monk discovered an icon of the Virgin miraculously dangling from a pine tree. The icon spends most of the year in the church of Trion Hierarchon, in Skiathos Town, but on November 20 the townspeople parade it to its former home for the celebration of the

Presentation of the Virgin the following day. You can enter the deserted monastery church any time, though its interior has been blackened by fire and its 18th-century frescoes are difficult to see. ⊠ *Troullos* ⊹ *4 km (2½ miles) north of Troullos* Ⓜ *Bus Stop 21.*

BEACHES

Agia Eleni and Krasa. Around the island's western tip are Ayia Eleni and Krasa, facing the nearby Pelion Peninsula. The beaches are also known as Big and Little Banana, perhaps because sun worshippers—mainly gay men on Little Banana—often peel their clothes off. Rocky coves provide some privacy. **Amenities:** food and drink; parking (free); showers; toilets; water sports. **Best for:** nudists; partiers; sunset; swimming. ⊠ *Troullos* ⊹ *1 km (½ mile) west of Koukounaries Beach, 13 km (8 miles) west of Skiathos Town* Ⓜ *Bus Stop 26.*

Fodor'sChoice
★ **Koukounaries.** Some fans call this scenic slice of shoreline "Golden Coast," after its fine, sparkling golden sand, but in high season, when sunseekers land by the boatload, you'll be lucky to find a free patch. The name, Greek for stone pines, comes from the forest that is almost watered by the waves. Enjoy a leisurely stroll behind the beach to Strofilia Lake, an impressive biotope where rare species of birds find shelter. **Amenities:** food and drink; lifeguard; parking (free); showers; toilets; water sports. **Best for:** partiers; snorkeling; sunrise; swimming; walking. ⊹ *4 km (2½ miles) northwest of Troullos, 12 km (8 miles) west of Skiathos Town* Ⓜ *Bus Stop 26.*

Mandraki Beach. A good 2½ km (1½ miles) from the main road—but accessible with a 4x4—this sandy stretch offers a sense of peace and privacy. Sometimes called Xerxes's harbor, the bay is where the notorious Persian king stopped on his way to ultimate defeat at the battles of Artemisium and Salamis. The reefs opposite are the site of a monument Xerxes allegedly erected as a warning to ships, the first such marker known in history. **Amenities:** food and drink; parking (free); toilets. **Best for:** nudists; snorkeling; solitude; swimming; walking. ⊠ *Troullos* ⊹ *5 km (3 miles) northwest of Troullos Bay, 12 km (7½ miles) west of Skiathos Town* Ⓜ *Bus Stop 23.*

Fodor'sChoice
★ **Megalos Aselinos and Mikros Aselinos.** At these side-by-side options, separated by a forested headland, expansive and laid-back Megalos Aselinos is a favorite of locals and tourists visiting by boat, while Mikros Aselinos is quieter and can be reached by car or bike. Neither, however, can be reached by bus. **Amenities:** food and drink; parking (free); toilets. **Best for:** snorkeling; solitude; sunset; swimming. ⊠ *Troullos Bay* ⊹ *7 km (4½ miles) north of Troullos, 12 km (7 miles) west of Skiathos Town* Ⓜ *No Bus.*

WHERE TO EAT

$$
MEDITERRANEAN
Fodor'sChoice
★ ✕ **Elia's.** An upstairs dining at the Mandraki Village hotel is as popular with outsiders as it is with guests, and the white, deep red, and magenta color scheme hints at the creativity of the cuisine, a thoughtful fusion of local Greek and Mediterranean flavors. An aubergine-and-goat's-cheese mille-feuille with pear might whisk you off to the south of France, while a gyro, that Greek street-food staple, comes with ramen noodles. **Known for:** airy and bold-yet-comfortable surroundings; innovative cuisine. Ⓢ *Average main: €20* ☎ *24270/493014* ⊕ *www.mandraki-skiathos.gr* Ⓜ *Bus Stop 21.*

$ ✕**Ratatouille Taverna-Grill House.** A popular and delightful terrace is the
GREEK setting for traditional Greek food and a great spot to prolong the relaxation after a lazy day on Troullos Beach. Succulent char-grilled chicken and lamb and *briam* (a Greek version of ratatouille) are the specialities and so good that tables fill up quickly, so it's best to reserve for dinner during peak summer months. **Known for:** souvlaki and other grilled meats; relaxed atmosphere. $ *Average main: €10* ✉ *Morfia Hotel ⚓ Just off the main road* ☎ *24270/49367* ⊕ *www.hotelmorfia.gr* Ⓜ *Bus Stop 18.*

WHERE TO STAY

$$ ⊡ **Mandraki Village.** Easy luxury and designer charm pervade these
HOTEL soothing accommodations done in warm, summery shades nestled in
FAMILY a "village" of eight buildings surrounded by an expansive garden of
Fodor'sChoice lemon trees and Mediterranean flowers. **Pros:** three tempting restaurants; attractive and soothing decor; beautiful garden setting. **Cons:**
★ some noise from room to room; not on the beach, but within walking distance to several; some rooms and bathrooms are small. $ *Rooms from: €161* ✉ *Koukounaries* ☎ *24270/49301* ⊕ *www.mandraki-skiathos.gr* ⇋ *38 rooms* ⦿| *Breakfast* Ⓜ *Bus Stop 21.*

$ ⊡ **Troulos Bay Hotel.** A big sandy beach steals the show here, and
HOTEL most of the clean, functional, and modern guest rooms look across
FAMILY lawns and a glimmering pool to the sea. **Pros:** good value for a beach hotel; best seaside location on the island; well suited to families. **Cons:** a bit basic; could-be-anywhere feel; few luxuries and amenities aside from beach and pool. $ *Rooms from: €110* ✉ *Troullos Bay* ☎ *24270/49390* ⊕ *www.troulosbayhotel.gr* ⊗ *Closed Nov.–Apr.* ⇋ *43 rooms* ⦿| *Breakfast* Ⓜ *Bus Stop 18.*

KASTRO ΚΑΣΤΡΟ

13 km (8 miles) northeast of Troullos, 9 km (5½ miles) northeast of Skiathos Town.

The ruins that are also known as the Old Town perch on a forbidding promontory high above the water, accessible only by steps. Skiathians founded this former capital in the 16th century when they fled from the pirates and the turmoil on the coast to the security of this remote cliff—staying until 1829. Its landward side was additionally protected by a moat and drawbridge, and inside the stout walls they erected 300 houses and 22 churches, of which only 2 remain. The little Church of the Nativity has some icons and must have heard many prayers for deliverance from the sieges that left the Skiathians close to starvation.

You can drive or take a taxi or bus to within 325 feet of the Old Town, or wear comfortable shoes for a walk that's mostly uphill. Better, take the downhill walk back to Skiathos Town; the trek takes about three hours and goes through orchards, fields, and forests on the well-marked paths of the interior.

LALARIA ΛΑΛΑΡΙΑ

2 km (1 miles) east of Kastro, 7 km (4½ miles) north of Skiathos Town.

Fodor'sChoice
★ The much-photographed, lovely Lalaria Beach, on the north coast, is flanked by a majestic, arched limestone promontory. The polished limestone and marble add extra sparkle to the already shimmering Aegean. There's no lodging here, and you can only reach Lalaria by taking an excursion boat or water taxi from the Old Port in Skiathos Town (the buses don't serve this beach). In the same area lie **Skoteini (Dark) cave, Galazia (Azure) cave,** and **Halkini (Copper) cave.** If taking a tour boat, you can stop for an hour or two here to swim and frolic. Bring along a flashlight to turn the water inside these grottoes an incandescent blue.

Evangelistria. The island's best-known and most beautiful monastery sits on Skiathos's highest point and was dedicated in the late-18th century to the Annunciation of the Virgin by the monks of Mt. Athos. It encouraged education and gave a base to revolutionaries, who pledged an oath to freedom and first hoisted the flag of Greece here in 1807. Looming above a gorge, and surrounded by fragrant pines and cypresses, the monastery has a high wall that once kept pirates out; today it encloses a ruined refectory kitchen, the cells, a small museum library, and a magnificent church with three domes. A gift shop sells the monastery's own Alypiakos wine, olive oil, locally made preserves, and Orthodox icons. In summer, a bus makes the run out to the monastery from the main station in Skiathos Town. ⊠ *Lalaria* ✛ *2 km (1 mile) south of Lalaria, 5 km (3 miles) north of Skiathos Town* 🖂 *Donations accepted.*

SKOPELOS ΣΚΟΠΕΛΟΣ

This triangular island's name means "a sharp rock" or "a reef"—a fitting description for the terrain on the northern shore. It's an hour away from Skiathos by hydrofoil and is the second largest of the Sporades. Most of its 122 square km (47 square miles), up to its highest peak on Mt. Delfi, are covered with dense pine forests, olive groves, and orchards. On the south coast, villages overlook the shores, and pines line the pebbly beaches, casting jade shadows on turquoise water.

Legend has it that Skopelos was settled by Peparethos and Staphylos, colonists from Minoan Crete, said to be the sons of Dionysus and Ariadne, King Minos's daughter. They brought with them the lore of the grape and the olive. The island was called Peparethos until Hellenistic times, and its most popular beach still bears the name Stafilos. In the 1930s a tomb believed to be Staphylos's was unearthed, filled with weapons and golden treasures (now in the Volos museum on the Pelion Peninsula).

The Byzantines were exiled here, and the Venetians ruled for 300 years, until 1204. In times past, Skopelos was known for its wine, but today its plums and almonds are eaten rather than drunk, and incorporated into the simple cuisine. Many artists and photographers have settled on the island and throughout summer are part of an extensive cultural program. Little by little, Skopelos is cementing an image as a green and artsy island, still unspoiled by success.

Although this is the most populated island of the Sporades, with two major towns, Skopelos remains peaceful and absorbs tourists into its life rather than giving itself up to their sun-and-fun desires. It's not surprising that ecologists claim it's the greenest island in the region.

GETTING HERE AND AROUND

AIR TRAVEL

There is no airport on Skopelos, but you can take an Athens–Skiathos flight, then taxi to Skiathos port, and from there take a hydrofoil to Skopelos.

BOAT AND FERRY TRAVEL

Ferries from the mainland leave from Agios Konstantinos or Volos, and ferries back to the mainland stop in Skiathos. Skopelos has two main ports: Skopelos Town and, at the northwestern end of the island, Loutraki (near the town of Glossa). In summer only there are three ferries weekly between Skopelos and Skyros; the trip takes about five hours.

Caïques leave from the docks in Skopelos Town and Loutraki for the most popular beaches. A lot of excursion boats also head over to Skiathos, as well as to nearby Alonissos; just walk along the docks, where captains post their destinations and departure times.

BUS TRAVEL

The main bus station on Skopelos is just above the harbor in Skopelos Town, in front of a large church at a junction for Agiou Riginou and Loutraki. Buses make a trip along the length of the island several times a day, more often in summer (hotels usually have schedules on hand). From Skopelos Town, buses cross the island to Stafilos then follow the west coast up to Glossa (€3.50, 1 hour), with stops along the way in Panormos, Elios, and other popular towns.

CAR TRAVEL

The only easy way to visit many beaches and see the forested interior is by car, and you'll probably want to rent one for at least part of your stay. The Local Route is a reliable car-rental company on Skopelos, and many international firms also have outlets. *See also Car Travel in Travel Smart.*

Contacts The Local Route. ✛ *50 meters to the right of the port* ☎ *24240/23682* ⊕ *www.thelocalroute.gr.*

TAXI TRAVEL

Taxis can be arranged through your hotel, or you can call operators directly.

Contacts Mr. G. Stamoulos. ☎ *69724/29568 mobile.*

TOURS

Skopelos Walks. To gain a unique perspective on Skopelos Town take one of the walking tours offered by Heather Parsons. She offers half- and full-day walking tours of the town and the island in May, June, September, and October lasting between three and five hours (longer tours have a lunchtime picnic stop). Most tours cost between €10 and €25. Advance reservations online or by phone are required. Parsons also arranges work weeks in which volunteers help clear *calderimia*, centuries-old stone paths that crisscross the island, sometimes with lodging and food provided in exchange for labor. ⊠ *Skopelos Town* ☎ *69452/49328* ⊕ *skopelos-walks.com.*

TRAVEL AGENCIES

Thalpos Holidays. Apart from providing the standard travel services, Thalpos can also arrange hiking, biking, cooking lessons, and other more personalized and alternative activities. ✉ *Paralia Skopelou, Skopelos Town* ☎ *24240/29036* ⊕ *www.holidayislands.com.*

VISITOR INFORMATION

Contacts Skopelos Municipality. ✉ *Waterfront, Skopelos Town* ☎ *24240/22205* ⊕ *www.skopelosweb.gr.*

SKOPELOS TOWN ΣΚΟΠΕΛΟΣ (ΠΟΛΗ)

3 hrs from Agios Konstantinos, ½ hr from Skiathos Town by ferry.

Pretty Skopelos Town, the administrative center of the Sporades, overlooks a bay on the north coast. Three- and four-story houses rise virtually straight up a hillside that is laced with steps and pebble-studded little lanes. The whitewashed houses look prosperous (18th-century Skopelos society was highly cultured and influential) and cared for, their facades enlivened by brightly painted or brown timber balconies, doors, and shutters, along with flamboyant vines and potted plants. Interspersed among the red-tile roofs are several with traditional gray fish-scale slate—too heavy and expensive to be used much nowadays. At the town's summit you're standing within the walls of the ruined 13th-century castle erected by the Venetian Ghisi lords who held all the Sporades as their fief. It in turn rests on polygonal masonry of the 5th century BC, as this was the site of one of the island's three ancient acropoli.

You will encounter many churches as you climb through the town—the island has more than 360, of which 123 are in the town proper, and their exteriors incorporate ancient artifacts, Byzantine plates or early Christian elements, and slate-capped domes. The uppermost, the 11th-century Ayios Athanasios, is said to be situated on the ruins of the ancient temple of Minerva and has a typically whitewashed exterior and an interior that includes 17th-century Byzantine murals.

EXPLORING

Evangelistria Monastery. A perch on Palouki Mountain provides views of the sea and the town. The impressive complex was founded in 1676 and completely rebuilt in 1712 by Ioannis Grammatikos, who believed he was saved from execution by an 11th-century icon of the Virgin. The miraculous object is housed in the church, with an intricately carved iconostasis. ✉ *Skopelos Town* ⊕ *On the mountainside opposite Skopelos Town, 1½ km (1 mile) northeast of town* ☎ *24240/23230* 🎫 *Free.*

Folklore Museum. For an impression of how upper-class Skopelians lived 200 years ago, step into this 18th-century mansion (1795) with hand-carved period furniture, decorative items, paintings, and embroideries. Don't miss the display of the elaborately sewn wedding dress in the bridal chamber. ✉ *Hatzistamati* ☎ *24240/23494* 🎫 *€3* ☯ *Closed weekends Oct.–May.*

Metamorphosis tou Sotera. The oldest monastery on the island (circa 1600), now occupied by a sole monk, features iconography in the old basilica that was painted by renowned Byzantine painter Agorastos. ✉ *Skopelos Town* ✛ *Follow the signs east of Skopelos Town, past Ayia Varvara* ⊗ *Closed Dec.–Mar.*

National Marine Park of Alonissos and Northern Sporades. Skopelos is at the edge of the largest swath of protected waters in the Mediterranean, covering 2,200 square km (849 square miles). Within the park, only neighboring Alonissos is inhabited; other islands and islets are the domain of goats and falcons, while dolphins and highly endangered Mediterranean monk seals swim in the pristine waters. Boats ply the waters of the park on day excursions from Skopelos, stopping at remote beaches and such outposts of civilization as the islet monastery of Megistis Lavras. Travel agencies and eager captains advertise the trips, easily arranged with a walk along the port. ✉ *Skopelos Town harbor.*

Prodromou (*Forerunner*). Dedicated to St. John the Baptist, Prodromou now operates as a convent. Besides being unusual in design, its church contains some outstanding 14th-century triptychs, an enamel tile floor, and an iconostasis spanning four centuries (half was carved in the 14th century, half in the 18th century). The nuns sell elaborate woven and embroidered handiwork. Opening days and hours vary. ✉ *Skopelos Town* ✛ *2½ km (1½ miles) east of Skopelos Town.*

Vakratsa. In this 19th-century mansion, furnishings, precious icons, and quotidian antiques from around the world make this a fine showcase of the life and traditions of a local family of high standing from a time when Skopelos was a hub for a well-traveled, politically influential, and highly cultured society. Andigoni Vakratsa and her father were doctors who offered free medical services to the poor. Head upstairs to view the living room (used only for very special occasions) where you can admire a traditional island engagement dress with its 4,000-pleat skirt. ✉ *Skopelos Town* ✛ *A short walk up from Ambrosia sweetshop* 🎫 *€3* ⊗ *Closed afternoons, but open mornings and evenings.*

BEACHES

FAMILY **Agnonda Beach.** This little seaside settlement fronts exceptionally clean waters and has numerous tavernas along its pebbled beach serving fresh seafood. Agnonda is named after a local boy who returned here victorious from Olympia in 569 BC brandishing the victor's wreath. **Amenities:** food and drink; parking (no fee); showers; toilets; water sports. **Best for:** snorkeling; solitude; swimming. ✉ *Agnonda* ✛ *8 km (5 miles) south of Skopelos Town.*

Stafilos Beach. Scattered farms and two tavernas, small houses with rooms for rent, and one or two pleasant hotels line the road to the seaside, where fragrant pines meet the cool, crystal-clear, calm waters. There's a simple canteen that serves snacks and refreshments (and even mojitos at sunset), and a lifeguard stand. Nearby, prehistoric walls, a watchtower, and an unplundered grave suggest that this was the site of an important prehistoric settlement. **Amenities:** food and drink; lifeguard, parking (no fee); showers. **Best for:** snorkeling; sunrise; swimming; walking. ✉ *Stafilos* ✛ *3 km (2 miles) southeast of Agnonda, 4 km (2½ miles) south of Skopelos Town.*

The Ayia Varvara Monastery is just one of 40 such medieval religious communities on Skopelos. Some are open to visitors: wear suitable dress (no bare arms or short skirts are allowed for women).

Velania. The name comes from the *valanium* (Roman bath) that once stood here on the coast due south of Skopelos Town. The bath has long since disintegrated under the waves, but the fresh spring water used for the baths still trickles out from a cave at the far end of the beach. To get here, follow the footpath that starts at Stafilos Beach over the forested hill. This extra hike is seemingly off-putting to many beachgoers, keeping Velania isolated and quiet. Today it's broadly favored by nudists. **Amenities:** none. **Best for:** nudists; snorkeling; solitude; sunrise; swimming; walking. ✥ *5 km (3 miles) south of Skopelos Town, 1 km (½ mile) east of Stafilos Beach.*

WHERE TO EAT

$ GREEK 🍴 **Alexander's Garden Restaurant.** At this little garden restaurant on the hillside, a 200-year-old well in the center of the elegant, leafy terrace produces its own natural spring water, a perfect addition to a traditional meal. Everything that comes from the kitchen is an old-time classic—bell peppers stuffed with cheese, garlic, and tomato, and the restaurant's *keftedakia,* meatballs made with a secret recipe. **Known for:** home cooking; lovely garden. [$] *Average main: €10* ✉ *Manolaki St.* ✥ *Turn inland after the corner shop Armoloi* ☎ *24240/22324* 🕓 *Closed Nov.–Mar. No lunch.*

$ GREEK 🍴 **Klimataria.** The blackfish *stifado* (stew) with onions is so delicious here you may find yourself doing the quintessentially Greek *papara*—sponging the plate clean with a piece of bread. Locals come to this harborside spot for other flavorsome local specialties, including such meat dishes as the pork cooked in a sauce of red wine, honey, and prunes (the sweet and sour fruit was once the island's star export), along with a soothing view of the moonlit sea. **Known for:** beautiful setting; reliably good cooking. [$] *Average main: €10* ✉ *Waterfront* ☎ *24240/22273* 🕓 *Closed mid-Oct.–mid-Dec.*

$ ✕ **Molos.** A favorite among the cluster of tavernas near the far end at the old port serves quality *magirefta* (dishes cooked ahead in the oven), along with a big dose of hospitality. Chef/owner Panayiotis sometimes takes time to liven things up with live music, stepping out from serving seafood pastas and such Skopelos specialties as stuffed courgette flowers. **Known for:** friendly atmosphere; traditional favorites. $ *Average main: €11* ✉ *Waterfront* ☎ *24240/22551* ⊘ *Closed Nov.–Mar.*

GREEK
Fodor's Choice
★

> **MAMMA MIA!**
>
> The 2008 movie *Mamma Mia!* used a lot of Skopelos as its dreamy setting, something many locals take great pride in. Film locations included the tiny Kastani Bay—where they constructed Meryl Streep's taverna and then dismantled it after the film—Milia Beach, and the breathtaking (literally) hilltop Ayios Ioannis Monastery overlooking Glossa.

4

$ ✕ **The Muses.** This romantic beachfront spot serves seafood and traditional Greek fare at the quiet edge of town, with the sea caressing the beach just a few feet from the tables. The freshest fish is grilled with a blend of mountain herbs and the succulent lamb *lemonato* (slow-roasted with garlic, salt, and lemon) falls off the bone. **Known for:** beachfront setting; good take on traditional cuisine. $ *Average main: €12* ✉ *Skopelos Beach* ⊹ *Southeast of the port, 350 feet along the beach road* ☎ *24240/24414.*

GREEK

$ ✕ **Ta Kymata.** Spirited brothers Andreas, Riginos, and Christophoros enthusiastically run the seafront taverna that has belonged to their family since 1896, serving traditional Skopelos recipes. The signature dish is *Tis Maharas*, an intense, pungent, yet surprisingly light mix of vegetables and cheeses with a creamy sauce, dedicated to the brothers' grandmother, whose name *Mahi* means battle and whose physical strength and towering height was said to ensure there was never any trouble at the taverna. **Known for:** fresh seafood and traditional cooking; nice harborside setting. $ *Average main: €10* ✉ *Skopelos Town* ⊹ *North end of the harbor* ☎ *24240/22381* ⊟ *No credit cards.*

GREEK

$ ✕ **To Perivoli.** The chef-owner of the aptly named "garden" prides himself on the fact that his menu has not changed at all in the last 20 years, and his regulars like it that way. A meal here, served on a patio beside an herb-and-flower garden, should include the filo pouches stuffed with mushrooms and end with the local specialty of *amygdalopitta* (almond cake) with ice cream. **Known for:** garden setting; traditional recipes with an innovative twist. $ *Average main: €12* ✉ *Off Platanos Sq., close to the waterfront* ☎ *24240/23758* ⊘ *Closed Oct.–May. No lunch.*

MODERN GREEK

WHERE TO STAY

$ ⬚ **Alkistis.** These simple but bright and airy apartments offer a feeling of a stay at a friend's summerhouse, with such idyllic touches as a beautifully maintained garden, abundant with bougainvillea and lemon trees, and an enormous swimming pool, with a retro swim-up bar. **Pros:** extremely restful atmosphere; nearby supermarket; friendly staff. **Cons:** isolated, although the hotel minibus takes guests to town; basic furnishings and amenities; not in town center. $ *Rooms from: €115* ✉ *Skopelos Town* ⊹ *2*

RENTAL
FAMILY

km (1 mile) southeast of town on road to Stafilos ☎ *24240/23006* 🌐 *www.alkistis-skopelos.gr* ⏲ *Closed Oct.–May* 🛏 *25 apartments* 🍴 *Breakfast.*

$ HOTEL 🏨 **Pension Sotos.** This cozy, restored old Skopelete house on the waterfront is inexpensive and casual, with tiny rooms looking onto one of the hotel's two courtyard terraces. **Pros:** low prices and good value; nice harbor-front location; loads of character. **Cons:** no breakfast; very few creature comforts; some stairs to climb. [$] *Rooms from: €40* ✉ *Skopelos Town* ✥ *On the waterfront* ☎ *24240/22549* 🛏 *12 rooms* 🍴 *No meals.*

$$ RESORT FAMILY 🏨 **Skopelos Village.** A chic, contemporary take on traditional Greek island charm comes with lots of breezy peacefulness, understated luxury, and comfort in delightful suites with plenty of outdoor space and, in many, sea views. **Pros:** lots of stylish comfort; great views; steps away from the beach. **Cons:** a 10-minute walk from the town center; neighborhood is quiet but not central; some bathrooms are small. [$] *Rooms from: €130* ✉ *Skopelos Town* ✥ *1 km (½ mile) east of the town center* ☎ *24240/22517* 🌐 *www.skopelosvillage.gr* ⏲ *Closed Nov.–Apr.* 🛏 *35 suites* 🍴 *Breakfast.*

$ HOTEL Fodor's Choice ★ 🏨 **Thea Home.** A wonderful choice for budget travelers, these clean, cozy, and graceful studios and maisonettes are a short walk up from the harbor—and come with a beautiful vista of the town from the large, living-room-like terrace. **Pros:** airy terraces; great views; small pool is a real plus in summer. **Cons:** steep uphill trek to reach the property (though free transport from port is provided); furnishings are fairly basic; some bathrooms are small and outdated. [$] *Rooms from: €65* ✉ *Ring road* ✥ *10-min walk up from the harbor* ☎ *24240/22859* 🌐 *www.theahomehotel.com* 🛏 *13 rooms* 🍴 *Breakfast.*

NIGHTLIFE

Nightlife on Skopelos is more relaxed than it is on Skiathos. A smattering of cozy bars play music of all kinds, and the *kefi* (good mood) is to be found at the western end of the waterfront in Skopelos Town. Take an evening *volta* (stroll); most bars have tables outside, so you really can't miss them.

MUSIC CLUBS

Anatoli. At this converted barn high up in town by the Kastro, tap into a Greek vein with proprietor Giorgo Xithari. Sometimes accompanied by local musicians and friends, he strums up a storm on his bouzouki and sings *rembetika,* traditional Greek acoustic blues. With an ouzo or two, the atmosphere can get heady, and soon you may discover new dancing talents inspired by old classics. ✉ *Kastro* ☎ *24240/22851.*

Anemos. Without a doubt the best cocktail bar on the island serves impeccably mixed cocktails not often found anywhere else; try the fragrantly sophisticated Paris Martini, or ask the barman to create one of his inspired concoctions to suit—or perfectly alter—your mood. The large stone terrace opens at 8 am for coffee and snacks. ✉ *Skopelos Town* ✥ *On the harbor front* ☎ *24240/23564.*

Mercurius. This perch just above the waterfront is ideal for a leisurely breakfast or invigorating sunset drinks with a stunning view and a sound track of world music. ✉ *Skopelos Town* ✥ *5-min walk up from the harbor* ☎ *24240/24593* 🌐 *www.mercurius.gr.*

Forget all those worries back home with one delicious dinner on the town square in Skopelos Town.

SHOPPING
LOCAL CRAFTS
Ploumisti. Kilims, bags, hand-painted T-shirts, ceramics, and jewelry are among the antique and new wares. ✉ *Paralia St., opposite the National Bank* ☎ *24240/22059.*

Yiousouri. Fans love the decorative ceramics. ✉ *Skopelos Town* ⚓ *On the waterfront near the Folklore Museum* ☎ *24240/23983.*

PANORMOS BAY ΟΡΜΟΣ ΠΑΝΟΡΜΟΥ

6 km (4 miles) west of Skopelos Town.

With a long beach and sheltered inner cove ideal for yachts, Panormos is fast becoming a holiday village, although so far this stretch of the coast retains a quiet charm. The little town has a long provenance and was founded in the 8th century BC by colonists from Chalkis; a few well-concealed walls are visible among the pinewoods on the acropolis above the bay. Inland, the interior of Skopelos is green and lush; not far from Panormos Bay, traditional farmhouses called *kalivia* stand in plum orchards. Some are occupied; others are used only for family holidays and feast-day celebrations. Look for the outdoor ovens, which baked the fresh plums when Skopelos was turning out prunes galore. This rural area is charming, but the lack of signposts makes it easy to get lost, so pay attention.

BEACHES

Adrina Beach. This strand of small pebbles has crystal-clear, turquoise water and, despite some sun beds and umbrellas, a feeling of seclusion. Dassia, the thickly forested islet across the bay, was named after a female pirate who (legend has it) was drowned there—but not before hiding her treasure. **■ TIP→ Access to the beach is somewhat difficult since you now have to go through the new resort to get to the shore.** **Amenities:** food and drink; showers; toilets; water sports. **Best for:** snorkeling; sunset; swimming. ✉ *Panormos Bay* ✣ *1 km (½ mile) west of Panormos Bay.*

Fodor's Choice ★ **Milia Beach.** Skopelos's longest beach is considered by many to be its best, with white sands, clear turquoise waters, and vibrant green trees. Though still secluded, the bay is up-and-coming—parasols and recliners are lined halfway across the beach and there's a large taverna tucked into the pine trees. **Amenities:** food and drink; parking (no fee); showers; toilets. **Best for:** snorkeling; sunset; swimming; walking; windsurfing. ✉ *Panormos Bay* ✣ *2 km (1 mile) north of Panormos Bay.*

WHERE TO STAY

$ HOTEL FAMILY **Afrodite.** Airy, light-filled rooms are steps from a lovely beach and are filled with views of the turquoise sea and lush mountains, all providing the essentials for a laid-back getaway. **Pros:** extremely friendly service; just steps from the beach; tavernas and shops a walk away. **Cons:** some nice amenities but few luxuries; holiday-village atmosphere (a plus for some); away from the action of Skopelos Town. $ *Rooms from: €85* ✉ *Panormos Bay* ☎ *24240/23150* 🌐 *www.afroditehotel.gr* *38 rooms* 🍽 *Breakfast.*

$ HOTEL **Panormos Beach Hotel.** The owner's attention to detail shows in the beautifully tended flower garden, the immaculate, attractive rooms with pine furniture and handwoven linens, the country dining room, and the museumlike lobby decorated with antiques and traditional costumes. **Pros:** friendly, homey environment; hospitality plus—with sweet offerings of homegrown fruit, wine, and sweets; lovely grounds. **Cons:** not all rooms have sea views; no elevator; no pool, but beach is nearby. $ *Rooms from: €80* ✉ *Panormos Bay* ✣ *1 block from the beachfront* ☎ *24240/22711* 🌐 *www.panormos-beach.com* ⏲ *Closed Nov.–Apr.* *34 rooms* 🍽 *Breakfast.*

GLOSSA ΓΛΩΣΣΑ

38 km (23 miles) northwest of Skopelos Town, 24 km (14 miles) northwest of Panormos Bay, 3 km (1½ miles) northwest of Klima.

Delightful Glossa is the island's second-largest settlement, where whitewashed, red-roof houses are clustered on the steep hillside above the harbor of Loutraki. Venetian towers and traces of Turkish influence remain; the center is closed to traffic. This is a place to relax, dine, and enjoy the quieter beaches. Just to the east, have a look at Ayios Ioannis Monastery, dramatically perched above a pretty beach. There's no need to tackle the series of extremely steep steps to the monastery, as it is not open to visitors.

WHERE TO EAT

$$ 🍴 **Agnanti Restaurant.** This long-established landmark entices with its playful and innovative takes on classic Greek dishes. While the awe-inspiring panoramic vista of the Aegean Sea would be enough to please customers, owner Nikos Stamatakis and his chef father, Stamatis, wow diners with the island's most exciting cuisine. **Known for:** amazing views; gracious ambience; innovative twists on traditional fare. [$] *Average main: €17* ✉ *Street of Tastes 3* ☎ *24240/33306* 🌐 *agnanti.com.gr* 🕒 *Closed Nov.–Apr.*

MODERN GREEK

Fodor's Choice ★

SKYROS ΣΚΥΡΟΣ

Even among these unique isles, Skyros stands out. The rugged terrain resembles that of an island in the Dodecanese, and the spectacularly sited main town—occupied on and off for the last 3,300 years and haunted by mythical ghosts—looks Cycladic. Surprisingly beguiling, this southernmost of the Sporades is the largest (209 square km [81 square miles]). A narrow, flat isthmus connects Skyros's two almost-equal parts, whose names reflect their characters—*Meri* or *Imero* ("tame") for the north, and *Vouno* (literally, "mountain," meaning tough or stony) for the south. The heavily populated north is virtually all farmland and forests. The southern half of the island is forbidding, barren, and mountainous, with Mt. Kochilas its highest peak (2,598 feet). The western coast is outlined with coves and deep bays dotted with a series of islets.

Until Greece won independence in 1831, the population of Skyros squeezed sardine-fashion into the area under the castle on the inland face of the rock. Not a single house was visible from the sea. Though the islanders could survey any movement in the Aegean for miles, they kept a low profile, living in dread of the pirates based at Treis Boukes Bay on Vouno.

The Skyrians have not had a seafaring tradition, and have looked to the land for their living. Their isolation has brought about notable cultural differences from the other Greek islands, such as pre-Christian Carnival rituals. Today there are more than 300 churches on the island, many of them private and owned by local families. An almost-extinct breed of pony resides on Skyros, and exceptional crafts—carpentry, pottery, embroidery—are practiced by dedicated artisans whose creations include unique furniture and decorative linens. There are no luxury accommodations or swank restaurants: this idiosyncratic island makes no provisions for mass tourism, but if you've a taste for the offbeat, you may feel right at home.

GETTING HERE AND AROUND

AIR TRAVEL

You can get to Skyros from Athens by air on Aegean Airlines in about 40 minutes. The airport is on the north of the island 15 km (9 miles) from Skyros Town, but a shuttle bus always meets the plane. Tickets on the shuttle cost €3 to €6; the trip takes 20 minutes.

Contacts Skyros Airport. ✣ *11 km (7 miles) northwest of Skyros Town* ☎ *22220/91684.*

In *Mamma Mia!*, Glossa's church of Ayios Ioannis was the beautiful backdrop for the wedding scene, but the interior was totally made up; the actual monastery is not open to visitors.

BOAT TRAVEL

Ferries to Skyros are operated by the Skyros Shipping Company (*see Boat and Ferry Travel in Travel Smart*) and leave from Kimi on the large island of Evia (connected to the mainland by bridges) and take 2½ hours; there are several ferries a day on weekends, and usually two daily ferries during the week. All boats dock at Linaria, far from Skyros Town. A shuttle bus always meets the boat; bus tickets cost €2 to €3. Taxis also meet the boats, but settle the fee before setting out. In summer only there are three ferries weekly between Skopelos and Skyros; the trip takes about five hours.

BUS TRAVEL

Contacts Skyros Bus Information. ☎ *22220/91600.*

CAR TRAVEL

Martina's is one of several reliable local agencies that rent cars on Skyros.

Contacts Martina's. ✉ *Maheras, Skyros Town* ☎ *22220/92022.*

TAXI TRAVEL

Arrange taxis through your hotel, or find them at the ports and town centers.

FESTIVALS

Apokries. This pre-Lenten Carnival revelry relates to pre-Christian Dyonisian fertility rites and is famous throughout Greece. Young men dressed as old men, maidens, or "Europeans" roam the streets teasing and tormenting onlookers with ribald songs and clanging bells. The "old men" wear elaborate shepherd's outfits, with masks made of baby-goat hides and belts dangling with as many as 40 sheep bells.

TRAVEL AGENCIES
Contacts Skyros Travel. ✉ *Agora, Skyros Town* ☎ *22220/91123, 22220/91600* ⊕ *www.skyrostravel.com.*

VISITOR INFORMATION
Contacts Greek National Tourism Organization (GNTO or EOT). ⊕ *www. visitgreece.gr.* **Skyros official website.** ☎ *22223/50300* ⊕ *www.skyros.gr.*

SKYROS TOWN ΣΚΥΡΟΣ (ΧΩΡΙΟ)

1 hr and 40 mins from Kimi to Linaria by boat, 30 mins from Linaria by car.

Fodor's Choice ★

From the southern landscapes, amid brown, desolate outcroppings with only an occasional goat as a sign of life, Skyros Town suddenly looms around a bend. Blazing white, cubist, dense, and otherworldly, clinging, precariously it seems, to the precipitous rock and topped gloriously by a fortress-monastery, this town more closely resembles a village in the Cyclades than any other you'll find in the Sporades.

Called *Chora* ("village") by the locals, Skyros Town is home to 90% of the island's 3,000 inhabitants. The impression as you get closer is of stark, simple buildings creeping up the hillside, with a tangle of labyrinthine lanes steeply winding up, down, and around the tiny houses, Byzantine churches, and big squares. As you explore the alleyways off the main street, try to peek discreetly into the houses. Skyrians are house-proud and often leave their windows and doors open to show off. In fact, since the houses all have the same exteriors, the only way for families to distinguish themselves has been through interior design. Walls and conical mantelpieces are richly decorated with European- and Asian-style porcelain, copper cooking utensils, wood carvings, and embroideries. Wealthy families originally obtained much of the porcelain from the pirates in exchange for grain and food, and its possession was a measure of social standing. Then enterprising potters started making exact copies, along with the traditional local ware, leading to the unique Skyrian style of pottery. The furniture is equally beautiful, and often miniature in order to conserve interior space.

The summit of the hill is crowned with three tiny cubelike churches with blue-and-pink interiors, and the ruined Venetian cistern, once used as a dungeon. From there you have a spectacular view of the town and surrounding hills. The roofs are flat, the older ones covered with a dark gray shale that has splendid insulating properties. The house walls and roofs are interconnected, forming a pattern that from above looks like a magnified form of cuneiform writing. Here and there the shieldlike roof of a church stands out from the cubist composition of white houses that fills the hillside—with not an inch to spare.

EXPLORING

Most commercial activity takes place in or near the Agora (the market street), familiarly known as Sisifos, as in the myth, because of its frustrating steepness. Found here are the town's pharmacies, travel agencies,

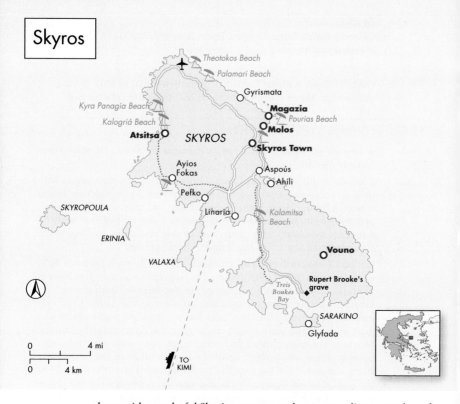

Skyros

Theotokos Beach
Palamari Beach
Gyrismata
Kyra Panagia Beach
Kalogriá Beach
Atsitsá   **SKYROS**   **Magazia**
                            Pourias Beach
                            Molos
Ayios   **Skyros Town**
Fokas   Aspoús
             Ahíli
Pefko
SKYROPOULA   Linariá   Kalamitsa
                          Beach
ERINIA
VALAXA   **Vouno**
                          Treis   **Rupert Brooke's**
                          Boukes   **grave**
                          Bay
                                     SARAKINO
                                     Glyfada

0   4 mi
0   4 km

TO
KIMI

shops with wonderful Skyrian pottery, and an extraordinary number of tiny bars and tavernas, but few boutiques and even less kitsch. In the summer heat, all shops and restaurants close from 2 pm to 6 pm, but the town comes alive at night.

Archeological Museum of Skyros. These two small rooms (on the way to Magazia Beach as you begin to descend from the town) contain rare weapons, pottery, and jewelry, mostly from graves dating from Neolithic to Roman times. Especially alluring are the pony motifs and the vase in the shape of a horse. ⊠ *Rupert Brooke Sq.* ☎ *2220/91327* ⊕ *odysseus.culture.gr* ☜ *€2* ⊗ *Closed Mon.*

Episkopi Church. Take the vaulted passageway from St. George's Monastery courtyard to this ruined church, the former seat of the bishop of Skyros, built in AD 895 on the ruins of a temple of Athena. The complex was the center of Skyros's religious life from 1453 to 1837. You can continue up to the summit from here. ⊠ *Skyros Town* ⊕ *Above St. George's Monastery.*

Fodor's Choice ★ **Faltaits Historical and Folklore Museum.** Built after Greek Independence by a wealthy family (who still owns the museum), the house is one of the most impressive in Skyros Town and is nearly overflowing with rare books, costumes, photographs, paintings, ceramics, local embroideries, Greek statues, and other heirlooms. Of particular note are the embroideries, which are famed for their flamboyant colors and vivacious renderings of mermaids, *hoopoes* (the Skyrians' favorite bird), and mythical human figures whose clothes and limbs sprout flowers. Top treasure among the museum's historical documents is a handwritten copy of the Proclamation of the Greek Revolution against the Ottoman Empire. The informative guided tour is well worth the extra euros. ✉ *Rupert Brooke Sq.* ☎ *2220/91150* ⊕ *www.faltaits.gr* 💶 *€2, tour €5.*

Fodor's Choice ★ **Monastery of St. George.** The best way to get an idea of the town and its history is to follow the sinuous cobbled lanes past the mansions of the Old Town to the Kastro, the highest point, and this fortified monastery founded in AD 962 and radically rebuilt in 1600. Today it is inhabited by a sole monk. A white marble lion, which may be left over from the Venetian occupation, is in the wall above the entrance to the monastery. The once splendid frescoes of the Monastery of St. George are now mostly covered by layers of whitewash, but look for the charming St. George and startled dragon outside to the left of the church door and, within, the ornate iconostasis. An icon of St. George on the right is said to have been brought by settlers from Constantinople, who came in waves during the iconoclast controversy of the 9th century. The icon has a black face and is familiarly known as Ayios Georgis o Arapis ("the Negro"); the Skyrians view him as the patron saint not only of their island but of lovers as well. ✉ *Skyros Town* ✛ *1 km (½ mile) above waterfront.*

MYTHIC SKYROS

In the legends of *The Iliad*, before the Trojan War, Theseus, the deposed hero-king of Athens, sought refuge in his ancestral estate on Skyros. King Lykomedes, afraid of the power and prestige of Theseus, took him up to the acropolis one evening, pretending to show him the island, and pushed him over the cliff—an ignominious end. In ancient times, Timon of Athens unearthed what he said were Theseus's bones and sword, and placed them in the Theseion—more commonly called the Temple of Hephaistion—in Athens, in what must be one of the earliest recorded archaeological investigations.

Rupert Brooke Memorial Statue. It'd be hard to miss the classical bronze statue, "To Brooke," an honorary tribute to the heroic Edwardian-era English poet Rupert Brooke, whose nude and very masculine depiction created quite a stir when unveiled in 1931. Every street seems to lead to the statue, with a 180-degree view of the sea as a backdrop. In 1915, aged 28, Brooke was on his way to the Dardanelles to fight in World War I when he died of septicemia in a French hospital ship off Skyros. Brooke was a socialist, but he became something of a paragon for war leaders such as Winston Churchill. ✉ *Rupert Brooke Sq.* ⊕ *www. rupertbrookeonskyros.com.*

BEACHES

Theotokos Beach. At the northwest side of Skyros above Ayios Petros, this is a relatively secluded beach reachable by dirt road followed by a little stroll down a goat path. Nearby is the off-limits military base. **Amenities:** none. **Best for:** nudists; snorkeling; solitude; swimming; windsurfing. ✛ *15 km (9 miles) northwest of Skyros Town.*

WHERE TO EAT

Skyros is especially noted for spiny lobster, almost as sweet as the North Atlantic variety.

$ ✕ **Anatolikos Anemos.** Come here to enjoy tasty *meze* bites and delicious
GREEK   simple dishes while sipping ouzo or cool white wine as the twilight colors the endless Aegean. This cozy little joint has a simple homey feel of a traditional Skyrian dwelling, with intricately carved dark brown walnut furnishings and colorful handmade embroideries adding verve to the boxy whitewashed interior spaces. **Known for:** views from the terrace; cozy atmosphere; cash only. $ *Average main: €10* ⊠ *Off Rupert Brooke Sq.* ☎ *22220/93622* ⊟ *No credit cards.*

$$ ✕ **O Pappous Ke Ego.** "My Grandfather and I," as the name translates in
GREEK   English, serves terrific Greek cuisine in an eclectic dining room decorated with hanging spoons, bottles of wine and ouzo, and whole heads of garlic. The proud grandson suggests that diners order a selection of *mezedes* (small plates) and share with others at the table. **Known for:** dishes based on local recipes; homey atmosphere; casserole of baby goat. $ *Average main: €18* ⊠ *Agora* ☎ *2220/93200* ☉ *Closed Nov. and Dec. No lunch.*

WHERE TO STAY

$$ ▦ **Nefeli Hotel.** The best hotel in Skyros Town is a bastion of taste and
HOTEL   comfort, with soothing Cycladic whites and soft green trim, a dazzling
Fodor's Choice   seawater pool, elegant bar terrace, and handsome furnishings in the
★   sophisticated guest rooms. **Pros:** stylish and comfortable; a library of more than a thousand books; easy walk to town and beach. **Cons:** often booked (reserve in advance); pricey by island standards; not on the water. $ *Rooms from: €140* ⊠ *Plageiá* ☎ *2220/91964* ⊕ *www.skyros-nefeli.gr* ⌦ *100 rooms* ▯◯▯ *Breakfast.*

NIGHTLIFE

Skyros Town's bars are seasonal affairs, offering loud music in summer.

Rodon Music Cafe. Takis, the owner, is also the DJ here, and he loves spinning the best tunes in town. ⊠ *Agora.*

SHOPPING

Want to buy something really unusual for a shoe lover? Check out the multithong *trohadia,* worn with pantaloons by Skyrian men as part of their traditional costume. Just as unique, elaborate Skyrian pottery and furniture are famous around the country. The pottery is both utilitarian and decorative, and the distinctive wooden furniture is easily recognizable by its traditionally carved style. The best places to shop are on the Agora. Skyrian furniture can be shipped anywhere. Don't try to shop between 2 and 6 pm, as all stores close for siesta.

FURNITURE

Thesis Wood. The workshop of Lefteris Avgoklouris and Emmanouela Toliou, carpenters with flair, is open to visitors. They will show off their chairs and other pieces and tell you about other master carpenters and craftspeople on the island who make original Skyrian furniture, famous around Greece for its intricate technique. They ship their distinctive pieces abroad. ⊠ *Lino* ✛ *On the beach south of Skyros Town* ☎ *22220/9106* ⊕ *www.thesiswood.com.*

MAGAZIA AND MOLOS ΜΑΓΑΖΙΑ ΚΑΙ ΜΩΛΟΣ

1 km (½ mile) northeast of Skyros Town.

Coastal expansions of the main town, these two resort areas are the places to stay if you love to swim. Magazia, where the residents of Skyros Town used to have their storehouses and wine presses, and Molos, a bit farther north, where the small fishing fleet anchors, are both growing fast. You can sunbathe, explore the isolated coastline, and stop at sea caves for a swim. Nearby are rooms to rent and tavernas serving the day's catch and local wine. From here, Skyros Town is 15 to 20 minutes away on foot, up the steps that lead past the archaeological museum to Rupert Brooke Square.

BEACHES

The coastline from **Molos** to **Magazia** is one long, sandy beach.

Palamari Beach. North of Molos, past low hills, fertile fields, and the odd farmhouse, a dirt road leads to this historical beach where ruins from a Neolithic fortress and settlement have been discovered. Palamari has cool, crystal waters and sandy shores that offer a sense of privacy. **Amenities:** none. **Best for:** nudists; snorkeling; solitude; sunrise; swimming; walking. ✥ *North of Skyros Town.*

Pourias Beach. A short walk south of Magazia, Pourias offers good snorkeling, and nearby on the cape is a small treasure: a sea cave that has been transformed into a chapel. There may be no amenities on the beach itself, but there is a little hotel nearby where one can get refreshments. **Amenities:** none. **Best for:** snorkeling; solitude; swimming; walking. ✉ *Magazia* ✥ *Just south of town.*

WHERE TO STAY

$ RESORT 🏨 **Perigiali.** Simply decorated, tasteful rooms and apartments come with many comforts—private terraces, a pretty, lush garden with plenty of shade, and a refreshing pool, all just steps from the beach and a 15-minute walk to Skyros Town. **Pros:** near Magazia Beach; nice outdoor spaces; friendly staff. **Cons:** no parking (but free parking two-minute walk away); no sea views; access difficult for travelers with limited mobility. [$] *Rooms from: €100* ✉ *Magazia* ✥ *On beachfront at foot of Skyros Town* ☎ *2220/91889* 🌐 *www.perigiali.com* 🛏 *11 rooms* 🍴 *Breakfast.*

$ RESORT 🏨 **Skiros Palace.** With a big pool and near a gorgeous, isolated beach, this cluster of white, cubist houses is a water lover's dream, though the simple, traditionally furnished guest rooms are pleasant, they don't quite live up to the hotel's name. **Pros:** very attractive grounds and pool; great views; Skyros Town is only a 20-minute walk away. **Cons:** half board required at some times; somewhat compoundlike in feeling; can be overrun with groups. [$] *Rooms from: €110* ✥ *North of Molos Town center* ☎ *2220/91994* 🌐 *www.skyroshotels.com* 🕓 *Closed Oct.–May* 🛏 *80 rooms* 🍴 *Breakfast.*

FESTIVALS

Panayia (*Festival of the Virgin*). On the major Greek Orthodox celebration of August 15 (Dormition of the Virgin), children gather at Magazia Beach to race on the island's domesticated small ponies, similar to Shetland ponies. ⊠ *Magazia Beach, Magazia.*

ATSITSA ΑΤΣΙΤΣΑ

14 km (9 miles) west of Molos.

On the northwest coast, pine forests grow down the rocky shore at Atsitsa. The beaches north of town—Kalogriá and Kyra Panayia—are sheltered from the strong northern winds called the *meltemi.*

EXPLORING

Skyros Centre. The first major center in Europe for holistic vacations has been bringing visitors to Skyros for 40 years. Participants come for a two-week session, staying in straw huts or in the main building, in a peaceful environment surrounded by pines and facing the sea. Studies and courses include windsurfing, creative writing with well-known authors, art, tai chi, yoga, massage, dance, drama, and sound-healing. Courses also take place in Skyros Town, where participants live in villagers' traditional houses. Skyros Centre's courses are highly reputed. Contact the London office well in advance of leaving for Greece. ⊠ *Atsitsa* ☏ *(0044)/01983–865566 in the UK* ⊕ *www.skyros.com.*

BEACHES

Ayios Fokas. The road south from Atsitsa deteriorates into a rutted track, nerve-racking even for experienced motorbike riders. If you're feeling fit and the weather's good, however, consider the challenging 6-km (4-mile) trek around the headland to Ayios Fokas. There are three lovely white-pebbled beaches and a small taverna where Kyria Kali serves fresh fish caught that very same day by her fisherman husband; the fish is garnished with her own vegetables, homemade cheese, and bread. She also rents out a couple of very basic rooms without electricity or plumbing. **Amenities:** food and drink; toilets. **Best for:** snorkeling; solitude; sunset; swimming; walking. ⊠ *Atsitsa* ✛ *5 km (3 miles) south of Atsitsa.*

Ayios Petros Beach. Close to the airport, this wonderful white-sand-and-pebble beach is surrounded by lush greenery and serenely backdropped, on the hill above, by the little chapel of Ayios Petros. Don't be put off by the 4 km (2½ miles) of dirt road leading to the beach, as the rough-going is definitely worth the effort. **Amenities:** none. **Best for:** snorkeling; swimming; walking; windsurfing. ⊠ *Atsitsa* ✛ *8 km (5 miles) north of Atsitsa, 15 km (9 miles) north of Skyros Town.*

VOUNO ΒΟΥΝΟ

Via Loutro, 5 km (3 miles) northwest of Linaria; access to southern territory starts at Ahilli, 4 km (2½ miles) south of Skyros Town and 25 km (15½ miles) from Atsitsa.

In the mountainous southern half of Skyros, a passable dirt road heads south at the eastern end of the isthmus, from Aspous to Ahilli. The little

bay of Ahilli (from where legendary Achilles set sail with Odysseus) is a yacht marina. Some beautiful, practically untouched beaches and sea caves are well worth the trip for hard-core explorers.

Thorny bushes warped into weird shapes, oleander, and rivulets running between sharp rocks make up the landscape; only goats and Skyrian ponies can survive this desolate environment. Many scholars consider the beautifully proportioned, diminutive horses to be the same breed as the horses sculpted on the Parthenon frieze. They are, alas, an endangered species, and only about 100 survive.

Rupert Brooke's Grave. Pilgrims to the poet's grave should follow the wide dirt road through the Vouno wilderness down toward the shore. As you reach the valley, you catch sight of the grave on your left. Brooke was buried the evening of the day in 1915 that he died of sepsis from an infected mosquito bite, aboard a French hospital ship anchored off Skyros, and his marble grave in an olive grove was immortalized with his prescient words, "If I should die think only this of me:/ That there's some corner of a foreign field/ That is forever England." Restored by the British Royal Navy in 1961, the grave site is surrounded by a stout wrought-iron and cement railing. You also can arrange for a visit by taxi or caïque in Skyros Town. ⊠ *Kalamitsa* ✛ *Southwest end of the island* ⊕ *www.rupertbrookeonskyros.com.*

BEACHES

Kalamitsa. The windy beach of Kalamitsa is 4 km (2½ miles) along the road south from Ahilli, and popular with windsurfers for obvious reasons. Nevertheless, this also means that the clean sands can be whipped up into a skin-cleansing frenzy on certain days, so whether you're a surfer or bather, check the winds first. ■ **TIP→ It's known for its clean waters.** There are three decent tavernas at this old harbor. **Amenities:** food and drink; parking (free); showers; toilets; water sports. **Best for:** snorkeling; sunset; surfing; swimming; windsurfing. ⊠ *Kalamitsa.*

CORFU

WELCOME TO CORFU

TOP REASONS TO GO

★ **Corfu Town:** Recognized by UNESCO as a World Heritage site, this sophisticated little gem of a city glows with a profusion of picturesque reminders of its Venetian, French, and British past.

★ **Pontikonisi:** As they savor the famous panorama of Pontikonisi, from the patio of the viewpoint in suburban Kanoni, how many of today's visitors know that tiny "Mouse island" was thought by the ancients to be Odysseus's ship turned to stone by Poseidon?

★ **Mon Repos:** Owned by the Greek royal family before they were deposed, the elegant neoclassical villa of Mon Repos, with its enchanting seaside gardens and secret beach, was originally built as a love gift from a British lord high commissioner to his wife.

★ **Paleokastritsa:** Once extolled by Odysseus, Homer's "city of the Phaeacians" remains a swimmable, sunbathed spectacle of grottoes, cliffs, white sand, and turquoise waters.

The islands in the Ionian Sea off the western coast of Greece had many occupiers over the millennia, but never the Turks. The residents of Corfu (*Kerkyra* in Greek), the main island, were greatly influenced by the urban lifestyles of Venetian settlers as well as the orderly formality of the 19th-century British protectorate. With its fairy-tale setting, Corfu is connected in high summer by ferries with Italy and Igoumenitsa on the Greek mainland. For many European travelers, Corfu is the gateway to Greece.

1 Corfu Town. Along the east coast mid-island, Corfu Town occupies a small peninsula anchored at its eastern tip by the massive Old Fortress and to the north by the New Fortress. Between the two is the gorgeous and lively Paleopolis (Old Town) crammed with Venetian and English Georgian houses, arcaded streets, narrow alleyways, and tiny squares, the entire urban ensemble buffered by the leafy Esplanade, used as a parade ground by the British and now a popular public park.

2 South Corfu. Just south of Corfu Town is a region that royals and their high-ranking officials once called home. Mon Repos, with its gorgeous seaside gardens, was the summer residence of the British lord high commissioners, later taken over by the Greek royal family, and was the birthplace of Prince Philip, Queen Elizabeth II's husband. Another 16 km (10 miles) south is Gastouri, site of the Achilleion, a late-19th-century Teutonic extravaganza built for Empress Elizabeth of Austria. To remind yourself you're really in Greece, head to Kanoni and take in the famed vista of the chapel-crowned Mouse island.

3 West-Central Corfu. Corfu Town is great for a day or three of sightseeing, but you really need to head into the interior and along the western and northeastern coastlines to discover the natural beauty and charms of Corfu. Many head to Paleokastritsa, on the west side of the island, home to one of Greece's best beaches; rent a boat to visit the nearby caves.

5

Pelekito

Kassiopi

Sidari

Roda

*Mt.
Pantokrator* ▲

Ano
Korakiana

Agni

Makrades

Kato
Korakiana

*Gulf of
Corfu*

Dassia

Paleokastritsa

3

C O R F U

PTIHIA

⭐ CORFU TOWN

1

Pelekas

◆ **Mon Repos**

Kanoni

◆ **Pontikonisi**

Achilleion

2

Gastouri

Pendati

Benitses

Moraitika

Boukari

I
O
N
I
A
N

S
E
A

Lefkimmi

0   15 mi

0   15 km

Updated by
Hilary Whitton
Paipeti

Temperate, multihued Corfu—of emerald mountains; turquoise waters lapping rocky coves; ocher and pink buildings; shimmering silver olive leaves; puffed red, yellow, and orange parasails; scarlet roses, bougainvillea, and lavender wisteria and jacaranda spread over cottages—could have inspired impressionism.

Kerkyra (Corfu) is certainly the lushest and, quite possibly, the loveliest of all Greek islands. Breathlessly blue waters lap rocky, pine-rimmed coves, and plants like bougainvillea, wisteria, and sweet-smelling jasmine spread over the countryside. Homer's "well-watered gardens" and "beautiful and rich land" were Odysseus's last stop on his journey home. Corfu is also said to be the inspiration for Prospero's island in Shakespeare's *The Tempest*. This northernmost of the major Ionian islands has, through the centuries, inspired other artists, as well as conquerors, royalty, and, of course, tourists.

Today more than a million—mainly British—tourists visit every year, and in summer they crowd the evocative capital city of Corfu Town (population 40,000). As a result, the town has a number of stylish restaurants and hotels and a sophisticated European atmosphere. The interior of Corfu, however, remains largely unspoiled, and the island has absorbed many layers of architectural history, offering an alluring mix of neoclassical villas, Venetian palazzo, pastel-painted hill towns, old farmhouses, and classy, city-sized resorts. You'll find all this plus ancient olive groves, pine-covered cliffs, and heart-stopping, beautiful vistas of sea and sky. Corfu remains an enchanting mixture of simplicity and sophistication.

The classical remains have suffered from the island's tempestuous history; architecture from the centuries of Venetian, French, and British rule is most evident, leaving Corfu and especially Corfu Town with a pleasant combination of contrasting design elements. And although it was bombed during the Italian and Nazi occupation in World War II, the town of Corfu remains one of the most charming in all of Greece.

PLANNING

WHEN TO GO

Corfu enjoys a temperate climate, with a relatively long rainy season that lasts from late fall through early spring. Winter showers bring spring flowers, and the countryside goes into floral overdrive starting in March, when the air is perfumed with the heady fragrance of orange blossoms and jasmine and wildflowers carpet the hillsides. In May, the weather clears and starts to get warm enough for swimming. July and August are the hottest months and can also be humid. September is gloriously warm and dry, with warm evenings and the occasional cool breeze. Swimming is often possible through mid-October. Late September through late October is good for hiking and exploring the countryside, as is the spring.

PLANNING YOUR TIME

Corfu is often explored in a day—many people pass through quickly as part of a cruise of the Greek islands. Two days allows enough time to visit Corfu Town and its nearby and most famous sites. With four days you can spend time exploring the island's other historic sites and natural attractions along both coasts. Six days allows you time to get a closer look at the museums, churches, and forts and perhaps even take a day trip to Albania.

Because Corfu is small, it's easy to make day trips to outlying villages and return to accommodations in or near Corfu Town. Alternatively, you could spend a night at the hilltop Pelekas or farther north at the seaside Paleokastritsa. To really get off the beaten path, take the coast road northeast from Corfu Town and around Daphnila bay to Agni and from there into the most mountainous part of the island, or head west from Corfu Town into the mountains and ancient olive groves to stay near Kato Korakiana, home to Etrusco, the best restaurant on Corfu, and many would say Greece itself. If you're planning a visit to the northwest, avoid the tatty beach towns of Sidari and Roda: both have been ruined by overdevelopment, and neither beach is particularly clean or inviting.

As for Corfu Town, where should you start upon your arrival? Catch your breath by first relaxing with a coffee or a gelato in Corfu Town's shaded Liston arcade, and then stroll the narrow lanes of the pedestrians-only quarter. For an overview of the immediate area, and a quick tour of Mon Repos palace, hop on the little tourist train that runs from May to September. Corfu Town has a different feel at night, so book a table at one of its famed tavernas to savor Corfu's unique cuisine.

GETTING HERE AND AROUND

You don't need or want a car in Corfu Town, which is compact and easily walkable. Buses run to the island's main towns and beaches, but if you want to visit some of Corfu's loveliest and most inaccessible places, all of them within an hour of Corfu Town, you'll need your own transportation. Corfu's gentle climate and rolling hills make it ideal motorbike country. You can rent cars and motorbikes at the airport or near the harbor in Corfu Town. If you plan to visit only a few of the major towns, the inexpensive local bus system will do. Taxis can be hired for day-trips from Corfu Town.

AIR TRAVEL

Olympic Air and Aegean Airlines offer multiple daily flights from Athens to Corfu. Fares change constantly, but the hour-long flight starts at about €180 round-trip from Athens. In Greece, Astra Airlines offers two flights per week from Thessaloniki to Corfu. Sky Express runs a service from Corfu to Preveza, Kefallonia, and Zakynthos three times a week. In the United Kingdom, easyJet has regularly scheduled flights to Corfu from Manchester, Bristol, Luton, and London's Gatwick. Jet2.com operates services from Glasgow, Manchester, Leeds Bradford, Newcastle, Edinburgh, London Stanstead, and East Midlands airports. Ryanair flies from East Midlands, London Stansted, Manchester, Leeds Bradford, Edinburgh, Birmingham, and Glasgow. British Airways flies directly from Heathrow every day in summer. *For information on all airlines, see Air Travel in Travel Smart.*

Corfu's Ioannis Kapodistrias International Airport is just south of Corfu Town, about a mile from the city center. A taxi from the airport to the center costs around €10; an airport bus runs hourly to the New Port via the Green Bus station and the town center. Taxi rates are on display in the arrivals hall.

Contacts Corfu International Airport (*CFU*). ⊕ *www.cfu-airport.gr*.

BOAT AND FERRY TRAVEL

There are no ferries from Piraeus to Corfu. Corfu's gateway to mainland Greece is the city of Igoumenitsa, from which ferries operated by the Kerkyra-Igoumenitsa-Paxi Consortium run almost hourly to Corfu Town throughout the day. Ferries four to five times daily also link Igoumenitsa with the port of Lefkimmi near Corfu's southern tip. Direct ferries from Italy (Brindisi, Bari, and Ancona) run only during July and August; outside of those months, you must change ferries in Igoumenitsa.

Most ferries dock at the New Port, in the northeast part of Corfu Town; from the ferry terminal you can easily walk into town or take a cab to your hotel. You can buy ferry tickets at the ports or book in advance through the ferry lines or travel agents. For the most up-to-date information on boat schedules (which change regularly and seasonally), call the port authority in the city of departure or check the Greek ferry information website.

One-way tickets for the ferry between Igoumenitsa and Corfu Town (1¼ to 2 hours) are about €11 per person and €40 per car.

Hydrofoils zip between Corfu and Paxos between one and three times daily. There is also a hydrofoil service to Saranda in Albania.

Contacts Greek ferry info. ⊕ *www.greekferries.gr*. **Igoumenitsa Port Authority.** ☎ *26650/22235*.

BUS TRAVEL

KTEL buses leave Athens Terminal A for Igoumenitsa, where there's a ferry to Corfu (11 hours, around €48 one-way, plus ferry fares).

On Corfu, bus services run from Corfu Town to the main towns and villages on the island; schedules and prices can change seasonally and yearly. There are two bus lines. The Green KTEL buses leave for distant towns from the Corfu Town terminal between the town center and the airport. Blue suburban buses (with stops including Kanoni and Gastouri) leave from in and around San Rocco Square. Get timetables at both bus depots. Tickets—farthest rides are just under €5—can be bought at the depots or on the bus.

Contacts Corfu Surburban (Blue) buses. ⊠ *San Rocco Sq., Corfu Town* ☎ *26610/31595* ⊕ *www.corfucitybus. com.* **Corfu KTEL (Green) buses.** ⊠ *Between Corfu Town and airport, Corfu Town* ☎ *26610/28900* ⊕ *www. greenbuses.gr.*

CAR TRAVEL

For those traveling with a car, the best route from Athens is National Road via Corinth to Igoumenitsa (472 km [274 miles]), where you take the ferry to Corfu. As on all Greek islands, exercise caution with regard to steep, winding roads, and fellow drivers equally unfamiliar with the terrain.

Corfu Town has several car-rental agencies, most of them clustered around the port, ranging from international chains to local agencies offering cheap deals; there is also an agency in Ermones. Depending on the season, prices can range from €35 a day to €230 a week for a compact, all insurance included. Chains have a bigger selection, but the locals will usually give a cheaper price. Don't be afraid to bargain, especially if you want to rent a car for several days. You can generally make arrangements to pick up your car at the airport.

A 50cc motorbike can be rented for about €15 a day or €100 a week, but you can bargain, especially if you want it for longer. Helmets are required by law. Check the lights, brakes, and other mechanics before you accept a machine.

Contacts Ansa International Rent a Car. ⊠ *Eleftheriou Venizelou 20, Corfu Town* ☎ *26610/21930.* **Corfu VIP Services Rent A Car.** ☎ *26610/71032* ⊕ *www.corfuvipservices.com.* **Ocean Car Hire.** ⊠ *Gouvia Marina, Gouvia* ☎ *26610/44017* ⊕ *www.oceancar.gr.* **Top Cars.** ⊠ *Donzelot 25, Corfu Town* ☎ *26610/35237* ⊕ *www.carrentalcorfu.com.*

TAXI TRAVEL

Taxis rates are reasonable—when adhered to. If you want to hire a cab on an hourly or daily basis, negotiate the price before you travel. In Corfu Town, taxis wait at San Rocco Square, the Esplanade, the airport, the Old Port Square, and the New Port. Many drivers speak English. Of course, long-distance trips on the island will pack a hefty price tag.

Contacts Radiotaxi Corfu. ☎ *26610/33811.*

BEST BETS FOR CRUISE PASSENGERS

Relax over a coffee at the Liston. This is a wonderful place to immerse yourself in modern Greek life.

Take pictures of Pontikonisi. Mouse island, as this tiny islet is also known, is one of the iconic Greek landscape views. Shimmering waters and verdant foliage contrast dramatically with the modest whitewashed chapel.

Explore Paleokastritsa. A breathtaking landscape of tiny rocky coves, azure waters, and fragrant woodland offers exceptional vistas surrounded by the sound of buzzing cicadas.

5

HOTELS

Corfu has bed-and-breakfast hotels in renovated Venetian town houses, sleek resorts with children's programs and spas, and, outside Corfu Town, simple rooms and studio apartments that can be rented out on the spot. The explosion of tourism in recent years has led to prepaid, low-price package tours, and the largest hotels often cater to groups. The availability of charter flights from the United Kingdom and other European cities means there's a steady flow of tourists from spring through fall. These masses can get rowdy and overwhelm otherwise pleasant surroundings, mainly in towns along the island's southeast and northwest coast. Budget accommodations are scarce, though rooms can sometimes be found in towns and villages. Many British companies offer villas and apartments for rent—some luxurious, others more basic—by the week or month. Corfu is popular from Easter (when the island is crammed with Greek tourists) through September, and reservations are strongly recommended during that period. Many hotels and restaurants are closed from the end of October to Easter.

RESTAURANTS

Traditionally, Corfiots tend to eat their main meal at midday, with simpler food in the evening. Though meat is eaten much more frequently these days, meals at home feature casseroles bulked out with lots of vegetables, such as the winter favorite *fassoulada,* a thick bean soup. Unless they cater to the local lunchtime trade, tavernas tend not to serve these home-style dishes, but prefer generic Greek dishes like moussaka and *stifado* (beef or rabbit cooked in a spicy sauce with small onions), plus the great Sunday-lunch and holiday dishes of the island, *pastitsada* (beef or rooster in a spicy tomato sauce served with pasta), *sofrito* (beef casserole with garlic and parsley), or the third great dish of Corfiot cooking, *bourdetto* (fish cooked in paprika, sometimes curry-hot). In the island's resorts, tavernas will also offer grills (such as pork chops and steaks), plus omelets and (often frozen) pizzas. Your main courses should be preceded by a variety of dips and small salads, and perhaps some *keftedes* (meatballs), which you all share.

Corfiot restaurants usually take the form of *psistaria,* or grillrooms, where all the meat is cooked on charcoal. Most of these places also run a takeaway service, so you'll eat in the company of neighborhood families waiting in line for souvlaki, whole spit-roasted chicken, or lamb chops. The most economical choice here is pita: a wrap enclosing meat, french fries, salad, *tzatziki,* and sauce. Desserts are not a strong suit on Corfu, although many love *karidopitta*—walnut cake drenched in syrup. Locals head to a *zacharoplasteio* (patisserie) for a creamy cake, some baklava, or *galaktoboureko* (custard pie in phyllo). In summer, the last port of call is the *gelatopoleio* (ice-cream parlor). Corfu produces wines mainly from *Skopelitiko* and *Kakotrigis* grapes, all drinkable and many excellent. Most tavernas have their own house wine, served in carafes or jugs, and usually this is a good choice. Bottled water can be bought everywhere—Corfu's salty tap water is *not* one of its pleasures. *Kali oreksi*! (Bon appetit!)

Restaurant and hotel reviews have been shortened. For full information, visit Fodors.com.

DINING AND LODGING PRICES IN EUROS			
	$	$$	$$$	$$$$
Restaurants	under €15	€15–€25	€26–€40	over €40
Hotels	under €125	€125–€225	€226–€275	over €275

Restaurant prices are the average cost of a main course at dinner or, if dinner is not served, at lunch. Hotel prices are the lowest cost of a standard double room in high season.

TOURS

From May through September, local travel agencies run half-day tours of Corfu's Old Town, and tour buses go daily to all the main sights on the island.

All-Ways Travel. One of the oldest travel agencies on the island, Greek- and English-run All-Ways Travel is reliable, especially helpful for any flight booking, including complicated connections. ⊠ *G. Theotoki Sq. 34, San Rocco* ☎ *26610/33955* ⊕ *www.allwaystravel.com.*

Anna Aperghi Travel. Aperghi Travel is an expert on hiking holidays and is a designated agent for accommodation and ground arrangements along the Corfu Trail (⊕ *www.thecorfutrail.com*), a bottom-to-top-of-the-island hike that offers lovely sections easily worth an hour or two of your time. ⊠ *Dimokratias Ave. and Polyla St. 1, Corfu Town* ☎ *26610/48713* ⊕ *www.aperghitravel.gr.*

Corfu Sunspots Travel. Sunspots runs a variety of coach tours, including the popular Grand Island Tour, as well as half-day trips to the north and south of the island. They specialize in Jeep safaris. ⊠ *National Paleokas-tritsa Hwy. 24, Corfu Town* ☎ *26610/39707* ⊕ *www.corfusunspots.gr.*

Ionian Cruises. Ionian Cruises offers boat day trips to other islands in the Ionian group, to mainland Greece, and to Albania. ⊠ *Eth. Antistaseos 4, Corfu Town* ☎ *26610/31649* ⊕ *www.ionian-cruises.com.*

Waterman Travel. Waterman is an expert in special-interest and active holidays, focusing on hiking (locally and in Zagoria on the mainland), mountain biking, and horseback riding, as well as arrangements for special groups. The office aims at sustainable and responsible travel that respects the local people and their way of life. ⊠ *Donzelot 9, Old Port, Corfu Town* ☎ *26613/03495* ⊕ *www.watermantravelcorfu.com.*

CORFU TOWN ΠΟΛΗ ΤΗΣ ΚΕΡΚΥΡΑΣ

34 km (21 miles) west of Igoumenitsa, 41 km (26 miles) north of Lefkimmi.

Corfu Town today is a vivid tapestry of cultures—a sophisticated weave, where charm, history, and natural beauty blend. Located about midway along the island's east coast, this spectacularly lively capital is the cultural heart of Corfu and has a remarkable historic center that UNESCO designated as a World Heritage site in 2007. All ships and planes dock or land near Corfu Town, which occupies a small peninsula jutting into the Ionian Sea.

Whether arriving by ferry from mainland Greece or Italy, from another island, or directly by plane, catch your breath by first relaxing with a coffee or a gelato in Corfu Town's shaded Liston Arcade, then stroll the narrow lanes of its pedestrians-only quarter. For an overview of the immediate area, and a quick tour of Mon Repos palace, hop on the little tourist train that runs from May to September. Corfu Town has a different feel at night, so book a table at one of its famed tavernas to savor the island's unique cuisine.

The best way to get around Corfu Town is on foot. The town is small enough so that you can easily walk to every sight. There are local buses, but they do not thread their way into the streets (many now car-free) of the historic center. If you are arriving by ferry or plane, it's best to take a taxi to your hotel. Expect to pay about €10 from the airport or ferry terminal to a hotel in Corfu Town. If there are no taxis waiting, you can call for one *(see Taxi Travel)*.

EXPLORING

Though beguilingly Greek, much of Corfu's Old Town displays the architectural styles of its conquerors—*molto* of Italy's Venice, a *soupçon* of France, and more than a tad of England; it may remind you of Venice or Bath. Many visitors will want to invest in the multi-attraction ticket, available at any of the sights, which includes admission to the Old Fortress, the Museum of Asian Art, the Antivouniotissa Museum, and Mon Repos palace.

TOP ATTRACTIONS

Antivouniotissa Museum. Panagia Antivouniotissa, an ornate church dating from the late 15th century, houses an outstanding collection of Byzantine religious art. More than 50 icons from the 13th to the 17th century hang on the walls. Look for works by the celebrated icon painters Tzanes and Damaskinos; they are perhaps the best-known artists of the Cretan style of icon painting, with unusually muscular, active depictions of saints. Their paintings more closely resemble Renaissance art—another Venetian legacy—than traditional, flat orthodox icons. ⊠ *Arseniou St. 25* ☎ *26610/38313* ⊕ *www.antivouniotissamuseum.gr* ⊠ *€4* ⊘ *Closed Mon.*

Fodor'sChoice ★ **Campiello.** This medieval quarter, part of a UNESCO-designated World Heritage site, is an atmospheric labyrinth of narrow, winding streets, steep stairways, and secretive little squares. Laundry lines connect balconied Venetian palazzi engraved with the original occupant's coat of arms to neoclassical 19th-century buildings constructed by the British. Small cobbled squares with central wells and watched over by old churches add to the quiet, mysterious, and utterly charming urban space. If you enter, you're almost sure to get lost, but the area is small enough so that eventually you'll come out on one of Corfu Town's major streets, or on the sea wall. ⊠ *Corfu Town* ✛ *West of the Esplanade, northeast of New Fortress.*

Fodor'sChoice ★ **Church of St. Spyridon.** Built in 1596, this church is the tallest on the island, thanks to its distinctive red-domed bell tower, and is filled with silver treasures. The patron saint's remains—smuggled here after the fall of Constantinople—are contained in a silver reliquary in a small chapel;

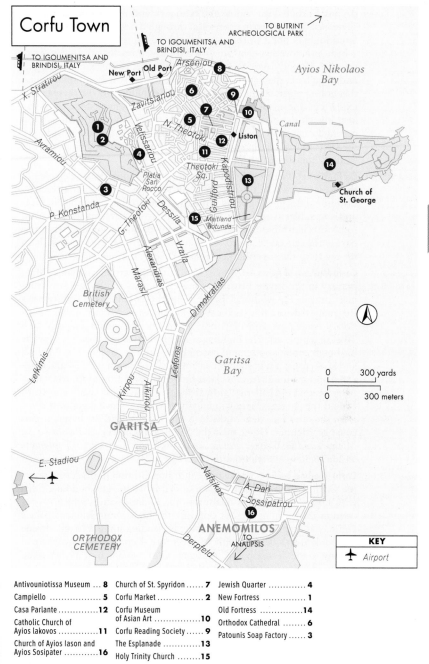

Corfu Town

5

devout Corfiots visit to kiss the reliquary and pray to the saint. The silver casket is carried in procession through the town four times a year. Spyridon was not a Corfiot but a shepherd from Cyprus, who became a bishop before his death in AD 350. His miracles are said to have saved the island four times: once from famine, twice from the plague, and once from the hated Turks. During World War II, a bomb fell on this holiest place on the island but didn't explode. Maybe these events explain why it seems every other man on Corfu is named Spiros. If you keep the church tower in sight, you can wander as you wish without getting lost around this fascinating section of town. Agiou Spyridonos, the street in front of the church, is crammed with shops selling religious trinkets and souvenirs. ⊠ *Agiou Spyridon.*

Fodor's Choice ★ **Corfu Market.** Picturesquely located in the dry-moat outer defenses of the New Fortress, Corfu's public market is laid out in an attractive, traditional design. The stalls showcase local produce, specifically fruits and vegetables (some of it ecologically grown), fresh fish, and local foodstuffs like olives, dry pulses, wine, and packaged goods. Two coffee bars in the central "square" provide refreshment at very low cost. It's a far cry from the supermarket! ⊠ *San Rocco* ☉ *Closed Sun.*

Fodor's Choice ★ **Corfu Museum of Asian Art.** It may seem a bit incongruous to admire Ming pottery in an ornate British colonial palace as the Ionian Sea shimmers outside the windows. But this elegant, colonnaded, 19th-century Regency structure houses the Museum of Asian Art, a notable collection of Asian porcelains, Japanese *ukiyo-e* prints, Indian sculpture, and Tibetan temple art. The building was constructed as a residence for the lord high commissioner and headquarters for the order of St. Michael and St. George; it was abandoned after the British left in 1864 and renovated about a hundred years later by the British ambassador to Greece. After visiting the galleries, stop at the Art Café in the shady courtyard behind the palace, where you may have trouble tearing yourself away from the fairy-tale view of the lush islet of Vido and the mountainous coast of Albania. Don't miss the **Municipal Gallery.** ⊠ *Palace of St. Michael and St. George, Palaia Anaktora* ✛ *At north end of Esplanade* ☏ *26610/30443* ⊕ *www.matk.gr* ☐ *€3.*

Fodor's Choice ★ **Corfu Reading Society.** The oldest cultural institution in modern Greece, the Corfu Reading Society was founded in 1836. The building, filled with books and archives relating to the Ionian islands, which is only open in the morning, stands opposite the high commissioner's palace and has an impressive exterior staircase leading up to a loggia. Inside is a book lover's delight, with 19th-century decor that is evocative testimony to the "English age" that gave Corfu so much of its character. ⊠ *Kapodistriou 120* ☏ *26610/39528* ☐ *Free* ☉ *Closed Sun.*

FAMILY Fodor's Choice ★ **The Esplanade.** Central to the life of the town, this huge, open parade ground and park just west of the Old Fortress is, many say, the most beautiful *spianada* (esplanade) in Greece. It is bordered on the west by a street lined with Venetian and English Georgian houses and a famous arcaded building called the **Liston,** built by the French under Napoleon and meant to resemble the Rue du Rivoli in Paris. Cafés spill out onto the passing scene, and Corfiot celebrations, games, and concerts take place here; at night, lovers promenade and children play in this festive public space. Sunday cricket matches, a holdover from British rule, are occasionally played on the northern half of the Esplanade, which was once a Venetian firing range. Standing in the center is an ornate **Victorian bandstand** and, just south of it, the **Maitland Rotunda,** a circular Ionic memorial built in honor of Sir Thomas Maitland, the not-much-loved first British lord high commissioner who was appointed in 1814 when the island became a protectorate of Britain. At the southernmost tip of the Esplanade a **statue of Ioannis Kapodistrias,** a Corfu resident and the first president of modern Greece, looks out over Garitsa bay. Kapodistrias was also, unfortunately, the first Greek president to be assassinated, in 1831. ⊠ *Corfu Town* ✛ *Between Old Fortress and Old Town.*

FAMILY **New Fortress.** Built during the period 1577–78 by the Venetians, the so-called "New" Fortress was constructed to strengthen town defenses—only three decades after the construction of Venetian fortifications on the "Old" Fortress. The French and the British subsequently expanded the complex to protect Corfu Town from a possible Turkish invasion. You can wander through the maze of tunnels and fortifications; the dry moat is the site of the town's fish-and-vegetable marketplace. A classic British citadel stands at its heart. The summit offers a fantastic view over the rooftops of the Old Town. ⊠ *Solomou* ✛ *On promontory overlooking New Port* ☎ *No phone* ☒ *Free.*

FAMILY **Old Fortress.** Corfu's entire population once lived within the walls of the Old Fortress, or Citadel, built by the Venetians in 1546 on the site of a Byzantine castle. Separated from the rest of the town by a moat, the fort is on a promontory mentioned by Thucydides. Its two heights, or *korypha* ("peaks"), gave the island its name. Standing on the peaks, you have a gorgeous view west over the town and east to the mountainous coast of Albania. A statue of Count Schulenburg, an Austrian mercenary who became a local hero in 1716 when he helped to defeat the invading Turks, stands at the fort's entrance; a plaque beside the statue tells Schulenburg's story. Inside, there's an exhibition of Byzantine art and a shop with museum copies, while a second hall hosts changing events. Most of the old Venetian fortifications inside the fortress were destroyed by the British, who replaced them with their own structures. The most notable of these is the **Church of St. George,** built to look like an ancient Doric temple. Near it, overlooking Garitsa bay, there is a shaded café where you can sit and enjoy the splendid view. ⊠ *Corfu Town* ✛ *On eastern point of Corfu Town peninsula* ☎ *26610/48310* ☒ *€6.*

WORTH NOTING

FAMILY **Casa Parlante.** A highly educational experience as well as an entertaining one, a visit to this living history museum allows you to meet three generations of a noble Corfiot family and their servants. The Count and his kin are not flesh and blood but realistic animated figures who occupy an old town house, fitted out with authentic 19th-century furniture and artifacts. A guided tour of the apartment, with intelligent and informative commentary that includes each character's backstory, brings Corfu's urban past to life, some of it rather graphically. ⊠ *N. Theotoki 16* ☎ *26610/49190* ⊕ *www.casaparlante.gr* ☒ *€5.*

CLOSE UP

Corfu's Changing Allegiances

It may be hard to believe that an island as small as Corfu could have had such a noteworthy role in the region's history. Corfu's proximity to Europe, 72 km (45 miles) from Italy and 2 km (1 mile) or so from Albania, and its position on an ancient trade route at the mouth of the Adriatic, assured a lively series of conquests and counter-conquests. In classical times, Corinth colonized the northern Ionian islands, but Corfu, growing powerful, revolted and allied itself with Athens, a fateful move that triggered the Peloponnesian War. Subjection followed: to the tyrants of Syracuse, the kings of Epirus and of Macedonia, in the 2nd century BC to Rome, and from the 11th to the 14th century to Norman and Angevin kings. Then came the Venetians, who protected Corfu from Turkish occupation and provided a 411-year period of development. Napoléon

Bonaparte took the islands after the fall of Venice. "The greatest misfortune which could befall me is the loss of Corfu," he wrote to Talleyrand, his foreign minister. Within two years he'd lost it to a Russo-Turkish fleet.

For a short time the French regained and fortified Corfu from the Russians, and their occupation influenced the island's educational system, architecture, and cuisine. Theirs was a Greek-run republic—the first for modern Greece—which whetted local appetites for the independence that arrived later in the 19th century. In 1814 the islands came under British rule and were administered by a series of British lord high commissioners; under their watch, roads, schools, and hospitals were constructed, and commercialism developed. The fight for national independence finally prevailed, and the islands were ceded to Greece in 1864.

Catholic Church of Ayios Iakovos. Built in 1588 and consecrated 50 years later, this elegant cathedral was erected to provide a grand place of worship for Corfu Town's Catholic occupiers. If you use the Italian name, San Giacomo, locals will know it. When it was bombed by the Nazis in 1943, the cathedral's original neoclassical facade of pediments, friezes, and columns was practically destroyed; only the bell tower remained intact. It's now been restored. Mass takes place daily at 7 pm and at 10:30 am on Sunday. Across the road is the office of the mayor, formerly a Venetian-built theater. Note the carvings and bas-reliefs on the walls. ⊠ *Dimarcheiou Sq.*

Church of Ayios Iason and Ayios Sosipater. The suburb of Anemomilos is crowned by the ruins of the Paleopolis church and by the 11th-century Church of Ayios Iason and Ayios Sosipater. It was named after two of St. Paul's disciples, St. Jason and St. Sosipater, who brought Christianity to the island in the 1st century. The frescoes are faded, but the icons are beautiful, and the exterior is dramatic among the unspoiled greenery. This is one of only two Byzantine churches on the island; the other is in the northern coastal village of Ayios Markos. ⊠ *Anemomilos* ✛ *At south end of Garitsa Bay* 🗃 *Donations accepted.*

Holy Trinity Church. Established in 1870 after the end of the British Protectorate (1815–1864), this Anglican church continues to serve the needs of the English-speaking community. All denominations are welcome to services and to other religious events and social activities in its sphere. Sunday morning service takes place at 10:30. ✉ *L. Mavili 21* ☎ *26610/31467* 🌐 *www.holytrinitycorfu.net* 🎟 *Donations accepted* 🕒 *Closed Mon.*

Jewish Quarter. This maze of streets was home to the area's Jewish population from the 1600s until 1944, when the community was decimated, most sent to Auschwitz by the occupying Nazis. Fewer than 100 of 3,000 Jews survived. At the southern edge of the ghetto, a 300-year-old synagogue with an interior in Sephardic style still stands. ✉ *Parados 4, Off Velissariou, 2 blocks from New Fortress.*

Orthodox Cathedral. This small, icon-rich cathedral, called Panagia Spiliotissa, was built in 1577. It is sacred to St. Theodora, the island's second patron saint. Her headless body lies in a silver coffin by the altar; it was brought to Corfu at the same time as St. Spyridon's remains. Steps lead down to the harbor from here. ✉ *Corfu Town* ✥ *Southwest corner of Campiello, east of St. Spyridon.*

Patounis Soap Factory. A Patounis has been producing olive oil soap by the traditional stamped method for over 100 years, and the family's factory—the only one left in Corfu—is listed as an Industrial Heritage site. Every weekday at noon, the current (fifth-generation) Patounis, Apostolos, runs an informative guided tour of the premises, during which you will see a demonstration of the traditional stamping and cutting process. You can also buy the merchandise, which is additive-free and hypoallergenic. ✉ *Ioannou Theotoki St. 9* ☎ 🌐 *www.patounis.gr* 🕒 *Closed Sun.*

WHERE TO EAT

$ MODERN GREEK

🍴 **Aegli.** Both local and international dishes are on the menu at this long-established and casually elegant restaurant on the Liston arcade. Start with a plate of steamed mussels or a salad, then move on to hearty Greek and Corfiot classics. **Known for:** home-baked sourdough bread; pastitsada, Corfu's rich beef stew; spectacular view of the Esplanade. [$] *Average main: €13* ✉ *Kapodistriou 23, Liston* ☎ *26610/31949* 🌐 *aeglirestaurant.com.*

$ GREEK

🍴 **Avli.** Avli specializes in *mezedes,* so you order a selection of these small dishes for sharing rather than your own main course. The young proprietors, Vasilis (front of house) and Christos (chef) source ingredients locally whenever possible and combine them in inventive and innovative ways, such as with the pork fillet, which comes accompanied by a sauce made from Corfu-grown kumquats. **Known for:** bread baked in-house daily; grilled Talagani cheese garnished with the unique local fig preserve; interesting fresh seafood dishes. [$] *Average main: €13* ✉ *Alk. Dari and Ath. Kavvada, Garitsa* ☎ *26610/31291* 🌐 *www.avlicorfu.com.*

$$ MODERN GREEK Fodor's Choice ★

🍴 **Corfu Sailing Club Restaurant.** Everyone—not just sailors—will appreciate the spectacular location of this classy restaurant, tucked under the northern wall of the Venetian-era Old Fortress beside the yacht club harbor. The food is Greek but offers twists on traditional concepts, such as a cheese pie topped with honey, in a dish straight out of ancient times.

Known for: wide-ranging wine list; excellent seafood combinations; location-appropriate Venetian calves liver. $ *Average main: €16* ⌧ *Old Fortress, Mandraki* ☎ *26610/38763* ⊕ *www.corfu-sailing-restaurant. com* ⊘ *Closed Nov.–Apr.*

$ ✕ **En Plo.** Blessed with a startlingly wonderful location by a wave-lapped

GREEK jetty in the little waterfront Faliraki area north of the Old Fortress, En Plo offers everything from snacks and pizzas to a full meal. Enjoy mezedes, a big variety of salads, and interesting pastas. **Known for:** unique location, where you can combine a swim with good food; spectacular view of the Old Fortress and the sea; very relaxed atmosphere. $ *Average main: €13* ⌧ *Faliraki* ✛ *On waterfront just north of Old Fortress* ☎ *26610/81813* ⊕ *www.enplocorfu.com* ⊘ *Closed Dec.–Mar.*

$$ ✕ **La Cucina.** To describe a restaurant's cuisine as "international" can

INTERNATIONAL imply that it is bland, but no one would ever say that about La Cucina. Renowned for its Italian cooking—and particularly handmade pasta— the menu also incorporates Thai curries, quirky takes on Corfiot staples, and even nods to British cuisine. **Known for:** handmade pasta and pizza; black Angus strip loin and Florentine T-bone steak on the grill; comprehensive and eclectic wine list. $ *Average main: €20* ⌧ *Moustoxidi 13 at Guilford* ☎ *26610/45799* ⊘ *No lunch.*

$$ ✕ **Rex.** A friendly Corfiot restaurant housed in a classic early-19th-

GREEK century building just behind the famous Liston arcade, Rex has been a

Fodor's Choice favorite of the locals since the early 20th century. Hearty local stews are

★ on the menu alongside examples of modern regional fare such as roast lamb knuckle with artichokes. **Known for:** signature dish of chicken with kumquat sauce; wonderful location for people-watching; elegant surroundings and service. $ *Average main: €16* ⌧ *Kapodistriou 66* ✛ *Behind the Liston arcade* ☎ *26610/39649* ⊕ *www.rexrestaurant.gr.*

$ ✕ **Rouvas.** A local favorite for lunch in town is located near San Rocco

GREEK Square in the center of Corfu's commercial district. It caters particularly to residents—many of them discerning civil servants and lawyers from local offices—who savor the chef's tasty and filling traditional dishes of the day, like fried fish with garlic sauce. **Known for:** superb pastitsio and rabbit stifado; bustling location near the market; classic taverna style, with food cooked on a traditional range in view of customers. $ *Average main: €10* ⌧ *Stamatis Desyllas 13* ☎ *26610/31182* ⊘ *No dinner.*

$$ ✕ **Salto.** This wine bar–and-bistro is as famous for its food as for a

MEDITERRANEAN very extensive wine list and a magnificent outlook across the Old Port to the massive walls of the New Fortress. Using pure ingredients from small producers all over Greece, the menu takes traditional Mediterranean dishes and moves them into trendsetting territory. **Known for:** exclusively Greek wine list, featuring the country's best vintages; crunchy cod bites with garlic mousse; creative and beautifully presented salads. $ *Average main: €15* ⌧ *Donzelot 23* ☎ *26613/02325* ⊘ *Closed Nov.*

$$ ✕ **Venetian Well.** The scene is as delicious as the food in this wonderfully

MEDITERRANEAN romantic restaurant arranged around a 17th-century well on the most

Fodor's Choice beautiful little square in the Old Town. Expect creative Greek and Medi-

★ terranean cuisine, with a menu that changes regularly according to the availability of the always-fresh ingredients. **Known for:** sous vide lamb

5

cooked for 24 hours; list of some 330 wines from all over the world; exquisite presentation and service. $ *Average main: €18* ✉ *Kremasti Sq., Campiello* ⊹ *Across from Church of the Panagia* ☎ *26615/50955* ⊕ *www.venetianwell.gr* ⊗ *No lunch.*

WHERE TO STAY

$ | ⊞ **Cavalieri Hotel.** This hotel occupies a landmark 18th-century build-
HOTEL | ing with a wonderful location equidistant between the Liston and the
Fodor's Choice | sea; it's one of the few hotels here to remain open year-round (and
★ | therefore caters to a lot of business travelers). **Pros:** beautiful historic building; great views over the Esplanade and the sea; short walk to the sights of the historic center. **Cons:** small public rooms; the area can be noisy; no dedicated parking. $ *Rooms from: €100* ✉ *Kapodistriou 4* ☎ *26610/39041* ⊕ *www.cavalieri-hotel.com* ⇨ *50 rooms* ⦿ *Breakfast.*

$$ | ⊞ **Corfu Palace.** Built in 1950 as the island's first resort hotel—and these
HOTEL | days showing it—the Corfu Palace is a grande dame in bad need of a face-lift, albeit in an unbeatable location and with some lingering grace notes. **Pros:** gorgeous garden and pool area; great breakfast buffet; has Corfu's only casino, open 24 hours a day. **Cons:** decor shows its age; no beach or sea swimming; limited parking space. $ *Rooms from: €220* ✉ *Leoforos Dimokratias 2* ☎ *26610/39485* ⊕ *www.corfupalace.com* ⇨ *112 rooms* ⦿ *Breakfast.*

$$ | ⊞ **Hotel Bella Venezia.** This elegant two-story Venetian town house cen-
HOTEL | trally located has been used as a hotel since the 1800s and remains one of the nicest small hotels in town. **Pros:** very friendly service; short walk to the sights of the historic center; lovely garden breakfast area. **Cons:** some rooms are small; views are urban rather than maritime; nearby parking hard to find. $ *Rooms from: €140* ✉ *Zambelli 4* ☎ *26610/20707, 26610/44290* ⊕ *www.bellaveneziahotel.com* ⇨ *31 rooms* ⦿ *Breakfast.*

$ | ⊞ **Hotel Hermes.** The old, no-frills Hermes was always popular with
HOTEL | backpackers, but since an upgrade it has more appeal for budget travelers in general. **Pros:** affordable rates; very helpful staff; plenty of restaurants nearby. **Cons:** adjacent market and main road are noisy in early morning; breakfast is not included; no parking nearby. $ *Rooms from: €60* ✉ *San Rocco, G. Markora 12-14* ☎ *26610/39268* ⊕ *www. hermes-hotel.gr* ⇨ *30 rooms* ⦿ *No meals.*

$$ | ⊞ **Siorra Vittoria Boutique Hotel.** Right in the heart of Corfu's historic
B&B/INN | center and just a minute's walk away from the Liston, this grand man-
Fodor's Choice | sion was built in 1823 by the aristocratic Metaxas clan and, happily, its
★ | conversion to a hotel succeeded in preserving its lovely and authentic Venetian style. **Pros:** exquisite accommodation with a real flavor of old Corfu; close to all the town's best facilities, yet tranquil; open all year. **Cons:** some rooms are small; most rooms lack balconies; not suitable for young children. $ *Rooms from: €180* ✉ *Stefanou Padova 36* ☎ *26610/36300* ⊕ *www.siorravittoria.com* ⇨ *9 rooms* ⦿ *Breakfast.*

NIGHTLIFE

Corfu Town is a late-night, café-crowded, club-happy city. During the summer months, the Greeks dine very late, often at 10 pm. The nightly *volta*, a pre- or post-dinner promenade along the Esplanade and the Liston, starts at about 9 pm. Couples stroll, families gather, kids play, and the cafés and restaurants fill up. The club and disco scene heats up much later, around midnight. Party Central lies about 2 km (1 mile) north of the town center, near the New Port, on Ethnikis Antistaseos (also known as "Bar Street"). This is where you'll find a string of plush lounge-bars (many with outdoor pools) and discos that really don't start swinging until after midnight. Clubs on Corfu come and go like tourists, with many featuring incredibly loud sound systems that throb with the latest Europop and dance hits. Most clubs have a cover charge, which includes the first drink.

Fodor's Choice
★ **Cavalieri Hotel Bar.** The rooftop bar at the Cavalieri Hotel is hard to beat for views. Hotel guests happily mingle with locals as the scene slowly enlivens from a mellow, early-evening cocktail crowd to a more-energetic party atmosphere. ⊠ *Cavlieri Hotel, Kapodistriou 4* ☎ *26610/39041* ⊕ *www.cavalieri-hotel-corfu-town.com.*

FAMILY **Liston Bar.** Hip but relaxed Liston Bar has chairs out on the flagstones and a good view of decked-out promenade strollers. ⊠ *Elefterias 10, Liston* ☎ *26610/45528* ⊕ *www.liston.gr.*

Nautilas. Anchored at Anemomylos ('Windmill'), where Garitsa meets Kanoni, Nautilas marks the southern terminus of the long seafront promenade that stretches from the Corfu Palace hotel to Mon Repos, and presides over what is possibly the best distant view of the Old Fortress. Around sundown it buzzes with locals and visitors enjoying the scene as the last rays of the sun blush the waters of the bay and the walls of the castle. To accompany drinks, the seafood platter is celebrated—it's an extravagance, but ample for six or eight people. ⊠ *Anemomylos* ✛ *Southern end of Garitsa Bar* ☎ *26610/20033* ⊕ *www.nautilas.net.gr.*

SHOPPING

Corfu Town has myriad tiny shops, and half of them seem to be selling jewelry. Designer boutiques, shoe shops, and accessory stores can be found in every nook and cranny of the town. The major tourist shopping streets are Nikiphorou Theotoki (designer boutiques, jewelry) and Agios Spyridonos (local souvenirs). The local fish-and-vegetable market is open Monday through Saturday from very early in the morning until around 2 pm. For traditional goods, head for the narrow streets of the historic

Fantasy island: Legend has it that Pontikonisi—here pictured behind Vlacherena Monastery—is really Odysseus's ship turned to stone by an enraged Poseidon.

center, where olive wood, lace, jewelry, and wineshops abound. For perishable products such as liqueurs and candies, you may do better checking out the supermarkets than buying in the Old Town. Most of the shops listed here are in the historic center and are open May to October, from 8 am until late (whenever the last tourist leaves); they're generally closed during winter. Stores in outlying shopping areas tend to close Monday, Wednesday, and Saturday afternoons at 2:30 pm, and all day Sunday.

Ceramic Art. The award-winning ceramic artists Kostas Panaretos and Klio Brenner create beautiful and unique pieces of ceramic art using the ancient Greek technique called Terra Sigillata. To achieve their striking orange colors, they make glazes from Greek soil and then proceed to fire the pieces with wood, imprinting the design through the action of the smoke. In their showroom in the Jewish Quarter you'll find everything from brightly colored bowls to remarkably sophisticated plates and pieces based on ancient Greek forms. ⊠ *Ayia Sophia 23* ☎ *26610/34631.*

Fos tis Anatolis. All goods in the "Light of the East" shop—including rugs, lamps, small pieces of furniture, clay ornaments, and jewelry—have a traditional Eastern style. ⊠ *Solomou 5* ☎ *26610/45273.*

Lazari Fine Jewellers. Kostas Lazaris uses 18- and 22-carat yellow gold and white gold to encapsulate precious stones in his original designs. He will endeavor to create anything you request. ⊠ *E. Voulgareos 40* ☎ *26610/20259.*

Nikos Sculpture and Jewellery. Corfu-born Nikos Michalopoulos creates original gold and silver jewelry and sculptures in cast bronze; they're expensive, but worth it. ⊠ *Paleologou 50* ☎ *26610/31107* ⊕ *www.nikosjewellery.com.*

Rolandos. Visit the talented artist Rolando and watch him at work on his jewelry. His mother does the paintings. ✉ *N. Theotoki 99* ☎ *26610/45004.*

Stella. This shop sells religious icons, ceramics, religious icons, stone sculptures, and dolls in traditional costume, all handmade and sourced from Greece. ✉ *Kapodistriou 62* ☎ *26610/24012.*

Terracotta. Contemporary Greek jewelry, ceramics, small sculptures, and one-of-a-kind art and craft objects are sold in this appealing shop. ✉ *N. Theotoki 70* ☎ *26610/45260.*

Workshop... by Tom. Located right in the heart of the Old Town, this is a genuine olive-wood workshop, where everything is made on the premises by Tom and his son. Salad servers, huge bowls, and various decorative items are among the goods on display next to the machines and tools— and outside in the tiny square. The shop is just off the main street, and you'll have to look carefully to discover it. There's also a showroom at Paleologou 58 (Jewish Quarter). ✉ *3rd Parados, N. Theotoki 8.*

SOUTH OF CORFU TOWN
ΝΟΤΙΑ ΤΗΣ ΠΟΛΗΣ ΤΗΣ ΚΕΡΚΥΡΑΣ

Outside Corfu Town, near the suburb of Kanoni, are several of Corfu's most unforgettable sights, including the lovely view of the island of Pontikonisi. The nearby palace and grounds of Mon Repos were once owned by Greece's royal family and are open to the public as a museum. A few villages south of Benitses (but not including this genteel former fishing village), and some on the island's southern tip, are usually over-run with raucous package-tour groups. Avoid them unless you seek a binge-drinking, late-night, party-people scene and beaches chockablock with shrieking crowds and tanning bodies. If you're looking for more solitary nature in the south, take a trip to Korission Lake with its juniper-covered dunes.

KANONI KANONI

5 km (3 miles) south of Corfu Town.

The suburb of Kanoni was once one of the world's great beauty spots, made famous by countless pictures. Today the landscape has been engulfed by development and a coffee bar has laid claim to the best spot to take in the legendary and still-lovely view, which looks out over two beautiful islets. If you truly want to commune with nature, visit the lush and lovely seaside gardens surrounding the country palace of Mon Repos.

Kanoni's famed vistas encompass the open sea separated by a long, narrow causeway that defines the lagoon of Halikiopoulou, with the intensely green slopes of Mt. Agii Deka as a backdrop. A shorter breakwater leads to the white convent of Moni Vlaherena on a tiny islet—one of the most picturesque islets in all of Greece and the one pictured on nearly all postcards of Mouse island. Nonetheless, it is the tiny island beyond that islet—the one in the middle of the lake with the tall cypresses—that is **Pontikonisi,** or Mouse island, a rock rising

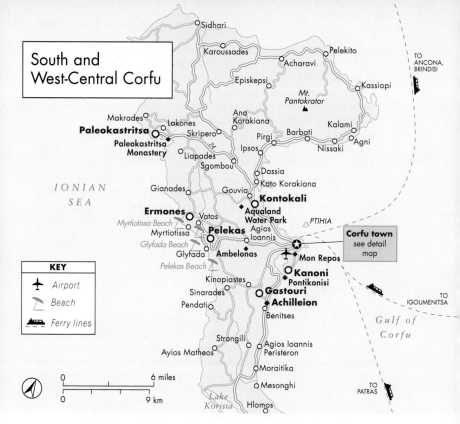

South and West-Central Corfu

Sidhari

Karoussades

Pelekito

TO ANCONA, BRINDISI

Acharavi

Episkepsi

Kassiopi

Mt. Pantokrator ▲

Makrades

Ano Korakiana

Lakones

Kalami

Paleokastritsa

Skripero

Pirgi

Barbati

Paleokastritsa Monastery

Liapades

Ipsos

Nissaki

Agni

Sgombou

Dassia

IONIAN SEA

Gianades

Kato Korakiana

Gouvia

Kontokali

Ermones

Vatos

Aqualand Water Park

PTIHIA

Myrtiotissa Beach

Agios Ioannis

Myrtiotissa

Pelekas

Corfu town see detail map

Glyfada Beach

Glyfada

Ambelonas

● **Mon Repos**

Pelekas Beach

Kinopiastes

Kanoni Pontikonisi

KEY

Sinarades

Gastouri

✈ Airport

Pendati

Achilleion

⟋ Beach

Benitses

Gulf of Corfu

🚢 Ferry lines

TO IGOUMENITSA

Strongili

Agios Ioannis Peristeron

Ayios Matheos

Moraitika

0   6 miles

Mesonghi

TO PATRAS

0   9 km

Lake Korisia

Hlomos

dramatically from the clear water and topped by a tiny 13th-century chapel. Legend has it that the island is really Odysseus's ship, which an enraged Poseidon turned to stone: the reason why Homer's much-traveled hero was shipwrecked on Phaeacia (Corfu) in *The Odyssey*. From June through August a boat service runs out to Pontikonisi. Keep in mind, though, that while the view *of* the islets has sold a thousand postcards, the view *from* the islets (looking back at Corfu) is that of a hilly landscape built up with resort hotels and summer homes and of the adjacent airport, where planes take off directly over the churches.

GETTING HERE AND AROUND

The local blue bus (line 2) offers frequent daily service (every 20 minutes Monday through Saturday, every 40 minutes on Sunday) to Kanoni from Plateia San Rocco in Corfu Town; the fare is about €1.50. A taxi to Kanoni costs approximately €15. The islet of Pontikonisi can be reached by a short boat trip from the dock at Vlaherena, 2 km (1 mile) below Kanoni and costs €2.50 round-trip. The best way to reach Mon Repos from Corfu Town is by walking; it takes about 30 minutes and you follow the seafront most of the way.

EXPLORING

Mon Repos. The former royal palace of Mon Repos is surrounded by gorgeous English-style gardens that lend magic to an idyllic setting. The compact neoclassical palace (really a villa) was built in 1831 by Sir Frederic Adam for his wife, and it was later the summer residence of the British lord high commissioners; the architect, Sir George Whitmore, also designed the Palace of St. Michael and St. George in Corfu Town. After Greece won independence from Britain in 1864, Mon Repos was used as a summer palace for the royal family of Greece. Queen Elizabeth II's husband, Prince Philip, was born here in 1921 (he was a royal prince of Greece and Denmark; the Corfiots, who have no love of royalty, call him "the penniless Greek who married a queen"). When King Constantine fled the country in 1967, the Greek government expropriated Mon Repos. Throughout the 1990s, the estate was entangled in an international legal battle over ownership; the Greek government finally paid Constantine a settlement and opened the fully restored palace as a museum dedicated to the area's archaeological history. Displays of items found in the area, as well as interpretive displays, rooms showcasing Regency design, contemporary antiques, and botanical paintings make for a truly eclectic museum collection The room where Prince Philip was born (on the kitchen table, it is said) houses a 3-D interactive map of Corfu Town and its environs.

After touring the palace, wander around the extensive grounds (entrance is free, so you can do this even if you don't visit the palace), which include the elusive remains of a Doric temple from the 7th and 6th centuries BC and the small but beautiful beach that was once used exclusively by the Greek royal family and is now open to the public. Bring your suit and join the locals on the long pier jutting out into the crystal-clear waters of the Ionian Sea. Opposite Mon Repos are ruins of Ayia Kerkyra, the 5th-century church of the Old City, and adjacent to the gate is an ancient Roman bathhouse. ✉ *Paleopolis ✛ 2 km (1 mile) south of the Old Fortress, following oceanfront walk* ⚐ *Grounds free; museum €4* ⊘ *Museum closed Mon.*

THE ACHILLEION AND GASTOURI ΑΧΙΛΛΕΙΟΝ ΚΑΙ ΓΑΣΤΟΥΡΙ

19 km (12 miles) southwest of Corfu Town.

GETTING HERE AND AROUND

The local blue bus (line No. 10) departs daily from Platia San Rocco in Corfu Town for Gastouri and the Achilleion about every two hours (check with the ticket window at Platia San Rocco for the exact schedule). Return times are approximately 20 minutes after arrival times; round-trip fare is €3—buy your return ticket at the same time as your outgoing one. A taxi costs about €20 (ask the driver for an approximate fare before entering the taxi).

EXPLORING

The village of Gastouri, overrun in summer by tour buses and day-trippers, is the site of the Achilleion.

Achilleion. This Teutonic palace, built in the late 19th century for Empress Elizabeth of Austria, is perhaps the most popular tourist attraction in Corfu and remains a monument of 19th-century historicism. The empress used the place as a retreat to escape court life and to ease her heartbreak over husband Franz Josef's numerous affairs and her son Archduke Rudolph's mysterious murder or suicide at Mayerling in 1889. Elizabeth named the palace after her favorite hero, Achilles, whom she inexplicably identified with Rudolph. After Elizabeth was assassinated in 1898, Kaiser Wilhelm II bought the villa and lived in it until the outbreak of World War I, during which time the Achilleion was used by French and Serbian troops as a military hospital. After the armistice, the Greek government received it as a spoil of war. During World War II, it was appropriated and used as a headquarters by the occupying Italian and German forces. In 1962 the palace was restored, leased as a gambling casino, and later used as the set for the casino scene in the James Bond film *For Your Eyes Only.* (The casino has since moved to the Corfu Palace Hotel.)

Today it's a museum, but not a terribly inspiring one. The interior is a series of rather ungainly, uninteresting rooms done in various styles (a pseudo-Byzantine chapel, a pseudo-Pompeian room, a pseudo-Renaissance dining hall), with a smattering of period furniture scattered about; the vulgar fresco called *Achilles in His Chariot,* behind a window on the upper level, tells you all you need to know about the empress's taste in pseudo-classical art. More appealing is the terrace, laid out like an Ionic peristyle with a number of 19th-century statues, the best of which is *The Dying Achilles.* The gardens, surrounded by olive groves and with a distant view of the sea, are pretty but, all in all, the whole place looks a bit vacuous and forlorn. Still and all, lovers of period style won't want to miss this. For a website on the estate, go to the Wikipedia entry (the easiest way to access it) and then hit the link to the Achilleion site in the footnotes. ✉ *Gastouri* ☎ *26610/56210* 🎟 *€8.*

WHERE TO EAT

$$ GREEK FAMILY Fodor's Choice ★

🍴 **Taverna Tripa.** This famous taverna (touristy but very quaint) in the charming hill village of Kinopiastes has been in business since 1936 and is still run by the same family. The fixed-price menu begins with an endless series of small meze plates, followed by a main course (usually spit-roasted lamb), and concludes with a selection of local and exotic fruits and desserts. **Known for:** gargantuan quantities of food and unlimited house wine; outstanding Greek nights with live music; popular with famous visitors. [$] *Average main: €30* ✉ *Kinopiastes* ✥ *2 km (1 mile) west of Gastouri* ☎ *26610/56333* 🌐 *www.corfu-tripas.com* 🕒 *No lunch.*

WHERE TO STAY

$ HOTEL FAMILY Fodor's Choice ★

🏨 **Grande Mare Hotel and Wellness.** Occupying a spectacular position on a hillside directly above the sea, the Grande Mare offers luxurious rooms and suites surrounded by gorgeous gardens. **Pros:** great restaurant, spa, and wellness center; waterpark for the kids; close to Benitses's swanky harbor. **Cons:** no kitchens; the road into Benitses can be busy; close to the shore but no good beach. [$] *Rooms from: €95* ✉ *Benitses* ✥ *2 km (1 mile) south of Gastouri* ☎ *26610/72672* 🌐 *www.grandemarehotel.gr* 🕒 *Closed Nov.–Apr.* 🛏 *88 rooms* 🍽 *Breakfast.*

NORTH OF CORFU TOWN
ΒΟΡΕΙΑ ΤΗΣ ΠΟΛΗΣ ΤΗΣ ΚΕΡΚΥΡΑΣ

West and north from Corfu Town, sweeping roads take you across the center of the island to the rugged west coast with its dramatic sandy es. Approaching Paleokastritsa, the road descends in tight bends to the sea, where two headlands, 130 feet high and covered with trees and boulders, form a pair of natural harbors. The beaches on this side of Corfu are lovely, but some of them, notably around Pelekas, have stronger surf and higher waves than the more-sheltered beaches on the east side of the island. The lush and fertile Ropa valley, once Corfu's agricultural heartland, lies between the sandy beaches of the west-central coast near Ermones and the olive-blanketed low hills of the island's center, with dramatic mountains in view to the north.

PELEKAS ΠΕΛΕΚΑΣ

11 km (7 miles) northwest of Gastouri, 13 km (8 miles) west of Corfu Town.

Inland from the coast at Glyfada is Pelekas, an attractive hilltop village that overflows with tourists because of its much-touted lookout point, called **Kaiser's Throne,** a rocky hilltop with spectacular views of the entire island and sea beyond. German Kaiser Wilhelm II enjoyed the sunset here when not relaxing at Achilleion Palace.

GETTING HERE AND AROUND
The local blue bus (line No. 11) has a regular all-day service from San Rocco Square for Pelekas, starting at 7 am, with the last bus at 10 pm (reduced services at weekends). In high season, the green KTEL bus has two morning departures for Glyfada, at 9 and 11 am, from the bus terminal between the town center and the airport. A taxi from Corfu Town to the Kaiser's Throne costs about €40 and will save you about 20 minutes' travel time.

EXPLORING
Ambelonas. Tucked away in the countryside between Corfu Town and Pelekas, this extensive wine estate has a large acreage under local-variety vines, in addition to olive groves and forest. At its center is an olive press and winery, reconstructed in traditional style, housing preindustrial olive presses and a large collection of associated agricultural equipment. Visitors can watch a video presentation showing the time-honored process of oil- and winemaking. Outside, in a yard shaded by pergolas, a restaurant serves a small but very select menu of seasonal local dishes—many resurrected from old recipe collections. A small shop selling local products showcases the owner's much-awarded preserves and the estate wines. Ambelonas also hosts public events such as cooking courses, concerts, and workshops. ⊠ *National Pelekas highway, Karoumbatika* ☎ *69321/58888* ⊕ *ambelonas-corfu.gr* ☒ *Free.*

FAMILY **Aqualand Water Park.** This giant, overpriced water theme park could be viewed as yet another example of how tourist-related developments are spoiling Corfu's lovely old landscapes, or you might see it as a great place to let your kids have a few hours of fun in the third-largest wave pool in the world. There are slides, rides, pools, playgrounds, restaurants and snack stands (food is mediocre in both), and stores everywhere you look, plus lots of noise. It's located midisland, on the main road to Glyfada, near Ayios Ioannis and can be reached by a number of different bus services, the easiest being the No. 8 Afra-Ayios Ioannis Blue Bus from San Rocco Square. ⊠ *National Pelekas highway, Agios Ioannis* ☎ *26610/58351* ⊕ *www.aqualand-corfu.com* 🎟 *€27* ⊘ *Closed Nov.–Apr.*

BEACHES

Glyfada Beach. Greeks have voted Glyfada Beach one of the top 10 in the country, and it's easy to see why when you visit this wide stretch of fine, golden sand. The central area, which is dominated by the giant Grand Glyfada hotel, has a number of funky beach bars that are more places to see and be seen. Here, the beach is highly organized, with rows of sun beds and umbrellas, sometimes rented from the nearest establishment. The northern end is more laid-back and has a small hotel, the Glyfada Beach hotel. If you've had enough of the sun, you can find shade among the trees that back the beach. A choice of water sports is available for the active, but swimmers should be aware of the strong undertow. **Amenities:** food and drink; lifeguards; parking; showers; water sports. **Best for:** partiers; swimming. ⊠ *Glyfada* ⊹ *3 km (2 miles) west of Pelekas.*

Myrtiotissa Beach. The writer Lawrence Durrell described Myrtiotissa as "the loveliest beach in the world." This statement may be hyperbolic, but few would argue that the strand is right up there with the best in Greece. Today, the beach is little changed from Durrell's time on Corfu in the 1930s, due to poor access keeping development at bay—there are no refreshment facilities directly on the beach, nor even organized sun bed or umbrella rentals. Most visitors park and walk down the steep road. The southern end of the beach, sheltered from view by rocks, is designated for nudists only, while at the more open northern end swimsuits are the norm. The sand is fine and golden. The sea can be rough with currents—it's only for experienced snorkelers. A small rustic restaurant stands a few minutes' walk from the far end of the beach. Another minute's walk takes you to a monastery, dedicated to the Virgin of the Myrtles, hence the name. **Amenities:** none. **Best for:** nudists; snorkeling. ⊠ *Pelekas* ⊹ *5 km (3 miles) north of Pelekas.*

FAMILY **Pelekas Beach.** Pelekas Beach could be two separate strands, and indeed there are two access roads down the long, steep hill. The busy southern section is overlooked by the huge Mayor Pelekas Monastery hotel complex with its satellite bars and restaurants. As you walk north, the development dwindles, and at the far northern end, the beach still possesses an atmosphere of the 1970s when it was the haunt of hippies. Most amenities, such as sun beds and water sports, are clustered in the vicinity of the hotel. **Amenities:** food and drink; lifeguards; showers; water sports. **Best for:** sunset; walking. ⊠ *Pelekas.*

WHERE TO EAT

$ ✕ **Jimmy's.** Only fresh ingredients and pure local olive oil are used at this
GREEK family-run taverna serving traditional Corfiot and other Greek food. Try *tsigarelli,* a combination of green vegetables and spices, or one of

the pastas and vegetarian dishes. **Known for:** locally grown vegetables; nice selection of sweets; exceptionally friendly and helpful proprietors. $ *Average main: €10* ✉ *Pelekas* ☎ *26610/94284* ⊕ *www.jimmyspelekas.com* ⊘ *Closed Nov.–Apr.*

$$
FRENCH

✕ **Spiros and Vassilis.** This restaurant, hidden from the road on farmland belonging to the Polymeris family, is something of a surprise because the menu is not Greek but classically French. The owner/chef, born in Corfu, worked for many years in Paris restaurants and is particularly adept with steaks. **Known for:** the best steaks on Corfu, sourced from organic local meat; classic frogs' legs; stylish and sophisticated dining in lovely country garden. $ *Average main: €16* ✉ *Agios Ioannis* ✛ *9 km (6 miles) west of Corfu Town on road to Pelekas* ☎ *26610/52552, 26610/52438* ⊕ *www.spirosvasilis.com* ⊘ *Closed Nov.–Apr.*

WHERE TO STAY

$
B&B/INN

🛏 **Levant Hotel.** Located at the top of Pelekas hill, next to the Kaiser's Throne lookout, this small hotel offers balconied guest rooms with breathtaking views (and sunsets) across silver-green olive groves to the shimmering Ionian Sea. Built in 1989, the Levant has a subdued, neo-classical look enlivened with touches of traditional Corfiot style. **Pros:** great views; personable service; good in-house restaurant with terrace. **Cons:** area particularly busy with tour groups; restaurant is open to nonresidents; quite a long walk to reach Pelekas village. $ *Rooms from: €75* ✉ *Pelekas* ✛ *Near Kaiser's Throne* ☎ *26610/94230* ⊕ *www.levanthotel.com* ⊘ *Closed Nov.–Easter* ⇆ *30 rooms* ⦿ *Breakfast.*

$$$$
RESORT

🛏 **Mayor Pelekas Monastery.** Built on a steep hillside directly above Pelekas Beach, this is one of the most attractive beach hotels on the island. **Pros:** great sea views from many rooms; contemporary decor in rooms and public areas; direct access to beach by funicular. **Cons:** lots of tour groups; not suitable for guests with mobility problems; tough climb to visit Pelekas village. $ *Rooms from: €294* ✉ *Pelekas Beach* ☎ *26611/80600* ⊕ *www.mayorhotels.com* ⊘ *Closed Nov.–Apr.* ⇆ *189 rooms* ⦿ *All-inclusive.*

$$
B&B/INN
Fodor's Choice
★

🛏 **Pelecas Country Club.** Some say this small, luxury hotel can be a bit snobbish; others insist that it lets you experience true Corfiot tradition in a unique setting: an old family mansion. **Pros:** lovely rooms and flower gardens; all rooms have a kitchen or kitchenette; quiet and traffic-free location. **Cons:** you need a car to get anywhere; country rather than seashore location; not for visitors who like modern, snazzy decor. $ *Rooms from: €150* ✉ *Pelekas* ☎ *26610/52918* ⊕ *www.country-club.gr* ⇆ *10 rooms* ⦿ *Breakfast.*

SHOPPING

The Witch House. Harry Potter would feel right at home in The Witch House, where every single item is made by multitalented sisters Katerina and Lakshen. Artifacts range from stoneware sculptures to "Phos" jewelry, which combines crystals with precious metals, and from witch-motif key rings to hand-sculpted ceramics glazed in subtle turquoise. ✉ *Main St.*

5

ERMONES ΕΡΜΟΝΕΣ

8 km (5 miles) north of Pelekas.

On the coast, 8 km (5 miles) north of Pelekas lies the small, low-key resort of Ermones, with pebbly sand beaches, heavily wooded cliffs, and a backdrop of green mountains. The Ropa River, which drains the vast central plain, flows into the Ionian Sea here; according to local legend, Nausicaa was rinsing her laundry at the river mouth when Odysseus came ashore, as told by Homer in *The Odyssey.* A short walk inland you find the island's only golf course; beyond that, the vast Ropa plain extends, a paradise for hikers, bird-watchers, and botanists. Also to the rear of the resort is the mountain village of Vatos, with its stunning views and traditional, picturesque neighborhoods.

WHERE TO EAT

$
GREEK
FAMILY

✕ **Navsika.** On a shady terrace above Ermones Beach, Navsika showcases home-cooked Corfiot dishes such as pastitsada and rice-and-herb-stuffed tomatoes and peppers, as part of a very extensive Greek and international menu. The stunning outlook takes in the full sweep of Ermones Bay with its forest-cloaked rocky hillsides. **Known for:** stupendous sunsets; perfectly cooked steaks; local ice cream in a variety of flavors. $ *Average main: €12* ✉ *Ermones Beach* ☎ *26610/94236* ⊗ *Closed Nov.–Apr.*

$
GREEK

✕ **Tristrato.** Set at a tree-shaded crossroads in the depths of the countryside, Tristrato was formerly an old wayhouse and still retains many of the building's original features. It now functions as a contemporary Greek gastropub where the proprietor brings you a variety of whatever they've got cooking, generally a choice between meat or fish mezes with salads and dips. **Known for:** food that quirkily combines local cooking style with exotic flavors; soothing rural outdoor dining with nice country view; cozy, publike interior. $ *Average main: €8* ✉ *Giannades–Marmaro crossroads, Giannades* ✛ *3 km (2 miles) north of Ermones* ☎ *26610/51580* ▭ *No credit cards.*

WHERE TO STAY

$$
RESORT
Fodor'sChoice
★

🏨 **Sensimar Grand Mediterraneo Resort & Spa by Atlantica.** This beachside resort, made up of low-rise buildings and bungalows cascading down a hillside, is now one of the most luxurious on Corfu's west coast. **Pros:** gorgeous scenery combining mountain and sea; very spacious rooms; luxurious spa for the use of guests. **Cons:** the beach is not Corfu's finest; the unfit and physically challenged may have difficulties with the terrain; no children under 16. $ *Rooms from: €175* ✉ *Ermones* ☎ *26610/95381* ⊕ *www.atlanticahotels.com* ⊗ *Closed Nov.–Apr.* ⇋ *279 rooms* ❙◎❙ *Breakfast.*

NIGHTLIFE

Dizi Bar. With its extensive shady deck terrace, Dizi Bar is a favorite summer rendezvous for locals. Many nights feature live music or DJ-led dancing until late. Call owner Kostas to find out what's happening and when. ✉ *Ermones* ☎ *26610/95080.*

SPORTS AND THE OUTDOORS

Corfu Golf Club. It's been called golf's best-kept secret, and, indeed, Corfu Golf Club combines a superb test of a golfer's skills with an outstanding natural environment. The course, in the delightfully rural Ropa valley and surrounded by lushly wooded mountains, was designed in the 1970s by the famous Swiss-based architect Donald Harradine, who blended the natural features of the landscape with man-made hazards to create a course that can be enjoyed by all categories of golfers. Players enter the course on footbridges crossing the Ropa River, and walk among lakes and streams and between copses and avenues of indigenous trees. Nature lovers may spot otters, terrapins, wild birds such as herons and kingfishers, and other native creatures. Back at the clubhouse, attractively built of local stone, the atmosphere is laid-back and welcoming, and the pro shop well stocked. A restaurant serves snacks and meals at reasonable prices. ✉ *Ermones* ☎ *26610/94220* 🌐 *www.corfugolfclub.com* 🎟 *€35 for 9 holes, €55 for 18 holes* ⛳ *18 holes. 6802 yards. Par 72.*

5

KONTOKALI ΚΟΝΤΟΚΑΛΙ

6 km (4 miles) north of Corfu Town.

Kontokali is best known for providing the main entry point to Corfu's biggest marina, a delightful place to stroll and admire the yachts, especially in the evening. Behind the marina stands a large roofless structure, built by the Venetians in the early 18th century as part of their shipyards. To the south of the marina lies the island's main cricket ground, incorporating a croquet field. The northern arm of the bay comprises the promontory of Kommeno, where expensive villas and large hotels are set among the trees. Tucked in the corner of the bay, on a tiny island at the approach to Kommeno, is the church of Ipapanti, one of Corfu's most picturesque spots.

GETTING HERE AND AROUND

A few kilometers north of Corfu Town, the village of Kontokali squeezes between the main road and the shoreline of Govino Bay. The area is heavily commercialized, but the village, which stretches along its own road parallel with the main one, is quiet and residential.

WHERE TO EAT

$$$ ECLECTIC Fodor's Choice ★ 🍴 **Etrusco.** The Botrini family restaurant is considered one of the best in Greece (the Athens branch has a Michelin star), and it certainly can be classed as among the most inventive, offering a menu of Italian- and Greek-inspired dishes. Chef Ettore Botrini demonstrates his flawless technique with a big blast of creativity on the molecular gastronomy front. **Known for:** elaborate tasting menus with wine pairings; homemade pappardelle with duck and blueberries; desserts, including goat-cheese ice cream and chocolate Bonnet. [$] *Average main: €40* ✉ *Kato Korakiana* ✥ *1 km (½ mile) west of Dassia* ☎ *26610/93342* 🌐 *www.etrusco.gr* 🕓 *No lunch.*

$$ SEAFOOD 🍴 **Fish Taverna Roula.** Choose from whatever fish is fresh that day—it could be sea bream, mullet, sole, squid, or snapper—or choose a pizza, steak, or chicken fillet. Sit on the waterfront terrace and watch the boats heading in and out of the marina. **Known for:** octopus carpaccio and other seafood

delicacies; seafood pizza and pasta dishes; magical marina view. $ *Average main: €16* ⊠ *Kontokali* ☎ *26610/91832* ⊕ *taverna-roula.gr.*

$$
SEAFOOD

✕ **Gerekos.** One of the island's longest-established and most famous fish restaurants, Gerekos pulls its catch daily from the family's own boats. The choice varies each day according to the season, but the friendly staff will show you what's available and guide your choice. **Known for:** octopus and other fish grilled on charcoal; secret-recipe fish soup; father-son team continuing a family tradition. $ *Average main: €20* ⊠ *Kontokali* ☎ *26610/91281.*

$
GREEK

✕ **Taverna Limeri.** Sitting in the "V" formed by the two streets in the village of Kato Korakiana, this taverna is where locals come to dine on wonderfully prepared local dishes. It's a good place to order several small plates and share a variety of tastes, like *gigantes* (giant beans stewed with tomato) or pork croquettes in cranberry sauce. **Known for:** exceptional house wines; beautiful steaks with a choice of classic sauces; village atmosphere off the tourist trail. $ *Average main: €10* ⊠ *Kato Korakiana* ✛ *1 km (½ mile) west of Dassia* ☎ *26610/97576* ☾ *No lunch.*

WHERE TO STAY

$$$
RESORT
Fodor'sChoice
★

🏨 **Corfu Imperial Grecotel Exclusive Resort.** One of the most sumptuous resorts on Corfu, the Imperial complex juts into Kommeno Bay atop a 14-acre peninsula and is beautiful both inside and out. **Pros:** beautifully maintained; excellent swimming; fine dining. **Cons:** so large you may feel anonymous; not within walking distance of restaurants and shops; access road has long-wait traffic lights. $ *Rooms from: €245* ⊠ *Limni* ✛ *10 km (6 miles) north of Corfu Town* ☎ *26610/88400* ⊕ *www.corfuimperial.com* ☾ *Closed Nov.– Apr.* ⇆ *274 room* ⦿ *Breakfast.*

$$$$
HOTEL

🏨 **Kontokali Bay Resort and Spa.** Built the same year as the superluxurious Corfu Imperial, this hotel-bungalow complex opened its doors in 1971 with a clean, modern look on a smallish sandy beach with a more relaxed feel than its primary competitor a few miles to the north. **Pros:** great spa; lovely grounds on seafront; contemporary decor. **Cons:** the surrounding area is rather bland; large and somewhat anonymous; the beach is not Corfu's finest. $ *Rooms from: €285* ⊠ *Nissi Gerekou* ☎ *26610/90500, 26610/99000* ⊕ *www.kontokalibay.com* ☾ *Closed mid-Oct.–Easter* ⇆ *261 rooms* ⦿ *Breakfast.*

PALEOKASTRITSA ΠΑΛΑΙΟΚΑΣΤΡΙΤΣΑ

21 km (13 miles) north of Pelekas, 25 km (16 miles) northwest of Corfu Town.

Fodor'sChoice
★

To quote one recent traveler: "I'd rather go to Paleokastritsa than to Heaven." Considered by many to be the site of Homer's city of the Phaeacians, this truly spectacular territory of grottoes, cliffs, and turquoise waters has a big rock named Kolovri, which the ancient Greeks said resembled the ship that brought Ulysses home. The jaw-dropping natural beauty of Paleo, as Corfiots call it, has brought hotels, tavernas, bars, and shops to the hillsides above the bays, and the beaches swarm with hordes of people on day trips from Corfu Town. You can explore the idyllic coves in peace with a pedal boat or small motorboat rented at the crowded main beach. There are also boat operators that go around to the prettiest surrounding beaches, especially those to the south, mostly inaccessible except from the sea; ask the skipper to let you off at a beach that appeals to you and to pick you up on a subsequent trip. Many visitors also enjoy a trip on the "Yellow Submarine," a glass-bottom boat that also runs night excursions (reservations are recommended—you can book at the Corfu Aquarium).

In the Paleokastritsa region, look for La Grotta bar, built grottolike into the rocks of a tiny cove. A mini-Acapulco, the high cliffs here tempt local youths to dive into the turquoise waters—great entertainment as you sip your cold beer or cocktail.

GETTING HERE AND AROUND

Depending on the day and the season, the green KTEL bus has four to six daily departures for Paleokastritsa from Corfu Town's bus terminal on Avramiou near the New Port (the daily 9 am departure is the fastest and most convenient). The trip takes about 45 minutes. A taxi from Corfu Town to Paleokastritsa costs about €50.

EXPLORING

FAMILY **Corfu Aquarium.** Although you might spot fish and other sea life when swimming in one of Paleokastritsa's stunning coves, you won't see the diversity of aquatic creatures as on display at the Corfu Aquarium, along with an assortment of reptiles. Located on the seashore at the foot of Paleokastritsa's monastery headland, the aquarium is home to a large number of species—crustaceans, starfish, and sea snails as well as fish—indigenous to Corfu's waters and the wider Mediterranean. The thrilling reptile room boasts boas, pythons, iguanas, and even a crocodile. The ticket price includes a very informative guided tour lasting around 30 minutes. You can book a concessionary dual ticket to the aquarium and on the Yellow Submarine tours at this location. ☎ 26630/41339 ⊕ www.corfuaquarium.com ☒ €6 ⊘ Closed Nov.–Mar.

Lakones. The village of Lakones, built on the steep mountain behind the Paleokastritsa Monastery, looks rather forbidding, but tourists flock there for the view. Kaiser Wilhelm was among many famous people who would make the ascent to enjoy the magnificent panorama of Paleokastritsa's coves from the cafés at Bella Vista, just beyond the village. In the village center is a small folk museum showcasing old photographs of the village. From nearby Krini you can climb up to the ruins of the 13th-century **Angelokastro**, a fortress built by a despot of Epirus during his brief rule over Corfu. On many occasions during the medieval period, the fort sheltered Corfiots from attack by Turkish invaders. Look for the chapel and caves, which served as sanctuaries and hiding places. ✛ 5 km (3 miles) northeast of Paleokastritsa.

Paleokastritsa Monastery. Paleokastritsa Monastery, a 17th-century structure, is built on the site of an earlier monastery, among terraced gardens overlooking the Ionian Sea. Its treasure is a 12th-century icon of the Virgin Mary, to whom the establishment is dedicated, and there's a small

Barely changed from the days of Homer, the Paleokastritsa region of Corfu is one of the most achingly beautiful landscapes in Greece.

museum with some other early icons. Note the Tree of Life motif on the ceiling. Be sure to visit the inner courtyard (go through the church), built on the edge of the cliff and looking down a precipitous cliff to the placid green coves and coastline to the south. There's a small gift shop on the premises. ⊠ *On northern headland* 🖃 *Donations accepted.*

WHERE TO EAT

$ ✕ **Corfu Dolce.** If Dolce is not the top patisserie-gelateria in Corfu, it's
CAFÉ certainly among the very best. The store distributes its own brand of ice cream islandwide, and its cakes are made on the premises. **Known for:** over 40 flavors of ice cream; overlooks one of the island's best views; cool mood music. $ *Average main: €5* ⊠ *Lakones Main St.* 🕾 *26630/49278* ⊕ *www.corfudolce.com* 🖃 *No credit cards.*

$ ✕ **Emeral Café and Pastry Shop.** Directly on the busy national road that
CAFÉ connects Corfu Town with Paleokastritsa, Emeral is a very popular
FAMILY place to stop for coffee, a sweet or savory pastry, or an ice cream. You'll have a hard time choosing from the variety of cream cakes, chocolate delicacies, and cookies in the display cases, to eat in or take away. **Known for:** fantastic cakes; variety of breads baked on the premises; great coffee. $ *Average main: €4* ⊠ *Km 10, Paleokastritsa National Rd., Korakiana* 🕾 *26610/91780* ⊕ *www.emeral.gr.*

$$ ✕ **Vrahos.** The stunning view from this restaurant overlooking the
GREEK cliff-enclosed bay at Paleokastrisa will make you want to linger. The menu offers a bit of everything, with lobster and spaghetti being the signature house dish. **Known for:** lobster spaghetti; prime location on Corfu's most famous bay; very polished service. $ *Average main: €16* 🕾 *26630/41233* ⊕ *www.vrachosp.gr* ☺ *Closed Nov.–Easter.*

CLOSE UP

The Corfu Trail

The Corfu Trail is a 220-km (137-mile) trekking route that begins at the island's southern tip and takes a winding course to its northernmost point. Though a relatively small island, Corfu possesses a diversity of scenery that astounds, and the walk—which requires around 10 days to complete in full—takes in many of its varied landscapes. Not only does each day offer a distinctive character, but even on a single day's walk the terrain changes constantly. At every corner, a new scene assaults the eye: a stunning view, a little church, a grove of ancient olive trees, a meadow carpeted with wild flowers. The trail takes in wild beaches, juniper-forested dunes, dense oak woodland, a karst plateau where nomad cattle roam, deep gorges, wetlands, mountain summits, and bucolic plains. The hand of modern man hardly encroaches, and only old monasteries, ruined olive presses, picturesque villages, and ancient fortresses intrude on nature. On-trail accommodation and daily luggage transfer may be booked through Aperghi Travel *(see Tours)*. For more information on the trail, see 🌐 *www.thecorfutrail.com.*

5

WHERE TO STAY

$ HOTEL Fodor's Choice ★ 🏨 **Akrotiri Beach Hotel.** Few hotels in Corfu are so superbly positioned to take in its natural splendor the way the Akrotiri is, which lords it over a paradisical little peninsula. **Pros:** the location could not be better; wonderful swimming; fabulous view from many of the rooms. **Cons:** public areas look a bit tired; road outside carries heavy traffic; a long walk to the main bays of Paleokastritsa. [$] *Rooms from: €120* ☎ *26630/41237* 🌐 *www.akrotiri-beach.com* 🕓 *Closed Nov.–May* 🛏 *125 rooms* 🍴 *Breakfast.*

$ RENTAL FAMILY Fodor's Choice ★ 🏨 **Casa Lucia.** There are far grander places to stay on Corfu but few with as much quiet, unpretentious charm as Casa Lucia, where the stone buildings of an old olive press have been converted into guest cottages and smaller studios. **Pros:** gorgeous gardens and pool; all units have a kitchen and terrace; family-friendly with no traffic. **Cons:** fairly basic bathrooms in studios; not by the sea; you need a car to access shops and sights. [$] *Rooms from: €60* ✉ *Corfu–Paleokastritsa road* ✥ *13 km (8 miles) northwest of Corfu Town* ☎ *26610/91419* 🌐 *www.casa-lucia-corfu.com* 🛏 *9 cottages* 🍴 *No meals.*

$ RENTAL 🏨 **Fundana Villas.** The charming suites and bungalows at this small hilltop lodging are built into and around a 17th-century stone-and-mortar Venetian storehouse; each has been turned into a comfortable hideaway. **Pros:** surrounded by lovely gardens and olive and orange groves; very quiet, traffic-free location; beautiful pool. **Cons:** short on in-room facilities; you need transport to access restaurants and shops; not by the sea. [$] *Rooms from: €75* ✉ *Km 15, Paleokastritsa National Rd.* ✥ *3 km (2 miles) east of Paleokastritsa* ☎ *26630/22532* 🌐 *www.fundanavillas.com* 🕓 *Closed Nov.–Mar.* 🛏 *12 rooms* 🍴 *Breakfast.*

$$
B&B/INN
Fodor's Choice
★

The Merchant's House. Owners Mark and Saskia have created their luxurious B&B from one of Perithia's former ruins with a sensitive and stylish renovation of the old stone structure. **Pros:** perfect for lovers of nature; warm and helpful personal service; homemade sourdough bread and jams for breakfast. **Cons:** no swimming pool; the village, though isolated, can be busy with day-trippers; hair-raising drive to get there. $ *Rooms from: €150* ☎ *26630/98444* ⊕ *www.merchantshousecorfu.com* ☾ *Closed Nov.–Mar.* ➟ *5 rooms* ⚹⃝ *Breakfast.*

THE CYCLADES

Tinos, Mykonos, Delos, Naxos, Paros,
Santorini, and Folegandros

WELCOME TO THE CYCLADES

TOP REASONS TO GO

★ **Santorini:** Volcanic, spectacular Santorini is possibly the last remnant of the "lost continent"—the living here is as high as the towns' cliff-top perches.

★ **Naxos:** Mythic haunt of the ancient Minoan princess Ariadne, Naxos is the largest of the Cyclades and is noted for its 16th-century Venetian homes.

★ **Mykonos:** The rich arrive by yacht, the middle class by plane, the backpackers by boat—but everyone is out to enjoy the golden sands and Dionysian nightlife.

★ **Paros:** The seaside villages of Paros, with their daytime charm and nighttime buzz, are among the most atmospheric in the Cyclades.

★ **Antiparos:** Hiding within the shadow of its mother island of Paros, this long-forgotten jewel has been discovered by Hollywood high-rollers like Tom Hanks and Brad Pitt.

Nearly 2,000 islands and islets are scattered like a ring (*Cyclades* is the Greek word for "circling ones") around the sacred isle of Delos, birthplace of the god Apollo, including many of Greece's top tourist destinations. Gateways include the airports on Mykonos and Santorini and the harbors of Paros and Naxos.

1 Tinos. Among the most beautiful of the Cyclades, Tinos's charms remain largely unheralded but include the "Greek Lourdes"—the Panayia Evangelistria church—1,300 traditional stone dovecotes, and idyllic villages like Pirgos.

2 Mykonos. Party central because of its nonstop nightlife, the chief village of Mykonos, called Mykonos Town, is the Cyclades' best preserved—a maze of flatstone streets lined with white houses and flower-filled balconies.

3 Delos. A short boat ride away from Mykonos is hallowed Delos, sacred to Apollo and now a vast archaeological site.

4 Paros. West of Naxos and known for its fine beaches and fishing villages, as well as the pretty town of Naousa, Paros often takes the summer overflow crowd from Mykonos. Today, crowds head here for Paros Town and its Hundred Doors Church and undeveloped beaches.

5 Naxos. Presided over by the historic castle of Naxos Town, largely the creation of the Venetian dukes of the archipelago, Naxos has a landscape graced with time-stained villages like Sangri, Chalki, and Apeiranthos, many with Venetian-era towers.

6 Folegandros. Tides of travelers have yet to discover this stark island, which makes it all the more alluring to Cyclades lovers, particularly those who prize its stunning cliff scenery.

7 Santorini. Once the vast crater of a volcano, Santorini's spectacular bay is ringed by black-and-red cliffs, which rise up 1,000 feet over the sea. The main towns of Fira and Ia cling inside the rim in dazzling white contrast to the somber cliffs. South lies the "Greek Pompeii" that is ancient Akrotiri.

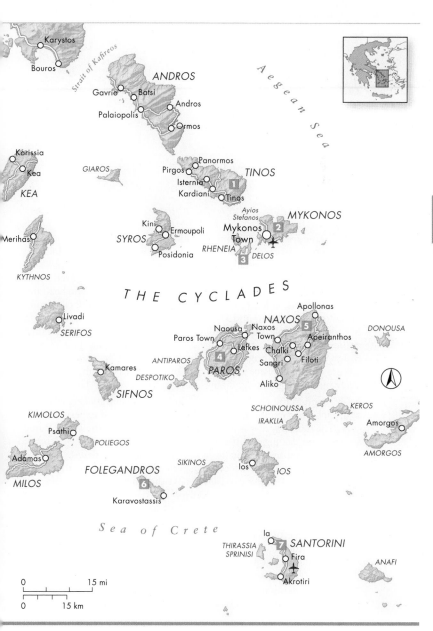

Karystos
Bouros
Strait of Kafireos
ANDROS
Aegean Sea
Gavrio Batsi
Palaiopolis
Andros
Ormos
Korissia
Kea
KEA
GIAROS
Panormos
Pirgos
Isternia
Kardiani
TINOS
1
Tinos
Ayios Stefanos
MYKONOS
Kini
SYROS Ermoupoli
Merihas
Posidonia
Mykonos Town
RHENEIA
2
DELOS
3
KYTHNOS
THE CYCLADES
Livadi
SERIFOS
Apollonas
NAXOS
Naousa Naxos Town
Paros Town Lefkes
Chalki
ANTIPAROS
Sangri
Kamares
DESPOTIKO
PAROS
Aliko
5
Apeiranthos
Filoti
DONOUSA
SIFNOS
KIMOLOS
Psathi
POLIEGOS
Adamas
MILOS
FOLEGANDROS
Karavostassis
6
SCHOINOUSSA
IRAKLIA
SIKINOS
Ios
IOS
KEROS
Amorgos
AMORGOS
Sea of Crete
THIRASSIA
SPRINISI
Ia
SANTORINI
7
Fira
Akrotiri
ANAFI

6

0   15 mi
0   15 km

Updated by Marissa Tejada

If the words *Greek islands* suggest blazing sun and sea, bare rock and mountains, olive trees and vineyards, white rustic architecture and ancient ruins, fresh fish, and fruity oils, the Cyclades are your isles of quintessential plenty, the ultimate Mediterranean archipelago.

"The islands with their drinkable blue volcanoes," wrote Odysseus Elytis, winner of the Nobel Prize for poetry, musing on Santorini. The major stars in this constellation of islands in the central Aegean Sea—Tinos, Mykonos, Naxos, Paros, and Santorini—remain the archetypes of the islands of Greece. No matter which of these islands you head for, it always seems, at least in summer, that Zeus's sky is faultlessly azure, Poseidon's sea warm, and Dionysus's nightlife buzzing (especially in Mykonos's clubs). The prevailing wind is the northern *vorias*; called *meltemi* in summer, it cools the always-sunny weather. In a blazing fusion of sunlight, stone, and aqua sparkle, the Cyclades offer both culture and hedonism: ancient sites, Byzantine castles and museums, lively nightlife, shopping, dining, and beaches plain and fancy.

Each island in the Cyclades differs significantly from its neighbors, so approach your exploration according to what sort of experience you seek. The most popular islands are Santorini, with its fantastic volcanic scenery and dramatic cliff-side towns of Fira and Ia, and Mykonos, a barren island that insinuates a sexy jet-set lifestyle, flaunts some of Greece's most famous beaches, has a perfectly preserved main town, and courts celebrities. These two islands have the fanciest accommodations. Naxos has the best mountain scenery and the longest, most pristine beaches. Tinos, the least visited and most scenic of the Cyclades, is the place to explore mountain villages, hundreds of churches, and fancifully decorated dovecotes. Throughout the Cyclades, many shuttered houses are being authentically restored, and much traditional architecture can still be found in Ia on Santorini and Apeiranthos on Naxos—villages that are part of any deep experience of the islands.

These arid, mountainous islands are the peaks of a deep, submerged plateau; their composition is rocky, with few trees. They are volcanic in origin, and Santorini, southernmost of the group, actually sits on the rim of an ancient drowned volcano that exploded about 1600 BC. The dead texture of its rock is a great contrast to the living, warm limestone of most Greek islands. Santorini's basic geological colors—black, pink, brown, white, pale green—are not in themselves beautiful; as you arrive by boat, little shows above the cliff tops but a string of white villages—like teeth on the vast lower

jaw of some giant monster. Still, the island was once called Kllisti, "Loveliest," and today appreciative visitors seek its mixture of vaulted cliff-side architecture, European elegance, and stunning sunsets.

A more-idyllic rhythm prevails on many of the other Cyclades (and, of course, off-season in Santorini). In the town of Mykonos, the whitewashed houses huddle together against the meltemi winds, and backpackers rub elbows with millionaires in the mazelike gray-stone streets. The island's sophistication level is high, the beaches fine, and the shopping varied and upscale. It's also the jumping-off place for a mandatory visit to tiny, deserted Delos. Apollo's windswept birth islet, still watched over by a row of marble lions, was once the religious and commercial center of the eastern Mediterranean.

Tinos has stayed authentically Greek, since its heavy tourism is largely owing to its miracle-working icon, not to its beautiful villages. Naxos, greenest of the Cyclades, makes cheese and wine, raises livestock, and produces potatoes, olives, and fruit. For centuries a Venetian stronghold, it has a shrinking aristocratic Roman Catholic population, Venetian houses and fortifications, and Cycladic and Mycenaean sites. Paros, a hub of the ferry system, has reasonable prices and is a good base for trips to other islands. It's also good for lazing on white-sand beaches and for visiting fishing villages.

Of course, throughout the Cyclades, there are countless classical sites, monasteries, churches, and villages to be explored. The best reason to visit them may be the beauty of the walk, the impressiveness of the location, and the hospitality you will likely find off the beaten track.

PLANNING

WHEN TO GO

The experience of the Cyclades is radically different in summer compared to winter. In summer all services are operating on overload, the beaches are crowded, the clubs noisy, the restaurants packed, and the scene hopping. Walkers, nature lovers, and devotees of classical and Byzantine Greece would do better to come in spring and fall, ideally in late April–June or September–October, when temperatures are lower

GETTING THERE: BOAT VS. PLANE

To get to the Cyclades, you either fly or take a boat. Flights from Athens are short and convenient, but if you want to understand what it means to be in the Aegean archipelago, and why an island has a special feeling, take the boat—after all, these are islands in the fabled Aegean, inhabited 5,000 years before Homer. Flights may cost three times the price of the slower ferries. Nevertheless, if you fly into Athens in time to make a flight connection (and especially if you don't want to visit the big city), it may be worth it. Seats are booked (sometimes overbooked) much in advance, and even in winter you need reservations. Single flights are much easier to get (even last-minute, owing to cancellations). High rollers can also hire a helicopter for €4,000, and you would be surprised how many travelers do this. Note that flights are often canceled owing to rough weather; the islands have small airports, and crosswinds (but not the prevailing north winds, which are fine, however strong) ground planes.

and tourists are fewer. But off-season travel means less-frequent boat service; in fact, there is sometimes no service at all between November and mid-March, when stormy weather can make the seas too rough for sailing. In winter, many shops, hotels, and restaurants are closed, and the open cafés are full of locals recuperating from summer's intensity. The villages can feel shuttered and the nightlife evaporates. Cultural organizations, film clubs, concerts of island music, and religious festivals become more important. The temperature will often seem colder than the thermometer indicates: if it is in the low 50s, cloudy, drizzling, and windy, you will feel chilled and want to stay indoors, and these islands are at their best outdoors.

PLANNING YOUR TIME

The Cyclades are more for lazing around than for book-nosed tourism. Start with the livelier islands (Mykonos, Santorini), add one or two of the larger islands (Naxos, Paros), and finish up with an untouristy one like Folegandros. Although it is true that feverish partying can overwhelm the young in summer, in other seasons the temptations are fewer, gentler, and more profound. If you move fast, you will see little, and the beauty is in the general impression of sea, sky, mountain, and village, and in the details that catch your eye: an ancient column used as a building block, an octopus hung to dry in the sun, a wedding or baptism in a small church you stopped by (Welcome, stranger!), a shepherd's mountain hut with a flagstone roof—they are endless. There are important sites such as Delos's ruins, but just enjoying the island rhythms often proves as soul-satisfying.

GETTING HERE AND AROUND

Transportation to the islands is constantly improving. Five of the Cyclades have airports, and high-speed ferry service between Athens and the islands and within the islands seems to increase with each season. But remember that boat schedules depend on Poseidon's weather whims, and service might be canceled when seas are rough. No matter how you travel, it's best to buy tickets well in advance of major spring and summer holidays.

AIR TRAVEL

Flight schedules change seasonally and are often revised; reservations are always a good idea. There are no airports on Tinos or Folegandros. Olympic Air has several daily flights to Mykonos, Naxos, Paros, and Santorini, with more in peak season. Aegean Airlines has daily flights to Mykonos and Santorini in summer. Many European airlines offer nonstop flights to both Mykonos and Santorini, and charter flights come from the Middle East and around Europe.

Airport Contacts Mykonos Airport (*JMK*). ✛ *4 km (2½ miles) southeast of Mykonos Town* ☎ *22890/22327* ⊕ *www.mykonos-airport.org.* **Naxos Airport** (*JNX*). ✉ *1 km (½ mile) south of Naxos Town* ☎ *22850/23969.* **Paros Airport** (*PAS*). ✛ *Near Alyki village, 9 km (5½ miles) south of Paros Town* ☎ *22840/92030.* **Santorini Airport** (*JTR*). ✛ *On east coast, 6 km (4 miles) from Fira* ☎ *22860/28400* ⊕ *www.santoriniairport.com.*

BOAT AND FERRY TRAVEL

Greek boats in general are efficient, stable, fast, and comfortable. Most boats leave from Athens's port of Piraeus and also from Rafina (accessible by KTEL bus from Athens); a few leave from Lavrio. The larger ferries are more stable, and islanders consider the various Blue Star Ferries their main connection to the mainland. Remember that some fast boats are small, and can roll uncomfortably in high seas. Also, high-speeds have little or no deck space; you are closed in. The Blue Star will give you a seat number for a small extra fee, and the fast boats have reserved seats only. In summer, you should always reserve seats in advance.

At Easter and around August 15, seats are hard to come by, and boat schedules change for the holidays. All ferries run much less frequently in winter, and many fast ferries don't run at all.

Seajets offers a comfy fast-boat connection between the two most popular islands in the Cyclades: Santorini and Mykonos.

Off-season you don't need reservations, and you can purchase tickets just before departure at offices on the dock in Piraeus. Ferries can be canceled owing to gales, and then schedules go haywire and hundreds of people and cars have to fight for new tickets (in effect, the ferry companies never cancel boats; the harbor police decide, according to international regulations).

For schedules (not too far in advance, please), check ⊕ *www.openseas. gr* or ⊕ *www.gtp.gr.*

Contacts Blue Star Ferries. ☎ *21089/19800* ⊕ *www.bluestarferries.com.* **Piraeus boat departures/arrivals.** ☎ *14541, 14944.* **Piraeus Port Authority.** ✉ *Akti Miaouli 10, Piraeus* ☎ *21045/50000* ⊕ *www.olp.gr.* **Rafina KTEL Buses.** ☎ *22940/23440 bus terminal* ⊕ *www.ktelattikis.gr.* **Seajets.** ☎ *21041/21001, 21041/21901* ⊕ *www.seajets.gr.*

BUS TRAVEL

For information about Bus Travel, consult the Getting Here and Around sections listed under each island.

CAR AND SCOOTER TRAVEL

To take cars on ferries, you must make reservations. Though there is bus service on all islands, you may find it more convenient to travel by car, especially on a larger island like Naxos. Although islanders tend to acknowledge rules, many roads on the islands are poorly maintained, and tourists sometimes lapse into vacation inattentiveness. Drive with caution, especially at night, when you may well be sharing the roads with motorists returning from an evening of drinking. All the major islands have car- and bike-rental agencies at the ports and in the business districts. Car rentals in summer cost about €40–€80 per day, with unlimited mileage and third-party liability insurance. Full insurance costs about €15 per day more. Many places now rent Smart Cars for about €60 a day: these two-seaters are a cool way to get around.

Often travelers opt for scooters or four-wheel semi-bikes (quads), but be careful—island hospitals get filled with people with serious-looking injuries due to poor roads, slipshod maintenance, careless drivers, and excessive partying. Quads, which Greeks call *gourounia* (piggies), look safer than scooters but in fact turn over easily. Choose a dealer that offers 24-hour service and a change of vehicle in case of a breakdown. Most will take you from and to your plane or boat.

FOOT TRAVEL

The Cyclades are justly famous for their hiking. Ancient goat and donkey trails go everywhere—through fields, over mountains, along untrodden coasts. Since tourists crowd beaches, clubs, and town promenades, walking is uncrowded even in July and August. Prime walking months, though, are April and May, when temperatures are reasonable, wildflowers seem to cover every surface, and birds migrate. October is also excellent for hiking—plus, olive groves provide their own sort of spectacle when dozens of gatherers spread their cloths.

HOTELS

Overall, the quality of accommodations in the Cyclades is high, whether they be tiny pensions, private houses, or luxury hotels. The best rooms and service (and noticeably higher prices) are on Mykonos and Santorini, where luxury resort hotels now rank among the world's favorites. Wherever you stay in the Cyclades, make a room with a view and a balcony a priority. If you're not interested in staying at luxury hotels and unless you're traveling at the very height of the season (July 15–August 30), you're unlikely to need advance reservations on some islands. Sometimes the easiest way to find something, in fact, is to head for a tourist office and describe your needs and price range. And remember: few hotels have elevators, and even Santorini's best often have breathlessly picturesque cliff-side staircases (though most have porters to carry your bags).

RESTAURANTS

Eating is a lively social activity in the Cyclades, and the friendliness of most taverna owners compensates for the lack of formal service. Unless you order intermittently, the food comes all at once. Restaurant schedules on the Cyclades vary; some places close for lunch, most close for siesta, and all are open late. Reservations are not required unless otherwise noted, and casual dress is the rule. But luxury restaurants are a different kettle of fish in some respects.

Greek food used to have a bad international reputation, and you can certainly find bad food in Greece. This is often a result of restaurants trying to adapt to the tastes and wallets of the throngs of tourists. Greece produces top-quality tomatoes, lamb chops, melons, olive oil, and farmer's cheese. When Greeks go out to eat, they expect good, simple food culled from these elements, as should you. Do likewise, and you will dine with much pleasure.

Dishes are often wonderfully redolent of garlic and olive oil; as a simple, plain alternative, order grilled seafood or meat—grilled octopus with ouzo is a treat. A typical island lunch is fresh fried calamari with a salad of tomatoes, peppers, onions, feta, and olives. Lamb on a skewer and *keftedes* (spicy meatballs) are also favorites. Of course, nouvelle Greek cuisine has made great strides since it was first introduced in the early 2000s at the luxury hotels of the Cyclades. At the finer hotels, and at certain outstanding restaurants, you can taste the collision of centuries-old traditional dishes with newer-than-now-nouvelle spices and preparations. There are just so many times one can eat lamb-on-a-skewer, so go ahead and splurge at top restaurants—if you have a chubby wallet, that is.

Greek wines have tripled in quality in the last decade. The volcanic soil of Santorini is hospitable to the grape, and Greeks love the Santorini wines. Santorini and Paros now proudly produce officially recognized "origin" wines, which are sought throughout Greece. Barrel or farmer's wine is common, and except in late summer when it starts to taste a bit off, it's often good.

Restaurant and hotel reviews have been shortened. For full information, visit Fodors.com.

DINING AND LODGING PRICES IN EUROS			
	$	$$	$$$	$$$$
Restaurants	under €15	€15–€25	€26–€40	over €40
Hotels	under €125	€125–€225	€226–€275	over €275

Restaurant prices are the average cost of a main course at dinner or, if dinner is not served, at lunch. Hotel prices are the lowest cost of a standard double room in high season.

SHOPPING

Mykonos is the best island in the Cyclades for shopping. You can buy anything from Greek folk items to Italian designer clothes, cowboy boots, and leather jackets from the United States. Although island prices are better than in the expensive shopping districts of Athens, there are many tourist traps in the resort towns, with high-pressure sales tactics and inflated prices for inferior goods. The Greeks have a word for a naive American shopper—*Americanaki*. It's a good sign if the owner of a shop selling traditional crafts or art lives on the island and is not a hot shot Athenian over for the summer to make a quick buck. Each island has a unique pottery style that reflects its individuality. Santorini potters like the bright shades of the setting sun, though the best pottery island is Paros. Island specialties are icons hand-painted after Byzantine originals; weavings and embroideries; local wines; and gold worked in ancient and Byzantine designs. Don't be surprised when the stores close between 2 and 5:30 in the afternoon and reopen in the evenings; even on the chic islands everybody takes a siesta.

VISITOR INFORMATION

Despite their popularity, most of the Cycladic islands do not have tourist offices. Instead, turn to local travel agencies, who can help you book tours, ferry tickets, and accommodations. General brochures and information about the Cyclades are available through the website and offices of the Greek National Tourism Organization (GNTO; EOT in Greece ⊕ *www.gnto.gr*).

TINOS ΤΗΝΟΣ

160 km (85 nautical miles) southeast of Piraeus harbor in Athens.

Tinos (or, as archaeologists spell it, Tenos) is among the most beautiful and most fascinating of the major Cyclades. The third largest of the island group after Naxos and Andros, with an area of 195 square km (121 square miles), it is inhabited by nearly 10,000 people, many of whom still live the traditional life of farmers or craftspeople. Its long, mountainous spine, rearing between Andros and Mykonos, makes it seem forbidding, and in a way it is. It is not popular among tourists for a few reasons: the main village, Tinos Town (Chora), lacks charm; the beaches are undeveloped; there is no airport; and the prevailing north winds are the Aegean's fiercest (passing mariners used to sacrifice a calf to Poseidon, ancient Tinos's chief deity, in hopes of avoiding shipwreck). On the other hand, Tinos is dotted with possibly the loveliest villages in the Cyclades.

Whether travelers head to Tinos or not, a visit here is essential for Greeks: its great Church of Panayia Evangelistria is the Greek Lourdes, a holy place of pilgrimage and miraculous cures; 799 other churches adorn the countryside. Encroaching development here is to accommodate those in search of their religious elixir and not, as on the other islands, the beach-and-bar crowd.

Tinos's magnificently rustic villages are, for some welcome reason, not being abandoned. The dark arcades of Arnados, the vine-shaded sea

views of Isternia, the gleaming marble squares of Pirgos: these, finally, are what make Tinos unique. A map, available at kiosks or rental agencies, will make touring these villages by car or bike somewhat less confusing, as there are nearly 50 of them. Of all the major islands, Tinos is the least developed for sports—the strong winds discourage water sports, and sports outfitters come and go.

GETTING HERE AND AROUND

In high season many boats stop at Tinos, since it is on the Mykonos line, and consequently it becomes crowded with travelers. But, owing to the famous church, it is also hugely popular with Greeks who arrive on Friday night and leave in time to get to work on Monday. The boats vary from big ferries to fast passengers-only boats, and it takes four to five hours, depending mostly on route and weather. Especially notice, as your boat rounds the point into the harbor, the high peak of Exambourgos with its acropolis and Venetian fort. For August weekends, reservations are recommended. For Easter and August 15, they are absolutely necessary, and the boats will be packed (the many cars in transit don't help). For these holidays, boat schedules do change; information much in advance is not trustworthy. Tinos has daily ferry connections with Andros, Mykonos, and Paros, less often with Naxos. Returning boats go either to Piraeus or to Rafina. When buying tickets at the quayside agencies, remember that not every office handles every boat, so check at more than one. For any queries or recommendations, contact Georgia, of Tinos Tours. There is a lot of information at ⊕ *www.greeka.com.*

On Tinos, buses (☎ *22830/22440*) run several times daily from the quay of Chora (Tinos Town) to nearly all the many villages in Tinos, including Kionia (15 minutes) and Panormos (1 hour); in summer buses are added for beaches. Prices range from €2 to €5 and service stops around 7 pm. The bus depot is near the new dock.

VISITOR INFORMATION

Contacts Tinos Tours. ✉ *Trion Ierarchon 30, Tinos Town* ☎ *22830/26011* ⊕ *www.tinostours.net.*

TINOS TOWN ΤΗΝΟΣ (ΧΩΡΑ)

14 km (9 miles) northwest of Mykonos Town.

Civilization on Tinos is a millennium older than Tinos Town, or Chora, founded in the 5th century BC. On weekends and during festivals, Chora is thronged with Greeks attending church, and restaurants and hotels cater to them. As the well-known story goes, in 1822, a year after the War of Independence began (Tinos was the first of the islands to join in), the Virgin sent the nun Pelagia a dream about a buried icon of the Annunciation. On January 30, 1823, such an icon was unearthed amid the foundations of a Byzantine church, and it started to heal people immediately.

EXPLORING

Archaeological Museum of Tinos. On the main street, near the church, is the small Archaeological Museum; its collection includes a sundial by Andronicus of Cyrrhus, who in the 1st century BC also designed Athens's Tower of the Winds. Here, too, are Tinos's famous huge, red storage vases, from the 8th century BC. ✉ *Megalohari* ☎ *22830/22670* 🕑 *€2* ⊗ *Closed Sat.–Mon.*

Cultural Foundation of Tinos. Founded in 2002, the Cultural Foundation of Tinos, housed in a large and splendid neoclassical building at the south end of the quay, remains active in promoting the fantastic art, history, and culture of the island. The center revolves around a full schedule of traveling exhibitions, lectures, performances, and other events. It has a permanent exhibit of work by Tinian sculptor, Iannoulis Chalepas. There's also a café. ✉ *Paralia Tinos* ☎ *22830/29070* ⊕ *www.itip.gr* 🕑 *€3* ⊗ *Closed Tues.*

To seek help for a sick relative from the icon within, a young woman must crawl a full kilometer from the harbor on her knees, then up these steps to the breathtaking Panayia Evangelistria.

Fodor's Choice **Panayia Evangelistria.** The Tinians built the splended Church of the
★ Annunciate Virgin on this site in 1823 to commemorate finding a
buried icon of the Annunciation in the foundations of an old Byzantine
church that once stood here. Imposing and beautiful, framed in gleaming yellow and white, it stands atop the town's main hill ("hora"),
which is linked to the harbor via Megalochari, a steeply inclined avenue lined with votive shops. Half Venetian, half Cypriot in style, the
facade (illuminated at night) has a distinctive two-story arcade and
bookend staircases. Lined with the most costly stones from Tinos,
Paros, and Delos, the church's **marble courtyards** (note the green-
veined Tinian stone) are paved with pebble mosaics and surrounded
by offices, chapels, a health station, and **seven museums.** Inside the
upper three-aisle church dozens of beeswax candles and precious tin-
and silver-work votives—don't miss the golden orange tree near the
door donated by a blind man who was granted sight—dazzle the eye.
You must often wait in line to see the little icon, encrusted with jewels,
which is said to have curative powers. To beseech the icon's aid, a
sick person sends a young female relative or a mother brings her sick
infant. As the pilgrim descends from the boat, she falls to her knees,
with traffic indifferently whizzing about her, and crawls painfully up
the faded red padded lane on the main street—1 km (½ mile)—to
the church. In the church's courtyards, she and her family camp for
several days, praying to the magical icon for a cure, which sometimes
comes. This procedure is very similar to the ancient one observed in
Tinos's temple of Poseidon. The **lower church,** called the Evresis, celebrates the finding of the icon; in one room a baptismal font is filled

Traditional Festivals in the Cyclades

All over Greece, villages, towns, and cities have traditional celebrations that vary from joyous to deeply serious, and the Cyclades are no exception. In Tinos Town, the healing icon from Panayia Evangelistria church is paraded with much pomp on Annunciation Day, March 25, and especially Dormition Day, August 15. As it is carried on poles over the heads of the faithful, cures are effected, and religious emotion runs high. On July 23, in honor of St. Pelagia, the icon is paraded from Kechrovouni Nunnery, and afterward the festivities continue long into the night, with music and fireworks. ⊕ www.tinoslitfestival.com).

If you're on Santorini on July 20, you can partake in the celebration of St. Elias's name day, when a traditional pea-and-onion soup is served, followed by walnut and honey desserts and folk dancing.

Naxos has its share of festivals to discover and enjoy. Naxos Town celebrates the Dionysia festival during the first week of August, with concerts, costumed folk dancers, and free food and wine on the square. During Carnival, preceding Lent, "bell wearers" take to the streets in Apeiranthos and Filoti, running from house to house making as much noise as possible with strings of bells tied around their waists. They're a disconcerting sight in their hooded cloaks, as they escort a man dressed as a woman from house to house to collect eggs. In Apeiranthos, villagers square off in rhyming-verse contests: on the last Sunday of Lent, the *paliomaskari*, their faces blackened, challenge each other in improvising *kotsakia* (satirical couplets). On July 14, Ayios Nikodemos Day is celebrated in Chora with a procession of the patron saint's icon through town, but the Dormition of the Virgin on August 15 is, after Easter and Christmas, the festival most widely celebrated, especially in Sangri, Filoti (where festivities take place on August 4), and Apeiranthos.

On Paros each year on August 23, eight days after the huge festival in Parikia at the Church of a Hundred Doors, Naousa celebrates the heroic naval battle against the Turks, with children dressed in native costume, great feasts, and traditional dancing. The day ends with 100 boats illuminated by torches converging on the harbor. On June 2, there is much feasting in Lefkes for the Holy Trinity.

with silver and gold votives. The chapel to the left commemorates the torpedoing by the Italians, on Dormition Day, 1940, of the Greek ship *Helle*; in the early stages of the war, the roused Greeks amazingly overpowered the Italians. ⊠ *Evangelistrias 1* ☎ *22830/22256* ⊕ *www. panagiatinou.gr.*

BEACHES

There is a series of beaches between Chora and Kionia (and beyond, for walkers).

Ayios Fokas Beach. This long sandy beach is the closest organized beach to Tinos Town, and it's also the island's largest beach overall. The coastline is marked with natural shade from tamarisk trees, but beach chairs and umbrellas are readily available for rent during the summer.

The main road behind the beach has a gathering of beach hotels, rooms, and tavernas. There are also a few beach bars and cafés along its 1½-km (1-mile) stretch. **Amenities:** food and drink. **Best for:** swimming; walking. ✉ *Ayios Fokas* ⊕ *3 km (2 miles) from Tinos Town.*

Stavros Beach. Within walking distance of Tinos Town, this beach is a peaceful little corner of Tinos. One or two tavernas are nearby, but Stavros beach is really known for its fine sand and its beautiful surroundings. The turquoise waters remain clear, and shady green trees dot the area surrounding Ayios Stavros, the pretty whitewashed church that gave the beach its name. ■ **TIP→ Come during sunset, as it makes for one of the most romantic settings on Tinos.** **Amenities:** food and drink. **Best for:** sunset; swimming. ✉ *Stavros Beach* ⊕ *1 km (½ mile) from Tinos Town.*

CALLING ALL FAITHFUL

Evangelistria, the street parallel to Panayia Evangelistria, the legendary church of Tinos Town, is closed to traffic and is a kind of religious flea market, lined with stores hawking immense candles, chunks of incense, tacky souvenirs, tin votives, and sweets. There are several good jewelers' stores on the market street, where, as always on Tinos, the religious note is supreme.

WHERE TO EAT

$$ MEDITERRANEAN Fodor's Choice ★ 🍴 **Itan Ena Mikro Karavi.** After entering off a main road in Tinos Town, take a short walk down a pastel-painted hallway to your open-air dining destination, where chef Antonis Psaltis serves his "creative Mediterranean" cuisine with superb results. This discreet entrance hides an impressively ambient setting with hanging bougainvillea, decorated with lively yet warm colors. **Known for:** beautiful setting; Mediterranean dishes. [$] *Average main: €20* ✉ *Trion Ierarchon* ☎ *22830/22818* 🌐 *www.mikrokaravi.gr* ⏲ *Closed Nov.–Apr.*

$ GREEK 🍴 **Metaxi Mas.** On a trellised lane by the harbor, this family-run taverna is a Tinos favorite, serving a wide range of Greek traditional and Tinian dishes. Main-course favorites include spicy lamb cooked in paper and calamari stuffed with cheese, tomatoes, and peppers. **Known for:** Tinian dishes; family-friendly atmosphere. [$] *Average main: €12* ✉ *Kontogiorgi* ☎ *22830/25945* 🌐 *www.metaximastinos.gr.*

$$ GREEK 🍴 **Symposion.** Giorgos Vidalis's café and restaurant occupies a sophisticated and well-preserved neoclassical building on a pedestrian-only street. Select from international- and Mediterranean-influenced dishes, to be enjoyed daytime on the upper terraces that overlook the Turkish fountain and the passing scene. **Known for:** beautiful interiors; good service. [$] *Average main: €18* ✉ *Evangelistrias 13* ☎ *22830/24368* 🌐 *www.symposion.gr* ⏲ *Closed Nov.–Mar.*

$ GREEK 🍴 **Zefki.** The Tsirou family cooks delicious Greek classics with a Tinian touch. Try the Tinian omelet with sausage and fresh potatoes, or for a more hearty dish go for the savory roasted local goat. **Known for:** reasonable prices; traditional Tinian dishes; live Greek music on summer Sundays. [$] *Average main: €12* ✉ *Alex. Lagourou 6* ⊕ *Walk up Evangelistria St. and take the 2nd right* ☎ *22830/22231* 💳 *No credit cards.*

WHERE TO STAY

$ | **⊤ Favie Suzanne Hotel.** Sleek, posh, and convenient, too—if you are will-
HOTEL | ing to give up a sea view, this is the best place to stay in Tinos Town, thanks, in good part, to the hotel's lovely decor, which, from fanlights to dovecotes, incorporates many Tinian details. **Pros:** there is an eleva-tor; swimming pool; conveniently located to Tinos Town sights. **Cons:** near the busy port; can feel crowded during high season; basic decor. $ *Rooms from: €70 ⊠ Antoniou Sochou 22 ☎ 22830/22693 ⊕ www. faviesuzanne.gr ☉ Closed Dec.–Feb. ⇘ 49 rooms |◎| Breakfast.*

$ | **⊤ Vincenzo Family Rooms.** Owner and manager Ioannis Vidalis has given
B&B/INN | Tinos just what it needs—a simple, friendly, convenient, and attractive hotel, right in Chora, with furnishings in traditional island style. **Pros:** walking distance to Tinos Town sights and a beach; a good budget hotel; parking is available. **Cons:** town can feel busy in high season; simple and basic accommodations; basic breakfast (included in price). $ *Rooms from: €90 ⊠ 25is Martiou 15 ☎ 22830/25888 ⊕ www.vin-cenzo.gr ⇘ 14 rooms |◎| Breakfast.*

NIGHTLIFE

Tinos has fewer bars and discos than the other big islands, but there's a lively late-night bar scene come summer. The action is behind the waterfront between the two boat docks.

Kaktos Bar. Jutting up next to a restored 16th-century Cycladic windmill, Kaktos is an open-air terrace bar where locals and visitors alike can sit back and enjoy a cocktail while taking in the view of Tinos Town and the Aegean Sea. The stone walls, wall hangings and artwork create an Old West–style atmosphere, complete with a few large cacti. Summer features a schedule of DJs that spin various house, mainstream, and dance beats. ⊠ *Leof. Tripotamou* ☎ *22830/25930* ⊕ *www.kaktos-bar.gr* ☉ *Closed Oct.–May.*

Koursaros Bar. *Koursaros*, which translates to "Pirate," gets its share of summer party crowds each year. Its decor is a soft mix of dark wood and stone with vintage maps and seafaring artifacts that play into the bar's nautical theme. Its location, at the very corner by the harbor, has made it one of the most visible landmark nightlife spots in Tinos since 1987. Café by day, a DJ turns up the music at night spinning rock, funk, or jazz. ⊠ *Akti Ellis 1* ☎ *22830/23963.*

Sivylla Club. Tinos Town has a nightlife district, but it only comes to life in the heat of the summer. Syvilla, located on one of the district's alleyways, churns out both Greek pop and international mainstream dance hits. ⊠ *Taxiarchon 17* ☎ *22830/22511* ⊕ *www.sivylla.gr.*

SHOPPING

Due to the island's landmark church, you'll find a wide variety of stores selling religious icons of every size and style, handmade from all types of material, including gold, silver, and wood. Tinos is still a rural island in many ways, so locally produced honey, cheese, and foodstuffs are of top quality and simply delicious. Finally, the island is particularly known for its marble arts and sculptures. If you're looking for something that may not be found anywhere else, beautiful Tinian artwork may be just the thing.

FOOD

Enosis (*Farmers' Cooperative*). Tinos produces a lot of milk. A short way up from the harbor, on the right, this little store sells milk, butter, and cheeses, including sharp *kopanistí,* a specialty of Tinos, that pairs perfectly with ouzo; local jams and honeys are for sale, too. ⊠ *Megalochori 16 ✛ The main street up from the harbor* ☎ *22830/23289.*

Halaris Sweet Shop. This shop and bakery is the local go-to for anything traditional and sweet. It's known for Tinian specialties such as almond paste candies called *psarakia tinou,* and cheesecake bites made with Tinian cheese called *gliko tiropitaki tsibiti.* You'll find yourself walking away with little gift boxes filled with your favorites, but before you go, try their homemade ice cream featuring flavors like Greek yogurt raspberry. ⊠ *Georgiou Plamari 3* ☎ *22830/23274.*

JEWELRY

Fodor'sChoice
★
Anna Maria. By the small park next to the Cultural Center, the entrance to the small arts shop Anna Maria is draped by blue morning-glory vines. The boutique showcases folklore jewelry by Greek artisans, with ancient and Byzantine motifs and also island-made marble pieces selected by owner and local Nikos Kangas. The crowded shop is a delight. ⊠ *Alvanou 6* ☎ *22830/23456.*

Ostria. The selection here is especially good; in addition to delicate silver jewelry, Ostria sells silver icon covers, silver plate, and 22-karat gold. ⊠ *Evangelistria 20* ☎ *22830/23893.*

MARKETS

Farmers' Market. Tinos is a rich farming island, and every day but Sunday, farmers from all the far-flung villages fill the square with vegetables, herbs, and *kritamos* (pickled sea-plant leaves). ⊠ *Tinos Town ✛ Between two docks* ☙ *Closed Sun.*

Fish Market. On a little square near the very center of town, local Tinian fishermen sell fresh seafood. Meanwhile, the local pelican (a rival to Mykonos's Petros the Pelican) can often be found cadging snacks from them. ⊠ *Tinos Town.*

RELIGIOUS ICONS

Dia Cheros. The walls of Xenofon Varveris's colorful neoclassical shop are filled with detailed religious icons that may look similar at first glance, but once you look closer you'll see that each piece is unique since each one has been handmade and hand-painted in Greece. Besides a fantastic selection of the icon plaques, Dia Cheros features collections of handmade Greek jewelry as well as traditional glass lamps. ⊠ *Evangelistrias 24.*

WEAVINGS

Biotechniki Scholi. The century-old weaving school, or Biotechniki Scholi, sells traditional weavings—aprons, towels, spreads—made by its students, local girls. The largest of its three high-ceiling, wooden-floor rooms is filled with looms and spindles. ⊠ *Evaggelistria ✛ A short walk up the main street from the sea* ☎ *22830/22894* ☙ *Closed Oct.–May.*

6

AYIOS IOANNIS BAY ΑΓΙΟΣ ΙΩΑΝΝΗΣ

7 km (4½ miles) east of Tinos Town.

Heading east from Tinos Town, you'll travel on a winding road surrounded by bare, rocky Cycladic island landscape. It eventually slopes down into Ayios Ioannis Bay (*O ormos tou Ayiou Ioanni* in Greek). The quiet beaches here offer clear seas that curve into picturesque bays. Around Ayios Ioannis Bay, several hotels, rooms for rent, and tavernas open each summer to cater to the season's travelers.

BEACHES

FAMILY **Ayios Ioannis Porto Beach.** Since it's secluded from the summer's temperamental gusty island winds, the sands that fill up the pretty curved beach of Ayios Ioannis Porto Beach stay put. Here you can spend the day under tamarisk trees for natural shade or rent beach chairs and umbrellas during peak season. Its shallow waters and calm nature make it a choice beach for families. Several beach hotels are in close proximity. A few tavernas are nearby for a beach break. **Amenities:** food and drink. **Best for:** swimming. ✉ *Ayios Ioannis.*

FAMILY **Ayios Sostis Beach.** Known for its shallow turquoise waters and excellent, clear view of Mykonos, the yellow sand-filled Ayios Sostis Beach is said to be a continuation of Ayios Kyriaki Beach. In the summer, beach chairs and umbrellas are available to rent. A few tavernas and cafés are within walking distance for a meal break or refreshments. There are several ways to get to the beach, including a few small roads lined with bougainvillea and tall reeds. **Amenities:** food and drink. **Best for:** swimming. ✉ *Ayios Sostis.*

Pachia Ammos Beach. Secluded in a cove east of Tinos Town, Pachia Ammos is named for its thick sand, which has a unique green hue that complements the surrounding short shrub hills that roll into the turquoise blue sea. It is completely undeveloped, and getting to the beach requires a 15- to 30-minute walk on an unmarked path, which isn't ideal for flimsy flip-flops while balancing your beach necessities. The effort, however, is rewarded with basking in one of the prettiest and most peaceful places on the island. To get there, drive 10 km (6 miles) on the main road east toward Ayios Ioannis Beach and turn off at the signs for Pachia Ammos. Park off the road and walk over the hill to your right; the beach isn't obvious right away but follow one of several trails and you'll see it appear before you. **Amenities:** none. **Best for:** solitude; swimming. ✉ *Past Porto, reached by a dirt road, Ayios Ioannis.*

WHERE TO STAY

$ RESORT FAMILY 🏨 **Akti Aegeou.** The family that runs this little resort is lucky to own such a valuable piece of property as Akti Aegeou, meaning "Aegean Coast," which is right on the uncrowded and pretty beach at Laouti. **Pros:** perfect for swimming in pool or beach; charming and welcoming environment; parking is available for guests. **Cons:** far from town; not within walking distance to major sights of Tinos; breakfast is extra. [$] *Rooms from: €80* ✉ *Laouti* ✥ *6 km (4 miles) east of Tinos Town* ☎ *22830/24248* 🌐 *www.aktiaegeou.gr* ⏲ *Closed Nov.–Mar.* 🛏 *35 rooms* 🍴 *No meals.*

$ **Porto Tango.** This ambitiously up-to-date and stylish resort-hotel
HOTEL strives for the best in decor and service—little wonder that Greece's
FAMILY late prime minister, Andreas Papandreou, stayed here during his last
visit to Tinos. **Pros:** great for families; nice spa amenities and services;
price includes breakfast and transfers. **Cons:** a bit out in the boonies;
necessary to have a car to get to Tinos sights; not much within walking distance. $ *Rooms from: €110* ⊠ *Ayios Ioannis* ☎ *22830/24411*
⊕ *www.portotango.gr* ⊘ *Closed Nov.–Mar.* ⤴ *57 rooms* ¶◯¶ *Breakfast.*

KIONIA KIONIA

2 km (1 miles) northwest of Tinos Town.

The little seaside town of Kiona is a short scenic drive, bike ride, or
hike west of Tinos Town. A few simple tavernas and rooms are set off
the main beach road, and on the main road the landmark Tinos Beach
Hotel directly overlooks Kiona beach. Kiona's main attraction is the
Sanctuary of Poseidon, which dates back to the 4th century BC.

Sanctuary of Poseidon. The reason to come to this small community
northwest of Tinos Town is to visit the large, untended Sanctuary of
Poseidon, also dedicated to the bearded sea god's sea-nymph consort,
Amphitrite. The present remains are from the 4th century BC and later,
though the sanctuary itself is much older. It was a kind of hospital,
where the ailing came to camp and solicit the god's help. The marble
dolphins in the museum were discovered here. According to the Roman
historian Pliny, Tinos was once infested with serpents (goddess symbols) and named Ophiousa (Serpenttown), until supermasculine Poseidon sent storks to clean them out. The sanctuary functioned well into
Roman times. ⊠ *Kionia.*

BEACHES

Kionia Beach. Just 3 km (2 miles) west of Tinos Town, Kionia Beach
remains one of the island's most visited beaches. It has both pebbles
and sand, but the long stretch of sand dominates, and a section of it
fronts the archaeological site of the Sanctuary of Poseidon. Kionia's
beachfront road is lined with cafés, tavernas, rooms for rent, and the
Tinos Beach Hotel, which are all within walking distance of the beach.
Beach chairs and umbrellas are available for rent during the summer.
Amenities: food and drink. **Best for:** swimming; walking. ⊠ *Kionia.*

WHERE TO EAT

$ ✕ **Tsambia.** Abutting the Sanctuary of Poseidon and facing the sea, this
GREEK multilevel taverna offers such tried-and-true indigenous specialties as
pork in red wine with lemon, or goat casserole with oregano. Starters
might include *louza* (smoked pork), local Tinian cheeses rarely sold in
stores (especially fried local goat cheese), and homegrown vegetables.
Known for: traditional food; fresh fish when available; local cheeses.
$ *Average main: €10* ⊠ *Epar. Od. Tinou-Kallonis.*

WHERE TO STAY

$ **Tinos Beach Hotel.** The winning points about this hotel is that it is
HOTEL big, comfortable, well appointed, and fronts Kionia's long beach. **Pros:**
FAMILY good hotel for families; property has elevators; right in front of a beach.

Cons: not convenient walking distance from town; some rooms may feel a bit outdated; not much to do at night in Kionia. $ *Rooms from: €94* ✉ *Kionia* ☎ *22830/22626* ⊕ *www.tinosbeach.gr* ⌁ *165 rooms* ⏐○⏐ *Breakfast.*

ISTERNIA ΙΣΤΕΡΝΙΑ

24 km (15 miles) northwest of Tinos Town.

The village of Isternia (Cisterns) is verdant with lush gardens. Many of the marble plaques hung here over doorways—a specialty of Tinos—indicate the owner's profession, for example, a sailing ship for a fisherman or sea captain. A long, paved road winds down to a little port, Ayios Nikitas, with a beach and two fish tavernas; a small boat ferries people to Chora in good weather.

BEACHES

Isternia Beach. The beach, located right at the foot of the little fishing village of Isternia Bay, is actually two beaches—one a pebbled area and one a sandy cove—but both are known for their peaceful seclusion, although two tavernas and a café are nearby. You can also take some time out to visit the inland village of Isternia about 5 km (3 miles) away. Whether you're lying on the beach or having a meal by the sea, you can look forward to enjoying one of the nicest sunset views in Tinos. **Amenities:** food and drink. **Best for:** solitude; swimming. ✉ *Isternia.*

WHERE TO EAT

$$

MEDITERRANEAN

Fodor's Choice

★

✕ **To Thalassaki.** The name means "the little sea" and this restaurant, specializing in Mediterranean seafood, has one of the island's best sea views. Set on a platform on Ormos Isternion Bay, right up against the Aegean Sea with views of Syros, chef and owner Antonia Zarpa produces innovative, well-thought-out dishes that capture the local flavors from her beloved island. **Known for:** seaside dining and fantastic sea views; excellent Greek-inspired cuisine with Tinian influences; innovative and delicious desserts. $ *Average main: €18* ✉ *Ornos* ⊗ *Closed Nov.–Mar.*

PIRGOS ΠΥΡΓΟΣ

32 km (20 miles) northwest of Tinos Town, 8 km (5 miles) north of Isternia.

The village of Pirgos, second in importance to Chora, is inland and up from the little harbor of Panormos. Tinos is famous for its marble carving, and Pirgos, a prosperous town, is noted for its sculpture school (the town's highest building) and marble workshops, where artisans make fanlights, fountains, tomb monuments, and small objects for tourists; they also take orders. The village's main square is aptly crafted of all marble; the five cafés, noted for *galaktoboureko* (custard pastry), and one taverna are all shaded by an ancient plane tree. The quarries for the green-vein marble are north of here, reachable by car. The cemetery here is, appropriately, a showplace of marble sculpture.

EXPLORING

Museum Iannoulis Chalepas. The marble-working tradition of Tinos survives here from the 19th century and is going strong, as seen in the two adjacent museums: Museum Iannoulis Chalepas and Museum of Tinos Artists, which house the work of Pirgos's renowned sculptor, and other works. ⊠ *Pirgos* ✛ *One block from bus stop* ☎ *22830/31262* 💷 *3€* 🕑 *Closed Oct.–Mar.*

Fodor'sChoice
★

Museum of Marble Crafts. In the highest building on Pirgos hill, the Museum of Marble Crafts is part of the Piraeus Bank Cultural Foundation's network of high-tech museums on the last century's traditional industries. Inside the strikingly modern building, exhibits show the process of quarrying and carving, and they are the best you'll ever see. The master artists' drawings for altarpieces and tomb sculpture are also on display, as are some of their works. ⊠ *Pirgos* ✛ *Take the staircase up from the main square of Pirgos* ☎ *22830/31290* ⊕ *www. piop.gr/en* 💷 *€3* 🕑 *Closed Tues.*

SHOPPING

Lambros Diamantopoulos. A number of marble carvers are, appropriately, found in Pirgos. You may visit the shop and view the work of probably the island's best master carver, Lambros Diamantopoulos, who accepts commissions for work to be done throughout Greece. His traditional designs are for sale, both to visitors and to other carvers, who may bring a portable slab home to copy. ⊠ *Pirgos* ✛ *Near main square* ☎ *22830/31365.*

PANORMOS BAY ΟΡΜΟΣ ΠΑΝΟΡΜΟΥ

35 km (22 miles) northwest of Tinos Town, 3 km (2 miles) north of Pirgos.

Panormos Bay, an unpretentious port once used for marble export, has ducks and geese, a row of seafood restaurants, and a good beach with a collapsed sea cave. More coves with secluded swimming are beyond, as is the islet of Panormos. There are many rooms to rent.

BEACHES

Panormos Beach. The sandy beach fronts the lovely fishing village of Panormos, which at one point was the island's main harbor. Located north of Tinos Town, most visitors also make it a point to visit the nearby inland village of Pirgos or beach-hop to little beaches to the east and west of Panormos Beach. When the island winds are right, windsurfers may take on the waters. **Amenities:** food and drink. **Best for:** swimming; windsurfing. ⊠ *Panormos.*

FAMILY

Rohari Beach. Located in the next cove southeast of Panormos Beach, Rohari remains just as popular in the summer as a favorite northern beach destination. Fully organized, the beachfront cantinas are the perfect spot for a cool drink; there are beach umbrellas and chairs for rent. It's within close proximity to the village of Panormos, which has a wide selection of tavernas and cafés for a beach-day break. **Amenities:** food and drink. **Best for:** swimming. ⊠ *Panormos.*

MYKONOS ΜΥΚΟΝΟΣ

From backpackers to the superrich, from day-trippers to yachties, from regular people to celebrities (who head here by helicopter), Mykonos has become one of the most popular of the Aegean islands. Today's scene is a weird but attractive cocktail of tradition, beauty, and glitz, but travelers from all over the world have long been drawn to this dry, rugged island—at 16 km (10 miles) by 11 km (7 miles), one of the smaller Cyclades—thanks to its many stretches of sandy beach, its thatched windmills, and its picturesque port town. One thing is certain: Mykonos knows how to maintain its attractiveness, how to develop it, and how to sell it. Complain as you will that it is touristy, noisy, and overdeveloped; you'll be back.

In the 1950s, a few tourists began trickling into Mykonos on their way to see the ancient marvels on the nearby islet of Delos, the sacred isle. For almost 1,000 years Delos was the religious and political center of the Aegean and host every four years to the Delian games, the region's greatest festival. The population of Delos actually reached 20,000 at the peak of its commercial period, and throughout antiquity Mykonos, eclipsed by its holy neighbor, depended on this proximity for income (it has been memorably described as Delos's "bordello"), as it partly does today. Anyone interested in antiquity should plan to spend at least one morning on Delos, which has some of the most striking sights preserved from antiquity, including the beautiful Avenue of the Lions or the startling, enormous stone phalli in the Sanctuary of Dionysus.

Today, the natives of Mykonos have happily fit cosmopolitan New Yorkers, Londoners, and Athenians gracefully into their way of life. You may see, for example, an old island woman leading a donkey laden with vegetables through the town's narrow streets, greeting the suntanned vacationers walking by. The truth is, Mykonians regard a good tourist season the way a fisherman inspects a calm morning's catch; for many, the money earned in July and August will support them for the rest of the year. Not long ago Mykonians had to rely on what they could scratch out of the island's arid land for sustenance, and some remember suffering from starvation under Axis occupation during World War II. How things have changed.

GETTING HERE AND AROUND

Mykonos is superpopular and easy to get to. It is totally jammed in season, in part thanks to 10 or more daily 45-minute flights from Athens in summer (there are almost as many in winter); there are also direct flights from Europe and the Middle East. The trip by ferry takes from two to five hours depending on your route, the boat, and Poseidon's weather ways. There are eight or more boats a day. For Easter and August 15, book early. In summer, reservations are necessary; off-season, you won't need one, but cars always need them. The boats usually pull in at the huge new dock area, from which you must take a bus or taxi, or get your hotel to pick you up (better hotels do this, and often charge you for it).

In Mykonos Town the Ayios Loukas bus depot in the Fabrica quarter at the south end of town has buses to Ornos, Ayios Ioannis, Platis Gialos, Psarou, Paradise Beach, the airport, and Kalamopodi. Another depot near the Archaeological Museum is for Ayios Stefanos, Tourlos, Ano Mera, Elia, Kalafatis, and Kalo Livadi. Schedules are posted (hotel concierges also should have this info); fares run from €2 to €10. Regular taxis line up at Plateia Manto Mavrogenous, while scooter-taxis greet new arrivals at the harbor; use them to get to your Mykonos Town hotel, usually hidden away on a pedestrian- and scooter-only street. Meters are not used on Mykonos; instead, standard fares for each destination are posted on a notice bulletin board; note there are only 13 regular cabs here even in August!

TOURS

Mykonos Accommodation Center. This center, in a picturesque old building (up a steep staircase), has grown to offer just about every service a visitor may need on Mykonos, including a wide variety of group tours. A guide takes a group every morning for a day tour of Delos (€50). The company also has half-day guided tours of the Mykonos beach towns, with a stop in Ano Mera for the Panayia Tourliani Monastery (€50). You can also take an excursion to nearby Tinos (€70), arrange private tours of Delos and Mykonos and off-road jeep trips (€70), charter yachts, and more. Owner John van Lerberghe is an expat who has lived on the island for decades, and he knows his stuff. ✉ *Enoplon Dynameon 10, Mykonos Town* ☎ *22890/23160* ⊕ *www.mykonos-accommodation.com.*

MYKONOS TOWN ΜΥΚΟΝΟΣ (ΧΩΡΑ)

177 km (110 miles) southeast of Piraeus harbor in Athens.

Although the fishing boats still go out in good weather, Mykonos largely makes its living from tourism these days. The summer crowds have turned one of the poorest islands in Greece into one of the richest. Old Mykonians complain that their young, who have inherited stores where their grandfathers once sold eggs or wine, get so much rent that they have lost ambition, and in summer sit around pool bars at night with their friends, and hang out in Athens in winter when island life is less scintillating.

Put firmly on the map by Jackie O in the 1960s, Mykonos Town—called Hora by the locals—remains the Saint-Tropez of the Greek islands. The scenery is memorable, with its whitewashed streets, Little Venice, the Kato Myli ridge of windmills, and Kastro, the town's medieval quarter. Its cubical two- or three-story houses and the churches, with their red or blue doors, domes and wooden balconies, have been long celebrated as some of the best examples of classic Cycladic architecture. Luckily, the Greek Archaeological Service decided to protect the town, even when the Mykonians would have preferred to rebuild, and so the Old Town has been impressively preserved. Pink oleander, scarlet hibiscus, and trailing green pepper trees form a contrast amid the dazzling whiteness, whose frequent renewal with whitewash is required by law.

Any visitor who has the pleasure of getting lost in its narrow streets (made all the narrower by the many outdoor stone staircases, which maximize housing space in the crowded village) will appreciate how its confusing layout was designed to foil pirates—if it was designed at all. After Mykonos fell under Turkish rule in 1537, the Ottomans allowed the islanders to arm their vessels against pirates, which had a contradictory effect: many of them found that raiding other islands was more profitable than tilling arid land. At the height of Aegean piracy, Mykonos was the principal headquarters of the corsair fleets—the place where pirates met their fellows, found willing women, and filled out their crews. Eventually the illicit activity evolved into a legitimate and thriving trade network.

Morning on Mykonos Town's main quay is busy with deliveries, visitors for the Delos boats, lazy breakfasters, and street cleaners dealing with the previous night's mess. In late morning the cruise-boat people arrive, and the shops are all open. In early afternoon, shaded outdoor tavernas are full of diners eating salads (Mykonos's produce is mostly imported); music is absent or kept low. In mid- and late afternoon, the town feels sleepy, since so many people are at the beach, on excursions, or sleeping in their air-conditioned rooms; even some tourist shops close for siesta. By sunset, people have come back from the beach, having taken their showers and rested. At night, the atmosphere in Mykonos ramps up. The cruise-boat people are mostly gone, coughing three-wheelers make no deliveries in the narrow streets, and everyone is dressed in their sexy summer best and starting to shimmy with the scene. Many shops stay open past midnight, the restaurants fill up, and the bars and discos make ice cubes as fast as they can.

Ready to dive in? Begin your tour of Mykonos Town (Hora) by starting out at its heart: Manto Mavrogenous Square.

EXPLORING

TOP ATTRACTIONS

Aegean Maritime Museum. The charming Aegean Maritime Museum contains a collection of model ships, navigational instruments, old maps, prints, coins, and nautical memorabilia. The backyard garden displays some old anchors and ship wheels and a reconstructed 1890 lighthouse, once lighted by oil. ⊠ *Enoplon Dynameon 10* ☎ *22890/22700* ⊕ *www. culture.gr* ✉ *€4.*

Archaeological Museum of Mykonos. Before setting out on the mandatory boat excursion to the isle of Delos, check out the Archaeological Museum, which affords insight into the intriguing history of its ancient shrines. The museum houses Delian funerary sculptures, many with scenes of mourning; most were moved to Rhenea when the Athenians cleansed Delos in the 6th century, during the sixth year of the Peloponnesian War, and, under instruction from the Delphic Oracle, the entire island was purged of all dead bodies. The most significant work from Mykonos is a 7th-century BC *pithos* (storage jar), showing the Greeks in the Trojan horse and the sacking of the city. ⊠ *Mykonos Town* ⚓ *Old Port of Chora Mykonos* ☎ *22890/22325* ⊕ *www.culture. gr* ✉ *€4* ⊗ *Closed Mon.*

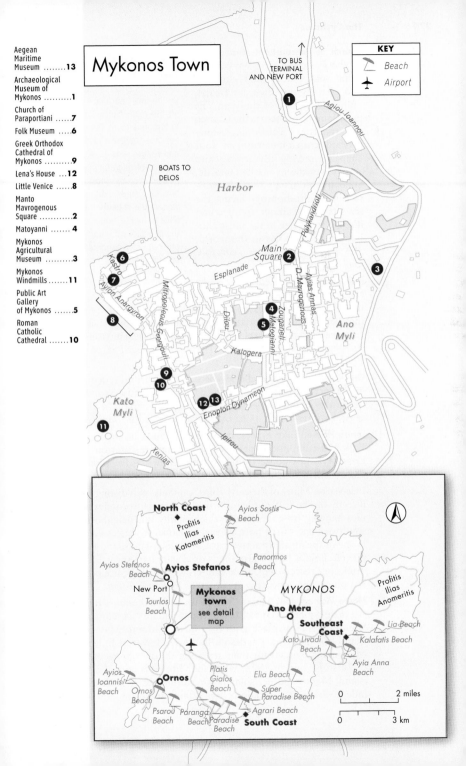

Mykonos Town

KEY

Beach

Airport

TO BUS TERMINAL AND NEW PORT

Agiou Ioannou

BOATS TO DELOS

Harbor

Palrikandrioti

Main Square ❷

❸

Esplanade

Kastro

❻

❼

Ayion Anargyron

❽

Mitropoleous Gorgouli

Dilou

Zouganeli

❹
Matoyanni

❺

Ayias Annas

D. Mavrogenous

Ano Myli

Kalogera

❾

❿

Kato Myli

⓬ ⓭

Enoplon Dynameon

⓫

Ipirou

Xenias

North Coast

Profitis Ilias Katomeritis

Ayios Sostis Beach

Ayios Stefanos Beach

Ayios Stefanos

Panormos Beach

New Port

Tourlos Beach

Mykonos town
see detail map

MYKONOS

Profitis Ilias Anomeritis

Ano Mera

Southeast Coast

Kato Livadi Beach

Lia Beach

Kalafatis Beach

Ayia Anna Beach

Ayios Ioannis Beach

Ornos

Ornos Beach

Platis Gialos Beach

Elia Beach

Super Paradise Beach

Agrari Beach

Psarou Beach

Paranga Beach

Paradise Beach

South Coast

0   2 miles

0   3 km

Fodor's Choice ★ **Church of Paraportiani** (*Our Lady of the Postern Gate*). Mykonians claim that exactly 365 churches and chapels dot their landscape, one for each day of the year. The most famous of these is the Church of Paraportiani. The sloping, whitewashed conglomeration of four chapels, mixing Byzantine and vernacular idioms, looks fantastic. Solid and ultimately sober, its position on a promontory facing the sea sets off the unique architecture; it's said to be one of the most photographed churches in the world. ✉ *Ayion Anargyron* ✥ *Near folk museum.*

THE PRANCE OF THE PELICAN

By the time morning's open-air fish market picks up steam in Mykonos Town, Petros the Pelican—the town mascot—preens and cadges eats. In the 1950s a group of migrating pelicans passed over Mykonos, leaving behind a single exhausted bird; Vassilis the fisherman nursed it back to health, and locals say that the pelican in the harbor is the original Petros (though there are several).

Folk Museum. Housed in an 18th-century house originally built for Captain Nikolaos Malouchos, this museum exhibits a bedroom furnished and decorated in the fashion of that period. On display are looms and lace-making devices, Cycladic costumes, old photographs, and Mykoniot musical instruments that are still played at festivals. ✉ *Kastro* ✥ *Old Port, near Paraportiani church* ⊙ *Closed Oct.–Apr.*

Greek Orthodox Cathedral of Mykonos. This cathedral is dedicated to Virgin Mary the Great (the name by which locals know it) and is noted for its number of old icons of the post-Byzantine period. ✉ *Alefkandra Sq.* ✥ *At the intersection of Anargyron and Odos Mitropolis.*

Lena's House. Take a peek into Lena's House, an annex of the local Folk Museum, and experience an accurate restoration of a middle-class Mykonos house from the 19th century. ✉ *Enoplon Dynameon* ☎ *22890/22390* ⊙ *Closed Nov.–Mar.*

Fodor's Choice ★ **Little Venice.** Many of the early ships' captains built distinguished houses directly on the seafront here, with elaborate buttressed wooden balconies hanging over the water, which is why this neighborhood, at the southwest end of the port, earned its name. Architecturally unique, it is one of the most attractive areas in all the islands, and many of these fine old houses now house shops or elegant bars specializing in sunset drinks or cabarets, which draw the crowds. Little Venice presents countless photo ops, especially at sunset. ✉ *Mykonos Town.*

Manto Mavrogenous Square. Start a tour of Mykonos Town (Hora) on the main square, Manto Mavrogenous Square (sometimes called Taxi Square). Pride of place goes to a bust of Manto Mavrogenous, the island heroine, atop a pedestal. In the 1821 War of Independence the Mykonians, known for their seafaring skills, volunteered an armada of 24 ships, and in 1822, when the Ottomans landed a force on the island, Manto and her soldiers forced them back to their ships. After independence, a scandalous love affair caused the heroine's exile to

Paros, where she died. An aristocratic beauty who becomes a great revolutionary war leader and then dies for love may seem straight out of Hollywood, but it is all true. ⊠ *Mykonos Town.*

Matoyanni. The main shopping street, Matoyanni, is lined with jewelry stores, clothing boutiques, chic cafés, and candy shops. Owing to the many cruise ships that disgorge thousands of shoppers daily in season—some unload 3,000 jostling tourists—the rents here rival 5th Avenue's, and the more-interesting shops have skedaddled to less-prominent side streets. ⊠ *Mykonos Town* ✢ *Perpendicular to harbor.*

A SEASIDE MILKY WAY

The best time to visit Mykonos's central harbor is in the cool of the evening, when the islanders promenade along the esplanade to meet friends and visit the numerous cafés. Mykonians, when they see the array of harbor lights from offshore, call it the String of Pearls, though more and more lights are fuzzing the dazzle.

Mykonos Windmills. Across the water from Little Venice, set on a high hill, are the famous Mykonos windmills, echoes of a time when wind power was used to grind the island's grain. The area from Little Venice to the windmills is called **Alefkandra,** which means "whitening": women once hung their laundry here. A little farther toward the windmills the bars chockablock on shoreside decks are barely above sea level, and when the north wind is up (often), surf splashes the tables. Farther on, the shore spreads into an unprepossessing beach, and tables are placed on sand or pebbles. After dinner (there are plenty of little tavernas here), the bars turn up their music, and knowing the beat thumps into the night, older tourists seek solace elsewhere. ⊠ *Alefkandra.*

WORTH NOTING

Mykonos Agricultural Museum. This museum displays a 16th-century windmill, traditional outdoor oven, waterwheel, dovecote, and more. ⊠ *Petassos* ✢ *At top of Mykonos Town* ☉ *Closed Oct.–May.*

Public Art Gallery of Mykonos. Located on Manto Mavrogenous Square, the Public Art Gallery of Mykonos changes exhibitions every 10 days giving Greek and international artists a great place to showcase their work. ⊠ *Matoyanni* ☎ *22890/27190.*

Roman Catholic Cathedral. Next to the Greek Orthodox Cathedral is the Roman Catholic Cathedral, the Virgin of St. Rosary, from the Venetian period. The name and coat of arms of the Ghisi family, which took over Mykonos in 1207, are inscribed in the entrance hall. ⊠ *Platia Alefkandra* ✢ *At the intersection of Anargyron and Odos Mitropolis.*

BEACHES

Swimming in quiet Aegean bays with clean blue water enclosed by rugged hills cannot be overpraised—so it is little wonder some of Greece's finest strands of sand are found on Mykonos. Mostly protected from the prevailing north winds, they can be conveniently grouped. In general the beaches charge €5–€15 for an umbrella and sun bed. Most of

The little church of Agios Nikolakis sits right on the Mykonos waterfront near the ferry to Delos and is one of the most photographed sights in Mykonos Town, whether it's in the background or the foreground.

the island's beaches lie along Mykonos's southern coast; from Mykonos Town, Ornos Beach is about 10 minutes, Kalafati is less than an hour. Mykonos Town does have a little beach that attracts local children or townies who just want a quick dip, but it's not going to be your beach of choice. All the others require transportation.

WHERE TO EAT

$$$ ✕ **Avra.** Set in an ambient, open garden space shaded by colorful bougainvillea in the heart of Mykonos Town, Avra offers mostly Mediterranean cuisine, as well as an international selection that features good Asian and Italian dishes. Excellent appetizers include fried feta in pastry topped with sesame seeds, grapes, and rose petal jelly. **Known for:** atmospheric garden dining area; international dishes done well. $ *Average main: €26* ⊠ *Kalogera 27* ☏ *22890/22298* ⊕ *www.avra-mykonos.com* ☾ *Closed Nov.–Apr.*

INTERNATIONAL

$$$ ✕ **Funky Kitchen.** Tucked in a quiet corner of Mykonos Town, on a picturesque whitewashed street lined with bougainvillea, you'll find talented chef Pavlos Grivas at work in his modern, open kitchen perfecting his innovative Mediterranean fusion dishes. Starters delight, reflecting the traditional products of Mykonos, including a uniquely flavorful panna cotta with kopanisti cheese, dried figs and Greek prosciutto. **Known for:** excellent service and reputation; quiet ambient dining in Mykonos Town; gluten-free options. $ *Average main: €26* ⊠ *Ignatiou Basoula 40* ☏ *22890/27272* ☾ *Closed Apr.–Oct.*

MEDITERRANEAN
Fodor'sChoice
★

$$ ✕ **Kounelas.** This long-established fresh-fish taverna is where many fishermen themselves eat, for solid, no-frills food; you can pick your own fish. The menu depends on the weather—low winds mean lots of fish.

SEAFOOD

Known for: fresh seafood and meats by the kilo, all grilled outside on a wood grill; after-dinner liqueur; casual, friendly atmosphere. $ *Average main: €25* ✉ *Mykonos Town* ✛ *Off the port, near Delos boats* ☎ *22890/28220* ⊕ *kounelas-myconos.com.*

$$$$
FRENCH
Fodor's Choice
★

✕ **La Maison de Katrin.** Hidden away in the Dilou quarter, this is one of the most reputable restaurants on the island, featuring the best of both French and Greek cuisine—which makes it well worth the search to find it. Fine food and excellent, hospitable service keep people coming, in spite of the prices. **Known for:** quality traditional Greek and French cuisine; excellent and professional service; rich and delightful desserts. $ *Average main: €60* ✉ *Ayios Gerasimos and Nikou, Dilou* ☎ *22890/22169* ⊘ *Closed Nov.–Apr.*

$$
INTERNATIONAL

✕ **Nice n Easy.** On a prime seafront location, chef Christos Athanasiadis keeps things "nice and easy" with farm-to-table Mediterranean cuisine using locally produced organic and gluten-free ingredients. The menu is plentiful, with diverse choices such as Mykonian chicken spaghetti with kopanisti cheese, fresh baked salmon with quinoa, and unique favorites like water buffalo meatballs with smoked tomato sauce (they have an organic buffalo farm in northern Greece). **Known for:** organic, farm-to-table dishes; fantastic sea views; sister restaurant to two successful Athens locations. $ *Average main: €20* ✉ *Platia Alefkandra* ✛ *By the Mykonos windmills* ☎ *22890/25421* ⊕ *www.niceneasy.gr.*

WHERE TO STAY

$$$$
HOTEL

▦ **Belvedere.** This is the hotel for those who seek stylish surroundings and hip fellow guests, and like to see what they are paying for. **Pros:** Mykonos Town's most "in" hotel; beautiful stylish and posh atmosphere; top restaurant on premises. **Cons:** you can pay plenty for a small room with no view; off a busy back road so can be noisy; not in easy reach to a beach. $ *Rooms from: €795* ✉ *Lakka Rohari* ✛ *School of Fine Arts District* ☎ *22890/25122* ⊕ *www.belvederehotel. com* ⊘ *Closed Dec. and Jan.* ⇆ *44 rooms* ⦿❘ *Breakfast.*

$$$$
HOTEL
Fodor's Choice
★

▦ **Bill and Coo.** From afar, Bill and Coo may look like any whitewashed Cycladic hotel, but inside a world of polished contemporary design and high-level service awaits. **Pros:** excellent service; beautiful infinity pool; one of the top restaurants on Mykonos is here. **Cons:** pricey summer suite rates; not in easy reach of the beach or party scene; not in easy walking distance to Mykonos Town sights. $ *Rooms from: €600* ✉ *Mykonos Town* ✛ *Megali Ammos area* ☎ *22890/26292* ⊕ *www.bill-coo-hotel.com* ⊘ *Closed Nov.–Apr.* ⇆ *30 rooms* ⦿❘ *Breakfast.*

$$
HOTEL

▦ **Hotel Mykonos Adonis.** Set on the edge of town not far from Little Venice and overlooking the sea, this is not only Mykonos's friendliest hotel but is also both convenient and nicely out of the fray. **Pros:** convenient to the party scene; good service; walking distance to major sights of Mykonos Town. **Cons:** on a street with traffic; proximity to town means possible noise from partiers at night; overall area can feel busy during high season. $ *Rooms from: €165* ✉ *Ayiou Ioannou* ☎ *22890/23433* ⊕ *www.myko-nosadonis.gr* ⊘ *Closed Nov.–Mar.* ⇆ *23 rooms* ⦿❘ *Breakfast.*

$$$$
HOTEL

▦ **Livin Mykonos.** Located on the outskirts of Mykonos Town, Livin Mykonos is a small boutique hotel where an ambient pool area enjoys an unexpectedly fantastic sunset view. **Pros:** excellent friendly service;

VERANDA

beautiful pool area; relaxing sunset view. **Cons:** rooms may be on the small side for the price paid; not much very close by; not in easy walking distance to sights, with uphill hike back to the hotel. $\boxed{\$}$ *Rooms from: €340 ⊠ Mykonos Town ☎ 22890/ 23474 ⊕ www.livinmykonos. gr* ⊗ *Closed Oct.–Apr.* ⊷ *26 rooms* ⦅◯⦆ *Breakfast.*

$$$ ⏇ **Myconian Korali.** This five-star addition to the Myconian Collec-
HOTEL tion Hotels and Resorts, and member of Relais & Châteaux, is a chic, modern option for a luxury stay with inspiring views, private pools, and fine service from smartly dressed, hospitable staff. **Pros:** beautiful design with a smart contemporary touch; excellent restaurant and breakfast buffet; sea views throughout the property. **Cons:** not within easy walking distance to Mykonos Town; pricey standard rooms in high season; a bit isolated, surrounded by other hotels. $\boxed{\$}$ *Rooms from: €250 ⊠ Mykonos Town ☎ 22890/22107 ⊕ www.myconiankorali.gr* ⊗ *Closed Nov.–Apr.* ⊷ *40 rooms* ⦅◯⦆ *Breakfast.*

$$ ⏇ **Philippi Hotel.** Of the inexpensive hotels scattered throughout town,
B&B/INN this is the most attractive, with rooms that have balconies overlooking the garden. **Pros:** conveniently located in Mykonos Town; clean accommodations with balconies; free Wi-Fi for guests. **Cons:** if you want to get away from it all, go elsewhere; some rooms in need of updating; smallish rooms. $\boxed{\$}$ *Rooms from: €220 ⊠ Kalogera 25 ☎ 22890/22294 ⊕ www. philippihotel.com* ⊗ *Closed Nov.–Mar.* ⊷ *15 rooms* ⦅◯⦆ *No meals.*

$$$$ ⏇ **Semeli.** Named after a Greek nymph, this quiet and convenient hotel
HOTEL is centrally located and many of its rooms offer beautiful sea views. **Pros:** cool and relaxing pool; conveniently in walking distance to town's sights; on-site restaurant and spa. **Cons:** stiff room rates; no elevators; location can feel crowded in high season. $\boxed{\$}$ *Rooms from: €460 ⊠ Mykonos Town ✛ Below ring road ☎ 22890/27471 ⊕ www.semeli-hotel.gr* ⊗ *Closed Dec. and Jan.* ⊷ *65 rooms* ⦅◯⦆ *Breakfast.*

$$ ⏇ **Villa Konstantin.** Styled in the traditional whitewashed Mykonian
B&B/INN architecture with cozy lounging areas, Villa Konstantin is a set of apart-
FAMILY ments and studios that offers a quiet atmosphere away from the bustle
Fodor's Choice of Mykonos Town but is still close enough to enjoy it. **Pros:** great
★ pool area; inexpensive for what you get, which is a lot; laid-back and relaxing atmosphere. **Cons:** the walk from town is uphill; not within very easy walking distance to Mykonos Town; Continental breakfast is extra for certain room types. $\boxed{\$}$ *Rooms from: €150 ⊠ Agios Vassilios ☎ 22890/26204 ⊕ www.villakonstantin-mykonos.gr* ⊗ *Closed Nov.–Mar.* ⊷ *19 rooms* ⦅◯⦆ *Breakfast.*

NIGHTLIFE

Whether it's bouzouki, jazz, mainstream dance, or techno, the nightlife on Mykonos beats to an obsessive rhythm until undetermined hours—little wonder the world's gilded youth comes here *just* to enjoy the night scene. That scene centers around two places: Mykonos Town and the southern beaches.

Nightlife begins in the late afternoon at beach bars that dot Paradise, Super Paradise, and Paranga. At 4 pm the music is pumping loudly as the hired, sexy dance crews top the tables, and cocktails flow freely. The beach scene dies down around 8 or 9, when the beach party animals rest up before the next round of nightlife.

The bars and clubs along Little Venice and throughout Mykonos Town start to fill up after 11 pm, as patrons sip their first drinks of the night. The gay scene is still alive on Mykonos. Those who prefer a quieter lounge-type experience remain seated outside a sea-view café with a glass of wine, watching it all go by.

For the true night owls, much happens after midnight. You can either choose to club-hop around town or head south to the glamorous, outdoor arena–style clubs along Paradise and Super Paradise beaches. In the summer, posters and leaflets flung throughout Mykonos Town advertise which of the hottest international DJs are booked to spin each night. That and the promise of a packed, friendly, flirtatious young crowd gets the international partygoers ready for the beach well into the night. What is "the" place of the moment? The scene is ever-changing, so you'll need to track the buzz once you arrive. But there are some ever-popular options.

Galleraki. For nearly 30 years Galleraki has gathered happy, stylish, summer crowds. One reason is that it serves some of the best cocktails on the island. But another compelling reason is its prime location, so close to the water in picturesque Little Venice, you may get sprayed when a boat passes. ⊠ *Mykonos Town* ☎ *22890/27188* ⊕ *www.galleraki.gr.*

Guzel. Ideally located on the Mykonos Town waterfront, you would probably pass the club during the day without a second thought to its plain, unimpressive exterior that still shows its former name, 9 Muses, beneath its new name. At night the club comes alive and the best thing about it is the music. A loud, fun, crazy, dance-encouraging mix from their summer DJ lineup gets everyone inside moving on the floor and on chairs. Pastel neon lights fling around in the dark, bubbly crowd to the latest international and Greek pop spins. ⊠ *Waterfront.*

Interni. This whitewashed, modern Cycladic-style garden setting in the heart of Mykonos Town is flanked on all sides by lovely large trees. It's a Mediterranean restaurant (dinner) and event space, but it really shines at night when it's lighted up and the summer crowd gathers to its central bar for cocktails and to enjoy the open airy space. Gathering a calmer crowd that likes to be seen, it's a place you can have a good drink, listen to music, and hear a person speaking next to you. ⊠ *Matogianni* ☎ *22890/26333* ⊕ *www.interni-restaurant.gr.*

Kastro Bar. Kostas Karatzas's long-standing Kastro Bar with heavy beamed ceilings and island furnishings creates an intimate environment for enjoying the evening sunset over the bay to classical music. ⊠ *Paraportiani* ✛ *Little Venice* ☎ *22890/23072.*

Montparnasse/The Piano Bar. For more than 30 years, Montparnasse has been simply known as The Piano Bar. It's lively, lovely and LGBT-friendly with a long-standing tradition of supporting the island's local artists. Check out the latest artwork on its walls and then admire the gorgeous sunset views that precede energy-filled evenings of live cabaret and musicals. ⊠ *Ayion Anargyron 24, Little Venice* ☎ *22890/23719* ⊕ *www.thepianobar.com.*

Rhapsody. Rubbing elbows with Montparnasse is Rhapsody, a cocktail bar open all year for Greek dancing. ⊠ *Mykonos Town ⚓ Little Venice* ☎ *22890/23412.*

Skandinavian Bar. Toward the end of Mykonos Town's main market street is the Skandinavian Bar, which spreads over two buildings, two floors (one for pub chats, one for dancing), and an outside seating area. The music in the three bars ranges from classic rock to pop to dance. ⊠ *K. Georgouli* ☎ *22890/22669* ⊕ *www.skandinavianbar.com.*

SPORTS AND THE OUTDOORS
WATER SPORTS
Water-sports facilities can be found at many beaches offering different types of equipment. The main hub for windsurfing in the southern part of the island is at Kalafati Beach. The north side of the island is also a wind lover's haven; Panormos and Ftelia is where they all head.

SHOPPING
Most stores are to be found in Mykonos Town, one right after the other among the warren of streets. In the peak of summer, many are open until midnight. The jet set is catered to quite well with an abundance of boutiques selling precious gems, fine jewelry, au courant fashion, swimwear, and shoes donning top international labels. Then, there are great local items that you'd only find in Greece—or in Mykonos—including handmade leather sandals, belts, and purses, and a selection of handicrafts and paintings created by local artists. Local food products and all-natural Greek cosmetics and soaps round out the best souvenirs options.

FASHION
Galatis. Designer Yiannis Galatis has outfitted such famous women as Julie Christie, Elizabeth Taylor, Ingrid Bergman, and Jackie Onassis. He will probably greet you personally and show you some of his costumes and hostess gowns. His memoirs capture the old days on Mykonos, when Jackie O was a customer. His art gallery is adjacent. ⊠ *Platia Manto Mavrogenous ⚓ Opposite Lalaounis* ☎ *22890/22255.*

Kalypso. Mother-and-daughter team Kalypso and Calliope Anastopoulou create their own collection of handmade leather sandals and women's clothing with colorful, island inspiration. Their shop, on busy Matoyianni Street, also has a selection of handmade jewelry. ⊠ *Andronikou 17* ☎ *22890/77149.*

Kampanas. For a wide selection of handmade leather goods, head to Kampanas. It will be hard to choose from the array of sandals for both men and women that line the walls. There are collections of purses and belts. The color choices are wide and the leather is top quality. ⊠ *Mitropoleos 3* ☎ *22890/22638* ⊕ *www.kampanas.gr* ☉ *Closed Sun.*

Parthenis. Opened by Dimitris Parthenis in 1978, Parthenis now features designs by his daughter Orsalia, all showcased in a large Mykonian-style building on the up side of Alefkandra Square in Little Venice. The collection of cotton and silk garments (mostly in neutral colors) is very popular for their soft draping and clinging wrap effect. ⊠ *Platia Alefkandra* ☎ *22890/22448* ⊕ *www.orsalia-parthenis.gr.*

Salachas. The small Salachas store is filled with linen and cotton garments of all-Greek materials and manufacture. Grandfather Joseph Salachas was a tailor in the 1960s, and once made clothes for Christian Dior and various celebrities. Today, his grandchildren keep up the tradition. ⊠ *K. Georgouli 58* ☎ *22890/22710.*

The Workshop. Walking into The Workshop you'll immediately realize that the owner, Christos Xenitidis, loves two things: music and jewelry. His handiwork is responsible for the lovely gold and silver necklaces, rings, and earrings behind the simple glass displays. Look above his jewelry workbench to see a line of the guitarlike *bouzoukias* that he fixes and collects. Sometimes, his musician Mykonian friends stop by and an impromptu concert will form before your eyes. ⊠ *Panahra 12* ☎ *22890/26455.*

Zonadiko. Head up the stairs off one of Mykonos's busiest pedestrian walkways to find Michalis Pavlos at work in his little leather workshop, where he creates leather belts, sandals, and purses. Since the late 1980s, Pavlos has been making his own goods and distributing them all over Greece, but he opened his own shop in 2014 to show and sell his work directly on his favorite island. The quality of the leather he uses is second to none and he takes bespoke orders, too. ⊠ *Matoyianni.*

FINE AND DECORATIVE ART

Anna Gelou. Anna Gelou's eponymous shop, started by her mother 50 years ago, carries authentic copies of traditional handmade embroideries, all using white Greek cotton, in clothing, tablecloths, curtains, and such. ⊠ *Ayion Anargyron 16, Little Venice* ☎ *22890/26825.*

Artists of Mykonos Studio. The Artists of Mykonos Studio features the work of several Mykonian artists including paintings by the expat artist Richard James North and pieces by Greek mosaicist Monika Derpapas. The collection is simply lovely, colorful, and expressive. ⊠ *Panachrantou 11* ☎ *22890/23527.*

Nikoletta. Mykonos used to be a weaver's island, where 500 looms clacked away. Only two active weavers remain today and Nikoletta Xidakis is one of them. She sells her skirts, shawls, and bedspreads made of local wool, as she has for more than 50 years. ⊠ *Scarpa* ✚ *Little Venice* ☎ *22890/27503.*

Ninemia. Maria Kouniou is a local artist and displays her own handmade and hand-painted woodcraft wall hangings in her little whitewashed shop. She's also proud to support other Greek artists and sells their fun, colorful jewelry and T-shirts that reflect the style and beauty of Greece. ⊠ *M. Axioti 51* ☎ *22894/00073* ⊕ *www.ninemia.net.*

JEWELRY

Ilias Lalaounis. Known internationally, this fine jewelry collection is based on ancient Greek and other designs but reinterpreted for the modern woman. With many of their earrings and necklaces as lovingly worked as art pieces, the shop is as elegant as a museum. New collections are introduced every year. ⊠ *Polykandrioti 14* ✚ *Near taxis* ☎ *22890/22444* ⊕ *www.lalaounis.gr.*

AYIOS STEFANOS ΑΓΙΟΣ ΣΤΕΦΑΝΟΣ

6 km (4 miles) north of Mykonos Town.

About a 45-minute walk north from Mykonos Town, Ayios Stefanos has water sports, restaurants, and umbrellas and lounge chairs for rent; kids love it, and you can watch the yachts and enormous cruise ships slide by. The south coast's many beaches include this one fit for families.

BEACHES

FAMILY **Ayios Stefanos Beach.** Like many beaches in Greece, Ayios Stefanos takes its name from the little chapel built on it. Just north of Mykonos Town, this sandy stretch attracts its share of families for its shallow waters and array of eating, lodging, and café options within reach. Although it's unsheltered from northern winds, it's always been an ideal beach to view the sunsets of Mykonos. **Amenities:** food and drink. **Best for:** sunset; swimming. ✉ *Ayios Stefanos* ✣ *Less than 2 km (1 mile) north from Mykonos Town.*

WHERE TO EAT

$$$$ GREEK 🍴 **Tagoo.** High Mykonian style can be yours at the eatery of this noted hotel, a creation of the popular Athens restaurant Spondi. The haute cuisine is served in either an all-white room or at outdoor tables, with Mykonos Bay on one side and an infinity pool on the other. **Known for:** gourmet plates; beautiful views; great service. [$] *Average main: €60* ✉ *Hotel Cavo Tagoo, Mykonos Town* ✣ *12 mins by foot south of Ayios Stefanos* ☎ *22890/20100* 🌐 *www.cavotagoo.gr* 🕒 *Closed Nov.–Apr.*

WHERE TO STAY

$$$$ HOTEL Fodor's Choice ★ 🏨 **Cavo Tagoo.** Many consider this to be the top hotel on Mykonos for luxury, service, and comfort—a whitewashed property climbing the hill over the bay in sensuous curves, with natural projecting rock on the winding path to the guest rooms. **Pros:** beautiful views from hotel; alluring Mykonos style; on-site spa and well-reputed restaurant. **Cons:** a 15-minute walk to town; high prices; not within easy walking distance to Mykonos Town sights. [$] *Rooms from: €750* ✉ *Ayios Stefanos* ✣ *Follow coast road, north of Old Port* ☎ *22890/20100* 🌐 *www.cavotagoo.gr* 🕒 *Closed Nov.–Apr.* 🛏 *89 rooms* 🍽 *Breakfast.*

$$$$ HOTEL Fodor's Choice ★ 🏨 **Grace Mykonos.** Small, charming, luxurious, and set above the beach of Ayios Stefanos, the Mykonos Grace is graced with a truly impressive setting, with an encompassing view of Mykonos harbor. **Pros:** impressive vistas; intimate atmosphere; professional service with nice on-site restaurant. **Cons:** not walking distance to Mykonos Town; not all rooms have direct access to elevator; smallish rooms for the price. [$] *Rooms from: €530* ✉ *Ayios Stefanos* ☎ *22890/20000* 🌐 *www.mykonosgrace.com* 🕒 *Closed Nov.–Mar.* 🛏 *31 rooms* 🍽 *Breakfast.*

$$$$ HOTEL 🏨 **Mykonos Princess.** Set on a slope above Ayios Stefanos Beach, the Mykonos Princess is a scenic and lively boutique hotel where courteous staff offer attentive service in the restaurant, around pool and pool bar, and for any local advice. **Pros:** scenic pool, restaurant, and pool bar area; attentive service; lively and energetic atmosphere. **Cons:** not within walking distance of Mykonos Town; not much within decent walking distance, except Ayios Stefanos Beach; rooms around the pool are noisy,

from pool lounge speakers and chatter. $ *Rooms from: €500* ✉ *Ayios Stefanos* ☏ *22890/23806* ⊕ *www.princessofmykonos.gr* ☉ *Closed Nov.–Mar.* ⌿ *34 rooms* ⎮◎⎮ *Breakfast.*

ORNOS ΟΡΝΟΣ

3 km (2 miles) south of Mykonos Town.

Ornos has always been more popular with Mykonians than tourists. The locals like its relaxed atmosphere for a family swim and beachside dining. There are several good restaurants, two fine hotels above the bay and several cheaper ones lower down, and chairs and umbrellas for rent. In calm weather, boats start here for the other southern beaches, so that they are all connected (45 minutes to the farthest southern beach, Elia), and you can beach-hop easily.

TOURS

Fodor's Choice
★

Mykonos On Board Sailing Tours. Another side to enjoying Mykonos is getting off the island to dive into the surreal aqua waters off the coast of its neighboring islands, which are best experienced by private sailing cruises. The hospitable captain, Artemis, and his team take up to eight guests on a comfortable, scenic, and sun-filled half-day journey to secluded secret swimming coves off Delos and Rhenia islands for swimming, relaxation, and his fresh and tasty Greek barbecue. The tour sets off from Ayios Ioannis Diakoftis Bay. ✉ *Ayios Ioannis* ☏ *69/3247–1055* ⊕ *www.mykonosonboard.com* ✉ *From €100 per person.*

BEACHES

FAMILY

Ayios Ioannis Beach. One of the best places on Mykonos to catch the sunset is the pebble-and-sand beach of Ayios Ioannis. Divided into two sections by large rocks, the waters usually remain calm but the summer winds can take their hold. The shallow bay is popular with families, and dining and lodging options are plenty thanks to the whitewashed beach town that grew around it. ■ **TIP→ The beach is also referred to as Shirley Valentine Beach, because the 1989 British movie of the same name was filmed here.** **Amenities:** food and drink. **Best for:** sunset; swimming. ✉ *Ayios Ioannis.*

FAMILY

Ornos Beach. A community has grown around this beach, which is now considered one of the most family-friendly on the island. It's pretty and sandy and there are umbrella and lounge chair rentals. A good selection of beach hotels, tavernas, restaurants, cafés, and shops make up Ornos Bay, and there's bus service from Mykonos Town. It's also the launch point to take a boat to other beaches or to Delos. **Amenities:** food and drink. **Best for:** swimming. ✉ *Ornos.*

WHERE TO EAT

$$
GREEK

✕ **Apaggio.** Tucked in a tranquil corner of Ornos Bay, Apaggio is simply decorated and lined with large open windows for a perfect, unobstructed view of the sea. Beautifully presented tavern-style specialties include local fish and familiar Greek favorites such as Greek salad and moussaka. **Known for:** traditional Greek specialities; sea view. $ *Average main: €20* ✉ *Ornos Beach* ⊕ *www.apaggio.gr.*

$$$ ✕**Buddha Bar Beach** . Set above the tranquil private beach at the exclusive
ASIAN FUSION Santa Marina Hotel, Buddha Bar Beach shows off its Greek-island side as
Fodor'sChoice part of the renowned upscale chain known for avant-garde world music,
★ celebrity DJs and chefs, and inspired cocktails. It's one of the most styl-
ish tables to book, and the Mediterranean-Greek fusion with Chinese,
Japanese, and Thai cuisines delivers on taste and presentation, enjoyed
in stylish moderation by a super-chic and well-heeled crowd. **Known for:**
beautiful beach and sea views; cosmopolitan and stylish crowd; excel-
lent Asian cuisine and fusion dishes. $ *Average main: €30* ⊠ *Ornos*
☎ *22890/23220* ⊕ *buddhabarbeachmykonos.gr* ☾ *Closed Nov.–Mar.*

$$ ✕**Hippie Fish.** Fronted by beautiful Ayios Ioannis Beach, Hippie Fish is
INTERNATIONAL one of the liveliest on-the-beach restaurants—an institution since the
Fodor'sChoice 1970s, serving a mix of international and Mediterranean cuisine with
★ excellent service. But what it will always be locally famous for is making the big screen as the 1989 setting for the movie *Shirley Valentine*,
about a dissatisfied housewife "finding herself" on Mykonos. **Known
for:** lively atmosphere; quality international and Mediterranean plates;
relaxed and scenic on-the-beach location. $ *Average main: €20* ⊠ *Ayios
Ioannis* ☎ *22890/22901* ⊕ *www.hippiefish-mykonos.com/.*

6

WHERE TO STAY

$$$$ 🛏**Deliades.** If you like comfort, large rooms, friendly service, a sea view,
HOTEL and quiet, Deliades is exactly for you. **Pros:** Ornos Bay views; large
rooms and bathtubs; relaxed atmosphere. **Cons:** not for those wanting to be in the thick of the Mykonos scene; no pets allowed; shuttle
necessary to conveniently get to Mykonos Town. $ *Rooms from: €300*
⊠ *Ornos Bay* ✛ *Far end of Ornos Beach, follow road up 30 yards*
☎ *22890/79430, 22890/79470* ⊕ *www.deliades.com* ☾ *Closed Oct.–
Apr.* ⤳ *30 rooms* ⦿*Breakfast.*

$$$$ 🛏**Kivotos Clubhotel.** The Kivotos Clubhotel is deluxe, architecturally
HOTEL ambitious, and stylishly arrayed around an impressive pool. **Pros:** exqui-
site design; quiet ambience; private section for guests on Ornos Beach.
Cons: isolated location; some rooms are small and lack views; those
high room rates. $ *Rooms from: €678* ⊠ *Ornos* ✛ *2 km (1 mile) from
Mykonos Town* ☎ *22890/24094* ⊕ *www.kivotosclubhotel.gr* ☾ *Closed
Nov.–Apr.* ⤳ *35 rooms* ⦿*Breakfast.*

$$$$ 🛏**Santa Marina.** With a sandy private beach, Santa Marina is the most
HOTEL exclusive hotel on Mykonos—in lush, tranquil island settings. **Pros:** top
Fodor'sChoice luxury amenities, services, and restaurants; beautiful views; excellent
★ spa offerings. **Cons:** very pricey; very upscale; transportation necessary
to get to other sights around the island. $ *Rooms from: €860* ⊠ *Ornos*
☎ *22890/23220* ⊕ *www.santa-marina.gr* ⤳ *101 rooms* ⦿*Breakfast.*

SOUTH COAST NOTIA AKTH

*The first beach is Psarou, 4 km (2½ miles) southeast of Mykonos Town;
the last beach is Elia, 12 km (7 miles) southeast of Mykonos Town.*

The popular south coast beaches stand on their own; hotels, restaurants,
cafés, and beach bars have sprung up around them, drawn to their
turquoise seas. It's the home of Psarou Beach, where yachts are always
moored in the distance and expensive sun beds are reserved in advance.

Platis Gialos is popular with families and has its own little village behind it. But it's truly known for what the international party crowd loves: the beach bar and club scene that revolves around Paraga, Paradise, and Super Paradise beaches. Agrari and Elia are less developed, have more nudity, and are quieter.

BEACHES

The south coast is where you'll find the famous party beaches of Mykonos. Psarou draws the jet set while nearby Platis Yialos is popular with families. The young and sexy crowd heads to the Paraga, Paradise, and Super Paradise. While they used to be primarily nude beaches, that is not the case any longer, but they are still busy and popular and have parties starting almost every afternoon. Paradise draws the sexy straight crowd, Super Paradise the sexy LGBT crowd, though in truth there's a lot of overlap. The rocky path between Paradise and Super Paradise, an hour's rough walk, was once a sexual no-man's land, but it is no longer. Farther along, Little Agrari and Elia are less developed, more nudist, and quieter, though they, too, have not escaped the voyeur's wandering eye.

Agrari Beach. Agrari is a low-key beach with yellow pebble sand flanked by a low hill of small whitewashed buildings to the left and a rocky island hill to the right. Umbrellas and sun beds are available for rent. You can grab a snack, drinks, or a full meal at the beach's own bar and restaurant, but there are more options just a walk away. Boats leave from Platis Gialos and Ornos Bay. It's also walkable via a footpath from neighboring Elia Beach, attracting nudists who stay in certain areas. ■TIP➔ **Driving east from Mykonos Town, watch out for a stunning view of the turquoise blue as you make that final turn to the beach.** **Amenities:** food and drink; water sports. **Best for:** swimming. ⊠ *Agrari.*

Elia Beach. Long, tranquil, and beautiful, Elia is a popular option for those who seek beach relaxation. Attracting a predominantly LGBT crowd, this southern beach is also popular with those who want to relax on a soft sand beach that's protected from the north winds that sweep through the island from time to time. Umbrellas and sun beds are for rent and water-sports facilities pop up during the peak summer months. Dining options are plentiful with several cafés and tavernas close by. **Amenities:** food and drink; showers; toilets. **Best for:** nudists; swimming. ⊠ *Elia.*

Paradise Beach. Famous the world over for its party scene, young, fun, international crowds hop straight to Paradise Beach. There's music, dancing, clubbing, and drinking at most hours of the day, but beach parties typically pick up around 4 pm and go on well into the next morning when everyone is dancing on tabletops, including sexy male and female models hired to get things moving. When partiers take a break, sun beds and umbrellas are available for lounging, and a full line of restaurants and fast-food options provide nourishment. Scuba diving and water-sport rental shops are open for business. The bus from Mykonos Town frequents the beach often and on time in the peak of summer. **Amenities:** food and drink; lifeguards; parking; showers; toilets; water sports. **Best for:** partiers. ⊠ *Paradise.*

Paraga Beach. Small and stunning, and surrounded by a picturesque rocky coastline that juts out against a sparkling turquoise bay, Paraga Beach is not only pretty, it's also one of Mykonos's liveliest party beaches. Several bars and beach clubs organize events every summer attracting a young, international crowd that gathers to mingle, dance, and drink. Hotels, rooms, and a large campground surround the beach. Umbrellas and chairs are available to rent at any of the beachside tavernas and cafés. A footpath to the east leads to neighboring party beach, Paradise, or offers you another view of the sea; it's about a 10-minute walk. **Amenities:** food and drink; lifeguards; toilets. **Best for:** partiers. ⊠ *Paraga* ⚓ *6 km (4 miles) southeast of Mykonos Town.*

FAMILY **Platis Gialos Beach.** Spacious, sandy, and pleasant, Platis Gialos is a calm southern beach getaway that's protected from the island's strong summer winds. Kids enjoy playing in the shallow waters, while adults head to deeper waters to try out the numerous water-sports rental options. The array of taverns, restaurants, and cafés is perfect for any food break. The beach is lined with rental umbrellas and chairs, and getting to it is easy by Mykonos Town beach boat and bus service. ■ TIP→ You can drive here, too, but parking spaces may be hard to find. **Amenities:** food and drink; water sports. **Best for:** swimming. ⊠ *Platis Gialos.*

Psarou Beach. With shiny yachts moored in its clear, pretty waters, sandy Psarou attracts vacationing international VIPs, Greek TV stars and singers, and the rich and/or famous. ■ TIP→ That oversized and high-priced beach bed and umbrella may be empty, but it may have been rented in advance by someone who doesn't want you to have it. If you know someone, you can make an advance reservation for one, too. You might bump into someone's bodyguard; several may be casing the beach. Sophisticated yet lively restaurants are plentiful, and they host afternoon and evening parties that are fun but not crazy. If you drive from Mykonos Town, a steep scenic road leads to the beach, but once you get there you'll notice parking options are slim. Many opt for valet parking run by private companies. You can also reach Psarou by taking a short walk from nearby Platis Gialos or hopping on a boat one stop away at Ornos Bay. **Amenities:** food and drink; parking (paid). **Best for:** partiers; swimming. ⊠ *Psarou* ⚓ *4 km (2½ miles) south of Mykonos Town.*

Super Paradise Beach. Young and wild, gay and straight: All crowds head to Super Paradise to let loose. The stunning sandy beach is one plus, but the beach bars and clubs truly dominate the scene. Summer months mean daily late-afternoon beach parties, where drinks and dancing rule. Hired bikini-clad models move to the beat of the music to encourage a crazy party atmosphere that includes people dancing everywhere and anywhere they can. For those not in the party mood (yet), umbrellas and sun beds can be rented and dining options are available for a meal; Super Paradise Rooms is right on the beach for those who need a place to crash. **Amenities:** food and drink; toilets; showers; lifeguards; water sports. **Best for:** partiers. ⊠ *Super Paradise* ⊕ *www.superparadise.com.gr.*

6

WHERE TO EAT

$$ MEDITERRANEAN 🍴 **Avli tou Thodori.** Overlooking pretty Platis Gialos Beach, Avli tou Thodori offers beachfront dining in a minimalist Cycladic setting, where cuisine presentation is excellent and the selection eclectic. To start, try the feta cheese wrapped in phyllo pastry covered with a light sweet sauce made with *rakomelo* (a spicy liqueur) and sprinkled with sesame seeds. **Known for:** good food for a beach restaurant; fresh prawns. [$] *Average main: €20* ✉ *Platis Gialos* 🌐 *www.avlitouthodori.gr* ⏲ *Closed Nov.–Mar.*

$$$$ MODERN GREEK 🍴 **Nammos.** This beach restaurant has become the in spot for well-to-do Athenians and for Mykonians who want to strut a bit on fashionable Psarou beach. All open-air, white wood, stone, bamboo, and palm trees, it serves Mediterranean fusion cuisine (their words) and is especially popular for a late lunch. **Known for:** late lunch; fresh sushi; good desserts. [$] *Average main: €50* ✉ *Psarou Beach, Psarou* ☎ *22890/22440* 🌐 *www.nammos.gr.*

NIGHTLIFE

Paradise Club. The international, young party people that flock to Mykonos pack this glamorous open-air club every summer season. It has three stages that are designed to feature the world's best DJs who fill its lineup each year. Paradise Club features a VIP area and a swimming pool. ✉ *Paradise Beach, Paradise* 🌐 *www.paradiseclubmykonos.com.*

Tropicana Beach Bar. One of the most popular beach bars in Mykonos is set on Paradise Beach where the party starts every afternoon in the peak summer season. The international, young, and looking-for-fun head to the outdoor bar to dance in the sand, on tables, and by the sea. The music is loud, mainstream, and fun, the people are happy, and the cocktail list is long. ✉ *Paradise Beach, Paradise* ☎ *22890/26990* 🌐 *www.tropicanamykonos.com.*

SPORTS AND THE OUTDOORS

DIVING

Mykonos Diving Center. Located on Paradise Beach, the Mykonos Dive Center offers a range of excursions for certified divers and training for all levels and experiences. They lead excursions from 30 different points on the island. ✉ *Paradise Beach, Paradise* ☎ *22890/24808* 🌐 *www.dive.gr.*

SOUTHEAST COAST ΝΟΤΙΟΑΝΑΤΟΛΙΚΗ ΑΚΤΗ

The first beach is Kalo Livadi, 11 km (7 miles) southeast of Mykonos Town; the last beach is Kalafatis Beach, 12 km (7½ miles) southeast of Mykonos Town.

The southeastern beaches, the farthest beaches from Mykonos Town, are favorites for those looking for something calm, yet organized, such as Kalo Livadi. Water-sports lovers head to Kalafatis, which is well organized for any sport.

BEACHES

Ayia Anna Beach. Somewhat hidden in the shadow of Kalafatis beach, Ayia Anna is a low-key beach, named after a little whitewashed chapel nearby. It's a place where you can observe windsurfers in the distance as fishing boats bob calmly in the wind-protected waters. Two hills protect the bay—the locals lovingly call them *divounia*, or Aphrodite's breasts. Summer beach chair and umbrella rentals are available and there is a handful of tavernas and cafés. There are also two easy hiking paths to neighboring Platis Gialos and Paraga beaches. **Amenities:** food and drink. **Best for:** swimming. ⊠ *Ayia Anna.*

Kalafatis Beach. This long stretch of picturesque beach with a line of shady trees is known for the water-sports and windsurfing crowds it attracts. The back road has an array of hotels, rooms-for-rent, tavernas, and beach bars, as well as a well-known windsurfing school and water-sports rental shop. A small dock to the left side of the beach houses a tavern, beach bar, and a diving center office that leads excursions out to nearby uninhabited islands. **Amenities:** food and drink; lifeguards; water sports. **Best for:** swimming; walking; windsurfing. ⊠ *Kalafati.*

FAMILY **Kalo Livadi Beach.** Mykonos's characteristic rocky hills surround Kalo Livadi's long sandy beach, at the edge of the island valley from which it got its name, meaning "good valley." Families head here to spend the day playing with their kids in the shallow waters and take a break at one of the many restaurants surrounding the beach. In summer the beach is divided into several areas that feature various styles of sun beds and umbrellas for rent. **Amenities:** food and drink. **Best for:** swimming. ⊠ *Kalo Livadi.*

Lia Beach. By Mykonos standards, Lia Beach is considered tranquil and quiet, perhaps because it's one of the farthest organized beaches from Mykonos Town. You can drive to the beach or get off at the last stop on the Mykonos Town boat that brings people to the beaches. Rows of beach chairs and umbrellas line the pebble and sand beach, which is surrounded on both sides by a rocky coastline and the typical bare yet beautiful hills of the island. Divers and snorkelers head here to explore the turquoise waters. ■TIP➔ **Once you're set up, see if you can spot Naxos and Paros in the distance. Amenities:** food and drink. **Best for:** snorkeling; solitude; swimming. ⊠ *Lia Beach ✛ 14 km (8½ miles) east of Mykonos Town.*

WHERE TO STAY

$$$ ⌂ **Aphrodite Beach Hotel.** Water-sports lovers head here to combine their
RESORT passion for sport with the upscale facilities of this resort located right
FAMILY off the wind-blessed beach of Kalafatis. **Pros:** fantastic location for water-sports lovers who want to be close to the beach; family-friendly; nice and relaxing sea views. **Cons:** far from Mykonos Town; away from Mykonos scene; a car may be necessary to see the sights of the island. $ *Rooms from: €250* ⊠ *Kalafati* ☎ *22890/71367* ⊕ *www.aphrodite-mykonos.gr* ☉ *Closed Nov.–Mar.* ⇱ *148 rooms* ⏏⊙⏐ *Breakfast.*

$$$$ ⌂ **Pietra e Mare.** Stacked on a quiet hillside by picturesque Kalo Livadi
HOTEL beach, this adults-only resort offers panoramic views and a chic yet laid-back atmosphere. **Pros:** good service; a combination of traditional and chic design; pool with a view. **Cons:** balconies are not private,

may be shared; not much in Kalo Livadi compared to other beach resort towns; pricey in high season. [$] *Rooms from: €500* ✉ *Kalo Livadi* ☎ *22890/71152* 🌐 *www.pietraemaremykonos.com* 🕓 *Closed Nov.–Apr.* 🛏 *31 rooms* 🍴 *Breakfast.*

SPORTS AND THE OUTDOORS

SCUBA DIVING

Kalafati Dive Center. For 20 years, the Kalafati Dive Center has offered diving excursions with excellent visibility around Mykonos, including various wrecks. Courses are available for beginners, advanced divers, and all those in between. Snorkeling trips are also available, as are equipment rental, children's courses, and private boat excursions. ✉ *Kalafati* ☎ *22890/71677* 🌐 *www.mykonos-diving.com.*

WATER SPORTS

Water-sports facilities, offering different types of equipment, can be found at many beaches. The main hub for windsurfing in the southern part of the island is at Kalafati Beach.

Kalafati Watersports. All the water-sports rentals to enjoy Kalafati's famous water-loving conditions can be found at Kalafati Watersports. Water ski, wakeboard, extreme tubes, and banana boat excursions are available, as well as speedboat island tours. **■ TIP→ Book in advance during the peak summer season.** ✉ *Kalafati* ☎ *69452/61242 cell phone* 🌐 *www.mykonoswatersports.com.*

WINDSURFING

Pezi Huber Windsurfing. Located right on the famed water-sports beach of Kalafati, where the meltemi winds blow "loyal and faithful," Pezi Huber runs his own windsurfing shop. He offers individual and group lessons for beginners and rentals for windsurfing. Rentals for stand-up paddleboards and other surf gear are also available. ✉ *Kalafati Beach, Kalafati* ☎ *22890/72345* 🌐 *www.pezi-huber.com.*

ANO MERA ΑΝΩ ΜΕΡΑ

8 km (5 miles) east of Mykonos Town.

Inland, the little town of Ano Mera has a couple of quiet tavernas and a monastery. The town only lights up during the monastery's festival day on August 15.

Monastery of the Panayia Tourliani. Monastery buffs should head to Ano Mera, a village in the central part of the island, where the Monastery of the Panayia Tourliani, founded in 1580 and dedicated to the protectress of Mykonos, stands in the central square. Its massive baroque iconostasis (altar screen), made in 1775 by Florentine artists, has small icons carefully placed amid the wooden structure's painted green, red, and gold-leaf flowers. At the top are carved figures of the apostles and large icons depicting New Testament scenes. The hanging incense holders with silver molded dragons holding red eggs in their mouths show an Eastern influence. In the hall of the monastery, an interesting **museum** displays embroideries, liturgical vestments, and wood carvings. A good taverna is across the street. The monastery's big festival—hundreds attend—is on August 15. ✉ *On central square* ☎ *22890/71249.*

NORTH COAST ΒΟΡΕΙΑ ΑΚΤΗ

The first beach is Ftelia, 7 km (4½ miles) southeast of Mykonos Town; the last beach is Ayios Sostis, 8 km (5 miles) northeast of Mykonos Town.

The beaches along the north coast are blessed with consistent winds suitable for windsurfing, and Ftelia is the island's center for that sport. But on calm days, Panormos and Ayios Sostis are worth a trip; both offer beautiful beach vistas without the crowds. If you are looking for uncrowded beaches (even in the busy summer season), these are your best bets.

BEACHES

Ayios Sostis Beach. All you'll find at Ayios Sostis is turquoise waters lapping against the sand and a small-pebble coast. Without natural shade, or any touristic development whatsoever, beachgoers who need shade should come prepared. This is a beach with hidden elements though, so be sure to go in search of the small unnamed beach tucked in between it and neighboring Panormos, which is accessible by footpath. Off another path that leads to the main road, you'll find the small church that this beach is named after. Next to the church, a crowd may gather outside a nearby garden tavern you might otherwise miss if it wasn't the peak summer season in July and August. **Amenities:** food and drink. **Best for:** solitude; swimming. ✉ *Ayios Sostis* ✣ *12 km (7½ miles) north of Mykonos Town.*

Ftelia Beach. Ftelia is famous for its winds, which attract windsurfers who love to test out the turquoise waters. The beach's smooth sand is free of any sun beds or umbrellas, so when you approach it, all you'll see is a wide-open stretch of yellow sand—if the wind isn't blowing it all about. Several tavernas and rooms-for-rent dot the area but are not directly on the beach. **Amenities:** none. **Best for:** windsurfing. ✉ *Ftelia.*

FAMILY **Panormos Beach.** A fine golden-sand beach with turquoise waters, Panormos caters to all kinds of beachgoers. Nudists head to the far right for peace and quiet, but there's an all-day beach bar and restaurant that offers music, food, and drinks to the left; it's popular with families, couples, and singles. This is a great spot when the southern winds attack; otherwise it's positioned to get the full brunt of the northern island winds. Water-sports equipment, umbrellas, and chairs are available for rent. **Amenities:** food and drink. **Best for:** nudists; swimming. ✉ *Panormos Beach.*

WHERE TO EAT

$$ GREEK 🍴 **Kiki's Taverna.** With no telephone number or signs, this simple little family-run garden taverna would likely be missed if there wasn't a constant line of people waiting to grab a table—in the summer, expect to wait up to an hour. The sea views of Ayios Sostis Beach are relaxing, and the perfect thing to gaze at as you wait for your meat and fish dishes that will be expertly grilled on a barbecue. **Known for:** pork cutlet; Greek salads and dips; long lines. [$] *Average main: €25* ✉ *Ayios Sostis* 💳 *No credit cards.*

DELOS ΔΗΛΟΣ

10 km (6 miles) southwest of Mykonos.

Arrive at the mythical, magical, and magnificent site of Delos and you might wonder how this barren islet, which has virtually no natural resources, became the religious and political center of the Aegean. One answer is that Dhlos—to use the Modern Greek transliteration—provided the safest anchorage for vessels sailing between the mainland and the shores of Asia; another answer is that it had no other use. A third is provided if you climb Mt. Kynthos to see that the isle (which is not more than 5 km [3 miles] long and 1 km [½ mile] wide) is shielded on three sides by other islands. Indeed, this is how the Cyclades—the word means "circling ones"—got their name: they circle around the sacred island.

Delos's amazing saga begins back in the times of myth: Zeus fell in love with gentle Leto, the Titaness, who became pregnant. When Hera discovered this infidelity, she forbade Mother Earth to give Leto refuge and ordered the Python to pursue her. Finally Poseidon, taking pity on her, anchored the poor floating island of Delos with four diamond columns to give her a place to rest. Leto gave birth first to the virgin huntress Artemis on Rhenea and then, clasping a sacred palm on a slope of Delos's Mt. Kynthos, to Apollo, god of music and light.

By 1000 BC the Ionians, who inhabited the Cyclades, had made Delos their religious capital. Homeric Hymn 3 tells of the cult of Apollo in the 7th century BC. One can imagine the elegant Ionians, whose central festival was here, enjoying the choruses of temple girls—Delian *korai*, who serve the "Far-Shooter"—singing and dancing their hymn and displaying their graceful tunics and jewelry. But a difficult period began for the Delians when Athens rose to power and assumed Ionian leadership. In 543 BC an oracle at Delphi conveniently decreed that the Athenians purify the island by removing all the graves to Rhenea, a dictate designed to alienate the Delians from their past.

After the defeat of the Persians in 478 BC, the Athenians organized the Delian League, with its treasury and headquarters at Delos (in 454 BC the funds were transferred to the Acropolis in Athens). Delos had its most prosperous period in late Hellenistic and Roman times, when it was declared a free port and quickly became the financial center of the Mediterranean, the focal point of trade, where 10,000 slaves were sold daily. Foreigners from as far as Rome, Syria, and Egypt lived in this cosmopolitan port, in complete tolerance of one another's religious beliefs, and each group built its various shrines. But in 88 BC Mithridates, the king of Pontus, in a revolt against Roman rule, ordered an attack on the unfortified island. The entire population of 20,000 was killed or sold into slavery. Delos never fully recovered, and later Roman attempts to revive the island failed because of pirate raids. After a second attack in 69 BC, Delos was gradually abandoned.

In 1872, the French School of Archaeology began excavating on Delos—a massive project, considering that much of the island's 4 square km (1½ square miles) is covered in ruins. The work continues today. Delos

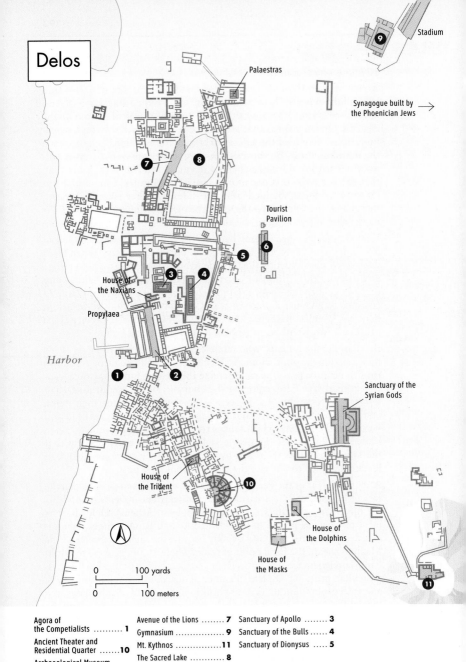

Delos

Stadium

Palaestras

Synagogue built by
the Phoenician Jews

Tourist
Pavilion

Archaeological Museum

House of
the Naxians

Propylaea

Harbor

Sanctuary of the
Syrian Gods

House of
the Trident

House of
the Dolphins

House of
the Masks

Mt. Kythnos

0   100 yards

0   100 meters

remains dry and shadeless; off-season, the snack bar is often closed; most guards leave on the last boat to Mykonos in the early afternoon. But if on the way to Mykonos you see dolphins leaping (it often happens), you'll know Apollo is about and approves.

GETTING HERE AND AROUND

Most visitors arrive from Mykonos on one of the excursions helpfully organized by tour companies whose offices are located at the west end of the harbor in Mykonos Town (tour boats also leave from Tinos, Paros, and Naxos). These boats leave around 9 am every day. If the sea is too rough, boats are cancelled. There are generally seven departures but the last boat returning from Delos is at 3 pm. Caïque boats (€15) also link Delos with Platis Gialos and Ornos beaches on Mykonos, but these excursions give you only about three hours on the sacred isle.

EXPLORING

Fodor'sChoice
★

Delos Archaeological Site. This tiny, sacred place—the fabled birthplace of Apollo—is a testament to Greece's glorious ancient civilization, home to one of the most fascinating and most important archaeological sites in Greece. When Delos was a thriving sacred city—it was the religious center of the Cyclades—one could never be born or die on the island. Today the isle is unpopulated, but with a little imagination you can understand how a grand, ancient city once ruled the region. All you'll find is ruins, and you'll have a few hours to explore them. Overnight stays are not allowed, and boats take you to the UNESCO World Heritage site just for the day to explore the 5 km- (3 mile-) long island. ⚠ The island has no shade, so don't forget to bring a hat, sunscreen, and plenty of water. ⊹ *Accessible only by boat from Mykonos Town* ☎ *22890/22259 archaeological museum, 22890/22218 Mykonos port (departures for Delos info)* ⊕ *www.culture.gr* ☒ *€12* ⊗ *Closed Mon. Nov.–Mar.*

Agora of the Competialists. The first monument you'll see, on the left from the harbor, is the Agora of the Competialists (circa 150 BC). The competialists were members of Roman guilds, mostly freedmen and slaves from Sicily who worked for Italian traders. They worshipped the *Lares Competales*, the Roman "crossroads" gods; in Greek they were known as *Hermaistai*, after the god Hermes, protector of merchants and the crossroads. ⊹ *West of the Archaeological Museum of Delos.*

Ancient Theater and Residential Quarter. Beyond the path that leads to the southern part of the island is this ancient theater, built in the early 3rd century BC. It once sat 5,500 people. Close by was the elegant residential quarter inhabited by Roman bankers and Egyptian and Phoenician merchants. Their one- and two-story houses were typically built around a central courtyard, sometimes with columns on all sides. Floor mosaics of snakes, panthers, birds, dolphins, and Dionysus channeled rainwater into cisterns below; the best-preserved can be seen in the House of the Dolphins, the House of the Masks, and the House of the Trident. ⊹ *South of the Archaeological Museum of Delos.*

Archaeological Museum of Delos. This museum is on the road south of the Gymnasium. It contains most of the antiquities found during excavations

As if posing for your camera, the ancient sculpted beasts of the Avenue of the Lions are Delos's most unforgettable photo op. They are copies; the originals are in Delos's museum.

on the island: monumental statues of young men and women, stelae, reliefs, masks, mosaics, and ancient jewelry. ☎ 22890/22259.

Avenue of the Lions. One of the most evocative and recognizable sights of Delos is the 164-foot-long Avenue of the Lions. The five marble beasts, which were carved in Naxos, crouch on their haunches, their forelegs stiffly upright, vigilant guardians of the Sacred Lake. They are the survivors of a line of at least nine lions that were erected in the second half of the 7th century BC by the Naxians. One statue, removed in the 17th century, now guards the Arsenal of Venice (though with a refurbished head); the remaining originals are in the Delos Archaeological Museum on the island. ✛ *West of the Agora of the Italians.*

Gymnasium. Northeast of the palaestras is the Gymnasium, a square courtyard nearly 131 feet long on each side. "Gym" means naked in Greek, and here men and boys stayed in shape (and, in those heavily Platonic days, eyed each other) as they exercised in the nude. The long, narrow structure farther northeast is the stadium, the site of the athletic events of the Delian Games. East of the stadium site, by the seashore, are the remains of a synagogue built by Phoenician Jews in the 2nd century BC. A road south from the gymnasium leads to the tourist pavilion, which has a meager restaurant and bar. ✛ *North of the Archaeological Museum of Delos.*

Mt. Kythnos. A dirt path leads up the base of Mt. Kynthos, which is the highest point on the island. Here lie the remains of many Middle Eastern shrines, including the Sanctuary of the Syrian Gods, which was built in 100 BC. A flight of steps goes up 368 feet to the summit of Mt. Kynthos (from which the name "Cynthia" was derived), where Greek mythology says Zeus watched the birth of his son, Apollo, on the slope. There are amazing views of Mykonos, Naxos, Paros, and Syros from the top of the mountain. The path is completely unshaded, so be prepared for the heat. ⊹ *Near the Sacred Way.*

The Sacred Lake. A short distance north of the Sanctuary of the Bulls is an oval indentation in the earth where the Sacred Lake once sparkled. It is surrounded by a stone wall that reveals the original periphery. According to islanders, the lake was fed by the river Inopos from its source high on Mt. Kynthos until 1925, when the water stopped flowing and the lake dried up. Along the shores are two ancient *palaestras* (buildings for physical exercise and debate). ⊹ *North of the Agora of the Italians.*

The Sacred Way. East of the Agora of the Competialists you'll find the entrance to the Sacred Way, which leads north to the temple of Apollo. The Way was once bordered by beautiful marbled statues and monuments created by various kingdoms and city states of Ancient Greece. It was also the route used by pilgrims during the holy Delian festival. ⊹ *Just east of the harbor.*

Sanctuary of Apollo. Beyond the Sacred Way is one of the most important sites on the island, the Sanctuary of Apollo. Three separate temples originally stood here flanked by altars, monuments, and statues, although not much remains of them. The main temple was grand, fittingly called the Great Temple of Apollo (circa 480 BC). Inside the sanctuary and to the right is the House of the Naxians, a 7th- to 6th-century BC structure with a central colonnade. Dedications to Apollo were stored in this shrine. Outside the north wall a massive rectangular pedestal once supported a colossal statue of Apollo (one of the hands is in Delos's Archaeological Museum, and a piece of a foot is in the British Museum in London). Near the pedestal a bronze palm tree was erected in 417 BC by the Athenians to commemorate the palm tree under which Leto gave birth. According to Plutarch, the palm tree toppled in a storm and brought the statue of Apollo down with it. In *The Odyssey,* Odysseus compares the Phaeacian princess Nausicaa to a palm he saw on Delos, when the island was wetter. ⊹ *West of the Archaeological Museum of Delos.*

Sanctuary of the Bulls. Southeast of the Sanctuary of Apollo is the ruins of the Sanctuary of the Bulls, an extremely long and narrow structure built, it is thought, to display a *trireme* (an ancient boat with three banks of oars) that was dedicated to Apollo by a Hellenistic leader thankful for a naval victory. Maritime symbols were found in the decorative relief of the main halls, and the head and shoulders of a pair of bulls were part of the design of an interior entrance. ⊹ *Southeast of the Sanctuary of Apollo.*

Sanctuary of Dionysus. Immediately to the right of the Archaeological Museum is the small Sanctuary of Dionysus, which was erected about 300 BC. Outside the sanctuary you'll find one of the more-boggling sights of ancient Greece: several monuments dedicated to Apollo by the winners of the choral competitions of the Delian festivals, each decorated with a huge phallus, emblematic of the orgiastic rites that took place during the Dionysian festivals. Around the base of one of them is carved a lighthearted representation of a bride being carried to her new husband's home. A marble phallic bird, symbol of the body's immortality, also adorns this corner of the sanctuary. ⊹ *East of the Sanctuary of the Bulls.*

PAROS AND ANTIPAROS
ΠΑΡΟΣ ΚΑΙ ΑΝΤΙΠΑΡΟΣ

168 km (104 miles) southeast of Piraeus harbor in Athens.

In the classical age, the great sculptor Praxiteles prized the incomparably snowy marble that came from the quarries at Paros; his chief rival was the Parian Scopas. Between them they developed the first true female nude, and gentle voluptuousness seems a good description of this historic island. Today, Paros is favored by people for its cafés by the sea, golden sandy beaches, and charming fishing villages. It may lack the chic of Mykonos and have fewer top-class hotels, but at the height of the season it often gets Mykonos's tired and detrending—Madonna (the singer, not Our Lady, who is always here) shows up every summer. The island is large enough to accommodate the traveler in search of peace and quiet, yet the lovely port towns of Paroikía (Paros Town), the capital, and Naousa also have an active nightlife (overactive in August). Paros is a focal point of the Cyclades ferry network, and many people stay here for a night or two while waiting for a connection. Paros Town has a good share of bars and discos, though Naousa has a chicer island atmosphere. And none of the islands has a richer cultural life, with concerts, exhibitions, and readings, than does Paros. For this, check the English-language monthly, *Paros Life,* available everywhere (⊕ *www.paroslife.gr*).

Paros is an island favorite among Greeks and visitors alike. The overflow of tourists is such that it has now washed up on Paros's sister, Antiparos: this island "forgetaway" still has an off-the-beaten-track vibe, even though the rich and famous—Tom Hanks is most prominent of them—have discovered it.

GETTING HERE AND AROUND

There are six Olympic Air flights a day to Athens in summer, three in winter. Early reservations are essential. If a dignitary wants a last-minute flight, you may get bumped. Paros is well served by ferries—there are at least 15 of them daily—many connecting Paros to other islands. Five daily ferries out of Piraeus stop at Paros. Blue Star Ferries are considered the most reliable. There are also at least two ferries departing from the port in Rafina. In summer there are daily connections to Tinos, Mykonos, Naxos, and Santorini. There are also regular connections to Milos, Kimolos, Anafi Ios, Iraklia, Donousa, Koufonisi, Schinousa, Crete, Folegandros, Sikinos, Sifnos, Serifos, Kea, Kastelorizo, Kimolos, Astypalea, Kalymnos, Rhodes, Kos, Nisyros, and Astypalea. There is also a speedboat for hire, much used by lawyers. For boat schedules check ⊕ *www.openseas.gr* and ⊕ *www.bluestarferries.com*.

From the Paros Town bus depot, just west of the dock, there is service every hour to Naousa and less-frequent service to Aliki, Pounta (about 10 buses a day to this departure point for Antiparos), and the beaches at Piso Livadi, Chrissi Akti, and Drios. Schedules are posted. Buy tickets at the booth; fares run from €2.50 to €8. There is a taxi stand across from the windmill on the harbor (☎ *22840/21500*).

Continued on page 303

Greece's Gods and Heroes

Superheroes, sex, adventure: it's no wonder Greek myths have reverberated throughout Western civilization. Today, as you wander ancient Greece's most sacred sites—such as Delos, island birthplace of the sun god Apollo—these ageless tales will come alive to thrill and perhaps haunt you.

Whether you are looking at 5th-century BC pedimental sculptures in Olympia or ancient red-figure vase paintings in Athens, whether you are reading the epics of Homer or the tragedies of Euripides, you are in the presence of the Greek mythopoetic mind. Peopled with emblems of hope, fear, yearning, and personifications of melting beauty or of petrifying ugliness, these ancient myths helped early Greeks make sense of a chaotic, primitive universe that yielded no secrets.

Frightened by the murder and mayhem that surrounded them, the Greeks set up gods in whom power, wisdom, and eternal youth could not perish. These gods lived, under the rule of Zeus, on Mount Olympus. Their rivalries and intrigues were a primeval, superhuman version of *Dynasty* and *Dallas*. These astounding collections of stories not only pervaded all ancient Greek society but have influenced the course of Western civilization: How could we imagine our culture—from Homer's *Iliad* to Joyce's *Ulysses*—without them?

Apollo, the sun god

ZEUS

Latin Name: Jupiter

God of: Sky, Supreme God

Attribute: Scepter, Thunder

Roving Eye: Zeus was the ruler of Mount Olympus but often went AWOL pursuing love affairs down on earth with nymphs and beautiful ladies; his children were legion, including Hercules.

HERA

Latin Name: Juno

Goddess of: Sky, Marriage

Attribute: Peacock

His Cheating Heart: Hera married her brother Zeus, wound up having a 300-year honeymoon with him on Samos, and was repaid for her fidelity to marriage by the many love affairs of her hubby.

APHRODITE

Latin Name: Venus

Goddess of: Love, Beauty

Attribute: Dove

And the Winner Is: Born out of the foam rising off of Cyprus, she was given the Golden Apple by Paris in the famous beauty contest between her, Athena, and Hera, and bestowed the love of Helen on him as thanks.

ATHENA

Latin Name: Minerva

Goddess of: Wisdom

Attribute: Owl, Olive

Top Billing: The goddess of reason, she gave the olive tree to the Greeks; her uncle was Poseidon, and the Parthenon in Athens was built in her honor.

APOLLO

Latin Name: Phoebus

God of: Sun, Music, and Poetry

Attribute: Bow, Lyre

Confirmed Bachelor: Born at Delos, his main temple was at Delphi; his love affairs included Cassandra, to whom he gave the gift of prophecy; Calliope, with whom he had Orpheus; and Daphne, who, fleeing from his embrace, changed into a tree.

ARTEMIS

Latin Name: Diana

Goddess of: Chastity, Moon

Attribute: Stag

Early Feminist: Sister of Apollo, she enjoyed living in the forest with her court, frowned on marriage, and, most notoriously, had men torn apart by her hounds if they peeked at her bathing.

YE GODS!

WHO'S WHO IN GREEK MYTHOLOGY

The twelve chief gods formed the elite of Olympus. Each represented one of the forces of nature and also a human characteristic. They also had attributes by which they can often be identified. The Romans, influenced by the arts and letters of Greece, largely identified their own gods with those of Greece, with the result that Greek gods have Latin names as well. Here are the divine I.D.s of the Olympians.

DEMETER

Latin Name: Ceres

Goddess of: Earth, Fecundity

Attribute: Sheaf, Sickle

Most Dramatic Moment: After her daughter Persephone was kidnapped by Zeus, Demeter decided to make all plants of the earth wither and die.

HERMES

Latin Name: Mercury

God of: Trade, Eloquence

Attribute: Wings

Messenger Service: Father of Pan, Hermes was known as a luck-bringer, harbinger of dreams, and the messenger of Olympus; he was also worshipped as the god of commerce and music.

POSEIDON

Latin Name: Neptune

God of: Sea, Earthquakes

Attribute: Trident

Water Boy: To win the affection of Athenians, Poseidon and Athena were both charged with giving them the most useful gift, with his invention of the bubbling spring losing out to Athena's creation of the olive.

ARES

Latin Name: Mars

God of: Tumult, War

Attribute: Spear, Helmet

Antisocial: The most famous male progeny of Zeus and Hera, he was an irritable man; considering his violent temper, few temples were erected in his honor in Greece.

HESTIA

Latin Name: Vesta

Goddess of: Hearth, Domestic Values

Attribute: Eternal Fire

Hausfrau: A famous virgin, she was charged with maintaining the eternal flame atop Olympus; the Vestal Virgins of ancient Romans followed in her footsteps.

HEPHAESTOS

Latin Name: Vulcan

God of: Fire, Industry

Attribute: Hammer, Anvil

Pumping Iron: The best-preserved Doric style temple in Athens, the Hephaestaion, was erected to this god in the ancient agora marketplace; today, ironmongers still have shops in the district there.

HERCULES

THE FIRST ACTION HERO

Greece's most popular mythological personage was probably Heracles, a hero who became a god, and had to work hard to do it. This paragon of masculinity was so admired by the Romans that they vulgarized him as Hercules, and modern entrepreneurs have capitalized on his popularity in silly sandal epics and sillier Saturday morning cartoons. His name means "glory of Hera," although the goddess hated him because he was the son of Zeus and the Theban princess Alcmene. The Incredible Bulk proved his strength and courage while still in the cradle, and his sexual prowess when he impregnated King Thespius' fifty daughters in as many nights. But the twelve labors are his most famous achievement.

To expiate the mad murder of his wife and his three children, he was ordered to:

1. Slay the Nemean Lion
2. Kill the Lernaean Hydra
3. Capture the Ceryneian Hind
4. Trap the Erymanthian Boar
5. Flush the Augean stables of manure
6. Kill the obnoxious Stymphalian Birds
7. Capture the Cretan Bull, a Minoan story
8. Steal the man-eating Mares of Diomedes
9. Abscond with the Amazon Hippolyta's girdle
10. Obtain six-armed Geryon's Cattle
11. Fetch the Golden Apples of the Hesperides, which bestowed immortality
12. Capture three-headed Cerberus, watchdog of Hades

In other words, he had to rid the world of primitive terrors and primeval horrors. Today, some revisionist Hellenistic historians considered him to be a historical king of Argos or Tiryns and his main stomping ground was the Argolid, basically the northern and southern Peloponnese. Travelers can today still trace his journeys through the region, including Lerna (near the modern village of Myli), not far from Nafplion, where the big guy battled the Hydra, now seen by some historians as a symbol for the malarial mosquitoes that once ravaged the area. Herc pops up in the myths of many other heroes, including Jason, who stole the Golden Fleece; Perseus, who killed Medusa; and Theseus, who established Athens' dominance. And his constellation is part of the regularly whirling Zodiac that is the mythological dome over all our actions and today's astrology.

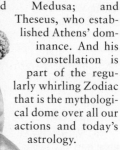

Hercules fighting with the centaur Nessus, sculpted by Giambologna

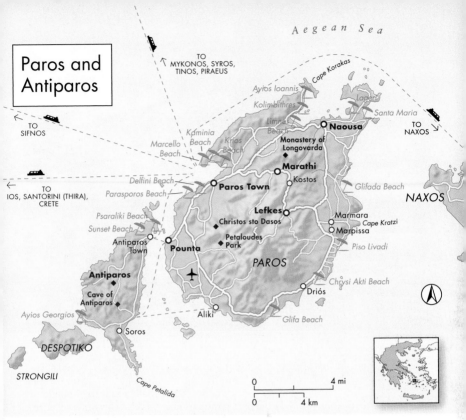

TOURS

Erkyna Travel. Many excursions by boat, bus, and foot are offered here. ✉ *Paros Town* ⚓ *Off the main harbor road where the ferries dock* ☎ *22840/22654, 22840/22655, 22840/53180* ⊕ *www.erkynatravel.com.*

Polos Tours. This agency handles all travel arrangements, from boat tickets to car rentals to excursions, with great efficiency. The company can also arrange boat tours to Antiparos. ✉ *Parikia, Paros Town* ⚓ *Next to dockside OTE office* ☎ *22840/22333* ⊕ *www.polostoursparos.com.*

Santorineos Travel Services. For yacht and other VIP services, check out Nikos Santorineos's office. ✉ *Paros Town* ⚓ *Opposite bus depot* ☎ *22840/24245* ⊕ *www.traveltoparos.gr.*

VISITOR INFORMATION

The most useful Paros website is ⊕ *www.parosweb.com.*

PAROS TOWN ΠΑΡΟΣ (ΠΑΡΟΙΚΙΑ)

168 km (104 miles) southeast of Piraeus, 35 km (22 miles) west of Naxos.

First impressions of Paroikía (Paros Town), pretty as it is, may not necessarily be positive. The port flashes too much concrete, too many boats dock, and the traffic problem, now that Athenian families bring two cars and local families own two cars, is insoluble. The waterfront is

Prince Charles (more than once) and many other architecture buffs have visited the great Church of Our Lady of the Hundred Doors, a proto-Byzantine landmark.

lined with travel agencies, a multitude of car and motorbike rental agencies, and *fastfood-adika*—the Greek word means just what you think it does. Then, if you head east on the harbor road, you'll see a lineup of bars, tourist shops, and coffee shops—many, as elsewhere on the more-prosperous islands, operated by Athenians who come to Paros to capitalize on the huge summer influx. Past them are the fishing-boat dock, a partially excavated ancient graveyard, and the post office; then start the beaches (shaded and over-popular), with their hotels and tavernas.

But go the other way straight into town and you'll find it easy to get lost in the maze of narrow, stone-paved lanes that intersect with the streets of the quiet residential areas. The marble plaza at the town's entrance is full of people strolling and children playing in the evening (during the day, you can fry eggs on this shadeless space). As you check your laptop (Paros Town has Wi-Fi) along the market street chockablock with tourist shops, you'll begin to traverse the centuries: ahead of you looms the seaside Kastro, the ancient acropolis. In 1207 the Venetians conquered Paros, which joined the Duchy of Naxos, and built their huge marble castle wall out of blocks and columns from three temples. At the crest, next to the church of Saints Constantine and Helen (built in 1689), are the visible foundations of a late-Archaic temple to Athena—the area remains Paros's favorite sunset spot.

EXPLORING

Archaeological Museum of Paros. The Archaeological Museum contains a large chunk of the famed Parian chronicle, which recorded cultural events in Greece from about 1500 BC until 260 BC (another chunk is in Oxford's Ashmolean Museum). It interests scholars that the historian inscribed detailed information about artists, poets, and playwrights, completely ignoring wars and shifts in government. Some primitive pieces from the Aegean's oldest settlement, Saliagos (an islet between Paros and Antiparos), are exhibited in the same room, on the left. A small room contains Archaic finds from the ongoing excavation at Despotiko—and they are finding a lot. In the large room to the right rests a marble slab depicting the poet Archilochus in a banquet scene, lying on a couch, his weapons nearby. The ancients ranked Archilochus, who invented iambic meter and wrote the first signed love lyric, second only to Homer. When he died in battle against the Naxians, his conqueror was cursed by the oracle of Apollo for putting to rest one of the faithful servants of the muse. Also there are a monumental Nike and three superb pieces found in the last decade: a waist-down kouros, a gorgon with intact wings, and a dancing-girl relief. ⊠ *Paros Town* ✛ *Behind Hundred Doors Church* ☎ *22840/21231* 💷 *€2* ⊘ *Closed Mon.*

OFF THE BEATEN PATH

Monastery of Longovarda. Halfway from Paros Town to Naousa, on the right, the 17th-century Monastery of Longovarda shines on its mountainside. The monastic community farms the local land and makes honey, wine, and olive oil. Only men, dressed in conservative clothing, are allowed inside, where there are post-Byzantine icons, 17th-century frescoes depicting the Twelve Feasts in the Life of Christ, and a library of rare books; it is usually open mornings. ✛ *3 km (2 miles) northeast of Paros Town* ☎ *22840/21202.*

Fodor'sChoice
★

Panayia Ekatontapyliani (*Hundred Doors Church*). The square above the port, to the northwest, was built to celebrate the church's 1,700th anniversary. From there note a white wall with two belfries, the front of the former monastic quarters that surround the magnificent Panayia Ekatontapyliani, the earliest remaining proto-Byzantine church in Greece and one of the oldest unaltered churches in the world. As such, it is of inestimable value to architecture buffs (such as Prince Charles, who has been spotted here).

The story began in 326, when St. Helen—the mother of Emperor Constantine the Great—set out on a ship for the Holy Land to find the True Cross. Stopping on Paros, she had a vision of success and vowed to build a church there. Though she died before it was built, her son built the church in 328 as a wooden-roof basilica. Two centuries later, Justinian the Great (who ruled the Byzantine Empire in 527–65) commissioned the splendid dome.

According to legend, 99 doors have been found in the church and the 100th will be discovered only after Constantinople is Greek again—but the name is actually older than the legend. Inside, the subdued light mixes with the dun, reddish, and green tufa (porous volcanic rock). The columns are classical and their capitals Byzantine. At the corners of the dome are two fading Byzantine frescoes depicting six-winged seraphim. The 4th-century iconostasis (with ornate later additions) is divided into five frames by marble columns. One panel contains the 14th-century icon of the Virgin, with a silver covering from 1777. The Virgin is carried in procession on the church's crowded feast day, August 15, the Dormition. During Easter services, thousands of rose petals are dropped from the dome upon the singing celebrant. The adjacent **Baptistery**, nearly unique in Greece, also built from the 4th to the 6th century, has a marble font and bits of mosaic floor. The church **museum**, at the right, contains post-Byzantine icons. ⊠ *Paros Town* ⊕ *750 feet east of dock* ☎ *22840/21243* ⊕ *www.ekatontapyliani.gr.*

BEACHES

From Paros Town, boats leave throughout the day for beaches across the bay: to sandy Marcellos and Krios and the quieter Kaminia. Livadia, a five-minute walk, is very developed but has shade. In the other direction, Delfini has a beach bar with live music, and Parasporos has a few beach bars. Sun lovers note: Paros is ringed with beaches.

> ## PRIDE GOETH BEFORE A FALL
>
> At one point, Justinian the Great (who ruled the Byzantine Empire in 527–65) had the Hundred Doors Church rebuilt. He appointed Isidorus, one of the two architects of Constantinople's famed Hagia Sophia, to design it, but Isidorus sent his apprentice, Ignatius, in his place. Upon inspection, Isidorus discovered the dome to be so magnificent that, consumed by jealousy, he pushed the apprentice off the roof. Ignatius grasped his master's foot and the two tumbled to their death together. Look for the folk sculpture of the two men at the sanctuary's closed left portal.

Delfini/Souvlia Beach. This small beach is known for its pretty water and "chill" atmosphere. It's also known around the island for Magaya, a colorful beach bar set right in front of the beach; it's a popular meeting spot for the island's expats. In the summer, beach chairs and umbrellas are available for rent, so grab one and settle in to enjoy the view of Paroikía Bay. ■TIP→ There's a small rocky islet with an underwater cave in the near distance, popular for swimmers to head to, but it's often full of sea urchins. **Amenities:** food and drink. **Best for:** swimming. ⊠ *Paros Town.*

Kaminia Beach. Sandy, long, and unorganized, Kaminia sits to the north of Paroikía Bay. Beachgoers seeking more solitude can head here, even though it's right next to the popular Krios Beach. See if you can find the cave of Archilochos, which is a small opening on the rock along the coast. The famous Ancient Greek poet was said to visit the cave for inspiration and wrote poetry there. **Amenities:** none. **Best for:** solitude; swimming. ⊠ *Paros Town.*

Krios Beach. Close to Paroikía, this sandy beach is a popular summer destination. Cliffs jut into the sand line, parting the coastline and providing protection from the summer island winds. From under a rented umbrella you can watch the boats and ferries slowly sail into the harbor. If you need to take a break, there's a selection of nearby tavernas. ■TIP→ To get here, you can hike the half-hour-long cliff-top trail, take a small boat from the harbor, or drive to the nearby parking area. **Amenities:** food and drink. **Best for:** swimming; walking. ⊠ *Paros Town.*

Livadia Beach. Considered the closest authentic Parian beach near Paroikía, Livadia is the first wide bay north of the harbor that's comprised of a series of smaller, white-sand beaches. Some areas are organized with beach chair and umbrella rentals while others are untouched by tourism, and only trees provide shade. Just a 10-minute walk from the town and harbor and near campgrounds, it can get crowded. **Amenities:** food and drink. **Best for:** swimming. ✉ *Paros Town.*

Marcello Beach. Marcello's famously cool waters attract Parians on the hottest summer days. You can spend the entire day eating, drinking, swimming, or watching the calm water lap against this long, sandy stretch of coastline, as the beach is well equipped with beach bars and cafés, tavernas, and umbrellaed lounge-chair rentals. Next to Krios Beach, it's accessible by car, ferry, or a 40-minute hike from Paroikía. **Amenities:** food and drink. **Best for:** swimming; walking. ✉ *Paros Town.*

Parasporos Beach. This large sandy beach is surrounded by a few shady trees, but umbrellas (and chairs) are available for rent in the summer season. The clear turquoise water gets deep fast, making it ideal for swimming. There are a few bars on-site that add a little beach-party fun. **Amenities:** food and drink. **Best for:** partiers; swimming. ✉ *Paros Town.*

WHERE TO EAT

$ SEAFOOD 🍴 **The Albatross.** You can expect great sunset views and well-prepared traditional dishes at one of Paros's most popular seafood tavernas. Properly it is an "ouzeri," serving mezedes with wine or ouzo, so you'll find there are many small plates to choose from. **Known for:** traditional Greek dishes; excellent ouzo; sunset waterfront views. [$] *Average main: €10* ✉ *Waterfront* ☎ *22840/21848* 🕒 *Closed Dec.–Mar.*

$$ GREEK FUSION Fodor's Choice ★ 🍴 **Levantis.** Chef George Mavridis is an expert at merging the flavors of traditional Greek dishes with contemporary tastes to offer an exciting menu that is beautifully presented. The dining space, a whitewashed indoor room and garden dining area, is inviting. **Known for:** contemporary takes on Greek classics; salt-cured mackerel; delicious baklava for dessert. [$] *Average main: €18* ✉ *Paros Town* ✣ *Off Lochagou Kourtinou* ☎ *22840/23613* 🌐 *www.levantisrestaurant.com* 🕒 *Closed Nov.–Apr.*

WHERE TO STAY

$ HOTEL 🏨 **Parian Village.** This shady, quiet hotel at the far edge of Livadia Beach has small rooms, all with balconies or terraces, most with spectacular views over Paroikía Bay. The pool is pretty, but the sea is close. **Pros:** pretty place near the sea; good vistas; some rooms have luxury mattresses. **Cons:** near crowded areas in high season; no on-site restaurant; sufficient walk for some to Paros Town. [$] *Rooms from: €100* ✉ *Paros Town* ✣ *25-min sea walk from center of Paroikía* ☎ *22840/23187* 🌐 *www.parianvillage.gr* 🕒 *Closed Dec.–Apr.* 🛏 *28 rooms* 🍽 *Breakfast.*

NIGHTLIFE AND PERFORMING ARTS

BARS

Turn right along the waterfront from the port in Paros Town to find the town's famous bars; then follow your ears. At the far end of the *paralia* is the laser-light-and-disco section of town, which you may want to avoid. In the younger bars, cheap alcohol, as everywhere in tourist Greece, is often added to the more-colorful drinks.

Entropy Bar. Year-round, Entropy offers a casual, fun atmosphere with a creative shot menu that will probably peak your curiosity. Mandarin

Jellybean, Disco Lemonball, or Shark Bite, anyone? The Paros Town seafront location attracts visitors from around the world with the enthusiasm to down colorful cocktails, too, such as the Watermelon Basil Smash, Aegean Blue Lagoon, and Tangerine Dream. ⊠ *Market St.* ☎ *22840/27323* ⊕ *www.entropybarparos.com.*

Pirate Bar. Located in the Old Town, this cozy bar combines whitewashed walls with a stone-and-wood design and soft lighting. The result is a sophisticated crowd that loves its jazz and blues music as well as its cocktails. Some nights, live bands are featured. ⊠ *Old Town.*

PERFORMING ARTS

Of all the islands Paros has the liveliest art scene (check ⊕ *paroslife. parosweb.com* for openings and events), with dozens of galleries and public spaces presenting exhibitions. Many artists, Greek and foreign, live on the island or visit regularly—painters Jane Pack and Neva Bergmann, sculptor Richard King, photographers Stavros Niflis and Elizabeth Carson, portrait artist Angelika Vaxevanidou, filmmaker Ioannis Tritsibidas, and ceramist Stelios Ghikas are just a few—and the Aegean Center has proved a strong stimulant.

Fodor'sChoice **The Aegean Center for the Fine Arts.** A small American arts college, the
★ Aegean Center for the Fine Arts hosts readings, concerts, lectures, and exhibitions in its splendidly restored neoclassical mansion. Director John Pack, an American photographer, lives on the island with his family. Since 1966 the center has offered courses (two three-month semesters) in writing, painting, photography, and classical voice training. ⊠ *Main cross street to Market St.* ☎ *22840/23287* ⊕ *www.aegeancenter.org.*

SPORTS AND THE OUTDOORS
WATER SPORTS
Many beaches offer water sports, especially windsurfing.

SHOPPING
CERAMICS
Yria Interiors. On Market Street, look for the house with the beautifully carved Parian marble facade to find Paros's most elegantly designed shop. Here, Stelios Ghikas, Monique Mailloux, and daughter Ramona display their pottery from Studio Yria, as well as a carefully chosen range of stylish household items, mostly from France. ⊠ *Market St.* ☎ *22840/24359* ⊕ *www.yriaparos.com.*

JEWELRY
Jewelry Workshop. Vangelis Skaramagas and Yannis Xenos, uncle and nephew, have been making their own delicate, precious jewelry here for more than 20 years. ⊠ *Paros Town* ✛ *End of Market St.* ☎ *22840/21008.*

Phaedra. Local Phaidra Apostolopoulou, who studied jewelry in Athens, has this tiny shop, where she shows her sophisticated silver and gold designs, and a line of lighthearted pieces for summer. ⊠ *Paros Town* ✛ *Near Zoodochos Pyghi church* ☎ *22840/23626* ⊕ *www.kosmimaphaedra.com.*

NAOUSA ΝΑΟΥΣΑ

10 km (6 miles) northeast of Paros Town.

Naousa, impossibly pretty, long ago discovered the benefits of tourism, and its outskirts are mushrooming with villas and hotels that exploit it further. Along the harbor—which thankfully maintains its beauty and function as a fishing port—red and navy blue boats knock gently against one another as men repair their nets and foreigners relax in the *ouzeri*—Barbarossa being the traditional favorite—by the water's edge. From here the pirate Hugue Crevelliers operated in the 1570s, and Byron turned him into the corsair. Navies of the ancient Persians, flotillas from medieval Venice, and the imperial Russian fleet have anchored in this harbor. The half-submerged ruins of the Venetian fortifications still remain; they are a pretty sight when lighted up at night. Compared to Paros Town, the scene in Naousa is somewhat chicer, with a more-intimate array of shops, bars, and restaurants, but in winter the town shuts down. The island's unobtrusive LGBT scene is here, if it is anywhere.

EXPLORING

Folklore Museum. Naousa's small Folklore Museum, about 500 feet from the main town square, is in a traditional house donated by Kanstantinos and Marouso Roussos. It's run by the Music, Dance and Theatre Group of Naousa and features folk costumes from Paros and the rest of Greece. The furniture and implements are also historic. ⊠ *Naousa* ☎ *22840/52284* ⌦ *€1* ⊘ *Closed Oct.–May.*

BEACHES

Ayios Ioannis. Served by the Kolimbithres boat, Ayios Ioannis's golden, sandy beach is peaceful, clean, and quiet. Also known by locals as Monastiri Beach, it is protected by a rocky cove and attached to the Paros Eco Park, which offers a snack bar and numerous amenities. The blue-domed, white-washed Ayios Ioannis Monastery sits to the right side of the beach, a short walk away. **Amenities:** food and drink; showers; toilets; water sports. **Best for:** swimming. ⊠ *Naousa* ✛ *In front of Paros Eco Park.*

FAMILY **Kolimbithres.** The beach, which is noted for its anfractuous rock formations, is also considered to be one of Paros's best, attracting its share of crowds to the small, sandy cove. The granite formations create shallow pools of water popular with the kids. It's within walking distance of two tavernas that overlook the region. Lounge chairs and umbrellas are available for rent from a seasonal café. Head to the top of nearby Koukounaries Hill to view the remains of an ancient site. You can get there by car, but there is no designated parking for the beach. People do park at area tavernas or along the road. Another way to reach the beach is by boat from Naousa. ■TIP➔ **A boat crosses the bay to Kolimbithres from Naousa Bay.** **Amenities:** food and drink. **Best for:** swimming. ⊠ *Naousa* ✛ *Directly across bay from Naousa.*

Lageri. A boat from Naousa regularly heads to Lageri, a long beach known for its fine sand, dunes, and calm, quiet atmosphere. Those are just a few of the reasons it attracts its share of nudists who prefer the less crowded Paros beaches. It's also accessible via a small footpath from the main road. **Amenities:** none. **Best for:** nudists; solitude; walking. ⊠ *Naousa* ✛ *North of Naousa.*

FAMILY **Santa Maria.** Several sandy footpaths from the main road lead you to one of Paros's most popular family-friendly beaches; the boat that travels to nearby Lageri also makes a stop in Santa Maria. Little fishing boats dock in the distance from the sandy cove, which is filled with sand dunes and lined with green brush. There's no natural shade, but in peak season it's well equipped with beach chair and umbrella rentals from seasonal cafés. Several tavernas are within walking distance. **Amenities:** food and drink. **Best for:** swimming. ⊠ *Naousa* ✛ *Northeastern shore of Paros.*

WHERE TO EAT

$$ ✕ **BlueFish.** By Naousa's charming harbor, with a stunning view of the sea, BlueFish brings a unique fusion of Greek and Japanese seafood cuisine to Paros—and it works divinely. The acclaimed menu is matched only by the sophisticated whitewashed and elegant setting. **Known for:** Greek-Japanese fusion; excellent service; beautiful harbor location. Ⓢ *Average main: €25* ⊠ *Naousa* ☎ *22840/51874* ☉ *Closed Nov.–Apr.*

FUSION
Fodor's Choice
★

$$ ✕ **Mario.** Good food is enhanced here by the pretty location, a few feet from the fishing boats on Naousa's harbor. The taverna specializes in fresh fish (from the fisherman a few feet away) and also fine cuisine. **Known for:** seafood specialties; excellent spot on the harbor. Ⓢ *Average main: €24* ⊠ *Naousa* ✛ *On fishing-boat harbor* ☎ *22840/51047.*

SEAFOOD

$$ ✕ **Mediterraneo.** For a calming view of Naousa harbor and a taste of Greek seafood specialties done to perfection, head to Mediterraneo. Here's the place to try traditional Greek taverna appetizers, including fresh grilled octopus and marinated anchovies, and dips like *taramosalata* (fish roe dip) and fava dip topped with caramelized onion, before mains that add a bit of contemporary creativity. **Known for:** view of Naousa harbor; excellent and fresh Greek-style seafood dishes. Ⓢ *Average main: €20* ⊠ *On the dock* ☎ *22840/53176.*

GREEK

$$ ✕ **Siparos.** Along the coast of Naousa Bay in the beach town of Santa Maria, this seaside restaurant serves fresh seafood and meat dishes using local products and traditional Greek recipes. Sunset and endless sea views make the fine-dining experience even more memorable. **Known for:** sunset views; excellent dishes. Ⓢ *Average main: €25* ⊠ *Xifara, Santa Maria* ☎ *22840/52785* ⊕ *www.siparos.gr.*

MEDITERRANEAN
Fodor's Choice
★

WHERE TO STAY

$$$$ ☷ **Astir of Paros.** Peaceful views of Naousa Bay are part of the experience at this graceful deluxe resort hotel, where green lawns, tall palm trees, subtropical gardens, and an art gallery contribute to its superlative reputation. **Pros:** good service; private beach and a beautiful pool; elegant setting. **Cons:** you need a vehicle to get anywhere, including Naousa; expensive for Paros; not much around the hotel to see, except the beach. Ⓢ *Rooms from: €295* ⊠ *Naousa* ✛ *Take Kolimbithres Rd. from Naousa* ☎ *22840/51976, 22840/51984* ⊕ *www.astirofparos.gr* ☉ *Closed Nov.–Mar.* ⇜ *57 rooms* ❄❄ *Breakfast.*

RESORT

$$ Kanale's. On a hillside, just steps from a beach just outside Naousa
HOTEL   harbor, Kanale's is a bright whitewashed hotel with modern touches.
Fodor'sChoice   **Pros:** near the beach; walking distance to Naousa; good on-site restau-
★   rant. **Cons:** no on-site spa; some stairs to climb, depending on room;
some rooms may not have a great view. $ *Rooms from: €180* ⊠ *Naousa*
☎ *22840/52044* ⊕ *www.kanales.gr* ⌦ *34 rooms* ⎛⊙⎞ *Breakfast.*

$$ Paliomylos. Close enough to the vibrant scene in Naousa, but far
HOTEL   enough for a pretty view of it, Paliomylos spa hotel has a choice of
suites and studios, with an overall design that reflects Cycladic island
style with contemporary elements. **Pros:** cool and relaxing scenic pool;
walking distance to beach and Naousa; nice on-site spa. **Cons:** near the
scene of Naousa—a busy place in high season; rooms may be on the
small side; early risers be aware: breakfast doesn't start until 8:30 am.
$ *Rooms from: €170* ⊠ *Naousa* ☎ *22840/51151* ⊕ *www.paliomylos.
com* ⊘ *Closed Oct.–Apr.* ⌦ *25 rooms* ⎛⊙⎞ *Breakfast.*

$ Svoronos Bungalows. The best budget choice in Naousa, these com-
B&B/INN   fortable bungalow apartments, near the beach but also convenient
Fodor'sChoice   for shopping and nightlife, always seem to be fully occupied. **Pros:**
★   charming and quiet; walking distance to beach; leafy-green property.
Cons: some rooms lack air-conditioning; far from Paros Town port, but
transfers may be included; no restaurant on-site. $ *Rooms from: €100*
⊠ *Naousa* ⊕ *Behind big church, one block in from Santa Maria Rd.*
☎ *22840/51211, 22840/51409* ⊕ *www.svoronosbungalows.wix.com/
paros* ⊘ *Closed Nov.–Apr.* ⌦ *20 bungalows* ⎛⊙⎞ *Breakfast.*

NIGHTLIFE AND PERFORMING ARTS

BARS

Agosta. In a pretty whitewashed building on the tip of the old harbor,
Agosta is considered a local favorite for drinks and dancing the night
away. Depending where you stand you'll get a stunning view of Naousa
harbor or Agios Dimitrios Beach. Past midnight everyone heads for the
two dance floors. ⊠ *Naousa* ⊕ *At fishing harbor.*

Linardo. In a whitewashed building that's more than 400 years old,
Linardo's interior is impeccably maintained and cooly decorated. It has
to be, considering that it's one of Naousa's top hot spots where crowds
gather until the early morning. The bar features DJs that typically spin
progressive house music. The party may spill out into the street where
you'll catch a charming view of the old harbor. ⊠ *Liminaki.*

Fodor'sChoice   **Sommaripa Consolato.** A prime spot above idyllic Naousa harbor is
★   where you'll find Sommaripa Consolato, which infuses Paros tradition
in its drinks. Instead of a mojito, try their creation—a sumito, which
replaces rum with the local homemade island liquor called suma.
Once the home of the Parian family, the family's younger generation
transformed it into a whitewashed, cool open space with artwork and
picture-perfect views of the bay. During the day, stop by for a Greek
coffee accompanied by one of Mama Sommaripa's homemade Greek
cookies or a slice of cake. ⊠ *Limanaki.*

DANCE PERFORMANCES

Music–Dance "Naousa Paros". The group Music–Dance "Naousa Paros," formed in 1988 to preserve the traditional dances and music of Paros, performs all summer long in Naousa in the costumes of the 16th century and has participated in dance competitions and festivals throughout Europe. Keep an eye out for posters; the schedule is online and venues change. ⊠ *Naousa* ☎ *22840/52284* ⊕ *www.users.otenet. gr/~parofolk/index_en.html.*

PERFORMANCE VENUES

Environmental and Cultural Park of Paros. Set on almost 200 acres of the beautiful Agios Ioannis Detis Peninsula, the Environmental and Cultural Park of Paros offers a full summer program of concerts in its outdoor theater. Locals, inspired to preserve the beautiful natural landscapes of the island, organized themselves to restore and showcase monuments. Lectures, festivals, ecological talks, marked and labeled pathways through the park's peninsula, a café, a beautiful church, and a protected beach for swimming all contribute to the natural preserve's splendor. ⊠ *Paros Park* ☎ *22840/53573* ⊕ *www.parospark.gr.*

SPORTS AND THE OUTDOORS

WATER SPORTS

Santa Maria Surfing Beach. The Santa Maria Surfing Beach complex is popular among sports lovers thanks to the fine facilities offered for windsurfing, waterskiing, tubing, and diving. There's a tennis court, and horseback riding excursions. Camping and accommodations services are also available. ⊠ *Santa Maria Beach* ✛ *Approximately 4 km (2½ miles) north of Naousa* ☎ *22840/52491* ⊕ *www.surfbeach.gr* ☞ *Closed Sept.–May.*

SHOPPING

ART AND JEWELRY

Paros is an art colony and exhibits are everywhere in summer. It is also home to quite a few creative jewelers.

Nid D'Or. A small shop, Nid D'Or showcases two lines: one is a collection by owner Aliki Meremetis, featuring rough-cut semiprecious stones; the second is by another well-known and respected Greek jeweler, Katerina Kotsaki. ⊠ *Naousa* ✛ *On 2nd street from harbor toward main church* ☎ *22840/51775.*

FASHION

Tango. Kostas Mouzedakis's stylish store has been selling classic sportswear for three decades, including its own Tangowear label, a men's line that reflects a Cycladic island lifestyle in cream, white, coral, and blue hues and various types of linen. ⊠ *Naousa* ✛ *On 2nd street from harbor toward main church.*

MARATHI ΜΑΡΑΘΙ

10 km (6 miles) east of Paros Town.

During the classical period, the island of Paros had an estimated 150,000 residents, many of them slaves who worked the ancient marble quarries in Marathi. The island grew rich from the export of this white, granular marble known among ancient architects and sculptors for its ability to absorb light. They called it *lychnites* ("won by lamplight").

Three Caverns. A short walk from main road, marked by a sign, three caverns are bored into the hillside, the largest of them 300 feet deep. This is where the world-famed Parian marble was mined. The most recent quarrying done in these mines was in 1844, when a French company cut marble here for Napoléon's tomb. ⊠ *Marathi.*

LEFKES ΛΕΥΚΕΣ

6 km (4 miles) south of Marathi, 10 km (6 miles) southeast of Paros Town.

Rampant piracy in the 17th century forced thousands of people to move inland from the coastal regions; thus for many years the scenic village of Lefkes, built on a hillside in the protective mountains, was the island's capital. It remains the largest village in the interior and has maintained a peaceful island feeling, with narrow streets fragrant with jasmine and honeysuckle. These days, the old houses are being restored, and in summer the town is full of people. Farming is the major source of income, evidenced by the well-kept stone walls and olive groves. For one of the best walks on Paros, take the ancient Byzantine road from the main lower square to the lower villages.

Two **17th-century churches** of interest are **Ayia Varvara** (St. Barbara) and **Ayios Sotiris** (Holy Savior). The big 1830 neo-Renaissance **Ayia Triada** (Holy Trinity) is the pride of the village.

BEACHES

Beyond Lefkes, the road continues on to Piso Livadi and a string of popular beaches.

Golden Beach. Golden Beach (or Chrysi Akti in Greek) is a series of tree-fringed sandy beaches that are well organized and in close proximity to an array of taverns, restaurants, and cafés. The area is famous for its water-sports activities and several centers are based here offering diving excursions and kitesurfing and windsurfing lessons. The Windsurfing World Cup has held events here. **Amenities:** food and drink. **Best for:** swimming; water sports; windsurfing. ⊠ *Golden Beach.*

Logaras Beach. Just around the bend from Piso Livadi is the long stretch of yellow sand known as Logaras Beach. A few tavernas are nearby, and in the distance the little whitewashed church of Ayios Georgios Thalassites, or St. George of the Sea, stands where it has since the 13th century. This quiet beach has chairs and umbrellas available for rent in the summer season. **Amenities:** food and drink. **Best for:** swimming; walking. ⊠ *Logaras Beach.*

FAMILY **Piso Livadi Beach.** One of the most popular beaches on Paros's southeastern coast, Piso Livadi has trees offering natural shade, but lounge chairs and umbrellas are also available to rent. The small resort town of Piso Livadi, once an ancient port for the marble quarries, surrounds the sandy stretch of well-developed beach and is filled with lodging options, tavernas, restaurants, and cafés. Boats depart from this port for Mykonos, Naxos, Amorgos, Ios, and Santorini. **Amenities:** food and drink. **Best for:** swimming. ⊠ *Piso Livadi* ✛ *On road past Lefkes* ⊕ *www.pissolivadi.com.*

WHERE TO EAT

$ 🍴 **Taverna Klarinos.** Andreas Ragoussis's family-run Greek tavern is about
GREEK tradition all the way. Like his parents who ran the tavern before him, he uses homegrown vegetables, local meat, and Parian cheese in each recipe and is always ready to serve his homemade wine. **Known for:** grilled meat; traditional vegetable dishes like fried zucchini and garlic beets; homemade wine. [$] *Average main: €12* ✉ *Main entrance street, opposite square, 2nd fl.* ☎ *22840/41608* 💳 *No credit cards* 🕓 *Closed Oct.–Apr.*

WHERE TO STAY

$$ 🏨 **Lefkes Village.** All the rooms in this elegant hotel have balconies with
HOTEL magnificent views down the olive-tree valley and over the sea to Naxos. **Pros:** village style upgraded; far-reaching views; in a charming village. **Cons:** Lefkes is far from the sea; not within convenient distance to other towns; Wi-Fi may not be strong. [$] *Rooms from: €130* ✉ *Lefkes* ✣ *East of Lefkes on main road* ☎ *22840/41827* 🌐 *www.lefkesvillage.gr* 🕓 *Closed Oct.–Apr.* 🛏 *20 rooms* 🍽 *Breakfast.*

SPORTS AND THE OUTDOORS

Aegean Diving College. Offering scuba lessons that take you to reefs, shipwrecks, and caves, the Aegean Diving College is headed by director Peter Nicolaides, who discovered the oldest shipwreck known and is a marine biologist involved in many of Greece's ecological projects. It's on the southeast corner of the island on Golden Beach. ✉ *Golden Beach* ☎ *22840/43347* 🌐 *www.aegeandiving.gr.*

SHOPPING

ART GALLERIES

Angelika Vaxevanidou Art Studio. A visit to the whitewashed studio and gallery of award-winning sculptor, mosaicist, and portrait artist Angelika Vaxevanidou is a glimpse into the world of a successful, internationally commissioned artist. The longtime local artist and resident is recognized internationally for her impressive, sensitive, and emotional large-scale colored-pencil portraiture, and on display are works past and present. The studio is open year-round. ✉ *Lefkes* ☎ *22840/44076* 🌐 *www.angelikavaxevanidou.com* 🕓 *Closed Sun.*

POUNTA ΠΟΥΝΤΑ

4 km (2½ miles) south of Paros Town.

Pounta is not even a village, just a few houses, three restaurants (one fine one), and a tiny harbor from which ferries leave for Antiparos. The road that turns left just before you get there continues on to many beaches. And beyond—it is a beautiful drive—are the peaceful harbor towns of Aliki and Dryos, both with fine beaches and restaurants, especially Faragas, now overdeveloped.

EXPLORING

OFF THE BEATEN PATH

Christos sto Dasos (*Christ in the Wood*). A 15-minute walk or 2-minute drive back toward Paros Town from the Valley of Butterflies leads to the convent known as Christos sto Dasos, from where there's a marvelous view of the Aegean. The convent contains the tomb of St. Arsenios (1800–77), who was a schoolteacher, an abbot, and a prophet. He was also a reputed rainmaker, whose prayers were believed to have ended a long drought, saving Paros from starvation. The nuns are a bit leery of tourists. If you want to go in, be sure to wear long pants or skirt and a shirt that covers your shoulders or the sisters will turn you away. ✣ *Between the Valley of Butterflies and Paros Town.*

Petaloudes Park. The Jersey tiger moth returns year after year to mate in Petaloudes (Butterflies Valley), a lush oasis of greenery in the middle of this dry island. In May, June, and perhaps July, you can watch them as they lie dormant during the day, their chocolate-brown wings with yellow stripes still against the ivy leaves. In the evening they flutter upward to the cooler air, flashing the coral-red undersides of their wings as they rise. A notice at the entrance asks visitors not to disturb them by taking photographs or shaking the leaves. ⊠ *Petaloudes Park* ☎ *22840/91554* ⊕ *www.parosbutterflies.gr* ⌧ *€2* ☾ *Closed mid-Sept.–mid-May.*

BEACHES

Pounta Beach. Pounta is Paros's party beach. A packed schedule of beach party events kicks off in the summer and continues daily. Mainstream pop music blares from the beach bars and cafés all day and all night. Dancing on the sand, and tabletops, is part of the scene. Greek pop stars perform in concerts here, too. Famous for its island winds, it's also an organized haven for windsurfers, kitesurfers, and extreme sport enthusiasts. **Amenities:** food and drink; toilets. **Best for:** partiers; surfing; windsurfing. ⊠ *Pounda* ✣ *On road past Piso Livadi* ⊕ *www.pundabeach.gr.*

WHERE TO EAT

$$ ✕ **Thea.** From the terrace of this fine restaurant you can enjoy the view
GREEK over the Antiparos strait and the little ferries that ply it, while inside it's all wood and hundreds of bottles of wine shelved from floor to high ceiling. Owner Nikos Kouroumlis is a wine fanatic, and Thea has the third most extensive wine list in all of Greece; his own wine is excellent. **Known for:** excellent Greek cuisine; long wine list. $ *Average main: €20* ⊠ *Pounta harbor* ☎ *22840/91220* ✐ *nikostheaparos@yahoo.gr.*

SPORTS AND THE OUTDOORS

SCUBA DIVING

Eurodivers. A proud Professional Association of Diving Instructors (PADI) 5-Star Resort, Eurodivers offers courses from beginner to professional levels. ⊠ *Pounta* ✣ *On west side of Paros* ☎ *22840/92071* ⊕ *www.eurodivers.gr.*

WINDSURFING

Paros Kite Pro Center. On the island's west coast, where turquoise waters meet windy conditions perfect for kitesurfing, the Paros Kite Pro Center offers International Kiteboarding Organization–certified lessons, equipment, and rentals. ⊠ *Pounta* ✣ *On the island's west coast* ⊕ *www.paroskite-procenter.com.*

ANTIPAROS ΑΝΤΙΠΑΡΟΣ

5 km (3 miles) southwest of Paros Town.

This smaller sister isle of Paros may have once been the best little secret of the Cyclades, but thanks to such gilt-edged visitors as Brad Pitt, Tom

Hanks, and Sean Connery, everybody now knows about this pretty little "forgetaway." And let's not overlook the fact that this green, inhabited islet belongs to the famously rich Goulandris family, benefactors of the Goulandris Cycladic Museum in Athens (and much else). As a result of all this glamour, Antiparos is developing all too rapidly. A great source of information about Antiparos, with a complete listing of hotels, can be found at ⊕ *www.antiparos-isl.gr.*

Two or three decades ago you would have gone to the Paros hamlet of Pounta, made your way to the church, opened its door (as a signal), and waited for a fishing caïque to chug over. Now, 30 car ferries ply the channel all day and a lovely 7-minute ride wafts you over to Antiparos (or you can take a 20-minute ferry ride from Paros Town). A causeway once crossed the Antiparos strait, which would be swimmable but for the current, and on one of its still emergent islets, Saliagos, habitations and objects have been found dating back almost to 5000 BC.

Antiparos's one town, also called Antiparos, has a main street and two centers of activity: the quay area and the main square, a block or two in. At both are restaurants and cafés. To the right of the square are houses and the Kastro's 15th-century wall. At the other end of the quay, from the ferry dock, a road goes to an idyllic sandy beach (it is 10 minutes by foot); you can wade across to the islet opposite, Fira, where sheep and goats graze.

It is pleasant to go around to the other side of Antiparos on the good road to Ayios Georgios, where there are three excellent taverns, perfect after a swim. On request a boat will take you to the nearby islet of **Despotiko**, uninhabited except for seasonal archaeologists excavating a late-Archaic marble temple complex to Apollo. In autumn the hills are fragrant with purple flowering heather.

EXPLORING

Cave of Antiparos. In the 19th century the most famous sight in the Aegean was the cave of Antiparos, and it still draws many visitors every year. Greece's oldest known cave sits on the southeastern part of Antiparos. It's filled with shapely stalactites and stalagmites of which the oldest is said to be 45 million years old. The natural wonder was first discovered by a French ambassador in the 16th century and myths, legends, and stories have been associated with it along the way. You'll need to take exactly 411 steps down into the cave's 100-meter-deep core to explore. Look for Lord Byron's autograph. Outside is the church of Agios Ioánnis Spiliótis, built in 1774. Audio tours are available. ⊠ *Agios Ioannis* ⌑ *€5* ☾ *Closed Nov.–Mar.*

Venetian Kastro. Close to the port you'll find yourself walking into the pedestrian paths of Antiparos Town, lined with whitewashed shops, restaurants, and cafés. Farther up, the arched stonework entrance to the historical center, known as the *camara,* leads to the centuries-old Venetian *kastro,* or castle, of Antiparos. Like other Cycladic islands, this architecture reflects the construction of fortresses built between the 13th and 16th century when Venetian and Ottoman influences took over the islands. You can walk the whitewashed streets of this small village, where Antiparians still live in small homes built on top of each other as one continuous block construction within the stone walls. There are also four churches within the settlement. ✉ *Antiparos Town* ⊕ *Northern tip of the island.*

BEACHES

Ayios Georgios Beach. Head 11 km (7 miles) south of Antiparos Town to the calm, southeastern beaches of Ayios Georgios. This series of small, fine-sand coves has a view of the uninhabited island of Despotiko. Here, three small fish tavernas sit on the edge of the tiny village road, overlooking the sea. Otherwise, what you see is what you get—a serene untouched landscape. **Amenities:** food and drink. **Best for:** solitude; swimming; walking. ✉ *Ayios Georgios.*

Camping Beach. This long, quiet sandy stretch of beach is located off a small path leading from the Antiparos Camping campground and just north of Antiparos Town. The view is peaceful: just the neighboring inlet of Diplos and a turquoise sea. On one section of the beach, umbrellas and lounge chairs can be rented and another area is frequented by nudists—it's one of Greece's recognized naturist beaches. **Amenities:** food and drink. **Best for:** nudists; solitude; walking. ✉ *Antiparos Town.*

FAMILY **Psaraliki Beach.** Within walking distance of Antiparos Town, this beach has two parts, referred to by locals as Psaraliki One and Psaraliki Two. Yellow, soft sand fills both and each is dotted with natural shade trees; lounge chairs and umbrellas are available during the summer months. The shallow waters make it a favorite for families, and its southeasterly placement on the island keeps it sheltered from gusty Cycladic winds. Several tavernas are close by. **Amenities:** food and drink. **Best for:** swimming; walking. ✉ *Antiparos Town.*

Sunset Beach. As its name implies, this is where Antiparians head to watch their island's fantastic sunsets. Clear water and golden sand are guaranteed, but ideal beach weather is not—located on the west coast, the beach isn't sheltered from the Cycladic winds that can stir things up. When the winds do die down, the conditions are ideal for snorkeling and swimming. **TIP→ The beach is also known as Sifneiko, because the neighboring island of Sifnos can be seen in the distance.** **Amenities:** food and drink. **Best for:** snorkeling; sunset; swimming. ✉ *Antiparos Town.*

WHERE TO EAT

$$ GREEK 🍴 **Akrogiali.** You can dine alfresco on Akrogiali's simple veranda and enjoy the view across the strait to the sacred isle of Despotikon. The restaurant is owned by the local Pipinos family, and the bells you'll hear in the background belong to the family's goats (yes, they occasionally end up on the table here). **Known for:** fresh seafood; homegrown ingredients. [$] *Average main: €15* ✉ *Ayios Georgios* ☎ *22840/22107* 💳 *No credit cards* 🕒 *Closed Oct.–Apr.*

$$ SEAFOOD Fodor's Choice ★ 🍴 **Captain Pipinos.** Dining here is on an elevated veranda right above the calm blue waters of Ayios Georgios Bay. The line of drying octopus may be out, evidence of Captain Pipinos pride in serving the freshest seafood on the island. **Known for:** fresh seafood from the family fishing boats; grilled thornback ray; psarasoupa (a fish soup). [$] *Average main: €15* ✉ *Ayios Georgios* 🌐 *www.captainpipinos.com.*

$$$ MEDITERRANEAN Fodor's Choice ★ ✕ **Tageri.** Perhaps Antiparos Town's best table, Tageri's menu delights with fresh seafood and Mediterranean plates that burst with flavor from local seasonal ingredients. The beautifully presented dishes have become local favorites, including a lobster pasta with fresh tomatoes and herbs, and a slow-baked fillet of lamb, stuffed with Parian cheese, garlic, spices, and herbs. **Known for:** gourmet dining; excellent service. [$] *Average main: €26* ✉ *Antiparos Town* ☎ *69/80803633 cell phone* 🌐 *www.tageri.com.*

WHERE TO STAY

$ RESORT FAMILY Fodor's Choice ★ 🏨 **Kastro Antiparos.** On a small hill and within comfortable walking distance to town and Psariliki Beach, this bright, open, whitewashed property has been consistently upgraded and expanded over the last 20 or so years by Antiparian couple Magda Kritsantoni and Markos Maouni. **Pros:** walking distance to town and beach; sea views from its open spaces; nice and refreshing pool. **Cons:** breakfast not included; may be busy with kids; not right in Antiparos Town. [$] *Rooms from: €100* ✉ *Antiparos Town* ☎ *22840/61011* 🌐 *www.antiparosgreece.com* 🕒 *Closed Nov.–Apr.* 🛏 *10 rooms* 🍴 *No meals.*

$ HOTEL 🏨 **Kouros Village Hotel.** The hotels on Antiparos tend to be simple, pleasant places to stay near the beach, and this two-story building, which offers a series of rooms, apartments, and suites, most overlooking a pool and beautiful Antiparos Bay, nicely fits the bill. **Pros:** attractive, convenient option; has all the usual amenities; balconies and terraces have fine sea views. **Cons:** in a busy port; may feel crowded in high season; breakfast not included. [$] *Rooms from: €70* ✉ *Antiparos harbor, Antiparos Town* ☎ *22840/61084* 🌐 *www.kouros-village.gr* 🕒 *Closed mid-Oct.–mid-Apr.* 🛏 *30 rooms* 🍴 *No meals.*

SHOPPING

Mariliza. Antiparos's trendiest concept boutique features a hip selection of clothing, purses, T-shirts, and accessories crafted by Greek designers. Also browse through creations made with care by the talented owner, Mariliza Dimakou, including stylish Greek leather sandals and handmade Greek-inspired jewelry. ✉ *Antiparos Town* 🌐 *www.marilizashop.gr.*

NAXOS ΝΑΞΟΣ

190 km (118 miles) southeast of Piraeus harbor in Athens.

"Great sweetness and tranquility" is how Nikos Kazantzakis, premier novelist of Greece, described Naxos, and indeed a tour of the island leaves you with an impression of abundance, prosperity, and serenity. The greenest, largest, and most fertile of the Cyclades, Naxos, with its many potato fields, its livestock and its thriving cheese industry, and its fruit and olive groves framed by the pyramid of Mt. Zas (at 3,295 feet, the Cyclades' highest), is practically self-sufficient. Inhabited for 6,000 years, the island has memorable landscapes—abrupt ravines, hidden valleys, long and sandy beaches—and towns that vary from a Cretan mountain stronghold to the seaside capital that strongly evokes its Venetian past.

Naxos is full of history and monuments—classical temples, medieval monasteries, Byzantine churches, Venetian towers—and its huge interior offers endless magnificent hikes, not much pursued by summer tourists, who cling to the lively capital and the developed western beaches, the best in the Cyclades.

GETTING HERE AND AROUND

Olympic Air flies three to five times a day from Athens to Naxos, and back; it takes 35 minutes (in winter connections are much fewer). There are no other air connections. Summer flights fill up fast, so book well in advance. Ferries to Naxos, many of which follow the Paros/Naxos/Santorini route, take from four to seven hours depending on route, boat, and pelagic happenstance. In summer there are five a day, in winter fewer. There are also daily connections with Paros and Santorini, and regular connections with Mykonos, Amorgos, Kythnos, Kea, Ios, and sometimes others. The Naxos Port Authority can give you information on ferries.

On Naxos, the bus system is reliable and fairly extensive. Daily buses go from Naxos Town, called Chora (near the boat dock), to Engares, Melanes, Sangri, Filoti, Apeiranthos, Koronida, and Apollonas. In summer there is added daily service to the beaches, including Ayia Anna, Pyrgaki, Ayiassos, Pachi Ammos, and Abram. Other villages have bus service but with much less frequency. Schedules are posted; hotel concierges also have this info, and schedules can be found online at ⊕ *www. naxosbeaches.gr* (under bus schedules). Fares run from €3 to €8. There is a taxi stand near the harbor.

Contacts Naxos Port Authority. ☎ *22850/22300.*

TOURS

Zas Travel. This agency runs several one-day tours of the island sights with different itineraries, each costing about €50, and one-day trips to Delos and Mykonos, as well as Santorini (about €60). ⊠ *At harbor, Naxos Town* ☎ *22850/23330, 22850/23331.*

NAXOS TOWN ΝΑΞΟΣ (ΧΩΡΑ)

140 km (87 miles) southeast of Piraeus, 33 km (21 miles) southeast of Mykonos, 35 km (22 miles) east of Paros.

As your ferry chugs into the harbor, you see before you the white houses of Naxos Town (Chora) on a hill crowned by the one remaining tower of the Venetian castle, a reminder that Naxos was once the proud capital of the Venetian semi-independent Duchy of the Archipelago.

The most ancient settlements of Naxos were directly on the square in front of the Greek Orthodox cathedral. You'll note that several of the churches on this square, including the cathedral itself, hint at Naxos's venerable history, as they are made of ancient materials. In fact, this square was, in succession, the seat of a flourishing Mycenaean town (1300–1050 BC), a classical agora (when it was a 167-foot by 156-foot square closed on three sides by Doric stoas, so that it looked like the letter "G"; a shorter fourth stoa bordered the east side, leaving room at each end for an entrance), a Roman town, and an Early Christian church complex. City, cemetery, tumulus, hero shrine: no wonder the Early Christians built here. For more of ancient Naxos, explore the nearby precinct of Grotta.

Naxos's most famous landmark is its "doorway to nowhere." The Portara is the sole remnant of a gigantic ancient Temple to Apollo.

EXPLORING

TOP ATTRACTIONS

Domus Venetian Museum. Located in the 800-year-old Dellarocca-Barozzi house, the Domus Venetian Museum lets you, at last, into one of the historic Venetian residences. The house, enclosed within the soaring walls of Chora's castle, adjacent to the "Traini," or Great Gate, was first erected in 1207. Inside, the house is like an Naxian attic filled with fascinating objects ranging from the Cycadic period to Victorian times. The museum's entertaining director, Nikos Karavias, personally leads tours through the house, telling stories of the French, Greek, and Venetian roots of the Dellarocca and Barozzi clans. The house's idyllic garden, built into the Kastro wall, provides a regular venue in season for a concert series, from classical to jazz to island music. ⊠ *Naxos Town* ✛ *At Kastro north gate* ☎ *22850/22387* ⊕ *www.naxosfestival.com* 🗹 *€5* ⊗ *Closed Sept.–May.*

Kastro. You won't miss the gates of the castle. The south gate is called the **Paraporti** (side gate), but it's more interesting to enter through the northern gate, or **Trani** (strong), via Apollonos Street. Note the vertical incision in the gate's marble column—it is the Venetian yard against which drapers measured the bolts of cloth they brought to the noblewomen. Step through the Trani into the citadel and enter another age, where sedate Venetian houses still stand around silent courtyards, their exteriors emblazoned with coats of arms and bedecked with flowers. Half are still owned by the original families; romantic Greeks and foreigners have bought up the rest.

The entire citadel was built in 1207 by Marco Sanudo, a Venetian who, three years after the fall of Constantinople, landed on Naxos as part of the Fourth Crusade. When in 1210 Venice refused to grant him independent status, Sanudo switched allegiance to the Latin emperor in Constantinople, becoming duke of the archipelago. Under the Byzantines, "archipelago" had meant "chief sea," but after Sanudo and his successors, it came to mean "group of islands," that is, the Cyclades. For three centuries Naxos was held by Venetian families, who resisted pirate attacks, introduced Roman Catholicism, and later rebuilt the castle in its present form. In 1564 Naxos came under Turkish rule but, even then, the Venetians ran the island, while the Turks only collected taxes. The rust-color Glezos tower was home to the last dukes; it displays the coat of arms: a pen and sword crossed under a crown. ⊠ *Naxos Town.*

Metropolis Site Museum. Built in the square in front of the Metropolitan Cathedral is a small museum that showcases the history of Naxos beginning with the Mycenean era. Displays include pottery, artifacts, and even a tomb from ancient times used to cover the graves of prosperous Naxians. ⊠ *Naxos Town* ☎ *22850/24151* ☾ *Closed Mon.*

Naxos Archaeological Museum. Today the historic convent and school of the Ursulines houses the Naxos Archaeological Museum, best known for its Cycladic and Mycenaean finds. During the Early Cycladic period (3200–2000 BC) there were settlements along Naxos's east coast and outside Naxos Town at Grotta. The finds are from these settlements and graveyards scattered around the island. Many of the vessels exhibited are from the Early Cycladic I period, hand-built of coarse-grain clay, sometimes decorated with a herringbone pattern. Though the museum has too many items in its glass cases to be appreciated in a short visit, you should try not to miss the white marble Cycladic statuettes, which range from the early "violin" shapes to the more-detailed female forms with their tilted flat heads, folded arms, and legs slightly bent at the knees. The male forms are simpler and often appear to be seated. The most common theory is that the female statuettes were both fertility and grave goddesses, and the males were servant figures. ⊠ *Kastro, Kastro* ☎ *22850/22725* ☒ *€3* ☾ *Closed Mon. and Nov.–Mar.*

Fodor's Choice
★

Old Town. A bewildering maze of twisting cobblestone streets, arched porticoes, and towering doorways, the Old Town plunges you alternatively into cool darkness and then suddenly into pockets of dazzling sunshine. The Old Town is divided into the lower section, **Bourgos,** where the Greeks lived during Venetian times, and the upper part, called **Kastro** (castle), still inhabited by the Venetian Catholic nobility. ⊠ *Naxos Town* ⊹ *Along quay, left at first big square.*

Portara. Although the capital town is primarily beloved for its Venetian elegance and picturesque blind alleys, Naxos's most famous landmark is ancient: the Portara, a massive doorway that leads to nowhere. The Portara stands on the islet of **Palatia,** which was once a hill (since antiquity the Mediterranean has risen quite a bit) and in the 3rd millennium BC was the acropolis for a nearby Cycladic settlement. The Portara, an entrance to an unfinished Temple of Apollo that faces exactly toward Delos, Apollo's birthplace, was begun about 530 BC by the tyrant Lygdamis, who said he would make Naxos's buildings the highest and most

Naxos

Aegean Sea

TO MYKONOS

TO PAROS TOWN

PAROS

Cape Stavri

Ayia

Apollonas

Ormos Abram Beach
Abram Village

Koronida/
Komiaki

Lionas

Pachia Ammos Beach

Galini

Engares

Koronos

Ayios
Thaleleos

Kourounochori

Naxos Town

Ayios Georgios

*Ayios
Prokopios*

Miloi

Flerio

Moni
Panayia Drosiani

Moutsouna

*Ayia
Anna*

Galanado

Chalki

Apeiranthos

Ayia Anna

Bellonia
Tower

Potamia

Plaka Beach

**Ayios
Mamas**

Filoti

Bazeos Tower

Sangri

Mikri Vigla Beach

Temple of
Demeter

Zas Cave

MOUNT ZAS

Mikri Vigla

TO
SANTORINI

Kastraki

Psili Ammos

Kastraki Beach

Cheimarros
Pirgos

Pyrgaki

Pyrgaki Beach

Panormos

KOUFONISI

Koufonisi Town

Kato Koufonisi Town

Kalantos

**KATO
KOUFONISI**

KEROS

Cape Katomeri

SHINOUSSA

Aghios
Georgios

Shinoussa
Town

IRAKLIA

0   2 mi

0   2 km

glorious in Greece. He was overthrown in 506 BC, and the temple was never completed; by the 5th and 6th centuries AD it had been converted into a church; and under Venetian and Turkish rule it was slowly dismembered, so the marble could be used to build the castle. The gate, built with four blocks of marble, each 16 feet long and weighing 20 tons, was so large it couldn't be demolished, so it remains today, along with the temple floor. Palatia itself has come to be associated with the tragic myth of Ariadne, princess of Crete.

Ariadne, daughter of Crete's King Minos, helped Theseus thread the labyrinth of Knossos and slay the monstrous Minotaur. In exchange, he promised to marry her. Sailing for Athens, the couple stopped in Naxos, where Theseus abandoned her. Jilted Ariadne's curse made Theseus forget to change the ship's sails from black to white, and so his grieving father Aegeus, believing his son dead, plunged into the Aegean. Seeing Ariadne's tears, smitten Dionysus descended in a leopard-drawn chariot to marry her, and set her bridal wreath, the Corona Borealis, in the sky, an eternal token of his love.

The myth inspired one of Titian's best-known paintings, as well as Strauss's opera *Ariadne auf Naxos*.

North of Palatia, **underwater remains of Cycladic buildings** are strewn along an area called **Grotta**. Here are a series of large worked stones, the remains of the waterfront quayside mole, and a few steps that locals say go to a tunnel leading to the islet of Palatia; these remains are Cycladic (before 2000 BC). ⊠ *Naxos Town* ✛ *At harbor's far edge.*

WORTH NOTING

Bazeos Tower. This 17th-century stonework tower, considered one of Naxos's most beautiful Venetian-era monuments, dominates the landscape as you approach the center of the island by car heading from Naxos Town. It has been renovated as a museum and a cultural space where a full calendar of exhibitions, concerts, and educational seminars take place every summer. ✛ *Between Naxos Town and Agiassos, 12 km (7.5 miles) from Chora toward Chalki* ☎ *22850/31402* ⊕ *www. bazeostower.gr* ▱ *€5* ⟳ *Closed Oct.–May.*

Catholic Cathedral of Naxos. Built by Sanudo in the 13th century, this grand cathedral was restored by Catholic families in the 16th and 17th centuries. The marble floor is paved with tombstones bearing the coats of arms of the noble families. Venetian wealth is evident in the many gold and silver icon frames. The icons reflect a mix of Byzantine and Western influences: the one of the Virgin Mary is unusual because it shows a Byzantine Virgin and Child in the presence of a bishop, a cathedral benefactor. Another 17th-century icon shows the Virgin of the Rosary surrounded by members of the Sommaripa family, whose house is nearby. ⊠ *Kastro.*

Greek Orthodox Cathedral. The Greek Orthodox cathedral was built in 1789 on the site of a church called Zoodochos Pigis (Life-giving Source). The cathedral was built from the materials of ancient temples: the solid granite pillars are said to be from the ruins of Delos. Amid the gold and the carved wood, there is a vividly colored iconostasis painted by a well-known iconographer of the Cretan school,

OFF THE BEATEN PATH

6

Dimitrios Valvis, and the Gospel Book is believed to be a gift from Catherine the Great of Russia. ✉ *Bourgos.*

Naxos Folklore Museum. This little museum shows costumes, ceramics, farming implements, and other items from Naxos's far-flung villages giving an insight into how life was on the island beginning in the 18th century. ✉ *Old Market St.* ☎ *22850/25531* 🌐 *www.naxos-folkmuseum.com* 🎟 *€3* 🕒 *Closed Oct.–Apr.*

SCHOLARLY IMPRINTS

The Convent and School of the Ursulines, a few steps beyond Naxos's cathedral, in the Kastro, was begun in 1739. In a 1713 document, a general of the Jesuits, Francis Tarillon, mentions that the proposed girls' school should be simple; grandeur would expose it to the Turks' covetousness. While it has now been recycled as part of the island's archaeological museum, wealthier Naxian women of a certain age still recall the good education the Ursulines provided.

BEACHES

The southwest coast of Naxos, facing Paros and the sunset, offers the Cyclades' longest stretches of sandy beaches. All the beaches have tavernas in case you get hungry or thirsty, and those directly on the beach may have chairs and umbrellas for rent.

FAMILY **Ayios Georgios Beach.** Essentially an extension of Naxos Town, the easily accessible Ayios Georgios Beach is a popular, developed destination that sees its throng of crowds during the peak summer months. Protected from summer winds, the sandy coastline edges up against shallow waters that make it ideal for kids. The bustle of the main town extends here; restaurants, tavernas, and café bars are all within easy walking distance with views of the sea. It's also an ideal beach scene to take in the sunset. **Amenities:** food and drink. **Best for:** sunset; swimming; walking. ✉ *Ayios Georgios.*

WHERE TO EAT

$$ MEDITERRANEAN 🍴 **Labyrinth.** Labyrinth's more-than-simple food, cozy flagstone garden, and good service are all praiseworthy. A good appetizer is the crunchy, sun-dried-tomato-and-feta tart. **Known for:** extensive wine selection; chicken with shrimp and potatoes; lemon mousse. [$] *Average main: €18* ✉ *Old Town* ☎ *22850/22253* 🕒 *Closed Oct.–Apr. No lunch.*

$$ ITALIAN 🍴 **L'Osteria Wine Bar Restaurant.** A walk up from Naxos harbor, tucked underneath the Old Town walls, L'Osteria offers authentic Italian dishes. Along with welcoming hospitality, dishes, served in a lush little courtyard, include such tasty options as well-plated Italian hams and cheeses, appetizing bruschetta, cool salads, classic pasta dishes, and fresh seafood choices. **Known for:** authentic Italian dishes; hospitable service. [$] *Average main: €20* ✉ *Kastro road* ☎ *22850/24080* 🌐 *www.osterianaxos.com* 🕒 *Closed Nov.–Mar.*

$$ GREEK 🍴 **Metaxi Mas.** In the winding alleys of the Palia Agora in Naxos Town, Metaxi Mas is the local favorite for home-cooked taverna specialties year-round, making the meaning of its name, "just between us," very appropriate. For more than a decade the Flerianos family has focused on the local flavors that Naxos has to offer, including cheese and fresh seafood.

Known for: hearty Naxian specialties; local taverna favorite. [$] *Average main: €18* ✉ *Naxos Town* ☎ *22850/26425* 🌐 *www.metaximas-naxos.gr.*

$$ GREEK 🍴 **Palatia Island.** Right under the island's famous ancient landmark, Apollo's Temple, Palatia Island's special location offers a beautiful summer dining experience. The open-air, elegant dining space showcases a stunning view of Naxos harbor, and as for the dishes, everything is fresh and local. **Known for:** beautiful location; excellent seafood and Naxian dishes. [$] *Average main: €22* ✉ *Naxos Town* ✣ *Near the port, under Apollo's Temple* ☎ *22850/26588* 🌐 *palatiaisland.com.*

$ GREEK Fodor's Choice ★ 🍴 **Popi's Grill.** The oldest family tavern in Naxos, established in 1948, remains true to the Margartis family traditions of cooking authentic Greek dishes with homegrown vegetables and local products. Order (and savor) the fried-cheese appetizer, Naxian *saganaki*, while its hot with a bit of lemon, or the chicken and pork souvlaki served with freshly cut fried Naxian potatoes. **Known for:** old-fashioned charm; good selection of Naxian liquor and local cheeses; complimentary yogurt with honey and lemon for dessert. [$] *Average main: €12* ✉ *Naxos Town* ✣ *On the harbor* ☎ *22850/23741* ⏲ *Closed Nov.–Mar.*

$ FAST FOOD 🍴 **Waffle House.** Offering a variety of creamy rich homemade ice cream, fresh waffles, and mini-sized "waffins," Waffle House has expanded since it opened in Naxos Town to the country's capital in Athens. Nevertheless, the Naxos original is a local favorite, and tables get packed here and at the island's second location in Plaka Beach. **Known for:** dessert waffles; house-made ice cream. [$] *Average main: €6* ✉ *Pigadakia* ✣ *500 meters up from harbor next to the Psari restaurant.*

WHERE TO STAY

$ B&B/INN 🏨 **Apollon.** In addition to being comfortable, charming, and quiet (it's a converted marble workshop), this hotel, in the Fontana quarter, is an easy walking distance to Naxos Town, and it even offers parking, which is a rarity. **Pros:** convenient walking distance to Naxos Town and Old Town; low prices; parking available. **Cons:** rooms can be small; breakfast not included; some rooms may need updating. [$] *Rooms from: €75* ✉ *Fontana area* ✣ *Behind Orthodox cathedral, car entrance on road out of town* ☎ *22850/26801* 🌐 *www.apollonhotel-naxos.gr* 🛏 *11 rooms* 🍽 *No meals.*

$ B&B/INN 🏨 **Chateau Zevgoli.** If you stay in Chora, try to settle in to Despina Kitini's fairy-tale pension, in a comfortable Venetian house that offers distinctive guest rooms and a lovingly appointed salon filled with dark antique furniture, gilded mirrors, old family photographs, and locally woven curtains and tablecloths. **Pros:** sweetly decorated; in a fetching neighborhood; traditional feeling. **Cons:** it is uphill and you must walk to it; no parking; breakfast may not be included. [$] *Rooms from: €75* ✉ *Naxos Town* ✣ *Follow the signs stenciled on walls* ☎ *22850/22993, 22850/26123* 🌐 *www.hotelzevgoli.gr* 🛏 *11 rooms* 🍽 *No meals.*

$$ HOTEL Fodor's Choice ★ 🏨 **Galaxy Hotel.** All whitewash and stone, this hotel is perfect if you want to be on the beach. **Pros:** a full resort hotel; great service; on the beach. **Cons:** too far from major sights, need a car or transfer; may feel crowded when beach is busy; not close to the main conveniences of Naxos Town. [$] *Rooms from: €180* ✉ *Ayios Georgios Beach*

☎ *22850/22422, 22850/22423* ⊕ *www.hotel-galaxy.com* ⊘ *Closed Nov.–Mar.* ⇨ *54 rooms* ⦿ *Breakfast.*

NIGHTLIFE

During the busy summer season, there are numerous cultural events in Naxos Town and also around the island. Important venues include the Catholic Cultural Center, the Domus Venetian Museum, and the Town Hall.

BARS

520. This cool, whitewashed Cycladic style space features a rooftop veranda perfect for sipping eclectic cocktails and traditional Greek liquors, such as masticha. Here's the place to try Greek vodka—yes, it exists. A range of drinks are named after the letters of the Greek alphabet and if you opt for Omega, the last letter, you get the bartender's special surprise. Siblings Argiro and Manos Fotis named this spot 520 for the bar code automatically marked on any products that are made in Greece. ⊠ *Naxos Town* ⊹ *On the harbor.*

Meli and Kanela. The Kioulafis family paid attention to every detail when renovating this family treasure, a simple Cycladic dwelling built more than a century ago. Tucked in the walls of Old Town, Meli and Kanela's bright turquoise door beckons you into its bar lounge and café space that's enhanced by soft lighting, creamy beige-and-white walls, and traditional charm. The name, which means honey and cinnamon in Greek, is a relaxing nightlife spot to chat over a *rakomelo* cocktail featuring honey and cinnamon, served with a large wedge of fresh orange. ⊠ *Naxos Town* ⊹ *On road to Kastro* ☎ *22850/26565* ⊕ *www.melikaikanela.com.*

Naxos Café. Tucked in the Old Town, this romantically lighted little café bar exudes the island's old-world charm and authenticity. It stays open late and sometimes the music is live. A few tables line the alleyway. The Greek coffee is famous here, and it's sometimes open during the day. Opt for a rakomelo at night. ⊠ *Bourgos* ☎ *22850/26343.*

Ocean Club. A lively chunk of Naxos nightlife is set on the south end of the Old Town, where happening bars face the waterfront and gather packed crowds of party people. This is one of them, with ambient decor and DJs that pump mainstream dance hits. Peak season, the party teeters to the edge of the street, right above the sea, where extra bars are set up to accommodate the happy crowds. ⊠ *Naxos Town* ☎ *22850/26766.*

SPORTS AND THE OUTDOORS

WATER SPORTS

Naxos-Surf Club. On Ayios Georgios Beach, just south of the Chora, the Naxos-Surf Club offers windsurfing lessons, equipment rentals, and other water-sports packages. Excursions to other prime windsurfing beaches, as well as mountain-biking trips, are available. ⊠ *Ayios Georgios* ⊹ *15-min walk south of Naxos Town* ☎ *22850/29170* ⊕ *www. naxos-surf.com.*

SHOPPING

The population of Naxos pours into Naxos Town to get their shopping done, so visitors can be sure to find what they are looking for, whether it's fashionable clothing or antiques. Naxians are especially proud of what their land gives them, and many shops sell local products, including honey, liqueurs like citron, and more. Meanwhile, the streets are filled with myriad stores and galleries run by local artists who showcase local artwork, including sculptures and handicrafts. Jewelry stores are also in abundance, selling traditional and more modern Greek designs in gold and silver.

ANTIQUES

Antico Veneziano. Eleni Dellarocca's shop is in the basement of her 800-year-old Venetian house. The columns inside come from Naxos's ancient acropolis. In addition to antiques, she has handmade embroideries, porcelain and glass, mirrors, old chandeliers, and vintage photographs of Naxos. One room is an art gallery, while the other is devoted to Greece's best CDs. ⊠ *Naxos Town* ✛ *In Kastro, down from museum* ☎ *22850/26206.*

BOOKS

Zoom. At Eleftherios Primikirios's bookstore there's an excellent selection of English-language books about Naxos and much else. No other island bookstore is this well stocked. ⊠ *Chora waterfront* ☎ *22850/23675.*

CLOTHING

The Loom. Vassilis and Kathy Koutelieris's store sells casual clothes made from organically grown Greek cotton such as the Earth Collection, which comes in muted natural colors. It features Greek designers, including Moraitis. ⊠ *Dimitriou Kokkou 8* ✛ *In old market, off main square, 3rd street on right* ☎ *22850/25531.*

JEWELRY

Nassos Papakonstantinou. The workshop of Nassos Papakonstantinou, on Old Town's main square, sells one-of-a-kind pieces both sculptural and delicate. His father was a wood-carver; Nassos has inherited his talent. ■TIP➔ **The shop has no sign—that is Nassos's style.** ⊠ *Ayiou Nikodemou* ☎ *22850/22607.*

TRADITIONAL CRAFTS

Argilos. Husband and wife Grigoris and Zetta Argilos are also local Naxian artists who love the island they grew up on. They created this shop to stylishly display their wares, which range from pottery to wall hangings and jewelry. The shop also promotes a diverse and colorful collection of art, jewelry, and ceramics handmade by other Greek artists from Naxos and the Cycladic islands. ⊠ *Naxos Town* ✛ *Entrance to Old Town* ☎ *22850/25244.*

Pocket Gallery. Anglo-Australian expat artist Tim Elkington's small craft and art shop in the Old Town showcases Greek and other expat artists who are inspired by the beauty and culture of Greece. Elkington is a painter, but also sells traditional and modern pottery, cards, ceramics, drawings, jewelry, and clothing that have a connection to Greece. ⊠ *Dimitriou Kokkou and Alexinoros* ☎ *22850/27106.*

Techni. *Techni* translates to "art" in Greek and that's what the shop showcases—locally and traditionally inspired handmade arts and crafts. The collections include jewelry in traditional designs, as well as embroidery and knitted items created by women in Greece's mountain villages. Handmade carpets and linens are also for sale. The family that runs Techni comes from a long line of goldsmiths and embroiderers. ✉ *Old Market* ☎ *22850/24767* ⊕ *www.naxos-art.gr.*

Promponas Wines and Liquors. A large selection of their famous *kitro* (citron liqueur) and preserves, as well as Naxos wines and thyme honey, packed in attractive gift baskets, can be found at Promponas Wines and Liquors, near the Naxos Town waterfront. It has been around since 1915, and free glasses of kitro are offered. ✉ *Dimitris Prombona 1* ☎ *22850/22258.*

AYIA ANNA ΑΓΙΑ ΑΝΝΑ

7 km (4½ miles) south of Naxos Town.

Ayia Anna is one of the island's ideal beach towns, where long stretches of sand front a main road lined with tavernas, restaurants, and cafés.

BEACHES

Ayia Anna Beach. South of Naxos Town, Ayia Anna is a sandy-smooth extension of Ayios Prokopios Beach. A small port, with connections to Paros, often has picturesque little boats docked here. At one point considered a main commercial harbor of the island, today it's a popular beach for water sports and those who want to enjoy the simplicity of its turquoise waters. The small village behind it is filled with restaurants, cafés, and beach bars. Beach chair and umbrella rentals are abundant. **Amenities:** food and drink; water sports. **Best for:** swimming; walking. ✉ *Ayia Anna.*

Ayios Prokopios Beach. This is one of the most popular beaches on the island due to its close proximity to Naxos Town and its long stretch of pure, fine white sand. It features a small leeward harbor with a unique view of small lagoons where herons find refuge. Its position protects it from island winds, so swimming is a calm experience that you don't always find on neighboring beaches. The small village surrounding it is lined with tavernas and cafés. Nudity is allowed in designated areas. **Amenities:** food and drink. **Best for:** nudists; swimming; walking. ✉ *Ayios Prokopios.*

FAMILY **Plaka Beach.** South of town, Plaka Beach is a natural extension of Ayia Anna Beach. It's a gorgeous two-and-half-mile stretch of sand filled with dunes and bamboo groves. Most of the beach is undeveloped, but you can still find sun beds to rent in organized areas. Come early to grab one in the peak season. There is a range of tavernas, restaurants, and café bars within walking distance. **Amenities:** food and drink; water sports. **Best for:** swimming; walking. ✉ *Ayia Anna.*

WHERE TO EAT

$$ ✕ **Gorgona.** Dimitris and Koula Kapris's beachfront taverna is popular
GREEK both with sun worshippers on Ayia Anna Beach and locals from Chora,
Fodor's Choice who come here year-round to get away and sometimes to dance until
★ the late hours, often to live music. The daily-changing menu is extensive and the fresh fish comes from the caïques that pull up at the dock right in front every morning. **Known for:** shrimp saganaki (with cheese); housemade wine; music until late. $ *Average main: €16* ✉ *Ayia Anna* ☎ *22850/41007* ▬ *No credit cards.*

$$ × **Palatia.** Dining by Naxos's pristine beaches is part of truly experiencing
GREEK the island, and Palatia on Ayia Anna Beach fits the bill with traditional fare
Fodor's Choice and a stunning view. Decorated in simple Cycladic style, with tables just
★ steps from the waves, the menu features fresh seafood specialties and Naxian plates created with locally sourced ingredients. **Known for:** scenic beach dining; Naxian specialties and fresh seafood. $ *Average main: €18* ⊠ *Ayia Anna* ☎ *22850/41591* ⊕ *www.palatiarestaurant.com* ☼ *Closed Nov.–Apr.*

WHERE TO STAY

$$ ⊡ **Medusa Beach Resort and Suites.** Rooms and suites here are arranged
HOTEL around a Zen-like garden, and some have sea views, but all guests are
just a stone's throw away from diving into the sea at one of the island's
prettiest sandy beaches. **Pros:** on the beach; lovely garden area; good
on-site restaurant and bar. **Cons:** far from Naxos Town; not much
within walking distance; transfers/car necessary to get to island sights.
$ *Rooms from: €190* ⊠ *Naxos Town* ☎ *22850/75555* ⊕ *www.medusaresort.gr* ☼ *Closed Oct.–May* ⇆ *21 rooms* ⦶*○⦶Breakfast.*

$$ ⊡ **Santana Beach.** This intimate complex of suites and apartments sits
HOTEL right on one of Naxos's most beautiful sandy beaches, Ayia Anna. **Pros:**
Fodor's Choice right on a very nice beach; good service; relaxing beach scene. **Cons:**
★ beach is popular, so can be noisy; not within walking distance to Naxos
Town; car/transfers necessary to get to island sights. $ *Rooms from:
€205* ⊠ *Ayia Anna Beach* ☎ *22850/42841* ⊕ *www.santanabeach.gr*
☼ *Closed Oct.–May* ⇆ *5 rooms* ⦶○⦶*Breakfast.*

SPORTS AND THE OUTDOORS
WINDSURFING
Plaka Watersports. The paradisiacal Plaka Beach is the summer playground for Plaka Watersports. The well-equipped water ski, wakeboard, kneeboard, canoeing, and sailing outfitter also organizes beginner and expert bike-riding tours throughout the most scenic areas of Naxos.
⊠ *Ayia Anna* ☎ *22850/41264* ⊕ *www.plaka-watersports.com.*

MIKRI VIGLA ΜΙΚΡΗ ΒΙΓΛΑ

18 km (11 miles) south of Naxos Town.

Mikri Vigla is a small village known for its nearby pristine beaches. Several small room rentals and a few cafés and beach bars dot the area. Windy days offer the ideal conditions for the windsurfing set.

BEACHES
South of Mikri Vigla are the two beaches farthest from Naxos Town, Kastraki and Pyrgaki.

Kastraki Beach. Although close to the popular beach destinations, Kastraki Beach has kept its tranquil, quiet, and low-key status in place. The long, sandy stretch of beach is essentially a continuation of Mikri Vigla but attracts those who prefer the experience of undeveloped and untouched Greek island beaches. Several designated areas are popular with nudists. **Amenities:** none. **Best for:** nudists; solitude; swimming; walking. ⊠ *Naxos Town.*

Mikri Vigla Beach. The pure white sand here is beautifully offset by a rocky hill, turquoise waters, and large, gentle sand dunes. The beach itself is edged by cedar trees. Here, the fierce island winds are welcome to kitesurfers and windsurfers; Flisvos Kite Centre offers equipment rentals and lessons. Not as developed as other beaches, a scattering of tavernas and cafés that mostly service sports aficionados can be found nearby. **Amenities:** food and drink. **Best for:** surfing; swimming; walking; windsurfing. ☒ *Mikri Vigla.*

Pyrgaki Beach. One of the island's quietest beaches is a stunning, wide cove of fine sand bordered by green cedar trees. Its name comes from a nearby hill that was used to scout for pirates back in the day. Today, its beauty remains untouched by development. Only a few tavernas and restaurants surround this corner of beach, which rarely gets crowded. **Amenities:** none. **Best for:** solitude; swimming. ☒ *Pyrgaki ✣ 18 km (11 miles) south of Naxos Town on a developed main road, then turn onto a dirt road signposted "To Pyrgaki".*

SPORTS AND THE OUTDOORS
WINDSURFING

Flisvos Kite Centre. Right behind Mikri Vigla Beach, the Flisvos Kite Centre takes advantage of the reliably windy days that bless this beach. For a decade, Michele Gasbarro has offered International Kiteboarding Organization–certified lessons, windsurfing lessons, and equipment rentals. The center also runs the Orkos Beach Hotel, which is on-site along with a restaurant and café. ☒ *Orkos Beach Hotel* ☏ *22850/75490* ⊕ *www.flisvos-kitecentre.com.*

GALANADO ΠΥΡΓΟΣ ΤΟΥ ΜΠΕΛΟΝΙΑ

5 km (3 miles) south of Naxos Town.

On a hill, Galando's village streets offer a pretty view toward Naxos Town. It's an agricultural village that is famous for the landmark Tower of Bellonia that faces the eastern side of the island.

EXPLORING

Bellonia Tower. The graceful Bellonia Tower (Pirgos Bellonia) belonged to the area's ruling Venetian family, and like other fortified houses, it was built as a refuge from pirates and as part of the island's alarm system. The towers were located strategically throughout the island; if there was an attack, a large fire would be lighted on the nearest tower's roof, setting off a chain reaction from tower to tower and alerting the islanders. Bellonia's thick stone walls, its Lion of St. Mark emblem, and flat roofs with zigzag chimneys are typical of these towers. ☒ *Galanado.*

"Double Church" of St. John. The unusual 13th-century "double church" of St. John exemplifies Venetian tolerance. On the left side is the Catholic chapel, on the right the Orthodox church, separated only by a double arch. A family lives in the tower, and the church is often open. From here, take a moment to gaze across the peaceful fields to Chora and imagine what the islanders must have felt when they saw pirate ships on the horizon. ☒ *Galanado ✣ In front of Bellonia tower.*

AYIOS MAMAS ΑΓΙΟΣ ΜΑΜΑΣ

3 km (2 miles) south of Galanado, 8 km (5 miles) south of Naxos Town.

A kilometer (½ mile) past a valley with unsurpassed views is one of the island's oldest churches (9th century), Ayios Mamas.

Ayios Mamas. St. Mamas is the protector of shepherds and is regarded as a patron saint in Naxos, Cyprus, and Asia Minor. Built in the 8th century, the stone church was the island's cathedral under the Byzantines. Though it was converted into a Catholic church in 1207, it was neglected under the Venetians and is now falling apart. You can also get to it from the Potamia villages. ⊠ *Ayios Mamas.*

SANGRI ΣΑΓΚΡΙ

3 km (2 miles) south of Ayios Mamas, 11 km (7 miles) south of Naxos Town.

Sangri is the center of an area with so many monuments and ruins spanning the Archaic to the Venetian periods it is sometimes called little Mystras, a reference to the famous abandoned Byzantine city in the Peloponnese.

EXPLORING

Kastro Apilarou. Above the village of Sangri, you can make out the ruins of Kastro Apilarou, the castle of the Italian conquerer, Marco Sanudo, who conquered Naxos after the 4th crusade. The castle was the defensive stronghold for the region, but locals today still say its a bit of a mystery about who the Apilarou family really was before Sanudo came and took over. If you do make the tough climb to view it up close, you'll be greeted with a fantastic view of the Naxian plains. ⊠ *Sangri* ✛ *On Mt. Profitis Ilias.*

Temple of Demeter. This marble Archaic temple, circa 530 BC, was lovingly restored by German archaeologists during the 1990s. Demeter was a grain goddess, and it's not hard to see what she is doing in this beautiful spot. There is also a small museum here (admission is free). ■ TIP➜ **The 25-minute walk here is splendid.** ⊠ *Sangri* ✛ *Take the asphalt road right before the entrance to Sangri.*

Timios Stavros Monastery (*Holy Cross*). The name Sangri is a corruption of Sainte Croix, which is what the French called the town's 16th-century monastery of Timios Stavros. The town is actually three small villages spread across a plateau. During the Turkish occupation, the monastery served as an illegal school, where children met secretly to learn the Greek language and culture. ⊠ *Sangri.*

CHALKI ΧΑΛΚΙ

6 km (4 miles) northeast of Sangri, 17 km (10 miles) southeast of Naxos Town.

You are now entering the heart of the lush Tragaia Valley, where in spring the air is heavily scented with honeysuckle, roses, and lemon blossoms and many tiny Byzantine churches hide in the dense olive groves.

Considered one of the most charming little villages on Naxos, Chalki has some of the most photographed lanes on Naxos. It doesn't take very long to walk through its bougainvillea-drenched lanes and maze of stone paths lined with gently refurbished neoclassical mansions that now serve as charming shops, galleries, and eateries.

EXPLORING

Frangopoulos Tower. Chalki itself is a pretty town, known for its neo-classical houses in shades of pink, yellow, and gray, which are oddly juxtaposed with the plain but stately 17th-century Frangopoulos Tower. Like other towers erected by the Venetians on the island, it was primarily used in its heyday for defense purposes. ⊠ *Main Rd., next to Panayia Protothrone* ⊘ *Hrs vary; enquire locally.*

Panayia Protothrone (*First Enthroned Virgin Church*). With its distinct red-roof, this is one of the most important Byzantine churches. Restoration work has uncovered frescoes from the 6th through the 13th century, and the church has remained alive and functioning for 14 centuries. The oldest layers, in the apse, depict the Apostles. ⊠ *Main Rd.* ⊘ *Closed afternoons.*

Vallindras Distillery. In the back of their quaint neoclassical house, the Vallindras family has supplied Naxos and Greece with citron liqueur from their distillery since 1896. Before you take the free tour, sample various flavors and strengths of the Greek aperitif that is marked with a Protected Destination of Origin (PDO) status. In the distillery room, examine the more-than-100-year-old copper equipment, which continues to produce the island's strong, traditional aperitif. ⊠ *Chalki* ☎ *22850/31220.*

SHOPPING

Era Products. Visit this little jam shop to sample natural jams and Greek fruit preserves, known as spoon sweets, handmade by Yannis Mandenakis; Mandenakis prides himself on only using three ingredients: fruit, sugar, and lemon. You may even catch him working his magic as he mixes, cans, and packages his in-season products right through the screened kitchen door in the shop. ⊠ *Sakelliades Ioannis* ✛ *Off the main street in town* ☎ *22850/31009.*

Fodor'sChoice
★
Fish and Olive Creations. Katherina sells her masterful ceramics and Alexander sells his sensitive jewelry—all with fish or olive motifs. The back room is an impressive little art gallery. ⊠ *Central Plateia* ☎ *22850/31771* ⊕ *www.fish-olive-creations.com.*

Handmade Textiles. Maria Maraki has been looming for decades, and if you're lucky, you may find her sitting at the wheel of her traditional silk and cotton weaving loom behind the shop window. Her creations—cotton table runners, curtains, placemats, and table covers—decorate every corner and wall of the shop. Maraki draws inspiration for her colorful designs from Greek history and her own imagination, but if she's in the shop, ask her to explain her designs. ⊠ *Sakelliades Ioannis* ☎ *22850/32938.*

Phos Gallery. When he's not shooting for the acclaimed Greek film director Theodoros Angelopoulos, photographer Dimitris Gavalas is busy at his own gallery, which he decided to build in his father's hometown of Chalki. His work includes landscapes, panoramics, and conceptual photography. ⊠ *Chalki* ☎ *22850/31118* ⊕ *www.phosgallery.gr.*

MONI ΜΟΝΗ

6 km (4 miles) north of Chalki, 23 km (14 miles) east of Naxos Town.

Off the fine asphalt Chalkiou-Keramotis road, Moni ("monastery") remains high in the mountains overlooking Naxos's greenest valley and has become a popular place for a meal or coffee on a hot afternoon. Local women make embroideries for Naxos Town's shops.

Panayia Drosiani. Just below Moni is one of the Balkans' most important churches, Panayia Drosiani, which has faint, rare Byzantine frescoes from the 7th and 8th centuries. Its name means Our Lady of Refreshment, because once during a severe drought, when all the churches took their icons down to the sea to pray for rain, only the icon of this church got results. The fading frescoes are visible in layers: to the right when you enter are the oldest—one shows St. George the Dragon Slayer astride his horse, along with a small boy, an image one usually sees only in Cyprus and Crete. According to legend, the saint saved the child, who had fallen into a well, and there met and slew the giant dragon that had terrorized the town. Opposite him is St. Dimitrios, shown killing barbarians. The church is made up of three chapels—the middle one has a space for the faithful to worship at the altar rather than in the nave, as became common in later centuries. Next to that is a very small opening that housed a secret school during the revolution. It is open mornings and again after siesta; in deserted winter, ring the bell if it is not open. ⊠ *Moni* ✛ *Off of Chalki–Keramotis road* ☎ *22850/31003.*

FILOTI ΦΙΛΟΤΙ

6 km (4 miles) south of Moni, 20 km (12 miles) southeast of Naxos Town.

Filoti, a peaceful village on the lower slopes of Mt. Zas, is the interior's largest. A three-day festival celebrating the Dormition starts on August 14. In the center of town is another Venetian tower that belonged to the Barozzi and the Church of Filotissa (Filoti's Virgin Mary) with its marble iconostasis and carved bell tower. There are places to eat and rooms to rent.

EXPLORING

Zas Cave. Filoti is the starting place for several walks in the countryside, including the climb up to Zas cave where obsidian tools and pottery fragments have been found; lots of bats live inside. Mt. Zas, or Zeus, is one of the god's reputed birthplaces; on the path to the summit lies a block of unworked marble that reads *Oros Dios Milosiou,* or "Boundary of the Temple of Zeus Melosios." (Melosios, it is thought, is a word that has to do with sheep.) The islanders say that under the Turks the cave was used as a chapel, and two stalagmites are called the Priest and the Priest's Wife, who are said to have been petrified by God to save them from arrest. ⊠ *Filoti* ✛ *Southeast of town on small dirt track.*

APEIRANTHOS ΑΠΕΙΡΑΝΘΟΣ

12 km (7 miles) northeast of Filoti, 32 km (20 miles) southeast of Naxos Town.

Apeiranthos is very picturesque, with views and marble-paved streets running between the Venetian Bardani and Zevgoli towers. As you walk through the arcades and alleys, notice the unusual chimneys—no two are alike. The elders, whose ancestors came from Crete, sit in their doorsteps chatting, while packs of children shout "Hello, hello" at any passerby who looks foreign.

Archaeological Museum. A very small Archaeological Museum, established by a local mathematician, Michael Bardanis, displays Cycladic finds, including statues and earthen pots dug up from the east coast. The most important of the exhibits are unique dark gray marble plaques from the 3rd millennium BC with roughly hammered scenes of daily life: hunters, farmers, and sailors going about their business. ⊠ *Off main square, Aperathos* 🖼 *€3.*

TOWERING VIEWS

The Cheimarros Pirgos (Tower of the Torrent), a cylindrical Hellenistic tower, can be reached from Filoti by a road that begins from the main road to Apeiranthos, outside town, or by a level, three-hour hike with excellent views. The walls, as tall as 45 feet, are intact, with marble blocks perfectly aligned. The tower, which also served as a lookout post for pirates, is often celebrated in the island's poetry: "O, my heart is like a bower/And Cheimarros's lofty tower!"

ABRAM VILLAGE ΧΩΡΙΟ ΑΜΠΡΑΜ

20 km (12 miles) northeast of Naxos Town.

Tucked in a quiet, rocky northern part of the island, Abram is a small village built around a shore that curves into attractive bays and small beaches surrounding Abram Bay. A few vineyards are scattered around the area, as well as a few small tavernas and lodging options.

WHERE TO STAY

$

B&B/INN

🖼 **Abram Village.** If you love island nature and dislike crowds, this is your place—set on Naxos's northern coast, Panyiotis Albertis's rooms and villas recline in a green garden on beautiful Abram Beach: the scenery is extraordinary and there are many coves with beaches. **Pros:** right on the sea; in a beautiful area; great for peace and quiet. **Cons:** isolated location; breakfast not included; not near the major sights of Naxos. 🖼 *Rooms from: €60* ⊠ *Abram* ✛ *20 km (12 miles) from Naxos Town* 🖀 *22850/63244* ⊕ *www.abram.gr* ⊘ *Closed Oct.–Apr.* ⤳ *8 rooms* ❢⦶ *No meals.*

FOLEGANDROS ΦΟΛΕΓΑΝΔΡΟΣ

180 km (112 miles) southeast of Piraeus harbor in Athens, 86 km (53 miles) northwest of Santorini.

If Santorini didn't exist, little, bare Folegandros would be world famous. Its gorgeous Cycladic main town of Chora, built between the walls of a Venetian fort, sits on the edge of a beetling precipice: this hilltop setting represents, with the exception of Santorini, the finest cliff-side scenery in the Cyclades. Beyond this, the island does not seem to have much to offer on paper—but in person it certainly does. Beautiful and authentic, it has become the secret island of Cyclades lovers, who find here a pure dose of the magic essence of the Aegean. Only 31 square km (12 square miles) in area and 64 km (40 miles) in circumference, it lacks ruins, villages, green valleys, trees, country houses, and graceful cafés at the edge of the sea. But what the island does have—one of the most stunning towns, deliberately downplayed touristic development, several good beaches, quiet evenings, traditional local food, and respectful visitors—make it addictive. There are no discos, no bank, but the sea is shining and, in spring, much of the island is redolent of thyme and oregano.

Visitors to Folegandros—historians are divided on whether the name immortalizes the Cretan explorer Pholegandrus or comes from the Phoenician term for "rock-strewn"—mostly stay in or near the main town, and hang around the town's three squares. A walk, a swim at the beach, a visit to the little Folklore Museum at Ano Meria, meeting other people who love the essence of the Greek islands: these require few arrangements. Unless you want to stop on the side of the road to look at views (the island does offer an array of interesting hiking trails), the bus is adequate. There are a number of beaches—Angali and Ayios Nikolaos are especially good. Because Folegandros is so small, it fills up fast in August, and despite the absence of raucous nightlife, it somewhat loses its special flavor.

GETTING HERE AND AROUND

Little islands like Folegandros used to get two or three boats a week. Tourism, however, has changed all that, at least in summer, and Folegandros is firmly in the loop. There are no flights here, but two daily boats from Piraeus in summer—fewer in winter—serve the island sufficiently. There are also regular connections to Anafi, Ios, Amorgos, Kea, Kimolos, Koufonisi, Kythnos Milos, Naxos, Paros, Serifos, Sifnos, Sikinos, and Santorini. For schedules check ⊕ *www.openseas.gr* or ⊕ *www.gtp.gr*. Faster boats are added on weekends but don't run in winter. The trip from Piraeus takes from 4 to 11 hours.

Buses, which meet the boats, go from the little port to Chora every hour or so throughout the day. Buses go almost as often to the southern beaches and to Ano Meria (which has a separate Chora bus stop near the Sottovento tourist office). Fares run from €1.50 to €2.50. Taxis (☎ *22890/22400 or 22860/41048*) meet boats and a stand is at the town entrance.

TOURS

Contacts Folegandros Travel. ☎ *22860/41273* ⊕ *www.folegandros-travel.gr.* **Sottovento.** ✉ *Main square, Chora* ☎ *69/39498972* ⊕ *www.folegandrosisland.com.*

A Water-Sports Paradise

When it comes to the Cyclades, anyone who invests in a mask, snorkel, and flippers has entry to intense, serene beauty. But even without this underwater gear, this archipelago is a swimmer's paradise.

Most of the Cycladic islands gleam with beaches, from long blond stretches of sand to tiny pebbly coves. The best beaches are probably those on the southwest coast of Naxos. Beaches on Tinos tend to be less crowded than those on other islands in the Cyclades. The strands on Santorini, though strewn with plenty of bathers, are volcanic; you can bask on sands that are strikingly red and black.

As for water sports, there are many options to entice sunseekers. Waterskiing, parasailing, scuba diving, and especially windsurfing have become ever more popular. Note that many water-sports venues change from season to season.

CHORA ΧΩΡΑ

42 km (26 miles) northwest of Santorini.

As the boat approaches the little port of Karavostasi, bare, sun-scoured cliffs—with a hint of relieving green in wet winter but only gray glare in summer—let you know where you are. Leaving the port immediately, since there is hardly anything here, visitors climb the road 3 km (2 miles) to Chora on buses (which meet all ferries). On the rugged way up, you'll see the spectacular, whitewashed **church of Komisis tis Theotkou** (or Dormition of the Mother of God) dominating the town on the high cliff where the ancient settlement first stood. On Easter Sunday the chief icon is carried through the town.

After a steep ride, cliff-top Chora comes into view. Its sky-kissing perch is well out of sight of the port, an important consideration in the centuries when the seas here were plagued by pirate raiders. Today, Chora—small, white, old, and preserved lovingly by the islanders—is less hidden and is known as the main reason to visit the island. Its main street, starting at the bus stop (no cars in town) meanders through five little squares—the middle three are the main ones—each with a few restaurants and cafés shaded by bougainvillea and hibiscus. Some of the buildings are set into the walls of the Venetian fort, or Kastro, built by the Venetian duke of Naxos in the 13th century. The second street circles the Kastro and the precipice on which the town stands and is strikingly lined with two-story cube houses that form a wall atop the towering cliff. The glory days of Venice came to an end in 1715, when the ruling Turks sacked Folegandros and sold the captives as slaves. The old families go back to 1780, when the island was repopulated.

WHERE TO EAT

$ ✕ **O Kritikos.** Set under a tree and abutting a Byzantine church, this
GREEK   simple little taverna serves exclusively local meats and vegetables. Souroto, a local cheese, makes a fitting appetizer. *Kontosouli* is usually pork on the spit; here it is a mixture of lamb and pork, and delicious.

Perched at a nearly angelic height, the Church of the Dormition of the Mother of God lords it over Folegandros's main town.

Known for: local specialities; pleasing location. [$] *Average main: €10* ✉ *Middle Sq.* ☎ *22860/41219* 💳 *No credit cards.*

$ GREEK 🍴 **Piatsa.** This middle-square eatery has tables set out under trees. Specialties include kalasouna cheese pies and homemade noodles (called *matsata*) with pork or lamb. **Known for:** local dishes; shady and relaxed outdoor dining. [$] *Average main: €10* ✉ *Middle Sq.* ☎ *22860/41274* 💳 *No credit cards.*

WHERE TO STAY

$$$ HOTEL Fodor's Choice ★ 🏨 **Anemomilos Apartments.** Perched on the towering cliff overlooking the sea and set amid a series of small garden terraces, this complex with truly breathtaking vistas of sea and sky, is the best place to stay in Folegandros. **Pros:** welcoming hospitality; beautiful pool; nice bar and restaurant. **Cons:** some apartments can feel closed in; quite expensive for the island; some rooms may need updating. [$] *Rooms from: €270* ✉ *Chora* ✣ *Edge of town* ☎ *22860/41309* 🌐 *www.anemomilosapartments.com* 🕓 *Closed Oct.–May* 🛏 *17 rooms* 🍽 *Breakfast.*

$ HOTEL 🏨 **Meltemi Hotel.** Whitewashed and spotless, these good-sized and simply furnished rooms open to verandas and are at the edge of Chora, making this little inn convenient to restaurants and the bus stop for the port, beaches, and other points on the island. **Pros:** pleasant and convenient; good basic accommodations; traditional-style rooms. **Cons:** no sea view; no pool; no amenities. [$] *Rooms from: €100* ✉ *Chora* ☎ *22860/41068* 💳 *No credit cards* 🕓 *Closed Nov.–Feb.* 🛏 *11 rooms* 🍽 *No meals.*

SHOPPING
JEWELRY

Creations Folegandros. Apostolos and Eleni have been creating their striking jewelry, fashioned from silver and gold and often with Greek stones, for more than 30 years. They also sell some work by other artists. ⊠ *Middle Sq.* ☎ *22860/41524* ⊕ *www.creations-folegandros. gr* ☉ *Closed Oct.–Apr.*

ANO MERIA ΑΝΩ ΜΕΡΙΑ

5 km (3 miles) northwest of Chora.

The paved road connects the port, the capital, and, after a short drive, Ano Meria. On the way there, you can see terraces where barley was coaxed seemingly from stone, though there is little farming now. The tiny town is a smaller version of Chora, and the cafés are perfect places for a drink.

Folklore Museum. Exhibits reconstruct traditional farming life. The adjacent church of Agios Panteliemon celebrates the feast day of Saint Panteliemon on July 27, and almost everyone goes. ⊠ *Ano Meria* ☎ *22860/41069* ☜ *€2.*

SANTORINI (THIRA) ΣΑΝΤΟΡΙΝΗ (ΘΗΡΑ)

235 km (146 miles) southeast of Piraeus harbor in Athens.

Undoubtedly the most extraordinary island in the Aegean, crescent-shaped Santorini remains a mandatory stop on the Cycladic tourist route—even if you must enjoy the sensational sunsets from Ia, the fascinating excavations, and the dazzling white towns with a million other travelers. Called Kllisti (the "Loveliest") as long ago as ancient times, the island has now reverted officially to its subsequent name of Thira, after the 9th-century-BC Dorian colonizer Thiras. The place is better known these days, however, as Santorini, a name derived from its patroness, St. Irene of Thessaloniki, the Byzantine empress who restored icons to Orthodoxy and died in 802.

Flying to Santorini from Athens and many other cities is the most convenient way to get here, but to enjoy a true Santorini rite of passage, opt instead for the boat trip, which provides a spectacular introduction. After the boat sails between Sikinos and Ios, your deck-side perch approaches two close islands with a passage between them. The bigger one on the left is Santorini, and the smaller on the right is Thirassia. Passing between them, you see the village of Ia adorning Santorini's northernmost cliff like a white geometric beehive. You are in the caldera (volcanic crater), one of the world's truly breathtaking sights: a crescent of cliffs rising 1,100 feet, with the white clusters of the towns of Fira and Ia perched along the top. The bay, once the high center of the island, is 1,300 feet in some places, so deep that when boats dock in Santorini's shabby little port of Athinios, they do not drop anchor (as if placed there to emphasize the depths, a sunken ocean liner lies eerily submerged beneath the surface). The encircling cliffs are the ancient rim of a still-active volcano, and you are sailing east across its flooded caldera. On your right are the Burnt Isles, the White Isle, and other volcanic remnants, all lined up as if some outsize display in a geology museum. Hephaestus's subterranean fires smolder still—the volcano erupted in 198 BC, about 735, and there was an earthquake in 1956.

Indeed, Santorini and its four neighboring islets are the fragmentary remains of a larger landmass that exploded about 1600 BC: the volcano's core blew sky high, and the sea rushed into the abyss to create the great bay, which measures 10 km by 7 km (6 miles by 4½ miles) and is 1,292 feet deep. The other pieces of the rim, which broke off in later eruptions, are Thirassia, where a few hundred people live, and deserted little Aspronissi ("White Isle"). In the center of the bay, black and uninhabited, two cones, the Burnt Isles of Palea Kameni and Nea Kameni, appeared between 1573 and 1925.

There has been too much speculation about the identification of Santorini with the mythical Atlantis, mentioned in Egyptian papyri and by Plato (who says it's in the Atlantic), but myths are hard to pin down. This is not true of old arguments about whether tidal waves from Santorini's cataclysmic explosion destroyed Minoan civilization on Crete, 113 km (70 miles) away. The latest carbon-dating evidence, which points to a few years before 1600 BC for the eruption, clearly indicates that the Minoans outlasted the eruption by a couple of hundred years, but most probably in a weakened state. In fact, the island still endures hardships: since antiquity, Santorini has depended on rain collected in cisterns for drinking and irrigating—the well water is often brackish—and the serious shortage is alleviated by the importation of water. Nevertheless, the volcanic soil also yields riches: small, intense tomatoes with tough skins used for tomato paste (good restaurants here serve them); the famous Santorini fava beans, which have a light, fresh taste; barley; wheat; and white-skin eggplants.

These days, unrestrained tourism has taken a heavy toll on Santorini. Fira, and now Ia, could almost be described as "a street with 40 jewelry shops"; many of the natives are completely burned out by the end of the peak season (the best times to come here are shoulder periods); and, increasingly, business and the loud ringing of cash registers have disrupted the normal flow of Greek life here. For example, if a cruise ship comes in during afternoon siesta, all shops immediately open. And you will have a pushy time walking down Fira's main street in August, so crowded is it. Still and all, if you look beneath the layers of gimcrack tourism, you'll find Greek splendor. No wonder Greece's two Nobel poets, George Seferis and Odysseus Elytis, wrote poems about it. For you, too, will be "watching the rising islands / watching the red islands sink" (Seferis) and consider, "With fire with lava with smoke / You found the great lines of your destiny" (Elytis).

GETTING HERE AND AROUND

The bay of Santorini is one of the world's great sights, and an incoming flight—45 minutes from Athens—gives a unique view of it. There are 12 daily flights, shared by Olympic Air, Athens Airways, and Aegean

Airlines. There are also flights from Thessaloniki and from other European cities. Reservations, the earlier the better, are essential.

As many as six daily boats from Athens's port of Piraeus ply the wine-dark Aegean to Santorini. The trip takes 4 to 10 hours, depending on route, boat, and the weather. Try to make sure your boat enters the harbor before sunset (usually an early-morning departure from Piraeus), since this is a spectacular sight, one crucial to savoring Santorini's vibe. There are also daily connections to Paros, Naxos, and Anafi, and there are regular summer connections to Folegandros, Crete, Ios, Karpathos, Kasos, Amorgos, Kea, Kimolos, Kos, Koufonisi, Kythnos, Milos, Mykonos, and Rhodes. Reservations are needed in summer and at Easter, and for cars year-round. The port town, Ormos Athinios, is only that, and you must proceed by vehicle to your destination. Buses generally meet the boats, and the drive up the volcano-cut cliff is amazing.

Buses leave from the main depot in central Fira just south of the town's main square. In high season, there are hourly buses for Akrotiri and buses on the half hour for Ia, Monolithos (airport), Kamari, and Perissa. Buses also connect with the main port of Athinios (at least a half-hour ride) as well as the popular Perissa and Kamari beaches. Schedules are posted; hotel concierges should also have this info. Fares run from €1.50 to €4. As might be expected, Santorini's buses can be as crowded as those of rush-hour Athens, so step lively! The main taxi station is near Fira's central square on Odos 25 Martiou. Connecting Fira with the harbor port of Fira Skala is the island's famed cable-car route, with its spectacular vistas. This is a must-do (a must-don't are the donkey treks up the cliff), even if you're not using the port facilities—but avoid times when cruise-ship passengers are trying to get back down to their tenders and lines can be impossibly long.

Contacts Fira Bus Station. ⊠ *Near main square, Fira* ☎ *22890/25404* ⊕ *ktel-santorini.gr.* **Fira Taxi Station.** ⊠ *Odos 25 Martiou, near main square, Fira* ☎ *22860/22555.* **Santorini Cable Car.** ⊠ *Town center, Fira* ⊕ *scc.gr.* **Santorini Port Authority.** ☎ *22860/22239* ⊕ *www.santorini-port.com.*

TOURS

Nomikos Travel. This agency has tours to the main sights along with some off-the-beaten-path attractions, including the island's wineries and the Monastery of Profitis Ilias. ⊠ *Fira* ☎ *22860/23887.*

Pelican Travel. This popular agency runs bus tours, wine tastings, and visits to Ia; it also has daily boat trips to the volcano and Thirassia and arranges private tours. ⊠ *Odus 25 Martiou, Fira* ☎ *22860/22220* ⊕ *www.pelican.gr.*

Santorini Wine Tours. Vaios Panagiotoulas, a professional sommelier, is your guide on an informative and fun tour of some of the island's leading wineries. Vaios chooses wineries that produce a variety of wines, giving a wide-ranging introduction to many distinct varieties. The tour includes a look at the wine-making process and a drive through vineyards, but the emphasis is on tasting and lively, highly enlightening discussion. The tour includes hotel pickup in a comfortable minibus. ⊠ *General Tourist Office, Fira* ☎ *22860/28358* ⊕ *www.santoriniwinetour.com.*

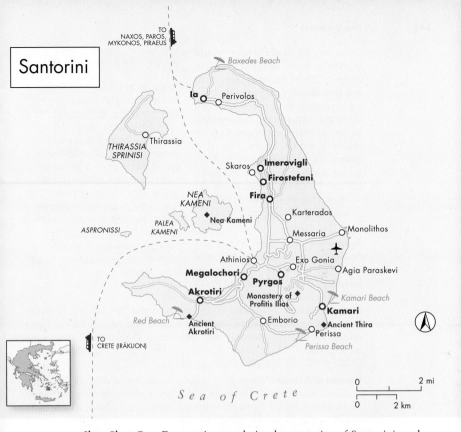

Shotz Photo Tour. For a unique and visual perspective of Santorini, and an opportunity to take great shots, too, book a half- or whole-day tour with professional photographer Olaf Reinen. Reinen, a New Zealand expat, lives on the island and aims to show off what has come to be one of the most photographed destinations in the world while offering tips on taking photographs using a DSLR or an iPhone. Tours are small and intimate (up to four people who are traveling together) and can cover a range of photo-enthusiast topics. ✉ *Ia* ☎ *22860/83278* ⊕ *www. santoriniphototours.com* ✉ *From €375 for 1 to 2 people.*

FIRA ΦHPA

76 km (47 miles) southeast of Paros, 10 km (6 miles) west of the Santorini airport, 14 km (8½ miles) southeast of Ia.

Tourism is Santorini's major industry and adds more than 1 million visitors per year to a population of 7,000. As a result, Fira, the capital, midway along the west coast of the east rim, is no longer only a picturesque village but a major tourist center, overflowing with bars, shops, and restaurants. Many of its employees—often Eastern Europeans or young travelers extending their summer vacations—hardly speak Greek. To experience life here as it was until only a couple of decades ago, walk down the much-photographed, winding staircase that descends from town to the water's edge—walk (carefully, trying to avoid the many slippery mule droppings) or take the spectacular cable car ride back up, avoiding the drivers who will try to plant you on the sagging back of one of their bedraggled-looking mules. It soon becomes clear what brings the tourists here: with its white, cubical houses clinging to the cliff hundreds of feet above the caldera, Fira is a beautiful place, an exhilarating Greek extravaganza.

EXPLORING

Archaeological Museum. This dusty collection of bits and pieces from island's millennia of history includes pottery, statues, and grave artifacts found mostly at excavations in ancient Thira and Akrotiri, from the Minoan through the Byzantine periods. Should you have time or inclination for only one museum visit on Santorini, the Museum of Prehistoric Thera is far more riveting. ⊠ *Stavrou and Nomikos, Mitropoleos, behind big church* ☎ *22860/22217* ⊕ *www.culture.gr* ⊠ *€3.*

> ### AVOID THE MULES
>
> Tourist touts still like to promote mules as a mode of transportation to take you up the zigzag cliff path to the island capital of Fira. But animal-rights groups would prefer you didn't, as would Fodor's, though the decision is ultimately up to the individual traveler. And you should be aware of another reason: the mules on Santorini are piously believed to contain souls of the dead, who are thus doing their purgatory. It is to say the least an arduous ascent, and best done with the tramway.

Museum of Prehistoric Thera. This is the treasure house that displays frescoes and other artifacts from the famed excavations at Akrotiri. Many of the finds have been sent off to the Archaeological Museum in Athens, but the most charming fresco remains here: a colorful depiction of women in dresses gathering saffron from the stamens of crocuses. Also in this small collection are fresco fragments with the famous painted swallows, the island's favorite design motif, that still flock to Santorini to roost on the cliffs. The fossilized olive leaves from 60,000 BC prove the olive to be indigenous. ⊠ *Fira* ✛ *Mitropoleos, behind big church* ☎ *22860/22217* ⊕ *www.odysseus.culture.gr* ⊠ *€2; €14 for combo ticket for the archaeological sites and museum in Thira* ☉ *Closed Tues.*

Panayia Ypapantis. The modern Greek Orthodox cathedral is a major landmark; many businesses in Fira list their addresses simply as "near the cathedral." You'll quickly note how the local priests, with somber faces, long beards, and black robes, look strangely out of place in summertime, tourist-jammed Fira. ⊠ *Fira* ✛ *Southern part of town.*

Petros M. Nomikos Conference Center. Upper Fira's exhibition hall, named for the famous ship owner, hosts many international conferences as well as concerts. Visitors can admire acclaimed seasonal exhibitions that reflect the culture and nature of the island through painting and sculpture. ⊠ *Caldera path, just north of cable car* ☎ *22860/23017* ⊕ *www.thera-conferences.gr* ⊠ *€4.*

OFF THE BEATEN PATH

Nea Kameni. To peer into a live, sometimes smoldering volcano, join one of the popular excursions to Nea Kameni, the larger of the two Burnt Isles. After disembarking, you hike 430 feet to the top and walk around the edge of the crater, wondering if the volcano is ready for its fifth eruption during the last 100 years—after all, the last was in 1956. Some tours continue on to the island of Therassia, where there is a village. Many operators on the island offer volcano tours.

WHERE TO EAT

$$ GREEK 🍴 **Naoussa.** Old-fashioned Greek fare, made with care and served by a friendly and accommodating staff, can be enjoyed on a breezy balcony; tables at one end get a caldera view. Starters include tomato fritters and rich fava dip. **Known for:** traditional Greek plates; beautiful view. [$] *Average main: €16* ✉ *Fira* ✣ *On caldera, near cathedral* ☎ *22860/21277* 🌐 *www.naoussa-restaurant.com.*

$$ GREEK 🍴 **Taverna Nikolas.** This sparsely decorated taverna right in the center of Fira has been serving strictly traditional fare since the days when the only way to town was on foot or the back of a donkey. The moussaka is reputed to be one of the best on the island, and lamb with lemon sauce is a regular special not to be missed. **Known for:** no-fuss traditional Greek plates; classic moussaka. [$] *Average main: €15* ✉ *Fira* ✣ *Near the main square* 💳 *No credit cards.*

WHERE TO STAY

When you book a room, remember that many of Santorini's hotel cliff-side balconies elbow each other out of the way for the best view and, with footpaths often running above and beside them, privacy is often hard to come by.

$$$$ RENTAL Fodor's Choice ★ 🏨 **Aigialos Hotel.** A cluster of buildings from the 18th and 19th centuries comprises the most comfortable and discreetly luxurious—as well as the most poetic and serenely quiet—place to stay in Fira. **Pros:** not a phony place set up for tourists; quiet elegance; friendly, discreet service. **Cons:** some steps, but fewer than elsewhere; the pool is tiny; for the price, not all rooms have a view. [$] *Rooms from: €450* ✉ *Fira* ✣ *South end of cliff-side walkway* ☎ *22860/25191* 🌐 *www.aigialos.gr* 🕓 *Closed Nov.–Mar.* 🛏 *15 rooms* 🍽 *Breakfast.*

$$$ B&B/INN 🏨 **Aroma Suites.** Caldera views come at an especially good value in either small white cave-rooms with vaulted ceilings or large cave suites, all nicely decorated with warm touches of color and sleek marble fixtures, and sharing a terrace overlooking the caldera. **Pros:** very attractive; small and friendly; perfect for guests who want a caldera view but aren't high rollers. **Cons:** those stairs; rooms are close together; breakfast is extra. [$] *Rooms from: €230* ✉ *Caldera walkway* ☎ *22860/24112* 🌐 *www.aromasuites.com* 🛏 *6 suites* 🍽 *No meals.*

$$$$ HOTEL 🏨 **Hotel Aressana.** Though there's no view of the caldera, a slant of sea view is effulgently wonderful—add in the large freshwater pool, excellent service, and location in central Fira, and the sum total makes these large, bright rooms a very popular option. **Pros:** driving to the door avoids steps; stylish whitewashed design; very comfortable and sparkling. **Cons:** no caldera view; some steps required to get around the hotel; no sea view at the pool. [$] *Rooms from: €325* ✉ *Fira* ✣ *South end of cliff-side walkway* ☎ *22860/23900* 🌐 *www.aressana.gr* 🕓 *Closed Nov.–Mar.* 🛏 *50 rooms* 🍽 *Breakfast.*

6

$$$
B&B/INN

🏠 **Hotel Villa Renos.** Huge terraces, shady porticoes, and a small but dramatic cliff-hanging pool all take advantage of spectacular caldera views, while the large, elegantly furnished rooms are pleasant retreats from the madness of the crowded center of Fira, just a few steps away. **Pros:** nice sense of quiet despite the central location; outstanding hospitality; fantastic views of the caldera. **Cons:** steps, but fewer than at many other properties; small pool; Fira is a busy place. $ *Rooms from: €240* ⊠ *Fira* ✛ *Off caldera walkway, near central square* ☎ *22860/22848* ⊕ *www. villarenos.com* ⊗ *Closed Nov.–Mar.* ⮑ *9 rooms* ⦿| *Breakfast.*

$$
B&B/INN

🏠 **Keti Hotel.** A stay in these traditional cave rooms puts you right in the center of Fira, but well below the bustle—a climb down a staircase leads to a quiet, intimate cliff-side aerie where charming vaulted rooms open to a welcoming veranda clinging to the cliff face above the old port. **Pros:** intimate little enclave with fantastic views; loaded with traditional charm; great rates for caldera view. **Cons:** lots of steps; no luxe amenities; transfers are extra. $ *Rooms from: €180* ⊠ *Fira* ✛ *Off caldera walkway below central square* ☎ *22860/22324* ⊕ *www.hotelketi.gr* ⊗ *Closed Nov.–Mar.* ⮑ *9 rooms* ⦿| *Breakfast.*

$$$
HOTEL

🏠 **Panorama Boutique Hotel.** These very pleasant rooms, in the center of Fira, combine traditional design with contemporary touches, proving that it's possible to enjoy a caldera view without breaking the bank—and without dealing with steps. **Pros:** convenient for taxis and buses; elevator makes access easy; nice design. **Cons:** some rooms are quite small; steps to the pool; busy surroundings. $ *Rooms from: €250* ⊠ *Fira* ✛ *On caldera, near central square* ☎ *22860/21760* ⊕ *www. panoramahotel.com.gr* ⊗ *Closed Dec.– Feb.* ⮑ *30 rooms* ⦿| *Breakfast.*

$$
HOTEL

🏠 **Pelican Hotel.** The neighborhood isn't pretty, but these rooms just down from the busy main (Theotokopoulou) square on Danezi Street are decent and the cost is very competitive for Santorini. **Pros:** very efficient and inexpensive; good restaurant next door; no steps to get to hotel. **Cons:** in a busy neighborhood away from the caldera; a city-hotel feeling; no caldera views. $ *Rooms from: €135* ⊠ *Fira* ✛ *On cobblestone road up from main traffic street, near town hall* ☎ *22860/23114* ⊕ *www.pelicanhotel.gr* ⮑ *18 rooms* ⦿| *Breakfast.*

NIGHTLIFE AND PERFORMING ARTS

BARS AND PUBS

Franco's Bar. Boasting a caldera view, the popular bar with a terrace plays classical music and serves Champagne cocktails. ⊠ *Fira* ✛ *Below cliff-side walkway* ☎ *22860/24428* ⊕ *www.francos.gr.*

DANCING

Casablanca Soul. Santorini's "second" club, after the more popular Koo, offers a live music program on weekends and music played by DJs other nights, always accompanied by excellent cocktails. ⊠ *Fira* ✛ *Near the central square* ☎ *22860/27188* ⊕ *www.casablancasoul.com.*

Koo Club. For Fira, this is Party Central and the township's most popular outdoor club by far. ⊠ *Fira* ✛ *North end of cliff-side walkway* ☎ *22860/22025* ⊕ *www.kooclub.gr.*

FESTIVALS

Santorini Jazz Festival. The island's big music festival fights for funds but keeps swinging, with performances near the beach in Kamari during July. ✉ *Kamari.*

Santorini Music Festival. Thank pianist Athena Capodistria for September's Santorini Music Festival, which always includes internationally known musicians. ✉ *Nomikos Conference Center, Firostefani* ☎ *22860/23166.*

SHOPPING

Despite the proliferation of shops displaying their wares on the street that can make Fira seem like a souk, you probably will not be too tempted by the goods on offers. T-shirts and cheap trinkets are, sadly, the norm, and shops selling fine jewelry and crafts for which the island was known in the early days of tourism are rare these days. With a little searching, however, you will come upon some treasures.

GALLERIES

AK Art Gallery. Christoforos Asimis studied painting at Athens University, and has had many exhibitions there and abroad. The nearby cathedral's murals are his. His paintings specialize in the light and landscape of his home island. His wife, Eleni Kollaitou, who also studied in Athens, creates some of Santorini's most elegant jewelry, bronze sculptures, and ceramics. ✉ *Ypapantis walkway* ☎ *22860/23041* ⊕ *www.ak-galleries.com.*

Mati. There's a Greek exuberance to the work of Yorgos Kypris, accentuated by a bright, airy perch high above the caldera. In his sculptural creations in glass, clay, and other natural materials, seabirds flock and fish swirl in schools; some designs are also available as jewelry and bowls. ✉ *Cathedral Sq.* ☎ *22860/23814* ⊕ *www.matiartgallery.com.*

Nikola's Art Gallery. Objets d'art are made from highly polished semi-precious stones and glow with color and form. Pantelis and Nikola Kaloteraki can also create jewelry in the stone of your choice. Vases, sculptures, and many other distinctive pieces also fill the shop, which has been a presence in Santorini for more than a quarter of a century. ✉ *Fira* ✛ *Town center* ☎ *22860/22283* ⊕ *www.nikolas-santorini.com.*

JEWELRY

Fodor's Choice
★

Bead Shop. Marina Tsiagkouri's shop has expanded with worry beads and some ready-made trinkets, but beads are still the main reason to go. Marina's unique beads are made from Santorini's volcanic rock, wood, and other natural materials. ✉ *Fira* ✛ *Opposite entrance to Museum of Prehistoric Thera* ☎ *22860/25176.*

Kostas Antoniou Jewelry. Many of Kostas's exquisite gold necklaces and bracelets take their inspiration from the art of ancient Thira and Crete. The shop also sells excellent wines from the family's Antoniou vineyards just south of Fira around Megalochori. ✉ *Fira* ✛ *In Spiliotica shopping area, near Archaeological Museum* ☎ *22860/22633* ⊕ *antoniousantorini.com.*

Sophia's Art Jewelry. Easily above the standard glitter of Santorini, Sophia's sells gold jewelry from several Greek workshops. Letting her work speak for itself, Sophia Koutsogiannopoulou has no website or email, nor does she stand at the doorway of her quiet shop (a block in from the cable-car) soliciting customers. ✉ *Fira* ✛ *Near cable car* ☎ *22860/23587.*

FIROSTEFANI ΦΗΡΟΣΤΕΦΑΝΙ

1 km (½ mile) northwest of Fira.

Firostefani used to be a separate village, but now it comprises the quieter, more pleasant northern end of Fira. The 10-minute walk between central Fira and Firostefani, along the caldera, is one of Santorini's highlights. From Firostefani's single white cliff-side street, walkways descend to traditional vaulted cave houses, which are fast becoming pensions. Though close to the action, Firostefani feels calm and quiet.

WHERE TO EAT

$$ GREEK 🍴 **Aktaion.** In his tiny taverna, Vangelis Roussos uses mostly recipes his family used when the place opened around a hundred years ago, including moussaka with white eggplant and a Salad Santorini made with caper leaves. Outdoor tables overlook the caldera; inside, the paintings on the walls are Vangelis's own. **Known for:** local favorite; traditional Santorini meals; nice view. [$] *Average main: €17* ✉ *Main square* ☎ *22860/22336* 🌐 *www.aktaionsantorini.com.*

WHERE TO STAY

$$$$ RESORT 🏨 **Agali Houses.** Firostefani is a 10-minute walk north from the center of Fira but a world apart; a quiet enclave with handsomely furnished, arch-roofed houses spreading down the cliff side on a series of dramatic terraces. **Pros:** lots of white curves and sumptuous sea views; large, attractive, well-appointed accommodations; privacy. **Cons:** many steps to reach the entrance; many steps to get around the hotel itself; Wi-Fi only in public areas. [$] *Rooms from: €357* ✉ *Firostefani* ✣ *Off the main street* ☎ *22860/22811* 🌐 *www.agalihouses.gr* 🕓 *Closed Nov.–Apr.* 🛏 *30 rooms* 🍽 *Breakfast.*

$ B&B/INN 🏨 **Reverie Traditional Apartments.** Only a suite and the roof garden have caldera views, but everything about the whitewashed and tiled surroundings in this former family home comprise a charming and relaxing island getaway. **Pros:** friendly and inexpensive; small but pleasant pool; no steps. **Cons:** most units do not have sea views; breakfast is extra; located in what can be a noisy area of town. [$] *Rooms from: €92* ✉ *Firostefani* ✣ *Between Firostefani walkway and main traffic road* ☎ *22860/23322* 🌐 *www.reverie.gr* 🕓 *Closed Nov.–Mar.* 🛏 *17 rooms* 🍽 *No meals.*

$$$$ B&B/INN Fodor's Choice ★ 🏨 **Tsitouras Collection, Firostefani on Santorini.** *Architectural Digest*–worthy decor and earthy Cycladic charm blend into what is truly Santorinian splendor; think sparkling white cubes with volcanic stone trimmings surrounding an 18th-century mansion. **Pros:** beautiful design; caldera views; lots of privacy. **Cons:** overdesigned; museum-like to some tastes; those prices, especially during high season. [$] *Rooms from: €980* ✉ *Firostefani* ✣ *Firostefani cliff face, next to St. Mark's* ☎ *22860/23747* 🌐 *www.tsitouras.com* 🕓 *Closed Nov.–Mar.* 🛏 *5 rooms* 🍽 *Breakfast.*

IMEROVIGLI ΗΜΕΡΟΒΙΓΛΙ

3 km (2 miles) northwest of Fira, 2 km (1 mile) northwest of Firostefani.

Set on the highest point of the caldera's rim, Imerovigli (the name means "watchtower") is quiet, traditional, and less expensive than other places on the caldera. The 25-minute walk from Fira, with incredible views, should be on everyone's itinerary. The lodgings, some of them traditional cave houses, are mostly down stairways from the cliff-side walkway. The big rock backing the village was once crowned by Skaros Castle, whence Venetian overlords reigned after 1207. It collapsed in an earthquake, leaving only the rock. A trail descending from the church of Ayios Georgios crosses the isthmus and encircles Skaros; it's only 10 minutes to the castle top. After 1 km (½ mile) it reaches the small chapel of Theoskepasti with a memorable caldera view.

WHERE TO EAT

$$ GREEK 🍴 **Blue Note.** You can't go wrong with the location: a deck extended over the cliff, a panoramic caldera view, and a sunset. For a starter try Gruyère flambé. **Known for:** panoramic view; friendly service. [$] *Average main: €20* ✉ *Spiliotica Apartments* ✣ *On cliff-side walkway, behind church of Panaghia Maltesa, near parking and bus stop* ☎ *22860/23771* 🌐 *www.spiliotica.com* 🕒 *Closed Nov.–Mar.*

$$ MEDITERRANEAN 🍴 **Mezzo.** Offering international and Greek cuisine, Mezzo's menu is diverse and exciting. A fantastic view goes with the experience, with three levels of dining terraces overlooking the caldera and out to Ia. **Known for:** caldera views; innovative cuisine; excellent service. [$] *Average main: €20* ✉ *Imerovigli* ☎ *22860/21874* 🕒 *Closed Apr.–Oct.*

WHERE TO STAY

$$$$ B&B/INN Fodor's Choice ★ 🏨 **Aenaon Villas.** On one of the island's highest points, these seven sumptuous villas offer a 21st-century interpretation of the classic Greek-island hideaway, built in a traditional style with careful respect for Cycladic architecture, with smooth white walls standing out brilliantly against the surrounding dark volcanic stone and the deep blues of the Aegean Sea. The villas are simple in design but entirely luxurious, with a fireplace, private veranda, and modern amenities, and a private plunge pool in one. **Pros:** beautiful private setting; owners make you feel like family; lovely infinity pool with views. **Cons:** no restaurant on-site; some steps, but not as many as other properties; only light snacks available to order. [$] *Rooms from: €400* ✉ *Imerovigli* ☎ *22860/27014* 🌐 *www.aenaonvillas.gr* 🕒 *Closed Oct.–May* 🛏 *5 villas* 🍽 *Breakfast.*

$ B&B/INN 🏨 **Annio Furnished Flats.** Accommodations in this cliff-side spot are attractive and simple, with local furnishings both new and old. **Pros:** beautiful caldera view at a very good price; good simple base; reflects local architecture. **Cons:** fairly basic; lots of stairs; no pool. [$] *Rooms from: €120* ✉ *Imerovigli* ☎ *22860/24714* 🌐 *www.annioflats.gr* 🕒 *Closed Nov.–Apr.* 🛏 *11 rooms* 🍽 *Breakfast.*

$$$ RESORT 🏨 **Astra Apartments.** Little cliff-side Imerovigli is a world apart from busy, nearby Fira, and this intimate enclave is an especially magical place to stay, with terraced, vaulted-ceilinged cave houses that are sophisticated and full of character. **Pros:** beautiful views; personalized service; infinity pool with a view is a cool retreat. **Cons:** a lot of steps to reach rooms; shared terraces; suites are pricey. [$] *Rooms from: €240* ✉ *Imerovigli* ✣ *Below caldera walkway* ☎ *22860/23641* 🌐 *www.astra-suites.com* 🕒 *Closed Nov.–Mar.* 🛏 *26 rooms* 🍽 *Breakfast.*

$$ B&B/INN 🏨 **Heliades Apartments.** Four split-level cave houses, each white with blue-green accents, are on top of one of the higher cliff ridges, so the verandas all have really breathtaking (literally) caldera views. **Pros:**

terraces with caldera views; few steps; kitchens included. **Cons:** on the simple side; breakfast is extra; nonprivate room balconies. $ *Rooms from: €180* ✉ *Imerovigli* ✛ *On cliff-side walkway, behind church of Panaghia Maltesa, near parking and bus stop* ☎ *22860/24102* ⊕ *www. heliades-apts.gr* ⊗ *Closed Nov.–Mar.* ⤲ *4 rooms* ⦶ *Breakfast.*

SPORTS AND THE OUTDOORS

SAILING

Santorini Sailing Center. This handy outfitter arranges charters and runs weekly two- to three-day sailing trips around the Cyclades for groups of up to 10. ☎ *22860/23891* ⊕ *www.sailingsantorini.com.*

IA OIA

14 km (9 miles) northwest of Fira.

At the tip of the northern horn of the island sits Ia (or Oia), Santorini's second-largest town and the Aegean's most-photographed village. Ia is more tasteful than Fira (for one thing, no establishment here is allowed to play music that can be heard on the street), and the town's cubical white houses (some vaulted against earthquakes) stand out against the green-, brown-, and rust-color layers of rock, earth, and solid volcanic ash that rise from the sea. Every summer evening, travelers from all over the world congregate at the caldera's rim—sitting on whitewashed fences, staircases, beneath the town's windmill, on the old Kastro—each looking out to sea in anticipation of the performance: the Ia sunset. The three-hour rim-edge walk from Ia to Fira at this hour is unforgettable.

In the middle of the quiet caldera, the volcano smolders away eerily, adding an air of suspense to an already awe-inspiring scene. The 1956 earthquake (7.8 on the Richter scale) left 48 people dead (thankfully, most residents were working outdoors at the time), hundreds injured, and 2,000 houses toppled. Santorini's west side—especially Ia, until then the largest town—was hard hit, and many residents decided to emigrate to Athens, Australia, and America. Although Fira, also damaged, rebuilt rapidly, Ia proceeded slowly, sticking to the traditional architectural style. In 1900, Ia had nearly 9,000 inhabitants, mostly mariners who owned 164 seafaring vessels and seven shipyards. Now there are about 500 permanent residents, and more than 100 boats. Many of these mariners use the endless flight of stairs to descend to the water and the small port of Armeni or take the road or steps to Ammoudi, where the pebble beach is home to some of the island's nicest fish tavernas and the port of embarkation for many excursion boats.

Ia is set up like the other three towns—Fira, Firostefani, and Imerovigli—that adorn the caldera's sinuous rim. There is a cliff-side walkway (Niko-laos Nomikou), which is old, and a more recent road for vehicles. Shops and restaurants are all on the walkway, and hotel entrances mostly descend from it—something to check carefully if you cannot negotiate stairs easily. Short streets leading from the road to the walkway have cheaper eateries and shops. There is a parking lot at either end, and the northern one marks the end of the road and the rim. Nothing is very far from anything else.

The main walkway of Ia can be thought of as a straight river, with a delta at the northern end, where the better shops and restaurants are. Many luxurious cave-house hotels are at the southern end, and a stroll by them is part of the extended evening promenade. Although Ia is not as crowded as Fira, where the tour boats deposit their thousands of hasty shoppers, relentless publicity about the town's beauty and tastefulness, accurate enough, are making the narrow lanes impassable in August. The sunset in Ia may not really be much more spectacular than in Fira, and certainly not better than in higher Imerovigli, but there is something tribally satisfying at the sight of so many people gathering in one spot to celebrate pure beauty. Happily, the night scene isn't as frantic as Fira's—most shop owners are content to sit out front and don't cotton to the few revelers' bars in operation. In winter, Ia feels pretty uninhabited.

EXPLORING

Naval Maritime Museum of Thera. In an old neoclassical mansion, once destroyed in the big earthquake, the museum has an enticing collection. Pieces include ships' figureheads, seamen's chests, maritime equipment, and models which reveal the extensive nautical history of the island, Santorini's main trade until tourism took over. ✉ *Town Center* ☎ *22860/71156* 🎟 *€4* 🕒 *Closed Tues.*

BEACHES

FAMILY **Baxedes.** The closest sand beach to Ia is handy when you don't feel like making the trip to more famous beaches on the south end of the island. It's not that there's anything second-rate about this beautiful spot: the cliff-backed strip of sand is rarely crowded; the sea floor is sandy, too, providing nice wading for kids and a pleasant experience when splashing around in the surf; and the cliffs provide welcome shade. A downside is the summertime meltemi winds, which churn up the surf and sand. Islanders used to grow fruits and vegetables down here, and the name comes from the Turkish word for garden, *baxes.* **Amenities:** food and drink; parking (free). **Best for:** surfing (at times); swimming. ✉ *Ia* ✥ *Near Paradissos, about 2 km (1 mile) north of Ia.*

WHERE TO EAT

$$ INTERNATIONAL 🍴 **Kandouni.** An enticing front garden, candlelit at night, and memento-filled salons of a centuries-old sea captain's home in the back lanes of Ia are a charming setting for a menu that includes some island favorites as well as some international ones, which may reflect the time the Korkiantis family spent in Canada. Whatever the origin, the sea bass in a salt crust and pasta with salmon and caviar are the delicious centerpieces of a meal here, accompanied by a good selection of local wines. **Known for:** charming environment; internationally influenced Greek dishes. [$] *Average main: €22* ✉ *Ia* ✥ *In back streets near bus station* ☎ *22860/71616.*

$$ GREEK 🍴 **Kastro.** This is a popular perch from which to witness a famous Ia sunset, and at that magical hour the terrace is always filled. Happily, the Greek cuisine here makes a fitting accompaniment including a starter of olives stuffed with cream cheese dipped in beer dough and fried, served on arugula with a balsamic sauce. **Known for:** sunset dining; pleasant environment. [$] *Average main: €20* ✉ *Ia* ✥ *Near Venetian castle* ☎ *22860/71045* 🌐 *www.kastro-ia.gr.*

Ia is world famous for its magnificent sunsets, which bathe the clifftop village in an ethereal light. Even if you aren't into sunset cocktails or dining with a view, Ia may convince you otherwise.

$$$ GREEK Fodor's Choice ★ 🍴 **Red Bicycle.** This sophisticated restaurant is at the north end of Ia's main walkway, just down the steps, and boasts a terrace with outstanding caldera views. Menu choices reflect local ingredients with a creatively appetizing touch. **Known for:** local fine-dining favorite; beautiful terrace views. [$] *Average main: €35* ✉ *Ia* ✥ *Off main walkway* ☎ *22860/71918* ⏲ *Closed Nov.–Mar.*

$ GREEK 🍴 **Roka.** Regulars are more than willing to forgo a caldera view for a meal in these simple rooms and two terraces, where the menu focuses on old-fashioned favorites. The best way to dine here is to order several small plates for the table to share—fried eggplant with tomato; apple and feta pie; fava puree (the best on the island, according to many locals); fresh sardines baked in lemon; and even simple tzatziki, especially good here because of the homegrown garlic and local yogurt. **Known for:** Santorinian specialities; a favorite with the locals. [$] *Average main: €12* ✉ *Ia* ✥ *In back streets near bus station* ☎ *22860/71896* 🌐 *www.roka.gr.*

$$$$ GREEK Fodor's Choice ★ 🍴 **Sigalas Winery.** Growing some of the best Greek grape varieties—since ancient times—has something to do with the land, and the enologists and sommeliers at Domaine Sigalas are ready to divulge every fascinating detail *and*present the Greek plates that perfectly accompany their best labels. Domaine Sigalas, a local, family-run winery, is a respected name in Greek wines and has opened up its lush island winery outside Ia for tastings and food pairing sessions. **Known for:** excellent wine tasting and food pairings; best wines from Santorini. [$] *Average main: €90* ✉ *Ia* ☎ *22860/71644* 🌐 *www.sigalaswinetasting.com.*

$$$
MEDITERRANEAN
Fodor's Choice
★

✕ **Sphinx Wine Restaurant.** In a elegantly decorated 19th-century "captain's house," mansions once built by the wealthy of the island, Sphinx centers its menu around well-presented gourmet Mediterranean cuisine. With an extensive wine list and knowledgeable sommeliers, the dining experience here is complete for any wine lover. **Known for:** excellent wine selection; romantic and historic setting. $ *Average main: €26* ⊠ *Ia* ☎ *22860/71450.*

$$
SEAFOOD
Fodor's Choice
★

✕ **Sunset Taverna.** The first of the Ammoudi fish houses opened in the 1980s and is still a standout among the several excellent tavernas that line the quay in this tiny fishing port just below Ia—you can walk down and take a cab back to town. Lapping waves, bobbing fishing boats, and tables so close to the water's edge that a clumsy move might add a swim to the evening's entertainment, testify to the freshness of the fish, which is simply grilled. **Known for:** beautiful waterfront harbor setting; sunset dining; excellent seafood. $ *Average main: €25* ⊠ *Waterfront* ✚ *Ammoudi* ☎ *22860/71614* ⊕ *www.sunset-ammoudi.gr.*

WHERE TO STAY

$$$$
HOTEL

🛏 **Armeni Suites.** Armeni's whitewashed rooms, inspired by the traditional cave houses of the island, impress with a contemporary touch. **Pros:** not as many steps as other caldera town hotels; great views; steps away from Ia's central street. **Cons:** there are steps to climb; nonprivate balconies for some rooms; no restaurant on-site. $ *Rooms from: €380* ⊠ *Ia* ☎ *22860/71439* ⊕ *www.armenivillage.com* ☾ *Closed Nov.–Mar.* ⇥ *15 rooms* ⦿| *Breakfast.*

$$$$
RESORT

🛏 **Canaves Hotel and Suites.** Two adjacent properties offer some of Santorini's most romantic accommodations, a collection of beautifully furnished rooms and suites, all done in crisp whites and handsome fabrics, meticulously maintained and enjoying stunning caldera views. **Pros:** extremely attractive; good dining poolside and in gourmet restaurant; elevator in suites section eliminates steps. **Cons:** in the busy center of Ia; steps in hotel section; pricey. $ *Rooms from: €750* ⊠ *Ia* ✚ *On caldera, center of town* ☎ *22860/71453* ⊕ *www.canaves.com* ☾ *Closed Nov.–Mar.* ⇥ *39 rooms* ⦿| *Breakfast.*

$$$$
B&B/INN
Fodor's Choice
★

🛏 **Esperas Hotel.** At this welcoming collection of sparkling white, arch-roofed cave houses that spill down the side of the caldera, homey suites and studios all have cozy sitting areas, well-equipped bathrooms and kitchenettes, and a private, view-saturated terrace overlooking dark cliffs and turquoise seas. **Pros:** wonderful caldera location; beautiful views; private balconies available. **Cons:** lots of steps to reach the hotel, though staff helps carry bags; more stairs inside to get to rooms; plain but traditional decor. $ *Rooms from: €320* ⊠ *Ia* ☎ *22860/71501* ⊕ *esperas-santorini.com* ☾ *Closed late Oct.–Apr.* ⇥ *21 rooms* ⦿| *Breakfast.*

$$$$
RESORT

🛏 **Ikies Traditional Houses.** A perch at the far eastern end of Ia provides wonderful views of the village as well as the caldera, which can be enjoyed from the private terraces of the handsomely furnished cave houses that were once used as workshops to repair and store fishing nets. **Pros:** nice sense of privacy in a small, off-the-beaten-track enclave; very attractive; low-key, attentive service. **Cons:** terraces are not entirely private; the inevitable steps; no elevator. $ *Rooms from: €360* ⊠ *Ia* ✚ *Off eastern end of caldera path* ☎ *22860/71311* ⊕ *www.ikies.com* ☾ *Closed Nov.–Mar.* ⇥ *11 rooms* ⦿| *Breakfast.*

6

$$$$ RESORT 🏨 **Katikies.** Sumptuously appointed, this immaculate white cliff-side complex layered on terraces offers ultimate luxury and sleek modern design, including Andy Warhol wall prints, stunning fabrics, and handsome furniture—chic as the surroundings are, the barrel-vaulted ceilings and other architectural details also lend a traditional air to the place. **Pros:** cliff-side infinity pool; all luxuries; quiet because no small children are allowed. **Cons:** many stairs; rather impersonal; on crowded part of caldera. [$] *Rooms from: €1,290* ✉ *Ia* ✥ *Ia cliff face, edge of main town* ☎ *22860/71401* 🌐 *www.katikies.com* 🕒 *Closed Nov.–Mar.* 🛏 *34 rooms* 🍴 *Breakfast.*

$$$$ RESORT 🏨 **Perivolas.** A cliff-hanging, much-photographed infinity pool that makes you feel you could easily swim off the edge into the caldera's blue bay 1,000 feet below is but one of the highlights at a luxury getaway that even the locals respect (big compliment). **Pros:** the best infinity pool on Santorini; attentive but relaxed service; beautiful and tranquil surroundings. **Cons:** lots of steps; a walk to town; no elevator. [$] *Rooms from: €650* ✉ *Nomikou* ✥ *Ia cliff face, east of center* ☎ *22860/71308* 🌐 *www.perivolas.gr* 🕒 *Closed Nov.–Mar.* 🛏 *20 houses* 🍴 *Breakfast.*

NIGHTLIFE

There are the usual cafés, bars, and pastry shops along the main street, but a peaceful note is struck by the fact that establishments are forbidden to play loud music.

Hassapiko. Nightlife may not be a thing in Ia, with its quiet romantic scene, but this is one bar that attracts locals and international visitors with its chill vibe, classic cocktails, and warmly lighted interiors. Also known by the owner's name, Mary Kay, it's "the place" to walk to—and stay awhile—after dinner in Ia. ✉ *Ia* ☎ *22860/71244* 🌐 *www.hassapiko.gr.*

Skiza. A balcony overlooking the caldera is a prime spot in Ia for drinks and light snacks, and the pastries are considered the best on the island. ✉ *Ia* ✥ *On caldera, near church* ☎ *22860/71569.*

SHOPPING

Ia mostly abjures the trinket madness of Fira, and instead offers a variety of handcrafted items. Since the shops are not so dependent on cruise ships, a certain sophistication reigns in the quiet streets. Art galleries, objets d'art shops, crafts shops, and icon stores set the tone.

ANTIQUES AND COLLECTIBLES

Dimitris Koliousis Workshop. Steps from the main street lead down to arched cave rooms, a stark setting for exuberantly rich and colorful pieces on wood that replicate Byzantine and Russian icons. ✉ *Main St.* ☎ *22860/71829.*

Loulaki. Manolis and Chara Kourtis sell antiques, ceramics, jewelry, and art in a delightful shop below their Red Bicycle restaurant; exploring their collection is a pleasure. Alexandra Solomos's painted plates are a favorite. ✉ *Main St.* ☎ *22860/71856.*

BOOKS

Fodor's Choice ★ **Atlantis Books.** A tiny English-language bookshop that would be at home in New York's Greenwich Village or London's Bloomsbury is an unexpected but wonderful treat in Ia. Built into a cave, only good literature makes it onto the shelves, and writers stop by to chat and give readings. ✉ *Ia* ✣ *North end of main shopping street* ☎ *22860/72346* 🌐 *www.atlantisbooks.org.*

SPORTS AND THE OUTDOORS

SAILING

Sunset Oia. Five-hour morning and afternoon sailings from Ammoudi include stops at the hot springs around the volcano and two beaches for swimming, with stunning caldera-cliff views along the way; afternoon cruises coincide with sunset. Meals and drinks are served onboard, and relatively small groups (especially in the company's "semiprivate" offerings) ensure a genuinely memorable experience. ✉ *Ammoudi* ☎ *22860/72200* 🌐 *www.sailing-santorini.com.*

PYRGOS ΠΥΡΓΟΣ

5 km (3 miles) south of Fira.

Though today Pyrgos has only 500 inhabitants, until the early 1800s it was the capital of the island. Medieval houses are stacked on top of one another and back-to-back for protection against pirates. Your reward for a climb up the picturesque streets ends at the ruined Venetian castle, where views extend across the vineyard-studded landscape to both coasts. In Pyrgos you are really in old Santorini—hardly anything has changed.

Monastery of Profitis Ilias. Standing on the highest point on Santorini, which rises to 1,856 feet at the summit, Santorini's largest monastery offers a cinematic vista: from here you can see the surrounding islands and, on a clear day, the mountains of Crete, more than 100 km (62 miles) away. You may also be able to spot ancient Thira on the peak below Profitis Ilias. Unfortunately, radio towers and a NATO radar installation provide an ugly backdrop for the monastery's wonderful bell tower.

Founded in 1711 by two monks from Pyrgos, Profitis Ilias is cherished by islanders because here, in a secret school, the Greek language and culture were taught during the dark centuries of the Turkish occupation. A **museum** in the monastery contains a model of the secret school in a monk's cell, another model of a traditional carpentry and blacksmith shop, and a display of ecclesiastical items. ✉ *Pyrgos* ✣ *At highest point on Santorini.*

WHERE TO EAT

$ GREEK Fodor's Choice ★ 🍴 **Franco's Cafe.** The hangout that is such a caldera-side hit in Fira also has a welcoming presence in Pyrgos, where cocktails and light snacks are served on breezy terraces overlooking the village, vineyards, and the sea. This spot is especially popular at sunset, but does a brisk business throughout the day, when the bar brews the island's best coffee well into the evening. **Known for:** snacks all day; sunset drinks; excellent coffee. [$] *Average main: €10* ✉ *Pyrgos* ✣ *Top of village near the fortress* ☎ *22860/33957.*

$$ **Metaxy Mas.** It seems that just
GREEK about everyone in Santorini looks
forward to a meal at this village
taverna. Even though the name
means "between us," the secret is
out and the place is so popular that
Greek customers will eat lunch at
5 pm or linger past midnight just
to get a table in the colorful, stone-
wall dining room or on one of the
terraces. **Known for:** hearty deli-
cious Greek plates; relaxed, simple
home-style cooking. $ *Average
main: €15* ⊠ *Exo Gonia* ✣ *Village
center* ☎ *22860/31323* ⊕ *www.
santorini-mataximas.gr.*

$$$$ **Selene.** One of the best Greek
GREEK island restaurants, with an elegant
Fodor'sChoice setting, attentive service, an exten-
★ sive wine list, and a fine-dining
menu that shows what is possible
with local ingredients in the hands
of a talented chef. Starters to savor
include shrimp ravioli with almond sauce, poached eggs with wild
greens, and potatoes in hay with brown butter. **Known for:** excel-
lent gourmet dishes inspired by Santorini tradition; terrace dining
and elegant indoor dining; great wine list; flawless service. $ *Average
main: €50* ⊠ *Pyrgos* ✣ *Village center* ☎ *22860/22249* ⊕ *www.selene.
gr* ⊘ *Closed Nov.–Mar.*

SANTORINI WINE

The locals say that in Santorini
there is more wine than water,
and it may be true; Santorini
produces more wine than any
other Cyclades island. The volca-
nic soil, high daytime tempera-
tures, and humidity at night are
favorable to 36 varieties of grape,
and these unique growing condi-
tions are especially ideal for the
production of distinctive white
wine. Farmers twist the vines into
a basketlike shape, in which the
grapes grow, protected from the
wind. A highlight of any Santorini
trip is a visit to one of its many
wineries—log on to ⊕ *www.
santorini.org/wineries* for a helpful
intro.

WHERE TO STAY

$$$$ **Zannos Melathron.** A delightful walled garden is the setting for this
HOTEL magical hideaway high above the island's medieval capital, where com-
fortable suites in two Cycladic-style manor houses sport stucco and stone
walls, vaulted ceilings, antique furnishings, and flowery terraces that look
out across the island to the sea. **Pros:** beautiful setting and surroundings;
elegant yet comfortable and welcoming; surrounded by winding lanes
of Pyrgos. **Cons:** in center of island away from sea; reached by steps
(but porters carry bags); far from caldera views Santorini is famous for.
$ *Rooms from: €375* ⊠ *Pyrgos* ✣ *Village center* ☎ *22860/28220* ⊕ *www.
zannos.gr* ⊘ *Closed Nov.–Easter* ⇆ *13 rooms* ⏐⊙⏐ *Breakfast.*

MEGALOCHORI ΜΕΓΑΛΟΧΩΡΙ

4 km (2½ miles) east of Pyrgos, 9 km (5½ miles) southwest of Fira.

Megalochori is a picturesque, half-abandoned town. Many of the vil-
lage's buildings were actually *canavas,* wine-making facilities. The tiny
main square is still lively in the evening.

EXPLORING

Boutari Winery. The island's first winery open to the public puts on a big show, with a bright, view-filled tasting room surrounded by vineyards and the chance to see stainless steel tanks, pneumatic presses, oak barrels, and temperature-controlled vats. A distinctly Santorini experience is a taste of Kallisti, a version of the Assyrtiko variety; the name, meaning "most beautiful," was given to the island in ancient times. ⊠ *Megalochori* ☎ *22860/81011* ⊕ *www.boutari-santorini.gr* 🍷 *Tasting and tour €12* ☉ *Closed Sun.*

Gavalas Winery. This winery has been exporting its distinguished produce since the days when mules carted wine-filled goatskins to the port in Fira. Tastings in the atmospheric old storage and pressing rooms include Voudomato, a dry rosé, and Nykteri, a sophisticated white from the island's indigenous Assyrtiko grapes—the name means "working the night away," because the grapes have traditionally been harvested at night to avoid damage from the heat. ⊠ *Megalochori* ☎ *22860/82552* ⊕ *www.gavalaswines.gr* 🍷 *Tasting €2 per glass* ☉ *Closed Nov.–Apr.*

WHERE TO STAY

$$$$

RESORT

🏨 **Vedema.** This distant and deluxe black-lava outpost is a world unto itself, where villas have been built around a beautiful 15th-century winery, almost like a gated community in Florida but with a minimalism-meets-Mediterranean leitmotif. **Pros:** cost is worth the luxury amenities; excellent service; nice design with stellar reputation. **Cons:** isolated from island life; pricey rooms; you need a car or to take bus to see the island sights. Ⓢ *Rooms from: €470* ⊠ *Megalochori* ☎ *22860/81796* ⊕ *www.vedema.gr* ☉ *Closed Nov.–Mar.* ➟ *42 rooms* ⍟*Breakfast.*

AKROTIRI ΑΚΡΩΤΗΡΙ

7 km (4½ miles) west of Pyrgos, 13 km (8 miles) south of Fira.

This village is most famous for its ancient ruins, but the little collection of houses surrounded by gardens and fields is a pleasant place in its own right, a pretty slice of rural Santorini. A stay here removes you from the hustle and bustle along the caldera and puts you within easy reach of sights, wineries, and the island's best beaches.

EXPLORING

Fodor's Choice
★

Ancient Akrotiri. If Santorini is known as the "Greek Pompeii," it is because of the archaeological site of ancient Akrotiri, near the tip of the southern horn of the island. The site now has a protective roof spanning the entire enclosed site—in fact a whole ancient city buried under the volcanic ashes. In the 1860s, workmen discovered the remains of an ancient town, frozen in time by ash from an eruption 3,600 years ago, long before Pompeii's disaster. In 1967 excavations began; it is thought that the 40 buildings that have been uncovered are only one-thirtieth of the huge site and that excavating the rest could take a century. Akrotiri was settled as early as 3000 BC and reached its peak after 2000 BC, when it developed trade and agriculture and settled the present town. Well-preserved frescoes found during excavations are now displayed in the National Archaeological Museum in Athens. ⊠ *Akrotiri* ✛ *South of* *modern Akrotiri, near tip of southern horn* ☎ *22860/81939* 🌐 *www.culture.gr* 🎫 *€12; €14 for combo ticket for the archaeological sites and museum in Thira* 🕓 *Closed Mon.*

BEACHES

Red Beach. A backdrop of red-and-black volcanic cliffs adds no small amount of drama to this strand of multicolored pebbles and red-hued sand, and the timelessness of the place is enhanced by the presence of nearby ancient Akrotiri. Crowds sometimes pile in during July and August, and a few too many loungers and umbrellas detract from the stunning scenery, but for the most part this is one of the quieter beaches on the south side of the island. There's a rough path from the parking area to the beach. The beach has been known to close due to rocks falling, and entering would be at your own risk. **Amenities:** food and drink; parking (about €2, not always imposed). **Best for:** snorkeling; swimming. ✉ *Akrotiri* ✥ *On southwest shore below Akrotiri.*

WHERE TO EAT

$$ SEAFOOD

🍴 **The Dolphins.** When the surf is rough, much of the outdoor dining room is surrounded by crashing waves, and on calm nights the moon playing off the water makes this quiet outpost on the southern end of the island one of the most romantic spots around. A meal is good enough, and the prices so reasonable, that you can almost forgive the sometimes sloppy service. **Known for:** dining on the beach; wonderful and fresh seafood plates. [$] *Average main: €20* ✉ *Akrotiri* ✥ *On the beach* ☎ *22860/81151.*

WHERE TO STAY

$$ HOTEL

🏨 **Hotel Goulielmos.** These very simple yet comfortable rooms, many with terraces, are among the island's unsung treasures, perched on the southern side of the caldera just outside Akrotiri, enjoying spectacular views up the rim to Fira and Ia. Nods to luxury are conspicuously absent—no pool or stylish public areas—and the experience of a stay in these tile-floored rooms with plain wood furnishings is much more like what you'll find in other parts of rural Greece, not on Santorini. **Pros:** nice grounds and views; quiet stay; some rooms have private balconies. **Cons:** some rooms need a bit of maintenance; few hotel amenities and services; far from caldera towns. [$] *Rooms from: €200* ✉ *Akrotiri* ✥ *On caldera off road into town* 🌐 *www.hotel-goulielmos.gr* 🕓 *Closed Nov.–Mar.* 🛏 *27 rooms* 🍽 *Breakfast.*

KAMARI ΚΑΜΑΡΙ

6 km (4 miles) east of Akrotiri, 6 km (4 miles) south of Fira.

Santorini's most popular beach resort is just that—a long line of hotels and tavernas strung out along a stretch of red-and-black sand on the island's southeastern coast. Tourism has all but consumed the onetime quieter pursuits of fishing and farming, though many residents still depend on both, and sun lovers descend en masse in July and August. Still, backed by fields and dramatic cliffs and headlands, Kamari is fairly low-key and a pleasant place to hit the beach.

EXPLORING

Ancient Thira. A Dorian city—with 9th-century BC tombs, an engraved phallus, Hellenistic houses, and traces of Byzantine fortifications and churches—floats more than 2,100 feet above the island. At the Sanctuary of Apollo, graffiti dating to the 8th century BC record the names of some of the boys who danced naked at the god's festival (Satie's famed musical compositions, *Gymnopédies,* reimagine these). To get here, hike up from Perissa or Kamari or take a taxi up **Mesa Vouna.** On the summit are the scattered ruins, excavated by a German archaeology school around the turn of the 20th century; there's a fine view. ⊠ *Kamari ⊹ On a switchback up mountain, right before Kamari* ☎ *22860/23217* ⊕ *www.culture.gr* ⊡ *€4* ⊘ *Closed Mon.*

Fodor's Choice ★ **Koutsoyannopoulos Wine Museum.** Founded in 1870, the Koutsoyannopoulos Winery offers a tour of its old facility, now a multiroom museum that is picturesque, authentic, and mostly underground. Tools, techniques, and the original business office are from a world long gone—but the wines, as the ensuing tasting proves, are contemporary and refined. The *Wine Spectator* rated their Assyrtiko among the world's top 100 whites. To add your own kudos, note that this admired winery is open year-round. ⊠ *Vothonas ⊹ On the road to Kamari* ☎ *22860/31322* ⊕ *www.volcanwines.gr* ⊡ *Tasting €10* ⊘ *Closed Sun. Dec.–Mar.*

BEACHES

Kamari Beach. Santorini's most popular beach, one of several excellent stretches of sand on the southern end of the island, manages to maintain its beauty despite an onslaught of sunseekers. The black sands are backed by dramatic cliffs, including the one topped by Ancient Thira. A steep path from one end of the beach leads up to the ruins, past a refreshing and very welcome natural spring, but most beachgoers don't venture beyond their umbrella-shaded loungers or the long line of beach bars and tavernas. **Amenities:** food and drink; showers; toilets; water sports. **Best for:** snorkeling; swimming; walking. ⊠ *Kamari ⊹ 8 km (5 miles) southeast of Fira.*

Perissa Beach. Separated from Kamari Beach by a huge slice of rock, Perissa is almost identical: a long black-sand beach that is popular with the summer crowds and where a lively beach resort town has grown to appreciate the view. **Amenities:** food and drink; showers; toilets; water sports. **Best for:** snorkeling; swimming; walking. ⊠ *Kamari.*

Perivolos Beach. Pretty much an extension of Perissa Beach, Perivolos features that famous volcanic black sand but with just a tad fewer restaurants, beach bars, and cafés, making it a quieter beach enclave to seek most times of the year. **Amenities:** food and drink; showers; toilets; water sports. **Best for:** snorkeling; swimming; walking. ⊠ *Kamari.*

WHERE TO EAT

$$ ⨯ **Forty One.** In a transformed historic tomato cannery off the Ayios
MEDITERRANEAN Georgios section of Perivolos Beach, Forty One is a chic, stylish destination for fine Mediterranean dishes with a calming sea view and ambient light. Besides creatively presented Mediterranean favorites like regional salads, risotto, pasta, and freshly grilled seafood plates, a charming

private dining room is used for special occasions and Santorini wine tastings and food pairings. **Known for:** Mediterranean dishes; wine tastings and food pairings; beachfront dining. [$] *Average main: €24* ✉ *Kamari* ☎ *22680/82710.*

WHERE TO STAY

$$$ B&B/INN Fodor's Choice ★

🏨 **Orabel Suites.** This romantically designed, adults-only getaway occupies what looks like the middle of nowhere—a quiet stretch of valley fronted by farmland and with a distant view of the sea. **Pros:** beautiful contemporary yet traditional design; perfect for couples; attentive service. **Cons:** no fantastic or famous Santorini view to boast of; no on-site restaurant (but breakfast service is excellent); not within walking distance of Santorini's major sights and villages. [$] *Rooms from: €230* ✉ *Kamari* ☎ *22860/85060* 🌐 *www.orabelsuites.gr* 🕒 *Closed Nov.–Mar.* 🛏 *11 rooms* 🍴 *Breakfast.*

CRETE

WELCOME TO CRETE

TOP REASONS TO GO

★ **Minoan Myths:** Explore the wonders of the 3,500-year-old civilization that flourished at Knossos.

★ **Beaches:** With its sandy strands and craggy coves, Crete has an array of fantastic beaches, all lapped by clean, turquoise waters.

★ **Charming Cities:** Chania, Rethymnon, and Ayios Nikolaos will seduce with their Venetian and Ottoman architecture, narrow lanes, and shady squares.

★ **The Outdoor Life:** From snowcapped peaks to deep gorges, wild Crete offers dramatic escapes for those who want to get away from it all.

★ **Luxury Living:** Live like royalty in a former Venetian palace, or indulge in the unabashed luxury of some of Greece's finest resort hotels.

Crete is long and narrow, approximately 257 km (160 miles) long and only 60 km (37 miles) at its widest. Most of the development is along the north shore; the southern coast largely remains blessedly unspoiled. The island's three major cities, Heraklion, Rethymnon, and Chania, are in the north and are connected by the island's major highway, an east–west route that traverses most of the north coast. Heraklion and Chania are served by ferry from Piraeus, and both have international airports. By car or bus, it's easy to reach other parts of the island from these gateways.

1 **Eastern Crete.** Knossos, the most spectacular of the Minoan palaces and Crete's most popular attraction, is here in the east. Just as this sprawling complex was the hub of island civilization 3,500 years ago, nearby Heraklion is Crete's bustling modern capital, and farther east along the coast is the Elounda Peninsula, the island's epicenter of luxury, where some of the world's most sumptuous resort getaways are tucked along a stunning shoreline. The east isn't all

clamor, glamour, and glitz, though; the beach at Vai is just one example of the natural beauty that abounds here in the east, and in mountain villages like those on the Lasithi Plateau, old traditions continue to thrive.

Sea of Crete

DIA

Fodhele

Rethymnon

Perama

Heraklion

◆ **Palace of Knossos**

Neapolis

Elounda

Gulf of Mirabello

Vai

1

LASITHI PLATEAU

Ayios Nikolaos

Siteia

MOUNT IDA

CRETE

DIKTI MOUNTAINS

Kritsa

Vori

Ayii Deka

MESARA PLAIN

Matala

Ierapetra

 CHRISI

KOUFONISI

Libyan Sea

7

```
0                          15 mi
0              15 km
```

2 Western Crete. The scenery gets more rugged as you head west, where the White Mountains pierce the blue sky with snowcapped peaks and then plunge into the Libyan Sea along dramatic, rocky shorelines. Mountain scenery and remote seacoast villages—some, like Loutro, accessible only on foot or by boat—attract many visitors to the west. Others come to enjoy the urban pleasures of Rethymnon and Chania, gracious cities that owe their harbors, architectural jewels, and exotic charms to Venetian and Ottoman occupiers.

Updated by Liam McCaffrey

Crete is a land of myth and imagination, where Theseus slayed the Minotaur, where Daedulus and Icarus set off on their ill-fated flight, and where Zorba danced on the sand. More than any other island, it is Greece in a nutshell—mountains, split with deep gorges and honeycombed with caves, rise in sheer walls from the sea; snowcapped peaks loom behind sandy shorelines, vineyards, and olive groves; delightful cities and quaint villages front the miles of beaches that fringe the coast. Yet it is still the mystery surrounding Europe's first civilization and empire that draws the great majority of visitors to Crete and its world-famous Minoan palaces.

Around 1500 BC, while the rest of Europe was still in the grip of primitive barbarity, one of the most brilliant civilizations the world was ever to know approached its final climax, one that was breathtakingly uncovered through the late 19th-century excavations of Sir Arthur Evans. He determined that the Minoans, prehistoric Cretans, had founded Europe's first urban culture as far back as the 3rd millennium BC, and the island's rich legacy of art and architecture strongly influenced both mainland Greece and the Aegean islands in the Bronze Age. From around 1900 BC the Minoan palaces at Knossos (near present-day Heraklion), Malia, Phaistos, and elsewhere were centers of political power, religious authority, and economic activity—all concentrated in one sprawling complex of buildings. Their administration seems to have had much in common with contemporary cultures in Egypt and Mesopotamia. What set the Minoans apart from the rest of the Bronze Age world was their art. It was lively and naturalistic, and they excelled in miniature techniques. From the scenes illustrated on their frescoes, stone vases, seal stones, and signet rings, it is possible to build a picture of a productive, well-regulated society. Yet new research suggests that prehistoric Crete was not a peaceful place; there may have been years of warfare before Knossos became the island's dominant power, in around 1600 BC. It is now thought that political upheaval, rather than the devastating volcanic eruption on the island of Santorini, triggered the violent downfall of the palace civilization around 1450 BC.

But there are many memorable places in Crete that belong to a more recent past, one measured in centuries and not millennia. Other invaders and occupiers—Roman colonists, the Byzantines, Arab invaders, Venetian colonists, and Ottoman pashas—have all left their mark on Heraklion, Chania, Rethymnon, and other towns and villages throughout the island. Today, Crete welcomes outsiders who delight in its splendid beaches, charming Old Town quarters, and array of splendid landscapes. Openly inviting to guests who want to experience the real Greece, Cretans remain family oriented and rooted in tradition, and you'll find that one of the greatest pleasures on Crete is immersing yourself in the island's lifestyle.

PLANNING

WHEN TO GO

The best times to visit Crete are May, when every outcrop of rock is ablaze with brilliant wildflowers and the sea is warm enough for a brisk dip, or September and October, when the sea is still warm and the light golden but piercingly clear.

Most of Crete, outside the major cities, is really only noticeably busy from mid-July through August, when the main sights and towns on the north coast come close to overflowing with tourists. Beaches get busier, and reservations can be essential in the most popular restaurants, too. Even in the height of summer, though, you can enjoy many parts of the east, west, and south coasts without feeling oppressed by crowds.

Crete can also be a pleasure in winter, when you can visit the museums and archaeological sites and enjoy the island's delightful towns without the crush of crowds. Remember, though, that rainfall can be heavy in January and February, and note that many hotels and restaurants, especially resorts, close from late October or November through mid-April or May.

PLANNING YOUR TIME

Inviting as Crete's beaches may be, there is much more to the island than lazing on the sand. Archaeological sites in Crete open at 8 or 8:30 in summer, so get an early start to wander through the ruins before the sun is blazing. You may also want to visit some of the folklife museums that pay homage to the island's traditional past, or simply head out and explore the magnificent mountain and coastal scenery. An evening should begin with a stroll around the shady squares that grace every Cretan town and village, or along a waterfront promenade—those in Chania, Ayios Nikolaos, and Sitia are especially picturesque and jammed with locals. Most evenings are spent over a long meal, almost always eaten outdoors in the warm weather. Retire for a contemplative drink of *raki* or, for entertainment, seek out a *kentron*, a taverna that hosts traditional Cretan music and dancing. The star performer is the *lyra* player, who can extract a surprisingly subtle sound from the small pear-shaped instrument, held upright on the thigh and played with a bow.

GETTING HERE AND AROUND

AIR TRAVEL

Olympic Air connects Athens, and other islands, with Heraklion, Chania, and Sitia. Aegean Airlines flies between Athens and Heraklion and Chania. Sky Express flies to both Heraklion and Sitia. Ryanair connects Chania to Athens, and to other European destinations. Fares on all are highest in the summer, often double that of a ferry.

The principal arrival point on Crete is Heraklion Airport, where up to 20 flights daily arrive from Athens and daily flights arrive from throughout Greece. Heraklion is also serviced directly by flights from other European cities.

There are several daily flights from Athens and, in summer, other European cities to Chania Airport, and several per week from Athens to Sitia, which is also connected to the Dodecanese islands with a few weekly flights in summer.

A bus just outside Heraklion Airport takes you to the town center. Tickets are sold from a kiosk next to the bus stop; the fare is €1.20. From Chania Airport, buses run hourly to the center for €2.50, but these are not running 24 hours. Tickets are available inside the airport. Cabs line up outside all airports to meet flights; the fare into the respective towns is about €10 for Heraklion, €23 for Chania, and €5 for Sitia.

Airport Contacts Chania Airport (*CHQ*). ✛ *15 km (9 miles) northeast of Chania, off the road to Sterne* ☎ *28210/83800* ⊕ *www.chq-airport.gr.* **Heraklion Airport (Kazantzakis International Airport)** (*HER*). ✛ *5 km (3 miles) east of town, off the road to Gournes* ☎ *28103/97800.* **Sitia Airport** (*JSH*). ✛ *1 km (½ mile) northwest of town, off the main coast road* ☎ *28430/24424.*

BIKE AND MOPED TRAVEL

You'll find rentals in just about any town on the tourist trail. Expect to pay about €25 a day for a 50cc moped, for which you will need to present only a valid driver's license; law requires a motorcycle license to rent larger bikes. Fees usually cover insurance, but only for repairs to the bike, and usually with a deductible of at least €500. The law mandates that you wear a helmet, despite what you may think from observing the locals. Be careful—the casualty departments of hospitals are full of over-eager tourists every year.

Bicycles are available to rent in most resorts, and are offered by many hotels and car rental companies. For the more adventurous, mountain bike and road tours are available.

Contacts Blue Sea Rentals. ✉ *Kosmo Zoutou 5–7, Heraklion* ☎ *28102/41097* ⊕ *www.bluesearentals.com.* **Olympic Bike.** ✉ *Adelianos Kampos 32, Rethymnon* ☎ *28310/72383* ⊕ *www.olympicbike.com.*

BOAT AND FERRY TRAVEL

Heraklion and Souda Bay (5 km/3 miles east of Chania) are the island's main ports. Most ferries are overnight, but there are daytime ferries from Piraeus to Heraklion and Chania in the summer. Ferries also connect Crete with other islands, mostly those in the Cyclades and Dodecanese. Service includes fast-ferries between Santorini and Heraklion (cutting travel time to just under two hours) and a ferry linking Sitia with the Dodecanese islands of Kassos, Karpathos, and Rhodes. There is also a ferry linking Sitia and Heraklion. There is an irregular service from Kalamata and Gythion in the Peloponnese to Kissamos (Kastelli) in the far west of the island. Ships also sail from Heraklion to Limassol, in Cyprus, and to Haifa, Israel. On the overnight runs, you can book either a berth or an airplane-style seat, and there are usually cafeterias, dining rooms, shops, and other services onboard. The most economical berth accommodations are in four-berth cabins, which are relatively spacious and comfortable and are equipped with bathrooms.

A one-way fare from Piraeus to Heraklion or Chania without accommodations costs about €38, and from about €55 with accommodations. A small discount is given for round-trip tickets. Car fares are about €80 each way, depending on vehicle size. In July and August, a boat service around the Samaria gorge operates along the southwest coast from Hora Sfakion to Loutro, Ayia Roumeli, Souyia, Lissos, and Paleochora, the main resort on the southwest coast. Ferries also sail from Paleochora to Gavdos, the most southerly island in Europe, and from Ierapetra to Krissi, an island also to the south. Most travel agencies sell tickets for all ferries and hydrofoils. Make reservations several days in advance during the July to August high season.

Ferry routes change often, but among the lines that serve Crete are Anek (Piraeus to Heraklion and Chania), Blue Star Ferries (Piraeus to Heraklion), Cretan Lines (Piraeus to Heraklion), Hellenic Seaways (Heraklion to Santorini, Paros, and Mykonos), and Minoan Lines (Piraeus to Heraklion). Ferry schedules are best checked at ⊕ *www.ferries.gr*.

Contacts Anek Lines. ⊠ *Akti Konili 24, Piraeus* ☎ *21041/97470* ⊕ *www.anek.gr*.

BUS TRAVEL

You can find schedules and book seats in advance at bus stations, and tourist offices are also well equipped with information about service. As efficient as the bus network is, you might have a hard time getting out of Heraklion, with its confusing number of stations. You'll find the bus station for western Crete, Bus Station A, opposite the port; this also serves places on the north coast east of Heraklion, such as Hersonissos, Archanes, Sitia, Ayios Nikolaos, and the Lasithi Plateau. The station for the south, Bus Station B, is outside the Chania Gate to the right of the Archaeological Museum; this is where you get buses for such places as Matala and Phaistos. Ask someone at the tourist information office to tell you exactly where to find your bus and to show you the spot on a map. You'll need to make reservations in advance for all buses. Alternatively, travel agents offer private bus transfers to the popular sights *(see Tour Options)*.

CAR TRAVEL

Roads on Crete are not too congested, yet the accident rate is high compared to other parts of Europe. Driving in the main towns can be nerve-racking, to say the least. Most road signs are in Greek and English, though signage is often nonexistent or inadequate. Be sure to carry a road map or GPS at all times, and to stop and ask directions when the need arises—otherwise, you may drive miles out of your way. Gas stations are not plentiful outside the big towns, and gasoline is more expensive in Crete than it is in the United States and on par with prices elsewhere in Europe—expect to pay about €1.55 a liter (about $6.45 a gallon).

Drive defensively wherever you are, as Cretan drivers are aggressive and liable to ignore the rules of the road. Sheep and goats frequently stray onto the roads, with or without their shepherd or sheepdog. In July and August, tourists on motor scooters can be a hazard. Night driving is not advisable.

As for car rentals, you can arrange beforehand with a major agency in the United States or in Athens to pick up a car on arrival in Crete, or work through one of the many local car-rental agencies that have offices in the airports and in the cities, as well as in some resort villages. For the most part, these local agencies are extremely reliable, provide courteous service, and charge very low rates. Many, such as the excellent Kappa Car Rental, will meet your ship or plane, or come to your hotel, and drop you off again at no extra charge.

Even without advance reservations, expect to pay about €40 or less a day in high season for a medium-size car with unlimited mileage. Weekly prices are negotiable, but with unlimited mileage rentals start at about €200 in summer. At many agencies, you are responsible for a €500 deductible for any damage, regardless of your insurance coverage.

Big international agencies, including Avis, Hertz, and Sixt, are well represented on Crete *(see Car Travel in Travel Smart for contact information)*

Contacts Kappa Car Rental. ✉ *Chania Airport, Chania* ☎ *28210/60120* ⊕ *www.auto-kappa.gr.*

HOTELS

Some of Greece's finest resorts line the shores of Elounda Peninsula, offering sumptuous surroundings and exquisite service. Although the atmosphere at these resorts is more international than Greek, in other places you'll find authentic surroundings in the Venetian palaces and old mansions that are being sensitively restored as small hotels, especially in Chania and Rethymnon. Many of the better hotels on Crete offer special rates and packages through their websites, and it's always worthwhile to check out what discounts might be available during your stay—special rates often bring even a luxurious hotel into affordable range, especially outside high season. For a more rustic yet authentic experience on Crete, opt for simple, whitewashed, tile-floor rooms with rustic pine furniture in the ubiquitous "room to rent" establishments in mountain and seaside villages. Another common term is studio, which implies the presence of a kitchen or basic cooking facilities. Standards of cleanliness are high in Crete, and service is almost always friendly.

RESTAURANTS

The Cretan diet has been the subject of much speculation recently. The reliance on fresh fruit and vegetables produced through the longest growing season in Europe, together with dairy, pulses, and mountain herbs, augmented by small amounts of fish and meat, all cooked in olive oil, has led to some of the healthiest, longest-living people on the planet. Organic is a way of life here, rather than a buzzword. Cretans are justifiably proud of their food, and you will eat well

Of course, all the Greek classics are present, but it is worth looking out for Cretan specialties that reflect the diverse heritage of the island. *Dakos* is a staple—twice-baked barley bread topped with tomatoes, crumbled *mizithra*, a creamy soft white cheese, drizzled with olive oil, and sprinkled with oregano. Pies are ubiquitous; *boureki*, with zucchini and potato, is the classic, but fennel, greens, and *sfakianes pitas*, with cheese and honey, are always popular. The olive oil is renowned for its quality and is liberally applied. Consider taking some back home—it makes a great reminder of your journey.

Meat and fish are often simply grilled, with lamb and goat served as a stew such as *tsigariasto*, a western Crete speciality slow-cooked in olive oil. A common way to eat is to sample the *mezedes* offered—small plates to share. Like a Greek version of tapas, it is a great way to sample the island's differing delicacies. Lunch is a fairly flexible concept; often taken between 1 and 4. Similarly, dinner is a movable feast that often starts at 10:30; indeed, as the tourists are finishing their meals, locals are just preparing to go out.

Cretan wine has made great inroads recently, and the quality is ever increasing. Boutique wineries are flourishing, offering neglected indigenous varieties. The house wine, confusingly sold by the kilo, is often not a bad option; the whites tend to be more palatable. The island's main alcoholic staple, however, is *tsikouthia*, commonly known as *raki*. This local firewater is an accompaniment to every occasion from breakfast to weddings! As a gesture of hospitality, restaurants will often offer a small flask, along with a small sweet, at the end of a meal.

Restaurant and hotel reviews have been shortened. For full information, visit Fodors.com.

DINING AND LODGING PRICES IN EUROS			
	$	**$$**	**$$$**	**$$$$**
Restaurants	under €15	€15–€25	€26–€40	over €40
Hotels	under €125	€125–€225	€226–€275	over €275

Restaurant prices are the average cost of a main course at dinner or, if dinner is not served, at lunch. Hotel prices are the lowest cost of a standard double room in high season.

TOUR OPTIONS

Most travel agents can arrange for personal guides.

BUS TOURS

Resort hotels and large agents organize guided tours in air-conditioned buses to the main Minoan sites; excursions to spectacular beaches such as Vai in the northeast and Elafonisi and Balos in the west; and trips to Santorini and to closer islands such as Spinalonga, a former leper colony off Ayios Nikolaos.

Crete Travel. Crete Travel is an excellent source for tour information, with insights into many of the island's attractions and tours, including hiking expeditions, gastronomic excursions, wine tastings, and visits to out-of-the-way monasteries, as well as the more obvious sights. Tailor-made itineraries are a specialty; if you ever wanted to make cheese in a shepherd's hut up a mountain or dreamed of skippering your own yacht, this is the place to come. ⊠ *Kallipoleos 11, Heraklion* ☎ *28102/13445* ⊕ *www.cretetravel.com.*

HIKING TOURS

Crete is excellent hiking terrain, and many trails crisscross the mountains and gorges, especially in the southwest. The Greek National Tourism Organization (GNTO or EOT) is a source of information.

Alpine Travel. This outfitter offers one-day, one-week, and two-week hiking tours throughout Crete, and arranges transportation and accommodations for individual trekkers as well. ⊠ *Chania* ☎ *28210/50939* ⊕ *www.alpine.gr.*

VISITOR INFORMATION

Tourist offices are more plentiful, and more helpful, on Crete than they are in many other parts of Greece. Offices of the Greek National Tourism Organization (GNTO or EOT), in the major towns, are open daily 8–2 and 3–8:30. The municipalities of Ayios Nikolaos, Sitia, and Ierapetra operate their own tourist offices, and these provide a wealth of information on the towns and surrounding regions, as well as help with accommodations and local tours; most keep long summer hours, open daily 8:30 am–9 pm.

EASTERN CRETE ΑΝΑΤΟΛΙΚΗ ΚΡΗΤΗ

Eastern Crete includes the towns and cities of Heraklion, Ayios Nikolaos, Sitia, and Ierapetra, as well as the archaeological sites of Knossos and Malia. Natural wonders lie amid these man-made places, including the palm-fringed beach at Vai and the Lasithi Plateau, and other inland plains and highlands are studded with villages where life goes on untouched by the hedonism of the coastal resorts. You may well make first landfall in Heraklion, the island's major port. You'll want to spend time here to visit the excellent Archaeological Museum and Knossos, but you're likely to have a more relaxing experience in Ayios Nikolaos, a charming and animated port town, or in the resorts on the stunning Elounda Peninsula. Sitia is slowly emerging as a visitor destination, but it still is, in essence, a provincial town that happens to have tourists, rather than a major destination. A pretty harbor front that feels almost

Cycladic with whitewashed buildings and narrow streets bears exploration, but it serves best as a gateway to the beautiful, undiscovered eastern end of the island.

HERAKLION ΗΡΑΚΛΕΙΟ

175 km (109 miles) south of Piraeus harbor in Athens, 69 km (43 miles) west of Ayios Nikolaos, 78 km (49 miles) east of Rethymnon.

In Minoan times, Crete's largest city, the fifth-largest city in Greece, was a harbor for Knossos, the grandest palace and effective power center of prehistoric Crete. The Bronze Age remains were built over long ago, and now Heraklion (also known as Iraklion), with more than 150,000 inhabitants, stretches far beyond even the Venetian walls. Heraklion is not immediately appealing: it's a sprawling and untidy collection of apartment blocks and busy roadways, often cast as the ugly sister to Chania's Cinderella. Many travelers looking for Crete's more rugged pleasures bypass the island's capital altogether, but the city's renowned Archaeological Museum and the nearby Palace of Knossos make Heraklion a mandatory stop for anyone even remotely interested in ancient civilizations.

Besides, at closer look, Heraklion is not without its charms. A walk down Daidalou and the other pedestrians-only streets provides plenty of amusements, and the city has more than its share of outdoor cafés where you can sit and watch life unfold. Seaside promenades and narrow lanes that run off them can be quite animated, thanks to ongoing restoration, and the inner harbor dominated by the Koules, a sturdy Venetian fortress, is richly evocative of the island's storied past.

GETTING HERE AND AROUND

Heraklion is Crete's major air hub, and Kazantzakis Airport has been greatly expanded in recent years. Flights on Olympic Air and Aegean Airlines arrive almost hourly from Athens, and many flights from other European cities use the airport. The airport is only about 5 km (3 miles) east of the city.

Frequent ferries connect Heraklion to Piraeus (at least five daily, including daytime ferries from May through August), Thessaloniki (three times weekly in the high season), and the Cyclades (Santorini, Mykonos, and others). Operators and schedules change frequently; for the latest information, check on your route at ⊕ *www.ferries.gr*, or stop by one of the travel agencies that operate near all Greek ports.

Heraklion is Crete's hub for bus travel, and you can get just about anywhere on the island from any of the city's bus terminals. Service to the main towns—Ayios Nikolaos, Rethymnon, and Chania—runs hourly. Buses to all these towns arrive at and leave from the two adjacent terminals on the harbor, just east of the city center.

EXPLORING

If you have just a day in Heraklion, your time will be tight. Get an early start and head for the Archaeological Museum before the crowds descend. Then, spend a couple of hours in the morning walking around the city, stepping into the churches if they're open and poking around the lively market. Nearby Knossos will easily occupy most of the

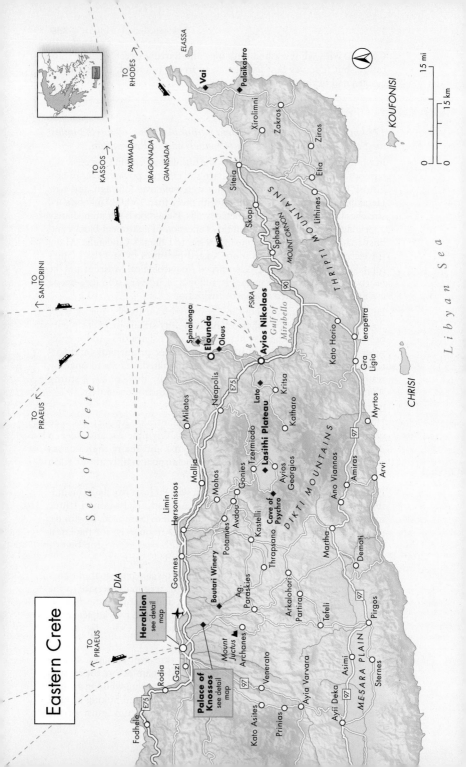

Eastern Crete

Sea of Crete

Libyan Sea

TO PIRAEUS
TO SANTORINI
TO KASSOS
TO RHODES

ELASSA
PAXIMADA
DRAGONADA
GIANISADA

Vai
Palaikastro
Xirolimni
Zakros
Siteia
Ziros
Skopi
Etia
Sphaka
Lithines

THRIPTI MOUNTAINS
MOUNTORNO

Ayios Nikolaos
Gulf of Mirabello
PSIRA
Kato Horio
Ierapetra
Gra Ligia

Spinalonga
Elounda
Olous
Neapolis
Lato
Krisa
Katharo
Myrtos

Milatos
Lasithi Plateau
Tzermiado
Ayios Georgios

DIKTI MOUNTAINS
Ano Viannos
Amiras
Arvi

Mallia
Mohos
Avdou
Cave of Psychro

Limin Hersonissos
Gonies
Kastelli
Thrapsano

Gournes
Potamies
Martha
Demati

Heraklion
see detail map
Boutari Winery
Ag. Paraskies
Arkalohori
Partira
Tefeli
Pirgos

DIA

Gazi
Rodia
Fodhele

Palace of Knossos
see detail map
Mount Juctus
Archanes
Venerato
Ayia Varvara

Kato Asies
Pinias
Ayii Deka
Asimi
Sternes

MESARA PLAIN

KOUFONISI

CHRISI

E75
E75
90
97
97
97
97

15 mi
15 km

afternoon. If you're staying overnight in or near Heraklion, take an evening stroll in the busy area around Ta Leontaria and Kornarou Square; half the population seems to converge here.

Heraklion's ever-improving road network is making it easier to avoid the all but impassable city center; however, if you're spending any time at all in Heraklion, it's best to wait until you are leaving the city to pick up a rental car.

TOP ATTRACTIONS

Fodor's Choice
★

Heraklion Archaeological Museum. Standing in a class of its own, this museum guards practically all of the Minoan treasures uncovered in the legendary excavations of the Palace of Knossos and other monuments of Minoan civilization. These amazing artifacts, many 3,000 years old, were brought to light in 20th-century excavations by famed British archaeologist Sir Arthur Evans and are shown off in handsome modern galleries. It's best to visit the museum first thing in the morning, before the tour buses arrive, or in late afternoon, once they pull away. Top treasures include the famous seal stones, many inscribed with Linear B script, discovered and deciphered by Evans around the turn of the 20th century. The most stunning and mysterious seal stone is the so-called Phaistos Disk, found at Phaistos Palace in the south, its purpose unknown. (Linear B script is now recognized as an early form of Greek, but the earlier Linear A script that appears on clay tablets and that of the Phaistos Disk have yet to be deciphered.)

Perhaps the most arresting exhibits, though, are the sophisticated frescoes, restored fragments of which were found in Knossos. They depict broad-shouldered, slim-waisted youths, their large eyes fixed with an enigmatic expression on the Prince of the Lilies; ritual processions and scenes from the bullring, with young men and women somersaulting over the back of a charging bull; and groups of court ladies, whose flounced skirts led a French archaeologist to exclaim in surprise, "*Des Parisiennes!,*" a name still applied to this striking fresco.

Even before great palaces with frescoes were being built around 1900 BC, the prehistoric Cretans excelled at metalworking and carving stone vases, and they were also skilled at producing pottery, such as the eggshell-thin Kamares ware decorated in delicate abstract designs. Other specialties were miniature work such as the superbly crafted jewelry and the colored seal stones that are carved with lively scenes of people and animals. Though naturalism and an air of informality distinguish much Minoan art from that of contemporary Bronze Age cultures elsewhere in the eastern Mediterranean, you can also see a number of heavy rococo set pieces, such as the fruit stand with a toothed rim and the punch bowl with appliquéd flowers.

The Minoans' talents at modeling in stone, ivory, and a kind of glass paste known as faience peaked in the later palace period (1700–1450 BC). A famous rhyton, a vase for pouring libations, carved from dark serpentine in the shape of a bull's head, has eyes made of red jasper and clear rock crystal with horns of gilded wood. An ivory acrobat—perhaps a bull-leaper—and two bare-breasted faience goddesses in flounced skirts holding wriggling snakes were among a group of treasures hidden

The Koules harbor fortress is a mighty reminder of the age when Venetians ruled Crete from their outpost in Heraklion.

beneath the floor of a storeroom at Knossos. Bull-leaping, whether a religious rite or a favorite sport, inspired some of the most memorable images in Minoan art. Note, also, the three vases, probably originally covered in gold leaf, from Ayia Triada that are carved with scenes of Minoan life thought to be rendered by artists from Knossos: boxing contests, a harvest-home ceremony, and a Minoan official taking delivery of a consignment of hides. The most stunning rhyton of all, from Zakro, is made of rock crystal. ⊠ *Xanthoudidou and Hatzidaki* ☎ *28102/279000* ⊕ *www.heraklionmuseum.gr* ⊠ *€10; combined ticket for museum and Palace of Knossos €16.*

Fodor'sChoice
★ **Historical Museum of Crete.** An imposing mansion houses a varied collection of Early Christian and Byzantine sculptures, Venetian and Ottoman stonework, artifacts of war, and rustic folklife items. The museum provides a wonderful introduction to Cretan culture, and is the only place in Crete to display the work of famed native son El Greco (Domenikos Theotocopoulos), who left the island—then part of the Venetian Republic—for Italy and then Spain around 1567; his *Baptism of Christ* and *View of Mount Sinai and the Monastery of St. Catherine* hang amid frescoes, icons, and other Byzantine pieces. Upon entering, look out for the *Lion of St. Mark* sculpture, with an inscription that says in Latin "I protect the kingdom of Crete." Left of the entrance is a room stuffed with memorabilia from Crete's bloody revolutionary past: weapons, portraits of mustachioed warrior chieftains, and the flag of the short-lived independent Cretan state set up in 1898. The 19th-century banner in front of the staircase sums up the spirit of Cretan rebellion against the Turks: *eleftheria o thanatos* ("Freedom or Death"). A small section is

dedicated to World War II and the German invasion of 1941. Upstairs, look in on a room arranged as the study of Crete's most famous writer, Nikos Kazantzakis (1883–1957), the author of *Zorba the Greek* and an epic poem, *The Odyssey, a Modern Sequel*; he was born in Heraklion and is buried here, just inside the section of the walls known as the Martinengo. The top floor contains a stunning collection of Cretan textiles, including the brilliant scarlet weavings typical of the island's traditional handwork, and another room arranged as a domestic interior of the early 1900s. ⊠ *Sofokli Venizelou 27* ☎ *28102/83219* ⊕ *www. historical-museum.gr* 🎫 *€5* ☉ *Closed Sun.*

Koules. Heraklion's inner harbor, where fishing boats land their catch and yachts are moored, is dominated by this massive fortress so named by the Turks but, in fact, built by the Venetians as the Castello del Molo in the 16th century and decorated with the three stone lions of St. Mark, the symbol of Venetian imperialism. On the east side of the fortress are the vaulted arsenal; here Venetian galleys were repaired and refitted, and timber, cheeses, and sweet malmsey wine were loaded for the three-week voyage to Venice. The view from the battlements takes in the inner as well as the outer harbor, where freighters and passenger ferries drop anchor, to the south rises Mt. Iouktas and, to the west, the pointed peak of Mt. Stromboulas. ⊠ *Inner harbor* ☎ *28102/43559* ⊕ *www.koules.efah.gr* 🎫 *€2.*

Loggia. A gathering place for the island's Venetian nobility, this open-air arcade, with a meeting hall above, was built in the early 17th century by Francesco Basilicata, an Italian architect. Restored to its original Palladian elegance, it adjoins the old Venetian Armory, now the City Hall. ⊠ *Avgoustou 25.*

NEED A BREAK

✗ **Kir-Kor 1922.** Stop into this venerable old *bougatsa* shop for an envelope of flaky pastry that's either filled with a sweet, creamy filling and dusted with cinnamon and sugar, or stuffed with soft white cheese. A double portion served warm with Greek coffee is a nice treat. **Known for:** Greek pastries; Cretan-style yogurt; opening early. ⊠ *Platia Liontarion* ☎ *28102/42705.*

Martinengo Bastion. Six bastions shaped like arrowheads jut out from the well-preserved Venetian walls. Martinengo is the largest, designed by Micheli Sanmicheli in the 16th century to keep out Barbary pirates and Turkish invaders. When the Turks overran Crete in 1648, the garrison at Heraklion held out for another 21 years in one of the longest sieges in European history. General Francesco Morosini finally surrendered the city to the Turkish Grand Vizier in September 1669. He was allowed to sail home to Venice with the city's archives and such precious relics as the skull of Ayios Titos—which was not returned until 1966. Literary pilgrims come to the Martinengo to visit the **burial place of writer Nikos Kazantzakis.** The grave is a plain stone slab marked by a weathered wooden cross. The inscription, from his writings, reads: "I fear nothing, I hope for nothing, I am free." ⊠ *Heraklion* ✛ *In walls south of city center, off Plastira.*

CLOSE UP

Beaches in Crete

With hundreds of miles of dramatic coastline, Crete has an almost endless supply of beaches. Many are soft and powdery, some are action-packed with water sports, and others are blissfully untrammeled. The most celebrated bookend the island: palm-shaded Vai to the east and Elafonisi to the west.

Lovers of sand and surf quickly discover that there are really two distinct types of beaches on Crete: the highly developed strands on the north coast and the rugged getaway beaches on the south coast. Northern beaches stretch along the flat, sandy coastal plain between the island's major cities and are easily reached by the east–west national highway, as well as by an extensive bus network. Most are packed with umbrellas and sun beds and backed by hotels.

Beaches on the south coast are tucked into coves and bays, often at the end of poor roads; a rental car and a good map are essential to explore them. Strike it lucky and you will see barely a soul, even in peak season.

Plateia Eleftherias. The city's biggest square is paved in marble and dotted with fountains. The Archaeological Museum is off the north end of the square; at the west side is the beginning of Daidalou, the main thoroughfare, which follows the line of an early fortification wall and is now a pedestrian walkway lined with tavernas, boutiques, jewelers, and souvenir shops. ⊠ *Heraklion* ✛ *Southeast end of Daidalou.*

Ta Liontaria. "The Lions," a stately marble Renaissance fountain, remains a beloved town landmark. It's the heart of Heraklion's town center—on Eleftheriou Venizelou Square, a triangular pedestrian zone filled with cafés and named after the Cretan statesman who united the island with Greece in 1913. The square is also known simply as Ta Liontaria or Plateia Liontarion and was the center of the colony founded in the 13th century, when Venice colonized Crete, and Heraklion became an important port of call on the trade routes to the Middle East. ⊠ *Dedalou and 25 Augousto.*

WORTH NOTING

Ayia Aikaterina. Nestled in the shadow of the Ayios Minas cathedral is one of Crete's most attractive small churches, named for St. Katherine and built in 1555. The church now houses a museum of icons by Cretan artists, who often traveled to Venice to study with Italian Renaissance painters. Look for six icons by Michael Damaskinos, who worked in both Byzantine and Renaissance styles during the 16th century. Crete's most famous artist, Domenikos Theotocopoulos, better known as El Greco, studied at the monastery school attached to the church in the mid-16th century. ⊠ *Kyrillou Loukareos* ☎ *28103/36316* ⊕ *www.iakm.gr.*

Ayios Minas. This huge, lofty cathedral, dating from 1895, can hold up to 8,000 worshippers, but is most lively on November 11, when Heraklion celebrates the feast of Minas, a 4th-century Roman soldier-turned-Christian. Legend has it that on Easter Sunday 1826 a ghostly Minas reappeared on horseback and dispersed a Turkish mob ready to slay the city's Orthodox faithful. Curiously, few of Heraklion's inhabitants

are named after Minas, which is unusual for a city's patron saint. The reason is that many years ago babies born out of wedlock were left on the steps of the church, and were named Minas by the clergy who took these children in and cared for them. Thus, the name Minas came to be associated with illegitimacy. ✉ *Kyrillou Loukareos.*

WHERE TO EAT

$　✗ **Erganos.** One of Heraklion's most traditional restaurants, just by
GREEK　Kazantzaki park, serves authentic local fare, mainly to a local crowd, far removed from the tourist havens in the center. Mouthwatering bite-sized *sfakianopita* (pies), filled with cheese and honey, are a classic true taste of Crete, and the lamb and goat are always popular, as are tremendous *keftedes* (meatballs). **Known for:** traditional Cretan cuisine; authentic atmosphere; hospitable staff. 💲 *Average main: €10* ✉ *G. Georgiadou 5* ☎ *28102/85629* ⊕ *www.erganos.gr.*

$　✗ **Ippokambos.** In a modern wood-and-glass conservatory overlooking
SEAFOOD　the Koules, this Heraklion institution serves some of the best fish in town, with the waves only a stone's throw away. Ask a local for a recommendation and they will invariably mention Ippokambos. **Known for:** the freshest local fish and seafood; generous portions; seafront setting. 💲 *Average main: €12* ✉ *Sofokli Venizelou 3* ☎ *28102/80240.*

$
GREEK
Fodor's Choice
★

✗ **Peskesi.** In a restored sea captain's mansion, stone walls and arches provide the backdrop to some of the best food in Crete: traditional cuisine brought to life with modern techniques and presentation. A 60-acre farm in Harasso is dedicated to supplying the restaurant with seasonal local produce, much of it organic, and the flavors really shine through. **Known for:** atmospheric location; truly knowledgeable and interested staff; delightful purely Cretan wines. $ *Average main: €12* ⊠ *Kapetan Haralabi 6-8* ☎ *28102/88887* ⊕ *www.peskesicrete.gr.*

WHERE TO STAY

$$
HOTEL

GDM Megaron. A handsome building, GDM Megaron stands sentinel over the harbor front, and from its humble roots as a citrus processing enterprise in the 1930s, it has risen to be the city's luxury choice; interiors are classic and elegantly furnished, with an impressive lobby and refined air. **Pros:** central seafront location overlooking Koules; most rooms have water views; wonderful rooftop restaurant. **Cons:** formal surroundings can feel a little hushed at times; rear rooms overlook the city; some noise from the nearby bus depot. $ *Rooms from: €130* ⊠ *D. Beaufort 9* ☎ *28103/05300* ⊕ *www.gdmmegaron.gr* ⋑ *58 rooms* ⦿l *Breakfast.*

$$
B&B/INN
Fodor's Choice
★

Kalimera Archanes Village. An especially appealing base for exploring Knossos and Heraklion is the well-kept wine village of Archanes, where three 19th-century stone houses tucked into a garden are fitted out with traditional furnishings and all the modern comforts. **Pros:** highly atmospheric and very comfortable; near many sights but provides a nice dose of Greek village life; beautiful interiors and outdoor spaces. **Cons:** beaches and Heraklion are a 15-minute drive away; a pool would be the icing on the cake; can be hard to find when you first approach. $ *Rooms from: €200* ⊠ *Theotokopoulou, Tsikritsi, Archanes* ✛ *Off Leof. Kapetanaki, left after Likastos Taverna* ☎ *28107/52999* ⊕ *www. archanes-village.gr* ⋑ *4 houses* ⦿l *Breakfast.*

$
HOTEL

Olive Green Hotel. Since opening in 2016, this city-center hotel has been shaking up the local hotel landscape with its supermodern design and facilities, allied to an eco-friendly approach. **Pros:** overlooks a tree-lined square; clean, neutral, tasteful design; supercentral location minutes from the seafront and main attractions. **Cons:** iPad control of room functions won't suit all guests; parking is a short walk around the corner and not free; cheapest rooms lack a balcony. $ *Rooms from: €105* ⊠ *Idomeneos 22* ☎ *28103/302900* ⊕ *www.olivegreenhotel.com* ⋑ *48 rooms* ⦿l *Breakfast.*

$
HOTEL

Veneziano Boutique Hotel. A landmark building in Heraklion, with both Venetian and Ottoman heritage dating back to 1510, has been given a careful renovation, resulting in one of the city's most stylish and chic accommodations. **Pros:** beautiful, elegant building handsomely restored; a two-minute walk from the heart of town; quiet backstreet location. **Cons:** steep flight of stairs to upstairs rooms; reception is a desk under those stairs; surrounding streets are a little dull. $ *Rooms from: €95* ⊠ *1770 and N. Kazantaki* ☎ *28103/44758* ⊕ *www.veneziano.gr* ⋑ *6 rooms* ⦿l *Breakfast.*

Palace of Knossos

0 ____ 40 yards

0 ____ 40 meters

KNOSSOS ΚΝΩΣΟΥ

5 km (3 miles) south of Heraklion.

Paintings of bull-leapers, sculptures of bare-breasted snake charmers, myths of minotaurs, and the oldest throne in Europe are just a few of the wonders that the British archaeologist Sir Arthur Evans brought up from the earth at Knossos at the close of the 19th century, to the astonishment of newspapers around the world. They provided telling evidence of the great elegance of King Minos's court (Evans chose the king's name to christen this culture), as the evocative ruins continue to do today.

GETTING HERE

Municipal bus No. 2 (€1.70) heads to the fabled Palace of Knossos every 20 minutes or so from Heraklion, where the main stops include Plateia Eleftherias.

EXPLORING

Boutari Winery. Established by one of the oldest wine-making families in Greece, this state-of-the-art winery marries tradition with innovation, producing over 100,000 bottles a year. In a modern tasting room with great views over the vines to the hills beyond, sample some of the estate's award-winning offerings. You can buy the wines

Although some critics claim that Sir Arthur Evans's restoration "Disneyfied" the Palace of Knossos, no one can deny the results are spectacular.

you have tasted, along with other local delicacies. ⊠ *Skalani, Heraklion* ☎ *28107/31617* ⊕ *www.boutari.gr* 🖃 *€5.*

Fodor's Choice
★

Palace of Knossos. This most amazing of archaeological sites once lay hidden beneath a huge mound hemmed in by low hills. Heinrich Schliemann, father of archaeology and discoverer of Troy, knew it was here, but Turkish obstruction prevented him from exploring his last discovery. Cretan independence from the Ottoman Turks made it possible for Sir Arthur Evans, a British archaeologist, to start excavations in 1899. A forgotten and sublime civilization thus came again to light with the uncovering of the great Palace of Knossos.

The magnificent Minoans flourished on Crete from around 2700 to 1450 BC, and their palaces and cities at Knossos, Phaistos, and Gournia were centers of political power and luxury—they traded in tin, saffron, gold, and spices as far afield as Spain—when the rest of Europe was a place of primitive barbarity. They loved art, farmed bees, and worshipped many goddesses. But what caused their demise? Some say political upheaval, but others point to an eruption on Thira (Santorini), about 100 km (62 miles) north in the Aegean, that caused tsunamis and earthquakes and brought about the end of this sophisticated civilization.

The Palace of Knossos site was occupied from Neolithic times, and the population spread to the surrounding land. Around 1900 BC, the hilltop was leveled and the first palace constructed; around 1700 BC, after an earthquake destroyed the original structure, the later palace was built, surrounded by houses and other buildings. Around 1450 BC, another widespread disaster occurred, perhaps an invasion: palaces and country villas were razed by fire and abandoned, but Knossos remained inhabited even though the palace suffered some damage. But around 1380 BC the palace and its outlying buildings were destroyed by fire, and around 1100 BC the site was abandoned. Still later, Knossos became a Greek city-state.

You enter the palace from the west, passing a bust of Sir Arthur Evans, who excavated at Knossos on and off for more than 20 years. A path leads you around to the monumental **south gateway.** The **west wing** encases lines of long, narrow storerooms where the true wealth of Knossos was kept in tall clay jars: oil, wine, grains, and honey. The **central court** is about 164 feet by 82 feet long. The cool, dark **throne-room complex** has a griffin fresco and a tall, wavy-back gypsum throne, the oldest in Europe. The most spectacular piece of palace architecture is the **grand staircase,** on the east side of the court, leading to the domestic apartments. Four flights of shallow gypsum stairs survive, lighted by a deep light well. Here you get a sense of how noble Minoans lived; rooms were divided by sets of double doors, giving privacy and warmth when closed, coolness and communication when open. The **queen's megaron** (apartment or hall) is decorated with a colorful dolphin fresco and furnished with stone benches. Beside it is a bathroom, complete with a clay tub, and next door a toilet, with a drainage system that permitted flushing into a channel flowing into the Kairatos stream far below. The east side of the palace also contained **workshops.** Beside the staircase leading down to the **east bastion** is a stone water channel made up of parabolic curves and settling basins: a Minoan storm drain. Northwest of the east bastion is the **north entrance,** guarded by a relief fresco of a charging bull. Beyond is the **theatrical area,** shaded by pines and overlooking a shallow flight of steps, which lead down to the **royal road.** This, perhaps, was the ceremonial entrance to the palace.

For a complete education in Minoan architecture and civilization, consider touring Knossos and, of course, the Archaeological Museum in Heraklion (where many of the treasures from the palace are on view), then traveling south to the Palace of Phaistos, another great Minoan site that has not been reconstructed.

■ TIP→ After a long day at the archaeological sites you may feel like you've earned a drink. Follow the signposts to one of the numerous vineyards that surround the pretty village of Archanes, 9 km (5½ miles) south of Knossos, and enjoy tasting some of the world's oldest wines. ✉ *Knossos* ☎ *28102/31940* ⊕ *odysseus.culture.gr* ✍ *€15; combined ticket with Archaeological Museum in Heraklion €16.*

LASITHI PLATEAU ΟΡΟΠΕΔΙΟ ΛΑΣΙΘΙΟΥ

47 km (29 miles) southeast of the Palace of Knossos, 52 km (32 miles) southeast of Heraklion.

The Lasithi Plateau, 2,800 feet high and the biggest of the upland plains of Crete, lies behind a wall of barren mountains. Windmills for pumping water rise above fields of potatoes and the apple and almond orchards that are a pale haze of blossom in early spring. The plateau is remote and breathtakingly beautiful, and ringed by small villages where shops sell local weaving and embroidery.

EXPLORING

Cave of Psychro. This impressive, stalactite-rich cavern is one of a few places in Crete that claim to be the birthplace of Zeus, king of the gods, and where he was reared in secret, out of reach of his vengeful father, Kronos. Approach the cave, once a Minoan sanctuary and now the plateau's most popular tourist attraction, on a short path from the large parking lot on foot or by donkey. ✉ *Lasithi* ✣ *Near village of Psychro* ☎ *28410/22462* 🎟 *€6.*

Cretan Traditional Folklore Museum. An old village house in Ayios Georgios stands as it was when generations of farmers lived here. The living quarters and stables, along with the delightful assemblage of simple furnishings, embroidery, and tools, provide a chance to see domestic life as it was, and indeed still is, for many residents of the plateau. ✉ *Ayios Georgios* ☎ *28440/31382* 🌐 *www.elsolas.gr* 🎟 *€3* 🕒 *Closed late Oct.–mid-Apr.*

WHERE TO EAT

$ GREEK

🍴 **Kronio.** The promise of a meal in this cozy, family-run establishment is alone worth the trip up to the plateau. The taverna is in its fifth decade and still offering delicious pies as well as casseroles and lamb dishes, accompanied by fresh-baked bread and followed up with homemade desserts. **Known for:** authentic Cretan home-cooked dishes served with bags of personality; mixed mezedes to share features 18 separate dishes; can get busy with tour parties. [$] *Average main: €10* ✉ *Tzermiado* ✣ *Center of the village on the Neapolis–Hersonissos road* ☎ *28440/22375* 🌐 *www.kronio.eu* 🕒 *Closed Nov.–Mar.*

EN ROUTE

A rewarding detour as you travel east from Heraklion toward the Lasithi Plateau and Malia takes you south to Kastelli, about 15 km (9 miles) southeast of Heraklion, where the lovely Byzantine church of Ayios Pandeleimon is decorated with elaborate frescoes. Interspersing the landscape here and there are segments of an aqueduct that served the nearby ancient Greek city of Lyttos, yet to be excavated. Thrapsano, about 7 km (4½ miles) farther southwest, is a famous pottery center, where workshops turn out earthenware jugs, pots, and decorative items for sale on the main square and at shops throughout town.

AYIOS NIKOLAOS ΑΓΙΟΣ ΝΙΚΟΛΑΟΣ

30 km (19 miles) east of the Lasithi Plateau, 69 km (43 miles) east of Heraklion.

Ayios Nikolaos is clustered on a peninsula alongside the Gulf of Mirabello, a dramatic composition of bare mountains, islets, and deep blue sea. Behind the crowded harbor lies the picturesque Lake Voulismeni, linked to the sea by a narrow channel. Hilly, with narrow, steep streets that provide sea views, the town is a welcoming and animated place, far more pleasant than Malia and the other resort centers in this part of Crete: you can stroll along waterside promenades, cafés line the lakeshore, and many streets are open only to pedestrians. Ayios Nikolaos and the nearby Elounda Peninsula provide an excellent base for exploring eastern Crete.

GETTING HERE AND AROUND

By ferry or by air, the best option is from Heraklion, less than an hour away by a bus service that runs at least every hour, and often more frequently during the day. The bus station in Ayios Nikolaos is just south of the town center, near the sea on Akti Atlantidos (off Platia Venizelou at the end of Venizelou Street). By car or taxi, Ayios Nikolaos is on the national highway and is easily reached from the capital. Parking in the town is difficult, and the easiest recourse is to opt for one of the inexpensive parking lots dotted around the pedestrians-only center.

VISITOR INFORMATION

Contacts Ayios Nikolaos Visitor Information. ⊠ *Akti Koundourou 21A* ✛ *On the lake bridge corner* ☎ *28410/22357* ⊕ *www.aghiosnikolaos.gr.*

EXPLORING

Folk Museum. This interesting little museum showcases exquisite weavings and embroidered pieces, along with walking sticks, tools, and other artifacts from everyday rural life in Crete. ⊠ *Kondylaki 2* ☎ *28410/25093* 🖃 *€3* ☾ *Closed Mon.*

Kritsa. This delightful village on a mountainside above Ayios Nikolaos is renowned for its weaving tradition, narrow lanes wide enough for only a donkey to pass, and whitewashed houses that surround a large, shady town square filled with café tables that afford views down green valleys planted with olive trees to the sea. The woven tablecloths and other wares are hard to miss—villagers drape them over every usable surface and hang them from storefronts and even trees. The lovely Byzantine church here, **Panayia Kera,** has an unusual shape, with three naves supported by heavy triangular buttresses. Built in the early years of Venetian occupation, it contains some of the liveliest and best-preserved medieval frescoes on the island, painted in the 13th century. ⊠ *Kritsa* ✛ *11 km (7 miles) west of Ayios Nikolaos* ☎ *28410/51525* 🖃 *€2* ☾ *Closed Mon.*

Lato. This ancient city in the hills just above Ayios Nikolaos was built by the Doric Greeks in a dip between two rocky peaks and named for the mother of Artemis and Apollo. Her image appears on coins found at the site. Make your way over the expanse of ancient masonry to the far end of the ongoing excavations for one of the best views in Crete: on a clear day you can see the island of Santorini, 100 km (62 miles) across the Cretan sea, as well as inland across a seemingly endless panorama of mountains and valleys. ⊠ *Ayios Nikolaos* ✛ *About 10 km (6 miles) west of Ayios Nikolaos, following marked road from village of Kritsa* ☎ *28410/22462* ⊕ *www.odysseus.culture.gr* 🖃 *€2* ☾ *Closed Mon.*

BEACHES

You can dip into the clean waters that surround Ayios Nikolaos from several good beaches right in town. Kitroplatia and Ammos are both only about a 5- to 10-minute walk from the center. Almyros, 2 km (1 mile) away, is the best and is rightly popular.

WHERE TO EAT

$$
MEDITERRANEAN

✕**Migomis.** Clinging to the cliff above the lake, this restaurant offers some of the best views in town. Food is on a par, too: Mediterranean-inspired dishes accompany Greek classics, and the steaks are rightly famous. **Known for:** dramatic and very romantic cliff-top setting; well presented dishes with an Italian flavor; good international wine list. $ *Average main: €20* ⊠ *Nikou Plastira 20* ☎ *28410/24353* ⊕ *www. migomis.com* ⊗ *Closed Nov.–Mar.*

$$
SEAFOOD

✕**Pelagos.** An enchanting courtyard garden and the high-ceilinged parlors of an elegant neoclassical mansion are the setting for what many consider to be the best fish tavern in Ayios Nikolaos. Simple is the keyword here: fresh catches from the fleet bobbing in the harbor just beyond are plainly grilled and accompanied by local vegetables and Cretan wines. **Known for:** simply prepared dishes in a lovely setting; friendly service from English-speaking staff; being busy, be prepared to wait in summer. $ *Average main: €15* ⊠ *Stratigou Koraka 11* ☎ *28410/82019* ⊗ *Closed Nov.–Mar.*

$
GREEK

✕**Taverna Stavrakakis.** Enhance the short trip out to Kritsa and Lato with a stop in the nearby village of Exo Lakonia to enjoy a meal at the homey *kafenion* of Manolis and Katerina Stavrakakis. Dishes are based on family recipes, and most are made from ingredients the couple grow themselves. **Known for:** authentic mezedes, not tourist taverna fare; great homemade pies; the friendliest welcome. $ *Average main: €8* ⊠ *Exo Lakonia* ✛ *About 8 km (5 miles) west of Ayios Nikolaos* ☎ *28410/22478.*

WHERE TO STAY

$$$$
RESORT
Fodor'sChoice
★

Daios Cove. Crashing onto the scene in 2010, this glamorous resort redefined the luxury concept with a mighty wow factor—spread over the sides of Vathi Bay (with a private sandy beach), every room has breathtaking views, and many have private terraces and pools. **Pros:** even the smallest rooms are twice the size of a regular hotel room; well-trained and friendly staff; design still feels fresh and new. **Cons:** a distance from Ayios Nikolaos and can feel a little isolated; food and drink costs are high; seemingly hundreds of steps (but funicular to beach helps). $ *Rooms from: €540* ⊠ *Vathi* ☎ *28418/88061* ⊕ *www. daioscovecrete.com* ⊗ *Closed Nov.–Apr.* ⤴ *290 rooms* ¶❘ *Breakfast.*

$
HOTEL

Hotel Du Lac. Right on the lake in the center of town, this good-value hotel has airy and spacious guest rooms that are nicely done with simple, contemporary furnishings; studios, with kitchens and large baths, are enormous and ideal for families. **Pros:** great lakeside views; good, budget option; pretty café below is handy for breakfast. **Cons:** large differential in size between rooms and studios; it's worth paying the extra; not 24-hour reception; parking (charge payable) is a short walk away. $ *Rooms from: €50* ⊠ *28is Oktovriou 17* ☎ *28410/22711* ⊕ *www.dulachotel.gr* ⤴ *23 rooms* ¶❘ *No meals.*

$$$$
RESORT
Fodor'sChoice
★

St. Nicolas Bay. Lovely and luxurious, this special resort is set within immaculate, verdant gardens overlooking the Gulf of Mirabello at the edge of Ayios Nikolaos—magical surroundings. **Pros:** smart, generous, and indulgent atmosphere; feels intimate but never crowded; superior dining options. **Cons:** away from the town center; not inexpensive; small beach can get busy. $ *Rooms from: €468* ⊠ *Thessi Nissi* ☎ *28410/90200* ⊕ *www. stnicolasbay.gr* ⊗ *Closed Nov.–late Apr.* ⤴ *102 rooms* ¶❘ *Breakfast.*

SHOPPING

Ceramica. Museum-standard copies of ancient amphora, pots, and pithoi are hand-painted by supremely talented artist Nic Gabriel. ⊠ *K. Palaeologou 28* ☎ *28410/24075.*

Chez Sonia. An appealing array of beads, quartz and silver jewelry, woven tablecloths and scarves, carved bowls, and other handicrafts fills Chez Sonia. ⊠ *28is Oktovriou 20* ☎ *28410/28475.*

ELOUNDA ΕΛΟΥΝΤΑ

11 km (7 miles) north of Ayios Nikolaos, 80 km (50 miles) east of Heraklion.

From its origins as a sleepy fishing village, Elounda has transformed into the de rigueur destination for luxury resorts. The shores of the Gulf of Korfos are thronged with villas and hotels offering the last word in indulgence. Spectacular views across to Spinalonga, broodily guarding the harbor, are a constant, as are a jet-set clientele. The beaches tend to be narrow and pebbly, but the water is crystal clear, and, in truth, many guests venture no farther than their private pool. Don't come here in search of Authentic Greece; expect to meet fellow international travelers. As an escape from the rigors of everyday life, though, there are few better-placed competitors.

EXPLORING

Olous. A sunken, ancient city is visible just beneath the turquoise waters off a causeway that leads to the Spinalonga Peninsula (not to be confused with the island of the same name), an undeveloped headland. Don't imagine you are going to discover Atlantis, but the outlines of a Roman settlement on the seabed and the warm, shallow waters make for an enjoyable diversion from the hotel pool. A mosaic floor from an Early Christian basilica with a striking fish motif can also be seen about 300 feet onshore. ⊠ *Elounda ✛ 3 km (2 miles) east of Elounda.*

OFF THE BEATEN PATH

Spinalonga. The Venetians built an imposing fortress on this small island in the center of the Gulf of Mirabello in the 16th century. It withstood Turkish invasion for more than 45 years after the mainland had fallen. Nevertheless, it is more recent history that gives this isle its eerie infamy; from the beginning of the last century it became a leper colony, imprisoning the unfortunate in primitive conditions until 1957. It is a poignant and evocative place with a sense of melancholy that remains to this day. The story is brought to life in the international best-selling novel *The Island* by Victoria Hislop. Boat excursions run from Ayios Nikolaos and Elounda. Most include a swim on a deserted island. There is also a shorter trip from Plaka, directly opposite Spinalonga. Expect to pay €10 from Elounda, €20 from Ayios Nikolaos, and €8 from Plaka. ⊠ *Gulf of Mirabello, Spinalonga* 🏛 *Fortress €8.*

WHERE TO EAT

$$

GREEK

✕**Kanali.** In an impossibly picturesque position next to the sunken ancient city of Olous, and the later canal from where it takes its name, Kanali serves elegant updates of Greek staples. Wooden furniture and an old stone building dressed with bold prints and lanterns lend it a shabby-chic air that would grace the seasides of Mykonos or Santorini. **Known for:** fish baked in a salt crust theatrically opened at your table; beautifully presented modern Greek cuisine; romantic, stylish setting. [$] *Average main: €20* ✉ *Elounda* ✥ *Next to the canal by Olous* ☎ *28410/42075* 🌐 *www.eloundakanali.gr* 🕒 *Closed Nov.–Mar.*

$ GREEK 🍴 **Marilena.** The choice among the many restaurants that cling to the harbor, it's an Elounda classic, having offered traditional Greek food for 40 years. The large rear garden, decked with grapevines, or the seafront-facing tables are charming places to sample the house mezedes, many with a Cypriot origin, or try some of the excellent grill dishes. **Known for:** long-serving unflustered staff; dramatic table-side flambé dishes; Cypriot twists on Greek classics. [$] *Average main: €12* ✉ *Harborside, main square* ☎ *28410/41322* 🌐 *www.marilenarestaurant.gr* 🕒 *Closed late Oct.–early Mar.*

WHERE TO STAY

$ HOTEL 🏨 **Akti Olous Beach.** Set on the edge of the gulf, with sweeping views across to the bay from its rooftop terrace pool, this hotel may be the answer to affordable accommodations in Elounda. **Pros:** seaside location within walking distance of town; same beautiful views as the fancy hotels along the bay; good value for Elounda. **Cons:** some rooms are a bit small and dark; pricier rooms have the front sea view; can be busy with tour groups. [$] *Rooms from: €120* ✉ *Akti Olountos* ☎ *28410/41270* 🌐 *www.eloundaaktiolous.gr* 🕒 *Closed Nov.–mid-Apr.* 🛏 *70 rooms* 🍽 *Breakfast.*

$$$$ HOTEL FAMILY 🏨 **Elounda Beach Hotel & Villas.** The original luxury resort hotel in Elounda, and one of Greece's most renowned, is set in 40 acres of gardens next to 1 km (½ mile) of seashore, and offers a dazzling array of delights. **Pros:** well-designed, comfortable accommodations; lovely gardens and seashore; first-class spa and kids' amenities. **Cons:** hard to shake the feeling better value may be had elsewhere; eye-wateringly expensive; very large, with a lot of rooms. [$] *Rooms from: €550* ✉ *Elounda* ✥ *3 km (2 miles) south of village* ☎ *28410/63000* 🌐 *www.eloundabeach.gr* 🕒 *Closed Nov.–Mar.* 🛏 *244 rooms* 🍽 *Breakfast.*

$$$$ RESORT 🏨 **Elounda Gulf Villas and Suites.** For those who value privacy and comfort, this may be the ultimate Elounda destination—with less of a resort feel than its larger neighbors, it is a second home to the jet set and the bright and the beautiful. **Pros:** beautiful accommodations in an intimate setting; personal, attentive service; excellent gourmet restaurants. **Cons:** not beachfront—private beach for guests is 10-minute drive away; pricier villas have the edge on suites; 20-minute walk into the town center. [$] *Rooms from: €380* ✉ *Elounda* ✥ *3 km (2 miles) south of village* ☎ *28102/27721* 🌐 *www.eloundavillas.com* 🛏 *33 villas* 🍽 *Breakfast.*

$$$$ HOTEL 🏨 **Elounda Mare.** This Relais & Chateaux property is one of the longest established in Elounda, and it blends charm and sophistication with a comfortably relaxed atmosphere. **Pros:** gorgeous setting and meticulously maintained grounds; Old Mill restaurant acknowledged as one of the best in Crete; golf course and Six Senses Spa at sister property open to guests. **Cons:** traditional decor beginning to feel a little dated; small beach; patchy Wi-Fi. [$] *Rooms from: €408* ✉ *Elounda* ✥ *3 km (2 miles) south of village* ☎ *28410/68200* 🌐 *www.eloundamare.gr* 🕒 *Closed Nov.–mid-Apr.* 🛏 *91 rooms* 🍽 *Breakfast.*

VAI ΒΑΪ

170 km (106 miles) east of Heraklion.

The appeal of the surrounding, fertile coastal plain was not lost on the ancient Minoans, who left behind ruins that are not as grand as those on the center of the island but are evocative nonetheless.

EXPLORING

Palaikastro. A sprawling Minoan town, formerly known as Rousso-lakkos, is currently being excavated by archaeologists. Palaikastro is missing any Knossos-type drama; here, for instance, there is no large palace structure, but you get a strong sense of everyday life amid the stony ruins of streets, squares, and shops. **■ TIP→ Nearby, Chiona and Kouremenos beaches make for pleasant diversions after clambering over the excavations.** ✉ *Palaikastro ✣ 2 km (1 mile) outside modern Palaikastro ☎ 28410/25115 🌐 www.odysseus.culture.gr 🎫 Free.*

BEACHES

Palm Beach at Vai. Even the classical Greeks recognized the beauty of this palm grove at the eastern end of the island, which is unique in Europe. It stood in for the Caribbean in a famous television commercial for a chocolate bar, and it's easy to see why. Nevertheless, the sandy stretch with nearby islets in clear turquoise water is such a stunner that many bus tours come all the way east just to show off the sand and palms, so Vai can get jammed in the summer. If the sand in front of the grove of 5,000 palms is too crowded, follow the path south over the headland to a slightly less crowded cove. **Amenities:** food and drink; parking (€2.50); showers; toilets; water sports. **Best for:** snorkeling; swimming. ✉ *Vai.*

WHERE TO STAY

$ HOTEL FAMILY **Sitia Bay Hotel.** In an area not renowned for its high-quality accommodations, this apartment-hotel stands out for its easy, relaxed feel. **Pros:** great position on the beachfront; superfriendly staff know all the best places to visit in the locality; good base for exploring this forgotten part of Crete. **Cons:** beach can get busy on weekends; don't expect luxurious furnishings; reception open only 8–8. 💲 *Rooms from: €100* ✉ *P. Vartholomaiou 27, Sitia ☎ 28430/24800 🌐 www.sitiabay.com ⏲ Closed Nov.–Apr. 19 apartments 🍴 Breakfast.*

7

WESTERN CRETE ΔΥΤΙΚΗ ΚΡΗΤΗ

Much of western Crete's landscape of soaring mountains, deep gorges, and rolling green lowlands remains largely untouched by mass tourism. Only the north coast is developed, leaving many interesting byways to be explored. This region is abundant in Minoan sites, including the Palace at Phaistos, as well as Byzantine churches and Venetian monasteries. Two of Greece's most-appealing cities are here: Chania and Rethymnon, both crammed with houses, narrow lanes, and minarets that hark back to Venetian and Turkish occupation. Friendly villages dot the uplands, and there are some outstanding beaches on the ruggedly beautiful and remote west and south coasts. Immediately southwest of Heraklion lies the traditional agricultural heartland of Crete: long, narrow valleys where olive groves alternate with vineyards of sultana grapes for export.

VORI ΒΟΡΙΟΝ

65 km (40 miles) southwest of Heraklion, 5 km (3 miles) north of Palace of Phaistos.

Vori, the closest town to Phaistos and Ayia Triada, is a pleasant farming community of whitewashed houses on narrow lanes; you might enjoy stopping here for some refreshment at one of the cafés on the lively main square and to visit the excellent folk museum.

Museum of Cretan Ethnology. A rich collection of Cretan folk items showcases exquisite weavings and pottery, basketry, farm implements, household furnishings, and clothing, all beautifully displayed and descriptively labeled in a well-designed building. Undoubtedly, the best museum of its kind on the island. ⊠ *Voroi Pirgiotissis* ✢ *Edge of village center* ☎ *28920/91110* ⊕ *www.cretanethnologymuseum.gr* ✆ *€3* ⊘ *Closed Oct.–Apr.*

PALACE OF PHAISTOS ΑΝΑΚΤΟΡΟ ΤΗΣ ΦΑΙΣΤΟΥ

50 km (31 miles) southwest of Heraklion, 11 km (7 miles) south of Vori.

On a steep hill overlooking olive groves and the sea on one side, and high mountain peaks on the other, the second-largest Minoan palace was the center of Minoan culture in southern Crete. Unlike Knossos, Phaistos has not been reconstructed, though the copious ruins are richly evocative. Nearby is another palace, Ayia Triada.

Ayia Triada. Another Minoan settlement was destroyed at the same time as Phaistos, which is only a few miles away on the other side of the same hill. Ayia Triada was once thought to have been a summer palace for the rulers of Phaistos but is now believed to have consisted of a group of villas for nobility and a warehouse complex. Rooms in the villas were once paneled with gypsum slabs and decorated with frescoes: the two now hanging in the Archaeological Museum in Heraklion show a woman in a garden and a cat hunting a pheasant. Several other lovely pieces, including finely crafted vases, also come from Ayia Triada and are now also on display in Heraklion. Though the complex was at one time just above the seashore, the view now looks across the extensive Messara Plain to the Lybian Sea in the distance. ⊠ *Ayia Triada, Tympaki, Phaistos* ✢ *Follow signs 3 km (2 miles) west from Phaistos* ☎ *28920/91360* ⊕ *www.odysseus.culture.gr* ✆ *€4.*

Fodor's Choice   **Palace of Phaistos.** The Palace of Phaistos was built around 1900 BC and
★   rebuilt after a disastrous earthquake around 1650 BC. It was burned and abandoned in the wave of destruction that swept across the island around 1450 BC, though Greeks continued to inhabit the city until the 2nd century BC, when it was eclipsed by Roman Gortyna.

You enter the site by descending a flight of steps leading into the west court, then climb a grand staircase. From here you pass through the **Propylon porch** into a light well and descend a narrow staircase into the **central court.** Much of the southern and eastern sections of the palace have eroded away. But there are large pithoi still in place in the old **storerooms.** On the north side of the court the recesses of an elaborate doorway bear a rare trace: red paint in a diamond pattern on a white ground. A passage from the doorway leads to the **north court** and the **northern domestic apartments,** now roofed and fenced off. The **Phaistos Disk** was found in 1903 in a chest made of mud brick at the northeast edge of the site and is now on display at the Archaeological Museum in Heraklion. East of the central court are the **palace workshops,** with a metalworking furnace fenced off. South of the workshops lie the **southern domestic apartments,** including a clay bath. From there, you have a memorable view across the Messara Plain. ✉ *Phaistos* ✛ *Follow signs and ascend hill off Ayii Deka–Mires–Timbaki road* ☎ *28920/42315* ⊕ *odysseus.culture.gr* ✉ *€8.*

EN ROUTE

The quickest route from Phaistos, Matala, and other places on the Messara Plain to the north coast is Heraklion Road, a small section of which is four lanes. But a very pleasant alternative leads northwest through Ayia Galini (the largest resort on this part of the southern coast) and the mountain town of Spili to Rethymnon. The route shows off the beauty of rural Crete as it traverses deep valleys and gorges and climbs the flanks of the interior mountain ranges. Just beyond Spili, follow signs to Moni Preveli, a stunningly located monastery perched high above the sea. A monument honors the monks here who sheltered Allied soldiers after the Battle of Crete and helped them escape the Nazi-occupied island via submarine. Below the monastery is Palm Beach, where golden sands are shaded by a palm grove watered by a mountain stream. It's lovely, but avoid this patch of paradise at midday during high season, when it is packed with day-trippers who arrive by tour boat from Ayia Galini.

MATALA ΜΑΤΑΛΑ

10 km (6 miles) southwest of Vori, 70 km (42 miles) southwest of Heraklion.

Renowned in the 1960s as a stopover on the hippie trail, with Joni Mitchell immortalizing it in song, Matala today is a small, low-key beach resort that retains its flower-power vibe, although tourism is increasing. The 2nd-century AD Roman tombs cut in the cliff side, where the beatniks made their home, now attract day-trippers from Heraklion and make an impressive sight from the pleasant town beach.

BEACHES

Kommos Beach. Fabulous, pine-and palm-fringed Kommos lies below the site of a Minoan harbor, once the port of Phaistos. At its far northern end lies the scrappy little resort of Kalamaki, where a few modest hotels and tavernas back the sand, but for the most part the beach is an unspoiled 2-km (1-mile) stretch of white sand washed by clear waters and backed by hills shaded with tamarisk trees. Kommos is especially popular with nudists, and it's also a nesting ground for the loggerhead sea turtle (*Caretta caretta*), so avoid taped-off areas where the females have laid their eggs. Lifeguards watch over the southern end of the beach. **Amenities:** food and drink; lifeguards; parking (free); showers, toilets. **Best for:** nudists; solitude; sunset; swimming; walking. ✉ *Off Mires–Matala road* ✛ *Near Pitsidia, 2 km (1 mile) from signposted turnoff.*

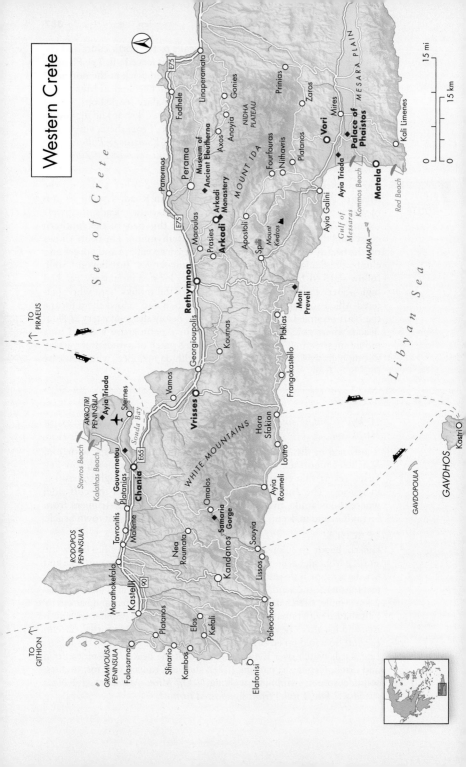

Western Crete

Sea of Crete

Libyan Sea

TO PIRAEUS

TO GITHION

RODOPOS PENINSULA

GRAMVOUSA PENINSULA

AKROTIRI PENINSULA

WHITE MOUNTAINS

MOUNT IDA

NIDHA PLATEAU

MESARA PLAIN

Gulf of Messaras

GAVDHOS

GAVDOPOULA

Falasarna
Sfinario
Kambos
Ketali
Elos
Platanos
Kastelli
Marathokefalo
Tavronitis
Maleme
Platanias
Nea Roumata
Kandanos
Paleochora
Elafonisi
Lissos
Souyia
Omalos
Samaria Gorge
Chania
Gouvernetou
Ayia Triada
Sternes
Stavros Beach
Kalathas Beach
Souda Bay
Vamos
Vrisses
Georgioupolis
Kournas
Kournas
Rethymnon
Panormos
Perama
Fodhele
Linoperamata
Museum of Ancient Eleutherna
Gonies
Axos
Anoyia
Maroulas
Prasies
Arkadi
Arkadi Monastery
Apostoli
Spili
Mount Kedros
Fourfouras
Nithavris
Platanos
Zaros
Prinias
Mires
Vori
Palace of Phaistos
Ayia Triada
Matala
Kommos Beach
Red Beach
Kali Limenes
Ayia Galini
Moni Preveli
Plakias
Frangokastello
Hora Sfakion
Loutro
Ayia Roumeli
MADIA
Kostri
GAVDHOS

0   15 mi
0   15 km

Red Beach. This beautiful crescent of sand is accessible by a 20-minute walk across a rocky promontory on a path from Matala, or by a boat that runs from Matala in summer. The trek includes a scramble up and over a headland and some steep climbs and descents, though it is manageable with moderate exertion. Your reward is a lovely, unspoiled crescent of golden sand washed by clear waters that is especially popular with nudists. Surf in the small bay can be rough, with riptides. Shade is scarce, though a small bar sometimes rents umbrellas and offers simple snacks. **Amenities:** food and drink (sometimes). **Best for:** nudists; solitude; swimming; walking. ⊠ *Matala* ✛ *1 km (½ mile) west of town.*

WHERE TO EAT

$ ✗ **Taverna Sigelakis.** Residents from villages for miles around come to the GREEK town of Sivas to enjoy a meal of *stifado* (meat in a rich tomato sauce) artichokes with *avgolemono* (egg and lemon sauce), and other specialties, including delicious roasted lamb and chicken, all served on the front terrace in warm seasons or in the stone-wall, hearth-warmed dining room when the weather's cold. A meal comes with friendly service, a visit from proprietor Giorgios, and a free glass of raki and a sweet. **Known for:** true traditional Cretan cooking; authentic surroundings; hospitable owner. $ *Average main: €10* ⊠ *Sivas, Sivas* ✛ *6 km (4 miles) northeast of Matala* ☎ *28920/42748* ⊕ *www.sigelakis-studios.gr.*

WHERE TO STAY

$ 🏨 **Thalori.** To enjoy a remote Cretan retreat without sacrificing comRESORT fort, it's hard to beat these beautifully renovated stone houses in an ages-old village that clings to a mountainside high above the Libyan Sea. **Pros:** beautiful surroundings; ideal for those who want to get away from it all and enjoy nature; very comfortable and unique. **Cons:** a half-hour drive to the nearest beach; thick stone walls plays havoc with the Wi-Fi; hair-raising road trip to reach the property. $ *Rooms from: €100* ⊠ *Kapetaniana* ☎ *28930/41762* ⊕ *www.thalori.com* ➥ *20 traditional houses* ✦ *Breakfast.*

ARKADI ARKADI

18 km (11 miles) southwest of Fodele, 30 km (19 miles) southwest of Heraklion.

As you approach Arkadi from the north, through the rolling lands at the base of Mt. Ida, one of the contenders in the dispute over the alleged Cretan birthplace of Zeus, you'll follow a gorge inland before emerging onto the flat pastureland that surrounds one of Crete's most beautiful and important monasteries. The approach is even more dramatic from the south, as you traverse the uplands of the beautiful Amari valley before dropping into the mountain plateau that the monastery and its vast holdings occupy. If you are heading east back to Heraklion, consider visiting Eleutherna, with stunning views of the local area, and pass through Fodele; a pretty village set in orange and lemon groves with a shady taverna-filled square and a small museum in the supposed birthplace of El Greco.

Crete has some of the best (and busiest) beaches of any of the Greek islands.

Arkadi Monastery. A place of pilgrimage for many Cretans, Moni Arkadi is also one of the most stunning pieces of Renaissance architecture on the island. The ornate facade, decorated with Corinthian columns and an elegant belfry above, was built in the 16th century of a local, honey-color stone. In 1866 the monastery came under siege during a major rebellion against the Turks, and Abbot Gabriel and several hundred rebels, together with their wives and children, refused to surrender. When the Turkish forces broke through the gate, the defenders set the gunpowder store afire, killing themselves together with hundreds of Turks. The monastery was again a center of resistance when the Nazis occupied Crete during World War II. ⊠ *Arkadi* ✙ *South of old Heraklion–Hania road* ☎ *28310/83135* ⊕ *www.imra.gr* 🖃 *€3.*

Museum of Ancient Eleutherna. In the foothills of Mt. Ida, Eleutherna was founded in the 9th century BC. It was one of the most important ancient cities, even minting its own coins. At a natural crossroad between Knossos to the east and Cydonia to the northwest, it controlled the ports of Stavromenos and Panormos and was near to the sacred cave of *Idaion Andron,* another one of the alleged birthplaces of Zeus. An archaeological-site museum was opened in 2016 in a modern building and it has been designed to be updated as new discoveries and finds are made. Housing objects from prehistoric through to Byzantine eras, the current collection spans 3000 BC to AD 1300, presented in a multimedia fashion. The archaeological site itself is accessible on rough stone paths with two large canopies covering the most important excavations. The *Orthi Petra* cemetery includes a funeral pyre for a warrior from 730–710 BC, and corroborates Homer's description in *The Iliad* of a similar burial. Elsewhere, roads, villas, public buildings, baths, and cisterns are to be seen, along with magnificent views of the countryside. ✉ *Eleutherna Mylopotamou, Rethymnon* ☎ *28340/92501* 🌐 *www.mae.com.gr* 🎟 *€4* 🕓 *Closed Mon.*

WHERE TO STAY

$$ HOTEL Fodor's Choice ★ 🏨 **Kapsaliana Village Hotel.** A 300-year-old hamlet set amid vast olive groves has been converted to one of Crete's most distinctive and relaxing lodgings with luxurious, stylishly appointed rooms, welcoming lounges, and an excellent dining room—all fashioned out of beautiful, ancient stone houses that were once part of the Arkadi Monastery holdings. **Pros:** unique insight into a way of life that has disappeared; a welcome alternative in an outstanding setting far from anonymous resorts; low-key sophistication is very charming. **Cons:** remote location makes a rental car a necessity; some distance from beaches; can feel a little isolated at night. [$] *Rooms from: €220* ✉ *Kapsaliana* ☎ *28310/83400* 🌐 *www.kapsalianavillage.gr* 🛏 *18 rooms* 🍴 *Breakfast.*

RETHYMNON ΡΕΘΥΜΝΟ

25 km (15 miles) west of Arkadi Monastery, 78 km (48 miles) west of Heraklion.

Rethymnon is Crete's third-largest town, after Heraklion and Chania. The population (about 40,000) steadily increases as the town expands—a new quarter follows the coast to the east of the Old Town, where the beachfront has been developed with large hotels and other resort facilities catering to tourists on package vacations. Nevertheless, much of Rethymnon's charm perseveres in the old Venetian quarter, which is crowded onto a compact peninsula dominated by the huge, fortified Venetian castle known as the Fortezza. Wandering through the narrow alleyways, you come across handsome carved-stone Renaissance doorways belonging to vanished mansions, fountains, archways, and wooden Turkish houses with latticework screens on the balconies to protect the women of the house from prying eyes.

GETTING HERE AND AROUND

There is no direct ferry connection to Athens from Rethymnon. However, this has a habit of changing year by year; ask at local agents for availability. If a boat is not operating when you wish to make the trip, a good option is to use the ferry terminal or airport at Chania, about 45 minutes and €90 away by taxi. Rethymnon is also served by an hourly bus service from Chania and Heraklion, each about an hour away, and the fare to either is about €8 each way. Rethymnon's bus terminal is on the west side of town, on the sea near the Venetian fortress, at Atki Kefaloyianithon. Rethymnon is on Crete's national highway, which runs along the north coast, and there is public parking on the seaside road around the Venetian fortress, next to the old harbor, and elsewhere around town.

EXPLORING

Archaeological Museum. Here's even more evidence of just how long Crete has cradled civilizations: a collection of bone tools from a Neolithic site at Gerani (west of Rethymnon); Minoan pottery; and an unfinished statue of Aphrodite, the goddess of love, from the Roman occupation (look for the ancient chisel marks). The museum is temporarily housed in the restored Venetian Chuch of St. Francisco while renovations are undertaken at the original site in the shadow of the Fortessa. ⊠ *Agios Fragiskos* ☎ *28310/54668* ⊕ *odysseus.culture.gr* ▨ *€3.*

Fortessa. The west side of the peninsula on which Rethymnon sits is taken up almost entirely with this massive fortress, strategically surrounded by the sea and thick ramparts. The high, well-preserved walls enclose a vast empty space occupied by a few scattered buildings—a well-restored mosque, two churches, and abandoned barracks that once housed the town brothels—and are surrounded by fields of wildflowers in spring. After a small fortress on the site failed to thwart a 1571 attack of 40 pirate galleys, Venetians conscripted 100,000 forced laborers from the town and surrounding villages to build the huge compound. It didn't fulfill its purpose of keeping out the Turks: Rethymnon surrendered after a three-week siege in 1646. ⊠ *Rethymnon* ✛ *West end of town* ☎ *28310/40150* ⊕ *www.rethymno.gr* ▨ *€4.*

Historical and Folk Art Museum. A restored Venetian palazzo almost in the shadow of the Neratze minaret houses a delightful collection of rustic furnishings, tools, weavings, and a re-creation of a traditional Cretan shopping street that provide a charming and vivid picture of what life on Crete was like until well into the 20th century. ⊠ *M. Vernardou 28–30* ☎ *28310/23398* ▨ *€4* ☉ *Closed Sun.*

Neratze. The most visible sign of the Turkish occupation of Rethymnon is the graceful minaret, one the few to survive in Greece, that rises above the Neratze. This large stone structure looming over the narrow lanes of the city center was a monastery, then church, under the Venetians, and was subsequently converted to a mosque under the Ottomans before being transformed into today's concert hall. ⊠ *Verna and Ethnikis Adistaseos.*

Venetian Harbor. Rethymnon's small inner harbor, with its restored 19th-century lighthouse, comes to life in warm weather, when restaurant tables clutter the quayside. Fishing craft and pleasure boats are crammed chockablock into the minute space. ⊠ *Waterfront.*

Venetian Loggia. The carefully restored clubhouse of the local nobility is now enclosed in glass and houses the Archaeological Museum's shop, selling a selection of books and reproductions of artefacts from its collections. This remnant of Venetian rule is enhanced by the nearby Rimondi Fountain, just down the street at the end of Platanos Square and is one of the town's most welcoming sights, spilling refreshing streams from several lions' heads. You'll come upon several other fountains as you wander through the labyrinth of narrow streets. ⊠ *Arkadiou* ☎ *28310/53270* ☉ *Closed weekends.*

WHERE TO EAT

$$ GREEK Fodor's Choice ★ 🍴 **Avli.** In an herb-filled multitiered courtyard that leads to a barrel-vaulted dining room, some of the finest food for miles is skillfully prepared. Refined, distinguished dishes are its calling card; sophisticated but true to their traditional roots. **Known for:** attentive, yet never overbearing service; tasting menu with matched local wines; enigmatic, inspiring surroundings. [$] *Average main: €22* ✉ *Xanthoudidou 22* ☎ *28310/26213* 🌐 *www.avli.gr.*

$ GREEK 🍴 **Kyria Maria.** On a blink-and-you'll-miss-it small alley behind the Rimondi Fountain, under an arbor of vines, with caged birds chirping away, this homely little taverna serves some accomplished traditional dishes in an atmospheric setting. Lamb in lemon sauce, stuffed calamari, moussaka, *yemista* (stuffed vegetables)—the menu is a roll call of all the comfort food you can think of, prepared as Grandma would have made it all those years ago. **Known for:** village-style dishes as you remember them; neighborhood setting on a back alley, steps from the center; friendly service, friendly prices. [$] *Average main: €9* ✉ *Moschovitou 20* ☎ *28310/29078* 🕓 *Closed Nov.–Apr.*

$ GREEK 🍴 **Raki Ba Raki 1600.** Opposite Avli, and part of the same stable, on one of Rethmynon's myriad pretty walkways, this is a modern reinvention of the classic Greek *rakadiko*—a place to eat small plates and drink raki. Don't assume the food is an afterthought to drinking, though, this is top-quality mezedes. **Known for:** best mezedes in town; creative Cretan flavors you won't find elsewhere; raki!—not just plain, but flavored with fruits and herbs. [$] *Average main: €8* ✉ *Arampatzoglou 17–19* ✣ *Opposite Avli* ☎ *28310/58250.*

$ MEDITERRANEAN 🍴 **Thalassographia.** The name means seascape, a poetic notion for this romantic gathering spot that spreads across a series of terraces wedged between the Fortessa and the azure waters below. Small plates are the order in this easy-going and relaxed place, with a strong selection of local wines and beers, and the best cocktails in town—the ideal spot for watching the sunset over the castle walls on a balmy summer evening. **Known for:** views of the mighty fortress and the sea beyond; eclectic Mediterranean-focused cuisine; romantic nighttime atmosphere. [$] *Average main: €10* ✉ *Kefalogianhidou 33* ☎ *28310/52569* 🕓 *Closed Nov.–Mar.*

WHERE TO STAY

$$ HOTEL 🏨 **Avli.** In a cluster of lovely 16th-century Venetian buildings, centered on a romantic leafy walled yard, accommodations are split between the various properties, and characterfully decorated with sparkling chandeliers, baroque gilt frames, and antique furniture against a backdrop of rough stone and wooden beams. **Pros:** evocative, intimate abode at the heart of town; personable staff—you are always a name, never a number; romantic courtyard. **Cons:** unique old buildings means stairs to all rooms; rooms facing restaurant garden can be a little noisy; parking is a couple of streets away, but staff will come and collect your bags. [$] *Rooms from: €160* ✉ *Xanthodidou 22 and Radamanthios* ☎ *28310/58250* 🌐 *www.avli.gr* 🛏 *12 rooms* 🍽 *Breakfast.*

$ HOTEL 🏨 **Leo Hotel.** Eleni Christonaki oversees this lovely little inn that occupies the 600-year-old house in which she was raised. **Pros:** attractive, comfortable surroundings; friendly service; central location on a quiet street

7

in the Old Town. **Cons:** steep stairs and no elevator may pose a problem for some guests; small common areas; not much in the way of amenities. $ *Rooms from: €115* ⊠ *Arkadiou and Vafe 2–4* 📞 *28310/261967* ⊕ *www.leohotel.gr* ⇆ *8 rooms* ⧠ *No meals.*

$
HOTEL
⌂ **Palazzino di Corina.** Rethymnon has several hotels occupying old palaces, but Corina is one of the most handsome, with pleasant, stylish surroundings that include a nicely planted courtyard surrounding a small plunge pool. **Pros:** cool courtyard is a perfect place to relax; informal, helpful staff; attached restaurant in pretty cloister next door. **Cons:** some rooms on upper floors require a climb; street-facing rooms are the noisiest; not all rooms have balconies. $ *Rooms from: €120* ⊠ *Damvergi and Diakou* 📞 *28310/21205* ⊕ *www.corina.gr* ⇆ *29 rooms* ⧠ *Breakfast.*

$$
HOTEL
⌂ **Rimondi Boutique Hotel.** Step through the heavy 16th-century wooden door of this hotel and you are transported to an oasis of civility away from the bustle of Rethymnon's busy streets, where two buildings split by a pretty pedestrian alleyway house some of the most sumptuous rooms in town. **Pros:** loving restoration of Venetian property is full of historical detail; tranquil, quiet atmosphere; garden areas with pools are a delight. **Cons:** some split-level suites with stairs; rooms in the modern annex are less attractive; parking is a five-minute walk away. $ *Rooms from: €180* ⊠ *Xanthoudidou 21* 📞 *28310/51001* ⊕ *www.hotelsrimondi.com* ⊗ *Closed Nov.–Mar.* ⇆ *34 rooms* ⧠ *Breakfast.*

SPORTS AND THE OUTDOORS

Fodor'sChoice
★
Happy Walker. This outfitter arranges easy day hikes in the mountains and gorges near Rethymnon, adding a welcome stop for a village lunch to each walk. The outfit also leads multiday treks through the remote regions of Crete. Walk costs from €35. ⊠ *Tombazi 56* 📞 *28310/52920* ⊕ *www.happywalker.com* ⊗ *Closed late Oct.–Mar.*

SHOPPING

Rethymnon's narrow lanes may remind you of a Middle Eastern souk—or a tacky shopping mall, depending on your frame of mind. If you are looking for something a bit more substantial than, say, playing cards with erotic images of gods and goddesses, you can also find small shops selling some genuinely high-quality goods, whether it's Cretan olive oil or the work of island craftspeople.

Agora—Avli Raw Materials. This amazing shop sells many of the best herbs, spices, oils, and other ingredients that Greece offers and that flavor the cuisine served just around the corner at the restaurant. Many of the offerings are unique to the shop and give a true taste of the local area. Oil and wine tastings are given, too. ⊠ *Arampatzoglou 38-40* 📞 *28310/58250* ⊕ *www.avli.gr.*

Kalymnos. For a souvenir that will be light to carry, stop in and browse shelves brimming with sponges harvested off the eponymous island and in other Greek waters. ⊠ *Arampatzoglou 26* 📞 *28310/50802.*

Continued on page 398

NECTAR OF THE GODS

The roots of Greek wine run deep: Naughty Dionysus partied his way through mythology as the God of Wine and became a symbol for celebration in Greece. During the ancient festivities called Dionysia, husbands and wives alike let loose and drank themselves into a heady joy. Now that you're in the land of the god, be sure to enjoy some liquid Dionysian delights. Greece's wine is flavorful and original, so much so that some of the wines here you won't find anywhere else.

This is one reason why few can resist taking some bottles home (a bottle of excellent Greek wine will cost at least €15 to €20, but good varieties can be found for around €10). Remember to ask the clerk to pad them with bubble wrap so they won't break in your suitcase on the journey back. Following are some tips about vintners who are leading the Greek winemaking renaissance, along with a rundown of the grape varietals that Greek wineries specialize in.

Hillside vineyard, Samos Island

THE GREEK WINES TO LOOK FOR

Former Yugoslav Republic of Macedonia

BULGARIA

ALBANIA

MACEDONIA

Assyrtiko
Athiri
Roditis
Xinomavro

TURKEY

EPIRUS

THESSALIA
Roditis

THE SPORADES

Limnos

Lesbos

CENTRAL GREECE

Assyrtiko
Athiri
Roditis
Savatiano

Rombola

Achaia

ATTICA

White Muscat

IONIAN ISLANDS

Agiorgitiko
Mavrodaphne
Moschofilero
Roditis
White Muscat

Athens

Samos

PELOPONNESE

THE CYCLADES

DODECANESE

Assyrtiko
Athiri

Santorini

Rhodes

Athiri
Mandilaria

Kotsifali
Mandilaria

CRETE

REDS

Agiorgitiko. The name means St. George and it's mainly found in the Nemea region of the Peloponnese. Richly colored and scented, with aromas of sour cherries and pomegranate, it goes well with red meat and yellow soft cheeses.

Kotsifali. Grown mainly in Crete, it is rich and aromatic, with hints of raisins, prunes, and sage. Pair with red meat, light red sauces, and yellow cheeses.

Mandilaria. Mainly cultivated in Rhodes and Crete, it is rich and intense, with hints of pomegranate. Pair with grilled and stewed meats with spicy sauces and mild cheeses.

Mavrodaphne. Found in the Peloponnese regions of Achaia and Ilia and the Ionian Islands, it is a lovely dessert wine. Drink alone or with a light dessert.

Xinomavro. Found in Macedonia, it is rich, acidic, and bursting with aromas such as gooseberry with hints of olives and spices. Pair with grilled meats, casseroles, and yellow spicy cheeses.

WHITES

Assyrtiko. One of Greece's finest white wines and found mainly in Santorini, Attica, and Macedonia, it is rich and dry with honeysuckle and citrus aromas and an earthy aftertaste. Pair with grilled fish, poultry, or pork and feta.

Athiri. An ancient variety found mainly in Santorini, Macedonia, Attica, and Rhodes, it is vibrant and fruity with tropical fruit and honey tones. Pair with poultry or pork, pasta, grilled fish, or white cheeses.

Moschofilero. Originating in the Peloponnese, it is vivid and has rich fruity and floral aromas. Pair with poultry, pasta, and seafood.

Roditis. Popular in Attica, Macedonia, Thessaly, and Peloponnese, it is light and has vibrant scents of pine

apple, pear, melon, and jasmine. Pair with poultry, fish, and mild cheeses.

Rombola. Grown in the Ionian island of Cephalonia, it is scented with citrus and peach and has a lemony aftertaste. Pair with fish or poultry.

Savatiano. Grown in Attica, it is full-bodied with fruity tones of apple, pear, and peach. Pair with poultry, pork, or fish as well as soft white cheeses.

White Muscat. Cultivated on the Aegean island of Samos and in the northern Peloponnese city of Patras, it is sweet and intense. Pair with desserts and ice cream.

PICK OF THE VINE

(left) Dionysos Kantharos, God of wine; (right) a toast with Santorini wine.

Wherever you head in Greece, wine-makers are perfecting the millennia-old traditions of Greek wine, with high-class estates such as Gaia, Boutari, and Porto Carras leading the way. These wineries can all be visited by appointment. A good introductory Web site is ⊕ *www.allaboutgreekwine.com.*

Peloponnese, Tetramythos Vineyards. While vineyards throughout the region produce Agiorgitiko, an aromatic and deeply colored red, those from Tetrmythos (⊕ *www.tetramythos.com*) on the northern slopes of Mt. Helmos, rising 7,775 feet above the Gulf of Corinth, are especially velvety and rich.

Cyclades, Haridimos Hatzidakis. On Santorini, his winery (⊕ *www.hatzidakiswines.gr*) near Pyrgos Kallistis comprises a celebrated set of organic vineyards. One of his top organic wines is the Aidani Assyritiko, a dry, fruity white.

Macedonia, Yiannis Boutaris. Up north, in Naoussa, Imathia wine lovers make a beeline to Yiannis's Ktima Kir-Yianni winery (⊕ *www.kiryianni.gr*). He split from his family's estate ten years ago to concentrate on producing standout dry reds.

DRINK LIKE A CRETAN

While Crete's viticultural history goes back 3,500 years, the island's wines are becoming newly popular. Vidiano, a complex, fruity, and full-bodied white, is quickly emerging from obscurity as a favorite of connoisseurs. Nikolaos Douloufakis is gaining attention with his bottlings of Vidiano and Vilana, a white grape with spicy aromas and notes of banana and clementine, and he also is known for his dry-red and sweet versions of Liatiko, another ages-old Cretan varietal. He comes from an established, nearly 80-years-old winemaking family in Dafnes (⊕ www.cretanwines.gr), a village near the island capital of Heraklion, which is well known among wine enthusiasts. Dafnes and nearby Archanes are surrounded by vineyards, and tasting rooms in and around both villages provide a satisfying introduction to Cretan wines.

7

IN FOCUS NECTAR OF THE GODS

VRISSES ΒΡΥΣΕΣ

26 km (16 miles) west of Rethymnon, 105 km (65 miles) west of Heraklion.

This appealing old village is famous throughout Crete for its thick, creamy yogurt—best eaten with a large spoonful of honey on top—that is served in the cafés beneath the plane trees at the center of town. Georgioupolis, on the coast about 7 km (4½ miles) due west, is another shady, lovely old town, where the Almiros River flows into the sea. Some of the coast here is undergoing rather unattractive development, but inland walks—including one through a eucalyptus-scented valley that links Vrisses and Georgioupolis—make it easy to get away from the fray.

CHANIA ΧΑΝΙΑ

52 km (32 miles) west of Vrisses, 78 km (48 miles) west of Rethymnon.

Fodor'sChoice
★

Chania surrendered its role as capital of Crete to Heraklion in 1971, but this elegant city of eucalyptus-lined avenues, miles of waterfront promenades, and shady, cobblestone alleyways lined with Venetian and Ottoman houses is still close to the heart of all Cretans. It was here that the Greek flag was raised in 1913 to mark Crete's unification with Greece, and the place is simply one of the most beautiful of all Greek cities.

GETTING HERE AND AROUND

Daily ferry service connects Chania with Pireaus, arriving at the harbor on Souda Bay every day at about 6 am and departing around 9 pm. The crossing takes roughly eight hours. During summer, ferries also provide daytime service between Pireaus and Chania, and crossings take six hours. Souda is a 20-minute taxi ride from the town center (€15), and municipal buses also run from Souda to Chania (€1.10). Chania's airport, also on Souda Bay, has daily service from Athens, as well as flights from many European cities, mostly charters, during high season. Buses run from the airport infrequently, so plan on taking a taxi or picking up your rental car at the airport. Hourly buses connect Chania with Rethymnon, about €7, and Heraklion, about €15. Less frequent bus service connects Chania with Kissamos, Paleochora, and many other places in western Crete. The well-organized bus station, with a helpful information desk, is at Kidonias 25, just off Halidon. The city center is well marked from National Road. For parking, drive to the center and make your way, following well-posted parking signs, to the west side of the Old City, where you'll find free parking near the sea. Be careful where you park, as some places are open only to residents, and violators are fined.

TRAVEL AGENTS

Contacts Diktynna Travel. ✉ *Archontaki 6* ☎ *28210/41321* ⊕ *www.diktynna-travel.gr.*

EXPLORING

The sizable Old Town is strung along the harbor, divided by a centuries-old seawall into outer and inner harbors, where tall Venetian houses face a pedestrians-only, taverna-lined waterside walkway, and fishing boats moor beside a long stretch of Venetian arsenals and warehouses. Well-preserved Venetian and Turkish quarters surround the harbors and a covered food-and-spice market, a remnant of Venetian trade and Turkish bazaars, is set amid a maze of narrow streets.

TOP ATTRACTIONS

Archaeological Museum. The former Venetian church of St. Francis, surrounding a lovely garden in the shadow of the Venetian walls, displays artifacts from all over western Crete, and the collection bears witness to the presence of Minoans, ancient Greeks, Romans, Venetians, and Ottomans. The painted Minoan clay coffins and elegant late-Minoan pottery indicate that the region was as wealthy as the center of the island under the Minoans, though no palace has yet been located. ⊠ *Chalidron 25* ☎ *28210/90334* ⊕ *www.chaniamuseum.culture.gr* ⊡ *€4* ⊙ *Closed Mon.*

Ayia Triada. Lands at the northeast corner of the Akrotiri Peninsula, which extends into the sea from the east side of Chania, are the holdings of several monasteries, including Ayia Triada (Holy Trinity) or Tzagarolon, as it is also known. The olive groves that surround and finance the monastery yield excellent oils, and the shop is stocked with some of the island's finest. Ayia Triada is a delightful place, where you can visit the flower-filled cloisters and the ornately decorated chapel, which dates from the monastery's founding in 1611. Today, just a handful of monks remain. ⊠ *Agias Triadas of Tzagarolon, Akrotiri* ✢ *16 km (10 miles) north of Chania, follow road from Chordaki* ☎ *28210/63572* ⊕ *www.holytrinity.gr.*

Byzantine and Post-Byzantine Collection of Chania. You'll get some insight into the Venetian occupation *and* the Christian centuries that preceded it at this small museum housed in the charming 15th-century church of San Salvadore alongside the city walls just behind the Firka. Mosaics, icons, coins, and other artifacts bring to life Cretan civilization as it was after the Roman Empire colonized the island and Christianity took root as early as the 1st century. ⊠ *Theotokopoulou 78–82* ☎ *28210/96046* ⊕ *odysseus.culture.gr* ⊡ *€2* ⊙ *Closed Mon.*

Fodor's Choice
★

Firka. Just across the narrow channel from the lighthouse, where a chain was connected in times of peril to close the harbor, is the old Turkish prison, which now houses the **Maritime Museum of Crete.** Exhibits, more riveting than might be expected, trace the island's seafaring history from the time of the Minoans, with a reproduction of an Athenian *trireme*, amphora from Roman shipwrecks, Ottoman weaponry, and other relics. Look for the photos and mementos from the World War II Battle of Crete, when Allied forces moved across the island and, with the help of Cretans, ousted the German occupiers. Much of the fighting centered on Chania, and great swaths of the city were destroyed during the war. Almost worth the price of admission alone is the opportunity to walk along the Firka's ramparts for bracing views of the city, sea, and mountains. ⊠ *Chania* ✢ *Waterfront at far west end of port* ☎ *28210/91875* ⊕ *www.mar-mus-crete.gr* ⊡ *€3.*

7

Gouvernetou. This 16th-century, Venetian-era monastery on the north end of the Akrotiri Peninsula is said to be one of the oldest and largest remaining religious communities on Crete. Delightful frescoes cover the wall of the courtyard chapel, while a path leads down the flanks of a seaside ravine past several caves used as hermitages and churches to the remote, 11th-century Katholiko, the monastery of St. John the Hermit, who pursued his solitary life in a nearby cave. Follow the path down to the sea along a riverbank for another mile or so to a secluded cove that is the perfect place for a refreshing dip. The return walk requires a steep uphill climb. ☒ *Stavros* ✚ *Northern end of Akrotiri Peninsula, 4 km (2½ miles) north of Ayia Triada; 19 km (12 miles) north of Chania, follow road north from Chordaki* ☎ *28430/63319* ☉ *Closed Wed. and Fri.*

Venetian Arsenali. As you follow the harbor front east from the mosque, you come to a long line of Venetian *arsenali* (warehouses) from the 16th and 17th centuries, used to store wares and repair craft. The seawalls swing around to enclose the harbor and end at the **old lighthouse** that stands at the east side of the harbor entrance; from here you get a magnificent view of the town, with the imposing White Mountains looming behind the animated harbor. ☒ *Akti Enoseos* ✚ *East end of old harbor.*

WORTH NOTING

Etz Hayyim Synagogue. This ancient landmark is tucked away in what was once the Jewish ghetto, a warren of narrow lanes known as Evraki, just off the harbor south of the Firka. The building was formerly the Venetian church of St. Catherine, became a synagogue under the Ottomans in the 16th century, and was sorely neglected and near collapse by the end of the 20th century. Venetian Gothic arches, a *mikveh* (ritual bath), tombs of three rabbis, and other architectural features have been beautifully restored and are a stirring memorial to Crete's once sizable Jewish population, obliterated during World War II; many Cretan Jews drowned when a British torpedo sank the ship carrying them toward Auschwitz in 1944. ☒ *Parodos Kondylaki* ☎ *28210/86286* ⊕ *www.etz-hayyim-hania.org* ☉ *Closed weekends.*

Janissaries Mosque. Kastelli hill creates a backdrop to the Janissaries Mosque, the oldest Ottoman building in Crete, built at the water's edge when Turks captured the town in 1645 after a two-month siege. You can enter the building only when the town uses it to host temporary art and trade exhibitions, but the presence of the domed structure at the edge of the shimmering sea lends Chania part of its exotic aura. ☒ *Chania* ✚ *East side of inner harbor.*

OFF THE BEATEN PATH

Samaria Gorge. South of Chania a deep, verdant crevice extends 16 km (10 miles) from near the village of Xyloskalo to the Libyan Sea. The landscape of forest, sheer rock faces, and running streams, inhabited by the elusive and endangered *kri-kri* (wild goat) is magnificent. The Samaria, protected as a national park, is the most traveled of the dozens of gorges that cut through Crete's mountains and emerge at the sea, but the walk through the canyon, in places only a few feet wide and almost 2,000 feet deep, is thrilling nonetheless. Reckon on five to six hours of downhill walking with a welcome reward of a swim at the end. Buses depart the central bus station in Chania at 7:30 and 8:30 am for Xyloskalo. Boats leave in the afternoon (5:30) from Ayia Roumeli, the mouth of the gorge, where it's an hour-long scenic sail to Hora Sfakion, from where buses return to Chania. Travel agents also arrange day trips to the gorge. Also from Chania, a couple of extremely scenic routes head south across the craggy White Mountains to the isolated Libyan Sea villages of **Paleochora**, the main resort of the southwest coast, and **Souyia**, a pleasant collection of whitewashed houses facing a long beach. Much of this section of the coast, including the village of **Loutro**, is accessible only by boat or by a seaside path. ✉ *Samaria* ✛ *35 km (22 miles) south of Chania, entrance near Omalos* ☎ ✉ *€5* ⊙ *Closed Oct. 15–May 1.*

BEACHES

A string of beaches extends west from the city center, and you can easily reach them on foot by following the sea past the old olive-oil factory just west of the walls and the Byzantine Museum. They are not idyllic, but the water is clean. Locals who want to spend a day at the beach often head out to some of the best beaches on Crete along the surrounding coastline.

Balos. You already know this beach from every postcard stand in Greece. Seemingly transported from the South Seas, an islet sits dramatically amid a shallow lagoon of bright blue-and-turquoise water framed by white sand. Approach by car along the 8-km (5-mile) very rough dirt road (€1 toll) and you will be rewarded by that picture-perfect panorama. Nevertheless, a half-hour descent on foot to the beach itself, and longer return, is the price to pay. Easier on the legs is to take the boat from Kissamos, which includes a stop at the deserted island Venetian fortress of Gramvousa. Like Vai, it can get very busy here; if you are coming by car, aim to arrive in the morning before the boats, or late in the afternoon once the crowds have left. **Amenities:** food and drink; parking (free); toilets. **Best for:** snorkeling; swimming; walking.

Elafonissi. A peninsula on the western end of the island, about 75 km (45 miles) west of Chania, extends into turquoise waters, with a lagoon on one side and isolated sands and coves on the other. The pink sands, rock formations, and colorful waters evoke the tropics. In places, the peninsula is broken by narrow channels, requiring beachgoers to wade through the warm, shallow waters, adding to the remote aura. The eastern, lagoon side of the peninsula has amenities and is popular with families (the water is never more than a few feet deep) while other parts, especially the western, ocean-facing side, are relatively isolated and frequented by nudists. **Amenities:** food and drink; lifeguards; parking (free); showers; toilets. **Best for:** nudists; snorkeling; solitude (western end); sunset; swimming; walking. ✉ *Elafonissi.*

Falassarna. Often cited as the best beach on the island, Falassarna stretches along the western edge of the island, about 60 km (37 miles) west of Chania. The long expanse of sand is broken into several coves and has a little bit of everything—amenities on the main section, Pacheia Ammos, plenty of isolation in other parts, and even ancient ruins behind the northern end. One small disadvantage is a steady wind from the west, which can make the water choppy (but is a boon for windsurfers). **Amenities:** food and

DID YOU KNOW?

Hiking the Samaria gorge, Europe's longest, you'll encounter wildflowers, streams (which can close the gorge in early spring), vultures, and maybe even the *kri-kri*, the Cretan wild goat.

drink; lifeguards; parking (free); showers; toilets, water sports. **Best for:** nudists; solitude; sunset; swimming; walking; windsurfing. ⊠ *Falassarna*.

Stavros. If this cove at the northern end of the Akrotiri Peninsula, about 15 km (9 miles) east of Chania, looks familiar, you may recognize it as the location of the 1964 movie *Zorba the Greek*. The onetime fishing village has grown a bit since then but it's still a charming place, especially with this white-sand beach on a lagoon backed by a steep mountain (it was here that Zorba did his Sirtaki dance); a slightly wilder, less crowded beach is just to the west. **Amenities:** food and drink; parking (free); showers; toilets; water sports. **Best for:** snorkeling; swimming. ⊠ *Stavros*.

WHERE TO EAT

$ | SEAFOOD · ✕ **Apostolis.** On the quieter end of the harbor next to the Venetian arsenals and removed from the tourist joints that surround the port, this lively taverna caters to locals and discerning tourists alike. Fresh fish and seafood are the standouts here, but also consider the stuffed aubergines, stifado, *kleftiko* (lamb), or the meats from the charcoal grill. **Known for:** the place the locals go to for the freshest fish; excellent, friendly staff; great people-watching spot right on the front. $ *Average main: €12* ⊠ *Akti Enoseos 10* ☎ *28210/43470.*

$ | MODERN GREEK · ✕ **Portes.** Relocated from the somewhat cramped alley it occupied in the city center to a pretty harborside spot in Nea Chora, Portes continues to offer some of the best cooking in Chania. Irish-born Susanna has a flare for hospitality, ably abetted by her son front-of-house, and the dishes on offer are always assured and pretty as a picture. **Known for:** diverse menu of Greek classics with a twist; super pies—octopus and fennel are stars; genial, generous atmosphere. $ *Average main: €10* ⊠ *Akti Papanikoli 1, Nea Chora* ☎ *28210/76261.*

$ | MEDITERRANEAN · ✕ **Tamam.** Steps away from the busy harbor, Tamam feels like a giant leap back in time—an ancient Turkish bath that now houses one of the most atmospheric restaurants in Chania's Old Town. Tamam means "alright" in Turkish, but the plates presented are certainly more than okay. **Known for:** atmospheric 600-year-old building; gently spiced dishes with a nod to Turkey; nice after-dinner treat of Turkish delight and raki. $ *Average main: €10* ⊠ *Zambeliou 49* ☎ *28210/96080* ⊕ *www.tamamrestaurant.com.*

$ | MEDITERRANEAN · ✕ **Well of the Turk.** In the old Ottoman district of Splantzia, opposite the underground church of Ayia Irene, this restaurant is somewhat difficult to find even with a map, but it is worth the endeavor. It serves a mixture of Greek and Turkish dishes with the odd trip to Northern Africa and the Middle East. **Known for:** fabulous food away from the crowds; adjoining flower-scented terrace, a nice option in summer; vegetarian moussaka—a revelation. $ *Average main: €12* ⊠ *Kalinikou Sarpaki 1–3, Splantzia* ☎ *28210/54547* ⊕ *www.welloftheturk.com.*

WHERE TO STAY

$$ | RESORT | FAMILY | Fodor's Choice ★ · ⊡ **Ammos Hotel.** Quite simply, one of the best family hotels in Greece, this is the classic Greek seaside hotel brought bang up-to-date with a chic and funky twist, where Cycladic and Scandinavian design references throughout create an atmosphere that is both modern and timeless. **Pros:** genuinely friendly and caring service; innovative food sourced

from local suppliers; fresh and fun design renovated every year. **Cons:** 5 km (3 miles) from Chania center (but on a bus route); pool can get busy; some rooms face the pretty gardens rather than the sea. $ *Rooms from: €180* ✉ *Irakli Avgoula, Glaros Beach* ☎ *28210/33003* ⊕ *www. ammoshotel.com* ☉ *Closed Nov.–early Apr.* ⤴ *33 rooms* ❘◎❘ *Breakfast.*

$$
HOTEL
Fodor'sChoice
★

Casa Delfino. If you have an ounce of romance in your body you'll love this gorgeous hotel—in 1835 Captain Delfino sailed from Genoa, only to founder on the rocks off Gramvousa, but, smitten by the beauty of Chania, he bought this Renaissance Venetian mansion as his home. **Pros:** prime position on Chania's achingly pretty harbor, opposite the lighthouse; superb breakfast in a mosaic pebbled courtyard with home-made specialties; stunning spa and rooftop terrace bar to indulge your senses. **Cons:** no parking in the town center (but hotel's golf buggy will collect you); historical building means some stairs; books up early in high season. $ *Rooms from: €200* ✉ *Theofanous 9* ☎ *28210/87400* ⊕ *www.casadelfino.com* ⤴ *24 suites* ❘◎❘ *Breakfast.*

$
HOTEL

Porto Veneziano. Nautical themes in blue and white make for a light, airy atmosphere in this harborside establishment, but the main draw are those views of the Venetian waterfront and the White Mountains. **Pros:** great position on the quieter end of the harbor; no smoking throughout the hotel; free bicycles to explore the delights of Chania. **Cons:** rooms at the rear overlook a pretty garden and not-so-pretty car park; rather plain common areas; standard rooms a little snug. $ *Rooms from: €120* ✉ *Old Venetian Harbor* ☎ *28210/27100* ⊕ *www.portoveneziano. gr* ⤴ *57 rooms* ❘◎❘ *Breakfast.*

$$
HOTEL

Samaria Hotel. Remodeled in 2013, this is something of a departure from the regular offerings on the Chania hotel scene, having the feel of a luxury business establishment, but with added personality. **Pros:** quiet, efficient service; contemporary decor is stylish and modern; city-center hotel with a pool—a rarity in Chania. **Cons:** small pool can get busy; not the prettiest of views from the balconies; some noise from the bus depot at the rear. $ *Rooms from: €155* ✉ *Kidonias 69* ☎ *28210/38600* ⊕ *www.samariahotel.gr* ⤴ *84 rooms* ❘◎❘ *Breakfast.*

SHOPPING

The most exotic shopping experience in town is a stroll through Chania's covered market to see local merchants selling rounds of Cretan cheese, jars of golden honey, lengths of salami, salt fish, lentils, and herbs.

Carmela. This enticing store just off the harbor sells the work of con-temporary jewelers and other craftspeople from Crete and throughout Greece, as well as the work of owner Carmela Iatropoulou and her artist husband. ✉ *Aggelou 7* ☎ *28210/90487.*

Top Hanak Old Cretan Blankets and Kilims. Many of these antique blankets and rugs were made for dowries from homespun wool and natural dyes. ✉ *Aggelou 3* ☎ *28210/98571.*

RHODES AND THE DODECANESE

Rhodes, Symi, Kos, Patmos

Visit Fodors.com for advice, updates, and bookings

WELCOME TO RHODES AND THE DODECANESE

TOP REASONS TO GO

★ **The Old Town of Rhodes:** The monuments built by the Knights of St. John some 700 years ago draw as many visitors to Rhodes as the beaches do; Rhodes's Old Town is a remarkably well-preserved and photogenic testimony to its Crusader past.

★ **The Asklepieion:** Kos's site of ancient healing, the Asklepieion, was the renowned medical school founded by Hippocrates, father of Western medicine.

★ **Natural Wonders:** The terrain yields butterflies (Rhodes), hot sea springs (Kos), countless coves (Patmos), and mountain paths (Symi).

★ **St. John's Patmos:** Called the "Jerusalem of the Aegean," Patmos is as peaceful as it was when the Apostle John glimpsed the Apocalypse in his cave here—the spiritual mystique of this little island is still strong.

The Dodecanese (Twelve Islands) are the easternmost holdings of Greece and are set around the shores of Turkey and Asia Minor. Here, classic, Byzantine, and Ottoman architectures blend, and multiculturalism is an old idea. Romans, Crusaders, Turks, and Venetians have all left their marks on Rhodes, in the south of the archipelago and the busiest, most populated, and most visited of the 12 islands. Just to the north is tiny, craggy Symi, sparsely inhabited and ringed by enticing coves. Kos, with its lush fields and sandy beaches, lies between Symi and Patmos, the northernmost island of the group, where arid hillsides are occasionally clad in great stands of cypress.

1 Rhodes. Start, like the crusading Knights of St. John did, with the walled city of Rhodes's Old Town with its monuments, shops, and restaurants. Heading south around the island, discover the moth-mecca of the Valley of the Butterflies in Petaloudes, then take the island's mountainous western road to ancient Kameiros city and medieval Monolithos fortress. The eastern road leads to lovely, car-free Lindos and many, many beaches.

2 Symi. *Picturesque* is the word for both Yialos Harbor, with its restaurants and shops, and Chorio, just above it. The inner island is littered with small churches. The impressive and popular Panormitis Monastery is serviced by boats.

3 Kos. The port town is an appealing blend of ancient stones and northern European partying teens. A short drive out of town, Asklepieion was once the greatest healing site of the ancient era. Large swaths of coast are perfect for swimming.

4 Patmos. Make your pilgrimage to Chora to see the cave St. John is said to have seen and recorded his revelation of the Apocalypse. Towering over Chora's skyline is the imposing, fortified Monastery of St. John the Theologian, and far below is Skala, Patmos's pleasant main town and harbor.

8

Updated
by Marissa
Tejada

Wrapped enticingly around the shores of Turkey and Asia Minor, the southernmost group of Greek islands called the Dodecanese (Twelve Islands) lies at the eastern edge of the Aegean sea. The Dodecanese archipelago first grabbed the spotlight when Rhodes was colonized by the crusading Knights of the Order of St. John in the 14th century. Today, of course, the Order of the Holy Holiday Maker now besieges its famed capital, Rhodes Town (and the island's overbuilt beach resorts), but happily Kos's native Hippocrates—father of Western medicine—seems to have immunized many of the inland landscapes of blissfully peaceful Symi and Patmos against tourists.

These islands have long shared a common history: Romans, Crusaders, Turks, and Venetians all built picturesque temples, castles, and fortresses in exotic towns of shady lanes and tall houses. Strategically located Rhodes has by far the most important place in history thanks to its starring role during the Crusades. Kos comes in second in popularity and has vestiges of antiquity; the Sanctuary of Asklepios, a center of healing, drew people from all over the ancient world. Today, parts of the coast have been transformed into an endless line of shops and restaurants. Retreat inland, however, to find hillsides crowded only with bleating goats.

Symi is a virtual museum of 19th-century neoclassical architecture almost untouched by modern development, while Patmos, where St. John wrote his *Book of Revelation*, became a renowned monastic center during the Byzantine period. Sometimes called the Jerusalem of the Aegean, this little island is as peaceful as it must have been when St. John lived here. It continues as a significant focal point of the Greek Orthodox faith, and today has become a favorite getaway for both

Greeks as well as an elite international crowd. Symi and Patmos both offer a sense of peace and quiet that in large part has been lost on much of overdeveloped Rhodes and Kos. But despite the invasion of sunseekers, there are still delightful pockets of local color on these islands, too.

PLANNING

WHEN TO GO

To avoid crowds, just before and after peak seasons (May, June, and September) are good times to visit. August is the busiest season on all these islands, when hotel reservations and even spots on interisland ferries can be hard to come by. Patmos and Rhodes are popular Easter getaways for Greeks, and celebrations include candlelight processions and fireworks late Saturday around midnight; island bakeries serve *tsoureki* (sweet braided bread). From October to May, most archaeological sites remain open, but many hotels, restaurants, and shops are closed, and boat travel is limited by curtailed schedules and the weather's whims.

PLANNING YOUR TIME

Rhodes and Kos are two of Greece's most popular resort islands, and for good reason: they offer not only some magnificent sandy beaches but also some real historical dazzlers and some rich, off-the-beach experiences. On Rhodes, cultural must-dos include visits to the Palace of the Grand Master and other sights in Rhodes's Old Town, as well as the Acropolis of Lindos. Kos's great archaeological treasure is the Asklepieion, the great healing center of antiquity. All open as early as 8 am in the summer and stay open well into the evening, and on an early or late visit you will avoid the heat and crowds.

On these busy islands it's also easy to wander off the beaten path to enjoy mountainous hinterlands carpeted in pine forests, vineyards, and groves of olives and oranges. A visit to either island should include a country drive (or bus excursion) and lunch in a village taverna; good stops are Siana in Rhodes and Kefalos or Zia on Kos. Symi and Patmos are geared to travelers looking for low-key retreats and a glimpse of authentic island life. It's easy to slip away to uncrowded beaches and coves on either, but also join islanders for their time-honored ritual of an evening stroll. On Symi, you can amble around the harbor in Yialos, then walk up the Kali Strata (Good Steps) to Chorio. In Patmos, the gathering spots are the main waterfront promenade and narrow lanes of Skala, which come alive in the evening.

GETTING HERE AND AROUND

AIR TRAVEL

Though you can get to the hubs of Rhodes or Kos in under 10 hours nowadays on the faster ferries, if you have limited time it's best to fly to these two islands. Aegean Airlines and Olympic Air fly between Athens and Rhodes, as do a number of other carriers, and Olympic and Aegean also run several daily flights between Athens and Kos. Flying time is about 45 minutes to either island. Aegean and Olympic also connect Rhodes and Kos with several other Greek islands, as does Sky Express. Finally, it's possible to fly directly to Rhodes and Kos from a number of

European capitals on Aegean and several European carriers, especially during the summer. Neither Patmos nor Symi has an airport.

AIRPORTS

Rhodes Diogoras Airport is in Paradissi, 15 km (9 miles) southwest of Rhodes Town and well connected by public bus (6 am–11 pm, €6) and taxi (approximately €25 for the half-hour drive). Parts of the Old Town are inaccessible to cars, so hotels will usually arrange to have a porter meet you near one of the gates.

Kos Airport is 26 km (16 miles) southwest of Kos Town. There is bus (€4) and taxi service from there to Kos Town and to some beach resorts; expect to pay about €45 for the taxi fare to Kos Town or the beach resorts.

Contacts Kos Airport. ☎ 22420/56000 ⊕ www.kosairportguide.com. **Rhodes Airport.** ☎ 22410/88700 ⊕ www.rhodes-airport.info.

BOAT AND FERRY TRAVEL

In August, for good rates and an assured spot, it is essential that you book as far as possible (at least two weeks) in advance. Boats at this time can be uncomfortably crowded, with deck-class passengers claiming key spots on the floor, in the lounge areas, and even—in peak season—on the metal deck under the stars. If you're taking an overnight boat in August, book a berth so you'll be assured a comfortable place to lay your head. If you are traveling to and around the Dodecanese islands outside the summer season, you'll find that service is curtailed.

When traveling from Piraeus to Rhodes by ferry (12–18 hours), you first make several stops, including at Patmos (6–10 hours) and Kos (10–16 hours). Bringing a car aboard can quadruple costs. Of the several ferry lines serving the Dodecanese, Blue Star Ferries has the largest boats and the most frequent service, sailing several times a week out of Piraeus. The Athens–Dodecanese ferry schedule changes seasonally, and ferries to Patmos do not run daily out of season, so contact ferry lines, the Greek National Tourism Organization (GNTO or EOT) in Athens, or a travel agency for details. An excellent source for ferry schedules is the Web-based tourist site, the Greek Travel Pages (GTP).

The easiest way to travel among the Dodecanese islands is by high-speed craft operated by Dodekanisos Seaways during the summer. Times and fares: Rhodes to/from Symi takes 50 minutes (€14); Rhodes to/from Kos takes 2¼ hours (€28); Rhodes to/from Patmos takes 5 hours (€50).

Contacts Dodekanisos Seaways. ✉ Thalassini Pili, Kolona Port ☎ 22410/70590 ⊕ www.12ne.gr. **Rhodes Port Authority.** ✉ Lohagou Fanouraki 26, Rhodes Town ☎ 22410/27242.

BUS TRAVEL

There is a decent bus network on all the islands, though there are more-infrequent routes on smaller islands. Buses from Rhodes Town leave from two different points on Averoff street for the island's east and west sides. Symi's and Patmos's bus stations are on the harbor. Kos Town is served by a city bus while KTEL buses service the rest of the island.

Contacts Kos KTEL Bus Depot. ✉ Cleopatras 7, Kos Town ☎ 22420/22292 ⊕ www.ktel-kos.gr. **Kos Town Bus Depot.** ✉ Akti Koundouriotou (main harbor),

Kos Town ☎ *22420/22292* ⊕ *ktel-kos.gr.* **Rhodes East-Side Bus Depot.**
✉ *Averoff, Rhodes Town* ⊹ *Near the end of Platia Rimini* ☎ *22410/26300.*
Rhodes West-Side Bus Station. ✉ *Averof, Rhodes Town* ⊹ *Next to the market*
☎ *22410/26300.*

CAR TRAVEL

A car is useful for exploring Rhodes or Kos, or to hop between Patmos's many beaches. In Symi, with its few roads, a car is of little use, and you should opt for the vans that serve as the island buses, make use of the island taxis, or walk along the paths that connect most places on the island.

You may take a car to the Dodecanese on one of the large ferries that sail daily from Piraeus to Rhodes and less frequently to the smaller islands. The relatively small network of roads on Rhodes is well maintained and detailed maps are available; traffic is likely to be heavy only from Rhodes Town to Lindos. In Kos, a car makes it easy to skirt the coast and make stops at the many sandy beaches, though resorts are serviced by bus. In Patmos, a car or motorbike makes it easy to tour the island, while sights and outlying restaurants are easily reached by bus or taxi, and a few beaches can be reached by either bus or boat. Symi, which has only one road suitable for cars, is best explored on foot or by bus or boat. Expect to pay at least €30–€40 a day to rent a car on one of the islands.

TAXI TRAVEL

Taxis are available throughout most of Rhodes. All taxi stands have a sign listing set fares to destinations around the island. Expect a delay when calling radio taxis in high season.

Contacts Kos Taxi. ☎ *22420/23333* ⊕ *www.kosradiotaxi.gr.* **Patmos Radio Taxi.** ☎ *22470/31225.* **Rhodes Radio Taxi.** ☎ *22410/69800* ⊕ *rhodes-taxi.gr.*

HOTELS

Rhodes has an array of resort hotels, with sea views and easy access to beaches. Many old houses in Rhodes's Old Town have been converted to boutique hotels, some modest and others quite luxurious. Mass tourist accommodations are also plentiful on Kos, but as in Rhodes, most lodging isn't especially Greek in style. Hotels on Symi are small and usually charming, since the island never encouraged the development of mammoth caravansaries. Similarly, Patmos has attractive, high-quality lodgings that tend to be both more elegant and traditional than its resort-magnet neighbors. High season can prove extremely crowded and you may have difficulty finding a room on any of these islands if you don't book well in advance. Many hotels throughout the Dodecanese are closed from November through March. Lodgings in water-poor Symi and Patmos may remind you to limit water use.

RESTAURANTS

Throughout the Dodecanese, you can find sophisticated restaurants, as well as simple tavernas serving excellent food. On Rhodes and Kos, beware of many completely mediocre eateries catering to tourists with fast food. It is sometimes best to wait until after 9 pm to see where the Greeks are eating. Because Rhodes and Kos produce most of their

8

own foodstuffs, in better restaurants you can count on fresh fruit and vegetables. Fish, of course, is readily available on all islands. Large fish goes by the kilo, so confirm the exact amount you'd like when ordering. Tiny, tender Symi shrimp, found only in the waters around this island, have such soft shells they can be easily popped in the mouth whole. They are used in dozens of local dishes. Wherever you dine, ask about the specialty of the day, and check the food on display in the kitchen of tavernas. Rhodes produces some excellent wines that appear on tables throughout the Dodecanese, and vintages from throughout Greece also show up on wine lists. With the exception of a few very high-end spots, dress on all the islands is casual; reservations are not necessary unless specified.

Restaurant and hotel reviews have been shortened. For full information, visit Fodors.com.

DINING AND LODGING PRICES IN EUROS			
$	**$$**	**$$$**	**$$$$**
Restaurants	under €15	€15–€25	€26–€40	over €40
Hotels	under €125	€125–€225	€226–€275	over €275

Restaurant prices are the average cost of a main course at dinner or, if dinner is not served, at lunch. Hotel prices are the lowest cost of a standard double room in high season.

TOURS

From April to October, local island boat tours take you to area sights and may include a picnic on a remote beach or even a visit to the shores of Turkey.

A1 Yacht Trade Consortium. This brokerage, rental agency, and outfitter organizes sailing tours around the Greek islands near the Turkish coast. ✉ *Commercial harbor, Rhodes Town* ☎ *22410/01000* ⊕ *www. a1yachting.com.*

Astoria Travel. On Patmos, Astoria Travel provides day bus trips to Patmos's St. John the Theologian Monastery and the Monastery of the Apocalypse. ✉ *Skala Harbor, Skala* ☎ *22470/31205* ⊕ *www.astoriatravel.com.*

Kalodoukas Tours. On Symi, Kalodoukas Tours runs boat trips to the Monastery of Panormitis, as well as to secluded beaches and islets, which include swimming and a barbecue lunch. ✉ *Harbor front, Yialos* ☎ *22460/71077* ⊕ *www.kalodoukas.gr.*

Symi Tours. The island's venerable tour organizer arranges boat excursions around the island and can help tourists book accommodations. ✉ *Harbor front, Yialos* ☎ *22460/71307* ⊕ *www.symitours.com.*

Triton Holidays. If you're not renting a car on Rhodes, it can be worth taking a bus tour to its southern points and interior. Starting at €35, Triton Holidays offers a guided bus tour to Thermes Kallitheas, Epta Piges, and Lindos; a bus tour to Kameiros, Filerimos, and Petaloudes; and a full-day trip through several points in the interior and south. They can also arrange a boat tour that leaves Mandraki Harbor in Rhodes Town in the morning, deposits you in Lindos for a day of sightseeing and beachgoing, with a return in the evening. ⊠ *Plastira 9, Rhodes Town* ☎ *22410/21690* ⊕ *www.tritondmc.gr.*

RHODES ΡΟΔΟΣ

Rhodes, at 1,400 square km (540 square miles) is the fourth-largest Greek island and, along with Sicily, Crete, and Cyprus, is one of the great islands of the Mediterranean. It lies almost exactly halfway between Piraeus and Cyprus, 18 km (11 miles) off the coast of Asia Minor, and it was long considered a bridge between Europe and the East. Geologically similar to the Turkish mainland, it was probably once part of Asia Minor, separated by one of the frequent volcanic upheavals this volatile region has experienced.

Today Rhodes retains its role as the center of Dodecanese trade, politics, and culture. Its diversity ensures it remains a polestar of tourism as well: Rhodes Town brings together fascinating artifacts, medieval architecture, an active nightlife, and is reputedly the sunniest spot in all of Europe. Like a gigantic historical pop-up book, Rhodes offers layers upon layers of sights: Romans, Crusaders, Turks, and Venetians built a remarkable array of temples, castles, and fortresses in exotic quarters of shady lanes and tall houses. But if you head out to the island's east coast you'll find it blessed with white-sand beaches and dotted with copses of trees, interspersed with fertile valleys full of figs and olives. And though some of the shore is beset by vast resort hotels and holiday villages, there are still some wonderfully unsullied sections of beach to be found all around the island; if you look for it, you'll even find a taste of rural life.

The island's history unfolds as an especially rich pageant. Rhodes saw successive waves of settlement, including the arrival of the Dorian Greeks from Argos and Laconia early in the 1st millennium BC. From the 8th to the 6th century BC, Rhodian cities established settlements in Italy, France, Spain, and Egypt and actively traded with mainland Greece, exporting pottery, oil, wine, and figs. Independence and expansion came to a halt when the Persians took over the island at the end of the 6th century BC and forced Rhodians to provide ships and men for King Xerxes's failed attack on the mainland (480 BC). A league of city-states rose under Athenian leadership. In 408 BC the united city of Rhodes was created on the site of the modern town; much of the populace moved there, and the history of the island and the town became synonymous. As the new city grew and flourished, its political organization became the model for the city of Alexandria in Egypt.

In 42 BC, Rhodes came under the hegemony of Rome, and through the years of the empire it was fabled as a beautiful city where straight roads were lined with porticoes, houses, and gardens. According to Pliny, who described the city in the 1st century AD, the town possessed some 2,000 statues, at least 100 of them of colossal scale. One of the most famous examples of the island's sculptural school is the world-famous *Laocöon*—probably executed in the 1st century BC—which showed

8

the priest who warned the Trojans to beware Greeks bearing gifts (it stands in the Vatican today). Sadly, the ancient glory of Rhodes has few visible remnants. The city was ravaged by Arab invaders in AD 654 and 807, and only with the expulsion of the Arabs and the reconquest of Rhodes by the Byzantine emperors did the city begin to revive—gloriously. Rhodes was a crucial stop on the road to the Holy Land during the Crusades. It came briefly under Venetian influence, then Byzantine, then Genoese. In 1309, when the Knights of St. John took the city from its Genoese masters, the island's most important modern era began.

The Knights of St. John, an order of Hospitalers, were organized to protect and care for Christian pilgrims. By the beginning of the 12th century the order had become military in nature, and after the fall of Acre in 1291, the knights fled from Palestine, withdrawing first to Cyprus and then to Rhodes. In 1312 the knights inherited the immense wealth of the Templars (another religious military order, which had just been outlawed by the pope) and used it to fortify Rhodes. But for all their power and the strength of their walls, moats, and artillery, the knights could not hold back the Turks. In 1522 the Ottomans, with 300 ships and 100,000 men under Süleyman the Magnificent, began what was to be the final siege, taking the city after six months.

During the Turkish occupation, Rhodes became a possession of the Grand Admiral, who collected taxes but left the Rhodians to pursue a generally peaceful and prosperous existence. They continued to build ships and trade with Greece, Constantinople (later Istanbul), Syria, and Egypt. The Greek mainland was liberated by the War of Independence in 1821, but Rhodes and the Dodecanese remained part of the Ottoman Empire until 1912, when the Italians took over. After World War II, the Dodecanese were formally united with Greece in 1947.

GETTING HERE AND AROUND

Rhodes is well served by regularly scheduled flights from Athens and Thessaloniki as well as both scheduled and charter flights from London, Rome, and other major European cities. Two daily ferries leave from Piraeus bound for Rhodes and the Dodecanese, a 15-hour overnight trip. You will find schedules and booking information for ferry service to and from Rhodes and other islands in the Dodecanese at ⊕ *www.ferries.gr* or ⊕ *www.gtp.gr*.

Regional ferries connect Rhodes, Kos, and Symi. Smaller boats, including those to other islands in the Dodecanese, dock at Rhodes Town's 2,500-year-old Mandraki Harbor; the larger overnight ferries use the adjacent new harbor.

Diogoras Airport is in Paradissi, 15 km (9 miles) southwest of Rhodes Town and well connected by public bus (running from 6 am to 11 pm, €6 and taxi, about €25 for the half-hour drive.

Rhodes Town's two bus terminals are hubs for service throughout the island—points on the western side of the island are served by buses from the West Side Station, near the shopping district of the New Town on Averof; most places on the eastern side are served from the East Side Station on Platia Rimini (Rimini Square), just down the street from the West Station next to the market on Mandraki Harbor. Bus service is

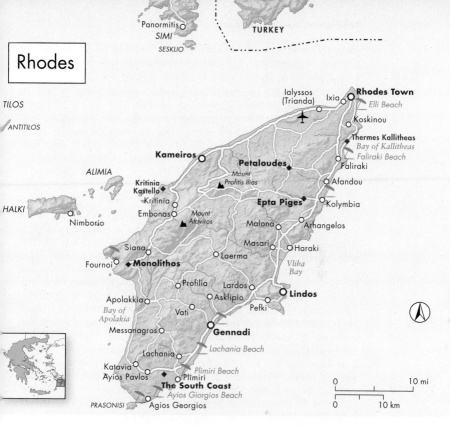

Rhodes

excellent, with, for example, buses to and from Lindos running almost hourly from the East Side Station; €6 each way, €65 by taxi.

VISITOR INFORMATION

The central Rhodes Municipal Tourism Office, near the bus station, is open May–October, daily 7:30 am–3 pm. The Rodos Tourism Promotion Organization maintains a helpful English website.

Contacts Rhodes Municipal Tourism Office. ✉ *Averof 3, Rhodes Town* ☎ *22410/35240* ⊕ *www.rhodes.gr.*

RHODES TOWN ΡΟΔΟΣ (ΠΟΛΗ)

463 km (288 miles) east of Piraeus harbor in Athens by ferry.

Fodors Choice ★

Early travelers described Rhodes as a town of two parts: a castle or high town (Collachium) and a lower city. Today Rhodes Town—sometimes referred to as Ródos Town—is still a city of two parts: the Old Town, a UNESCO World Heritage site that incorporates the high town and lower city, and the modern metropolis, or New Town, spreading away from the walls that encircle the Old Town. The narrow streets of the Old Town are for the most part closed to cars and are lined with Orthodox and Catholic churches, Turkish houses (some of which follow the ancient orthogonal plan), and medieval public buildings with exterior staircases and facades elegantly constructed of well-cut limestone from Lindos. Careful reconstruction in recent years has enhanced the harmonious effect.

Spreading out in all directions from the original city walls, the New Town is "new" only in relative terms—islanders began settling outside the walls of the Old Town with the arrival of the Turks in 1522. Italians added a great deal of flair in the first part of the 20th century, adding the art deco administrative buildings clustered near the harbor. Later growth has also been relatively kind to New Town, and the streets of low-rise modern apartment blocks are tree-lined and many commercial streets are attractive pedestrian walkways.

EXPLORING

TOP ATTRACTIONS

Archaeological Museum of Rhodes. The Hospital of the Knights (now the island's archaeological museum), completed in 1489, surrounds a Byzantine courtyard, off which are the refectory and wards where the wealthy institution once administered to the knights and townspeople. These wonderful surroundings are enhanced with findings from around Rhodes and nearby islands, among them two well-known representations of Aphrodite: the *Aphrodite of Rhodes,* who, while bathing, pushes aside her hair as if she's listening; and a standing figure, known as *Aphrodite Thalassia,* or "of the sea," as she was discovered in the water off the northern city beach. Two 6th-century BC *kouros* (statues of idealized male youth) were found in the nearby ancient city of Kameiros, and in a beautiful 5th-century BC funerary stela, a young woman named Crito, hair cut short in mourning, gives a farewell embrace to her mother, Timarista, who is already moving outside the frame, as she leaves the world. Another stela of three-year-old Ploutos is inscribed, "loosening the support of a cart which had upon it a heavy load of stakes I passed over the threshold of Hades." ⊠ *Platia Mouseou* ☎ *22410/75674* ⊕ *odysseus.culture.gr* ⌧ *€8* ☉ *Closed Nov.–Mar.*

Inn of France. The most elaborate of the striking inns on this famously historic street today houses a French language institute (appropriately enough). The facade is ornately carved with the fleur-de-lis and heraldic patterns and bears an inscription that dates the building to between 1492 and 1509. ⊠ *Rhodes Town* ✛ *About halfway down Street of Knights from Loggia of St. John.*

Loggia of St. John. This 19th-century neo-Gothic structure stands on the site of the 14th-century Church of St. John, patron of the Knights of St. John and the final resting place of many members of the order. Used as an ammunition storehouse during Turkish occupation, the church was reduced to rubble in an explosion sparked by lightning in 1856. ⊠ *Rhodes Town* ✛ *Next to Palace of Grand Masters.*

Mosque of Murat Reis. The 17h-century mosque was named after Murat Reis, an Ottoman naval commander who served in Süleyman the Magnificent's navy. The shady peaceful grounds surrounding it are a network of traditional and ornate cobblestone courtyards and a battered but proud cemetery where the marbled Ottoman grave markers remain. British expat novelist Lawrence Durrell once lived on the grounds, inspired by the tranquil beauty of the place. ⊠ *Georgiou Papanikolaou 30, New Town.*

The Colossus of Rhodes may be long gone, but the Palace of the Grand Masters remains a colossal landmark of the Old Town quarter.

Fodor's Choice
★

Palace of the Grand Master of the Knights of Rhodes. This massive affair with fairy-tale towers, crenellated ramparts, and more than 150 rooms crowns the top of the Street of Knights and is the place to begin a tour. Unscathed during the Turkish siege of Rhodes in 1522, the palace was destroyed in 1856 by an explosion of ammunition stored nearby in the cellars of the Church of St. John. The present structure—a Mussolini-era Italian reconstruction—was rebuilt in a storybook, pseudo-medieval style all the rage in the early 20th century and was later used as a holiday abode for King Vittorio Emmanuele III of Italy. Today, the palace's collection of antiques and antiquities includes Hellenistic and Roman mosaic floors from Italian excavations in Kos, and in the permanent exhibition downstairs extensive displays, maps, and plans showing the layout of the city will help you get oriented before wandering through the labyrinthine Old Town. ⊠ *Ippoton, Old Town* ☎ *22410/23359* ⊕ *odysseus.culture.gr* ⌂ *€12* ⊘ *Closed Nov.–Apr.*

Fodor's Choice
★

Street of Knights. The Knights of St. John built most of their monuments along this cobblestone lane, also known as Ippoton, which descends from the Palace of the Grand Masters—at the highest spot of the medieval city—toward the commercial port. The lane is a little more than a third of a mile long and follows the route that once connected the ancient acropolis to the harbor. It is bordered on both sides by the Inns of the Tongues, where the knights supped and held their meetings. ⊠ *Ippoton, Old Town.*

Turkish Library. A rare collection of Turkish, Persian, and Arab manuscripts, including many rare Korans, founded in 1794, is a striking reminder of the Ottoman presence. The collection and the adjacent

Mosque of Süleyman are still used by those members of Rhodes's Turkish community who stayed in Rhodes after the 1923 population exchange, a mass repatriation of Greek and Turkish migrants. ⊠ *Sokratous* ✛ *Opposite Mosque of Süleyman* ☎ *22410/74090* ◷ *Closed Sun.*

Walls of Rhodes. One of the great medieval monuments in the Mediterranean, the walls of Rhodes are wonderfully restored and illustrate the engineering capabilities as well as the financial and human resources available to the Knights of St. John. For 200 years the knights strengthened the walls by thickening them, up to 40 feet in places, and curving them so as to deflect cannonballs. The moat between the inner and outer walls never contained water; it was a device to prevent invaders from constructing siege towers. You can get a sense of the enclosed city's massive scale by walking inside the moat.

Parts of the walkway that runs the 4 km (2½ miles) along the top of the walls is sometimes accessible through the Palace of the Grand Master by a city tour; check with the Rhodes tourist office for times. ⊠ *Rhodes Town* ✛ *Old Town* ☜ *Tours €3.*

WORTH NOTING

The Acropolis of Rhodes. About 2 km (1 mile) to the west of Rhodes's town center, atop Mt. Smith, are the freely accessible ruins of the Acropolis of Rhodes, a fine example of the stately sanctuaries that the ancient Greeks built atop many of their cities. The complex includes a theater that the Italians restored in the early 20th century, a stadium, three restored columns of the Temple of Apollo Pythios, the scrappy remains of the Temple of Athena Polias, a Nymphaia, and an Odeon. For a dramatic view, make your way to the westernmost edge of the summit, which drops via a sharp and almost inaccessible cliff to the shore below, now lined with enormous hotels. ⊠ *New Town* ⊕ *www.culture.gr.*

Byzantine Museum. Icons and frescos from churches throughout Rhodes Town (most of them long since destroyed) are displayed within the 11th-century Lady of the Castle Church, once the Byzantine cathedral and, under the Turks, a mosque. ⊠ *Off Platia Mouseou* ☎ *22410/38309* ☜ *€3* ◷ *Closed Mon.*

Evangelismos Church. The town's cathedral is a 1920s Italian-built replica of the Knights Church of St. John in the Old Town and rises next to the harbor. ⊠ *Rhodes Town* ✛ *Near Mandraki Harbor* ☎ *22410/77916.*

Fort Ayios Nikolas. This circular fortress, built by the Knights of St. John in the 15th century, guards the entrance to Mandraki Harbor, near a row of picturesque but disused windmills. ⊠ *Rhodes Town* ✛ *North of Old Town walls, bordering Mandraki Harbor.*

Mandraki Harbor. What was once the main harbor, in use since the 5th century BC, adjoins the commercial harbor on the east side of Old Town and is home to the city's municipal buildings and an open-air bazaar. ⊠ *Rhodes Town.*

Our Lady of the Bourg. Soaring vaults are all that remains of what was once a magnificent Gothic church, completed by the Knights of St. John in 1456. The knights believed that Mary, the mother of Jesus, provided them and Rhodes special protection against the ever-present threat of

Continued on page 427

THE MARCH OF GREEK HISTORY

The 21st-century Greeks are one of the oldest peoples on the face of the earth: they have seen *everything*. While Greeks are now subjected to an annual full-scale invasion by an army of camera-toting legions, their ancestors were conquered by numberless encroachers for the past four millennia. During this epic time span, Greece was forged, torn asunder, and remade into the vital nation it is today.

Paradox is a Greek word and highly applicable to Greek history. Since the rehabilitation of Homer by Hermann Schliemann's excavations, Agamemnon, Great King of Mycenae, and the earliest heroes of ancient Greece have moved from legend into history. Today, the remote 13th century BC sometimes appears more familiar than most Greek events in better documented later periods. Not that subsequent ages were any duller—the one epithet that is utterly unsuitable in Greece—but they lacked the master touch of the great epic poet.

However, while ancient temples still evoke Homer, Sophocles, Plato, and the rest, today's Greeks are not just the watered-down descendants of a noble people living in the ruined halls of their ancestors. From time immemorial the Greeks have been piling the present on top of the past, blithely building, layering, and overlapping their more than 30 centuries of history to create the amazing fabric that is modern Greece.

(top) The Parthenon atop the Acropolis in Athens

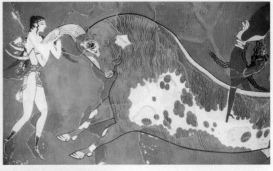

(top) Cycladic female figure; (top right) Bull fresco from Minoan ruins on Crete; (bottom) Fresco of ladies from Minoan ruins on Crete

3000 BC–1900 BC

Cycladic Origins

Greece is far older than the glory days of the Classical age—the 5th century BC—which gave us the Parthenon. It has been inhabited almost continuously for the past 13,000 years. Tools made on the island of Milos around 11,000 BC have been found in a cave in the Peloponnese, suggesting that even in those long-ago reaches of history Greeks were sailing across the sparkling Aegean between islands and mainland shores. Around 3000 BC, about the time cultures were flourishing in Egypt and Mesopotamia, small cities were springing up throughout the Cycladic islands—the first major

Greek settlements, today known as the Keros-Syros culture. These early Cycladic people lived by sea and, as the need for protection from invaders intensified, in fortified towns in the uplands. Objects found in mass graves tell us they made tools, crockery, and jewelry. The most remarkable remnants of Cycladic civilization are flat, two-dimensional female idols, strikingly modern in appearance.

■ Sights to see: Museum of Cycladic Art (Goulandris Foundation), Athens.

2000 BC–1150 BC

Minoan Bronze Age

By 2000 BC, a great culture—Europe's oldest state (as opposed to mere tribal groupings)—had taken root on the island of Crete. What these inhabitants of Greece's southernmost island actually called themselves is not known; archaeologist Sir Arthur Evans named the civilization Minoan after Minos, the legendary king of the famous labyrinth who probably ruled from the magnificent palace of Knossos. Their warehouses were filled with spices traded throughout the Mediterranean, and royal chambers were decorated with sophisticated art—statuary, delicate rythons,

(top) Replica of Trojan Horse; (top, right) Lion Gate at Mycenae; (bottom) Mycenean gold funeral mask

IN FOCUS THE MARCH OF GREEK HISTORY

8

and, most evocative of all, alluring frescoes depicting fanciful secular scenes as well as the goddesses who dominated the matriarchal Minoan religion. A system of writing, known as Linear A and Linear B script, appears on seal stones. The cause of the downfall of the Minoans remains a mystery—political unrest, invasions from the mainland, a volcano on nearby Santorini and subsequent earthquakes? Enter the mainland Mycenaeans.

■ Sights to see:
Palace of Knossos, Crete. Archaeological Museum, Heraklion.

1600 BC–1100 BC

The Mycenaeans

By the 14th century BC, the Mycenaeans wielded power throughout mainland Greece and much of the rest of the known world, from Sicily to Asia Minor. Their capital, Mycenae (in the Peloponnese), was one of several great cities they built around palaces filled with art and stories of the new Olympian gods and heavily fortified. As civilized as the Mycenaeans were, they were also warlike. Their exploits inspired the *Iliad* and *Odyssey*, and Agamemnon, legendary hero of the 12th-century Trojan Wars—the starting point in the endless ping-pong match between Europe and Asia—is said to have ruled from

Mycenae. For all their might, the Mycenaeans fell into decline sometime around 1100 BC. Soon the Dorians, from northern Greece, moved south, pushing the Mycenaeans into a dark age during which art and writing were lost. But Greeks who sailed across the Aegean to flee the Dorians established Ephesus, Smyrna, and other so-called Ionian cities in Asia Minor, where a rich culture soon flourished.

■ Sights to see:
Lion Gate, Mycenae, the Argolid. Cyclopean Walls, Tiryns. Nestor's Palace, Messinia.

(top) Ancient vase depicting Olympic athletes; (left) Bust of Homer; (right) Statue of King Leonidas

The Age of Homer

1000 BC–800 BC

By the 8th century BC, Greeks were living in hundreds of *poleis*, city-states that usually comprised a walled city that governed the surrounding country-side. Most poleis were built around a raised acropolis and an agora (a market-place), as well temples and often a gymnasium; limited power lay with a group of elite citizens—the first inklings of democracy. As the need for resources grew, Greeks began to establish colonies in Sicily and Gaul and on the Black Sea, and with this expansion came contact with the written word that laid the founda-tions of the Greek alphabet.

Two essential elements of Greek culture led the new Greek renaissance that forged a nation's identity: Homeric legends began circulating, recounting the deeds of heroes and gods, and athletes showed off their strength and valor at the Olympic Games, first staged in 776 BC. Participa-tion in these games meant support of Hellenism—the concept of a united Greece.

■ Sights to see:
Greek colonies set up in Asia Minor, Sicily (Agrigento, Syracuse), and southern Italy (Paestum).

Persian Invasions

499 BC–449 BC

The most powerful poleis, Athens and Sparta, would soon become two of history's most famous rivals—but for a brief time in the fifth cen-tury, they were allies united against a common foe, the Persians, who, in 490 BC, launched an attack against Athens. Though far outnum-bered, the Athenians dealt the Persians a crippling blow on the Marathon plain. Ten years later, the Persians attacked again, this time with a massive army and navy commanded by King Xerxes. The Spartan King Leonidas and his "300"—the men of his royal guard (along with an unknown

(top) Phoenician sailors building a pontoon bridge on the Hellespont for the Persian invasion of Greece in 480 BC; (top right) Bust of Pericles; (right) Relief sculpture fragment depicting the king of Persia; (bottom) Greek helmet

IN FOCUS THE MARCH OF GREEK HISTORY

8

number of slaves, or Helots)—sacrificed their lives to hold the Persians off at Thermopylae, allowing the Athenians time to muster ships and sink much of the Persian fleet. Xerxes returned the following year, in the summer of 479 BC, to sack Athens, but an army drawn from city-states throughout Greece and under the command of Pausanias, a Spartan general, defeated the Persians and brought the Persian Wars to an end.

■ Sights to see:
Marathon Tomb, Marathon, Attica.

460 BC–431 BC
Pericles' Golden Age

Athens thrived for much of the fifth century BC under the leadership of Pericles. The city became the center of the Hellenic world—and the cradle of Western civilization. The Parthenon was built; Socrates engaged in the dialogues that, recorded by Plato, became the basis of European philosophy; Aeschylus, Aristophanes, Euripides, and Sophocles wrote dramas; Praxiteles sculpted his masterpieces; and Herodotus became the "father of history."

■ Sights to see:
The Parthenon, Athens. Sanctuary of Apollo, Delphi.

431 BC–404 BC
Peloponnesian War

Athens was leader of the Delian League, a confederation of 140 Greek city-states, and Sparta headed the Peloponnesian League, a formidable alliance of city-states of southern and central Greece. From 431 to 404 BC these two powers engaged in battles that plunged much of Greece into bloodshed. Sparta emerged the victor after Athens suffered two devastating defeats: the destruction of a massive force sent to attack Syracuse, a Spartan ally in Sicily, and the sinking of the Athenian fleet.

■ Sights to see:
Archaeological Museum, Sparta, Laconia.

(top) Alexander the Great listening to his tutor Aristotle; (top right) Byzantine basilica; (bottom) Alexander the Great on horseback

Alexander the Great

338 BC– AD 323

In the years following the Peloponnesian War, Sparta, Athens, and an emerging power, Thebes, battled for control of Greece. Eventually, the victors came from the north: Macedonians led by Philip II defeated Athens in the Battle of Chaeronea in 338 BC. Philip's son, Alexander the Great, who had been tutored by Aristotle, quickly unified Greece and conquered Persia, most of the rest of the Middle East, and Egypt. In the ensuing 11 years of unparalleled triumphs he spread Greek culture from the Nile to the Indus. Alexander died in Babylon of a mysterious illness in 323 BC and the great empire he amassed soon fell asunder. Roman armies began moving toward Athens, Greece became the Roman province of Achaia in 27 BC, and for the next 300 years of peace Rome readily adapted Greek art, architecture, and thought. This cultural influence during the Pax Romana compensated for the loss of a much-abused independence.

■ Sights to see: Birthplace, Pella, Central Macedonia. Royal Tombs, Vergina, Central Macedonia. Roman Agora, Athens. Archaeological Museum, Marathon, Attica.

Byzantine Greece

324–1204

With the division of the Roman Empire into East and West, Greece came under the control of the Eastern Empire, administered from the Greek city of Byzantium (later Constantinople), where Emperor Constantine moved the capital in 324. The empire had embraced Christianity as its official religion, and Byzantium became the seat of the Eastern Orthodox Church, which led to the Great Christian Schism of 1094. Byzantium's Greek culture evolved into a distinct architectural style and religious art forms best represented by mosaics and icon paintings. For centuries Byzantine

841 Parthenon transformed
into cathedral

Fourth Crusade
invades Greece

800   1000   1200   1400

IN FOCUS THE MARCH OF GREEK HISTORY

8

(top) Gold-leaf mosaics;
(left) Palace of the
Grand Masters, Rhodes;
(right) Portrait of
Mehmet II

Greece fended off invasions from Visigoths, Vandals, Slavs, Muslims, Bulgars, and Normans. As an ally of the empire, the Republic of Venice developed trading strongholds in Greece in the 11th century. Interested in the control of maritime routes, the Venetians built a network of fortresses and fortified towns along the Ionian coast of Greece. Venice later extended its possessions over several Aegean islands and Crete, which it held until 1669.

■ Sights to see:
Little Mitropolis, Athens.
Byzantine Museum, Rhodes.

1204–1453
Crusaders and Feudal Greece

The Byzantine Empire, and Greece with it, finally succumbed to Crusaders who pillaged Constantinople in 1204. Frankish knights created vassal feudal states in Thessalonica, the Peloponnese, and Rhodes, while other short-lived kingdoms in Epirus and on the shores of the Black Sea became the refuge of Byzantine Greek populations. Soon, however, a new threat loomed as Ottoman Turks under Sultan Mehmet II began marching into Byzantine lands, occupying most of Asia Minor, Macedonia, and Thessaly.

■ Sights to see:
Palace of the Grand Masters, Rhodes.

1453–1821
Ottoman Age

Constantinople fell to the Ottomans in 1453, and by the 16th century Sultan Suleyman the Magnificent had expanded his Empire from Vienna through the Middle East. Greece was the stage of many battles between East and West. In 1687, Athens was besieged and the Parthenon heavily damaged by Venetian bombardments. Only in 1718 all of Greece was conceded to the Ottoman Empire, just in time for a resurgence of Hellenist culture in Europe, Neoclassicism in the arts, and a brand-new interest in Greek archaeology.

■ Sights to see:
Old Town, Rethymnon.

| 1522 Knights of St. John surrender Rhodes to the Attomans | Lord Elgin removes marbles | Olympic Games in Athens |
| | Greeks drive Turks out | |

1600   1800   2000

(top) 2004 Olympic Stadium, Athens; (far left) Portrait of Eleftherios Venizelos; (left) Portrait of Lord Byron

A Greek Nation

1821–1935

Ottoman rulers allowed a degree of autonomy to Greece, yet uprisings became increasingly fierce. In 1821 the bloody War of Independence, which started as a successful rebellion in the Peloponnese, spread across the land. Western Europeans, including the Romantic poet Lord Byron, rushed to the Greek cause. After years of setbacks and civil wars, Britain, France, and Russia mediated with the Ottomans to establish Greece as an autonomous region. Otto of Bavaria, only 17, was named sovereign of Greece in 1831, the first of the often-unpopular monarchs who reigned intermittently until 1974. Public favor soon rested with prime ministers like Eleftherios Venizelos, who colonized Crete in 1908. In 1919 Venizelos, a proponent of a "Greater Greece," sought to conquer ethnic Greek regions of the new Turkish nation, but his forces were defeated and hundreds of thousands, on both sides, were massacred. The subsequent peace decreed the massive population exchange of two million people between the two countries, resulting in the complete expulsion of Greeks from Asia Minor, after 3,000 years of history.

■ Sights to see: Achilleion Palace, Corfu. National Garden, Athens.

A New Republic

1936–PRESENT

Greece emerged from the savagery of Axis occupation during World War II in the grip of civil war, with the Communist party battling right-wing forces. The right controlled the Greek government until 1963, when Georgios Papandreou became prime minister and proposed democratic reforms that were soon put down by a repressive colonels' junta led by Georgios Papadopoulos. A new republic was proclaimed in 1973, and a new constitution replaced the monarchy with an elective government—democratic ideals born in Greece more than 2,000 years earlier.

■ Sights to see: 2004 Olympic Stadium, Athens.

a Muslim invasion. ⊠ *Old Town* ⊹ *Inside remains of walls, access through Gate of the Virgin.*

OFF THE BEATEN PATH

Thermes Kallitheas. As you travel south along the east coast, a strange sight meets you: an assemblage of buildings that look as if they have been transplanted from Morocco. In fact, this spectacular mosaic-tile bath complex was built in 1929 by the Italians. As far back as the early 2nd century BC, area mineral springs were prized; the great physician Hippocrates of Kos extolled these springs for alleviating liver, kidney, and rheumatic ailments. Though the baths are no longer in use, the ornate rotunda has been restored (art exhibitions are often on view), as have peristyles and pergolas, and you can wander through the beautifully landscaped grounds—note the pebble mosaics, an ancient folk tradition come alive again, with mosaics of fish, deer, and other images—and have a drink or snack in the attractive café. A pretty beach rings a nearby cove. ⊠ *Rhodes Town* ⊹ *10 km (6 miles) south of Rhodes Town* ☎ *22410/65691* ⊕ *www.kallitheasprings.gr* ▣ *€3* ⊘ *Closed Nov.–Mar.*

> **SEE MORE AND SAVE**
>
> Plan on hitting all of Rhodes's Old Town attractions? Purchase a multisight ticket (€10), which gets you admission to the Palace of the Grand Masters, Archaeological Museum, Museum of Decorative Arts, and Byzantine Museum. It's available at any of the sights.

BEACHES

Elli Beach. Though the beach is pebbly rather than sandy, a handy location right at the edge of Old Town makes this seaside strip immensely popular, and it's lined with chairs and umbrellas. An offshore diving platform is a huge hit with kids and what seems to be most of the teenage population of Rhodes. What you won't find here is solitude, and what semblance of peace and quiet you might find will likely be interrupted by an endless stream of hawkers selling everything from trinkets to cold drinks. **Amenities:** food and drink; lifeguards; toilets; showers; water sports. **Best for:** swimming; walking. ⊠ *Rhodes Town* ⊹ *North of Old Town, near Rhodes Yacht Club.*

Faliraki Beach. The most popular beach in Rhodes will be your idea of paradise or hell, depending on what you think of crowded sands backed by fun parks, supermarkets, all-inclusive resorts, and fast-food joints. Stretches of the 5 km (3 miles) of fine sand are a little less cramped than others, the southern end part especially, officially designated as a naturist beach. Buses run between Rhodes Town and Faliraki throughout the day and late into the evening. **Amenities:** food and drink; lifeguards; parking (free); showers; toilets; water sports. **Best for:** nudists; partiers; swimming; walking. ⊠ *Faliraki* ⊹ *14 km (8½ miles) south of Rhodes Town.*

WHERE TO EAT

$$$

SEAFOOD

Fodor's Choice

★

✕ **Alexis 4 Seasons.** Known for the best seafood on Rhodes, Alexis 4 Seasons is also known for its handsomely decorated old rooms, beautiful walled garden, and a panoramic view from the roof terrace. Mussels in wine, scallops in vodka sauce, shrimp risotto in an ouzo sauce, as well as simply grilled fish fill the menu. **Known for:** gourmet

8

Mighty fortifications, like this Palace of the Grand Master of the Knights of Rhodes, remind us that the Crusaders dominated Rhodes until the Ottoman era.

seafood; city-view terrace. $ *Average main: €30* ⊠ *Aristotelous 33* ☎ *22410/70522* ⊕ *www.alexis4seasons.com.*

$$$
SEAFOOD
✕ **Dinoris.** Tucked away down an Old Town lane, this elegant and spacious restaurant's foundations date back to AD 310, when it was a hospital, and it was converted into a stable for the Knights of St. John in 1530. Seafood specialties are the main attraction on the menu, including the variety platter, which includes *psarokeftedakia* (fish fritters) as well as mussels, shrimp, and lobster. **Known for:** excellent seafood; charming outdoor-dining setting in the Old Town. $ *Average main: €30* ⊠ *Platia Mouseou 14a* ☎ *22410/25824* ⊕ *www.dinoris.com* ☾ *Closed Jan.*

$$
MODERN GREEK
✕ **Marco Polo Cafe.** One of the most enchanting places to dine is the garden of a little guesthouse, where you'll want to linger amid the foliage and flowers for an entire evening. The menu features a rich lamb souvlaki and a delectable sesame-encrusted tuna. **Known for:** romantic dining; good service. $ *Average main: €25* ⊠ *Agiou Fanouriou 42, Old Town* ☎ *22410/25562* ⊕ *www.marcopolomansion.gr* ☾ *Closed Nov.–Feb.*

$
GREEK
✕ **To Steno.** When Rhodians want a traditional meal, they head to this simple little taverna on a residential street in the New Town. Dining is in a plain room and on a sparkling-white terrace in warmer months, where you can compose a meal of such delicious mezedes as *bakaliaros* (salted cod) in garlic sauce, pumpkin fritters, and zucchini flowers filled with feta cheese. **Known for:** good and simple Greek taverna food; relaxed atmosphere. $ *Average main: €7* ⊠ *Agion Anargiron 29* ☎ *22410/35914.*

CLOSE UP

The Great Colussus

At the end of the 4th century BC the Rhodians commissioned the sculptor Chares, from Lindos, to create the famous Colossus, a huge bronze statue of the sun god, Helios, and one of the Seven Wonders of the Ancient World. Two bronze deer statues mark the spot where legend says the Colossus once straddled the Mandraki Harbor entrance. The 110-foot-high statue stood only for half a century. In 227 BC, when an earthquake razed the city and toppled the Colossus, help poured in from all quarters of the eastern Mediterranean. After the calamity, the Delphic oracle advised the Rhodians to let the great Colossus remain where it had fallen. So there it rested for some eight centuries, until AD 654 when it was sold as scrap metal and carted off to Syria, allegedly by a caravan of 900 camels. After that, nothing is known of its fate.

WHERE TO STAY

$$$$
B&B/INN
🏨 **Kokkini Porta Rossa.** As befits Rhodes's muticultural heritage, the opulent, intriguing rooms of this hotel surround a garden, beautifully blending Ottoman and Greek heritage with sumptuous antiques, rich fabrics, fine woods, and contemporary fittings to provide warm surroundings that seem like a posh private home. **Pros:** superbly designed; large and comfortable accommodations; feel of a private home with excellent service. **Cons:** most easily reached on foot, but just inside gates; not for those looking for low-key casual surroundings; public parking for cars is 400 feet away. $ *Rooms from: €380* ⊠ *Rhodes Town* ✢ *Next to Gate of St. John* ☎ *22410/75114* ⊕ *kokkiniporta.com* ⇆ *5 suites* ‖◎‖ *Breakfast.*

$$
HOTEL
Fodor's Choice
★
🏨 **Marco Polo Mansion.** Entering this renovated 15th-century Ottoman mansion in the maze of the Old Town's colorful Turkish section is like stepping into another world. **Pros:** exotic ambience; warm hospitality; the courtyard restaurant is wonderful. **Cons:** rooms are reached via several sets of stairs; hotel can only be reached on foot; come here to live like a pasha, not to indulge in modern amenities. $ *Rooms from: €130* ⊠ *Aghiou Fanouriou 40–42* ☎ *22410/25562* ⊕ *www.marcopolomansion.gr* ⊙ *Closed Nov.–Apr.* ⇆ *10 rooms* ‖◎‖ *Breakfast.*

$
B&B/INN
🏨 **Medieval Inn.** These simple, whitewashed lodgings with bright accents are sparkling clean and surround a flowery courtyard. **Pros:** excellent location; very clean and comfortable; friendly service. **Cons:** basic comforts; some bathrooms, while private, are outside the room; can only be reached on foot. $ *Rooms from: €65* ⊠ *Timachida 9, Old Town* ☎ *22410/22469* ⊕ *www.medievalinn.com* ⇆ *9 rooms* ‖◎‖ *No meals.*

$$
RESORT
FAMILY
🏨 **Mitsis Grand Hotel.** Located steps away from Rhodes Town Beach, the Grand resort is a large complex that makes full use of its resort space, including several pools, 13 restaurants, and cozy lounge bars. **Pros:** steps away from the beach; good for families and large groups; great amenities, restaurants, and services. **Cons:** impersonal feel; extra charges apply for in-room Wi-Fi; peak season may feel crowded. $ *Rooms from: €190* ⊠ *Akti Miaouli and Papanikolaou, New Town* ☎ *22410/54700* ⊕ *grandhotel.mitsishotels.com* ⇆ *402 rooms* ‖◎‖ *All-inclusive.*

8

$$ HOTEL **S. Nikolis Hotel.** All the atmosphere of Rhodes's medieval Old Town is captured here at this charmingly restored 14th-century house. **Pros:** atmospheric rooms and surroundings; beautiful garden; warm hospitality. **Cons:** some rooms are small; no parking; reachable only by foot. [$] *Rooms from: €180* ✉ *Odos Ippodamou 61* ☎ *22410/34561* 🌐 *www.s-nikolis.gr* 🛏 *16 rooms* 🍴 *Breakfast.*

$$$ HOTEL **Spirit of the Knights.** A restored Ottoman house on the quiet back lanes of the Old Town is one of Rhodes's most distinctive getaways. **Pros:** lovely courtyard with Jacuzzi; quiet location; excellent breakfast and service. **Cons:** can only be reached on foot; no elevator; no parking. [$] *Rooms from: €270* ✉ *Alexandridou 14* ☎ *22410/39765* 🌐 *www.rhodesluxuryhotel.com* 🛏 *6 rooms* 🍴 *Breakfast.*

NIGHTLIFE AND PERFORMING ARTS

BARS AND DISCOS

A stylish nightlife has sprung up amid the medieval buildings and flower-filled courtyards of the Old Town. Some bars and cafés here are open all day for drinks, and many—often those with beautiful medieval interiors—stay open most of the year. Nighttime-only spots in the Old Town open up around 10 pm and close around 3 or 4 am. The action centers on narrow, pebble-paved Miltiadou street, where seats spill out from trendy bars set in stone buildings. Another hot spot is Arionos Square. Those wanting to venture to the New Town's throbbing discos should head to Orfanidou street, where bronzed, scantily clad tourists gyrate till dawn at massive clubs.

Colorado. The biggest dance club on the island is a three-stage complex with live rock bands, as well as dance hits and R&B. ✉ *Orfanidou 57, New Town* ☎ *22410/75120* 🌐 *www.coloradoclub-rhodes.com.*

Macao. A haven for grown-up lounge lizards, Macao is all about dark, moody lighting, a romantic terrace, mellow music, and worldly cocktails. ✉ *Archelaou 5* ☎ *69364/00305* 🌐 *www.macaobar.gr.*

CASINOS

Casino Rodos. Housed in a 1920s, Italian-built faux-palace of Byzantine and Arabesque design, Rhodes's municipal casino evokes the island's mid-20th-century heyday as a gathering spot for the international elite. Aside from gaming, the casino also offers concerts and other events. To enter, you must be at least 21 years old and present a passport. Also, respectable casual attire is required. ✉ *Hotel Grande Albergo Delle Rose, Georgiou Papanikolaou 4, New Town* ☎ *22410/97400* 🌐 *www.casinorodos.gr* 🎟 *€6.*

FESTIVALS

Medieval Rose Festival. You can get a glimpse of life in medieval Rhodes in late May when jesters, jugglers, and fire-eaters parade through the cobblestone streets of Old Town. 🌐 *www.medievalfestival.gr.*

SPORTS AND THE OUTDOORS

Dive Med College. A "Discover Scuba" program includes a 30-minute theory lesson and practice in shallow water, then a 20-minute descent. Longer, open-water dive training sessions are also available. ✉ *45 Kritika* ☎ *22410/61115* 🌐 *www.divemed.gr.*

SHOPPING

In Rhodes Town you can buy good copies of Lindos ware, a delicate pottery decorated with green and red floral motifs. The Old Town's shopping area, on Sokratous, is lined with boutiques, some of which sell furs, jewelry, and other high-ticket items.

Astero Antiques. Owner Mahalis Hatziz travels throughout Greece each winter to fill his shop with some of the most enticing goods on offer on the island. ⊠ *Ayiou Fanouriou 4* ✢ *Off Sokratous* ☎ *22410/34753.*

EPTA PIGES ΕΠΤΑ ΠΗΓΕΣ

30 km (19 miles) south of Rhodes Town.

Epta Piges. A deeply shaded glen watered by seven mountain springs (*epta piges* in Greek) is made all the more photogenic thanks to the imported peacocks that flaunt their plumage in the woods around the pools. The waters are channeled through a 164-yard-long tunnel, which you can walk through, emerging at the edge of a cascading dam and a small man-made lake where you can swim. Here an enterprising local shepherd began serving simple fare in 1945, and his sideline turned into the busy waterside taverna and tourist site of today. Despite its many visitors, the beauty of the springs remains unspoiled. ⊠ *Archangelos* ✢ *To get here, turn right on the inland road near Kolymbia and follow signs.* ☎ *22410/56259* ⊕ *eptapiges.com.*

LINDOS ΛΙΝΔΟΣ

19 km (12 miles) southwest of Epta Piges, 48 km (30 miles) southwest of Rhodes Town.

Lindos, cradled between two harbors and dominated by its massive hilltop acropolis, is incredibly scenic and remarkably well preserved. Many 15th-century houses are still in use, and the Crusader architecture you see in Rhodes Town is everywhere: substantial houses of finely cut Lindos limestone, with windows crowned by elaborate arches. Many floors are paved with black-and-white pebble mosaics. Intermixed with these Crusader-era buildings are whitewashed Cycladic-style houses with square, blue-shuttered windows.

Before the existence of Rhodes Town, Lindos was the island's principal maritime center, possessing a revered sanctuary, consecrated to Athena, whose cult probably succeeded that of a pre-Hellenic divinity named Lindia; the sanctuary was dedicated to Athena Lindia. By the 6th century BC, an impressive temple dominated the settlement, and after the foundation of Rhodes, the Lindians set up a *propylaia* (monumental entrance gate) on the model of that in Athens. In the mid-4th century BC, the temple was destroyed by fire and almost immediately rebuilt, with a new wooden statue of the goddess covered by gold leaf, and with arms, head, and legs of marble or ivory. Lindos prospered into Roman times, during the Middle Ages, and under the Knights of St. John. Only at the beginning of the 19th century did the age-old shipping activity cease.

One of the most magnificent examples of Crusader era architecture is the great fortress at Lindos.

Like Rhodes Town, Lindos is enchanting off-season but can get unbearably crowded when summertime pilgrims make the trek from Rhodes Town daily, and passage through narrow streets lined with shops selling clothes and trinkets slows to a snail's pace. At these times, an overnight visit allows you to enjoy the town's beauties after the day-trippers leave. Only pedestrians and donkeys are allowed in Lindos because the town's narrow alleys are not wide enough for vehicles. If you're arriving by car, park in the lot above town and walk the 10 minutes down (about 1,200 feet) to town.

EXPLORING

FAMILY
Fodor's Choice
★

Acropolis of Lindos. A 15-minute climb (on the back of a donkey if you prefer) from the village center up to the Acropolis of Lindos leads past a gauntlet of Lindian women who spread out their lace and embroidery like fresh laundry over the rocks. The final approach ascends a steep flight of stairs, past a marvelous 2nd-century BC relief of the prow of a Lindian ship, carved into the rock.

The entrance takes you through the medieval castle built by the Knights of St. John, then to the Byzantine Chapel of St. John on the next level. The Romans, too, left their mark on the acropolis, with a temple dedicated to Diocletian. On the upper terraces, begun by classical Greeks around 300 BC, are the remains of elaborate porticoes and stoas, commanding an immense sweep of sea and making a powerful statement on behalf of Athena and the Lydians (who dedicated the monuments on the Acropolis to her); the lofty white columns of the temple and stoa on the summit must have presented a magnificent picture. The main portico of the stoa had 42 Doric columns, at the center of which an opening led to the staircase up to the Propylaia (or sanctuary). The Temple of Athena Lindia at the very top is surprisingly modest, given the drama of the approach. As was common in the 4th century BC, both the front and the rear are flanked by four Doric columns. Numerous inscribed statue bases were found all over the summit, attesting in many cases to the work of Lindian sculptors, who were clearly second to none. ✉ *Lindos* ✣ *Above the village* ☎ *22440/31258* 🌐 *www.culture.gr* 🎟 *€12.*

EASY AS 1-2-3

Most of Lindos's mazelike streets don't have conventional names or addresses; instead, buildings are numbered, from 1 through about 500. Lower numbers are on the north side of town, higher numbers on the south.

Church of the Panayia. A graceful building with a beautiful bell tower probably antedates the Knights of St. John, though the bell tower bears the arms of Grand Master d'Aubusson with the dates 1484–90. Frescoes in the elaborate interior were painted in 1779 by Gregory of Symi, and the black-and-white pebble floor is a popular Byzantine design. ✉ *Lindos* ✣ *Off main square.*

Tomb of Kleoboulos. Escape the crowds by trekking to the Tomb of Kleoboulos, which is incorrectly named after Lindos's 6th-century BC tyrant Kleoboulos; it's actually the final resting place of a wealthy family of the 1st to 2nd century BC. After about 3 km (2 miles), a 30-minute scenic walk on a stony path across the headland (on the north side of Lindos Bay), you encounter the small, rounded stone tomb. You can peer inside and see the candle marks, which testify to its later use as the Church of St. Emilianos. ✉ *Lindos* ✣ *Look for sign at parking lot near beach above main square. Follow the dirt path along the hill on opposite side of bay from Acropolis.*

8

WHERE TO EAT

$$ GREEK Fodor's Choice ★

🍴 **Mavrikos.** With a large terrace overlooking the sea and Lindos Square, Mavrikos offers elegant simplicity through its flavorful Greek dishes, such as the chickpeas in orange zest, swordfish in caper sauce, black butter beans in carob syrup, and squid risotto. Third-generation chef Dimitris Mavrikos owns this institution along with his brother Michalis, a family-run restaurant that has kept a stellar reputation since the 1930s. **Known for:** quality local dishes; open-air terrace dining. [$] *Average main: €25* ✉ *Main square* ☎ *22440/31232* 🕓 *Closed Nov.–Mar.*

WHERE TO STAY

$$$$ RESORT

🏨 **Lindos Blu Hotel.** Sea views seem to fill every inch of this small, sun-drenched, adults-only resort, where many of the stylishly contemporary guest rooms and suites have their own pools tucked onto terraces. **Pros:** attentive, personalized service; resort amenities in an intimate atmosphere; all rooms have sea view. **Cons:** decor is a bit generic; not within walking distance to sights in Lindos Town; pricey in high season. [$] *Rooms from: €430* ✉ *Vlicha Lindos* ✣ *2 km (1 mile) outside village center* ☎ *22440/32110* 🌐 *www.lindosblu.gr* 🕓 *Closed Nov.–Apr.* 🛏 *70 rooms* 🍽 *Breakfast.*

$$$$ HOTEL Fodor's Choice ★ **Melenos Lindos.** Overlooking Lindos Bay and set at the foot of the Acropolis, each room is furnished for 17th-century Lindian elegance including raised beds, hand-carved cedar woodwork, Turkish tiles, and wall tapestries. **Pros:** terraces with sea views; exquisite service; great restaurant. **Cons:** no elevator; reachable only by foot; no parking. [$] *Rooms from: €370* ✉ *Lindos* ✥ *At edge of Lindos, on path to Acropolis* ☎ *22440/32222* 🌐 *www.melenoslindos.com* 🕒 *Closed Nov.–Mar.* 🛏 *12 rooms* 🍴 *Breakfast.*

NIGHTLIFE

Most of Lindos's bars cater to a young, hard-drinking crowd; few are without a television showing soccer. Many are open year-round to serve the locals.

Fodor's Choice ★ **Gelo Blu.** The most popular hangout in town serves homemade ice cream by day and drinks day and night in the cool, blue-cushioned interior and pebbled courtyard and on the rooftop terrace of a sea captain's house. ✉ *Lindos* ✥ *Near Theotokou Church* ☎ *22440/31761.*

Rainbird. Coffee and drinks are served all day, but the views from the romantic terrace make this spot especially popular around sunset. ✉ *Lindos* ✥ *On lane to Acropolis* ☎ *22440/32169.*

GENNADI AND THE SOUTH COAST
ΓΕΝΝΑΔΙ ΚΑΙ ΝΟΤΙΑ ΠΑΡΑΛΙΑ

20 km (12 miles) south of Lindos, 68 km (42 miles) south of Rhodes Town.

The area south of Lindos, with fewer beaches and less fertile soil, is less traveled than the stretch to its north. Though development is increasing, the still pretty and inexpensive coastal village of Gennadi has pensions, rooms for rent, and a handful of tavernas, nightclubs, and DJ-hosted beach parties.

BEACHES

Lachania Beach. Stretching uninterrupted for several miles, Lachania Beach lies below the unspoiled, whitewashed village of the same name, one of the most picturesque in Rhodes. Though stretches of the sand are lined with sun beds, it's easy to find a fairly secluded spot backed by scrub-covered dunes. **Amenities:** food and drink; water sports. **Best for:** solitude; swimming; walking. ✉ *Lachania* ✥ *9 km (5½ miles) south of Gennadi.*

Plimiri Beach. A lovely bay is ringed by soft and quiet sands, where it's easy to find a relatively secluded spot. The clear, calm waters are ideal for swimming, though winds tend to pick up in the afternoon, a boon for windsurfers. A few tavernas prepare delightfully simple seafood meals. **Amenities:** food and drink. **Best for:** nudists; solitude; swimming; windsurfing.

MONOLITHOS TO KAMEIROS ΜΟΝΟΛΙΘΟΣ ΠΡΟΣ ΚΑΜΕΙΡΟΣ

28 km (17 miles) northwest of Gennadi, 74 km (46 miles) southwest of Rhodes Town.

Rhodes's west coast is more forested, with fewer good beaches than its east coast—but if you're looking to get away from the hordes, you'll find peace and quiet among the sylvan scenery, august ruins, and vineyards.

EXPLORING

Kameiros. One of the three ancient cities of Rhodes, excavated by the Italians in 1929, lies on three levels on a slope above the sea. Most of the city, apparently never fortified, that is visible today dates to the classical period and later, and includes an acropolis, a large reservoir, a gridlike pattern of streets lined with houses and shops, and several temples. The hill hides many more ruins, yet to be unearthed. ⊠ *Rhodes Town ✛ Off main Rhodes road, 23 km (14 miles) northeast of Siana; turn at sign for Ancient Kameiros* ☎ *22410/40037* ⊕ *www.culture.gr* 🎫 *€6* ☉ *Closed Mon. Nov.–Mar.*

Kritinia Kastello. This ruined-yet-still impressive fortress, built by the Knights of St. John in the late 15th century, rises high above the sea on the coast just north of Mt. Avrios, with good views in every direction. ⊠ *Kritinia ✛ 13 km (8 miles) northeast of Siana.*

Fodor's Choice ★ **Monolithos.** A medieval fortress of Monolithos—so named for the jutting, 750-foot monolith on which it is built—rises above a fairy-tale landscape of deep-green forests and sharp cliffs plunging into the sea. Inside the Venetian stronghold (accessible only by a steep path and series of stone steps) there is a chapel, and the ramparts provide magnificent views of Rhodes's emerald inland and the island of Halki. The small pebble beach of Fourni beneath the castle is a delightful place for a swim. ⊠ *Monolithos ✛ Take western road from middle of Monolithos village; near hairpin turn there's a path up to fortress.*

Siana. This small town perches on the wooded slopes of Mt. Acramitis above a vast, fertile valley. A popular stop on the tourist trail, Siana is known for its fragrant honey and for *souma* (a very strong, sweet wine that resembles a grape-flavor schnapps); look for stands selling both. ⊠ *Siana ✛ 5 km (3 miles) northeast of Monolithos.*

EN ROUTE
Beyond Siana, the road continues on a high ridge through thick pine forests, which carpet the precipitous slopes dropping toward the sea. To the east looms the bare, stony massif of Mt. Ataviros, Rhodes's highest peak, at 3,986 feet. If you follow the road inland rather than continue north along the coast toward Kritinia, you'll climb the flanks of the mountains to the traditional, arbor-filled village of Embonas in Rhodes's richest wine country *(see "Nectar of the Gods" in Chapter 7).*

8

PETALOUDES ΠΕΤΑΛΟΥΔΕΣ ΚΑΙ ΙΑΛΥΣΟΣ

22 km (14 miles) east of Kameiros, 25 km (15 miles) southwest of Rhodes Town.

Shady lanes and babbling brooks winding through the forested grounds of a former Venetian estate would be quite enticing even without the presence of some of Rhodes's most famous inhabitants, brown and red tiger moths that swarm to create a much-observed spectacle. You'll find more rustic retreats elsewhere on Rhodes, but a walk through the cooling woods can be refreshing—and especially rewarding during prime swarm times, dusk in July and August.

FAMILY   **Petaloudes.** The "Valley of the Butterflies" lives up to its name, especially in July and August. In summer the *callimorpha quadripunctaria*, actually a moth species, cluster by the thousands around the low bushes of the pungent storax plant, which grows all over the area. Through the years the numbers have diminished, partly owing to busloads of tourists clapping hands to see them fly up in dense clouds—an antic that causes the moths to deplete their scant energy reserves and is strongly discouraged. Access to the valley involves an easy walk up an idyllic yet crowded trail through a pretty wood past a stream and ponds. ⊠ *Rhodes Town* ✛ *Turn off coastal road south and follow signs leading to the site with its own parking lot* ☎ *22410/82822* ⬛ *€5* ⊙ *Closed Nov.–Mar.*

SYMI ΣΥΜΗ

45 km (28 miles) north of Rhodes by ferry.

The island of Symi is an enchanting place, where island life centers around sparkling Yialos Harbor, and Chorio, a 19th-century town of neoclassical mansions, crowns a hillside above. The island has few beaches and almost no flat land, so it is not attractive to developers. As a result, quiet Symi provides a peaceful retreat for travelers, who tend to fall in love with the island on their first visit and return year after year.

GETTING HERE AND AROUND

Little Symi is well served by boats, either on one-day excursion trips from Mandraki Harbor in Rhodes Town (check with any travel agent like Triton Holidays *(see Tours)* or one of the shills on the harbor; the trip takes less than an hour. All boats arrive in Yialos, Symi's main harbor, and catamarans also make a stop in Panormitis or Pedi, though these remote places are of most interest to day-trippers who just want a day at a remote beach.

A sturdy bus makes the hourly trip from Yialos Harbor up to Chorio and on to Pedi Bay, €0.80. But once on Symi, you'll learn that the easiest way to get around is by foot, as roads are few and often quite rough. If you are staying in Nimborios or another outlying place, make arrangements in advance for your hotel to pick you up, as taxis refuse to make the trip on unimproved roads.

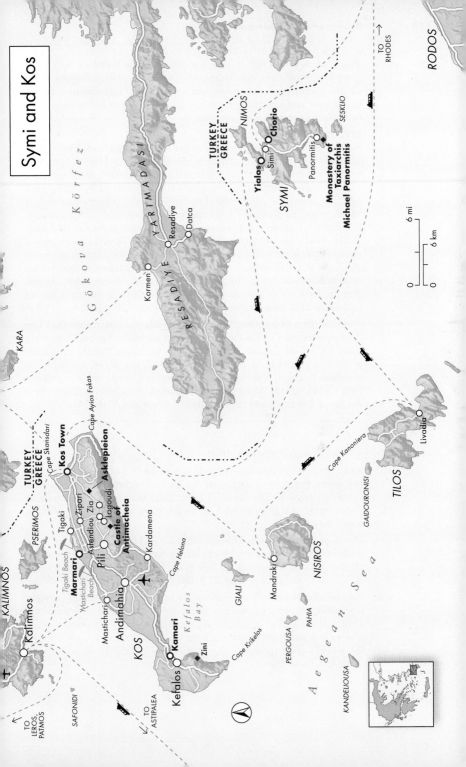

Symi and Kos

KARA

GÖKOVA Körfez

KALIMNOS

TURKEY
GREECE

PSERIMOS

Kalimnos

TO
LEROS,
PATMOS

SAFONIDI

Cape Skansdari

Kos Town

Tigaki Beach

Tigaki

Marmari

Mastichari Beach

Zipari

Astendiou Zia

Mastichari

Pili

Lagoudi

Castle of
Antimacheia

KOS

Andimahia

Kefalos

Kamari

Zini

Kefalos
Bay

Cape Krikelos

Cape Heloma

TO
ASTIPALEA

Cape Ayios Fokas

Asklepieion

Kardamena

Cape Kanoniera

YARIMADASI

Kormen

RESADIYE

Resadiye

Datca

NIMOS

Yialos

Simi

Chorio

SYMI

Panormitis

Monastery of
Taxiarchis
Michael Panormitis

SESKLIO

TURKEY
GREECE

TO
RHODES

RODOS

GIALI

Mandraki

NISIROS

PERGOUSA

PAHIA

KANDELIOUSA

GAIDOURONISSI

TILOS

Livadia

Aegean Sea

0   6 mi

0   6 km

VISITOR INFORMATION

The region's only English-language newspaper is found on Symi. The *Symi Visitor* (⊕ *www.symivisitor.com*), available at tourist spots, is full of information on events, news, and activities, and includes an overview of the sites and bus and ferry schedules; the website has accommodations listings and weather updates.

EXPLORING

Nireus, the ancient king of Symi noted for his looks, sailed with three vessels to assist the Greeks at Troy, as mentioned by Homer. Symi was later part of the Dorian Hexapolis dominated by Rhodes, and it remained under Rhodian dominance throughout the Roman and Byzantine periods. The island has good natural harbors, and the nearby coast of Asia Minor provided plentiful timber for the Symiotes, who were shipbuilders, fearless seafarers and sponge divers, and rich and successful merchants. Under the Ottomans their harbor was proclaimed a free port and attracted the trade of the entire region. The Symiotes' continuous travel and trade and their frequent contact with Europe led them to incorporate foreign elements in their furnishings, clothes, and cultural life. At first they lived in Chorio, high on the hillside above the port, and in the second half of the 19th century spread down to the coast at Yialos.

Proof of their prosperity exists in the neoclassical mansions that line the narrow streets of Chorio and the main harbor in Yialos. There were some 20,000 inhabitants at this acme, but under the Italian occupation at the end of the Italo-Turkish war in 1912, the island declined; the Symiotes lost their holdings in Asia Minor and were unable to convert their fleets to steam. Many emigrated to work elsewhere, and now there are just a few thousand inhabitants in Chorio and Yialos.

YIALOS ΓΙΑΛΟΣ

45 km (28 miles) north of Rhodes Town.

As the boat from Rhodes to Symi rounds the last of many rocky barren spurs, the port of Yialos, at the back of a deep, narrow harbor, comes into view. The shore is lined with mansions, their ground floors converted to cafés with waterside terraces perfect for whiling away lazy hours.

Church of Ayhios Ioannis. This church built in 1838 incorporates in its walls fragments of ancient blocks from a temple that apparently stood on this site and is surrounded by a plaza paved in an intricate mosaic, fashioned from inlaid pebbles. ⊠ *Yialos* ✛ *Near center of Yialos Village.*

FAMILY **Symi Nautical Museum.** Sponge-diving tools, model ships, antique navigation tools, and vintage anchors give a good taste of life in Symi in the 19th and early 20th centuries. It's hard to miss the ornamental blue-and-yellow building—a landmark on Yialos Harbor, it was once one of the world's great sponge-diving centers. ⊠ *Yialos* ✛ *Yialos waterfront* €3 ⊙ *Closed Mon.*

WHERE TO EAT

$$$ GREEK 🍴 **Tholos.** A seaside perch at the end of Yialos Harbor is the picturesque setting for an excellent meal, which often begins with such traditional appetizers as stuffed zucchini or boiled greens (the taramasalata here might just be among the best in Greece) and includes fresh grilled fish and other daily home-cooked offerings. You may want to arrive early enough to enjoy sunset views of the harbor. **Known for:** sunset views; excellent Mediterranean dishes. [$] *Average main: €30* ✉ *Waterfront* ☎ *22460/72033* ⏲ *Closed mid-Oct.–Mar.*

WHERE TO STAY

$$ HOTEL Fodor's Choice ★ 🏨 **Aliki Hotel.** At this three-story, 1895 mansion on the waterfront, guest rooms are furnished with a tasteful mix of antiques and newer pieces—the best, of course, are those that face the water. **Pros:** lovely old house with plenty of atmosphere; waterfront location; beautiful terrace. **Cons:** rooms are reached by a climb up steep stairs; no elevator; no parking. [$] *Rooms from: €130* ✉ *Yialos waterfront* ☎ *22460/71665* 🌐 *www.hotelaliki.gr* 🛏 *15 rooms* 🍽 *Breakfast.*

$$ B&B/INN 🏨 **Niriides.** A little fishing village of Nimborios, about a mile from Yialos, is the setting for a get-away-from-it-all retreat in these pleasant apartments overlooking the sea and the coast of Turkey and surrounded by gardens. **Pros:** wonderful relaxing atmosphere; great hospitality; spacious, attractive accommodations; beautiful rural location. **Cons:** remote location; steps to get to rooms; not within close distance to major sights of Symi. [$] *Rooms from: €135* ✉ *Yialos* ✣ *Nimborios* ☎ *22460/71784* 🌐 *www.niriideshotel.com* ⏲ *Closed Nov.–Apr.* 🛏 *11 rooms* 🍽 *Breakfast.*

$$$ HOTEL 🏨 **The Old Markets.** Symi's historic sponge trading halls—one of many landmarks that surround the old harbor—have been restored as an intimate and atmospheric inn where centuries-old surroundings are accented by stone walls, painted ceilings, exquisite antiques, and such 21st-century touches as high-tech lighting and supremely comfortable beds. **Pros:** extremely comfortable accommodations, including a lavish suite; personal service; walking distance to major sights of Symi. **Cons:** harbor location puts you amid the one busy spot on the island; steps to reach the hotel; no elevator. [$] *Rooms from: €240* ✉ *Kali Strata* ☎ *22460/71440* 🌐 *theoldmarkets.com* ⏲ *Closed Nov.–Apr.* 🛏 *10 rooms* 🍽 *Breakfast.*

BEACHES

One reason Symi's beaches are so pristine is that almost none are reachable by car. From the main harbor at Yialos, boats leave every half hour between 10:30 am and 12:30 pm to the beautiful beaches of **Aghia Marina, Aghios Nikolas, Aghios Giorgos,** and **Nanou Bay**. Return trips run from 4 to 6 pm. The round-trips cost €5 to €10. In summer, there are also small boats for hire from the clock tower.

For a swim near Yialos, you can go to the little strip of beach beyond the **Yialos Harbor**—follow the road past the bell tower and the Aliki Hotel and you come to a seaside taverna that rents umbrellas and beach chairs for €5 a day. If you continue walking on the same road for about 2 km (1 mile), you come to the pine-shaded beach at Nimborios Bay, where there is another taverna.

Aghios Giorgos. The half-hour boat trip down the rugged east coast of the island from Pedi Bay is part of the pleasure of an excursion to this beautiful strip of sand, backed by sheer cliffs. The absence of amenities requires a bit of preparation—bring water, food, and an umbrella, as there are few shade-providing trees. **Amenities:** none. **Best for:** nudists; snorkeling; solitude; swimming. ⊠ *Pedi Bay.*

FAMILY **Aghios Nikolas.** Accessible only by water taxi from Pedi Bay or a half-hour-walk along a rough path, this sandy beach along a little bay slopes gently, providing shallow waters that are excellent for children, and is backed by a grove of shade-giving trees. Despite the relative isolation, the beach attracts summertime crowds and is well equipped with food vendors and other facilities. **Amenities:** food and drink; toilets; water sports. **Best for:** snorkeling; swimming. ⊠ *Pedi Bay ⊕ 3 km (2 miles) east of Pedi Bay.*

FESTIVALS

Symi Festival. Free dance, music, theater performances, and movie screenings come to the island every year from June through September. Most events take place in the main harbor square in Yialos, but some are scheduled in the Monastery of Taxiarchis Michael Panormitis and other historic places around the island. A schedule of events is posted at the square, and programs can be found at local stores, travel agents, and the town hall.

CHORIO ΧΩΡΙΟ

1 km (½ mile) east of Yialos.

It's a 10-minute walk from the main harbor of Yialos up to the hilltop town of Chorio, along a staircase of some 400 steps, known as Kali Strata (Good Steps). There is also a road that can be traveled in one of the island's few taxis or by bus, which makes a circuit with stops at the harbor in Yialos, Chorio, and the seaside community of Pedi. The Kali Strata are flanked by elegant neoclassical houses with elaborate stonework, lavish pediments, and intricate wrought-iron balconies. Just before the top of the stairs (and the welcome little Kali Strata bar), a line of windmills crowns the hill of Noulia. Most of Chorio's many churches date to the 18th and 19th centuries, and many are ornamented with richly decorated iconostases and ornate bell towers. Donkeys are often used to carry materials through the narrow streets for the town's steady construction and renovation work.

EXPLORING

Archaeological Museum of Symi. The collection at the Archaeological Museum, housed in a neoclassical dwelling amid the maze of Chorio's lanes, displays Hellenistic and Roman sculptures and inscriptions as well as more recent carvings, icons, costumes, and handicrafts; the re-creation of a simple Symi dwelling is especially charming. ⊠ *Chorio ⊕ Follow signs from central square to Lieni neighborhood* ☎ *22460/71114* ⊡ *€3* ⊗ *Closed Mon.*

Kastro (*Castle*). Incorporating fragments of an ancient acropolis within its walls, the castle was built by the Knights of St. John in a short-lived attempt to expand their holdings in Rhodes. A church and several chapels dot the sparse hillside around the remnants of its walls. The hilltop view takes in both sides of the narrow peninsula that Chorio crowns, with the villages of Yialos and Pedi (and their sparkling harbors) far below. ✉ *Chorio* ✣ *At top of town, in the ancient acropolis.*

WHERE TO EAT

$$ GREEK 🍴 **Georgio and Maria's Taverna.** Meals at this simple taverna, as popular with locals as it is with tourists, are served in a high-ceilinged, whitewashed dining room or on a terrace that is partially shaded by a grape arbor and affords wonderful views over the sea and surrounding hills. Fish is a specialty, and simply prepared *mezedes* (small dishes), such as roasted peppers topped with feta cheese and fried zucchini, are a great start to a meal here. **Known for:** local favorite; sea views; best place to eat in Chorio. [$] *Average main: €15* ✉ *Chorio* ✣ *Off the main square at top of the Kali Strata* ☎ *22460/71984.*

WHERE TO STAY

$ B&B/INN 🏨 **Hotel Fiona.** At this bright, cheerful perch on the hillside in Chorio, just about all the large, white-tile-floored rooms have a sea-facing balcony. **Pros:** friendly service; excellent views over the harbor far below; simple and comfortable. **Cons:** strenuous climb down and back up 400 steps to Symi Town; reached only by foot; no parking. [$] *Rooms from: €55* ✉ *Chorio* ✣ *Near main square* ☎ *22460/72088* 🌐 *www.fionahotel.com* ⏲ *Closed Nov.–Apr.* 🛏 *17 rooms* 🍽 *Breakfast.*

MONASTERY OF TAXIARCHIS MICHAEL PANORMITIS
ΜΟΝΗ ΤΑΞΙΑΡΧΗ ΜΙΧΑΗΛ ΠΑΝΟΡΜΙΤΗ

7 km (4½ miles) south of Chorio.

The tiny hamlet of Panormitis on the south end of the island is a remote and idyllic setting for this holy assemblage, a popular place of pilgrimage and a pleasure to visit simply for the scenery. A trip to the monastery can be accompanied by a refreshing swim at the designated edges of the deep-blue harbor. There's bus service twice a day from Yialos, which passes through Chorio, or you can take one of the daily boats from Yialos or Rhodes. You can also hike to the monastery along a well-marked route from Chorio; it's about 10 km (6 miles), but can certainly seem longer if you don't set out early enough to avoid the heat of the day. Several tour companies organize day trips to the monastery, with time for a swim and a hike in the surrounding countryside, for about €25, including lunch. *(See Tours for more information.)*

Fodor's Choice ★ **Monastery of Taxiarchis Michael Panormitis.** The main reason to venture to the atypically green, pine-covered hills surrounding the little Gulf of Panormitis is to visit this unexpectedly grand monastery dedicated to Symi's patron saint, the protector of sailors. The site's entrance is surmounted by an elaborate **bell tower,** of the multilevel wedding-cake variety on display in Yialos and Chorio. A black-and-white pebble mosaic adorns the floor of the **courtyard,** which is surrounded by a vaulted stoa. The interior of the **church,** entirely frescoed in the 18th century, contains a marvelously ornate wooden iconostasis, which is flanked by a heroic-size 18th-century representation of Michael, all but his face covered with silver. There are two small **museums** devoted to Byzantine and folk art. The Byzantine includes a collection of votive offerings, including an enchanting collection of wooden ship models and bottles with notes containing wishes and money in them, which, according to local lore, travel to Symi on their own after having been thrown into the sea.

If a day trip isn't enough for you, the monastery rents 70 spartan rooms (from €15 per night) with kitchens and private baths. Though the price doesn't include a towel or air-conditioning and there are insects (some rather large), the spiritual aspect makes for an enriching experience. A nursing home as well as a market, bakery, restaurant, and a few other businesses make up the rest of the settlement. The monastery is at its busiest for the week leading up to November 8, Michael's feast day, an event that draws the faithful from throughout the Dodecanese and beyond. ✛ *Symi's south side, at harbor* ☎ *22460/71581 museums, 22460/72414 rooms* ⊕ *www.imsymis.org* ✉ *Monastery free; museums €1.50.*

KOS ΚΩΣ

92 km (57 miles) north of Rhodes.

Aglow with flowering oleanders and hibiscus, the island of Kos is the third largest in the Dodecanese. It certainly remains one of the most verdant in the otherwise arid archipelago, with lush fields and tree-clad mountains, surrounded by miles of sandy beach. Its highest peak, part of a small mountain range in the northeast, is a respectable 2,800 feet. All this beauty has not gone unnoticed, of course, and Kos undeniably suffers from the effects of mass tourism: its beaches are often crowded, most of its seaside towns have been recklessly overdeveloped, and the main town is noisy and busy between June and September.

In Mycenaean times and during the Archaic period, the island prospered. In the 6th century BC it was conquered by the Persians but later joined the Delian League, supporting Athens against Sparta in the Peloponnesian War. Kos was invaded and destroyed by the Spartan fleet, ruled by Alexander and his various successors, and was twice devastated by earthquakes. Nevertheless, the city and the economy flourished, as did the arts and sciences. The painter Apelles, the Michelangelo of his time, came from Kos, as did Hippocrates, father of modern medicine. Under the Roman Empire, the island's Asklepieion and its renowned healing center drew emperors and ordinary citizens alike. The Knights of St. John arrived in 1315 and ruled for the next two centuries, until the Ottomans replaced them. In 1912 the Italians took over, and in 1947 the island was united with Greece.

GETTING HERE AND AROUND

Kos is a major air hub, with regular service from Athens and, during high season, from many other European cities. The airport is about 25 km (15 miles) outside Kos Town, about an hour by bus (€5) and half-hour by taxi (€30), so keep the time and taxi-cost factors in mind when booking an early-morning outgoing flight.

Kos is also well served by ferries, with at least two boats arriving from Pireaus daily in high season (10 hours) and at least two arriving from Rhodes (about 2½ hours). Boats also arrive from Mykonos, Paros, and other islands in the Cyclades about twice a week. Schedules change all the time, so check with ⊕ *www.ferries.gr*, ⊕ *www.gtp.gr*, or with any of the many travel agencies along the waterfront in Kos Town for the latest info on boat service. Kos Harbor is adjacent to the city center, so convenient to services and bus connections.

An excellent bus network serves most of the island, putting most resort towns around the island within easy reach of Kos Town by public transportation; as many as six buses a day connect Kos Town in the north and Kefalos in the south, for example, and the trip takes about an hour and costs €4.

VISITOR INFORMATION

Contacts Kos Municipal Tourism Office. ⊠ *Vasileos Georgiou 1, Kos Town* ☎ *22420/360400* ⊕ *www.kos.gr.*

KOS TOWN ΚΩΣ ΠΟΛΗ

92 km (57 miles) north of Rhodes.

The modern town lies on a flat plain encircling spacious Mandraki Harbor and is a pleasant assemblage of low-lying buildings and shady lanes, with a skyline pierced by minarets and palm trees. The fortress, which crowns the west side of town, is a good place to begin your exploration of Kos Town. Hippocrates is supposed to have taught near here, in the shade of a plane tree that is said to have grown on one side of little Platanou Square—but this is merely legend, as the Koan capital, called Astypalaia, was at the far, western end of the island and Thucydides recounts its destruction by an earthquake. A loggia, actually a mosque built in 1786, now graces the square. A combination ticket (€13) offers entrance to the four major archaeological sites of Kos over a period of three days including the Archaeological Museum, Casa Romana, Castle of the Knights, and the Asklepieion. The ticket can be purchased at any of the sites.

EXPLORING

Agora and Harbor Ruins. Excavations by Italian and Greek archaeologists have revealed ancient agora and harbor ruins that date from the 4th century BC through Roman times. Remnants include parts of the walls of the old city, of a Hellenistic stoa, and of temples dedicated to Aphrodite and Hercules. The ruins are not fenced and, laced with pine-shaded paths, are a pleasant retreat in the modern city. In spring the site is covered with brightly colored flowers, which nicely frame the ancient gray-and-white marble blocks tumbled in every direction. ⊠ *Kos Town* ⊕ *Over bridge from Platia Platanou, behind Castle of the Knights.*

Archaeological Museum. The island's archaeological museum houses Hellenistic and Roman sculpture by Koan artists, much of it unearthed by Italians during their tenure on the island in the early 20th century. Among the treasures are a renowned statue of Hippocrates—the great physician who practiced on Kos—and Asclepius, god of healing; a group of sculptures from various Roman phases, all discovered in the House of the Europa Mosaic; and a remarkable series of Hellenistic draped female statues mainly from the Sanctuary of Demeter at Kyparissi and the Odeon. ⊠ *Platia Eleftherias* ✢ *West of agora through gate leading to Platia Platanou* ☎ *22420/28326* ⊕ *www.culture.gr* 🎫 *€6* ⊙ *Closed Mon.*

FAMILY **Casa Romana** (*Roman House*). The Roman House is a lavish restoration of a 3rd-century Roman mansion, with 36 rooms grouped around three atriums. The house provides a look at what everyday life of the well-to-do residents of the Roman town might have been like and also houses some beautiful frescoes and mosaics. The Greek and Roman ruins that surround the house are freely accessible, however, and are just as evocative. ⊠ *Pavlou and Grigoriou* ☎ *22420/23234* 🎫 *€6* ⊙ *Closed Dec.–Mar. and Mon. Apr.–Nov.*

Castle of the Knights. Built by the Knights of St. John in the 15th century and taken by the Turks in 1522 (with the rest of the knights' Dodecanese holdings), the castle/fortress is an imposing presence on the harbor. It's best to let that remain the impression you have of this massive structure: Little remains inside the walls but a field littered with fragments of ancient funerary monuments and other sculptural material from the island's Greek and Roman inhabitants. ⊠ *Kos Town* ✢ *Over bridge from Platia Platanou* ☎ *22420/27927* 🎫 *€4* ⊙ *Closed Mon.*

West Excavations. These excavations laced through a quiet residential district have uncovered a portion of one of the main Roman streets with many houses, including the **House of the Europa Mosaic**, and part of the **Roman baths** (near main Roman street) that was later converted into a basilica. The **gymnasium** is distinguished by its partly reconstructed colonnade, and the so-called **Nymphaion** is a lavish public latrine that has been restored. In the **Odeon**, 18 rows of stone seats remain intact. The West Excavations are always open, with free access, and significant finds are labeled. ⊠ *Kos Town* ✢ *Southwest of agora and harbor ruins.*

BEACHES

If you must get wet but can't leave Kos Town, try the narrow pebble strip of beach immediately south of the main harbor.

WHERE TO EAT

$$
MODERN GREEK
✕**Petrino.** Three brothers have created a calm oasis a few streets in from the hustle and bustle of Kos Harbor. A 150-year-old stone house provides cozy dining in cool months, and in summer, tables pepper a garden full of private nooks, fountains, and gentle music. **Known for:** atmospheric dining; a local favorite. 💲 *Average main: €16* ⊠ *Platia Ioannou Theologou* ☎ *22420/27251* ⊕ *www.petrino-kos.gr.*

$$
GREEK
✕**Platanos.** Set on the shady square where Hippocrates once taught, the most storied place in Kos, this island institution maintains high standards for excellent cooking and top-notch service. Occupying an early-20th-century Italian club, the surroundings of tiled rooms

and candlelit balconies are elaborate. **Known for:** romantic and historic setting; excellent dishes. $ *Average main: €25* ✉ *Platia Platanos* ☎ *22420/28991* ⊕ *www.platanoskos.gr* ⊙ *Closed Nov.–Mar.*

WHERE TO STAY

$$$$
RESORT
Fodor's Choice
★

🛏 **Aqua Blu.** Who says chic can't be supremely comfortable—as these truly exciting all-suite lodgings prove, with sea views, private pools, fireplaces, hardwood floors, handsome built-ins, and all sorts of other extras. **Pros:** small and intimate yet extremely luxurious; polished and friendly service; excellent food. **Cons:** outside town; not a full-scale resort (can be a plus); no kids allowed. $ *Rooms from: €320* ✉ *Ephelondon Paleon Polemiston* ✛ *Lambi Beach* ☎ *22420/22440* ⊕ *www.aquabluhotel.gr* ⊙ *Closed Nov.–Mar.* ⟿ *53 rooms* ⦿ *Breakfast.*

$$$
HOTEL

🛏 **Aktis Art Hotel.** With a perch right on the beach at the edge of the Old Town, these modernist guest rooms seem to be afloat in the Aegean, whose azure waters fill the floor-to-ceiling windows and glass-fronted balconies. **Pros:** excellent location on the sea; relaxing and stylish decor and ambience; near all in-town attractions. **Cons:** full range of resort amenities is not available; hotel doesn't have its own swimming pool; no local style. $ *Rooms from: €242* ✉ *Vasileos Georgiou 7* ☎ *22420/47200* ⊕ *www.kosaktis.gr* ⟿ *42 rooms* ⦿ *Breakfast.*

$$$$
RESORT

🛏 **Grecotel Kos Imperial.** The grounds of this huge resort, set next to an idyllic Aegean beach, are laced with seawater and freshwater pools, artificial rivers and lagoons, glimmering glass-tile hydrotherapy pools, and dozens of spa treatment basins. **Pros:** finest of the big resorts on Kos; excellent amenities; attractive and comfortable guest rooms. **Cons:** big-resort feel; a distance from Kos Town; Wi-Fi may not be strong. $ *Rooms from: €300* ✉ *Psalidi* ✛ *4 km (2½ miles) east of Kos Town* ☎ *22420/58000* ⊕ *www.grecotel.com* ⟿ *385 rooms* ⦿ *Breakfast.*

$
HOTEL

🛏 **Hotel Afendoulis.** Plain, whitewashed rooms with dark-wood furniture are spotless, attractive, and of far better quality than most in this price range (the best open to little balconies with sea views), and the genuinely warm, attentive service far exceeds the norm. **Pros:** pleasant, quiet surroundings; in-town location; excellent hospitality includes laundry service. **Cons:** no pool; no parking; no resort amenities. $ *Rooms from: €50* ✉ *Evripilou 1* ☎ *22420/25321* ⊕ *www.afendoulishotel.com* ⟿ *23 rooms* ⦿ *No meals.*

NIGHTLIFE

Things start cooking before 7 pm and in many cases roar on past 7 am on Akti Koundourioti and in the nearby Exarhia area, which includes rowdy Nafklirou and Plessa streets. Competing bars try to lure in bar-hoppers with ads for cheap beer and neon-colored drinks.

H2O. This loungey seaside club on the beachfront has a small, sleek interior as well as outdoor seating, and excellent meals are served in the adjoining restaurant of the same name. ✉ *Aktis Art Hotel, Vasileos Georgiou 7* ☎ *22420/47107.*

To Spitaki. The name means little house, and this is a local favorite for evening cocktails and drinks by the sea. A restaurant and café by day, its open-air wooden deck, outfitted with tables and chairs, is more popular at night, especially during the summer. ✉ *Vasileos Georgiou 9* ☎ *22420/27655.*

SPORTS AND THE OUTDOORS

BIKING

Kos, particularly the area around the town, is good for bicycle riding. Ride to the Asklepieion for a picnic, or visit the Castle of Antimacheia. Note: be aware of hazards such as cistern openings—very few have security fences around them. You can rent bicycles everywhere—in Kos Town and at the more-popular resorts. Try the many shops along Eleftheriou Venizelou street in town. Renting a bike costs about €8 per day.

ASKLEPIEION ΑΣΚΛΗΠΙΕΙΟΝ

4 km (2½ miles) west of Kos Town.

The ruins of one of the great healing centers of antiquity still impress and fire the imagination, framed by a thick grove of cypress trees and laid out on several broad terraces connected by a monumental staircase.

Fodor's Choice ★ **Asklepieion.** Hippocrates began to teach the art of healing on Kos in the 5th century BC, attracting health seekers to the island almost up to the time of his death, allegedly at age 103, in 357 BC. This elaborate, multitiered complex dedicated to the god of medicine, Asklepios, was begun shortly after Hippocrates's death and flourished until the decline of the Roman Empire as the most renowned medical facility in the Western world. The lower terrace probably held the Asklepieion Festivals, famed drama and dance contests held in honor of the god of healing. On the middle terrace is an **Ionic temple,** once decorated with works by the legendary 4th-century BC painter Apelles, including his renowned depiction of Aphrodite (much celebrated in antiquity, it was said the artist used a mistress of Alexander the Great as a model). On the uppermost terrace is the **Doric Temple of Asklepios,** once surrounded by colonnaded porticoes. ✉ *Platani* ✣ *Take the local bus from Kos Town to the hamlet of Platani and walk to the ruins from there* ☎ *22420/28326* 🌐 *odysseus.culture.gr* 🎫 *€8* 🕒 *Closed Mon. Nov–Mar.*

EN ROUTE

Leaving the main road southwest of the Asklepieion (turnoff is at Zipari, 9 km [5½ miles] southwest of Kos Town), you can explore an enchanting landscape of cypress and pine trees on a route that climbs to a handful of lovely, whitewashed rural villages that cling to the craggy slopes of the island's central mountains. The busiest of them is Zia, with an appealing smattering of churches; crafts shops selling local honey, weavings, and handmade soaps; and open-air tavernas where you can enjoy the views over the surrounding forests and fields toward the sea.

WHERE TO EAT

$ GREEK Fodor's Choice ★ 🍴 **Taverna Ampavris.** The surroundings and the food are both delightful at this charming, rustic taverna, outside Kos Town on a lane leading to the village of Platani. Meals are served in the courtyard of an old farmhouse, and the kitchen's emphasis is on local country food—including wonderful stews and grilled meats, accompanied by vegetables from nearby gardens. **Known for:** charming atmosphere; local Greek dishes. [$] *Average main: €12* ✉ *Ampavris* ✣ *On the way from Kos Town to Platani* ☎ *22420/25696* 🌐 *www.ampavris.gr* 💳 *No credit cards* 🕒 *No lunch.*

MARMARI ΜΑΡΜΑΡΙ

10 km (6 miles) west of Asklepieion, 14 km (9 miles) west of Kos Town.

You won't find much that's authentically Greek in this unattractively overbuilt resort town surrounded by holiday villages. Even so, the surrounding beaches are beautiful, and without too much effort you can find a deserted strip of sand to call your own.

BEACHES

Mastichari Beach. In this north-coast resort 32 km (20 miles) west of Kos Town, the wide sand beaches backed by shade-providing pines are much discovered, backed by tavernas, rooms for rent, and luxurious all-inclusive resorts. The beach is lined with chairs and umbrellas and the launching pad for pedal boats and jet skis. Mastichari also has a fishing pier, from where boats set sail on day trips to the uncrowded islet of Pserimos. **Amenities:** food and drink; showers; toilets; water sports. **Best for:** snorkeling; swimming; walking. ⊠ *Mastichari.*

Tigaki Beach. This appealing sandy beach sits on the north coast, 13 km (8 miles) west of Kos Town. Some resort hotels line the sands, but much of the inland terrain behind the beach dunes remains rural. Beachgoers can enjoy the amenities of some of the more built-up sections. The more isolated, western edge of the beach is popular with gay men. **Amenities:** food and drink; showers; toilets; water sports. **Best for:** nudists; solitude; swimming; walking. ⊠ *Tigaki.*

CASTLE OF ANTIMACHEIA ΚΑΣΤΡΟ ΑΝΤΙΜΑΧΕΙΑΣ

11 km (7 miles) southwest of Marmari, 25 km (15 miles) southwest of Kos Town.

This proud fortress standing high above the sea is not just a symbol of the former might of the Knights of St. John. These days it also reminds us that overbuilt, tourist-oriented Kos has a proud past and had some historical clout. Plus, the cool stone interiors and views over verdant hillsides to the sparkling sea are a refreshing tonic and nice break from the beach.

Castle of Antimacheia. The thick, well-preserved walls of this 14th-century fortress look out over the sweeping Aegean and Kos's green interior. Antimacheia was another stronghold of the Knights of St. John, whose coat of arms hangs above the entrance gate. Within the walls, little of the original complex remains, with the exception of two stark churches; in one of them, Ayios Nikolaos, you can make out a primitive fresco of St. Christopher carrying the infant Jesus. ⊠ *Antimachia.*

KAMARI ΚΑΜΑΡΙ

10 km (6 miles) south of the Castle of Antimacheia, 35 km (22 miles) southwest of Kos Town.

On Kefalos bay, the little beach community of Kamari is pleasant and less frantic than the island's other seaside resorts. On a summit above is the lovely Old Town of Kefalos, a pleasant place to wander for its views and quintessential Greekness. Close offshore is a little rock formation holding a chapel to St. Nicholas. Opposite are the ruins of a magnificent 5th-century Christian basilica.

BEACHES

Ayios Stefanos Beach. A chunk of beautiful Ayios Stefanos Beach, just north of Kefalos, is now occupied by a Club Med; the rest belongs to beach clubs renting umbrellas and chairs and offering activities that include waterskiing and jet-skiing. Expect to pay about €45 for a waterskiing session, €60 for jet skiing. Two early Christian basilicas crown a promontory at the southern end of the beach, adding to the allure of this lovely spot. **Amenities:** food and drink; parking (free); showers; water sports. **Best for:** snorkeling; swimming. ⊠ *Kefalos.*

Polemi Beach. This long stretch of lovely sand is about 10 km (6 miles) north of Kefalos, just far enough away to remain wonderfully undeveloped. Backed by scrub-covered dunes, the sands offer little except some sun bed concessions and are washed by calm, crystal-clear waters. **Amenities:** parking (free). **Best for:** nudists; solitude; swimming; walking. ⊠ *Kefalos.*

WHERE TO STAY

$

HOTEL

🏨 **Hotel Kokalakis Beach.** Many guests return annually to this simple hotel to enjoy the peaceful proximity to pebble and sand beaches and the hospitality of the Kokalakis family. **Pros:** close to beach; nice pool area; extremely welcoming hosts. **Cons:** fairly basic accommodations; very basic breakfast (included); small rooms. $ *Rooms from: €45* ⊠ *Kefalos* ✛ *Behind waterfront* ☎ *22420/71466* ▭ *No credit cards* ☾ *Closed Nov.–Apr.* ⬎ *32 rooms* ❍❘ *Breakfast.*

PATMOS ΠΑΤΜΟΣ

8

161 km (100 miles) north of Kos.

For better or worse, it can be difficult to reach Patmos—for many travelers, this lack of access is definitely for the better, since the island retains the air of an unspoiled retreat. Rocky and barren, the small, 34-square-km (13-square-mile) island lies beyond the islands of Kalymnos and Leros, northwest of Kos. Here on a hillside is the Monastery of the Apocalypse, which enshrines the cave where St. John received the "revelation" in AD 95. Scattered evidence of Mycenaean presence remains on Patmos, and walls of the classical period indicate the existence of a town near Skala. Most of the island's approximately 2,800 people live in three villages: Skala, medieval Chora, and the small rural settlement of Kambos. The island is popular among the faithful, who make pilgrimages to the monastery, as well as among vacationing Athenians and stylish international vacationers, who have bought homes in Chora and elsewhere around the island. Happily, administrators have carefully contained development, and as a result, Patmos retains its charm and natural beauty—even in the busy month of August.

GETTING HERE AND AROUND

Patmos has no airport, and outside of July and August, ferries wending through the Dodecanese from Athens call only every other day or so, with daily service in high season; the trip from Athens takes only seven hours, but boats arrive at the ungodly hour of 2 am. It's much easier to fly to Kos and board one of some four daily boats for the two-hour trip up to Patmos. On days when ferries do not call at Patmos, the boat to Kos with a transfer to Patmos is also an option. A convenient way to reach beaches around the island is to board a water taxi from Skala Harbor.

The island's limited bus route provides regular service from Skala to Chora, Kambos, and other popular spots. It's easy to move around by taxi—and fairly inexpensive since distances are short.

VISITOR INFORMATION

Contacts **Patmos Municipal Tourism Office.** ⊹ *Near ferry dock* ☎ *22470/31666* ⊕ *www.patmosweb.gr.*

SKALA ΣΚΑΛΑ

161 km (100 miles) north of Kos.

Skala, the island's small but sophisticated main town, is where almost all the shops and restaurants are located. It's a popular port of call for cruise ships, and in summer the huge liners often loom over the rooftops. There's not much to see in the town, but it is lively and very attractive. Most of the town center is closed to cars and, since strict building codes have been enforced, even new buildings have traditional architectural detail. The medieval town of Chora and the island's legendary monasteries are perched above Skala on a nearby hill. Take a 20-minute hike up to Kastelli, on a hill overlooking Skala, to see the stone remains of the city's 6th- to 4th-century BC town and acropolis.

BEACHES

The small island is endowed with at least 24 beaches. Although most of them, which tend to be coarse shingle, are accessible by land, sun worshippers can sail to a few (as well as to the nearby islet cluster of Arkoi) on the caïques that make regular runs from Skala, leaving in the morning. Prices vary with the number of people making the trip (or with the boat); transportation to and from a beach for a family for a day start around €45.

FAMILY **Kambos Beach.** The most popular beach on the island stretches for 1.6 km (1 mile) or so along Kambos Bay, with a gently sloping sea floor that's ideal for young waders and swimmers. Sun beds line the strand of fine pebbles and sand, and pines behind the beach provide plenty of shade. The many amenities include windsurfing, waterskiing, and pedal-boat rentals. Regular bus service connects Kambos with Skala, about 6 km (4 miles) away. **Amenities:** food and drink; parking (free); showers; water sports. **Best for:** snorkeling; swimming; windsurfing. ⊠ *Skala.*

Psili Amos Beach. It's well worth the effort required to reach the most beautiful (and remote) beach on the island, a lovely scallop of sand backed by pines and rough, goat-filled hills. Getting there requires a 45-minute caïque ride (€15) from Skala or a 20-minute walk on a footpath from Diakofti (the narrowest point on the island), where visitors can park their cars. While nudism is not officially allowed on Patmos, this is one beach where nude bathing is tolerated and common, at the far edges. An extremely basic taverna sometimes serves light fare, but you'll want to bring water and snacks for an outing to this pristine spot. **Amenities:** food and drink; parking (free); toilets. **Best for:** nudists; snorkeling; solitude; swimming.

WHERE TO EAT

$$
MEDITERRANEAN
Fodor's Choice
★

✕**Benetos.** A native Patmian, Benetos Matthaiou, and his American wife, Susan, operate this lovely restaurant abutting a seaside garden that supplies the kitchen with fresh herbs and vegetables. These home-grown ingredients find their way into a selection of Mediterranean-style dishes that are influenced by the couple's travels and include phyllo parcels stuffed with spinach and cheese, the island's freshest Greek salad, and a juicy grilled swordfish in citrus sauce. **Known for:** good service; excellent Mediterranean dishes. ⓢ *Average main: €25* ✉ *Sapsila* ⊹ *On harborside road between Skala and Grikos* ☎ *22470/33089* ⊕ *www.benetosrestaurant.com* ⊘ *Closed Mon. and mid-Oct.–May. No lunch.*

$
GREEK

✕**Tzivaeri.** The excellent island cooking here is spiced up by the sea views, which you can savor from a seaside balcony table or right on the beach below. The mezedes menu includes such traditional favorites as leek pie, fried eggplant, and smoked pork. **Known for:** beautiful sea views; beachside dining; live music. ⓢ *Average main: €10* ✉ *Harborside road* ☎ *22470/31170* ▭ *No credit cards* ⊘ *No lunch.*

$$$
GREEK

✕**Vegghera.** A handsome mansion overlooking the harbor is the setting for an exquisite meal that combines traditional Greek and international influences. Fresh seafood tops the menu, but pastas, herb-flavored chops, and traditional vegetable dishes are a delight as well. **Known for:** fine dining; marina views; diverse menu of Mediterranean tastes. ⓢ *Average main: €30* ✉ *Skala* ⊹ *At the marina* ☎ *22470/32988* ⊘ *Closed Nov.–Easter. No lunch.*

WHERE TO STAY

$$$$
HOTEL
Fodor's Choice
★

▦ **Hotel Petra.** One of Greece's truly special retreats sits high above Grikos Bay south of Skala and provides a luxurious yet informal getaway, with large and sumptuous guest quarters, delightful outdoor lounges, a welcoming pool, and soothing sea views. **Pros:** wonderful outdoor spaces; superb service and hospitality; beach is just steps away. **Cons:** the hotel climbs a series of terraces reached only by steps; no elevator; not within walking distance to main sights of Patmos. ⓢ *Rooms from: €365* ✉ *Grigos* ☎ *22470/34020* ⊕ *www.petrahotel-patmos.com* ⊘ *Closed mid-Oct.–May* ⬐ *11 rooms* ⦿| *Breakfast.*

$
HOTEL

▦ **Hotel Skala.** Skala's best in-town option places you in the center of the action, steps from the municipal beach yet removed from the harbor noise and offering simple but comfortable guest rooms that surround a bougainvillea-filled garden. **Pros:** top location; attractive terrace and pool; elevator. **Cons:** occasionally hosts large groups; high-season rates are high, given quality of accommodations; lack of design. ⓢ *Rooms from: €120* ✉ *Harbor front* ☎ *22470/31343* ⊕ *www.skalahotel.gr* ⊘ *Closed Nov.–Mar.* ⬐ *78 rooms* ⦿| *Breakfast.*

$
HOTEL
Fodor's Choice
★

▦ **Porto Scoutari.** It seems only fitting that Patmos should have a hotel that reflects the architectural beauty of the island while providing luxurious accommodations, and the enormous, suitelike guest rooms and a verdant garden (with a swimming pool) help it fit the bill nicely. **Pros:** beautiful grounds; near beach; excellent service. **Cons:** only ground-floor rooms are suitable for travelers with mobility issues; 5-km (3-mile) drive from Patmos Town; not within walking distance of major sights. ⓢ *Rooms from:*

8

€120 ⊠ *Skala* ⊹ *1 km (½ mile) northeast of Skala Center* ☎ *22470/33123* ⊕ *www.portoscoutari.com* ☯ *Closed Nov.–Mar.* ⤳ *34 rooms* ⦿| *Breakfast.*

SHOPPING

Patmos has some elegant boutiques selling jewelry and crafts, including antiques, mainly from the island.

CRAFTS

Katoi. Head here to explore a wide selection of ceramics, icons, and silver jewelry of traditional design. ⊠ *Skala* ⊹ *On Skala–Chora road* ☎ *22470/31487.*

Selene. Whether made of ceramic, glass, silver, or wood, each work—by one of 40 different Greek artists—displayed in a former boatbuilding shop is unique. ⊠ *Harbor front* ☎ *22470/31742.*

CHORA ΧΩΡΑ

5 km (3 miles) south of Skala.

Atop a hill due south of Skala, the village of Chora, clustered around the walls of the Monastery of St. John the Theologian, has become a preserve of international wealth even as the whitewashed houses, Byzantine mansions, and quiet, twisting lanes retain a great deal of dignity and charm. Though the short distance from Skala may make walking seem attractive, a steep incline can make this challenging. A taxi ride is about €8, and there is frequent bus service (€2 from Skala and other points on the island).

EXPLORING

Monastery of the Apocalypse. In AD 95, during the Emperor Domitian's persecution of Christians, St. John the Theologian was banished to Patmos, where he lived until his reprieve two years later. He writes that it was on Patmos that he "heard … a great voice, as of a trumpet," commanding him to write a book and "send it unto the seven churches." According to tradition, St. John wrote the text of *Revelation* in the little cave, the Sacred Grotto, now built into the Monastery of the Apocalypse. The voice of God spoke through a threefold crack in the rock, and the saint dictated to his follower Prochorus. A slope in the wall is pointed to as the desk where Prochorus wrote, and a silver halo is set on the stone that was the apostle's pillow. The grotto is decorated with wall paintings from the 12th century and icons from the 16th.

The monastery, which is accessible via several flights of outdoor stairs, was constructed in the 17th century from architectural fragments of earlier buildings, and further embellished in later years; the complex also contains chapels to St. Artemios and St. Nicholas. ⊠ *Chora* ⊹ *2 km (1 mile) south of Chora on Skala–Chora road.* ☎ *22470/31276 monastery* ⛬ *€2.*

Fodor'sChoice ★ **Monastery of St. John the Theologian.** On its high perch at the top of Chora, the Monastery of St. John the Theologian is one of the world's best-preserved fortified medieval monastic complexes, a center of learning since the 11th century, and today recognized as a UNESCO World Heritage site. Hosios Christodoulos, a man of education, energy, devotion, and vision, established the monastery in 1088, and the complex soon

The luckiest monks on Patmos—famed for its vibrant community of monks—get to call the Monastery of St. John the Theologian (seen in the background here) home.

became an intellectual center, with a rich library and a tradition of teaching. Monks of education and social standing ornamented the monastery with the best sculpture, carvings, and paintings and, by the end of the 12th century, the community owned land on Leros, Limnos, Crete, and Asia Minor, as well as ships, which carried on trade exempt from taxes.

A broad staircase leads to the entrance, which is fortified by towers and buttresses.

The complex consists of buildings from a number of periods: in front of the entrance is the 17th-century **Chapel of the Holy Apostles**; the **main Church** dates from the 11th century, the time of Christodoulos (whose skull, along with that of Apostle Thomas, is encased in a silver sarcophagus here); the **Chapel of the Virgin** is 12th century.

The **Treasury** contains relics, icons, silver, and vestments, most dating from 1600 to 1800. An 11th-century icon of St. Nicholas is executed in fine mosaic work and encased in a silver frame. Another icon is allegedly the work of El Greco. On display, too, are some of the library's oldest codices, dating to the late 5th and the 8th centuries, such as pages from the Gospel of St. Mark and the Book of Job. For the most part, however, the **Library** is not open to the public and special permission is required to research its extensive treasures: illuminated manuscripts, approximately 1,000 codices, and more than 3,000 printed volumes. The collection was first cataloged in 1200; of the 267 works of that time, the library still has 111. The archives preserve a near-continuous record, down to the present, of the history of the monastery as well as the political and economic history of the region. ⊠ *Chora* ☎ *22470/20800* ⊕ *www.patmosmonastery.gr* ▧ *€4.*

WHERE TO EAT

$$
GREEK

✕ **Vagelis.** Choose between a table on the main square (perfect for people-watching) or the raised terrace out back with stunning views of the sea. Fresh grilled fish and lemon-and-oregano-flavored goat are specialties of the traditional kitchen, and other simple dishes such as mint-flavored *dolmades* (stuffed grape leaves) and *tzatziki* (yogurt and cucumber dip) are the way to go. **Known for:** stunning sea views; excellent traditional Greek dishes. $ *Average main: €15* ⊠ *Main square* ☎ *22470/31967* ═ *No credit cards.*

FESTIVALS

Patmos Festival of Sacred Music. In late August or early September, the Monastery of the Apocalypse hosts this festival, with world-class Byzantine and ecclesiastical music performances in an outdoor performance space. ⊠ *Monastery of the Apocalypse* ☎ *22470/31666* ⊕ *patmosfestival.gr.*

THE NORTHERN AEGEAN ISLANDS

Lesvos, Chios, and Samos

WELCOME TO
THE NORTHERN AEGEAN ISLANDS

TOP REASONS TO GO

★ **Historic Stars of Samos:** Math genius Pythagoras, freedom-loving Epicurus, and the fabled Aesop were just a few of this island's brightest stars.

★ **Mesmerizing Mastic Villages:** Pirgi in Chios is known for the resin it produces, but with its Genoese houses patterned in black and white, it's the Escher-like landscape that's likely to draw you in.

★ **Sappho's Island:** If it's poetic truth you seek, head to Skala Eressos, a popular and appealing seaside village on Lesvos and onetime home to the ancient lyric poet, who wrote much of her verse in praise of female beauty.

★ **Sailing to Byzantium:** Colorful Byzantine mosaics make Chios's 11th-century Nea Moni monastery an important piece of history—and a marvel to behold.

★ **Dizzyingly Good Ouzo:** Though you can get this potent potable anywhere in Greece, Lesvos's is reputedly the best—enjoy it with famed salt-baked Kalloni sardines.

About the only thing the islands of Samos, Chios, and Lesvos share is their proximity to Turkey: from their shores, reaching from Macedonia down to the Dodecanese along the coast of Asia Minor, you can see the very fields of Greece's age-old rival. No matter that these three islands may be a long haul from Athens: few parts of the Aegean have greater variety and beauty of landscape—a stunning blend of pristine shores and craggy (Homer's word) mountains.

1 Samos. This famously fertile island, in classical antiquity a center of Ionian culture and luxury, is still renowned for its fruitful land and the delectable Muscat wines it produces. The island attracts active archaeology fanatics and lazy beach lovers alike, leaving visitors spoiled for choice among a plethora of ancient sights (such as the Temple at Heraion—once four times larger than the Parthenon) and long sandy beaches with crystal waters.

2 Lesvos. Often called Mytilini after its historic (but today somewhat boisterous) capital, Lesvos is the third-largest island in Greece. Known as the "sweet home" of lesbians from around the world, this was the land of origin of the ancient poet Sappho, whose romantic lyrical poetry was said to be addressed to women. Sapphic followers who flock to the island mostly stay in Skala Eresou, but Lesvos has something for everyone: exquisite cuisine and ouzo, beautiful beaches, monasteries with miraculous icons, and lush landscapes.

3 Chios. You'll find something of authentic Greece here. Go beyond the busy, almost souklike main town to discover starkly haunting countryside and quaint village squares. The 11th-century monastery of Nea Moni is celebrated for its Byzantine art. Chios is the "mastic island," producing the highly beneficial resin that is used in chewing gum and cosmetic products; the most noted mastic village is Pirgi, famed for the geometric patterns on its house facades.

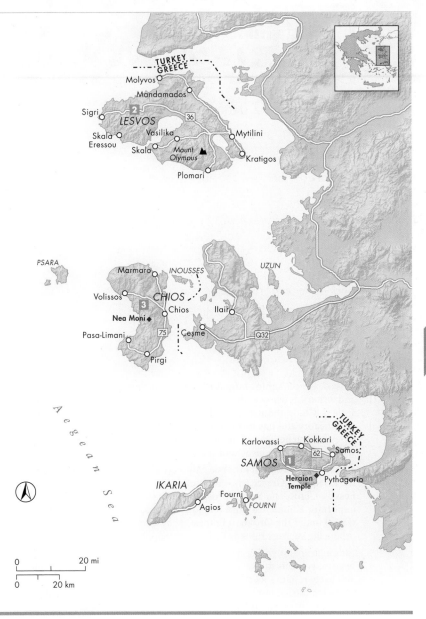

TURKEY
GREECE

Molyvos

Mandamados

Sigri

2 LESVOS

36

Skala
Eressou

Vasilika

Mytilini

Skala

Mount
Olympus ▲

Kratigos

Plomari

PSARA

Marmaro

INOUSSES

UZUN

Volissos

CHIOS

Nea Moni ◆

Chios

Ilair

Pasa-Limani

75

Çesme

Q32

Pirgi

9

A
e
g
e
a
n

S
e
a

TURKEY
GREECE

Karlovassi

Kokkari

SAMOS **1**

62

Samos

IKARIA

Heraion
Temple ◆

Pythagorio

Fourni

Agios

FOURNI

| 0 | | 20 mi |
| 0 | | 20 km |

Updated by Stephen Brewer

Quirky, seductive, fertile, sensual, faded, sunny, worldly, ravishing, long-suffering, hedonistic, luscious, mysterious, legendary—these adjectives only begin to describe the islands of the northeastern Aegean. This startling and rather arbitrary archipelago includes a sizable number of islands, such as Ikaria, Samothraki, and Thassos, but the three largest (and most visited) are Lesvos, Chios, and Samos. Closer to Turkey's coast than to mainland Greece, and quite separate from one another, these islands are hilly, sometimes mountainous, with dramatic coastlines and uncrowded beaches, brilliant architecture, and unforgettable historic sites.

Lesvos, Greece's third-largest island and birthplace of legendary artists and writers, is dense with gnarled olive groves and dappled with mineral springs. Chios, though ravaged in parts by fire in recent years, retains an eerie beauty and has fortified villages, old mansions, Byzantine monasteries, and stenciled-wall houses. Samos, the lush, mountainous land of wine and honey, whispers of the classical wonders of antiquity.

Despite their proximity to Asia Minor, the Northern Aegean islands are the essence of Greece, the result of 4,000 years of Hellenic influence. Lesvos, Chios, and Samos prospered gloriously in the ancient world as important commercial and religious centers, though their significance waned under the Ottoman Empire. They also were cultural hothouses, producing such geniuses as Pythagoras, Sappho, and (probably) Homer.

Although many young backpackers and partiers bypass the Northern Aegean, you can still carve out plenty of beach time by day and wander into lively restaurants and bars at night, but these islands reveal a deeper character, tracing histories that date back to ancient, Byzantine, and post-Byzantine times, and offer landscapes that are both serene and unspoiled.

Visitors to the northern islands should come with the spirit of discovery and open themselves to opportunities to interact with rich, enduring cultures.

More than 1 million refugees, mostly from Syria and Afghanistan, have passed through the islands in recent years. While many have moved on to Athens and beyond, some remain, and their presence has not only enhanced the cosmopolitan nature of these crossroads islands but has also shown off the generous hospitality of the islanders.

PLANNING

WHEN TO GO

From early May to early June, the weather is usually sunny and warm and the sea is still a bit chilly. From mid-June until the end of August, the weather goes through quite a sweeping change and can become very hot, although the waters of the Aegean can prove sufficiently refreshing. In September the weather begins to mellow considerably, and by mid-October is usually at its warmth limit for swimming, although sunshine can continue throughout the year on and off. Between November and March these islands can make for an enjoyable trip; unlike the holiday-oriented islands there are enough restaurants, museums, and sites open to keep visitors happy, though the weather can make ferry travel unreliable.

PLANNING YOUR TIME

If you have only a week to devote to this region, try to visit two islands. Start by exploring Mytilini, the capital of Lesvos, a bustling center of commerce and learning, with its grand old mansions overlooking the harbor. From there, head to the countryside to the northern destinations: Molyvos, a medieval town sprawling under the impressive Molyvos Castle; Skala Eresou with its fine beach and bars; and the hilltop Agiassos, immersed in verdant forests. For your second stop, take a ferry to Chios, where you can enjoy the nightlife in the main town, and don't miss the Old Quarter. Travel via Lithi—derived from *Alithis limin*, meaning "true haven," which is rather apt for this beautiful fishing village—to enjoy a good fish lunch. Next, go to Pirgi (famous for its unique mosaics) and Mesta, part of the "masticohoria" or mastic villages, world renowned for their cultivation of mastic trees, which preserve a Greece of centuries past.

If you have a little more time, take the ferry from Chios to Samos. Circle the island, stopping at its lovely beaches and at Pythagorio, the ancient capital, or the temple at Heraion, one of the Wonders of the Ancient World. Consider visiting the popular traditional fishing village of Kokkari, which has managed to keep its architectural authenticity, then head for the beaches Tsamadou and Lemonakia, where the green pine slopes meet the cobalt-blue waters of the Mediterranean. If you're drawn to the shores of Turkey, Samos makes a convenient stopover, as there's a daily ferry service to Kusadasi.

GETTING HERE AND AROUND

AIR TRAVEL

Even if they have the time, many people avoid the 8- to 10-hour ferry ride from Athens and fly, which takes less than an hour. Aegean Airways and its subsidiary Olympic have at least a dozen flights a week (three or four daily) from Athens to Lesvos and Chios in summer and at least four daily flights to Samos. There are several flights a week from Chios to Lesvos, Limnos, Rhodes, and Thessaloniki; and several each week from Lesvos to Chios, Limnos, and Thessaloniki. From Samos there are several weekly flights to Limnos, Rhodes, and Thessaloniki; there are also flights (usually at least one per week) between Samos and the other northern islands, some operated by Sky Express. Overbooking is not uncommon; if you have a reservation, you should be entitled to a free flight if you get bumped. *For airline contact information, see Air Travel in Travel Smart.*

AIRPORTS

Lesvos Airport is 7 km (4½ miles) south of Mytilini. Chios Airport is 4½ km (3 miles) south of Chios Town. The busiest airport in the region is on Samos, 17 km (10½ miles) southwest of Samos Town, with many international charters arriving in summer.

Contacts Chios National Airport. ☎ *22710/81400.* **Odysseas Elitis Airport.** ☎ *22510/38700.* **Samos International Airport.** ☎ *22730/87800.*

BOAT AND FERRY TRAVEL

Ferries between any of the Northern Aegean islands and Piraeus, Athens's port, take 8 to 11 hours (Piraeus–Samos, approximately €45).

There is usually one daily overnight ferry from Piraeus to Lesvos (€43, 10–11 hrs); there is one weekly ferry from Thessaloniki to Lesvos (€38, 16 hrs). These ferries call at Chios first (€38, 8–9 hrs).

Five to nine ferries travel each week from Piraeus to Samos (€39, 15 hrs), arriving in either Samos Town or Karlovassi (28 km [17 miles] northwest of Samos Town), some stopping at Syros, Mykonos, and Evdilos/Ikaria.

Ferries and hydrofoils to Kusadasi, on the Turkish coast, leave from Samos Town for excursions to the classical ruins at Ephesus; ferries also make a popular excursion from Samos to Patmos. At least once-a-day ferry service connects Chios with Çesme, one of Turkey's most popular resorts; the crossing takes less than a half hour. From Lesvos, a ferry runs at least once a week to and from Ayvalik, the Turkish port near the classical cities of Troy, Assos, and Pergamon; the crossing takes 1½ hours.

Service between the various Northern Aegean islands is not as frequent as one might wish, making island-hopping a bit of a challenge. There is daily service between Lesvos and Chios. The cost is about €19 and the trip takes 2½ hours. As many as three ferries per week run between Lesvos and Samos (7 hours, €18) and three a week between Samos and Chios (3 hours, €13). Unfortunately for relaxing vacationers, departures and arrivals are often in the predawn hours.

Contacts Chios Port Authority. ☎ *22710/44433, 22710/44434 in Chios Town* ⊕ *www.hcg.gr/node/186.* **Mytilini Port Authority.** ☎ *22510/40827 in Mytilini, 22510/37447, 22510/24115* ⊕ *www.hcg.gr/node/176.* **Piraeus Port Authority.** ☎ *210/455–0000, 210/455–0100* ⊕ *www.olp.gr.* **Samos Port Authority.** ☎ *22730/27318 in Samos Town, 22730/30888 in Karlovassi, 22730/61225 in Pythagorio* ⊕ *www.hcg.gr/node/215.*

BUS TRAVEL

The public (KTEL) bus system on the Northern Aegean islands is generally reliable, cheap (a few euros one-way), and obliging.

CAR TRAVEL

Lesvos, Chios, and Samos are large, so a car is useful. Expect to spend about €35 to €80 per day for a compact car with insurance and unlimited mileage. An international driving permit (available at your local AAA office) is required to rent a car in Greece, although many agencies allow you to rent with your national license; however, if you are stopped by the police or get into an accident and cannot produce an international or EU license, you might have problems. Discover, on Lesvos, has newer cars and is cheaper than other agencies. Vassilakis on Chios has reliable, well-priced vehicles. Aramis Rent-a-Car, part of Sixt, has fair rates and reliable service on Samos.

Contacts Aramis Rent-A-Car. ✉ *Directly across from port, Samos Town* ☎ *22730/23253* ⊕ *samos-rentacar.com* ✉ *Town center, opposite Commercial Bank, Kokkari* ☎ *22730/92385.* **Discover.** ✉ *Aristarchou 1, Mytilini* ✛ *Across from port* ☎ *2251/020391* ⊕ *www.rentacarlesvos.gr.* **Vassilakis.** ✉ *92 El. Venizelou, Chios Town* ☎ *22710/43880* ⊕ *www.rentacarinchios.com.*

TAXI TRAVEL

Due to the small number of taxis, prices are high: expect to shell out around double what you'd pay in Athens, but always check the rates in advance. If you do spring for a ride, it's a good idea to ask for a card with the driver's number in case you need a lift later in your trip. On Lesvos, Michalis Parmakelis is a recommended driver who speaks fluent English.

Contacts Michalis Parmakelis. ☎ *69744/63299.*

HOTELS

Restored mansions, village houses, sophisticated hotels, and budget accommodations are all options on the Northern Aegean islands. Reserve early in high season for better-category hotels, especially in Pythagorio on Samos and Molyvos on Lesvos. Off-season you can usually bargain down the official prices. Lodging in general is cheaper here than elsewhere in Greece, but many hotel rooms are basic, with simple pine furniture and sparse, locally built furnishings. Hotels are usually small and family-operated, and except for a few exceptions on Samos and Lesvos, there are few large resorts. Islanders are extremely friendly hosts, and while they may become more standoffish when the multitudes descend in August, they treat you as a guest rather than a billfold. On Lesvos, stay in Mytilini if you like a busy, citylike setting, in Molyvos for its dramatic medieval beauty, or in Skala Eresou for its laid-back beach style. On Chios avoid staying in the main town unless

9

you're just stopping over briefly, as it's not terribly relaxing, and opt to stay in the outlying Kambos District or the picturesque mastic village of Mesta instead. Vathi (aka "Samos Town") is a good central option in Samos, but Pythagorio and Kokkari are more resortlike.

RESTAURANTS

On Lesvos, sardines—the tastiest in the Mediterranean, traditionally left in sea salt for a few hours and eaten at a sushi-like consistency—from the Gulf of Kalloni are famous nationwide, as is the island's impressive ouzo variety. Apart from classic salads and vegetable dishes like seasonal *briam* (a kind of ratatouille), and oven-baked or stewed Greek-Turkish dishes, meat dishes may reflect more of a Turkish influence. Try *soutzoukakia* (meatballs spiced with cumin and cinnamon), or *keskek* (chopped meat mixed with wheat, served most often at festivals).

Local figs, almonds, and sun-ripened raisins are delicious; a Lesvos dessert incorporating one of those native treats is *baleze* (almond pudding). Besides being recognized for its mastic products, Chios is also known for mandarins—try the "mandarini" ice cream or juice in the main town. You'll also find a great variety of mastic-flavor sweets as well as savory foods.

Thyme-scented honey, *yiorti* (the local version of keskek), and *revithokeftedes* (chickpea patties) are Samos's edible claims to fame.

Unless noted, reservations are unnecessary, and casual dress is always acceptable. Go to the kitchen and point to what you want (the Greek names for fish can be tricky to decipher), or be adventurous and let the waiter choose for you (although you may wind up with enough food to feed a village). Remember, however, that fresh fish is very expensive across the islands, €50 and up per kilo, with a typical individual portion measured at about half a kilo. The price for fish is not factored into the price categories below (and lobster is even more expensive). Many restaurants close from October to May.

Restaurant and hotel reviews have been shortened. For full information, visit Fodors.com.

DINING AND LODGING PRICES IN EUROS			
	$	$$	$$$	$$$$
Restaurants	under €15	€15–€25	€26–€40	over €40
Hotels	under €125	€125–€225	€226–€275	over €275

Restaurant prices are the average cost of a main course at dinner or, if dinner is not served, at lunch. Hotel prices are the lowest cost of a standard double room in high season.

TOURS

Masticulture. Masticulture in Chios orients visitors to a hearty perspective of local traditional life and the island's natural beauty. Organizing everything from walking tours, cooking classes, tending mastic trees, grape pressing, and offering original accommodations to suit every taste, the friendly staff is happy to provide plugged-in tips on what to see and do locally. They stand out for nicely providing what eclectic—and especially environmentally minded—travelers might be looking for. ⊠ *Mesta* ✛ *On main square* ☎ *22710/76084* ⊕ *www.masticulture.com.*

Pandora Travel Lesbos. A thoughtful and knowledgeable staff caters to the cruise-ship crowd on the island for a few hours as well as to other tourists who may be on Lesvos for a longer time and want to experience the many sides of this rich island. They lead hikes, bird-watching expeditions, fishing and diving expeditions, and much more. ⊠ *Agora, Lisvori* ☎ *22520/42080, 69/8672–9992* ⊕ *www.pandoralesvos.com.*

Petra Tours. This action-oriented firm is located in Petra, a beach town just south of Molyvos. The staff plans bird-watching, botanical, walking, and scuba-diving excursions, and also arranges distinctive accommodation. ⊠ *Petra* ☎ *22530/41390, 22530/42011* ⊕ *www.petratours-lesvos.com.*

Rhenia Tours. An efficient staff puts together informative and fun tours of the classical sites on Samos and the island's natural wonders and also arranges excursions to Ephesus in Turkey and the island of Patmos. ⊠ *15 Sofouli, Samos Town* ☎ *22730/88800* ⊕ *www.rhenia.gr.*

VISITOR INFORMATION
Please see the Visitor Information listing in the pages devoted to each island for Lesvos and Chios.

LESVOS ΛΕΣΒΟΣ

The Turks called Lesvos the "garden of the empire" for its fertility: in the east and center of the island, about 12 million olive trees line the hills in seemingly endless, undulating groves, interspersed with fragrant pine forests. The western landscape is filled with oak trees, sheep pastures, rocky outcrops, and mountains. Wildflowers and grain cover the valleys, and the higher peaks are wreathed in dark green pines. Adding to the allure—and much to the delight of hedonists—are the hot, mineral-rich waters that bubble to the surface and in places are channeled into thermal baths. This third-largest island in Greece is filled with beauty, and its other treasures are the creative artists and thinkers it has produced and inspired through the ages.

Lesvos was once a major cultural center known for its Philosophical Academy, where Epicurus and Aristotle taught. It was also the birthplace of the philosopher Theophrastus, who presided over the Academy in Athens; of the great lyric poet Sappho; of Terpander, the "father of Greek music"; and of Arion, who influenced the later playwrights Sophocles and Alcaeus, inventors of the dithyramb (a short poem with an erratic strain). Even in modernity, artists have emerged from Lesvos: Theophilos, a poor villager who earned his ouzo by painting some of the finest native modern art Greece has produced; novelists Stratis Myrivilis and Argyris Eftaliotis; and the 1979 Nobel Prize–winning poet Odysseus Elytis.

The island's recorded history stretches back to the 6th century BC, when its two mightiest cities, Mytilini and Mythimna (now Molyvos), settled their squabbles under the tyrant Pittacus, considered one of Greece's Seven Sages. Thus began the creative era, but later times brought forth

9

TO
THESSALONIKI

Lesvos

the same pillaging and conquest that overturned other Greek islands. In 527 BC the Persians conquered Lesvos, and the Athenians, Romans, Byzantines, Venetians, Genoese, and Turks took turns adding their influences. After the Turkish conquest, from 1462 to 1912, much of the population was sent to Turkey, and traces of past civilizations that weren't already destroyed by earthquakes were wiped out by the conquerors. Greece gained sovereignty over the island in 1923. This led to the breaking of trade ties with Asia Minor, diminishing the island's wealth, and limiting the economy to agriculture, making this one of the greener islands of Greece.

Lesvos has more inhabitants than either Corfu or Rhodes with only a fraction of the tourists, so here you can get a good idea of real island life in Greece. Many Byzantine and post-Byzantine sites dot the island's landscape, including castles and archaeological monuments, churches, and monasteries. The traditional architecture of stone and wood, inspired by Asia Minor, adorns the mansions, tower houses, and other homes of the villages. Beach composition varies throughout the island from pebble to sand. Some of the most spectacular sandy beaches and coves are in the southwest of the island, quite markedly divided into east and west at its centerpoint by the long Gulf of Kalloni.

GETTING HERE AND AROUND

From Athens there are two to four direct Aegean Airlines flights every day, which take 40 minutes and cost between €70 and €130 one-way. Seaside Mytilini Airport is 8 km (5 miles) south of town. Taxi fare into town is about €15.

One or two ferries leave from Piraeus for Lesvos daily in summer, a few times a week the rest of the year, and take between 9 and 11 hours and cost €42–€43. These also stop at Chios in both directions, so there are regular links to this neighboring island (€14–€20, 2½ hours). Once a week there is a ferry from Thessaloniki to Lesvos (€42–€43, 16 hours).

Lesvos's bus network is fairly extensive and efficient; there are five a day from Mytilini to Molyvos (€6.90 one way) via Kaloni, as well as service between other larger towns on the island. The main bus station is at Aghias Eirinis 2 in central Mytilini.

VISITOR INFORMATION

Contacts Lesvos Municipal Tourist Office. ⊠ *Harbor front, Aristarchou 6, Mytilini* ☎ *22510/42511, 22510/44165* ⊕ *www.mytilene.gr.*

MYTILINI ΜΥΤΙΛΗΝΗ

350 km (217 miles) northeast of Piraeus by ferry, 218 km (135 miles) southeast of Thessaloniki by ferry.

Built on the ruins of an ancient city, Mytilini (so important through history that many call Lesvos by the port's name alone) is, like Lesvos, sculpted by two bays, one to the north and one to the south, making the town's waterfront resemble a jigsaw-puzzle piece. This busy main town and port, with stretches of grand waterfront mansions and a busy old bazaar area, was once the scene of a dramatic moment in Greek history. Early in the Peloponnesian War, Mytilini revolted against Athens but surrendered in 428 BC. As punishment, the Athens assembly decided to put to death all men in Lesvos and enslave the women and children, so a trireme set sail to issue the order. The next day a less vengeful mood prevailed in Athens; the assembly repealed its brutal decision and sent a double-manned trireme after the first one. The second trireme pulled into the harbor just as the commander of the first ship finished reading out the death sentence. Just in time, Mytilini was saved. To the south the modern town flows along the seafront into the elegant suburb and artistic enclave of Varia, once home to the modern "naive" artist Theophilos; Stratis Eleftheriadis, "Tériade," famous publisher of modern art journals; and the 20th-century poet Odysseus Elytis.

EXPLORING

The bustling waterfront just south of the headland between the town's two bays is where most of the town's sights are clustered.

Ancient Theater. This vestige of ancient Mytilini is within a pine grove and freely accessible. One of the largest theaters in ancient Greece is from the Hellenistic period and seated an estimated audience of 10,000. Pompey admired it so much that he copied it for his theater in Rome. Though the marbles are gone, the shape, carved into the mountain, remains beautifully intact. ✉ *Mytilini* ✚ *In pine forest northeast of town, off Synoiksmos* ⊕ *odysseus.culture.gr.*

Archaeological Museum of Mytileni. In a 1912 neoclassical mansion, the island's archaeological museum displays finds from the neolithic through the Roman eras, a period of some 5,000 years. Quite telling is a tablet showing a woman on horseback—a rarity in ancient Roman art—and a suggestion that Lesvos has always been an enlightened place. A garden in the back displays the famous 6th-century Aeolian capitals from the columns of Klopedi's temples. The museum's modern "wing" (on the corner of Noemvriou and Melinas Merkouri), contains finds from prehistoric Thermi, mosaics from Hellenistic houses, reliefs of comic scenes from the 3rd-century Roman house of Menander, and temporary exhibits. ✉ *Mansion, Argiri Eftaliotis 7* ✚ *Behind the ferry dock* ☎ *22510/28032* ⊕ *odysseus.culture.gr* ☜ *€3* ⊙ *Closed Mon.*

Ayios Therapon. The enormous five-domed post-baroque church of Ayios Therapon, completed in 1935, was designed by architect Argyris Adalis, an islander who studied under Ernst Ziller, the prolific architect of so many of the municipal buildings in Athens. The church is dedicated to Saint Therapon, whose name means "healer," and it's been visited by many people who came to Lesvos to recuperate from illness. It has an ornate interior, a frescoed dome, and there's a Byzantine museum in the courtyard that's filled with religious icons. ✉ *Mytilini* ✚ *Southern waterfront* ☎ *22510/22561* ☜ *Museum €2 (free on 1st Sun. of month)* ⊙ *Museum closed Sun. (except for 1st Sun of the month).*

Ermou. Stroll the main bazaar street, Ermou, which goes from the port on the north side of town to the port on the south side. Walk past the fish market on the southern end, where men haul in their sardines, mullet, and octopus. Narrow lanes are filled with antiques shops and grand old mansions. ✉ *Ermou.*

Gera Bay Hot Springs. The island's most deluxe hot springs are just east of town on the Gulf of Gera and include indoor-outdoor soaking tubs, a spa, and a chic outdoor café. Especially alluring are the delightfully warm waters that cascade from marble spouts to provide a soothing massage. Best of all, soakers can emerge from the tubs onto a beach for a refreshing dip in the waters of the gulf. ✉ *Mytilini* ✚ *On shores of Gulf of Gera off Kalloni Rd., 8 km (4 miles) west of Mytilini* ☎ *22510/41503* ☜ *€4.*

Kastro. The pine-covered headland between the bays—a nice spot for a picnic—supports a Kastro, a stone fortress with intact walls that seem to protect the town even today. Built by the Byzantines on a 600 BC temple of Apollo, it was repaired with available material (note the ancient pillars crammed between the stones) by Francesco Gateluzzi of the famous Genoese family. Look above the gates for the two-headed eagle of the Palaiologos emperors, the horseshoe arms of the Gateluzzi family, and inscriptions made by Turks, who enlarged it; today it is a military bastion. Inside the castle there's only a crumbling prison and a Roman cistern, but you should make the visit for the fine view. In the harbor just to the north, you can see waves crashing over the breakwater the Romans built 2,000 years ago. The grounds are always accessible, even when the citadel is closed. ✉ *Mytilini* ✢ *On a hill, northeast of port* 🌐 *odysseus.culture.gr* 🎟 *€2* ⏱ *Closed Mon.*

Musée–Bibliothèque Tériade. The home of Stratis Eleftheriadis, better known by his French name, Tériade, houses a luminous collection of French art, much of which appeared in Tériade's highly influential Paris publications *Minotaure* and *Verve*. Among the works on display are lithographs done for the publisher/collector/critic by Picasso, Matisse, Chagall, Rouault, Giacometti, and Miró. The house is set among the olive trees of Varia and is also home to the Museum of Theophilos. ✉ *Vareia* ✢ *4 km (2½ miles) southeast of Mytilini* ☎ *22510/23372* 🌐 *www.museumteriade.gr* 🎟 *€3.50* ⏱ *Closed Mon.*

Museum of Theophilos. This museum, sitting amid olive groves, houses a large number of the eponymous artist's "naive," precise neo-Hellenic works, detailing the everyday life of local folk such as fishermen and farmers, and polytheical fantasies of another age. Theophilos lived in poverty but painted airplanes and cities he had never seen. He painted in bakeries for bread, and in cafés for ouzo, and walked around in ancient dress and for a time lived inside a tree that can be seen in the hamlet of Karini. ✉ *Vareia* ✢ *4 km (2½ miles) southeast of Mytilini, next to the Tériade Museum* ☎ *22510/41644* 🎟 *€3* ⏱ *Closed weekends.*

WHERE TO EAT

$ GREEK

🍴 **Antonis Ouzeri.** This friendly spot in the hill village of Kagiani, next to Varia and just south of Mytilini, has wonderful views of Mytilini Town, the Aegean, and Asia Minor beyond. Grilled octopus, perfectly fried crispy red mullet, and other meat and fish favorites are served in traditional Lesvos style, as small plates to accompany ouzo. **Known for:** fantastic views; delicious mezedes. [$] *Average main: €8* ✉ *Up the hill from Varia, Taxiarhes, Vareia* ☎ *22510/61951* 🌐 *antonis-kagiani.gr.*

$ GREEK Fodor's Choice ★

🍴 **Ermis Ouzeri.** This centuries-old landmark on the main thoroughfare between the old and new harbors dates back to Ottoman times and is the best place in town to sip ouzo, on the vine-shaded terrace with marble-top tables. Accompanying the ouzo selection are delicious "aperitif" mezedes, such as soutzoukakia, octopus in wine sauce, long-cooked chickpeas, and homemade sausages. **Known for:** old-world ambience; opening early (and staying open late); cash only. [$] *Average main: €6* ✉ *Ermou 2, toward the north end of the street* ☎ *22510/26232* 💳 *No credit cards.*

$ GREEK

🍴 **Kalnterimi.** An ever-popular ouzeri and grill on shady Thassou Street in the Old Town is an almost mandatory stop while shopping along adjoining Ermou Street. Fresh grilled baby calamari and lightly fried courgette flowers stuffed with cheese are among many enticing bites that accompany the generous selection of ouzo. **Known for:** ouzo and atmosphere; rembetiko music some nights. [$] *Average main: €7* ✉ *Thasou 2* ☎ *22510/46557.*

$ GREEK

🍴 **Polytechnos.** Locals and visiting Athenians pack the outdoor tables of what's essentially a fast-food and drinks joint across from the municipal building at the southern end of the harbor, a favorite stop on a walk along the quay. Souvlaki and gyros are perennial favorites, though the selection of fish dishes is also impressive. **Known for:** souvlaki and other casual fare; fried seafood; cash only. $ *Average main: €8* ⊠ *Fanari quay* ☎ *22510/44128* ▭ *No credit cards.*

WHERE TO STAY

$$
HOTEL
FAMILY

🛏 **Loriet Hotel.** Some of the island's most atmospheric digs are in an 1880s stone mansion, where high frescoed ceilings, friezes, and antique furniture set the mood—little wonder you'll sometimes find visiting dignitaries booking the fancy suites. **Pros:** beautifully restored mansion with historic atmosphere; nice pool; convenient to airport and town. **Cons:** the long stretch of beach in front is rather unappealing; a bit run-down in places; regular rooms are small and basic. $ *Rooms from: €150* ⊠ *Vareia* ✛ *2 km (1 mile) south of Mytilini* ☎ *22510/43111* ⊕ *www.loriet-hotel.com* ⌲ *35 rooms* ⋈ *Breakfast.*

$
HOTEL

🛏 **Pyrgos of Mytilene.** A restored 1916 mansion in the ornate Second Empire style, replete with amazing white-and-Grecian-blue tile work, fuses modern-day amenities and 19th-century nostalgia, with the emphasis on the latter in the frilly guest rooms. **Pros:** handsome exterior looking out onto the sea; excellent breakfast; some rooms have expansive sea views. **Cons:** room decor verges on kitsch, with too much gilt and gold; no pool; a little fussy for casual travelers. $ *Rooms from: €100* ⊠ *Eleftherios Venizelou 49* ☎ *22510/27977, 22510/25069* ⊕ *www.pyrgoshotel.gr* ⌲ *12 rooms* ⋈ *Breakfast.*

NIGHTLIFE

The cafés along the harbor turn into bars after sunset, generally closing at 3 am.

Bracciera. This outdoor beach bar next to the airport has an upscale, artistic vibe and is a great place to spend time while waiting for a flight or to while away a day or evening. ⊠ *Aeorodromio-Kratigos* ✛ *7 km (4½ miles) south of Mytilini, on beach past Mytilini Airport* ☎ *22510/63104.*

Hacienda. For a relaxed Caribbean-style start to your night, begin with a cocktail at this port-side bar and café. ⊠ *91 Koudourioti Paviou, at the southeastern end of the main harbor* ☎ *22510/46850.*

SHOPPING

Much of the best shopping is along the Ermou Street bazaar. Here you can buy a little of everything, from food (especially olive oil and ouzo) to pottery, wood carvings, and embroidery.

Veto. Lesvos produces 50 brands of ouzo, and George Spentzas's shop, Veto, right on the main harbor, has made its own varietals on the premises since 1948. It also sells local food products such as olive oil, olives, dried fruit, and *hilopites* (pasta). It's open Monday through Saturday, 7 am to 10 pm. ⊠ *Aristarchou 1* ☎ *22510/24660* ⊕ *www.ouzoveto.gr.*

MORIA ΜΟΡΙΑ

7 km (4½ miles) northwest of Varia, 6 km (4 miles) northwest of Mytilini.

On the coast as you head north from Mytilini, Moria is best known for its Roman aqueduct. But the town is also famed for its annual Feast of Ayios Dimitrios. The celebrations begin the night of October 25 and continue well into the next day, with the killing and all-night cooking of a bull, accompanied by the entire village singing, dancing, and participating in daylong horse races.

Roman aqueduct. Moria's Roman aqueduct dates back to the 2nd century, and the 17 arches that remain demonstrate how magnificent the structure was in its heyday. Constructed from gray Lesviot marble, the aqueduct stretched 26 km (16 miles) from Olympos mountain at Tsingos to Mytilini. It was in Lesvos that Julius Caesar first made his mark. Sent to Bythinia to drum up a fleet, he hung around so long at King Nicodemus's court that he was rumored to be having an affair with the king, but he finally distinguished himself by saving a soldier's life. ✉ *Moria* ✣ *Just outside town; follow the signs.*

PAMFILA ΠΑΜΦΙΛΑ

4 km (2½ miles) north of Moria, 8 km (5 miles) north of Mytilini.

In the 19th century, Pamfila's traditional tower mansions were used by wealthy families as summer homes. The views across the straits to Turkey are wonderful. Equally beautiful are the old stone factories in this area, some of which are still in use.

PIRGI THERMIS ΠΥΡΓΟΙ ΘΕΡΜΗΣ

8 km (5 miles) northwest of Mytilini.

Pirgi Thermis is known for its tower mansions and for its 12th-century church, Panayia Tourlot, near the outskirts of town. The town's one-time big attractions, thermal baths, and a lavish spa hotel set in seaside gardens are now closed; the latter is in a state of sad but romantic ruin.

WHERE TO STAY

$ HOTEL Fodor's Choice ★ 🏨 **Votsala Hotel.** This alluring, Bauhaus-style retreat surrounded by wonderfully peaceful gardens that run down to the water is a beloved island institution, a favorite of scores of return visitors. **Pros:** friendly, welcoming atmosphere; excellent homemade dishes at breakfast and other meals; lovely seaside grounds. **Cons:** no in-room TVs or phones, a plus for many guests; no pool but a jetty and beach for swimming; few luxuries, offset by wonderful bohemian vibes. [$] *Rooms from: €85* ✉ *Pirgi Thermis* ☎ *22510/71231* 🌐 *www.votsalahotel.com* 🕓 *Closed Nov.–Mar.* 🛏 *45 rooms* 🍴 *Breakfast.*

9

MANDAMADOS ΜΑΝΤΑΜΑΔΟΣ

7 km (4½ miles) northwest of Pirgi Thermis, 36 km (22½ miles) northwest of Mytilini.

Pretty Mandamados has stone houses, wood carvings, and the ruins of a medieval castle. The village is famous for its pottery, *koumari* urns (they keep water cool even in scorching heat), and an icon.

Taxiarchis Michail. The black icon of Archangel Michael is in the 17th-century monastery dedicated to the island's patron saint, Taxiarchis Michail. The gruesome legend has it that the icon was carved by a monk who used mud and the blood of his comrades, slain in an Ottoman attack, to darken it. Believers used to make a wish and press a coin to the archangel's forehead; if it stuck, the wish would be granted. Owing to wear and tear on the icon, the practice is now forbidden. ⊠ *North end of village.*

SKALA SIKAMINIAS ΣΚΑΛΑ ΣΥΚΑΜΙΝΙΑΣ

35 km (22 miles) northwest of Mytilini.

At the northernmost point of Lesvos, past Pelopi, is the exceptionally lovely fishing port of Skala Sikaminias, a miniature gem—serene and real, with several good fish tavernas on the edge of the dock. The novelist Stratis Myrivilis used the village as the setting for his *Mermaid Madonna.* Those who have read the book will recognize the tiny chapel at the base of the jetty. The author's birthplace and childhood home are in Sikaminia, the village overlooking Skala Sikaminias—and the Turkish coast—from its perch high above the sea.

WHERE TO EAT

$

GREEK

✕ **Skamnia.** Sit at a table of Skala Sikaminias's oldest taverna, under the same spreading mulberry tree beneath which novelist Stratis Myrivilis wrote, to sip a glass of ouzo and watch the fishing boats bob. Stuffed zucchini blossoms or cucumbers and tomatoes tossed with local olive oil are food for thought: light, tasty, and ideal for snacking. **Known for:** idyllic views; chicken in grape leaves; fish and other seafood. $ *Average main: €12* ⊠ *On the waterfront* ☎ *22530/55319, 22530/55419.*

MOLYVOS ΜΟΛΥΒΟΣ

17 km (10½ miles) southwest of Skala Sikaminias, 61 km (38 miles) west of Mytilini.

Fodor's Choice

★

Also known by its ancient name, Mythimna, this is a place that has attracted people since antiquity. Legend says that Achilles besieged the town until the king's daughter fell for him and opened the gates; then Achilles killed her. Before 1923, Turks made up about a third of the population, living in many of the best stone houses. Today these balconied buildings with center staircases are weighed down by roses and geraniums; the red-tile roofs and cobblestone streets are required by law. Attracted by the town's charms, many artists live here. Don't miss a walk down to the picture-perfect harbor front.

EXPLORING

Fodor's Choice ★ **Kastro.** A 13th-century Byzantine-Genoese fortified castle is a magnetic presence when seen from below, and a drive or walk to the hilltop landmark affords a hypnotic view down the tiers of red-tile roofs to the glittering sea. At dawn the sky begins to light up from behind the mountains of Asia Minor, casting silver streaks through the placid water as weary night fishermen come in. Purple wisteria vines shelter the lanes that descend from the castle and pass numerous Turkish fountains, some still in use. ✉ *Above town* ☎ *22530/71803* 🎟 *€2* 🕒 *Closed Mon.*

OFF THE BEATEN PATH **Leimonos Monastery.** This stunning 16th-century complex houses 40 chapels and an impressive collection of precious objects. Founded by St. Ignatios Agalianos on the ruins of an older Byzantine monastery, Leimonos earned its name from the "flowering meadow of souls" surrounding it. The intimate St. Ignatios church is filled with colorful frescoes and is patrolled by peacocks. A folk-art museum with historic and religious works is accompanied by a treasury of 450 Byzantine manuscripts. Women are not allowed inside the main church. ✉ *Kalloni* ✣ *Up a marked road 5 km (3 miles) northwest of Kalloni, 15 km (9 miles) southwest of Molyvos* ☎ *22530/22289* 🎟 *Museum and treasury €2.*

BEACHES

Eftalou. Just to the east of Molyvos is this nice, empty stretch of coastline, blessed not just with a beach but with thermal mineral baths. You can soak in the enclosed tubs for a small fee or find a spot just below the old baths where the hot water bubbles into the sea. An easy walk east from there takes you past a pleasant beachside taverna to a long expanse of sand and pebbles, remote enough in parts to attract nudists. **Amenities:** food and drink, parking (no fee). **Best for:** nudists; solitude; swimming; walking. ✉ *Molyvos* ✣ *3½ km (1 mile) east of Molyvos.*

WHERE TO EAT

$ SEAFOOD Fodor's Choice ★ 🍴 **Captain's Table.** At the end of a quay, this harborside favorite serves mouthwatering seafood caught on its own trawler, moored opposite. It's best to enjoy the fresh fish and seafood, along with garden-grown vegetables, as small mezedes dishes to be shared. **Known for:** fresh seafood; harbor views; Captain's Platter for two. [$] *Average main: €9* ✉ *Molyvos* ✣ *Molyvos harbor, across from Ayios Nikolaos chapel* ☎ *22530/71241* 🕒 *Closed Mid-Oct.–mid-Apr. No lunch.*

$ GREEK 🍴 **Gatos.** Gaze over the island and harbor from the veranda of this yellow-and-green-dressed charmer, or sit inside and watch the cooks chop and grind in the open kitchen: the beef fillet is tender, the lamb chops nicely spiced, and the salads fresh. **Known for:** grilled meats; terrace views; popular spot for coffee. [$] *Average main: €9* ✉ *Molyvos* ✣ *Center of old market* ☎ *22530/71661* 🌐 *www.gatos-restaurant.gr* 🕒 *Closed mid-Oct.–Mar.*

9

WHERE TO STAY

$ HOTEL 🏨 **Belvedere Hotel.** A little away from the buzz of Molyvos, this cluster of traditional red-roof buildings offers ample chance to relax, with nice grounds, pleasant beachside rooms opening to verandas, and a swimming pool—hard to find in Molyvos proper. **Pros:** hotel shuttle service into town; playground and many activities for children; nice pool area with Jacuzzi. **Cons:** nearby beach is rather mediocre; unexceptional hotel decor; a somewhat generic resort feel. [$] *Rooms from: €100* ✉ *Molyvos* ✣ *On road to Eftalou* ☎ *22530/71772* 🌐 *www.belvedere-lesvos.gr* 🕒 *Closed Nov.–Mar.* 🛏 *74 rooms* 🍴 *Breakfast.*

$$ HOTEL FAMILY 🏨 **Clara Hotel.** In these handsome red-roofed bungalows, soothing color palettes and lots of wood accents invite relaxation, while views from the verandas take in the sea, Petra, and Molyvos, and a small beach follows the bay beneath the L-shaped pool—all suggesting an aura of relaxed efficiency. **Pros:** great facilities and lots of activities; aesthetically pleasing architecture and decor; extremely comfortable rooms. **Cons:** hotel beach is clean but has some seaweed; no elevator and many steps; resortlike atmosphere is nice but can seem a bit generic. [$] *Rooms from: €125* ✉ *Petra* ✣ *South of Petra* ☎ *22530/41532* 🌐 *www.clarahotel.gr* 🕒 *Closed Nov.–Mar.* 🛏 *51 rooms* 🍴 *Breakfast.*

$ HOTEL Fodor's Choice ★ 🏨 **Sea Horse Hotel.** Most of the character-filled rooms and their balconies at this delightful stone-fronted presence on Molyvos harbor overlook the photogenic quay; the lobby even extends into a lively waterfront café that's a great place to linger over a drink or a meal. **Pros:** port setting gives you real Greek fishing village experience; enchanting bay views; lots of character. **Cons:** even though small, hotel attracts group bookings; rooms can be noisy from harborside comings and goings; amenities are nice but limited. [$] *Rooms from: €80* ✉ *Molyvos* ✣ *Molyvos quay* ☎ *22530/71320, 22530/71630, 69/4633–4935 during annual closure* 🌐 *www.seahorse-hotel.com* 🕒 *Closed Mid-Oct.–mid-Apr.* 🛏 *16 rooms* 🍴 *Breakfast.*

NIGHTLIFE

Congas Beach Bar. This breezy indoor/outdoor lounge, a few steps from the waters' edge, has been a favorite hangout for some time, filling with locals and tourists alike, who come for a drink, a meal, dessert, or to dance the night away. Cool grooves, great cocktails, and colorful sunsets are the signature features. ✉ *Molyvos* ☎ *22530/72181* 🌐 *www.congas.gr.*

Molly's Bar. Music to unwind to in a friendly environment is enhanced by waterside views. This popular predinner stop and late-night spot is open from 6 pm until the early hours. ✉ *Molyvos* ✣ *On street above harbor* ☎ *22530/71772.*

SHOPPING

Elleni's Workshop. Stop by this shop and studio on the way to Efthalou hot springs for handmade olive wood artworks and ergonomic utensils. You'll find gifts of all shapes and sizes, for all budgets. ✉ *Molyvos* ✣ *On the road to Eftalou* ☎ *22530/72004.*

Evelyn. A wide variety of local goods is available here on the main square of Molyvos, including ceramics, pastas, olive oil, wines, ouzo, sauces, and marmalades. It's open daily from 10 am to midnight. ✉ *Kyriakou Sq.* ☎ *22530/72197.*

Mythos Art Gallery. Beautiful silver jewelry, statuettes, pendants, and other items fashioned by artistan Theofolis Mantzoros fill his airy, light-filled, and hospitable shop above the sea. ✉ *17 November St. 1, at Poseidon* ☎ *22530/71711* 🌐 *www.myth.gr.*

AGIASSOS ΑΓΙΑΣΟΣ

55 km (33 miles) southeast of Molyvos, 28 km (17½ miles) southwest of Mytilini.

The prettiest hill town on Lesvos sits in an isolated valley amid thousands of olive trees, near the foot of Mt. Olympus, the highest peak. (In case you're confused, 19 mountains in the Mediterranean are named Olympus, almost all of them peaks sacred to the local sky god, who eventually became associated with Zeus.) Exempted from taxes by the Turks, the town thrived. The age-old charm of Agiassos can be seen in its gray-stone houses, cobblestone lanes, medieval castle, and local handicrafts, particularly pottery and woodwork.

Panayia Vrefokratousa (*Madonna Holding the Infant*). This walled compound in the village center was founded in the 12th century to house an icon of the Virgin Mary, believed to be the work of St. Luke, and it remains a popular place of pilgrimage. Built into the foundation are shops whose revenues support the church, as they have through the ages. The church museum has a little Bible from AD 500, with legible, elegant calligraphy. ✉ *Central square* 🎟 *Church free; museum €1* 🕑 *Closed daily 1–5:30.*

WHERE TO EAT

$ GREEK

🍴 **To Stavri.** Up the hill toward the top of the village you will find this popular village gathering spot with tables straddling a bridge that crosses the main thoroughfare. The menu consists of local favorites and most of the delicious produce is homegrown. **Known for:** local flavor; home cooking; cash only. [$] *Average main: €8* ✉ *Agiassos* ✣ *Top of the village* ☎ *22520/22936* 💳 *No credit cards.*

PLOMARI ΠΛΩΜΑΡΙ

20 km (12½ miles) south of Agiassos, 42 km (26 miles) southwest of Mytilini.

The second-largest town on Lesvos is on the southern coast, between the Gulf of Gera to the east and the Gulf of Kalloni to the west, dramatically set in a cliff face overlooking a wide harbor and Aegean sunsets. This was once a major port, but today the town is a cheerful mix of resort and quiet fishing village with narrow, cobbled lanes and houses spilling down to the sea. Plomari is famous throughout Greece for its ouzo, and there's a lively night scene on the harbor, where visitors gather after a long day at one of the surrounding beaches.

BEACHES

Plomari is surrounded by some enticing beaches that stretch along the southern edge of the island.

FAMILY **Agios Isidoris.** The beach strip just east of Plomari is backed by low-key hotels and tavernas. Though the setting is hardly remote, the sea washing onto the long stretch of golden sand is sparkling clean. A bonus for swimmers and snorkelers is the bountiful sea life that flourishes on the rocky shelf just below the surface of the turquoise waters. **Amenities:** food and drink; parking (no fee); water sports. **Best for:** snorkeling; swimming; walking. ✉ *Agios Isidoris.*

VATERA ΒΑΤΕΡΑ

53 km (33 miles) west of Mytilini.

This appealing place rambles along a 9-km-long (5½-mile-long) sandy strip of sparkling water, lined with tamarisk trees and framed by green hills. You can sit and enjoy the view of the cape of Ayios Fokas, with its excavated Temple of Dionysus. As is often the case in succeeding cultures, the temple's marble fragments were recycled, built into the center aisle of a town basilica.

EXPLORING

Hot Springs of Polichnitos. Tucked into the mountains along the main road you'll follow into Vatera are some of the hottest springs in Europe. They bubble up into a pastel-colored, mineral-saturated stream bed outside the atmospheric Old Town of Polichnitos and are channeled into pools inside a bathhouse. You'll probably start to wither after five minutes or so in the steamy waters that are said to be a remedy for ailments from rheumatism to digestion problems. Between bouts you can cool off with a beverage on the pleasant café terrace. ✣ *Eastern edge of Polichnitos, 10 km (6 miles) north of Vatera* 🎟 *€5.*

BEACHES

To find an idyllic place to sit on the sand or swim, just follow the coast road east from Vatera.

FAMILY **Vatera Beach.** This long stretch of sand could in itself put Lesvos on the map for beach lovers, yet it's often easy to find a patch all to yourself—the farther east you drive or walk from the settlement of Vatera, the more remote the setting becomes. The curving, southern exposure is idyllic, and swimming is good for water enthusiasts of all ages. **Amenities:** food and drink; parking (no fee). **Best for:** solitude; swimming; walking. ✉ *Vatera.*

WHERE TO STAY

$ HOTEL FAMILY 🏨 **Vatera Beach Hotel.** Staying in one of these low-key white-and-blue beachside houses is like having your own little seaside bungalow, with the beach just beyond your own outside entrance and endless sea views from the balconies. **Pros:** excellent location right on the beach; warm and friendly service; lots of outdoor spaces, including nice balconies. **Cons:** not all rooms have a sea view; furnishings are basic (but comfortable); few amenities, though the beach is the main draw. [$] *Rooms from: €80* ✉ *Vatera Beach* ☎ *22520/61212, 22520/61165* 🌐 *www.vaterabeach.gr* 🕓 *Closed Nov.–Mar.* 🛏 *24 rooms* 🍴 *Breakfast.*

SKALA ERESSOU ΣΚΑΛΑ ΕΡΕΣΟΥ

58 km (35 miles) southwest of Molyvos, 89 km (55 miles) west of Mytilini.

The poet Sappho, according to unreliable records, was allegedly born here circa 612 BC. She most likely presided over a finishing school for marriageable young women, and she appears to have been married herself and to have had a daughter. Dubbed the Tenth Muse by Plato because of her skill and sensitivity, Sappho wrote songs that erotically praise girls and celebrate their marriages. Sappho's works—proper and popular in their time—were burned by Christians, so that mostly fragments survive; one is "and I yearn, and I desire." Sapphic meter was in great favor in Roman and medieval times; both Catullus and Gregory the Great used it, and in the 19th century, so did Tennyson. Since the 1970s, many gay women have been coming to Skala Eresou to celebrate Sappho (the word "lesbian" derives from Lesvos), although the welcoming town is also filled with plenty of heterosexual couples and other travelers who come to enjoy the delightful setting and appealing, laid-back scene.

EXPLORING

Acropolis of Eresos. Ancient Eresos crowned a hillside overlooking the sea, and sections of the pre-classical walls, medieval castle ruins, and the AD 5th-century church, Ayios Andreas, remain from the storied and long-inhabited site. The church has a mosaic floor and a tiny adjacent museum housing local finds from tombs in the ancient cemetery. ⊠ *Skala Eressou ✛ 1 km (½ mile) north of Skala Eresou* ☎ *22530/53332, 22530/53037* ⊕ *odysseus.culture.gr* ✉ *Free* ⊗ *Closed Mon.*

Eresos. The old village of Eresos, separated from the coast by a large plain, was developed to protect its inhabitants from pirate raids. Along the mulberry tree–lined road leading from the beach you might encounter a villager wearing a traditional head scarf (*mandila*), plodding by on her donkey. This village of two-story, 19th-century stone and shingle houses is filled with superb architectural details. Note the huge wooden doors decorated with nails and elaborate door knockers, loophole windows in thick stone walls, elegant pediments topping imposing mansions, and fountains spilling under Gothic arches. ⊠ *Skala Eressou ✛ 11 km (7 miles) inland, north of Skala Eresou.*

BEACHES

Some of the island's best beaches are in this area, though some of them have been built up rapidly—and not always tastefully.

Skala Eresou Beach. The 4-km-long (2½-mile-long) town beach at Skala Eresou is a wide stretch of dark sand lined with tamarisk trees. A small island is within swimming distance, and northerly winds lure windsurfers along with the swimmers and sunbathers. There are many rooms to rent within walking distance of the beach, and in the section that skirts the town, many appealing bars and cafés front the sands. **Amenities:** food and drink; parking (no fee); showers; toilets; water sports. **Best for:** partiers; snorkeling; sunset; swimming; walking; windsurfing. ⊠ *Skala Eressou.*

9

WHERE TO EAT

$ CAFÉ 🍴 **Parasol.** Totem poles, colored coconut lamps, and other knickknacks from exotic travels make this beach bar endearing in its evocation of the South Pacific, as if the setting weren't transporting enough. The owner and his wife serve omelets, fruits, yogurt, and sweet Greek coffee for breakfast, and simple dishes like pizzas, veggie spring rolls, sandwiches, and cheese platters the rest of the day. **Known for:** exotic beachside terrace; great cocktails; cash only. [$] *Average main: €10* ✉ *Skala Eresou Beach* 💳 *No credit cards* 🕓 *Closed Nov.–Apr.*

$$ SEAFOOD 🍴 **Soulatso.** The enormous anchor and octopi drying on a line outside are signs that you're in for some seriously good seafood. Tables set on a wooden deck are just a skipping-stone's throw from the break of the waves. **Known for:** great seafood; outdoor seaside dining; cash only. [$] *Average main: €15* ✉ *Skala Eresou Beach* ✣ *At beach center* ☎ *22530/52078* 💳 *No credit cards* 🕓 *Closed Nov.–Apr.*

WHERE TO STAY

$ HOTEL FAMILY Fodor'sChoice ★ 🏨 **Heliotopos.** A delightfully peaceful and lovingly maintained large garden set in olive and citrus groves behind the beach surrounds homey and sparkling guest bungalows, all with lots of outdoor space. **Pros:** peaceful setting; lush garden; delightful hominess. **Cons:** no breakfast served; not on the beach; surroundings are comfortable rather than luxurious. [$] *Rooms from: €55* ✉ *Skala Eressou* ☎ *6948/510257* 🌐 *www.heliotoposeressos.gr* 🕓 *Closed mid-Nov.–Feb.* 🛏 *8 units* 🍽 *No meals.*

SIGRI ΣΙΓΡΙ

26 km (16 miles) northwest of Skala Eresou, 93 km (58 miles) west of Mytilini.

This welcoming cluster of white houses surrounding a lovely cove is set in stark, mountainous countryside at the far western end of the island.

FAMILY Fodor'sChoice ★ **Natural History Museum of the Lesvos Petrified Forest.** Don't miss these excellent displays, where you can learn how trees in the nearby forest were petrified and where petrified tree trunks can be touched; the exhibits are scrupulously labeled and laid out. There are also some unique and amazing fossils of animals like the Deinotherium, an early ancestor of the elephants, and vegetation preserved on volcanic rock that resembles delicate Zen art. ✉ *Main Rd.* ☎ *22530/54434* 🌐 *www.lesvos.com/petrifiedforestinformation.htm* 🎟 *€3* 🕓 *Closed Nov.–May.*

Fodor'sChoice ★ **Petrified Forest.** Conifer trees fossilized by volcanic ash up to 20 million years ago litter a hillside above Sigri. If you're expecting a thick woods, you might be taken aback by this seemingly barren site that at first appears like a bunch of stumps leaning every which way among shrubs and rock. But a walk along well-organized trails reveals delicate colors and a stark, strange beauty. You can also study the specimens at Ipsilou, a large monastery on the highest peak in this wild, moonscape-like volcanic landscape, overlooking western Lesvos and Asia Minor across the Aegean. ✉ *Sigri* ✣ *Between Sigri and Eresou* ☎ *22510/54434* 🌐 *www.petrifiedforest.gr* 🎟 *€2* 🕓 *Closed Mon. Nov.–June.*

BEACHES

Among the charms of Sigri are the surrounding, isolated beaches of exceptionally dark sand.

Faneromeni. An end-of-the-world atmosphere prevails at this lovely stretch of sand at the far west of the island just north of Sigri, punctuated by a rocky outcropping and fronting a green river valley, where you're likely to see birds and turtles. **Amenities:** parking (no fee). **Best for:** nudists; solitude; sunset; swimming; walking; windsurfing. ⊠ *Sigri* ✚ *4 km (2½ miles) north of Sigri.*

CHIOS ΧΙΟΣ

"Craggy Chios" is what local boy Homer, the island's first publicist, so to speak, called this starkly beautiful outcropping that almost touches Turkey's coast and shares its topography. The island has suffered its share of misfortunes: the bloody Turkish massacre of 1822 during the fight for Greek independence; major earthquakes, including one in 1881 that killed almost 6,000 Chiotes; severe fires, which in recents years have burned pine forests and coveted mastic shrubs; and, through the ages, the steady stripping of forests to ax-wielding boatbuilders. Yet despite these setbacks, the island remains a wonderful destination, with friendly inhabitants, and villages so rare and captivating that just one of them alone would make this island a gem.

The name Chios comes from the Phoenician word for "mastic," the resin of the *Pistacia lentisca,* evergreen shrubs that with few exceptions thrive only here, in the southern part of the island. Every August, incisions are made in the bark of the shrubs; the sap leaks out, permeating the air with a sweet fragrance, and in September the output is harvested. This aromatic resin, which brought huge revenues until the introduction of petroleum products, is still used in cosmetics, chewing gum, and mastiha liqueur sold on the island today. Pirgi, Mesta, and other villages where the mastic is grown and processed are enchanting. In these towns you can wind your way through narrow, labyrinthine Byzantine lanes protected by medieval gates and lined with homes that date back half a millennium.

Chios is also home to the elite families that control Greece's private shipping empires: Livanos, Karas, Chandris; even Onassis came here from Smyrna. The island has never seemed to need tourists or to draw them. Yet Chios intrigues, with its deep valleys, uncrowded sandy and black-pebble beaches, fields of wild tulips, Byzantine monasteries, and haunting villages—all remnants of a poignant history.

GETTING HERE AND AROUND

Aegean and Olympic Airlines offer four flights daily between Athens and Chios (50 minutes; from €69 to €128 one-way). There are also daily Astra Airlines flights from Thessaloniki (1 hour, €37.60 to €87.60). Chios Airport is 4½ km (3 miles) south of Chios Town; a taxi ride runs around €6 to €10.

Daily ferries connect Chios and Piraeus in summer (8 hours; €38 to €39), less frequently at other times; these ferries usually go on to Lesvos

Many of the churches on the Northern Aegean islands are picture-perfect, thanks to their beautiful frescoes.

(3 hours; €14 to €20). Several times a week there is a ferry to and from Thessaloniki (up to 20 hours, €38). For schedule information, see ⊕ *www.gtp.gr.*

BUS TRAVEL ON CHIOS

Buses leave the town of Chios several times per day for Mesta and Pirgi. The main station for local buses is in Chios Town at Vlatarias 13, north of the park by Platia Plastira. A second bus station, which services the long-distance KTEL buses, is found to the south of the park adjacent to the main taxi stand on the central square. Bus fares run €1.50 to €5. KTEL also offers island tours daily at 9:30 and 10 am, finishing at 5 pm, for €8 to €15 depending on the route.

VISITOR INFORMATION

Contacts Chios Municipal Tourist Office. ⊠ *18 Kinari St., Chios Town* ☏ *22710/51723, 22710/51726* ⊕ *www.chios.gr.*

CHIOS TOWN ΧΙΟΣ ΠΟΛΗ

285 km (177 miles) northeast of Piraeus, 55 km (34 miles) south of Mytilini.

The main port and capital, Chios Town, or Chora, is a busy commercial settlement on the east coast, across from Turkey. By day, the streets are clamorous with a bazaarlike atmosphere, and when the lights come on in the evening, the scene is softened by a mingling of blue hues, the cafés begin to overflow with ouzo and good cheer, and locals promenade along the bay side. The outskirts straggle into vast olive groves that stretch toward the mountains, and particularly appealing is the Kambos district, where beautiful Genoese are surrounded by lush gardens behind honey-colored walls.

EXPLORING

TOP ATTRACTIONS

Byzantine Museum. The only intact mosque in this part of the Aegean, complete with a slender minaret, dates from the 19th century and houses the Byzantine Museum. The museum seems to be perpetually under renovation, but the porch and courtyard are littered with richly inscribed Jewish, Turkish, and Armenian gravestones, including one depicting St. George slaying the dragon. Also on display are column capitals unearthed across the island and some delightful 18th-century Byzantine murals in which three sleeping girls await the miracle of St. Nicholas. ⊠ *Vounakiou Sq.* ☎ *22710/26866* ⌲ *€2* ⊘ *Closed Mon.*

Chios Archaeological Museum. Among classical pottery and sculpture is a letter, on stone, from Alexander the Great addressed to the Chiotes and dated 332 BC. Also on display is some remarkably intact prehistoric pottery from the 14th century BC. ⊠ *Michalon 8* ☎ *22710/44239* ⌲ *€2* ⊘ *Closed Mon.*

FAMILY **Citrus.** The Kambos district is famed as one of the most superlatively fertile orchard regions of Greece—orange and lemon groves set behind honey-hued stone walls are given the status of museums and landmarks. It is only fitting that the owners of the Perleas Mansion hotel have opened this beautifully fragrant estate to showcase the history of citrus products on the island and entice visitors with a shop and delightful café selling citrus-inspired sweets. The estate buildings are gorgeous, centered on a farm where English-language placards explain the layout and workings of a historic citrus estate and beautiful stone barns and houses are set with hunter-green window shutters. The fragrant grounds are replete with a folkloric-painted watermill, grazing animals, and an exceedingly picturesque arbor. ■ TIP→ **Call in advance to check visiting hours as they can vary, sometimes dramatically.** ⊠ *Artgenti St. 9–11, Kambos* ☎ *22710/31513* ⊕ *www.citrus-chios.gr* ⊘ *Closed Mon.*

OFF THE BEATEN PATH

Nea Moni. Almost hidden among the olive groves, the island's most important monastery—with one of the finest examples of mosaic art anywhere—is the 11th-century Nea Moni. Byzantine emperor Constantine IX Monomachos ("the Dueler") ordered the monastery built where three monks found an icon of the Virgin Mary in a myrtle bush. The octagonal *katholikon* (medieval church) is the only surviving example of 11th-century court art—none survives in Constantinople. The monastery has been renovated a number of times: the dome was completely rebuilt following an earthquake in 1881, and a great deal of effort has gone into the restoration and preservation of the mosaics over the years. The distinctive three-part vaulted sanctuary has a double narthex, with no buttresses supporting the dome. This design, a single square space covered by a dome, is rarely seen in Greece. Blazing with color, the church's interior gleams with marble slabs and mosaics of Christ's life, austere yet sumptuous, with azure blue, ruby red, velvet green, and skillful applications of gold. The saints' expressiveness comes from their vigorous poses and severe gazes, with heavy shadows under the eyes. On the iconostasis hangs the icon—a small Virgin and Child facing

left. Also inside the grounds are an ancient refectory, a vaulted cistern, a chapel filled with victims' bones from the massacre at Chios, and a large clock still keeping Byzantine time, with the sunrise reckoned as 12 o'clock. ✉ *Nea Moni ✢ In mountains 17 km (10½ miles) west of Chios Town, beyond Karies* ☎ *22710/79391* ⊕ *www.neamoni.gr* ✑ *Donations accepted* ⊙ *Closed Mon. and early afternoon.*

Fodor's Choice
★
Old Quarter. An air of mystery pervades this old Muslim and Jewish neighborhood, full of decaying monuments, fountains, baths, and mosques, within the walls of the **Kastro** (castle) fortifications, built in the 10th century by the Byzantines and enlarged in the 14th century by the Genoese Giustiniani family. Under Turkish rule, the Greeks lived outside the wall, and the gates closed daily at sundown. A deep dry moat remains on the western side. Note the old wood-and-plaster houses on the narrow backstreets, typically decorated with latticework and jutting balconies. Scattered among the precinct are several stone towers and, inside the old gate, the cells where the Turks jailed then hanged 75 leading Chiotes during the fight for independence in 1822, when Chios joined the rest of Greece in rebellion against occupying Turks. The revolt here on the island failed, and the sultan retaliated: the Turks killed 30,000 Chiotes and enslaved 45,000, an event written about by Victor Hugo and depicted by Eugène Delacroix in *The Massacre of Chios*. The painting, now in the Louvre, shocked Western Europe and increased support for Greek independence. Copies hang in many places on Chios. In the quarter's Frouriou Square, look for the Turkish cemetery and the large marble tomb (with the fringed hat) of Kara Ali, chief of the Turkish flagship in 1822. ✉ *Chios Town ✢ Northern end of port.*

WORTH NOTING

Bazaar District. The capital is crowded with half the island's population, and the heart of Chios life is this sprawling district behind the port. Merchants hawk everything from local mastic gum and fresh dark bread to kitchen utensils in the morning, but most stalls close in the afternoon. ✉ *Chios Town ✢ South and east of Vounakiou Sq. (the main square).*

Chios Maritime Museum. Livanos, Karas, Chandris, Onassis: many of the world-famous shipping families were based or born on Chios. Exquisite ship models and portraits of vessels that have belonged to Chios owners over time celebrate the sea-based heritage of the island. One exhibit highlights the Liberty ships and others constructed during World War II that contributed to Greece's booming postwar shipping industry. ✉ *Stefanou Tsouri 20* ☎ *22710/44139* ⊕ *www.chiosnauticalmuseum.gr* ✑ *€2.50* ⊙ *Closed afternoons and Sun. (except Sun. in Aug.).*

OFF THE
BEATEN
PATH
Daskalopetra (*Teacher's Rock*). This rocky outcropping, where Homer is said to have taught his pupils, stands just above the port of Vrontados, 4 km (2½ miles) north of Chios Town. Archaeologists think an ancient altar to Cybele once stood on the rock; you can sit on it and muse about how the blind storyteller might have spoken here of the fall of Troy in *The Iliad.* ✉ *Vrontados.*

Giustiniani Museum. A 15th-century palace of the Genoese, who ruled Chios until the Turks drove them out in 1566, is one of the most venerable landmarks on the island, with a loggia and external staircase.

9

Inside are some glorious Byzantine murals of the prophets from the 13th century, as well as icons and sculptures. ✉ *Kalothetou* ✥ *At the eastern edge of the Old Quarter* ☎ *22710/22819* 🎟 €2 🕒 *Closed Mon.*

Fodor's Choice ★ **Kambos District.** In medieval times and later, wealthy Genoese and Greek merchants built ornate, earth-colored, three-story mansions on this fertile plain of tangerine, lemon, and orange groves south of Chios Town. On narrow lanes behind stone walls adorned with coats of arms, each estate is a world of its own, with multicolored sandstone patterns, arched doorways, and pebble-mosaic courtyards. Some houses have crumbled, but many still stand, surrounded by fragrant citrus groves and reminders of the wealth, power, and eventual downfall of an earlier time. These suburbs of Chios Town are exceptional, but the unmarked lanes can be confusing, so leave time to get lost and to peek behind the walls into another world. ✥ *4 km (2½ miles) south of Chios Town.*

Philip Argenti Museum. The second floor above the impressive Korais Library, Greece's third largest, houses artifacts celebrating life on Chios. Meticulously designed costumes, embroideries, pastoral wood carvings, furniture of a village home, and rare books and prints are the legacy of Philip Argenti (1891–1974), a Renaissance man who studied at Oxford, was a diplomat and scholar, and for many years chronicled island history from his estate in Kambos. ✉ *Korais 2* ✥ *Near the cathedral* ☎ *22710/44246* 🌐 *www.koraeslibrary.gr* 🎟 €2 🕒 *Closed Sun.*

BEACHES

Karfas Beach. This popular and often-crowded beach fronts a shallow bay, and its golden brown sands and warm waters make it a good spot for young families. Many tavernas and hotels geared to package tours line the overbuilt shoreline, and in summer there's transportation to and from town. **Amenities:** food and drink; showers; toilets; water sports; parking (no fee). **Best for:** snorkeling; sunrise; swimming. ✥ *8 km (5 miles) south of Chios Town.*

WHERE TO EAT

$ MEDITERRANEAN 🍴 **Bakses** (*O Mpakses*). Stepping into the garden or intimate rooms of this traditional farmhouse is quite an experience, because you'll feel like you've been invited into a private home. The simple and traditional Greek and Mediterranean dishes, including moussaka and hearty braised beef in a rich tomato sauce, do nothing to dispel the notion. **Known for:** pretty, flower-filled garden; light Mediterranean fair; intimate, homelike surroundings. [$] *Average main: €12* ✉ *Kalvokoresi 80* ☎ *697/202–7947* 🕒 *Closed Mon. and Tues. No lunch Wed.–Fri.*

$ GREEK Fodor's Choice ★ 🍴 **O Hotzas.** Family portraits and brass implements hang below a wood-beam ceiling at this spacious taverna that shows off its 19th-century origins. In addition to deep-fried dishes, there's also succulent lamb with lemon sauce and several vegetable choices. **Known for:** old-world atmosphere; delicious home-style cooking; squid. [$] *Average main: €8* ✉ *Yioryiou Kondili 3* ☎ *22710/42787* 🕒 *Closed Sun. and Mon. No lunch.*

$ GREEK FAMILY 🍴 **Taverna tou Tassou.** Dependably delicious traditional food is why so many locals eat here in a garden courtyard beneath a canopy of trees. Fresh fish and seafood, lamb chops and other meats, stuffed

The spectacular north coast of Samos is lined with beautiful beaches, including Lemonakia. Though the beach itself is more pebbles than sand, the water has a gorgeous blue-green hue.

peppers and cooked greens—you can't go wrong with the home-style cooking and friendly welcome from Dimitrius Doulos and his son, who is the chef. **Known for:** friendly atmosphere; traditional Greek dishes. $ *Average main: €8* ⊠ *Livanou 8* ⊹ *South side of town* ☎ *22710/27542* ⊘ *Closed Nov.*

WHERE TO STAY

$ ⛲ **Chios Chandris.** A perch on a point of land between the harbor and
HOTEL open sea comes with endless sea views, enjoyed from the balconies that open off each of the generic but airy and bright guest rooms done in shades of Aegean blue and yellow. **Pros:** quiet edge-of-town setting not too far from the center; pool (albeit a small one); magnificent views. **Cons:** a bit worn; rooms and public areas have little character; overall maintenance not what it could be. $ *Rooms from: €120* ⊠ *2nd Eugenia's Chandris St.* ⊹ *Between the port and beach* ☎ *22710/44401* ⊕ *www.chandris.gr* ⇨ *139 rooms* ⓘⓄⓘ *Breakfast.*

$ ⛲ **Chios Rooms.** A 19th-century neoclassical building on the waterfront
B&B/INN at the southern edge of town holds simple but character-filled rooms that are a welcome throwback to the days of old-fashioned pensions and come with the homey presence of hosts Don and Dina. **Pros:** very friendly, advice-dispensing management makes you feel right at home; rooms open to balconies or terrace; use of communal kitchen. **Cons:** some street noise out front; not all baths are en suite; no credit cards accepted. $ *Rooms from: €40* ⊠ *Leoforos Aigaiou 110* ☎ *22710/20198* ⊕ *www.chiosrooms.com* ⊟ *No credit cards* ⇨ *10 rooms* ⓘⓄⓘ *No meals.*

$ **Grecian Castle Hotel.** With warmly appointed guest rooms, a pretty
HOTEL   pool, and carefully landscaped grounds, this sophisticated retreat sets a
Fodor'sChoice   high standard for Chios, as you'll see once you pass the impressive stone
★   gateway and head up a regal, tree-lined lane into an enclave that subtly
evokes a medieval castle. **Pros:** urbane ambience; professional service;
lovely grounds and pool. **Cons:** a few dark and not-so-spacious rooms;
beach across the road is not appealing; somewhat out-of-the-way location. **$** *Rooms from: €120 ⊠ Leoforos Enosseos ✛ 1 km (½ mile) south
of town toward the airport ☎ 22710/44740 ⊕ www.greciancastle.gr
↘ 55 rooms ⦿l Breakfast.*

$ **Kyma Hotel.** A neoclassical villa that was once the headquarters of
HOTEL   Nikolaos Plastiras, a general in the 1920s conflicts with Turkey who
later became prime minister, is these days a welcoming and character-
filled waterside inn that's both quirky and comfortable. **Pros:** friendly,
professional staff; good waterside location with great sea views;
character-filled salons and guest rooms. **Cons:** not all rooms have
a sea view; some bathrooms are small; some renovation is in order.
$ *Rooms from: €80 ⊠ Chandris 1 ☎ 22710/44500 ⊕ hotelkyma.com
↘ 59 rooms ⦿l Breakfast.*

$ **Perleas Mansion.** Guests soon feel like aristocrats from a lost era on
B&B/INN   the 16th-century Kambos neighborhood estate of Genoese merchants,
Fodor'sChoice   where their lovely mansion of rough-hewn stone is surrounded by gar-
★   dens fragrant with orange blossoms. **Pros:** utterly delightful surroundings; the real deal when it comes to living like gentry; fresh orange juice
and homemade citrus preserves at breakfast. **Cons:** 10-minute drive
from nearest beach; old-fashioned charm might not appeal to those
looking for modern luxuries; no pool, but a lily pond is most soothing. **$** *Rooms from: €120 ⊠ Vitiadou St. ✛ 4 km (2½ miles) south
of Chios Town ☎ 22710/32217, 22710/32962 ⊕ www.perleas.gr ↘ 7
rooms ⦿l Breakfast.*

NIGHTLIFE

Design-centered nightspots along the harbor are trendier than those on
most of the other Northern Aegean islands, and many of the clubs are
filled with well-off young tourists and locals. You can just walk along,
listen to the music, and size up the crowd; most clubs are open to the
harbor and dramatically lighted.

Cosmo. This inviting cocktail lounge plays international and Greek
music. ⊠ *Aigaiou 100 ☎ 22710/81695.*

Kronos Ice Cream Parlor. A favorite stop on an evening stroll is this spiffy
shop that has been making its best-selling praline ice cream since 1930.
It's open from early morning well into the wee hours. ⊠ *Philipos Argenti
2 ☎ 22710/82982 ⊕ www.pagotakronos.gr.*

Metropolis Lounge Cafe Bar. Stop by for cold coffee and chill music during
the day, then return at night for exotic mixed spirits and high-tempo
beats. ⊠ *Aegaeou 92 ☎ 22710/43883.*

Odyssey Wine Bar. Accompanying the generous wine list is the occasional
live blues and jazz night as well as avant-garde Greek music performed
by local talent. ⊠ *Aigaiou 102 ☎ 22710/20585.*

SHOPPING

The resinous gum made from the sap of the mastic tree is a best buy in Chios. It makes a fun and notoriously healthy souvenir and conversation piece; the brand is Elma. You can also find mastic (digestif) liqueur called *mastiha,* and *gliko koutaliou,* sugar-preserved fruit served in small portions with a spoon. Stores are typically closed Sunday, and open mornings only on Monday, Wednesday, and Saturday.

Mastic Spa. At the elegant outlet of this local business with an international outreach, all the beauty and health products contain the local balm. ⊠ *Agoiu 84* ⚓ *On the waterfront* ☎ *22710/33101.*

Moutafis. Try this place for its fine array of mastiha, fruit preserves, and other sweets and spirits. ⊠ *Venizelou Eleftheriou 7* ☎ *22710/25330.*

Zaharoplasteion Avgoustakis. This traditional candy store specializes in *masourakia* (crispy rolled pastries dripping in syrup and nuts) and *rodinia* (melt-in-your-mouth cookies stuffed with almond cream). ⊠ *Psychari 4* ☎ *22710/44480.*

VOLISSOS ΒΟΛΙΣΣΟΣ

42 km (26 miles) northwest of Chios Town.

Homer's birthplace is thought to be here at Volissos, though Smyrna, Colophon, Salamis, Rhodes, Argos, and Athens also claim this honor. Once a bustling market town, this pretty village is today half empty, with only a few hundred inhabitants. There are few services for tourists, save a casual restaurant here and there in the village and on the beach. Solid stone houses march up the mountainside to the Genoese fort, where Byzantine nobles were once exiled. Atop the hill is the place for sunset lovers.

BEACHES

Limia. Some of the best beaches on the island are in the vicinity, including Limia, with calm, turquoise waters. **Amenities:** none. **Best for:** snorkeling; solitude; sunset; swimming. ⊠ *Volissos* ⚓ *2 km (1 mile) south of Volissos.*

PIRGI ΠΥΡΓΙ

25 km (15½ miles) south of Nea Moni, 25 km (15 miles) south of Chios Town.

Beginning in the 14th century, the Genoese founded 20 or so fortified inland villages in southern Chios. These villages shared a defensive design with double-thick walls, a maze of narrow streets, and a square tower, or *pyrgos,* in the middle—a last resort to hold the residents in case of pirate attack. The villages prospered on the sales of mastic gum and were spared by the Turks because of the industry. Today they depend on mastic production, unique to the island—and tourists.

Pirgi is the largest of these mastic villages, and aesthetically, the most wondrous. It could be a graphic designer's model or a set of a mad moviemaker. Many of the buildings along the tiny arched streets are adorned with *xysta* (like Italian *sgraffito*); they are coated with a mix of cement and volcanic sand from nearby beaches, then whitewashed and stenciled, often top to bottom, in patterns of animals, flowers, and geometric designs. The effect is both delicate and dazzling. This exuberant village has more than 50 churches.

EXPLORING

Armolia. In the small mastic village of Armolia, 5 km (3 miles) north of Pirgi, pottery is a specialty. In fact, the Greek word *armolousis* ("man from Armola") is synonymous with potter. To the west, above the village, there is an impressive Byzantine castle that was built in 1446, and to the east is the wonderful 18th-century baroque-styled Vrettou Monastry. ✉ *Armolia.*

Ayioi Apostoli (*Holy Apostles*). The fresco-embellished 12th-century church Ayioi Apostoli is a very small replica of the *katholikon,* or major church, at the Nea Moni Monastery. Cretan artist Antonios Domestichos created the 17th-century frescoes that completely cover the interior, and they have a distinct folk-art leaning. ✉ *Pirgi* ✣ *Northwest of main square* ⏲ *Closed Mon.*

FAMILY Fodor's Choice ★ **The Chios Mastic Museum.** The mastic shrub has dominated Chios life, economy, culture, and destiny for centuries, and its role is explained in depth in well-designed exhibits in a stunning glass, stone, and wood pavilion overlooking a wide sweep of mastic groves. Aside from learning about how the valuable resin is cultivated and processed, you'll see artifacts and photographs of village life and learn about the island's tumultuous history, including times when hoarding even a sliver of mastic gum was a crime punishable by death. ✉ *Pirgi* ✣ *3 km (2 miles) south of Pirgi off Pirgi–Emborio road* ☎ *22710/72212* 🎟 *€3* ⏲ *Closed Tues.*

Kimisis tis Theotokou (*Dormition of the Virgin Church*). This towering church just off the main square was built in 1694 and is embellished with a lavishly decorated portico. ✉ *Pirgi* ✣ *Off main square.*

BEACHES

Fodor's Choice ★ **Mavra Volia** (*Black Pebbles*). This glittering volcanic black-pebbled beach is just next to the attractive seaside village of Emborio, where the waterfront is lined with tavernas serving seafood. The cove comprises three beaches, which are backed by jutting volcanic cliffs and fronted by calm dark-blue water colored by the deeply tinted seabed. Here, perhaps, was an inspiration for the "wine-dark sea" that Homer wrote about. **Amenities:** parking (no fee). **Best for:** solitude; sunrise; swimming; walking. ✉ *Emborio* ✣ *8 km (5 miles) southeast of Pirgi.*

WHERE TO STAY

$ HOTEL 🏨 **Emporios Bay.** The closest thing Chios has to a a fancy resort is this attractive white enclave of airy and comfortable accommodations clustered around gardens and a sparkling pool at the back of a south-coast seaside village near Pirgi. **Pros:** attractive rooms and pool terrace; chance to experience village life; near the beach and southern sights. **Cons:** a bit large and generic for the village setting; some tour groups; not right on the seafront. [$] *Rooms from: €65* ✉ *Emborio* ✣ *Behind the waterfront* ☎ *22710/70180* 🌐 *www.emporiosbay.gr* 🛏 *40 rooms* 🍴 *Breakfast.*

SHOPPING

Lagini. At this ceramics studio and shop in the outlying village of Armolia, you can see the potter ply her trade, as well as buy the traditional handmade pottery. ✉ *Armolia–Pirgi road, Armolia ✣ 5 km (3 miles) north of Pirgi* ☎ *22710/72634.*

MESTA ΜΕΣΤΑ

11 km (7 miles) west of Pirgi, 30 km (18½ miles) southwest of Chios Town.

Fodor's Choice ★ Pirgi may be the most unusual of the mastic villages, but Mesta is the island's best preserved: a labyrinth of twisting vaulted streets links two-story stone-and-mortar houses that are supported by buttresses against earthquakes. The enchanted village sits inside a system of 3-foot-thick walls, and the outer row of houses also doubles as protection. In fact, the village homes were built next to each other to form a castle, reinforced with towers. Most of the narrow streets, free of cars and motorbikes, lead to blind alleys; the rest lead to the six gates. The one in the northeast retains an iron grate. Artists and craftspeople are attracted to the town, so you'll unearth art galleries and craft boutiques with a little hunting.

EXPLORING

Megas Taxiarchis (*Great Archangel*). The 19th-century church that commands the main square of Mesta (and one of two churches of the same name in the town) is one of the wealthiest in Greece; its vernacular baroque is combined with the late-folk-art style of Chios. The church was built on the ruins of the central refuge tower. **■ TIP→ If the church is closed, ask at the square and someone may come and open up for you.** ✉ *Main square.*

BEACHES

Escape to the string of secluded coves, between Elatas and Trahiliou bays, for good swimming.

Apothika. This remote spot, at the end of a well-marked road that leads southeast toward the coast from Mesta, is one of the best beaches on Chios. The clear waters lap against the sand and pebbles that make up this small stretch of coast. A canteen looks down upon the unspoiled beach. **Amenities:** food and drink; parking (no fee); showers; toilets; water sports. **Best for:** snorkeling; solitude; sunset; swimming; walking; windsurfing. ✉ *Mesta ✣ On marked road that leads from the north end of Mesta.*

WHERE TO EAT

$ SEAFOOD 🍴 **Limani Meston.** The fishing boats bobbing in the water only a few feet away supply the kitchen with a rich daily fish selection. The friendly, gracious owner may well persuade you to munch on some of his smaller catches, such as sardines served with onions and pita, accompanied by calamari and cheese balls. **Known for:** fresh seafood; harbor views; cozy wintertime ambience. [$] *Average main: €8* ✉ *Limenas ✣ 3 km (2 miles) north of Mesta village* ☎ *22710/76389* 💳 *No credit cards.*

$ ✕**O Mesaonas.** A traditional Greek kitchen turns out delicious food
GREEK served on outdoor tables in the small village square, adjacent to Megas
Taxiarchis. You dine surrounded by medieval homes and magical lights
at night, but the setting is lovely even for a daytime coffee and relaxed
conversation. **Known for:** traditional cooking; village square setting.
Ⓢ *Average main: €8* ⊠ *Main square* ☎ *22710/76050.*

WHERE TO STAY

$ ▦ **Lida Mary Hotel.** A lovingly restored complex set in mazelike village
HOTEL lanes stylishly combines modern luxuries and a mysterious medieval
Fodor'sChoice atmosphere with vaulted ceilings and thick stone walls. **Pros:** memora-
★ bly unique experience; exciting, tasteful, and welcoming surroundings;
chance to experience village like a resident. **Cons:** some steps; a walk
over cobbles to reach; some rooms are a bit dark. Ⓢ *Rooms from: €78*
⊠ *Mesta* ☎ *22710/76217* ⊕ *www.lidamary.gr* ⇨ *8 rooms* ⏍ *Breakfast.*

NIGHTLIFE

Maona. The nightlife at Mesta is not exactly rocking, but this café and
bar offers some relief to the restless souls who want to extend their
evening. ⊠ *Main square* ☎ *22710/76004.*

SPORTS AND THE OUTDOORS

FAMILY **Masticulture.** The ecotourist specialists on Chios lead all kinds of tours.
Fodor'sChoice Trek through the mastic tree groves, where local farmers show you
★ how they gather mastic through grooves carved into the trees' bark.
Learn how wine, *souma* (a type of ouzo made from distilled figs), and
olive oil are produced, and go on fascinating custom-designed walks
discovering the unique flora and fauna of Chios. Go kayaking or sailing. Greek cooking courses are also available, which focus on seasonal
foods in accordance with the Mediterranean diet. Check the website for
dates, times, and prices. ⊠ *Off main square* ☎ *22710/76084* ⊕ *www.
masticulture.com.*

Tortuga Diving School. Based at the stunning beach of Apothika, Tortuga
offers scuba-diving excursions, free-diving and snorkeling courses, sea
kayak rentals, and a snack bar. ⊠ *Apothika Beach* ☎ *69/74725459
mobile* ⊕ *tortuga.gr.*

SAMOS ΣΑΜΟΣ

The southernmost of this group of three Northern Aegean islands lies
the closest to Turkey of any Greek island, separated by only 3 km (2
miles). Samos was, in fact, a part of Asia Minor until it split off during
the Ice Age. Samos means "high" in Phoenician, and the abrupt volcanic
mountains soaring dramatically like huge hunched shoulders from the
rock surface of the island are among the tallest in the Aegean, geologically part of the great spur that runs across western Turkey. As you
approach from the west, Mt. Kerkis seems to spin out of the sea, and
in the distance Mt. Ambelos guards the terraced vineyards that produce
the famous Samian wine. The felicitous landscape has surprising twists,
with lacy coasts and mountain villages perched on ravines carpeted in
pink oleander, red poppy, and purple sage.

When Athens was young, in the 7th century BC, Samos was already a political, economic, and naval power. In the next century, during Polycrates's reign, it was noted for its arts and sciences and was the expanded site of the vast Temple of Hera, one of the Seven Wonders of the Ancient World. The Persian Wars led to the decline of Samos, however, which fell first under Persian rule, and then became subordinate to the expanding power of Athens. Samos was defeated by Pericles in 439 BC and forced to pay tribute to Athens.

Pirates controlled this deserted island after the fall of the Byzantine Empire, but in 1562 an Ottoman admiral repopulated Samos with expatriates and Orthodox believers. The island languished under the sun until tobacco and shipping revived the economy in the 19th century.

Small though it may be, Samos has a formidable list of great citizens stretching through the ages. The fabled Aesop, the philosopher Epicurus, and Aristarchos (first in history to place the sun at the center of the solar system) all lived on Samos. The mathematician Pythagoras was born in Samos's ancient capital in 580 BC; in his honor, the town was renamed Pythagorio in AD 1955 (it only took a couple of millennia). Plutarch wrote that in Roman times Anthony and Cleopatra took a long holiday on Samos, "giving themselves over to the feasting," and that artists came from afar to entertain them.

Since the late 1990s Samos has become popular with European package tourists, particularly in July and August. The curving terrain allows you to escape the crowds easily and feel as if you are still in an undiscovered Eden.

GETTING HERE AND AROUND

Olympic and Aegean airways operate four flights daily between Athens and Samos (55 minutes, €69 to €121). Astra Airlines has daily flights to Samos from Thessaloniki (1 hour, €40 to €90). The Samos airport is 3 km (2 miles) from Pythagorio; taxis from the airport cost €20 to Vathi (the main town, also known as Samos) or €15 to Pythagorio.

The main port of Samos is Vathi. Ferries from the Piraeus and the Cyclades usually stop at both Samos Town (Vathi) and Karlovassi (Samos's second port). During high season, there are usually seven weekly ferries from Pireaus (8 hours, €38); two to Chios (4 hours, €12); three to Mykonos (5½ hours, €48), with transfers available for Santorini and Naxos. Ferries arrive and depart from a facility directly across the harbor from the Vathi waterfront and *not* the docks right in town. There is usually a service most days to Patmos from Pythagorio.

BUS TRAVEL ON SAMOS

Samos has reliable bus service, with frequent trips (as many as eight daily) between Pythagorio, Samos Town (Vathi), and Kokkari. The island's main bus station is at Ioannou Lekati and Kanari in central Samos Town. Fares range from €1.50 to €3. Taxis can be hailed on Platia Pythagora.

TOURS

Pure Samos. "Don't just visit—experience!" That's what this travel agency, created by locals, lets visitors to Samos do, thanks to their wide array of experiential vacations: from yoga workshops to wine tours, from horseback-riding to spear-fishing and scuba diving, visitors can experience a memorable tailor-made holiday (which can include unique accommodations such as country cottages). ⊠ *Iras 2, Pythagorio* ☎ *22730/62760, 69/3874–4978* ⊕ *www.puresamos.gr.*

SAMOS TOWN ΣΑΜΟΣ ΠΟΛΗ

278 km (174 miles) east of Piraeus, 111 km (69 miles) southeast of Mytilini.

Also known as Vathi, the capital is tucked into the head of a sharply deep bay on the northeast coast. Red-tile roofs sweep around the arc of the bay and reach toward the top of red-earth hills. In the morning at the sheltered port, fishermen grapple with their nets, spreading them to dry in the sun, and in the early afternoon everything shuts down. Slow summer sunsets over the sparkling harbor match the relaxed pace of the town.

EXPLORING

Ano Vathi. In the quaint 17th-century old settlement just above the port, wood-and-plaster houses with pastel facades and red-tile roofs are clustered together, their balconies protruding over narrow cobbled paths. From here savor a beautiful view of the gulf. ⊠ *Samos Town* ✛ *Southern edge of Samos Town, beyond museum, to right.*

Fodor's Choice ★ **Archaeological Museum of Vathi of Samos.** Samian sculptures from past millennia were considered among the best in Greece, and examples here show why. The newest wing holds the impressive **kouros from Heraion,** a colossal statue of a male youth, built as an offering to the goddess Hera and the largest freestanding sculpture surviving from ancient Greece, dating from 580 BC. The work of a Samian artist, this statue was made of the typical Samian gray-and-white-band marble. Pieces of the kouros were discovered in various peculiar locations: its thigh was being used as part of a Hellenistic house wall, and its left forearm was being used as a step for a Roman cistern. The statue is so large (16½ feet tall) that the gallery had to be rebuilt specifically to house it. The museum's older section has a collection of pottery and cast-bronze griffin heads (the symbol of Samos). An exceptional collection of tributary gifts from ancient cities far and wide, including bronzes and ivory miniatures, affirms the importance of the shrine to Hera. ⊠ *Dimarhiou Sq.* ☎ *22730/27469* ⊕ *www.culture.gr* ⊠ *€4* ☉ *Closed Mon.*

Museum of Samos Wines. Samos is famous for its (internationally awarded) wines, particularly its delectable *vin doux* liqueur or other sweet wines such as Nectar and Anthemis, and more recently its dry whites such as Phyllas, made with organic muscat grapes. All wines produced on Samos are by law made by the Union of Vinicultural Cooperatives, who created this museum on the winery's grounds in tribute to the island's wine-making past and present, and it's the best place to dive into the island's wine culture. Start by looking at the photo exhibition of local wine making over the last century and proceed to see the large and small tools used in production, as well as early-20th-century casks, and finally the French oak barrels used today. Then proceed to the main hall to indulge in a wine tasting of the union's wines, which are also sold at the museum shop. ⊠ *Malagari* ✛ *Opposite side of bay* *from port* ☎ *22730/87551* 🌐 *www.samoswine.gr* ⏲ *Closed some days in winter; call ahead.*

OFF THE BEATEN PATH

From Samos Town (as well as from Pythagorio and from Ormos Marathokambos), you can easily take a ferry to Turkey. Once you're there, it's a 13-km (8-mile) taxi or bus ride from the Kusadasi port on the Turkish coast, where the boats dock, to Ephesus, one of the great archaeological sites and a major city of the ancient world. (The Temple of Artemis in Ephesus is a copy of the Temple of Hera in Heraion, which now lies in ruins.) Many travel agencies have guided round-trip full-day tours to the site (about €120), although you can take an unguided ferry trip for about €55 with same-day return.

BEACHES

Kerveli Bay. Calm, turquoise waters wash onto this beach of sand and pebbles that is shaded by pine trees. Time here provides a quiet escape from the beaches near the more populated centers, and getting here involves riding into a pleasurable final stretch through some of the loveliest forested parts in eastern Samos. Tavernas on the beach dish out light summer salads, fresh seafood, and heartier *magirefta* (cooked dish) of the day, like *pastitsio* (a rich pasta bake). **Amenities:** food and drink; parking (no fee); showers; toilets. **Best for:** snorkeling; sunrise; swimming; walking. ✉ *Kerveli* ✥ *On the coast, 9 km (5½ miles) east of Samos Town.*

Psili Ammos. One of the island's more popular beaches is pristine and sandy, protected from the wind by cliffs. There are two tavernas here, and the beach can get extremely busy during high season. **Amenities:** food and drink; parking (no fee); showers; toilets. **Best for:** sunrise; swimming. ✥ *9½ km (6 miles) southeast of Samos Town, near Mesokambos.*

WHERE TO EAT

$ GREEK 🍴 **Ta Kotopoula.** Chicken is the star on the menu of this affordable grill restaurant, which serves simple yet delicious, seasonal dishes throughout the day in a laid-back atmosphere. Payment is by cash only. **Known for:** grilled meats; shady terrace; friendly gathering spot. [$] *Average main: €10* ✉ *Vlamaris and Mykalis Sts.* ☎ *22730/28415* 💳 *No credit cards.*

$ SEAFOOD 🍴 **Zen.** Sometimes it seems like everyone in town gathers at this friendly harborside spot, where the emphasis is on fresh seafood and traditional home cooking. Fresh, locally grown vegetables and Samos wines accompany the meals, which are served with care by the friendly staff. **Known for:** harbor views; nicely prepared dishes; friendly service. [$] *Average main: €10* ✉ *Kefalopoulou 6* ☎ *22730/80983.*

WHERE TO STAY

$ HOTEL 🏨 **Hotel Samos.** Simple but pleasant rooms are equipped with some nice amenities, including soundproof windows facing the harbor and a roof garden with a pool and hot tub. **Pros:** more luxurious than it may seem at first sight; roof garden and pool make this an in-town retreat; excellent value. **Cons:** no parking; could do with a touch-up; small bathrooms. [$] *Rooms from: €60* ✉ *Them. Soufouli 11* ☎ *22730/28377* 🌐 *www.samoshotel.gr* 🛏 *100 rooms* 🍽 *Breakfast.*

$ HOTEL 🏨 **Ino Village Hotel.** A tranquil setting on the outskirts of Vathi comes with a refreshing pool and nice views—enjoyed from many of the private balconies—of Samos Bay and the mountains beyond. **Pros:** some very nice rooms; pool provides a nice getaway; good dining. **Cons:** a 15-minute walk uphill from the town center (hotel will arrange transport); a car is almost necessary (parking is easy); some rooms are worn. $ *Rooms from: €75* ⊠ *Samos Town* ✢ *1 km (½ mile) north of Samos Town center* 🕾 *22730/23241* ⊕ *www.inovillagehotel.com* ⟿ *65 rooms* ❑ *Breakfast.*

NIGHTLIFE

Bars generally are open May to September from about 8 or 10 pm to 3 am.

Escape Music Club. The spacious patio just above the water is the place to party until the early hours. The music and dancing in this hip spot doesn't begin until 10 pm and lasts until 4 am. Friday is theme night and there are full-moon parties. ⊠ *Samos Town* ✢ *Past port police station, on main road out of town, near hospital* 🕾 *22730/28345.*

PYTHAGORIO ΠΥΘΑΓΟΡΕΙΟ

14 km (8½ miles) southwest of Samos Town.

Samos was a democratic state until 535 BC, when the town now called Pythagorio (formerly Tigani, or "frying pan") fell to the tyrant Polycrates (540–22 BC). Polycrates used his fleet of 100 ships to make profitable raids around the Aegean, until he was caught by the Persians and crucified in 522 BC. His rule produced what Herodotus described as "three of the greatest building and engineering feats in the Greek world." One is the Heraion, west of Pythagorio, the largest temple ever built in Greece and one of the Seven Wonders of the Ancient World. Another is the ancient mole protecting the harbor on the southeast coast, on which the present 1,400-foot jetty rests. The third is the Efpalinio tunnel, built to guarantee that water flowing from mountain streams would be available even to besieged Samians. Pythagorio remains a picturesque little port, with red-tile-roof houses and a curving harbor filled with fishing boats. There are more busy restaurants and cafés here than elsewhere on the island.

EXPLORING

Archaeological Museum of Pythagoreion. This tiny but impressive collection shows off local finds, including headless statues, grave markers with epigrams to the dead, human and animal figurines, in addition to some notably beautiful portrait busts of the Roman emperors Claudius, Caesar, and Augustus. ⊠ *Pythagora Sq., in the municipal building* 🕾 *22730/62811* ⊕ *www.culture.gr* 🖾 *€4* ⊘ *Closed Mon.*

Kastro *(castle, or fortress).* At the eastern corner of Pythagorio lie the crumbling ruins of the Kastro, probably built on top of the ruins of the Acropolis. Revolutionary hero Lykourgou Logotheti built this 19th-century edifice; his statue is next door, in the **courtyard** of the church built to honor the victory. He held back the Turks on Transfiguration Day, and a sign on the church announces in Greek: "Christ saved Samos 6 August 1824." On some nights the villagers light votive candles in the church cemetery, a moving sight with the ghostly silhouette of the fortress and the moonlit sea in the background. Nearby are some fragments of the wall that the ruler Polycrates built in the 6th century BC. ⊠ *Pythagorio.*

Panayia Spiliani Church. Enter this spacious cave and descend 95 steps to the tiny church of Panayia Spiliani (Virgin of the Grotto). Half-church, half-cavern, this most unique landmark is also called *Kaliarmenissa* ("for good travels"), as it houses an antique icon of the Virgin Mary that, according to legend, was stolen from Samos, carried to a far-off land, and fell from a boat and broke into pieces, all of which washed ashore on Samos. A pool in the grotto, once the sanctuary of a Roman cult, is considered to contain miracle-working water. ⊠ *Pythagorio* ⊹ *Above the village, near the Roman theater.*

To Efpalinio Hydragogeio (*Tunnel of Eupalinos*). Considered by Herodotus as the world's Eighth Wonder, this famed underground aqueduct was completed in 524 BC with archaic tools and without measuring instruments. The ruler Polycrates, not a man who liked to leave himself vulnerable, ordered the construction of the tunnel to ensure that Samos's water supply could never be cut off during an attack. Efpalinos of Megara, a hydraulics engineer, set perhaps 1,000 slaves into two teams, one digging on each side of Mt. Kastri. Fifteen years later, they met in the middle with just a tiny difference in the elevation between the two halves. The tunnel is about 3,340 feet long, and it remained in use as an aqueduct for almost 1,000 years. More than a mile of (long-gone) ceramic water pipe once filled the space, which was later used as a hiding place during pirate raids. Today the tunnel is exclusively a tourist attraction, and though some spaces are tight and slippery, you can walk part of the length—also a wonderful way to enjoy natural coolness on swelteringly hot days. Though the tunnel has been closed for necessary engineering work, a partial opening is set for 2018. At some point, with ongoing work, it will be possible to traverse the tunnel in its entirety. On a hillside above the tunnel entrance are the scant remains of a Greek and Roman theater, and a wooden platform over the shell is occasionally used for performances. ⊠ *Pythagorio* ⊹ *Just north of town* ☎ *22730/62811* ☜ *€4* ☉ *Closed Mon.*

WHERE TO EAT

$ | **✕ Elia.** A standout among the affable places along the harbor front is a little more sophisticated than its neighbors in its surroundings and, with a Swedish chef, offers a refreshingly eclectic take on Greek cuisine, with a big nod to local flavors. Prawns are sautéed in ouzo; chicken is stuffed with spinach, feta, and topped with a tarragon sauce; and the pork is cooked with Samos wine. **Known for:** innovative takes on Greek cuisine; pleasant waterside terrace. $ *Average main: €12* ⊠ *Pythagorio* ⊹ *Harbor front* ☎ *22730/61436* ⊕ *eliarestaurant-samos.gr.*

MODERN GREEK

$ | **✕ Maritsa.** A regular Pythagorio clientele frequents this simple fish taverna in a garden courtyard on a quiet, tree-lined side street. You might try the shrimp souvlaki or squid garnished with garlicky *skordalia* (a thick lemony sauce with pureed potatoes, vinegar, and parsley), though the kitchen also does justice to lamb on the spit. **Known for:** fresh seafood; nice garden. $ *Average main: €12* ⊠ *Pythagorio* ⊹ *Off Lykourgou Logotheti, one block from waterfront* ☎ *22730/61957.*

GREEK

9

WHERE TO STAY

$$ RESORT FAMILY 🏨 **Doryssa Bay Hotel-Village.** A "stage set" of traditional Samian houses surrounds a rusticated main square, while beachfront accommodations are in the gigantic and plush main block; guest rooms in both are filled with elegant contemporary furnishings. **Pros:** good for families; lots of amenities; great beach (but there's a charge for sun beds!). **Cons:** lots of tour groups in summer; next to the airport with associated noise; seems to be a world removed from the real Greece. [$] *Rooms from: €170* ✉ *Pythagorio Beach* ✣ *Near the airport road* ☎ *22730/88300, 22730/88400* 🌐 *www.doryssa-bay.gr* 🕒 *Closed Nov.–Mar.* 🛏 *302 rooms* 🍴 *Breakfast.*

$ HOTEL 🏨 **Fito Bay Hotel.** White bungalows glistening with terra-cotta roofs stand along winding paths lined with roses and lavender next to a sparkling pool, making it easy to settle into this friendly enclave just steps from Pythagorio Beach. **Pros:** close to beach and town; nice pool area; beautifully kept grounds. **Cons:** at end of airport runway; no sea view; no-frills rooms. [$] *Rooms from: €65* ✉ *Pythagorio Beach* ✣ *On the road to the airport* ☎ *22730/61314* 🌐 *www.fitobay.gr* 🕒 *Closed Oct.–Apr.* 🛏 *88 rooms* 🍴 *Breakfast.*

$$ RESORT FAMILY Fodor's Choice ★ 🏨 **Proteas Blu Resort.** Fresh, contemporary bungalows climb through Mediterranean gardens from a gorgeous pool and a beautiful, secluded beach, while airy, pastel-hued guest quarters, some with their own plunge pools, look out to sparkling sea views and purple-hued Turkish mountains from their balconies. **Pros:** great place for quiet and pampered stay; excellent meals with professional service; beautiful beach. **Cons:** not all rooms have sea views; intimate but still somewhat generic; a drive outside town. [$] *Rooms from: €220* ✉ *Pythagorio Rd.* ☎ *22730/62200* 🌐 *www.proteasbluresort.gr* 🕒 *Closed Oct.–mid-May* 🛏 *92 rooms* 🍴 *Breakfast.*

NIGHTLIFE

Beyond. Owner Mike makes his casual but sophisticated lounge a showcase for his superb skill in crafting cocktails and elegant finger food. Try his tantalizing Beyond Basil Bliss—a play on a mojito that replaces mint with basil and rum with tequila—as you sit at the space-age white-and-neon bar or perch over the waterfront on the second-floor terrace. ✉ *Pythagorio* ✣ *In the middle of Pythagorio's seaside promenade* ☎ *69/9416–3663* 🌐 *beyondsamos.com.*

SPORTS AND THE OUTDOORS

Samosail. Based in Pythagorio, this local yacht charter has a modern fleet of sailboats for rent for one- or two-week trips, with or without a captain. They can tailor trips to suit any needs. ✉ *Pythagorio* ☎ *22730/61739* 🌐 *www.samosail.com.*

IREO ΗΡΑΙΟ

6 km (4 miles) southwest of Pythagorio, 20 km (12½ miles) southwest of Samos Town.

Although Samos was a center for trade and commerce for a long time prior, it was Polycrates "the Tyrant" who really put the island on the map in the mid-6th century BC. The monumentality that he embarked on at the Heraion was a show to all—trader, pirate, ally, and would-be conqueror—that Samos's might under the watchful gaze of her Patron Goddess Hera was undisputable.

Heraion of Samos. The early Samians worshipped the goddess Hera, wife of Zeus, believing she was born here beneath a bush near the stream Imbrassos. Several temples were built on the site in her honor, the earliest dating back to the 8th century BC. Polycrates rebuilt the **To Hraio,** or Temple of Hera, around 540 BC, making it four times larger than the Parthenon and the largest Greek temple ever conceived, with two rows of columns (155 in all). The temple was damaged by fire in 525 BC and never completed, owing to Polycrates's untimely death. In the intervening years, masons recycled the stones to create other buildings, including a basilica (foundations remain at the site) to the Virgin Mary. Today you can only imagine the To Hraio's massive glory; of its forest of columns only one remains standing, slightly askew and only half its original height, amid acres of marble remnants in marshy ground thick with poppies.

At the ancient celebrations to honor Hera, the faithful approached from the sea along the **Sacred Road,** which is still visible at the site's northeast corner. Nearby are replicas of a 6th-century BC sculpture depicting an aristocratic family; its chiseled signature reads "Genelaos made me." The kouros from Heraion was found here, and now is in the Archaeological Museum in Samos Town. Hours may be shortened in winter. ✣ *11 km (7 miles) east of Pythagorio* ☎ *22730/62811* ⊕ *www.culture.gr* 🖃 *€3* ⊗ *Closed Mon.*

KOKKARI KOKKAPI

5 km (3 miles) southwest of Samos Town.

A spectacular stretch of coast road west of Samos Town is lined with olive groves and vineyards and ends in the fishing village of Kokkari, one of the most lively spots on the island during the summer. Until 1980, not much was here except for a few dozen houses between two headlands, and tracts of onion fields, which gave the town its name. Though now there are hotels and European tourists, you can still traipse along the rocky, windswept beach and spy fishermen mending trawling nets on the paved quay. Cross the spit to the eastern side of the headland and watch the moon rise over the lights of Vathi (Samos Town) in the next bay. East of Kokkari you pass by Malagari, the winery where farmers hawk their harvested grapes every September.

BEACHES

Acclaimed coves of the north coast are ringed with small pebbly beaches washed by gorgeous blue-green waters.

FAMILY **North Coast Beaches. Lemonakia, Tsamadou,** and **Tsabou** all are just a few minutes' drive from one another, forming a continuous string of sand and pebbles separated by pine-clad headlands. They're all delightful places to lounge and swim, and well supplied with sun beds and concessions. The stretch is to be avoided when the summertime *meltemi* (northern winds) blow, unless you're a windsurfer. **Amenities:** food and drink; parking (no fee); toilets; water sports.

9

Best for: swimming; walking; windsurfing. ⊠ *Kokkari ⊹ Northwest of Kokkari.*

WHERE TO EAT

$ ✕**Ammos Plaz.** What many locals consider to be the best traditional
GREEK   Greek food in Kokkari is served in an ideal location—smack on the beach. Expect the dishes to change daily, but you may find choices like lamb fricassee and stuffed calamari. **Known for:** beachfront setting; fresh seafood; octopus in sweet Samos wine and grilled lobster. $ *Average main: €12 ⊠ Kokkari Promenade* 🕾 *22730/92463* ⊗ *Closed Nov.–Mar.*

WHERE TO STAY

$ 🛏 **Armonia Bay Hotel.** Tucked away in pine trees above Tsamadou Beach,
HOTEL   this utterly delightful villa combines sophistication and informal style
Fodor'sChoice   and is one of the island's most special retreats, with beautiful gardens
★   and terraces, handsomely furnished guest rooms that open to balconies and lawns, and a sparkling pool, all overlooking the sea below. **Pros:** stylishly relaxing surroundings; excellent service and food; the aura of being in a private seaside villa. **Cons:** not right on the beach; will want a car for convenience; too hard to leave this paradise. $ *Rooms from: €100 ⊠ Kokkari ⊹ Off the coast road above Tsamadou Beach* 🕾 *22730/92583* ⊕ *www.armoniahotels.com* ⊗ *Closed Nov.–Apr.* ⇌ *24 rooms* ❙⊙❙ *Breakfast.*

$ 🛏 **Hotel Olympia Village.** Surrounded by big, flowery gardens, these
HOTEL   immaculate, attractive, and comfortably furnished apartments open
FAMILY   to wide verandas and seem a world removed from the beach scene just down the lane. **Pros:** large, well-appointed units; lovely garden hideaway; beach, shops, restaurants are just steps away. **Cons:** sea views are limited; some noise from other units; no pool. $ *Rooms from: €95 ⊠ Northwest beach road* 🕾 *22730/92420, 22730/92420* ⊕ *www.olympia-hotels.gr* ⊗ *Closed Nov.–Apr.* ⇌ *22 apartments* ❙⊙❙ *Breakfast.*

SPORTS AND THE OUTDOORS

FAMILY   **Kokkari Surf and Bike Center.** This professional and well-equipped windsurfing outfitter rents windsurfing equipment, sea kayaks, and mountain bikes during the summer months. They also provide windsurfing instruction for all, from absolute beginners to advanced freestyle levels, and run treks for hikers. ⊠ *Kokkari ⊹ On road to Lemonakia Beach* 🕾 *22730/92102* ⊕ *www.samoswindsurfing.gr.*

ATTICA AND DELPHI

WELCOME TO ATTICA AND DELPHI

TOP REASONS TO GO

★ **Delphi, "Navel of the World":** Delphi's Sanctuary of Apollo invites you to imagine a time of oracles, enigmatic prophecies, and mystical emanations.

★ **Sunset at Sounion:** Perched over the water, the spectacular Temple of Poseidon still summons strong emotions in this land of seafarers.

★ **Mighty Marathon:** Dare you retrace Pheidippides's first marathon when he ran 26 hilly miles from this town to Athens in 490 BC?

★ **Cape Vouliagmeni:** Enjoy a sun-kissed day on the beach at the heart of the eternally glamorous Athens Riviera.

★ **Naval Galaxidi:** The town the shipbuilders built back in the 18th century today oozes old-world charm and quaint character.

Attica, the southeastern tip of central Greece, is much more than the home of Athens—it is also a fertile land, with fabled temples and beautiful Byzantine monasteries. Bordered by three mountain masses—Mt. Hymettos to the east, Mt. Aigaleo and Mt. Parnitha to the west, and Mt. Pendeli to the north—Attica mainly lies east and north of the Athens basin. A tramline from downtown Athens to Glyfada allows travelers easy access to the famed Athens Riviera and the Apollo Coast, with its Temple of Sounion and luxurious resorts. Cradled in the mountains, the Delphi region is set around Mt. Parnassus and Arachova.

1 Attica. Head for the rolling hills (and a few mountains) for a welcome change from the capital's hectic pace. Explore the archaeological sites, beautiful beaches, small vineyards, riding clubs, serene monasteries, and hot nightlife at the seaside resorts of Glyfada and Vouliagmeni. Top sights here include

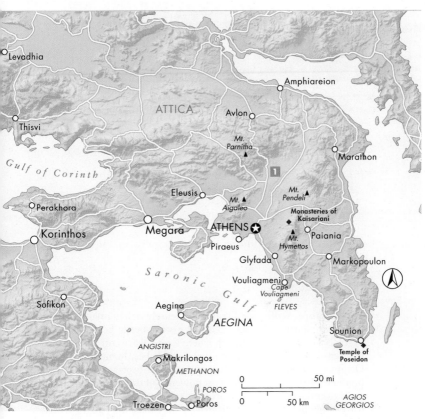

Levadhia

Amphiareion

ATTICA

Avlon

Thisvi

Mt.
Parnitha ▲

Marathon

Gulf of Corinth

Eleusis

Mt. ▲
Aigaleo

Mt.
Pendeli ▲

Monasteries of
Kaisariani ◆

Perakhora

Korinthos

Megara

ATHENS ✪

Paiania

Piraeus

Mt.
Hymettos ▲

Glyfada

Markopoulon

Saronic

Vouliagmeni
Cape
Vouliagmeni

Sofikon

Aegina

FLEVES

Gulf

AEGINA

Sounion

ANGISTRI

Makrilongos

Temple of
Poseidon

METHANON

0   50 mi

POROS

0   50 km

Troezen

Poros

AGIOS
GEORGIOS

10

ancient treasures like the Temple of Poseidon at Sounion, the Marathon Tomb, and Eleusis's Sanctuary of Demeter, plus the Byzantine monastery of Kaisariani and the trails of Mount Hymettos.

2 Delphi and Environs. Not far from Athens, Delphi's ancient rocks signal a time of ancient worship and secret ritual. Steeped in history, this region is today popular not only with tourists who flock to the sublime Sanctuary of Apollo, its renovated museum, and the nearby monastery of Osios Loukas, but also with

skiers, who have turned Arachova into the most cosmopolitan winter resort in the country.

Updated by Stephen Brewer

If anything was ever truly "classical," it is the landscape of Attica. Attikí is a mountainous region, bounded on three sides by the sea and an indented coastline fringed with innumerable beaches. On stony foothills pungently aromatic shrubs grow: thyme, myrtle, and lentisk. Higher up, the feathery Aleppo pine of Attica becomes supplanted by dark firs. Inland, gently undulating hills are laced with vineyards and, over all hangs the famed light, the purest of lights sharply delineating a majestic land.

It is the proper setting for a region immensely rich in mythological and historical allusions. In fact, recorded history began here, in the towns of the Boeotian plain, although where legend leaves off and fact begins is often a matter of conjecture (witness Thebes, home to the luckless Oedipus). Nevertheless, the story of Attica has been almost inextricably bound to that of Athens, the most powerful of the villages that lay scattered over the peninsula. By force and persuasion Athens brought these towns together, creating a unit that by the 5th century BC had become the center of an empire.

The heart of the region was the sacred precinct of Delphi. For the ancient Greeks, this site was the center of the universe, home to Apollo and the most sacred oracle, and, today, its archaeological site remains a principal place of pilgrimage.

For more worldly pleasures, travelers head to the sun-gilt sea bordering the Athens Riviera and the "Apollo Coast"—home to the famed Temple to Poseidon atop Cape Sounion.

PLANNING

WHEN TO GO

Athens's nightlife shifts to the southern coast in the summer, typically from July through August. Après-ski town Arachova is the place to be in winter (though expensive), but it's only a stepping stone to Delphi in summer. Attica's northeastern coast is beautiful anytime, though in winter things can feel dead. In Delphi, be prepared to go head-to-head with the crowds and the heat in summer. The beaches, of course, are most enjoyable in full summer, but even chic and pricey Astir Beach gets engulfed by a rising tide of tourists. A much better time to visit is April to June, when wildflowers carpet the arid hillsides of Attica and the Marathon plain. September and October is another beautiful stretch since the sea remains warm, with temperatures that are still ideal for swimming.

PLANNING YOUR TIME

A week in this region would allow plenty of time for exploring, letting you hit the major archaeological sites of Delphi and Sounion as well as traverse Marathon at less than breakneck speed. Short on time? In two to three days, you can explore Attica's coasts and visit a few key sites. The ancient Greeks believed Delphi was the center of the world, so you could do worse than making it the focus of a trip. With stunning mountain scenery, a world-famous archaeological site, and an excellent museum, touring Delphi can easily take up two days. (Note: Although it's possible to drive from Athens to Delphi and back in a day, we don't recommend it. A night in the crisp mountain air is a pleasant alternative to falling asleep behind the wheel.) If you do need to see Delphi in a day, however, be sure to leave Athens early (it's a three- to four-hour trip). A second day could be spent hiking around the mountain village of Arachova, or even skiing (in season). Or head to the pretty port town of Galaxidi.

GETTING HERE AND AROUND

Athens and Attica system buses (and trams) run from Athens's center to the southern and northeastern coast, and points from Marathon to Eleusis. Taking a bus to Arachova, Delphi, and Galaxidi may help you avoid road fatigue. Attica's public bus service is extensive, though buses can be infrequent; for ambitious exploring in the area, a car is invaluable. The roads to Arachova, Mt. Parnassus, and Galaxidi are decent, but include hairpin turns and can get icy in winter.

BUS TRAVEL

Places close to Athens can be reached with the blue city bus lines: Bus A16 from Koumoundourou Square for Daphni and Eleusina via Iera Odos; Bus A2, A3, or B3 from Syntagma Square for Glyfada; Bus A2 to Voula; Bus A2 to Glyfada, then connect with Bus 114, or 116 to Vouliagmeni. For detailed public transit information, call ☎ *11185* or go to ⊕ *www.oasa.gr*.

To reach other destinations, if you don't rent a car, the most efficient mode of travel is the regional KTEL bus system in combination with taxis. The extensive network serves all points in Attica from Athens, and local buses connect the smaller towns and villages. KTEL buses for eastern Attica leave hourly from their main station in downtown Athens (Aigyptou Square at the corner of Mavromateon and Leoforos Alexandras). KTEL buses depart regularly for Marathon, Ayia Marina (stopping at Rhamnous on the way), and Sounion. All these fares are inexpensive as these are all considered local routes.

The Greek National Tourism Organization (EOT) distributes a list of bus schedules, as does the Attica KTEL terminal in Aigyptou Square (☎ 21088/08000 ⊕ ktelattikis.gr). KTEL buses servicing Delphi, Arachova, Osios Loukas, and Galaxidi depart from Terminal B in Athens. To Delphi (via Arachova), there are four departures (eight on Friday and Sunday), beginning at 7:30 am. The journey takes about three hours. Three buses daily (four on Sunday) make the four-hour trip to Galaxidi, starting at 7:30 am. For more information on these journeys, call KTEL (☎ 22650/29900 ⊕ www.ktel-fokidas.gr). To get to Terminal B from downtown Athens, catch Bus 24 on Amalias in front of the National Garden. Tickets for these buses are sold only at this terminal. *For more detailed contact information, see Bus Travel in Travel Smart.*

CAR TRAVEL

Points in Attica and Delphi can be reached from the main Thessaloniki–Athens and Athens–Patras highways, with the National Road (Ethniki Odos) the most popular route, now connecting to the Athens ring road (Attiki Odos), which has a toll.

From the Peloponnese drive east via Corinth to Athens, or from Patras cross the Rio–Antirrio bridge to visit Delphi. Most roads off these highways are two-lane secondary arteries. Several of these—notably from Athens to Delphi and Itea and from Athens to Sounion—are spectacularly scenic.

Local and international car rental agencies have offices in downtown Athens—most are on Syngrou Avenue—as well as at the arrivals level at Eleftherios Venizelos Athens International Airport, in Spata.

TAXI TRAVEL

You will find "Piatsa" taxi ranks next to all the airports, and taxis will be lined up even late at night if there is a boat or flight coming in. On the other hand, your hotel can usually arrange a taxi for you, but if you need one in the wee hours of the morning make sure you book it in advance.

HOTELS

The standards are high at the hotels along Attica's much-traversed coast, and they fit roughly into three groups: those catering to families on a budget, those aimed at corporate travelers, and those servicing luxury lovers. It's no surprise why corporate moguls from all over the world often rent over-the-top bungalows at some of these resorts for the whole season, with their stunning seaside views, state-of-the-art spas, and dazzling public spaces. But no matter how many face-lifts they endure, Attica's luxury hotels cannot remove their predominant mid-20th-century "shipping tycoon" style. Conversely, in Delphi, Arachova, and Galaxidi, accommodations tend to be homey, and in some places you may even have the sensation of being part of a family, as rooms are decorated with personal heirlooms and breakfast includes homemade goodies. In Delphi and Arachova, peak demand is during ski season and Easter (many places close for summer in Arachova).

RESTAURANTS

The cuisine of Attica resembles that of Athens, central Greece, and the Peloponnese. Local ingredients dominate, with fresh fish perhaps the greatest (and most expensive) delicacy. Since much of Attica's vegetation used to support herds of grazing sheep and the omnivorous goat, the meat of both animals is also a staple in many country tavernas. Although it is becoming increasingly difficult to find the traditional Greek taverna with large stewpots full of the day's hot meal, or big *tapsi* (pans) of *pastitsio* (layers of pasta, meat, and cheese laced with cinnamon) or *papoutsakia* (eggplant slices filled with minced meat), market towns and villages in Attica still harbor the occasional rustic haunt, offering tasty, inexpensive meals. Always ask to see the *kouzina* (kitchen) to look at the day's offerings, or even to peer inside the pots. Regional cuisine in Delphi and Arachova relies heavily on meats, including game, while in the coastal town of Galaxidi, fresh fish and seafood courses dominate. Informal dress is appropriate at all but the very fanciest of restaurants, and unless noted, reservations are not necessary.

DINING AND LODGING PRICES IN EUROS			
$	**$$**	**$$$**	**$$$$**
Restaurants	under €15	€15–€25	€26–€40	over €40
Hotels	under €125	€125–€225	€226–€275	over €275

Restaurant prices are the average cost of a main course at dinner or, if dinner is not served, at lunch. Hotel prices are the lowest cost of a standard double room in high season.

VISITOR INFORMATION

See the main offices listed under "Visitor Information" in the larger towns in this chapter. Also note the tour outfitters that are found under Tours, below.

10

TOURS

Taking a half-day trip from Athens to the breathtaking Temple of Poseidon at Sounion avoids the hassle of dealing with the crowded public buses or paying a great deal more for a taxi. A one-day tour to Delphi with lunch is possible, but it's a very long day; a two-day tour (with an overnight in a first-class hotel) gives you more time to explore this wonder.

RECOMMENDED OPERATORS

Dolphin Hellas. With headquarters within walking distance of the Acropolis, this full-service agency provides a range of services for individual and group travelers: hotel accommodations, villa rentals, ferry tickets, air tickets, organized coach tours, car rentals, fly and drive programs, transfer and guide services. ✉ *Syngrou Ave. 16, Makriyianni* ☎ *210/922–7772* ⊕ *www.dolphin-hellas.gr*.

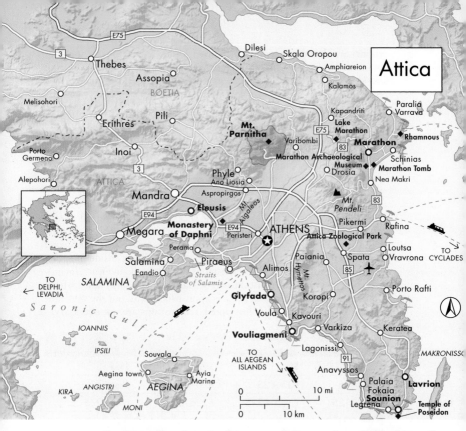

Key Tours. Showing travelers around Greece since 1963, this well-respected firm offers more than 20 different scheduled excursions, including one-day trips to Delphi from Athens. ✉ *Athanasiou Diakou 26, Athens* ☎ *210/923–3166* ⊕ *www.keytours.gr.*

ATTICA ΑΤΤΙΚΗ

This triangular peninsula, focused on sprawling Athens and more or less the center of the classcial world, spreads from Mt. Parnitha in the north to the Temple of Poseidon and Cape Sounion at the southern tip. In between are busy beach resorts, the famed Sanctuary of Demeter at Eleusis, the Monastery of Daphni, the fabled plain of Marathon, and small towns set amid rolling hills, olive groves, vineyards.

GLYFADA ΓΛΥΦΑΔΑ

17 km (10½ miles) southeast of Athens.

Gateway to the Athens Riviera and the Apollo Coast—which stretches from Pireaus south to Cape Sounion's famed temple to Poseidon—Glyfada is loved for its palm-fringed coastal promenade lined with parks, beautiful villas, golf courses, shopping, dance clubs, and seaside dining spots.

GETTING HERE AND AROUND

Buses A2, A3, and B3 leave Athens's center (Akadimia and Syntagma Square) and stop at Glyfada's main square. The buses run regularly (two to five an hour) in both directions until midnight. The ride can take an hour or more. Express Bus E22 (Akadimia–Saronida) also stops in Glyfada. On summer weekends only, OASA bus line 790 operates through the night (12 to 4:30 am) to serve clubbers who come to party and escape the Athens heat; it leaves from Glyfada Square and heads into Peristeri through the center of Athens.

The tram offers a more scenic, if often slower, route. Take the Asklipeio Voulas tram from Syntagma Square; it passes through the Zappion park and endless city blocks before it reaches Palio Faliro, where it curves to the left, following Poseidonos Avenue along the sea to Glyfada. Most trams run until 1 am daily, except for Friday and Saturday, when they run until 2:30 am (and a couple even later than that, but be sure to check the timetable before you depart). The Athens metro serves the nearby suburb Elliniko, making it even more accessible from the metropolitan center. *For more information on Athens public transportation options, including all relevant contact information, see Getting Here and Around in Athens.*

EXPLORING

Since the old international airport here closed, Glyfada is much quieter and less touristy. Athenians come to swim, stroll, shop, and spend quiet moments gazing at the sea. On summer nights, however, the area transforms itself into a pulsing dance club scene. A large expat community seeks out exquisite local cuisine and ample international offerings in Glyfada's center. Glyfada has several fine hotels and, with Athens city center just a tram ride away, makes a good base for travelers who prefer being near the beach.

FAMILY **Sea Turtle Rescue Center.** Since 1983, the primary objective of Archelon, the Sea Turtle Protection Society of Greece, has been to protect the sea turtles and their habitats in Greece. At the Glyfada rescue center, housed in five disused train wagons donated by the Hellenic Railways Organization (OSE), you can watch the team of volunteers in action (caring for turtles at the last stage of rehabilitation), lend a helping hand by bringing much needed supplies, and learn about ongoing rescue efforts throughout Greece. ⊠ *3rd Marina* ☎ *210/898-2600* ⊕ *www.archelon.gr* ☉ *Closed Aug.*

10

BEACHES

Attica's southwestern coast is mainly rock, with some short, sandy stretches in Alimos, Glyfada, and Voula that have been made into public pay beaches. Along with beach bars, changing rooms, beach umbrellas, and rental water-sport equipment for windsurfing and waterskiing, there are gardens, parking, and playgrounds. These beaches have received Blue Flags for cleanliness from the European Union despite their proximity to Athens. Most are open from 8 am to 8 pm in summer, and most charge entry fees. At some beaches, fees go up on weekends, and at others you may have to pay extra for a lounge chair or parking. In July and August, when temperatures climb past 100°F (38°C), public

In the summer, many of Athens's trendiest clubs and restaurants relocate to be closer to Glyfada's popular beaches, many of which have received a coveted Blue Flag for cleanliness.

beaches often stay open until midnight. The beaches at Asteria, on the north side of Glyfada, and Voula, just to the south, are free.

Alimos Beach (*Akti tou Iliou*). The town of Alimos has the nearest developed—and clean—beach to Athens. The so-called Beach of the Sun extends over 60,000 square meters and has umbrellas and lounge chairs for rent, three beach bars, a couple of tavernas, and one minimarket. Expect it to be packed over the hot summer months. There is an entry fee (slightly higher on weekends); expect to be charged extra for the sun beds during weekends as well. **Amenities:** food and drink; lifeguards; parking (fee); showers; toilets. **Best for:** swimming; walking. ⊠ *Poseidonos, opposite no. 62, Alimos* ⊕ *10 km (6 miles) south of Athens, 5 km (3 miles) north of Glyfada* ☎ *210/985–5169* ✉ *€3 weekdays, €5 weekends.*

Asteras Beach. This sprawling, upmarket complex really stands out in Glyfada, drawing a hip young crowd as well as families with children, who enjoy different sides of the beach. Built around a fine sand beach and landscaped grounds shaded by elegant pergolas, Asteras offers lounge chairs, umbrellas, pools, lockers, changing rooms, showers, trampolines, a playground, a self-service restaurant, three bars, and water sports. You can keep going all day and night at the youthful Balux poolside café-club, where you can cool off on abundant pillows with a chilled coffee in hand or sip a cocktail long after sundown. **Amenities:** food and drink; parking (fee); showers; toilets; water sports. **Best for:** partiers; swimming; walking; windsurfing. ⊠ *Poseidonos 58* ⊕ *15 km (9 miles) south of Athens* ☎ *210/894–1620, 210/894–41189* ⊕ *www. asterascomplex.com* ✉ *€5.*

WHERE TO EAT

$$ STEAKHOUSE 🍴 **George's Steak House.** This spot (affectionately called *Biftekakia* or "burger joint" by the locals) started out as the local butcher shop in 1951, so it's little wonder that the menu is limited to grilled meats, like steaks (George learned how to carve a T-bone from a visiting American) and *biftekia* (thick, grilled, hamburger-like patties of ground beef and pork served without a bun), plus a limited selection of side dishes like fries, tzatziki, seasonal boiled greens, and Greek salad. The service is fast, so don't be disappointed if all the tables are taken when you arrive; there's a continuous stream of diners coming and going. **Known for:** grilled meats; great value; cash only. [$] *Average main: €15* ✉ *Konstantinoupoleos 4–6* ☎ *210/894–6020* 🌐 *www.georgessteakhouse.gr* 💳 *No credit cards.*

$$ MODERN GREEK Fodor's Choice ★ 🍴 **Mentzelo's Slow Food and Drinks.** Chef Mentzelos Drosopoulos is an ardent proponent of the Slow Food movement and wants his customers at this colorful Glyfada eatery (where a long bookcase painted in intense Aegean-blue hues dominates the interior) to share his enthusiasm for locally sourced products, which are prepared as responsibly and as naturally as possible. The menu focuses on classic Greek dishes that are always cooked with a modern twist. **Known for:** nice modern takes on classics; daily specials. [$] *Average main: €25* ✉ *Pandoras St. 16* ☎ *210/894–1071.*

WHERE TO STAY

$$ HOTEL 🏨 **Blazer Suites.** A clublike panache, friendly and personal service, and location—a short walk from Glyfada's shopping and restaurants (and near a tram line that takes you right into the Athens center)—make this a good choice for combining sightseeing with languid days by the pool or nearby beach. **Pros:** nice pool area; five-minute walk from cosmopolitan Glyfada center; spacious, comfortable guest quarters. **Cons:** located on a busy six-lane avenue, which can get noisy; surrounding area is not that attractive; geared to business travelers. [$] *Rooms from: €220* ✉ *Karamanli 1, Voula* ☎ *210/965–8801* 🌐 *www.blazersuites.gr* 🛏 *28 suites* 🍽 *Breakfast.*

$$$$ RENTAL 🏨 **Brasil Suites Hotel Apartments.** These modern, clean, minimalist suites are large (the smallest is 50 square meters/538 square feet), and all include a fully equipped kitchen. **Pros:** spacious and comfortable; good choice for families; very friendly staff. **Cons:** a bit of a journey to reach major tourist sites in downtown Athens; some noise from surrounding clubs; expensive given location. [$] *Rooms from: €280* ✉ *Eleftherias 4* ☎ *210/894–2124* 🌐 *www.brasilhotel.gr* 🛏 *15 suites* 🍽 *Breakfast.*

$ HOTEL FAMILY 🏨 **Emmantina Hotel.** Although the decor could use a little updating, this reasonably priced option offers clean rooms, a friendly staff, sea views, and a rooftop pool. **Pros:** reasonable prices; simple but pleasant accommodations; the center of Glyfada just 10 minutes away on foot. **Cons:** busy and noisy six-lane avenue just outside the door with narrow sidewalks; a bit "tired" looking; Athens center 45 minutes away on the tram. [$] *Rooms from: €90* ✉ *Poseidonos 33* ☎ *210/898–0683* 🌐 *www.emmantina.gr* 🛏 *80 rooms* 🍽 *Breakfast.*

NIGHTLIFE

Glyfada is renowned as a summer party spot, since some of Athens's most popular clubs close up shop downtown and move here in summer. Places seem to change their name and style each season to keep up with trends; ask at your hotel for the latest information. Most clubs have a cover charge that includes a drink; if you're a large party, take a tip from the Greeks and share a bottle (whiskey, vodka) to save on the cost of ordering single drinks. It is sensible to make a reservation for a table beforehand.

Akrotiri Club Restaurant. Easygoing music gives way to lively post-midnight clubbing at one of Glyfada's hottest nightspots. An outdoor bar area surrounds a huge swimming pool. The club is open nightly, but during high season, from April to October, reservations for both the club section and the restaurant section are essential and should be made well in advance. ⊠ *Vas. Georgiou II 5* ☎ *210/985–9147* ⊕ *www.akrotirilounge.gr.*

Fodor'sChoice ★ **Balux Cafe—The House Project.** A creative design as an open-plan house, complete with playroom and pool area, ensures a feeling of "home away from home." By day, a contemporary Greek menu is served, and once the sun sets, the café becomes the perfect spot to slowly sip a cocktail right on the beachfront, enjoying one of the bands performing live (usually on Thursday), or the dance music played by top local DJs. It's open year-round. ⊠ *Asteras Seaside Complex, Poseidonos 58* ☎ *210/898–3577* ⊕ *www.baluxcafe.com.*

Noa Bay Club. This open-air club has a dance stage, four bars, an additional cocktail bar, a balcony with beach access, impressive sound and light installations, and a VIP area. ⊠ *Voula Beach, Karamanli 4, opposite Asklipieion Hospital, Voula* ☎ *213/000–8790.*

SHOPPING

Boutique 52. Bohemian-chic fashions, including flowing sundresses and Grecian-style evening gowns are by such international and Greek designers as the up-and-coming Stelios Koudounaris. ⊠ *Kyprou 52* ☎ *210/894–4250* ⊕ *www.boutique52.gr.*

SPORTS AND THE OUTDOORS

BOATING AND SAILING

Many yacht brokers charter boats and organize scuba tours and flotilla cruises in small rented sailboats around the islands.

Vernicos Yachts. Headquartered in a seaside suburb between Glyfada and Athens, this is the best place to go near Athens if you want to rent a boat to sail down to the islands. The company hosts crewed, weeklong cruises and also charters boats. ⊠ *Poseidonos 11, Alimos* ☎ *210/989–6000* ⊕ *www.vernicosyachts.com.*

GOLF

Konstantinos Karamanlis Glyfada Golf Course. With many distinguished politicians (including the legendary Greek politician it is named after), businessmen, and members of the diplomatic community on its roster, this green oasis of rolling hills is lovingly landscaped with tall trees and shrubbery. You need to make reservations for the weekend by

Wednesday, while the greens are open Tuesday–Sunday from 7:30 am until sunset and Monday 1 pm (noon in winter) until sunset. ⊠ *Glyfada* ✢ *Off Saki Karagiorga and end of Pronois* ☎ *210/894–6820* ⊕ *www. golfglyfada.gr* ⊠ *€60 daily, €50 for 18 holes, €30 for 9 holes* ⅄ *18 holes. 6847 yards. par 72.*

SCUBA DIVING

Athina Diving. Take lessons or go on scheduled dives with experienced instructors. Not to be missed: the night diving available upon request, either from shore or by boat. Equipment rentals are also available. ⊠ *Km 38, Athina–Sounio road, Lagonissi* ☎ *22910/25434* ⊕ *www. athinadiving.gr.*

VOULIAGMENI ΒΟΥΛΙΑΓΜΕΝΗ

8 km (5 miles) southwest of Glyfada, 25 km (16 miles) south of Athens.

A classy seaside residential suburb, Vouliagmeni is the most prestigious address for an Athenian's summer home or business.

GETTING HERE AND AROUND

Express Bus E22 is the easiest way to get to Vouliagmeni from Athens. It runs two to three times an hour, but only until 10 pm. (The last bus returning to Athens leaves at 9:45 pm.) Several buses, including 114, 115, and 170, originate in Glyfada and pass through Vouliagmeni on the way to Athens. Bus 114 stops outside the Astir Hotel Complex (with a good 15-minute walk to the front gate), but runs only until 7:10 pm, with just one bus an hour. Bus 115 does very few runs but caters to night owls, between 9:30 pm and midnight. *For more information, see Bus and Tram Travel in Athens.*

EXPLORING

Vouliagmeni is coveted for the large yacht harbor (including the exclusive Nautical Club that caters to water-sports lovers) and the scenic promontory, Laimos Vouliagmenis, which is covered with umbrella pines and includes an area called Kavouri, where there are several seaside fish tavernas. Vouliagmeni can serve as a convenient base from which to explore Attica, but it is far less crowded and more exclusive than Glyfada.

BEACHES

Here, beaches are quieter, and cleaner, than the beaches farther north toward Athens.

FAMILY **Akti Vouliagmenis.** A reasonable fee gives you access to elegant wooden lounge chairs, white umbrellas, and shiny beach bars. Also on-site at this public beach are basketball, volleyball, and tennis courts as well as a playground for pre- or post-swimming fun. There's also Wi-Fi and a first-aid station during the summer. **Amenities:** food and drink; lifeguards; parking (free); toilets. **Best for:** swimming; walking. ⊠ *2 Poseidonos, at Apollonos* ☎ *210/896–0697* ⊕ *vouliagmeni-akti.gr* ⊠ *€4 per person, €5 on weekends.*

Astir Beach. This beach club on the Laimos Vouliagmenis promontory is on the premises of the Arion Resort & Spa of the Astir Hotel Complex, but is open to the public daily from 8 am to 9 pm. Its more

10

exclusive location has always commanded a hefty entry fee, which means the green lawns and sandy stretch are usually not so crowded. Sand sports are played on the beach, including at two beach volleyball courts. A range of services (including shopping, dining, water sports, and yoga on the beach) are offered at an extra cost. **Amenities:** food and drinks; water sports. **Best for:** swimming; walking. ⊠ *Apollonos 40* ☎ *210/890–1619* ⊕ *astir-beach.com* ▨ *€28 weekends, €18 weekdays, reduced during low season.*

Kavouri Beach. This public beach extends north from Vouliagmeni to Voula and is one of the most easily accessible free, public beaches with fine golden sand near the city. This is a good choice for families, and there are a few modest cafés along the beach as well as some shops, while umbrellas and sun beds are available for rent. **Amenities:** food and drink; parking (free); showers; toilets. **Best for:** swimming; walking. ⊠ *Vouliagmeni* ✛ *Western shore of Vouliagmeni headland* ▨ *Free.*

Vouliagmeni Lake. The part-salt, part spring-fed warm waters of Vouliagmeni Lake are reputed to have curative powers, and thus are popular with older Greeks. At the lakeshore beach, with a dramatic, rocky backdrop that provides one of the most exotic settings in Attica, you can rent umbrellas, and there are showers, as well as a pleasant and popular café-restaurant. Most of the lake has a gradual slope and sandy bottom (although caution is recommended, as it deepens suddenly in parts). **Amenities:** food and drink; parking (no fee); showers. **Best for:** sunset; swimming; walking. ⊠ *Vouliagmeni* ✛ *2 km (1 mile) southeast of Vouliagmeni* ☎ *210/896–2237* ⊕ *www.limnivouliagmenis.gr* ▨ *€8.*

FAMILY **Yabanaki Beach Varkiza.** Beach-club amenities—umbrellas and sun beds for rent, water sports, bars, restaurants (including a popular *souvlaki* eatery), a children's water park, and cabins where you can change—spread across 25 acres behind a long stretch of sand. Varkiza is popular with windsurfers and waterskiers. **Amenities:** food and drink; lifeguards; parking (no fee); water sports. **Best for:** walking; windsurfing. ⊠ *Varkiza* ✛ *5 km (3 miles) east of Vouliagmeni* ☎ *210/897–2414* ⊕ *www.varkizaresort.gr* ▨ *€6.*

WHERE TO EAT

$$$ ✕ **Garbi.** Athenians flock year-round to share a seafood platter and bottle
SEAFOOD of white wine or feast on a fisherman's version of bouillabaisse made up of *kakavia* fish (when available). There's meat on the menu, too, but most opt for the fresh grilled fish that is brought daily from Kalimnos, Patmos, and Leros islands and a selection of appetizers with subtle influences from the cuisine of Istanbul Greeks. **Known for:** fresh seafood; seaside terrace and views. Ⓢ *Average main: €35* ⊠ *Iliou 21 and Selinis, Patras* ✛ *3 km (2 miles) west of Vouliagmeni* ☎ *210/896–3480* ☽ *No lunch.*

$$$ ✕ **Lambros.** Perched next to the waters of scenic Vouliagmeni Lake, this
SEAFOOD traditional fish taverna has been serving the best of Greek fishermen's catches since 1889. With wonderful views of crystalline, aquamarine waters, Lambros remains legendary for its mussel rice (*mydopilafo*), its seafood pasta, and its grilled fresh fish that arrives daily from all parts of Greece. **Known for:** waterside dining; fresh fish and seafood dishes; mydopilafo (mussel rice). Ⓢ *Average main: €35* ⊠ *Poseidonos 20* ☎ *210/896–0144* ☽ *Closed Mon.*

$$$ MODERN GREEK 🍴 **Moorings Vouliagmeni.** Wonderful views over the best of the Athenian Riviera, the Vouliagmeni marina, and a small church shrine can make for an unforgettably romantic evening. The hip lounge atmosphere of this seafront café-restaurant is complemented by the Nouveau Greek menu created by chef Andreas Sxinas, with the healthy seafood and Mediterranean options standing out from the rest. **Known for:** romance-inducing views; salads and other light fare; seafood. [$] *Average main: €40* ✉ *Marina Vouliagmenis* ☎ *210/967–0659, 210/896–0310* 🌐 *www.moorings.gr.*

WHERE TO STAY

$$$$ RESORT FAMILY 🏨 **Grand Resort Lagonissi.** With its own beaches, pools, restaurants, bars, and open-air cinema and a sports center, all augmenting deluxe accommodations, you may have little need to stray from this hedonistic seaside paradise. **Pros:** incredible sea views; standard accommodations can be a relatively good-value; good for romantic getaways. **Cons:** some suites are ridiculously expensive; food and beverages can also be expensive; some decor could use an update. [$] *Rooms from: €350* ✉ *Km 40, Athens–Sounio road, Lagonissi* ✣ *17 km (10 miles) southeast of Vougliameni* ☎ *22910/76010* 🌐 *www.lagonissiresort.gr* 🛏 *430 rooms* 🍽 *Breakfast.*

$$$$ HOTEL Fodor's Choice ★ 🏨 **The Margi.** A sculptural stone fireplace in the lobby, a rich brown leather headboard in one guest room, an antique dressing table in another: no detail escapes notice at this upscale retreat whose chic, truly spectacular pool and handsome guest rooms attract young and trendy Athenians. **Pros:** romantic atmosphere; nicely decorated pool area; cool vibe. **Cons:** smallish rooms; expensive for what's on offer; some furniture getting a bit tired. [$] *Rooms from: €400* ✉ *Litous 11* ☎ *210/892–9000* 🌐 *www.themargi.gr* 🛏 *96 rooms* 🍽 *Breakfast.*

$ HOTEL FAMILY 🏨 **Stefanakis Hotel and Apartments.** If you can sacrifice style for value, you can get a good location, balconies, basic amenities, and a breakfast buffet, along with Varkiza's wonderful sandy beach and café-lined waterfront just a short walk away. **Pros:** very good value; 100 feet from the beach; nice pool and outdoor areas. **Cons:** basic amenities; limited breakfast options; somewhat tired 1970s-style decor. [$] *Rooms from: €80* ✉ *Aphroditis 17, Varkiza* ✣ *3 km (2 miles) east of Vouliagmeni* ☎ *210/897–0528* 🌐 *www.stefanakishotel.gr* ⏲ *Closed Nov.–Mar.* 🛏 *52 rooms* 🍽 *Breakfast.*

SHOPPING

Georgiadou Bakery. Athenians flock here for the *piroshki,* a Russian turnover filled with spicy ground meat, but leave carrying bags filled with all types of baked goods, from baguettes and hearty peasant loaves to honey-drenched cakes. A branch of this historic bakery (founded in 1910) recently opened right in the center of Athens, on Ermou Street, a few yards away from the Greek Parliament. ✉ *Vas. Konstantinou 98, at Afroditis 2, Varkiza* ✣ *5 km (3 miles) southeast of Vouliagmeni* ☎ *210/897–5602* 🌐 *www.georgiadou.gr.*

EN ROUTE

South of Vouliagmeni the road threads along a rocky and heavily developed coastline dotted with inlets where intrepid bathers swim off the rocks, after leaving their cars in the roadside parking areas and scrambling down to the inviting *limanakia* (coves) below. (If you're not driving, you can take the urban E22 Saronida Express from the

Akadimias terminal in central Athens to Saronida or a KTEL bus from various points in Athens.) If you are a good swimmer and want to join them, take along your snorkel, fins, and mask so you can enjoy the underwater scenery, but avoid the stinging sea urchins (you won't have to be reminded a second time) clustered on rocks.

SOUNION ΣΟΥΝΙΟ

50 km (31 miles) southeast of Vouliagmeni, 70 km (44 miles) southeast of Athens.

Poised at the edge of a rugged 195-foot cliff, the Temple of Poseidon hovers between sea and sky, its "marble steep, where nothing save the waves and I may hear mutual murmurs sweep" unchanged in the centuries since Lord Byron penned these lines. Today the archaeological site at Sounion is one of the most photographed in Greece. The coast's raw, natural beauty has attracted affluent Athenians, whose splendid summer villas dot the shoreline around the temple. There is a tourist café-restaurant by the temple, and a few minimarts on the road, but no village proper. Arrange your visit so that you enjoy the panorama of sea and islands from this airy platform either early in the morning, before the summer haze clouds visibility and the tour groups arrive, or at dusk, when the promontory has one of the most spectacular sunset vantage points in Attica.

In antiquity, the view from the cliff was matched emotion for emotion by the sight of the cape (called the "sacred headland" by Homer) and its mighty temple when viewed from the sea—a sight that brought joy to sailors, knowing upon spotting the massive temple that they were close to home. Aegeus, the legendary king of Athens, threw himself off the cliff when he saw the approaching ship of his son, Theseus, flying a black flag. The king's death was a Greek tragedy born of misunderstanding: Theseus, returning from a mission to slay the Minotaur in Crete, had forgotten to change his ship's sails from black to white—the signal that his mission had succeeded. So the king thought his son had been killed. To honor Aegeus, the Greeks named their sea, the Aegean, after him.

GETTING HERE AND AROUND

Orange KTEL buses leave from Aigyptou Square, off Pedion Areos park, in Athens for Sounion (also spelled Sounio). It's a two-hour journey on modern buses from Athens. Buses (every two hours) run between 8 am and 7 pm daily, hitting spots including Varkiza, Anavyssos, and Legrena. For sunset gazers, the last bus returns from the site at 9 pm (in summer). *For more information on Athens buses and bus stations, see Bus and Train Travel in Athens.*

EXPLORING

Fodor's Choice
★

Temple of Poseidon. Although the columns at the Temple of Poseidon appear to be gleaming white from a distance, when you get closer you can see they are made of gray-veined marble, quarried from the Agrileza Valley 2 km (1 mile) north of the cape. Climb the rocky path, and beyond the scanty remains of an ancient propylon (gateway), you enter the temple compound. On your left is the temenos (precinct) of Poseidon; on your right, a stoa (arcade) and rooms. The temple itself (now roped off) was commissioned by Pericles, the famous leader of Greece's golden age, and was built between 444 and 440 BC on the site of an earlier cult to Poseidon; two colossal statues of youths, carved more than a century before the temple's construction, were discovered in early excavations (now at the National Archaeological Museum). The 15 Doric columns that remain stand sentinel over the Aegean. The view from the summit is breathtaking. ✉ *Cape Sounion* ☎ *22920/39363* 🌐 *www.culture.gr* 🎟 *€8.*

BY THE LIGHT OF THE SILVERY MOON

On summer full-moon nights, the Temple of Poseidon opens free of charge to the public.

BEACHES

FAMILY **Anavyssos Beach.** The broad, sandy beach at Anavyssos is very popular with windsurfers (especially the stretch called Alykes). There's a children's playground and beach volleyball courts, as well as sun beds and umbrellas for hire. **Amenities:** food and drink; showers; toilets; water sports. **Best for:** solitude; swimming; windsurfing. ✉ *Anavyssos* ✣ *13 km (8 miles) northwest of Sounion.*

Legrena Beach. On your approach to the Temple of Poseidon, there is a decent sandy beach at Legrena. The fine golden sand is reminiscent of the Cycladic islands, while an added bonus is the usual lack of crowds. A few miles before you arrive (from Athens), look for the sight of the small island of Patroklos. It is uninhabited today, has ancient fortress ruins, and is said to belong to a wealthy Greek family. **Amenities:** food and drink. **Best for:** solitude; swimming; walking. ✉ *Legrena* ✣ *4 km (2½ miles) north of Sounion, before the turnoff for Haraka.*

Sounion Beach. If you are spending the morning visiting the Temple of Poseidon, you might also want to take a swim on the free public beach just below it. Of course, this sandy strip—known locally as Kavokolones—becomes uncomfortably crowded in summer. **Amenities:** none. **Best for:** sunset; swimming. ✉ *Km 68, Athens–Sounion ave.*

WHERE TO EAT

$$ SEAFOOD 🍴 **O Ilias.** Every table at this fish taverna founded in 1944 has a view of the Temple of Poseidon, while the traditional menu centers around *psari* (fish), from "small frys" like marida, atherina, and anchovy to large ones by the kilo. Try the homemade french fries or fried peppers to start and some *ravani* (a traditional Greek honey-covered cake) to top off the meal. **Known for:** views of Temple of Poseidon; fresh fish; Greek ravani honey cake for dessert. [$] *Average main: €20* ✉ *Sounion* ✣ *On beach below Temple of Poseidon* ☎ *22920/39114* ⏲ *No dinner weekdays Nov.–Mar.*

$ GREEK 🍴 **Syrtaki.** Sit among the pines, take in the view of the sea, and try the traditional *pites* (homemade pastry pies, these with cheese-and-spinach filling); the fava; and, of course, the fresh fish. Grilled meats are also excellent here. **Known for:** sea views; good choice of mezedes (small plates). [$] *Average main: €15* ✉ *Km 69, Athens–Sounion avenue* ✣ *4 km (2½ miles) north of Sounion* ☎ *22920/39125.*

$$ **✕ Theodoros-Eleni.** A Greek-British husband-and-wife team build their
SEAFOOD menu around huge portions of fresh fish and seafood, like the steamed mussels with feta in wine cheese sauce or the seafood pastas. At the end of the dinner, the plate of seasonal fruit or the homemade chocolate *kormos* (log-shaped) cake is on the house. **Known for:** mussels and fresh fish; tasty seafood pastas. $ *Average main: €25* ✉ *Legrena* ✛ *3 km (2 miles) south of Sounion, off the road into Legrena village* ☎ *22920/51936* ☾ *Closed Nov.–Mar.*

WHERE TO STAY

$$ ⏰ **Aegeon Beach Hotel.** Nothing can beat the location—much objected
HOTEL to by environmentalists and archaeologists—*on* the beach beneath the Temple of Poseidon, above the very harbor where ancient ships once navigated, and all guest rooms have balconies, most have sea views, and a few gaze up at the temple. **Pros:** views of temple and one of the best sunsets in the world; nice beach bar; beautiful water just outside the doors. **Cons:** beach especially crowded with Athenians during summer weekends; decor is minimal and a bit dated; food is uninspired. $ *Rooms from: €150* ✉ *Athens–Sounion Ave. Km 68* ☎ *22920/39200* ⊕ *www.aegeon-hotel.com* ⇆ *45 rooms* ⦿⦿ *Breakfast.*

$$$$ ⏰ **Grecotel Cape Sounio.** One of the most elaborate hotels in Greece
HOTEL perches amid the verdant pine forest of Sounion National Park with
FAMILY stunning views of the Temple of Poseidon from bungalows and villas,
Fodor's Choice all arranged in tiers along a hill. **Pros:** grandiose architecture; family-
★ friendly; beautiful grounds and beach. **Cons:** decor is not as luxurious as the prices might suggest; food is good but expensive; service and maintenance are not always at five-star standards. $ *Rooms from: €350* ✉ *Km 67, Athens–Sounion avenue* ☎ *22920/69700* ⊕ *www.capesounio. com* ☾ *Closed Nov.–Apr.* ⇆ *153 rooms* ⦿⦿ *Breakfast.*

$$ ⏰ **Plaza Resort Hotel.** These bright rooms right next to Anavyssos Beach
RESORT are done in soothing white-on-white minimalist decor, and most are
FAMILY reasonably spacious (some are smaller than others), while outdoors is an 80-foot-long pool just a two-minute stroll away from the beach. **Pros:** impressive lobby; pleasant surroundings; private sandy beach with pool. **Cons:** nearby town a bit dull; a few maintenance issues; high restaurant and beach bar prices. $ *Rooms from: €160* ✉ *Km 52, Athens– Sounion avenue, Anavyssos* ✛ *13km (8 miles) northwest of Sounion* ☎ *22910/75000* ⊕ *www.plaza-resort.com* ⇆ *135 rooms* ⦿⦿ *Breakfast.*

SPORTS AND THE OUTDOORS

Kouros Surf Club. This outfit on Anavyssos's Alykes Beach offers beginner and advanced windsurfing, kitesurfing, wakeboarding, stand-up paddling, and sailing lessons, a pro shop, and a relaxed beach bar-restaurant. ✉ *Km 50, Athens–Sounion avenue, Anavyssos* ☎ *22910/40804* ⊕ *www.kourosclub.gr.*

LAVRION ΛΑΥΡΙΟ

10 km (6 miles) north of Sounion, 80 km (50 miles) southeast of Athens.

After Sounion, the road twists and turns along the coast, winding past holiday homes, before hitting a rather dreary stretch by Lavrion's boatyard, where there always seems to be marina construction work under way. There is increasing activity in the post of Lavrion during the summer, as many boats for nearby Cycladic islands (Kythnos, Kea [Tzia], etc.) depart from here, and an increasing number of cruise ships also stop here for easy access to the Temple of Poseidon at Sounion. Lavrion, an industrial town with a few remnants of belle epoque architecture, was celebrated in antiquity for its silver mines. Several thousand ancient shafts have been discovered in the area—devoid of the riches they once yielded. Themistocles could not have built the fleet that saved Greece from the Persians, nor Pericles the monuments on the Acropolis, without the area's riches. Easy access to the airport at Spata via the Markopoulou highway has begun to attract investment, including a joint public-private venture to create a technological and cultural park on the grounds of the now-defunct mining company (worth a visit if only for its architectural value).

EXPLORING

Lavrion Mineralogical Museum. Not only geology buffs can fully appreciate the small mineralogical museum, whose 700 exhibits—including several rare and beautiful specimens such as laurionite and azurite—are housed in a charming late-19th-century building then used by the French Mining Company to wash minerals. Coins made from the silver that the ancient Greeks mined around Lavrion are also on display. ✉ *Iroon Polytechniou Sq.* ☎ *22920/25295* 🖱 *€2.*

MARATHON ΜΑΡΑΘΩΝΑΣ

165 km (102 miles) northwest of Sounion, 42 km (26 miles) northeast of Athens.

Athenians enter the fabled plain of Marathon to enjoy a break from the capital, visiting the freshwater lake created by the dam, or sunning at the area's beaches while enjoying views across the bay to the island of Euboia. The beauty of the region endures, despite some large-scale forest fires in recent years. When the Athenian *hoplites* (foot soldiers), assisted by the Plataians, entered the plain in 490 BC, it was to crush a numerically superior Persian force. Some 6,400 invaders were killed fleeing to their ships, while the Athenians lost 192 warriors. This, their proudest victory, became the stuff of Athenian legend; the hero Theseus was said to have appeared himself in aid of the Greeks, along with the god Pan. The Athenian commander Miltiades sent a messenger, Pheidippides, to Athens with glad tidings of the victory; it's said he ran the 42 km (26 miles) hardly taking a breath, shouted *Nenikikamen!* ("We won!"), then dropped dead of fatigue (more probably of a heart attack)—the inspiration for the marathon race in today's Olympics. To the west of the Marathon plain are the quarries of Mt. Pendeli, the seemingly inexhaustible source for a special marble that weathers to a warm golden tint.

GETTING HERE AND AROUND

Head to the outdoors Attica KTEL bus terminal in Aigyptou Square in Athens to check routes and plan your Marathon trip. The journey takes about 1½ hours (depending on the traffic along the busy Mesogeion and Marathonos avenues). Buses depart approximately every half hour, starting at 5:30 am. *For more information on Athens buses and bus stations, see Bus and Train Travel in Athens.*

EXPLORING

FAMILY **Attica Zoological Park.** Youngsters tired of trekking through museums may appreciate the distraction of this 32-acre zoo, home to more than 2,000 animals, 46 mammal species, 30 types of reptiles, and 238 species of birds, from a jaguar and wallaby to a brown bear, African penguin, and snowy owl. Take the Spata exit if you're coming from the airport, or the Rafina exit if you're coming from the direction of Eleusis. ✉ *Ya-lou region, Spata* ☎ *210/663–4724* ⊕ *www.atticapark.com* 🏷 *€18.*

Lake Marathon. The huge man-made reservoir formed by the Marathon Dam (built by an American company in 1925–31) warrants a visit if only to see the only dam in the world said to be faced with real marble. At the downstream side is a marble replica of the Athenian Treasury of Delphi. This is a main source of water for Athens, supplemented with water from Parnitha and the Boeotia region. If you are looking for a drink or snack (pasta dishes and pies with phyllo pastry are the chef's specialty), stop at the café-restaurant Fragma (*www.fragma.gr*) on the east side of the dam. Wonderful views glimpsed from the tall front windows help make this a perfect and refreshing stop on your way back to Athens from Sxinias Beach. ✉ *Marathon* ⊹ *8 km (5 miles) west of Marathon, down a side road from village of Ayios Stefanos.*

Marathon Archaeological Museum. Five rooms contain very well preserved objects from excavations in the area, ranging from neolithic pottery from the cave of Pan to Hellenistic and Roman inscriptions and statues (labeled in English and Greek). Eight larger-than-life sculptures came from the gates of a nearby sanctuary of the Egyptian gods and goddesses. In the center of one of the rooms stands part of the Marathon victory trophy—an ionic column that the Athenians erected in the valley of Marathon after defeating the Persians. Next to the museum, the Middle Hellenic cemetery is well sheltered from the forces of nature and very visitor-friendly. ✉ *Plataion 114* ⊹ *Approximately 6 km (4 miles) southwest of Marathon* ☎ *22940/55155* ⊕ *www.culture.gr* 🏷 *Combined ticket with Marathon Tomb €6* ☽ *Closed Mon.*

Marathon Run Museum. Medals, photos, and other memorablia are an homage to the Athens Marathon, run since 1896, as well as other marathons around the world. The experience of a visit seems all the more poignant since the museum is near the site where the courier Pheidippides is said to have set off on his impressive feat of running 26 miles to Athens to bring home the news of victory over the Persians in 490 BC. ✉ *Marathonos, at 25th Martiou St.* ☎ *22940/67617* ⊕ *www.marathon-runmuseum.com* 🏷 *€2* ☽ *Closed Mon.*

Marathon Tomb. This 30-foot-high mound is built over graves containing the cremated remains of the 192 Athenians who died in the 490 BC battle against Persian forces. At the base, the original gravestone depicts the Soldier of Marathon, a hoplite, which has been reproduced here (the original is in the National Archaeological Museum in Athens). The battle is plotted on illustrated panels. ✉ *Marathon* ⊹ *5 km*

10

(3 miles) south of Marathon ☎ *22940/55462* 🎫 *Combined ticket with Archaeological Museum* €6 ⊘ *Closed Mon.*

Rhamnous. This isolated, romantic spot on a small promontory overlooks the sea between continental Greece and the island of Euboia. It is a bit off the beaten track but if you want to escape the crowds of Athens and make it a day trip together with a swim at nearby Sxinias, this is definitely worth the drive (especially if you have your own vehicle). From at least the Archaic period, Rhamnous was known for the worship of Nemesis, the great leveler, who brought down the proud and punished the arrogant. The scenic site, excavated during many years, preserves traces of temples from the 6th and 5th centuries BC. The smaller temple from the 6th century BC was dedicated to Themis, goddess of Justice. The later temple housed the cult statue of Nemesis, envisioned as a woman, the only cult statue remaining from the high classical period. Many fragments have turned up, including the head, in the British Museum. The acropolis stood on the headland, where ruins of a fortress (5th and 4th centuries BC) are visible. As you wander over the usually serene, and always evocative, site you discover at its edge little coves where you can enjoy a swim. For those going by public transportation, take a KTEL bus from Athens toward the Ayia Marina port, get off at the Ayia Marina and Rhamnous crossroads, and follow the signs, about 3 km (2 miles) down the road. Or take a taxi from Marathon village. ✉ *Grammatiko* ✛ *15 km (9 miles) northeast of Marathon* ☎ *22940/63477* ⊕ *www.culture.gr* 🎫 €4 ⊘ *Closed Mon.*

BEACHES

Rhamnous Beach. The coves at Rhamnous, approached via a rough road about 2,000 feet before the entrance to the archaelogical site, are cozy and remote. These are favorite swimming spots of nudists and free campers, although the latter is technically forbidden. Beware of spiny sea urchins when swimming off the rocks from this pebbly beach. **Amenities:** parking (free). **Best for:** nudists; solitude; walking. ✉ *Grammatiko* ✛ *15 km (9 miles) northeast of Marathon.*

FAMILY
Fodor's Choice
★

Schinias Beach. The best beach in the north of Attica, just beyond Marathon, is this long, sandy, pine-backed stretch called Schinias. It's crowded with Athenians on the weekend, has a few simple tavernas along the sand and quite a lot of beach bars, and is frequently struck by strong winds that windsurfers love in summer. A dirt-and-sand track skirts the pine groves behind the beach, providing access to some relatively remote stretches. Campers like to settle in the Schinias forest during the summer, taking care not to disturb its precious natural habitat, which is enviromentally protected. **Amenities:** food and drink; lifeguards; parking (free); showers; toilets; water sports. **Best for:** sunset; swimming; walking; windsurfing. ✉ *Schinias* ✛ *10 km (6 miles) southeast of Marathon.*

Sessi Beach. The smaller Sessi Beach on the left is about 400 meters long and has a small canteen, while the main pebble beach with its crystal clear waters has a couple of tavernas and a beach bar. There are also a few smaller stretches of sand accessible on foot that are fairly private.

Bring your own sun beds and umbrellas because there's nothing for rent here. **Amenities:** food and drink. **Best for:** solitude; swimming. ✉ *Grammatiko ✛ 6 km (4 miles) northeast of Marathon.*

Varnavas Beach. This fine-pebbled beach is reached from Varnavas village, north of Marathon. There is a lifeguard here during the summer months and a few tavernas nearby where you can enjoy a post-swim snack. It's a popular spear-fishing spot. **Amenities:** food and drink; lifeguards; parking (free). **Best for:** swimming; snorkeling. ✉ *Varnavas ✛ 15 km (9 miles) northeast of Marathon.*

WHERE TO EAT

$$
ARGENTINE
✕ **Argentina.** While living in South America, owner Nikos Milonas learned how to carve beef, how high to fire up the grill, and exactly how to time a perfect medium-rare steak (size XXL!). The meat-loving population of Greece has been benefiting from his expertise ever since. **Known for:** steak; long waits (up to an hour) if you don't call in advance. $ *Average main: €25* ✉ *Bitakou 3, Vothonas ✛ About 1½ km (1 mile) after Marathon dam crossing* ☎ *22940/66476* ☉ *Closed Mon. and two weeks in Aug. No dinner Sun.*

$$
MEDITERRANEAN
✕ **Cavo Seaside Bar & Restaurant.** One of the most popular seaside spots in Attica is set under the pine trees right next to the beach in Mati, a pleasant seaside town near Marathon. Excellent cocktails accompany such creative Mediterranean delights as smoked salmon with mango salad, octopus canelloni, and risotto with chicken and lime sauce. **Known for:** chic vibe; innovative cuisine. $ *Average main: €25* ✉ *Poseidonos 105, Mati* ☎ *22940/39018.*

$$
SEAFOOD
✕ **Isidora Fish Tavern.** Front tables at this lively and friendly spot, a perfect stop after a day at the beach, are nearly immersed in the sea, and others are tucked into a Mediterranean garden. Family matriarch Isidora orchestrates the delicious homemade meals, many including fresh fish of the day, accompanied by rich seasonal salads and fresh village bread. Just remember: it's cash only. **Known for:** beachside setting; fresh fish; cash only. $ *Average main: €20* ✉ *Perikleous 5* ☎ *22940/56467* ▭ *No credit cards* ☉ *Closed weekdays Nov.–Apr.*

WHERE TO STAY

$
HOTEL
▦ **Cabo Verde.** A convenient spot in the seaside suburb of Mati, near the airport and the port of Rafina, comes with a pool and spa that compliment spacious, comfortable guest rooms, with delightful sea views that include Evia island's profile directly across the strait. **Pros:** relaxing views of the harbor; 20 minutes from the airport; simple but stylish rooms. **Cons:** few luxuries; lackluster restaurant (but nice pool bar); hard to reach by public transport. $ *Rooms from: €80* ✉ *Poseidonos 41, Mati ✛ 7 km (4½ miles) south of Marathon* ☎ *22940/33111, 22940/33113* ⊕ *www.caboverde.gr* ⤳ *38 rooms* ⦿❘ *Breakfast.*

$$
HOTEL
FAMILY
▦ **Marathon Beach Resort.** A retro-Florida vibe permeates this sprawling, beautifully maintained mini-resort where simple but stylish rooms, done in dazzling whites with bright accent colors, surround an enormous garden and pool terrace, all just steps from the beach. **Pros:** simple but comfortable and pleasant rooms; beautiful pool area; good choice of affordable

10

dining options. **Cons:** no elevator; few luxuries; not all rooms have sea views. $ *Rooms from: €140* ✉ *Poseidonos 12, Nea Makri* ☎ *22940/95022* ⊕ *www.marathonbeachresort.com* ⤳ *74 rooms* ⦿| *Breakfast.*

SPORTS AND THE OUTDOORS

RUNNING

Athens Authentic Marathon. Held every year in early November (over roughly the same course taken in 490 BC by the courier Pheidippides, when he carried to Athens the news of victory over the Persians), the 42-km (26-mile) race is open to men and women of all ages. Starting in Marathon, it finishes at the Panathenaic Stadium in Athens. In recent years, the event has been updated to include pasta parties and other events for runners. If following in all of Pheidippides's footsteps is too much for you, the 5-km (3-mile), 10-km (6-mile), or power-walking races are good options. Even if you don't have the stamina for the race, cheer on the runners at the end of the route in Athens—they represent many ages, nationalities, and physiques. Those who finish the course sprint triumphantly into the marble stadium, where the first modern Olympics were held in 1896. ✉ *Marathonos, at 25th Martiou St.* ☎ *22940/67617* ⊕ *www.athensauthenticmarathon.gr.*

WATER SPORTS

Moraitis Sports Center. This part of Attica is ideal for all kinds of water sports, and accredited instructors at Moraitis specialize in windsurfing. The beach volleyball tournament is also popular with local players, while many triathletes use the center as a basis for their year-round training. ✉ *Schinias Beach* ☎ *22940/55965* ⊕ *www.moraitisbeach.com.*

MT. PARNITHA ΠΑΡΝΗΘΑ

62 km (38 miles) west of Marathon, 33 km (20½ miles) northwest of Athens.

The summit of Mt. Parnitha, Attica's highest mountain, affords splendid views of the plain of Athens. Tragically, large swaths of the mountain's protected national park, particularly its western side, have been destroyed by wildfires in recent years; however, lovely nature walks threading through the Mt. Parnitha massif are still possible. In April and May the forest blooms with wildflowers, red poppies, white crocuses, purple irises, and numerous species of orchid. Many Athenians come year-round, especially on Sunday, to enjoy the clean air, mountain bike, or picnic, but some are equally attracted by the gaming tables at the nearby casino.

EXPLORING

Regency Casino Mont Parnes. This popular casino welcomes visitors while in the process of a gradual renovation. The view-filled ascent with the funicular is free of charge, and for many visitors that's the highlight of a visit to this dim, smokey gaming room with an expensive restaurant. The casino can also be reached by car. ✉ *Mt. Parnitha, Acharnés* ☎ *210/242–1234* ⊕ *www.regencycasinos.gr* ⤳ *€6.*

WHERE TO EAT

$$
BARBECUE
Fodor's Choice
★

✕ **Pappas.** This family-run taverna at the foot of Mt. Parnitha is popular for its mountain views and cozy fireplace in the winter, as well as for its serene garden with tall plane trees providing a much needed respite from the summer heat. The menu is built around grilled meat, mostly ribs and chops, served by the kilo on heaping platters. **Known for:** homey atmosphere; refreshing garden; grilled meats. $ *Average main: €20* ⊠ *Thessalonikis 2, off Athens–Lamia road, Acharnés* ☎ *210/243–1232.*

SPORTS AND THE OUTDOORS

HIKING

There are 12 marked hiking trails, with varying degrees of difficulty, on Mt. Parnitha.

Bafi Refuge. A 2.2-km (1.4-mile) ascent from the church of Ayia Triada (takes approximately 40 minutes) leads to the Bafi Refuge, run by the EOS Athinon (Hiking Club of Athens), where basic board and lodging are available. The refuge has a fireplace and kitchen; water is piped in from a nearby spring. The refuge remains open all year long. ⊠ *Parnithos Rd., Mt Parnitha* ☎ *210/240–3566* ⊕ *www.mpafi.gr.*

Church of Ayios Petros. One of the milder, and most pleasant, hikes on Mt. Parnitha follows a marked trail from the church of Ayia Triada through the national park to the church of Ayios Petros at Mola forest. The path leads past the Skipiza spring, providing spectacular views of western Attica and the town of Thebes along the way. The 6-km (4-mile) walk takes about two hours, and you might spot deer darting among the trees. ⊠ *Mola forest, Off Parnithos Rd., Mt. Parnitha, Acharnés.*

EOS Athinon Alpine Club. The Hiking Club of Athens runs huts where you can spend the night in the Bafi Refuge, and the organization can also give you information on the trails. In most cases, when you call you'll be able to find someone who speaks English. ☎ *210/321–2355 in Athens* ⊕ *eosathinon.gr.*

Flambouri Refuge. From Bafi, one trail turns south, tracing the fir and pine woods along the Houni ravine, skirting the craggy Flambouri peak—a favorite nesting place of the park's raptors. This trail intersects with another path leading to the Flambouri Refuge, a basic hikers' hut run by EOS Acharnon Hiking Club. You can stay the night or enjoy their views of Mt. Parnitha and hearty food, before exploring more trails. ⊠ *Off Parnithos Rd., Acharnés* ☎ *210/246–4666.*

10

MONASTERY OF DAPHNI ΜΟΝΗ ΔΑΦΝΙΟΥ

61 km (38 miles) southwest of Mt. Parnitha, 11 km (7 miles) west of Athens.

Daphni means "laurel tree," which was sacred to Apollo, whose sanctuary once occupied this site on the Sacred Way between Athens and Eleusis. The original temple was destroyed in AD 395 after the anti-pagan edicts of the Emperor Theodosius, and the Orthodox monastery that stands here now was probably established in the 6th century, incorporating materials of Apollo's sanctuary in the church and walls. Reoccupied by Orthodox monks only in the 16th century, the Daphni complex has since been host to a barracks and mental institution. The monastery, a UNESCO World Heritage site, is once again open to the public even though restoration work is ongoing. You can reach the site on the A16 bus from Koumoundourou Square.

Fodor'sChoice **Monastery of Daphni.** Sacked by Crusaders, inhabited by Cistercian
★ monks, and desecrated by Turks, this UNESCO World Heritage site remains one of the most splendid Byzantine monuments in Greece. Dating from the 11th century, the golden age of Byzantine art, the church contains a series of miraculously preserved mosaics without parallel in the legacy of Byzantium: powerful portraits of figures from the Old and New Testaments, images of Christ and the Virgin Mary in the *Presentation of the Virgin,* and, in the golden dome, a stern *Pantokrator* ("ruler of all") surrounded by 16 Old Testament prophets who predicted his coming. The mosaics, made of chips of four different types of marble, are set against gold. An ongoing long-term restoration project makes it hard to see some of the mosaics, but this doesn't take away much of the awe inspired by the craftmanship of the Byzantine masters. ✛ *At the end of Iera Odos, at Athinon* ☎ *210/581–1558* ⊕ *www.culture.gr* ✉ *Free* ☉ *Closed Mon., Wed., Thurs., Sat., and Sun.*

ELEUSIS ΕΛΕΥΣΙΝΑ

11 km (7 miles) west of the Monastery of Daphni, 22 km (14 miles) west of Athens.

The growing city of Athens co-opted the land around Eleusis, placing shipyards in the pristine gulf and steel mills and petrochemical plants along its shores. It is hard to imagine that there once stretched in every direction fields of corn and barley sacred to the goddess Demeter, whose realm was symbolized by the sheaf and sickle. You can reach the site, like nearby Daphni Monastery, on the A16 bus from Koumoundourou Square.

EXPLORING

Sanctuary of Demeter. This once sacred place lies on an eastern slope, at the foot of the ancient acropolis protecting the settlement of Eleusis, hardly visible amid the modern buildings of the main square of Elefsina (or Eleusis, as it was called in the ancient Greek world). The legend of Demeter and her daughter Persephone explained for the ancients the cause of the seasons and the origins of agriculture.

It was to Eleusis that Demeter traveled in search of Persephone after the girl had been kidnapped by Hades, god of the underworld. Zeus himself interceded to restore her to the distraught Demeter but succeeded only partially, giving mother and daughter just half a year together.

Nevertheless, in gratitude to King Keleos of Eleusis, who had given her refuge in her time of need, Demeter presented his son Triptolemos with wheat seeds, the knowledge of agriculture, and a winged chariot so he could spread them to mankind. Keleos built a *megaron* (large hall) in Demeter's honor, the first Eleusinian sanctuary.

The worship of Demeter took the form of mysterious rites, part purification and part drama, and both the Lesser and the Greater Eleusinian rituals closely linked Athens with the sanctuary. The procession for the Greater Eleusinia began and ended there, following the route of the Sacred Way (along the avenue still called Iera Odos today).

Much of what you see now in the sanctuary is of Roman construction or repair, although physical remains on the site date back to the Mycenaean period. Follow the old Sacred Way to the great *propylaea* (gates) and continue on to the Precinct of Demeter, which was strictly off-limits on pain of death to any but the initiated. The *Telesterion* (Temple of Demeter), now a vast open space surrounded by battered tiers of seats, dates to 600 BC, when it was the hall of initiation. It had a roof supported by six rows of seven columns, presumably so the mysteries would be obscured, and it could accommodate 3,000 people.

The museum, just beyond, contains pottery and sculpture, particularly of the Roman period. Although the site is closed at night, you can see the sacred court and propylaea from a distance thanks to special lighting by Pierre Bideau, the French expert who also designed the lighting for the Acropolis in Athens. ⊠ *Gkioka 1, Eleusis (Elefsina)* ☎ *210/554–6019* ⊕ *www.visit-ancient-greece.com/eleusis.html* 🎫 *€6* ☙ *Closed Mon.*

DELPHI AND ENVIRONS ΔΕΛΦΟΙ

According to legend, and so described by Sophocles in *Oedipus Rex,* the infant Oedipus was left to die by his father, Laius, on a mountainside near Thebes, now a bustling market town between Athens and the famous archaeological site of Delphi. An oracle predicted that Oedipus would murder his father and marry his mother, but some shepherds, ignorant of the curse, rescued him, and he was raised by the king of Corinth. The saga unfolded when, as a young man, Oedipus was walking from Delphi and met his father, Laius, king of Thebes, near the Triple Way. The latter, having struck Oedipus with his whip in order to make room for his chariot to pass, was in turn attacked and accidentally killed by the young man, who did not recognize his father, not having seen his parents since his birth. Journeying to Thebes, he solved the riddle of the terrible Sphinx and, as a reward, was offered the throne and the hand of Jocasta (who was, unbeknownst to him, his mother). When they discovered what had happened, Oedipus blinded himself and Jocasta hanged herself.

10

The preferred route from Athens follows National Road to the Thebes turnoff, at 74 km (46 miles). Take the secondary road south past Thebes and continue west through the fertile plain—now planted with cotton, potatoes, and tobacco—to busy Levadia, capital of the province of Boeotia. If you detour in Levadia by following the signs for the *piges* (hot springs), you come to the banks of the ancient springs of Lethe and Mnemosyne, or Oblivion and Remembrance (these springs are about a 10-minute walk from the main square); in antiquity the Erkinas (Hercyne) gorge was believed to be the entrance to the underworld. Today, the plane- and maple-tree-shaded river is spanned by an old stone arch bridge built in Ottoman times. Almost halfway between Levadia and

Delphi, the Triple Way (where the roads from Delphi, Daulis, and Levadia meet) is where Oedipus fatefully met his father.

If you turn south toward Distomo at the junction, you can visit the monastic complex at Osios Loukas. National Road continues to Mt. Parnassus, where the formerly quiet mountain village of Arachova is now a successful confluence of traditional Greek village and Athenian style, thanks to the proximity of ski lifts. The sublime ruins at Delphi are captivating whether you have little knowledge of ancient Greece or have long awaited a chance to see where the Pythian priestesses uttered their cryptic prophecies. After the Acropolis of Athens, Delphi is the most powerful ancient site in Greece. Its history reaches back at least as far as the Mycenaean period; in Homer's *Iliad* it is referred to as Pytho. Southwest of the Delphi ruins on the coast, picturesque Galaxidi now caters to wealthy Athenians who have restored many of the mansions once owned by shipbuilders.

OSIOS LOUKAS ΟΣΙΟΣ ΛΟΥΚΑΣ

150 km (93 miles) northwest of Athens.

The monastic complex at Osios Loukas, still inhabited by a few monks, is notable for its exquisite mosaics and its dramatic location, looming on a prominent rise with a sweeping view of the Elikonas peaks and the sparsely inhabited but fertile valley. The outside of the buildings is typically Byzantine, with rough stonework interspersed with an arched brick pattern. The spot is especially beautiful in February when the almond branches explode with a profusion of delicate oval pinkish-white blooms.

GETTING HERE AND AROUND

Osios Loukas is located near the town of Distomo in the Voiotia prefecture, about 160 km (99 miles) north of Athens. Driving is easiest, but there are also buses. Take one of the KTEL buses that depart daily from bus Terminal B in Athens for Livadeia. The one-way journey takes 2½ hours. From there, you can take the local bus to Osios Loukas, for an additional fare. *For more information on Athens buses and bus stations, see Bus and Train Travel in Athens.*

EXPLORING

Fodor'sChoice   **Osios Loukas.** Luke (Loukas) the Hermit—not the evangelist who wrote
★   a book of the New Testament—was a medieval oracle who founded a church at this site and lived here until his death in AD 953. He was probably born in Delphi, after his family fled from Aegina during a raid of Saracen pirates. This important monastery was founded by the emperor Romanos II in AD 961, in recognition of the accuracy of Loukas's prophecy that Crete would be liberated by an emperor named Romanos. The *katholikon*, a masterpiece of Byzantine architecture, was built in the 11th century over the tomb of Luke. It follows to perfection the Byzantine cross-in-a-square plan under a central dome and was inspired by Ayia Sophia in Constantinople; in turn, it was used as a model for both the Monastery of Daphni and Mystra churches. Impressive mosaics in the narthex and in portions of the domed nave are set against a rich gold background and done in the somber but

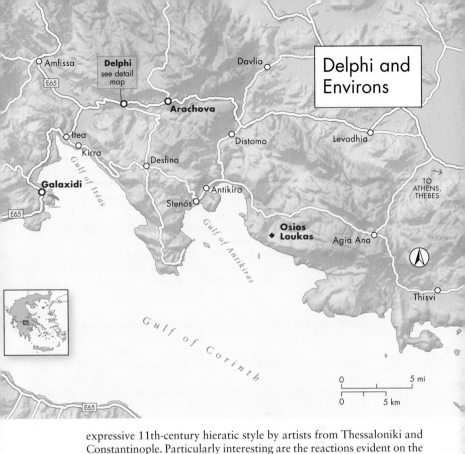

Delphi and
Environs

Amfissa

Delphi
see detail
map

E65

Davlia

Arachova

Itea

Kirra

Distomo

Levadhia

Desfina

TO
ATHENS,
THEBES

Galaxidi

Antikira

Stenós

Gulf of Iteas

Gulf of Antikiras

Osios
Loukas

Agia Ana

E65

Thisvi

Gulf of Corinth

0   5 mi

0   5 km

expressive 11th-century hieratic style by artists from Thessaloniki and Constantinople. Particularly interesting are the reactions evident on the faces of the apostles, which range from passivity to surprise as Christ washes their feet in the mosaic of *Niptir,* to the far left of the narthex.

In the second niche of the entrance is a mosaic showing Loukas sporting a helmet and beard, with his arms raised. The engaging *Nativity, Presentation in the Temple,* and the *Baptism of Christ* mosaics are on the curved arches that support the dome. Two priceless icons from the late 16th century, *Daniel in the Lion's Den* and *Shadrach, Meshach, and Abednego in the Flames of the Furnace,* by Damaskinos, a teacher of El Greco, were stolen a few years back from the white marble iconostasis in the little apse and have been replaced with copies. The tomb of Osios Loukas is in the crypt of the katholikon; his relics, formerly in the Vatican, were moved here in 1987, making the monastery an official shrine. A highlight of the complex, evocatively clinging to a pine-scented hillside, is the Theotokos (Mother of God), a small communal church dedicated to the Virgin Mary, on the left as you enter. On the periphery are the monks' cells and a refectory, now restored, which has been used as a sculpture museum since 1993. To visit you must wear either long pants or a skirt. Bring a small flashlight to help see some of the frescoes. ✉ *On rise above valley of Mt. Elikon* ☎ *22670/22797* ⊕ *www.culture.gr* ✉ *€4.*

ARACHOVA ΑΡΑΧΩΒΑ

24 km (16 miles) northwest of Osios Loukas, 157 km (97 miles) northwest of Athens.

Arachova's gray-stone houses with red-tile roofs cling to the steep slopes of Mt. Parnassus, the highest mountain in Greece after Mt. Olympus. Winter weekends bring sophisticated Athenians heading for the slopes: hotel prices soar and rooms are snapped up; cobblestone streets fill with SUVs carrying skis aloft; and village taverns get crowded after dark as people warm their weary bones before the fires. In summer, meanwhile, there are hardly any Greek tourists in Arachova and not everything may be open.

GETTING HERE AND AROUND

KTEL buses servicing Arachova depart from the Terminal B bus station in Athens. The journey takes about three hours. It is the same regional bus that continues on to Delphi and there are five daily departures, beginning at 7:30 am. *For more information on Athens buses and bus stations, see Bus and Train Travel in Athens.*

EXPLORING

St. George's Day. If you're lucky enough to be in Arachova for the festival on St. George's Day—April 23 (or the Monday after Easter if April 23 falls during Lent)—you're in for the time of your life. St. George, the dragon slayer, is the patron saint of Arachova, and the largest church on the top of the highest hill in town is dedicated to him. So, naturally, the festival here lasts three days and nights, starting with a procession behind the generations-old silver icon from the church, in which the villagers don the local costumes, most of them ornately embroidered silken and brocaded heirlooms that testify to the rich cultural heritage of the town. The festival is kicked off in fine form with the race of the *yeroi*, the old men of the town, who are astonishingly agile as they clamber up the hill above the church without so much as a gasp for air. The following days are filled with athletic contests, cooking competitions, and, at night, passionate dancing in the tavernas until long after the goats go home. Visitors are welcome to partake of a feast held outside St. George (Ayios Georgios) church that features Mt. Parnassus's legendary roast lamb and feta cheese and a steady flow of Arachova wine. ☎ 22670/31241 *Ayios Georgios church* ⊕ *www.panigiraki.gr.*

WHERE TO EAT

$$$
GREEK
✕ Panagiota. It is well worth climbing the 263 steps leading from the main road up to the church of Ayios Georgios, where the lovely smells wafting from the kitchen of this hilltop institution, from the 1930s, will prepare you for a tasty meal. Start with local specialty *opsimotyri* (tart yogurt dip) and the house salad of shredded red cabbage, carrot, and grilled mushrooms. **Known for:** homey atmosphere; traditional mountain dishes. 💲 *Average main: €28* ⊠ *Ano Arachova, behind Ayios Georgios* ☎ 22670/32735 ⊘ *Closed Mon.–Wed. in June–Aug.*

$$
GREEK
✕ Taverna To Agnandio. In the winter you can warm yourself at your choice of several fireplaces in this old stone house that's been deemed a historic building by the state, and look out at the excellent views of the mountains. *Tirokafteri*, a piquant cheese spread, is the perfect accompaniment

For Byzantine splendor, look no further than the paintings covering the crypt of the great monastery at Osios Loukas.

to the stone-ground country bread to start. Follow with a sampling of the large purplish Amphissa olives, *fava* (mashed yellow split peas, lemon, and raw onions), or the potent skordalia. **Known for:** cozy fireside dining; mountain views. $ *Average main: €18* ⊠ *Delfon* ⚓ *Next to town hall and clock tower* ☎ *22670/32114* ⊘ *Closed June–Aug.*

WHERE TO STAY

$$

HOTEL

Fodor's Choice

★

Boutique Hotel Skamnos. This ski hotel and mountain lodge offers some of the region's best views, along with alluring, wood-ceilinged guest rooms, plus such luxurious perks as a heated indoor pool, outdoor Jacuzzi, and a spa. **Pros:** incredible mountain views, perfect for relaxation; relatively good value for the money; attractive surroundings. **Cons:** some smallish rooms; a bit of a drive to Arachova for nightlife and food; can be very busy in season. $ *Rooms from: €135* ⊠ *Voiotia* ⚓ *On road between Arachova and Parnassus Ski Center* ☎ *22670/31927* ⊕ *www.skamnos.com* ⇲ *22 rooms* ⎮⊙⎮ *Breakfast.*

NIGHTLIFE

On winter weekends Arachova streets are jammed with Athenians who come almost as much for the nightlife as for the skiing. Clubs change frequently, but favorites remain.

Aquarella Restaurant Bar. Greek music—sometimes live—sets the tone: drop by for a drink or tuck into a large gourmet menu of meaty offerings Friday and Saturday nights. Later at night, you can still get finger food, and some center tables might be removed to make room for dancing and, even better, for some legendary "flower wars" among happy club goers. Smart dress is strongly recommended. ⊠ *Lakka Sq.* ☎ *22670/32660.*

Café Bonjour. Catch a coffee or freshly squeezed mixed-fruit juice by day or a drink by night at at this popular hangout in tree-covered Lakka Square—and don't forget their croissants: the best in town! ⊠ *Delfon, Lakka Sq.* 🕾 *22670/32330* ⊕ *www.cafebonjour.gr.*

FAMILY
Fodor's Choice
★

Emboriko Tsitsi. This charming gathering spot is housed in a beautiful mountain chalet in the Livadi area (just outside Arachova). It's especially popular later in the evening, when there are tasty cocktails offered at the bar and occasional live performances. Throughout the day, Emboriko draws for pre- and post-skiing food; it also offers organized Segway and bike rides and sells delicious homemade sweets and wine. There's ample parking. ⊠ *Livadi* 🕾 *22670/31218* ⊕ *www.tsitsi.gr.*

Flox All-Day Bar Restaurant. Located off the Ayios Georgios steps, this trendy restaurant-bar, open from October through March, is transformed into a club after midnight. Red wine flows on chilly nights within the carefully lighted rock-wall interior. ⊠ *Ayios Georgios* 🕾 *22670/31007.*

Isidora Gallery. Don't be misled by the name: a wine bar, not a gallery (although temporary exhibitions of up-and-coming Greek artists are often shown here) combines the traditional village aura of an old mansion (built in 1760) with a monklike austerity accentuated by tall candles. A selection of excellent Greek wine is on offer, or you can opt for one of the cocktails. The cheese platters are an ideal accompaniment to your drink, while the jazzy notes in the background will not obstruct your conversation. It opens nightly at 7 pm. ⊠ *Odyssea Androutsou 297* 🕾 *6980/195968.*

Red Six Bar. This rowdy split-level club is quite a scene, with mainstream music, young things dancing on the bar, and a doorman to keep out the unhip. It is still as popular with *après* skiers as it was 25 years ago when it first opened its doors. ⊠ *Lakka Sq.* 🕾 *6940/777444.*

SPORTS AND THE OUTDOORS

HIKING

Arachova and its environs are made for exploring on foot, either by simply walking a country lane to see where it leads or picking up one of the hiking trails like the E4 through Parnassus National Park or the ancient footpath down the mountain. The 8,061-foot summit of Mt. Parnassus is now easily accessible, thanks to roads opened up for the ski areas. The less hardy can drive almost up to the summit.

Arachova Hiking and Skiing Club. This local club for outdoors enthusiasts welcomes visitors and organizes regular group hiking outings; give them a call to join the next one. 🕾 *22670/311118* ⊕ *www.shoarahovas.com.*

SKIING

Parnassos Ski Center. The center, just 40 minutes from Arachova, comprises 17 ski runs, as well as 7 ski routes and 10 trails, spreading across two areas: Fterolakka has a good restaurant and several more-challenging runs; Kelaria is good for beginners. Perks include night ski parties. ⊠ *Kelaria* ✛ *25 km (17 miles) north of Arachova* 🕾 *22340/22700* ⊕ *www.parnassos-ski.gr* 🎿 *From €30 weekends, €15 weekdays.*

SHOPPING

Arachova was known even in pre-ski days as a place to shop for wool, with stores selling rugs and weavings lining the main street. The modern mass-produced bedspreads, *flokatis* (woolen rugs, sometimes dyed vivid colors), and kilim-style carpets sold today are reasonably priced. If you poke into dark corners in the stores, you still might turn up something made of local wool; anything that claims to be antique bears a higher price. Also look for anything made of carved wood, from eating utensils to furniture, as well as local foodstuffs like the delicious Parnassus honey, the local cheese *formaella* (often served warm), and the fiery hot *rakomelo* (a combination of anise liqueur and honey), which is served in most of the bars and cafés on a cold winter's night to warm those who've been outside all day.

Klaoudatos Ski Shop. This well-known outdoors-sports-goods retailer caters to all levels, from beginners to pros; it also runs ski bus tours, two mountain refuges, and organizes ski camps. ⊠ *Distomo-Arachova intersection* ☎ *22670/31457* ⊕ *www.klaoudatos-ski.gr.*

Pappos-Baldoumis Snow Republic Ski Shop and Ski School. The biggest ski school in Greece operates a couple of well-equipped ski shops, including one in Arachova's main square and a second one along the main road, going towards Athens. ⊠ *Lakka Sq.* ☎ *22670/31552* ⊕ *www.skischool.gr.*

DELPHI ΔΕΛΦΟΙ

10 km (6 miles) west of Arachova, 189 km (118 miles) northwest of Athens.

Up in the mountains, modern Delphi is perched dramatically on the edge of a grove leading to the sea, west of an extraordinary ancient site. The hospitable people of modern Delphi take great pride in their town. They maintain a tradition of comfortable, small hotels and a main street thick with restaurants and souvenir shops. Ancient Delphi, the home of a famous oracle in antiquity, can be seen from the town's hotels or terraced village houses. It's easily reached from almost any point in the central town, at most a 10- to 15-minute walk. When the archaeological site is first seen from the road, it would appear that there is hardly anything left to attest to the existence of the ancient religious city. Only the Treasury of the Athenians and a few other columns are left standing, but once you are within the precincts, the plan becomes clearer and the layout is revealed in such detail that it is possible to conjure up a vision of what the scene must have once been when Delphi was the holiest place in all Greece.

GETTING HERE AND AROUND

Surprisingly, there are no trains to Delphi, just buses. In fact, the same KTEL buses from Athens that go to Arachova continue on to Delphi, for no additonal fare. The journey lasts 3½ hours. The first KTEL bus leaves Athens Terminal B at 7:30 am; the last one at 5:30 pm, and 8 pm on Friday and Sunday. *For more information on Athens buses and bus stations, see Bus and Train Travel in Athens.*

10

EXPLORING

At first the settlement probably was sacred to Gaia, the mother goddess; toward the end of the Greek Dark Ages (circa 1100–800 BC), the site incorporated the cult of Apollo. According to Plutarch, who was a priest of Apollo at Delphi, the oracle was discovered by chance, when a shepherd noticed that his flock went into a frenzy when it came near a certain chasm in the rock. When he approached, he also came under a spell and began to utter prophecies, as did his fellow villagers. Eventually a *Pythia,* an anointed woman over 50 who lived in seclusion, was the one who sat on the three-footed stool and interpreted the prophecy.

On oracle day, the seventh of the month, the Pythia prepared herself by washing in the Castalian Fountain and undergoing a purification involving barley smoke and laurel leaves. If the male priests of Apollo determined the day was propitious for prophesying, she entered the Temple of Apollo, where she drank the Castalian water, chewed laurel leaves, and presumably sank into a trance. Questions presented to her received strange and garbled answers, which were then translated into verse by the priests. A number of the lead tablets on which questions were inscribed have been uncovered, but the official answers were inscribed only in the memories of questioners and priests. Those that have survived, from various sources, suggest the equivocal nature of these sibylline emanations: perhaps the most famous is the answer given to King Croesus of Lydia, who asked if he should attack the Persians. "Croesus, having crossed the Halys river, will destroy a great realm," said the Pythia. Thus encouraged, he crossed it, only to find his *own* empire destroyed.

During the 8th and 7th centuries BC, the oracle's advice played a significant role in the colonization of southern Italy and Sicily (Magna Graecia) by Greece's Amphictyonic League. By 582 BC the Pythian Games had become a quadrennial festival similar to those held at Olympia. Increasingly an international center, Delphi attracted suppliants from beyond the Greek mainland, including such valued clients as King Midas and King Croesus, both hailing from wealthy kingdoms in Asia Minor. During this period of prosperity, many cities built treasure houses at Delphi. The sanctuary was threatened during the Persian War but never attacked, and it continued to prosper in spite of the fact that Athens and Sparta, two of its most powerful patrons, were locked in war.

Delphi came under the influence first of Macedonia and then of the Aetolian League (290–190 BC) before yielding to the Romans in 189 BC. Although the Roman general Sulla plundered Delphi in 86 BC, there were at least 500 bronze statues left to be collected by Nero in AD 66, and the site was still full of fine works of art when Pausanias visited and described it a century later. The emperor Hadrian restored many sanctuaries in Greece, including Delphi's, but within a century or two the oracle was silent. In AD 385 Theodosius abolished the oracle. Only in the late 19th century did French excavators begin to uncover the site of Apollo.

Fodor's Choice
★

Ancient Delphi. After a square surrounded by late-Roman porticoes, pass through the main gate to Ancient Delphi and continue on to the Sacred Way, the approach to the Altar of Apollo. Thanks to the 2nd-century AD writings of Pausanias, archaeologists have identified treasuries built by the Thebans, the Corinthians, the Syracusans, and others—a roster of 6th- and 5th-century BC powers. The **Treasury of the Athenians** was built with money from the victory over the Persians at Marathon; the **Stoa of the Athenians** housed an immense cable with which the Persian king Xerxes roped together a pontoon bridge for his army to cross the Hellespont from Asia to Europe. The **Temple of Apollo** is from the 4th century BC, as is the well-preserved **theater**, though it was restored in about 160 BC, and later restored again by the Romans. Also worth the climb is the view from the **stadium** at the highest point of the ancient town. ⊠ *Delphi ✛ Road to Arachova, immediately east of modern Delphi* ☎ *22650/82313* ⊕ *www.culture.gr* ⊠ *€12, includes the Sanctuary of Athena and Delphi Museum.*

Fodor's Choice
★

Delphi Museum. Visiting this museum is essential to understanding the site and sanctuary's importance to the ancient Greek world, which considered Delphi its center (literally—look for the copy of the omphalos, or Earth's navel, a sacred stone from the adytum of Apollo's temple). The museum is home to a wonderful collection of art and architectural sculpture, principally from the Sanctuaries of Apollo and Athena Pronoia. Highlights include the *Charioteer,* one of the greatest surviving ancient bronzes on display, from about 470 BC; two life-size Ionian *chryselephantine* (ivory heads with gold headdresses) from the Archaic period, probably from statues of Apollo and his sister Artemis; an exquisitely detailed marble frieze of the same gods battling with giants, from the 6th century BC; the *caryatids* (supporting columns in a female form) from the treasury's entrance; and the *metopes,* marble sculptures depicting Greece's two greatest heroes, Heracles and Theseus, from the Treasury of the Athenians. There's also a pleasant outdoor café. ⊠ *Delphi ✛ East of Ancient Delphi* ☎ *22650/82313* ⊕ *www.culture.gr* ⊠ *€12, includes Ancient Delphi and the Sanctuary of Athena.*

Fodor's Choice
★

Sanctuary of Athena. Start your tour of the Old Delphi in the same way the ancients did, with a visit to the Sanctuary of Athena, before going on to the Ancient Delphi site. The most notable among the numerous remains on this terrace is the **Tholos** (Round Building), a graceful 4th-century BC ruin of Pendelic marble. By the 2nd millennium BC, the site was already a place of worship of the earth goddess Gaia and her daughter Themis, one of the Titans. The gods expressed themselves through the murmuring of water flooding from the fault, from the rustle of leaves, and from the booming of earth tremors. The Tholos remains one of the purest and most exquisite monuments of antiquity. Beneath the Phaedriades, in the cleft between the rocks, a path leads to the **Castalian Fountain**, a spring where pilgrims bathed to purify themselves, though today access is prohibited. ⊠ *Delphi ✛ Below road to Arachova, before Phaedriades* ⊕ *www.culture.gr* ⊠ *€12, includes Ancient Delphi and the Delphi Museum.*

10

Stoa of the Athenians 2
Temple of Apollo 3
Treasury of the Athenians 1

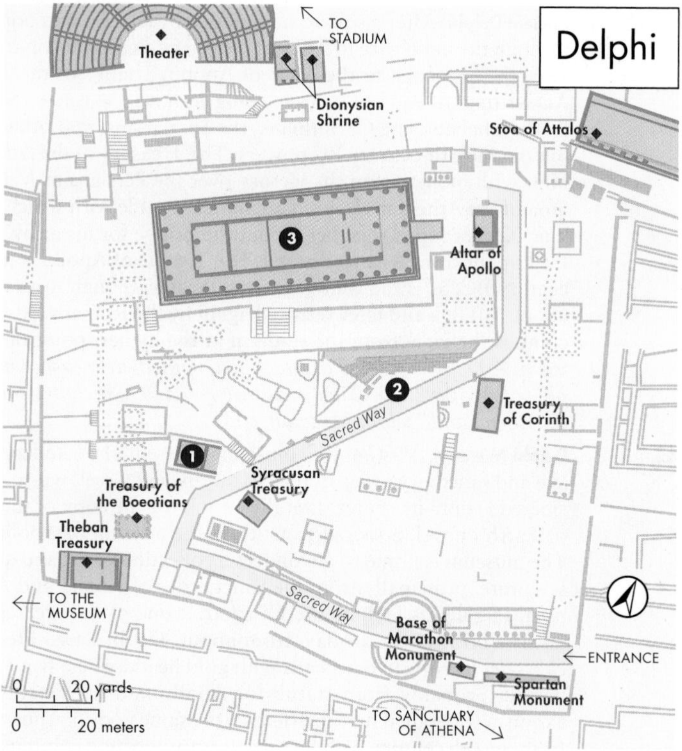

WHERE TO EAT

$$ GREEK
🍴 **Epikouros.** Nothing in the simple restaurant design detracts from the view of the beautiful Itea gorge from the large, open veranda. Even in the colder months, a glass canopy protects the seating area and allows diners to look out year-round. **Known for:** views from the terrace; hearty meat dishes. [$] *Average main: €20* ✉ *Vas. Pavlou and Friderikis 33* ☎ *22650/83250* 🌐 *www.epikouros.net.*

$$ GREEK
🍴 **Iniohos.** Local specialties and small dishes, such as zucchini croquettes, grilled mushrooms, and the *bekri* ("drunk's") *meze*—a meat appetizer meant to be consumed slowly with the region's red Brusco wine—are served at this excellent restaurant of the King Iniohos Hotel. Residents stop by late at night to have a nightcap or a snack—fried formaella cheese, *sfongato* (country vegetable omelet), or a sweet baklava. **Known for:** small dishes; sweeping views; good-value set menus. [$] *Average main: €20* ✉ *Vas. Pavlou and Friderikis 19* ☎ *22650/83101* 🌐 *www.delphi-hotels-iniohos.gr.*

$$ GREEK
Fodor's Choice ★
🍴 **Taverna Vakchos.** Owner Ilias Theorodakis, his wife, and their two sons keep a watchful eye on the kitchen and on the happiness of their customers, who can choose between the spacious dining room or the large sheltered veranda with a stunning valley view. The menu is heavy on meat dishes, either grilled, boiled, or simmered in the oven, but vegetarians can put together a small feast from boiled greens and other

homemade meatless Greek classics, like sweet peas in tomato sauce and stuffed cabbage leaves. **Known for:** friendly family atmosphere; homemade dishes. $ *Average main: €15* ✉ *Apollonos 31* ☎ *22650/83186* ⊕ *www.vakhos.com.*

$$ ✕ **To Patriko Mas.** A traditional stone house built in 1850 in the center
GREEK of Delphi is the setting for hearty lunches and dinners—no wonder this place has long been a favorite with meat-loving skiers. In winter dine near the fireplace and relish hot soups, homemade pies with wild greens, and *kolokythokeftedes* (zucchini balls). **Known for:** game dishes; fireside dining in winter; good local wines. $ *Average main: €20* ✉ *Vas. Pavlou and Friderikis 69* ☎ *22650/82150* ⊕ *www.topatrikomas.gr.*

WHERE TO STAY

$ ⊞ **Acropole.** Feel completely secluded, though you're in the heart of
HOTEL Delphi town's action, as you look from a room filled with handsome wood furniture, traditional linens, and paintings over a sea of olive trees and the Itea gorge (just make sure you ask for a room with a view of the Corinthian gulf). **Pros:** charming and family-run; awesome views; ample-sized rooms. **Cons:** compact bathrooms with shower only; no parking; some decor is a bit dated. $ *Rooms from: €65* ✉ *Filellinon 13* ☎ *22650/82675* ⊕ *www.delphi.com.gr* ⤳ *42 rooms* ⦿⊣ *Breakfast.*

$ ⊞ **Amalia Hotel Delphi.** Clean-cut retro chic predominates at this sleek,
HOTEL low-lying 1965 landmark built by well-known Greek architect Nicos
Fodor'sChoice Valsamakis as a part of one of the country's oldest hotel chains, with
★ comfortable contemporary rooms and 35 acres of gardens that spread down the mountainside to olive groves and pines with, in the distance, a breathtaking vista of the Corinthian gulf. **Pros:** great vintage architecture and decoration; charming gardens and public areas; beautiful swimming pool. **Cons:** a bit off-center of town compared to other hotels; caters mostly to tour groups; slightly impersonal service. $ *Rooms from: €80* ✉ *Apollonos 1 and Osiou Louka 47* ☎ *22650/82101, 210/607–2000 in Athens* ⊕ *www.amaliahoteldelphi.gr* ⤳ *184 rooms* ⦿⊣ *Breakfast.*

$ ⊞ **Fedriades.** A simple, functional look at this attractive spot in the
B&B/INN center of town is accented by warm colors and a touch of Greek mountain style, while avoiding the "ancient kitsch" of several other nearby hotels. **Pros:** spic-and-span cleanliness; center-of-town location convenient to ruins; comfort at a good price. **Cons:** smallish rooms; can be noisy due to traffic on the main street; not all rooms have views. $ *Rooms from: €55* ✉ *Karamanli 46* ☎ *22650/82370* ⊕ *www. fedriades.com* ⤳ *24 rooms* ⦿⊣ *Breakfast.*

FESTIVALS

Fodor'sChoice **Delphi Summer Arts Festival.** Sit in the ancient stadium of Delphi or at
★ the Frynichos theater under the stars and watch everything from the National Beijing Opera Theater's *The Bacchae* to the tragedies of Aeschylus and Euripides, and even folk and traditional music improvisations at the Summer Arts Festival, organized by the European Cultural Center of Delphi. All performances, which begin around 8:30 pm, are open to the public and charge a small fee. ✉ *Ancient Delphi site* ☎ *22650/82731* ⊕ *www.eccd.gr.*

10

GALAXIDI ΓΑΛΑΞΕΙΔΙ

35 km (22 miles) southwest of Delphi.

Sea captains' homes with classic masonry and an idyllic seaside location reminiscent of an island make Galaxidi a terribly appealing place, all the more so since the little port below Delphi is relatively undiscovered. The heyday of the harbor town was in the 19th century—thanks to shipbuilding and a thriving mercantile economy—but after the invention of steamships it slipped into decline. Today the Old Town is classified a historical monument and undergoes continual renovation and restoration.

GETTING HERE AND AROUND

Three buses daily make the four-hour trip from Athens to Galaxidi (four on Sunday), starting at 7:30 am. KTEL buses servicing Galaxidi depart from Terminal B in Athens. This is the same bus that also reaches Delphi and Arachova, usually with a vehicle change in the coast town of Itea. *For more information on Athens buses and bus stations, see Bus and Tram Travel in Athens.*

FESTIVALS

Kathara Deftera (*Clean Monday*). If you happen to be in Galaxidi at the start of Greek Orthodox Lent, *Kathara Deftera,* duck. Locals observe the holiday with flour fights in the town's streets, a custom dating back to the 18th century. The common baking flour is tinted with food dye and by the end of the day everyone and everything in sight—buildings, cars, shrubs—is dusted with a rainbow of colors that match spring's bright palette. The custom has pagan roots: every year the dead were thought to be allowed to leave Hades for a day and return to Earth; if they had a good time, a good crop was assured. Remember to wear your old, unwanted T-shirt and jeans for the day—nobody will ask for your permission before they throw!

EXPLORING

If you are a shore person rather than a mountain person, Galaxidi is a good alternative to Delphi as a base for the region. Stroll Galaxidi's narrow streets with their elegant stone mansions and squares with geraniums and palm trees, and then take a late-afternoon swim in one of the pebbly coves around the headland to the north, dine along the waterfront, and enjoy the stunning views of Galaxidi, with a mountain backdrop, reflected in the still waters.

Ayios Nikolaos. The cathedral, perched atop a hill above the harbor and Old Town, is named after the patron saint of sailors and possesses a beautifully carved 19th-century altar screen. ⊠ *Old Town.*

Maritime Museum of Galaxadi. Housed in an 1868 neoclassical building, this collection includes paintings with nautical themes and many local artifacts from Greek ships and from old sea captains' houses. A small archaelogical collection is also on view. ⊠ *Mouseiou 4* ☎ *22650/41558* 💲*€5.*

DID YOU KNOW?

Set along the grand Sacred Way of Delphi—which leads to the Altar of Apollo—are several beautifully preserved treasuries, which were built by the Athenians, Thebans, and other groups to store their precious offerings to the god.

Easter Week in Delphi

Orthodox Easter Week is the most important holiday in Greece, and Delphians celebrate it with true passion. The solemn Good Friday service in Ayios Nikolaos church and the candlelight procession following it, accompanied by the singing of haunting hymns, is one of the most moving rituals in all of Greece. By Saturday evening, the mood is one of eager anticipation as the townspeople are decked out in their nicest finery and the earnest children are carrying *lambades,* beautifully decorated white Easter candles. At midnight the lights of the cathedral are extinguished, and the priest rushes into the sanctuary shouting *Christos anesti!* (Christ is risen!). He lights one of the parishioner's candles with his own and the flame is passed on, one to the other, until the entire church is illuminated with candlelight, which is reflected in the radiant faces of the congregation.

Firecrackers are set off by the village schoolboys outside to punctuate the exuberance of the moment. After the liturgy is finished, each person tries to get his or her candle home while still lighted, a sign of good luck for the following year, whereupon the sign of the cross is burned over the door. Then the Easter fast is broken, usually with *mayiritsa* (Easter soup made with lamb) and brilliantly red-dyed hard-boiled eggs. On Easter Sunday, the entire village works together to roast dozens of whole lambs on the spit. It is a joyous day, devoted to feasting with family and friends, but you are welcome and may be offered slices of roast lamb and glasses of the potent dark red local wine. In the early evening, a folk-dance performance is held in front of the town-hall square, followed by communal dancing and free food and drink.

WHERE TO EAT

$
GREEK

×**Albatros.** It's hard not to feel at home in this tiny and cozy taverna tucked away on one of the inland streets. Eleni, the owner, prepares excellent dips to start and cooks traditional Greek fare like stuffed tomatoes with rice, fried eggplant, and chicken in lemon sauce with thick-cut chips. **Known for:** homey, intimate surroundings; nicely prepared traditional dishes. $ *Average main: €15* ✉ *Kon. Satha 36* ☎ 22650/42333.

$$
GREEK
Fodor'sChoice
★

×**O Bebelis.** The wine barrel by the front door is the first hint that this cozy *ouzeri,* tucked into a side street off the harbor, is a place to sit back, relax, order the house wine, and taste the little treats laid before you, like home-cured olives, steamed mussels, and other small dishes prepared and served by the genial owner. Daily specials present some innovative takes on classics; the stuffed onions and the pork with plums are especially delicious. **Known for:** laid-back ambience; innovative dishes. $ *Average main: €18* ✉ *Nikolaou Mama 20–22* ✛ *Near the start of the harbor* ☎ 22650/41677.

$$
SEAFOOD

×**O Tassos.** Locals and tourists pack the waterfront terrace, drawn in year-round by the quality of the seafood in this basic taverna with reasonable prices. Farm-raised crawfish (*karavides*) are simply boiled and sprinkled with lemon—a true delicacy. **Known for:** fresh seafood;

harbor views; good local wine. $ *Average main: €24* ⊠ *Akti Ianthis 69* ✛ *At far end of harbor on waterfront* ☎ *22650/41291.*

$$ × **Porto.** Some tasteful antique decorative touches lend this portside
GREEK house a quaint feeling, but in warm weather the terrace is the place to be, to watch the world pass by while enjoying a wide-ranging menu. Aside from a good choice of grilled meats and fish, there are some wonderful seafood and vegetarian pastas, along with a nice selection of salads. **Known for:** good selection of dishes; pleasant portside terrace. $ *Average main: €20* ⊠ *Akti Oianthis* ☎ *22650/41182.*

$$ × **To Barko tis Maritsas.** A captains' *kafeneio* (coffeehouse) from 1850 is
SEAFOOD elegantly decorated in a nautical theme with classic Chesterfield sofas, a character-filled setting in which to enjoy mussels—what Galaxidi is known for—served here in a saganaki, steamed, and in a pilaf. There's also seafood risotto and lobster pasta, as well as traditional non-seafood dishes such as homemade pies. **Known for:** many preparations of mussels; character-filled surroundings. $ *Average main: €25* ⊠ *Akti Ianthis 34* ✛ *On the waterfront* ☎ *22650/41059* ⊙ *Closed weekdays Nov.–Apr.*

WHERE TO STAY

$ 🛏 **Archontiko Art Hotel.** Yiannis Schizas, who established this homey and
B&B/INN comforting hotel with his wife, Argyroula, has a knack for collecting odd items, and each guest room is decorated differently (and tastefully) with his finds—bathroom fixtures might be from ships, or a sewing machine might be used as a table in one room and a bed-in-a-boat in another. **Pros:** quirky and charming; lovely home-away-from-home feeling; nice garden. **Cons:** may be a bit hard to find ; parking is limited; not all rooms have sea views. $ *Rooms from: €60* ⊠ *Parodos, Eleftherias 80* ☎ *22650/42292* ⊕ *archotikoarthotel.gr* ⤵ *8 rooms* ⦿ *Breakfast.*

$ 🛏 **Hotel Ganimede.** A 19th-century sea captain's mansion and two other
B&B/INN houses surround a lush garden, combining welcoming outdoor spaces and
FAMILY homey interiors where unpretentious antiques are interspersed with weav-
Fodor'sChoice ings, small sculptures, and paintings, giving each room personality. **Pros:**
★ homebaked breakfast served in luscious garden; gracious hospitality; welcome drinks served in the garden. **Cons:** no elevator; some bathrooms are small; parking is on street outside. $ *Rooms from: €70* ⊠ *N. Gourgouris 20* ☎ *22650/41328* ⊕ *www.ganimede.gr* ⤵ *7 rooms* ⦿ *Breakfast.*

$ 🛏 **Hotel Miramare.** Everything about this seaside house is bright, from
B&B/INN the flower-filled garden to the huge, tile-floored rooms, all with kitch-
FAMILY enettes, filled with light and sea views and opening to breezy terraces. **Pros:** very large rooms; bright, cheerful surroundings; lovely garden. **Cons:** no elevator; some noise from nearby bars; bathrooms are a bit basic. $ *Rooms from: €50* ⊠ *Platoni and Piniatidou* ✛ *Near the seafront* ☎ *22650/41328* ⊕ *www.ganimede.gr/services/hotel-miramare* ⤵ *9 rooms* ⦿ *Breakfast.*

SHOPPING

Avra Grocery. A traditional grocery shop on the waterfront that not only stocks all the essentials, most of them locally sourced, but also transports you back in time with its old-fashioned, romantic decor. It has been lovingly created by the owners of the Archontiko Art Hotel. ⊠ *Oianthis 95* ☎ *22650/42295.*

10

Nikotakis. At this traditional pastry shop in the heart of town, you'll taste local sweet delicacies like syrupy sponge cake with rice, almond paste, and the fresh cream pastry *galaktoboureko.* ⊠ *Nik. Mama 28* ☎ *22650/42001* ⊕ *www.nikotakis.com.*

Ostria. Clearly, artists are behind the dazzling selection of gift items at Ostria. Beautifully displayed pieces include nautical objects like brass compasses and model ships, but also an array of toys, clocks, icons, and jewelry. There's also a huge selection of ceramics, some by owner Petros Skourtis. He and co-owner Katie Kapi, who is a painter, also invite customers to visit their nearby workshop, where they can even take a pottery course. ⊠ *Akti Ianthis 101* ✛ *On the waterfront* ☎ *22650/41206.*

EPIRUS AND THESSALY

Ioannina, Metsovo, and the
Meteora Monasteries

WELCOME TO EPIRUS AND THESSALY

TOP REASONS TO GO

★ **Meteora Monasteries:** Even more wondrous than the Meteora's soaring rock pinnacles are the medieval monasteries perched atop them—walk, climb, or drive to these still-inhabited spots where eagles once nested.

★ **Zagorohoria Region:** Dotting the dramatic Vikos gorge are 46 traditional villages filled with picturesque Ottoman houses—this is some of the best hiking countryside in all of Greece.

★ **Dodona:** Visiting the ancient site of Dodona in Epirus is a must; many mystical ceremonies took place in this ancient sanctuary of Zeus.

★ **Experience Metsovo's Traditions:** This mountain village has held on hard to its traditional character—discover its stone houses, customary foods, and winding alleyways (each with its own story).

★ **Haunts of Ali Pasha:** Even Lord Byron was drawn to Ioannina to trace the haunted spirit of the legendary pasha who once made Epirus his own personal potentate.

Travelers in search of wild and romantic country will be more than delighted with these two regions of northern Greece. In the markedly Balkan region of Epirus, the route east from Ioannina leads to the thriving traditional village of Metsovo and over the Katara pass on one of the most dramatic roads in Greece. Westward lies the fertile province of Thessaly, where spectacular rock-pinnacle monasteries are shadowed by the Pindos, Plion, and Olympus mountain ranges.

1 Ioannina. Strongly infused by the influences of Greeks, Jews, and Turks, Ioannina rests on the banks of Lake Pamvotis. Picturesquely medieval and founded by Emperor Justinian in 527, the town is shadowed by two historic mosques, which reflect the area's marked oriental character. Although it has an extensive, multicultural history, Ioannina also has a vibrant modern scene. To the north lies the Zagorohoria, whose combo of picturesque houses and arresting gorge landscape make this a must-do.

2 Metsovo. Studded with traditional houses filled with Epirote arts and crafts, this mountain township is famously inhabited by Vlachs who speak their distinct dialect. After visiting the noted Tositsa Museum, head to the hills for an idyllic skiing vacation, nature walks, or wine tours.

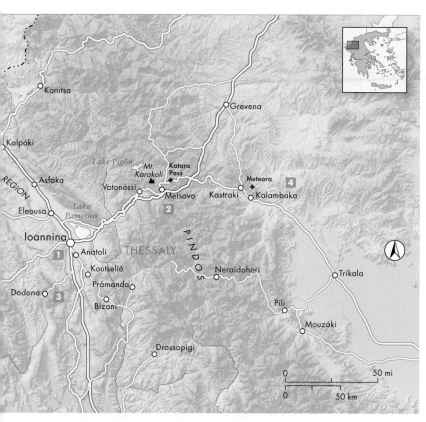

3 Dodona. Mentioned by Homer in the 10th book of the *Iliad*, the Dodona oracle once presided here, only eclipsed by Delphi in classical times. View the remains of the sanctuary of Zeus and the majestic ancient theater, which once held 17,000 spectators and is still the venue of Greek drama presentations.

4 Meteora. Looming out of the edge of Thessaly's main plain, the sky-kissing medieval monasteries of Meteora seem to float in midair, built atop bizarrely shaped pinnacles that tower over the town of Kalambaka. You can enjoy relaxed, fun nights in this "town near Meteora" on its central Dimoula Square, with the Meteora rocks as a backdrop.

Updated by
Adrian Vrettos

As travelers journey through the provinces of northern Greece, they quickly realize that Epirus and Thessaly may have far fewer miles of drop-dead-gorgeous coastline than the south, but if visitors have brought their hiking boots as well as their bathing suits, the north's spectacular mountains, folkloric villages, and lush valleys more than make up for it.

The land changes abruptly from the delicately shaded green of the idyllic olive and orange groves near the shore to the tremendous solidity of the bare mountains inland. This was the splendid massive landscape that came to cast its spell over Lord Byron, who traveled here to meet tyrant Ali Pasha (1741–1822). The Epirote capital of Ioannina still bears many vestiges of this larger-than-life figure, who seems to have stepped from the pages of *The Arabian Nights*.

Going back in time, and taking an easy trip southwest of Ioannina, you can visit Dodona, the site of the oldest oracle in Greece. North of Ioannina, in the mountainous region known as Zagorohoria, or the Zagori, dozens of tiny, unspoiled villages contain remnants of the Ottoman period, and outdoor activities such as hiking are abundant. The route east from Ioannina leads to the thriving traditional village of Metsovo in the Pindos Mountains and over the Katara pass on one of the most dramatic roads in Greece. It ends in the fertile province of Thessaly, where, on the edge of the plain, the Byzantine-era monasteries of Meteora seem to float in midair, built atop bizarrely shaped pinnacles that tower over the town of Kalambaka. At this spiritual center of Orthodox Greece, the quiet contemplation of generations of monks is preserved in wondrously frescoed buildings. Nearby, spectacular mountain passes reveal shepherd villages with richly costumed women speaking the Vlach vernacular.

All in all, northwestern Greece, which stretches from the northern shore of the Gulf of Corinth to the Albanian frontier west of the Pindos range, was aroused from its centuries-old slumber several decades ago with the advent of the ferryboats from Italy. The nautical crossing from Corfu to Igoumenitsa, the westward gateway town to mainland Greece, is

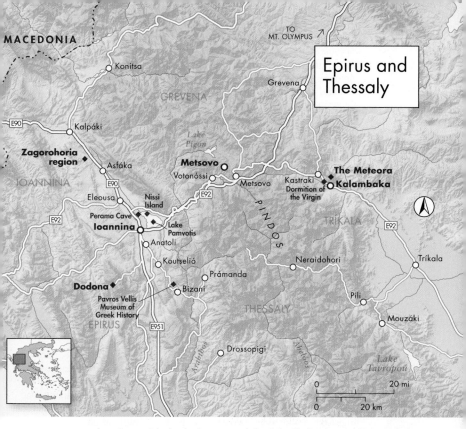

enchanting, with the lush green of the island slowly receding and the stark outlines of the mainland dramatically ahead. The bay is at its best in the early morning, but sunset will do, when the gray rocks likewise flame with deep pinks and violets in an unforgettable welcome. Igoumenitsa is generally unappealing as a port of entry, which means everyone quickly pushes on into the interior and discovers the often-overlooked wonders of Epirus and Thessaly.

PLANNING

WHEN TO GO

Ioannina is easy to visit year-round, but excursions to the countryside are best May through October, when most places are open. Winter is great for skiing and curling up by the fire, although spring, when the abundant and broadly variable natural surroundings blossom, is captivating, especially in the fabled Zagorohoria region. Metsovo can be blissfully cool even in high summer (especially at night). This helps make the town *panagyri* (saint's day festival) for Ayia Paraskevi, held July 26, quite pleasant, but the heat is oppressive elsewhere in this region at this time. The Meteora monasteries attract considerably fewer people in winter, but keep in mind the Thessalian plain can bake during summer in the vast oven formed by the surrounding high mountains. Maximum enjoyment will be obtained in the spring, especially at the Meteora monasteries. At this point, the mountains are still snow covered and blend harmoniously with the green fields, the red poppies, and the white and pink fruit trees.

In Epirus, local tourist offices and most hotels will provide information about festivals, including the famous Ioannina International Folk Festival showcasing the region's music and dancing, which takes place in July. For those seeking the haunting traditional *klarino* (clarinet) music and graceful circle dances of Epirus such as the *pogonisios* and *beratis,* this is a fascinating event. Local groups also perform eerie polyphonic singing, another unique folk tradition rooted in the region.

PLANNING YOUR TIME

Coming either from Thessaloniki, or from the northwestern port of Igoumenitsa, it's reasonable to make the lively town of Ioannina and its glittering lake your starting point. Two nights there should be enough to get a good taste of this city, leaving ample time to take in the top attractions and regional tastes on offer. From there head to the Zagorohoria villages, a unique destination that draws visitors from around the world. Two days here will offer you a good introduction to the area but will definitely leave you wanting more. The Vikos gorge, the deepest in Europe, is a highlight of this stunning area.

Metsovo is the next noteworthy destination in Epirus. A couple of nights are more than enough to enjoy this unique Vlach mountain town. From Metsovo the meandering mountain roads first wind their way up out of Epirus and then down into Thessaly and the town of Kalambaka. It's next to the breathtaking Meteora monasteries perched atop giant limestone stacks, where you should linger a couple of days.

GETTING HERE AND AROUND

Although it's not a major tourist destination, Volos is the major port city of the Thessaly region, and bus, train, and boat routes often use it as a base.

AIR TRAVEL

Olympic Air and Aegean Airlines are the only carriers that service this region. The Ioannina airport, the primary airport in the region, is 8 km (5 miles) north of town. *For detailed information about these airlines, see Air Travel in Travel Smart.*

Contacts Ioannina Airport, aka King Pyrros. ⊠ *Km 8, Ethnikos Odos Ioanninon–Trikalon road, Ioannina* ☎ *26510/83600, 26510/83602.*

BUS TRAVEL

About seven buses a day make the 7-hour trip from Athens's Terminal A (Kifissou) to Ioannina's main Papandreou Station. One of these takes the longer route east through Kalambaka and Trikala rather than the usual southern route to the Rion–Antirion ferry over the suspension bridge, which is the largest in Europe. From Athens's dismal Terminal B (Liossion), seven buses leave daily for the 5-hour journey to Kalambaka. Most routes require you to hop on a different bus for the final leg from Trikala, but one morning bus goes direct. From Thessaloniki to Ioannina there are six buses a day, and, thanks to the Engatia highway, the trip takes a mere 3½ hours and costs €28. Thessaloniki to Kalambaka takes 2¾ hours (€20) with four buses leaving daily. Around four KTEL buses leave Ioannina daily for Metsovo (about 1 hour) and two buses for Kalambaka (2 hours); frequencies are the same in the opposite direction. Buses also head to Dodona. The several-times-weekly bus heading for Melingi village passes the ancient site. Other bus options drop you off 1 km (½ mile) or ½ km (¼ mile) from the site; ask for information based on the day you want to go. On Sunday, service is reduced for all towns. Regular bus service runs from Ioannina's main terminal to the towns in the Zagorohoria. There is also regular and frequent bus service from Athens to Volos, of little interest to travelers but a major transportation hub in the region; from Volos, you can easily connect to Thessaloniki and other destinations in the region. *For detailed information about travel by bus, see Bus Travel in Travel Smart.*

Contacts Ioannina Bus Station. ⊠ *Papandreou 45, Ioannina* ☎ *26510/25014 for Metsovo, Kalambaka, and Dodona, 26510/26286* ⊕ *www.ktelioannina.gr.* **Kalambaka Bus Station.** ⊠ *Ikonomou 9, Kalambaka* ☎ *24320/22432 in Trikala.*

CAR TRAVEL

This region is best explored by car, and if you plan to go beyond the main sights, your own wheels are essential. Driving to Kalambaka or Ioannina from Athens takes the greater part of a day. To reach Ioannina take National Road west past Corinth in the Peloponnese, crossing the magnificent Rion–Antirion bridge. The total trip is 445 km (276 miles). For Kalambaka, take National Road north past Thebes; north of Lamia there's a turnoff for Trikala and Kalambaka (a total of 330 km [205 miles]). The drive from Thessaloniki takes around 5 hours and winds you over the mountains and river valleys of Kozani and Grevena on National Road.

The road from Ioannina to Metsovo to Kalambaka is one of the most scenic in northern Greece, but it traverses the famous Katara pass, which is curvy and can be hazardous, especially December through March (snow chains are necessary). If you are traveling with a few people, it might be more relaxing and almost as economical to hire a taxi to drive you around, at least for a day.

You can rent a car from either Avis, Budget, or Hertz at the Ioannina Airport. Avis also has an office in town. *For information about major agencies, see Car Travel in Travel Smart.*

Contacts Avis Car Hire. ⊠ *Dodonis 71, Ioannina* ☎ *26510/46333* ⊕ *www.avis. gr/greece/car-rental/Ioannina_car_hire.htm.*

TAXI TRAVEL

If you see a cab along the street, step into the road and shout your destination. The driver will stop if he or she is going in your direction. You can ask your hotel reception desk to phone for a taxi and help you negotiate with a taxi driver, especially if you want a tour. You can find taxis at the local bus station, on the central square and at other spots around town. Minimum tariffs are €3.

TRAIN TRAVEL

Kalambaka is reachable by train. Locals normally prefer to travel by bus, because trains generally take longer. Nevertheless, train travel makes sense on the Athens Larissis Station–Kalambaka route if you take the daily express intercity (5 hours) at 8:30 am—ironically €10 cheaper than the slow trains. It costs around the same as a bus—about €25 class A, €18.50 class B for the train and €28 for the bus. Investing in a class A seat (*proti thesi*) means more room and comfort. The nonexpress train is agonizingly slow (at least 7 hours) and requires a change at Palaiofarsalo.

There are also frequent trains between Athens and Volos (a 5-hour journey that leaves six to seven times per day and costs €35–€43) via Larissa. From Volos, buses and trains connect with Thessaloniki every 2 hours (a journey lasting around 2½ hours and costing €18.40); the train trip requires a change at Larissa. Trains to Larissa leave about every hour on the 2- to 3-hour journey; tickets cost €12–€27.

For detailed information about taking the train, see Train Travel in Travel Smart.

Contacts Kalambaka Train Station. ✉ *Pindou, Kalambaka* ☎ *24320/22451.*

HOTELS

Rooms are usually easy to find in Ioannina and, except at the best hotels, are simply decorated. Reservations might be necessary for Kalambaka, which is packed with tour groups to the Meteora monasteries in late spring and summer, and in Metsovo during ski season or the town's July 26 festival. In these two towns, private rooms are likely to be far cheaper than comparable hotel rooms—look for advertisements as you arrive. Off-season, prices drop drastically from those listed here, and you should always try to negotiate. Ask to see the room first, and don't assume anything; if you have special requests, such as a mountain view, a *diplo drevati* (double bed) rather than a *diklino* (twin bed); a balcony; or a bathtub, speak up. In some cases, prices will skyrocket for Greek Easter and Christmas. In Epirus, most small hotels are built in the charming and traditional style—usually recognizable by the heavy use of wood and stone, most suited to the cold winter months, when these accommodations make the perfect base for skiing, hiking, and other activities.

RESTAURANTS

In all but the fanciest restaurants, check out what's cooking because menus change seasonally here. These regions, perhaps because of their dramatic winters, are known for some of the heartiest, rib-stickingest meals around Greece. Informal dress is usually appropriate. Metsovites are particularly known for their meat specialties, such as *kontosouvli* (lamb or pork kebab) and boiled goat, their *trahanas*soup (made from cracked wheat boiled in milk and dried then reboiled up with tomatoes), and their sausages or meatballs stuffed with leeks, as well as their costly but delectable smoked Metsovone cheese. *Pites* (pies, or pita) are pastry envelopes filled with local and seasonal produce, from savory meats and vegetables to sweet dairy creams and honey. Head to the lakesides, most famously those in Ioannina, to feast on aquatic delights: frogs' legs, trout, eel, and crayfish. Wherever you head, Epirote restaurants generally offer an interesting blend of Greek, Turkish, and Jewish flavors, usually prepared with fresh local produce. Some of their tried-and-true recipes are *moschari kokkinisto* (a tomato-base veal stew with carrots, onions, and peas), lamb in lemon sauce, and *lathera* (stove-top vegetable stew made with artichoke hearts, beans, okra, and tomatoes). And the best wine to wash it all down with is Katogi red wine, pressed from French Bordeaux grapes grown locally in Metsovo.

DINING AND LODGING PRICES IN EUROS			
$	**$$**	**$$$**	**$$$$**
Restaurants	under €15	€15–€25	€26–€40	over €40
Hotels	under €125	€125–€225	€226–€275	over €275

Restaurant prices are for one main course at dinner, or for two mezedes (small dishes). Hotel prices are for a standard double room in high season, including taxes.

VISITOR INFORMATION

The Greek National Tourism Organization (GNTO or EOT) in Ioannina is open weekdays 7:30–2:30 and 5:30–8, Saturday 9–1 in July and August; hours vary other months. Mornings are the best time to catch someone in. In summer a tourist information booth is usually erected on the main square of Kalambaka, but it's best to visit the town hall for information.

Contacts Greek National Tourism Organization. ⊠ *Dodonis 39, Ioannina* ☎ *26510/48866, 26510/41142, 26510/48866* ⊕ *www.visitgreece.gr.* **Kalambaka Municipality.** ⊠ *Vlahava 3, Kalambaka* ☎ *24323/50245, 24323/50246.*

EPIRUS ΗΠΕΙΡΟΣ

Ipiros (Epirus) fully justifies its name, "continent," by an overwhelming concentration of mountains, contrasting with the islands—Corfu, Paxi, Lefkada—strung along its littoral. The abrupt changes from the delicately shaded green of the idyllic olive groves on the coast to the tremendous solidity of the bare mountains have been faithfully depicted by that versatile Victorian Edward Lear (of limerick fame). But few travelers would nowadays put up with the discomfort, hardship, and very real danger from bandits that Lear seems to have enjoyed. The scenery has kept its grandeur but has become easily accessible by a good road network and plenty of hotels.

Ancient Epirus was once a huge country that stretched from modern-day Albania (an area the Greeks still call northern Epirus and one in which Greek is still spoken by large communities) to the Gulf of Arta and modern Preveza. The region is bordered by the Ionian Sea to the west, the islands of Lefkada to the south, and Corfu to the north. Inland it is defined by a tangle of mountain peaks and upland plains, and the climate is markedly Balkan.

Although invaded by Normans in 1080, Epirus gained in importance after the influx of refugees from Constantinople and the Morea beginning in 1205 and was made a despotate, a principality ruled by a despot. Ioannina was subsequently made the capital of Epirus and fortified by Michalis Angelos, the first despot. After an invasion by Serbs, Ioannina surrendered to the Ottomans in 1431 and Epirus remained a part of its empire until it became part of Greece in 1913. Besides this great Turkish influence, Metsovo and the surrounding area contain the largest concentration of the non-Greek population known as the Vlachs, nomadic shepherds said to be descendants of legionnaires from garrisons on the Via Egnatia, one of the Roman Empire's main east–west routes. The Vlachs speak a Romance language related to Italian and Romanian.

IOANNINA ΙΩΑΝΝΙΝΑ

305 km (189 miles) northwest of Athens, 204 km (127 miles) west-southwest of Thessaloniki.

On the rocky promontory of Pamvotis Lake lies Ioannina, its fortress punctuated by mosques and minarets whose reflections, along with those of the snowy peaks of the Pindos range, appear in the calm water. The lake contains tiny Nissi, or "island," where nightingales still sing and fishermen mend their nets (and now noted as the hometown of Karolos Papoulias, the previous (2005–15) president of the Greek Republic). Although on first impression parts of the city may seem noisy and undistinguished, the Old Quarter preserves a rich heritage. Outstanding examples of folk architecture remain within the castle walls and in the neighborhoods surrounding them; Ioannina's historic mansions, folk houses, seraglios, and bazaars are a reminder of the city's illustrious past. Set at a crossroads of trading, the city is sculpted by Balkan, Ottoman, and Byzantine influences. Thanks to a resident branch of the Greek national university, today the bustling provincial capital city (population 100,000) has a thriving contemporary cultural scene (and a proliferation of good restaurants and popular bars). Things get particularly lively the first two weeks of July, when the city's International Folk Festival takes place.

The name Ioannina was first documented in 1020 and may have been taken from an older monastery of St. John. Founded by Emperor Justinian in AD 527, Ioannina suffered under many rulers: it was invaded by the Normans in 1082, made a dependency of the Serbian kingdom in 1345, and conquered by the Turks in 1431. Above all, this was Ali Pasha's city, where, during its zenith, from 1788 to 1821, the despot carved a fiefdom from much of western Greece. His territory extended from the Ionian Sea to the Pindos range and from Vaona in the north to Arta in the south. The Turks ended his rule in 1821 by using deception to capture him; Ali Pasha was then shot and decapitated by Greek monks.

GETTING HERE AND AROUND
Olympic Air offers tickets from €27 to €105 one-way from Athens. Direct charter flights from any European capital to Ioannina Airport are also available.

There is no train service to Ioannina, but it is well served by bus. Ioannina KTEL bus station (✉ *Georgiou Papandreou 45,* ☎ *26510/27442*) offers routes connecting with Konitsa (2 hours), Igoumenitsa (2½ hours), Athens (6½ hours), Thessaloniki (3½ hours), and many other towns. From Athens, buses depart weekdays every couple hours from 6:30 am to 10:30 pm, Sunday from 8:30 am to 10:30 pm; tickets are €39. Buses connect with Metsovo twice a day weekdays and once a day on weekends; tickets are €5.80. Buses connect with Trikala's bus station (☎ 24310/73130), a major hub of Thessaly, twice daily; the ride takes 2½ hours and costs €14.70.

Boats depart for Nissi island in Lake Pamvotis every hour in the winter and every 45 minutes in the summer months. The boats leave from the gate of the Kastro fortress; tickets are €1.80.

EXPLORING

TOP ATTRACTIONS

Archaeological Museum of Ioannina. Located in the center of town, this museum is the best in the area. It houses exhibits from the greater Epirus, such as Paleolithic tools, inscriptions, statues, headstones, and a collection of coins, all presented in a contemporary exhibition space with multimedia facilities. ⊠ *25th Martiou Sq.* ☎ *26510/01089* ⊕ *www. culture.gr* ☞ *€4* ☞ *€8 ticket valid for: Archaeological Museum of Ioannina, Byzantine Museum of Ioannina, Dodona.*

Byzantine Museum. Within the larger citadel is the fortress, called Its Kale by the Turks, where Ali Pasha built his palace; these days the former palace serves the city as the Byzantine Museum. The museum's small collection of artworks, actually almost all post-Byzantine, includes intricate silver manuscript Bible covers, wall murals from mansions, and carved wooden benediction crosses covered in lacy silver, gathered from all over the countryside of Epirus. It's carefully arranged in the front half of the museum with good English translations. The second half of the museum houses an important collection of icons and remarkable iconostases, painted by local masters and salvaged from 16th- and 17th-century monasteries. The most interesting section is devoted to silver works from Ali Pasha's treasury from the seraglio. Within the fortress grounds is a very pleasant little café—why not enjoy some light snacks and desserts as you take in the views of the lush gardens around the Byzantine Museum and the impressive old ruins? Nearby is the **Fethiye (Victory) Mosque,** which purports to contain Ali Pasha's tomb. ⊠ *Ioannina* ✛ *Eastern corner of Its Kale fortress* ☎ *26510/39580* ⊕ *odysseus.culture.gr* ☞ *€4.*

Kastro (*Castle*). One of Ioannina's main attractions is the Kastro, with massive, fairly intact stone fortress walls that once dropped into the lake on three sides; Ali Pasha completely rebuilt them in 1815. The city's once-large Romaniote Jewish population, said to date from the time of Alexander the Great, lived within the walls, alongside Turks and Christians. The Jews were deported by the Nazis during World War II, to meet their deaths at extermination camps; the population of 4,000-plus around the turn of the 20th century is now fewer than 100. The area inside the walls is now a quaint residential area with a few hotels, cafés, restaurants, and stores. Outside the citadel walls, near the lake, a **monument** at Karamanli and Soutsou streets commemorates the slaughter of the Jewish community. ⊠ *Ioannina* ✛ *Lakeside end of Odhos Averoff.*

Fodor'sChoice **Nissi Island.** Look back at the outline of the citadel and its mosques in
★ a wash of green as you take the 10-minute ride from the shore toward
small Nissi island. The whitewashed lakeside island village was founded
in the late 16th century by refugees from the Mani (in the Peloponnese). No outside recreational vehicles are allowed, and without the din
of motorcycles and cars, the picturesque village seems centuries away
from Ioannina. Ali Pasha once kept deer here for hunting. With its
neat houses and flower-trimmed courtyards, pine-edged paths, runaway
chickens, and reed-filled backwater, it's the perfect place to relax, have
lunch, visit some of the monasteries (dress appropriately and carry a
small flashlight to make it easier to see the magnificent frescoes), and
have a pleasant dinner. Frogs' legs, eel, trout, and carp (displayed live
in large tanks) take center stage, although traditional fare is also served
at most tavernas here. To cap off your visit, stop by quiet Aleion Square
for a relaxed coffee and a leisurely game of backgammon. ⊠ *Ioannina*
⊹ *Ferry below citadel, near Mavili Sq.* ⊠ *Ferry €2.*

WORTH NOTING

Agios Nikolaos ton Filanthropinon. Of Nissi's several monasteries, Agios
Nikolaos ton Filanthropinon has the best frescoes. The monastery was
built in the 13th century by an important Byzantine family, the Filan-
thropinos, and a fresco in the northern exonarthex (the outer narthex)
depicts five of them kneeling before St. Nikolaos (1542). Many of the
frescoes are by the Kontaris brothers, who later decorated the mighty
Varlaam in Meteora. Note the similarities in the bold coloring, expressiveness, realism, and Italian influence—especially in the bloody scenes
of martyrdom. Folk tradition says the corner crypts in the south chapel
were the meeting places of the secret school of Hellenic culture during
the Ottoman occupation. A most unusual fresco here of seven sages of
antiquity, including Solon, Aristotle, and Plutarch, gives credence to
this story. It is not really feasible, however, that the school would have
been kept a secret from the Ottoman governors for long; more likely,
the reigning Turkish pasha was one who allowed religious and cultural
freedom (as long as the taxes were paid). ⊠ *Ioannina* ⊹ *On Nissi, follow signs* ⊠ *Donations accepted.*

Ali Pasha Museum. The main attraction on Nissi is the 16th-century
Pandelimonos Monastery, now the Ali Pasha Museum. Ali Pasha was
killed here in the monks' cells on January 17, 1822, after holding out
for almost two years. In the final battle, Ali ran into an upstairs cell,
but the soldiers shot him through its floorboards from below. (The
several "bullet" holes in the floor were drilled there when the original
floor had to be replaced.) A wax version of the assassination can be
seen at the Pavlos Vrellis Museum of Greek History in Bizani, south of
Ioannina. A happier Ali Pasha, asleep on the lap of his wife, Vasiliki,
can be seen in the museum's famous portrait. The Ali Pasha Museum
also houses the crypt where Vasiliki hid, some evocative etchings and
paintings of that era, an edict signed by Ali Pasha with his ring seal (he
couldn't write), and his magnificent narghile (water pipe) standing on
the fireplace. The community-run museum is generally open as long as
boats are running; if the doors are shut, ask around to be let in. The
local ticket taker will give a brief tour of the museum in Greek and

broken English (supplemented by an English-language printed guide). A tour is free, but do leave a tip. ⊠ *Ioannina* ✢ *On Nissi, go left from boat landing and follow signs* ☎ *26510/81791* 🔖 *€3.*

Kostas Frontzos Museum of Epirote Folk Art. In a finely restored Ottoman house, this small museum has a collection of richly embroidered local costumes, rare woven textiles made by the nomadic tent-dwelling Sarakatsanis, ceramics, and cooking and farm implements. ⊠ *Michail Angelou 42* ☎ *26510/23566* 🔖 *€2.*

Lake Pamvotis. Despite the fact that the water level is so low (the streams that feed it are drying up) and it has become too polluted for swimming, Lake Pamvotis remains picturesque. It has the longest rowing course in Greece, and teams from all over the Balkans use it for training. The Valkaniadia rowing championships are periodically hosted here. Legend has it that the notorious Ali Pasha drowned his son's lover (after she rejected the Pasha's wishes for her to become his own mistress) in this lake along with other local women, and that their spirits haunt it to this day. ⊠ *Ioannina.*

Mavili Square. This waterfront square is lined with large, noisy cafés that fill with locals and travelers waiting for the next boat to the nearby isle of Nissi. In the evening the seawall is *the* place to hang out—the youth of Ioannina while away the hours here sipping turbo-charged frappé iced coffees or aperitif drinks. The *volta* (ritual promenade) is still a favorite way of passing the time and keeping up to date with all the action and gossip, particularly at night when the town shifts into high gear. ⊠ *Ioannina.*

Municipal Museum. The collections in the well-preserved Aslan Mosque, now the Municipal Museum, recall the three communities (Greek, Turkish, and Jewish) that lived together inside the fortress from 1400 to 1611. The vestibule has recesses for shoes, and inscribed over the doorway is the name of Aslan Pasha and "there is only one god, allah, and muhammed is his prophet." The mosque retains its original decoration and *mihrab*, a niche that faces Mecca. Exhibited around the room are a walnut-and-mother-of-pearl table from Ali Pasha's period, ornate inlaid hamman (Turkish bath) shoes on tall wooden platforms, treasure chests, traditional clothing, a water pipe, and a collection of 18th- and 19th-century guns. ⊠ *Ioannina* ✢ *North end of citadel* ☎ *26510/26356* ⊕ *www.ioannina.gr* 🔖 *€2.*

Old Bazaar. Vestiges of 19th-century Ioannina remain in the Old Bazaar. On Anexartisias are some Turkish-era structures, such as the Liabei arcade (where cool and trendy bars and clubs now dominate), across from the bustling municipal produce market and, on Filiti, a smattering of the copper-, tin-, and silversmiths who fueled the city's economy for centuries. Some workshops still have wares for sale. ⊠ *Ioannina* ✢ *Around citadel's gates at Ethnikis Antistasios and Averoff.*

FAMILY **Pavlos Vrellis Museum of Greek History.** Want to see a tableau of Ali Pasha's legendary murder? Head to this museum to be shocked and amused, by turns, by its collection of historical Epirote waxwork figures from the past 2,500 years, all leading players in more than 30 historical "settings," including streets, mountains, caves, churches, and more. All

To assert their rule over Ioannina, the Turks built the Its Kale fortress; but it was transformed into Ali Pasha's palace in the early 19th century.

the figures were sculpted in wax by artist Pavlos Vrellis, a local legend who embarked on this endeavor at the ripe age of 60. His studio is on the premises, a modern building that has stayed true to Eipirotic architectural style. ⊠ *Neo Bizani ✛ 12 km (7 miles) south of Ioannina, Ethnikos Odos Ioanninon–Athinon road* ☎ *26510/92128* ⊕ *www.vrellis.gr* ▱ *€6.*

OFF THE BEATEN PATH

Perama Cave. The cave's passageways, discovered in the early 1940s by locals hiding from the Nazis, extend for more than 1 km (½ mile) under the hills. You learn about the high caverns and multihued limestone stalagmites during the 45-minute guided tour in English. Printed English-language information is also available. Be prepared for the many steps you must walk up on the way out. At the information center you can see some of the paleontological finds from Perama and learn more about the geology of caves. Bus No. 16 from Ioannina's clock tower gets you here. ⊠ *Ioannina ✛ E92, 4 km (2½ miles) north of Ioannina* ☎ *26510/81521* ⊕ *spilaio-perama.gr* ▱ *€7.*

WHERE TO EAT

$

GREEK

✕ **Fisa Roufa.** This is the best place in Ioannina to enjoy Grandma's home-style cooking, such as pork and celery in a velvety egg-lemon sauce, chicken in yogurt sauce, and *patsa* (tripe) and beef in tomato sauce—simply head to the counter at the back of the charming little *magirion*, a canteen variety of taverna, and point to the dishes that strike your fancy. Beer is served cold and the wine by the kilo (or half, if you must). **Known for:** old-style Greek eatery; good value for money; warm and friendly staff. Ⓢ *Average main: €6* ⊠ *Averof 55* ☎ *26510/26262.*

$ | **Gastra.** For more than 30 years
GREEK | Mr. Vassilis has run this friendly place, where you can discover how Greek grandmothers cooked before the comforts of electricity were introduced to Epirus. The *gastra* is basically a large clay or iron container placed on a fire with hot coals scattered on the iron lid over the pot. **Known for:** succulent slow-cooked meats; traditional local taverna. $ *Average main: €11* ⊠ *Opposite the Dodonis factory, Eleousa ⊹7 km (4½ miles) north of Ioannina (past the airport)* ☎ *26510/61530* ⊕ *www.estiatorio-gastra.gr* ⊘ *Closed Mon.*

THE PRETTIEST WALK

Set at the lakeside end of Odhos Averoff, tree-lined Dionyssiou Skylosofou, which circles the citadel along the lake, is ideal for a late-afternoon stroll. The street was named for a defrocked Trikala bishop who led an ill-fated uprising against the Turks in 1611 (and was flayed alive as a result). A moat, now filled, ran around the southwest landward side, and today the walls divide the Old Town—with its rose-laden pastel-color houses, overhanging balconies, cobblestone streets, and birdsong—from the new.

$ | **Mirovolos.** One of the last in Ioan-
GREEK | nina's main and famous row of
Fodor's Choice | lakeside tavernas, family-run and
★ | welcoming Mirovolos serves great food. Graze while you gaze at the lovely view of the minaret of Aslan Mosque reflecting on the calm waters of Lake Pamvotis. **Known for:** al fresco lakeside dining; slightly elevated and international take on local Greek cuisine. $ *Average main: €12* ⊠ *Strat. Papagou 28* ☎ *26510/78695.*

$ | **Stoa Louli.** The old-fashioned aura created by the old stone building,
GREEK | the interior of which is a stoa with an arched (partly glass) ceiling and doors, is the most alluring feature of this place. Stoas are covered courtyards or walkways used in Greek architecture since ancient times and commonly created for public use, and this one is no different—except that here you can enjoy tasty and well-presented local food along with some excellent wine with an accompaniment of acoustic live music. **Known for:** great character and mood; live music; good wine list. $ *Average main: €13* ⊠ *Anexartisias 78* ☎ *26510/71322.*

WHERE TO STAY

$ | **Epirus Palace.** Indulging oneself in the city of that sybarite Ali Pasha
HOTEL | seems entirely fitting, and you can do so in style at this stunning and
FAMILY | lavish hotel, which was opened in 1999 by the innovative brothers Natsis. **Pros:** special deals can make your five-star stay very affordable; good poolside restaurant; bus service into town. **Cons:** 10 minutes from Ioannina by car; staff is accommodating, but it's a little disorganized for a five-star hotel; breakfast is nothing to write home about. $ *Rooms from: €120* ⊠ *Ethnikos Odos Ioanninon–Athinon ⊹7 km (4½ miles) south of Ioannina* ☎ *26510/93555, 26510/91072* ⊕ *www.epiruspalace.gr* ⇆ *200 rooms* ⦿❘ *Breakfast.*

$ | **Heritage Hotels Kalari.** Here's your chance to stay at an appealing
HOTEL | 16th-century Ottoman market converted into a 21st-century boutique hotel. **Pros:** expertly renovated historic building; excellent wine-bar restaurant in hotel; good value for a five-star boutique-hotel experience. **Cons:** central location means that it is a little noisy at certain

times; no hotel parking; early booking advised to avoid disapointment. $ *Rooms from: €125* ⊠ *Kallari 21* ☎ *26510/27007* ⊕ *www.heritage-hotels.gr* ➳ *13 rooms* ⏷ *Breakfast.*

$

HOTEL

Fodor'sChoice

★

⊞ **Kastro Hotel.** The stylish vibe of old aristocracy coupled with minimalist good taste infuses this neoclassical mansion, which features delightful wood beams, painted wooden ceilings, and fireplaces in the sitting and breakfast rooms—and it's one of the few options within the walls of the historic citadel. **Pros:** welcoming and helpful owners; beautiful antique decor throughout; historical location. **Cons:** can get booked up year-round; sometimes difficult to find parking; breakfast not always included in price, so specify this when booking. $ *Rooms from: €60* ⊠ *Andronikou Paleologou 57* ☎ *26510/22866* ⊕ *hotelkastro.gr* ➳ *7 rooms* ⏷ *Breakfast.*

NIGHTLIFE AND PERFORMING ARTS

Even in a relatively small city like Ioannina, the *magazia* (club-cafés) are always changing names and owners; they may close for winter and open elsewhere for summer, usually under the stars. Karamanli, adjacent to the citadel, is lined with trendy *mezedopoleia* (Greek-style tapas bars) and smart pubs, as is the area around Garivaldi Street running along the outside of the eastern wall of the citadel past Gate D.

Blue Gin Bar. A vaulted cellar has been converted into this chic little bar-club, on a trendy street next to the western wall of the Its Kale fortress. Local DJs and fun events nights make it popular with the town's students, but typically it only starts buzzing after 10 pm. Known for great cocktails—try one with a Greek twist. ⊠ *Eth. Antistaseos 40* ☎ *6932/020361.*

Denoar. In a creatively restored Ottoman-period marketplace, this cool bar-club is a mainstay of Ioannina nightlife. Theme nights, imaginative drinks, and a mixture of funk, rock, and dance music keep eclectic night owls flocking in. ⊠ *Maramenou Stoa, Anexertasias 40* ☎ *26510/69945.*

Fodor'sChoice

★

Stoa Liabei. This Ottoman-era arcade has been transformed into the nightlife hub of the city. Bars and clubs, all with differing styles and music, now occupy every nook and cranny, and attract Ioannina's hip and trendy crowd. One can hop from Stoa Bar, playing deep house and funky sets, to Route 66 with its alternative, soul, and funky grooves. If it's cool yuppie vibes you're after, head to trendy Montage with its breezy uptown decor. In summer the action gets combustible, as these bars merge and mingle, since most of the action is outside. In winter they become more autonomous, shutting doors and pumping up that volume. ⊠ *Stoa Liabei* ✛ *Between Anexatrisias and Kannigos Sts.*

SHOPPING

Ioannina has long been known throughout Greece for its silver craftsmanship and for its jewelry, copper utensils, and woven items. You can find delicate jewelry on the island of Nissi, but there are also many stores selling silver on Odhos Averoff (the better place for larger items, like trays, glasses, and vases), near Neomartiros Georgiou Square. Avoid the shinier and brighter items in stores near the entrance to the citadel.

Presiding over some of the most beautiful folkloric villages of the Zagorohoria region are grand monasteries, such as Agia Paraskevi in Monodendri.

CRAFTS

Center of Traditional Handcraft of Ioannina (Kepavi). A silversmiths' cooperative, Kepavi's sells the silverware and jewelery produced by 44 regional workshops. Items vary in style and technique, including many traditional Epirote pieces as well as some interesting modern ones. The prices are good, and there's something to suit all pockets. ■**TIP→ You can also take a tour of some of the workshops and watch the smiths practicing their fine skills.** ⊠ *Archipiskopou Makariou 11* ✛ *On the road bordering Lake Pamvotis* ☎ *26510/27660* ⊕ *www.kepavi.gr* ☉ *Closed 2:30–6 Mon.–Fri.*

Pagouri est. in Ioannina. This is a really interesting and modern little gift shop, with handmade and painted objects like sunglasses, tote bags and clutches, painted postcards, and lighting frames of the town made by local artists. They also sell herbal olive oil soaps. ⊠ *Karamanli 35* ☎ *6946/153431.*

CERAMICS

Vasilis Gatzias Ergastiri Kataskevis Kosminatos. On Nissi, you will find a handful of quaint little stores selling replicas of traditional objects, such as Turkish water pipes and ornate knives, silver pillboxes encrusted with semiprecious stones, ceramic vases, and jewelry. Those interested in more-original work should head here, to the only boutique that creates unique, handmade pieces. ⊠ *Nissi* ☎ *26510/81878.*

ZAGOROHORIA REGION ΖΑΓΟΡΟΧΟΡΙΑ

40 km–60 km (25 miles–37 miles) north of Ioannina.

One of the most beguiling and untamed sections of Greece is the region of Zagorohoria (pronounced zah-go-ro- *hor*-ee-ah), also known as Zagori or Zagoria, which comprises 46 villages to the north and northwest of Ioannina. During the last decade, the Zagorohoria region has become incredibly popular among Greeks, but it's a place that only foreigners "in the know" visit. Its cultured people, stunning landscapes, cozy guesthouses, World Heritage–protected architecture, and sparkling rivers make it a unique destination.

Here you can see *arhontika* (stone mansions with walls and roofs made of gray slate from surrounding mountains), winding cobblestone streets, graceful arched Turkish bridges, churches with painted interiors, *kalderimi* (old mule trails), and forests of beech, chestnut, and pine. If you have only a day to spare, rent a car or bargain with a taxi driver in Ioannina to transport you to some of the many villages connected by well-paved roads. If you opt to spend the night in one of the villages, you have the chance to truly soak up the local color, get a look at the interiors of some of the Ottoman-style living quarters, and partake of some excellent food. Wonderful hikes are another pleasure for those who choose to stay and explore awhile. Some of the villages, such as Megalo, Mikro Papingo, Monodendri, and Konitsa, are likely to be busy with travelers in July and August, particularly on weekends and major holidays. Book ahead or, better yet, stay in some of the (even) lesser-known villages, some of which have only 10 permanent residents.

Kipi, 40 km (25 miles) north of Ioannina in the central Zagori, is famous for its three-arch packhorse bridge, and the community runs a fascinating folklore museum. **Tsepelovo,** 5 km (3 miles) northeast of Kipi, is one of the most authentic villages. Perched on the slopes of Mt. Tymphai, at 3,960 feet, it was built using the gray-brown tile-like rock that makes up most of the surroundings. A must-see village, **Monodendri,** 44 km (27 miles) north of Ioannina, is a well-preserved settlement perched on the rim of a breathtaking gorge on the boundary of the Vikos–Aoos National Park. There's a stunning vista from the abandoned 15th-century monastery, Agia Paraskevi.

Papingo, 59 km (37 miles) north of Ioannina, has delightful architecture—many houses are still topped with the silvery blue slate that used to be so common throughout Epirus—varied scenery, and friendly locals, although it was among the first villages here "discovered" by wealthy Greeks. It's divided into two towns. **Megalo Papingo,** aka Big Papingo, is near the Voidomatis River, which has excellent rafting and canoeing. **Mikro Papingo,** aka Little Papingo, is 1.5 km (1 mile) up the road from Megalo Papingo, below some limestone rocks; it's really small—the population is fewer than 100—but appealing. **Dilofo** (31 km [19 miles] from Ioannina), aka Two Hills, is one of the best-preserved, quietest, and most picturesque villages in the region, and among the very few where cars can park at its entrance. Your kids (and you) can run safe and free along its cobblestone footpaths.

Buses, which depart from G. Papandreou Avenue 45, Ioannina for the region's larger villages, are few and far between, going only once or twice a week: to Kipi, Monday 6 am and 1:30 pm and Thursday 5:30 am and 1:30 pm; and to Papingo, Tuesday 5:30 am and 2:30 pm. Renting a car is the ideal way to visit, or take a taxi—your hotel should be able to let you know ballpark figures for where you want to go and may arrange the taxi for you.

WHERE TO STAY

$ · **Ameliko.** An imposing stone mansion lovingly restored, with a beautiful garden, Ameliko is an ideal place to stay for those exploring Zagorohoria. **Pros:** management arranges excellent tours and activities in the area; lovely garden; great location. **Cons:** gets busy during winter breaks; Wi-Fi is slow; breakfast could have more variety. $ *Rooms from: €75* ⊠ *Ano Pedina* ☎ *26530/71501* ⊕ *www.ameliko.gr* ⇗ *13 rooms* ⎮◎⎮ *Breakfast.*

HOTEL
FAMILY

$ · **Gaia.** A comfortable, elegant, and well-designed guesthouse, Gaia rose from the ruins of an 1862 mansion thanks to the efforts of devoted owners, architect Yiannis Anastasakis and his wife, Thomais, who literally built Gaia with their own hands after buying it on a passionate whim because they fell in love with the area on a trip. **Pros:** homey and comfortable; very good breakfast with homemade products; guides available for walks. **Cons:** few in-room amenities; Dilofo is a very quiet village; rooms fill fast in high season, so book early. $ *Rooms from: €85* ⊠ *Dilofo* ✣ *Off main square* ☎ *26530/22570* ⊕ *www.gaia-dilofo.gr* ⇗ *7 rooms* ⎮◎⎮ *Breakfast.*

B&B/INN

$ · **Hotel Bourazani.** The old Bourazani hunting lodge has been revamped into this accommodating hotel, one of the few places to stay in this immediate region, which has been given over to nature; the only noises to be heard at night are the distant rustling of the river Aoos and the song of nightingales. **Pros:** owners are gold mines of info about activities; excellent river fishing nearby; great breakfast. **Cons:** access difficult without a car—and call first for detailed directions; mounted animal heads on the walls won't appeal to everyone; patchy Wi-Fi. $ *Rooms from: €85* ⊠ *Bourazani, Konitsa* ☎ *26550/61283, 26550/61320* ⊕ *www.bourazani.gr* ⇗ *20 rooms* ⎮◎⎮ *Breakfast.*

HOTEL

$ · **Zarkada.** Most of the guest rooms in this pension in the heart of the picturesque village of Monodendri have fireplaces—an essential luxury during the long and cold winter nights—and three rooms have saunas, while another seven have hot tubs. **Pros:** feel-good amenities; helpful service; central location, in one of the bigger villages of the area. **Cons:** not all the rooms have fireplaces; some bathrooms are in need of a makeover; some rooms have poor Wi-Fi signal. $ *Rooms from: €60* ⊠ *Monodendri* ✣ *Off main square* ☎ *26530/71305* ⊕ *www.monodendri.gr/?land=en* ⇗ *18 rooms* ⎮◎⎮ *Breakfast.*

B&B/INN

SPORTS AND THE OUTDOORS

Hiking is one of the real pleasures of the Zagorohoria region, but trails can be challenging, not to mention dangerous. Your safest bet is to go on a guided walk; a number of outfitters schedule gorge hikes and other invigorating activities. Make sure you have proper footwear, hiking gear, food and water, and emergency supplies and provisions, and *never* hike in heavy rains or go far in groups of fewer than four. Staff at most hotels can provide basic maps and put you in touch with local guides or trekking clubs. If you want to go it alone, the Greek Alpine Club is a good source of information for a safe hike; it is also a good idea, as a precaution, to let your hotel know where you are going and when you expect to return.

If you're a physically fit hiker, you may want to hike at least part of the steep and long **Vikos gorge**. To get to the famed gorge—the deepest in the world—you follow a precipitous route from the upper limestone tablelands of Monodendri down almost 3,300 feet to the clear, rushing waters of the Voidomatis trout stream (no swimming allowed) as it flows north into Albania. It's a strenuous but exhilarating eight-hour hike on which you are likely to see dramatic vistas, birds of prey, waterfalls, flowers and herbs, and hooded shepherds tending their flocks.

RESOURCES

Greek Alpine Club. ⊠ *Smirnis 15, Ioannina* ✢ *Close to Pargis Sq.* ☎ *26510/22138 Mon.–Sat. 7 pm–9 pm only* ⊕ *www.orivatikos.gr.*

MAPS

Anavasi. One of the best hiking maps of Zagori are by Anavasi. It's GPS compatible and includes shorter and longer walks in the area. ☎ *210/3218104, 210/3210152* ⊕ *www.anavasi.gr.*

OUTFITTERS

FAMILY
Fodor's Choice
★

No Limits. Specialists in the Zagorohoria region, No Limits tours are a fun way to see and explore this spectacular little corner of Europe. As well as rafting, rock climbing, and hiking, they also have horseback-riding trips through the breathtaking Epirote countryside. ⊠ *Central square, Konitsa* ☎ *6944/751418* ⊕ *www.nolimits.com.gr* 🖃 *From €45 for a two-day excursion.*

Robinson Expeditions. This Ioannina outfitter specializes in outdoor tours and can make arrangements for single travelers or groups to hike the Vikos gorge; other programs are hang gliding, canyoning, rafting, mountain biking, kayaking, and nature study. The company also schedules rock-climbing excursions around the Meteora. ⊠ *Kipi (Gardens), Zagorohoria* ☎ *26511/15502, 6949/802702* ⊕ *www.robinson.gr* 🖃 *From €33.*

FAMILY
Fodor's Choice
★

Trekking Hellas. This well-established and reliable outfitter offers activities and excursions throughout Greece and uses the best local experts as guides. In Zagorohoria, activities range from a leisurely 90-minute walk from Vitsa to Kokaris bridge—ideal for families—to a full eight-day expedition in the region, which includes hiking and rafting. They also lead exciting adventure tours in Meteora and Metsovo, and offer multiday guided and self-guided hikes in the area. ⊠ *Spirou Labrou 7, Ioannina* ☎ *26510/71703, 6945/154101* ⊕ *www.trekking.gr* 🖃 *From €52.*

METSOVO ΜΕΤΣΟΒΟ

58 km (36 miles) east of Ioannina, 293 km (182 miles) northwest of Athens.

The traditional village of Metsovo cascades down a mountain at about 3,300 feet above sea level, below the 6,069-foot Katara pass, which is the highest in Greece and marks the border between Epirus and Thessaly. Even in summer, the temperatures may be in the low 20s C (70s F), and February's average highs are just above freezing. Early evening is a wonderful time to arrive. As you descend through the mist, dazzling lights twinkle in the ravine. Stone houses with gray-slate roofs and sharply projecting wooden balconies line steep, serpentine alleys. In the square, especially after the Sunday service, old men—dressed in black flat caps, dark baggy pants, and wooden shoes with pom-poms—sit on a bench, like crows on a tree branch. Should you arrive on a religious feast day, many villagers will be decked out in traditional costume. Older women often wear dark blue or black dresses with embroidered trim every day, augmenting these with brightly colored aprons, jackets, and scarves with floral embroidery on holidays. Note that there is no EOT (tourist office) in Metsovo.

GETTING HERE AND AROUND

A bus or car from Ioannina takes about 45 minutes; bus tickets are €5.80. There is no train service to Metsovo.

EXPLORING

Although most such villages are fading away, Metsovo, designated a traditional settlement by the Greek National Tourism Organization (GNTO or EOT), has become a prosperous, self-sufficient community with a growing population. In winter it draws skiers headed for Mt. Karakoli, and in summer it is—for better or worse—a favorite destination for tourist groups. For the most part Metsovo has preserved its character despite the souvenir shops selling inauthentic "traditional handicrafts" and the slate roofs that have been replaced with easy-to-maintain, cheaper tile.

The natives are descendants of nomadic Vlach shepherds, once believed to have migrated from Romania but now thought to be Greeks trained by Romans to guard the Egnatia highway connecting Constantinople and the Adriatic. Metsovo became an important center of finance, commerce, handicrafts, and shepherding, and the Vlachs began trading farther afield—in Constantinople, Vienna, and Venice. Ali Pasha abolished the privileges in 1795, and in 1854 the town was invaded by Ottoman troops led by Abdi Pasha. In 1912 Metsovo was freed from the Turks by the Greek army. Many important families lived here, including the Averoffs and Tositsas, who made their fortunes in Egyptian cotton. They contributed to the new Greek state's development and bequeathed large sums to restore Metsovo and finance small industries. For example, Foundation Baron Michalis Tositsa, begun in 1948 when a member of the prominent area family endowed it (although he was living in Switzerland), helped the local weaving industry get a start.

Agia Paraskevi. The freely accessible 18th-century church of Agia Para-skevi has a flamboyantly decorated altar screen that's worth a peek. Note that July 26 is its saint's day, entailing a big celebration in which the church's silver icon is carried around the town in a morning procession, followed by feasting and dancing. ⊠ *Main square.*

Averoff Museum. This fascinating museum of regional paintings and sculptures showcases the outstanding art collection amassed by politician and intellectual Evangelos Averoff (1910–90), whose effect on Metsovo is still lauded today. The 19th- and 20th-century paintings depict historical scenes, local landscapes, and daily activities. Most major Greek artists, such as Nikos Ghikas and Alekos Fassianos, are represented. One painting known to all Greeks is Nikiforos Litras's *Burning of the Turkish Flagship by Kanaris,* a scene from a decisive battle in Chios. Look on the second floor for Pericles Pantazis's *Street Urchin Eating Watermelon,* a captivating portrait of a young boy. Paris Prekas's *The Mosque of Aslan Pasha in Ioannina* depicts what Ioannina looked like in the Turkish period. ⊠ *Main Sq.* ☎ *26560/41210* ⊕ *www. averoffmuseum.gr* 🎫 *€3* 🕐 *Closed Tues.*

Katogi-Averoff Winery. Enjoy a tour around this important winery and discover the wine-making process, animated with video projections and sound and art installations. The journey ends in the wine-tasting area, so just try leaving without a few bottles of the exquisite, full-bodied, musky red Katogi-Averoff wine. For those who can't seem to tear themselves away, the four-star Katogi-Averoff Hotel awaits. ⊠ *Metsovo* ✛ *Eastern edge of village, in Upper Aoos valley* ☎ *26560/31490, 22910/41650* ⊕ *www.katogi-strofilia.gr* 🎫 *Free* 🕐 *Closed weekends* ☞ *Book at least one day in advance.*

Fodor's Choice ★ **Tossizza Museum.** For generations the Tossizza family had been one of the most prominent in Metsovo, and to get a sense of how Metsovites lived (and endured the arduous winters in style), visit their home, a restored late-Ottoman-period stone-and-timber building that is now the Tossizza Museum of popular art and local Epirote crafts. Built in 1661 and renovated in 1954, this typical Metsovo mansion has carved woodwork, sumptuous textiles in rich colors on a black background, and hand-crafted Vlach furniture. In the stable you'll see the gold-embroidered saddle used for special holidays and, unique to this area, a fanlight in the fireplace, ensuring that the hearth would always be illuminated. The goatskin bag on the wall was used to store cheese, one of the area's most noted products. Wait for the guard to open the door prior to the tour. Guides usually speak some English. ⊠ *Metsovo* ✛ *Up stone stairs to right off Tositsa (main road) as you descend to main town square* ☎ *26560/41084* 🎫 *€3* 🕐 *Closed Thurs.*

OFF THE BEATEN PATH **Ayios Nikolaos Monastery.** Visit a restored 14th-century monastery, about a 30-minute walk (each way) into the valley. Two images of the *Pantocrator* (Godhead), one in each dome—perhaps duplicated to give the segregated women their own view—stare down on the congregation. You can also see the monks' cells. The guided tour in English explains the 18th-century frescoes created in Epirote style. ⊠ *Metsovo* ✛ *Down* *into valley via footpath (follow signs near National Bank of Greece; turn left where paving ends) ✉ Donations accepted.*

WHERE TO EAT

$
GREEK
Fodor'sChoice
★

✕ **To Koutouki Tou Nikola.** *Koutouki* ("little box"), aptly named for its diminutive interior, is a good value, just one reason this place is so popular with the locals. All the taverna favorites are here, but order something made with the local cheese, or the amazing *hilopotes* (local pasta) cooked in a chicken broth, or the divine celery-leek-and-beef meatballs. **Known for:** excellent local cuisine; really good quality at a low price; warm and friendly service. Ⓢ *Average main: €7* ✉ *Aghiou Georgiou, Averof Georgiou 44200* ✛ *Next to the post office* ☎ *26560/41732* ▭ *No credit cards.*

$
GREEK

✕ **To Paradosiako.** The name means "traditional," and that's what this comfortable spot decorated with colorful weavings and folk crafts is. Vasilis Bissas, the chef-owner, has revived many of the more esoteric regional specialties. **Known for:** hearty winter fare; good friendly service. Ⓢ *Average main: €10* ✉ *Tositsa 44* ☎ *26560/42773* ▭ *No credit cards.*

WHERE TO STAY

$
HOTEL

🏨 **Apollon Hotel.** Family-run and centrally located, looking out on the Pindos mountain range, Apollon is built in traditional style, topped by picturesque coves, and offers comfortable, modern amenities along with old-world accents. **Pros:** friendly, obliging, family-run business; located right in the center of town; organizes excursions. **Cons:** not all rooms have good views; weak Wi-Fi signal in some rooms; basic bathrooms. Ⓢ *Rooms from: €60* ✉ *Main square* ☎ *26560/41844* ⊕ *www.metsovo-hotels.com* ⇄ *40 rooms* �|◯| *Breakfast.*

$
HOTEL
FAMILY
Fodor'sChoice
★

🏨 **Hotel Bitouni.** Local craftsmen created the elegantly carved wooden ceilings in this traditional-style Metsovo mansion—at its heart a large fireplace in the main reception room nicely warms the cozy hotel. **Pros:** great breakfast with many homemade treats; excellent and helpful service; great value lodging also has free parking. **Cons:** luxury lovers, look elsewhere; only a few basic amenities in room; not all rooms have the mountain views. Ⓢ *Rooms from: €55* ✉ *Tositsa St.* ✛ *On the main street leading up from main square* ☎ *26560/41217* ⊕ *www.hotelbitouni.com* ⇄ *30 rooms* ⚲ *Breakfast.*

$$
HOTEL

🏨 **Grand Forest Metsovo.** Your view of the verduous and imposing nature that surrounds you is everything in this top-notch hotel, that can make for an idyllic getaway throughout the year. **Pros:** five-star amenities at an excellent price; wonderful spa and pool area; stunning mountain vistas. **Cons:** one of the floors is not serviced by an elevator; tricky to get to—you definitely need a car; the last stretch of road to the hotel is winding and narrow. Ⓢ *Rooms from: €130* ✉ *Interchange 7A to Anilio* ✛ *Off Egnatia Odos Hwy.* ☎ *26560/29001, 26563/00500* ⊕ *www.grand-forest.gr* ⇄ *62 rooms* ⚲ *Breakfast.*

SPORTS AND THE OUTDOORS

Metsovo is one of the few places in Greece to offer winter skiing, when the entire region is covered in snow and the area's famed Vlach shepherds even have to move their flocks from the mountains to the lowlands around Trikala.

Anilio Ski Resort. Opened in 2012, Anilio has 12 ski runs, the longest winding 1 km (½ mile) down the mountain face, and five ski lifts. A chalet serves a few bites and a good variety of soothing hot drinks. Snow cover suitable for skiing is usually from mid-November to early March. There is also an ice-skating rink nearby. ✉ *Metsovo* ⚓ *Take the E92 and then left onto the E90 following the signs for Anilio; hotel is 6 km (4 miles) south of Metsovo* ☎ *6980/760850.*

SHOPPING

Metsovo is known for its fabrics, folk crafts, silver, and smoked cheese. Although many of the "traditional" arts and crafts here are imported low-quality imitations, with a little prowling and patience you can still make some finds, especially if you like textiles and weavings. Some are genuine antiques that cost a good deal more than the newer versions, but are far superior in quality. Everything's available on the main square.

Aris Talaris. This is actually two shops: one sells quality silver jewelry made in Talaris's own workshop, and the other displays gold pieces. The Metsovo silverwork trade is one of the oldest in the region; members of the Talaris family have been silversmiths for many generations (and now they have branched out as hoteliers, owning the hotel where their shops are). ✉ *Hotel Egnatia, Tositsa 19* ☎ *26560/41263, 26560/41900.*

Pigi. This colorful shop overflows with cheeses of all shapes and sizes. Metsovo is renowned for its cheese, and you will find any local variety your heart (or palate) desires, from the smoky *metsovitico* ewe's and cow's milk cheese to the zingy *metsovela* and even a local Parmesan that rivals any from Italy. ✉ *Tositsa 17* ⚓ *On the left of the main road leading to the main square* ☎ *26560/42163.*

DODONA ΔΩΔΩΝΗ

22 km (14 miles) southwest of Ioannina.

The only thing to do, or see for that matter, at the somewhat isolated Dodona are the ancient ruins. This archaeological site, steeped in history and mystery, is worthy of the time and effort it takes to visit, and dedicating a whole day is most rewarding.

Said to be the oldest oracle in Greece, the Dodona flourished for well over a millennium, from at least the 8th century BC until the 4th century AD, when Christianity succeeded the cult of Zeus. Homer, in the *Iliad*, mentions "wintry Dodona," where Zeus's pronouncements, made known through the burbling brook and the wind-rustled leaves of a sacred oak, were interpreted by priests "whose feet are unwashed and who sleep on the ground." The oak tree was central to the cult, and its image appears on the region's ancient coins. Here Odysseus sought forgiveness for slaughtering his wife's suitors, and from this oak the Argonauts took the sacred branch to mount on their ship's prow. According to one story, Apollo ordered the oracle moved here from Thessaly; Herodotus, however, writes that it was locally believed a black dove from Thebes in Egypt landed in the oak and announced, in a human voice, that the oracle of Zeus should be built.

There is a little canteen at the entrance to the site where visitors can get refreshments, but bringing a simple packed lunch—some bread, cheese, olives, and a tomato—is a pleasant alternative. You can sit and listen for whispers from long-forgotten Zeus, father of gods.

GETTING HERE AND AROUND

The most efficient way to get here from Ioannina is with a rented car or a taxi; the driver will wait an hour or so at the site. Negotiate with one of the drivers near Ioannina's clock tower or ask your hotel to call a cab. Only on Mondays and Fridays are there buses from Ioannina's Bizaniou Station, one at 6:30 am and the other at 8:30 pm.

EXPLORING

Fodor's Choice ★ **Dodona.** Vestiges of two of ancient Greece's important cosmological and cultural institutions, divining and drama, are here—you can see the space of the ancient oracle and the superbly preserved and impressive theater. As you enter the archaeological site, you pass the **stadium** on your right, built for the Naïa games and completely overshadowed by the **theater** on your left. One of the largest and best preserved on the Greek mainland, the theater once seated 17,000; it is used for summer presentations of ancient Greek drama. Its building in the early 3rd century BC was overseen by King Pyrrhus of Epirus. The theater was destroyed, rebuilt under Philip V of Macedon in the late 3rd century, and then converted by the Romans into an arena for gladiatorial games. Its retaining wall, reinforced by bastions, is still standing. East of the theater are the foundations of the **bouleuterion** (headquarters and council house) of the Epirote League, built by Pyrrhus, and a small rectangular temple dedicated to Aphrodite. The remains of the **acropolis** behind the theater include house foundations and a cistern that supplied water in times of siege.

The remains of the **sanctuary of Zeus Naios** include temples to Zeus, Dione (goddess of abundance), and Heracles; until the 4th century BC there was no temple. The Sacred Oak was here, surrounded by abutting cauldrons on bronze tripods. When struck, they reverberated for a long time, and the sound was interpreted by soothsayers. ⊠ *On main Ioaninon–Dodonis road, signposted off E951, Dodoni* ☎ *26510/82287* ⊕ *odysseus.culture.gr* ▨ *€4* ⊘ *Closed Mon.*

THESSALY ΘΕΣΣΑΛΙΑ

Though Thessaly, with part of Mt. Olympus within its boundaries, is the home of the immortal gods, a Byzantine site holds pride of place: Meteora, the amazing medieval monasteries on top of inaccessible needles of rock. The monasteries' extraordinary geological setting stands in vivid contrast to the rest of Thessaly, a huge plain in central Greece, almost entirely surrounded by mountains: Pindos to the west, Pelion to the east, Othrys to the south, and the Kamvounian range to

Today the theater at Dodona—one of Greece's grandest—remains the enthralling site for summer concerts and performances.

the north. It is one of the country's most fertile areas and has sizable population centers in Lamia, Larissa, Trikala, and Volos. Thessaly was not ceded to Greece until 1878, after almost five centuries of Ottoman rule; today vestiges of this period remain. Kalambaka and Meteora are in the northwest corner of the plain, before the Pindos Mountains. The best time to come here, especially to the Meteora monasteries, is spring, when the mountains are still snow covered and blend harmoniously with the green fields, the red poppies, and the white and pink flowering fruit trees.

KALAMBAKA ΚΑΛΑΜΠΑΚΑ

71 km (44 miles) east of Metsovo, 154 km (95 miles) southwest of Thessaloniki.

Kalambaka may be dismissed as one more drab modern town, useful only as a base to explore the fabled Meteora complex north of town. Yet an overnight stay here, complete with a taverna dinner and a stroll around the main squares, offers a taste of everyday life in a provincial Thessalian town. This will prove quite a contrast to an afternoon spent at nearby Meteora, where you can get acquainted with the glorious history and architecture of the Greek Orthodox Church. Invariably, you return to modern Kalambaka and wind up at a poolside bar to sip ouzo and contemplate the asceticism of the Meteora monks. If you'd rather stay in a more attractive place slightly closer to the monasteries, head to Kastraki, a hamlet with some pleasing folk-style houses about 2.5 km (1½ miles) north of Kalambaka.

GETTING HERE AND AROUND

> **NOT SO CRYSTAL CLEAR**
>
> The Dodona oracle had its ups and downs. Consulted in the heroic age by Heracles, Achilles, and all the best people, it went later into a gentle decline because of its failure to equal the masterly ambiguity of Delphi.

The famous Meteora monasteries, set just outside Kalambaka, are easily accessible by both train and slightly more expensive bus, but, as most trips, it is by far preferable to take the bus rather than the slow and creaky trains that service the area. Buses connecting Kalambaka with Trikala take 45 minutes and leave Trikala at 5 am then hourly until 1 pm, and 2:15 then hourly until 10:15 pm; tickets are €2.10. Buses to and from Athens take 5 hours and require a change at Trikala; tickets are €29 one-way, €44 round-trip. Buses to the major port of Volos depart Kalambaka at 7 am, 11:30 am, 3 pm, and 7 pm; tickets are €15. The Kalambaka–Ioannina bus (3 hours) departs at 8:30 am and 3 pm; tickets are €15.

There are seven trains daily from Athens to Kalambaka (€18–€38). Trains often connect with Trikala (15 minutes, €1.80–€2.60), the major transportation hub of Thessaly; there are four trains daily. Kalambaka is currently the last stop on this OSE route.

EXPLORING

Dormition of the Virgin. Burned by the Germans during World War II, Kalambaka has only one building of interest, the centuries-old cathedral church of the Dormition of the Virgin. Patriarchal documents in the outer narthex indicate that it was built in the first half of the 12th century by Emperor Manuel Comnenos, but some believe it was founded as early as the 7th century, on the site of a temple of Apollo (classical drums and other fragments are incorporated into the walls, and mosaics can be glimpsed under the present floor). The latter theory explains the church's paleo-Christian features, including its center-aisle *ambo* (great marble pulpit), which would usually be located to the right of the sanctuary; its rare *synthronon* (four semicircular steps where the priest sat when not officiating) east of the altar; and its Roman-basilica style, originally adapted to Christian use and unusual for the 12th century. The church has vivid 16th-century frescoes, work of the Cretan monk Neophytos, son of the famous hagiographer Theophanes. The marble baldachin in the sanctuary, decorated with crosses and stylized grapes, probably predates the 11th century. ✉ *Kalambaka* ✥ *North end of town, follow signs from Riga Fereou Sq.* ☎ *24320/22752* 🌐 *odysseus.culture.gr/h/2/eh251.jsp?obj_id=1703* 🎟 *€1.50.*

WHERE TO EAT

$ GREEK 🍴 **Estiatorio Meteora.** At this spot on the main square, a local favorite since 1925, the Gkertsos family serves food prepared by the matriarch, Ketty. Meteora is known for hearty main courses—try Ketty's special wine-and-pepper chicken, veal, or pork *stifado* (stew)—and some specialties from Asia Minor, including *tzoutzoukakia Smyrneika,* aromatic meatballs in a red sauce laced with cumin. **Known for:** traditional local recipes; family-run service. [$] *Average main: €10* ✉ *Ekonomou 4* ✥ *On*

Continued on page 573

Nearer to Heaven

THE METEORA
MONASTERIES

Ayia Triada

Here in the most remote corner of Greece, landscape and legend conspire to twist reality into fantasy. Soaring skyward out of dense orchards looms a different kind of forest: gigantic rock pinnacles, the loftiest of which rises 984 feet. But even more extraordinary than these stone pillars are the monasteries that perch atop the stalagmitic skyscrapers. Funded by Byzantine emperors, run by ascetic monks, and once scaled by James Bond, these saintly castles-in-air are almost literally "out of this world."

The name Meteora comes from the Greek word *meteorizome* ("to hang in midair"). These world-famous monasteries seem to do just that. The origin of these rocks, which loom up between the Pindos range and the Thessalian plain, is an enigma. Some geologists say a lake that covered the area 30 million years ago swept away the soil and softer stone as it forced its way to the sea. Others believe the inexorable flow of the Peneus River slowly carved out the towering pillars, now greatly eroded by wind and rain. Legend created, as it often does, a more colorful story: the rock needles are meteors hurled to earth by an angry god.

THE MONASTIC BUILDERS

Man first staked claim to the Meteora peaks when the inaccessible pinnacles served as refuge to pious hermits in the turbulent 14th century. As soon as the Turkish rulers of Trikkala began warring with the Byzantine emperors of Constantinople for rights to the fertile valley, these anchorite monks were forced to retreat to the heights of the impregnable rocks. In 1336 they were joined by St. Athanasios, who hailed from fabled Mt. Athos. Notwithstanding the legend that says that the saint flew up to the rocks on the back of an eagle, Athanasios began the backbreaking task of building the Megalo Meteoro (1356–72)—the biggest of the Meteora monasteries—using pulleys and ropes to haul construction materials.

By the 16th century, 13 monasteries had been established here as bastions of Christianity. During the late-Byzantine period, they are said to have helped "save" Western civilization from the inroads of Turkish domination. In the end, however, the Meteora monasteries came to poignantly epitomize both the glory and the decline of Eastern monasticism. Once the former abodes of emperors and kings, they are now largely supported by tourism.

A VISIT TODAY

For centuries, jointed ladders and descending nets were the only way to ascend the rocky peaks. Tourists who may yearn for the days when travelers made the ascent squeezed into an outsize string-bag are cured of their nostalgia after one look at the rusty windlass, especially if accompanied by the gruesome story that the rope was only ever changed "when it broke." Today, stone bridges, rock-hewn stairs, and *monopati* (old paths) guide visitors up hundreds of steps to the heavenly monasteries.

VISITING THE MAIN MONASTERIES

Monks at Megalo Meteoro use cable cars to avoid tourist crowds on the stairs

Set atop the Meteora's "heavenly columns" are six sky-kissing monasteries. While their dizzying perch seems attributable only to divine intervention, their architecture can be dated from the 14th to 17th centuries. Restricted by space, the buildings rise from different levels. Some are whitewashed; others display the pretty Byzantine pattern of stone and brick, the multiple domes of the many churches dominating the wooden balconies that hang precariously over the frightening abysses.

NIKOLAOS ANAPAFSAS: THE ROAD LESS TRAVELED

Even though **Ayios Nikolaos Anapafsas** (Holy Monastery of St. Nicholas Anapausas) is the first monastic complex you see and is accessed by a relatively unchallenging path, many travelers hurry on to the large, Megalo Meteoro, leaving this one relatively uncrowded. Its *katholikon* (church), built 1388, faces north rather than the usual east because of the rock's peculiar shape and the rock's small area precluded the construction of a cloister, so the monks studied in the larger-than-usual narthex. While the monastery dates from the end of the 15th century, its superb frescoes are from the 16th century and the work of Theophanis Strelitzas. Though conservative, his frescoes are lively and expressive: mountains are stylized, and plants and animals are portrayed geometrically. Especially striking are the treatments of the Temptation and the scourging of Christ.

Ayios Nikolaos Anapafsas
☎ 24320/22375 ▦ €3 ⏱ Apr.–Oct., Sat.–Thurs. 9–3:30; Nov.–Mar., Sat.–Thurs. 9–1

VARLAAM: FABLED FRESCOES

The monastery closest to the Megalo Meteoro is the **Varlaam**, which sits atop a ravine and is reached by a bridge and a climb of 195 steps. Originally here were the Church of Three Hierarchs (14th century) and the cells of a hermitage started by St. Varlaam, who arrived shortly after St. Athanasios. Two brothers from the wealthy Aparas family of Ioannina rebuilt the church in 1518, incorporating it into a larger katholikon called Agii Pandes (All Saints). A church document relates how it was completed in 20 days, after the materials had been accumulated atop the rock over a period of 22 years. The church's main attraction, the 16th-century frescoes—including a disturbing Apocalypse with a yawning hell's mouth—completely covers the walls, beams, and pillars. The frescoes' realism, the sharp contrasts of light and dark, and the many-figured scenes show an Italian influence, though in the portrayal of single saints they follow the Orthodox tradition. Note the

Greek Icon, Meteora

Pantocrator peering down from the dome. These are the work of Frangos Katellanos of Thebes, one of the most important 16th-century hagiographers. Set around a pretty garden, other buildings include a chapel to Sts. Cosmas and Damien. By the large storerooms is an ascent tower with a net and a winch.

Varlaam ☎ 24320/22277 🏷 €3
🕐 May–Oct., Sat.–Thurs. 9–4; Nov.–Apr., Sat.–Wed. 9–3

AYIA BARBARA: GET THEE TO A NUNNERY

On the lowest rock—thought an appropriate tribute to male superiority by the early monks (who first refused to have women in the Meteora)—the compact monastery of **Ayia Barbara** (Holy Monastery of Rousanou) was the only nunnery in the complex centuries ago. With its colorful gardens in and around red-and gray-stone walls, it is a favorite for picture-taking. Set on a large mesa-like rock, the squat building was abandoned in the early 1900s and stood empty until a new order of nuns moved in some years ago and restored it. The monastery was thought to have been founded in 1288 by the monks Nicodemus and Benedict. The main church has well-preserved frescoes dating from the

mid-16th century. Most depict gory scenes of martyrdom, but one shows lions licking Daniel's feet during his imprisonment. The nunnery is accessible via steps and a new bridge.

Ayiya Barbara ☎ 24320/2269 🏷 €3
🕐 Apr–Oct., daily 9–6; Nov–Mar., daily 9–2

MEGALO METEORO: HIGHEST AND GRANDEST

Superlatives can be trotted out to describe the **Megalo Meteoro** (Church of the Metamorphosis [Transfiguration])—the loftiest, richest, biggest, and most popular of the monasteries. Founded by St. Athanasios, the monk from Athos, it was built of massive stones 1,361 feet above the valley floor and is reached by a stiff climb of more than 400 steps. As you walk toward the entrance, you see the chapel containing the cell where St. Athanasios once lived. This monastery, known as the Grand Meteoron, gained imperial prestige because it counted among Athanasius's disciples the Hermit-King Ioasaph of Serbia and John Cantacuzene, expelled by his joint emperor from the Byzantine throne. Dating from 1387—1388, the sanctuary of the present church was the chapel first built by St. Athanasios, later added to by St. Ioasaph. The rest of the church was erected in 1552 with an unusual transept built on a cross-in-square plan with lateral apses topped by lofty domes, as in the Mt. Athos monasteries. To the right of the narthex are the tombs of Ioasaph and Athanasios; a fresco shows the austere saints holding a monastery in their hands. Also of interest are the gilded iconostasis, with plant and animal motifs of exceptional workmanship; the bishop's throne (1617), inlaid with mother-of-pearl and ivory; and the beautiful 15th-century icons in the sanctuary. In the narthex are frescoes of the Martyrdom of the Saints, gruesome scenes of persecution under the Romans. Note the kitchen, blackened by centuries of cooking, and the wine cellar, filled with massive wine barrels. The gift shop is noted for its icons and incense. From November to March the monastery may close early.

Megalo Meteoro ☎ 24320/22278 🖃 €3 ⊗ Apr.–Sept., Wed.–Mon. 9–4; Oct.– Mar., Thurs.–Mon. 9–3

AYIA TRIADA: FOR YOUR EYES ONLY?

The most spectacularly sited of all the Meteora monasteries, **Ayia Triada** (Monastery of the Holy Trinity) is shouldered high on a rock pinnacle isolated from surrounding cliffs; it is reached via rock tunnels and 130 stone-hewn steps (see opening photo). Primitive and remote, the monastery will also be strangely familiar: James Bond fans will recognize it from its starring role in the the 1981 movie *For Your Eyes Only* (the famous winch is still in place, and you may be shown it in a tour by the one monk who lives here). According to local legend, the monk Dometius was the first to arrive in 1438; the main church, dedicated to the Holy Trinity, was built in 1476, and the narthex and frescoes were added more than 200 years later. Look for the fresco with St. Sisois gazing upon the skeleton of Alexander the Great, meant to remind the viewer that power is fleeting. The apse's pseudo-trefoil window and the sawtooth decoration around it lend a measure of grace to the structure. Ayia Triada is fabled for its vistas, with Ayios Stephanos and Kalambaka in the south and Varlaam and Megalo Meteoro to the west. Conveniently, a well-traveled footpath near the entrance (red arrows) descends to Kalambaka, about 3 km (2 miles) away.

Ayia Triada ☎ 24320/22220 ✉ €3 ⊙ May–Sept., Fri.–Wed. 9–5; Oct.–Apr., Fri.–Tues. 10–4

AYIOS STEPHANOS: AGING GRACEFULLY

At the far end of the eastern sector of the Meteora is **Ayios Stephanos**, the oldest monastery—a permanent bridge has replaced the movable one that once connected the monastery with the hill opposite, making this perhaps the most easily accessible, with a car road passing not far below the entrance. According to an inscription that was once on the lintel, the rock was inhabited before 1200 and was the hermitage of Jeremiah. After the Byzantine emperor Andronicus Paleologos stayed here in 1333 on his way to conquer Thessaly, he made generous gifts to the monks, which funded the building of a church in 1350. Today Ayios Stephanos is an airy convent, where the nuns spend their time painting Byzantine icons, writing, or studying music; some are involved in the community as doctors and professors. The katholikon has no murals but contains a carved wooden baldachin and an iconostasis depicting the Last Supper. You can also visit the 15th-century frescoed church of Ayios Stephanos as well as a small icon museum.

Ayios Stephanos ☎ 24320/22279 ✉ €3 ⊙ Apr.–Oct., Tues.–Sun. 9–1:30 and 3:30–5:30; Nov.–Mar., Tues.–Sun. 9:30–1 and 3–5

PLANNING YOUR METEORA VISIT

HOW MANY MONASTERIES CAN I SEE IN A DAY?
All monasteries can be visited in a single journey from Kalambaka—a 21-km (13-mile) round-trip by car—but most visitors prefer to do only two or three, especially if they are hiking along the old monopati (old paths) that connect the monasteries. Most of the stairs upwards are in fine shape but some of the paths are crumbling in places and require the skill of an inordinately sure-footed goat (no heels, please!). ■TIP→ Megalo Meteoro and Varlaam are the two most rewarding monasteries to visit if time is tight. Whatever your mode of transport, buy a map of the monasteries in Kalambaka.

WHAT IS THE GENERAL GEOGRAPHIC LAYOUT?
Heading out from Kalambaka, the comfortable Patriarhou Dimitriou road serpentines past the village of Kastraki and then winds its way ingeniously through the sandstone Meteora labyrinth. The first monastery is Ayios Nikolaos Anapafsas. Beyond it lies the mammoth Megalo Meteoro and, vis-à-vis, Varlaam. Southward is Ayia Barbara and, after a major curving detour, Ayia Triada and Ayios Stephanos. Along the main road, arrowed signposts indicate the turn-offs for the various monasteries. Note, however, that you have to journey along side roads that run for at least one mile (sometimes as much as two) to get to the feet of the monasteries.

HOW CHANGEABLE ARE THE OPENING HOURS?
We list official opening hours, but as these can vary depending on the season (winter hours are usually more limited), confirm the information with your hotel receptionist in Kalambaka. And leave plenty of time before setting off up the hundreds of steps: if you don't, you may find the monastery door closed at the top once you get there!

IS THERE A DRESS CODE?
When visiting you are expected to dress decorously: men must tuck up long hair and wear long pants, women's skirts (no pants allowed) should fall to the knee, and always cover shoulders. Some monasteries provide appropriate coverings at their entrances.

IS THERE ANYPLACE TO EAT?
Once on the monastery circuit, there are just a few overpriced concession stands; if you plan to make a day of it, stock up on picnic goods in town.

CAN I GET TO THE MONASTERIES BY BUS?
A bus leaves Kalambaka for Megalo Meteoro five times daily (once daily in winter); the bus returns to town in late afternoon.

Map:

0 — 2 mi
0 — 2 km

Megalo Meteoro
Varlaam
Ayios Nikolaos
Ayia Barbara
METEORA
Ayia Triada
KASTRAKI
Ayios Stefanos
KALAMBAKA
Patriarhou Dimitriou
E92
E92

Dimarchiou Sq. ☎ *24320/22316* 🌐 *meteora-restaurant.gr* 💳 *No credit cards* 🕒 *Closed Dec.–Jan. Lunch only Oct.–Nov. and Mar.–May.*

$ GREEK FUSION 🍴 **Meteoron Panorama Restaurant.** Come here just for the knockout views of Meteora and the Kalambaka plain below, and the food isn't bad either. Of course, to make sure you get a prime position on the veranda it's best to book in advance. **Known for:** great views of Meteora; attentive service. [$] *Average main: €10* ✉ *Patriarchou Dimitriou 54* ☎ *24320/78128* 🌐 *www.meteoronpanorama.gr.*

$ GREEK FAMILY 🍴 **O Kipos Tou Ilia.** Also know as Elias's Garden restaurant, this simple taverna with a traditional Greek menu and a waterfall in the garden attracts everyone from visiting royalty to Olympic-medal winners. Kids get their own *pethika piata* (kids' plates). **Known for:** al fresco dining in a lovely shaded garden; fun, engaging, and slightly eccentric owner. [$] *Average main: €9* ✉ *Trikalon 149* ✣ *At terminus of Ayia Triada, before entrance to Kalambaka* ☎ *24320/23218* 🌐 *www.gardenrestaurant.gr.*

$ GREEK 🍴 **Paradisos.** When a Greek cooks with *meraki* (good taste and mood), the world does indeed find *paradissos* (paradise). Owner Kyriakoula Fassoula serves meat dishes cooked *tis oras* (to order), such as grilled pork and lamb chops. **Known for:** tasty regional cuisine; friendly service. [$] *Average main: €8* ✉ *Kastraki* ✣ *On main road to Meteora across from Spania Rooms* ☎ *24320/22723* 🕒 *Closed Nov.*

WHERE TO STAY

$ HOTEL 🏨 **Amalia.** At this low-lying, clay-color complex just outside Kalambaka on the road to Trikala, guests can relax in the sitting room with striking antiques, floral murals, and fireplace—you can also enjoy fireplaces in the bar and restaurant—or chill out at the poolside bar, with glistening blue tiles and rustic rafters. **Pros:** spacious, elegant public rooms; lush green garden setting; large swimming pool. **Cons:** a little outside the city; no stores nearby; somewhat unreliable Wi-Fi. [$] *Rooms from: €80* ✉ *Theopetra* ✣ *14 km (9 miles) along Ethnikos Odos Trikalon–Ioanninon road* ☎ *24320/72216* 🌐 *www.amaliahotel-kalambaka.gr* 🛏 *172 rooms* 🍽 *Breakfast.*

$ HOTEL FAMILY 🏨 **Dellas Boutique Hotel.** A good quality hotel in very close proximity to Meteora's famous rocks and the rich surrounding nature makes this a solid choice. **Pros:** free hotel parking; lovely views of the surrounding area; very helpful staff. **Cons:** weak and slow Wi-Fi; no elevator (but only two floors); small bathrooms. [$] *Rooms from: €80* ✉ *Kastraki* ✣ *On the road between Kalambaka and Kastraki* ☎ *24320/78260* 🌐 *dellasboutiquehotel.com* 🛏 *18 rooms* 🍽 *Breakfast.*

$ B&B/INN Fodor's Choice ★ 🏨 **Doupiani House.** Reside in a traditional stone-and-wood hotel set amid vineyards in the upper reaches of the idyllic village of Kastraki, where each room—with a luxurious carved double bed, oak floors, and closets—has a balcony with panoramic views of both Meteora and Kastraki. **Pros:** excellent and helpful staff have extensive local knowledge; ideal combo of comfort and tradition; wonderful hearty breakfast. **Cons:** not all rooms have the stunning view of the monasteries; patchy Wi-Fi; a little out of the way, but close to the monasteries. [$] *Rooms from: €65* ✉ *Kastrakiou, Kastraki* ✣ *Left off main road to Meteora, near Cave Camping* ☎ *24320/75326* 🌐 *www.doupianihouse.gr* 🛏 *17 rooms* 🍽 *Breakfast.*

$ HOTEL **Kastraki.** This is one of the last hotels on the road to the Meteora monasteries. **Pros:** some amazing views; right next to Meteora; on-site parking. **Cons:** some rooms exposed to noise from the sometimes very busy road leading up to Meteora; no elevator, and you have to ask staff to assist you with your bags; weak Wi-Fi signal in some rooms. [$] *Rooms from: €60* ✉ *Patriarchou Dimitriou, Kastraki* ✢ *On Kalambaka–Meteora road* ☎ *24320/75336* 🌐 *www.hotelkastraki.gr* 🛏 *27 rooms* 🍴 *Breakfast.*

$$ HOTEL FAMILY **Pyrgos Adrachti.** Immersed in greenery and directly overlooking the massive monolithic pillars of Meteora that monks have made their home and people come from across the world to admire, Pyrgos Adrachti makes for a unique stay. **Pros:** proximity to the monasteries makes this an ideal base for visitors; very friendly and helpful staff; free parking. **Cons:** not all rooms have the magnificent views, so request when booking; a little out of the way; the steep driveway can be tricky to navigate. [$] *Rooms from: €140* ✉ *Kastraki* ✢ *Right turn off the main road of Kastraki immediately after Hotel Gogos. 1 1/2 km (1 mile) to the end of that road.* ☎ *24320/22275* 🌐 *www.hotel-adrachti.gr* 🛏 *10 rooms* 🍴 *Breakfast.*

NIGHTLIFE

Kalambaka isn't the most cosmopolitan town, but you may find some fun places for ice cream or coffee along the main drag, Trikalon. Dimoula Square is all abuzz on weekends, as locals descend from the surrounding villages.

Melydron Cafe. If you're taking the bus up to Meteora, this busy café on the square next to the Kalambaka town hall is a good spot for that extra coffee boost, as it's right next to the bus stop. Melydron is also a decent watering hole at night. ✉ *Patriarchou Dimitriou 2* ☎ *24320/75003.*

Rapsodia Cafe Bar. This is Kalambaka's hot spot, with live bands and pool tables drawing in the local youth. It's a good place to head if you need a break from the quiet austerity of monastic visits. ✉ *Eleftheriou Venizelou 4* ☎ *24320/77741* 🌐 *www.rapsodia.gr.*

THE METEORA ΜΕΤΕΩΡΑ

3 km (2 miles) north of Kalambaka, 178 km (110 miles) southwest of Thessaloniki.

Fodor's Choice ★ As you drive through the mighty Pindos range, strange rock formations rise ever higher from the plain. Just beyond the dramatic sheer cliff that shelters the town of Kalambaka, the legendary monasteries of the Meteora—one of the wonders of the later Middle Ages—begin to appear along a circular road as it winds 6 km (4 miles) through an unearthly forest of gigantic rock pillars. The ancients believed these formations to be meteors hurled by an angry god. Ascending to 1,820 feet above sea level, these towers, in fact, owe their fantastic shapes to river erosion. But they owe their worldwide fame (and Hollywood moment of glory—remember the James Bond *For Your Eyes Only* climax?) to what perches atop six of them: the impregnable monasteries built here by pious hermits in the turbulent 14th century. *For a complete overview of these fascinating retreats, see our special illustrated feature, "Nearer to Heaven: The Meteora Monasteries."*

THESSALONIKI AND
CENTRAL MACEDONIA

WELCOME TO THESSALONIKI AND CENTRAL MACEDONIA

TOP REASONS TO GO

★ **Mt. Olympus:** Bask in a gods'-eye view from the top of Greece's highest peak, often covered in clouds and lighting as if to prove Zeus still holds sway. Ascend skyward thanks to numerous enchanting trails.

★ **Thrilling Thessaloniki:** In this great commercial hub, the Armani suits and €5 coffees are in contrast to the ruins of the ancient city walls, Byzantine monuments, and the spirited bartering of the city's bazaar.

★ **Between Heaven and Earth:** Lush Mt. Athos, pinpointed with monasteries, is Greece's most solemn precinct; off-limits to women, it is an exclusive Orthodox bastion as well.

★ **Alexander the Great Sites:** The fabled ancient ruler made this region the crossroads of the ancient world. Walk in his footsteps in Pella (his birthplace) and Vergina (home to the royal tomb of his father, Philip II).

At the crossroads of East and West, Macedonia bears the traces of many civilizations: Macedonian, Hellenic, Roman, Byzantine, and Ottoman. Greece's second city, cosmopolitan Thessaloniki lies in the strategic center of Macedonia, nestled gracefully in the wide but protective arms of the Thermaic Gulf and buttressed on its inland side by a low-lying mountain range around which the Axios River flows south to the Aegean. Macedonia's famed three-fingered peninsulas, tipped by famed Mt. Athos monasteries, are only a few hours away by car on good highways.

1 Thessaloniki. Named after Alexander the Great's stepsister, this bustling, commercial center is Greece's second city and has always played a supporting role. Rather than wallow in this eternal bridesmaid status, Thessaloniki has excelled as a cultural and business center, with some of Greece's best food and nightlife (it is known as the country's Liverpool for the jazz and rock groups that were formed here), much of which is concentrated

around its beautifully planned and architecturally rich city center.

2 Alexander the Great Country. Just southwest of Thessaloniki, central Macedonia dazzles with natural beauty and archaeological wonders, especially at Dion and Vergina, where Philip II of Macedonia, father of Alexander the Great, was buried.

3 **Mt. Olympus.** Don't miss an excursion to Greece's highest and most storied peak, which dramatically ascends from greenery to rock to cloud, with no rolling hills to muddle the effect. Look up or down at this fabled peak and you'll understand why people settled at its foot and dreamed up the 12 Greek gods believed to live in the folds of the mountain.

4 **Halkidiki.** East of Thessaloniki, the road leads to the three fingers of Halki-diki. Known as "Heaven's City," Ouranoupoulis is close to several small and fetch-ing islets on Proviakas Bay. Beyond is famed sacred Mt. Athos. Monks got to North-ern Greece long before tour groups, and the sites they chose for their monasteries are truly beautiful. In this region of extraordinary Byzantine architecture, one of the most impressive monastic complexes in the world is the Ayion Oros (Holy Mountain) on Mt. Athos, a males-only commu-nity for Greek and Eastern Orthodox monks.

Updated by
Adrian Vrettos

A land shaped by gods, warriors, and ghosts, Northern Greece sparkles with the sights, sounds, scents, and colors of its melting-pot history and epic geography. Here you will find remnants of the powerful civilizations that battled each other: temples and fortifications built by Athens and Sparta, Macedonian tombs, the arches and rotundas of imperial Rome, the domes of Byzantium, and the minarets and hammams of the Ottomans. Today, these sights rank among the most splendid sightseeing delights in Greece.

Burnished by history, the area that is often called Northern Greece borders Albania, the Former Yugoslav Republic of Macedonia (FYROM, also known as Skopje), Bulgaria, and Turkey. From north to south, this land is heritage-rich. "Even today, house-owners sometimes dream that beneath their cellars lie Turkish janissaries and Byzantine necropolises," wrote historian Mark Mazower in his 2004 book *Salonica: City of Ghosts*. "One reads stories of hidden Roman catacombs, doomed love-affairs, and the unquiet souls who haunt the decaying villas near the sea."

Around 316 BC, the Macedonian leader Cassander founded what is now the area's major city, Thessaloniki, which grew into a culturally rich and politically strategic metropolis where Christians, Muslims, and Jews lived together for hundreds of years. Today it remains the second-largest city in Greece, is an anchor for arts and culture in the Balkans, and also brims with antiquities, old-style street markets, and old-world European flavor. Beyond Thessaloniki lies Central Macedonia, where you can explore ancient monasteries, admire the frescoed tomb of Philip II of Macedon, hike the bloom-filled trails leading to Mt. Olympus, commune with farmers over grilled wild mushrooms, and enjoy some of Greece's finest beaches and seaside resorts.

The region was established as the state of Macedonia in the 8th century BC, and an illustrious monarchy was ensconced by about the 7th century BC. Philip II (382–336 BC) and his son Alexander the Great conquered most of the rest of Greece—except Sparta—and all of Persia. After Alexander's death, his brother-in-law, Cassander, established Thessaloniki as the capital (316 BC), naming it for his new bride, Thessalonica, Alexander's half sister and daughter of the much-married Philip. (Philip had named her after his famous *nike*, or "victory," in Thessaly, where her mother had been one of the prizes.) The Romans took Macedonia as Alexander's successors squabbled, and by 146 BC, the rest of Greece had fallen under Roman rule. After the assassination of Julius Caesar, Marc Anthony defeated Brutus and Cassius at the battles of Philippi in Macedonia in 42 BC. Under Pax Romana, St. Paul twice traveled through on his way to Corinth.

Greek and Macedonian culture bloomed again during the Byzantine Empire (circa AD 312–1453), when the center of Greek civilization shifted from Athens to Constantinople (modern-day Istanbul). Thessaloniki became the second-most important city in the empire, and it remained so during the Ottoman domination that lasted from the fall of Constantinople until the 1912–13 Balkan Wars. That's when Macedonia became part of Greece, and the 1923 Treaty of Lausanne established the present borders with Thrace. The collapse of Yugoslavia in the 1990s rekindled ethnic and religious animosities. Today's northern Greeks are fiercely nationalist, and they strongly oppose the Former Yugoslav Republic of Macedonia's (FYROM) insistence on calling itself "Macedonia" and using ancient Macedonian symbols such as the star of Vergina on its flag, in an attempt to create a speedy and easily identifiable post-Communist national identity. Tempers flared again in December 2006, when FYROM announced plans to name its international airport in Skopje after Alexander the Great.

Name-game squabbling aside, Northern Greece is flourishing. It's a hub for southeast European commerce and culture, and is home to Aristotle University, Greece's largest. The area is also expected to benefit from the Egnatia Odos, a 669-km (416-mile) road project that connected the Greek–Turkish border with the western port of Igoumenitsa. An influx of immigrants, many of them from Eastern Europe and the Middle East, is once again giving a multicultural flavor to Thessaloniki.

PLANNING

WHEN TO GO

Travel throughout Northern Greece is best from May through October. Fall is beautiful; the air is cool and clear and the forests are dressed in burnished hues of orange, red, and copper. Spring is also lovely, especially in Dion, with its blooming fields of wildflowers scenting the breeze. Winters are mild, though there's usually enough snow in the north to keep ski resorts in business. July and August are the most crowded, but best for sunning, swimming, and chatting with Northern Europeans and Greek families on holiday. In summer, Thessaloniki gets hot and humid but rarely reaches the scorching temperatures that sizzle southern Greece. As a whole, Northern Greece is rainier and cooler than the rest of Greece, especially in mountainous areas.

Autumn and winter rains, besides turning some roads to mud, do not enhance the appearance of Thessaloniki, a city designed for the sun.

PLANNING YOUR TIME

Thessaloniki makes a great base for a trip to Northern Greece. Most of the city's sights are concentrated within the easily walkable center, and the city is also the main hub for regional buses and rental cars. There are wonderful museums and a great counterculture vibe. You could easily spend days exploring Greece's second-largest city, especially if you're an ecclesiastical buff (the five-aisled basilica Ayios Dimitrios is Greece's largest church) or a foodie (Thessaloniki has outstanding restaurants). From Thessaloniki, go west to Pella, the birthplace of Alexander the Great. Then go south to the town of Vergina, home of the magnificent Royal Tombs, and the ancient city of Dion, tucked into the lush foothills of Mt. Olympus. You'll need at least two days to hike the great summit of the gods, including an overnight stay in the pretty village of Litochoro.

GETTING HERE AND AROUND

Thessaloniki doesn't have good public transportation, and a new metro was not open at this writing—it's scheduled to open sometime in 2020. Nevertheless, getting around the city on foot is fairly easy, since most of the sights are relatively close together. Taxis are also an option, and at reasonable prices. If you choose to drive, know that the traffic here can be as bad as the gridlock in Athens. That changes once you get out of Thessaloniki. The national highway is easy to navigate, and the smaller roads in Central Macedonia are well paved. If you wish to rent a car, there are several reliable car rental agencies in Thessaloniki. There are also buses daily that go to major sites in Central Macedonia, many belonging to the giant KTEL company.

AIR TRAVEL

Thessaloniki Macedonia International Airport (SKG) is at Mikras, 13 km (8 miles) southeast of the city center on the coast; it's about a 20-minute drive. In addition to international flights from primarily European destinations, there are frequent daily flights to and from Athens; flying time is 45 minutes. Domestic carriers including Aegean Air and its subsidiary Olympic Air connect Thessaloniki with a number of other cities in mainland Greece as well as Mykonos, Santorini, Crete, Rhodes, Corfu, Limnos, Chios, and Lesvos.

Bus 78 to and from the airport originates at the KTEL bus terminal, stops at the train station, and makes a stop at Aristotle Square (along Egnatia). Taxis charge according to the meter, with a €3.60 surcharge from the airport; expect to pay around €25 to the Town Center (after midnight the charge doubles).

Contacts Thessaloniki Macedonia International Airport. ⊠ *Km 16, Ethnikos Odos, Thessaloniki–Perea road, Thessaloniki* ☎ *2310/985000* ⊕ *www.thessalonikiairport.gr.*

BOAT AND FERRY TRAVEL

Hellenic Seaways, Nel, Minoan, and other sea lines connect Thessaloniki to Chios, Lesvos, Samos, Heraklion (Crete), Kos, Rhodes, Skiathos, Skopelos, Naxos, Mykonos, Paros, and Santorini. Buy tickets at the Karacharisis Travel and Shipping Agency, Zorpidis Travel Services (Sporades and Cyclades only), Alexander Travel, or another travel agency. You can connect to Piraeus from Kavala, 136 km (85 miles) east of Thessaloniki (confirm schedules with the Kavala Port Authority). In summer, you should reserve ferries a month in advance. The Greek Travel Pages (⊕ *www.gtp.gr*) list ferry schedules online.

Contacts Karacharisis Travel and Shipping Agency. ⊠ *Salaminas 10, Port* ☎ *2310/513005, 2310/524544* ⊕ *thesferry.gr.* **Kavala Port Authority.** ⊠ *Averof 1, Kavala* ☎ *2510/223691, 2510/225192* ⊕ *www.portkavala.gr.* **Zorpidis Travel Services.** ⊠ *Egnatia 76, Kentro* ☎ *2310/231170, 2310/244400* ⊕ *www.zorpidis.gr.*

BUS TRAVEL

The trip to Thessaloniki from Athens takes about 6 hours and costs €45 one way and €65 return (with 10 buses per day), with one rest stop. Intercity KTEL buses connect Thessaloniki with cities throughout Greece. There are small ticket-office terminals (*praktorio*) for each line and separate ticket offices and telephone numbers for each destination. You can browse the KTEL website to get an idea of timetables (it's in Greek, so use Google to translate the page), or call KTEL Thessaloniki Main Terminal, but it's best to make ticket inquiries in person. The KTEL Main Terminal is on Thessaloniki's southwestern outskirts, off National Road (Ethnikos Odos). Buses to Halkidiki leave from another KTEL terminal (⊕ *www.ktelmacedonia.gr*) every half-hour from 4 am until 10:45 pm. All of this can be confusing, so definitely confirm both the time of your bus and the terminal from which it leaves when you buy your ticket.

Contacts KTEL Main Terminal. ⊠ *Giannitson 244, Thessaloniki* ☎ *2310/595400 call center, 2310/595421 reservations for buses in Thessaloniki, 2310/595413 reservations for buses to Athens, 2310/595428 reservations for buses to Litochoro, 2310/595435 reservations for buses to Veria* ⊕ *ktelmacedonia.gr.*

CAR TRAVEL

Driving to Greece through the Former Yugoslav Republic of Macedonia is possible but often time-consuming owing to many border problems. The Athens–Thessaloniki section of the Ethnikos Odos (National Road), the best in Greece, is 500 km (310 miles); the drive takes 5 to 7 hours. The roads in general are well maintained and constantly being improved and widened throughout the region. A good four-lane highway that begins in Athens goes to the border with Turkey. Posted speed limits are up to 120 kph (75 mph). When there's traffic, vehicles regularly use the shoulder as an extra lane, even though this is illegal. Driving in Thessaloniki is not recommended because of the congestion, frequent traffic jams, and scarcity of parking. Walking and taking a local bus or taxi are much easier on the nerves.

Having a car to get out of town and explore the smaller villages is helpful. Major car-rental agencies have offices at the Thessaloniki airport (some also have in-town locations). Aeolos is a good location option.

Contacts Aeolos. ⊠ *Agelaki 23, Kentro* ☎ *2312/201888* ⊕ *www.e-aeolos.eu.*

TRAIN TRAVEL

Thessaloniki is the primary entry point for train travel to Northern Greece. Of the six Athens–Thessaloniki trains that run per day, five are express (taking 5 hours 23 minutes). Make reservations in advance at Athens Larissis Station's (Stathmos Larissis) south office (far-left facing, not the main entrance ticket booths, which are for same-day tickets only), or in Thessaloniki. The fastest intercity train will set you back €55.40 for a class-A seat or €45.40 for class B, and it's worth paying the difference for the extra comfort. Other express options begin at €35.10 for class A, €25.10 class B, and take 7 hours. Thessaloniki Station also has a left-luggage office (€2 for 8 hours, €3 for 24 hours) where you can store your bags before checking into or after checking out of your hotel.

Contacts OSE Thessaloniki Train Station. ✉ *Monastiriou 28, West Thessaloniki* ☎ *14511 Customer Service (6 am–11 pm)* ⊕ *www.ose.gr.*

HOTELS

In the past, Thessaloniki's hotels were nothing to write home about and were mostly geared to the needs of transient business travelers, with little emphasis on capturing the spirit-of-place so appealing to tourists. Today, there are some more fetching options out there. The selection of hotels throughout Northern Greece varies from exclusive seaside resorts in Chalkidiki to modest family-managed hostels on the slopes of Mt. Olympus to luxe outposts in Thessaloniki. Throughout the countryside, hotels are usually small, somewhat spartan affairs whose charm comes mainly from their surroundings. Note that some establishments—particularly in Chalkidiki—close for the winter (we've noted when it's otherwise); it is best to make arrangements ahead.

RESTAURANTS

Traditional Thracian and Macedonian cooks adapt to the seasons: in winter, rich game such as boar and venison is served; in summer, there are mussels and other seafood from the Aegean, as well as fruits and vegetables from the fertile plains. The relatively cooler climate here is reflected in rich soups like *patsas* (tripe), roast chicken, stuffed vegetables, and stewed lamb and pork. Local restaurants also reflect Jewish, French, Ottoman, and Balkan culinary traditions.

Small plates (*mezedes*) are a fundamental part of the Thessaloniki dining experience. Specialties include *midia* (mussels), which come from farms outside the bay and are served in styles that include *saganaki* (sauteed in a pan with tomatoes, peppers, and melted feta) and *achnista* (steamed in broth with herbs). Also look for *soutzoukakia* (Anatolian-style meatballs in a rich tomato sauce seasoned with cumin). *Pinerli* (an open-faced boat of bread filled with cheese and ham) is a Black Sea specialty brought here by the Pontii, Greeks who emigrated from that area. Thessaloniki's street food and indulgent sweets are also famous throughout the country.

Meals are complemented by generous amounts of wine, ouzo, and especially *tsipouro*, the local version of grappa. Try the excellent barrel or bottled local wines, especially reds under labels such as Naoussa or Porto Carras or a little bottle of Malamatina retsina, considered the best bottled version in Greece, as is the Boutari label, created by passionate winemaker and popular Mayor Yiannis Boutaris. Throughout

12

the city, little shops and cellars specialize in a Macedonian treat called submarine (or *ipovrihio*), a spoonful of sugary fondant often flavored with vanilla or mastic and dipped in an ice cold glass of water, or other spoon sweet such as *visino* (black) cherries in syrup. As for dinnertime, you can arrive around 8, earlier than most Greeks like to eat dinner (many places do not open before then)—but it's much more fun to come at 9 or 10 and mix with the locals until the late hours.

Restaurant and hotel reviews have been shortened. For full information, visit Fodors.com.

DINING AND LODGING PRICES IN EUROS			
	$	$$	$$$	$$$$
Restaurants	under €15	€15–€25	€26–€40	over €40
Hotels	under €125	€125–€225	€226–€275	over €275

Restaurant prices are the average cost of a main course at dinner or, if dinner is not served, at lunch. Hotel prices are the lowest cost of a standard double room in high season.

TOURS

Dolphin Hellas. Dolphin Hellas leads organized five-day tours of Northern Greece that begin in Athens and take in the ancient archaeological sites; these are offered approximately once a month. Like other agencies, the company also arranges tailored tours and books hotels and car rental. Going through an agency often nets a cheaper rate than those quoted to individual walk-ins. ☎ *210/9227772 in Athens* ⊕ *www.dolphin-hellas.gr.*

Dopios. A super new initiative connecting locals with visitors. Dopios is wonderful new way of exploring the different facets of life and culture in Thessaloniki and its environs with a *dopios* (local) as a guide. Check out the website to see what kind of tour may interest you, whether it be a gastro tour, barhopping, or the more standard sightseeing. ⊕ *www.dopios.com.*

Thessaloniki Tourist Guide Association. To hire a sightseeing guide, you can contact the Thessaloniki Tourist Guide Association. Prices vary depending on the tour and the place, but count on roughly €120 for a half-day and €160 for a full-day tour in Thessaloniki itself. Note that the TTGA offices do not have regular opening hours, so leave a message or send an email and they will get back to you. ☎ *2310/546037* ✉ *guideskg@otenet.gr.*

Eat and Walk Food Day Tours. These tours provide an excellent way to see the sights of the city while also tasting and learning about how food, which is colorfully woven into the historic and cultural tapestry of the area, has made Thessaloniki such a culinary center. Prices start at €20, for the short walks and tasting tour. ⊠ *Mitropoleos 53, Kentro* ☎ *2310/278027* ⊕ *www.eatandwalk.gr.*

Zorpidis Travel. Many tours in the region leave from Halkidiki, but major tour operator Zorpidis runs half-day tours to Vergina–Pella from Thessaloniki, and even arranges honeymoon trips. ⊠ *Mitropoleos 24, Kentro* ☎ *2310/231168* ⊕ *www.zorpidis.gr.*

VISITOR INFORMATION

In Thessaloniki, the Greek National Tourism Organization (GNTO or EOT) central regional office on Tsimiski is open year-round from 8:30 to 3 on weekdays, and 8:30 to 2 on Saturday. Opening hours may be longer in summer but are not guaranteed. There's also a branch at the airport.

Contacts Greek National Tourism Organization *(GNTO/EOT). ☒ Tsimiski 136, at Dagkli, Kentro ☎ 2310/254839, 2310/252170 ⊕ www.visitgreece.gr.*

THESSALONIKI ΘΕΣΣΑΛΟΝΙΚΗ

At the crossroads of East and West, where North blends into South, Thessaloniki (accent on the "ni") has seen the rise and fall of many civilizations: Macedonian, Hellenic, Roman, Byzantine, Ottoman, and that of the Jews and the modern Greeks. Each of its successive conquerors has plundered, razed, and buried much of what went before. In 1917 a great fire destroyed much of what was left, but the colorful past can still be seen and sensed. The vibrant city with close to 1.5 million inhabitants today—also known as Thessalonike, Saloniki, Salonika, or Salonica—has a spacious, orderly layout that is partly a result of French architect Ernest Hébrard, who rebuilt the city after the fire.

Though Thessaloniki has suburbanized since the 1990s, sprawling to the east and west, the old part of the city is fairly centralized and easy to get used to. Whether you're in Ano Polis (Upper City) or along the lively seaside promenade, long, leisurely walks here are well rewarded; you will come across parks, squares, old neighborhoods with narrow alleyways and gardens, courtyards draped with laundry, neoclassical mansions, and some of the more than 50 churches and 40 monasteries. Thessaloniki's Early Christian and Byzantine monuments, with their distinctive architecture and magnificent mosaics, are UNESCO World Heritage sites. The ever-changing nature of the city continues as neighborhoods like Ladadika, a former warehouse district (which got its name from the olives and olive oil or *ladi* stored here), have been recycled into pedestrian zones of restaurants and clubs. The neighborhood is filled with young and old, strolling by fountains, snapping fingers to the music in the air, and savoring mezedes and microbrews at tables spilling onto the stone squares.

One of the most alluring aspects of Greece's "second capital" is its vibrant cultural scene—annually people travel here from across the globe to attend the city's two major film festivals, the Thessaloniki International Film Festival and the International Documentary Film Festival, both of which offer numerous parallel events like exhibitions, workshops, and performances, as well as several other independent film, music, theater, dance, and gastronomy festivals throughout the year. Its intricate cultural character is also reflected in its quarters, such as the Jewish section, and the impressive museums, buildings, restaurants, and shops associated with them.

GETTING HERE AND AROUND

You can get to Thessaloniki from Athens easily by train or bus in about 6 hours (sometimes faster by express train), or you can fly. There are also international trains daily from Thessaloniki to Istanbul, Belgrade, and Bulgaria.

Buses traveling throughout the city streets of Thessaloniki are frequent, and the routes are useful. Bus 1 goes between the train station and the KTEL Main Terminal; Bus 78 goes from the KTEL Main Terminal to the train station and the airport; Bus 36 from Voulgari and Egnatia corner (in the eastern part of the city) goes to the KTEL Halkidiki Terminal (for Ouranoupolis, etc.). Tickets cost €0.80 at bus company booths and at some kiosks (*periptera*) or corner stores; or €0.90 on the bus and the ticket is reusable for any trip up to 90 minutes after the initial validation. You can also buy a 24-hour ticket for €4.

Thessaloniki's official taxis are blue with white hoods, and there are plenty cruising the streets by day, though fewer at night, and they can be hailed anywhere. The "Taxi" sign is lit up showing the availability. The minimum fare is €3, but make sure that the meter is on (rates double after midnight). On the whole the drivers are not only honest but also helpful, and tipping, though not essential, is the norm. Despite the heavy traffic (every hour seems to be rush hour in Thessaloniki) taking a taxi is cheap in comparison to most other places in Europe and the United States. You can also call for a pickup or use Taxibeat, a brilliant free online service that hails the taxi of your choice in the vicinity. On Taxibeat, each taxi is rated and has useful information about the driver/taxi (e.g., languages spoken, Wi-Fi on board, pet-friendly, etc.).

Bus Contacts O.A.S.T.H. ⊠ *Papanastasiou 90, 3rd floor, West Thessaloniki* ☎ *11085* ⊕ *www.oasth.gr.*

Taxi Contacts Lefkos Pyrgos (*White Tower*). ☎ *2310/214900* ⊕ *taxiway.gr.* **Makedonia.** ☎ *2310/550500.* **Taxibeat.** ⊕ *taxibear.gr.*

EXPLORING

The appeal of Thessaloniki lies in part in its warmth, accessibility, and languid pace. The afternoon *mesimeri*, or siesta, is still sacrosanct (don't call people between 3 and 5 pm). Take your time exploring in-town archaeological sites and Byzantine treasures, making sure to stop for café-style people-watching. It's best simply to wander through the streets responding to whatever you encounter. It is hard to get lost, since the entire city slopes downhill to the bay, where you can always align yourself with the White Tower and the city skyline.

KENTRO

The lively shopping streets, bustling markets, and cafés of the Kentro (City Center) and adjacent areas reward you with the unexpected encounters and sensual treats of a great city. A stroll along the recently developed seafront is also enjoyable and a good way to walk off a big lunch. Walking eastward along the promenade, the landscaped areas and lush gardens are found at the end towards the concert hall. If you're feeling sporty, then join the locals who come here for a jog. Exploring the area from the White Tower west along the seaside to Aristotelous Square reveals icons of the city's history: grand monuments of Emperor Galerius, artifacts from the Neolithic period through the Roman occupation housed in the Archaeological Museum, and prominent churches, as well as the city's most important landmark, the tower itself.

TOP ATTRACTIONS

Arch of Galerius. The imposing *kamára* (arch) is one of a number of monuments built by Galerius around AD 305, during his reign as co-emperor of Diocletian's divided Roman Empire. It commemorated the Roman victory over Persia in AD 297, and you can still see scenes of those battles on the badly eroded bas-reliefs. Originally, the arch had four pediments and a dome and was intended to span not only the Via Egnatia, the ancient Roman road, but also a passageway leading north to the Rotunda. Only the large arches remain. ⊠ *Sintrivaniou Sq., Egnatia, Kentro.*

Fodor's Choice ★ **Archaeological Museum of Thessaloniki.** The unpretentious, single-story white structure gives no hint from the outside of the treasures within. A superb collection of artifacts from Neolithic times; sculptures from the Archaic, classical, and Roman eras; and remains from the Archaic temple at Thermi all reside under this roof. Objects discovered during construction of the Egnatia and Thessaloniki–Skopje highways were added in 2005 to the collection, which is displayed in eight galleries. *Thessaloniki, the Metropolis of Macedonia* traces the city's history through artifacts and a multimedia collection. *Towards the Birth of Cities* offers remains from settlements from Kastoria to Mt. Athos that date to as early as the Iron Age. ⊠ *Manoli Andronikou 6, Kentro* ☎ *2313 /310201* ⊕ *www.amth.gr* 💲 *€8; combined ticket with Byzantine Museum €8.*

Ayia Sofia. The founding date of this church, a UNESCO World Heritage site and the focal point of the city's Easter and Christmas celebrations, has been the subject of disagreements over the centuries. Ecclesiastics think it was built after the first Council of Nicea (AD 325), when Jesus was declared a manifestation of Divine Wisdom; other church historians say it was contemporaneous with the magnificent church of Ayia Sofia in Constantinople, completed in AD 537, on which it was modeled. From its architecture the church is believed to date to the late 8th century, a time of transition from the domed basilica to the cruciform plan. The rather drab interior contains two superb mosaics: one of the Ascension and the other of the Virgin Mary holding Jesus in her arms. This latter mosaic is an interesting example of the conflict in the Orthodox Church (AD 726–843) between the iconoclasts (icon smashers, which they often literally were) and the iconodules (icon venerators). At one point in this doctrinal struggle, the Virgin Mary in the mosaic was replaced by a large cross (still partly visible), and only later, after the victory of the iconodules, was it again replaced with an image of the Virgin Mary holding baby Jesus. The front gate is a popular meeting spot. ⊠ *Ermou and Ayias Sofias, Kentro* ☎ *2310/270253* ⊕ *www.agiasofia.info.*

Ayios Dimitrios. Magnificent and covered in mosaics, this five-aisle basilica is Greece's largest church and a powerful tribute to the patron saint

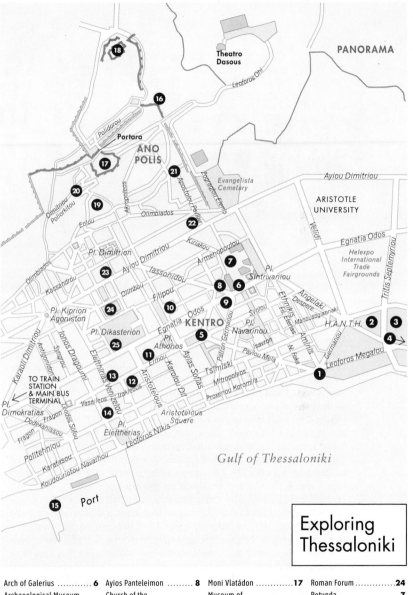

Exploring Thessaloniki

One of the major crossroads of Thessaloniki, Aristotelous Square is a bustling *platia* set near the sea.

of Thessaloniki. It was rebuilt and restored from 1926 to 1949, with attention to preserving the details of the original; the marks left by a fire can still be seen throughout. In the 4th century, during the reign of Emperor Galerius, the young, scholarly Dimitrios was preaching Christianity in the coppersmith district, in contravention of an edict. He was arrested and jailed in a room in the old Roman baths, on the site of the present church. While he was incarcerated in AD 303, Dimitrios gave a Christian blessing to a gladiator friend named Nestor, who was about to fight Galerius's champion, Lyaios. When Nestor fought and killed Lyaios, after having made Dimitrios's blessing public, the enraged Galerius had Nestor executed on the spot and had Dimitrios speared to death in his cell. His Christian brethren were said to have buried him there. A church that was built on the ruins of this bath in the 5th century was destroyed by an earthquake in the 7th century. The church was rebuilt, and gradually the story of Dimitrios and Nestor grew to be considered apocryphal until the great 1917 fire burned down most of the 7th-century church and brought to light its true past. The process of rebuilding the church uncovered rooms beneath the apse that appear to be baths; the discovery of a reliquary containing a vial of bloodstained earth gave credence to the idea that this is where St. Dimitrios was martyred. You enter through a small doorway to the right of the altar. Work your way through the crypt (which tends to close a little earlier than the church itself), containing sculpture from the 3rd to 5th century AD and Byzantine artifacts. The church's interior was plastered over when the Turks turned it into a mosque, but eight original mosaics remain on either side of the altar. ⊠ *Ayiou Dimitriou 97, Kentro* ☎ *2310/270008, 2310/260915* ⊕ *www.inad.gr* ✉ *Free.*

Ayios Panteleimon. A prime example of 14th-century Macedonian religious architecture, Ayios Panteleimon is an eye-catching church that draws you in to take a closer look. Restored in 1993 after an earthquake in 1978, the facade reveals the ornamental interplay of brick and stonework, and a dome displays typically strong upward motion. ⊠ *Iasonidou and Arrianou, near Egnatia, Kentro* ☎ *2310/204150.*

12

FAMILY **Museum of Byzantine Culture.** Much of the country's finest Byzantine art—priceless icons, frescoes, sculpted reliefs, jewelry, glasswork, manuscripts, pottery, and coins—is on exhibit here. Ten rooms contain striking treasures, notably an exquisite enamel-and-gold "woven" bracelet (Room 4), and an enormous altar with piratical skull-and-crossbones. A mezzanine (Room 7) shows how early pottery was made. Check the museum's website for the current temporary exhibitions. ⊠ *Leoforos Stratou 2, Kentro* ☎ *2313/306400* ⊕ *www.mbp.gr* 🔖 *Nov.–May €4; Apr.–Oct. €8; combined ticket with Archaeological Museum €15.*

Panagia Chalkeon. The name *Chalkeon* comes from the word for copper, and the beautiful "Virgin of the Copper Workers" stands in what is still the traditional copper-working area of Thessaloniki. Completed in 1028, this is one of the oldest churches in the city displaying the domed cruciform style and is filled with ceramic ornaments and glowing mosaics. Artisans and workers frequently drop by during the day to light a candle to this patron of physical laborers. Inside the sunken walls is a pretty and well-tended garden. The area around Panagia Chalkeon has many shops selling traditional copper crafts at low prices. ⊠ *Chalkeon 2, Kentro* ✛ *Corner of Egnatia and Aristotelous* ☎ *2310/272910.*

Rotunda. Also known as Ayios Giorgios, this brickwork edifice has become a layered monument to the city's rich history. Built in AD 306, it was probably intended as Roman emperor Galerius's mausoleum. When he died in Bulgaria, however, his successor refused to have the body brought back. Under Theodosius the Great, the Byzantines converted the Rotunda into a church dedicated to St. George, adding the impressive 4th-century AD mosaics of early saints. The Ottomans made it a mosque (the minaret still stands). It was restored after damage suffered in a 1978 earthquake and is still undergoing restoration at this writing. Once a month and on major holidays a liturgy is held here, as are occasional art exhibits and concerts. ⊠ *Plateia Agiou Georgiou, Kentro* ☎ *2310/968860* 🔖 *€2.*

Fodor'sChoice **White Tower.** The city's most famous landmark, and a symbol of Macedonia, the White Tower is the only medieval defensive tower left standing along the seafront (the other remaining tower, the Trigoniou, is in the Upper City). Now a part of the Museum of Byzantine Culture, its six floors offer a wonderful multimedia introduction to the city's history. Much of that history occurred within these walls—for centuries this was a prison—and *on* its walls: formerly known as "Blood Tower" it got its current name in 1896 when a convict exchanged his sentence for whitewashing the entire structure (which was removed in a 1980s renovation). The displays teach you that formidable seawalls and intermittent towers encircled the medieval city and were erected in the 15th century on the site of earlier walls. In 1866, with the threat of piracy diminishing and European commerce increasingly imperative, the Ottoman Turks began demolishing them, except for the White Tower. At the top of your climb of 96 steps you are rewarded with a lovely museum café, whose rooftop setting provides sweeping vistas of the city. ⊠ *Leoforos Nikis and Pavlou Melas, Kentro* ☎ *2310/267832* ⊕ *www.lpth.gr* ☜ *€3.*

WORTH NOTING

Atatürk Museum. The soldier and statesman who established the Republic of Turkey and became its president, Atatürk (Mustafa Kemal) was born here in 1881. He participated in the city's Young Turk Movement, which eventually led to the collapse of the sultanate

ALL ROADS LED TO THESSALONIKI

It was during the Byzantine period that Thessaloniki came into its own as a commercial crossroads, because the Via Egnatia, which already connected the city to Rome (with the help of a short boat trip across the Adriatic), was extended east to Constantinople. Today, the avenue called Egnatia Odos virtually follows the same path; it is Thessaloniki's main commercial thoroughfare (Tsimiski, which runs parallel to it two blocks to the south, is a bit more upscale).

and the formation of the modern Turkish state. About eight blocks east of the Ayios Dimitrios church, the modest pink house is decorated in Ottoman style. It has been turned into a museum, with personal items and documents of Turkey's founding father. ⊠ *Apostolou Pavlou 17 and Isaia St., Kentro* ✛ *At Ayiou Dimitriou, behind the Turkish Consulate* ☎ *2310/248452.*

Athonos Square. A warren of side streets around a tiny square with a fountain is filled with tavernas and crafts stores. The area is frequently referred to, but it rarely appears on street maps: everyone knows where it is. ⊠ *Kentro* ✛ *East of Aristotelous, between Gennadiou and Karolou Dil, between Egnatia and Ermou.*

Church of the Metamorphosis. This sunken church, part of which is (as the name would suggest) below ground level, is an example of 14th-century Macedonian ecclesiastical architecture, with a decorative mix of brick and stonework and a dome thrusting upward. Originally dedicated to the Virgin Mother, it was later dedicated to the Transfiguration of the Savior. ⊠ *Egnatia and P.P. Germanou, Kentro.*

Jewish Museum of Thessaloniki. Among the displays in this museum dedicated to the history of the local Jewish community are tombstones from the city's ancient necropolis, which was on the grounds now inhabited by Aristotle University. Also on exhibit are objects rescued from the 32 synagogues that existed around the city, some of which were destroyed by the Nazis. The neoclassical building is one of the few Jewish structures that were spared in the great fire of 1917. ⊠ *Ayiou Mina 13, Kentro* ☎ *2310/250406* ⊕ *www.jmth.gr* ☜ *€3.*

Memorial to Grigoris Lambrakis. If you've read the 1966 novel *Z* by Vassilis Vassilikos (or seen the 1969 Costas-Gavras film about the murder of Lambrakis, a leftist member of Parliament, by rightists in 1963), this monument is especially moving. The murder precipitated the events leading to the 1967–74 dictatorship of the colonels. A dramatic bronze head and arm, above which flutters a sculpted dove, marks the spot. ✉ *Corner of Ermou and Eleftheriou Venizelou, Kentro.*

Modiano Market. Overhauled in 1922 by the Sephardic architect Eli Modiano, this old landmark is basically a rectangular building with a glass roof and pediment facade. Inside, the rich aromas of food—fish, meats, vegetables, fruits, breads, and spices—compete with music and the noisy, colorful market characters, from the market owners to the bargain hunters. In the little tavernas nearby, ouzo and mezedes are sold at all hours. It is worth a visit—as is the generally cheaper **open-air market** (on the north side of Ermou)—even if you have no intention of buying anything. ✉ *Block bounded by Aristotelous, Ermou, Irakliou, and Komninon, Kentro.*

Panagia Acheiropoietos. The name *Achiropiitos* means "made without hands" and refers to the icon representing the Virgin that miraculously appeared in this 5th-century Byzantine church during the 12th century. An early example of the basilica form, the church has marvelous arcades, monolithic columns topped by elaborate capitals, and exquisite period mosaics of birds and flowers. It is the second-oldest church in Thessaloniki and probably the oldest in continuous use in the eastern Mediterranean. An inscription in Arabic on a column states that "Sultan Murat captured Thessaloniki in the year 1430," which was the year the church was converted temporarily into a mosque. ✉ *Ayias Sofias 56, Kentro* ☎ *2310/272820.*

Roman Forum. The forum in the ancient agora, or market, dates back to the end of the 2nd century AD. The small amphitheater here, which hosted public celebrations and athletic and musical contests in ancient times, is now often the site of romantic concerts on balmy summer evenings. In 2011 a new museum opened here, with items from the Hellenic area through the 4th century AD. ✉ *Kentro* ✚ *Between Olimbou and Filipou, behind Dikasterion Sq.* ☎ *2310/221266, 2313/310400* ⊕ *odysseus.culture.gr* 🎫 *€4.*

Thessaloniki Center of Contemporary Art. This moody box of experimental and conceptual art, inside a remodeled warehouse on Thessaloniki's port, features a wide range of new-media art and video installations. It showcases some of the most exciting young Greek artists around and hosts cutting-edge, temporary exhibitions. ✉ *Thessaloniki Port, Warehouse B1, Kentro* ☎ *2310/593270, 2310/546683* ⊕ *www.cact.gr* 🎫 *€3.*

DEPOT

The Depot neighborhood was once where the wealthy, mainly Jewish, merchants lived in impressive 19th-century villas. Very close to the port and the city center, this area was just outside the Old City walls. Nowadays, the few remaining villas are mostly owned by foundations, and high-rise apartment blocks dominate the area.

TOP ATTRACTIONS

Pinakothiki (*Municipal Art Gallery*). This art gallery has a distinctive icon collection from the Byzantine and post-Byzantine periods, engravings that highlight the development of the craft of icon making in Greece, and a representative collection of modern Greek art. One section shows the work of three generations of Thessalonian artists, documenting modern art in the city from the turn of the 20th century to 1967. The museum collection, once housed in the nearby Villa Mordoh, is now in Casa Bianca, a large three-story art nouveaux villa. ✉ *Casa Bianca, Vasilissis Olgas 180 and Them Sofouli, Depot ✛ East of Kentro* ☎ *2310/427555* ⊕ *www.thessaloniki.gr* ✉ *Free.*

LADAKIKA

A particularly large number of restaurants can be found in the Ladadika district in central Thessaloniki, near the port, which was named after the oil vendors who moved to the area after the great fire of 1917. Protected as a historic district from the building frenzy of the mid-1980s, the Ladadika was instead colonized by entrepreneurs who opened cheap tavernas (filling tables with inviting mezedes and carafes of ouzo) and bars in the restored turn-of-the-20th-century buildings. Locals thronged to the lively area, and more and more establishments opened up and spilled over into the surrounding streets and alleys. Though a bit subdued after the financial crisis, the Ladadika still has buckets of charm and still hosts many of the city's best restaurants and drinking establishments.

ANO POLIS

Ano Polis, where many fortified towers once bristled along the city's upper walls, is what remains of 19th-century Thessaloniki. It's filled with timber-framed houses with their upper stories overhanging the steep streets. The views of the modern city below and the Thermaic Gulf are stunning, but other than Byzantine churches, there are few specific places of historical interest. This elevated northern area of the city gained its other name, Ta Kastra (The Castles), because of the castle of Eptapyrghion and the fortified towers that once dominated the walls. The area within and just outside the remains of the walls is like a village unto itself, a pleasing jumble of the rich, the poor, and the renovated. Rustic one-story peasant houses, many still occupied by the families that built them, sit side by side with houses newly built or restored by the wealthier class. As the area continues to be upgraded, tavernas, café-bars, and restaurants spring up to serve visitors, both Greek and foreign, who flock there for a cool evening out. It's an experience in itself to navigate the steps, past gossipy women, grandfathers playing backgammon in smoky cafés, and giggling children playing tag in tiny courtyards filled with sweet-smelling flowers, stray cats, and flapping laundry.

Getting here can be a chore, as taxi drivers often try to avoid the cramped, congested streets and fear missing a fare back down. Have your hotel find a willing driver, or take a local bus. Bus 23 leaves from the terminal at Eleftherias Square (two blocks west of Aristotelous Square, on the waterfront side) every 10 to 15 minutes and follows an interesting route through the narrow streets of Ano Polis. Or you can stroll the 30 minutes north from the White Tower, along Ethnikis Aminis, to get to Ano Polis.

TOP ATTRACTIONS

Moni Vlatádon. The Vlatades Monastery, shaded with pine and cypress, is a cruciform structure that displays a mixture of architectural additions, from Byzantine times to the present. It's known for its Ecumenical Foundation for Patriarchal Studies, the only one in the world. The small central church to the right of the apse has a tiny **chapel dedicated to Sts. Peter and Paul,** which is seldom open. It is believed to have been built on the spot where Paul first preached to the Thessalonians, in AD 49. Go through the gate entrance to get a panoramic view of the city of Thessaloniki. ⊠ *Eptapyrghiou 64, Ano Polis* ☎ *2310/209913.*

Old Turkish Quarter. During the Ottoman occupation, this area, probably the most picturesque in the city, was considered the best place to live. In addition to the superb city views, it catches whatever breeze there is in summer. More recently, it was the home of some of the poorest families in Thessaloniki. Now the area is gentrifying, thanks to European Union development funds (which repaired the cobblestones), strict zoning and building codes, and the zeal of young couples with the money to restore the narrow old houses. The most notable houses are on Papadopolou, Kleious, and Dimitriou Poliorkitou streets. ⊠ *Ano Polis* ✛ *South of Dimitriou Poliorkitou.*

NEED A BREAK

✕ **Tsinari Ouzeri.** A tree shades the terrace and blue, multipaned storefront of the Tsinari Ouzeri, the last remaining Turkish-style coffeehouse (opened in 1850) and the only one to have survived the fire of 1917. During the 1920s it became the social hub for the refugees from Asia Minor who lived here. **Known for:** local meze; good ouzo; popular with groups of locals. ⊠ *Papadopoulou 72, at Kleious, Ano Polis* ☎ *2310/284028.*

Fodor's Choice ★ **Osios David** (*Blessed David*). This entrancing little church with a commanding view of the city was supposedly built about AD 500 in honor of Galerius's daughter, who was secretly baptized while her father was away fighting. It was later converted into a mosque, and at some time its west wall—the traditional place of entrance (in order to look east when facing the altar)—was bricked up, so you enter Osios David from the south. No matter; this entirely suits the church's rather battered magic. You can still see the radiantly beautiful mosaic in the dome of the apse, which shows a rare beardless Jesus, as he seems to have been described in the vision of Ezekiel: Jesus is seen with a halo and is surrounded by the four symbols of the Evangelists—clockwise, from top left, are the angel, the eagle, the lion, and the calf. To the right is the prophet Ezekiel and, to the left, Habakuk. To save it from destruction, the mosaic was hidden under a layer of calfskin during the iconoclastic ravages of the 8th and 9th centuries. Plastered over while a mosque, it seems to have been forgotten until 1921, when an Orthodox monk in Egypt had a vision telling him to go to the church. On the day he arrived, March 25 (the day marking Greek independence from the Ottomans), an earthquake shattered the plaster, revealing the mosaic to the monk—who promptly died. ⊠ *Timotheou 7, Ano Polis* ✛ *Near intersection of Dimitriou Poliorkitou and Ayias Sofias* ☎ *2310/221506.*

WORTH NOTING

Ayios Nikolaos Orfanos. Noted frescoes here include the unusual *Ayion Mandilion* in the apse, which shows Jesus superimposed on a veil sent to an Anatolian king, and the *Niptir,* also in the apse, in which Jesus is washing the disciples' feet. The artist is said to have depicted himself in the right-hand corner wearing a turban and riding a horse. The 14th-century church, which became a dependency of the Vlatádon Monastery in the 17th century, has an intriguing mix of Byzantine architectural styles and perhaps the most beautiful midnight Easter service in the city. ⊠ *Kallithea Sq. and Apostolou Pavlou, enter on Irodotou, Ano Polis* ☎ *2310/214497.*

Eptapyrghion. In modern times, this Byzantine fortress—its name means "the seven towers" even though there are ten towers—was an abysmal prison, closed only in 1988. There's not much to see here except wall ruins and a small museum that documents the building's history. The area is an untended green space, not an unpleasant place to sit and survey Thessaloniki below. The surrounding tavernas accommodate throngs of locals in the evening. ⊠ *Eptapyrghiou, Ano Polis* ☎ *2313/310400.*

Tower of Trigoniou. From this survivor of the city walls, you can see the city spread out below you in a graceful curve around the bay, from the suburbs in the east to the modern harbor in the west and, on a clear day, even Mt. Olympus, rising near the coastline at the southwest reaches of the bay. There is, however, little of historic interest to see within the walls. ⊠ *Eptapyrghiou, Ano Polis.*

SFAGEIA

The nightlife district Sfageia is a short hike or cheap taxi ride southwest of the train station, along 26th Oktovriou Street. Many of the restaurants here offer live *rembetika* (Greek blues) and other Greek music.

WHERE TO EAT

The cosmopolitan, multiracial character of Thessaloniki—building on its historic Byzantine and Ottoman influences—has created a subtly sophisticated, multifaceted cuisine; many Greeks feel Thessaloniki has the best food in the country. It is distinguished by its liberal use of fragrant Levantine spices, including sweet red peppers from Florina called *florines* and hot peppers known as *boukovo*. Thessaloniki is especially known for its *mezedes*, or small plates; every little *ouzeri* (casual bar serving ouzo and mezedes) or taverna has at least one prized house recipe. Leisurely lunches consisting of a multitude of mezedes are the focal point of a typical Thessaloniki day.

KENTRO

$$
GREEK FUSION
FAMILY
✕ **Duck Private Cheffing.** A gourmet dining experience based on fresh, seasonal ingredients with an ever-changing menu, Duck offers the opportunity to sample an array of local seafood prepared in contemporary ways. You might be served fish carpaccio or shrimp *kritharoto* (made with barley pasta) as well as traditional favorites like dolmades and taramosalata. **Known for:** fresh, seasonal ingredients ; a wine list with over

12

50 labels; reservations-only dining. $ *Average main: €15* ⊠ *Chalkis 3, Patriarchika Pileas, Aerodromio* ✢ *Near the airport* ☎ *2315/519333.*

$

GREEK

✕ **O Loutros.** Diners at this side-street Thessaloniki institution rub shoulders with lawyers, students, out-of-towners, and workers from the Bezesteni market. Complete with an outside terrace, this family-run taverna sits opposite an old Turkish bath (*loutra* means "baths"). **Known for:** fresh fish and other seafood; no frills; traditional taverna. $ *Average main: €12* ⊠ *M. Kountoura 5, Bezesteni, Kentro* ☎ *2310/228895.*

$

GREEK

Fodor'sChoice

★

✕ **Ouzeri Aristotelous.** Behind a wrought-iron gate opening to a stoa, artists, scholars, couples, old friends, and businesspeople pack marble-topped tables. This convivial atmospheric place epitomizes the quality and spirit of Thessaloniki dining, down to the traditional spoon desserts. **Known for:** cuttlefish gemista (stuffed with cheese); smart, professional service; hidden oasis in the center of town. $ *Average main: €13* ⊠ *Aristotelous 8, in the stoa, Kentro* ☎ *2310/230762.*

$

MEDITERRANEAN

✕ **Ouzeri Melathron.** "Ouzo's Mansion," established as Greece's first ouzeri franchise in 1993, attracts a mainly young crowd. The chefs here are trained in a style that is essentially Mediterranean, with some French and Turkish influences. **Known for:** irreverently named dishes; popular and buzzy; takeout available. $ *Average main: €10* ⊠ *Eleftheriou Venizelou 23 at Ermou, Kentro* ✢ *In Stoa Karypi* ☎ *2310/275016.*

$$

SEAFOOD

Fodor'sChoice

★

✕ **7 Thalasses.** One of the better and most creative seafood restaurants in Thessaloniki offers a menu that maintains the delicate flavors of its ingredients but also manages to add a modern twist. For instance, the marinated sea bass tartare, seasoned with fleur de sel, lemon, and olive oil, is then covered with a sprinkling of roe, bringing to mind a wave gently breaking against your tongue. **Known for:** elevated dining in a modern setting; mithopilafo (mussels with rice); good desserts. $ *Average main: €22* ⊠ *Kalapothaki 8–10, Kentro* ☎ *2310/233173* ⊕ *7thalasses.eu.*

$$

GREEK

✕ **Ta Nissia.** The food may be costly, but Ta Nissia doesn't seem overpriced thanks to the quality of ingredients and careful preparations by owner-chef Yiannis Alexiou. You're in the city here, but the lightness and decor of this place may make you feel as if you've been transported to some Cycladic isle. **Known for:** two decades of fine dining in Thessaloniki; fish and meat with Mediterranean flavors; house rosé. $ *Average main: €17* ⊠ *Proxenou Koromila 13, Kentro* ☎ *2310/224477, 2310/285991* ⊕ *www.tanisia.com* ☾ *No dinner Sun. Closed July and Aug.*

$

GREEK

✕ **To Meteoro Vima Tis Garidas.** This casual, friendly place in the midst of busy Modiano Market is known for great *garides* (prawns), served in many different ways, and its humor: the name translates as "the meteoric step of the prawn." The locals also come time and again for the *tamaras* (white cod roe), butter beans with chestnut, and homemade *dolmadakia* (stuffed vine leaves). Order your ouzo and a selection of mezedes, and take in the bustle of market life. **Known for:** fresh seafood straight from the market; charming old-school taverna atmosphere; mezedes menu. $ *Average main: €10* ⊠ *Modiano Market, Irakliou 31, Kentro* ☎ *2310/279867* ☾ *Closed mid-July–mid-Aug. No dinner.*

$$ ✕**Zythos Dore.** Crowded and lots of fun, this café has a good buzz
GREEK in a converted 1920s-era Viennese-style coffeehouse, and it offers a
great view of the White Tower if you chose to sit on the terrace out
front. Decent Greek and international dishes range from *pastourma* pie
(with spicy air-cured dried beef) to homemade lamb sausages. **Known
for:** mini-chain in two great central locations; imported beers; views
from the terrace. $ *Average main: €16* ✉ *Tsiroyiannis Sq. 7, Kentro*
☎ *2310/279010* ⊕ *www.zithos.gr.*

LADADIKA

$ ✕**Bakaliarakia Tou Aristou.** Serving Thessaloniki's most well known
SEAFOOD fish-and-chips since 1940, this is a classic hangout where you can get
FAMILY your fingers greasy as you dig into crispy fried cod and fresh-cut fries.
Your fish-and-chips are always accompanied by pungent *skordalia* gar-
lic dip and casually served on grease-proof paper. **Known for:** locally
sourced fish; historical atmosphere; casual and affordable food. $ *Aver-
age main: €7* ✉ *Katouni 3 and Fasianou 2, Ladadika* ☎ *2310/548668*
⊕ *www.mpakaliarakia-aristou.gr.*

$ ✕**Omikron.** This lovely, unpretentious little restaurant in the trendy
GREEK FUSION Ladadika district has become a local favorite. Delightful Greek-Med-
iterranean dishes are tastefully presented to reflect the chef-owner's
culinary stint in France. **Known for:** popular locally; good prices for
well-prepared dishes; seafood risotto. $ *Average main: €6* ✉ *Oplopoiou
3, Ladadika* ☎ *2310/532774.*

$ ✕**To Full Tou Meze.** Ordering your meal at this establishment in the heart
GREEK of the bustling Ladadika district is quite an experience. The waiters
bring their own eccentric individuality to this often mundane ritual, and
the menu is printed on a "newspaper" with photos from old Greek films
and articles heralding the dishes you're about to munch on. **Known
for:** eccentric (but somewhat erratic) waiters; tasty traditional Greek
mezedes; deli-style decor. $ *Average main: €10* ✉ *Katouni 3, Ladadika*
☎ *2310/524700* ⊕ *www.fullmeze.gr.*

WHERE TO STAY

The majority of hotels are located in the Kentro (center) of Thessaloniki.
There are lodgings to suit all budgets, but the area is busy and noisy all
day and much of the night, so the most upscale establishments have cre-
ated a quiet oasis within their walls, insulated from the chaos outside.
Look to the more tranquil Faliro neighborhood for a quieter locale.

KENTRO

Stay in Kentro and all the city action will be on your doorstep, and
you'll find most attractions, shopping, and good restaurants within
walking distance. More important, Kentro is close enough to the water-
front that top-floor rooms may have sea views. Parking is difficult,
however, and noise can be a problem, especially at cheaper hotels.

$ ⬚**Aegeon Hotel.** Don't despair over the garish neon sign outside—this
HOTEL place is actually one of the warmest and best-priced hotels along busy
Egnatia Street, conveniently close to the train station, port, city center,
and Ladadika districts. **Pros:** double glazing does a lot to minimize the
commotion on noisy Egnatia; good location; decent low-price option.

Noted for its mosaics, the Ayios Dimitrios is Greece's largest church and is the shrine of the city's patron saint.

Cons: directly on the busy main road; few room amenities; breakfast nothing to write home about. [$] *Rooms from: €55* ✉ *Egnatia 19, Kentro* ☎ *2310/522921* 🌐 *www.aegeon-hotel.gr* 🛏 *59 rooms* 🍴 *Breakfast.*

$ HOTEL 🏨 **Hotel Olympia.** Location counts at this boutique hotel on a corner close to the flea market, copper market, Roman Forum, and Ayios Dimitrios—but there are many other pluses at this nicely stylish place, which enjoys quality service and offers an excellent, American-style breakfast. **Pros:** service is excellent; check for discounts; bicycles available for rental. **Cons:** limited parking spaces for guests; location means lower floors have traffic noise; small bathrooms. [$] *Rooms from: €67* ✉ *Olymbou 65, at Papageorgiou, Kentro* ☎ *2310/366466* 🌐 *www.hotelolympia.gr* 🛏 *97 rooms* 🍴 *Breakfast.*

$ HOTEL 🏨 **Hotel Orestias Kastorias.** Blink and you may miss this circa-1920 hotel—a favorite of budget travelers—on a quiet, narrow street leading from the top corner of the Roman Forum to Ayios Dimitrios church. **Pros:** pretty good value for those on a budget; good service; views onto the Roman forum. **Cons:** breakfast is not served (although guests can help themselves to coffee and biscuits in the reception area); very limited parking available; no elevator. [$] *Rooms from: €55* ✉ *Agnostou Stratiotou 14, Kentro* ☎ *2310/276517* 🌐 *www.okhotel.gr* 🛏 *37 rooms* 🍴 *No meals.*

$ HOTEL FAMILY 🏨 **Le Palace Art Hotel.** On one of the city's main thoroughfares, this updated art deco–style hotel is popular with savvy business travelers and Greek tourists. **Pros:** sleep like a baby on Coco-Mat luxury natural mattresses; convenient and central location; friendly staff. **Cons:** can be noisy; check bill carefully for unexpected charges, such as parking; in need of some renovations. [$] *Rooms from: €75* ✉ *Tsimiski 12, at Eleftheriou Venizelou, Kentro* ☎ *2310/257400* 🌐 *www.lepalace.gr* 🛏 *57 rooms* 🍴 *Breakfast.*

$ **Tourist Hotel.** An impressively elegant, turn-of-the-20th-century build-
HOTEL   ing houses this modest family-run hotel that's very popular with regular foreign visitors—from business-trippers to families—who enjoy the
guest rooms with high ceilings, plus some nifty historic touches, such as
time-burnished wainscoting and an attractive 1920s-era elevator. **Pros:**
prime location, just west of Aristotelous Square; great budget option;
good breakfast. **Cons:** room windows are double-glazed, but ask for a
room at the back if sensitive to main-road noise; can get a little stuffy
in summer; few hotel amenities. $ *Rooms from: €60* ⊠ *Mitropoleos
21, at Komninon, Kentro* ☎ *2310/270501* ⊕ *www.touristhotel.gr* ↩ *37
rooms* ⫼ *Breakfast.*

LADADIKA

The trendy Ladadika neighborhood (very close to the Kentro) is where
most of the city's tavernas and bars are located. There are only a handful
of places to stay here, most in restored old buildings. These places book
up quickly, so finding a room here may be a little more challenging. The
neighborhood is still very central and architecturally interesting, and
it's quiet in the mornings. Views, though not expansive, are engaging.
But late-night noise—especially on weekends—can be a problem, and
parking is almost nonexistent (the nearest parking lots are five minutes'
walk and cost at least €10/day); no hotels have parking here.

$$ **The Bristol Hotel.** An elegant retreat with a touch of history, this exqui-
HOTEL   site boutique hotel occupies one of the few buildings that survived the
Fodor's Choice   great fire of 1917 untouched—during Ottoman rule the structure served
★   as the city's post office—and, today, a mixture of handmade furniture,
hand-picked antiques, and works of art makes this place special. **Pros:**
small intimate hotel; excellent location; á la carte breakfast. **Cons:** no
parking; patchy Wi-Fi signal; no spa, gym, or pool. $ *Rooms from:
€135* ⊠ *Oplopiou 2, at Katouni, Ladadika* ☎ *2310/506500* ⊕ *www.
bristol.gr* ↩ *20 rooms* ⫼ *Breakfast.*

$$ **Mediterranean Palace.** From the abundance of amenities at this tra-
HOTEL   ditionally decorated, six-story hotel near the port and Ladadika, it's
easy to see that the Mediterranean Palace caters to business travelers,
who will appreciate the consistently good service and many amenities.
Pros: top location; top-of-the-line hotel services; free parking. **Cons:**
rooms on the street side of hotel can be noisy; noisy, but much needed,
makeover in progress; the only rooms on the higher floors and in the
front of hotel have sea views. $ *Rooms from: €130* ⊠ *Salaminos 3, at
Karatasou, Ladadika* ☎ *2310/240400* ⊕ *www.mediterranean-palace.gr*
↩ *118 rooms* ⫼ *Breakfast.*

FALIRO

Faliro, a modern, residential area, is south of the city center and the
White Tower. The hotels here are usually in large, high-rise buildings
owned by trusted brands with good amenities (including swimming
pools) and offering high standards of service. You're still very close
to the waterfront, so it's easy to get a room with a sea view, and since
there's space, hotels tend to have parking and more on-site amenities.
However, you'll be slightly out of the city center (20 minutes by foot),
and Faliro obviously lacks the character and sparkle of the central areas.

$$ ▢ **Daios Luxury Living Hotel.** A minute's walk from the White Tower, this
HOTEL upscale contemporary hotel in shimmering glass stands out for all the
Fodor's Choice right reasons: a prime seafront location, cool and chic interiors, and
★ exemplary, discrete service. **Pros:** right in the heart of the city with
outstanding views of the Thermaikos Gulf; free minibar in all rooms;
the best luxury suites in town at good prices out of season. **Cons:**
some rooms partially overlook the city to the side; expensive nightly
parking fee; some road noise in the lower-floor rooms. $ *Rooms from:*
€150 ▢ *Nikis 59, Faliro* ☎ *2311/180655* ⊕ *www.daioshotels.com* ⤵ *49
rooms* ❑ *Breakfast.*

$$ ▢ **Makedonia Palace.** You might see a rock star or the president of Albania
HOTEL here; it's that kind of place—just note the excellent location on the water-
FAMILY front, southeast of the White Tower, with stunning views of the sunset
and Mt. Olympus, or the slew of amenities (mini-stereos, dual-voltage
outlets, multimedia convention center) the Grecotel chain has installed
behind the hotel's 1970s-era facade. **Pros:** top location right on the beachfront; discounts possible in summer; major renovations started in 2016.
Cons: rooms on the lower floor might be a bit noisy from the traffic;
still a few discreet but ongoing renovations; make sure to book a room
with a sea view. $ *Rooms from: €125* ▢ *Megalou Alexandrou 2, Faliro*
☎ *2310/897197* ⊕ *makedoniapalace.com* ⤵ *276 rooms* ❑ *Breakfast.*

NIGHTLIFE

The Thessaloniki bar-and-club scene is eclectic, dynamic, and energized.
Students, academics, and artists haunt the bars on Zefxidos Street near
Ayia Sofia church while music lovers crowd the stages at Mylos, a
former flour mill that is now Northern Greece's most coveted arts-and-
entertainment complex. In summer most clubs close, as their clients
flock to the beaches of Halkidiki, which functions as an outer suburb of
the city. The discos on the road to the airport go in and out of fashion
and change names (and concept) from one season to the next, so ask
at your hotel for the newest and best.

When you hear locals talking about Paralia, they are referring to the
road that lines the city center's waterfront, Leoforos Nikis. The cafés
and bars here buzz at all hours of the day and night. Walk east along
Proxenou Koromila, one block up from the waterfront, to find more
intimate, cool bars.

KENTRO

BARS AND CLUBS

Pastaflora Darling! Pastaflora Darling! is a whimsically decorated hangout for students and artists philosophizing about the latest global trend.
Drinks are excellent and inexpensive. It's open all day until late in the
evening (or morning, rather). ▢ *Zefxidos 6, Kentro* ☎ *2310/261518.*

Urban. Urban is a former art gallery–turned–glam bar for counterculture
scenesters, young academics, and lifelong artists. The music is fantastic,
as is the people-watching. The music starts kicking after 9 pm. ▢ *Zefxidos 7, Kentro* ☎ *2310/272821.*

SFAGEIA

BARS AND CLUBS

Fodor'sChoice **Mylos.** Mylos, in a former mill on the southwest edge of the city, has
★   become perhaps the best venue in Greece for jazz, folk, and pop acts,
both Greek and foreign. This fabulous complex of clubs, bars, and
ouzeri-tavernas, as well as art galleries and a concert stage, shows how
a respectful architectural conversion can become a huge success. Don't
miss the Xylourgeio stage, which has some of the best alternative acts
around. The lively place starts to get busy as early as 11 pm. ✉ *An-
dreadou Georgiou 56, Sfageia* ☎ *2310/551836* ⊕ *www.mylos.gr.*

PERFORMING ARTS

Thessaloniki is an outstanding town for all things cultural: large orchestras and string trios, drama and comedy, and performances by international and local favorites are all part of the scene. For current happenings
or information about festivals in the city or area, check with your hotel.

CONCERTS

Megaron Moussikis Thessaloniki (*Thessaloniki Concert Hall*). The Megaron Moussikis Thessaloniki is a large venue that hosts ballet, opera, and
other high-brow musical and cultural events. Graced by international
and local orchestras (including the Municipal Orchestra of Thessaloniki), there are classical, folk, and jazz nights, as well as seminars
and lectures. ✉ *25 Martiou and Paralia, Kalamaria* ☎ *2310/895800,
2310/895938, 2310/895939 box office* ⊕ *www.tch.gr.*

FESTIVALS

Helaxpo, the large international trade fair that is held mid-September,
makes hotel reservations very difficult to come by, as does the Thessaloniki Film Festival in November.

Apokriés. Apokriés—what Greeks call their Carnival celebrations—
mark the period preceding Lent and ending on the night before
"Clean Monday," the beginning of Lent for Eastern Orthodox and
Catholics. These costume-and-parade affairs are particularly colorful
(and often bawdy) in Northern Greece. You are welcome to join in
the fun in Thessaloniki and other towns. Sohos, 32 km (20 miles)
northeast of Thessaloniki, hosts a festive event in which people
cavort in animal hides with sheep bells around their waists and
phallic headdresses. In Naoussa, 112 km (70 miles) west of Thessaloniki, some participants wear *foustanellas* (short, pleated white
kilts), special masks, and chains of gold coins across their chests,
which they shake to "awaken the Earth." The whole town dons costumes and takes to the streets behind brass marching bands, which
have a tradition of playing New Orleans–style jazz.

Dimitria Festival. St. Dimitrios's feast day is celebrated on October 26. Its
secular adjunct, the Dimitria Festival, has developed into a major series
of cultural events that include theater, dance, art exhibits, and musical
performances. They are held from September to December at venues
around Thessaloniki. ✉ *Thessaloniki* ☎ *2310/228414, 2313/318222*
⊕ *www.dimitria.thessaloniki.gr.*

FILM

Alex. A must-do in summer, especially for film lovers, is to see a movie at an open-air cinema. There are usually two showtimes (around 8 and 11 pm, the later one usually at lower volume, depending on the neighborhood). Call ahead or check the website to see what's playing—some screen oldies and foreign art films, and others run the latest from Hollywood. Most films are subtitled, but note that animated movies are almost always dubbed. Alex is the most central theater. ⊠ *Ayias Sofias and Olympou, Kentro* ☎ *2310/269403* ⊕ *www.cine.gr/prog.asp.*

Fodor's Choice ★ Thessaloniki International Film Festival. Each November, the best films by new directors from around the world are screened and awarded prizes at the Thessaloniki International Film Festival. Southeast Europe's most noted cinematic festival, it attracts well-known regional talent and some internationally aclaimed stars. Films are usually subtitled, and tickets can be hard to come by. In March, there's also an international documentary film festival. ⊠ *Olympion Bldg., Aristotelous Sq. 10, Kentro* ☎ *2310/378400* ⊕ *www.filmfestival.gr.*

THEATER

Performances are in Greek, although there are occasional visits by English-speaking groups.

Kratiko Theatro (*State Theater*). The National Theater presents plays, ballets, and special performances of visiting artists year-round. ⊠ *Ethnikis Aminis 2, Kentro* ✛ *Opposite the White Tower* ☎ *2315/200000, 2315/200200 box office* ⊕ *www.ntng.gr.*

Theatro Dasous (*Forest Theater*). Theatro Dasous stages theatrical performances in foreign languages in summer, as well as other events, such as concerts. ⊠ *Oxi avenue, Ayios Pavlos* ✛ *In Seich-Sou forest* ☎ *2315/200200, 2130/288000.*

PLAYING WITH FIRE

Anastanarides (fire dancers) are a famous part of Northern Greece. Starting on the feast day of Saints Constantine and Eleni, May 21, religious devotees in the villages of Langadha (25 km [15 miles] north of Thessaloniki) and Ayia Eleni (80 km [50 miles] northeast of Thessaloniki) take part in *pirovassia* (literally, "fire dancing"). During the three-day rite, participants dance unharmed on a bed of hot coals while holding the saints' icons. The rite is derived from the eastern Thracian village of Kosti, where the villagers are said to have rescued the original icons from a burning church around 1250.

12

SHOPPING

ANTIQUES

Antiques shops on Mitropoleos between Ayias Sofias and the White Tower are perfect for leisurely browsing; look also on the streets around Athonos Square. But one block west of the Roman Forum, Tositsa is the best source for junk, antiques, and roaming peddlers in the city, with good finds in everything from brass beds to antique jewelry. The *paliatzidiko* (flea market) here has a marvelous jumble of fascinating, musty old shops, with the wares of itinerant junk collectors spread out on the sidewalks, intermingled with small, upscale antiques shops.

Bazaar. On Wednesday the narrow streets surrounding the Rotunda are taken over by a bazaar with knickknacks and the occasional interesting heirloom, antique, or folk art piece for sale. ⊠ *Rotunda.*

CLOTHING

Thessalonians are noted for being tastefully and stylishly dressed. Clothing here is high quality (but notice that sizes are a lot smaller than their American counterparts). The best shopping streets are Tsimiski, with its brand-name boutiques, Mitropoleos, Proxenou Koromila, Mitropolitou Iosif, Karolou Dil, and P.P. Germanou. Cheaper children's clothing (normally extortionate) can be found on Syngrou, south of Egnatia.

GREEK SOUVENIRS

Athonos Square has shops with traditional, handmade items; craftspeople themselves own many of the stores on the narrow streets between Aristotelous and Ayias Sofias. The streets around Panayia Chalkeon have shops selling copper items. Try at the Archaeological Museum for Macedonian-focused souvenirs.

Korres. Greece's leading producer of excellent natural cosmetics and beauty products now has a shop in Thessaloniki south of the city center. Even though most pharmacies stock Korres, this shop has the full range of products. For those who want to order these and other top Greek beauty products online and have them sent to your home there are good some websites providing this service, the best of which is www.mysecretkshopper.com. ⊠ *Agisilaou 19, Kifissia* ☎ *2310/314662.*

Mastihashop. Mastihashop carries products containing mastic—a tree resin produced on the Aegean island of Chios. The face cream, preserves, sweets, and other items come in extremely attractive, easy-to-pack tins. ⊠ *Vogatsikou 12, Kentro* ⊹ *Across from the Holy Metropolis of Thessaloniki* ☎ *2310/250205* ⊕ *www.mastihashop.com.*

SWEETS

Thessaloniki is well known for its food, including a vast array of Balkan and Eastern-oriented pastries and desserts. Sit down, sample, and decide which you think is best.

Agapitos Patisserie. With eight outlets in Thessaloniki, Agapitos Patisserie, which aptly translates as "loved one," is indeed one of the best loved confectionary shops in the city. Best known for chocolate-covered *tsourekia* (a sweet bread traditionally served at Easter) and the syrupy pastries from Asia Minor. ⊠ *Tsimiski 10, Kentro* ☎ *2310/225950* ⊕ *www.agapitospatisserie.com.*

Averof. Averof is the only patisserie in Thessaloniki that creates kosher pastries. ⊠ *Vasilissis Georgiou 11, Kentro* ☎ *2310/814284* ⊕ *www.averof.gr.*

Hatzis. Sample Thessaloniki's fabled Anatolian sweets at central Hatzis. Specialties include the buffalo milk cream-based *kazan dipi,* a kind of flan; *trigono,* a cream-filled triangle of phyllo; and *kataïfi* (logs of crushed and sugared walnuts wrapped in honey-drenched shredded phyllo) served with *kaïmaki* (mastic-flavored ice cream). Choose a beverage—like iced coffee, granita, or *boza* (a thick, sweet, millet-and-corn drink)—and people-watch from the pedestrian side street that faces the gardens of Panagia Chalkeon church. ⊠ *Eleftheriou Venizelou 50, Kentro* ☎ *2310/279058* ⊕ *www.chatzis.gr.*

Terkenlis. Terkenlis serves an unforgettable *tsoureki* (sweet bread flavored with *mahlepi,* a spice made from the ground-up pits of a Persian cherry) and then filled and dipped in chocolate. This delicacy is so delicious that it disappears within hours from this extremely popular patisserie's shelves. ⊠ *Tsimiski 30, Kentro* ☎ *2310/271148* ⊕ *www. terkenlis.gr.*

12

ALEXANDER THE GREAT COUNTRY

Macedonia, one of the less visited areas of Greece, is a region of legend and history, full of architectural treasures and remnants of the reign of Alexander the Great. Happily, many of these places are within easy reach of Thessaloniki. Few places in the world have greater ancient sites than Pella, Vergina, and Dion, which are famously connected to Alexander the Great and his father, Philip II, heroes of the ages. Even one would be worth a detour, but they are so close to Thessaloniki that it is easy to see all of them. You can rush and explore all three in a harried day trip from Thessaloniki; better would be scheduling a relaxed day for each, allowing time for contemplation, or after seeing the first two, spending the night near Dion or Mt. Olympus and visiting both of these the next day.

In the 7th century BC the Dorian Makedonoi (Macedonian) tribe moved out of the Pindos mountains (between Epirus and Macedonia), settled in the fertile plains below, and established a religious center at the sacred springs of Dion at the foot of Mt. Olympus. Perdikkas, the first king of the Macedonians, held court at a place called Aigai, now known to have been at Vergina; and in the 5th century BC, the king of that time, Archelaos (413–399), moved his capital from Aigai to Pella, which was then on a rise above a lagoon leading to the Thermaic Gulf.

In 359 BC, after a succession of kings and near-anarchy exacerbated by the raids of barbarian tribes from the north, the 23-year-old Philip II was elected regent. Philip II pulled the kingdom together through diplomacy and marital alliances and then began expanding his lands, taking the gold mines of the Pangeon mountains and founding Philippi there. In 356 BC, on the day that Alexander the Great was born, Philip II was said to have simultaneously taken the strategic port of Potidea in Halkidiki, received news of his horse's triumph in the Olympic Games, and learned of a general's victory against the Illyrians. That was also the day the temple of Artemis at Ephesus was destroyed by fire, which later prompted people to say that the goddess was away on that day, tending to Alexander's birth. In 336 BC, Philip II was assassinated in Vergina at a wedding party for one of his daughters. (His tomb there was discovered in 1977 by the Greek archaeologist Manolis Andronikos.) Alexander, then 20, assumed power, and within two years he had gathered an army to be blessed at Dion, before setting off to conquer the Persians and most of the known world.

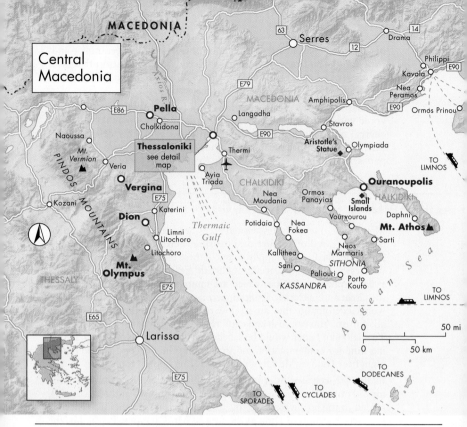

PELLA ΠΕΛΛΑ

40 km (25 miles) west of Thessaloniki.

Pella was Alexander's birthplace and the capital of the Macedonian state in the 4th century BC. The modern-day village is not the most alluring, nor is there anywhere to stay, and hides the fact that Pella was once a thriving city-state with the largest agora market of its time. It housed workshops, administrative buildings, shops, and much more. The city was built using the sophisticated Hippodamian grid plan—by none other than the great Hippodamos himself. On the hill to the north, one can visit the vast palatial complex where King Philip and Alexander the Great once lived.

GETTING HERE AND AROUND

If coming by train, get off at Edessa and take the KTEL bus to the site. If coming by bus, get off the Thessaloniki–Edessa KTEL bus right at the site; there are buses every hour from 6 to 6. Zorpidis Travel, among others, arranges day trips from Thessaloniki that cover both Pella and Vergina.

EXPLORING

Pella Archaeological Site. The ancient village ruins and its museum—both best known for their intricate, artful, beautifully preserved floor mosaics, mainly of mythological scenes—are on either side of the main road toward Edessa (where waterfalls invite a possible further trip). It's best to first get an overview at the **Archaeological Museum,** which contains a model of the 4th-century BC dwelling that stood across the road, as well as fascinating artifacts of Neolithic, Bronze, and Iron Age settlers, some as old as the 7th century BC. Note also the unique statuette of a horned Athena (apparently influenced by Minoan Crete), the statue of Alexander sprouting the horns of Pan, and the adorable sleeping Eros (Cupid), reproductions of which can be bought at the gift shop. Descriptions are sparse, but the attendants, pointedly not experts, are happy to share what they know.

In 1914, two years after the Turks' departure, the people who lived on the land were moved to a village north of here, and excavations of the **archaeological site** began. These include portions of the walls; the sanctuaries of Aphrodite, Demeter, and Cybele; the marketplace; cemetery; and several houses. In 1987, on a small rise to the north, the remains of the **palace** came to light; at present there is a restoration program at the site. ⊠ *Pella ⌖ Off E86, Thessaloniki–Edessa road* ☎ *23820/31160* ⊕ *www.pella-museum.gr* ✉ *€8 includes site and museum.*

VERGINA ΒΕΡΓΙΝΑ

40 km (25 miles) south of Pella, 135 km (84 miles) southwest of Thessaloniki.

The modern city of Vergina wasn't established in its present form until 1922, but the ancient city of Aigai, the original capital of Macedonia, was founded in the 8th century BC and at its height in the 4th century BC. It's here that Philip II, the father of Alexander the Great, was assassinated in 336 BC and where he was buried among the Royal Tombs, which are a UNESCO World Heritage site. For years, both archaeologists and grave robbers had suspected that the large mound that stood on this site might contain something of value but, try as they might, neither of these groups was successful in penetrating its secret. Serious excavations begin in the mid-19th century, and although discoveries were made, the most important discoveries didn't happen for almost 100 years. Many locals still remember playing ball on the mound as children. Professor Manolis Andronikos, who discovered the tombs, theorized in his book *The Royal Tombs of Vergina* that one of Alexander's successors, wanting to protect Philip's tomb from robbers, had it covered with broken debris and tombstones to make it appear that the grave had already been plundered, and then built the tumulus so that Philip's tomb would be near the edge rather than the center. When Andronikos discovered it, on the final day of excavation, in 1977, he had been trying one of the last approaches, with little hope of finding anything—certainly not the tomb of Philip II, in as pristine condition as the day it was closed. It was the first intact Macedonian tomb ever discovered.

GETTING HERE AND AROUND

The easiest way to get to Vergina is by car. Be attentive, however, because the route is not well marked from Pella. You can also get here with public transport via Veria, 11 km (7 miles) away, using trains or buses. KTEL buses, more convenient than train services, run from Thessaloniki to Veria every hour starting early in the morning; the trip takes one hour. From Veria take a bus to Vergina (20 minutes, every other hour from 6:50 am to 8 pm). Ask to be let off at the Vergina archaeological sites. For the tombs look for a low hillock in the center of town with souvenir shops nearby. The palace and the theater are about 1 km (½ mile) southeast of the village up a low hill. Veria is also on the bus route from Athens to Naousa.

There are regular trains from Thessaloniki to Veria from 5:50 am (one hour); however, the station is 3 km (2 miles) outside of Veria, so you will need to take a taxi to the bus station in the center.

EXPLORING

FAMILY

Fodor's Choice

★

Aigai Archaeological Site. Some of antiquity's greatest treasures await you at the Royal Tombs of Vergina, opened to the public in 1993, 16 years after their discovery. Today the complex, including a museum, is a fitting shrine to the original capital of the kingdom of Macedonia, then known as Aigai. The entrance is appropriately stunning: you walk down a white-sandstone ramp into the partially underground structure, roofed over by a large earth-covered dome approximately the size of the original tumulus (mounded grave). Here on display are some of the legendary artifacts from the age of Philip II of Macedonia.

This was the first intact Macedonian tomb ever found—imposing and exquisite, with a huge frieze of a hunting scene, a masterpiece similar to those of the Italian Renaissance but 1,800 years older, along with a massive yet delicate fresco depicting the abduction of Persephone (a copy of which is displayed along one wall of the museum). Two of the few original works of great painting survive from antiquity. On the left are two tombs and one altar that had been looted and destroyed in varying degrees by the time Andronikos discovered them. Macedonian Tomb III, on the right, found intact in 1978, is believed to be that of the young Prince Alexander IV, Alexander the Great's son, who was at first kept alive by his "protectors" after Alexander's death and then poisoned (along with his mother) when he was 14. To the left of Tomb III is that of Philip II. He was assassinated in the nearby theater, a short drive away; his body was burned, his bones washed in wine, wrapped in royal purple, and put into the magnificent, solid-gold casket with the 16-point sun, which is displayed in the museum. His wife, Cleopatra (not the Egyptian queen), was later buried with him.

The tombs alone would be worth a special trip, but the golden objects and unusual artifacts that were buried within them are equally impressive. Among these finds, in excellent condition and displayed in dramatic dimmed light, are delicate ivory reliefs; elegantly wrought gold laurel wreaths; and Philip's crown, armor, and shield. Especially interesting are those items that seem most certainly Philip's: a pair of greaves (shin guards), one shorter than the other—Philip was known to have a

Burial places for famed rulers such as Philip II and Alexander IV—the father and son of Alexander the Great—the Royal Tombs of Vergina are archaeological landmarks.

limp. To the right of the tombs, a gift shop sells books and postcards; the official gift shop is outside the entrance gate (across from Philippion restaurant), on the same side of the road. Macedonian souvenirs available here are scarce elsewhere.

The winding road to the site of Philip's assassination goes through rolling countryside west of modern Vergina, much of it part of the vast royal burial grounds of ancient Aigai. On the way you pass three more **Macedonian tombs** of little interest, being rough-hewn stone structures in typical Macedonian style; the admission to the Royal Tombs includes these. In the field below are the remnants of the **theater,** discovered by Andronikos in 1982. It was on Philip's way here, to attend the wedding games that were to follow the marriage of his daughter to the king of Epirus, that he was murdered and where his son, Alexander the Great, was crowned. ✉ *Vergina* ✣ *Off E90, near Veria* ☎ *23310/92347* 🌐 *www.aigai.gr* 🎟 *€12.*

WHERE TO EAT

$ GREEK Fodor's Choice ★ 🍴 **Ap'Allou.** With mouthwatering dishes inspired by Asia Minor and Greece and ingredients from both the land (seasonal vegetables, with plenty of vegetarian options, quality meats) and the sea (fresh shellfish and seafood), this place is a satisfaction-guaranteed stop for lunch or dinner. The menu changes with the season, but luscious desserts, such as the delicious profiteroles and homemade ice cream are a must-try year-round. **Known for:** good prices for high-quality food; friendly service and familial ambience; excellent selection of regional wines. [$] *Average main: €10* ✉ *Patriarchi Ioakim 5* ✣ *Veroia, 15-min drive west of Vergina* ☎ *23310/20199.*

$ 🍴 **Philippion.** Choose from traditional foods such as moussaka or try GREEK the highly recommended fresh local pasta. The regional vegetables are especially delicious, and fresh frozen yogurt is made with local fruits. **Known for:** quick bites before or after visit to Royal Tombs; self-service; decent Greek fare. [$] *Average main: €11* ✉ *Vergina* ✣ *Immediately outside the archaeological site* ☎ *23310/92892.*

WHERE TO STAY

$ 🏨 **Archontiko Dimitra.** B&B/INN FAMILY On a quiet street a five-minute walk from the ancient archaeological site at Vergina is this beautiful two-story hotel, built in 2003—you'll want to consider making this your base for area excursions, as the hotel is designed with accents of fetching wood trim and antique brass chandeliers, with each of the eight light-filled and spacious studio suites showcasing its own classic style and private balcony. **Pros:** discounts available for extended stays; free parking; good location near both the Royal Tombs and the buzzy little town. **Cons:** small, so book early; no 24-hour reception; weak Wi-Fi signal in certain rooms. [$] *Rooms from: €60* ✉ *Athinas 5* ☎ *23310/92900* 🛏 *8 rooms* 🍽 *Breakfast.*

$ 🏨 **Kalaitzis Estate.** B&B/INN Fodor's Choice ★ Though not within Vergina itself, this countryside retreat is well worth the effort to reach and is especially delightful in the snow-covered winter months because of its plush, cozy, and sumptuous decor. **Pros:** wonderful and friendly service; tranquil coutryside retreat; the wine is a must. **Cons:** 5 to 10 minutes' drive from Vergina; only a few rooms, so do book in advance; all nightlife in nearby Veria. [$] *Rooms from: €80* ✉ *Metochi* ☎ *23310/92092* 🌐 *www.ktima-kalaitzi.gr* 🛏 *11 rooms* 🍽 *Breakfast.*

$ 🏨 **Vergina Pension.** B&B/INN Between the modern and ancient village sits a two-story, pine-furniture-and-crisp-sheets accommodation like those found all over the country. **Pros:** very convenient for buses to Veria; big breakfasts; good low-budget option. **Cons:** owners do not speak very good English; lacking in charm; patchy Wi-Fi. [$] *Rooms from: €40* ✉ *Aristotelous 55* ☎ *23310/92510* 🛏 *10 rooms* 🍽 *Breakfast.*

DION ΔΙΟΝ

90 km (56 miles) south of Vergina, 87 km (54 miles) southwest of Thessaloniki.

At the foothills of Mt. Olympus lies ancient Dion. Even before Zeus and the Olympian gods, the mountain was home to the Muses and Orpheus, who entranced the men of the area with his mystical music. The story says that the life-giving force of Dion came from the waters in which the murderers of Orpheus (the women of Mt. Olympus, jealous for attention from their men) washed their hands on the slopes of the sacred mountain to remove the stain of their own sin. The waters entered the earth and rose, cleansed, in the holy city of Dion. (Zeus is Dias in Greek; the city was named for him.) Ancient Dion was inhabited from as early as the classical period (5th century BC) and last referred to as Dion in the 10th century AD according to the archaeological findings.

12

Today a feeling of tranquility prevails at Dion, at the foot of the mountain of the gods. Few people visit this vast, underrated city site. The silence is punctuated now and then by goats, their bells tinkling so melodically you expect to spy Pan in the woods at any moment. Springs bubble up where excavators dig, and scarlet poppies bloom among the cracks—this is the essence of Greece.

GETTING HERE AND AROUND

Litochoro, an hour by KTEL bus from Thessaloniki (hourly from 7 am), is the gateway to both Dion and Mt. Olympus. The bus stop is in Litochoro's central *platia* (square). From Litochoro's central square, call a taxi for the 11-km (7-mile) trip, which costs €13 one-way, to the splendid archaeological park. You can also call Mr. Sakis or Mr. Zaharis, both local cabbies with good English, to come and pick you up. You take a KTEL bus from Thessaloniki to Katerini, where you can take the local "blue" bus to the Dion site (€1.20). There are buses to Katerini from Thessaloniki every half hour.

Contacts Litochoro Taxi. ☎ 6937/176867 Mr. Sakis, 6987/320800 Mr. Zaharias, 23520/82333 Taxi Rank.

EXPLORING

FAMILY

Fodor's Choice

★

Dion Archaeological Site. Being at the base of sacred Olympus, Dion was a sacred city for the Macedonians, devoted primarily to Zeus and his daughters, the Muses. A city was built adjacent to the ancient city during the reign of Alexander. Unearthed ruins of various buildings include the villa of Dionysos, public baths, a stadium (the Macedonian Games were held here), shops, and workshops. The road from the museum divides the diggings at the archaeological site into two areas. On the left is the **ancient city** of Dion itself, with the juxtaposition of public toilets and several superb floor mosaics. On the right side are the **ancient theaters** and the **sanctuaries of Olympian Zeus, Demeter, and Isis.** In the latter, which is a vividly beautiful approximation of how it once looked, copies of the original statues, now in the museum, have been put in place. ⊠ *Dion ✛ 7 km (4½ mile) north of Litochoro, off E75/1A, Thessaloniki–Athens road* ☎ *23510/53484* ⊕ *www.ancient-dion.org* ✉ *€8 incl. museum.*

FAMILY

Museum of Dion. The splendid museum is an important stop to help you get an idea of the history and importance of the city to the ancient Macedonians. Be sure to see the video (in English) prepared by the site's renowned archaeologist, Dimitris Pandermalis, which describes the excavations, the finds, and their significance. (His efforts to keep the artifacts in the place where they were found have established a trend for the decentralization of archaeological finds throughout Greece.) The second floor contains a topographical relief of the area and the oldest surviving pipe organ precursor—the 1st-century BC hydraulis. The basement learning area has an Alexander mosaic, a model of the city, and ancient carriage shock absorbers. ⊠ *Dion ✛ Adjacent to archaeological site* ☎ *23510/53206* ⊕ *www.ancientdion.org* ✉ *€8.*

WHERE TO EAT

$ 🍴 **Dionysos.** Excellent food and true Greek *filoxenia* (hospitality) await
GREEK at the combination tourist shop, café, and three-meal-a-day restaurant. Recommended are the *loukanika* (sausages); rolled, spiced, and spit-roasted meat; and the excellent *yemista* (stuffed tomatoes and peppers) and *papoutsakia* (eggplant halves baked with cheese, spiced ground beef, and garlicy tomato sauce). **Known for:** quick, ready-made food; grilled meats; hima krasi (homemade wine) and tsipouro (Greek grappa). [$] *Average main: €11* ✉ *Village center* ✣ *Directly opposite the museum* ☎ *23510/53730.*

WHERE TO STAY

$ 🏨 **Safeti.** The mauve-color Safeti, opened in 2005, was a most welcome
RENTAL addition to Dion, offering three gorgeous, modern apartments, one of
FAMILY which has a hot tub (another a fireplace). **Pros:** family-run and friendly; near both Mt. Olympus and the sea; next to the museum and very cose to the archaeological park. **Cons:** only for those looking to self-cater; limited number of accommodations; no breakfast. [$] *Rooms from: €70* ✉ *Opposite Museum of Dion, on main road, Olympos* ☎ *23510/46272* 🌐 *www.safetis.gr* 🛏 *3 apartments* 🍽 *No meals.*

MT. OLYMPUS ΟΡ. ΟΛΥΜΠΟΣ

17 km (10 miles) southwest of Dion, 100 km (62 miles) southwest of Thessaloniki.

To understand how the mountain must have impressed the ancient Greeks and caused them to shift their allegiance from the earth-rooted deities of the Mycenaeans to those of the airy heights of Olympus, you need to see it clearly from several different perspectives. On its northern slope, the Olympus range catches clouds in a turbulent, stormy bundle, letting fly about 12 times as many thunder-and-lightning storms as anywhere else in Greece. From the south, if there is still snow on the range, it appears as a massive, flat-topped acropolis, much like the one in Athens; its vast, snowy crest hovering in the air, seemingly capable of supporting as many gods and temples as the ancients could have imagined. As you drive from the sea to Mt. Olympus, the mountain appears as a conglomeration of thickly bunched summits rather than as a single peak. The truly awe-inspiring height is 9,570 feet.

Nearby, Litochoro is the lively town (population 7,000, plus a nearby army base) nestled at the foot of the mountain. It's the gateway to Mt. Olympus. Souvenir shops, restaurants, local-specialty bakeries (stock up before a hike), and hotels vie for customers.

GETTING HERE AND AROUND

Trains from Athens and Thessaloniki (1 hour) stop at Litochoro, but you must then take a bus into town to catch another to the site. The train station is about 5 km (3 miles) from the town, near the seaside and motorway. It is better to take the train to Katerini or to Larissa and then a bus from there, or to simply take a bus from Litchoro *(see Dion)*.

Depending on which way you decide to ascend Mt. Olympus, take a taxi to Prionia, a tiny settlement 18 km (11 miles) from Litochoro.

EXPLORING

Mt. Olympus has some of the most beautiful nature trails in Europe. Hundreds of species of wildflowers and herbs bloom in spring, more than 85 of which are found only on this mountain. There are basically three routes to Zeus's mountaintop, all beginning in Litochoro. The most-traveled road is Via Prionia; the others are by Diastavrosi (literally, "crossroads") and along the Enipeos. You can climb all the way on foot or take a car or negotiate a taxi ride to the end of the road at Prionia (there's a taverna) and trek the rest of the way (six hours or so) up to snow-clad Mytikas summit—Greece's highest peak at 9,570 feet. The climb to Prionia takes about four hours; the ride, on a bumpy gravel road with no guardrails between you and breathtakingly precipitous drops, takes little less than an hour, depending on your nerves. If you can manage to take your eyes off the road, the scenery is magnificent. The trail is snow-free from about mid-May until late October.

Fodor's Choice ★ **Spilios Agapitos.** During any Mt. Olympus hike, you could take a lunch break or stay overnight at Spilios Agapitos. The refuge is run by the daughter of Kostas Zolotas, a venerable climbing guru. To bunk down for the night costs €13 per person (€11 with an international mountaineering card); there are blankets but no sheets. Bring your own flashlight, towel, and soap. Campers can pitch tents for €4.20 (€3.20 with card) per person and can use the refuge's facilities (note that cooking is not permitted in the refuge). The restaurant is open all day until 9 pm. It's 6 km (4 miles), about 2½–3 hours, from Prionia to Refuge A. From here it's 5 km (3 miles), about 2½–3 hours, to the Throne of Zeus and the summit. The trail is easy going to Skala summit (most of the way), but the last bit is scrambling and a bit hair-raising. Some people turn back. If you plan to hike up Mt. Olympus, be sure to take a map; the best are produced by Anavasi. If you would prefer a guided hike up Mt. Olympus, the staff at Refuge A can arrange a guide for you, and Trekking Hellas organizes treks for various-size groups. ✉ *Refuge A, Litochoro* ☎ *23520/81800* 🌐 *www.mountolympus.gr.*

WHERE TO EAT

$$ GREEK Fodor's Choice ★ 🍴 **Gastrodromio En Olympo.** Self-taught chef Andreas Gavris creates seasonal delights fit for the gods in his justifiably popular restaurant. Standouts include the *bourani,* a rich rice dish with nettles, wild mushrooms, and a Gruyère-like cheese from Crete; and the mountain lamb, cooked with olives and tomatoes and seasoned with rosemary. **Known for:** tastefully elevated Greek cuisine; professional and friendly service; an extensive wine list. [$] *Average main: €16* ✉ *Agios Nikolaou 36, Litochoro* ✣ *Opposite the town hall* ☎ *23520/21300* 🌐 *www.gastrodromio.gr.*

$ ✕ **To Pazari.** This homey restaurant is known for its outstanding sea-
GREEK   food—it's always fresh, artfully prepared, and surprisingly cheap. The
grilled meats are good, too, as are the fresh bread and the dips—especially the *kopanisti* (the punchy spiced cheese dip) and the *melitzanosalata* (lovingly made from roasted eggplant and garlic). **Known for:**
old-style taverna; traditional Greek fare; no-frills but well-prepared
food. Ⓢ *Average main: €8* ✉ *Martiou 25, Litochoro* ☎ *23520/82540.*

WHERE TO STAY

$$ 🏨 **Dion Palace Beauty and Spa Resort.** Enjoy excellent views of the sea or
RESORT   the peaks at the Dion Palace, which also offers great proximity to the
FAMILY   beach, Mt. Olympus, and the archaeological site at Dion, and let's not
forget the luxury spa, as well as many activities for kids. **Pros:** enjoy
the luxury of a spa while you're here; some rooms have a private pool;
the restaurant has good food. **Cons:** near the National Highway so you
will need a vehicle to get around; on foot, little is close by; patchy Wi-Fi.
Ⓢ *Rooms from: €150* ✉ *Limni Litochoro, Litochoro* ✢ *6 km (4 miles)
northeast of Litochoro* ☎ *23520/61431 to 614314* ⊕ *www.dionpalace.
com* ⤴ *196 rooms* ⦿| *Breakfast.*

$ 🏨 **Ktima Faki.** This guesthouse, expanded and with a new swimming
B&B/INN   pool, is 700 meters (½ mile) up on the slopes of Mt. Olympus, 5 km (3
FAMILY   miles) from Litochoro, on the road to the church of St. John (Agios Ioan-
Fodor'sChoice   nis), a local landmark. **Pros:** acres of gardens for children to explore;
★   tasteful decor; lovely swimming pool. **Cons:** a car is essential, as it is
out of the way; breakfast starts late (at 8:30 am); books out especially
on weekends, and some rooms can only be booked for two or more
nights. Ⓢ *Rooms from: €100* ✉ *Litochoro* ✢ *Road to the church of
Agios Ioannis, 5 km (3 miles) from Litochoro* ☎ *23520/83750* ⊕ *www.
ktimafaki.gr* ⤴ *21 rooms* ⦿| *Breakfast.*

$ 🏨 **Olympus Mediterranean.** Pretty and friendly, this spa hotel—built in
HOTEL   2004—is a great value considering the quality of luxury and comfort
on offer. **Pros:** in town and a great base for hikers visiting the mountain;
indoor swimming pool and sauna; good service. **Cons:** not all rooms
have great views, so make sure to ask when booking if that's important
to you; patchy Wi-Fi; tricky to find. Ⓢ *Rooms from: €121* ✉ *Dionys-
sou 5, Litochoro* ☎ *23520/81831* ⊕ *www.mediterraneanhotels.gr* ⤴ *23
rooms* ⦿| *Breakfast.*

$ 🏨 **Villa Pantheon.** You know you're somewhere special when you see
B&B/INN   this family-run establishment at the trailhead for Mt. Olympus; views
stretch to the sea and the mountains—not surprisingly, given the loca-
tion and the relatively low price for what you get here, reservations are
a must, especially on weekends and holidays. **Pros:** only a five-minute
walk to the gorge; good value for the money; nice vistas of the village.
Cons: only the suites have a fireplace; 10-minute walk into town; poor
Wi-Fi signal in some of the rooms. Ⓢ *Rooms from: €65* ✉ *Litochoro*
✢ *At the end of Ayiou Dimitriou* ☎ *23520/83931, 23520/81019 after
10 pm* ⊕ *www.villapantheon.gr* ⤴ *12 rooms* ⦿| *Breakfast.*

SPORTS AND THE OUTDOORS

Hellenic Alpine Club. The Hellenic Alpine Club can help with information on hiking Mt. Olympus. ⊠ *Enipeas gorge entrance, Litochoro* ☎ *23520/82444, 6940823886* ⊕ *eoslitohorou.blogspot.gr.*

Olympos Trek. Guided treks to the summit of Mt. Olympus, rafting, and climbing are just some of the activities organized by this reputable outdoor adventure agency. ⊠ *Katerini* ☎ *6932/545001, 2410/921244* ⊕ *www.olympostrek.gr* ⊠ *From €35.*

Personality Journeys. This top adventure travel company will plan and arrange your whole expedition to Mt. Olympus and other unmissable mountain destinations in Greece. ☎ *2152/151629* ⊕ *www.personality-journeys.com* ⊠ *From €1,300 for trekking tours.*

Trekking Hellas. Trekking Hellas runs hiking, rafting, mountain biking, and other outdoor excursions in the region, including some great trips up the mythical Mt. Olympus by foot (or bike) from Litochoro. ⊠ *Litochoro* ☎ *210/3310323 head office in Athens* ⊕ *www.trekking. gr* ⊠ *From €60.*

HALKIDIKI

Eastern Macedonia's sandy coves and Mediterranean landscape have had a considerably less violent, but no less intricate and long, history than the western end of the realm. The region of Halkidiki, the birthplace of the great Aristotle, is best known as Thessaloniki's summer playground. It consists primarily of three peninsulas with endless coastlines, Kassandra, Sithonia, and Agion Oros. Kassandra is well developed with many hotels and high-end resorts attracting holiday makers who enjoy their creature comforts, while Sithonia is less traveled, with fewer resorts and more campsites hugging its picturesque shores, luring the bohemian traveler. The last (and most easterly, with Ouranoupolis and its offshore islands) is Mt. Athos; a peninsula of natural and spiritual beauty that is dotted with the famous fortified Orthodox Christian monasteries, places for holy days, rather than holidays.

OURANOUPOLIS ΟΥΡΑΝΟΥΠΟΛΗ

110 km (68 miles) east of Thessaloniki, 224 km (189 miles) north and east of Mt. Olympus.

Meaning "heaven's city" in Greek, Ouranoupolis (also spelled Ouranopolis) is an appealing cul-de-sac on the final point of land that separates the secular world from the sacred sanctuaries of Mt. Athos. The village, noted for its rug and tapestry weaving, is particularly entrancing because of the bay's aquamarine waters, and the town is full of families on holiday in summer. The narrow village beaches can become overcrowded. There are many pensions and rooms-to-let around town, but the hotels on an islet or slightly outside the main town are quietest.

If you make your own way to Ouranoupolis from Thessaloniki via Route 16, stop at Aristotle's statue in Stagira (west of the modern village, watch for the easy-to-miss road sign), the region of this remarkable

A thrill for many is to hike up Mt. Olympus, the legendary home of the ancient Greek gods—these are among Greece's most beautiful nature trails.

man's birthplace. Aristotle's theories and inventions are re-created in engaging hands-on exhibits (there's a small fee) around a grassy knoll with a surveying view.

GETTING HERE AND AROUND

Ouranoupolis is reachable by KTEL bus from the Halkidiki terminal in Thessaloniki. There are six buses departing Thessaloniki daily (five on Sunday) with the first heading off at 5:30 am (6:15 on Sunday) and the last leaving at 5:45 pm. The trip takes two hours.

Taking a taxi takes two hours but will set you back well over €100 from the Kentro or Thessaloniki airport. Renting a car may be the better option as prices tend to be reasonable here. *See Car Travel for more information on car rentals.*

TOURS

Athos Sea Cruises. Some travelers prefer to cruise past 12 monasteries since they are off-limits to women. Athos Sea Cruises sails for the Mt. Athos area from April to October at 10:30 am, with an additional afternoon departure at 1:45 pm from May to October; tours last three hours. There is a commentary in English, French, Russian, and German. Tickets can be bought from the Ouranoupolis central square. ⊠ *Ouranoupolis* ⊕ *Near tower on main road* ☎ *23770/71370, 23770/71606, 23770/71071* ⊕ *www.athos-cruises.gr* ⊠ *From €20.*

Tower of Prosforion. Ouranoupolis was settled by refugees from Asia Minor in 1922–23, when the Greek state expropriated the land from Vatopedi Monastery on Mt. Athos. The settlement, known as Prosforion, was until then occupied by farming monks, some of whom lived in the Byzantine Tower of Prosforion, its origins dating from the 12th century. The tower subsequently became the abode of Joice and Sydney Loch, a couple who worked with Thessaloniki's noted American Farm School to help the refugees develop their rug-weaving industry. The tower was burned, altered, and restored through the centuries. Now it's a breezy and open place to take in the view on a sweltering day. ⊠ *Main Sq.* ✢ *At waterfront* ☎ *23770/71651* ⊕ *www.dimosaristoteli.gr* 🎫 *€2.*

OFF THE BEATEN PATH

Small Islands. Floating on the Proviakas Bay's turquoise waters are tiny emerald islands that are reachable from Tripiti (6 km [4 miles] north of Ouranoupolis) via a 15-minute caïque or ferry ride that runs every half hour or so in summer—and by small outboard motorboats, which you can rent by the day. All the islets have glorious white-sand beaches, and two—**Gaidoronisi** (part of the Drenia group) and the fishing hamlet of **Amouliani Town**—have places to eat.

WHERE TO EAT

$$

SEAFOOD

Fodor's Choice

★

✕ **O Kritikos.** Want sublime seafood pasta? Head to a place like this one, where the owner is a local fisherman and everything served is the catch of the day. **Known for:** fresh fish and seafood; excellent service; being busy (so reservations strongly recommended). $ *Average main: €22* ⊠ *Main road, away from the tower* ☎ *23770/71222* ⊕ *www.okritikos. com.*

WHERE TO STAY

$

HOTEL

🏨 **Akrogiali.** Built in 1935, this was the town's first hotel, and the only one across the street from the beach—the three-story building is nothing special to look at, but the sea-view rooms are just fine for basic beach holidays. **Pros:** closest hotel to the beach; decent and clean; most rooms have great sea views. **Cons:** on a busy road; Wi-Fi signal is poor; front-facing rooms can get some street noise. $ *Rooms from: €60* ⊠ *Beach road* ☎ *23770/71201* ⊕ *www.ouranoupolis-akrogiali.gr* 🛏 *15 rooms* ⦿ *No meals.*

$$$$

RESORT

FAMILY

Fodor's Choice

★

🏨 **Eagle's Palace.** The monastic architecture and lush gardens of this Small Luxury Hotels member is deeply inspired by the mystical Orthodox peninsula of Mt. Athos, which lies just a stone's throw away. **Pros:** endless golden-sand beaches in front of the resort; flawless service; free activities and shuttle to nearby villages. **Cons:** pack mosquito repellent; beware of hidden costs; not all the six restaurants are open all the time. $ *Rooms from: €350* ⊠ *Skala Neon Rodon* ☎ *23770/31070, 23774/40070* ⊕ *www.eaglespalace.com* 🛏 *157 rooms* ⦿ *Some meals.*

$

B&B/INN

Fodor's Choice

★

🏨 **Skités.** Find peace and privacy on a bluff off a gravel road south of town at this charming complex of garden bungalows, comprised of small and pleasant rooms, and staffed by folks who want to make you feel comfortable. **Pros:** private and peaceful; very personal service; those delicious vegetables from the owner's own plot. **Cons:** don't come here if it's buzzy nightlife you're after; the rustic bohemien style is not to everyone's taste; Wi-Fi patchy in certain areas. $ *Rooms from: €121* ⊠ *1 km (½ mile) south of town* ✢ *If you need directions, ask for the hotel of Mrs. Pola Bohn* ☎ *23770/71140* ⊕ *www.skites.gr* ⊗ *Closed Nov.–late Apr.* 🛏 *25 rooms* ⦿ *Breakfast.*

MT. ATHOS ΟΡ. ΑΘΩΣ

50 km (31 miles) southeast of Ouranoupolis, 120 km (74 miles) southeast of Thessaloniki.

The third peninsula of Halkidiki, Mt. Athos is called *Ayion Oros* (Holy Mountain) in Greek, although it does not become a mountain until its southernmost point (6,667 feet). The peninsula is prized for its pristine natural beauty, seclusion, and spirituality; its monasteries contain priceless illuminated books and other treasures.

The Virgin Mary, it is said, was brought to Athos by accident from Ephesus, having been blown off course by a storm, and she decreed that it be venerated as her own special place. This story has since become the rationale for keeping it off-limits to all women but the Virgin herself. Hermits began settling here and formed the first monastery in the 10th century. By the 14th century, monasteries on the 650-square-km (250-square-mile) peninsula numbered in the hundreds. In 1924 the Greek state limited the number of monasteries, including Russian, Bulgarian, and Serbian Orthodox, to 20, but a number of hermitages and separate dependencies called *skits* also exist. The semiautonomous community falls under the religious authority of the Istanbul-based Orthodox Ecumenical Patriarch.

Only men may visit the monasteries, and the numbers are strictly limited. You must apply for a permit at the Holy Executive of the Holy Mt. Athos Pilgrims' Bureau in Thessaloniki several months in advance. Mt. Athos is a place of religious pilgrimage: proper attire is long pants and shirts with sleeves at least to midarm; wearing hats inside the monasteries is forbidden. Video cameras and tape recorders are banned from the mountain, but taking photographs is allowed.

GETTING HERE AND AROUND

From Ouranoupolis, boats leave twice daily to Dafni (the main port on the west coast of Athos). The 6:30 am boat sails direct to Dafni, but the 9:45 am boat stops at each harbor or monastery (the trip can take as long as 90 minutes). From Dafni there's a connecting service farther south to Ayias Annas. Fares vary depending on the speed of the boat. You can also take a bus to Ierissos, from where boats leave at 8:30 am (daily in summer; Thursday–Monday from September to June) for the monastery of Iviron, which is midway down the east coast here. Boats stop at each monastery en route, with the journey taking around two hours. Make sure to double-check times and travel options at the Holy Executive of the Holy Mt. Athos Pilgrims' Bureau in Thessaloniki, or inquire at the Thessaloniki bureau of the Greek National Tourism Organization for more information.

PERMITS

Holy Executive of the Holy Mt. Athos Pilgrims' Bureau. Men who want to visit Mt. Athos should contact the Holy Executive of the Holy Mt. Athos Pilgrims' Bureau (Grafio Proskyniton Ayiou Orous) four to six months in advance of arrival. ■TIP→ **Cancellations are quite common, and you may get a pass immediately if there has been a cancellation, so it's always worth asking if you want to go but haven't made the proper arrangements in advance.** You must obtain a written permit (free) from this office, which issues 10 permits a day for non-Orthodox visitors, and 100 permits a day for Orthodox visitors (Greek or foreign). You will need to pick it up in person, presenting your passport. Enquire about making reservations for a specific monastery, which must be done in advance (some might be closed for renovations). The permits are valid for a four-day visit on specific dates, which may be extended by authorities in Karyes. When you arrive at Ouranoupolis, you also need to pick up a *diamonitirio,* or visiting permit (€35). Boats headed for the monasteries depart Ouranoupolis for Daphni on the peninsula at 9:45 am; it's a two-hour sail and costs €7.50. There are faster boats also that take 45 minutes; these leave at 8:45 am and 10:30 am and cost €12.50. You need to book a seat as soon as you receive your permit (visit ⊕ *www.microathos.gr* or call ☎ *2377/071400* for boat tickets and timetables). Local transport takes you the last 13 km (8 miles) to Karyes and to monasteries beyond from there. ✉ *Egnatia 109, Kentro* ☎ *2310/252578 for non-Greeks, 2310/252575 for Greeks* ⊕ *www. athosfriends.org.*

THE PELOPONNESE

Monemvassia, Mycenae, Nafplion,
the Mani, and Olympia

WELCOME TO THE PELOPONNESE

TOP REASONS TO GO

★ **Ancient Ruins A to Z:** Some of Greece's greatest classical ruins, including Corinth, Mycenae, and Olympia, are packed into this region.

★ **Nafplion Grace:** The favorite Greek city of many seasoned travelers has a magnificent setting on the Gulf of Argolis, imposing remains, an animated waterfront, and street after street of old houses, churches, and mosques.

★ **Majestic Mani:** True connoisseurs of Greece flaunt the fact that they've traveled to this far-from-the-madding-crowds peninsula, famed for its silent villages, stark coastal landscapes, and feeling of mystery.

★ **High Drama:** The theater at Epidaurus, the setting for a highly acclaimed drama festival, still boasts of acoustics so perfect that every word can be heard—even from the very last of its 55 tiers.

★ **Byzantine Glory:** Two remarkable strong-holds, Mystras and Monemvasia, display a rich Byzantine legacy.

The northern Peloponnese runs westward along the Gulf of Corinth to the big transportation hub of Patras and the Adriatic coast, while in the east, the Gulf of Argolis is the setting for beautiful Nafplion, famed for its Venetian, Ottoman, and German neoclassic houses. The southern Peloponnese is bisected with rugged mountain ranges and meets the sea in fingerlike peninsulas that dangle from the southernmost extremes of the Greek mainland.

1 Argolid and Corinthiad. Forgotten civilizations left their mysteries here in the northern Peloponnese, most strikingly at the ruined city of Mycenae, with giant tombs to the heroes of Homer's *Iliad*. Nearby Nafplion, with its medieval edifices jutting into the Gulf of Argolis, is perhaps the most beautiful city in Greece, with fabled ancient sites like Epidauros and Corinth within easy reach. To the south, beyond the mountain valleys of Elis, is famed Ancient Olympia, birthplace of the ancient Olympic games.

2 Arcadia. Two of Greece's most appealing mountain villages, Stemnitsa and Dimitsana, are here in this still somewhat remote region, as is the spectacular Temple of Apollo at Bassae.

3 Laconia. Surrounded on three sides by mountains and by the sea on the other, Laconia was home to the harsh Spartans and also to the civilized Byzantines, who left splendid cities at Mystras, now in ruin, and Monemvasia, an intact medieval stronghold that clings to a rock above the sea. To the south lies the hauntingly beautiful Mani Peninsula, and its stark and sublime villages.

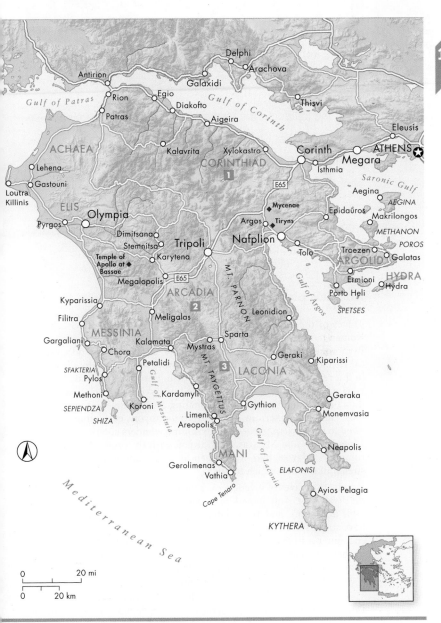

13

Delphi
Arachova
Antirion
Galaxidi
Gulf of Patras
Rion
Egio
Diakofto
Patras
Aigeira
Gulf of Corinth
Thisvi
Eleusis
ACHAEA
Kalavrita
Xylokastro
Corinth
Megara
ATHENS
CORINTHIAD
Isthmia
Saronic Gulf
1
E65
Aegina
Lehena
Gastouni
ELIS
Loutra
Killinis
Olympia
Mycenae
Epidauros
AEGINA
Makrilongos
Pyrgos
Dimitsana
Stemnitsa
Karytena
Tripoli
Argos
Tiryns
Nafplion
Tolo
METHANON
POROS
Troezen
Galatas
Temple of
Apollo at
Bassae
Megalopolis
E65
ARCADIA
ARGOLID
HYDRA
Ermioni
Hydra
Porto Heli
MT. PARNON
Gulf of Argos
Kyparissia
2
Meligalas
Leonidion
SPETSES
Filitra
MESSINIA
Gargaliani
Chora
Kalamata
Mystras
Sparta
Geraki
Kiparissi
SFAKTERIA
Petalidi
MT. TAYGETUS
3
LACONIA
Pylos
Methoni
Kardamyli
Geraka
SEPIENDZA
Koroni
Gythion
Monemvasia
SHIZA
Limeni
Areopolis
MANI
Gulf of Laconia
Neapolis
Gerolimenas
Vathia
ELAFONISI
Ayios Pelagia
Cape Tenaro
Gulf of Messinia
Mediterranean Sea
KYTHERA

0   20 mi
0   20 km

Updated
by Stephen
Brewer

Over the millennia the rugged terrain of the Peloponnese—a vast region that hangs like a large leaf from the stem of the Corinthian isthmus—has nourished kingdoms and empires. The stony landmarks of these ancient achievers litter the ground liberally, from Epidaurus to Olympia to Ancient Messe. This, indeed, is the fabulous Greece of history and myth: if Hercules walked the earth (some historians now believe he was an actual early king of Argos or Tiryns), his main stomping grounds were here.

Traces of these lost realms—ruined Bronze Age citadels, Greek and Roman temples and theaters, and the fortresses and settlements of the Byzantines, Franks, Venetians, and Turks—attest to this land's historical richness. Four thousand years of history are more fully illustrated in this region than nearly anywhere else in Europe. No wonder visitors who spend less than a week here wind up asking themselves why they didn't allot more time to this fascinating area of Greece, the country's most ruin-packed terrain, ground zero for anyone even remotely interested in the ancient past—with Byzantine wonders entering the mix at Monemvasia and Mystras. Plus, if you wish to forgo clamoring over ruins for a day or two, it's easy to find a mountain path or isolated stretch of sand on which to relax.

Despite the waves of invaders over the centuries this land is considered the distillation of all that is Greek, with its indulged idiosyncrasy, intractable autonomy, and appreciation of simple pleasures. Time seems to have stood still in the smaller towns here, and even in the cities you'll encounter a lifestyle that remains more traditionally Greek than that of some of the more developed islands. The joy of exploring this region comes as much from watching life transpire in an animated square as it does from seeing the impressive ruins.

"Pelopónnisos" means "Island of Pelops," though only the narrow Corinth canal separates it from the mainland. Pelops was the son of the mythical Tantalos, whose tragic descendants dominate the half-legendary Mycenaean centuries. The myths and legends surrounding Pelops and his family—Atreus, Agamemnon, Orestes, and Electra, among others—provided the grist for poets and playwrights from Homer to Aeschylus and enshroud many of the region's sites to this day.

A walk through the Lion Gate into Mycenae, the citadel of Agamemnon, brings the Homeric epic to life, and the massive walls of nearby Tiryns glorify the age of might. Eastward lies Corinth, the economic superpower of the 7th and 6th centuries BC, and also Epidaurus, the sanctuary of Asklepios, god of healing, where in summer Greek dramas are re-created in the ancient theater, one of the finest and most complete to survive.

In the western side of the Peloponnese is one of Greece's greatest ancient sites, Olympia, the sanctuary of Zeus and site of the ancient Olympic Games. Ancient Messene, with its mammoth fortifications from the 4th century BC, is on the sandy cape of Messinia, in the southern part of the region.

Fast forward almost two millennia. By the 13th century the armies of the Fourth Crusade (in part egged on by Venice) had conquered the Peloponnese after capturing Constantinople in 1204. But the dominion of the Franks was brief, and Byzantine authority was restored under the Palaiologos dynasty. Soon after Constantinople fell in 1453, the Turks, taking advantage of an internal rivalry, crushed the Palaiologoi and helped themselves to the Peloponnese. In the following centuries the struggle between the Venetians and the Ottoman Turks was played out in Greece. The two states alternately dominated the Peloponnese until the Ottomans ultimately prevailed as Venetian power declined in the early 1700s. The Turkish mosques and fountains and the Venetian fortifications of Nafplion recall this epic struggle. Rebellion against Turkish rule ignited in the Peloponnese, and after the Turks withdrew in 1828 in the wake of the Greek War of Independence, Nafplion was the capital of Greece from 1829 until the move to Athens in 1834.

PLANNING

WHEN TO GO

As in much of Greece, late April and May provide optimum conditions for exploration—hotels, restaurants, and sites have begun to extend their hours but the hordes of travelers have not yet arrived, and days are long. September and October are also excellent times because the weather is warm but not oppressive, the sea is at its balmiest, and the throngs of people have gone home. In summer, morning and early-evening activity will avoid the worst of the heat, which can be a formidable obstacle. Mosquitoes are out in force around seaside villages, which are often surrounded by fields and groves, so bring repellent and, more important, seek out a hotel room with air-conditioning. Remember that snow renders many of the mountain regions hard to access in winter.

PLANNING YOUR TIME

The remains of the ancient world are what draw many visitors to the Peloponnese—Mycenae, Epidaurus, and Olympia certainly top of the list of must-see sights of anyone with an interest in archaeology. Nafplion, a delightful city, with Byzantine, Venetian, and Turkish roots, makes an ideal base from which to explore these well-preserved ruins of ancient Greece. After Nafplion, Ancient Olympia, a don't-miss destination, beckons the Peloponnesian traveler. Continuing southward, one enters Laconia. The rewards here include exploring the stark Mani Peninsula and ancient splendors at Messene and elsewhere, and the trip down there is easy: Highway E65 allows travelers to speed from Athens to Kalamata or Sparta and Gythion in a few hours. Resort life is relatively low-key in the southern Peloponnese. Monemvasia, however, is a popular weekend destination for Greeks, and the narrow lanes can seem jammed; the town is much less crowded and more pleasant to visit during the week, when the medieval atmosphere regains a hold. The Mani, another favorite "remote" seaside getaway for Athenians, is rarely crowded, except on August weekends.

GETTING HERE AND AROUND

Nafplion is the major city in the east of the region, on the Gulf of Argolis, about 150 km (90 miles) south of Athens. Though it's possible to travel by train from Athens to the northern Peloponnesian, ongoing and often delayed improvements can make this less than a magic-carpet ride. The easiest way to get around the often-rural Peloponnese is therefore by car, on the region's well-maintained and well-marked roads. The bus network between towns is excellent, though service to smaller villages tends to be infrequent. It's easy to get to most places in the Peloponnese via the E65, a north–south highway that cuts through the region and is four lanes for much of its length, connecting Corinth, Tripoli, Sparta, and Kalamata with Athens. Another leg, E55, drops down to the western coast near Pylos. From Nafplion, an excellent base for exploring the region, you can easily reach such ancient sites as Epidaurus and Mycenae.

AIR TRAVEL

The main airport in the Peloponnese is the small field 9 km (5 miles) outside Kalamata. It's not terribly well served, though Aegean Airlines offers daily one-hour flights to and from Athens. The airport also handles charter flights to and from northern Europe in summer.

Airport Contacts Kalamata Airport. ✉ *Off Hwy. E2, 9 km (5 miles) west of city center, Kalamata* ☏ *27210/63805.*

BOAT AND FERRY TRAVEL

The big city of Patras (the tourist office is near the harbor) is the port for boats to and from Corfu and the other Ionian islands, as well as boats to and from Italy. Minoan, ANEK, and Blue Star all run boats between Patras and the Ionians, and Superfast and Minoan have the most extensive services between Patras and Ancona, Bari, and Venice in Italy. Lane Sea Lines runs service in summer between Gythion and Neapoli, in the Southern Peloponnese, and Kythera and Kissamos (Kastelli), Crete. The Nafplion Port Authority and Patras Port Authority can advise you about entry and exit in their ports for yachts. *For detailed information on ferry companies and port authorities, see Boat Travel in Travel Smart.*

BUS TRAVEL

Bus service between Athens and the Peloponnese is excellent—so good that you might consider taking a bus to your destination and renting a car locally, saving tolls and high fuel charges. Take advantage of the English speakers at the ticket offices to get information on traveling throughout the Peloponnese by bus—they have at their disposal a wealth of information that is otherwise hard to get. The association of regional bus companies (KTEL) no longer provides schedules on its national website, only on a pay-per-minute phone line in which information is available only in Greek. Nevertheless, you can usually find regional schedules online by searching for buses from an origin city to a destination, such as Gythion to Kalamata or Nafplion to Epidaurus. Within the Peloponnese, bus schedules are posted at local KTEL stations, usually on the main square or main street. You will often find English-speaking staff behind the desk in stations in the larger towns. Service from Athens to Corinth and Patras operates as frequently as every half hour from 6 am to late evening; it takes only an hour to Corinth and three or so to Patras. From Corinth, you can continue or connect for service to Nafplion, from where a local network serves the nearby classical sights, and to Sparta, with connections or onward service to such places as Monemvasia and the Mani. From Patras, you can make boat connections or connect to buses to Olympia and other places in the southwest Peloponnese. From Athens, direct buses also run several times daily to Gythion, Kalamata, and Tripoli and at least once a day to Andritsena, Monemvasia, and Pylos.

CAR TRAVEL

For pure pleasure, traveling by car through the Peloponnese really delivers. Four wheels are not only the easiest way to get around, but a car also provides a chance to enjoy dramatic scenery and get to out-of-the-way spots. The very best driving routes? Some point to the mountain roads that lead to Stemnitsa and Demitsana—on this journey, you'll encounter thick forests, stone villages clinging to steep hillsides, and brooding Frankish castles. Others tout the road from Kalamata to Mystras: this scenic route rises from the Messinia plains onto the forested flanks of the Taygettus range and the ruined city of Mystras and modern Sparta. For some, the road down the Mani Peninsula can't be beat: setting out from Kalamata, the landscape becomes starker the farther south you travel (on a highway that is barely more than one lane in places) until you reach Cape Tenaro, the mythical entrance to the underworld.

Note that even if highways have assigned numbers, no Greek knows them by any other than their informal names, which usually refer to their destination. A well-maintained toll highway, known simply as Ethnikos Odos, or National road (officially E65), runs from Athens to the isthmus of Corinth (84 km [52 miles], 1hour), and from there continues south to Nafplion and Kalamata (you can veer off to Sparta, Monemvasia, the Mani, and other places in the southern Peloponnese).

A branch, E55, heads east from Corinth toward Patras and Olympia and connects with the Rion bridge across the Gulf of Corinth. Have change ready, as a toll of about €1 to €2 is collected intermittently on parts of the system. From Corinth the trip to Patras takes about 1½ hours, and to Kalamata and Sparta less than 2 hours.

Narrow roads cross mountainous terrain throughout the region, providing many a scenic route when not closed due to snow in winter. You'll need a GPS device and/or a good map to navigate the back roads, as well as a transliteration of the Greek alphabet—many signs on remote roads are in Greek only. Gas stations are few and far between in some places, so top off the tank when you have the chance.

If you're renting a car in Athens, do so at the airport and drive south from there; the E94 ring road around Athens allows you to avoid the harrowing city traffic and connects with E65 south to the Peloponnese. On the other hand, bus travel into the region is so easy that you may want to travel by bus to your destination in the Peloponnese and rent a car for local exploring. You may rent a car in Patras if you are arriving on a boat from Italy or one of the Ionian islands. *For detailed information on renting a car, see Car Travel in Travel Smart.*

TAXI TRAVEL

If you have trouble reaching a site—for example, there is no public transportation to Ancient Messene—take a taxi from a town's main square, which is always near the bus station. In rural areas drivers don't usually speak English, though they will often find someone near the taxi stand who does to help you negotiate the ride.

In rural areas drivers may not switch on the meter if the destination has a fixed price, but make sure you agree on the cost before getting in. When leaving town limits, the driver may switch his meter to the higher rate (Tarifa 2).

TRAIN TRAVEL

The good news is that train travel from Athens to the Peloponnese is improving all the time—or, at least, is scheduled to improve. The bad news is that extensive track work is ongoing on the Peloponnesian lines, service interruptions are common, and Greece's financial woes have severely curtailed improvements. There are plans for a fast network to be running from Athens to Patras, Kalamata, and other cities in the Peloponnese, but no one is counting on such a network actually being in place soon. If you are traveling from Athens to anywhere other than Corinth, you will probably find bus travel to be faster, more reliable, and in many cases your only option for public transportation. Trains run to and from Corinth and Athens every hour between 8 and 8. The trip takes one hour and costs €9 to and from Athens, €11 to and from the airport. *For detailed information on traveling by train, see Train Travel in Travel Smart.*

Contacts Greek Railways Organziation (OSE). ⊕ *www.ose.gr.*

HOTELS

Hotels in Nafplion, Sparta, and other large towns and cities tend to be open year-round. Monemvasia is a year-round getaway and hotels stay open there as well. In beach resorts, such as the Mani villages, and in Olympia, many hotels close in late October and reopen in late March or early April. In Nafplion, many old houses have been converted to pleasant small hotels and do a brisk weekend business as a getaway for Athenians, and here you'll also be likely to find the region's more luxurious and expensive lodgings. Overall, lodging is a good value in the Peloponnese, and even in high season you can usually manage to find a clean and pleasant room for two, with breakfast, for less than €100.

RESTAURANTS

While you can enjoy elegant and nouvelle dining in some of the finer restaurants of the Peloponnese's beauty spots, such as Nafplion and Monemvasia, one of the great pleasures of traveling in this region is enjoying a meal on a square or seaside terrace in a simple village. In fact, villages here were the source of such international favorites as avgolemono soup and lamb fricassee. There are several other local specialties to watch for: in the mountain villages near Tripoli, order *stifado* (beef with pearl onions), *arni psito* (lamb on the spit), *kokoretsi* (entrails on the spit), and thick, creamy yogurt. In Sparta, look for *bardouniotiko* (a local dish of chicken stuffed with cheese, olives, and walnuts), and, around Pylos, order fresh ocean fish (priced by the kilo). In the rest of Laconia, try *loukaniko horiatiko* (village sausage), and in the Mani ask for ham.

Vegetables are almost always locally grown and fresh in this region famous for its olives and olive oil as wells as figs, tomatoes, and other produce. Seafood is plentiful, though sometimes frozen—menus will usually indicate what's frozen and what's fresh (and frozen usually hails from beyond Greece). A fresh catch is usually available at seaside tavernas, and an octopus or two will usually be drying out front. Inland, many tavernas serve grilled pork from local farms, as well as chicken and roosters plucked that morning. As for wine, beyond those *varelisio* (from the barrel), there are great reds from the region around Nemea and a top light white from Mantinea. After dinner, try *mavrodaphne,* a heavy dessert wine, or *dendoura,* a clove liqueur, as a digestive. Dress is casual and reservations usually unnecessary, although you might be asked to wait for a table if you're dining at 9 pm or later.

DINING AND LODGING PRICES IN EUROS			
	$	$$	$$$	$$$$
Restaurants	under €15	€15–€25	€26–€40	over €40
Hotels	under €125	€125–€225	€226–€275	over €275

Restaurant prices are for one main course at dinner, or for two mezedes (small dishes). Hotel prices are for a standard double room in high season, including taxes.

TOUR OPTIONS
Many operators organize whirlwind one-day tours from Athens to Corinth, Mycenae, Epidaurus, and Nafplion; the cost is about €85. These no-frills tours, aimed at those who don't expect much handholding, can be booked at travel agencies and at larger hotels. CHAT and other operators also offer a more leisurely two-day tour of Corinth, Mycenae, and Epidaurus, with an overnight stay in Nafplion; cost is about €140. If you are in Nafplion, many local travel agencies can arrange day tours of the classical sites.

VISITOR INFORMATION
The Peloponnese is woefully underserved by tourist offices. Nafplion has a locally run tourist office, but most towns in the region do not have tourist offices of any sort. For tourist information and general help in places without tourist offices, it's best to go to the Greek National Tourism Organization website (⊕ *visitgreece.gr*) or to contact the local tourist police, who often speak English and can be extremely helpful.

ARGOLID AND CORINTHIAD
ΑΡΓΟΛΙΔΑ ΚΑΙ ΚΟΡΙΝΘΙΑ

The plain of Argolid is littered with ancient ruins that include the city of Mycenae and the classical theater at Epidaurus; the beautiful Turkish-Venetian city of Nafplion lies at the edge of the plain, on the Gulf of Argolis. The Corinthiad is a hilly region overlooked by Ancient Corinth.

ANCIENT CORINTH ΑΡΧΑΙΑ ΚΟΡΙΝΘΟΣ

81 km (50 miles) southwest of Athens.

The isthmus is where the Peloponnese begins. Were it not for this narrow neck of land less than 7 km (4½ miles) across, the waters of the Gulf of Corinth and the Saronic Gulf would meet and would make the Peloponnese an island; hence the name, which means "Pelops's island."

For the ancient Greeks the isthmus was strategically important for both trade and defense; Corinth, with harbors on either side of the isthmus, grew wealthy on the lucrative east–west trade. Ships en route from Italy and the Adriatic to the Aegean had to sail around the Peloponnese, so in the 7th century BC a paved roadway called the Diolkos was constructed across the isthmus, over which ships were hauled using rollers. You can still see remnants near the bridge at the western end of the modern canal.

West of the isthmus, the countryside opens up into a low-lying coastal plain around the head of the Gulf of Corinth. Modern Corinth, near the coast about 8 km (5 miles) north of the turnoff for the ancient town, is a regional center of some 23,000 inhabitants. Concrete pier-and-slab is the preferred architectural style, and the city seems to be under a seismic curse: periodic earthquakes knock the buildings down before they have time to develop any character. Corinth was founded in 1858 after one of these quakes leveled the old village at the ancient site; another flattened

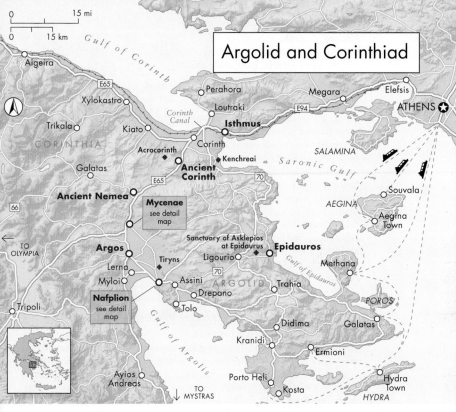

the new town in 1928; and a third in 1981 destroyed many buildings. Most tourists tend to avoid the town altogether, visiting the ruins of Ancient Corinth and moving on.

EXPLORING

Acrocorinth. Looming some some 540 meters (1,772 feet) above Ancient Corinth, the Acrocorinth is one of the best naturally fortified citadels in Europe. Citizens retreated in times of invasions and earthquakes, and armies could keep an eye out for approaches by land over the isthmus and by sea from the Saronic Gulf and the Gulf of Corinth. The moat and three rings of wall are largely Byzantine, Frankish, Venetian, and Turkish—but the right-hand tower of the innermost of the three gates is apparently a 4th-century BC original. Corinth's famous Temple of Aphrodite, which had 1,000 prostitutes in attendance, stood here at the summit, too. On the slope of the mountain is the Sanctuary of Demeter, which you can view but not enter. Take the road next to the ticket office in Ancient Corinth; if you don't have your own car, you can hire one of the taxis that often wait for visitors for the trip up to the tourist pavilion and café (about €5 round-trip), from which it's a 10-minute walk to Acrocorinth gate. ⊠ *Corinth* ✛ *Off E94, 7 km (4½ miles) west of Corinth* ☎ *27410/31207* ⊕ *www.culture.gr* ▣ *€2.*

Ancient Corinth. Excavations of one of the great cities of classical and Roman Greece have gone on since 1896, exposing ruins on the slopes of Acrocorinth and northward toward the coast. In ancient times, goods and often entire ships were hauled across the isthmus on a paved road between Corinth's two ports—Lechaion on the Gulf of Corinth and Kenchreai on the Saronic Gulf—ensuring a lively trade with colonies and empires throughout Europe and the Middle East. Most of the buildings that have been excavated are from the Roman era; only a few from before the sack of Corinth in 146 BC were rehabilitated when the city was refounded under orders of Julius Caesar.

The **Glauke Fountain** is past the parking lot on the left. According to the Greek traveler Pausanias, Glauke, Jason's second wife, also known as Creusa, threw herself into the water to obtain relief from a poisoned dress sent to her by the vengeful Medea. Beyond the fountain is the **museum,** which displays examples of the black-figure pottery—decorated with friezes of panthers, sphinxes, bulls, and warriors—for which Corinth was famous.

Seven of the original 38 columns of the **Temple of Apollo** (just above the museum) are still standing, and the structure is by far the most striking of Corinth's ancient buildings—as well as one of the oldest stone temples in Greece (mid-6th century BC). Beyond the temple are the remains of the **North Market,** a colonnaded square once surrounded by many small shops, and south of the temple is the main forum of Ancient Corinth. A row of shops bounds the forum at the far western end. East of the market is a series of small temples, and beyond is the forum's main plaza. A long line of shops runs lengthwise through the forum, dividing it into an **upper (southern)** and **lower (northern) terrace,** in the center of which is the bema (large podium), perhaps the very one where in AD 52 St. Paul delivered his defense of Christianity before the Roman proconsul Gallio.

The southern boundary of the forum was the **South Stoa,** a 4th-century-BC building, perhaps erected by Philip II of Macedonia to house delegates to his Hellenic confederacy. There were originally 33 shops across the front, and the back was altered in Roman times to accommodate such civic offices as the council hall, or *bouleuterion,* in the center. The road to Kenchreai began next to the bouleuterion and headed south. Farther along the South Stoa were the entrance to the **South Basilica** and, at the far end, the **Southeast Building,** which probably was the city archive.

THE ISTHMUS CANAL

Nero was the first to begin cutting a canal, supposedly striking the first blow, with a golden pickax, in AD 67, a task he then turned over to 6,000 Jewish prisoners. But the canal project died with Nero the following year, and the roadway was used until the 13th century. The modern canal, built 1882–93, was cut through 285 feet of rock to sea level. The impressive sight is a fleeting one if you are speeding by on the highway, so keep a sharp lookout. A well-marked turnoff leads to the tourist area, which has many restaurants (best avoided) and souvenir shops, as well as an overlook above the canal.

In the lower forum, below the Southeast Building, was the **Julian Basilica,** a former law court. Continuing to the northeast corner of the forum, you approach the facade of the **Fountain of Peirene.** Water from a spring was gathered into four reservoirs before flowing out through the arcadelike facade into a drawing basin in front. Frescoes of swimming fish from a 2nd-century Roman refurbishment can still be seen. The Lechaion road heads out of the forum to the north. A colonnaded courtyard, the **Peribolos of Apollo,** is directly to the east of the Lechaion road, and beyond it lies a **public latrine,** with toilets in place, and the remains of a **Roman-era bath,** probably the Baths of Eurykles described by Pausanias as Corinth's best known.

Along the west side of the Lechaion road is a large basilica entered from the forum through the **Captives' Facade,** named for its sculptures of captive barbarians. West of the Captives' Facade the row of **northwest shops** completes the circuit.

Northwest of the parking lot is the **odeon** (a roofed theater), cut into a natural slope, which was built during the 1st century AD, but burned around 175. Around 225 the theater was renovated and used as an arena for combats between gladiators and wild beasts. North of the odeon is the **theater** (5th century BC), one of the few Greek buildings reused by the Romans, who filled in the original seats and set in new ones at a steeper angle. By the 3rd century they had adapted it for gladiatorial contests and finally for mock naval battles.

North of the theater, inside the city wall, are the **Fountain of Lerna** and the **Asklepieion,** the sanctuary of the god of healing with a small temple (4th century BC) set in a colonnaded courtyard and a series of dining rooms in a second courtyard. Terra-cotta votive offerings representing afflicted body parts (hands, legs, breasts, genitals, and so on) were found in the excavation of the Asklepieion, and many of them are displayed at the museum. ⊠ *Corinth ✛ Off E94, 7 km (4½ miles) west of Corinth* ☎ *27410/31207* ⊕ *www.culture.gr* ⊠ *€8.*

Corinth Historical and Folklore Museum. If you find yourself in the new town, it's well worth your time to step into this collection with its well-done displays of beautiful costumes, works of embroidery, and furniture from throughout Greece. ⊠ *Near town wharf, Ermou 1, Corinth* ☎ *27410/25352* ⊕ *www.culture.gr* ⊠ *€2.*

EPIDAURUS ΕΠΙΔΑΥΡΟΣ

62 km (38 miles) south of the isthmus, 25 km (15 miles) east of Nafplion.

What is now a pleasant little agricultural village surrounded by orange and olive groves has been on the Greek map for millennia. Epidaurus was known for its theater and healing center as early as the 4th century BC. Today the beautifully preserved theater standing proud in a pine-scented glade is a magnificent sight, one of the most popular of all the ruins of ancient Greece.

EXPLORING

FAMILY

Fodor's Choice

★

Sanctuary of Asklepios at Epidaurus. What was once the most famous healing center in the ancient world is today best known for the **Theater at Epidaurus,** remarkably well preserved because it was buried at some time in antiquity and remained untouched until it was uncovered in the late 19th century. Built in the 4th century BC by the architect Polykleitos the Younger, the 14,000-seat theater was never remodeled in antiquity, and because it was rather remote, the stones were never quarried for secondary building use. The extraordinary qualities of the theater were recognized even in the 2nd century AD. Pausanias of Lydia, the 2nd-century AD traveler and geographer, wrote, "The Epidaurians have a theater in their sanctuary that seems to me particularly worth a visit. The Roman theaters have gone far beyond all the others in the world... but who can begin to rival Polykleitos for the beauty and composition of his architecture?" In addition, the acoustics are so perfect that even from the last of the 55 tiers every word can be heard. It's the setting for a highly acclaimed **summer drama festival,** with outstanding productions.

The **Sanctuary of Asklepios** is dedicated to the god of healing, the son of Apollo who was allegedly born here. The most important healing center in the ancient world drew visitors in search of a cure from throughout Greece and the colonies. The sanctuary is in the midst of a decades-long restoration project, but you can see the ruins of the Sleeping Hall, where clients slept in order to be visited by the gods in their dreams and told which cure to follow, as well as the enormous Guest House, with 160 rooms, and the Tholos, where serpents that were said to cure with a flick of the tongue were housed in a maze of labyrinths. Some copies of sculptures found among the ruins are in the **site museum** (the originals are in the National Archaeological Museum in Athens) along with ancient medical instruments, votives, and inscriptions expressing the gratitude of the cured. Heading south from the isthmus on Highway 70, don't take the turnoffs for Nea Epidaurus or Palaio Epidaurus; follow the signs that say "Ancient Theater of Epidaurus." ⊠ *Epidaurus ♁ Off Hwy. 70, near Ligourio* ☎ *27530/23009* ⊕ *www.culture.gr* ⊒ *€12.*

PERFORMING ARTS

Athens and Epidaurus Festival. In the theater at Epidaurus, this festival offers memorable performances from late June through August, Friday and Saturday only, at 9 pm. All productions are of ancient Greek drama in modern Greek, many presented by the national theater troupe. Actors are so expressive (or often wear ancient masks to signal the mood) that you can enjoy the performance even if you don't know a word of Greek. Get to the site early (and bring a picnic lunch or have a drink or a light meal at the decent Xenia Café on-site), because watching the sun set behind the mountains and fields of olives and pines is unforgettable. You can buy tickets at the Festival Box Office in Athens (at Panepistimiou 39), by phone, or online, and a short time before performance days at the theater box office. Many tour operators in Athens and Nafplion offer tours that include a performance at Epidaurus. On the days of performances, four or five buses run between Nafplion and the theater, and there's service back to Nafplion after the play. Look for buses that say "Theater" or "Epidaurus," not "Nea Epidaurus" or "Archea Epidaurus." Buses also run to and from Athens on days of performances. ✉ *Ancient theater, Epidaurus* ☎ *210/928–2900 general information, 210/372–2000 tickets* ⊕ *www.greekfestival.gr* ✉ *Tickets €10–€50.*

NAFPLION ΝΑΥΠΛΙΟ

65 km (40½ miles) south of Corinth, 27 km (17 miles) west of Epidaurus.

Fodor's Choice
★

Oraia (beautiful) is the word Greeks use to describe Nafplion. The town's old section, on a peninsula jutting into the Gulf of Argolis, mixes Greek, Venetian, and Turkish architecture; narrow streets, often just broad flights of stone stairs, climb the slopes beneath the walls of Acronafplia, the massive hilltop castle. Tree-shaded plazas surround neoclassical buildings. The Palamidi fortress—an elegant display of Venetian might from the early 1700s—guards the town. Nafplion deserves at least a leisurely day of your undivided attention, and you may want to spend several days or a week here and use the city as the base from which to explore the many surrounding ancient sights.

GETTING HERE AND AROUND

A favorite outing for Athenians is to whisk down to Nafplion on the toll road. The trip takes two hours (less for some drivers). You may want to take a more leisurely trip and stop at the isthmus and Ancient Corinth along the way. Once in Nafplion you can usually find a space in the enormous free parking lot alongside the port next to the Old Town. From there you can walk to most Nafplion accommodations.

Travelers to Nafplion can also take advantage of the new suburban rail links between Athens and Corinth, a trip of about an hour. From there you can transfer to one of the four daily trains to Nafplion (€10 each way), for a total trip time of three to four hours, or continue to Nafplion by taxi for about €50.

Bus service, either directly from Athens or with a connection in Corinth, is good. Buses to Nafplion run about every hour, and you should allow about three hours for the trip, which costs about €12 each way and often requires a change in Corinth.

EXPLORING

Little is known about ancient Nafplion, and the town did not grow in importance until Byzantine times, when it was fought over by the Byzantines and the Frankish crusaders. Then the duke of Athens, the Venetians, and the Turks held Nafplion; it was liberated in the War of Independence and briefly became the capital of Greece. Today Nafplion is once again just a provincial city, busy only in the tourist season and on weekends when Athenians arrive to get away from city pressures.

A full exploration of this lovely town takes an entire day; a quick tour, with some omissions, could be done in three hours. Although a step-by-step itinerary can lead you to all the main sights, you can get a good sample of Nafplion just by following your nose through its winding streets and charming squares. Around Syntagma (Constitution) Square are some of Nafplion's top sights, including the Peloponnesian Folklore Foundation Museum, St. Spyridon Church, and the archaeological museum. The most picturesque avenue is Vasileos Konstantinou; the more-commercial Amalias is lined with shops. Westward you'll find the Church of the Virgin Mary's Birth, an elaborate post-Byzantine structure. Continuing north, you come to quayside and Philhellenes Square and St. Nicholas Church.

From St. Nicholas westward along the quayside (called Akti Miaouli) is an unbroken chain of restaurants, most just average, and, farther along, pastry shops, which are better and especially pleasant in the afternoon for postcard writing, an iced coffee or ouzo, and conversation. From the quay, you can embark on a boat trip out to the miniature fortress of the Bourtzi in the harbor. Or you can continue walking along the waterfront promenade to the Five Brothers bastion, and then follow the winding Kostouros Street up to Psaromachalas, the picturesque fishermen's quarter. Return to the Five Brothers to continue on the promenade that follows the sea along the south side of the Nafplion Peninsula, or, instead, go through the tunnel that looks like a James Bond movie set from the parking lot off Kostouros Street and take the elevator to the Nafplia Palace hotel and the top of the Acronafplia fortress. The hotel bar is an excellent place to enjoy a sunset. Above all looms the town's Venetian-era Palamidi fortress, another top sunset spot (when weekday hours permit).

TOP ATTRACTIONS

FAMILY
Fodor'sChoice
★

Acronafplia. The Turks called this imposing hilltop of ruined fortifications Its Kale (Inner Citadel). The heights are crowned with a series of castles: a Frankish one on the eastern end of the hill, a Byzantine one on the west, and a massive Castello del Torrione (or Toro for short), also at the eastern end, built by the Venetians around 1480. During the second Venetian occupation, the gates were strengthened and the huge Grimani bastion was added (1706) below the Toro. The Acronafplia is accessible from the west side via the elevator next to the Nafplia Palace hotel, which sits on the ruins of the Frankish fort, and from the east via Potamianou Street, whose flights of steps ascend the hillside from St. Spyridon Square. Most of the remains of fortifications can be explored free of charge on overgrown paths that provide stupendous views over Nafplion and the sea. ⊠ *Nafplion.*

Bourtzi. Nafplion's pocket-size fortress is a captivating presence on a speck of land in the middle of the harbor generously called St. Theodore's Island. The Venetians built a single tower in 1471, and they enlarged it with a second tower and bastion when they recaptured Nafplion in 1686. Freedom fighters captured the Bourtzi during the War of Independence in 1822 and used the island to bombard the Turks defending the town. The new Greek government retreated to the island in the unsettled times following the revolution; after 1865, the fortress was the residence of the town executioners, and from 1930 until 1970 it was run as a hotel. Boats leave on no fixed schedule from the eastern end of Akti Miaouli. ⊠ *In harbor* 🛥 *Castle free; ferry €5.*

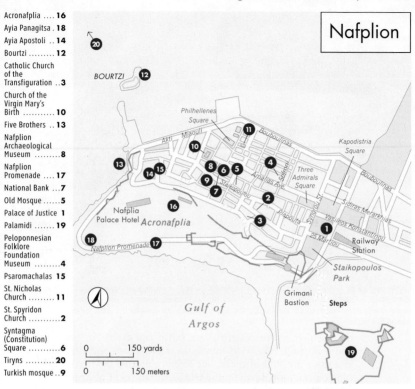

13

Nafplion Archaeological Museum. The thick walls of this red-stone building, built in 1713 to serve as the storehouse for the Venetian fleet, ensure the coolest interior in town. The museum houses artifacts from such nearby sites as Mycenae, Tiryns, Asine, and Dendra; the loot from Mycenaean tombs is especially rich and includes wonderful masks and a suit of armor. ⊠ *West side of Syntagma Sq.* ☎ *27520/27502* ⊕ *www. culture.gr* ⊠ *€6* ⊗ *Closed Mon. Nov.–Mar.*

Fodor's Choice ★ **Nafplion Promenade.** A seaside promenade skirts the Nafplion Peninsula, paved with reddish flagstones and opening every so often to terraces planted with a few rosebushes and olive and cedar trees. Along the south side of the peninsula, the promenade runs midway along a cliff— it's 100 feet up to Acronafplia, 50 feet down to the sea—and leads to Arvanitia Beach, a lovely place for a dip. Here and there a flight of steps goes down to the rocky shore below. (Be careful if you go swimming here, because the rocks are covered with sea urchins, which look like purple-and-black porcupines and whose quills can inflict a painful wound.) ⊠ *Nafplion.*

Palamidi. Whether in harsh sunlight or under floodlights at night, this mighty fortress is a beautiful sight, with red-stone bastions and flights of steps that zigzag down the 700-foot-tall cliff face. You can drive up

Surviving nearly intact from the 4th century BC, the arena at Epidaurus remains the most famous ancient theater in the world.

the less-precipitous eastern slope, but if you are in reasonable shape and it isn't too hot, try climbing the stairs. Most guidebooks will tell you there are 999 of them, but 892 is closer to the mark. From the top you can look down on the Old Town, the Gulf of Argolis, and the entire Argive plain.

Built in 1711–14, the Palamidi comprises three forts and a series of freestanding and connecting defensive walls. The name is taken from the son of Poseidon, Palamedes, who, legend has it, invented dice, arithmetic, and some of the Greek alphabet. Sculpted in gray stone, the lion of St. Mark looks outward from the gates. The Palamidi fell to the Turks in 1715 after only eight days, allegedly because the Venetians assumed the fortress was impregnable and saw no need to garrison a large number of troops within the walls. During the Turkish occupation the fortress was used as a prison; its inmates included the revolutionary war hero Theodore Kolokotronis, whose cell is indicated by a sign. ⊠ *Nafplion* ⊹ *Above town* ☎ *27520/28036* 🖅 *€4.*

Fodor'sChoice ★ **Peloponnesian Folklore Foundation Museum.** This exemplary collection focuses on textiles and displays outstanding costumes, handicrafts, and household furnishings. Many of the exhibits are precious heirlooms that have been donated by Peloponnesian families, and several rooms are painstaking re-creations of 19th-century Nafplion homes. Top hats from the 1950s and contemporary fashion sandals are among items that bring the overview into the present day. The gift shop has some fascinating books and a good selection of high-quality jewelry and handicrafts, such as weavings, kilims, and collector's items such as *roka* (spindles) and wooden *koboloi* (worry beads). ⊠ *Vasileos Alexandrou 1* ✛ *On block immediately north of Amalias, going up Sofroni* ☎ *27520/28379* ⊕ *www.pli.gr/en* ✎ *€4.*

Syntagma (Constitution) Square. The center of the Old Town is one of Greece's prettiest *platias* (squares), distinguished by glistening, multi-color marble paving bordered by neoclassical and Ottoman-style build-ings. In summer the restaurants and patisseries on the square—a focal point of Nafpliote life—are boisterous with the shouts and laughter of children and filled with diners well into the evening. ⊠ *Along Amalias and Vasileos Konstantinou.*

OFF THE
BEATEN
PATH

Tiryns. Homer describes the 3,500-year-old Mycenaean acropolis of Tiryns, facing the Gulf of Argolis just north of Nafplion, as "the wall-girt city." The modern writer Henry Miller was repelled by the place, as he records in *The Colossus of Maroussi*: "Tiryns is prehistoric in char-acter. Tiryns represents a relapse. Tiryns smells of cruelty, barbarism, suspicion, isolation." Today the well-preserved site seems harmless, surrounded by citrus trees and home to a few lizards that timidly sun themselves on the stones. The citadel makes use of a long, low outcrop, on which was set the circuit wall of gigantic limestone blocks of the type called "cyclopean" because the ancients thought they could have been handled only by the giant cyclops—the largest block is estimated at more than 15 tons. Via the **cyclopean ramp** the citadel was entered on the east side, through a gate leading to a narrow passage between the outer and inner walls. You could then turn right, toward the residential section in the **lower citadel,** or to the left toward the **upper citadel** and **palace.** The heavy **main gate** and **second gate** blocked the passage to the palace and trapped attackers caught between the walls. After the second gate, the passage opens onto a rectangular **courtyard,** whose massive left-hand wall is pierced by a **gallery of small vaulted chambers,** or casemates, opening off a **long, narrow corridor** roofed by a **corbeled arch.** (The chambers were possibly once used to stable horses, and the walls have been worn smooth by the countless generations of sheep and goats that have sheltered there.)

An elaborate entranceway leads west from the court to the upper citadel and palace, at the highest point of the acropolis. The complex included a colonnaded **court;** the great *megaron* (main hall) opened onto it and held the royal throne. Surviving fragments suggest that the floors and the walls were decorated, the walls with frescoes (now in the National Archaeological Museum in Athens) depicting a boar hunt and women riding in chariots. Beyond the megaron, a large **court** overlooks the houses in the lower citadel; from here, a long **stairway** descends to a small **postern gate** in the west wall. At the excavated part of the lower acropolis a significant discovery was made: two parallel **tunnels,** roofed in the same way as the galleries on the east and south sides, start within the acropolis and extend under the walls, leading to **subterranean cis-terns** that ensured a continuous water supply. ⊠ *Tiryns* ✛ *Off road to Argos, 5 km (3 miles) north of Nafplion* ☎ *27520/22657* ⊕ *odysseus. culture.gr* ✎ *€4.*

WORTH NOTING

Ayia Panagitsa (*All Holy Chapel*). While following the seaside promenade, before you reach the very tip of the peninsula (marked by a ship's beacon), there is a little shrine at the foot of a path leading up toward the Acronafplia walls above. The tiny church of the Little Virgin Mary, or Ayia Panagitsa, hugs the cliff on a small terrace and is decorated with icons. During the Turkish occupation the church hid one of Greece's secret schools. ⊠ *Nafplion* ✛ *End of promenade.*

Ayios Apostoli (*Chapel of the Apostles*). This pretty, miniature whitewashed chapel, perched near the top of a quiet neighborhood, has six small springs that trickle out the side of Acronafplia. ⊠ *Nafplion* ✛ *Off parking lot of Psaromachalas.*

Catholic Church of the Transfiguration. In the 19th century King Otho returned this 13th-century Venetian-built landmark, converted to a mosque under the Turks, to Nafplion's Catholics. The church is best known for the wooden arch erected inside the doorway in 1841, with the names carved on it of philhellenes (Greek admirers) who died during the War of Independence (Lord Byron is number 10). A mihrab (Muslim prayer recess) behind the altar and the amputated stub of a minaret are evidence of the church's use as a mosque. The church has a small museum and an underground crypt in which can be found sculptural work commemorating the defeat of the Turks at the hands of the Greeks and philhellenes. ⊠ *Zigomala* ✛ *Two blocks south of St. Spyridon.*

Church of the Virgin Mary's Birth. This post-Byzantine three-aisle basilica is by tradition linked to St. Anastasios, a Nafpliote painter. Anastasios was supposedly engaged to a local girl, but he abandoned her because she was immoral. Becoming despondent as a result of spells cast over him by her relatives, he converted to Islam. When the spell wore off, he cried out, "I was a Christian, I am a Christian, and I shall die a Christian." An Ottoman judge ordered that he be beheaded, but a Turkish mob stabbed Anastasios to death. His corpse was then allegedly hanged on an ancient olive tree that rises next to the church and that never again bore fruit. The basilica was the main Orthodox church during the Venetian occupation and has an elaborate wooden reredos carved in 1870. ⊠ *Nafplion* ✛ *West of Syntagma Sq.*

Five Brothers. Above the harbor at the western edge of town are the ruins of a fortification known as the Five Brothers, the only remaining part of the lower wall built around Nafplion in 1502. The name comes from the five guns placed here by the Venetians around 1690; they remain in place, all bearing the winged lion of St. Mark. ⊠ *Nafplion* ✛ *Near promontory of peninsula.*

NEED A BREAK

Beyond the Five Brothers, a few pleasant cafés and bars line the seaside promenade that follows the southern edge of the peninsula. These are good places to sit with an ouzo and watch the sun set behind the mountains across the gulf; some establishments have created little swimming areas alongside the tables, so it's not unusual to see patrons bobbing around in the water.

National Bank. This contemporary structure displays an amusing union of Mycenaean and modern Greek architectural elements fashioned with concrete. Take a look at the sculptures of a winged lion of St. Mark (which graced the main gate in the city's landward wall, long since demolished) and of Kalliope Papalexopoulou (a leader of the revolt against King Otho), whose house once stood in the vicinity. They're in the square next to the bank. ⊠ *Nafplion ⊹ South of Syntagma Sq.*

Old Mosque. This venerable mosque near the southeast corner of Syntagma Square has been put to various purposes since Nafplion was liberated from the Turks: as a school, a courthouse, municipal offices, and a movie theater. (The writer Henry Miller, who did not care for Nafplion, felt that the use of the building as a movie theater was an example of the city's crassness.) The landmark occasionally hosts temporary exhibits and performances. ⊠ *Syntagma Sq.*

13

Palace of Justice. The gracelessness of this building is magnified by its large size, but the effect is softened by an adjacent **square** with a statue honoring Nikitaras the Turk-Eater, who directed the siege of Nafplion during the War of Independence. ⊠ *Syngrou ⊹ Two blocks down from Kapodistria Sq.*

NEED A BREAK

✕ **Antica Gelateria di Roma.** Traditional Italian gelato (ice cream), in many flavors and dished up in colorful old surroundings, supplies a tempting excuse for a break. ⊠ *Farmakopoulou 3* ☎ *27520/23520.*

Psaromachalas. The fishermen's quarter is a small district of narrow lanes running between cramped little houses that huddle beneath the walls of Acronafplia. The old houses, painted in brownish yellow, green, and salmon red, are embellished with additions and overhangs in eclectic styles. The walk is enjoyable, but keep a low profile to respect the privacy of the locals. ⊠ *Along Kostouros.*

St. Nicholas Church. This church near the waterfront was built in 1713 for sailors by Augustine Sagredo, the prefect of the Venetian fleet, and is furnished with a Venetian reredos and pulpit, and a chandelier from Odessa. ⊠ *Off Philhellenes Sq.*

St. Spyridon Church. This one-aisle basilica with a dome (1702) has a special place in Greek history: it was in its doorway that the statesman Ioannis Kapodistrias, the first president of an independent Greece, was assassinated in 1831 by the Mavromichalis brothers from the Mani, the outcome of a long-running vendetta. The mark of the bullet can be seen next to the Venetian portal. On the south side of the square, opposite St. Spyridon, are two of the four Turkish fountains that remain in Nafplion. A third is a short distance east on Kapodistria Street, at the steps that constitute the upper reaches of Tertsetou Street. ⊠ *St. Spirdonas Sq.*

Turkish mosque. Now known as the Vouleftiko (Parliament), this former mosque was where the Greek National Assembly held its first meetings. The mosque is built of carefully dressed gray stones, and legend has it that the lintel stone from the Treasury of Atreus was used in the construction of the large, square-domed prayer hall. ⊠ *Staikopoulou ⊹ Next to Nafplion Archaeological Museum and behind National Bank.*

Enjoy a boat ride out to the Bourtzi fortress, built by 15th-century Venetians to protect the beautiful port town of Nafplion.

BEACHES

Arvanitia Beach. This in-town swimming spot is not really a beach but a seaside perch of smooth rocks, pebbled shoreline, and concrete plat-forms, all backed by fragrant pines. This is a good place for a morning wake-up swim or a refreshing plunge after a day of sightseeing. At times the popular and well-maintained spot, with a pleasant beach bar, seems as sociable as the town square, so don't be surprised to hear other bathers gossiping and exchanging recipes as they bob in the delightful water. You can walk to Arvanitia by following the seaside promenade that hugs the cliffs beneath the Acronafplia south of town. **Amenities:** food and drink; parking (no fee); showers; toilets. **Best for:** swimming. ⊠ *Nafplion ✛ South side of town, below Acronafplia.*

FAMILY **Karathona.** The closest sandy beach to Nafplion, Karathona is easy to reach by road (just keep following 25 Maritou Street) or a pleasant walk first along the seaside promenade and then a dirt track (you can also get there by bus in summer). The pine-backed sands are favored by Greek families with picnic baskets, and this is an ideal spot for kids, since the waters remain shallow far out into the bay. Sun loungers and umbrellas are available for rent, though a pine grove behind the sands provides plenty of nice shady spots. Several tavernas back the beach. **Amenities:** food and drink; parking (no fee); showers; toilets; water sports. **Best for:** swimming; walking. ⊠ *Nafplion ✛ About 3 km (2 miles) south of town.*

Psili Ammos. The resort town of Tolo, 12 km (7½ miles) south of Naf-plion, is a short inexpensive bus ride from Nafplion's main station or a more expensive taxi ride; beware, though, that in the warm months the beach of fine sand is packed solid with sunburned northern Europeans and abuzz with every water sport and beach activity ever invented, from taking in the sun in the endless rows of loungers to volleyball. A long parade of bars and tavernas backs the beach, and some tables are set right on the sands. Two uninhabited islands in the bay, Romvi and Koronissi, can be reached by excursion boat. **Amenities:** food and drink; parking (fee); showers; toilets; water sports. **Best for:** partiers; swimming; walking. ⊠ *Tolo road, Tolo.*

WHERE TO EAT

It's a Nafplion tradition to have dessert at one of the cafés on Syntagma Square or the *zacharoplasteia* (pastry shops) on the harbor. Lingering over an elaborate ice-cream concoction or after-dinner drink is a memorable way to wrap up an evening.

$$
SEAFOOD

✕ **Arapakos.** Nafplion locals are demanding when it comes to seafood, so it's a credit to this attractive, nautical-themed taverna on the waterfront that locals pack in to enjoy expert dishes made from fresh catches. The kitchen sends out such traditional accompaniments as a memorable *taramosalata* (fish roe dip) and *tzatziki* (yogurt garlic cucumber dip), as well as a few meat dishes, including exquisitely seasoned and grilled lamb chops. **Known for:** fresh seafood; affable service in pleasant surroundings. $ *Average main: €15* ⊠ *Bouboulinas 81* ☎ *27520/27675* ⊕ *www.arapakos.gr* ⊘ *Closed Tues. in winter.*

$
GREEK

✕ **Paleo Archontiko.** Seating here is in the ground floor of an old stone mansion or on the narrow street in front. Tassos Koliopoulos and his wife, Anya, oversee the ever-changing menu, which highlights good home cooking, such as beef *stifado* (stew slow-cooked with tomatoes and small onions) and *krassato* (rooster in wine sauce). **Known for:** homey setting; popular with locals on weekends. $ *Average main: €10* ⊠ *Siokou 7, at Ipsilantou* ☎ *27520/22449* ⊘ *No lunch weekdays and in winter.*

$
GREEK

✕ **Ta Fanaria.** Staikopoulou Street is one long outdoor dining room, with dozens of tourist-oriented tavernas serving night and day, and this popular place is leagues ahead of its neighbors. The kitchen concentrates on excellent versions of such staples as *ladera* (vegetables cooked in olive oil), charcoal-grilled lamb ribs, and *imam bayilda* (eggplant stuffed with onions), and serves them beneath a bougainvillea arbor in a quiet lane next to the restaurant. **Known for:** simple home-style fare; pleasant dining beneath an arbor. $ *Average main: €7* ⊠ *Staikopoulou 13* ☎ *27520/27141* ⊕ *www.fanaria.gr.*

$
GREEK FUSION

✕ **Taverna Byzantio.** Charcoal-grilled meats are the specialty in this snug, high-ceilinged old room tucked away in the backstreets off the harbor. The cuisine strays from Greece into the neighboring Balkans, with some wonderful schnitzels, cheese-filled pork roast, and other dishes that provide a nice change from a steady diet of Greek fare. **Known for:** grilled meats; attractive room and sidewalk terrace; cash only. $ *Average main: €10* ⊠ *Alexandrou 15* ☎ *27520/21631* ⊕ *www.taverna-byzantio.gr* ⊟ *No credit cards.*

WHERE TO STAY

$
B&B/INN

Aetoma. A 19th-century neoclassical mansion on a quiet square has been delightfully transformed into a petite B&B with extremely comfortable guest rooms and alluring public spaces. **Pros:** friendly, attentive service; each room has a balcony; the top-floor room has a terrace; excellent breakfast. **Cons:** stairs may pose an obstacle for some travelers; parking is limited but free spots available nearby; not all rooms have views. $ *Rooms from: €85* ✉ *Spiridomas Sq.* ☎ *27520/27373* ⊕ *www. nafplionhotel.gr* ⊅ *5 rooms* |○| *Breakfast.*

$$
HOTEL

Amphityron. Sea views fill every window in the airy, stylish, and contemporary guest rooms here, all of which open to teakwood decks—though the Old Town is just a few steps away, you may feel as if you're in the middle of the sea on a ship, and a pretty swanky one at that. **Pros:** at the edge of the Old Town and convenient to sights; comfortable rooms; sea views. **Cons:** food and drink are expensive; some complaints about maintenance; some street noise. $ *Rooms from: €220* ✉ *Spiliadou* ☎ *27520/70700* ⊕ *www.amphitryon.gr* ⊅ *45 rooms* |○| *Breakfast.*

$
HOTEL

Byron Hotel. A great deal of charm prevails here, from the simply but tastefully decorated rooms, with Turkish carpets and the odd sloping ceiling, to the outdoor patio set atop an old Turkish hammam. **Pros:** old-fashioned atmosphere; lovely patio; tucked away in the heart of Old Town. **Cons:** some rooms are cramped; outlooks from some rooms are limited; lots of indoor and outdoor stairs could be a real hardship for guests with mobility issues. $ *Rooms from: €60* ✉ *Platonos 16, Kapodistria Sq.* ☎ *27520/22351* ⊕ *www.byronhotel.gr* ⊅ *18 rooms* |○| *Breakfast.*

$
HOTEL

Hotel Athina. One of the best-value lodgings in Nafplion commands a prime spot on Syntagma Square, and the scene can be enjoyed from the narrow balconies or from the quiet comfort of the simply furnished rooms. **Pros:** excellent location; good value for comfort; generous and tasty breakfast. **Cons:** some rooms are dark; rooms facing square can be noisy; modern decor can be a bit stark. $ *Rooms from: €100* ✉ *Syntagma Sq.* ☎ *27250/26647* ⊕ *www.athina-hotel.gr* ⊅ *14 rooms* |○| *Breakfast.*

$
B&B/INN
Fodor'sChoice
★

Hotel Latini. This handsomely restored old house, just off the waterfront in the center of town, feels like a well-appointed private home, and the extremely comfortable guest rooms are graciously appointed and have sparkling bathrooms; all have views of the bay or a palm-filled square. **Pros:** convenient location in the Old Town near the port and parking; pleasing decor; comfortable, homelike atmosphere. **Cons:** no elevator; some views are limited; street noise at times. $ *Rooms from: €50* ✉ *Othonos 47* ☎ *27520/96470* ⊕ *www.latinihotel.gr* ⊅ *10 rooms* |○| *Breakfast.*

$
HOTEL
FAMILY
Fodor'sChoice
★

Hotel Perivoli. Surrounded by orange groves, this hilltop retreat is just a few minutes outside Nafplion but provides a resortlike getaway, with handsome, contemporary-style rooms and large terraces overlooking a shimmering pool and, in the near distance, the Gulf of Argolis. **Pros:** attractive; attentive, friendly service; one of the few Nafplion hotels with a pool. **Cons:** reachable only by car; not near restaurants, though an evening meal is served; a drive to beaches, but the pool is beautiful.

$ *Rooms from: €110* ✉ *Pirgiotika* ✛ *8 km (5 miles) east of Nafplion* ☎ *27520/47905* ⊕ *hotelperivoli.com* ⤳ *12 rooms* ⦿ *Breakfast.*

$ ⌂ **King Othon I.** This gracious neoclassical mansion has decorative
B&B/INN   rosette ceilings and a curving wooden staircase leading to high-ceilinged rooms that are pleasantly decorated in a turn-of-the-20th-century style. **Pros:** historic character; beautiful garden; excellent location near the harbor. **Cons:** some rooms are small; bathrooms tend to be cramped; breakfast is a bit meager. $ *Rooms from: €70* ✉ *Farmakopoulou 4* ☎ *27520/27585* ⊕ *www.kingothon.gr* ⤳ *11 rooms* ⦿ *Breakfast.*

$ ⌂ **Pension Marianna.** These extremely comfortable and character-filled
B&B/INN   rooms seem to be on top of the world, tucked away at the very top
FAMILY   of the Old Town, just below the Acronafplia, and facing the sea from breezy balconies and gardens. **Pros:** extremely hospitable; great communal outdoor spaces; lovely perch at the top of town. **Cons:** takes some stair climbing to reach; parking is not adjacent; a few rooms are dark. $ *Rooms from: €90* ✉ *Ilia Potamianou 9* ☎ *27520/24256* ⊕ *www.hotelmarianna.gr* ⤳ *20 rooms* ⦿ *Breakfast.*

NIGHTLIFE

Nafplia Palace Bar. An elevator whisks you from the Old Town up to the extensive grounds of this rather neglected hotel perched high above Nafplion on the ruins of the Frankish fortification atop Acronafplia. At first glance, the 1970s-era public spaces tend to be cavernous and austere, but the delightful pine-scented terrace hanging high above the town and bay is a prime spot for a sunset cocktail. ✉ *Nafplia Palace, Acronafplia* ☎ *27520/70800* ⊕ *nafpliapalace.gr.*

SHOPPING

Shopping in Nafplion is pleasant business, with a nice array of wares filling attractive shops tucked into old houses on shady lanes. Many shops sell clothing and decorative items geared to well-heeled Athenians who visit Nafplion for a day or weekend, while others specialize in some distinctly Greek goods.

Karonis. This family-run business has dispensed fine wines, ouzo, and other spirits since 1869 and offers tastings and a great deal of knowledge about local vineyards. Karonis also has a distillery on the outskirts of the Old Town. ✉ *Amalias 5* ☎ *27520/24446* ⊕ *www.karonis.gr.*

Komboloi Museum Shop. A shop on the ground floor of this museum in an old home sells antique and new worry beads and attractive beaded key chains. The museum's exhibits of historic worry beads are fascinating and provide a little insight into the national male pastime of fiddling with a string of them. ✉ *Staikopoulou 25* ☎ *27520/21618* ⊕ *www.komboloi.gr* ⊡ *Museum €2.*

Peloponnesian Folklore Foundation Museum Shop. This enticing shop on the ground floor of the excellent museum stocks an appealing array of merchandise that includes jewelry, candlesticks, and other gift items. ✉ *Vasileos Alexandrou 1* ☎ *27520/28379* ⊕ *www.pli.gr.*

13

ARGOS ΑΡΓΟΣ

12 km (7½ miles) northwest of Nafplion, 7 km (4½ miles) northwest of Tiryns.

The city of Argos (population 21,000), set amid citrus groves on the western edge of the Argive plain, is the economic hub of the region, a workaday town with a long past. The fall of Mycenae and Tiryns at the close of the late Bronze Age proved favorable for Argos, and under King Pheidon in the 7th century BC, it became the chief city in the Peloponnese. In the mid-5th century BC, the city consolidated its hold on the Argive plain by eradicating Mycenae and Tiryns. But like Corinth, Argos was never powerful enough to set its own course, following in later years the leadership of Sparta, Athens, and the Macedonian kings.

> **THE HEROINES OF ARGOS**
>
> Twice in the history of Argos, women are said to have defended the city: once in 494 BC when Telesilla the poetess (who may be mere legend) armed old men, boys, and women to hold the walls against the Spartans; and again in 272 BC when Pyrrhus, king of Epirus, who was taking the city street by street, was felled from above by an old woman armed with a tile.

Archaeological Museum. A small but interesting collection of finds from the classical city and surrounding sites includes a mosaic floor representing the zodiac from a Roman villa and a squat clay statue female figure unearthed at nearby Lerna. It may have been fashioned as early as 2500 BC; it's also said to be one of the earliest known representations of the human figure to be found in Europe. ⊠ *Off main square, Ayios Petros* ☎ *27510/68819* ⊕ *www.culture.gr* ⊡ *€2* ⊗ *Closed Mon.*

Argos Kastro. This Byzantine and Frankish structure incorporates remnants of classical walls and was later expanded by the Turks and Venetians. You can drive almost to the entrance, and the grounds provide an unsurpassed view of the Argive plain. ⊠ *Argos* ⊹ *On top of hill above town* ⊡ *Free.*

Classical Argos. Remains of the classical city are scattered throughout the modern one, and you can see in a small area the extensive ruins of the Roman bath, odeon (a roofed theater), and agora, or market. The theater is especially striking, and its well-preserved seats climb a hillside. ⊠ *Tripoleos* ⊡ *Free.*

SHOPPING

On Saturday morning the main square is transformed into a huge household-merchandise and produce market (dwarfing that at Nafplion). You can often find unusual household items, such as wooden stamps used to impress designs on bread loaves, at prices that haven't been inflated. Argos is also well known throughout Greece for its ouzo.

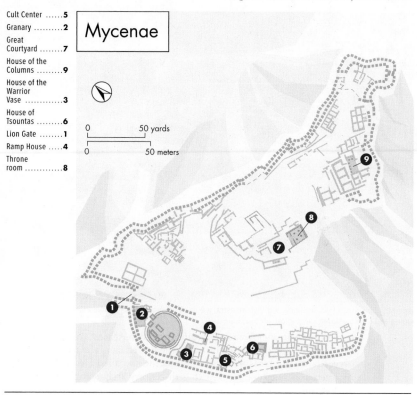

Mycenae

0 — 50 yards

0 — 50 meters

13

MYCENAE ΜΥΚΗΝΕΣ

21 km (13 miles) north of Nafplion.

The ancient citadel of Mycenae, which Homer wrote was "rich in gold and once ruled much of the Mediterranean world," stands on a low hill, wedged between sheer, lofty peaks on the edge of two deep ravines. The gloomy, stony ruins are hauntingly suggestive of what becomes of might and power.

GETTING HERE AND AROUND

Once in Nafplion, you can reach Mycenae and other nearby ancient sights via a decent local bus network; buses leave from Nafplion's Kapodistria Square. The small office is often staffed by an English speaker, and times are usually also posted at the Municipal Tourist Office at Martiou 25 (open only mornings and evenings and, curiously, often staffed with only non-English speakers).

EXPLORING

Fodor's Choice ★ **Mycenae.** The gloomy, gray ruins are hardly distinguishable from the rock beneath; it's hard to believe that this kingdom was once so powerful that it ruled a large portion of the Mediterranean world, from 1500 BC to 1100 BC. The major archaeological artifacts from the dig are

Haunted by the spirits of Agamemnon and Clytemnestra, the royal graves of Mycenae make it one of the most brooding and memorable archaeological sites in Greece.

now in the National Archaeological Museum in Athens, so seeing those first will add to your appreciation of the ruined city. The most famous object from the treasure found here is the so-called Death Mask of Agamemnon, a golden mask that 19th-century archaeologist Heinrich Schliemann found in the last grave he excavated at Mycenae. He was ecstatic, convinced this was the mask of the king of Homeric legend who launched the Trojan War with his brother, Menelaus—but it is now known that this is impossible, since the mask dates from an earlier period. The Archaeological Museum in Nafplion also houses artifacts from this once-great city.

In 1841, soon after the establishment of the Greek state, the Archaeological Society began excavations of the **ancient citadel,** and in 1874 Heinrich Schliemann began to work at the site.

Today the citadel is entered from the northwest through the famous **Lion Gate.** The triangle above the lintel depicts in relief two lions, whose heads, probably of steatite, are now missing. They stand facing each other, their forepaws resting on a high pedestal representing an altar, above which stands a pillar ending in a uniquely shaped capital and abacus. Above the abacus are four sculptured discs, interpreted as representing the ends of beams that supported a roof. The gate was closed by a double wooden door sheathed in bronze. The two halves were secured by a wooden bar, which rested in cuttings in the jambs, still visible. The holes for the pivots on which it swung can still be seen in both sill and lintel.

Inside on the right stands the **Granary,** so named for the many *pithoi* (clay storage vessels) that were found inside the building, holding carbonized wheat grains.

Beyond the granary is the grave circle, made up of six **stone slabs,** encircled by a row of upright stone slabs interrupted on the northern side by the entrance. Above each grave stood a vertical stone stele. The "grave goods" buried with the dead were personal belongings including gold face masks, gold cups and jewelry, bronze swords with ivory hilts, and daggers with gold inlay, now in the National Archaeological Museum of Athens. South of the stone slabs lie the

remains of the **House of the Warrior Vase,** the **Ramp House,** the **Cult Center,** and others; farther south is the **House of Tsountas** of Mycenae. The palace complex covers the summit of the hill and occupies a series of terraces; people entered through a monumental gateway in the northwest side and, proceeding to the right, beyond it, came to the **Great Courtyard** of the palace. The ground was originally covered by a plaster coating above which was a layer of painted and decorated stucco. East of the Great Courtyard is the **throne room,** which had four columns supporting the roof (the bases are still visible) and a circular hearth in the center. Remains of an **Archaic temple** and a **Hellenistic temple** can be seen north of the palace, and to the east on the right, on a lower level, are the **workshops** of the artists and craftsmen employed by the king. On the same level, adjoining the workshops to the east, is the **House of the Columns,** with a row of columns surrounding its central court. The remaining section of the east wall consists of an addition made in around 1250 BC to ensure free communication from the citadel to the subterranean reservoir cut at the same time. ⊠ *Mycenae ⊹ 21 km (13 miles) north of Nafplion* ☎ *27510/76585* ⊕ *www. culture.gr* ✉ *Combined ticket with Treasury of Atreus and Mycenae Archaeological Museum €12.*

Mycenae Archaeological Museum. Most of the great treasures of Mycenae have been removed to the National Archaeological Museum in Athens, but you'll see copies of death masks and other great artifacts in the small but well-done museum at the site. Cult offerings and other original finds are also on view. Of most interest are the model of the ancient city, helping put the ruins in context, and reconstructions of several rooms of the palace. ⊠ *Mycenae ⊹ Near entrance to site* ☎ *27510/76585* ✉ *Combined ticket with Mycenae and Treasury of Atreus €12.*

Treasury of Atreus. On the hill of Panagitsa, on the left along the road that runs to the citadel, lies this most imposing example of Mycenaean architecture. The construction of this huge *tholos* (or beehive tomb) took place around 1250 BC, contemporary with that of the Lion Gate, during the last century of Mycenaean prominence. Like other tholos tombs, it consists of a passageway cut into the hillside that was built of huge squared stones. The passage leads into a vast domed chamber. The facade of the entrance had applied decoration, but only small fragments have been preserved, and traces of bronze nails suggest that similar decoration once existed inside. The tomb was found empty, already robbed in antiquity, but it must at one time have contained rich and valuable grave goods. Pausanias wrote that the ancients considered this to be the Tomb of Agamemnon, and the treasury is still often referred to as such. ⊠ *Mycenae* ✛ *Across from citadel of Mycenae* ☎ *27510/76585* ⊕ *www.culture.gr* ☒ *Combined ticket with Mycenae and Mycenae Archaeological Museum €12.*

ANCIENT NEMEA ΑΡΧΑΙΑ ΝΕΜΕΑ

18 km (11 miles) north of Mycenae.

This quiet little town, surrounded by undulating vineyards, was once as famous as Olympia, site of biennial games that attracted athletes from throughout ancient Greece.

Ancient Nemea. The ancient storytellers proclaimed that it was here Hercules performed the first of the Twelve Labors set by the king of Argos in penance for killing his own children—he slew the ferocious Nemean lion living in a nearby cave. Historians are interested in Ancient Nemea as the site of a sanctuary of Zeus and the home of the biennial Nemean games, a Panhellenic competition like those at Isthmia, Delphi, and Olympia (today there is a society dedicated to reviving the games).

The main monuments at the site are the **Temple of Zeus** (built about 330 BC to replace a 6th-century BC structure), the **stadium,** and an **early Christian basilica** of the 5th to 6th century AD. Several columns of the temple still stand. An extraordinary feature of the stadium, which dates to the last quarter of the 4th century BC, is its vaulted tunnel and entranceway. The evidence indicates that the use of the arch in building may have been brought back from India with Alexander (arches were previously believed to be a Roman invention). A spacious **museum** displays finds from the site, including pieces of athletic gear and coins of various city-states and rulers. ■TIP➡ **Around Nemea, keep an eye out for roadside stands where local growers sell the famous red Nemean wine of this region.** ⊠ *Nemea* ✛ *North of E65, near modern village of Nemea* ☎ *27460/22739* ⊕ *www.culture.gr* ☒ *Site and museum €4.*

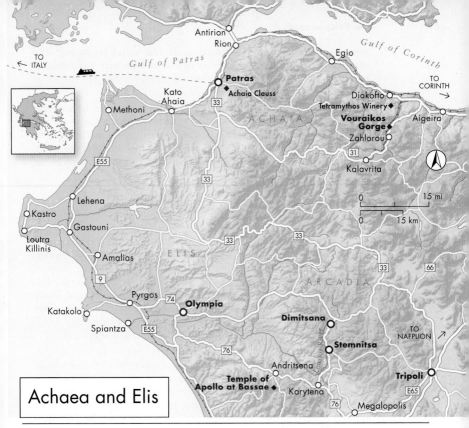

TO
← ITALY

TO
CORINTH
→

Gulf of Patras

Gulf of Corinth

Antirion
Rion

Egio

Patras
Achaia Clauss

Kato
Ahaia
33

Methoni

Diakofto
Tetramythos Winery ♦
**Vouraikos
Gorge** ♦
Zahlorou

Aigeira

31

Kalavrita

E55

33

Lehena

0   15 mi
0   15 km

Kastro

Gastouni

E L I S

33

33

Loutra
Killinis

Amalias

33   66

9

A R C A D I A

Pyrgos 74

Olympia

Dimitsana

Katakolo

Spiantza E55

76

Stemnitsa

TO
NAFPLION ↗

Andritsena

Tripoli

**Temple of
Apollo at Bassae** ♦

Karytena

E65

76   Megalopolis

Achaea and Elis

ARCADIA TO OLYMPIA
ΑΡΚΑΔΙΑ ΠΡΟΣ ΟΛΥΜΠΙΑ

In these relatively remote reaches of the Peloponnese, ancient ruins and historic towns and monuments pervade the landscape. Despite the waves of invaders over the centuries—Franks, Venetians, and Turks—this land is considered the distillation of all that is Greek, with its indulged idiosyncrasy, intractable autonomy, and appreciation of simple pleasures.

Arcadians are believed to be among the oldest inhabitants of the Peloponnese; this group of tribes first united when they entered the Trojan War. They later founded the powerful Arcadian League, but after Corinth fell to Rome in 146 BC, the region slipped into decline. When the Goths invaded in AD 395, Arcadia was almost entirely deserted. Several centuries later the Franks conquered the area and built many castles; they were succeeded by the Byzantines and then the Turks, who ruled until the War of Independence. No conqueror ever really dominated the Arcadians. Even under the Turks, mountain villagers lived much as they pleased, maintaining secret schools to preserve the rudiments of Greek language and religion and harassing the Turks in roaming bands. Forested mountainsides and valley farms still lend themselves to a decidedly rural way of life, and the very word *arcadia* has come to suggest the sorts of pastoral pleasures you will encounter here.

The province of Elis, farther to the south, is even more bucolic and peaceful. This is a land of hills green with forests and vegetation, and it is not surprising that the Greeks chose this region as the place in which to hold the Olympic Games. Crowning this region is the fabled archaeological site of Olympia, one of the most visited places in Greece.

TRIPOLI ΤΡΙΠΟΛΗ

150 km (93 miles) southwest of Athens, 70 km (43 miles) southwest of Corinth.

History, along with the practicalities of the road network in this part of Greece, makes it very likely that you'll at least pass through the outskirts of Tripoli when you're in the area. In the days of the Ottoman Empire, this crossroads was the capital of the Turkish pasha of the Peloponnese, and during the War of Independence it was the first target of Greek revolutionaries. They captured it in 1821 after a six-month siege, but the town went back and forth between the warring sides until 1827, when Ibrahim Pasha's retreating troops burned it to the ground.

Tripoli is a workaday town with few attractions to keep you here, although if you do hang around, you'll get an eyeful of Greek life. Its most attractive feature is the mountain scenery, with attendant hillside villages, that surrounds it; you will soon understand why this region is nicknamed "the Switzerland of Greece." Unless you run out of daylight, you'll probably want to move on from Tripoli to one of these villages.

Areos Square. You can observe Greek life in the squares in the center of town, especially Areos, one of the largest and most beautiful *platias* (central squares) in Greece—definitely the place to while away the time if you're marooned in Tripoli. ✉ *Tripoli.*

WHERE TO STAY

$ HOTEL 🏨 **Mainalon Resort.** The fairly luxurious amenities here, the best place to stay if you need to spend a night in Tripoli, include a tasteful mix of traditional and contemporary furnishings, silk fabrics in the guest rooms, and large marble bathrooms. **Pros:** in the center of things; quite comfortable; nice café on premises. **Cons:** oddly anonymous and business-like; could use some updating; rooms in front can be noisy. [$] *Rooms from: €70* ✉ *Areos Sq.* ☎ *2710/230300* 🌐 *www.mainalonhotel.gr* 🛏 *32 rooms* 🍴 *Breakfast.*

VOURAIKOS GORGE ΦΑΡΑΓΓΙ ΤΟΥ ΒΟΥΡΑΙΚΟΥ

Diakofto, the coastal access point is 81 km (49 miles) west of Corinth; Kalavrita is 25 km (15 miles) south of Diakofto.

The Vouraikos gorge is a fantastic landscape of towering pinnacles and precipitous rock walls that you can view on an exciting train ride. In addition, a road goes directly from Diakofto, on the coast, to mountaintop Kalavrita; the spectacular 25-km (15-mile) drive negotiates the east side of the gorge.

Diakofto is a peaceful seaside settlement nestled on a fertile plain with dramatic mountains as a background; the village straggles through citrus and olive groves to the sea. If you're taking a morning train up the gorge, plan on spending the night in Diakofto, maybe enjoying a swim off one of the pebbly beaches and a meal in one of several tavernas. After dinner, take a stroll on Diakofto's main street to look at the antique train car in front of the train station, then take a seat at an outdoor table at one of the cafés surrounding the station square and enjoy a *gliko* (sweet). This is unembellished Greek small-town life.

The Kalavrita Express, a narrow-gauge train, makes a dramatic 25-km (15-mile) journey between Diakofto and Kalavrita, which is a refreshingly cool retreat in summer and a ski center in winter. Italians built the railway between 1889 and 1896 to bring ore down from Kalavrita, and these days a diminutive train, a diesel engine sandwiched between two small passenger cars, crawls upward, clinging to the rails in the steeper sections with a rack and pinion, through and over 14 tunnels and bridges, rushing up and down wild mountainside terrain. Beyond the tiny hamlet of Zakhlorou, the gorge widens into a steep-sided green alpine valley that stretches the last 11 km (7 miles) to Kalavrita, a lively town of about 2,000 nestled below snowcapped Mt. Helmos. Greeks remember Kalavrita primarily as the site of the Nazis' most heinous war crime on Greek soil. On December 13, 1943, the occupying forces rounded up and executed the town's entire male population over the age of 15 (1,436 people) and then locked women and children into the school and set it on fire. They escaped, but the Nazis later returned and burned the town to the ground. The clock on the church tower is stopped at 2:34 pm, marking the time of the execution.

GETTING HERE AND AROUND

The Kalavrita Express makes the round-trip from Diakofto three times daily on weekdays, five times daily on weekends. The trip takes about an hour, and the first train leaves at 8:10 am. Comings and goings are timed so that you can do some exploring; in a day's outing, for example, you can alight at Zakhlorou, make the trek to Mega Spileo, continue on to Kalavrita, explore that town, and return to Diakofto by the last train of the day. Check with the EOT in Athens to make sure the train is operating—repairs can close the line for months at a time; the Chris-Paul Hotel in Diakofto is another good source of information.

VISITOR INFORMATION

Kalavrita Visitor Information. ⊕ *www.ekalavrita.gr*.

EXPLORING

Mega Spileo. This mountainside monastery, altitude 3,117 feet, was founded in the 4th century and is said to be the oldest in Greece, though it has been burned down many times, most recently in 1934. The community once had 450 monks and owned vast tracts of land in the Peloponnese, Constantinople (now Istanbul), and Macedonia, making it one of the richest in Greece. Mega Spileo sits at the base of a huge (360-foot-high) curving cliff face and incorporates a large cavern (the monastery's name means "large cave"). You can tour the monastery to see a charred black-wax-and-mastic icon of the Virgin, supposedly painted by St. Luke, found in the cave after a vision of the shepherdess Euphrosyne led some monks there in AD 362. Also on display are ornate vellum manuscripts of early gospels and the preserved heads of the founding monks. **■ TIP→ Modest dress is required; wraps are available at the entrance.**

If you're taking the Kalavrita Express, 45 minutes into its trip you can alight at the stream-laced mountain village of Zakhlorou, from where you can hike up a steep path through evergreen oak, cypress, and fir to the monastery. This hour-long trek (one-way) along a rough donkey track gives you superb views of the Vouraikos valley and distant villages on the opposite side. The occasional sound of bells, from flocks of goats grazing on the steep slopes above, is carried on the wind. It's also possible to take a cab from the village, though they are not always available; if you're driving, the monastery is just off the road between Diakofto and Kalavrita and is well marked. ✉ *Zakhlorou* 🎫 *€2.*

OFF THE BEATEN PATH

Tetramythos Winery. If you're driving from Diakofto to Kalavrita, make a stop at Tetramythos. The winery attributes the high quality and refined flavor of its reds and whites to the location of its vineyards on the northern slopes of Mt. Helmos, which protects the grapes from hot winds. Tours and tastings are available year-round. ✉ *Ano Diakofto* ✥ *5 km (3 miles) south of Diakofto* ☎ *26910/97500* 🌐 *www.tetramythoswines.com* 🎫 *Free.*

WHERE TO EAT

$ GREEK

🍴 **Taverna Kostas.** Grilled chicken is the main attraction at this *psistaria* (grill house) run by a hospitable Greek-Australian family, and regulars come from miles around to enjoy it. *Horta* (boiled wild greens), huge *horiatiki* (village, i.e., "Greek") salads with a nut-flavored feta cheese, and stuffed zucchini are other reasons to enjoy a meal on the large terrace in warm months or the cozy dining room in winter. **Known for:** grilled meats; lively terrace dining scene; cash only. [$] *Average main: €8* ✉ *Diakofto* ✥ *Main road coming into town, opposite National Bank* ☎ *697/595–1711* 💳 *No credit cards.*

WHERE TO STAY

$ HOTEL

🏨 **Chris-Paul Hotel.** Guest rooms in this appealing hotel, just around the corner from the train station, are attractive and well maintained, and each has a balcony overlooking the surrounding orchards. **Pros:** handy base for gorge visit *Kalavrita Express*; nice pool; soothing gardens. **Cons:** simple accommodations; in need of updating; no elevator. [$] *Rooms from: €50* ✉ *Diakofto* ✥ *Clearly signposted, in an orchard close to the train station* ☎ *26910/41715* 🌐 *www.chrispaul-hotel.gr* 🛏 *24 rooms* 🍽 *Breakfast.*

PATRAS ΠΑΤΡΑ

5 km (3 miles) west of Rion, 135 km (84 miles) west of Corinth.

Patras is the third-largest city in Greece and a major harbor. Unless you come to town to catch a ferry to Italy or Corfu, you might want to zoom right by. The municipality has launched an extensive improvement plan, paving the harbor roads and creating pedestrian zones on inner-city shopping streets. Even so, earthquakes and mindless development have laid waste to most of the elegant European-style buildings that earned Patras the nickname "Little Paris of Greece" in the 19th and early 20th centuries. The E65 toll road connects Athens and Patras in less than three hours, and bus service between the two runs about every half hour to 45 minutes throughout the day.

Patras has the international, outward-looking feel common to port cities. The waterfront is pleasant enough. You'll find lots of mediocre restaurants, some decent hotels, the bus station, and numerous travel agents (caveat emptor for those near the docks). Back from the waterfront, the town gradually rises along arcaded streets, which provide welcome shade and rain protection. Of the series of large platias, tree-shaded Queen Olga Square is the nicest. Patras is built on a grid system, and it is easy to find your way around. If you have time for a stroll, take Ayios Nikolaos Street upward through the city until it comes to the long flight of steps leading to the Kastro, the medieval Venetian castle overlooking the harbor. The narrow lanes on the side of Ayios Nikolaos are whitewashed and lined with village-style houses, many of which are being restored.

GETTING HERE AND AROUND

Bus service between Athens and Patras is excellent, with buses running about every half hour to 45 minutes throughout the day. The bus station in Patras is near the port at Othonos-Amalias and is currently being reconstructed.

Within the next five years direct express-train service is expected to be in operation from Athens to Patras and then down the west coast of the Peloponnese. Before the express train begins, you're better off taking the bus.

EXPLORING

Like all respectable Greek cities, Patras has an ancient history. Off the harbor in 429 BC, Corinthian and Athenian ships fought inconclusively, and in 279 BC the city helped repel an invasion of Celtic Galatians. Its acropolis was fortified under Justinian in the 6th century, and Patras withstood an attack by Slavs and Saracens in 805. Silk production, begun in the 7th century, brought renewed prosperity, but control passed successively to the Franks, the Venetians, and the Turks, until the War of Independence. Thomas Palaiologos, the last Byzantine to leave Patras before the Turks took over in 1458, carried an unusual prize with him—the skull of the apostle St. Andrew, which he gave to Pius II in exchange for an annuity. St. Andrew had been crucified in Patras and had been made the city's patron saint. In 1964 Pope Paul VI returned the head to Patras, and it now graces St. Andrew's Cathedral, seat of the Bishop of Patras.

Achaia Clauss. The oldest winery in Greece was founded by the Bavarian Gustav Clauss in 1861 and continues to produce a distinctive line of wines. Mavrodaphne, a rich dessert wine, is the house specialty, and oak barrels still store vintages from Gustav's day. The winery is set on a hilltop amid fragrant pines. ⊠ *Patras* ✛ *Exit 3 off E55, 8 km (5 miles) west of Patras* ☎ *2610/580100* ⊕ *www.achaiaclauss.gr.*

Olga Square. In this quintessentially Greek meeting place, the most appealing of the city center's energetic platias, locals sip their ouzo and observe their fellow townspeople as they eat, drink, shop, and play. Other popular squares nearby include **Martiou 25 Square** and **Ypsila Alonia Square.** ⊠ *Patras* ✛ *Two blocks uptown from Othonos-Amalias, off Kolokotronis.*

Archaeological Museum of Patras. Stunning galleries are laden with Mycenaean-through-Roman-period finds, including tools, cups, and jewelry reflecting everyday life in the Peloponnese. More than 15 mosaics from Roman villas around Patras have been reassembled, and many items are from the ancient Roman odeon in town. A large collection of burial items includes several reconstructed tombs. ⊠ *Amerikis, at Athens–Patras road* ✛ *7 km (4 miles) east of center* ☎ *2610/420645* 🎫 *€2* ⊙ *Closed Mon.*

Patras Kastro. In the evening the Frankish and Venetian citadel atop a bluff overlooking Patras draws many Greek couples seeking a spectacular view; a long flight of stone steps ascends toward the Kastro from the southern edge of the Old Town. The sight of the shimmering ships negotiating the harbor stirs even the most travel-weary. ⊠ *End of Ayios Nikolaos.*

Patras Roman Odeon. A Roman odeon remains in use in Patras, almost 2,000 years after it was built. Today the productions of summer arts festivals are staged in the well-preserved theater, which was discovered in 1889 and heavily restored in 1960. ⊠ *Patras* ✛ *Off Martiou 25 Sq.*

St. Andrew's Cathedral. One of the largest churches in Greece dates from the early 20th century but is built next to a spring that's been used for thousands of years. In antiquity, the waters were thought to have prophetic powers. St. Andrews is an important pilgrimage sight—the cavernous interior houses the head of the namesake saint, who spread Christianity throughout Greece and was crucified in Patras in AD 60. ⊠ *Patras* ✛ *At end of Trion Navarhon, at western edge of city center.*

BEACHES

Ayios Vassilios. The closest beach to Patras is a long stretch of pebbles washed by crystal clear waters. Even so, crowds, a sea of beach umbrellas, freighter traffic, and the looming presence of the Rion suspension bridge spanning the narrows leading into the Gulf of Corinth make for a less than idyllic experience. **Amenities:** food and drink; parking (free); showers; toilets; water sports. **Best for:** partiers; swimming. ⊠ *Patras* ✛ *Off E65, near Rion, 5 km (3 miles) east of Patras.*

13

Kalogria. This long, sandy stretch backed by a pine forest and a grassy plain where cattle graze is much favored by Patras residents on weekends and in August. Bracing winds that can whip up a wild surf don't seem to deter beachgoers and are a boon for windsurfers. A river behind the beach forms estuaries that are great for bird-watching. People swim in them as well, but you may feel like Hercules if you are joined by yard-long snakes (they are nonvenomous). **Amenities:** food and drink; parking (free); showers; toilets; water sports. **Best for:** swimming; walking; windsurfing. ✉ *Kalogria* ✥ *Off E55, about 40 km (25 miles) west of Patras, near Sageika.*

WHERE TO EAT

For lighter fare or after-dinner ice cream, coffee, and pastries, choose one of the cafés along upper Gerokostopoulou Street, which is closed to traffic; in Olga Square; or in Ypsila Alonia Square—a favorite watering hole of locals near the Kastro, which, as a bonus, has a panoramic view of the harbor. The streets, including Papadiamatopoulou, leading through the Old Town up to the south end of the Kastro, have many small *mezedopoleia,* which serve *mezedes,* Greek-style tapas.

$ GREEK 🍴 **Krini.** The sloping streets heading up to the Kastro are the setting for this *oinopoleia,* or wineshop, which sells wine from barrels to a loyal clientele and serves simple but excellent fare. The rustic taverna room and rear garden are the places to sample delicacies like the spicy sausage meatballs known as *soutzoukakia* or rabbit braised with white wine and rosemary. **Known for:** old-fashioned atmosphere; good home cooking; cash only. [$] *Average main: €7* ✉ *Pandokratoros 57* 💳 *No credit cards* ⏲ *Closed last 2 wks of Aug. No lunch.*

WHERE TO STAY

$ HOTEL 🏨 **Byzantino.** A neoclassical mansion in the heart of town bursts with style—thanks to stone and hardwood floors, antiques, and old kilims—and the large, high-ceilinged guest rooms have been brought efficiently up to date with good lighting and well-equipped bathrooms. **Pros:** city center location; character-filled surroundings; rooms are comfortable even if a bit outdated. **Cons:** some street noise in front rooms; bathrooms are rather basic; limited views from many rooms. [$] *Rooms from: €75* ✉ *Riga Fariou 106* ☎ *2610/243000* 🌐 *www.byzantino-hotel.gr* 🛏 *30 rooms* 🍽 *Breakfast.*

$$ HOTEL 🏨 **Primarolia.** Step through the doors of the most distinctive hotel in town (located in a former distillery), and the workday town seems far away: modernist furniture by Greek artists fills the soothing public rooms, and dramatic fabrics and wallpapers add flair to the handsome, well-equipped guest rooms. **Pros:** très chic and stylish; convenient to ferries and town center; helpful staff. **Cons:** not all rooms have balconies with harbor views, so ask for one that does; some street noise; comfort level not always up to snuff. [$] *Rooms from: €130* ✉ *Othonos Amalias 33* ☎ *2610/624900* 🌐 *www.arthotel.gr* 🛏 *15 rooms* 🍽 *Breakfast.*

NIGHTLIFE AND THE ARTS

BARS AND CAFÉS

On the northern side of Martiou 25 Square are the steps at the head of Gerokostopoulou street, below the odeon. Closed to traffic along its upper reaches, this street has many cafés and music bars, making it a good choice for a relaxing evening.

FESTIVALS

Patras Carnival. If you're in Patras in late January to February, you're in for a treat: the carnival, which lasts for several weeks before the start of Lent, is celebrated with masquerade balls, fireworks, and the Sunday Grand Parade competition for the best costume. Room rates can double or even triple during this time. ⊠ *Patras* ☎ *2610/226063* ⊕ *www.carnivalpatras.gr.*

Patras Summer Arts Festival. Patras holds a lively summer arts festival with concerts and dance performances at the Roman odeon. It usually runs from mid-June to early October. ☎ *2610/390937* ⊕ *www. festivalpatras.gr.*

SHOPPING

Patras is a major city, and you'll find fashionable clothing, jewelry, and other products here. The best shops are on Riga Fereou, Maizonas, and Korinthou streets, near Olga Square. Patras also has shops that sell handmade and machine-made Greek icons, which make beautiful decorations. At night in the narrow streets surrounding the Kastro, Greek craftspeople burn the midnight oil in their workshops and stores painting images of saints on wood and stone.

Marks and Spencer. An outlet of the venerable London department store is a good stop if you realize you're missing a vacation essential. ⊠ *Mezonos 68* ☎ *2610/623247.*

DIMITSANA ΔΗΜΗΤΣΑΝΑ

40 km (25 miles) west of Tripoli, 40 km (25 miles) southwest of Olympia.

Leave your car at the entrance of this stone village stunningly set amid the Arcadian mountains and stroll the maze of narrow cobbled lanes. If you want to add some ancient history to your enjoyment of this romantic place, be advised that archaeologists found ruins of a cyclopean wall (irregular stones without mortar) and classical buildings near the town; the ruins belonged to the acropolis of Teuthis, an ancient city.

EXPLORING

Dimitsana Ecclesiastical Museum. Manuscripts, a 35,000-volume library, and other artifacts here are from surrounding churches, monasteries, and the School of Greek Letters that flourished in Dimitsana in the 19th century. The school educated Germanos, a bishop of Patras, and other young men who went on to become Greek scholars and church leaders. ⊠ *Dimitsana* ✢ *Off main square* ☎ *27950/31360* 🖃 *€2* ⊙ *Closed Mon.–Fri.*

Dimitsana Town Library. The town library displays manuscripts, rare books, and memorabilia from the Greek revolutionary period, when

Dimitsana was a center for revolutionary activity against the Turks. Many of the books were printed clandestinely, against Turkish law, in Greek. The collection is a fraction of its former size, as most of the books were destroyed during the War of Independence, when the pages were used to wrap gunpowder. Also on display are household items, costumes, and other reminders of 19th-century life in Dimitsana. ⊠ *Main Sq.* ☎ *27950/31219* ⊙ *Closed Sat.–Sun.*

E2 Hiking Path. A leg of the European trail system passes through Dimitsana. You can follow the path south along the gorge of the river Lousios or east into the surrounding mountains. The trek south brings you to several small monasteries tucked into the walls of the gorge and the scanty ruins of the ancient city of Gortys. ⊠ *Dimitsana.*

Open Air Water Power Museum. A water mill, tannery, and gunpowder mill on the river Lousios below town provide displays and demonstrations that reveal why water power was the force behind the region's economy until the first part of the 20th century. Mills like the one here operated up and down the river and helped supply the forces who successfully fought the Turks during the War of Independence in 1821. ⊠ *Dimitsana* ⚓ *Off main road, south of town* ☎ *27950/31630* ⊕ *www. piop.gr* 🎫 *€3* ⊙ *Closed Tues.*

EN
ROUTE
The winding road between Dimitsana and Stemnitsa reveals extensive views over the forested rises and valleys of the Arcadian mountains. About halfway between the two villages you'll come to a widening in the road that's a perfect place to stop: a mountain spring supplies cool, refreshing water (make sure you have containers to fill), and a viewpoint overlooks miles of mountain scenery.

STEMNITSA ΣΤΕΜΝΙΤΣΑ

10 km (6 miles) south of Dimitsana.

Also called Ipsous, Stemnitsa is one of the most beautiful towns in southern Greece, wondrously perched 3,444 feet above sea level amid a forest of fir and chestnut trees. For centuries the stone village was one of the Balkans' best-known metalworking centers, and today a minuscule school is still staffed by local artisans. Above the lively square rises the bell tower of the church of Ayios Georgios, and at the top of a nearby hill is the monument to fighters in the 1821 War of Independence against the Turks. Stemnitsa, in fact, claims to have been the capital of Greece for a few weeks in 1821, when it was the center for rebels who successfully routed the Turks. The views throughout the town are phenomenal, and at night the village lies beneath a canopy of bright stars.

Moni Ayiou Ioannitou. From the north side of town, a well-marked path leads through the mountains to the isolated monastery of Moni Ayiou Ioannitou, with a little chapel, covered in frescoes, that is generally open. From the monastery other paths lead through a beautiful, wooded valley to the banks of the river Lousios. Several other monasteries, closed to visitors, are nestled alongside the riverbank. ⊠ *Stemnitsa.*

A Little Night Music

Dance performances, accompanied by traditional music, are common in the region. In the *tsakonikos,* the dancers wheel tightly around each other and then swing into bizarre spirals; this dance resembles the sacred dance of Delos, first performed by Theseus to mime how he escaped from the Labyrinth. The popular *kalamatianos* is a circular dance from Kalamata. The *tsamikos,* from Roumeli in central Greece, is an exclusively male dance showcasing agility. You will see your fill of dancing at local festivals to celebrate a town or village's patron saint, usually in summer. Dancing is also part of a Greek wedding, and it's not entirely unlikely that you might attend one. The guest list usually includes the entire population of a village or section of town, and if you happen to be staying there at the time of a wedding, you may well be invited.

Stemnitsa Folklore Museum. This unusual collection devotes one floor to models of workshops for indigenous crafts such as candle making and bell casting; the other two floors house re-created traditional rooms and a charmingly haphazard collection of costumes, weapons, icons, and plates. ⊠ *Stemnitsa* ⊹ *Off main road* ☏ *27950/81252* ⊕ *www.stemnit-samuseum.gr* 🎟 *€1* ⊘ *Closed Feb.*

OLYMPIA ΟΛΥΜΠΙΑ

112 km (69 miles) south of Patras, 85 km (53 miles) west of Stemnitsa.

Ancient Olympia, with the Sanctuary of Zeus, was famously the site of the ancient Olympic Games. Scenically located at the foot of the pine-covered Kronion hill and set in a valley near two rivers, today the ancient ruins are among the most popular attractions in Greece. Modern Olympia, an attractive mountain town surrounded by pleasant hilly countryside, has hotels and tavernas, convenient for visitors to the ancient site.

GETTING HERE AND AROUND

From Athens, buses head to Olympia three times daily for a trip that takes about six hours; the trip sometimes requires a change in Pyrgos. The fare is about €15. From Patras, you can take one of the almost hourly KTEL buses to Pyrgos, then change there for the short trip inland to Olympia; total trip time is about an hour and costs about €4.

In Pyrgos you can also hop aboard one of the trains that connect Katakolon, the cruise ship port, and Olympia. Trains run four times a day, but only when cruise ships are in port. The trip from Katakolon to Olympia with a stop in Pyrgos takes about 45 minutes and costs €10 round-trip (€15 for two). The website for Katakolon Port has information on the train.

Travel directly from Athens to Olympia by car on a trip that lasts about five hours via toll roads to Corinth and Patras, then down the west coast to Olympia. Free parking is ample in Olympia, either on the street or in the lots near the entrance to the ancient site.

Nestled within the lofty Arcadian mountains, the stone village of Dimitsana offers amazing vistas over the valley of Megalopolis.

VISITOR INFORMATION

Contacts **Katakolon Port Information.** ⊕ *www.katakolon.org.*

EXPLORING

FAMILY
Fodor's Choice
★

Ancient Olympia. One of the most celebrated archaeological sites in Greece is located at the foot of the pine-covered Kronion hill and set in a valley where the Kladeos and Alpheios rivers join. Just as athletes from city-states throughout ancient Greece made the journey to compete in the ancient Olympics—the first sports competition—visitors from all over the world today make their way to the small modern Arcadian town. The Olympic Games, first staged around the 8th century BC, were played here in the stadium, hippodrome, and other venues for some 1,100 years. Today, the venerable ruins of these structures attest to the majesty and importance of the first Olympiads. Modern Olympia, an attractive mountain town surrounded by pleasant hilly countryside, has hotels and tavernas, convenient for visitors to the ancient site.

As famous as the Olympic Games were—and still are—Olympia was first and foremost a sacred place, a sanctuary honoring Zeus, king of the gods, and Hera, his wife and older sister. The sacred quarter was known as the Altis, or the Sacred Grove of Zeus, and was enclosed by a wall on three sides and the Kronion hill on the other. Inside the Altis were temples, altars, and 12 treasuries of various city-states.

To honor the cult of Zeus established at Olympia as early as the 10th century BC, altars were first constructed outdoors, among the pine forests that encroach upon the site. But around the turn of the 6th century BC, the earliest building at Olympia was constructed, the Temple of Hera, which originally honored Zeus and Hera jointly, until the Temple of Zeus was constructed around 470 BC. The Temple of Zeus was one of the finest temples in all of Greece. Thirteen columns flanked the sides, and its interior housed the most famous work of ancient Greece—a gold and ivory statue of Zeus. Earthquakes in 551 and 552 finished off the temple.

After the Treasuries, the Bouleuterion, and the Pelopeion were built, the 5th and 4th centuries BC—the golden age of the ancient games—saw a virtual building boom. The monumental Temple of Zeus, the Prytaneion, and the Metroon went up at this time. The enormous Leonidaion was built around 300 BC, and as the games continued to thrive, the Palaestra and Gymnasion were added to the complex.

FRANKS IN THE PELOPONNESE

Franks, in the personages of itinerant French noblemen on their way to the Fourth Crusade, began settling in the Peloponnese in the early years of the 13th century. One of them, Geoffrey de Villehardouin, made landfall in Methoni and was enchanted by his surroundings. Meanwhile, his colleagues had sacked Constantinople, making it easy for Villehardouin and other nobles to take control of the Peloponnese, capturing such Byzantine strongholds as Mystras and Monemvasia.

The history of the Olympic Games is long and fabled. For almost 11 centuries, free-born Greeks from the various city-states gathered to participate in the games, held every four years in August or September. These games became so much a part of the culture that the four-year interval between the games became a standard unit of time, an Olympiad. An Olympic truce—the Ekecheiria—allowed safe passage for athletes from the different city-states traveling to the games, and participation in them meant allegiance to a "Panhellenic" ideal of a united Greece. The exact date of the first games is not known, but the first recorded event is a footrace, a *stade,* run in 776 BC. A longer race, a *diaulos,* was added in 724 BC, and wrestling and a pentathlon—consisting of the long jump, the javelin throw, the discus throw, a foot race, and wrestling—in 708 BC. Boxing and chariot racing were 7th-century BC additions, as was the *pankration,* a no-holds-barred match (broken limbs were frequent and strangulation sometimes the end)—Plato, the great philosopher, was a big wrestling fan. By the 5th century BC, the games featured nine events, held over four days, with the fifth day reserved for the ceremonies. Most of the participants were professional athletes, for whom winning a laurel wreath at Olympia ensured wealth and glory from the city-states that sponsored them.

Today's tranquil pine-forested valley at Olympia, set with weathered stones of peaceful dignity, belies the sweaty drama of the first sporting festivals. Stadium foot races run in the nude; pankration wrestling was so violent that today's Ultimate Fighting matches look tame; weeklong bacchanals—serviced by an army of prostitutes—held in the Olympic Village: little wonder this ancient event is now called the "Woodstock of its day" by modern scholars (wrestlers, boxers, and discus throwers being the rock stars of ancient Greece).

For today's sightseer, the ruins of many of Olympia's main structures are still visible. The **Altis** was the sacred quarter, also known as the Sacred Grove of Zeus. In the **Bouleuterion,** the seat of the organizers of the games, the Elean senate, athletes swore an oath of fair play. In the **Gymnasion,** athletes practiced for track and field events in an open field surrounded by porticoes. In the **Hippodrome,** horse and chariot races were run on a vast racecourse. The **House of Nero** was a lavish villa built for the emperor's visit to the games of AD 67, in which he competed. The **Leonidaion** was a luxurious hostel for distinguished visitors to the games; it later housed Roman governors. The **Metroon** was a small Doric temple dedicated to Rhea (also known as Cybele), mother of the Gods. The **Nymphaion,** a semicircular reservoir, stored water from a spring to the east that was distributed throughout the site by a network of pipes. The **Palaestra** was a section of the gymnasium complex used for athletic training; athletes bathed and socialized in rooms around the square field. The **Pelopeion,** a shrine to Pelops, legendary king of the region now known as the Peloponnese, housed an altar in a sacred grove. **Pheidias's Workshop** was the studio of the great ancient sculptor famed for his enormous statue of Zeus, sculpted for the site's Temple of Zeus. The **Prytaneion** was a banquet room where magistrates feted the winners and a perpetual flame burned in the hearth. The **Stadium** held as many as 50,000 spectators, who crowded onto earthen embankments to watch running events. The starting and finishing lines are still in place. The **Temple of Hera,** one of the earliest monumental Greek temples, was built in the 7th century BC. The **Temple of Zeus,** a great temple and fine example of Doric architecture, housed Pheidias's enormous statue of the god, one of the seven wonders of the ancient world. The famous **Treasuries** were templelike buildings that housed valuables and equipment of 12 of the most powerful of the city-states competing in the games.

You'll need at least two hours to fully see the ruins and the Archaeological Museum of Olympia (to the north of the ancient site), and three or four hours would be better. ⊠ *Off Ethnikos Odos 74 ✛ ½ km (¼ mile) outside modern Olympia)* ☎ *26240/22517* ⊕ *www.culture.gr* ✇ *€12, combined ticket with Archaeological Museum; €6 Nov.–Mar.*

Fodor'sChoice **Archaeological Museum of Olympia.** Of all the sights in ancient Olympia,
★ some say the modern archaeological museum gets the gold. Housed in a handsome glass and marble pavilion at the edge of the ancient site, the magnificent collections include the sculptures from the Temple of Zeus and *Hermes Carrying the Infant Dionysus,* sculpted by the great Praxiteles, which was discovered in the Temple of Hera in the place noted by Pausanias. The central gallery of the museum holds one of the greatest sculptural achievements of classical antiquity: the pedimental sculptures and metopes from the Temple of Zeus, depicting Hercules's Twelve Labors. The *Hermes* was buried under the fallen clay of the temple's upper walls and is one of the best-preserved classical statues. Also on display is the famous *Nike of Paionios.* Other treasures include notable terra-cottas of Zeus and Ganymede; the head of the cult statue of Hera; sculptures of the family and imperial patrons of Herodes Atticus; and bronzes found at the site, including votive figurines, cauldrons, and

armor. Of great historical interest are a helmet dedicated by Miltiades, the Athenian general who defeated the Persians at Marathon, and a cup owned by the sculptor Pheidias, which was found in his workshop on the Olympia grounds. ✉ *Off Ethnikos Odos 74* ✢ *½ km(¼ mile) outside modern Olympia* ☎ *26240/22742* 🌐 *www.culture.gr* 🎟 *€12, combined ticket with Ancient Olympia; €6 Nov.–Mar.*

WHERE TO EAT

$ GREEK 🍴 **Aegean.** Don't let the garish signs depicting the menu put you off: the far-ranging offerings are excellent. You can eat lightly—a gyro or pizza—but do venture into some of the more serious fare, especially such local dishes as the fish that's been oven-baked with onion, garlic, green peppers, and parsley. **Known for:** good, traditional fare; friendly atmosphere. [$] *Average main: €7* ✉ *Praxiteli Kondyli 35* ☎ *26240/22540.*

$ GREEK 🍴 **Taverna Bacchus.** The best restaurants in Greece are often in small villages, and this appealing family-run taverna and inn set amid fields, a favorite among Olympians, is one such example. The poolside terrace is a lovely place to spend an afternoon or evening, though locals don't start arriving until 10 pm or so for dishes that include a delicious chicken with oregano, grilled lamb, and farm-fresh vegetables that appear in such deliciously simple preparations as baked eggplant with tomatoes and feta. **Known for:** nice terrace; country setting just outside town. [$] *Average main: €8* ✉ *Ancient Pissa (Mirika)* ✢ *5 km (3 miles) west of Olympia* ☎ *26240/22298* 🌐 *www.bacchustavern.gr* ⏲ *Closed Dec.–Feb.*

$ GREEK 🍴 **Taverna Thea.** Olympians flock out to the little village of Floka, about 5 km (3 miles) west of town, at dinnertime to enjoy traditional fare in this country setting. Dining is in a homey room or on the summertime terrace with wide views across the landscape, and the specialties are the expertly grilled meats. **Known for:** village setting; grilled meats; cash only. [$] *Average main: €9* ✉ *Flokas* ☎ *26240/23264* 💳 *No credit cards* ⏲ *No lunch Nov.–Apr.*

WHERE TO STAY

$ B&B/INN 🏨 **Bacchus Pension.** One of the region's most popular eateries also provides attractive and character-filled guest rooms, all with balconies overlooking the countryside. **Pros:** great restaurant; beautiful pool and terrace area; pleasant, attractive rooms. **Cons:** outside town, although just a short drive to ancient site; rooms vary in size; some noise from restaurant. [$] *Rooms from: €65* ✉ *Ancient Pissa (Mirika)* ☎ *0624/22298* 🌐 *www.bacchustavern.gr* ⏲ *Closed Dec.–Feb* 🛏 *8 rooms* 🍽 *Breakfast.*

$ HOTEL Fodor's Choice ★ 🏨 **Hotel Europa.** White stucco, pine, and red tiles are handsome accents to gracious guest rooms that are all extremely large, with queen-size beds in many, and marble bathrooms and small terraces; most have sunken sitting areas and face either the pool, which is set in an olive-shaded garden, or the countryside. **Pros:** attractive, well-maintained rooms; fine restaurants; beautiful pool and garden. **Cons:** slightly out of town center and can be reached easily only by car; can seem a bit anonymous; popular with large groups. [$] *Rooms from: €110* ✉ *Oikismou Drouba* ☎ *26240/22650* 🌐 *www.hoteleuropa.gr* 🛏 *80 rooms* 🍽 *Breakfast.*

$ ▢ **Hotel Pelops.** Suzanna and Theo Spiliopoulou and their family set
HOTEL   the gold standard for a small hotel, providing stylish and comfortable
rooms that have wood floors, overlook the nearby mountains, and
have small terraces. **Pros:** convenient to town and ruins; helpful hosts;
attractive and welcoming. **Cons:** located in town (but in a quiet and
pleasant neighborhood); no pool, but guests can use pool at Hotel
Europa; simple but quite comfortable. $ *Rooms from: €70* ⊠ *Varela*
2 ☎ *26240/22543* ⊕ *www.hotelpelops.gr* ⤶ *18 rooms* ⦿ *Breakfast.*

$$$$ ▢ **Mandola Rosa.** This extremely elegant retreat, tucked into the sprawl-
RESORT   ing multihotel Olympia Riviera Resort on the coast beneath the ancient
city, pampers guests with handsome and comfortable suites in a luxurious Mediterranean-style villa and in lavish bungalows tucked into lush
seaside gardens. **Pros:** an extremely attractive and comfortable place
to stay; beautiful beach and wealth of amenities; superb and friendly
service. **Cons:** the cost is as high as Mt. Olympus; part of big resort complex; a distance from ancient site. $ *Rooms from: €550* ⊠ *Kastro 50,*
Kyllini ✛ *60 km (36 miles) west of Olympia* ☎ *26230/64400* ⊕ *www.*
mandolarosa.com ⤶ *55 rooms* ⦿ *Breakfast.*

SHOPPING

Atelier Exekias. Sakis Doylas sells exquisite handmade and hand-painted
ceramic bowls and urns, fashioned after finds in Ancient Olympia; the
glazes and colors are beautiful. ⊠ *Kondoli* ☎ *6936/314054.*

Olympia Archaeological Museum Shop. The shop of the Archaeological
Museum carries an appealing line of figurines, bronzes, votives, and
other replicas of objects found in the ruins. ⊠ *Off Ethnikos Odos 74*
✛ *North of Ancient Olympia site* ☎ *26240/22742.*

TEMPLE OF APOLLO AT BASSAE
ΝΑΟΣ ΤΟΥ ΑΠΟΛΛΩΝΑ ΣΤΙΣ ΒΑΣΣΕΣ

38 km (23 miles) southeast of Olympia, 54 km (32 miles) south of
Dimitsana.

The launching point for the drive up to the Temple of Apollo is Andritsena, a pleasant collection of stone houses that cling to the side of a deep
gorge. A small library in town, found 100 yards past the town square on
the main road, houses 15th-century Venetian and Vatican first editions
and documents relating to the War of Independence.

Temple of Apollo Epikourios at Bassae. One of the great majesties of ancient
Greek architecture is isolated amid craggy, uncompromising scenery.
Unfortunately, these days the temple looks more like the Sydney Opera
House, thanks to a modernistic shed that has cocooned the structure in
an attempt to prevent further weather damage during ongoing restoration. The covering destroys the sense of place that was so important to
this temple, which sits in miles of empty, hilltop fields. For many years
it was believed that this temple was designed by Iktinos, the Parthenon's architect. Although this theory has recently been disputed, Bassae
remains one of the best-preserved classical temples in Greece, super-
seded in its state of preservation only by the Hephaistion in Athens. The
residents of nearby Phygalia built it atop an older temple in 420 BC to

13

thank Apollo for delivering them from an epidemic; *epikourios* means "helper." Made of local limestone, the temple has some unusual details: exceptional length compared to its width; a north–south orientation rather than the usual east–west (probably because of the slope of the ground); and Ionic half columns linked to the walls by flying buttresses. Here, too, were the first known Corinthian columns with the characteristic acanthus leaves—only the base remains now—and the earliest example of interior sculptured friezes illustrating the battles between the Greeks and Amazons (now in the British Museum). As for the restoration, it will be ongoing for at least another decade. **■ TIP→ Climb to the summit northwest of the temple for a view overlooking the Nedhas River, Mt. Lykaeon, and, on a clear day, the Ionian Sea.** ✉ *Bassae* ✣ *Off Rte. 76, and then up a one-lane road* ☎ *26260/22254* 🌐 *www.culture.gr* 🎟 *€6.*

WHERE TO STAY

$ HOTEL 🏨 **Theoxenia Hotel.** This serviceable stopover point for an early-morning visit to the Temple of Apollo at Bassae is geared only to basic comfort, but the old-fashioned rooms are large and offer vistas of mountains and woods. **Pros:** airy rooms with views; handy for visiting the Temple of Apollo; within easy walking distance of village center. **Cons:** fairly outdated with basic bathrooms; no elevator; cash only. [$] *Rooms from: €40* ✉ *Main road, Andritsaina* ✣ *On edge of village as you enter from Karitena* ☎ *26260/22219* 💳 *No credit cards* ⏲ *Closed Nov.–Feb* 🛏 *28 rooms* 🍴 *No meals.*

ANCIENT MESSENE ΑΡΧΑΙΑ ΜΕΣΣΗΝΗ

35 km (21 miles) south of Temple of Apollo at Bassae.

The ruins of this remarkably fortified ancient city, about 20 km (12 miles) north of the modern town of the same name, are set amid a lush landscape of olive groves and pine forests on the slopes of majestic Mt. Ithomi (also known as Voulkanos).

EXPLORING

Ancient Messene. In terms of footprints, this is one of the most awe-inspiring sites of ancient Greece, thanks to mile-long bulwark walls, famed entry gates, vast theater arenas, and temples. One temple alone, the Asklepion, was thought to be an entire town by archaeologists until recently (see *www.ancientmessene.gr* for an excellent scholarly take on the site). Epaminondas, the Theban leader, built the ancient town, which today incorporates the village of **Mavromati,** in 370–369 BC as a defense against the Spartans, whom the Messenians had battled during two Messenian wars, in 743–724 BC and 650–620 BC.

The most striking aspect of the ruins is the city's **circuit wall,** a feat of defensive architecture that rises and dips across the hillsides for an astonishing 9 km (5½ miles). Four gates remain; the best preserved is the north or **Arcadian Gate,** a double set of gates separated by a round courtyard. On the ancient paving stone below the arch, grooves worn by chariot wheels are still visible. The heart of the walled city is now occupied by the modern village, but excavations have uncovered the most important public buildings, including a **theater,** whose seats have

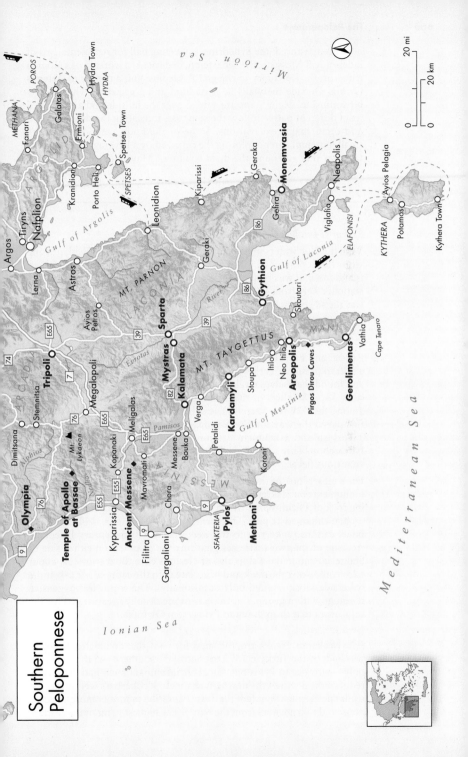

Southern Peloponnese

now been restored; the **Synedrion,** a meeting hall for representatives of independent Messene; the **Sebasteion,** dedicated to worship of a Roman emperor; the **sanctuary to the god Asklepios;** and a **temple to Artemis Orthia.** Outside the walls lie a **stadium** and a **cemetery.** The site is a bit confusing, as the ruins are spread over the hillside and approached from different paths; follow the signposts indicating the theater, gates, and other major excavations. Some of the finds are in the village's **small museum.** After exploring the ruins, enjoy a beverage in one of the tavernas that surround the main square of Mavromati. ✉ *Mavromati ✛ From modern town of Messene, turn north at intersection of sign-posted road to Mavromati* ☎ *27240/51201* ⊕ *www.culture.gr* 🎫 *€12.*

PYLOS

22 km (14 miles) south of Chora.

With the blue waters in its port and the bougainvillea-swathed, pristine white houses fanning up Mt. St. Nicholas, Pylos may remind you of an island town. It was built according to a plan drawn by French engineers stationed here from 1828 to 1833 with General Maison's entourage and was the site of a major naval battle in the War of Independence. Ibrahim Pasha chose Sfakteria, the islet that virtually blocks Pylos Bay, as the site from which to launch his attack on the mainland. For two years Greek forces flailed under Turkish firepower until, in 1827, Britain, Russia, and France arrived to support the Greek insurgents. They sent a fleet to persuade Turkey to sign a treaty, were accidentally fired upon, and found themselves retaliating. At the end of the battle the allies had sunk 53 of 89 ships of the Turko-Egyptian fleet without a single loss among their 27 war vessels. The sultan was forced to renegotiate, and this paved the way for Greek independence. A column rising between a Turkish and a Venetian cannon in the town's main square, Trion Navarchon (Three Admirals) Square, commemorates the leaders of the victorious fleets.

For a closer look of the bay, take an hour-long boat tour to see various monuments on Sfakteria, some sunken Turkish ships, and the neighboring rock of Tsichli-Baba, which has a vast, much photographed natural arch, nicknamed Tripito. This former pirate hideout has 144 steps. The boats can also take you to the weed-infested 13th-century Paleokastro, one of the two fortresses guarding the channels on either side of Sfakteria, and make a stop also at Nestor's cave. Boat trips cost about €25; walk along the dock and negotiate with the captains, or ask at the waterside kiosk (staffed only occasionally). The trip is less expensive if you go with a group, but these trips are usually prearranged for the tour buses that drop down to Pylos from Olympia.

EXPLORING

Pylos Neokastro. Neokastro, the "new fortress" that dominates the town, was built by the Turks in 1573 to control the southern—at that time, the only—entrance to Pylos Bay (an artificial embankment had drastically reduced the depth of the northern channel). Neokastro's well-preserved walls enclose the Church of the Transfiguration (a former mosque), cannons, and two anchors from the battle. The highest point of the castle is guarded by a hexagonal fort flanked by towers. A prison in the 18th and 19th centuries, the fort was more secure than most other Greek prisons because it sometimes housed convicts from the Mani, who continued their blood feuds while behind bars. ✉ *Pylos* ✥ *Access is by trail from south side of town or off road to Methoni* 🎟 €2.

WHERE TO STAY

$$$$ RESORT FAMILY 🏨 **Costa Navarino Resort.** This vast complex incorporates two adjoining resorts, the Westin and the slightly more upscale Romanos, and sprawls along a swath of coast in the southwestern Peloponnese, providing sparkling rooms—some with their own pools—and a long list of amenities, including more bars and restaurants than most guests will have time to sample and two impressive golf courses, making this Greece's leading resort for duffers. **Pros:** a huge choice of dining options in 16 restaurants; beautiful sandy beach and great golf; close to Ancient Messene and other attractions. **Cons:** rather generic surroundings; removed from real Greek experience; food, drink, and other amenities can be pricey. [$] *Rooms from: €375* ✉ *Navarino Dunes* ☎ *27230/95000* 🌐 *www.costanavarino.com* 🛏 *760 rooms* 🍴 *Breakfast.*

13

METHONI ΜΕΘΩΝΗ

11 km (7 miles) south of Pylos.

Methoni, a small fishing and farming village and quiet resort on a cape south of Pylos, has delighted visitors for some time: it was one of the seven towns Agamemnon offered Achilles to appease him after his beloved Briseis was carried off. According to Homer, Pedasos, as it was called, was "rich in vines," and tradition says that the town got its modern name because *onoi* (donkeys) carrying the town's wine became *methoun* (intoxicated) from the aroma. The small fishing and farming village is still fairly intoxicating, with long beaches backed by olive groves and vineyards. Modern Methoni is two towns: a low-key settlement huddled on the beach beneath the fortress, and, just above, an animated Old Town on the crest of a rise—a laid-back, pleasant place to rest for a day or two.

EXPLORING

Fodor's Choice ★ **Methoni Fortress.** Methoni's principal attraction is its kastro, an imposing, well-kept citadel that the Venetians built when they took control of the town in 1209. The town already had a long history: after the Second Messenian War in the 7th century BC, the victorious Spartans gave Methoni to the Nafplions, who had been exiled from their homeland for their Spartan alliance. With its natural harbor, the town was an important stop on trade routes between Europe and the East during the Middle Ages. A stone bridge leads over the dry moat to the citadel; various coats of arms mark the walls, including those of Genoa and Venice's Lion of St. Mark. A second bridge joins the kastro with the Bourtzi, an octagonal tower built above the crashing surf on a tiny islet during the Turkish occupation (shortly after 1500). ✉ *South end of town* 🎟 €2.

WHERE TO EAT

$ GREEK 🍴 **Nikos's.** "The only time this kitchen closes is if I'm sick," says Nikos Vile, who insists on cooking everything from *mamboulas* (a moussaka made with tomatoes) to *maridakia* (lightly fried whitebait) each day. You can sip an aperitif at the bar or hide out in the vine-covered courtyard. **Known for:** good, home-style food; warm hospitality. [$] *Average main: €8* ✉ *Methoni* ✥ *Near entrance to fortress* ☎ *27230/31282.*

$ GREEK 🍴 **Taverna Kilmataria.** Many of the dishes that come to the table in this rustic room or on the flowery terrace are based on homegrown produce, so count on the freshest greens and succulent eggplant and zucchini appearing in moussaka and other traditional favorites. The stuffed grape leaves and stuffed zucchini flowers are excellent starters, and the lamb is grilled perfectly. **Known for:** nice garden with castle views; good vegetable dishes; cash only. [$] *Average main: €8* ✉ *Methoni* ✥ *Near entrance to fortress* ☎ *27230/31544* 💳 *No credit cards* 🕒 *Closed Nov.–Apr.*

WHERE TO STAY

$ HOTEL 🏨 **Ulysses.** From the shady, well-manicured side garden to the attractive traditional furnishings in the spotless rooms, every part of this hotel is welcoming. **Pros:** nice village location near beach; lavish breakfast; comfortable, homey rooms. **Cons:** cash only; rather basic bathrooms; not luxurious but charming. [$] *Rooms from: €55* ✉ *Kiprou 17* ☎ *27230/31600* 🌐 *www.ulysseshotel.com* 💳 *No credit cards* 🕒 *Closed Nov.–Apr* 🛏 *9 rooms* 🍽 *Breakfast.*

EN ROUTE

Though not Greece's most attractive city, Kalamata warrants a quick stop as you head toward the Mani. The city of olive fame has the animated air of a busy port and market town as well as a long beachfront promenade and a string of lively squares. The oldest remnants of the city, all but leveled in a devastating earthquake in 1986, huddle beneath the 13th-century kastro built by Frankish knight Geoffrey de Villehardouin. Along the old streets below is the convent of the Kalograies, who weave beautiful silk scarves and table linens, for sale in a shop just inside the entrance; ask to step into the tranquil cloister. Nearby is the small 13th-century Ayii Apostoli ("Holy Apostles"), dedicated to the Virgin of Kalamata ("of the good eye"), from whom the town may get its name. This is one of Greece's double churches, with two naves—one for the Roman Catholics and one for the Orthodox—that resulted from 13th- and 14th-century ecumenical efforts.

THE MANI MANH

Kardamyli, the western entrance to the Mani, is about 70 km (50 miles) southeast of Ancient Messene.

Isolated and invincible, stark yet unforgettable, the Mani region may be an acquired taste, but it remains one of the must-dos of the Peloponnese for intrepid travelers. For Greeks, it has always been something of a frontier, a bit like the American West, as well as a rugged seaside getaway yet to be spoiled by large-scale development. Given its good looks, it's little wonder that the Mani is becoming increasingly popular with Athenians, who come to the region for weekends or longer getaways.

The bare mountains, rugged coastline, and simple villages suggest a different time and remind us that this was a land of bandits and blood feuds. Just look at the 19th-century stonework town of Vathia: this icon of the Mani is set over the sea and bristles with enough forbidding tower houses to look like a primeval Manhattan. The Dorians never reached this far south, Roman occupation was perfunctory, and Christianity was not established here until the 9th century. Neither the Venetians nor the Turks could quell the constant rebellions that arose when clans began building defensive tower houses (the oldest dates to the 15th century) up to four stories high and fighting for precious land in this barren landscape. The object in battle was to annihilate the enemy's tower house, as well as its entire male population. Feuds could last for years, with the women—who were safe from attack—bringing in supplies. Mani women were famous throughout Greece for their singing of the *moirologhi* (laments), like the ancient choruses in a Greek tragedy.

A temporary truce had to be called during the harvest, but a feud ended only with the complete destruction of a family or its surrender, called *psychiko* (a thing of the soul), in which losers filed out of their tower house one by one, kissing the hand of the enemy clan's parents. The victor then decided under what conditions the humbled family could remain in the village. When King Otho tried to tame this incorrigible bunch in 1833, his soldiers were ambushed, stripped naked, and held for ransom. Today few people live in the Mani. If you have the good luck to share a shot of fiery raki with a Maniote, you may notice a Cretan influence in his dress—older men still wear the baggy breeches, black headbands, and decorated jackets wrapped with heavy belts.

On its western side, the Mani Peninsula—the middle of the three fingers that dangle from the southern Peloponnese—stretches from Kardamyli to the Tenaro cape, the mythical entrance to the underworld, and on its eastern side from the Tenaro cape up to Gythion. The western half is the Messenian Mani, while the eastern half is the Laconian Mani.

KARDAMYLI ΚΑΡΔΑΜΥΛΙ

122 km (76 miles) southwest of Tripoli.

The gateway to the Mani on the Messenian side is Kardamyli, 31 km (19 miles) southeast of the market town of Kalamata. Kardamyli is considered part of the outer Mani, an area less bleak and stark than the inner Mani, which begins at Areopolis. Here the foothills of the Taygettus range are still verdant, and the sun is more forgiving. The quiet and attractive stone town has become a tourist destination for travelers attracted to its pleasant seaside lanes and squares, the stark beauty of the mountainous backdrop, and the hiking paths in the surrounding hills. Kardamyli's most famous resident was for many years the late Patrick Leigh Fermor, an Anglo-Irish writer who wrote extensively on Greece and on the Mani in particular. The old section of Kardamyli, above the modern town, is on a pine-scented hillside dotted with small clusters of tower houses, some of which are being restored; stone-paved paths cut through the enclave.

WHERE TO EAT

$

✕ **Elies Hotel Restaurant.** For a lot of travelers a perfect day in Kardamyli includes lunch beneath the olive trees in the Elies garden, which stands directly across from the beach. The setting is memorable at night, too, and at any time a meal includes tasty daily preparations of lamb, chicken, and fish, infused with herbs and prepared with local olive oil. **Known for:** idyllic seaside garden setting; nice preparations of local favorites. $ *Average main: €12* ✉ *Kardamyli Beach* ✛ *On the beach road* ☎ *27210/73140* ⊕ *www.elieshotel.gr* ⊗ *Closed Nov.–Mar.*

GREEK
FAMILY

$

✕ **Lela's Taverna.** The late Mrs. Lela, once housekeeper for author Patrick Leigh Fermor, was famous for her simple, old-fashioned cooking using fragrant homemade olive oil and exceedingly fresh tomatoes and herbs. Her taverna is an institution in these parts, and dinner beneath the trees on the seaside terrace of an oleander-covered stone house is a high point of a visit to the Mani. **Known for:** lovely seaside terrace; nicely prepared traditional dishes; cash only. $ *Average main: €9* ✉ *Kardamyli* ✛ *On the seaside, above the rocky beach near the old soap factory* ☎ *27210/73541* ⊕ *www.lelastaverna.com* ▭ *No credit cards* ⊗ *Closed Tues. No lunch.*

GREEK
Fodor's Choice
★

WHERE TO STAY

$

🏨 **Hotel Patriarcheas.** The marble-floored rooms in this pleasant stone hotel in the Old Town are unusually large—those in the front face the sea but also hang above the main road, so you might want to forgo the sea view and choose one of the rear rooms to enjoy the quiet setting from your balcony. **Pros:** old-fashioned in a good way; bright and sunny rooms; pleasant communal terrace. **Cons:** noise from road in front rooms; basic comforts with only a modest breakfast; cash only. $ *Rooms from: €50* ✉ *Old Town* ☎ *27210/73366* ▭ *No credit cards* ⇱ *16 rooms* ⦿| *Breakfast.*

HOTEL

$

🏨 **Lela's Taverna Rooms.** Four plain but comfortable rooms above Lela's famous taverna have soothing sea views and handsome furnishings that include extremely comfortable Cocomat beds; all have balconies, and the terrace below is a pleasant place to lounge when the restaurant is not serving. **Pros:** beautiful seaside location; very simple but comfortable; two rooms are suites, well-suited to families. **Cons:** few hotel services and amenities, as well as basic bathrooms; taverna noise can be a nuisance into the night; cash only. $ *Rooms from: €65* ✉ *Kardamyli* ✛ *On the seaside, above the rocky beach near the old soap factory* ☎ *27210/73541* ⊕ *www.lelastaverna.com* ▭ *No credit cards* ⇱ *4 rooms* ⦿| *No meals.*

B&B/INN

$

🏨 **Notos Hotel.** These bright, attractive lodgings, scattered across hillside gardens in handsome stone cottages, are furnished in handmade, bleached-wood pieces and attractive muted fabrics—each unit has a large terrace or two overlooking the sea and kitchens are well equipped. **Pros:** extremely attractive and well-equipped units; friendly atmosphere; lovely views across countryside and sea. **Cons:** village is a hearty walk away; advisable to have a rental car to enjoy area; no pool, but the beach is just down the hill. $ *Rooms from: €80* ✉ *Kardamyli* ✛ *Above the beach, about 1 km (½ mile) north of the town center* ☎ *27210/73730* ⊕ *www.notoshotel.gr* ⇱ *14 apartments* ⦿| *No meals.*

B&B/INN
Fodor's Choice
★

BEACHES

Kardamyli's main beach, at the northern edge of town, is a long stretch of sand and pebbles backed by stands of pines. You can also swim off the dock in the clear, deep waters of the town's small harbor. Other beaches are tucked into coves as you drive south on the main road. Stoupa, about 10 km (6 miles) south of Kardamyli, is a low-key collection of seaside tavernas and rooms for rent that stretches along a beautiful sandy beach; it's hardly idyllic but a good place to come for lunch and a swim. Neo Itilo sits on a beautiful large bay with a white-pebble beach. Enjoy a swim as you watch the fishermen fixing their nets, checking their ship hulls, and talking among themselves amid the din of their portable radios.

FAMILY **Foneas.** A sand-and-pebble beach rings a sparkling cove, where the languid, turquoise waters are perfect for swimming and, with offshore rocky outcroppings, a playground for snorkelers. A swim-through sea cave just off the beach is a perfect retreat in which to float and escape the sun. **Amenities:** food and drink; parking (no fee); showers; toilets. **Best for:** snorkeling; swimming. ⊠ *Kardamyli ✛ Off Coast road, 4 km (2½ miles) south of Kardymili.*

Stoupa. This long stretch of clean sand along a curving bay is undeniably the most popular beach in the Mani, though far from the quietest and most scenic spot in this rugged region. You'll share the company of frolicking young Greeks and sun-worshipping northern Europeans, but given that this is the Mani, this is a relatively low-key beach resort, and it's quite possible to find a quiet stretch. **Amenities:** food and drink; parking (free); showers; toilets; water sports. **Best for:** partiers; snorkeling; swimming; walking. ⊠ *Stoupa.*

AREOPOLIS ΑΡΕΟΠΟΛΗΣ

44 km (26 miles) southwest of Kardamyli.

In Areopolis, the typical Maniote tower houses begin to appear in earnest as spooky sentinels in the harsh landscape. The town was renamed after Ares, the god of war, because of its role in the War of Independence: Petrobey Mavromichalis, governor of the Mani, initiated the local uprising against the Turks here (his statue stands in the square, and his descendants have turned the family's seaside mansion in nearby Limeni into a stunning small hotel). Areopolis now enjoys protection as a historical monument by the government, but although the town seems medieval, most of the tower houses were built in the early 1800s. The Taxiarchis (Archangels) church, which looks as if it has 12th-century reliefs over the doors, was actually constructed in 1798. It's easy to slip vicariously into a time warp as you meander along dark cobblestone lanes past the tower houses with their enclosed courtyards and low-arched gateways.

EXPLORING

FAMILY **Pirgos Dirou Caves.** Carved out of the limestone by the slow-moving
Fodor's Choice underground river Vlychada on its way to the sea, the vast Pirgos Dirou
★ caves—actually two main caves, Glyfada and Alepotrypa—are one of Greece's more popular natural attractions, and a visit is an entertaining

and surreal experience. The eerie caverns, places of worship in Paleolithic and Neolithic times, were believed to be entrances to the underworld by the ancient Greeks, and served as hiding places millennia later for Resistance fighters during World War II.

Today you climb aboard a boat for a 25-minute tour of Glyfada's grottoes—with formations of luminous pink, white, yellow, and red stalagmites and stalactites that resemble buildings and mythical beasts. The cave system is believed to be at least 70 km (43 miles) long, with more than 2,800 waterways, perhaps extending as far as Sparta. At the end of the tour you walk for several hundred yards (about a fifth of a mile) before emerging on a path above the crashing surf. The close quarters in the passageways are not for the claustrophobic, and even in summer the caves are chilly. During high season you may wait up to two hours for a boat, so plan to arrive early. In low season you may have to wait until enough people arrive to fill up a boat. Opening hours change frequently. ✉ *Pirgos Dirou* ✣ *10 km (6 miles) southwest of Areopolis, 5 km (3 miles) west of Areopolis–Vathia road* ☎ *27330/52222* 🎟 *€12.*

WHERE TO EAT

$ SEAFOOD 🍴 **Takis.** The fish and seafood, priced by the kilo and served at the water's edge in Limeni, are some of the freshest in the region—and best when simply grilled, usually with mountain herbs. You may end up dining next to the boat that brought in the fresh catch, or for that matter, near a crew cleaning the fish that will soon appear on your plate (it's much more charming than it sounds). **Known for:** fresh fish right off the boat; nice harborside perch; cash only. [$] *Average main: €12* ✉ *Limeni* ✣ *On Limeni waterfront, 5 km (3 miles) north of Areopolis* ☎ *27330/51327* 💳 *No credit cards.*

$ GREEK 🍴 **Taverna Barba Petros.** A simple, high-ceilinged room and terrace are the settings for the traditional meals here. The kitchen uses only market-fresh vegetables and locally raised meat, which appear in simple and delicious ways. **Known for:** traditional Mani dishes, including grilled meats; nice summertime terrace; cash only. [$] *Average main: €9* ✉ *Main street, Areopoli* ☎ *27330/51026* 💳 *No credit cards.*

$ GREEK 🍴 **To Katoi.** Once used as a stable, this vaulted, stone-walled room is pleasant and welcoming and extends to a terrace on the street in good weather. The kitchen specializes in home cooking with the freshest local ingredients, including such traditional favorites as rooster roasted with potatoes and vegetables and a hearty omelet made with smoked pork. **Known for:** welcoming atmosphere; delicious lamb with lemon and other traditional dishes; cash only. [$] *Average main: €8* ✉ *Areopoli* ✣ *Across from the Taxiarchis church* ☎ *27330/51201* 💳 *No credit cards* 🕒 *No lunch in winter.*

WHERE TO STAY

$ HOTEL 🏨 **Trapela.** In this beautiful, traditionally styled house just off the main square, large, stone-floored, stone-walled, wood-ceilinged rooms combine distinctive, traditional ambience with modern comforts. **Pros:** lovely terraces and a garden; pleasant decor; stylish and comfortable base for visiting the Mani. **Cons:** limited service; a distance from a beach; no elevator. $ *Rooms from: €90* ✉ *Areopoli* ✛ *Near the center of town* ☎ *27330/52690* ⊕ *www.trapela.gr* ⤴ *9 rooms, 4 suites* ⦿ *Breakfast.*

$$ ⛨ **Pirgos Mavromichali.** The fortified, seaside stronghold of the Mav-

B&B/INN romichali clan, noted for its role in Greek independence, is now an

Fodor's Choice enchanting inn with 13 character-filled rooms and suites set within

★ the walls of a centuries-old tower building and clustered around sun-drenched terraces that drop down to the turquoise waters of Limeni harbor, just north of Areopolis. **Pros:** panoramic, historic surroundings at the edge of the sea; extremely attentive service; an ideal base for exploring the rugged Mani landscape. **Cons:** steps may be difficult for guests with mobility issues; some rooms are a bit dark; a car is a necessity. $ *Rooms from: €135* ✉ *Harborfront, Limeni* ✛ *5 km (3 miles) north of Areopolis* ☎ *27330/51042* ⊕ *www.pirgosmavromichali.gr* ⤴ *13 rooms* ⦿ *Breakfast.*

GEROLIMENAS ΓΕΡΟΛΙΜΕΝΑΣ

22 km (14 miles) south of Areopolis.

Located at the end of a long natural harbor, Gerolimenas was an important port in the late 19th and early 20th centuries. Sleepy as it now is, it's the most tourist-friendly place in this stark part of the southernmost Mani, with several hotels, tavernas, and shops and a lively town beach. About 3 km (2 miles) north of Gerolimenas is the hamlet of Stavri, from where you can make a memorable one-hour trek to the Castle of Mina, built by the Franks in 1248 into the rock face at the end of a long promontory surrounded by crashing surf. The most photogenic sight around here, however, is picture-perfect **Vathia,** 10 km (6 miles) south of Gerolimenas. Although now virtually a ghost town, its small clusters of looming tower houses perched against the sea are one of the postcard icons of Greece. The two- and three-story stone tower houses here all have small windows and tiny openings over the doors through which boiling oil was poured on the unwelcome.

The landscape becomes more rugged and even more forbidding south of Vathia, on the way to **Tenaro cape** at the tip of the peninsula. The road winds around the mountainsides to Porto Kayio, where a few tavernas face a lovely beach, and then to more beaches at Marmari. A narrow road leads south to barren Cape Tenaro, where the ruins of a small Roman settlement include a mosaic that is perilously open to the elements. An underwater cave here, to which you might be able to convince a boatman to take you, is one of several alleged entrances to the classical underworld. From the cape you can look out over the Mani Peninsula and the Gulf of Laconia and Gulf of Messinia.

WHERE TO STAY

$$ ⛨ **Kyrimai Hotel.** The Kyrimis family have lovingly restored a welcoming

HOTEL assemblage of 19th-century stone warehouses into a beautiful retreat,

Fodor's Choice with comfortable guest rooms furnished with antiques and a tasteful

★ mix of traditional and contemporary pieces; many have balconies and sleeping lofts. **Pros:** atmospheric surroundings; excellent swimming from hotel jetty; pleasant seaside terraces. **Cons:** some rooms are dark

13

and do not have views; parking can be difficult; service can be hit or miss. $ *Rooms from: €135* ⊠ *Waterfront* ☎ *27330/54288* ⊕ *www. kyrimai.gr* ⌀ *26 rooms* ⦿ *Breakfast.*

LACONIA ΛΑΚΩΝΙΑ

The Laconian plain is surrounded on three sides by mountains and on one side by the sea. Perhaps it was the fear that enemies could descend those mountains at any time that drove the Spartans to make Laconia their training ground, where they developed the finest fighting force in ancient Greece. A mighty power that controlled three-fifths of the Peloponnese, Sparta contributed to the Greek victory in the Second Persian War (5th century BC). Ultimately, Sparta's aggressiveness and jealousy of Athens brought about the Peloponnesian War, which drained the city's resources but left the Spartans victorious. The Greek world found Sparta to be an even harsher master than Athens, and this fact may have led to losses in in 222–221 BC at the hands of the Achaean League, who liberated all areas Sparta had conquered. A second period of prosperity under the Romans ended with the barbarian invasions in the 3rd century AD, and Sparta declined rapidly.

Laconia can also claim two important magnificently medieval sites: Mystras and Monemvasia. The former was an intellectual and political center, the latter a sea fortress meant to ward off invaders from the east.

GYTHION ΓΥΘΕΙΟΝ

79 km (49 miles) north of Vathia, 50 km (30 miles) northeast of Gerolimenas.

At the foot of the Taygettus range on the northeastern edge of the Mani, Gythion seems terribly cosmopolitan, compared to the stark countryside that surrounds it. Graceful pastel 19th-century houses march up the steep hillside and line the busy harbor, where a fishing fleet bobs alongside ouzeri and little shops. As Laconia's main port, Gythion is the region's gateway to the Mani Peninsula. It claims Hercules and Apollo as its founders, and survives today by exporting olives, oil, rice, and citrus fruits. Kranae, a tiny islet at the eastern end of the harbor, is where Paris and Helen (wife of the Mycenaean king Menelaos) allegedly consummated their love affair after escaping Sparta, provoking the Trojan War described in the *Iliad*. A causeway now joins Marathonissi to the mainland.

MONEMVASIA ΜΟΝΕΜΒΑΣΙΑ

140 km (85 miles) northeast of Gythion.

Fodor's Choice
★

The Byzantine town of Monemvasia clings to the side of the 1,148-foot rock that was once a headland but in AD 375 was separated from the mainland by an earthquake. The town was first settled in the 6th century AD, when Laconians sought refuge after Arab and Slav raids. Monemvasia—the name *moni emvasia* (single entrance) refers to the narrow passage to this walled community—once enjoyed enormous prosperity, and for centuries dominated the sea lanes from Western Europe to the Levant. During its golden age in the 1400s, Monemvasia was home to families made wealthy by their inland estates and the export of malmsey wine, a sweet variety of Madeira praised by Shakespeare. When the area fell to the Turks, Monemvasia was controlled first by the pope and then by the Venetians, who built the citadel and most of the fortifications. The newer settlement that has spread out along the water on the mainland is not as romantic as the Old Town, but it's pleasant and well equipped with shops and services.

Well-to-do Greeks once again live on the rock, in houses they have turned into vacation homes. Summer weekends are crowded, but off-season Monemvasia is nearly deserted. Houses are lined up along steep streets only wide enough for two people abreast, among remnants of another age—escutcheons, marble thrones, Byzantine icons. It's a delight to wander through the back lanes and along the old walls, and to find perches high above the town or the sea, and an overnight stay here allows you to enjoy this strange place when the tour groups have departed.

EXPLORING

Ayia Sofia. For solitude and a dizzying view, pass through the upper town's wooden entrance gates, complete with the original iron reinforcement. Up the hill is a rare example of a domed octagonal church, founded in the 13th century by Emperor Andronicus II and patterned after Dafni Monastery in Athens. Under Venetian rule the Byzantine complex served as a convent. Follow the path to the highest point on the rock for a breathtaking view of the coast. ⊠ *Monemvasia* ✛ *At top of mountain.*

Ayios Pavlos. This humble stone structure is one of the oldest churches in Greece, dating to the 10th century. Although Ayios Pavlos was converted into a mosque under the Ottoman occupation, it was allowed to function as a church: an unusual indulgence. ⊠ *Monemvasia* ✛ *Across from Tzamiou Sq.*

Christos Elkomenos (*Christ in Chains*). The town's 13th-century cathedral is reputedly the largest medieval church in southern Greece. Carved peacocks on its portal are symbolic of the Byzantine era; the detached bell tower—like those of Italian cathedrals—is a sign of Venetian rebuilding in the 17th century. ⊠ *Tzamiou Sq., along main street.*

BEACHES

Some people swim off the rocks at the base of the Old Town and along the road leading to the main gate, but the pebble beach in the New Town is safer and more appealing. For the most rewarding beach experience, head to the sandy strands at Pori, about 5 km (3 miles) northwest of Monemvasia.

WHERE TO EAT

$ ✕ **Marianthi.** You'll feel as if you're dropping into someone's home at
GREEK   dinner here: family photos of stern, mustachioed ancestors hang on the walls along with local memorabilia, and the service, at tables on the street in good weather, is just as welcoming (perhaps too much so, as cats can be as numerous as diners). A memorable meal makes the most

of local ingredients—wild mountain greens, any of the fish but especially the fresh red mullet, the addictive potato salad (you may have to order two plates), and the marinated octopus sprinkled with oregano. **Known for:** character-filled surroundings; excellent small plates; cash only. $ *Average main: €9* ✉ *Main street* ☎ *27320/61371* ▭ *No credit cards.*

$

GREEK

✕ **To Kanoni.** After you roll out of bed, wander over to the Kanoni, which opens early for the day to serve breakfast on a terrace overlooking the square's cannon. Choose from omelets, ham and eggs, or thick, creamy yogurt and honey, then come back at lunch or dinner for a nicely varied menu that often includes eggplant baked with other fresh vegetables and feta and *yiouvetsi* (beef baked in a clay pot with orzolike pasta). **Known for:** nice view-filled terrace; wide-ranging menu. $ *Average main: €9* ✉ *Main Sq.* ✛ *Old Town* ☎ *27320/61387* ⊕ *tokanoni.com.*

WHERE TO STAY

$

B&B/INN

Byzantino. All of these unusual accommodations, tucked into several stone buildings in the Old Town, are different and full of character—all are embellished with stone- and tile work and other distinctive decorations, and some are multilevel. **Pros:** character-filled accommodation in medieval houses; some units have nice terraces and sea views; warm hospitality. **Cons:** steep streets and stairs to reach some rooms; ask about accessibility when booking; rooms vary greatly, so ask to see a few if available; noise from nearby bars in some rooms. $ *Rooms from: €90* ✉ *Monemvasia* ✛ *The hotel office is on the main street near the town entrance gate* ☎ *27320/61351* ⊕ *www.hotelbyzantino.com* ↪ *25 rooms* ❖*No meals.*

$

HOTEL

Hotel Pramataris. If there's no room at the Old Town's inns, or if you don't like the idea of carting your baggage up and down narrow lanes, then this sparkling New Town choice with bright, tile-floored rooms overlooking the sea and the Gibraltar-like rock is a wonderful alternative and a real bargain. **Pros:** pleasant seaside location; friendly service; nice outdoor spaces. **Cons:** not in the atmospheric Old Town; some noise at night; premises could use some updating. $ *Rooms from: €60* ✉ *New Town* ✛ *On the seafront* ☎ *27320/61833* ⊕ *www.pramatarishotel.gr* ↪ *18 rooms* ❖*Breakfast.*

$

B&B/INN

Kellia. Accommodations in this old monastery (*kellia* means "cells") are fairly simple, but they are extremely appealing and face an airy square above the sea. **Pros:** beautiful seaside location, tucked away from the busy main street and squares; atmospheric surroundings; friendly hosts. **Cons:** hard to reach over the cobblestone streets; a steep climb to steps in some rooms; some rooms are a bit dark. $ *Rooms from: €75* ✉ *Monemvasia* ✛ *On the lower square, opposite the Church of Panagia Chrissafitissa* ☎ *27320/61520* ⊕ *www.keliamonemvasia.com* ↪ *11 rooms* ❖*Breakfast.*

$$$$

HOTEL

Fodor'sChoice

★

Kinsterna Hotel and Spa. An Ottoman estate has been brought back to life as one of Greece's most distinctive hotels, where courtyards, terraces, domes, vaulted ceilings, arches, stone work, fireplaces, and other architectural elements are put to dazzling effect—the outdoor dining room overhangs a centuries-old cistern and a river-like swimming pool winds through the garden. **Pros:** architecturally distinctive

CLOSE UP

The Spartan Ethic

The Spartans' relentless militarism set them apart from other Greeks in the ancient world. They were expected to emerge victorious from a battle or not at all, and for most of its existence Sparta was without a wall, because according to Lykourgos, who wrote Sparta's constitution sometime around 600 BC, "chests, not walls, make a city." The government was an oligarchy, with two kings who also served as military leaders. Spartan society had three classes: a privileged elite involved with warfare and government; farmers, traders, and craftspeople, who paid taxes; and the numerous Helots, a serf class with few rights.

Selected boys in the reigning warrior class were taken from their parents at the age of seven and submitted to a training regimen without parallel in history for its ruthlessness. Their diet involved mostly herbs, roots, and the famous black broth, which included pork, the blood of the pig, and vinegar. Rich foods were thought to stunt growth. Forbidden to work, boys and young men trained for combat and practiced stealing, an acceptable skill—it was believed to teach caution and cunning—unless one was caught. One legend describes a Spartan youth who let a concealed fox chew out his bowels rather than reveal his theft. Girls also trained rigorously in the belief they would bear healthier offspring; for the same reason, newlyweds were forbidden to make love frequently.

The kingdom's iron coinage was not accepted outside Sparta's borders, creating a contempt for wealth and luxury (and, in turn, rapacious kings and generals). Sparta's warrior caste subjugated the native Achaean inhabitants of the region. Today all that remains of this realm founded on martial superiority is dust.

surroundings; beautifully furnished and well-equipped rooms and suites; attractive pool and gardens. **Cons:** countryside setting that can only be reached by car; food can be expensive; rooms vary in character. [$] *Rooms from: €300* ✉ *Agios Stefanos* ☎ *27320/66300* 🌐 *www.kinsternahotel.gr* 🛏 *27 rooms* 🍴 *Breakfast.*

$ B&B/INN 🏨 **Malvasia Traditional Hotel.** A complex of restored buildings at the far edge of the Old Town (reached on a trek over sometimes steep and uneven pavement) provides atmospheric and comfortable lodgings tucked into nooks and crannies under cane-and-wood or vaulted brick ceiling. **Pros:** appealing and nicely designed bright rooms with character; many private terraces and sea views; pleasant public indoor and outdoor spaces. **Cons:** reached via a trek through town on rough streets; reserve well in advance for July and August; steps to reach some rooms. [$] *Rooms from: €75* ✉ *Monemvasia* ✥ *End of Old Town* ☎ *27320/63007* 🌐 *www.malvasiahotel-traditional.gr* 🛏 *16 rooms* 🍴 *Breakfast.*

SPARTA ΣΠΑΡΤΗ

96 km (60 miles) northwest of Monemvasia.

For those who have read about ancient Sparta, the bellicose city-state that once dominated the Greek world, the modern city on the broad Eurotas River might be a disappointment, since ruins are few and far between. Given the area's earthquakes and the Spartans' tendency to live more like an army camp than a city-state, no elaborate ruins remain, a fact that so disconcerted Otto, Greece's first king, that in 1835 he ordered the modern city built on the ancient site. The modern town is not terribly attractive, but it's pleasant enough, with a lively pedestrian-only city center.

At least seven buses a day connect Athens and Sparta, a trip of about four hours that costs about €18 each way. From Sparta's bus station (☎ 27310/26441), located downtown at the junction of Lykourgou and Dafnou, you can catch one of six daily buses to Monemvasia (about 2 hours, €5) and also continue on to the Mani region (service several times a day to Gythion and Aeropolis) and other places in the southern Peloponnese.

By car, follow the toll highway south from Athens through Corinth and Tripoli to a well-marked exit onto Highway 70 for Sparta. The trip from Athens takes about three hours of reasonable driving.

EXPLORING

FAMILY   **Museum of the Olive and Greek Olive Oil.** Olives are thick on the ground in these parts, so it's only fitting that Sparta is home to a quirky and appealing collection of apparatus and culture related to the staple of Greek economy since ancient times, housed in a stunning renovation of the city's first electricity works. ⊠ *Othonos-Amalias 129, Sparta* ☎ *27310/89315* ⊕ *www.oliveoilmuseums.gr* 🖃 *€3* ⊗ *Closed Tues.*

Sparta Acropolis. What little remains of Ancient Sparta's acropolis is now part archaeological site, part park. Locals can be seen here strolling, along with many young couples stealing a romantic moment amid the fallen limestone and shady trees. The sparse ruins include a **theater,** a **stadium,** and a **sanctuary to Athena.** ⊠ *Sparta* ✛ *North end of town.*

Sparta Archaeological Museum. This eclectic collection reflects Laconia's turbulent history and is worth an hour to see Neolithic pottery; jewels and tools excavated from the Alepotrypa cave; Mycenaean tomb finds; bright 4th- and 5th-century Roman mosaics; and objects from Sparta. Most characteristic of the relatively few pieces of Spartan art that have survived are the bas-reliefs with deities and heroes; note the one depicting a seated couple bearing gifts who are framed by a snake (540 BC). ⊠ *Ayios Nikonos, between Dafnou and Evangelistria, Sparta* ☎ *27310/21516* ⊕ *www.culture.gr* 🖃 *€2.*

Statue of Leonidas. Stop a moment and contemplate the statue of the stern Spartan leader. During the Second Persian War in the 5th century BC, with 30,000 Persians advancing on his army of 8,000, Leonidas, ordered to surrender his weapons, jeered, "Come and get them." For two days he held off the enemy, until a traitor named Efialtes (the word has since come to mean "nightmare" in Greek) showed the Persians a way to attack from the rear. When forced to retreat to a wooded knoll, Leonidas is said to have commented, "So much the better, we will fight in the shade." His entire troop was slaughtered. ✉ *End of Konstantinou, Sparta.*

Temple of Artemis Orthia. At this temple outside town, young Spartan men underwent *krypteia* (initiations) that entailed severe public floggings. The altar had to be splashed with blood before the goddess was satisfied. Traces of two such altars are among sparse vestiges of the 6th-century BC temple. The larger ruins are the remains of a grandstand built in the 3rd century AD by the Romans, who revived the flogging tradition as a public spectacle. ✉ *Tripoli Rd., Sparta* ✥ *Down path to Eurotas River.*

WHERE TO EAT

$ GREEK 🍴 **Diethnes.** Locals claim this is one of Sparta's best restaurants, but then again, most head out to village tavernas for a big meal and leave this place to the tour-bus crowd. Even so, the food is excellent, the best you're likely to find in town. **Known for:** shady rear garden; traditional dishes; cash only. [$] *Average main: €9* ✉ *Paleologou 105, Sparta* ☎ *27310/28636* 💳 *No credit cards.*

WHERE TO STAY

$ B&B/INN FAMILY 🏨 **Eumelia.** A working farm near a village 45 minutes outside of Sparta provides a rare chance to experience rural Greece, while enjoying handsome bunglow accommodations, homecooked organic meals, yoga sessions, and easy excursions to Monemvasia and other places of interest in the southeastern Peloponnese. **Pros:** well designed and attractive; environmentally friendly; genial, English-speaking host. **Cons:** remote location not suitable for everyone; not on the coast (though beaches are within easy driving distance); may be a bit too laid-back for some guests. [$] *Rooms from: €100* ✉ *Gouvai* ☎ *2735/300419* 🌐 *www.eumelia.com* 🛏 *5 bungalows* 🍽 *Breakfast.*

$ HOTEL 🏨 **Maniatis Hotel.** The sleek style here begins in the modern marble lobby and extends through fittingly spartan yet handsome guest rooms, with their contemporary, light-wood furnishings and soft, soothing colors. **Pros:** attractive accommodations; good in-house restaurant; central location. **Cons:** small rooms and bathrooms; relatively few luxuries; some street noise. [$] *Rooms from: €70* ✉ *Paleologou 72, Sparta* ☎ *27310/22665* 🌐 *www.maniatishotel.gr* 🛏 *80 rooms* 🍽 *Breakfast.*

$ HOTEL 🏨 **Menelaion Hotel.** The pool sparkling in the leafy courtyard is a welcome sight after a hot day of exploring the ruins of nearby Mystras, and the well-equipped guest rooms are quite stylish. **Pros:** attractive public areas; good in-house restaurant and bar; courtyard with pool. **Cons:** rooms are stylish but lack a little character; street noise in front-facing rooms; no garage and difficult parking. [$] *Rooms from: €100* ✉ *Paleologou 91, Sparta* ☎ *27310/22161* 🌐 *www.menelaion.com* 🛏 *30 rooms* 🍽 *Breakfast.*

Magnificently redolent of the Byzantine era, Mystras is a town filled with churches and monasteries, many adorned with 12th-century paintings.

MYSTRAS ΜΥΣΤΡΑΣ

8 km (5 miles) west of Sparta, 64 km (40 miles) southwest of Tripoli.

While little remains to attest to Spartan power and might, residents of the Byzantine capital just to the west left behind a treasure trove of architectural splendors. A visit to Sparta requires a fertile imagination; in Mystras all you need is a good pair of walking shoes and some water as you scramble amid the copious remnants of the last days of the Byzantine Empire.

In spring Mystras is resplendent with wildflowers and butterflies, but it can be oppressively hot in summer, so get an early start to avoid exploring the site in the midday sun. That said, it's easy to spend half a day here, so wear sunscreen, a hat, and sturdy shoes for traction on slippery rocks. And watch out for the occasional snake.

FAMILY
Fodor's Choice
★

Mystras Archaeological Site. In this Byzantine city, abandoned gold-and-stone palaces, churches, and monasteries line serpentine paths; the scent of herbs and wildflowers permeates the air; goat bells tinkle; and silvery olive trees glisten with the slightest breeze. An intellectual and cultural center where philosophers like Chrysoloras, "the sage of Byzantium," held forth on the good and the beautiful, Mystras seems an appropriate place for the last hurrah of the Byzantine emperors in the 14th century. Today the splendid ruins are a UNESCO World Heritage site and one of the most impressive sights in the Peloponnese. A pleasant modern town adjoins the ruins.

In 1249 William Geoffrey de Villehardouin built the castle in Mystras in an attempt to control Laconia and establish Frankish supremacy over the Peloponnese. He held court here with his Greek wife, Anna Comnena, surrounded by knights of Champagne, Burgundy, and Flanders, but in 1259 he was defeated by the Byzantines. As the Byzantines built a palace and numerous churches (whose frescoes exemplified several periods of painting), the town gradually grew down the slope.

Surrender to the Turks in 1460 signaled the beginning of the end. For a while the town survived because of its silk industry, but after repeated pillaging and burning by bands of Albanians, Russians, and Ibrahim Pasha's Egyptian troops, the inhabitants gave up and moved to modern Sparta.

Among the most important buildings in the lower town (Kato Chora) is **Ayios Demetrios**, the *mitropolis* (cathedral) founded in 1291. Set in its floor is a stone with the two-headed Byzantine eagle marking the spot where Constantine XII, the last emperor of Byzantium, was consecrated. The cathedral's brilliant frescoes include a vivid depiction of the Virgin and the infant Jesus on the central apse and a wall painting in the narthex of the Second Coming, its two red-and-turquoise-winged angels sorrowful as they open the records of Good and Evil. One wing of the church houses a **museum** that holds fragments of Byzantine sculptures, later Byzantine icons, decorative metalwork, and coins.

In the Vrontokion monastery are **Ayios Theodoros** (AD 1295), the oldest church in Mystras, and the 14th-century **Church of Panagia Odegetria**, or **Afendiko**, which is decorated with remarkable murals. These include, in the narthex, scenes of the miracles of Christ: *The Healing of the Blind Man, The Samaritan at the Well,* and *The Marriage of Cana.* The fluidity of the brushstrokes, the subtle but complicated coloring, and the resonant expressions suggest the work of extremely skilled hands.

The **Pantanassa monastery** is a visual feast of intricate tiling, rosette-festooned loops, and myriad arches. It is the only inhabited building in Mystras; the hospitable nuns still produce embroidery that you can purchase. Step out onto the east portico for a view of the Eurotas River valley below.

Every inch of the tiny **Perivleptos monastery,** meaning "attracting attention from all sides," is covered with exceptional 14th-century illustrations from the New Testament, including *The Birth of the Virgin,* in a lush palette of reds, yellows, and oranges; *The Dormition of the Virgin* above the entrance (with Christ holding his mother's soul represented as a baby); and, immediately to the left of the entrance, the famous fresco the *Divine Liturgy.*

In the upper town (Ano Chora), where most aristocrats lived, stands a rare Byzantine civic building, the **Palace of Despots,** home of the last emperor. The older, northeastern wing contains a guardroom, a kitchen, and the residence. The three-story northwest wing contains an immense reception hall on its top floor, lighted by eight Gothic windows and heated by eight huge chimneys; the throne probably stood in the shallow alcove that's in the center of a wall.

In the palace's **Ayia Sofia chapel,** the Italian wives of emperors Constantine and Theodore Palaiologos are buried. Note the polychromatic marble floor and the frescoes that were preserved for years under whitewash, applied by the Turks when they transformed this into a mosque. Climb to the **castle** and look down into the gullies of Mt. Taygettus, where it's said the Spartans, who hated weakness, hurled their malformed babies. ⊠ *Ano Chora* ☎ *27310/23315* ⊕ *odysseus. culture.gr* 🎫 *€12.*

WHERE TO STAY

$$$

B&B/INN

Pyrgos of Mystras. A stone mansion set in a fragrant garden at the edge of the modern town is the setting for this stylish country retreat, where luxurious rooms, all decorated with rich colors and fabrics, overlook orange groves and Mt. Taygettus. **Pros:** beautiful decor; extremely comfortable; pleasant terrace. **Cons:** not a full-service hotel; a bit fussy for country setting; no pool. $ *Rooms from: €190* ⊠ *Manousaki 3* ☎ *27310/20870* ⊕ *www.pyrgosmystra.gr* 🛏 *7 rooms* ⦿ *Breakfast.*

UNDERSTANDING
GREECE

GREEK VOCABULARY

VOCABULARY

GREEK	ROMAN	GREEK	ROMAN
A, α	a	N, ν	n
B, β	v	Ξ, ξ	x or ks
Γ, γ	g or y	O, o	o
Δ, δ	th, dh, or d	Π, π	p
E, ε	e	P, ρ	r
Z, ζ	z	Σ, σ, ς	s
H, η	i	T, τ	t
Θ, θ	th	Y, υ	i
I, ι	i	Φ, φ	f
K, κ	k	X, χ	h or ch
Λ, λ	l	Ψ, ψ	ps
M, μ	m	Ω, ω	o

THE GREEK ABC'S

The proper names in this book are transliterated versions of the Greek name, so when you come upon signs written in the Greek alphabet, use this list to decipher them.

The phonetic spelling used in English differs somewhat from the internationalized form of Greek place names. There are no long and short vowels in Greek; the pronunciation never changes. Note, also, that the accent is a stress mark, showing where the stress is placed in pronunciation.

ENGLISH	GREEK

BASICS

ENGLISH	GREEK
Do you speak English?	Miláte angliká?
Yes, no	Málista or Né, óchi
Impossible	Adínato
Good morning, Good day	Kaliméra
Good evening, Good night	Kalispéra, Kaliníchta
Good-bye	Yá sas
Mister, Madam, Miss	Kírie, kiría, despiní
Please	Parakaló
Excuse me	Me sinchórite or signómi
How are you?	Ti kánete or pós íste
How do you do (Pleased to meet you)	Chéro polí
I don't understand.	Dén katalavéno.

ENGLISH	GREEK
To your health!	Giá sas!
Thank you	Efcharistó

NUMBERS

one	éna
two	dío
three	tría
four	téssera
five	pénde
six	éxi
seven	eptá
eight	októ
nine	enéa
ten	déka
twenty	íkossi
thirty	triánda
forty	saránda
fifty	penínda
sixty	exínda
seventy	evdomínda
eighty	ogdónda
ninety	enenínda
one hundred	ekató
two hundred	diakóssia
three hundred	triakóssia
one thousand	hília
two thousand	dió hiliádes
three thousand	trís hiliádes

DAYS OF THE WEEK

Monday	Deftéra
Tuesday	Tríti
Wednesday	Tetárti
Thursday	Pémpti
Friday	Paraskeví

ENGLISH	GREEK
Saturday	Sávato
Sunday	Kyriakí

MONTHS

January	Ianouários
February	Fevrouários
March	Mártios
April	Aprílios
May	Maíos
June	Ióunios
July	Ióulios
August	Ávgoustos
September	Septémvrios
October	Októvrios
November	Noémvrios
December	Dekémvrios

TRAVELING

I am traveling by car ...	Taxidévo mé aftokínito ... me
train ... plane ... boat.	tréno ... me aeropláno ...me vapóri.
Taxi, to the station ...	Taxí, stó stathmó ...
harbor ... airport	limáni ... aerodrómio
Porter, take the luggage.	Akthofóre, pare aftá táprámata.
Where is the filling station?	Pou íne tó vensinádiko?
When does the train leave for ... ?	Tí óra thá fíyi to tréno ya ... ?
Which is the train for ... ?	Pío íne to tréno gía ... ?
Which is the road to ... ?	Piós íne o drómos giá ... ?
A first-class ticket	Éna isitírio prótis táxis
Smoking is forbidden.	Apagorévete to kápnisma.
Where is the toilet?	Póu íne í toaléta?
Ladies, men	Ginekón, andrón
Where? When?	Póu? Póte?
Sleeping car, dining car	Wagonlí, wagonrestorán
Compartment	Vagóni

ENGLISH	GREEK
Entrance, exit	Íssodos, éxodos
Nothing to declare	Den écho típota na dilósso
I am coming for my vacation.	Érchome giá tis diakopés mou.
Nothing	Típota
Personal use	Prossopikí chríssi
How much?	Pósso?
I want to eat, to drink, to sleep.	Thélo na fáo, na pió, na kimithó.
Sunrise, sunset	Anatolí, díssi
Sun, moon	Ílios, fengári
Day, night	Méra, níchta
Morning, afternoon	Proí, mesiméri, or apóyevma
The weather is good, bad.	Ó kerós íne kalós, kakós.

ON THE ROAD

Straight ahead	Kat efthían
To the right, to the left	Dexiá, aristerá
Show me the way to …	Díxte mou to drómo …
Please	Parakaló
Where is … ?	Pou íne … ?
Crossroad	Diastávrosi
Danger	Kíndinos

IN TOWN

Will you lead me? take me?	Thélete na me odigíste? Me pérnete mazí sas?
Street, square	Drómos, platía
Where is the bank?	Pou íne i trápeza?
Far	Makriá
Police station	Astinomikó tmíma
Consulate (American, British)	Proxenío (Amerikániko, Anglikó)
Theater, cinema	Théatro, cinemá
At what time does the film start?	Tí óra archízi ee tenía?
Where is the travel office?	Pou íne to touristikó grafío?
Where are the tourist police?	Pou íne i touristikí astinomía?

ENGLISH	GREEK

SHOPPING

I would like to buy	Tha íthela na agorásso
Show me, please.	Díxte mou, parakaló.
May I look around?	Boró na ríxo miá matyá?
How much is it?	Pósso káni? (or kostízi)
It is too expensive.	Íne polí akrivó.
Have you any sandals?	Échete pédila?
Have you foreign newspapers?	Échete xénes efimerídes?
Show me that blouse, please.	Díxte mou aftí tí blouza.
Show me that suitcase.	Díxte mou aftí tí valítza.
Envelopes, writing paper	Fakélous, hartí íli
Roll of film	Film
Map of the city	Hárti tis póleos
Something handmade	Hiropíito
Wrap it up, please.	Tilixteto, parakaló.
Cigarettes, matches, please.	Tsigára, spírta, parakaló.
Ham	Zambón
Sausage, salami	Loukániko, salami
Sugar, salt, pepper	Záchari, aláti, pipéri
Grapes, cherries	Stafília, kerássia
Apple, pear, orange	Mílo, achládi, portokáli
Bread, butter	Psomí, voútiro
Peach, figs	Rodákino, síka

AT THE HOTEL

A good hotel	Éna kaló xenodochío
Have you a room?	Échete domátio?
Where can I find a furnished room?	Pou boró na vró epiploméno domátio?
A single room, double room	Éna monóklino, éna díklino
With bathroom	Me bánio
How much is it per day?	Pósso kostízi tin iméra?
A room overlooking the sea	Éna domátio prós ti thálassa
For one day, for two days	Giá miá méra, giá dió méres

ENGLISH	GREEK
For a week	Giá miá evdomáda
My name is ...	Onomázome ...
My passport	Tó diavatirió mou
What is the number of my room?	Piós íne o arithmós tou domatíou mou?
The key, please.	To klidí, parakaló.
Breakfast, lunch, supper	Proinó, messimergianó, vradinó
The bill, please.	To logariasmó, parakaló.
I am leaving tomorrow.	Févgo ávrio.

AT THE RESTAURANT

Waiter	Garsón
Where is the restaurant?	Pou íne to estiatório?
I would like to eat.	Tha íthela na fáo.
The menu, please.	To katálogo, parakaló.
Fixed-price menu	Menú
Soup	Soúpa
Bread	Psomí
Hors d'oeuvre	Mezédes, orektiká
Ham omelet	Omelétta zambón
Chicken	Kotópoulo
Roast pork	Psitó hirinó
Beef	Moschári
Potatoes (fried)	Patátes (tiganités)
Tomato salad	Domatosaláta
Vegetables	Lachaniká
Watermelon, melon	Karpoúzi, pepóni
Desserts, pastry	Gliká or pástes
Fruit, cheese, ice cream	Fróuta, tirí, pagotó
Fish, eggs	Psári, avgá
Serve me on the terrace.	Na mou servírete sti tarátza.
Where can I wash my hands?	Pou boró na plíno ta héria mou?
Red wine, white wine	Kokivó krasí, áspro krasí
Unresinated wine	Krasí aretsínato

ENGLISH	GREEK
Beer, soda water, water, milk	Bíra, sóda, neró, gála
Greek coffee	Ellenikó kafé
Coffee with milk, without	Kafé gallikó me, gála skéto
sugar, medium, sweet	métrio, glikó

AT THE BANK, AT THE POST OFFICE

Where is the bank?	Pou íne i trápeza?
post office	to tachidromío
I would like to cash a check.	Thélo ná xargiróso mía epitagí.
Stamps	Grammatóssima
By airmail	Aëroporikós
Postcard, letter	Kárta, grámma
Letterbox	Tachidromikó koutí
I would like to telephone.	Thélo na tilephonísso.

AT THE GARAGE

Garage, gas (petrol)	Garáz, venzíni
Oil	Ládi
Change the oil.	Aláksete to ládi.
Look at the tires.	Rixte mia matiá sta lástika.
Wash the car.	Plínete to aftokínito.
Breakdown	Vlávi
Tow the car.	Rimúlkiste tó aftokínito.
Spark plugs	Buzí
Brakes	Fréna
Gearbox	Kivótio tachitíton
Carburetor	Karbiratér
Headlight	Provoléfs
Starter	Míza
Axle	Áksonas
Shock absorber	Amortisér
Spare part	Antalaktikó

TRAVEL SMART
GREECE

GETTING HERE AND AROUND

■ AIR TRAVEL

Flying time to Athens is 3½ hours from London, 10½ hours from New York, 12 hours from Chicago, 16½ hours from Los Angeles, and 19 hours from Sydney.

There are only four nonstop flights from the United States to Athens, on Delta (from New York–JFK), American Airlines (from Philadelphia), United (from Newark–EWR), and Emirates (from New York–JFK). There are five nonstop routes from Canada, on Air Canada (from both Toronto and Montreal) and on Air Transat (from Toronto, Montreal, and Calgary). Therefore, most U.S. travelers will need to connect in an airport in Europe; further, most travelers originating in the United States will need to transfer in Athens to reach any other destination in Greece. There is a large number of charter flights, especially from Northern Europe, that fly directly to resort destinations in Greece during the high season. Nevertheless, many discount carriers fly from (mostly) secondary airports in Europe nonstop to Greece, and these flights may be relevant, particularly for those travelers who plan to visit another country in addition to Greece.

Strikes, either for several hours or days, can be a sporadic problem in Greece, so it's always a good idea to keep your eyes on the local headlines while traveling. Athens International Airport (Eleftherios Venizelos) posts real-time flight information on its website (*see Airports, below*). You can contact the Hellenic Civil Aviation Authority at the main Athens airport if you have complaints or concerns about flight cancellations or flight delays or are denied boarding.

Airline Security Issues Transportation Security Administration. ☎ 866/289–9673 ⊕ www.tsa.gov.

Air Travel Resources in Greece Hellenic Civil Aviation Authority. ✉ Vas. Georgiou 1, Glyfada ☎ 210/891–6000 weekdays 9–2 ⊕ www.hcaa.gr.

AIRPORTS

Athens International Airport at Spata, 33 km (20 miles) southeast of the city center, opened in 2001 as the country's main airport. Officially named Eleftherios Venizelos, after Greece's first prime minister, the airport is modern and quite user-friendly (there's also a very nice, albeit expensive, Sofitel if you need to stay over). The main terminal building has two levels: upper for departures, ground level for arrivals. Unless you are flying directly to one of the islands, you'll likely pass through the Athens airport during your trip to Greece. It's quite easy to switch from international to domestic flights or get to Greece's main harbor, Piraeus, about a one-hour train ride south of the airport. Greece's second-largest city has another busy international airport: Thessaloniki Makedonia Airport, which handles both international and domestic flights. So does the airport on Rhodes (in the Dodecanese islands). Two other airports, in Heraklion and Corfu, also have a large number of international flights. Airports on many smaller islands (Santorini, Mykonos, Karpathos, Kos, and Paros among them) receive international charter flights during the busier summer months.

Contacts Athens International Airport– Eleftherios Venizelos (*ATH*). ✉ End of Attiki Odos, Spata ☎ 210/353–0000 flight information and customer service, 210/353–0515 lost and found ⊕ www.aia.gr. **Heraklion International Airport–Nikos Kazantzakis** (*HER*). ☎ 2810/397800, 2810/397368 lost property. **Kerkyra Airport–Ioannis Kapodistrias** (*CFU*). ✉ Anapafseos 1, Corfu Town ☎ 26610/89600. **Rhodes International Airport Diagoras** (*RHO*). ☎ 22410/88700 ⊕ www.rhodes-airport.org. **Thessaloniki International Airport–Makedonia** (*SKG*). ✉ Kalamaria ☎ 2310/985000 ⊕ www.thessalonikiairport.com.

GROUND TRANSPORTATION

See the respective destination chapters for detailed information on airport transfers. While both Athens and Thessaloniki have public transportation, other places in Greece, especially the islands, do not.

FLIGHTS

In addition to Delta, American, United, and Emirates (and Air Canada and Air Transat from Canada), many carriers offer one-stop connections to major destinations in Greece (but particularly Athens) from the United States. And most of the larger European airlines, including Air France, British Airways, KLM, and Lufthansa, also offer code-share flights with their U.S. partners. Some European budget carriers, including EasyJet and Ryanair, offer flights to a wide range of destinations throughout Greece.

FLIGHTS WITHIN GREECE

In Greece, when faced with a boat journey of six hours or more, consider flying since domestic flights have good prices for many destinations. The frequency of flights varies according to the time of year (with an increase between Greek Easter and November), and it is essential to book well in advance for summer or for festivals and holidays, especially on three-day weekends. There is usually a fee to check bags; only hand luggage (with strictly enforced limits) is free.

Scheduled domestic air travel in Greece is provided by Aegean Airlines and its subsidiary Olympic Air (both of which operate out of Athens International Airport in Spata), Astra Airlines and Ellinair (which fly from Thessaloniki), and Sky Express (which has a more diffuse network of flights around Greece). Aegean Airlines and Olympic Air have the largest route network around Greece, with flights to virtually every destination you might need, with the best connections through Athens. If you fly into Athens, you'll be able to transfer quite easily to a domestic flight.

Contacts Aegean Airlines. ☎ 801/112–0000 toll-free in Greece, 210/626–1000 from abroad/mobile phones, 855/323–4326 U.S. only ⊕ www.aegeanair.com. **Air Canada.** ☎ 888/247–2262 toll-free for U.S. and Canada ⊕ www.aircanada.com. **Air France.** ☎ 800/237–2747 in the U.S. ⊕ www.airfrance. us. **Air Transat.** ☎ 877/872–6728 ⊕ www. airtransat.com. **Alitalia.** ☎ 06/656–49 ⊕ www. alitalia.com. **American Airlines.** ☎ 800/433–7300 in U.S. and Canada (24 hrs) ⊕ www. aa.com. **Astra Airlines.** ☎ 2310/489391 ⊕ www.astra-airlines.gr. **British Airways.** ☎ 800/247–9297 in the U.S. ⊕ www.britishairways.com. **Delta Airlines.** ☎ 800/241–4141 international reservations in the U.S., 210/998–0090 in Greece, 210/353–0116 office at El. Venizelos Airport ⊕ www.delta. com. **easyJet.** ☎ 0033/365–5000 in the U.K., 211/198–0013 in Athens ⊕ www.easyjet.com. **Ellinair.** ☎ 2311/224–700 in Greece ⊕ www. ellinair.com. **Emirates.** ☎ 800/777–3999 toll-free reservations in the U.S. (24 hrs) ⊕ www. emirates.com. **Iberia Airlines.** ☎ 800/772–4642, 211/198–0095 in Athens ⊕ www. iberia.com. **Jet2.com.** ☎ 203/059–8336 in the U.K. ⊕ www.jet2.com. **KLM Royal Dutch Airlines.** ☎ 211/180–9473 in Athens ⊕ www. klm.com. **LOT.** ☎ 213/038–2141 in Athens, 212/789–0970 in the U.S. ⊕ www.lot.com. **Lufthansa.** ☎ 800/645–3880 in the U.S., 210/617–5200 in Athens ⊕ www.lufthansa. com. **Monarch Airlines.** ☎ 0333/003–1793 in the U.K. ⊕ www.monarch.co.uk. **Norwegian.** ☎ 800/357–4159 in the U.S. ⊕ www. norwegian.com. **Olympic Air.** ☎ 210/355–0500 in Athens, 801/80110101 toll-free within Greece, 210/355–0500 El. Venizelos Airport desk ⊕ www.olympicair.com. **Qatar Airways.** ☎ 210/950–8700 in Athens ⊕ www.qatarairways.com. **Royal Jordanian.** ☎ 210/924–2600 in Athens ⊕ www.rj.com. **Ryanair.** ☎ 871/246–0002 in the U.K. (fee per min) calling from U.S. ⊕ www.ryanair.com. **SAS Scandanavian Airlines.** ☎ 210/961–8411 in Greece ⊕ www.flysas.com. **Sky Express.** ☎ 28102/23800 ⊕ www.skyexpress.gr. **Swiss International Airlines.** ☎ 877/359–7947 in the U.S., 210/617–5320 in Athens, 210/353–0382 in Athens airport ⊕ www.swiss.com. **Tarom.** ☎ 21/204–6464 in Romania ⊕ www. tarom.ro. **United Airlines.** ☎ 800/864–3331 ⊕ www.united.com.

■ BOAT AND FERRY TRAVEL

Ferries, catamarans, and hydrofoils make up an essential part of the national transport system of Greece, reaching every inhabited island. There are fast and slow boats and ferries that are more modern than others. When choosing a ferry, take into account the number of stops and the estimated arrival time. Sometimes a ferry that leaves an hour later gets you there faster.

With so many private companies operating, so many islands to choose from, and complicated timetables—and with departures changing not just by season but also by day of the week—the most sensible way to arrange island-hopping is to select the islands you would like to visit, then consult a travel agent to ask how your journey can be put together. Dolphin Hellas, a full-service tour and travel company based in Athens *(see Travel Agents)*, has a unique online portal to view various schedules and purchase ferry tickets.

If the boat journey will be more than a couple of hours, it's a good idea to take along water and snacks. Greek fast-food franchises operate on most ferries, charging high prices. On longer trips ferries have both cafeteria-style and full-service restaurants.

Ferries may be delayed by weather conditions, especially when the northern winds called *meltemia* hit in August, so stay flexible—one advantage of not buying a ticket in advance. If your ship's departure is delayed for any reason (with the exception of force majeure), you have the right to stay on board in the class indicated on your ticket or, in case of prolonged delay, to cancel your ticket for a full refund. If you miss your ship, you forfeit your ticket; if you cancel in advance, you receive a partial or full refund, depending on how far in advance you cancel.

Websites like ⊕ *www.ferries.gr*, ⊕ *www.viva.gr*, and ⊕ *www.greekferries.gr* are also quite helpful to check schedules and book tickets.

MAJOR FERRY PORTS

Of the major ferry ports in Greece, Piraeus, Rafina, and Lavrion are fairly well connected to Athens by bus, and the latter two are close enough to the Athens airport in Spata to be reached by taxi and KTEL buses. For the Cycladic, Dodecanese, and Ionian islands, small ferry companies operate local routes that are not published nationally; passage can be booked through travel agents on the islands served.

PIRAEUS

Greece's largest and busiest port is Piraeus, which lies 10 km (6 miles) south of Central Athens, at the end of metro Line 1, which is close to gates E5 and E6. The train ride from Central Athens takes about 25 minutes, and you can board at Thisseion, Monastiraki, or Omonia; change at Monastiraki if you get on or want to go to Syntagma.

A taxi can take longer than the metro and will cost around €20. Often, drivers wait until they fill their taxi with debarking passengers headed in roughly the same direction, which leads to a longer, more circuitous route to accommodate everyone's destination. It's often faster to walk to the main street and hail a passing cab. Expect the new taxi apps such as Uber and Taxibeat to offer better reduced rates (about €15 from Central Athens to the port of Piraeus).

From Piraeus you can reach the Saronic islands (Aegina, Hydra, Poros, Angistri, and Spetses); Peloponnesian ports (Hermioni and Porto Heli); the Cyclades (Amorgos, Folegandros, Anafi, Ios, Milos, Mykonos, Naxos, Paros, Santorini, Serifos, Sifnos, Syros, and Tinos); and the northern Aegean islands (Samos, Ikaria, Mytileni, and Chios).

Be aware that Piraeus port is so vast that you may need to walk some distance to your gate (quay) of departure once you arrive, so be sure to arrive with plenty of time to spare. Changes may occur at the last moment. Just confirm at an information kiosk. Usually, the gates serve the following destinations:

E1 the Dodecanese

E2 Crete, Chios, Mytilini (Lesvos), Ikaria, Samos

E3 Crete, Kithira

E4 Kithira

E5 Main pedestrian entrance

E6 Cyclades, Rethymnon (Crete)

E7 Cyclades, Rethymnon (Crete)

E8 Saronic islands

E9 Cyclades, Samos, Ikaria

E10 Cyclades, Samos, Ikaria

RAFINA

From Greece's second-busiest port, which is 35 km (22 miles) northeast of Athens, you can reach Evia (Euboea) daily, as well as some of the Cyclades (Mykonos, Paros, Tinos, Santorini, Naxos, Ios, and Andros). Ferry timetables change in winter and summer, and special sailings are often added around holiday weekends in summer when demand is high.

To get to Attica's second port, Rafina, take a KTEL bus, which leaves approximately every half hour (or every 15 minutes during rush hour; inquire about their schedule before your departure). Usually KTEL buses run from 5:30 am to 9:30 pm from Aigyptou Square near Pedion Areos park, which is within walking distance from the Viktoria (green line) station. The KTEL bus takes about an hour to get to Rafina; the port is slightly downhill from the bus station. There is also a KTEL bus that connects the port of Rafina to the El. Venizelos Airport about 20 km (12 miles) away. The journey takes about 30 minutes and costs €3. Buses depart from the airport every hour and the bus stop is located between exits 2 and 3 at the Arrivals level (opposite Sofitel hotel).

From Athens, it's also possible to take a taxi (a 40-minute trip), but it is fairly expensive.

LAVRION

From the port of Lavrion, 61 km (38 miles) southeast of Athens and close to Sounion, you can reach Kea (Tzia) and Kythnos, and (less regularly) Syros, Mykonos, Paros, Naxos, Anafi, Ios, Sikinos, Folegandros, Kimolos, Milos, Tinos, Andros, Ag. Efstratios, Limnos, Kavala, and Alexandroupolis. There are hourly buses from the Athens airport directly to Lavrion (bus change at Markopoulo), or it's about 35 to 40 minutes by taxi.

PATRAS

From Patras, on the western coast of the Peloponnese, 210 km (130 miles) west of Athens, you can reach Italy (Ancona, Bari, Brindisi, Ravenna, Trieste, and Venice) as well as the Ionian islands (Corfu, Ithaki, Paxoi, and Kefalonia). The drive from Athens takes about three hours.

KILLINI

From Killini, 73 km (45 miles) south of Patras, you can reach the Ionian islands of Kefalonia and Zakynthos.

IGOUMENITSA

From Igoumenitsa, on Greece's northwest coast 482 km (300 miles), you can reach Italy (Ancona, Bari, Brindisi, Ravenna, Trieste, and Venice) and Corfu (several ferries daily). Given its distance from Athens, it is generally more realistic to fly.

OTHER PORTS

From northern mainland towns of **Kavala** and **Alexandroupolis** you can reach the Dodecanese islands of Limnos, Samothrace (Samothraki), Lesvos, Samos, and Thassos.

From **Agios Konstantinos, Volos,** or **Thessaloniki** you can reach the Sporades islands of Alonissos, Skiathos, and Skopelos. Thessaloniki also has frequent seasonal connections to Mykonos and Santorini.

From **Kimi,** on the east coast of Evia, you can reach Skyros, Skopelos, And Alonissos.

From **Heraklion** you can reach the islands of Mykonos, Paros, Naxos, Ios, Santorini, Karpathos, Rhodes, Kasos, Anafi, Chalki, and Milos (summer only).

Contacts **Agios Konstantinos Port Authority.** ☎ 22350/31759. **Igoumenitsa Port Authority.** ☎ 26650/99300 ⊕ www.olig. gr. **Kimi Port Authority.** ☎ 22220/22606 ⊕ www.olne.gr. **Lavrion Port Authority.** ☎ 22920/27711, 22920/22089 ⊕ www.oll. gr. **Patras Port Authority.** ☎ 2613/615400 ⊕ www.patrasport.gr. **Piraeus Port Authority.** ☎ 210/455-0000 ⊕ www.olp.gr. **Rafina Port Authority.** ☎ 22940/23605, 22940/22840 ⊕ www.rafinaport.gr. **Thessaloniki Port Authority.** ☎ 2310/593118, 2310/593121 ⊕ www.thpa.gr. **Volos Port Authority.** ☎ 24210/31888, 2410/32975 ⊕ www.port-volos.gr.

BUYING FERRY TICKETS

It's best to buy your ticket at least two or three days ahead if you are traveling between July 15 and August 30, when most Greeks vacation, if you need a cabin (good for long trips), or if you are taking a car. If possible, don't travel by boat around August 15, when most ferries are very crowded. The ferry schedule systems are fairly seasonal, so by the end of April it is usually possible to book tickets for the busy summer months.

You can buy tickets from a travel agency or *praktoreio* at the port, online through travel websites (popular sites include ⊕ *www.directferries.gr,* ⊕ *www.greekferries.gr,* and ⊕ *www.ferries.gr*). Although you can also buy tickets directly from the ferry company offices and websites, it's usually easier to use a travel agent. Last-minute tickets can always be purchased from a ferry company kiosk at every port. Always book your return upon arrival if you are pressed for time. You can also buy ferry tickets from ⊕ *www.viva.gr,* which is a comprehensive, multilingual, ticket-selling website in Greece.

Generally you can pay by either credit card or cash. On islands the local office of each shipping line posts a board with departure times.

FERRY TYPES

Greek ferries can be either slow or fast. On longer trips, the experience is a bit like a minicruise. You can relax on board, enjoy the sea views, snap photos from the deck at ports of call (there may be multiple calls on some routes) and as you approach your destination. Slow ferries from Piraeus to Lesvos, Rhodes, Crete, and Santorini can last eight hours or more, so there's also the option to rent a cabin for the journey that may run overnight.

If boat rides equal boredom for you, high-speed ferries, catamarans, and hydrofoils (seajets)—or in Greek *iptamena delphinia* (flying dolphins)—are a pricier option that cuts travel time in half. Catamarans are the larger of these fast ferries, with more space to move around, although passengers are not allowed outside when the boat is not docked. If the sea is choppy, these boats often cannot travel. Although they are faster, they lack the flavor of the older ferries with the open decks.

Schedules vary between both the slower and faster boats. It's best to check what fits your time frame and budget.

INTERNATIONAL FERRIES

From Greece you can opt to travel to neighboring Italy and Turkey. Travel time to Turkey from most destinations in Greece is relatively short, usually less than 90 minutes. Travel to various stops in Italy can take from 9 to 21 hours.

TRAVEL TO TURKEY

You can cross to Turkey from the northeastern Aegean islands. The journey takes anywhere from one hour to 90 minutes, depending on the destination. Ferries sail between the Greek islands of Rhodes, Kos, Samos, Simi, Chios, and Lesvos to the Turkish destinations of Bodrum, Marmaris, Kusadasi, Turgutreis, Datca, Fethiye, Dikely, Ayvalik, and Cesme.

Note that British and American passport holders must pay $20 or €18 to obtain an Electronic Visa for visiting Turkey. New Zealanders don't need a visa. Canadian and Australian citizens need to pay $60 or

€53. The Electronic Visa (e-Visa) Application System was launched in 2013 by the Turkish Ministry of Foreign Affairs and has now become mandatory for port entry (some airports still provide sticker visas at border crossings). This system allows visitors traveling to Turkey to obtain their e-Visas online in advance (⊕ *www. evisa.gov.tr*). The online application process takes approximately three minutes. Just be aware that visa rules can change, so you should always verify the current requirements before you decide to make a last-minute trip to Turkey from Greece.

Ferry lines that sail between Greece and Turkey include the following: Erturk, Turyol, Marmaris Ferry, Meander Travel, SeaDreams, Bodrum Ferryboat, Dodecanese Flying Dolphins, Tuana Maritime, Dodecanisos Seaways, and Yesil Marmaris Lines.

TRAVEL TO ITALY

There are also frequent ferries between Greece and Italy. From Igoumenitsa, Patras, Zante, and Corfu you can find ferries that head to Ancona, Bari, Brindisi, Trieste, and Venice. The fastest ferry crossing is from Corfu to Otranto in Italy, which takes about 2½ hours with Liberty Lines.

The most respected and competitively priced is Minoan Lines (which is now a subsidiary of Italy's Grimaldi Lines). Its modern, well-maintained vessels are outfitted with bars, a self-service restaurant, a pool, a spa, a gym, an Internet café, a casino, shops, and even a conference center.

Prices depend on the season and your class of service (deck, seat, or cabin). High season runs from mid-July to late August; prices drop considerably in low and middle season. Some companies offer special family or group discounts, while others charge extra for pets or offer deep discounts on return tickets, so comparing rates does pay. When booking, also consider when you will be traveling; an overnight trip can be offset against hotel costs, and you will spend more on incidentals like food and drink when traveling during the day.

Ferry lines that sail between Greece and Italy include the following: Anek, Blue Star Ferries, European Seaways, Minoan Lines, Superfast Ferries, Grimaldi Lines, Liberty Lines, and Ventouris.

Ferry Lines Aegean Flying Dolphins. ☎ 210/422–1766 in Athens ⊕ www. aegeanflyingdolphins.gr. **Aegean Speed Lines.** ☎ 210/969–0950 in Athens ⊕ www. aegeanspeedlines.gr. **Alpha Ferries.** ☎ 210/452–9330 in Athens ⊕ www.alphaferries.gr. **Anek Lines.** ☎ 210/419–7400 phone bookings, 210/419–7470 phone bookings, 210/419–7420 customer service ⊕ www.anek. gr. **ANEM Ferries.** ☎ 22420/59124 ⊕ www. anem.gr. **ANEN Lines.** ☎ 2810/346185 ⊕ www.ferries.gr/anen-lines. **Anes Ferries.** ☎ 210/523–7613 phone bookings ⊕ www. anes.gr. **Blue Star Ferries.** ☎ 210/891–9800 in Athens, 210/891–9010 customer service in Athens ⊕ www.bluestarferries.gr. **Bodrum Ferryboat.** ☎ 252/316–0882 in Bodrum ⊕ www.bodrumferryboat.com. **Dodecanese Flying Dolphins.** ☎ 22410/37401 in Rhodes, Greece ⊕ www.12fd.eu. **Dodecanisos Seaways.** ☎ 22410/70590 in Rhodes ⊕ www.12ne.gr. **Erturk Lines.** ☎ 232/712–6768 in Cesme, Turkey ⊕ www.erturk.com. tr. **European Seaways.** ☎ 210/956–1630 in Athens ⊕ www.europeanseaways.com. **Fast Ferries.** ☎ 210/418–2005 phone bookings ⊕ www.fastferries.com.gr. **Golden Star Ferries.** ☎ 80122/24000 in Greece, 212/222–4000 from abroad ⊕ www.golden-starferries.gr. **Grimaldi Lines.** ☎ 081/496444 in Naples ⊕ www.grimaldi-lines.com. **Hellenic Seaways.** ☎ 210/419–9000 ticket information in Athens ⊕ www.hellenicseaways.gr. **Ionian Group.** ☎ 210/949–9400 phone bookings ⊕ www.ioniangroup.com. **Lane Sea Lines.** ☎ 2736/037055 bookings ⊕ www.lane-kithira. com. **Liberty Lines.** ☎ 0923/873–813 ⊕ www. libertylines.it. **Marmaris Ferry.** ☎ 252/413–0230 in Turkey ⊕ www.marmarisferry.com. **Meander Travel.** ☎ 256/612–8888 in Turkey ⊕ www.meandertravel.com. **Minoan Lines.** ☎ 2810/399899 bookings, 801/11–75000 in Greece ⊕ www.minoan.gr. **SAOS Ferries.**

☎ 22510/38503 ⊕ www.saos.gr. **Saronic Ferries.** ☎ 210/411–7341 in Athens ⊕ www.saronicferries.gr. **Sea Dreams–Aegean Shipping Company.** ☎ 22410/74535 in Rhodes ⊕ www.seadreams.gr. **Seajets.** ☎ 210/412–0001 in Athens, 210/412–1901 in Athens ⊕ www.seajets.gr. **Skyros Shipping Company.** ☎ 22220/92164 ⊕ www.sne.gr. **Strinzis Ferries.** ☎ 210/422–5000 in Athens ⊕ www.strintzisferries.gr. **Superfast Ferries.** ☎ 210/891–9800 bookings in Greece ⊕ www.superfast.gr. **Tuana Maritime.** ☎ 252/612–4242 in Turkey ⊕ www.tuanmaritime.com. **Turyol.** ☎ 266/331–67000 in Turkey ⊕ www.turyolonline.com. **2 Way Ferries.** ☎ 210/625–0131 ⊕ www.2wayferries.gr. **Ventouris Ferries.** ☎ 210/482–8001 through 210/482–8004 in Athens ⊕ www.ventourisferries.com. **Yesil Marmaris Lines.** ☎ 252/412–2290 in Turkey ⊕ www.yesilmarmarislines.com.

▮ BUS TRAVEL

For information on guided bus tours, see Tours in the Planning section of individual chapters.

Greece's nationwide bus network is extensive, with routes to even the most far-flung villages. It's divided into a fairly reliable regional bus system (KTEL) made up of local operators. Buses from Athens travel throughout the country, and other Greek cities have connections to towns and villages in their own regions. Routes are listed on KTEL's website, but unless you speak Greek or know someone who does, it won't make sense. If you plan to visit Thessaloniki, you can visit the Macedonia KTEL site ⊕ www.ktelmacedonia.gr, which has an English-language version that will enable you to plan your bus trip and purchase the ticket online. In most other cities you will need to head to the main KTEL terminal to inquire about schedules and rates. In Thessaloniki there is also a downtown ticket office at 119 Egnatia Street (more info on website).

BUYING TICKETS

There is no centralized website in English to buy KTEL tickets in advance, though most regional KTEL networks now have their own informative websites (and some of them sell tickets online, too). It's easiest to purchase your bus tickets in person at the KTEL station or on the bus. Reservations are unnecessary on most routes, especially those with several round-trips a day. If you are traveling on holiday weekends, it's best to go to the station and buy your ticket a couple of days in advance. To give you a sense of costs and schedules, the bus from Athens to Corinth costs €9 and takes about 1 hour (no e-ticket yet through this website ⊕ *www.ktelkorinthias.gr*); to Nafplion, €14.40 (e-ticket available at ⊕ *www.ktelargolida.gr*), 2½ hours; to Patras, €20.70, 2½–3 hours (e-ticket available but unfortunately their website ⊕ *www.ktelachaias.gr* does not have an English version yet); and to Thessaloniki, €45, 6 hours 15 minutes.

CATCH YOUR BUS

Athens has three bus stations. In Athens, KTEL's Terminal A is the arrival and departure point for bus lines to northern Greece, including Thessaloniki, and to the Peloponnese destinations of Epidauros, Mycenae, Nafplion, and Corinth. Terminal B serves Evia, most of Thrace, and central Greece, including Delphi. Most KTEL buses to the east Attica coast—including those for Sounion, Marathon, and the ports of Lavrion and Rafina—leave from the downtown KTEL terminal near Pedion Areos park.

The buses, which are punctual, span the range from slightly dilapidated to luxurious and air-conditioned with upholstered seats. There is just one class of ticket. Board early, because Greeks have a loose attitude about assigned seating, and ownership counts here. Although smoking is forbidden on KTEL buses, the driver will stop every two hours or so at a roadside establishment; smokers can light up then.

PUBLIC TRANSPORTATION BUSES

In large cities, you can buy individual tickets for urban buses at terminal booths, convenience stores, or at selected *periptera* (street kiosks). *See our Athens chapter Getting Here and Around section for information on the city's convenient multiday transportation passes (good for buses, trolleys, and the metro).*

Bus Information KTEL. ⊕ *www.ktelbus.com.*

Athens Bus Stations Downtown Athens KTEL terminal. ✉ *Aigyptou Sq., Mavromateon and Leoforos Alexandras, near Pedion Areos park, Athens* ☎ *210/880–8080, 210/818–0221* ⊕ *www.ktelattikis.gr.* **Terminal A–KTEL Kifissou.** ✉ *Kifissou 100, Kolonos* ☎ *210/512–4910.* **Terminal B–KTEL Liossion.** ✉ *Rikaki 6, Kato Patissia* ☎ *210/831–7186.*

▌ CAR TRAVEL

Road conditions in Greece have improved in the last decade, yet driving in Greece still presents certain challenges. In Athens, traffic is mind-boggling most of the time and parking is scarce, so public transportation or taxis are much better options than a rental car. If you are traveling by ferry, taking along a car will increase your ticket costs substantially and limit your ease in hopping onto any ferry (fast ferries do not accommodate cars). On islands, you can always rent a taxi or a car for the day if you want to see something distant, and domestic flights are fairly cheap, especially if you book well in advance. The only real reason to drive is if it's your passion, if you are a large party with many suitcases and many out-of-the-way places to see, or if you need the freedom to change routes and make unexpected stops not permitted on public transportation.

DOCUMENTS

International driving permits (IDPs), required for drivers who are not citizens of an EU country, are available from the American, Australian, Canadian, and New Zealand automobile associations. These international permits, valid only in conjunction with your regular driver's license, are universally recognized; having one may save you a problem with local authorities.

GASOLINE

Gas pumps and service stations are everywhere, and lead-free gas is widely available. Nevertheless, away from the main towns, especially at night, open gas stations can be very far apart *(see Hours of Operation, below).* Don't let your gas supply drop to less than a quarter tank when driving through rural areas. Gas costs about €1.50 a liter for unleaded ("ah- *mo*-lee-vdee"), €1.25 a liter for diesel ("*dee*-zel"). Prices may vary by as much as €0.50 per liter from one region to another, but a price ceiling has been imposed on gas prices during the busy summer months in popular tourist destinations. You aren't usually allowed to pump your own gas, though you can do everything else yourself. If you ask the attendant to give you extra service (check oil, air, and water or clean the windows), leave a small tip. Gas stations are now required by law to issue receipts, so make sure you pick up yours from the attendant. The word is *apodiksi.* Credit cards are usually accepted at big gas stations (BP, Shell, Elinoil, EKO, Avin, Aegean, Revoil, etc.), less so at stations found in remote areas.

INSURANCE

In general, auto insurance is not as expensive as in other countries. You must have third-party car insurance to drive in Greece. If possible, get an insurance "green card" valid for Greece from your insurance company before arriving. You can also buy a policy with local companies; keep the papers in a plastic pocket on the inside right front windshield. To get more information, or to locate a local representative for your insurance company, call the Hellenic Union of Insurance Firms/Motor Insurance Bureau.

Contacts Hellenic Union of Insurance Firms/Motor Insurance Bureau. ✉ *Xenofontos 10, Athens* ☎ *210/333–41000* ⊕ *www.eaee.gr.*

PARKING

The scarcity of parking spaces in Athens is one good reason not to drive in the city. Although a number of carparks operate in the city center and near suburban metro stations, these aren't enough to accommodate demand. They can also be quite expensive, with prices starting at €6 for an hour. Pedestrians are often frustrated by cars parked on sidewalks, and police have become stricter about ticketing. "Controlled parking" zones in some downtown districts like Kolonaki, Pangrati, and Acropolis have introduced some order to the chaotic system; a one-hour card costs €2, with a maximum of three hours permitted (for a total cost of €6). Buy a parking card from the kiosk and display it inside your windshield. Be careful not to park in the spots reserved for residents, even if you have a parking card, as you may find your license plates mischievously gone when you return!

Outside Athens, the situation is slightly better. Many villages, towns, and islands have designated free parking areas just outside the center where you can leave your car.

ROAD CONDITIONS

Driving defensively is the key to safety in Greece, one of the most hazardous European countries for motorists. In the cities and on the highways, the streets can be riddled with potholes; motorcyclists seem to come out of nowhere, often passing on the right; and cars may even go the wrong way down a one-way street. In the countryside and on islands, you must watch for livestock crossing the road, as well as for tourists shakily learning to use rented motorcycles.

The many motorcycles and scooters weaving through traffic and the aggressive attitude of fellow motorists can make driving in Greece's large cities unpleasant—and the life of a pedestrian dangerous. Greeks often run red lights or ignore stop signs on side streets, or round corners fast without stopping. It's a good idea at night at city intersections and

at any time on curvy country lanes to beep your horn to warn errant drivers.

In cities, you will find pedestrians have no qualms about standing in the middle of a busy boulevard, waiting to dart between cars. Make eye contact so you can both determine who's going to slow. Rush hour in the cities runs from 7 to 10 am and 1:30 to 3:30 pm on weekdays, plus 8 to 10 pm on Tuesday, Thursday, and Friday. Saturday morning brings bumper-to-bumper traffic in shopping districts, and weekend nights guarantee crowding around nightlife hubs. In Athens, the only time you won't find traffic is very early morning and most of Sunday (unless you're foolish enough to stay at a local beach until evening in summer, which means heavy end-of-weekend traffic when you return). Finally, perhaps because they are untrained, drivers seldom pull over for wailing ambulances; the most they'll do is slow down and slightly move over in different directions.

Highways are color-coded: green for the new, toll roads and blue for old national roads. Tolls are usually €2.50–€4. The older routes are slower and somewhat longer, but they follow more-scenic routes, so driving is more enjoyable. The national roads can be very slick in places when wet—avoid driving in rain and on the days preceding or following major holidays, when traffic is at its worst as urban dwellers leave for villages.

ROADSIDE EMERGENCIES

You must put out a triangular danger sign if you have a breakdown. Roving repair trucks, owned by the major road assistance companies, such as Interamerican, Intersalonica, Mondial, Europ Assistance, etc., patrol the major highways, except the Attiki Odos, which has its own contracted road assistance company. This provides assistance for free, provided it is something that can be fairly easily repaired roadside. You can call them on ☎ 1866 in case of need. You can also call the emergency telephone line provided by the Greek Animal Friends Society ☎ 210

602–0202 if you spot a dead or wounded animal on a national road.

RULES OF THE ROAD

Remember to always buckle your seat belt when driving in Greece, as fines are very costly if you don't. Children 10 years old or younger are required to sit in the backseat. You have to be at least 18 to be able to drive in Greece. Motorcycle helmets are compulsory, though Greeks tend to ignore these rules, or comply with them by "wearing" the helmet strapped to their arms.

International road signs are in use throughout Greece. You drive on the right, pass on the left, and yield right-of-way to all vehicles approaching from the right (except on posted main highways). Cars may not make a right turn on a red light. The speed limits are 120 kph (74 mph) on a national road, 90 kph (56 mph) outside urban areas, and 50 kph (31 mph) in cities, unless lower limits are posted. But limits are often not posted, and signs indicating a lower limit may not always be visible, so if you see Greek drivers slowing down, take the cue to avoid speed traps in rural areas.

In Central Athens there is an odd-even rule to avoid traffic congestion. This rule does not apply to rental cars, provided the renter has a foreign passport. If you are renting a car, ask the rental agency about any special parking or circulation regulations in force. Although sidewalk parking is illegal, it is common. And although it's tempting as a visitor to ignore parking tickets, keep in mind that if you've surrendered your ID to the rental agency, you won't get it back until you clear up the matter. You can pay your ticket at the rental agency or local police station. Under a driving code aimed at cracking down on violations, fines start at €50 (for illegal parking in places reserved for the disabled) and can go as high as €1,200 if you fail an alcohol test; fines for running a red light or speeding are now €700, plus you have your license revoked for 60 days and your plates revoked for 20 days. If fines are paid in cash within 10 days, there is a 50% discount in the amount that you actually pay.

If you are involved in an accident, don't drive away. Accidents must be reported (something Greek motorists often fail to do) before the insurance companies consider claims. Try to get the other driver's details as soon as possible; hit-and-run is all too common in Greece. If the police take you in (they can hold you for 24 hours if there is a fatality, regardless of fault), you have the right to call your local embassy or consulate for help getting a lawyer.

DRIVING IN AND OUT OF ATHENS

Greece's two main highways, the newly redesigned Athens–Corinth and Athens–Thessaloniki (connecting through national road *Ethniki Odos* and the Attiki Odos), circulate traffic around the metropolis. Avoid using them during periods of mass exodus, such as Friday afternoon or Sunday evening. These highways and the Egnatia Odos, which goes east to west across northern Greece, along with the secondary roads, cover most of the mainland, but on islands, some areas (beaches, for example) are accessible via dirt or gravel paths. With the exception of main highways and a few flat areas like the Thessalian plain, you will average about 60 km (37 miles) an hour: expect some badly paved or disintegrating roads; stray flocks of goats; slow farm vehicles; detours; curves; and, near Athens and Thessaloniki, traffic jams. At the Athens city limits, signs in English mark the way to Syntagma and Omonia squares in the center. When you exit Athens, signs are well marked for the National Road, usually naming Lamia and Thessaloniki for the north and Corinth or Patras for the southwest.

CAR RENTAL

When you reserve a car, ask about cancellation penalties, taxes, drop-off charges (if you're planning to pick up the car in one city and leave it in another), and surcharges (for being under or over a certain age, for additional drivers, or for driving across state or country borders or beyond a specific distance from your point of rental). Don't forget to check if the rental price includes unlimited mileage. All these things can add substantially to your costs. Request car seats and extras such as GPS when you book.

Rates are sometimes—but not always—better if you book in advance or reserve through a rental agency's or an airline's website. There are other reasons to book ahead, though: for popular destinations, during busy times of the year, or to ensure that you get certain types of cars (vans, SUVs, exotic sports cars).

■ TIP➡ Make sure that a confirmed reservation guarantees you a car. Agencies sometimes overbook, particularly for busy weekends and holiday periods.

Because driving in Greece can be harrowing, car-rental prices can be higher than in the United States, and transporting a car by ferry hikes up the fare substantially. The exception is on large islands where the distance between towns is greater and taxi fares are higher; you may want to rent a car or a moped for the day for concentrated bouts of sightseeing. Official rates in Greece during high season (July–September) are much cheaper if you rent through local agents rather than the large international companies.

In summer, renting a small car with standard transmission will cost you about €230 to €340 for a week's rental (including tax, insurance, and unlimited mileage). Four-wheel-drives can cost anywhere from €100 to €180 a day, depending on availability and the season. Luxury cars are available at some agencies, such as Europcar, but renting a BMW or a Mercedes can fetch a hefty price—anywhere from €100 per day in low season to €300 a day in high season. This does include the 24% V.A.T. (V.A.T. is 17% in the islands). Convertibles ("open" cars) and minibuses are also available. Probably the most difficult car to rent, unless

you reserve from abroad, is an automatic. Note that car rental fees really follow laws of supply/demand so there can be huge fluctuations and, in low season, lots of room for bargaining. Off-season, rental agencies are often closed on islands and in less-populated areas.

If you're considering moped or motorcycle rental, which is cheaper than a car, especially for getting around on the islands, try Motorent or Andeli Mototouring, both in Athens. On the islands, independent moped rentals are available through local agents.

You can usually reduce prices by reserving a car through a major rental agency before you leave. Or opt for a midsize Greek agency and bargain for a price; you should discuss when kilometers become free. These agencies provide good service, and prices are at the owner's discretion. It helps if you have shopped around and can mention another agency's offer. If you're visiting several islands or destinations, larger agencies may be able to negotiate a better total package through their local offices or franchises. Some hotels or airlines may also have partner agencies that offer discounts to guests.

In Greece your own driver's license is not acceptable unless you are a citizen of the European Union. For non-EU citizens an international driver's permit (IDP) is necessary (see Car Travel, above). To rent, you must have had your driver's license for one year and be at least 21 years old. For some companies you need to be at least 23 years old to rent or you face additional insurance surcharges); for some car categories and for some agencies, you must be 25. Presenting a credit card is recommended for the pre-authorization of the renter's liability. You need the agency's permission to ferry the car or cross the border (Europcar does not allow across-the-border rentals). A valid driver's license is usually acceptable for renting a moped, but you will need a motorcycle driver's license if you want to rent a larger bike.

Most major car-rental agencies have several offices in Athens and also at the Athens airport, in major cities like Thessaloniki, and often throughout the country. Some apply a surcharge for delivering the vehicle at the Athens airport, where there is also usually an additional surcharge for delivering your vehicle between 11 pm and 6 am. You will need to read the General Terms and Conditions carefully to discover the particular surcharges that apply to you.

Contacts Avis. ☎ *210/687–9800 in Athens* ⊕ *www.avis.gr.* **Budget Rent a Car.** ☎ *213/021–3120 in Athens* ⊕ *www.budget. gr.* **Enterprise Rent a Car.** ☎ *210/349–9030 in Athens* ⊕ *www.enterprise.gr.* **Europcar Car Rental.** ✉ *2 Varis-Koropiou Ave. and Ifaistou* ☎ *210/973–5000* ⊕ *www.europcar-greece.gr.* **Hertz.** ☎ *210/626–4000 in Athens* ⊕ *www. hertz.gr.* **Sixt Car Rental.** ☎ *210/5770–006 in Athens* ⊕ *www.sixt.gr.*

▌ TAXI TRAVEL

In Greece, as everywhere, unscrupulous taxi drivers sometimes try to take advantage of out-of-towners. All taxis must display the rate card; it's usually on the dashboard, though taxis outside the big cities don't bother. Ask your hotel concierge or owner before engaging a taxi what the fare to your destination ought to be. It should cost between €35 and €50 from the airport (depending on whether you are traveling with Rate 1 or Rate 2 taxi charges) to the Athens city center (this includes tolls) and about €10 to €20 from Piraeus port to the center. It does not matter how many are in your party (the driver isn't supposed to squeeze in more than four); the metered price remains the same. Taxis must give passengers a receipt (*apodiksi*) if requested.

Make sure that the driver turns on the meter to Rate (Tarifa) 1 (€0.60), unless it's between midnight and 5 am, when Rate (Tarifa) 2 (€1.05) applies. Remember that the meter starts at €1.05 and the minimum is €2.80 in Athens and Thessaloniki (€3 for the rest of the country).

A surcharge applies when taking a taxi to and from the airport (€3.40) and from (but not to) ports and bus and train stations (€0.95). There is also a surcharge of €0.35 for each item of baggage that's over 10 kilograms (22 pounds). If you suspect a driver is overcharging, demand to be taken to the police station; this usually brings them around. Complaints about service or overcharging should be directed to the tourist police; at the Athens airport, contact the Taxi Syndicate information desk. When calling to complain, be sure to report the driver's license number.

Taxi rates are inexpensive compared to fares in most other European countries, mainly because they operate on the jitney system, indicating willingness to pick up others by blinking their headlights or slowing down. Would-be passengers shout their destination as the driver cruises past. Don't be alarmed if your driver picks up other passengers (although he should ask your permission first). Drivers rarely pick up additional passengers if you are a woman traveling alone at night. Each new party pays full fare for the distance he or she has traveled.

A taxi is available when a white-and-red sign (*eleftbero*) is up or the light is on at night. Once the driver indicates he is free, he cannot refuse your destination, so get in the taxi before you give an address. He also must wait for you up to 15 minutes, if requested, although most drivers would be unhappy with such a demand. Drivers are familiar with the major hotels, but it's good to know a landmark near your hotel and to have the address and phone number written in Greek.

You can download the popular TaxiBeat or Uber apps from home, which let you order a nearby taxi that is equipped with GPS (to easily find your destination), and choose your taxi driver based on languages spoken and customer rating. The driver will come right to your destination, recognizable by his license plates. The service is at no extra cost and is available in Athens and Thessaloniki (Athens only for Uber).

On islands and in the countryside, the meter may often be on Rate (Tarifa) 2 (outside city limits). Do not assume taxis will be waiting at smaller island airports when your flight lands; often, they have all been booked by arriving locals. If you get stuck, try to join a passenger going in your direction, or call your hotel to arrange transportation.

When you're taking an early-morning flight, it's a good idea to reserve a radio taxi the night before, for an additional charge of €3 to €5 (depending on whether it is daytime or night tariff). These taxis are usually quite reliable and punctual; if you're not staying in a hotel, the local tourist police can give you some phone numbers for companies. Taxis charge €9.60 per hour of waiting.

Taxi Complaints in Athens Taxi Syndicate. ☎ 210/523-6904 for Greece, 210/523-9524 for Attica (incl. Athens) ⊕ www.satataxi.gr. **Tourist police.** ☎ 1571.

▌ TRAIN TRAVEL

Traveling by train is a convenient, cost-effective, and scenic way to reach certain destinations in Greece and to connect to other European countries. The Greek Railway Organization (TrainOSE) runs the national train network and the *proastiakos* light-rail line is part of the network (⊕ *www.trainose.gr*). In Athens, the main train station is Larissis Station, off Diliyianni Street west of Omonia Square *(see Train Travel in Athens in Chapter 2 for more information)*. In Thessaloniki the station is located on Monastiriou Avenue, which is a 15-minute drive from Aristotle Square.

ABOUT TRAVEL IN GREECE

Trains are generally on time. At smaller stations, allow about 15–20 minutes for changing trains; on some routes, connecting routes are coordinated with the main line.

All trains have both first- and second-class seating. On any train, it is best during high season, around holidays, or for long distances to travel first class, with a reserved seat, as the difference between the first- and second-class coaches can be significant: the cars are cleaner, the seats are wider and plusher, and, most important, the cars are emptier.

The assigned seating of first class (*proti thesi*) is a good idea in July and August, for example, when many trains are packed with tourists. Many travelers assume that rail passes guarantee them seats on the trains they wish to ride: Not so. You need to book seats ahead even if you are using a rail pass *(see Rail Passes, below)*; seat reservations are required on some European trains, particularly high-speed trains, and are a good idea on trains that may be crowded—particularly in summer on popular routes. You also need a reservation if you purchase sleeping accommodations. On high-speed (IC) trains, you pay a surcharge (not applicable for Eurail holders) and there may be other surcharges that you might need to incur.

You can pay for all train tickets purchased in Greece with cash (euros) or with credit cards (Visa and MasterCard only). The online system is available up to 24 hours before departure at ⊕ *www.trainose.gr*. You can also book and pay by telephone. Note that any ticket issued on the train costs 50% more. You can get train schedules from TrainOSE offices and online.

POPULAR TRAIN ROUTES

The main line running north from Athens divides into two lines at Thessaloniki, continuing on to Skopje and Belgrade; and Sofia and Bucharest.

Within Greece, some popular routes include Athens to Thessaloniki, Alexandroupoli (Dikaia), Florina, Kalambaka, Volos, and Chalkida. There is also an InterCity Express service from Athens to Thessaloniki that takes four hours instead of six. At this writing, the IC train costs €42 for A class, versus €35 for B class. In Athens, the light-rail also runs regularly from the airport connecting to the

Doukissis Plakentias station, where you can change trains and continue to the city center (Metro Line 3 to Ayia Marina), using the same ticket. The service can also take you to Kiato, east of Corinth.

A few historic train lines have been kept up and continue to be popular with travelers. The one-hour journey from Diakofto to Kalavryta in the northern Peloponnese travels up a pine-crested gorge in the Peloponnese mountains. It is one of the oldest rail lines in Greece, assigned by PM Harilaos Trikoupis in 1889. The 90-minute trip aboard the steam train of Pelion departs from Ano Lehonia, stops in Ano Gatzea, and arrives in Milies, crossing breathtaking landscapes in central and northern Greece. Finally, the 45-minute journey from Katakolo to Ancient Olympia passes through Pirgos.

BUYING TICKETS

You can head to the TrainOSE website to view train schedules in English as well as to book tickets online. You can also purchase tickets in person at any train station, or by telephone. Light-rail (*Proastiakos*) tickets are available at stations and cost €1.40 for a basic ticket and €10 one-way for the airport (from Athens). Validating machines are on the platform, not on board.

Some sample train fares for popular trips include: €6.50 Athens to Chalkida, and €42 Athens to Thessaloniki (on B-class, this is the web discounted price, which is cheaper compared to buying from the ticket kiosk). First-class costs about 30% more than second-class (*thefteri thesi*).

Contacts TrainOSE Customer Service.
✉ *Karolou 1, Omonia Sq.* ☎ *210/529–7628, 14511 customer service (6 am–11 pm)* ⊕ *www. trainose.gr.*

RAIL PASSES

Greece is one of 28 countries in which you can use Eurail passes, which provide unlimited first-class rail travel, in all of the participating countries, for the duration of the pass. Trenose's current international destinations include Sofia, Skopje, Bucharest, Beograd, and Italy, where you can connect with other networks. If you plan to rack up the miles in several countries, get a standard Eurail Global Pass. These are available for 15 days of travel within two months ($846), 15 days continuous ($549), 22 days continuous ($707), one month ($866), two months ($1,221), and three months ($1,505).

In addition to standard Eurail passes, ask about special rail-pass plans. Among these are the Eurail Pass Youth (for those under age 26), the Eurail Saver Pass (which gives a discount for two or more people traveling together), and the Eurail Flexi Pass (which allows a certain number of travel days within a set period). Among those passes you might want to consider: the Greece Pass allows first-class rail travel throughout Greece; the standard three days' unlimited travel in a month costs $141 first class, and the rate rises per day of travel added. The Greece–Italy Pass gives you four days' travel time over a span of two months; the cost is $311 for first class, $251 for second. Youths (18–25 years of age) pay about 50% less, and there are special rates for groups and families.

Passes can be shipped to anywhere you are in Europe, as well as worldwide, but can't be shipped to a particular train station. Shipping is by registered mail. Residents of Canada must purchase their tickets from the Rail Europe's Canadian site at ⊕ *www.raileurope.ca.*

Rail Passes Rail Europe. ☎ *800/622–8600 in the U.S., 800/361–7245 in Canada* ⊕ *www. raileurope.com.*

ESSENTIALS

■ ACCOMMODATIONS

When it comes to making reservations, it is wise to book several months in advance for the high season, from June through August, especially when booking top-end hotels in high-profile destinations like Mykonos, Santorini, and Hydra. Accommodations may be hard to find in smaller summer resort towns in winter (when many hotels close for repairs) and at the beginning of spring.

Many hotels have reduced their prices to remain competitive in the face of the country's ongoing economic crisis. Sometimes during off-season you can bargain down the official prices even further (rumor has it to as much as a quarter of the officially quoted price). So be sure to ask if there are any additional discounts for the off-season. The response you get will depend largely on the length of your stay, the hotel's policy, and the season in question. You can also reduce the price by eliminating breakfast or by going through a booking website or local travel agency, particularly for larger hotels on major islands and in Athens and Thessaloniki. A 13% (9% in the islands) government Value-Added Tax and 0.5% municipality tax are added to all hotel bills, though usually the rate quoted includes the tax; be sure to ask. When booking, it's worth asking whether or not the hotel provides transportation from the airport/port as part of their services.

Plumbing in rooms and most low-end hotels (and restaurants, shops, and other public places) is delicate enough to require that toilet paper and other detritus be put in the wastebasket and not flushed.

The lodgings we list are the cream of the crop in each price category. When pricing accommodations, always ask what's included and what's not. Common items that may add to your basic room rate are breakfast, parking, use of certain facilities such as tennis courts, the spa, or gym, Wi-Fi, etc.

Note that some resort hotels also offer half- and full-board arrangements for part of the year. And all-inclusive resorts are mushrooming. Inquire about your options when booking.

For price charts detailing our array of hotel price categories, see Planning in every regional chapter.

HOTELS

The EOT (GNTO) authorizes the construction and classification of hotels throughout Greece. It classifies them into five categories, A–E, which govern the rates that can be charged. Ratings are based on considerations such as room size, hotel services, and amenities including the furnishing of the room. Within each category, quality varies greatly, but prices don't. Still, you may come across an A-category hotel that charges less than a B-class. The classifications can be misleading—a C-rated hotel in one town might qualify as a B in another.

For category A expect the equivalent of a five-star hotel in the United States, although the room will probably be somewhat smaller. A room in a C-class hotel can be perfectly acceptable; with a D the bathroom may or may not be shared. Ask to see the room before checking in. You can sometimes find a bargain if a hotel has just renovated but has not yet been reclassified. A great hotel may never move up to a better category just because its lobby isn't the required size.

Official prices are posted in each room, usually on the back of the door or inside the wardrobe. The room charge varies over the course of the year, peaking in the high season when breakfast or half-board (at hotel complexes) may also be obligatory.

A hotel may ask for a deposit of the first night's stay or up to 25% of the room rate. If you cancel your reservations at least 21 days in advance, you are entitled to a full refund of your deposit.

Unless otherwise noted, *in this guide*, hotels have air-conditioning (*klimatismo*), room TVs, and private bathrooms (*banio*). Bathrooms mostly contain showers, though some older or more luxurious hotels may have tubs. Beds are usually twins (*diklina*). If you want a double bed, ask for a *diplo krevati*. In upper-end hotels, the mattresses are full- or queen-size.

Use the following as a guide to making accommodations inquiries: to reserve a double room, *thelo na kleiso ena diklino*; with a bath, *me banio*; without a bath, *horis banio*; or a room with a view, *domatio me thea*. If you need a quiet room (*isiho domatio*), get one with double-glazed windows (*dipla parathyra*) and air-conditioning, away from the elevator and public areas, as high up (*psila*) as possible, and off the street.

RENTAL ROOMS

For low-cost accommodations, consider Greece's ubiquitous "rooms to rent": bed-and-breakfasts without the breakfast. You can count on a clean room, often with such amenities as a terrace, air-conditioning, and a private bath, at a very reasonable price, in the range of €40–€50 for two. Look for signs in any Greek town or village; or, let the proprietors find you—they have a knack for spotting strangers who look like they might need a bed for the night. When renting a room, take a good look first and be sure to check the bathroom before you commit. If there are extra beds in the room, clarify in advance that the amount agreed on is for the entire room—owners occasionally try to put another person in the same room.

When approached by one of the touts who meet the island ferries, make sure he or she tells you the location of the rooms being pushed, and look before you commit. Avoid places on main roads or near all-night discos. Around August 15 (an important religious holiday of the Greek Orthodox Church, commemorating the Assumption of the Virgin Mary), when it seems all Greeks go on vacation, even the most-basic rooms are almost impossible to locate, although you can query the tourist police or the municipal tourist office. On some islands, the local rental room owners' association sets up an information booth.

AIRBNB IN GREECE

Renting out spare rooms and empty apartments and homes on Airbnb (⊕ *www. airbnb.com*) have become a favorite practice of many Greek home owners, who amidst a tough and persistent economic climate are looking for ways to increase their income. In addition, the notion of letting out, for a limited period of time, one's home or summer house agrees with the Greek notion of hospitality *philoxenia*, hence Airbnb's popularity with Greek hosts. More than 300 properties are currently listed on the website and it is worth checking out the accommodation on offer, if feeling "at home" even when abroad is what you are after. The range of accommodation on offer varies from affordable basic to high-end luxury.

▌ ADDRESSES

To make finding your way around as easy as possible, it's wise to learn to recognize letters in the Greek alphabet. Most areas have few road signs in English, and even those that *are* in English don't necessarily follow the official standardized transliteration code (⊕ *www.elot.gr*), resulting in odd spellings of foreign names. Sometimes there are several spelling variations in English for the same place: Agios, Aghios, or Ayios; Georgios or Yiorgos. Also, the English version may be quite different from the Greek, or even what locals use informally: Corfu is known as Kerkyra; island capitals are often just called Chora (town), no matter what their formal title; and Panepistimiou, a main Athens boulevard, is officially named Eleftheriou

CUSTOMS OF THE COUNTRY

Greeks are friendly, passionate, and openly affectionate. It is not uncommon, for example, to see women strolling arm in arm, or men two-cheek kissing and hugging each other. Displays of anger are also quite common. To the person who doesn't understand Greek, the loud, intense conversations may all sound angry—but they're not. But there's a negative side to Greeks' outgoing nature. Eager to engage in conversation over any topic, they won't shy away from launching into political discussions about the state of the economy or foreign policy (best politely avoided) or asking personal questions like how much money you earn. The latter isn't considered rude in Greece, but don't feel like you need to respond. Visitors are sometimes taken aback by Greeks' gestures or the ease in which they touch the person to whom they're speaking—take it all in stride. If a pat on the hand becomes a bit too intimate, just shift politely and the other person will take a hint. On the other hand, kissing someone you've just met good-bye on the cheek is quite acceptable—even between men.

GREETINGS AND GESTURES

When you meet someone for the first time, it is customary to shake hands, but with acquaintances the usual is a two-cheek kiss hello and good-bye. One thing that may disconcert foreigners is that when they run into a Greek with another person, he or she usually doesn't introduce the other party, even if there is a long verbal exchange. If you can't stand it anymore, just introduce yourself. Greeks tend to stand closer to people than North Americans and Northern Europeans, and they rely more on gestures when communicating. One gesture you should never use is the open palm, fingers slightly spread, shoved toward someone's face. The *moutza* is a serious insult. Another gesture you should remember, especially if trying to catch a taxi, is the Greek "no," which looks like "yes": a slight or exaggerated (depending on the sentiment) tipping back of the head, sometimes with the eyes closed and eyebrows raised. When you wave with your palm toward people, they may interpret it as "come here" instead of "good-bye"; and Greeks often wave good-bye with the palm facing them, which looks like "come here" to English speakers.

OUT ON THE TOWN

Greeks often eat out of communal serving plates, so it's considered normal in informal settings to spear your tomato out of the salad bowl rather than securing an individual portion. Sometimes in tavernas you don't even get your own plate. Note that it is considered *tsigounia*, stinginess, to run separate tabs, especially because much of the meal is to be shared. Greeks either divide the bill equally among the party, no matter who ate what, or one person magnanimously treats. A good host insists that you eat or drink more, and only when you have refused a number of times will you get a reprieve; be charmingly persistent in your "No." Always keep in mind that Greeks have a loose sense of time! They may be punctual if meeting you to go to a movie, but if they say they'll come by your hotel at 7 pm, they may show up at 8 pm.

Venizelou, but if you ask for that, no one will know what you're talking about. A long street may change names several times, and a city may have more than one street by the same name, so know the district you're headed for, or a major landmark nearby, especially if you're taking a taxi. In this guide, street numbers appear after the street name. Finally, there are odd- and even-numbered sides of the streets, but No. 124 could be several blocks from No. 125.

▌ COMMUNICATIONS

INTERNET

Major hotels have high-speed Internet connections in rooms, and most smaller ones have at least a terminal in the lounge for guests' use. Telecom privatization has helped Greece close the Internet gap with other European countries and, especially on touristed islands, you'll find most cafés offer Wi-Fi, often for free.

The city of Athens offers free Wi-Fi access in Syntagma Square, Thissio (Ayion Asomaton Square), Metaxourgeio Square, Gazi-Technopolis, and Platia Kotzia (Kotzia Square), and a number of rural towns also have free Wi-Fi in public areas. There are also countless cafés and bars that offer free Wi-Fi to guests, just look for the sign. There is also free Wi-Fi inside the Acropolis Museum, the Onassis Cultural Center, and other tourist destinations. Wi-Fi is also available at the bigger airports (Athens, Thessaloniki, Mykonos, etc.), some shopping centers etc. Head to the national electronic store chains Plaisio, Public, and Germanos to purchase mobile Internet access within Greece by the day, week, or month.

Computer parts, batteries, and adaptors of any brand are expensive in Greece and may not be in stock when you need them, so carry spares for your laptop. Also note that many upscale hotels will rent you a laptop.

PHONES

Greece's phone system has improved markedly. You can direct dial in most better hotels, but there is usually a huge surcharge, so use your calling card, cell phone, or a card telephone. You can make calls from most large establishments, kiosks, card phones (there are about 25,000 of them all over Greece, but steadily declining in numbers), and from the local office of Greece's major telephone company, known as OTE ("oh-teh"). International roaming charges for cell phones have decreased in recent years but you still need to check with your provider before you leave the United States. Sometimes mobile phones need to be activated or "unlocked"in order to work abroad.

Doing business over the phone in Greece can be frustrating—the lines always seem to be busy, and while most people speak some basic English, it might not always be enough for efficient communication. You may also find people too busy to address your problem—the independent-minded Greeks are still learning how to be service-conscious. Things have improved in recent years especially in the tourism industry.

The country code for Greece is 30. When dialing Greece from the United States, Canada, or Australia, first dial 011, then 30, the country code, before punching in the area code and local number. From continental Europe, the United Kingdom, or New Zealand, start with 0030.

CALLING WITHIN GREECE

For Greek directory information, dial 11888; many operators speak English. In some cases you must give the surname of the shop or restaurant proprietor to be able to get the phone number of the establishment. The people behind 11888 also operate the website ⊕ *www.vrisko.gr*, which is a Greece-based online directory inquiries resource.

Pronunciations for the numbers in Greek are: one (*"eh*-na"); two (*"dthee*-oh");

three ("*tree*-a"); four ("*tess*-ehr-a"); five ("*pen*-de"); six ("*eh*-ksee"); seven ("ef-ta"); eight ("och- *toh*"); nine ("eh- *nay*-ah"); ten ("*dtheh*-ka").

All telephone numbers in Greece have 10 digits. Area codes now have to be dialed even when you are dialing locally. For cell phones, dial both the cell prefix (a four-digit number beginning with 69) and the telephone number from anywhere in Greece.

You can make local calls from the public OTE phones using phone cards, not coins.

Keep in mind since there are more cell phone users than ever, OTE hasn't bothered to repair or replace broken phone booths, hence their declining numbers. A few kiosks may also have metered telephones, which allow you to make local or international calls.

CALLING OUTSIDE GREECE

To place an international call from Greece, dial 00 to connect to an international network, then dial the country code (for the United States and Canada, it's 1), and then the area code and number. If you need assistance, call 13888. Most people these days prefer to connect through their own mobile phones, making use of Wi-Fi, cellular connectivity and apps such as Skype, Facetime, or Facebook Messenger. You will need an international cellular plan through a U.S. or local provider. From a Greek landline, you can also call the United States through AT&T's international access code for Greece.

Contacts AT&T. ☎ 314/925–6925 *support for travel outside the U.S. (available 24/7), free from mobile phone* ⊕ *www.att.com.* **Sprint.** ☎ 817/698–4199 *travel support outside the U.S. (not toll-free)* ⊕ *www.sprint.com.* **Verizon.** ☎ 800/711–8300 *help with travel inside the U.S., 908/559–4899 help with travel outside the U.S. (within Greece)* ⊕ *www.verizonwireless.com.*

Access Codes AT&T USADirect access codes. ☎ 00/800–1311 *for Greece, 800/225–5288 in U.S.* ⊕ *www.att.com.* **Sprint**

International Travel. ☎ 888/226–7212 *international helpline in the U.S.* ⊕ *www.sprint.com.*

CALLING CARDS

OTE phone cards worth €6, €13, or €25 can be purchased at kiosks, convenience stores, or the local OTE office and are the easiest way to make calls from anywhere in Greece. These phone cards can be used for domestic and international calls (the €6 Chronocarta phone card allows one to talk for up to 630 minutes to U.S. and Canadian landlines and mobile phones). Once you insert the phone card, the number of units on the card will appear; as you begin talking, the units will go down. Once all the units have been used, the card does not get recharged—you must purchase another.

MOBILE PHONES

If you have a multiband phone (some countries use different frequencies from what's used in the United States) and your service provider uses the world-standard GSM network (as do T-Mobile, AT&T, Sprint, and Verizon), you can probably use your phone abroad. Before traveling call your provider for specific info. International roaming fees can be steep; however, they are on the decline at about 30¢ a minute. And overseas you normally pay the toll charges for incoming calls. It's almost always cheaper to send a text message than to make a call, since text messages have a very low set fee (often less than 2¢). In Greek mobile phone contracts, only the caller and not the person receiving the call can be charged for local phone calls (both are charged for international calls, however).

You can completely avoid roaming charges if you connect to a local Wi-Fi network and use one of many Wi-Fi calling apps (including Skype, Google Hangouts, Facebook Messenger, Viber, and WhatsApp). All four major U.S. carriers (T-Mobile, Sprint, AT&T, and Verizon) provide built-in Wi-Fi calling, but make sure you check if there are any additional costs incurred before you travel (in the form of international calling plan rates).

As of June 15, 2017, roaming charges were abolished within the EU. This means you can use your regular allowance of calls, texts, and data for no extra cost from anywhere in the European Union. To minimize roaming charges to other countries, use free Wi-Fi whenever possible and check if your mobile provider has a roaming add-on (an extra allowance for data, texts, and minutes to use abroad as a one-off) at a small cost.

If you just want to make local calls, consider buying a new SIM card (note that your provider may have to unlock your phone for you to use a different SIM card) and a prepaid service plan in the destination. You'll then have a local number and can make local calls at local rates. If your trip is extensive, you could also simply buy a new cell phone in your destination, as the initial cost will be offset over time.

■ TIP→ **If you travel internationally frequently, save one of your old mobile phones or buy a cheap one on the Internet; ask your cell phone company to unlock it for you, and take it with you as a travel phone, buying a new SIM card with pay-as-you-go service in each destination.**

If you take your cell phone with you, call your provider in advance and ask if it has a connection agreement with a Greek mobile carrier. If so, manually switch your phone to that network's settings as soon as you arrive. To do this, go to the Settings menu, then look for the Network settings and follow the prompts.

If you're traveling with a companion or group of friends and plan to use your cell phones to communicate with each other, buying a local prepaid connection kit is far cheaper for voice calls or sending text messages than using your regular provider. The most popular local prepaid connection kits are Cosmote's What's Up, Vodafone's Unlimited and CU, or Wind's F2G or Card To All—these carriers all

have branded stores, but you can also buy cell phones and cell phone packages from the Germanos and Plaisio chain stores as well as large supermarkets like Sklavenitis.

Contacts Cellular Abroad. ☎ *800/287-5072, 310/862-7100* ⊕ *www.cellularabroad.com.* **Mobal.** ☎ *888/888-9162* ⊕ *www.mobal. com.* **Planet Fone.** ☎ *888/988-4777* ⊕ *www. planetfone.com.*

■ CUSTOMS AND DUTIES

Any visitor entering or leaving the EU and carrying cash of the value of €10,000 or more is required to declare that sum to the customs authorities of the Member State through which he/she is entering or leaving the EU. For persons traveling in a group the €10,000 limit applies to each person individually. The obligation to declare cash also applies to minors through their parents or legal guardians, and to mentally incompetent persons or protected adult persons through their legal representation. If you are unsure if you have to declare or not, it is important to spontaneously approach and seek advice from the authorities at the point of entry or exit of the EU.

Only one per person of such expensive portable items as cameras, camcorders, computers, and the like is permitted into Greece. It is recommended that you register these with Greek Customs upon arrival to avoid any problems when taking them out of the country again (although few visitors choose to do so). Sports equipment, such as bicycles and skis, is also limited to one (or one pair) per person. One windsurf board per person may be imported/exported duty-free.

To bring in a dog or a cat, your pet must have a pet passport and be identified by the electronic identification system (microchip) according to ISO standard 11794 or 11785. They must also have been vaccinated against rabies. Traveling pets must also be accompanied by a health certificate for noncommercial movement of pets (regulation EC No. 998/2003) endorsed by a USDA state veterinarian.

For more information on Greek Customs, check with your local Greek Consulate or the Greek Ministry of Finance in Athens, which has more-detailed information on customs and import/export regulations.

Finally, there are also limits to the amount of goods you can bring back to the United States duty-free. The U.S. Customs and Border Protection department maintains accurate information on those limits.

Contacts in Greece European Commission Taxation and Customs Union. ⊕ *ec.europa. eu/taxation_customs/home_en.* **Ministry of Finance–Customs Office.** ☏ *210/480–2449 foreign exchange declaration* ⊕ *www.gsis.gr.*

Contacts in the United States U.S. Customs and Border Protection. ⊕ *www.cbp.gov.*

▌EATING OUT

MEALS AND MEALTIMES

Greeks don't really sit down for breakfast, so with the exception of hotels, few places serve that meal. You can pick up a cheese pie, a baguette sandwich, and rolls at a bakery or a sesame-coated bread ring called a *koulouri* sold by city vendors; order a *tost* ("toast"), a sort of dry grilled sandwich, usually with cheese or paper-thin ham slices, at a café; or dig into a plate of yogurt with honey. Local bakeries may offer fresh doughnuts in the morning. On the islands in summer, cafés serve breakfast, from Continental to combinations that might include Spanish omelets and French coffee. Caffeine junkies can get a cup of coffee practically anywhere.

Greeks eat their main meal at either lunch or dinner, so the offerings are the same. For lunch, heavyweight meat-and-potato dishes can be had, but you might prefer a real Greek salad (no lettuce, a slice of feta with a pinch of oregano, and ripe tomatoes, cucumber, onions, and green peppers) or souvlaki or grilled chicken from a taverna. For a light bite you can also try one of the popular Greek chain

eateries such as Everest or Grigori's for grilled sandwiches or spanakopita and *tiropita* (cheese pie); or Goody's Burger House, the local equivalent of McDonald's, where you'll find good-quality burgers, pasta dishes, and salads.

Coffee and pastries are eaten in the afternoon, usually at a café or *zaharoplastio* (pastry shop). The hour or so before restaurants open for dinner—around 7—is a pleasant time to have an ouzo or glass of wine and try Greek hors d'oeuvres, called *mezedes,* in a bar, *ouzeri,* or *mezedopoleio* (Greek tapas place). Dinner is often the main meal of the day, and there's plenty of food. Starters include dips such as *taramosalata* (made from fish roe), *melitzanosalata* (made from smoked eggplant, lemon, oil, and garlic), and the well-known yogurt, cucumber, and garlic *tzatziki.* A typical dinner for a couple might be two to three appetizers, an entrée, a salad, and wine. Diners can order as little or as much as they like, except at very expensive establishments. If a Greek eats dessert at all, it will be fruit or a modest wedge of a syrup-drenched cake like *ravani* or semolina halvah, often shared between two or three diners. Only in fancier restaurants might diners order tiramisu or crème brûlée with an espresso. One option for those who want a lighter, shared meal is the mezedopoleio.

In most places, the menu is broken down into appetizers (*orektika*) and entrées (*kiria piata*), with additional headings for salads (Greek salad or *horta,* boiled wild greens; this also includes dips like tzatziki) and vegetable side plates. But this doesn't mean there is any sense of a first or second "course," as in France. Often the food arrives all at the same time, or as it becomes ready.

Breakfast is usually available until 10:30 or 11 at many hotels and until early afternoon in beach cafés. Lunch is between 1 and 6 (especially during summer months), and dinner is served from about 8 to midnight, or even later in the big cities and resort islands. Most Greeks dine very late, around 10 or 11 pm. Unless otherwise noted, the restaurants listed in this guide are open daily for lunch and dinner.

PAYING

For restaurant price categories, see the Planning section in every regional chapter. For guidelines on tipping, see Tipping below.

RESERVATIONS AND DRESS

Regardless of where you are, it's a good idea to make a reservation if you can. In some places (especially the more upmarket restaurants), it's expected. We only mention them specifically when reservations are essential (there's no other way you'll ever get a table) or when they are not accepted. For popular restaurants, book as far ahead as you can and reconfirm on the day of your reservation. (Large parties should always call ahead to check the reservations policy.) We mention dress only when men are required to wear a jacket or a jacket and tie, which is rare in Greece and almost unheard of on the islands.

▌ ELECTRICITY

The electrical current in Greece is 220 volts, 50 cycles AC. Wall outlets take Continental-type plugs with two round oversize prongs. If your appliances are dual-voltage, you'll need only an adapter; if not, you'll also need a step-down converter/transformer (United States and Canada).

Consider making a small investment in a universal adapter, which has several types of plugs in one lightweight, compact unit. Most laptops and mobile phone chargers are dual voltage (i.e., they operate equally well on 110 and 220 volts) so require only an adapter. These days the same is true of small appliances such as hair dryers. Always check labels and manufacturer instructions to be sure. Don't use 110-volt outlets marked "for shavers only" for high-wattage appliances such as hair dryers.

Contacts Walkabout Travel Gear. ⊕ *www. walkabouttravelgear.com.*

▌ EMERGENCIES

Regrettably, vacations are sometimes marred by emergencies, so it's good to know where you should turn for help. In Athens and other cities, hospitals treat emergencies on a rotating basis; an ambulance driver will know where to take you. Or, since waving down a taxi can be faster than waiting for an ambulance, ask a cab driver to take you to the closest *"e-phee-me-re-von"* (duty) hospital. Large islands and rural towns have small medical centers (*iatreio* or *kentro ygeias*) that can treat minor illnesses or arrange for transport to another facility.

Medications are sold only at pharmacies, which are by law staffed by licensed pharmacists who can treat minor cuts, take blood pressure, and recommend cold medication. Pharmacies are marked with a green-and-white cross and there's one every few city blocks. Outside standard trading hours, there are duty pharmacies offering 24-hour coverage. These are posted in the window of every pharmacy. The tourist police throughout Greece can provide general information and help in emergencies and can mediate in disputes.

Foreign Embassy Embassy of the United States of America. ⊠ *Vasilissis Sofias 91, Mavili Sq.* ☎ *210/721–2951 switchboard* ⊕ *athens.usembassy.gov.*

▌ HEALTH

Greece's strong summer sun and low humidity can lead to sunburn or sunstroke if you're not careful. A hat, a light-colored long-sleeve shirt, and long pants or a sarong are advised for spending a day at the beach or visiting archaeological sites. Sunglasses, a hat, and sunscreen are necessities, and be sure to drink plenty of water. Most beaches present few dangers, but keep a lookout for the occasional jellyfish and, on rocky coves, sea urchins. Should you step on one, don't break off the embedded spines, which may lead to infection, but instead remove them with heated olive oil and a needle. Food is seldom a problem, but the liberal amounts of olive oil used in Greek cooking may be indigestible for some. Tap water in Greece is fine in most urban areas, and bottled spring water is readily available. Avoid drinking tap water in many rural areas.

In greener, wetter areas, mosquitoes may be a problem. In addition to wearing insect repellent, you can burn coils ("spee-*rahl*") or buy plug-in devices that burn medicated tabs ("pah- *steel*-ya"). Hotels usually provide these. Lemon eucalyptus sprays are a more natural way to keep insects away. The only poisonous snakes in Greece are the adder and the sand viper, which are brown or red, with dark zigzags. The adder has a V or X behind its head, and the sand viper sports a small horn on its nose. When hiking, wear high tops and hiking socks and don't put your feet or hands in crevices without looking first. If bitten, try to slow the spread of the venom until a doctor comes. Lie still with the affected limb lower than the rest of your body. Apply a tourniquet, releasing it every few minutes, and cut the wound a bit in case the venom can bleed out. Do NOT suck on the bite. Whereas snakes like to lie in the sun, the scorpion (rare) likes cool, wet places, in woodpiles and under stones. Apply Benadryl or Phenergan to minor stings, but if you have nausea or fever, see a doctor at once.

For minor ailments, go to a local pharmacy first, where the licensed staff can make recommendations for over-the-counter drugs. Pharmacies are open in the morning (8–2) and three evenings per week (Tuesday, Thursday, and Friday 5–8), and each posts the name of the nearest pharmacy open off-hours and on weekends. Most state hospitals and rural clinics won't charge you for tending to minor ailments, even if you're not an EU citizen; at most, you'll pay a minimal fee. For a doctor or dentist, check with your hotel, embassy, or the tourist police.

Do not fly within 24 hours of scuba diving.

▌ HOURS OF OPERATION

Most business and retail stores are typically open Monday and Wednesday 9 am to 3 pm; Tuesday, Thursday, and Friday 9 am to 2 pm; and 5:30 pm to 9 pm and Saturday 9 am to 8 pm; and are closed on Sunday. However, these longtime standards are changing quickly, and you can find some supermarkets and big chains open on Sunday as well. Still, each establishment has its own particular timetable, and establishments in tourist resorts may remain open longer, even after midnight.

For certain categories such as pharmacies, banks, and government offices, hours have always been standardized, but again there are some establishments in tourist resorts that follow extended hours.

Many small businesses and shops in main urban hubs close for at least a week around mid-August, and most tourist establishments, including hotels, shut down on the islands and northern Greece from November until mid-spring. Restaurants, especially tavernas, often stay open on holidays; some close in summer or move to cooler locations. Christmas, New Year's, Orthodox Easter, and August 15 are the days everything shuts down, although, for example, bars work full force on Christmas Eve, since it's a social occasion and not particularly family-oriented. Orthodox

Easter changes dates every year, so check your calendar. On Orthodox Easter Week, most shops follow a different schedule while on Good Friday, shops open after church services, around 1 pm.

Banks are normally open Monday through Thursday 8 to 2:30, Friday 8 to 2, but a few branches of Alpha and Eurobank are open until 6 weekdays and on Saturday morning. Hotels also cash traveler's checks on weekends, and the banks at the Athens airport have longer hours.

Government offices are open weekdays from 8 to 2. For commercial offices, the hours depend on the business, although most private companies have by now adopted the 9 to 5 schedule.

All gas stations are open daily 6 am to 9 pm (some close Sunday). These hours are extended during the high season (usually from May 1 to September 30) from 6 am to 10:30 pm and some stations pump all night in the major cities and along the National Road and Attica highway. They do not close for lunch.

Pharmacies are open Monday, Wednesday, and Friday from about 9 to 2 and Tuesday, Thursday, and Friday from 9 to 2 and 5 until 8 at night. The pharmacy at Athens International Airport operates 24 hours. According to a rotation system, there is always at least one pharmacy open in any area *(See Emergencies, above).*

If it's late in the evening and you need an aspirin, a soft drink, cigarettes, a newspaper, or a pen, look for the nearest open kiosk, called a *periptero*; these kiosks on street corners everywhere brim with all kinds of necessities. Owners stagger their hours, and many towns have at least one kiosk that stays open late, occasionally through the night. Neighborhood mini-markets also stay open late.

NATIONAL HOLIDAYS

January 1 (New Year's Day); January 6 (Epiphany); Clean Monday (first day of Lent); March 25 (Feast of the Annunciation and Independence Day); Good Friday; Greek Easter Sunday; Greek Easter Monday; May 1 (Labor Day); Pentecost; Holy Spirit Day (Whit Monday, the day after Pentecost); August 15 (Assumption of the Holy Virgin); October 28 (Ochi Day); December 25–26 (Christmas Day and Boxing Day).

Only on Orthodox Easter and August 15 do you find that just about *everything* shuts down. It's harder getting a room at the last minute on these days (especially the latter), and traveling requires stamina if you want to survive on the ferries and the highways. On the other hand, the local rituals and rites associated with these two celebrations are interesting and occasionally moving (like the Epitaphios procession on Good Friday).

▌ MAIL

Letters and postcards take about five days to reach the United States by airmail, but it can take longer in August, when postal staff is reduced, and during Christmas and Easter holidays. If what you're mailing is important, send it registered, which costs about €3.40 in Greece (for a 20-gram envelope). Within Greece, for about €2.20 for a 20-gram envelope (with the cost increasing depending on the weight), you can send your letter "express"; this earns you a red sticker and faster local delivery. The ELTA post office also operates three courier-type services, domestic Porta-porta, international EMS Express, and SPM. Delivery to the continental United States takes about two to four days with EMS, and costs €29 for up to 0.5 kgr of weight (possible customs charges not included). Packages take three to five days, and cost depends on the weight. For guaranteed next-business-day delivery to principal destinations in Europe and in the United States (24-hour), use ELTA's SPM (Special Priority Mail). An envelope of up to 0.5 kgr of weight costs €27. Postcards can be sent on a priority basis for €0.80 each.

Post offices are open weekdays 7:30 to 2, although in city centers they may stay open in the evenings and on weekends.

The main post offices in Athens, Thessaloniki, and Piraeus are open weekdays 7:30 am to 8:30 pm, Saturday 7:30 to 2:30, and Sunday 9 to 1:30 (only for the main post office in Athens, at Syntagma Square, and in Thessaloniki). The post offices at Athens International Airport and the Acropolis are open weekends, too. Throughout the country, mailboxes are yellow and sometimes divided into domestic and international containers; express boxes are red.

Airmail letters to destinations other than Europe and weighing up to 20 grams cost €0.90, and €1.45 for 50 grams (€0.90 and €1.30, respectively, to other European countries, including the United Kingdom).

Contacts Hellenic Post (ELTA). ☎ *800/118–2000 toll-free, 210/335–3777* ⊕ *www.elta.gr.*

▮ MONEY

Although costs have risen astronomically since Greece switched to the euro currency in 2002, the country will seem reasonably priced to travelers from the United States and Great Britain. Popular tourist resorts (including some of the islands) and the larger cities are markedly more expensive than the countryside. Though the price of eating in a restaurant has increased, you can still get a bargain. Hotels are generally moderately priced outside the major cities, and the extra cost of accommodations in a luxury hotel, compared to in an average hotel, often seems unwarranted.

ITEM	AVERAGE COST
Cup of Coffee	€2–€5 (in a central-city café; Greek coffee is a bit cheaper)
Glass of Wine	€4–€8
Glass of Beer	€3; €5–€9 in a bar
Sandwich	€2.50–€4
1-mile (½-km) Taxi Ride in Capital City	€3.00
Archaeological Site Admission	€2–€12

Other typical costs: soft drink (can) €1, in a café €2; spinach pie, €1.80; souvlaki, €2.20; local bus, €1.20; foreign newspaper, €3–€5.30.

Prices throughout this guide are given for adults. Discounts are almost always available for children, students, and senior citizens.

ATMS AND BANKS

Your own bank will probably charge a fee for using ATMs abroad; the foreign bank you use may also charge a fee. Nevertheless, you'll usually get a better rate of exchange at an ATM than you will at a currency-exchange office or even when changing money in a bank. And extracting funds as you need them is a significantly safer option than carrying around a large amount of cash for your entire trip. However, it's normally a bad idea to use your debit card to make purchases abroad; if there's any kind of fraud or problem, that money is gone from your bank account until you can contact the bank and dispute the transaction. Save your debit card for cash withdrawals, and use a credit card for purchases.

▮TIP→ PIN numbers with more than four digits are not recognized at ATMs in Greece. If yours has five or more, remember to change it before you leave. Letters do not generally appear on Greek ATM keypads.

ATMs are widely available throughout the country. Virtually all banks, including the National Bank of Greece (known as *Ethniki*), have machines that dispense money to Cirrus or Plus cardholders, but in the rare instance that you still have an ATM card without a chip, you may need one to access your account at many European banks. You may find bank-sponsored ATMs at harbors and in airports as well. Other systems accepted include Visa, MasterCard, and less often American Express, Diners Club, and Eurocard. The farther away from the capital you go, the less likely you are to encounter card machines and ATMs, so make sure you always carry some cash with you, particularly when traveling to smaller islands or mainland towns. The word for PIN is pronounced "peen," and ATMs are called *Ei Ti Em* after the letters, or just *to mihanima,* "the machine." Machines usually let you complete the transaction in English, French, or German and seldom create problems, except Sunday night, when they sometimes run out of cash. For most machines, the minimum amount dispensed is €20. Sometimes an ATM may refuse to "read" your card. Don't panic; it's probably the machine. Try another bank.

■ TIP→ At some ATMs in Greece you may not have a choice of drawing from a specific account. If you have linked savings and checking accounts, make sure there's money in both before you depart.

CREDIT CARDS

It's a good idea to inform your credit-card company before you travel, especially if you don't travel internationally very often. Otherwise, the credit-card company might put a hold on your card owing to unusual activity—not a good thing halfway through your trip. Record all your credit-card numbers—as well as the phone numbers to call if your cards are lost or stolen—in a safe place, so you're prepared should something go wrong. Both MasterCard and Visa have general numbers you can call (collect if you're abroad) if your card is lost, but you're better off calling the number of your issuing bank, since MasterCard and Visa usually just transfer you to your bank; your bank's number is usually printed on your card.

Most credit-card transactions in Europe now require a chip-and-PIN or chip-and-signature card. Most credit cards in the United States now have these, and you can sometimes get a PIN from your bank to make transactions abroad easier. If you plan to use your credit card for cash advances from an ATM (which we strongly advise against), you'll certainly need to apply for a PIN at least two weeks before your trip. Although it's usually cheaper (and safer) to use a credit card abroad for large purchases (so you can cancel payments or be reimbursed if there's a problem), some credit-card companies and the banks that issue them add substantial percentages to all foreign transactions, whether they're in a foreign currency or not. Check on these fees before leaving home, so there won't be any surprises when you get the bill.

■ TIP→ Before you charge something, ask the merchant whether or not he or she plans to do a dynamic currency conversion (DCC). They will normally ask you if you want to "pay in euros or dollars." In such a transaction the credit-card processor (shop, restaurant, or hotel, not Visa or MasterCard) converts the currency and charges you in your home currency rather than euros. It's an expensive transaction since in most cases you'll pay the merchant an additional 3% fee for this service on top of any credit-card company and issuing-bank foreign-transaction surcharges.

It's always safer to use a credit card for purchases while traveling. A credit card allows you to delay payment and gives you certain rights as a consumer, including the right to dispute a fraudulent charge before you have to make a payment on your account and a limit of $50 for fraudulent charges to a lost or stolen card (provided you report the loss as soon as you discover it). A debit card deducts funds directly from your checking account and helps you stay within your budget, but you may not receive an automatic credit if you dispute a charge. When you want to rent a car, though, you may still need an old-fashioned credit card.

Shop owners in Greece often give you a lower price if you pay with cash rather than credit, because they want to avoid the credit-card bank fees.

Reporting Lost Cards American Express.
☎ *800/917–8047 in U.S., 273/696–933 collect from abroad* ⊕ *www.americanexpress.com.*

com. **Diners Club.** ☎ *800/234–6377 in U.S., 514/881–3735 collect from abroad* ⊕ *www. dinersclub.com.* **Discover.** ☎ *800/347– 2683 in U.S., 801/902–3100 collect from abroad* ⊕ *www.discover.com.* **MasterCard.** ☎ *800/627–8372 in U.S., 636/722–7111 collect from abroad, 800–11/8870303 toll free in Greece* ⊕ *www.mastercard.com.* **Visa.** ☎ *800/847–2911 in U.S., 303/967–1096 collect from abroad, 800–11/638–0304 toll-free in Greece* ⊕ *www.visa.com.*

CURRENCY AND EXCHANGE

Greece uses the euro. Under the euro system, there are eight coins: 1 and 2 euros, plus 1, 2, 5, 10, 20, and 50 euro cents. Euros are pronounced "evros" in Greek; cents are known as "lepta." All coins have the euro value on one side; the other side has each country's unique national symbol. Greece's images range from triremes to a depiction of the mythological Europa being abducted by Zeus transformed as a bull. Bills (banknotes) come in six denominations: 5, 10, 20, 50, 100, and 200 euros. Bills are the same for all EU countries.

Off Syntagma Square in Athens, the National Bank of Greece, Alpha Bank, and Pireos Bank have automated machines that change your foreign currency into euros. When you shop, remember that it's always easier to bargain on prices when paying in cash instead of by credit card.

If you do use an exchange service, good options are American Express and One-Exchange (formerly Eurochange). Watch daily fluctuations and shop around. Daily exchange rates are prominently displayed in banks and listed in the global edition of the *New York Times* (⊕ *www.global. nytimes.com*). In Athens, around Syntagma Square is the best place to look. In some tourist resorts you might be able to change money at the post office, where commissions may be lower than at banks. To avoid lines at airport exchange booths, get a bit of local currency before you leave home.

■TIP➔ Even if a currency-exchange booth has a sign promising no commission, rest assured that there's some kind of substantial, hidden fee that can be as much as 8%, often in the form of a bad rate. And as for rates, you will always get a better exchange rate for euros at an ATM.

Contacts Bank of Greece. ⊠ *21 Panepistimiou (El. Venizelou) Avenue, Syntagma* ⊹ *Customer side entrance from Stadiou 14* ☎ *210/320–1111.* **Kapa Change.** ⊠ *Filellinon 1, Syntagma* ☎ *210/331–3830* ⊕ *www. kapachange.gr.* **National Bank of Greece.** ⊠ *Karageorgi Servias 2, Syntagma* ☎ *210/334– 8015* ⊕ *www.nbg.gr.* **OneExchange.** ⊠ *Karageorgi Servias 2, Syntagma* ☎ *210/322–0005* ⊕ *www.onexchange.gr.*

■ PASSPORTS AND VISAS

All citizens (even infants) of the United States, Canada, Australia, and New Zealand need only a valid passport to enter Greece, which is a party to the Schengen Agreement, for stays of up to 90 days. Your passport should be valid for at least three months beyond the period of your stay (the U.S. Department of State recommends six months). If you leave after 90 days and don't have a visa extension, you will be fined anywhere from €600 to €1,300 (depending on how long you overstay) by Greek airport officials, who are not flexible on this issue. Even worse perhaps, you must provide *hartosima* (revenue stamps) for the documents, which you don't want to have to run around and find as your flight is boarding. If you want to extend your stay beyond 90 days, there is heavy bureaucracy involved but eventually you will be able to do it for a cost of about €150. Inquire at your local police station for details.

If you are going to visit Greece, you can enroll to the Smart Traveler Enrollment Program of the U.S. Embassy in Greece. Then, you can be kept up-to-date with important safety and security announcements. Enrolling also will help friends and family get in touch with you in an emergency.

■ TIP→ Before your trip, make two copies of your passport's data page (one for someone at home and another for you to carry separately). Or scan the page and email it to someone at home and/or yourself.

Contacts **U.S. Department of State.** ☏ *877/487–2778* ⊕ *travel.state.gov/passport.* **Smart Traveler Enrollment Program.** ⊕ *step. state.gov.*

▌ TAXES

Taxes are typically included in all quoted prices.

Value-Added Tax, 6% for books and 24% (V.A.T. is 17% on some remote Aegean islands) for almost everything else, called FPA (pronounced "fee-pee-ah") by Greeks, is included in the cost of most consumer goods and services, including most groceries. If you are a citizen of a non-EU country, you may get a V.A.T. refund on products (except alcohol, cigarettes, or toiletries) worth €120 or more bought in Greece in one shopping spree from licensed stores that usually display a Tax-Free Shopping sticker in their window. Note that the V.A.t. refund may also apply to hotel bills, package tours, car rentals, and other services, so make sure you ask in advance. Ask the shop to complete a refund form called a Tax-Free Check receipt for you, which you show at Greek customs.

Have the form stamped like any customs form by customs officials when you leave the country or, if you're visiting several European Union countries, when you leave the EU. Be ready to show customs officials what you've bought (pack purchases together, in your carry-on luggage); budget extra time for this. After you're through passport control, take the form to a refund-service counter for an on-the-spot refund, or mail it back in the pre-addressed envelope given to you at the store. You receive the total refund stated on the form, but the processing time can be long, especially if you request a credit-card adjustment. Note that there are no cash refunds issued in the United States anymore.

If you are leaving from the Eleftherios Venizelos Airport for a country outside the EU, after your Tax-Free Check form has been stamped, you can go directly to the Onexchange bureau de change (extra-Schengen area, Gates 1–4, opening hours 6 am–10 pm) and get your refund cash.

A refund service can save you some hassle, for a fee. Global Blue is a Europe-wide service with 300,000 affiliated stores and more than 200 international tax refund offices at major airports and border crossings. The service issues refunds in the form of cash, check, or credit-card adjustment, minus a processing fee. If you don't have time to wait at the refund counter, you can mail in the form instead. Maximum refunded V.A.T. per transaction is up to the equivalent of €1,500 will be refunded in cash, but in a currency other than euros.

V.A.T. Refunds Global Blue. ☏ *+421/232– 111111* ⊕ *www.globalblue.com.*

▌ TIME

Greek time is Greenwich Mean Time (GMT) plus two hours. To estimate the time back home, subtract 7 hours from the local time for New York and Washington, 8 hours for Chicago, 9 for Denver, and 10 for Los Angeles. Londoners subtract two hours. Those living in Sydney or Melbourne add eight hours. Greek Daylight Saving Time starts on the last Sunday in March and ends the last Sunday in October. Stay alert—newspapers barely publicize the change.

▌ TIPPING

How much to tip in Greece, especially at restaurants, is confusing and is usually up to the discretion of the individual.

TIPPING GUIDELINES FOR GREECE	
Bartender	10% maximum
Bellhop	€1 per bag
Hotel Concierge	€3–€5, if he or she performs a service for you
Hotel Maid	Up to €10 per stay
Hotel Room-Service Waiter	€2–€3 per delivery, even if a service charge has been added
Porter at Airport or Train Station	€1 per bag
WSW Skycap Services at Airport	€1–€3 per bag checked
Taxi Driver	Round up the fare to the nearest €0.50 or €1
Tour Guide	5% of fee
Waiter	By law a 13% service charge is figured into the price of a meal; however, it is customary to round up the bill if the service was satisfactory. During the Christmas and Greek Easter holiday periods, restaurants tack on an obligatory 18% holiday bonus to your bill for the waiters.
Others	For restroom attendants €1–€2 is appropriate. People dispensing programs at theaters get about €2.

▌ TRAVEL AGENTS

Many travel arrangements in Greece are still made (and indeed better made) through travel agencies. There are countless travel agents in Greece, and as is the case anywhere, the service you get makes a difference. Some agents simply want to confirm as many bookings as possible then move on, but when you find an agent who understands that bespoke personalized attention is great for you and for future business, you'll find no more helpful professional. Greek travel agents who do the job right can take the headache out

of figuring out the logistics behind your dream Greek itinerary. They know the ins and outs of the ferry systems from timetables to schedules, they can suggest which accommodations suit your style, and they can propose tours that interest you. And they can often get you better prices than you can find on your own, even through popular online discounters.

If you are traveling in July and August, travel agencies can come to the rescue with preset packages for the islands you want to visit or suggest other options from archaeological sites, mountain trips, or coastal villages. *See the individual destination chapters for more local recommendations.*

Dolphin Hellas Travel. Dolphin Hellas has been working with travelers worldwide since 1970. They pride themselves on tailor-made trip planning. They specialize in group, honeymoon, and individual travel that includes hotel and villa rentals, cruises, and transportation services. Through their website clients can check online ferry schedules and make reservations. If you are planning a trip to Greece, contact this agency in advance, especially before booking your hotels, to see if their prices are better than what you can find on your own. ⊠ *Syngrou 16, Athens* ☎ *210/922–7772 in Athens* ⊕ *www.dolphin-hellas.gr.*

Fantasy Travel. Since 1983, Fantasy Travel's agents aim to offer personalized service when planning travel for their clients that visit Greece. They specialize in cruises, tours, island-hopping itineraries, bespoke vacation packages, and more. ⊠ *Filillenon 19, Athens* ☎ *210/331–0530* ⊕ *www.fantasy.gr.*

Navigator. If you are looking for a Greece-based travel agency through which to book a cruise, you can do no better than Navigator. With decades of experience in the travel agency business, the agency specializes in Greek island cruises. ⊠ *Akadimias 32, Athens* ☎ *210/360–9801 in Athens* ⊕ *www.navigator.gr.*

▌ VISITOR INFORMATION

Tourist police, stationed near the most-popular tourist sites, can answer questions in English about transportation, steer you to an open pharmacy or doctor, and locate phone numbers of hotels, rooms, and restaurants. You can download maps, brochures, and guides from the Greek National Tourism Organization website. The complete *Greek Travel Pages* is available online and is a valuable resource for all travel in Greece.

Contacts Greek National Tourism Organization (*GNTO*). ✉ *800 3rd Ave., 23rd floor, New York* ☎ *212/421–5777* ⊕ *www.visitgreece. gr.* **Greek Travel Pages.** ✉ *International Publications Ltd., Psylla 6, at Filellinon, Athens* ☎ *210/324–7511* ⊕ *www.gtp.gr.*

INDEX